Current Biography
Yearbook
1981

CURRENT BIOGRAPHY

YEARBOOK

1981

EDITOR

Charles Moritz

ASSOCIATE EDITORS

Evelyn Lohr

Henry Sloan

Kieran Dugan

Judith Graham

ASSISTANT EDITOR

Lore Croghan

THE H. W. WILSON COMPANY

NEW YORK

FORTY-SECOND ANNUAL CUMULATION—1981

PRINTED IN THE UNITED STATES OF AMERICA

International Standard Serial No. (0084-9499)

Library of Congress Catalog Card No. (40-27432)

PREFACE

The aim of CURRENT BIOGRAPHY YEARBOOK 1981 like that of the preceding volumes in this series of annual dictionaries of contemporary biography, now in its fifth decade of publication, is to provide the reference librarian, the student, or any researcher with brief, objective, accurate, and well-documented biographical articles about living leaders in all fields of human accomplishment the world over. Whenever feasible, obituary notices appear for persons whose biographies have been published in *Current Biography*.

CURRENT BIOGRAPHY YEARBOOK 1981 carries on the policy of including new and updated biographical sketches that supersede earlier, outdated articles. Sketches have been made as accurate and objective as possible through careful researching by CURRENT BIOGRAPHY writers in newspapers, magazines, authoritative reference books, and news releases of both government and private agencies. Immediately after they are published in the eleven monthly issues, articles are submitted to biographees to give them an opportunity to suggest corrections in time for CURRENT BIOGRAPHY YEARBOOK. To take account of major changes in the careers of biographees, sketches have also been revised before they are included in the yearbook. With the exception of occasional interviews, the questionnaire filled out by the biographee remains the main source of direct information.

In the back of the volume under *Organizations* can be found the names of those who head organizations. Some persons who are not professional authors but who have written books are included under *Nonfiction* in addition to their vocational fields. The annual bestowal of Nobel Prizes has added articles to the volume. The pages immediately following contain: *Explanations; Key to Reference Abbreviations; Key to Pronunciation;* and *Key to Abbreviations*. The indexes at the end of the volume are *Biographical References; Periodicals and Newspapers Consulted; Classification by Profession;* and *Cumulated Index—1981*. The 1940-1950 index can be found in the 1950 yearbook; the 1951-1960 index, in the 1960 yearbook, the 1961-1970 index in the 1970 yearbook, and the 1971-1980 index in the 1980 yearbook.

For their assistance in preparing CURRENT BIOGRAPHY YEARBOOK 1980, I should like to thank the associate and assistant editors.

Charles Moritz

Explanations

Authorities for biographees' full names, with some exceptions, are the bibliographical publications of The Wilson Company. When a biographee prefers a certain name form, that is indicated in the heading of the article: for example, Niemöller, (Friedrich Gustav Emil) Martin means that he is usually referred to as Martin Niemöller. When a professional name is used in the heading, as, for example, Anne Bancroft, the real name (in this case Annemarie Italiano) appears in the article itself.

The heading of each article includes the pronunciation of the name if it is unusual, date of birth (if obtainable), and occupation. The article is supplemented by a list of references to sources of biographical information, in two alphabets: (1) newspapers and periodicals and (2) books. (See the section *Biographical References,* found in the rear of this volume.)

Key to Reference Abbreviations

References to some newspapers and periodicals are listed in abbreviated form; for example, "Sat Eve Post 217:14 S 30 '44 por" means *Saturday Evening Post,* volume 217, page 14, September 30, 1944, with portrait. (For full names, see the section *Periodicals and Newspapers Consulted,* found in the rear of this volume.)

January—Ja	July—Jl	Journal—J
February—F	August—Ag	Magazine—Mag
March—Mr	September—S	Monthly—Mo
April—Ap	October—O	Portrait—por
May—My	November—N	Weekly—W
June—Je	December—D	Review—R

KEY TO PRONUNCIATION

ā	āle	ō	ōld	ü	Pronounced approximately as ē, with rounded lips: French u, as in *menu* (mə-nü); German ü, as in grün
â	câre	ô	ôrb		
a	add	o	odd		
ä	ärm	oi	oil		
		o͞o	o͞oze		
ē	ēve	o͝o	fo͝ot		
e	end	ou	out		
				ə	the schwa, an unstressed vowel representing the sound that is spelled a as in sofa e as in fitted i as in edible o as in melon u as in circus
g	go				
		th	then		
ī	īce	*th*	thin		
i	ill				
ᴋ	German ch as in *ich* (iᴋ)	ū	cūbe		
		û	ûrn; French eu, as in *jeu* (zhû), German ö, oe, as in schön (shûn), *Goethe* (gû'te)	zh	azure
ɴ	Not pronounced, but indicates the nasal tone of the preceding vowel, as in the French *bon* (bôɴ).			′	= main accent
				″	= secondary accent
		u	tub		

Key To Abbreviations

AAAA	Amateur Athletic Association of America	ECA	Economic Cooperation Administration
A.A.U.	Amateur Athletic Union	ECOSOC	Economic and Social Council
ABA	American Bar Association	EDC	Economic Defense Community
ABC	American Broadcasting Company	EEC	European Economic Community
ACA	Americans for Constitutional Action	ERA	Equal Rights Amendment
A.C.L.U.	American Civil Liberties Union	ERP	European Recovery Program
ADA	Americans for Democratic Action	ESA	Economic Stabilization Administration
AEC	Atomic Energy Commission		
AEF	American Expeditionary Force		
AFL	American Federation of Labor	FAO	Food and Agriculture Organization
AFL-CIO	American Federation of Labor and Congress of Industrial Organizations	FBI	Federal Bureau of Investigation
		FCC	Federal Communications Commission
ALA	American Library Association	FEPC	Fair Employment Practice Committee
AMA	American Medical Association		
A.P.	Associated Press	FHA	Federal Housing Administration
ASCAP	American Society of Composers, Authors and Publishers	FOA	Foreign Operations Administration
		FPC	Federal Power Commission
ASNE	American Society of Newspaper Editors	FSA	Federal Security Agency
		FTC	Federal Trade Commission
		GATT	General Agreement on Tariffs and Trade
B.A.	Bachelor of Arts	G.B.E.	Knight or Dame, Grand Cross Order of the British Empire
BBC	British Broadcasting Corporation		
B.D.	Bachelor of Divinity	G.C.B.	Knight Grand Cross of the Bath
B.L.S.	Bachelor of Library Science	G.O.P.	Grand Old Party
B.S.	Bachelor of Science		
		H.M.	His Majesty; Her Majesty
CAA	Civil Aeronautics Administration	HUD	Housing and Urban Development
CAB	Civil Aeronautics Board		
C.B.	Companion of the Bath	IBM	International Business Machine Corporation
C.B.E.	Commander of (the Order of) the British Empire		
		ICBM	Intercontinental Ballistic Missile
CBS	Columbia Broadcasting System	ICC	Interstate Commerce Commission
C.E.	Civil Engineer	I.C.F.T.U.	International Confederation of Free Trade Unions
CEA	Council of Economic Advisers		
C.E.D.	Committee for Economic Development	IGY	International Geophysical Year
		I.L.A.	International Longshoremen's Association
CENTO	Central Treaty Organization		
CIA	Central Intelligence Agency	I.L.G.W.U.	International Ladies' Garment Workers' Union
CIO	Congress of Industrial Organizations		
C.M.G.	Companion of (the Order of) St. Michael and St. George	I.L.O.	International Labor Organization
		IMF	International Monetary Fund
Com.	Commodore	INS	International News Service
CORE	Congress of Racial Equality	IRA	Irish Republican Army
		IRO	International Refugee Organization
D.A.R.	Daughters of the American Revolution	J.D.	Doctor of Jurisprudence
D.C.L.	Doctor of Civil Law		
D.D.	Doctor of Divinity	K.B.E.	Knight of (the Order of) the British Empire
D.Eng.	Doctor of Engineering		
DEW	Distant Early Warning Line	K.C.	King's Counsel
D.F.C.	Distinguished Flying Cross	K.C.B.	Knight Commander of the Bath
D.J.	Doctor of Jurisprudence		
D.Litt.	Doctor of Literature	L.H.D.	Doctor of Humanities
D.Mus.	Doctor of Music	Litt.D.	Doctor of Letters
DP	Displaced Person	LL.B.	Bachelor of Laws
D.Pol.Sc.	Doctor of Political Science	LL.D.	Doctor of Laws
D.Sc.	Doctor of Science		
D.S.C.	Distinguished Service Cross	M.A.	Master of Arts
D.S.M.	Distinguished Service Medal	M.B.A.	Master of Business Administration
D.S.O.	Distinguished Service Order	MBS	Mutual Broadcasting System

M.C.E.	Master of Civil Engineering	REA	Rural Electrification Administration
M.D.	Doctor of Medicine	RFC	Reconstruction Finance Corporation
M.E.	Master of Engineering	RKO	Radio-Keith-Orpheum
METO	Middle East Treaty Organization	ROTC	Reserve Officers' Training Corps
MGM	Metro-Goldwyn-Mayer		
M.Lit.	Master of Literature		
M.P.	Member of Parliament	SAC	Strategic Air Command
M.P.P.D.A.	Motion Picture Producers and Distributors of America	SALT	Strategic Arms Limitation Talks
		S.J.	Society of Jesus
MRP	Mouvement Républicain Populaire	SCAP	Supreme Command for the Allied Powers
MSA	Mutual Security Agency	SEATO	Southeast Asia Treaty Organization
M.Sc.	Master of Science	SEC	Securities and Exchange Commission
Msgr.	Monsignor, Monseigneur		
		SHAEF	Supreme Headquarters, Allied Expeditionary Force
NAACP	National Association for the Advancement of Colored People	SHAPE	Supreme Headquarters, Allied Powers Europe
NAB	National Association of Broadcasters	S.J.D.	Doctor of Juridical Science
		SLA	Special Libraries Association
NAM	National Association of Manufacturers	S.T.B.	Bachelor of Sacred Theology
		S.T.D.	Doctor of Sacred Theology
NASA	National Aeronautics and Space Administration		
NATO	North Atlantic Treaty Organization	TVA	Tennessee Valley Authority
NBC	National Broadcasting Company	T.W.U.A.	Textile Workers Union of America
NEA	National Education Association		
NLRB	National Labor Relations Board		
N.M.U.	National Maritime Union	UAR	United Arab Repubic
NOW	National Organization for Women	U.A.W.	United Automobile, Aircraft, and Agricultural Implement Workers of America
NRA	National Recovery Administration		
NRPB	National Resources Planning Board		
NYA	National Youth Administration	UMT	Universal Military Training
		U.M.W.A.	United Mine Workers of America
O.A.S.	Organization of American States	U.N.	United Nations
O.B.E.	Officer of (the Order of) the British Empire	UNESCO	United Nations Educational, Scientific, and Cultural Organization
OCD	Office of Civilian Defense	UNICEF	United Nations Children's Fund
OEEC	Organization for European Economic Cooperation	UNRRA	United Nations Relief and Rehabilitation Administration
OMB	Office of Management and Budget	U.P.I.	United Press and International News Service
OPA	Office of Price Administration		
OPEC	Organization of Petroleum Exporting Countries	USO	United Service Organizations
		U.S.S.R.	Union of Soviet Socialist Republics
OPM	Office of Production Management	U.S.W.A.	United Steel Workers of America
OWI	Office of War Information		
		VA	Veterans Administration
PBS	Public Broadcasting Service	V.F.W.	Veterans of Foreign Wars
P.E.N.	Poets, Playwrights, Editors, Essayists and Novelists (International Association)		
		W.F.T.U.	World Federation of Trade Unions
Ph.B.	Bachelor of Philosophy	WHO	World Health Organization
Ph.D.	Doctor of Philosophy	WMC	War Manpower Commission
PLO	Palestine Liberation Organization	WPA	Work Projects Administration
PWA	Public Works Administration	WPB	War Production Board
Q.C.	Queen's Counsel		
		YMCA	Young Men's Christian Association
		YMHA	Young Men's Hebrew Association
RAF	Royal Air Force	YWCA	Young Women's Christian Association
RCA	Radio Corporation of America		

Current Biography Yearbook 1981

Agam, Yaacov (ə-gäm′ yä-kof′)

May 11, 1928- Israeli artist. Address: b. c/o Galerie Denise René, 124 rue La Boétie, Paris 8°, France

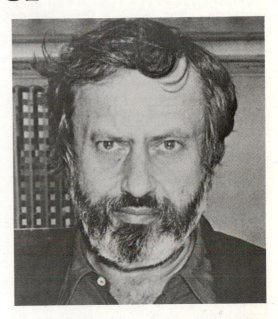

Yaacov Agam, the world-renowned Israeli artist who lives and works in Paris, pioneered in kinetic and optical art in the 1950's and has continued to experiment ceaselessly in many modes and media of the visual arts. Best known for the innovative three-dimensional paintings he calls polymorphic and contrapuntal, he has also created several types of transformable paintings and sculptures, as well as films, fountains, prints, theatre projects, and electronically controlled constructions. Although his works often beguile the eye with the decorative appeal of their simple geometric shapes and bright colors or gleaming metals, Agam intends them as expressions—through their movement or movability—of the transience of all human experience. He seeks to define himself essentially as a Jewish artist, not only by reflecting in his art a Jewish view of reality, but also by resolving through his use of a totally nonrepresentational subject matter the ancient Hebrew ban on graven images.

Yaacov Agam was born Yaacov Gibstein on May 11, 1928 in Rishon le Zion, an early Jewish settlement in what was then the British mandate of Palestine. His father, Yehoschua Gibstein, a Russian immigrant, was an Orthodox rabbi and student of Hebrew mystic texts; his mother, the former Yochevet Pombrovsky, was the daughter of a prosperous Jewish merchant in Poland. The Gibsteins were not wealthy, and the rabbi, absorbed in his holy books, cared little for the outside world. In boyhood Yaacov had few playthings but was free to amuse himself by roaming the colony and the surrounding hills and dunes. He did not enter school until he was thirteen because the settlement had no regular religious school, and his father would not send him to a secular one.

Referring to those years of involuntary hooky, Agam recalled in an interview for the New York *Post* (June 8, 1966), "I was thrown back on an inner world. I learned to use intuition, reason and reflexes." Significantly for the character that his art acquired, "the changing sky of Israel replaced the walls and ceiling of a classroom." Learning to draw at an early age, he saw the pictures that he traced on the sand transformed by the wind before they disappeared. Also important to his artistic development was his early instruction in music,

especially harmony. At the age of twelve he began playing the clarinet in an orchestra. He was also twelve when he read *Lust for Life*, Irving Stone's novel about the painter Van Gogh. "It showed me that painting was not just something decorative to be hung on the wall but was itself life. Everything could be expressed in a picture," he told Frank Popper, author of the biographical and critical study *Agam* (1976). Despite Talmudic strictures on representing images, Agam's family encouraged his talent in drawing.

At seventeen Agam was imprisoned for eighteen months by the British authorities as a suspected underground Zionist activist. When he was released from prison in 1946, he went to Jerusalem to study art at the Bezalel Academy of Arts and Design, where his teacher was Mordecai Ardon, who had been trained at the Bauhaus in Dessau, Germany. In 1949, on Ardon's recommendation, Agam went to Zurich to study with Johannes Itten, a former Bauhaus teacher, Siegfried Giedion, and Max Bill. Agam's sense of design and his use of shapes and colors derive largely from his early grounding in the Bauhaus tradition, which linked arts with crafts, favored geometric forms, and insisted that design take into consideration the nature of materials used.

In 1951 Agam left Zurich with the intention of studying—on Giedion's advice—at the Illinois Institute of Technology in Chicago. En route he passed through Paris and decided to stay. He found a teaching job, enrolled at the Académie de la Grande Chaumière, met the cubist painter Léger and the sculptor Brancusi, and mingled in surrealist circles. Max Ernst, a doyen of the surrealists, was the first to buy one of Agam's works.

Agam's first one-man show, held in 1953 at the Galerie Craven in Paris, was the first recorded one-man show of kinetic painting in art history. The exhibition included his transformable paintings, which a viewer can rearrange into an infinite number of variations by moving its several elements—such as a set of flat, colored shapes—around a background plane. With others in the Parisian avant-garde Agam participated from 1956 to 1958 in making experimental films, including *Recherche* (Search) and *Le Désert Chante* (Song of the Desert).

During the 1950's Agam perfected his techniques for creating a special kind of optical and kinetic art, a kind of relief painting he called polymorphic and contrapuntal, which presents several shifting, merging simultaneous images. He constructs the paintings with narrow, parallel, vertical, lathe-like strips, triangular in section, made of wood or aluminum, attached to a base plane so that they form a ridged, tightly pleated, or corrugated, surface. The two sides of the ribs—ranging from less than one inch to about four inches wide, depending on the painting's scale—are painted in various patterns, so that one design appears when the painting is viewed from the left, another when it is viewed from the right, another when viewed from the center, and an infinite series of views appears as the spectator moves back and forth. Agam sometimes paints two vertical strips on each rib face. One polymorphic painting can contain as many as nine separate patterns.

The merging of independent concurrent color designs corresponds to the interweaving of distinguishable melodic themes into one harmonic structure, as in counterpoint. Bach's fugues are believed to have inspired Agam's use of the word "contrapuntal" to describe his relief paintings, one of which, from the early 1960's, he titled *Homage to J. S. Bach*. The artist himself has explained, as quoted in *Look* (April 18, 1967), that his several types of painting "have in common a single objective—the introduction of the concept of time, duration through a new technique and a new aesthetic." His relief paintings move, change, and evolve in time as the spectator walks past them and, like reality itself, are perceptible only in stages and in part.

Time as well as motion is integral to Agam's variable, transformable, vibratory, or tactile paintings, the pictures with which he began his career and on which he has continued to experiment, sometimes introducing sound and lighting effects. He creates works that a viewer can alter manually by spinning them around, by brushing a hand over elements mounted on

springs, by moving pieces on pegs from one hole to another in a board, or by swiveling certain elements on pivot attachments. Agam has even produced a machine that blows color bubbles of a size and at a rate determined by a viewer's handling of a control mechanism.

In all of his work Agam wants to involve the viewer directly in an act of artistic creation, which he regards as God-like. He encourages viewers to engage his constructions directly by moving around them, touching them, altering them. That aspect of his painting and sculpture reflects Agam's desire to create an art, as he told Frank Popper, "based on the concept of no longer representing fixed situations but simply *possibilities* in the midst of a constant being. . . . I only create things that are constantly changing. There is no single image." The totally abstract—nonemotional, nonrepresentational—character of Agam's work reflects not only his use of Bauhaus ideas, but his effort to come to grips, as a devout Jew, with the Mosaic proscription of graven images. "For me," he has said, "it is neither poetry nor representation that counts but the visual representation of the essence of Jewish spiritualism."

Since his solo exhibition at the Galerie Craven, Agam has had more than twenty others. One of the major shows was a 1972 retrospective in Paris organized jointly by the Musée National d'Art Moderne and the Centre National des Arts Contemporains and shown thereafter at the Stadtisches Museum in Düsseldorf, the Stedelijk Museum in Amsterdam, and the Tel Aviv Museum. Agam has also been included in several significant group shows. In 1955 he was represented in the first group show of kinetic art, "Le Mouvement," at the Galerie Denise René, Paris, with Jésus Soto, Pol Bury, Jean Tinguely, Alexander Calder, and other avant-garde champions of motion in art. In 1963 he represented Israel at the seventh Bienal of São Paulo, Brazil, where he received an award for artistic research.

Reviewing "The Responsive Eye," a 1965 group exhibition of optical art at the Museum of Modern Art in New York, John Canaday, art critic of the New York *Times* (February 28, 1966), praised the "brilliant show" for its "display of craftsmanship in the service of a new idea as to what art should be about in this century." He singled out for description Agam's giant vibratory relief painting *Double Metamorphosis II*, which was soon afterward acquired by the museum for its permanent collection. Canaday's comment that the op art constructions in the show "have the glorious virtue of being free from association" is clearly relevant to Agam.

A large display of more than a hundred works at Manhattan's Marlborough-Gerson Gallery in 1966, Agam's first one-man show in the United States, drew mixed reactions locally. In her review of the exhibition in the New York *Post* (May 28, 1966), Charlotte Willard called Agam "a man to watch—and applaud" and declared that his paintings "sparkle and glint with color, brilliant, subtle, and completely masterful." On the other hand, in the New York *Times* (May 14, 1966) critic Hilton Kramer wrote that Agam's originality is "mainly technical" and that the very extensiveness of the show pointed up Agam's "general paucity of pictorial or sculptural invention."

Determinedly explorative, nevertheless, in 1966 Agam began to experiment with transformable sculpture, multiple-unit works that can be manipulated into an endless variety of forms. His sculptures of that type are all based on the same principle, a repetition of simple shapes, usually in a graded series of sizes, that can be moved around each other to form varying though related shapes. Often made of tubing of highly polished chrome steel or other metals, they range from table-top models to monuments sixty feet tall. One of them, *Three by Three Interplay*, transformable by means of a winch, has been installed in front of the Juilliard School of Music at Lincoln Center, New York (1971); another is in front of Israel's Presidential Palace in Jerusalem (1972); another is an enormous musical fountain in Paris' Quartier de la Défense (1976).

Even for an artist as energetic and prolific as Agam, the number of his commissions during the past two decades has almost overwhelmed his capability. His major commissions include a twenty-seven-foot-high mural for the Israeli ship *Shalom* (1964); a ten-by-197-foot ceiling mural for the National Convention Center in Jerusalem (1965); a kinetic "environment"—a room for which he designed murals, ceiling, carpet, and doors—in the Elysée Palace, Paris (1972), now installed in the Centre Pompidou; and a thirty-foot-square mural in Birmingham, Alabama (1979).

One of Agam's largest commissions is an encircling, hexagonal mural that he completed in 1970 for a concert hall in the cultural center of Leverkusen, West Germany. It comprises six polymorphic paintings, each eighteen by thirty-three feet, covered with 1,000 pounds of paint in 347 colors, completely enclosing a windowless space. Even the door is treated as part of the mural. The end result exhilarated some viewers but disturbed others, such as some city fathers, who feared that the mural's shifting images would distract both performers and audiences. Agam, however, does not intend his art to be restful. To him, the Leverkusen mural is a "living wall." "Like reality," he was quoted in *Time* (May 18, 1970) as explaining, "it is changing, disappearing, ever present. Its impact comes from its attempt to accept change."

"Agam: Beyond the Visible," a show of twenty-five works at the Guggenheim Museum in New York in 1980, included two pieces created expressly for the exhibition: *Aenitral*, a forty-eight-foot-high, four-foot-square tower, which was to be rebuilt in a Miami hotel, and *Panoramagam*, a relief mural running along a section of the face of the museum's interior spiral. The show also displayed a sculpture made up of 180 cubes in a variety of designs that were intended to serve also as movable seats during performances of a play by Eugène Ionesco in a theatre, conceived by Agam in 1962, in which the dramatic action surrounds the spectators as several scenes take place simultaneously on several stages. The play never officially opened, reportedly because of a disagreement between Agam and Ionesco, who felt that simultaneous presentation of different scenes, rather than the same scene, would create cacophony.

When Theodore F. Wolff reviewed the Guggenheim show for the *Christian Science Monitor* (October 22, 1980), he praised it as "extremely attractive," assuring his readers, "The shapes are clean and well defined, the colors are bright and clear, the movements beautifully choreographed." But he protested that despite "the declarations of profound intent given to these works by Mr. Agam, . . . the works themselves exist as extremely handsome and lively decoration—and very little else." Agam's characteristic response to criticism of his work appears in Popper's book: "If you have nothing childlike in you, you shouldn't be looking at paintings. . . . I am trying to make things that are very, very serious, and what comes out of it is things that are quite friendly, gay, and sometimes even amusing." One such intriguing piece is a pulsing heart-shaped mobile, which Agam gave to President Ronald Reagan, along with three other sculptures, when he moved into the White House in 1981. (Agam was introduced to Reagan by Walter Annenberg and his wife, Leonore Annenberg, chief of protocol, who are collectors of his creations.)

The apparent contradiction between the simplicity and gaiety of his colorful designs and his philosophical message lessens when a distinction is made between the *content* of his works, which produces almost purely visual pleasure, and their *form*, which expresses the mutability and transience of existence. In Agam's words: "I have tried to express the marvels of life, while remaining true to the vision that eternity does not exist."

Yaacov Agam is a stocky, bearded man, self-assured and exuberant in discussing his work. On November 29, 1956 he married Clila Lusternik, a native of Rehavot, Israel. They have two sons, Ron (born in 1958) and Orram (born in 1963), and a daughter, Orrit (born in 1969). Several years ago he moved with his family to a country estate but kept his Paris apartment and his studio at Montparnasse.

As a guest lecturer at Harvard University in 1968, Agam conducted a seminar in his theory of visual communication. He also lectured, as visiting distinguished professor of art, at Washington University in the fall of 1980, when a large exhibition of his painting and sculpture was held at the Neiman-Marcus store in St. Louis, Missouri. A collection of his writings, *Y. Agam*, was published in Neuchâtel in 1962. His honors include the Chevalier de l'Ordre des Arts et Lettres (1974), an honorary Ph.D. degree from Tel Aviv University (1975), and the Medal of the Council of Europe (1977). France also honored him in 1980 by issuing a postage stamp of his design.

References: Art in America 67:163 My '79 por; Christian Sci Mon p21 D 21 '72; N Y Post p47 Je 8 '66, p31 Jl 23 '74 por; N Y Times II p29 My 22 '66 por; People 15:105+ Ap 20 '81 pors; Time 95:66+ My 18 '70; Contemporary Artists (1977); Dictionnaire des Peintres, Sculpteurs, Dessinateurs et Gravures (1976); Metken, Günter. Agam (1977)

Ashley, Merrill

1950- Dancer. Address: b. c/o New York City Ballet, New York State Theatre, Lincoln Center for the Performing Arts, New York City, N.Y. 10023

With her precisely articulated footwork, blinding speed, effortless grace, and innate musicality, Merrill Ashley is the quintessential "dancer's dancer." A member of George Balanchine's iconoclastic New York City Ballet since 1967, she is arguably its most brilliant technician. Her peerless allegro technique in such virtuosic ballets as *Ballo della Regina*, *Divertimento No. 15*, and *Square Dance* has stunned balletomanes and obliged critics to reach for superlatives. She is, as Arlene Croce has observed, "the modern liberated woman as ballerina—aggressive, work-proud, mistrustful of glamour, dependent on no one for effects." Indeed, Miss Ashley's independence is such that when her partner, Robert Weiss, became

disabled in the middle of *Ballo della Regina* on the opening night of the spring 1980 New York season, she coolly modified some of the steps and finished the ballet alone.

Merrill Ashley was born Linda Merrill in St. Paul, Minnesota in 1950, the daughter of Harvie and Mardelle (Edwards) Merrill. (She took the professional name Merrill Ashley when she joined the New York City Ballet, which at the time numbered among its ranks another dancer named Linda Merrill.) A short time later, Miss Ashley moved with her family to Rutland, Vermont, where she spent most of her childhood. An athletic child, she learned to ice skate, ski, and ride horseback, and she reveled in the basic gymnastics course she took at the neighborhood elementary school.

Miss Ashley first became interested in dance when she visited her older sister's ballet class. At the age of seven, she too began taking weekly ballet lessons from Sybil de Neergaarde, a local teacher. Encouraged by her parents, who were, in her words, "fostering always, but never pushing," she continued her training with Phyllis Marmein, in Schenectady, New York and with professional teachers in New York City and at summer dance camps. After completing an intensive summer program at the School of American Ballet, the New York City Ballet's official school, in 1964, Miss Ashley was awarded a Ford Foundation scholarship to study full time at the school.

In addition to committing themselves to several hours of daily ballet instruction, students at the School of American Ballet were required to take a regular course of study at the nearby Professional Children's School, but for Merrill Ashley, ballet was "all there was." As she told Tobi Tobias years later in an interview for *Dance* magazine (June 1979), "During those early teens, it was just fine with me to be absorbed in ballet. Later on, perhaps, you realize the parts of being young you've missed. There are those big blank spaces. Suddenly you want to meet people and do things in the outside world—and you don't know how. But at the time, wrapped up in that intense, narrow life of the work in the school, I was perfectly happy."

Miss Ashley received her high school diploma from the Professional Children's School in 1967, and in October of that year, at the invitation of George Balanchine, the director of City Ballet, she joined the company's corps de ballet. Although she was assigned several solo roles during her first few years with the company, she soon experienced the frustrations common to most talented corps dancers. Admittedly impatient to take on leading roles, she nonetheless sensed that something was "terribly lacking" in her performances. For Tobi Tobias, she analyzed what she saw as her shortcomings: "Technically I was a whiz, and maybe that was the problem. I was all legs and feet. From the waist up, though, I wasn't very exciting. Onstage I was too mild, and one-dimensional. . . . I was almost completely unknowledgeable about the performing aspect of dancing. I had no natural instinct for it, I guess, and the school didn't emphasize it at all in its teaching." Jaded New York dance critics occasionally agreed with her assessment. For example, in his New York Times (January 25, 1970) review of her performance as the lead girl in the energetic fourth movement of John Clifford's Stravinsky Symphony, Don McDonagh noted tersely, "Miss Ashley launched herself into the role with the subtlety of a kamikaze pilot, accompanied by a concomitant disregard of the nuances of performance that might be expected."

With the help of Jacques d'Amboise, a veteran principal dancer known for his finely etched interpretations, Miss Ashley gradually learned the difference between "giving a performance and just going out there and doing the steps," as she put it. For several years, she performed regularly with d'Amboise's small touring group, dancing such roles as Polyhymnia and Terpsichore in Apollo, the pas de deux from A Midsummer Night's Dream, and leading parts in Who Cares? and Raymonda Variations. The experience she gained eventually led to more important roles with the parent company, among them solos in d'Amboise's Irish Fantasy and Saltarelli, a sprightly trio that he created especially for her, in Balanchine's Cortège Hongrois, and in Jerome Robbins' Dances at a Gathering.

Miss Ashley found Robbins' inventive, flowing choreography, which she has compared to time-lapse photography, particularly difficult to master. Looking back on her first, tentative portrayals of the Girl in Mauve in his Dances at a Gathering, she conceded to Tobi Tobias that she had been "too bold" and "too strong in a forced way." In time, however, she captured the emotional essence of the role, giving it a "quiet grace" and "muted elegance" that "lent poignancy to the ballet as a whole," as John Gruen observed in the New York Times (May 1, 1977).

Promoted to soloist in 1974, Miss Ashley added to her repertory such principal roles as the exuberant "Liberty Bell-El Capitán" pas de deux in Stars and Stripes, the "Sanguinic" movement of The Four Temperaments, Dew Drop and the Sugar Plum Fairy in the company's traditional Christmas offering of The Nutcracker, the waltz variation in La Ventana, the angular, flashy "Rubies" section of Jewels, and the technically demanding "Theme and Variations" from Suite No. 3. She also took leading parts in such City Ballet staples as Tchaikovsky Concerto No. 2, Agon, Who Cares?, Divertimento No. 15, Donizetti Variations, Symphony in C, Brahms-Schönberg Quartet, Symphony in Three Movements, and Square Dance, all choreographed by Balanchine, and in Jacques d'Amboise's Tchaikovsky Suite No. 2, with its intimidating series of whirlwind double pirouettes.

Miss Ashley's long-awaited debut in the lively and witty Square Dance, in Washington, D.C. in March 1977, did not disappoint the growing contingent of Ashley cultists among New York City Ballet regulars. "It is the performance the ballet has been waiting for—full of sharp, bright photoflash pictures," Arlene Croce wrote in the New Yorker (March 21, 1977). "The old version of the role was more complex than the version Ashley has been given to do; she could be the one to restore the exploding passage of beats in the finale or, in the pas de deux, the opening into arabesques that ends each sequence of double turns under the boy's arms."

In September 1977 Merrill Ashley was elevated to the rank of principal dancer. To display the quicksilver speed and unparalleled allegro technique of his newest ballerina, Balanchine created for her the ballet that has become her signature piece: Ballo della Regina. Set to the ballet music from Verdi's opera Don Carlo, Ballo is a choreographic trial by fire—a technically taxing series of solos and duets demanding brisk, precision footwork, dizzying off-balance turns, staccato hops on point, sharp split leaps, and sudden shifts in direction. Miss Ashley carried it off with astonishing ease and queenly authority. "[Balanchine] could not have done Ballo five years ago," Peter Martins, an admiring City Ballet colleague said, as quoted in Time magazine (February 6, 1978). "It is all Merrill. She executed steps at speeds that seem impossible. And she never takes a short cut."

By her own admission, Miss Ashley is happiest "dancing alone" in allegro roles, such as Ballo or the dazzling, neoclassical Allegro Brillante. "I've always liked quick things, but I have trouble moving slowly," she confessed in an interview for Ballet News (June 1979). "I always feel I'm not doing enough." To help her extend her range, Balanchine deliberately cast against type and assigned her partnered adagio roles, including the cool, elegant "Emeralds" section and the Petipa-influenced "Diamonds" pas de deux in Jewels; Robbins' lyrical In the Night, a companion piece to Dances at a Gathering; and his own personalized, one-act version of Swan Lake.

Always in command of the technical requirements of Swan Lake, Miss Ashley gradually acquired the deliquescent legato phrasing and mastered the dramatic nuances of the role of the enchanted Swan Queen. Her tender portrayal makes of the central pas de deux a "silent unfolding of body and soul," as Linda Small noted in a review for Dance magazine (October 1981). "[She] projects a tragic fragility by holding back the more rounded, full effect she's capable of. . . . With Ashley's concentration and Balanchine's spareness of design, this spiritual essence of Swan Lake makes the idea of detailed story ballet, with extraneous characters and dances, seem indulgent and unnecessary." Despite her success in the role, Miss Ashley has no desire to play the dual role of Odette/Odile in the full-length Petipa-Ivanov Swan Lake or, for that matter, to dance in any of the nineteenth-century classics. "Balanchine and Robbins have created classics of their own, and they're just as demanding and just as challenging as *Swan Lake, Giselle,* or *The Sleeping Beauty,*" she insisted to one interviewer.

Since becoming a principal dancer, Miss Ashley has annexed to her large and varied repertory the "Voices of Spring" segment of the crowd-pleasing *Vienna Waltzes;* the "Flower Festival" pas de deux in *Bournonville Divertissements;* Jerome Robbins' *In G Major, The Goldberg Variations,* and *The Four Seasons; La Source,* a sophisticated, extended pas de deux; *Raymonda Variations,* a choreographic exercise in pure, nineteenth-century classical style; *An Evening's Waltzes;* the "Pas Degas" section of *Tricolore;* and the sultry "My One and Only" solo from *Who Cares?* Partnered by fellow City Ballet principals Adam Lüders and Robert Weiss, she performed two of her newer roles, *Tchaikovsky Pas de Deux* and *Valse-Fantaisie,* at the White House in May 1978 for President Jimmy Carter and his distinguished guests from the NATO countries.

In the spring of 1980 Balanchine created for Merrill Ashley a tailor-made exercise in lyricism called *Ballade.* Like many technically superlative "pure" dancers, Miss Ashley had always found it difficult to relax onstage. As a result, her dancing was, by her own estimation, "too neat," "methodical," and "lifeless." To coax a more personal performance out of his ballerina, Balanchine, in making *Ballade,* focused not on steps, as he had done in *Ballo della Regina,* but on the highly individual way in which Miss Ashley executes steps. As Arlene Croce observed in her long and thoughtful analysis of the ballet for the *New Yorker* (June 2, 1980), *"Ballade* reshapes her technique so that the way she dances becomes a legitimization and a rationalization of the way she *looks* when she dances. . . . The choreography not only permits but caters to Ashley's characteristic angularity and to something effaced and averted in her temperament."

After several viewings, Miss Croce reported that Miss Ashley had easily met the technical challenge of *Ballade,* "dancing with a virtuosity more serene at every performance," but that she had as yet failed to give the work an emotional flavor. The critic was especially bothered by the apparent lack of rapport between Miss Ashley and her partner, Ib Andersen. "She never really looks at him," Miss Croce complained. "Is she running from him? Making him up in her mind? When Ashley decides that the placing and weighing of Andersen's presence in the ballet is her responsibility, she'll have matured as a performer. A prodigious dancer will have become a ballerina."

Miss Ashley danced the premiere of *Ballade,* in May 1980, in considerable pain. Prone to injuries, she had lost, by her count, "at least two full years" of her professional career because of torn ligaments, tendonitis, pulled

muscles, and bruised bones, and she was loath to lose additional time. Because the persistent pain in her left hip did not affect her dancing, she continued to perform and even occasionally filled in for other ailing ballerinas. By July 1980, however, the pain had become so severe that she was forced to stop.

Having diagnosed her injury as a tear of the left tensor fascia lata, the muscle that controls turnout, several orthopedic specialists recommended surgery, but Miss Ashley preferred a less radical course. Over the next few months, she tried rest, physical therapy, acupuncture, isometric exercises, chiropractic, and ultrasound treatments. Her recovery was frustratingly slow. Although she was limited in what roles she could do, she finally returned to the company in December 1980. "I was literally bursting with joy to be onstage, savoring every instant out there," she told a writer for *Ballet News* (June 1981). "It reminded me how much it means to perform, and that it's worth all the hard work."

To Miss Ashley's dismay, the strenuous activity eventually aggravated her injury, and the pain returned. In April 1981 she flew to England, where she was operated on by Dr. Eivind Thomasen, the Danish orthopedic surgeon who has saved the careers of several prominent ballerinas. Just a few weeks later, she was back on the stage of the New York State Theatre, dancing two of her most demanding roles—*Divertimento No. 15* and *Ballo della Regina*—and, for the Tchaikovsky Festival that was the highlight of the City Ballet's 1981 New York summer season, *Swan Lake* and the "Diamonds" pas de deux, retitled *Andante Elegiac* for the occasion.

With her long, lean legs, Merrill Ashley appears to be even taller than her five feet seven inches. She has a sharp-featured, elfin face, large, almond-shaped hazel eyes, and long, chestnut-brown hair. Although she admits to having "a terrible sweet tooth," she does not need to follow a strict diet to keep her weight at about 115 pounds as long as she is dancing regularly. Like most dancers, Miss Ashley leads a disciplined, regimented life structured around daily morning classes, afternoon rehearsals, and evening performances. "Doing what I do, I've got to run my body like an efficient machine, putting it in gear to work hard during the day while still conserving enough energy to let loose in the evening, when it really counts," she explained to Harry Stein in an interview for an *Esquire* magazine (September 1979) profile. After performances, she usually unwinds by having a late dinner with her husband, Kibbe Fitzpatrick, a simultaneous interpreter of French and Spanish into English at the United Nations, whom she married on September 6, 1980. "I like it that he's not a dancer," she told Harry Stein. "Mine is often a very closed world; it's terribly refreshing to be able to step into his."

Recognizing that dancers have a short professional career, Miss Ashley has vowed never to be seen onstage as a "broken-down ballerina," but she has also questioned the wisdom of early retirement. "It's always seemed to me terribly unfair—and silly, too—that people in my business have to retire after they've accrued all those years of experience simply because they can no longer consistently execute the most difficult movements," she explained to Harry Stein. "There are plenty of roles where the technical requirements aren't so demanding. Why not have companies of older dancers performing those ballets? I know when the time comes, I'd join one of them in a second—and go on for just as long as I could." Miss Ashley lives with her husband in an apartment on Manhattan's Upper West Side, within walking distance of the Lincoln Center for the Performing Arts, the home base of the New York City Ballet.

References: Dance 53:49+ Je '79 pors; Esquire 92:73+ S '79 por; N Y Post p39+ N 11 '77 por; N Y Times II p1+ Ja 4 '81 pors; Time 111:64+ F 6 '78 por; Vogue 170:84 N '80 por

---

Austin, Tracy

Dec. 12, 1962- Tennis player. Address: b. c/o United States Tennis Association, 51 E. 42nd St., New York City, N.Y. 10017

Ranked among the top ten women players in the world when she was only fifteen, Tracy Austin made international headlines as a pint-sized, pigtailed tennis prodigy when she took on the invincible Chris Evert Lloyd in the 1977 Wimbledon tennis tournament. In 1979, just one year after she had turned professional, she became the youngest player, male or female, ever to win the United States Open. A fiercely competitive player who combines the baseline steadiness of Chris Evert Lloyd with the aggressive attack of Billie Jean King, the young right-hander is known for her speed, footwork, and her extraordinary court know-how.

The youngest of the five children of George and Jeanne Austin, Tracy Ann Austin was born on December 12, 1962 in Redondo Beach, California. Her father, a nuclear physicist in the aerospace industry, and her mother were avid tennis players, as were her four older siblings, three of whom—Jeff, John, and Pam—attained some distinction as touring professionals on the international tennis circuit. Succumbing to the family passion, Tracy Austin began swinging a cut-down tennis racket when she was just two years old. Mrs. Austin frequently took her daughter to the local Jack Kramer tennis club, and while she worked in the pro shop, the little girl practised hitting balls against a wall. Vic Braden, then the head teaching pro at the club, was so impressed by the child's extraordinary eye-hand coordination that he began coaching her. By the time she was five years old, she was good enough to rally with college students.

Miss Austin entered her first tennis tournament when she was only seven. Undeterred by her first-round loss to a twelve-year-old player, she continued to practise daily and, the following year, she won both the ten-year-old-and-under and the twelve-year-old-and-under singles championships for the city of Los Angeles, California. Robert Lansdorp, a former member of the Netherlands' Davis Cup squad and Braden's successor as head pro, took over as Miss Austin's coach in about 1970. Under his guidance, she took the national girls' title for twelve-year-olds, in 1974, and for fourteen-year-olds, in 1975 and 1976, and the indoor singles championship for girls aged sixteen and under, in 1976. Over the next few months, she continued to defeat older and physically stronger players. She even bested former United States Open winners Bobby Riggs and Jack Kramer in exhibition matches. Although she regularly spent up to four hours a day on the tennis court, Miss Austin maintained a straight "A" average at the Dapple Gray Intermediate School, where she also played on the girls' basketball, softball, and volleyball teams.

By the beginning of 1977 Miss Austin had won ten national junior titles and nearly 200 trophies. Ready to test her skill against the professionals, she entered the Avon Futures tournament in Portland, Oregon in January 1977 and won it with comparative ease, thus becoming the youngest player ever to take a pro singles title. With 128 tournament victories to her credit, Miss Austin decided, in June 1977, to compete in the women's singles event at Wimbledon, England. In her first-round match, before a standing-room-only crowd, she stunned Elly Vessies-Appel, 6-3, 6-3, and totally captivated Britons, who were as taken by her pigtails, braces, and gingham pinafores as they were by her superior court coverage and unusually strong baseline volleys. Miss Austin's next opponent was Chris Evert, the reigning Wimbledon champion and her longtime idol. Relying heavily on well-placed drop shots, Miss Evert needed just forty-nine minutes to take the match, 6-1, 6-1, but because eight of the fourteen games went to deuce, the match was closer than the final score indicates.

Miss Austin was not expected to survive the first few rounds of the United States Open in September 1977, but after a nervous, three-set, first-round victory over Heidi Eisterlehner, she beat her next two opponents handily. A come-from-behind victory over Virginia Ruzici earned her a berth in the quarterfinals, but the diminutive teenager was no match for the strong and experienced Betty Stove. Miss Stove, who was then a foot taller and seventy pounds heavier than Miss Austin, simply overpowered the younger girl, 6-2, 6-2, with an astonishing thirty-seven winners.

Over the next few months Miss Austin took time out from her classes at Rolling Hills High School in Rolling Hills, California to play in several important junior tournaments, winning the sixteen-and-under national singles title and the girls' eighteen-division crown at the Rolex International Junior Tennis Tournament. Her eighteen national championships and her 153 tournament victories earned her *Tennis* magazine's Rookie of the Year award for 1977. To qualify for the 1978 Wimbledon and United States Open tournaments, Miss Austin entered a number of women's events, most notably the Maureen Connolly Brinker Charity Open in March 1978, in which she halted Martina Navratilova's thirty-seven-match winning streak before falling to Evonne Goolagong Cawley in the final, 6-4, 0-6, 2-6, and the *Family Circle*-sponsored tourney in April 1978, in which she became Chris Evert's 117th consecutive victim in clay-court singles matches. Since the 1977 Wimbledon contest, Miss Austin herself had lost only eight singles matches, all to top professionals.

Four inches taller and fifteen pounds heavier than she had been in the summer of 1977, Miss Austin, playing an especially aggressive game, reached the fourth round at Wimbledon, where she lost to a determined Martina Navratilova. Disappointed by her defeat, the teenager took some consolation in winning the Wimbledon junior crown and, in August 1978, her second consecutive girls' eighteen-and-under national singles title. At home on the clay-type composition courts at Forest Hills, she breezed through her early rounds at the United States Open to advance to the quarterfinals against Chris Evert. Equally matched in the first set, the younger girl visibly tired in the second set and lost to Miss Evert, 5-7, 1-6.

After discussing the matter with her family, Miss Austin decided, in October 1978, to turn professional. "I've been playing on the pro tour as an amateur for more than a year now, and it just seemed like the right time," she said, as quoted in the *Christian Science Monitor* (October 31, 1978). "I don't feel that becoming a professional will change my life that much. I'm used to the practice and traveling, only instead of roses now when I win, I'll get money." In her first outing as a professional, she subdued Betty Stove, 6-3, 6-3, in the final of an international invitational tourney in Stuttgart, West Germany, then teamed with her erstwhile adversary to capture the doubles title. A few weeks later, she routed Miss Navratilova, 6-1, 6-1, in the final of an eight-player tournament in Tokyo, Japan. Using her consistent baseline play to good advantage, she also helped the United States women's team to its third consecutive Federation Cup, in December 1978.

As the women's winter tour progressed, Miss Austin continued to play with supreme confidence, even against such formidable antagonists as Miss Navratilova. In an Avon contest in Washington, D.C. in January 1979, for example, she upset the top-seeded Czech, 6-3, 6-2, by keeping her impeccable baseline returns deep and by hammering away at Miss Navratilova's weak backhand. In the eight-player, double-elimination Avon Championship in New York City's Madison Square Garden in March 1979, she relied on slashing drives and well-paced groundstrokes to defeat Wendy Turnbull, Dianne Fromholtz, and for the first time in her career, Chris Evert, and thus gain a spot in the final. Troubled by a faulty forehand, she eventually crumbled under Miss Navratilova's powerful twisting serve and penetrating forehand, 3-6, 6-3, 2-6. As runner-up, Miss Austin collected $52,000, bringing her total winnings in her first six months on the tour to $173,000.

In a grim baseline duel at the Colgate Women's Italian Open in May 1979, Miss Austin brought Chris Evert's string of clay-court victories to an end at 125 with a 6-4, 2-6, 7-6 triumph in the semifinals. Fatigued by that grueling contest, she faltered briefly in the second set of the final against Sylvia Hanika of West Germany, but recovered sufficiently to win her first major international title, 6-4, 1-6, 6-3.

Going into the 1979 Wimbledon tourney, the fourth-seeded Miss Austin, who was then ranked third in the world, had a professional match record of fifty-seven wins and eleven losses in singles competition and fourteen and seven in doubles. Hobbled by a leg injury, she played rather tentatively in the first few rounds, but nonetheless managed to put together a string of respectable victories, including a 6-4, 6-7, 6-2 quarterfinal conquest of Billie Jean King, a six-time Wimbledon singles champion. Her winning string was snapped in straight sets in the semifinals by Miss Navratilova's overwhelming serve-and-volley game.

Under the watchful eye of her longtime coach, Robert Lansdorp, Miss Austin steadily improved her consistent baseline game, but her deep groundstrokes, beautifully timed passing shots, deft drop shots, and sharply angled crosscourt backhands were often undermined by her weak serve. To help her turn it into an equally formidable weapon, she enlisted the aid of Roy Emerson, a two-time Wimbledon champion known for his blistering serves. Relying heavily on her newly perfected serve, Miss Austin, the third seed at the 1979 United States Open, lost only one set—to Kathy Jordan, in a hotly contested match marred by questionable and late calls—on her way to the semifinals against Martina Navratilova. Nervous after several double faults, Miss Austin squandered a 5-2 lead in the first set, then settled down to play her nearly flawless baseline game. Her 7-5, 7-5 win earned her the right to challenge Chris Evert Lloyd, who was trying for an unprecedented fifth consecutive Open singles titles, in the championship.

In the rather uneventful final, which the New York *Times*'s Neil Amdur called "a looking-glass war," the two well-matched young women traded service breaks and unforced errors during routine baseline rallies that were, in Amdur's words, "won more on mental attrition than physical superiority." Cashing in on Mrs. Lloyd's critical mistakes, Miss Austin took the match, 6-4, 6-3, and with it, the United States Open singles titles. The victor attributed her win to "mental toughness." "I play my game," she told reporters in the traditional post-match press conference. "I wasn't going to change a winning game. [Mrs. Lloyd's] won it four times, and I think it was time to give me a chance. . . . It would be reaching a bit to say I'm number one, but I'm close up there, maybe two or three."

As if proving her claim, Miss Austin, over the next few months, whipped Mrs. Lloyd and Miss Navratilova in an international tournament in Stuttgart and Mrs. King and Miss Navratilova in the all-star invitational Emeron Cup meet in Tokyo. She was especially effective against the Czech, trouncing her in two finals matches, 6-2, 6-0 and 6-2, 6-1. In November 1979 her superlative performances contributed significantly to the United States squad's triumph over Great Britain in the fifty-first Wightman Cup competition. In the course of that contest, Miss Austin stunned Virginia Wade and Sue Barker in straight sets in singles play and, paired with Ann Kiyomura, ousted a relatively inexperienced British doubles team, 6-3, 6-1.

Throughout that period, Miss Austin continued to maintain an "A-minus" average at Rolling Hills High School. Usually alternating a week on tour with two weeks at school, she carried a minumum load of three academic courses and earned additional credits in a special "work experience" program by playing tennis. Miss Austin's mother accompanied her on road trips, and her coach often joined her for major tournaments. Because of the age difference, she found it difficult to make friends with the other players on the tour, but a few of the older women—Wendy Turnbull, Betty Stove, Françoise Durr—have become her confidantes and, occasionally, her doubles partners. In her first full year as a pro, Miss Austin grossed $568,457 and won the titles of Most Improved Player of the Year from *Tennis* magazine and Female Athlete of the Year from the Associated Press.

Continuing her domination of Chris Evert Lloyd, Miss Austin overwhelmed her former idol no less than three times in two weeks in January 1980. In desperation, Mrs. Lloyd, a fellow baseliner, repeatedly tried to alter the pace of the games with drop shots, but more often than not, Miss Austin, cannily anticipating the tactic, returned forcing shots. She was generally less successful against Martina Navratilova. In the final of the Colgate Series Championship in January 1980, Miss Navratilova displayed such awesome power and technical brilliance that Miss Austin lost the first point in every service game and won a total of only eight points in the entire second set. She avenged that embarrassing 6-2, 6-1 rout two months later, in the final of the $300,000 Avon Championships. Playing an aggressive and daring game, she relentlessly fired backhand bullets down the line and sliced crosscourt winners at extreme angles to keep her adversary hustling and off-balance. Forced by an erratic serve to play Miss Austin's game, Miss Navratilova succumbed, 2-6, 6-2, 2-6. A week later Miss Austin repeated the humiliation with a straight set victory over Miss Navratilova in the final of the Clairol Championship in Carlsbad, California.

Miss Austin warmed up for the 1980 Wimbledon competition by topping Wendy Turnbull, 7-6, 6-2, in the final of the $125,000 BMW tournament in Eastbourne, England. Aided by a favorable draw, she easily advanced to the Wimbledon semifinals only to lose, 3-6, 6-0, 4-6, to Evonne Goolagong Cawley. Within hours, however, she and her brother John had outlasted the Australian team of Dianne Fromholtz and Mark Edmonson, 4-6, 7-6, 6-3, to secure the mixed doubles title. In preparation for her defense of her United States Open crown, Miss Austin worked on a new serve, which was, by her estimation, "maybe one mile [per hour] faster." Occasionally bothered by a sore serving arm, she played rather erratically in her early-round Open matches against Anne Smith, Rosie Casals, and Pam Shriver, and quickly fell behind Mrs. Lloyd, who had recovered her old form, in the semifinals, 6-4, 1-6, 1-6.

Plagued by recurrent injuries, Miss Austin temporarily withdrew from tournament play in January 1981 to recover from a severely inflamed sciatic nerve. She got off to a shaky start when she finally returned to the women's tour four months later, but with the help of Marty Riessen, her new adviser and practice partner, she quickly regained her old form, winning the Eastbourne BMW and Canadian

Open titles. In September 1981 she bounced back from a 1-6 deficit in the first set to edge out Martina Navratilova, 1-6, 7-6, 7-6, for her second United States Open title.

In mid-1980 Miss Austin became the youngest player ever to win $1,000,000. Her finances, tournament contracts, and business interests are looked after by Sara Kleppinger, a sports attorney with the firm of Dell, Craighill, Fentress, & Benton, from whom Miss Austin draws a small allowance. She has only a few endorsement contracts, with Wilson rackets and Pony tennis shoes, and she has accepted just three commercial commitments, for Canon AE-1 cameras, a Japanese textile firm, and Knudsen's, a California dairy. "I don't want to spend what free time I have making TV commercials or promoting products," she said, as quoted in the Washington *Post* (August 19, 1979). "I want to live as normally as I can, which under the circumstances is not too easy."

Blue-eyed, freckled-faced Tracy Austin stands about five feet four inches tall and weighs around 110 pounds. She has long legs and unusually large feet for a young woman of her height. During matches, she wears her shoulder-length strawberry-blond hair pulled back in a ponytail. Considering her fame and accomplishments, she is surprisingly unaffected. Although she is sometimes reticent with reporters, she is garrulous and impishly humorous with her friends. When she is not following the pro circuit, Miss Austin relaxes by going to movies and by listening to music, especially discs and tapes by Billy Joel, Blondie, and Donna Summer. Like many teenagers, she is inordinately fond of junk food and is admittedly addicted to mint chip ice cream. She makes her home with her parents in Rolling Hills, California.

References: Christian Sci Mon p6 F 4 '77 por; N Y Daily News p76 Ap 7 '77 por; Newsday p10+ Ag 26 '79 pors; Newsweek 94:68 S 24 '79 por; People 8:90 D 26 '78 por; Sports Illus 47:49+ Jl 4 '77 por, 50:80 Ja 15 '79 por; Time 114:73 S 24 '79 pors; Washington Post E p1+ S 28 '79 por; World Tennis 26:35+ Ag '78; Aaseng, Nathan. Little Giants of Pro Sports (1980); Gutman, Bill. More Modern Women Superstars (1979); World of Tennis, 1978

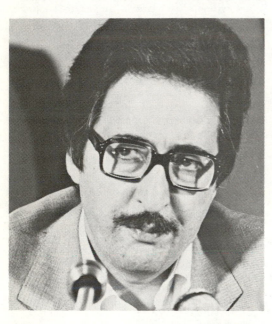

Bani-Sadr, Abolhassan (bä'nē sä'dər)

1933- Former President of the Islamic Republic of Iran; economist. Address: Auvers-sur-Oise, France

As the first President of the oil-rich and strategically important Islamic Republic of Iran, Abolhassan Bani-Sadr confronted problems that seemed virtually unsolvable. Heading a government in which he had no real authority, he was the nominal ruler of a developing nation that has profound economic and social problems and is torn by factional strife. In late 1980 Iran was at war with neighboring Iraq as well as in a continuing conflict with its former ally, the United States. A long-time opponent of Shah Mohammed Riza Pahlevi, Bani-Sadr spent a number of years in exile in France, where he become a member of the "inner circle" of the Ayatollah Ruholla Khomeini, spiritual head of Iran's dominant Shi'ite Muslim sect and the symbolic leader of the opposition to the Shah. After the Shah was driven into exile in early 1979, Bani-Sadr was among the few chosen to accompany Khomeini back to Iran to help consolidate the revolution.

An economist by training, Bani-Sadr is noted for his formulation of an "Islamic economics" that seeks to harmonize the principles of socialism and the Muslim religion. More Westernized than most of Iran's leaders, he remained in office as long as he did only by sufferance of the Ayatollah Khomeini and the right-wing religious leaders who are the dominant force in Iranian politics. Removed from the Presidency in June 1981, Bani-Sadr returned to exile in France in the following month.

Abolhassan Bani-Sadr, one of the seven children of the Ayatollah Sayed Nasrollah Bani-Sadr, was born in 1933 in Hamadan province, in northwestern Iran. As the son and grandson of wealthy landowners who were eminent members of the Muslim clergy and who expected him to become a clergyman too, Bani-Sadr was given a devoutly religious upbringing. He also imbibed a family tradition of hatred for Iran's ruling Pahlevi dynasty, and as a teenager, he reportedly once predicted to his mother that he was destined someday to replace the Shah as the country's leader.

While studying Muslim theology, economics, and sociology at Teheran University in the early 1950's, Bani-Sadr first became politically active as a supporter of Dr. Mohammed Mossadegh's nationalist government, although he avoided affiliating himself with any specific party or group. When a coup backed by the United States Central Intelligence Agency in 1953 ousted Mossadegh's government and returned the Shah, who had fled the country, to the Iranian throne, Bani-Sadr joined the underground opposition movement, aligning himself with its Islamic religious wing.

Over the following decade Bani-Sadr was on two occasions arrested by SAVAK, the Shah's secret police. In 1963 he was critically wounded and arrested again, in the holy city of Qom, while taking part in a protest against the Shah's modernization program known as the "White Revolution." After serving four months in prison he left Iran and settled in Paris, where he became closely associated with French leftist circles and with the many disaffected Iranians in Western Europe. With the aid of a scholarship, Bani-Sadr undertook graduate studies at the Sorbonne, and after earning his doctorate with a dissertation on agrarian reform in Iran he became a member of the Sorbonne's faculty, teaching economics and sociology and devoting his remaining time almost exclusively to reading and study. According to a nephew quoted in *People* (March 3, 1980), Bani-Sadr was not enticed by the blandishments of Parisian life; "To him, France was nothing but a library."

In the following years Bani-Sadr increasingly involved himself in the Iranian émigré community's opposition to the Shah's regime, eventually becoming one of the émigré dissident movement's chief publicists and theoreticans. He wrote many articles and pamphlets in French and Farsi on the Iranian political and economic situation and the goals of the Iranian revolution. In collaboration with the Marxist economist Paul Vieille he published the book *Pétrole et Violence; Terreur Blanche et Résistance en Iran* (Oil and Violence; White Terror and Resistance in Iran) (Editions Anthropos, 1974) as well as an essay on "Iran and the multinationals." The authors argued that Iran had become "a tributary of foreign economies," since its economy was based on oil exports and a growing consumption of imported goods. Bandi-Sadr's published works also include a book on the "economics of divine unity," expounding his unique program for an "Islamic economy" in which Iran would base its national development on an amalgam of socialism and traditional Muslim values as set forth in the Koran. Although Bani-Sadr's compound of Islam, nationalism, and socialism seemed outlandish to some Western commentators, it was described sympathetically by Robert Stephens in the London *Observer* (February 3, 1980), who compared it to the Christian Socialism advocated in nineteenth-century England by William Morris. Some of Bani-Sadr's writings from his period of exile were published in English translation in the late 1970's in the collection *Iran Erupts*, edited by Ali Reza Nobari.

While in France, Bani-Sadr entered into a correspondence with the Ayatollah Ruhollah Khomeini, an old friend of his father's and the charismatic religious leader who for many Iranians personified the opposition to the Shah. The two men met for the first time in 1972 at the funeral of Bani-Sadr's father, in the Iraqi holy city of An Najaf, where Khomeini was then living in exile. Before very long Khomeini had become Bani-Sadr's spiritual mentor. In 1978, when the Ayatollah came to France, Bani-Sadr arranged for him to settle in the Paris suburb of Neauphlè-le-Château and became his secretary. He was soon established as one of Khomeini's most trusted advisers and spokesmen, representing him in meetings with Iranian émigrés throughout Europe. In January 1979 the Shah went into exile in the wake of demonstrations largely stimulated by agitation from Khomeini's Paris headquarters. When the triumphant Khomeini returned to Iran on February 1, to become, in effect, the country's new ruler, Bani-Sadr was one of the select group of associates chosen to accompany him.

During the first few months after his return, with the country in a state of chaotic euphoria, Bani-Sadr spent much of his time visiting universities and factories to expound his economic program, which included, among other things, the raising of oil prices and lowering of oil production, the increase of taxes on imported goods to help the development of Iranian industry, the establishment of workers' committees to run nationalized industries, the cancellation of Iran's foreign debts, the nationalization of banks, and the abolition of interest. He apparently preferred to exercise his influence behind the scenes, and although he was a member of Khomeini's Council of the Islamic Revolution, for some months he refused invitations to join the Cabinet of Prime Minister Mehdi Bazargan. Finally, in July 1979, he joined the government as Minister of Economic Affairs and Finance.

In his new post, Bani-Sadr immediately devoted himself to inaugurating the initial stages of an "Islamic economy." One of his first and perhaps most unusual projects entailed establishing a computerized microfilm filing system that correlated modern economic concepts with relevant chapter and verse from the Koran as a means of ensuring that his program would accord with Muslim tradition. Bani-Sadr's widely recognized Muslim piety made him extremely popular with the Iranian masses, as did his Koranic-based abolition of interest on loans, which went into effect soon after his accession to office, and his insistence, also in conformity with Koranic principles, that agricultural reform must be based on private ownership of land rather than collectivization.

Further public acclaim greeted Bani-Sadr's nationalization of Iran's banking and insurance industries in the summer of 1979, at which time he became a member of the governing board of the country's new Central Bank. His popularity was also enhanced by the newspaper he edited, *Inqilab-e-Islam* ("Islamic Revolution"), whose pages provided a daily forum in which he was able to affirm his commitment to the necessity of preserving the Iranian people's newly won democratic rights, and his advocacy of a middle course that would avoid entanglements with either the United States or the Soviet Union.

The disorganization and factional strife that characterized Iran in the period after the Shah's overthrow was exacerbated when on November 4, 1979 a group of political militants, apparently acting on their own but with the approval of Khomeini, stormed the United States Embassy in Teheran and held its staff of some sixty persons as hostages. Although the country was unified, after a fashion, by hostility to the United States and the desire to have the Shah returned to Iran to stand trial, it was in other respects in a state of political chaos. As the crisis heightened, Bani-Sadr was appointed Minister of Foreign Affairs on November 10, but dismissed eighteen days later, because his negotiating position vis-à-vis the United States was believed to be too conciliatory.

It had been Bani-Sadr's contention that the holding of hostages violated both international law and Islamic tradition and merely served to line up world opinion behind the United States. Instead, he proposed to win international support by presenting Iran's grievances against the Shah before the United Nations Security Council, but his plan was vetoed by Khomeini, who maintained that the world body was under American domination. Nevertheless, before being replaced as Minister of Foreign Affairs by Sadeq Ghotbzadeh, Bani-Sadr managed to obtain the release of five women and eight black men from among the hostages held in the American Embassy. Retaining his position as Minister of Economic Affairs and Finance, Bani-Sadr also served on the Council of Experts charged with drafting Iran's new constitution, which was overwhelmingly approved by voters in December 1979.

Many observers expected that the situation in Iran would begin to improve after January 1980, when the first democratic presidential election in the nation's 2,500-year history was scheduled to take place, especially if the winner emerged with an overwhelming popular mandate. As the election drew near, the vast field of prospective candidates, representing virtually every faction in the country's variegated political scene, narrowed down to eight chief contenders.

Among them was Bani-Sadr, who was widely regarded as Khomeini's choice, although the Ayatollah had made no public statement to that effect. Bani-Sadr's position was strengthened considerably when his two foremost rivals were disqualified. Jalaluddin Farsi, the candidate of the powerful and reactionary Islamic Republican party, had to withdraw when he was revealed to be of Afghan ancestry, and Masoud Rajavi, representing the progressive Mujaheddeen Khalq, was eliminated because he opposed the new constitution. In the election, on January 25, 1980, Bani-Sadr garnered 10,709,330 votes, or 75 percent of the total, while his nearest rival, Admiral Ahmad Madani, received 14.6 percent. Among the factors contributing to Bani-Sadr's victory, political observers cited the fact that, unlike other Westernized leaders, such as Bazargan, he was perceived as a genuinely pious Muslim. Also, voters distressed by the increasing politicization of Iranian society, and the concomitant inability of any government to function, were drawn to Bani-Sadr because he was not seen as a partisan ideologue bound to any particular faction. Futhermore, he enjoyed strong support from Teheran's slum dwellers and the poor peasants of the countryside, to whom he promised a greater share of the nation's wealth in his campaign speeches.

Inaugurated on February 4, 1980 for a four-year term as President in a ceremony held at the Teheran hospital where Khomeini was recuperating from a heart attack, Bani-Sadr became chairman of the Council of the Islamic Revolution three days later, and on February 19 Khomeini designated him supreme commander of the armed forces. Despite his overwhelming victory, however, Bani-Sadr was little more than a figurehead. He had no party of his own to provide him with a personal political base, and his powers as President were not clearly defined, since under the Iranian constitution supreme authority was vested in Khomeini and a council of religious leaders. Furthermore, since a national parliament had not yet been elected or convened, there was no body that represented even nominally the interests of the nation as a whole. Therefore, Bani-Sadr was forced to mediate between competing political parties of various shades that were striving to gain control of the government.

During the next few months, to use the phraseology of Ned Temko in the *Christian Science Monitor* (April 22, 1980), the popular but powerless Bani-Sadr ruled, when at all, by "desperate improvisation" in a whirlpool of "permanent revolution," trying to accommodate both the radical left and the fundamentalist Muslim right. Meanwhile, Iran's economy continued to deteriorate, Bani-Sadr's efforts to find a face-saving solution to the crisis involving the American hostages were of no avail, and the Soviet occupation of neighboring Afghanistan since late 1979 continued to cause concern in Iran. In the face of such problems, as well as the growing unrest among Kurds and other ethnic minorities virtually excluded from a voice in the nation's affairs by the Shi'ite Muslim orientation of its constitution, Bani-Sadr's position steadily eroded, and it was weakened even more as a result of the parliamentary elections concluded in May 1980, in which the fundamentalist Islamic Republican party won a majority of the 270 contested seats in the new unicameral Islamic Consultative Assembly. According to political analysts, Bani-Sadr had made a crucial error in failing to organize a slate of candidates loyal to his administration, and as a result he found himself deprived of the authority, once promised to him by Khomeini, to name his own prime minister. Futhermore, although he succeeded in putting down a planned military coup in the summer of 1980, his enemies were able to use the incident as a pretext for purging the military and the civil service to eliminate officials who had been counted among Bani-Sadr's supporters.

Although Bani-Sadr's election had for a time raised hopes that an orderly governmental system might emerge from the country's extended post-revolutionary chaos, his Presidency was in a shambles by the summer of 1980, given more deference, perhaps, in the Western press and diplomatic circles than in Iran itself. His waning influence, coinciding with the ascendancy of the politicized Islamic right, was clearly demonstrated in August when, after his earlier compromise choice had been rejected by the Parliament, he was compelled to name Mohammed Ali Rajai, the candidate of the hard-line Islamic Republican party. He was, however, able to exercise some authority in rejecting seven of the Prime Minister's twenty-one Cabinet appointees.

Bani-Sadr's position seemed to be strengthened by the upsurge of patriotism that followed the outbreak of war with Iraq in September 1980, since he was popular with the army and nominally its commander-in-chief. Appointed head of the newly established Supreme Defense Council and given special war powers by Khomeini, Bani-Sadr visited the battlefront in the early stages of the war and personally directed Iranian military operations. But despite the semblance of unity engendered by the war, the conflict between liberals and Islamic militants appeared to be sharpening. At the end of 1980, Bani-Sadr was still able to function as President only by accommodating himself to the hardline Muslim clerics who dominated the Islamic Republican party, and the fundamental weakness of the presidential office remained unchanged.

The release of the American hostages in January 1981 failed to ease tensions in Iran, and during the months that followed, Bani-Sadr was fighting for his political life in his conflict with the fundamentalist clergy. On June 10, 1981 Khomeini dismissed Bani-Sadr as commander-in-chief of the armed forces. Twelve days later, following a nearly unanimous parliamentary vote declaring him unfit to hold office, Bani-Sadr was divested of his presidential powers by the Ayatollah.

Meanwhile, amid clashes between his supporters and opponents, mob cries for his death, and official efforts to arrest him, Bani-Sadr dropped out of sight. He reemerged on July 29, 1981 in Paris, where French authorities granted him asylum on condition that he refrain from political activity, and he declared that he would stay in France "until the people of Iran follow the path of democracy."

When Abolhassan Bani-Sadr returned to Iran in 1979, his wife, Ozra, and their three children remained in their home in the Paris suburb of Cachan. In Teheran, Bani-Sadr shared a modest apartment with his sister and mother and led an austere private life, sleeping on a thin mattress on the floor and praying to Allah five times a day. He is said to be quiet, even diffident, combining a professorial way of expressing himself with the informality of manners typical of the Left Bank of Paris. Short, stocky and somewhat boyish in his appearance, Bani-Sadr wears glasses, has a brush mustache, and is said to bear resemblance to Peter Sellers or Charlie Chaplin. His taste in clothing runs to French-tailored suits, but he eschews neckties as "a symbol of hierarchy." United States officials, quoted in the New York Times (November 12, 1979), described Bani-Sadr as "unpredictable," a "maverick," and "something of a lightweight and a kook," whose ideas are "more theoretical than practical." Oriana Fallaci, writing in the New Republic (May 10, 1980), asserted that Bani-Sadr counted "for nothing and was "impotent . . . , a puppet in the hands of Khomeini," but according to Robert Stephens, writing in the London Observer (February 3, 1980), "Bani-Sadr has never been lacking in optimism or self-confidence."

References: London Observer p12 F 3 '80 por; Los Angeles Times I p8+ Ja 26 '80; N Y Times A p8 Ja 28 '80, IV p1 F 17 '80 por; People 13:30+ Mr 3 '80 pors; International Who's Who, 1980-81

Beatrix, Queen of the Netherlands

Jan. 31, 1938- Address: Paleis Noordeinde, The Hague, the Netherlands

Continuing Holland's royal matriarchy, Beatrix of the Netherlands was invested as Queen on April 30, 1980, at the end of the thirty-one-year reign of her mother, Queen Juliana, whose own mother, Queen Wilhelmina, had held the throne for fifty years. The ceremony followed the abdication of Queen Juliana on the occasion of her seventy-first birthday. Although the Dutch are governed by a parliament (called the States-General) and a Cabinet under a

Queen Beatrix of the Netherlands

constitution adopted in 1814 and later revised, the hereditary monarch possesses certain powers: "the right to be consulted, the right to encourage, the right to warn," as well as the responsibility to sign all bills passed by the parliament. In practice, the monarchs of the Netherlands have functioned as advisers and mediators in a country of over fourteen million people. Because of the representation of eleven political parties in the States-General, the monarch's role has also been that of a unifying force.

A highly industrialized country with considerable wealth derived from its geographical position bordering the North Sea, making it a gateway to Europe, from its productive agricultural methods, and its traditional hospitality to business interests, the Netherlands has nevertheless begun to share in recent years many of the ills of the rest of Europe. The loss of its Indonesian colonies and, later, of Surinam brought substantial emigration from those former territories. Although the terrorist incidents of the mid-1970's, spawned by the political aspirations of the South Moluccans, have now abated, unemployment, inflation, and especially housing shortages continue to plague the nation. As Crown Princess, after spending five war years in Canada, Beatrix was carefully educated in law, languages, and other subjects chosen to give her an understanding of her people and of contemporary world problems. She has shown particular interest in social welfare and in conditions of the Third World and is expected to be an active ruler rather than merely a figurehead.

The traditional fifty-one gun salute, signaling to the nation a royal female, proclaimed

the birth of Princess Beatrix at **Soestdijk Palace** in Baarn, near the center of Holland, on January 31, 1938. As the firstborn of Crown Princess Juliana (Louise Emma Marie Wilhelmina, Princess of Orange-Nassau, Duchess of Mecklenburg) and Prince Bernhard (Leopold Frederic Everhard Jules Curt Charles Godfrey Pierre von Lippe-Biesterfeld), Beatrix was in a direct line after her mother, Queen Wilhelmina's only offspring, to ascend to the throne of the Netherlands. Beatrix was to be the third woman to inherit the crown of the House of Orange-Nassau, founded in the sixteenth century by William the Silent. Her birth was greeted not only with the cheers of the Dutch people but with sighs of relief from the country's souvenir manufacturers, who had dated thousands of commemorative items January 1938, leaving a blank space for the day of birth.

In mid-May 1938 a grand procession of coaches carried a glittering party of royalty from Queen Wilhelmina's official residence, Paleis Noordeinde, to the Groote Kerk, a Dutch Reformed Church in The Hague, where the new Princess was christened Beatrix Wilhelmina Armgard van Orange-Nassau, Princess van Lippe-Biesterfeld, with the title Princess of of the Netherlands. The name "Beatrix," meaning "she who brings happiness," was a break with the Orange custom of naming the royal children after ancestors, although her other given names—"Wilhelmina," after the reigning Queen, and "Armgard," after Prince Bernhard's mother—represented some concession to tradition. The baby's godparents were King Leopold of Belgium, Princess Alice (the sister of Queen Wilhelmina's mother, Queen Emma), and Countess Kotzebue (Prince Bernhard's aunt).

On August 5, 1939 Princess Juliana gave birth to another girl, Irene. During the following year the Nazi threat spread turmoil throughout Europe, and on May 10, 1940 the Germans invaded the Netherlands. Two days later, acting on Queen Wilhelmina's orders, Princess Juliana, Prince Bernhard, and the two baby princesses escaped to England, accompanied by a small party and carrying the crown jewels of the Netherlands.

The family stayed in Gloucestershire in a home owned by Lord Bledisloe, while Queen Wilhelmina, who had followed on May 13, established a temporary government headquarters in London. When even England, however, proved not to be a haven for the next generation of the House of Orange, the family accepted an invitation to Ottawa from Beatrix' godmother Princess Alice, whose husband, the Earl of Athlone, was to become governor-general of Canada. On June 2, Princess Juliana, Beatrix and Irene and a small entourage, eleven in all, sailed aboard the Dutch cruiser *Sumatra* for Halifax, Nova Scotia. Queen Wilhelmina and Prince Bernhard stayed behind in England to work in the war effort.

Princess Beatrix, called Trix by everyone, thus spent her early years in Ottawa and had her first schooling in Canada. The family made occasional visits to the United States, and beginning in 1941 Prince Bernhard joined them from time to time. In January 1943 a third princess, Margriet, was born in Ottawa. Not until August 4, 1945 was the family reunited in its liberated homeland. By then Beatrix was a lively, blond seven-year-old. In February 1947 Maria Christina, the last of Beatrix' three sisters, was born.

A practical woman, Princess Juliana wanted her children to experience as nearly as possible the sort of life lived by the average Dutch child. The highly progressive Werkplaats school run by Kees Boeke in Bilthoven was chosen as the place where the young princesses might learn about housework as well as study regular school subjects. When she was twelve, Beatrix was transferred to a small special branch of the local grammar school at Baarn near Soestdijk Palace, where she followed a rigorous preuniversity curriculum. Besides demonstrating ability in her studies, Beatrix showed talent as a painter and sculptor, enjoyed such sports as horseback riding and especially sailing, and was known as a natural leader.

When Princess Beatrix turned eighteen in 1956, she was confirmed as a member of the Dutch Reformed Church and was, as is legally required in the Netherlands, installed by Queen Juliana as a member of the Council of State. In celebration of that special occasion the Dutch people gave their Crown Princess a yacht, a sailing sloop accommodating six, which Beatrix, who designed the interior herself, named the *Green Dragon*. From that moment she became entitled under the constitution to act as regent and assume the powers of the crown in case of necessity and to receive her own income of 300,000 guilders (then about $75,000) a year.

In September 1956 Princess Beatrix enrolled in the University of Leiden, which had been founded by her forebear Wiliam the Silent and which Queen Juliana had also attended. At Leiden, Beatrix studied sociology, parliamentary history, and law as well as economics and international affairs. She earned a doctorate in political science at the law faculty in 1961. As a student she lived with a few classmates, bicycled to class, and traveled about with fellow students, leading as normal a student life as a princess and the daughter of one of the richest families in the world could be permitted. In May 1959 she caused a stir by buying, without consultation with her parents, a residence of her own, the seventeenth-century Drakensteyn (Dragon-stone) Castle near her parents' Soestdijk Palace. Royalty watchers speculated that the purchase signified the possibility of a romance, but no eligible young man appeared.

A crowd of 200,000 and a traditional New York City ticker-tape parade welcomed Princess Beatrix on September 11, 1959, when the Crown Princess, age twenty-one, made an official visit to the United States. Sailing on the maiden voyage of a new Dutch ship of innovative design, S.S. *Rotterdam,* she entered America via the harbor discovered 350 years before by Henry Hudson, the Dutch explorer. Celebrations of the anniversary of his discovery, at which she represented the crown, were main events of her ten-day stay in the United States. Her visit also included a brief trip to Washington for a luncheon at the White House and many official functions in New York, relieved by occasional private shopping and theatre excursions. It was only the second official overseas visit for the Princess, who had made a tour of Surinam and the Netherlands Antilles in 1958, but she carried out all her duties with aplomb, charming her American hosts with her good humor and directness. When asked at a meeting with newsmen what was the greatest challenge of being a princess, Beatrix replied, "Press conferences." Her formal speeches, however, showed her careful preparation as future Queen. In New York she said, "We feel a close friendship to the people of this city and of this country, because we share the same belief in human dignity, in the freedom of man and in the right of the individual to life, liberty and the pursuit of happiness."

Although reports of romance appeared in the press, for years gossip columnists searched in vain for a potential prince for Beatrix. They found much to discuss, however, in 1964, when Beatrix' sister Irene secretly became a Roman Catholic in order to marry Prince Carlos-Hugo de Bourbon Parma, pretender to the Spanish throne. The government in power in the Netherlands at that time insisted that Irene choose between love and her right to succession to the throne. Irene renounced her claim as next in line after Beatrix.

Having moved into her Drakensteyn Castle in 1963, Princess Beatrix continued her preparations for ascension to the throne, made worldwide official visits, and sponsored a European equivalent of the American Peace Corps. Then in May 1965 a photographer snapped pictures of the Crown Princess walking hand in hand at Drakensteyn with a tall young man. Soon afterward a romance that had been secretly brewing since the couple met at a German noble wedding the previous June became public. Beatrix' choice was thirty-eight-year-old Claus Georg Wilhelm Otto Friedrich Gerd von Amsberg, a member of the minor German nobility and a diplomat with the West German government. A storm of controversy broke when it became known that he had served as a member of the Hitler Youth and then of the German army in Italy during World War II.

Princess Beatrix was forthright about the situation at a press conference, saying of her opponents, "We realize these are people who have genuine rights to be unhappy about our engagement. We are not shocked by the fact there is a controversy. This a democratic country and everybody has the right to speak out." Hostility towards the marriage lessened gradually, but many found it still hard to accept, as reflected in a Gallup poll showing that only 71 percent of the Dutch people still supported the monarchy, an all-time low for the popular House of Orange. Some observers suggested that a combination of memories of the oppressive German occupation, the perception of Beatrix as willful and uncaring of public opinion, and the increasing cost of the monarchy were perhaps bringing republican sentiments to the fore.

Intensive investigations convinced the Dutch parliament, whose approval was needed if Beatrix was to retain her right of succession to the throne, that von Amsberg was not a Nazi sympathizer. By an overwhelmingly favorable vote on a bill of consent, the parliament gave its formal approval of the wedding in the fall of 1965. The royal couple's decision, however, that the ceremony would take place in Amsterdam, rather than the traditional site of The Hague, rekindled the controversy. Exceptional security measures caused further tension as reports surfaced of protests planned along the route to Westerkerk, where the wedding was to be held. The city's rabbis, a number of Amsterdam's municipal councillors, and some of Europe's royalty boycotted the wedding. Nevertheless, on March 10, 1966, despite smoke bombs marring the scene, the golden coach of the Netherlands, accompanied by a rich royal display, made its way from the palace to the town hall, where Burgomeister Gijsbertus van Hall performed the civil ceremony, and onward to Westerkerk, where the Reverend Hendrik Jan Kater solemnized the marriage. Van Amsberg, who adopted the Dutch spelling of his name, then became Prince of the Netherlands. The Princess and her bridegroom flew off in a United States Air Force plane to a Mexican honeymoon.

No discord whatever dampened the celebration signaled by the 101-gun-salute for the birth of the first male heir to the Dutch throne in 116 years. The first son of Princess Beatrix and Prince Claus was born at the Academic Hospital in Utrecht on April 27, 1967 and was named Prince Willem-Alexander Claus George Ferdinand. Two more boys were born to the royal couple: Prince Johan Friso Bernhard Christiaan David on September 25, 1968 and Prince Constantijn Christof Frederik Aschwin on October 11, 1969. The probable succession of a king to the Dutch throne in the future brought new popularity to the monarchy.

Over the years the press reported indications that Princess Beatrix was becoming increasingly impatient to assume the crown. Queen Juliana, however, did not abdicate in favor of her daughter as expected when she reached age sixty-five, despite scandals over Prince Bernhard's questionable financial dealings. Finally, on her seventy-first birthday, on April 30, 1980, she signed an Act of Abdication, and at that moment Princess Beatrix became Queen of the Netherlands. Violent protests, this time mainly over Amsterdam's critical housing shortages, punctuated the pomp and pageantry of the investiture of the new Queen, which took place in the fifteenth-century Nieuwe Kerk, where an ermine-clad Beatrix swore to "defend and preserve the territory of the state." Part of her first official day as monarch was spent with Prince Claus at the Amsterdam University Clinic, visiting those who had been injured in the street riots.

The Netherlands' Queen stands five feet seven inches tall and has blue eyes and auburn hair, darkened from the blondness of her childhood. Prince Claus's rapid acquisition of accent-free Dutch, his quiet demeanor, and serious interest in Third World problems have gained him respect and popularity that have increased her subjects' sense of loyalty to her. More than her mother, whose down-to-earth style reflected that of her people, Queen Beatrix appears to have the steel of Queen Wilhelmina, according to press reports. As head of state, the new Queen has a keen interest in the affairs of state, but in keeping with the Dutch constitution, she cannot play a direct role in government. She will, however, after a general election or resignation of a Cabinet, having heard her advisers, such as leaders of political parties, appoint a so-called *formateur* to form a government.

References: London Observer p5 Mr 13 '66 por; N Y Times A p6 F 1 '80 por, A p8 My 1 '80; Newsweek 67:46+ Mr 21 '66 por; People 10:28+ Jl 10 '78 pors; Time 87:51 Mr 18 '66 por; Toronto Globe and Mail p20 Je 1 '57 por; U S News & World Report 88:61 My 5 '60 por; Washington Post B p7 Je 29 '65; Hoffman, Betty and Netherlands News Agency. Born to Be Queen (1955); Hoffman, William. Queen Juliana (1979); Who's Who in the World, 1974-75

Bennett, Michael

Apr. 8, 1943- Choreographer; director. Address: b. 890 Broadway, New York City, N.Y. 10003

Dance, Michael Bennett once said, is "the essence of the Broadway musical." To celebrate dance and the dedication of unsung chorus dancers, Bennett, a former Broadway "gypsy" himself, conceived, directed, choreographed, and coproduced *A Chorus Line*, and with it made Broadway history. One of the longest-running musicals in the annals of the American stage, *A Chorus Line* won nine Tony awards and the 1976 Pulitzer Prize for drama. Before creating *A Chorus Line*, Bennett, an energetic and productive choreographer, had made his mark with the distinctive dances he had devised for such musicals as *Promises, Promises, Company,* and *Follies.* Like his idol, Jerome Rob-

Michael Bennett

bins, Bennett is a master at making dances that are both integral to the plot and satisfying in themselves. "My approach to everything in dancing is not in the step kick, step kick, back, change, step kick," he once said. "That's not my bag. What I want to do is to make the movement give a psychological insight into a character, to advance the story, and make a point quickly, as in a cartoon."

Michael Bennett was born Michael Bennett DiFiglia on April 8, 1943 in Buffalo, New York, the son of Salvatore Joseph and Helen (Ternoff) DiFiglia. His father was a machinist at a local Chevrolet plant; his mother was a secretary at a neighborhood Sears, Roebuck store. To provide a creative outlet for their son's energy, the Bennetts enrolled the boy in a children's dancing school when he was only three. By the time he was twelve, he had taken lessons in tap, ballet, modern, and folk dance and had often performed in the variety shows put on by Mrs. John Dunn's Little Stars of Tomorrow. With the support of his parents, he regularly spent his summers in New York City, where he studied with such professional dance instructors as Aubrey Hitchins and Mat Maddox. Bennett always enjoyed dancing, but as he explained to Olga Maynard in an interview for *After Dark* (August 1975), it was never more than "a personal pleasure, something for [his] own joy." "What I wanted to do, what I wanted to *work* at, was putting on big shows—not just dancing, but singing, acting, dancing shows, and I wanted to make these shows on other people, not on myself," he said.

While attending Hutchison Central High School for Boys in Buffalo, Bennett choreographed and directed a number of student productions, appeared in community theatre presentations, and invariably spent his summer vacations serving as an apprentice in a touring stock company. He usually worked behind the scenes, painting backdrops and changing sets, but his perseverance was finally rewarded when, at the age of fifteen, he was assigned the role of Baby John in a stock production of *West Side Story*. The following year, Bennett auditioned for and won the same part in the professional company that Jerome Robbins, who had directed and choreographed the musical on Broadway, was assembling for an upcoming European tour. Although his high school graduation was just a few months away, Bennett immediately dropped out of school to accept the role.

On his return to New York City after twelve months abroad, Bennett danced in the choruses of the musical comedies *Subways Are for Sleeping*, *Here's Love*, and *Bajour*, all of which enjoyed respectable runs on Broadway, and acted as a kind of unofficial assistant to the choreographer for *How Now, Dow Jones*, *Your Own Thing*, and *By Jupiter*. His first solo effort as a choreographer was *A Joyful Noise*, a rags-to-riches-to-rags tale about a country and western singer who turns his back on his success. Originally conceived as a summer stock show, the musical played for nearly three months on the East Coast strawhat circuit before moving to the Mark Hellinger Theater on Broadway on December 15, 1966, where it closed after just twelve performances. According to most critics, Bennett's bouncy choreography was one of the show's few bright spots, and it earned him his first Tony award nomination. In addition to working on Broadway, Bennett also appeared on and choreographed such television programs as *Hullabaloo*, the *Ed Sullivan Show*, the *Dean Martin Show*, and *Hollywood Palace*, and he staged the musical numbers for *What's So Bad About Feeling Good?* (Universal, 1965), a flimsy comedy film directed by George Seaton.

Henry, Sweet Henry was Bennett's next Broadway offering and, like *A Joyful Noise*, it was a case of "a choreographer in search of a show," as Richard Philp observed in *Dance* (June 1975). Adapted by Nunnally Johnson from the novel *The World of Henry Orient*, *Henry, Sweet Henry* opened on Broadway on October 23, 1967 to generally unfavorable reviews. Only Bennett's choreography escaped critical condemnation. Clive Barnes, who reviewed the production for the New York *Times* (October 24, 1967), called the "briskly modern dances" the "most original aspect of the show." In Barnes's opinion, Bennett's inventive choreography not only showed a genuine sense of choreographic structure but also revealed an intuitive understanding of the Broadway musical. Michael Bennett, he concluded, was "the most hopeful new name around Broadway dance." *Henry, Sweet Henry* closed after a two-month run, but it earned Bennett his second Antoinette Perry Award nomination for choreography.

With *Promises, Promises*, Neil Simon's adaptation of Billy Wilder's 1960 Academy award-winning film, *The Apartment*, Bennett finally had a smash hit. From its opening night performance on December 1, 1968 to its closing on June 26, 1971, the show played to capacity crowds whose enthusiasm was generated not only by the music and lyrics of Burt Bacharach and Hal David but also by the dance routines that Bennett devised to the intricate rhythms of its score. The nightly showstopper was "Turkey-Lurkey Time," a frenetic number for a tipsy secretary at an office Christmas party, danced by Donna McKechnie. Michael Bennett received his third consecutive Tony nomination for his contribution to *Promises, Promises*.

While *Promises, Promises* was still in the first year of its long run, Bennett set to work on *Coco*, the Alan Jay Lerner-André Previn musical biography of the French couturière Gabrielle ("Coco") Chanel that starred Katharine Hepburn. He staged all of its musical numbers, including the elaborate fashion-show sequences that one critic described as being "in the tradition of Busby Berkeley, but without the feathers." *Coco* opened on December 18, 1969 to the biggest box-office advance in Broadway history, but it failed to impress many critics, some of whom complained about its unmemorable music and its lackluster direction, among other deficiencies. Still, even John Simon, the acidulous drama critic for *New York* magazine, singled out its choreography as one of the play's strongest assets.

With yet another Tony nomination to his credit, Bennett immediately went into rehearsals for *Company*, Stephen Sondheim's plotless, episodic play about a thirty-five-year-old bachelor and his friendship with five married couples. A daring departure from conventional American musical theatre, *Company* presented few opportunities for the lavish production numbers of traditional musical comedies. Rising to the challenge, the inventive Bennett used timeworn choreographic devices in unexpected ways that fused perfectly with Harold Prince's directorial concept. In *Company*, as in *Promises, Promises*, the highlight of the evening was a dance solo—"Tick Tock"—by his "favorite instrument," Miss McKechnie. *Company* ran on Broadway for eighteen months and captured the majority of the 1971 Tony awards, although Bennett lost the citation for choreography to Donald Saddler for *No, No Nanette*.

Michael Bennett finally won his first Tony for *Follies*, Sondheim's hit musical about the reunion of some faded Ziegfeld beauties on the stage of the theatre—now awaiting the wrecker's ball—where they once performed. As the ex-showgirls run through their old routines, their youthful "ghosts" mirror their actions in the background. When *Follies* opened on April 4, 1971, critics were sharply divided on their assessment of the show, which Bennett codirected with Harold Prince, but they unani-mously praised its imaginative choreography. "I think it is . . . safe to say that Michael Bennett is the best choreographer working in the theatre today," Craig Zadan observed in *After Dark* (May 1971). "Rather than recreate the Follies era he *creates* it with total originality, freshly and inventively stopping the show time and time again." In addition to his award for choreography, Bennett acquired a Tony for best direction of a musical.

Because he did not want to become known simply for his choreography, Bennett founded Plum Productions and, in 1971, coproduced and directed *Twigs*, George Furth's comedy about three frustrated sisters and their domineering mother. Although the gifted Sada Thompson had read for the part of only one of the sisters, Bennett decided to take advantage of her enormous range by casting her in all four roles. The result turned out to be a *tour de force* for Miss Thompson and an impressive directorial debut for Bennett. His staging of *God's Favorite*, Neil Simon's reworking of the Biblical story of Job, which ran for three months during the 1974-75 Broadway season, was less successful. According to most critics, however, the fault lay more in Simon's occasionally offensive script than in Bennett's workmanlike direction.

In February 1973, just six weeks before its scheduled New York opening, Bennett was called in to salvage *Seesaw*, the Cy Coleman-Dorothy Fields musical version of the 1958 stage hit *Two For the Seesaw*. The project seemed hopeless, but Bennett, who had insisted on complete artistic control, overhauled the entire production, changing everything from its sets and costumes to its leading lady. *Seesaw*, which opened on schedule to a standing ovation and critical approval, ran for nine months. Bennett's dance numbers, which unerringly caught the pulsating, carnal rhythms of New York City, earned him his second Tony for choreography.

Between *Seesaw* and *God's Favorite*, Bennett worked briefly on a new musical, tentatively called "Pin-ups," then, bored with his work, he took several months off to reflect on his career. "I turned thirty and hadn't danced for about a year . . . and I thought: 'What have I done? I've given up something that I love!'" he explained to Richard Philp in an interview for a *Dance* magazine (June 1975) profile. "I started wondering why I got out of dancing. And, then, what drove me to get into the business in the first place. What drives anybody to get into the business?" In an all-night marathon bull session in January 1974, the choreographer and a group of dancers he had worked with over the years talked candidly about their careers, their childhoods, their lifestyles, and their goals, both personal and professional. That freewheeling, tape-recorded discussion furnished the basic story for *A Chorus Line*.

After talking over his idea with Joseph Papp, the producer, who offered to fund a workshop for the project, Bennett chose his cast—about half from the original group of dancers—and began forging the raw material into a show. He hired Marvin Hamlisch to compose the score and Edward Kleban to write the lyrics and enlisted the aid of Nicholas Dante, a dancer turned writer, and James Kirkwood to rework and polish the script. The eagerly anticipated premiere of *A Chorus Line* on May 21, 1975 at Papp's 299-seat Newman Theater in the New York Shakespeare Public Theater complex on Lafayette Street caused a sensation. "The conservative word for *A Chorus Line* might be tremendous, or perhaps terrific," Clive Barnes wrote in the New York *Times* (May 22, 1975). "Bennett's choreography and direction burn up superlatives as if they were inflammable. In no way could it have been better done." To a man, his colleagues agreed, hailing the play as the most exciting and original American musical since *West Side Story*. An established hit by midsummer, the show moved to the Shubert Theater on Broadway, where it continued to play to near-capacity audiences into the decade of the 1980's.

As the curtain rises on *A Chorus Line,* two dozen nervous dancers are lined up in a drab rehearsal studio, where they have come to compete for eight openings in the chorus of a new musical. After putting them through their paces, Zach, the director, asks each contestant to talk about himself, and one by one, they do —in monologues, songs, and dance routines. As each character speaks, his ambitions and frustrations, hopes and fears, victories and defeats become synonymous with those of Everyman. "The point we are making . . . [is] nobody has the right to judge anybody else," Bennett told Olga Maynard. "You have the right to be what you are, to succeed on your terms, even if your kind of 'success' is everybody else's idea of 'failure.'" After Zach has selected the four men and four women for the chorus, all the dancers return, in resplendent costumes, for a rousing song-and-dance finale. Bennett intended that number, called "One," to be "a comment on the audience" as well as on the state of the art of musical-comedy dancing: "I want the audience to walk out of the theatre saying, 'Those kids shouldn't be in the chorus!' And I want . . . every chorus kid in the country to say, 'If those chorus kids can do it, maybe I can do it!' If just everybody had the guts to try harder, to push out, to do."

For almost five years Bennett was busy with *A Chorus Line.* He auditioned, rehearsed, and directed the national, international, and new Broadway companies, and he signed a contract with Universal Studios, which had purchased the film rights to *A Chorus Line* for $5,500,000, to direct the motion picture version. In early 1979, however, he withdrew from the film. "If I did the movie it means for sure another three years," he told reporters. "Then that's my whole career, and I don't want my whole career to be that."

In mid-1978, with *A Chorus Line* companies still performing on Broadway and all over the world, Bennett finally turned to a new project. After raising $2,000,000 by, as he put it, "hocking everything I have," he produced, directed, and choreographed a musical—a "real schmaltzy romance," to use his words—based on *Queen of the Stardust Ballroom*, Jerome Kass's sentimental television play about a lonely middle-aged widow who falls in love with an unhappily married man she meets at the Stardust Ballroom. Bennett cast the veteran actors Dorothy Loudon and Vincent Gardenia in the leading roles and recruited a huge chorus line of forty-to-sixty-year-old dancers, many of whom had performed in the original Broadway productions of *Oklahoma!* and *Carousel*. For the professional dancers he choreographed spinning, swirling variations of traditional ballroom dances; his steps for the central characters, newcomers to the ballroom scene, were simpler—"like an apple tossed into a basket of pomegranates," as Jack Kroll remarked in his review for *Newsweek* (January 1, 1979).

Ballroom opened on December 14, 1978 to mixed notices from critics, who agreed with Kroll that Bennett had failed to give his essentially sound concept "enough support in the book and music." When the show closed on March 24, 1979, Bennett accepted its failure philosophically. As he told Carol Lawson in an interview for the New York *Times* (December 29, 1979), "Everyone was waiting to see what I'd do after *Chorus Line*. I went out of my way to be sure I didn't do *Chorus Line II*. So now I've done this, and my halo is knocked off a bit. But now I'm free. People know I'm liable to do anything. It will be easier next time." Although *Ballroom* was a commercial and critical failure, Bennett took some consolation in the Tony award that he and Bob Avian, his longtime collaborator, shared for the production's dance arrangements.

A slight, elfin figure standing about five feet seven inches in height, Michael Bennett has a dancer's lithe body, a "bonily ascetic" face, and piercing dark eyes. He usually wears his hair cut very short, and he frequently sports a moustache and beard. Although he is a wealthy man (his income reportedly reached $90,000 a week at the height of *A Chorus Line*'s run), Bennett lives frugally on a small, self-imposed weekly allowance issued by his business manager. In a rare burst of extravagance after *A Chorus Line* swept the Tony awards, he purchased a 1965 Rolls-Royce, the first car he had ever owned.

Aside from skiing, Bennett once joked that his only hobby was psychoanalysis, which he has undergone, off and on, for a decade. The theatre is both his vocation and his avocation. "I don't do anything else," he admitted to Allan Wallach in an interview for *Newsday* (April 22, 1979). "I know how to go out and have a nice time for an evening and stuff like that . . . , but there's always something more important to do. . . . I'm lucky; I work at something I love to do, so it's never really been work. I would do all of this for nothing, and would have my whole life." Bennett and Donna McKechnie were married on December 4, 1976, but the marriage broke up within months under the strain of their joint careers. Since their divorce, the choreographer has lived alone in an apartment in midtown Manhattan.

References: After Dark 8:38+ Ag '75; Dance 44:72+ F '70, 49:62+ Je '75 pors; N Y Post p13 S 20 '75 por; N Y Times II p5 Je 15 '75 por; N Y Times Mag p18+ My 2 '76 por; Newsday mag p19 Ap 22 '79 por; Time 106:47 Jl 28 '75 por, 108:44 D 20 '76 por; Who's Who in America, 1980-81; Who's Who in the Theatre (1977)

Bergman, (Ernst) Ingmar

July 14, 1918- Film writer and director. Address: b. c/o Swedish Film Institute, Box 27 126, S-102 52 Stockholm, Sweden

NOTE: This biography supersedes the article that appeared in Current Biography in 1960.

Since his emergence in the 1950's as the "thinking" filmgoer's favorite writer-director, Sweden's Ingmar Bergman has created a body of work that for boldness of visual concept and luminosity of performance is unmatched in the history of the motion picture. Besides being "a poet with the camera" and the possessor of "a mesmeric ability to extract hidden resources from his cast," he has so consistently used the movie medium as a means of personal expression that his oeuvre has a rare cohesiveness; most of his films explore aspects of the same theme: mankind's search for love in a universe where God remains inexplicably silent.

The recipient of innumerable awards, Bergman ranks with Federico Fellini as a major influence on the style and content of post-World War II movies. More prolific and more austere than Fellini, and much less self-indulgent. Bergman has, in the words of Village Voice reviewer Andrew Sarris, "ennobled the cinema by entrusting to it the gravest issues of Western civilization" and "has managed not infrequently to be as entertaining as he is edifying." European theatre critics hold him in equally high esteem as a stage director.

Ernst Ingmar Bergman was born in Uppsala, Sweden on July 14, 1918. His father, a Lutheran clergyman who eventually became chaplain to the Swedish royal family, believed in strict discipline, including caning and the locking of children in closets; his mother seemed to share her husband's rigid views. From the time he was six, movies afforded Bergman an avenue of escape. With his older brother, he was allowed to attend Saturday night screenings of films for children at the Ostermalm Grammar School in Stockholm. Later, while entrusted to the care of his grandmother in Dalarna, a rural province in central Sweden, he cultivated a friendship with the projectionist at the local cinema and from a perch alongside him would sit entranced, peering down at the flat-white surface on which the flickering images played. At nine he bartered a set of tin soldiers for a magic lantern and began collecting snippets of film that he glued together and narrated as the makeshift reel unwound. Another toy that he prized was a cardboard puppet theatre for which he devised special scenic and lighting effects. A younger sister was the captive audience for all his shows.

In 1937 Bergman entered the University of Stockholm to study art history and literature, but when he was offered the chance to direct a campus drama group, he leapt at it. Following a bitter confrontation with his parents, Bergman left his rectory home, dropped out of school, and accepted a job as a glorified errand boy at the Royal Opera House in Stockholm. "I was assistant to everybody," he has been quoted as saying, "and paid nothing . . . but it helped me to learn my craft." In the fall of 1942 Bergman got a job in the script department at Svensk Filmindustri, preparing adaptations of literary properties, but his name did not appear among studio credits until October 2, 1944, when Hets had its Swedish premiere. That film, which dealt with a sadistic teacher's determination to sabotage the love affair of a schoolboy and his shopgirl sweetheart, represented Bergman's first successful attempt to create an original screenplay. Hets won eight "Charlies" (the Swedish equivalent of an American Oscar); it also captured the Grand Prix du Cinema at the 1946 Cannes Film Festival, turned its leading lady, Mai Zetterling, into an international star and, on its release in the United States under the title *Torment* in 1947, proved popular in the fledgling art house circuit.

By 1945 Bergman was so eager to expand his role in the movie-making process that when Svensk Filmindustri proposed assigning him the unwelcome task of adapting to the screen and directing a Danish soap opera to which the studio had misguidedly acquired the rights, he agreed, with the stipulation that he be granted autonomy on his next project. *Crisis (Kris)*, the picture with which he made his debut as an "auteur" in 1945, was, in Bergman's opinion, "lousy," but a perceptive Swedish critic of the day regarded it as "a daring shot by an eager hunter—in the right direction but shy of the mark." Bergman made several more near-misses: *The Devil's Wanton (Fängelse)* and *Three Strange Loves (Törst)* in 1949; *Illicit Interlude (Sommarlek)* in 1951; *Secrets of Women (Kvinnors Vantan)* in 1952; *Monika (Sommaren med Monika)* and *The Naked Night (Gycklarnas Afton)* in 1953. Finally, in 1955, he hit the "mark" with his stylish period piece *Smiles of a Summer Night (Sommarnattens Leende)* which, after winning the prize for Most Poetic Humor at the 1956 Cannes Film Festival, charmed reviewers wherever it was exhibited. Cinema historian Georges Sadoul maintains in his *Dictionary of Films* that "though superficially a farce in the Feydeau manner," *Smiles of a Summer Night* "is in fact a profound satire of mores and social conventions." With Bergman's approval, Broadway composer-lyricist Stephen Sondheim and librettist Hugh Wheeler based their hit musical, *A Little Night Music*, on the movie.

The Seventh Seal (Det Sjunde Inseglet), at once an allegory of man's relation to God and a lyrical disquisition on his mode of coping with the idea of death, earned Bergman a special jury prize at the 1957 Cannes Film Festival and, while it failed to generate much business at Swedish box offices, began a Bergman cult in art theatres throughout the rest of the world. In 1972, when the editors of the British publication *Sight and Sound* conducted an international survey of critics to determine their choices of the best motion pictures of all time, *The Seventh Seal* occupied tenth place on the list of twelve compiled by Richard Corliss, the influential American film reviewer.

The harrowing journey across a plague-stricken medieval landscape on which Bergman had induced audiences to accompany him in *The Seventh Seal* was given a contemporary, psychoanalytical twist in *Wild Strawberries (Smultronstället)*, produced in 1957. Constructed around dream sequences filled with funerary portents and with flashbacks suffused with an octogenarian's nostalgia, the movie traveled through a philosophical terrain as difficult to negotiate as that of its predecessor, but its modern setting rendered it more accessible. The presence of its sympathetic protagonist lent it greater emotional impact, since few viewers could avoid identifying with the elderly professor who, honored by his peers but estranged from his intimates, recalls in the course of a day-long journey the events of the past that have led to his sense of isolation and loss in the present.

In Europe, *Wild Strawberries*, or *The Garden of His Dreams*, as it was then known, won first prize at the Berlin International Film Festival in 1958. Released in the United States the following year, it was named the best foreign picture of 1959 by the National Board of Review, which also honored the performance of its venerable star, Victor Sjöström, as the year's best by an actor in any language and cited Bergman for his versatility and for his handling of unusual subject matter. Bergman also received an Academy Award nomination in the category of best story and screenplay written directly for the screen, but the Oscar went instead to the writers of *Pillow Talk*, a frivolous commercial blockbuster that starred Doris Day and Rock Hudson.

Two other Bergman-directed features reached American screens during 1959. In *The Magician (Ansiktet)* Max von Sydow, whose portrayal of a knight in *The Seventh Seal* had been one of its principal strengths, played the complex title role, that of an itinerant nineteenth-century showman with a demonic facade and a flair for duplicity. Arguments raged as to what the film meant. Did it constitute Bergman's spiritual autobiography? Could a parallel be drawn between it and the Passion Play? Or was *The Magician* merely an opaque illustration of the religion-versus-rationalism contest? Although the movie's merits were also hotly debated, it won a special jury prize at the 1959 Venice Film Festival. Around *Brink of Life (Nära Livet)*, however, little controversy developed. From a script by Ulla Isaksson about some women in a maternity ward, Bergman crafted a drab film. The acting of Eva Dahlbeck, Ingrid Thulin, Bibi Andersson, and Babro Ornas was splendid (the four shared the 1958 Best Actress award at Cannes), but the movie remained a clinical and claustrophobic exercise.

Equally distressing to the queasy was Bergman's graphic treatment of a medieval gang-rape and murder in *The Virgin Spring (Jungfrukällan)*. In the wake of its hideousness, an audience could comprehend, if not condone, the primitive vengeance exacted by the father of the victim. By balancing beauty and horror, and by juxtaposing the pagan urge to retaliate and the Christian will to forgive, Bergman had once again produced a profound and poetic masterwork. He received the International Critics Prize at the 1960 Cannes Film Festival, and at the Oscar presentation ceremonies in Hollywood, *The Virgin Spring* was honored as the best foreign picture of the year.

In a deliberate change of pace, Bergman next, in 1960, brought forth a comedy that took liberties with the legend of Don Juan by casting him as a latter-day emissary of Satan returned to earth to seduce the chaste young daughter of a Swedish parson. Entitled *The Devil's Eye (Djaäulens Öga)* and released in the United States in the fall of 1961, the film was patronized by the majority of reviewers, who acknowledged its cleverness but insisted that it was strictly minor Bergman.

For the next major Bergman opus, American movie critics had to wait until his Strindbergian *Through a Glassy Darkly (Sasom i en Spegel)* opened in Manhattan in March 1962. In its relentless analysis of a single day in the lives of four members of a disintegrating family, the picture signaled a shift in Bergman's approach: always observant, his supersensitive camera was now capable of recording "the subtlest nuances of the soul," and he demonstrated a new economy of technique, minus flashbacks or any other narrative embellishment. That absence of artifice extended to the acting, especially the wrenching performance of Harriet Andersson, a Bergman "regular," as the schizophrenic Karin, who wearies of battling the demons that threaten her sanity and welcomes her descent into total madness. *Through a Glass Darkly* won an Academy Award as 1961's best foreign language feature.

Through a Glass Darkly is so intimately linked with the two films that followed that cinema historians have grouped them together as "a kind of trilogy." In *Winter Light (Nattsvardsgästerna)*, the second in his suite of so-called Chamber Plays, the strain of "masterly asceticism" intensified. The somber tale of a village pastor whose faith in God has faltered, and whose rapport with his parishioners has dwindled to the point where he is powerless to prevent the suicide of one troubled communicant, *Winter Light* was icily allegorical, with its pivotal figure, portrayed with his customary brilliance by a Bergman standby, Gunnar Björnstrand, doggedly going through the motions of his religious role. Enormously responsive to music, Bergman has said that he drew his inspiration for *Winter Light* from Stravinsky, and for *The Silence (Tystnaden)*, the concluding segment in his so-called trilogy, from Bartók. The truth of his assertion is attested to by the hypnotic rhythm of the finished film with its ominously stated themes and counter-themes and by the visual shocks that correspond to the explosions of dissonance favored by some contemporay composers.

Because some conservative critics voiced outrage over Bergman's frank depiction of "perverted" sexual acts in *The Silence*, sensation-seekers flocked to the film. They were disapointed when, instead of the orgy of voyeurism they had anticipated, what they saw was an exploration of terminal despair, a trip to a nightmarish world of noncommunication where the human specimens subjected to microscopic scrutiny were a dying woman, her indolent and sensual younger sister, and the latter's seven-year-old son. American reviewers rated the movie as another artistic masterpiece.

Weary of having to defend *The Silence* against the watchdogs of public morals, Bergman opted next for another radical change-of-pace maneuver. But *All These Women (För Att Inte Tala Om Alla Dessa Kvinnor)*, which had the double distinction of being Bergman's first color film and his first out-and-out farce, was neither as clever or as comic as the epigrammatic *The Devil's Eye*. A mélange of slapstick sight gags that misfired and of juvenile gibes at those who, in the past, had misread his intentions, it was a sour and dispiriting affair.

In the wake of that debacle, Bergman adopted a policy of retrenchment. In the summer of 1965, instead of making a movie, he wrote the script for a four-hour, two-part film entitled "The Cannibals" that he planned to direct the following year, but a series of illnesses that he suffered in 1966 forced him to cancel that project. Then, while undergoing treatment for a viral infection of the inner ear that had made him subject to vertigo, Bergman began to gestate the idea of a film with more modest proportions.

Just before his illness, Bibi Andersson, a long-time member of his screen "stock" company, had introduced him to a new friend of hers named Liv Ullmann. On impulse, Bergman had suggested that the young Norwegian actress accept a small role in "The Cannibals," which had not yet been shelved and in which Bibi Andersson had already agreed to appear. Later, when he happened to see a photograph taken of the two women as they sat sunning themselves against a wall, it struck Bergman that, in a "strange sort of way," they were "devilishly alike!" Afterwards, with little else to occupy his mind as he lay in a hospital bed, he reflected that "it would be wonderful to write something about two people who lose their identities in each other." Out of that concept germinated the idea for *Persona*.

The plot that Bergman invented to capitalize on the resemblance between the two women had Andersson embody a "normal" nurse and Ullmann her speech-bereft patient; within their neurotic intimacy, he charted the growth of a bond that was both mental and physical and that culminated in a bizarre commingling of their personalities. The National Society of Film Critics voted Bergman the year's best director, *Persona* the year's best picture, and Bibi Andersson the year's best actress. More importantly, *Persona*, which was released in 1967, heralded the beginning of the still continuing collaboration of Bergman and Liv Ullmann.

To Bergman's next three films Liv Ullmann contributed performances that were models of controlled emotionality. It was her portrayal, for example, of a deranged painter's desperate wife that gave distinction to *Hour of the Wolf* (1968), a surreal study of the plight of the artist in society. *Shame*, a indictment of war that focused on a married couple concerned with sheer survival, was released in the United

States only eight months after *Hour of the Wolf.* For his direction of the two pictures, Bergman was named best director of the year by the National Society of Film Critics, which also selected *Shame* as the best picture of 1968, and, for her performance in it, Liv Ullmann as best actress.

With *The Passion of Anna* (1970), which concerned itself with the destruction left in her wake by a willful idealist, played by Liv Ullmann, many reviewers felt that the art of Ingmar Bergman had reached its zenith. Bergman's second picture to be shot in color, it brought him yet another best-director-of-the-year award from the National Society of Film Critics. His next film, *The Touch* (1970), was the first to use an American actor (Elliott Gould) in a leading role and the first to require that his Swedish stars (Bibi Andersson and Max von Sydow) speak English. In *Life* (September 10, 1970) Richard Schickel summed up *The Touch,* which handled the eternal triangle theme with Bergman's usual depth and maturity, as "an exquisitely detailed, beautifully modeled portrait of modern women in crisis."

Ironically, *Cries and Whispers* (1972), an already undisputed classic that is widely held to be among Bergman's most remarkable accomplishments, had difficulty finding an American distributor until Roger Corman's New World Pictures took a gamble on releasing it. The fear that American audiences would shun a film that dealt so unflinchingly with the agonies of terminal illness and its corrosive impact on intimate family relationships proved groundless, and it enjoyed a considerable commercial success, thanks to the extravagant praise of such influential reviewers as Vincent Canby of the New York *Times.* The National Society of Film Critics voted Bergman's screenplay and Sven Nykvist's cinematography the year's best, and the New York Film Critics bestowed on *Cries and Whispers* awards for best motion picture, best direction, and best actress (Liv Ullmann).

Derived from a six-part miniseries that Bergman made for Swedish television, *Scenes from a Marriage* (1974) received even more rapturous reviews than those that had greeted *Cries and Whispers.* Paul D. Zimmerman of *Newsweek* (September 23, 1974) hailed *Scenes from a Marriage,* which starred Liv Ullmann and Erland Josephson, and which chronicled the crumbling of an ostensibly "perfect" union, as "a monumentally ambitious journey to the center of a modern marriage: shattering, touching, exhaustingly honest, with a sweep and candor that put American television—not to say movies—to shame." Writing in *Time* (September 30, 1974), T. E. Kalem accounted it "a work of magnetic force, searing intelligence, and an oppressive melancholy lightened by flashes of erotic ecstasy." And once again a Bergman film monopolized the awards that the National Society of Film Critics and the New York Film Critics had in their power to bestow that year.

As the world's foremost exponent of serious movie-making, Bergman seemed miscast as a purveyor of holiday cheer, but *The Magic Flute,* his exuberant version of the Mozart opera that was the Christmas offering at a number of American art theatres in 1974, constituted evidence to the contrary. Visually and vocally, it was beguiling, chiefly because Bergman insisted on using singers who could act convincingly even within the confines of a closeup and whose looks were appropriate to their roles. The sumptuousness of the production belied its origin as a film for television that the Swedish State Broadcasting System had commissioned to help celebrate the fiftieth anniversary of Swedish Radio.

On January 30, 1976, while rehearsing a new production of Strindberg's *Dance of Death* at the Royal Dramatic Theater in Stockholm, Bergman was approached by plainclothes policemen who whisked him off to the public prosecutor's office. There he learned that income tax fraud charges had been lodged against him, and he was interrogated for several hours. Suffering from what his doctor diagnosed as "deep depression occasioned by shock," Bergman had to be hospitalized. Not until March was he officially absolved of wrongdoing, but by that time he had decided to go into self-imposed exile abroad. In October, following trips to New York, Los Angeles, and various European capitals to inspect their film-production facilities, he announced his intention of settling permanently in Munich.

To compound his woes, his next film, *Face to Face* (1976), which diagramed the mental breakdown of a female psychiatrist, did not evoke the kind of reception accorded *Cries and Whispers, Scenes from a Marriage,* and *The Magic Flute.* "The film has power," Jack Kroll of *Newsweek* (April 12, 1976) conceded, "but it's the airless, electric power of an intensive-care unit where the life signs are monitored but humanity lies mortally stricken." Equally dissatisfied was *Time's* Jay Cocks (April 12, 1976), who suggested that in *Face to Face,* Bergman had been "working at less than full capacity." Nevertheless, *Face to Face* evoked the usual ritualistic round of awards from various organizations, this time from the Hollywood Foreign Press Association, the Los Angeles Film Critics Association, the New York Film Critics, and the National Board of Review.

The Serpent's Egg, Bergman's first movie as an expatriate, came perilously close to being as complete a fiasco as *All These Women.* Critics agreed that the fault lay in "the peculiar sense of dislocation within his English-language screenplay" which, set in the Berlin of 1923, tried to examine the roots of Nazism but did so in a manner that was "dull and didactic." Even Liv Ullmann, in a role that was "shadowy and unsuitable," seemed to lack her customary radiance, and David Carradine, the American actor who appeared opposite her, seemed to move through the film like a sleepwalker.

With the release of *Autumn Sonata* in 1978, Bergman demonstrated that his unique gift for what a *Newsweek* reviewer once called "merciless compassion" had not deteriorated, that his intuitive grasp of emotional truth could still be relied upon, and that his reputation as a great director of actors was still intact. Filmed in Norway, and fortified with performances by Ingrid Bergman and Liv Ullmann, *Autumn Sonata* was praised for its searching analysis of the ambivalent relationship between a mother and daughter and was generally greeted as the best Bergman film in years. It quite understandably won awards from the Hollywood Foreign Press Association, the National Board of Review, the New York Film Critics, and the National Society of Film Critics.

Bergman's most recent film, *From the Life of the Marionettes,* appropriated the characters of the battling husband and wife from the dinner party sequence of *Scenes from a Marriage* and dissected their unhealthy alliance within the framework of a psychological thriller. *Newsweek*'s Jack Kroll (November 17, 1980) praised the way in which Bergman had articulated his bleak vision of man "as a spiritual double agent" and declared unequivocally that, for his "powerful and troubling explorations of . . . atomic fission in the human soul," he "should be the first filmmaker to win the Nobel Prize." In spite of its acknowledged merits and its exemplary cast of German actors, *From the Life of the Marionettes* was a commercial failure.

Although Bergman is no publicity seeker, journalists to whom he has granted interviews report that he is far from inaccessible. Modest about his achievements, and friendly, he has a mellifluous voice, eloquent gestures, and a sprightly sense of humor that offsets the sadness in his eyes. Bergman has been married at least four times (since 1971 to the former Ingrid Karlebo von Rosen) and has fathered eight children, one of whom, his daughter Linn, was born out of wedlock during his liaison with Liv Ullmann. His relations with his ex-wives and ex-mistresses remain cordial.

No longer a man without a country, Bergman returned to his homeland in December 1977 to accept the Swedish Academy of Letters Great Gold Medal, one of only seventeen persons who have received it in this century. In 1978 he resumed his directorship of Stockholm's Royal Dramatic Theatre, the same year in which the Swedish Film Institute established a prize for excellence in filmmaking in his name. Through all the vicissitudes of recent years, he has held on to his beloved retreat on the remote Baltic island of Farö.

References: *Life* 71:60+ O 15 '71 pors; *London Observer* p25+ Ja 25 '76 por; *New York* 13:33+ O 27 '80 por; *N Y Times Sunday Mag* p12+ Jl 1 '73 pors; Bawden, Liz-Anne, ed. *The Oxford Companion to Film* (1976); Bjorkman, Stig et al. *Bergman on Bergman* (1972); Donner, Jorn. *The Films of Ingmar Bergman* (1964); Katz, Ephraim. *The Film Encyclopedia* (1979); Sadoul, Georges. *Dictionary of Films* (1972); Sarris, Andrew. *Interviews with Film Directors* (1968); Steinberg, Cobbett. *Film Facts* (1980)

Bonynge, Richard (bon'ing)

Sept. 29, 1930- Australian conductor; musicologist. Address: b. Australian Opera, PO Box J 194, Brickfield Hill, NSW 2000, Australia

Although in his own right Richard Bonynge enjoys ever growing, if at times grudging, recognition as an opera conductor and musicologist, he is more widely known for shaping the career of his wife, Joan Sutherland, the star coloratura soprano. He possesses what she calls "a sort of ESP where singers are concerned," which may have guided him in the 1950's when he sensed her potential for performing the vocal gymnastics required in coloratura roles. A great lover of the eighteenth- and early nineteenth-century bel canto operas that feature coloratura singing, Bonynge persuaded Joan Sutherland to shift from the dramatic roles of the Wagnerian soprano to the bel canto repertoire of Handel, Bellini, Donizetti, Rossini, and other composers. Since then he has continued to be the driving force behind her career, serving as her vocal coach, adviser, and agent. "Theirs," the music critic Stephen E. Rubin has pointed out, "is one of the greatest meetings of musical talents in current history."

In the early 1960's Bonynge began conducting most of his wife's performances, even though his musical training had been in piano, not conducting. Since then he has conducted for other opera stars, too. Bonynge is also acknowledged as the foremost expert on bel canto opera. Researching early operatic scores, he revised modern performances to conform more closely to the composers' intentions and resuscitated many nearly forgotten operas in the bel canto repertoire. During the 1970's he expanded his expertise to French opera of the middle and late nineteenth century.

Richard Bonynge was born in Sydney, Australia on September 29, 1930, the only child of E.A. Bonynge of Epping, New South Wales. Music came naturally: "I didn't chose it; it chose me," he has said, as quoted in Opera News (December 31, 1966). At the age of three he began picking out chords and tunes on the piano, and at six he began taking piano lessons. Regarded as a child prodigy, he entered the Sydney Conservatorium of Music when he was twelve, although his parents would have preferred him to become a linguist. He acquired an interest in opera from his conservatory piano teacher, Lindley Evans, who had been accompanist to the famous Australian prima donna Dame Nellie Melba. Soon Bonynge became the official accompanist of the conservatory's opera school and also began accompanying his cousin, who sang coloratura opera roles.

Because of his outstanding work at the Sydney Conservatorium, Bonynge was believed to have a great future as a pianist. With the help of Sir Eugene Goosens, the conservatorium's director, he won a scholarship at nineteen to the Royal Academy of Music of London. Soon after arriving there, in 1950, Bonynge developed a strong dislike for the school. He was not permitted to study Mozart or conducting, as he had planned. He found theory boring and began cutting classes, studying privately instead under piano teacher Herbert Fryer. But Fryer, by arousing his pupil's enthusiasm for Chopin, indirectly reawakened his interest in opera, for it was only a short step from Chopin to the romantic music of the early nineteenth-century Italian bel canto operas of Donizetti, Bellini, and Rossini. Besides, as Bonynge recalled in a conversation with Stephen E. Rubin of Stereo Review (November 1972), "when it came to sitting down and practicing three hours a day, my concentration started to go.... I was very passionate about music, but not about the piano as such."

In the meantime, Joan Sutherland, an aspiring Australian operatic singer, arrived in London in 1951 to study at the Royal Academy. Bonynge as a teenager had met her when he

served as accompanist at many of her concerts for Australia's Affiliated Music Clubs. In London he became a frequent visitor at her flat and companion at operas and concerts. Bonynge gave concerts and television performances during the early 1950's. But believing, as he later told Jo Anne Levine of the Christian Science Monitor (January 21, 1977), that the voice "is the greatest instrument of all," he paid increasing attention to developing Miss Sutherland's singing. Moved by a growing love for bel canto music and guided by his uncanny ability to judge the capability of singers, Bonynge worked toward directing her career from the heavily dramatic roles of the Wagnerian soprano for which she was preparing to the florid, lighter, more complex, and more delicate roles of the coloratura soprano.

Voices of Joan Sutherland's power were almost unheard of in coloratura singing, which required great vocal agility, as well as the capacity for extremely high notes. She was therefore at first scornful of his efforts. But the persistent Bonynge cited Maria Callas, who had initiated a revival of the long-out-of-fashion bel canto operas, as an example of how a large-voiced soprano could handle intricate coloratura roles. During practice sessions he sometimes used deception to extend her range upward, telling her she was singing lower notes than she actually was. He corrected her breathing and taught her to relax so as to float her head voice properly. Often he found it necessary to bully Miss Sutherland, who lacked confidence in her ability to become a coloratura singer. "He makes me feel that I can do things that I think I can't do," she told John and Sarah Dunn and Sarah Moore Hall of People (April 30, 1979).

Having come to rely more and more on Bonynge's coaching, by 1954 Joan Sutherland was studying with him rather than with the repetiteurs of London's Covent Garden Opera Company, of which she had become a member in 1952. They were married in 1954, and the following year Bonynge gave up his career as a pianist to dedicate himself full time to her career. He extended his concern to every minute detail that would enhance her performance, including grooming. Covent Garden assigned Miss Sutherland a variety of roles without having any coherent plan for her future. Largely because of Bonynge's importunate insistence that she be offered more coloratura roles, the management finally agreed to give her the lead in Donizetti's Lucia di Lammermoor. With the help of the ornamentation that he wrote for her Mad Scene aria, she performed brilliantly in a February 1959 performance. Gaining overnight renown as a coloratura singer, she was flooded with offers from opera managers in Europe and America.

So successful was her coloratura debut that Bonynge took complete control of his wife's career and decided when, where, and how she would sing without the interference of opera managements. Lacking great ambition, she would have been satisfied to remain a member of the Covent Garden Company. Bonynge, however, launched her on an endless series of worldwide tours that made her an international star of bel canto opera. Within three years she had performed at the three other great citadels of opera besides Covent Garden: La Scala in Milan, L'Opéra in Paris, and the Metropolitan Opera in New York.

Although recognized as the major force behind his wife's professional work, Bonynge became somewhat bored with being in the background and tired of being called "Mr. Sutherland." To play a more visible role in her career, he made his debut as her conductor with the Santa Cecilia Orchestra in Rome in January 1962 and since then has conducted most of her performances. He first appeared in America at the Hollywood Bowl in 1962. His debut at Covent Garden occurred in 1964 and at New York's Metropolitan Opera in 1966. As artistic director and chief conductor of the Sutherland/Williamson International Grand Opera Company, he contributed much to the triumph of Joan Sutherland's three-month tour of Australia in mid-1965.

The operatic repertoire of Bonynge and Joan Sutherland during the 1960's and early 1970's included Mozart, Haydn, Gounod, Délibes, and Verdi. But they were best known for their bel canto successes, which they scored in such early nineteenth-century Italian operas as Donizetti's *Lucia di Lammermoor*, *La Fille du Régiment*, *Maria Stuarda*, and *Lucrezia Borgia*; Bellini's *I Puritani*, *Beatrice di Tenda*, *Norma*, and *La Sonnambula*; and Rossini's *Semiramide* and *Il Barbiere di Siviglia*; and the eighteenth-century baroque-era operas, Handel's *Alcina* and Gluck's *Orfeo ed Euridice*.

Since Bonynge had had no training as a conductor, Joan Sutherland was accused of foisting him upon opera impresarios. Nevertheless, she insisted that he was the perfect conductor for her because of his remarkable understanding of the problems of singers and his knowledge of how she felt and what she was capable of doing. Particularly in his early years of conducting, many critics offered sharply negative evaluations of his work, citing erratic tempo and weak rhythm. But Winthrop Sargeant, one of his severest critics, acknowledged that he had special endowments for conducting bel canto opera, in which the vocal acrobatics of the singer are of overwhelming importance and dramatic values count for less. In the *New Yorker* (April 1, 1972) Sargeant wrote, "From a singer's point of view —and especially from the point of view of a bel canto singer—he is the ideal maestro. He never pushes the vocalist with insistent rhythms. He follows the vocal line, allowing the singer to set his own pace, which may differ from one performance to another, depending on the agility of the moment or the supply of breath. He is acutely conscious of breathing problems, and he tailors his orchestral accompaniments to suit."

As he gained in experience, Bonynge began getting an increasing number of operatic engagements with singers other than his wife in the 1970's. Among the major singers who have enjoyed working with him are Martina Arroyo, Marilyn Horne, Huguette Tourangeau, and Spiro Malas. One musical observer told Herbert Kupferberg of the *National Observer* (April 27, 1974) that "for a while with Richard it was earn while you learn, but he is developing into a conductor with ideas of his own and a much sharper sense of rhythm." His approach was to rely on his instincts and feelings rather than intellect or technical considerations. As he told Rubin, "I'd rather be exciting and theatrical than correct and dull."

Within the opera world Bonynge became known as the outstanding authority on eighteenth- and early nineteenth-century bel canto opera. A collector of old scores, he began examining them to discover how the operas were originally meant to be performed. "We can find out much about performance practice from original and early editions and from scores marked up by singers," he explained to Raymond Ericson of the New York *Times* (November 3, 1968). He applied the knowledge acquired from old scores to his wife's performances. For a 1973 production of Offenbach's *Tales of Hoffmann* at the Metropolitan Opera, Bonynge removed spurious recitatives and substituted spoken dialogue. To the Metropolitan's 1976 presentation of Bellini's *I Puritani*, he added Elvira's long-forgotten final aria, restored from early scores of the opera that he had recently discovered. For eighteenth-century operas of Handel and Mozart, he reduced the orchestra to conform more closely to the smaller size that those composers probably employed. That change was necessary, he believed, so that the coloratura singer could decorate the vocal line properly.

In his search for old scores Bonynge dug up unknown or rarely performed operas, such as Rossini's *Semiramide*, thereby expanding the bel canto repertoire. During the 1970's he was in the forefront of the revival of French opera of the middle and late nineteenth century with his recovery of neglected works such as Massenet's *Esclarmonde*, *Thérèse*, and *Le Roi de Lahore* and Bizet's *Les Pêcheurs de Perles* (*Pearl Fishers*) and *Djamileh*. Joan Sutherland's career followed in the direction of his new interest, so that she sang fewer coloratura roles in favor of more dramatic performances requiring big sounds and an emotional delivery.

Another form of theatre that attracted Bonynge as a subject for research was the ballet, performances of which are among the vivid memories of his youth in Australia. In England during the 1950's he started a collection of books on the history of the dance that helped to prepare him for the dance recordings he began conducting in the mid-1960's. He gave his closest attention to the romantic era of ballet contemporaneous with bel canto opera. Some of his best reviews have been for his ballet recordings, on the London Records label, which have included *Giselle* and *Le Diable à Quatre,* by Adam, *Coppélia,* by Délibes, *La Favorita,* by Minkus, *Swan Lake,* by Tchaikovsky, and *The Swan* by Saint-Saëns. But because Joan Sutherland and Bonynge, as her conductor, are generally booked for opera performances up to four years in advance, he has not been able to conduct much live ballet.

Bonynge and Joan Sutherland have recorded, mainly for London Records also, most of their repertoire in addition to a few other operas such as Donizetti's *L'Elisir d'Amore,* Verdi's *Il Trovatore,* and Leoni's *L'Oracolo,* and several operettas, including *Fledermaus* and *The Merry Widow.* They have, futhermore, collaborated on a recording of Noël Coward songs. In 1974 Bonynge conducted her Public Broadcasting System television series, *Who's Afraid of Opera?,* and on January 22, 1979 he conducted her joint concert with tenor Luciano Pavarotti on the PBS television program *Live from Lincoln Center.*

Appointed artistic director of the Vancouver Opera Association in 1974 and musical director of the Australian Opera in Sydney in 1975, at both institutions Bonynge had responsibilities that included supervision of casting, repertoire, and artistic standards and conducting some of the operas. Because of financial difficulties in Vancouver resulting in part from Bonynge's expensive productions, he left his post there in 1978. He retained his position in Sydney, where he was required by contract to be present six months each year.

Richard Bonynge is a tall, handsome man with a quiet manner and an unaffected charm and presence that have been assets to him as a conductor. He speaks in a refined Australian accent modified by years of living in England and the United States. His lack of apparent ego was indicated by his remarks in an interview for *People* about his decision to change the course of his lifework to benefit his wife: "From the beginning it was clear that hers was the greater talent. I knew I had to sacrifice my career to hers. I saw that helping her would be a full-time occupation." The Bonynges have a spacious chalet above Montreux in Switzerland and an apartment in Sydney. For their visits to New York they rent two floors of a mansion in Brooklyn Heights. Their twenty-five-year-old son, Adam Bonynge, works in Switzerland in hotel management. Bonynge likes to garden and to paint and, especially, to collect antiques and opera memorabilia, including old scores and books, Staffordshire porcelain, and autographed letters.

References: *Gramophone* 54:761+ N '76 por; *New Yorker* 48:40+ Ap 1 '72; *People* 11:129+ Ap 30 '79 por; *Stereo R* 29:74+ N '72 por, 37: 68+N '76; Braddon, Russell. *Joan Sutherland* (1962); *Notable Australians* (1978); Rubin, Stephen E. *The New Met in Profile* (1972)

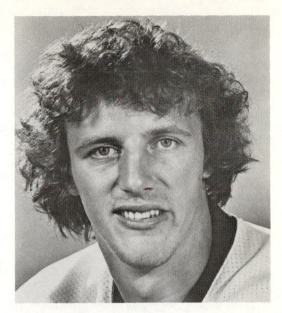

Bossy, Mike

Jan. 22, 1957- Hockey player. Address: b. New York Islanders, 1155 Conklin St., Farmingdale, N.Y. 11735

The fastest hands in professional hockey are arguably those of Mike Bossy, the nonpareil right wing of the New York Islanders, who is aptly known as "the phantom of the rinks." "You're always looking for Bossy, wondering where he is," Phil Myre, the Philadelphia Flyers' goalie, has testified. "Sometimes you never see him until he's scored on you." Bossy can be a dazzling puck carrier by himself, but it has largely been in combination with center Bryan Trottier that he has transformed the Islanders from a defense-oriented team into a championship scoring machine, winner of the Stanley Cup in 1979-80 and 1980-81. In 1977-78 Bossy set a National Hockey League mark for goals by a rookie, with fifty-three, and he went on to amass 100 and 200 goals sooner than any other NHL player, in 129 and 255 games respectively. He was also unique in scoring fifty-plus goals in each of his first three seasons, including the 1978-79 tally of sixty-nine, which surpassed by eight the previous record for a right wing, held by Reggie Leach of the Flyers. In 1980-81 Bossy led the league in goals, with sixty-eight, tied league marks by scoring twenty-eight times on the power play and racking up fifty goals in fifty games, and set a new record for most "hat tricks," or three-goal games, in a season, with nine. His career total of 241 goals in 307 regular-season games gives him a scoring percentage of .785, the highest in NHL history among players with more than 200 goals. Bossy became the highest paid player in the history of the NHL on October 27, 1981, when the Islanders signed him to a seven-year contract worth an estimated $4,500,000.

The fifth of ten children of Borden and Dorothy Bossy, Michael Bossy was born in Montreal, Quebec, Canada on January 22, 1957. Although he is of English descent, with an admixture of Ukrainian and Austrian, he grew up bilingual in the French-speaking section of Montreal, and the false impression that he is French-Canadian is widespread. That impression was fostered by the *Québecois* press, which Gallicanized him in his amateur years, referring to him as "Michel." The name stuck all the way up to his first year as a pro, when he was initially listed on the Islanders' roster as Michel Bossy.

Sports is a Bossy family tradition. An uncle, Leo, once coached the Montreal Junior Canadiens, the hockey team, and Mike's father, an industrial engineer by profession, was an Olympic-calibre paddler in his youth. Mike began skating when he was three, on the rink his father created each winter by flooding the backyard. By the age of six he was the best hockey player among the "Mites" of Montreal's St. Alphonse Parish, and later, as a "Peewee," he scored 170 goals in forty games. His superiority over his peers came partly from his ability to flick his stick without having to take time to balance himself. That unusual equilibrium is still one of his key assets.

In 1973 Bossy joined the Laval Nationals of the Quebec Junior Hockey League. He scored seventy goals in his first year with the Nationals, led the league with eighty-four in his second, and tallied seventy-nine in his third and seventy-five in his fourth. He was voted the league's Most Gentlemanly Player in the 1976-77 season, his last, and over the four years he had 221 assists. His 309 goals as a junior were just five short of Guy Lafleur's junior record.

His coaches in the juniors, content with his superiority on offense, did not press Bossy to develop his defensive skills. As a result, as he has admitted, he "got lazy" and acquired a negative reputation with professional scouts for checking, playing defense, and dispensing or taking punishment. Probably no other junior player with such outstanding offensive statistics ever wound up in such a poor draft position as did Bossy in 1977. Fourteen teams, including his hometown Canadiens, passed him by in the first round before the New York Islanders, desperate for offensive talent, snapped him up. "It was important that I got picked on the first round for my pride, my self-confidence," he later commented.

Al Arbour, the coach of the Islanders, put Bossy on a line with center Bryan Trottier and left wing Clark Gillies, and that line, dubbed the "Trio Grande" by sportswriters, quickly became the most formidable in the National Hockey League. "Bryan is the perfect center for me," Bossy told a reporter two months after the 1977-78 season began. "He can get the puck to me 95 percent of the time

when I am open and Clark gets the puck out of the corners to Bryan 95 percent of his chances."

Although Bossy came to the Islanders with an innate scoring knack, he had to acquire a sense of direction, as he recently recalled in an interview with Larry Brooks for *Sports Illustrated* (January 19, 1981): "In the juniors I pretty much carried the puck all the time except for one year when I played with a center named Jean Trottier. But when I came to the Islanders, Bryan had the puck most of the time, or Clarkie was digging for it in the corners, so I had to find a way to get into position to take a pass if I wanted it. If I stand in one place, the other team will hook, hold, and clutch me, but by moving around the way I do, all they can do is whack at me, and that won't stop me. It's hard work, it's tiring, . . . but I want to be in position where I can get the puck and shoot it."

Thirty-eight assists added to his record-breaking fifty-three goals as a rookie brought Bossy's total points in 1977-78 to ninety-one. The Islanders finished first in the Campbell Conference's Patrick Division and third overall in the NHL, and in the playoffs—which Bossy opened with a hat trick—they lost to Toronto in the quarterfinals. In winning the *Sporting News* Rookie of the Year award, Bossy received 142 of a possible 246 votes in a league-wide poll of his fellow players. In addition, he received the Calder Memorial Trophy as the NHL's top rookie.

With a league-leading sixty-nine goals and a total of 126 points, Bossy in 1978-79 paced the Islanders to their first regular-season NHL championship, and on the way he reached the 100-goal mark in 129 games, faster than any other player in NHL history. In the Stanley Cup playoffs, he contributed five goals to the Islanders' victory over Chicago in the quarterfinals but was held to one goal by the victorious New York Rangers in the semifinals. In the finals the Rangers were repulsed by the Montreal Canadiens, holders of the Stanley Cup since 1976.

In 1979-80 Bossy scored fifty-one goals and the Islanders finished second in the Patrick Division. In the playoffs, a jammed right thumb kept him out of the first three games of the quarterfinals against the Boston Bruins. Returning to action in the fourth Boston game, he scored twice and went on to become an important factor in the six-game finale against the Philadelphia Flyers. He tallied a total of ten goals and thirteen assists, making him the second-highest scorer, and the Islanders won the Stanley Cup for the first time.

On January 18, 1981 Bossy broke the old NHL hat trick record, with his eighth of the season. Five days later, in his fiftieth game of the season, he scored his fiftieth goal of the season, tying the unofficial mark set by Maurice ("Rocket") Richard in 1944-45. Asked to compare himself to Bossy, Richard told a reporter:

"[Bossy] gets the same good shots in front of the net that I did. But the real secret is having a great centerman and left winger feeding you the puck. I had Elmer Lach and Toe Blake with me, and Mike's got Bryan Trottier and Clark Gillies. . . . I think we shoot the same way. Mike has a good backhand shot, a great wrist shot, and he doesn't use the slap shot—well, maybe just a half-slap sometimes. But he very seldom is off target. He is usually right on net with his shots, and that's important."

Outside of regular season play, Bossy participated in the thirty-third NHL All-Star game, in Los Angeles on February 10, 1981, and on that occasion he contributed an assist to the Campbell Conference's 4-1 victory over the Wales Conference. Back in the regular schedule, Bossy set his sights on the record of seventy-six goals in seventy-eight games set by Phil Esposito in 1970-71. Falling into a slump, and again hampered by a sprained right thumb, he ended up eight goals short of his objective, but with his sixty-eighth goal, on March 29, 1981, he gave the Islanders a comeback 5-4 victory over the Washington Capitals and put them in first place in the overall NHL standings. He ended the season with sixty-eight goals and fifty-one assists, for 119 points. While leading the league in goals, he was fourth behind Wayne Gretzky of the Edmonton Oilers in points. In the playoffs, Bossy had an unprecedented eight power-play goals going into the final series, in which the Islanders defeated the Minnesota North Stars to win their second straight Stanley Cup.

In warmups and practice, Bossy tries nine or ten different kinds of slapshots, wristers, flicks, and backhands. An adept passer and stick handler, he has been working diligently at making himself a rounded, versatile, two-way player. But however good he becomes at backchecking, his defensive style is unlikely ever to match his natural offensive knack, which he has never tried to analyze by studying films or videotapes of himself shooting the puck or making plays. To him, "scoring goals is just something [he has] always been able to do."

Any analysis of Bossy's effectiveness on the ice might well begin with the observation that he eschews—as well as loudly denounces—the violent physical contact that gives hockey a bad name. Among the fastest skaters in the National Hockey League, he eludes and fazes rather than confronts the opposition, skating toward it at blinding forty-five degree angles when he himself is carrying the puck forward. More often, his pacifism reinforces the deceptive impression of casual aloofness he gives as he circles from one side of the net to the other when anticipating a pass from a linemate and positioning himself for a shot. He is virtually invisible—until suddenly he comes out of nowhere firing the puck into the one unprotected inch of net without even looking up. "Bossy has the knack of hitting the open spot in the net, just like my brother Phil," Tony Esposito, the Chicago Black Hawks's goalie, has observed. "You can't teach that. You have to be born with that instinct for the spot where the goalie isn't." John Davidson, the New York Rangers' goalie, has explained, "You can't set up for Bossy's shot because he gets it off before the puck is on his stick." And Charlie Simmer, the Los Angeles Kings's left wing, rates him as "the best shooter around from twenty-five feet out." Under his first contract with the Islanders, Bossy made $65,000 a year, and he now makes approximately three times that much. The figure is expected to reach superstar size when he signs a new contract in 1982.

Six feet tall and weighing 185 pounds, Mike Bossy is sinewy of limb and angular of face, with a pale complexion and eyes that reflect his unspoiled, unassuming disposition. Soft-spoken, he is cautious but candid in expressing his opinions, and he seldom loses his composure, on or off the ice. "You can't needle him and get results as much anymore," according to his linemate Bryan Trottier. Homesick, sensitive, and not making friends easily when he arrived in Long Island, Bossy found a kindred spirit in the quiet Trottier. "Ever since, Bryan has been my closest friend on the team," Bossy has said. "Without somebody like him, maybe my life would have been unbearable here. . . . We're not the night-life type. When we go on the road, we like to watch television. We might be classified as boring by some people's standards."

"When I am hurting," Bossy once said, referring to his wife, "she is the only one I reach out to." He and Lucie Creamer, his French-Canadian childhood sweetheart, were married on July 23, 1977. With their daughter, Josiane, they live in a modest rented duplex in East Northport, Long Island, twenty miles from the Nassau Veterans Memorial Coliseum in Uniondale, the Islanders' home rink, during the hockey season, and in a home they own in the Montreal suburb of Laval in the off-season. The Bossys speak French among themselves and he translates for his wife in English conversation with others, although she is reportedly fairly fluent in the language herself. "We don't go out much," Bossy has said of his and his wife's social life. The last known entertainment trip they made into Manhattan, aside from hockey games at Madison Square Garden, was to see *Beatlemania* quite a while ago.

Bossy makes no secret of the facts that his family is "the only thing that's important" and that he "hurts for home," meaning suburban Montreal. At least partly for those reasons, he has been quoted as saying, he intends to quit hockey by age thirty. Among possible second careers, golf would probably be his preference. In the meantime, he thanks God for "the natural ability He gave me" and continues to find in hockey a simple joy rare in a professional superstar. "When I score a goal," he has said, "the feeling I get is something I'd wish on people," and what he means is evident in the exultant upward thrust of his arms each time the puck finds its mark.

References: N Y Daily News SE p4 D 12 '80 por; N Y Times V p1+ N 2 '80 por; Newsweek 91:73 Mr 13 '78 por; Sports Illus 54:36+ Ja 19 '81 pors; People 11:49+ Mr 26 '79 pors; Sporting News p3 F 28 '81 pors; Time 117:76 F 2 '81 pors; Toronto Globe and Mail mag p16+ Ap 21 '79 pors

Brandt, Bill

1904- British photographer. Address: b. c/o Marlborough Gallery Inc., 40 W. 57th St., New York City, N.Y. 10019

For nearly half a century British photographer Bill Brandt has been an artist of international reputation. Since the 1930's, the days of his renowned depictions of upper- and lower-class London life, Brandt has devoted himself to the creation of enduring photographic images through the combined exercise of personal emotion, idiosyncratic vision, and aesthetic control. In more recent years Brandt has also become known as a distinguished portrait and landscape photographer. Moreover, he has stirred excitement with his inspired reinterpretation of the female nude. Although now in his late seventies, Brandt continues his career with unabated artistry.

Bill Brandt was born in South London in 1904 (some sources say 1905) to British parents of Russian descent. He spent most of his childhood and youth in Germany and in Switzerland, where he went to recover from a bout of tuberculosis. Because of his delicate health in his early years, Brandt was advised to give up his plan of becoming an architect. He decided instead to become a portrait photographer. Brandt studied in a Swiss portrait studio and in 1928 made his first photographic efforts in London before being introduced to the surrealist photographer Man Ray. For three months in 1929, Brandt worked as Man Ray's assistant at his studio in Paris. Although he received little direct instruction from Man Ray, Brandt has said that he gained "a new excitement about photography and about the world as well" from his exposure to his teacher's unique vision. Brandt also learned much from the Parisian art of the period, such as the films of Luis Buñuel and Salvador Dali and the photographs of Brassaï, Eugène Atget, and André Kertesz. In 1930 Brandt contributed free-lance photographs to Paris magazine before returning, in 1931, to the city of his birth.

Instead of becoming a portrait photographer, during the 1930's Bill Brandt turned his attention to capturing the nuances of London's hierarchic social life. Brandt depicted the habitations, occupations, and amusements of rich and poor with an observant eye for significant detail. He usually worked when prompted by specific assignments, which has been his practice throughout his career. As he has explained, "The sheer having to do a job supplies an incentive, without which the taking of photographs just for fun seems to leave the fun rather flat." In the 1930's Brandt's commissions came from such British newspapers and magazines as News Chronicle, Weekly Illustrated, Lilliput, Picture Post, and Vogue as well as the French art magazines Verve and Minotaure. In 1937 Brandt visited the North of England on his own initiative to chronicle the life of the industrial towns hit by economic hardship.

Although some critics see Bill Brandt's pictures of the 1930's as simple documentaries, most look upon them as art works that are the products of a poet's intuition and an outsider's detachment. According to Ian Jeffrey of Studio International (March/April 1977), Bill Brandt has said that in taking those photographs he was influenced by the Edwardian illustrations in the books he looked at during childhood. Norman Hall, in a catalogue essay for Brandt's 1976 retrospective at the Marlborough Gallery in New York City, pointed to French illustrator Gustave Doré's book London, A Pilgrimage (1872) as a particularly strong influence on Brandt's 1930's photos.

During the 1930's Brandt compiled his social photographs into two books. The first one, The English at Home, was published in 1936 by B. T. Batsford Ltd. in England and by Charles Scribner's Sons in the United States. In that collection of some sixty photographs, produced in the soft, warm tones of Brandt's early printing style, the similarities and differences between the lives of rich and poor are revealed through depictions of their habitual activities. For example, two companion photos, *Workmen's Restaurant* and *Clubmen's Sanctuary*, present contrasting groups of men reading and meditating in the tranquil solitude of the refuges to which their respective social classes assign them. Sometimes a series of photographs offers multiple impressions of class distinctions, as in the case of a sequence that suggests the differences between the crowds at Ascot and Epsom racetracks. That series culminates in a picture that combines the contrasting social worlds in a single image. The focus of *Ascot Enclosure: Within and Without* is the bright white fence across the photo's middle ground, which divides the carefully-dressed ladies and gentlemen who watch the race from the stolid worker who watches them and from the sleeping vagrant who lies oblivious among discarded newspapers.

The second of Brandt's books of social photographs, *A Night in London,* was published in 1938 by Country Life Ltd. in England and by Charles Scribner's Sons in the United States. Its pictures, once again produced in the glowing, full-bodied shades of Brandt's early printing style, are arranged chronologically from sunset to sunrise in an all-embracing composite of disparate experiences during a London night. Brandt looks at Londoners amusing themselves at society balls in Mayfair, card games in Kensington, and literary gatherings in Bloomsbury; at Londoners working in bakeries, subways, and markets; and especially at Londoners retiring for the night in the snug beds of children's nurseries, on the hard steps of public stairways, and in the coffin-like boxes of charity shelters. *A Night in London* reveals its meanings, as John Taylor observed in *Creative Camera* (March/April 1981), not only through single pairs of contrasting images, but also through the careful arrangement of its sixty-four photographs into a sequence that "flows like an extended frieze or papyrus roll." In 1938 Arts et Métiers Graphiques published *Londres de Nuit,* the book's French edition, and mounted Brandt's first solo exhibition at the Galerie du Chasseur d'Images in Paris.

Brandt captured a very different vision of nights in London during the blitzkrieg of World War II, when he took to the empty streets to photograph the unearthly glow of moonlight on the damaged city. Those pictures exude the brooding solemnity of a post-apocalyptic silence in which deserted buildings remain amidst surrounding rubble. Brandt also went underground to document, for the British Home Office, the use of subway stations and church crypts as air-raid shelters. Brandt's poignant studies of the subterranean shelters were published, together with British sculptor Henry Moore's sketches of the same subject, in *Lilliput* in 1942. That same year a number of Brandt's war photographs were published in the magazine *Horizon*.

At the end of World War II, Brandt turned his attention to the three major subjects that have occupied him ever since: artists' portraits, British landscapes, and female nudes. His first postwar book, however, is another study of his favorite city. *Camera in London,* published in 1948 in England and the United States by the Focal Press, includes a selection of the war photographs in addition to a variety of peacetime images. The book is noteworthy because its introduction, written by Bill Brandt himself, offers a rare explanation of his professional theories.

In his introduction to *Camera in London,* Brandt declared that a photographer must have "an emotional response" to his subject matter in order to make powerful pictures. For his own part, he responds most readily to "atmosphere" as a subject. "I found *atmosphere* to be the spell that charged the commonplace with beauty. And I am still not sure what atmosphere is," he explained. "...I only know it is a combination of elements, perhaps most simply and yet most inadequately described in technical terms of lighting and viewpoint, which reveals the subject as familiar and yet strange." Brandt tries to convey atmosphere so emphatically in his pictures that viewers will also respond to it; as a photographer, he insisted, it is his job to enable other people "to see the world anew." To fulfill that task, Brandt asserted, the photographer must possess extraordinary vision, with "something of the receptiveness of the child who looks at the world for the first time or of the traveller who enters a strange country."

Brandt began his postwar portrait work in the 1940's, when he accepted commissions from *Lilliput* and *Picture Post* to photograph notable British artists. He continued his work in the 1950's with a series of portraits of international artists for *Harper's Bazaar*. (Since the war's end Brandt has also carried out assignments for the New York *Times Magazine* and *Holiday*.) To make his portraits of writers, poets, painters, sculptors, and actors, Brandt went to the work environment of each subject, taking with him a companion to talk to his sitter while he gathered impressions and decided how to capture most effectively the personality of the artist and his surroundings.

Critics have expressed their admiration for the power of Brandt's portraits, which include such images as British writer Robert Graves turning his haunted gaze upon the viewer from within the sanctuary of his cottage; British painter Francis Bacon losing himself in grim meditation during a walk down Primrose Hill; and French painter Jean Dubuffet standing before the inspirational stones of the Col de Vence. Norman Hall, writing in *Popular Photography* (September 1967), observed that the portraits possess "a probing quality which seems to unmask the sitter and reveal not just the way he looks, but a sort of understanding about how he thinks and what he fears." Hilton Kramer of the New York *Times* (September 28, 1969) asserted that the portraits "show us figures and faces almost unbearably vulnerable.

... The world these figures inhabit is shown to be a harsh place; an unbenevolent fate seems ready to close in the moment the shutter has closed."

After World War II Brandt also began working on studies of British landscapes, intrigued, as Tom Hopkinson pointed out in an article for *Photography* magazine (April 1954), not "by natural beauty, but . . . with space, and the possibilities of conveying impressions of space by photographic means." In his landscapes Brandt also concerned himself with the evocation of atmosphere that elicits an emotional response from both photographer and viewer. To capture the atmosphere of a particular locale, Brandt exercised great patience in waiting for ideal lighting and weather conditions.

Brandt's landscape book, *Literary Britain,* was published in England in 1951 by Cassell and Company Ltd. Its pictures reveal the quintessential moods of the places where seven centuries of British writers or their fictional creations lived and worked. For example, a slender ribbon receding through long grass recalls the trek of the pilgrims in Geoffrey Chaucer's *Canterbury Tales;* a stunted pony ambles across the close-mown gorse of Egdon Heath, where Thomas Hardy set the major events of *The Return of the Native;* a shadowy expanse of lawn encompasses Gad's Hill Place, the house that Charles Dickens longed for in his childhood and lived in during the tormented and productive years of his later life. Brandt also selected and arranged the photographs of a second landscape book, *The Land: Twentieth Century Landscape Photographs,* published in England in 1975 by Gordon Fraser Ltd., and prepared the comprehensive exhibition of works by European, American, and Japanese photographers from which the book's pictures were culled. The Victoria and Albert Museum mounted the show in London in late 1975 and sent it in 1976 to Edinburgh, Ulster, and Cardiff.

Brandt's interest in the exploration of space inspired him in his studies of nudes as well as landscapes. During the 1940's Brandt took his first photographs of nudes in Victorian rooms when commissioned by the editor of the annual publication *Saturday Book* to do an extensive feature on the subject. The editor never got to use the pictures because his publisher embarked on what Brandt has called "a purity campaign," but Brandt decided to continue his work independently until he produced enough material for a book. For over a decade he experimented with an old wooden Kodak whose wide-angle lens, focused on infinity, could encompass the full sweep of a room in a single photograph. In the elongated spaces of Brandt's alien interiors, the female body takes on threatening and alluring new forms. In the late 1950's Brandt abandoned his ancient camera and took his models to the seashores of East Sussex, Normandy, and the Côte d'Azur to create images in which the nudes become organic elements of the natural settings.

Brandt first revealed his innovative photos to the general public in 1961, fifteen years after he began work on them, in a volume entitled *Perspective of Nudes.* The book was published in England by Bodley Head and in the United States by Amphoto. It generated considerable controversy because some critics, ignorant of Brandt's spatial and formal concerns, dismissed the pictures as ugly, misogynistic images. More perceptive reviewers praised the pictures as celebrations of "pure, plastic form." As Mark Haworth-Booth later declared in his introduction to Brandt's book *Shadow of Light* (1977), the nude studies have extended the language of photography. After the publication of *Perspective of Nudes,* Brandt turned his attention away from nudes until 1977, when he embarked on a series of increasingly sinister images of distorted figures, with faces frequently obscured by cloth gags or tangled tresses. Brandt combined a number of those nightmarish nudes with selections from his earlier studies to create a second book, *Nudes 1945-1980,* which was published in 1980 by Gordon Fraser Ltd. in England and by the New York Graphic Society in the United States.

Brandt's nudes also appear in his book *Shadow of Light,* a retrospective survey of the different phases of his career. The first version, published in 1966 by Bodley Head in England and by Viking Press in the United States, was heralded as a welcome volume of masterful work. Brandt selected a considerable number of additional images for its second version, published in 1977 by Gordon Fraser Ltd. in England and by Da Capo Press in the United States. For both editions of the book Brandt printed older and newer photographs alike in a distinctively stark, high-contrast style that eliminates most soft, gray details.

Brandt also used high-contrast prints in his major retrospective exhibitions of recent years. In 1969 New York City's Museum of Modern Art presented Brandt's first retrospective, which was shown the following year at London's Hayward Gallery and at a series of museums in cities throughout the United Kingdom. In 1976 Marlborough Gallery's New York and London branches both mounted comprehensive solo shows of Brandt's work, and in 1981 the New York branch offered a major exhibition of his nudes. Also in 1981, the Royal Photographic Society inaugurated its National Centre of Photography in Bath with an exhibition of fifty years of Brandt's pictures. His work has been honored as well by a score of smaller shows in the past decade or so, in such far-flung cities as Paris, Stockholm, San Francisco, Houston, Boston, and Washington, D.C.

Bill Brandt is an elegant, austere man who scorns self-aggrandizement and refuses to discuss his private life with the press. "The person is of no importance. It is the picture that is important," he told Tom Picton of *Camerawork* (November 1976). Brandt's pictures are indeed considered important by London's Victoria and

Albert Museum, New York City's Museum of Modern Art, Rochester's International Museum of Photography, and Paris' Bibliothèque Nationale, which all have major collections of his prints. Because of his distinguished work, Brandt was named a Royal Designer for Industry by the Royal Society of Arts in 1978 and was awarded the Silver Progress Medal of the Royal Photographic Society for 1979. When he is not preoccupied by photography, Brandt spends his time making three-dimensional collages from found objects. In recent months, he has begun work on a new series of commissioned portraits.

References: Camera 51:14+ My '72; Sat R 22:52+ O 11 '69; Washington Post C p1+ O 30 '69; Brandt, Bill. Shadow of Light (1977); Who's Who, 1981-82

Brett, George

May 15, 1953- Baseball player. Address: b Kansas City Royals, P. O. Box 1969, Kansas City, Mo. 64141

In his first seven seasons with the Kansas City Royals of the American League West, the free-spirited third baseman and team spark plug George Brett established himself as the Royals' runs-batted-in and hitting leader, with career figures of 578 and .319 in those categories. Brett, whose many offensive distinctions include two American League batting titles, had his best season thus far in 1980, when he was named Most Valuable Player in the league. In leading Kansas City to its first pennant that year, he

tallied a batting average of .390, the best in the major leagues since 1941. Carl Yastrzemski, the Boston outfielder, at that time rated Brett "the best hitter in the American League right now, and maybe in all of baseball," and Gene Mauch, the California Angels' manager, said: "Taking everything into consideration, his great abilities plus the intangibles, Brett is probably the best player in the game today."

The youngest of four sons of a finance officer for the Datsun automobile company, George Howard Brett was born in Glendale, West Virginia on May 15, 1953. All three of his brothers played baseball professionally, but only one made the majors—Kenneth, now a pitcher with Kansas City. John is in the construction business, and Robert is in real estate.

Brett grew up in Hermosa Beach, California and starred in football as well as baseball at El Segundo (California) High School. "My father . . . backed us all the way," he recounted in an interview with Ron Fimrite for Sports Illustrated (August 11, 1980). "We got the best $40 gloves, although mine were hand-me-downs from Bobby and John. We were middle-class. My father said we didn't have to get jobs in the summer. That was the time to enjoy yourself, he told us. I don't recall ever getting an allowance, but if I needed something, I got it. There was no stereo or TV in my room, but if I wanted $3 to go to the movies, I'd get it."

Brett recalled watching his brother Ken pitch in the World Series for the Boston Red Sox in 1967, when he, Ken, was nineteen. "I saw him in Busch Stadium," Brett told Fimrite. "I was only fourteen. What a thrill! At that time, he could really blow the ball. He'd come home, driving a GTO and pulling out a roll of $10 bills—there might have been only three or four, but it looked like a roll. I'd say, 'Look, he's got it made.' That's when I decided if there was anything I wanted to be, it was a ballplayer."

After graduating from high school, Brett briefly attended El Camino Junior College in Torrance, California. Drafted as a shortstop by the Royals in 1971, he was sent to the Kansas City farm team in Billings, Montana, where he was switched to third base. With Billings he hit .291 and batted in forty-four runs in sixty-eight games. He was the shortstop on the 1971 All-Pioneer League team and the National Association All-Rookie squad.

With San Jose in 1972, Brett hit .274 and drove in sixty-eight runs in 117 games. The following year he was assigned to Omaha, where he had a .284 batting average and 117 RBI's. During that year with Omaha he was selected to the American Association All-Star team. As a minor leaguer, Brett tried to be a pull hitter, always going for the long ball, as he has recalled: "As a kid I wanted to be like Brooks Robinson, only I was left-handed. So I made Carl Yastrzemski my hero. All through the minor leagues I tried to hit like Yaz. But I wasn't half as strong as he was. And I couldn't pull the ball either."

Brett first saw major-league action as a replacement for injured third baseman Paul Schaal for two weeks in August 1973, when he batted .125 in thirteen games. He opened the 1974 season at Omaha but was summoned back to Kansas City on May 3 as starting third baseman, after Schaal was traded to California.

By the All-Star break in July 1974, Brett was batting below .200 and was beginning to think that he was not going to last in the majors. Then Charley Lau, at that time the Royals' special hitting instructor, took him aside and changed his stance and style at the plate. Lau taught him to extend his arms at the moment of contact, and at the same time to take his top hand off the bat. He also taught him to increase his power by standing off from the plate and keeping his weight on the balls of his feet. "Charlie got me to hold the bat parallel to the ground, to wait for the pitch and to hit to the opposite field," Brett told a reporter. "It used to be that the only time I hit a ball to left field was when I swung late."

Thus, under Lau's tutelage, Brett was transformed from a mediocre power pull hitter, a would-be slugger, into a consistent spray-the-field single puncher. Complementing his change at the plate was a new-found aggressiveness on the base paths, learned from his teammate Hal McRae. "I could see him stretching singles into doubles, and I'd say, 'Hey, I can do that,'" Brett recounted in the *Sports Illustrated* interview with Ron Fimrite. "I'd never played that way in the minor leagues. I was lackadaisical. Now I don't think I can play any other way but all out. Baseball's no fun if you don't go out there and be . . . well . . . berserk, if that's the word. I enjoy the game so much because I'm putting so much into it. It makes you feel great inside when you're standing on second or third base knowing you've just stretched a hit."

Brett finished the 1974 season with a .282 batting average, and the following year he led the Royals with a .308 average and the American League with 195 hits and 634 times at bat. Also in 1975, he tied for league leadership in triples, with thirteen, and led league third basemen in all offensive categories except homers.

In 1976 Brett had a brilliant season, leading the American League in batting (.333), hits (215), triples (fourteen), total bases (298), and at-bats (546). In the league playoffs against the New York Yankees in 1976, his three-run homer tied the fifth game, which the Yankees ultimately won on a dramatic hit by Chris Chambliss in the ninth inning. For his performance in 1976 he was selected for the *Sporting News* and UPI All-League teams and the Associated Press All-Major team.

In 1977 Brett's statistics included a .312 batting average and eighty-eight runs-batted-in. That year the Royals again reached the playoffs, where they were again stopped by the Yankees. The following year—when he played much of the season with a painfully bruised left shoulder and bone chips in the thumb of his throwing hand—he batted .294 and led the league in doubles, with forty-five. In the 1978 playoffs—where the Royals were for a third time eliminated by the Yankees—he set a play-off record by hitting three home runs off Catfish Hunter. His batting average in the fourteen playoff games in which he had played to that point was a robust .375.

Following surgery on his thumb, Brett missed spring training in 1979, and he wore a protective device on the thumb at the plate for most of the season. Through the middle of May, his fielding was hampered and his batting average never rose above the mid-.200's. Then returning to his best form, he finished the season with a .329 batting average (second in the league to Fred Lynn's .334), forty-two doubles, twenty-three homers, 119 runs, and 107 runs-batted-in. He led the league in triples, with twenty, and hits, with 212, and he stole seventeen bases. Kansas City finished second in the American League West that season.

An All-Star for four successive years beginning in 1976, he was at bat a total of ten times for the American League. He tallied his first run against the National League in 1978, and his second, along with his first hit, in 1979. In 1980 he was again selected for the All-Star game, but he did not appear because of injuries to his right ankle and heel that also forced him to sit out thirty-seven regular-season games.

In May 1980 Brett was hitting .247, and by the All-Star break he was batting .337. After the break he went into a thirty-game hitting streak, from July 18 to August 18, the momentum of which made him a continuous media event through to the end of the season, with "Brett for President" bumper stickers displayed all over Kansas City and its environs. On August 17 his average passed the .400 mark, and in Milwaukee on August 26 he went five for five to raise it to a season peak of .407. He did not slip below .400 until September 20, and the .390 with which he finished the season was the highest in the majors since 1941, when Ted Williams hit .406 with the Red Sox. It equaled the previous highest for a third baseman, the .390 recorded by John McGraw with Baltimore of the National League in 1899. The previous best for an American League third baseman was .347, set by Frank Baker with Philadelphia in 1912.

Among Brett's other 1980 season statistics were a slugging percentage of .664, the highest in the majors since Mickey Mantle's .687 in 1971; an on-base percentage of .461, which led both leagues; 118 RBI's in 117 games, making him the first player in thirty years to drive in at least one run per game; twenty-four home runs, his career high; and twenty-two strikeouts, only three more than Rich Dauer of Baltimore, who had the fewest strikeouts in the American League.

In the American League playoffs against the Yankees following the 1980 season, Brett had three hits in eleven times at bat. Two of the hits were home runs, and one of the homers put the Royals into the World Series. Brett smacked that four-bagger off Goose Gossage as the Royals were trailing 2-1 in the third game of the playoffs with two men on base. Altogether, he drove in four runs, bringing his league championship series total of RBI's to fourteen.

After the playoff victory over the Royals' perennial nemesis, New York, the World Series was a letdown, especially for Brett, who was suffering with a severe hemorrhoidal problem. In the first game against Philadelphia his bad judgment allowed a run to score in the Phillies' 7-6 victory. The pain he was experiencing became so bad that he had to leave the field after the sixth inning of the second game, which Philadelphia won 6-4. Following surgery, he returned for game three, in which his first-inning homer started the Royals toward a 4-3 win. He contributed a hit (and ducked a controversial pitch by Dickie Noles) in the fourth game, which Kansas City won 5-3. With the series tied at two games apiece, the Royals were ahead 3-2 in the ninth when Mike Schmidt, the Philadelphia third baseman, came to bat. Brett was positioned for the possibility of a bunt, but Schmidt hit a hard line drive to Brett's left. Brett, in a dive, knocked the shot down but couldn't make a play on it. Schmidt's single sparked a rally that enabled the Phillies to win 4-3, and they wrapped up the Series two days later. In addition to the American League MVP title, Brett's 1980 post-season honors included the American League Silver Bat Award, the Joe Cronin Award, the Fred Hutchinson Award, and the Major League Player of the Year awards of the *Sporting News, Sport* magazine, and the Associated Press.

In 1981 the Royals declined alarmingly and Brett lost his stride. By June 12, when the major league players went out on strike, the team was in fifth place in the American League West, with a 20-30 record. Brett's .323, tied for tenth best in the league, was a good batting average by general standards but not by Brett's. His other statistics included thirteen RBI's and one homer. Also, Brett's happy-go-lucky attitude disappeared, especially in his relations with the press, at which he lashed out angrily on several occasions. On one of the occasions, when he had a sprained ankle, he swung a crutch at a bothersome photographer.

Following the settlement of the strike, the 1981 baseball season reopened on August 10, 1981. Playing more than he had in the first half of the season, Brett had a final average of .314 and a total of forty-three runs-batted-in. The Royals had a record of 50-53, and they were eliminated by Oakland in the division playoff.

Whitey Herzog, former manager of the Royals, now with the St. Louis Cardinals, ranks Brett the easiest player he has ever managed— "You just let him play." Regarding Brett's defensive play, the only area in which he is vulnerable to criticism, a teammate, pitcher Paul Splittorff, has said: "His fielding is really pretty good, but it doesn't measure up to his hitting. What could? He's just an amazing clutch player." What impresses Jim Frey, the manager of the Royals, most about Brett is how hard and zestfully he plays. "He breaks up the double play, he takes the extra base, he dives for balls," Frey said in the *Sports Illustrated* interview with Ron Fimrite. "Like Brooks Robinson, he just loves being a ballplayer."

Frey believes that Brett's handling of the hot corner is underrated. "His hands are good," he told Fimrite, "his range is good, and he's improved in throwing over the last two years. The guy people are talking about when they say he isn't a good fielder is the guy who played three or four years ago, the guy who might backhand a ball and then throw it away. George does a helluva job defensively now." Explaining the thirty errors he made in 1980, Brett himself said: "Sometimes my mind wanders and I sort of forget."

Brett arrives at the ballpark earlier than most of his teammates. Among his superstitions is the wearing of a lucky T-shirt. Brett bats left and throws right. He uses a Louisville Slugger T85 bat, unvarnished, thirty-four-and-a-half inches long, and weighing thirty-two ounces, and he is one of the few players in baseball who does not use a batting glove. His secret at the plate is a combination of ease and concentration. "We all come here with talent," his teammate Hal McRae has explained. "But the stars are the ones who don't have to work at concentrating. The superstars are the ones who are unconscious." McRae describes the state that Brett is in at bat as "a trance."

The trance begins when Brett steps into the on-deck circle. He talks to himself, saying things like "I'm hot," "This guy can't get me out," or "I'm going to hit this pitcher." "As I walk up to the batter's box I suck up the applause," he told Frank W. Martin of *People* (September 15, 1980). "Then I concentrate on that little white ball and relax. You don't get hits by trying hard. You try easy." Once he contacts the ball, however, he burns the path to first.

Blue-eyed, sandy-haired George Brett is six feet tall, weighs about 200 pounds, is a casual dresser, and always seems to be in motion, on or off the field. A bachelor, Brett has a reputation as a wooer of women, but lately he has been trying to cut down on his nightlife to make more room for such other recreations as golf, hunting, fishing, pool, hockey, photography, rounding up cattle on a friend's ranch, and place-kicking a football (one of his high school fortes).

The tobacco-chewing Kansas City superstar drives a Mercedes and a Bronco and lives in a $225,000 home on Lake Quivira, twenty-five miles west of Kansas City. He also owns real estate in California, has investments in diamonds, oil, and gas, and does public relations work for a savings and loan association in

Kansas City. The five-year contract he signed with the Royals in 1977 was for a total of $1,000,000. In 1980 he negotiated a new five-year contract assuring him $1,000,000 a year and adding $250,000 to each of the two remaining years under the old contract. Brett's teammates have testified that success "hasn't affected him at all," that "he's the same guy who was making $500 a month." "The best thing about him," pitcher Andy Hassler of the Angels, a former teammate, has said, "is that he doesn't take himself too seriously, not like a lot of superstars."

References: Newsweek 96:81+ S 1 '80 por; People 14:52+ S 15 '80 pors; Sport 72:65 Ja '81 por; Sports Illus 53:36+ Ag 11 '80 por, 54:66+ F 12 '81 pors, 54:20+ Ap 13 '81 pors; Time 116:61 S 1 '80 por

Brokaw, Tom

Feb. 6, 1940- Broadcast journalist. Address: b. NBC News, 30 Rockefeller Plaza, New York City, N.Y. 10020

A no-nonsense newsman with solid journalistic credentials and more than twenty years' experience in television news broadcasting, Tom Brokaw has been the host of NBC's early morning Today show since August 1976. Before joining the staff of that durable weekday wake-up program of news, interviews, and features, Brokaw worked as a reporter and anchorman for NBC affiliate stations in Nebraska, Georgia, and California, and from 1973 to 1976, as the network's White House correspondent. Widely respected by his colleagues in the press corps for his resourcefulness and persistence and by viewers for his authoritative delivery and easy-going amiability, Brokaw helped Today to recover from the ratings onslaught mounted by ABC's chirpy Good Morning, America. By the fall of 1980, Today had regained its position as the most popular of the three network morning news programs. Under the terms of Brokaw's new multi-year contract with NBC, which he signed in July 1981, he was slated to co-anchor, with Roger Mudd, the network's nightly news broadcast beginning in April 1982.

Thomas John Brokaw was born in Webster, South Dakota on February 6, 1940 to Anthony Orville Brokaw, a foreman on a United States Army Corps of Engineers dam, and Eugenia (Conley) Brokaw. Raised in Yankton, South Dakota, where he attended the local public schools, Brokaw developed an interest in politics and world affairs at an early age. "One of the advantages of a South Dakota childhood is that there is so little around you intellectually that you reach out for broader sources of material," he explained to Betty White in an interview for a Saturday Evening Post (May/June 1978) profile. "I was always aware of what was going on in New York, or other power centers. . . . I was known as the town talker. I was always involved in whatever arguments were going, agitating things constantly, always had an opinion on everything." For a time, he intended to become a lawyer, but his growing admiration for Chet Huntley and David Brinkley, who coanchored the Huntley-Brinkley Report, NBC-TV's award-winning nightly newscast, in the late 1950's and 1960's, prompted him to shift his attention to broadcast journalism. By the time he was fifteen, he had found an after-school job as an announcer at KYNT, a Yankton radio station.

Following his graduation from high school in 1958, Brokaw enrolled at the University of South Dakota. He paid for his college education by working as a roving reporter for several radio stations in the university area. After taking his B.A. degree in political science in 1962, Brokaw signed on as newscaster and morning news editor at KMTV, the NBC affiliate television station in Omaha, Nebraska. There he covered a wide variety of stories, ranging from murder trials to sanitation strikes to natural disasters. Because the station had such a small staff, he learned all phases of news broadcasting. He shot and edited his own film, wrote his own scripts, and even put on his own makeup before going on the air. In 1965 he joined WSB-TV in Atlanta as editor and anchorman of the 11:00 P.M. nightly news broadcast. Since NBC did not then have a network-staffed bureau in the South, he also contributed occasional reports on the burgeoning civil rights movement to the Huntley-Brinkley Report.

The following year Brokaw moved to the West Coast to become a reporter for and, later, anchorman of the late-night newscasts at KNBC-TV, the network's owned-and-operated station in Los Angeles, California. Among the stories he covered during his tenure there were the assassination of Senator Robert F. Kennedy, the 1971 earthquake, and the gubernatorial campaigns of Ronald Reagan and Edmund G. Brown Jr. His cool, straightforward delivery so impressed network news executives that in April 1971 they chose him to anchor an edition of *First Tuesday,* NBC's monthly prime-time news magazine.

A self-described "political junkie," Brokaw jumped at the chance to become, in 1973, NBC's White House correspondent, even though it meant taking a sizable pay cut. At first scorned by veterans in the Washington press corps as an inexperienced lightweight, Brokaw quickly established himself as a combative and persistent reporter. As Ann Compton, the White House correspondent for ABC News, explained to Michael Ryan and Sally Bedell in an interview for *TV Guide* (May 14, 1977), "Tom always asked good questions at briefings. He always had a good angle on something that everybody else had missed." By the summer of 1974 Brokaw was making significant inroads into the popularity of his CBS counterpart, Dan Rather, and after Rather's reassignment later that year, he was widely regarded as the most dynamic reporter on the White House beat.

Like his colleagues in both print and broadcast journalism, during his first fifteen months as a White House correspondent Brokaw devoted much of his time to the Watergate scandals. Looking back on the news media's coverage of that extraordinary period, he told Arthur Unger, who interviewed him for a *Christian Science Monitor* (September 3, 1976) profile, "They called it adversary journalism, but adversary is too weak a word. It reached the heights of hostility, and I'm not sure that either side—the press or the President—was well served." Still, he maintained that if the reporters had erred, "it was on the side of caution."

Special events relating to the Presidency continued to command Brokaw's attention in the months following Nixon's resignation. In January 1975, for instance, he and John Chancellor conducted an exclusive one-hour live interview with President Gerald R. Ford. With his characteristic forthrightness, Brokaw bluntly asked the President about the widespread public conception that he was not intelligent enough for his job. While assigned to the White House, Brokaw also covered the 1974 off-year gubernatorial elections, anchored the Saturday evening edition of the *NBC Nightly News* and the 1973 sports documentary *The Long Winter of Henry Aaron,* and served as an on-camera reporter for the three-hour prime-time NBC News special *New World—Hard Choices: American Foreign Policy, 1976,* which was broadcast on January 5, 1976. During the summer of 1976 he was one of NBC's

floor reporters at both the Democratic and Republican National Conventions. Working on the convention floor was "something I've always wanted to do," he told one interviewer, "like a kid wanting to grow up and play second base for the Yankees."

In the summer of 1974 Brokaw's tenure at the White House nearly ended following his week-long tryout as cohost, with Barbara Walters, of NBC's early morning *Today* show. NBC executives, who were looking for a successor to Frank McGee, Miss Walters' former cohost, were impressed by his intelligence, poise, and humor as well as his journalistic experience, but Richard Wald, the president of NBC News, preferred to keep the correspondent in Washington. Partly because of Brokaw's lucid White House reports to the *NBC Nightly News,* that newscast was, for the first time in years, seriously challenging the ratings dominance of the *CBS News With Walter Cronkite.* For his part, Brokaw steadfastly refused to read commercials, a condition for the *Today* assignment. "I find doing commercials repulsive," he explained, as quoted in *Time* (July 15, 1974). "If that is a job requirement, it would not be negotiable with me." Moreover, he was unwilling to give up the fast-breaking Watergate story, so he let the opportunity pass, despite the prospect of a reported $225,000 annual salary increase. "I've never done anything purely for the money," he explained to Gary Deeb, the television reporter for the Chicago *Tribune* (January 12, 1977).

After Barbara Walters' celebrated defection to ABC News in April 1976, NBC officials again asked Brokaw to join the *Today* show, this time as its sole host. Steadily losing ground in the early morning ratings race to ABC's slick new entry, *Good Morning, America,* the program needed a boost, and since it was such a huge moneymaker, earning about $20,000,000 a year—more than enough to keep the entire NBC news operation in the black—in advertising revenue, network executives were not prepared to take any chances. After the network dropped the requirement that the reporters do commercials, Brokaw agreed, in May 1976, to take over as host of *Today,* succeeding Jim Hartz. According to unofficial NBC sources, his five-year contract called for an annual salary of $400,000, with increases to $500,000.

Assuming his new post on August 30, 1976, Brokaw quickly won critical approval for his intelligent and informed interviewing technique and his relaxed and personable manner. His adroitness and poise served him well, for as host his responsibilities included, in addition to interviewing newsmakers, carefully monitoring the clock to maintain the smooth flow of the program's precisely timed segments and ad-libbing with the other regulars, among them Gene Shalit, the resident arts critic, news reader Floyd Kalber, Lew Wood, the weatherman and features reporter, and beginning in

October 1976, Jane Pauley. Brokaw himself eventually read the morning news bulletins. Otherwise, unlike his predecessors, he worked without a script, relying instead on the information passed to him by reporters and researchers and on his own journalistic instincts.

During Brokaw's first few months on the job Paul Friedman, *Today's* new producer, made a number of changes in the program's style and format. He shortened and tightened interviews, hired specialists in such fields as science, finance, and travel, added segments that offered practical advice in health care and consumer affairs, and scrapped the formal, conventional desks for a homier modular arrangement of swivel chairs in a boldly colored set. To many viewers, it appeared that *Today* was imitating its entertainment-oriented competitor, *Good Morning, America.* Denying that charge, Brokaw explained that the alterations were designed not to trivialize the show, but to make it livelier and more responsive to "the needs and tastes of the times." As he told Gary Deeb, he opposed "loading up on soft features that amuse people" without providing any useful information. "To me it's an issue of information versus diversion," he said. "Almost everything we do . . . is information. Very little of it is just diversion. And that is the basic difference between our show and *Good Morning, America* on ABC."

To insure that *Today* continued to offer information instead of froth, Brokaw insisted on taking an active part in the behind-the-scenes long-range planning discussions and in the daily production and story conferences. He frequently suggested topics for feature segments on such subjects as the economy, environmental protection, the social aspects of increased leisure, and special interest political groups. In his first few months as host, for example, he reported on the widespread use of marijuana, the high prices of homes in Southern California, and the causes and effects of the oil crisis. He also managed to slip useful bits of information into entertainment features, as when he added to a fashion segment news on the rising consumer prices of ready-to-wear clothing.

More recently, Brokaw has reported on legal gambling, the changing life-styles of American teenagers, inflation and the "fast buck," and the strategic deterrent capabilities of the United States armed forces. He went to Vienna to cover the signing of the SALT II accord, to Panama to discuss the Canal treaties with Brigadier General Omar Torrijos Herrera, the country's strongman, and to the atomic research laboratory at Los Alamos, California to look into recent developments in nuclear weapons.

As *Today's* principal interrogator, Brokaw earned his colleagues' respect for eliciting enlightening answers from even the most recalcitrant guests. He serves as, in his words, "a kind of midwife" to nervous interviewees, gently coaxing information from them, but he can be tough with people who, as he put it, "seem to be avoiding the issue or trying to peddle something that is not made of whole cloth." "I never throw softballs," he told Arthur Unger. "I just don't think there are any other kinds of interviews to do. I won't hammer people out of bed in the morning, but I feel they are ready for some real information and persistent interviews."

Among the wide variety of persons Brokaw has interviewed in the course of his career as the host of the *Today* show are former Vice President Walter F. Mondale, Studs Terkel, the author and oral historian, journalist Richard Reeves, Burt Reynolds, the actor and director, Governor James R. Thompson of Illinois, former Senator Eugene J. McCarthy, and Chicago Symphony Orchestra conductor Sir Georg Solti. He has talked about the ethics of the press with Clifton Daniel, the former associate editor of the New York *Times;* homosexual rights and fundamentalist religion with Anita Bryant; the proliferation of survivalist groups with Peter Arnett, a special correspondent of the Associated Press; and Soviet-American relations with Anatoly F. Dobrynin, the Russian ambassador to the United States. Most media critics agree with Arthur Unger that Brokaw "revels" in hard-news interviews. "My idea is not to be provocative, but to try to get the story," Brokaw explained to Betty White. "The best interviews are those that leave people with a sense that they have learned something."

Doing a two-hour, live early morning broadcast five days a week is a great strain, but Brokaw has compared his job favorably with his former post as White House correspondent. "The difference is that there I was concentrating on one man and one institution," he told Greg McGarry of the Los Angeles *Times* (November 8, 1977), "but here I'm covering a much greater range of issues and personalities and situations. I think it's more broadening, personally, doing what I'm doing now." Despite his busy schedule, Brokaw occasionally accepts special news assignments, such as representing NBC on a live one-hour television interview with President Jimmy Carter, in December 1977, and acting as one of the network's floor reporters at the national political conventions, in 1980.

Concerned about the future of his profession, which he once described as "documenting history," Brokaw taught a course in television news at Yale University during the 1978-79 academic year. He also wrote a perceptive introduction to *The Best of Photojournalism, 5: People, Places and Events of 1979* (University of Missouri Press, 1980). The majority stockholder of Tom Tom Communications, Inc., Brokaw realized his "ultimate dream" when, in 1974, he purchased KTOQ, a radio station in Rapid City, South Dakota. The journalist is the recipient of the Golden Mike Award from the Radio and Television News Association of Southern California, an Alumni Achievement Award from the University of South Dakota, and an honorary doctor of humane letters degree, also from his alma mater. He is a member of the Sierra Club, Sigma Delta Chi, the journalism fraternity, the American Federation of Television and Radio Artists, and the advisory board of the Reporters Committee for Freedom of the Press.

A personable man who looks years younger than his chronological age, Tom Brokaw has brown eyes, modishly styled brown hair, a winning smile, and an aura of midwestern wholesomeness. He speaks in a low, authoritative voice and often displays a self-deprecating wit. According to friends and colleagues, he is "the quintessential nice guy," always willing to do a favor or lend a helping hand. A self-confessed "sports nut," he plays tennis, skis, and jogs daily in Central Park. "I'm not a wonderful athlete, but I'm one of the best Walter Mittys that I know," he wrote in a recent article for the New York Daily News (January 30, 1981). "If I could perform as well as my mind thinks I can, well, Jim Thorpe would be an also-ran." His enthusiasm for jazz is reflected in the frequent appearances on the Today show of such musicians as Lionel Hampton, Eubie Blake, and Dave Brubeck.

Brokaw married Meredith Lynn Auld, a former Miss South Dakota, on August 17, 1962. Mrs. Brokaw, a teacher of English as a second language by training, is the co-owner of Penny Whistle, a toy shop on Manhattan's Upper East Side, within walking distance of the apartment she and her husband share with their three daughters, Jennifer Jean, Andrea Brooks, and Sarah Auld. Brokaw finds life in New York City to be "adventurous," "exciting," and at times, "mildly exasperating." When he begins to feel "closed in," he and his family flee to the mountains of Colorado for a backpacking vacation.

References: Chicago Tribune p61 D 12 '76; Christian Sci Mon p22 S 3 '76 por; Los Angeles Times IV p15 N 8 '77 por; N Y Daily News p91 Ag 20 '76 por; Sat Eve Post 250:78+ My/Je '78 pors; TV Guide 25:14+ My 14 '77 por; Washington Post B p1+ Jl 22 '81 por; Who's Who in America, 1980-81

Brown, Charles L(ee, Jr.)

Aug. 23, 1921- Corporation executive. Address: b. 195 Broadway, New York City, N.Y. 10007

On February 1, 1979 Charles L. Brown succeeded John D. deButts as chairman of the board of the American Telephone and Telegraph Company, operator of the Bell Telephone system and parent company to the Bell Telephone Laboratories and Western Electric. With its 1,000,000 employees, assets of $100 billion, annual sales of $45.4 billion, and annual profits of $5.7 billion, AT&T ranks among the world's largest business enterprises. During his thirty-five year career with AT&T, which he joined as a summer employee and maintenance man in the 1940's, Brown has held more than a score of different jobs, including that of the presidency of the Illinois Bell Telephone Company. Later, as chief financial officer of AT&T, he played a key role in cutting back the company's debt. As president, he helped to reorganize the Bell System along entirely new lines, in one of the biggest corporate reorganization efforts in business history.

Since assuming the chairmanship, Brown has adopted a realistic attitude toward government-sponsored change in the communications industry and has moved decisively to adapt AT&T to the altered competitive environment brought about by the advent of new technologies, antitrust measures, and deregulation. "I think it's important that the company continue on the positive trajectory that it's been on for some time," Brown told Sonny Kleinfield, author of The Biggest Company on Earth: A Profile of AT&T, "both in terms of service and financial aspects. . . . We will continue to be the Bell System with our traditional goal of providing a channel that will transport any kind of information from any place to anywhere."

Charles Lee Brown Jr. was born on August 23, 1921 in Richmond, Virginia, the son of Charles Lee and Mary (McNamara) Brown. His mother had been a telephone operator and supervisor before her marriage; his father, a college teacher of mathematics, later became a district traffic manager in the Long Lines department of AT&T and spent thirty-seven years with the phone company. "An atmosphere . . . was caught by me," Brown told Sonny Kleinfield. "An atmosphere that here was a good place to work, a place that set high goals, a place that employed people who were good people. But I was never consciously shoved in the direction of phone work by my parents." Brown lived with his parents in a series of rented apartments before the 1930's, when the family moved into its first home, but although the Depression imposed some hardships, the family did not suffer from poverty. In the Kleinfield interview, Brown described his childhood as "conventional, stable, middle-class" and "uneventful."

In high school, Brown worked most of his summers as a lifeguard, but during the summers of 1939 and 1941 he earned $13 a week digging ditches and laying and splicing cable for AT&T's Long Lines department in Cleveland, Ohio. "I enjoyed it tremendously," he told Kleinfield. "I was living in hotels with a crew of people who were hard manual workers, with people who had substantial responsibility." In the fall of 1939 he enrolled at the University of Virginia, at Charlottesville, where he majored in electrical engineering, played on the varsity baseball and basketball teams, served as a professor's assistant and as a counselor in the dormitories, and maintained a B-average in course work. In his senior year, a doctor discovered that Brown suffered from a minor if unusual eye disorder: short-sightedness in one eye and long-sightedness in the other.

After graduation from the University of Virginia with a bachelor of science degree in 1943, Brown immediately enlisted as a radio man in the United States Navy, where he remained until the end of World War II; he served in the Pacific Theatre aboard the U.S.S. Mississippi, among other assignments. After his discharge from the service, in April 1946, with the rank of lieutenant, Brown considered several employment options, including working for the airlines and for an electrical equipment manufacturer. In May 1946, however, he decided to accept a job as equipment maintenance man with the AT&T Long Lines department in Hartford, Connecticut. "It just looked to me like a good place to start," Brown told Kleinfield. "It was a close decision. I was not at all sure that I was going to stay. I merely decided I would give it a whirl."

The Long Lines department, for which Charles L. Brown was to work some fifteen years, was a departmental operating arm of AT&T, not a separate company like AT&T's other major divisions, whose primary task was to coordinate, route, and service the Bell System's long distance calls. After spending six months in Hartford, Brown was transferred to the job of equipment engineer in New York City, and from March to September 1949 served as a traffic equipment supervisor. Between September 1949 and March 1952 Brown left Long Lines briefly to work as a plant extension engineer and as a systems planning engineer for AT&T. Both assignments were in New York.

In July 1952 Brown returned to Long Lines as district plant superintendent in Birmingham, Alabama, and during the next decade he held a series of assignments for Long Lines around the country: commercial manager in Atlanta, Georgia (1954-56); division plant superintendent in Philadelphia (1956-58); assistant to the general manager (1958-59) and area traffic manager (1959-60) in Cincinnati, Ohio; and area commercial manager (1960-61) and area sales manager (June 1961) in Kansas City. Between 1961 and early 1962 Brown again left Long Lines to become the first head of AT&T's Cooperstown, New York Data Communications School, the company's first attempt to train its communications employees to service a data processing market.

Returning to Long Lines a second time, in April 1962 Brown became general manager of the central area in Cincinnati, and in February 1963 he was transferred to the post of general manager of the southeastern area in Atlanta. Then, only five months later, he was offered the position of vice-president and general manager of the Illinois Bell Telephone Company in Chicago. "I was very distraught," Brown told Kleinfield. "I had lived in Atlanta previously and liked the city, liked the job I had there, what little taste I had gotten of it. I was disappointed and concerned. I considered turning the move down, but in the end I looked at what was probably best for the company and went ahead and took it." Brown explained further, "I always took the next move. I'm not saying it wasn't difficult. It often was. You leave old friends behind, you have to find new schools for the youngsters. But you surmount those kinds of things."

From the position of vice-president and general manager at Illinois Bell, Brown was promoted to its vice-president of operations and made a director in March 1965. He was finally elevated to the presidency of the Illinois Bell Telephone Company on April 24, 1969, retaining his post as director. Reflecting on his many assignments over the years, Brown told Kleinfield, "I certainly expected to climb in the business, but I didn't really worry that much about it. . . . I found out early in my work that if I enjoyed myself on the job, the next step would take care of itself. I went into every job on the basis that that was where I was going to be, and I had better do it well."

One of the major tasks facing Brown as president of Illinois Bell was to adapt the company to the Federal Communications Commission's Carterfone decision, which encouraged greater competition in the production and sale of telephone switchboards and instruments. Reacting to that decision by establishing Illinois Bell's first marketing section and promoting Bell equipment and products aggressively in the marketplace, he even made a few sales calls himself, in the company of Bell salesmen, to emphasize the need for serious marketing efforts within the organization, and to demonstrate to business customers the importance he placed in their continued patronage.

As president of Illinois Bell, Brown was so cost-conscious that although company limousines were available to the president and other top officers, he walked to meetings in the downtown area whenever possible, often arriving about the time other executives were pulling up in their limousines. One characteristic anecdote about him concerns an employee walkout at Illinois Bell in the late 1960's. During the course of the strike Brown sometimes went out on telephone repair calls on weekends to help make up for the loss of service induced by the work stoppage. One weekend, reportedly, some members of the country club to which Brown belonged contacted the company with a request for repair service and were surprised to see the Illinois Bell president respond in person.

In 1972 Charles L. Brown made national headlines when he completed, with Edward Heveran, president of the Oak Brook (Illinois) Bank, the country's first intercity subscriber picturephone call, over a distance of twenty miles. The picturephone is a device that links a video image of a caller to the voice image. Brown and Heveran chatted over the phone for several minutes, observing one another on 5½-inch by 5½-inch screens. But the picturephone, after making its promising and highly publicized debut, proved too expensive for widespread consumer use and was eventually employed only in long-distance conference calling and, internally, within the Bell System itself.

On July 1, 1974, after serving for five years as president and director of Illinois Bell, Brown was promoted to the top corporate management of AT&T in New York, as executive vice-president. A month later, on August 1, he took on the additional title of chief financial officer for AT&T, after John J. Scanlon had resigned from that post. On April 1, 1976 he was promoted from executive vice-president to vice-chairman of the board and a directorship, while retaining the title of chief financial officer.

During his three-year tenure as chief financial officer, Brown played a leading part in lowering AT&T's high 46.4 percent debt-to-capital ratio to 38.3 percent. He also devised a program to encourage AT&T's 2.9 million stockholders to reinvest their dividends in the company by offering a 5 percent discount—a program that generated $800 million in additional equity for the company in 1978 alone. "I consider it [the financial post] as important as the presidency in preparing me for becoming chief executive officer," Brown later remarked, as quoted by the Los Angeles Times (June 26, 1979).

Finally, on April 1, 1977, Charles L. Brown was elected president and chief operating officer of AT&T. Shortly before and during his term as president, the company began encountering increased competition as a result of a number of governmental actions. A series of regulatory agency and court decisions ended the Bell monopoly on equipment production and long-distance service; the United States Congress began debate on sweeping deregulatory measures; the Justice Department continued to press an antitrust suit, initiated in 1974, that aimed at severing Bell's manufacturing arm, the Western Electric Company, from AT&T; and revolutionary changes in technology began to blur the line between data processing and communications, placing AT&T more directly into competition with such manufacturing giants as IBM.

Partly in response to those changing conditions, AT&T chairman John D. deButts put Charles L. Brown in charge of one of the most sweeping reorganizations in corporate history. Under its old system, AT&T was structured along functional lines—customer services, installations and repairs, collections and billing, and so on. Under the new system, the company was divided into three organizations along customer lines. One division dealt with residential customers, another with business customers, and a third with the nationwide network as a whole. "We have decided that we can better serve the customer market by this sort of organization," Brown told a reporter for the New York Times (February 24, 1978), "and we've got a competitive situation that makes it desirable that we understand what the customer wants." Begun in 1978, the reorganization continued for more than a year.

Although the announcement in October 1978 that John D. deButts would step down from the chairmanship of AT&T a year before his sixty-fifth birthday occasioned some surprise, his choice of Charles L. Brown as his successor did not. Brown officially assumed the role of chairman of the board of AT&T, which has been called "corporate America's top post," on February 1, 1979. In his first public address as chairman, delivered that same month to the National Telephone Cooperative Association in Atlanta, Brown announced AT&T's more conciliatory attitude toward competition, a policy that he has adhered to ever since. "I am a competitor," he said, "and I look forward with anticipation and confidence to the excitement of the marketplace." In the past the company had generally used the courts and regulatory agencies to preserve and extend its communications monopoly. Brown qualified his support of competition, however, by announcing his strong opposition to the government's antitrust suit, which sought to dismember AT&T, and to anything beyond limited deregulation.

Two years later, in assessing Brown's incumbency, Andrew Pollack of the New York Times (February 6, 1981) noted: "Mr. Brown has not made any seminal decisions, or abrupt departures in company policy. His strength . . . has been in carrying out the policies set in motion by Mr. deButts and adapting to change brought about by technological advances and Government decisions." One innovation Brown has introduced is the Office of the Chairman, which is composed of himself, the president, two vice-chairmen, and AT&T's general counsel; it is now the highest executive unit in the organization.

In 1980 Juanita M. Kreps, former United States Secretary of Commerce in the Carter Administration, became the second woman to join AT&T's board of directors. Under Charles L. Brown, the company extended its innovative technical advances, preparing for a time when the telephone is expected to become the heart of an information and communications revolution in both home and office, and experimenting with such new technologies as mobile phones, glass fiber transmission lines, and voice-activated computers.

But the main concern of corporate activity at AT&T has continued to focus on the rapidly changing communications marketplace. In April 1980 the Federal Communications Commission ordered AT&T to set up a fully separate subsidiary by March 1982 in order to compete fairly in computer-based services. In response, that summer AT&T announced plans for a second major restructuring to comply with the FCC's decision. It would split into two units, one to handle the still regulated phone business, and the other to handle newly allowed computer-related activities. Nicknamed "Baby Bell," the latter unit was to receive approximately $12 billion of AT&T assets and 150,000 employees. Brown regards the establishment of Baby Bell as one of his major accomplishments. "As far as I can see," he told Pollack, "there are very few businesses that have embarked on a structure change, shift in attitude and skills on such a massive scale in such a short time."

One reason why AT&T responded with such alacrity to the FCC decision was its hope that the move would dissuade the United States Congress and the Justice Department from pressing for a division of the company into independent operating units. By late 1980, in addition to the Justice Department's major suit, AT&T faced antitrust suits filed by thirty-seven private companies. One of those suits, filed by the tiny MCI Communications Corporation in Washington, D.C., resulted in a staggering $1.8 billion judgment against AT&T by a Chicago federal court, a judgment that the company is appealing. MCI had charged that AT&T had delayed in supplying it with telephone hookups vital to the operation of its rival long-distance telephone system. And early in July 1981 a New York City jury held that AT&T, having unfairly forced Litton Industries out of the telephone equipment business, should award the aerospace and electronics conglomerate $92,000 in damages. Again, AT&T planned to appeal.

Lean of build, and five feet ten inches tall, Charles L. Brown has been described in a New York *Times* profile (November 20, 1978) as an "intense man, with penetrating eyes, a determined chin and a profile somewhat on the order of the Presidential busts carved on Mount Rushmore." He is chauffeured to work in New York City each morning from his home in Princeton, New Jersey, an 80-minute drive. He arrives at his office by 8 A.M. and usually leaves around 5:45 P.M. Brown takes a three- or four-week vacation, usually at a cottage he owns near Palm Beach, Florida. He reads an average of one book a week and has a special interest in world history. His relatively modest corporate "perks" include, besides the limousine and access to a company jet, free home telephone calls to a limit of $35 a month and paid membership in three clubs. His salary and bonuses amount to approximately $624,000 a year.

Charles L. Brown married his second wife, Ann Lee Saunders, on July 25, 1959. By his first marriage, he has one son, Charles A. Brown, a physician practising in California. Chairman Brown is a director of AT&T, E. I. du Pont Nemours, Chemical Bank and Chemical New York Corporation, and the Associates of the Harvard University Graduate School of Business Administration; he is a trustee of Columbia-Presbyterian Hospital, the Institute for Advanced Study in Princeton, New Jersey, the Colonial Williamsburg Foundation, and the University of Virginia Endowment Fund; he is a member of Delta Upsilon, Theta Tau, Omicron Delta Kappa, the Business Council, the Business Roundtable, and nine clubs. His past affiliations include many social, cultural, and religious organizations. Brown's hobbies are golf and tennis.

References: Bsns W p120 N 6 '78 por; Fortune 98:15 N 20 '78 por; N Y Times D p1 N 20 '78 por; Kleinfield, Sonny. The Biggest Company on Earth: A Profile of AT&T (1981); Who's Who in America, 1980-81; Who's Who in the East, 1979-80

Brundtland, Gro Harlem

Apr. 20, 1939- *Former Prime Minister of Norway; political leader; physician. Address:* b. Det Norske Arbeiderpartiet, Oslo, Norway; h. Theodor Lövstadsvei 19, Oslo 2, Norway

On February 4, 1981, Mrs. Gro Harlem Brundtland took office as Prime Minister of Norway's constitutional monarchy, the first woman to occupy that office in her country's history and, at forty-one, the youngest of her sex to head a modern government. She was chosen for the post to restore voter confidence in Norway's ruling Labor party (Det Norske Arbeiderpartiet), which had been steadily losing ground under her predecessor, Odvar Nordli. A physician by profession, Mrs. Brundtland had been active in the Labor party and a champion of

Gro Harlem Brundtland

its democratic socialism since her student years. As Minister of Environmental Affairs in Norway's Cabinet from 1974 to 1979, she became known as the "green goddess" because of her passionate defense of a high quality of life for her country's 4,000,000 people. But although Mrs. Brundtland inspired considerable hope in many of her compatriots, she did not succeed in her efforts to maintain the Labor party in power in the national election of September 13 and 14, 1981. While retaining the party chairmanship, which she had occupied since April, she was succeeded as Prime Minister in mid-October by Conservative party leader Kare Willoch.

A member of a politically committed family, Gro Harlem Brundtland was born in Oslo, Norway on April 20, 1939 to Gudmund and Inga Harlem. Her father served as personal physician to the prime ministers of the Labor party and was a member of Norway's Cabinet from 1955 to 1965, first as Minister for Social Affairs and then as Minister of Defense. When she was only two, she was smuggled across the border to neutral Sweden to escape Nazi Germany's occupation of Norway, and she spent the World War II years in Stockholm while her father served with Norway's anti-Nazi Resistance.

Back in Oslo after the war, Gro Harlem joined a children's group affiliated with the Labor party when she was seven, and during her student years she became involved in political work. In senior secondary school she served on the executive committee of the students' socialist union, and later, while studying medicine at the University of Oslo, she was vice-chairman of the socialist students' association, a branch of the Labor party. In

1960 Gro Harlem married Arne Olav Brundtland, a political scientist.

After graduating in 1963 with a doctor of medicine degree from the University of Oslo medical school, where her dissertation dealt with the onset of menstruation at puberty, Mrs. Brundtland came to the United States for additional graduate work at the Harvard University School of Public Health. There, her studies of pollution problems aroused her interest in environmental protection. On obtaining her master of public health degree from Harvard in 1965 she returned to Oslo, where she became a consultant to the Ministry of Health and Social Affairs and, in 1966, a junior medical officer with the office of hygiene at the National Directorate of Health. From 1968 to 1974 Mrs. Brundtland was assistant chief physician with Oslo's municipal health board, and from 1969 to 1974 she was, in addition, deputy director of the city's school health services. She has also served as a physician in the children's department at Ulleval Hospital and at the Rikshospital in Oslo, and she has written articles on such topics as school health, preventive medicine, and human growth.

Inspired by the burgeoning feminist movement of the 1960's and 1970's, Mrs. Brundtland became a champion of the increased participation of women in politics, and she spoke out in favor of the liberalization of abortion laws and on other controversial matters. Her deep concern for the quality of the environment prompted Prime Minister Trygve Bratteli, a friend of her father, to appoint her to his Cabinet as Minister of Environmental Affairs in September 1974, a post in which she remained after Odvar Nordli succeeded Bratteli in the Prime Ministership in January 1976. She became increasingly active in Labor party affairs and in 1975 was elected the party's vice-chairman.

Mrs. Brundtland, whose tenure as Norway's Minister of the Environment coincided with a growing worldwide interest in ecology, proved to be a dedicated champion of environmental quality. She promoted a popular program for the establishment of nature preserves, and she campaigned for protection of the environment from damage by offshore drilling operations for Norway's newly discovered North Sea oil reserves. Although industrial safety laws were not directly within her province, she fought for safer conditions in offshore oil drilling and in other industries. Some of her environmental proposals were opposed by industrialists.

In September 1977 Mrs. Brundtland was elected to Norway's parliament, the Storting, as a representative for Oslo. Her Storting seat was at first occupied by her proxy while she continued to serve as Minister of the Environment, but in October 1979 she left the government to devote her efforts, as Labor party vice-chairman, to the party's revitalization, because of the setbacks that it had suffered in recent local elections. Within the Storting, Mrs. Brundtland became a member of the standing committees on finance, foreign affairs, and the constitution, as well as deputy leader of the Labor party parliamentary group.

Meanwhile, the decline in popularity suffered by the Labor party as a result of problems regarding the management of the economy, disputes about national defense, and power struggles among its leadership caused concern that the party might lose control of the government in the national elections scheduled for mid-September 1981. It was only with the help of the two members of the small Socialist Left party that the Labor party had been able to maintain a bare majority of one in the Storting. The plurality of 42 percent of the vote that Labor had garnered in the 1977 national election had dwindled to 36 percent in the local elections of 1979. According to opinion polls, by early 1981 it commanded the support of only 31 percent of the electorate and was running neck and neck with the opposition Conservative party.

Although Norway, with an annual per capita income in excess of $10,000, remains one of the world's more prosperous countries, it has, like a number of European nations, been plagued by inflation and recession in recent years. One major problem facing the Norwegian government has been the question of how to utilize the steadily growing proceeds from the country's oil resources in ways that would maintain the stability of the economy. Prime Minister Nordli's efforts to limit government spending while trying to hold down wages and prices, and his moves to shift the financing of the welfare state from an unpopular income tax to various indirect sales taxes, failed in the long run to placate his critics.

The question of national defense set off a major national debate in early 1981. Although Norway is a charter member of the North Atlantic Treaty Organization, its policy has been to bar nuclear armaments and foreign troops from its soil, except in the event of hostilities. But in January 1981 Nordli's Labor government signed an accord with the United States to permit the stockpiling of arms, ammunition, and other equipment in Norway for use by United States Marines in case of an attack by the Soviet Union. Although the agreement received overwhelming support in the Storting, it provoked loud protests from the left wing of the Labor party, represented by party chairman Reiulf Steen, and the dispute underscored dissatisfaction with the government of Nordli, who represented the center-right faction of the party.

On January 30, 1981, Odvar Nordli announced his resignation of the Prime Ministership of Norway, citing his poor health as the reason, but according to informed political observers, he was persuaded to step aside by his party colleagues, who felt that he failed to provide decisive leadership. On February 3 the Labor party's central committee unanimously selected Gro Harlem Brundtland to succeed Nordli as Prime Minister. According to her supporters, she not only had the popularity, competence, self-assurance, and optimism needed to restore the Labor party to health, but also represented a consensus of party opinion and enjoyed loyal support at the grassroots level. It was largely as a result of the influence of local leaders that the national party leadership accepted her as Prime Minister, reportedly in preference to Rolf Hansen, her successor as Minister of Environmental Affairs.

Although Mrs. Brundtland was not a member of any particular faction of the Labor party, she was generally aligned with the party's left wing in matters of social and economic policy. But despite her past skepticism toward the North Atlantic Treaty Organization she stood with Nordli in support of NATO. At the same time she favored "working more actively for nuclear disarmament" and consistently proposed the establishment of a nuclear weapon-free zone in Scandinavia.

On February 4, 1981, at the royal palace of King Olav V, Gro Harlem Brundtland was formally installed as Norway's twenty-second Prime Minister. On taking office, Mrs. Brundtland declared that she would carry on the government's policies of full employment and social welfare and that the national security would continue to be based on Norway's membership in NATO, but that her most immediate task was to unite and strengthen the Labor party for the forthcoming parliamentary election. On stepping down, outgoing Prime Minister Nordli congratulated his successor and said that she merited the sympathy and good will of every Norwegian. Her seventeen-member Cabinet, installed on the same day, included only three new ministers who had not been members of the Nordli government.

When she was interviewed a month after she took office by Marshall Ingwerson of the *Christian Science Monitor* (March 5, 1981), Mrs. Brundtland reaffirmed her government's commitment to NATO but asserted that Europeans would demand a stronger and more independent role within the Atlantic Alliance in the future. She pointed out that some policies of the United States, such as American support for the civilian-military junta in El Salvador, have evoked deep misgivings among Europeans, and she dismissed as unrealistic recent statements emanating from the Administration of President Ronald Reagan to the effect that the United States could virtually disregard Europe. Mrs. Brundtland called for more mutual decision-making among the NATO partners, and she noted that a growing fear of nuclear war had instilled in her countrymen a greater sense of international responsibility.

At its annual party congress in April 1981, the Labor party moved towards greater party unity by electing Mrs. Brundtland to succeed Reiulf Steen in the top-ranking party position, uniting the posts of Prime Minister and party chairman in the same official for the first time since 1975. According to opinion polls, in the months following Mrs. Brundtland's inauguration as Prime Minister, the Labor party's fortunes seemed at first to have experienced an upswing. "This woman is a vote-getter," Professor Henry Valen of the University of Oslo, an authority on Norwegian politics, observed, as quoted in the *Christian Science Monitor* (March 5, 1981). "You can feel the change of opinion, the optimism, around here."

But as the national parliamentary election drew nearer, pollsters provided scant encouragement to those who hoped that the Labor party would remain in power. According to R. W. Apple Jr., writing in the New York *Times* (September 14, 1981), despite Mrs. Brundtland's personal popularity, "her directness and aggressiveness have offended many of her Labor colleagues in a country where confrontation is a dirty word," and she failed to capture enough support from women and youth—her natural constituency—to ensure her party's victory. There was considerable discontent with Norway's mounting rate of inflation, which under the impact of increasing oil revenues had reached an annual rate of nearly 14 percent by mid-1981. Despite her efforts to capitalize on an anti-inflationary price-freeze announced by her government in August, and her argument that the rightist opposition was seeking to dismantle the welfare state, many Norwegians looked for economic improvement to the Conservatives, who promised to reduce personal income taxes, hold down public expenditures, place the government's oil distribution company under private ownership, institute commercial television, and thin the ranks of the bureaucrats.

Norway's voters trooped to the polls on September 13 and 14, 1981 to elect their representatives to the national parliament. With sixty-eight seats—a loss of eight from its previous strength—Labor remained the strongest single party in the 155-member Storting, but the Conservatives and their right-wing allies, with about 55 percent of the popular vote against the 45 percent received by the left, proved strong enough to form a government. Mrs. Brundtland relinguished her post as Prime Minister on October 14, 1981 to Conservative party leader Kare Willoch, an advocate of "supply-side" economics and an admirer of President Ronald Reagan.

Gro Harlem Brundtland and Arne Olav Brundtland live in a luxury villa in Oslo with their two youngest sons, Ivar and Jörgen, and their daughter, Kaja. The oldest son, Knut, is employed on a North Sea oil rig. While Mrs. Brundtland was preoccupied with affairs of state, the other members of the family shared in the household chores. The fact that her husband, an international relations expert, is a leading member of the Conservative party poses no problem in peaceful coexistence for Mrs. Brundtland. "I think this situation is going to happen increasingly—that couples have different political standpoints," she told John

Vinocur of the New York *Times* (February 4, 1981). "And I'd like to do what I can to de-dramatize it." Dark-haired and of medium height, she was described in the London *Times* (February 4, 1981) as having an "easy charm disguising a forceful personality" and a "clear, straightforward way of saying things." According to the New York *Times* profile, Mrs. Brundtland is "a woman with an easy smile and a delightful laugh" who is known as "an excellent administrator and organizer" but is "a bit of a nit-picker and occasionally self-righteous." She considers herself "absolutely typically Norwegian" and enjoys outdoor activities, especially cross-country skiing. Among the women in history whom she most admires are Joan of Arc and Golda Meir.

References: London Observer p7 F 8 '81 por; London Times p6 F 4 '81; N Y Times A p6 F 4 '81 por; Dictionary of Scandinavian Biography (1976); International Who's Who, 1981-82

Calvo Sotelo (y Bustelo), Leopoldo

Apr. 14, 1926- Prime Minister of Spain.
Address: b. Palacio de la Moncloa,
Madrid, Spain

On February 25, 1981, the day after the suppression of an attempted military coup, the Spanish Cortes, or Congress of Deputies, endorsed Leopoldo Calvo Sotelo as the third Prime Minister of Spain's five-year-old constitutional monarchy. A conservative technocrat who served as Deputy Prime Minister under his predecessor, Adolfo Suárez González,

Calvo Sotelo thus assumed office while the country's fragile democratic institutions underwent their severest test since their inception following General Francisco Franco's death in 1975.

Calvo Sotelo, whose high-level experience in business and government dates back to the Franco dictatorship, is a cofounder of the Unión Centro Democrática (UCD), under whose banner Suárez González had governed Spain for four-and-a-half years. As Prime Minister, Calvo Sotelo faces grave problems, including the prospect of another military coup attempt, economic stagnation, terrorism, provincial separatist demands, and a gloomy electorate disenchanted with ineffective political solutions. Nevertheless, he is determined to maintain his leadership of the country at least until the next scheduled elections in 1983.

Leopoldo Calvo Sotelo y Bustelo was born in Madrid on April 14, 1926 into a family with roots in Galicia, the northwestern region of Spain that produced both Franco and Suárez. The Bustelos, his ancestors on his mother's side, included political rebels and leftists. More in line with the industrial-political oligarchy with which his family name is associated was his uncle José Calvo Sotelo, a right-wing monarchist Finance Minister in the Second Republic, whose assassination in July 1936 helped to trigger General Franco's nationalist uprising. After the Civil War a number of streets in Spanish cities bore the Calvo Sotelo name in his memory.

Although Leopoldo Calvo Sotelo, who was only ten when the Civil War broke out, belonged to a generation that was relatively untouched by the violent political convictions that had brought about that conflict, he identified himself with the monarchist cause early in life and at sixteen joined the Juventudes Monárquicas (Young Monarchists). He attended schools in Madrid and at Ribadeo in the northwestern province of Lugo. In 1946 he entered the elite civil engineering college Escuela de Ingenieros de Caminos, Canales y Puertos in Madrid and, a few years later, graduated first in his class.

After obtaining his doctorate in engineering in 1951, Calvo Sotelo went to work in the chemical industry. From 1963 to 1967 he was the general director of the Union Española de Explosivos, S. A. In line with the Franco regime's plans, developed in the late 1950's to alter Spain's weak commercial structure by replacing bureaucratic management with skilled technocrats drawn from industry, Calvo Sotelo served in 1967 and 1968 as head of RENFE, the Spanish national railway network, one of the official monopolies established to facilitate economic growth. Under the Franco regime's second and third development plans, Calvo Sotelo presided over a subcommittee on basic chemical industries and a work group on industrial localization.

Calvo Sotelo is generally identified with those younger-generation politicians who sup-

ported Franco's Movimiento Nacional but who pressed steadily for restoration of the monarchy, in line with the regime's 1947 law of succession. In 1957, he was a founding member of the Unión Española, a monarchist group of professionals seeking the early enthronement of Juan Carlos, the grandson of Alfonso XIII, Spain's last king. In 1969 Franco designated Juan Carlos as his successor.

From 1971 to 1975, Calvo Sotelo served in the Franco regime's "rubber stamp" Cortes, or parliament, as a *procurador* representing the entrepreneurs in the chemical industry's trade association, which spoke for both management and labor. He was also president of the legislative chamber's public works commission. In November 1972 he became chairman of SODIGA, a society established to promote industrial development in Galicia, and about fourteen months later he was appointed president of the chemical industries' commission under the economic and social development plan of the Ministry of Development Planning. In 1974 Calvo Sotelo was appointed to the board of directors of the Banco Urquijo, and in early 1975 he was made a full member of the higher council of chambers of commerce, industry, and navigation.

After Franco's death, in November 1975, Prime Minister Carlos Arias Navarro, who had headed the government since late 1973, appointed Calvo Sotelo Minister of Commerce in the first royal Cabinet under newly enthroned King Juan Carlos I. The Cabinet was sworn in on December 13, 1975. In the monarchy's crucial first year of transition and liberalization, Calvo Sotelo's growing influence in the government was linked with his early support of Juan Carlos and his close association with the rising political star of Adolfo Suárez González, who worked with him in the Arias Navarro Cabinet in the influential post of Minister Secretary-General of the Movimiento Nacional. In July 1976, dissatisfied with Arias Navarro's slow progress in replacing the old regime's political structure, the King called for his resignation and appointed Suárez Prime Minister. Calvo Sotelo was Suárez' choice in the new Cabinet as Minister of Public Works and Town Planning. Under Suárez there followed a rapid series of reforms that included political amnesty, restoration of civil rights, de-politization of the military, total reconstruction of the Cortes, legalization of a party system that eventually included Socialists and Communists, and the restoration of free general and parliamentary elections, the first of which were scheduled for June 1977.

In the scramble among more than 200 political groups to assemble candidates and organize coalitions in time for the elections, Calvo Sotelo emerged as Suárez' "right-hand man" and election manager. Suárez was originally aligned with the Democratic Center, a party formed in September 1976 of liberals and centrist Christian Democrats whose goal was to counteract the Francoist Alianza Popular

(AP) on the right and the Socialists and Communists on the left. As election time neared, Calvo Sotelo organized a strong slate of eighty relatively young "independent" candidates for the Cortes who had been Franco bureaucrats and then supported Suárez. Having resigned his Cabinet post in early May 1977 to devote himself full time to the political campaign, Calvo Sotelo hastily organized the Unión Centro Democrática (UCD) with Interior Minister Martín Villa. Suarez then merged his Democratic Center with the UCD, running as its first candidate from Madrid, while Calvo Sotelo ran as second candidate and became official representative of the coalition. Ignoring the Francoist past and stressing political reform under Suárez, the UCD campaign ended on June 15, 1977 in a victory for Suárez and King Juan Carlos, with the UCD winning 46 percent of the Cortes seats, a workable minority, to the second-place Socialists' 34 percent. The right-wing AP's lowly 4.6 percent and the Communists' 5.7 percent indicated the voters' rejection of extremes on both ends of the political spectrum.

Although Calvo Sotelo won election to the Cortes, he was not a member of the second Cabinet appointed by Suárez in July 1977. Instead, he was placed on the UCD's seven-member executive committee, which was charged with the task of transforming a loose coalition into a unified party. Describing the first period of Suárez' leadership, from 1976 to 1979, in Current History (May 1981), Meir Serfaty observed that it was an age of change "marked by euphoria and good will" as leaders of various political persuasions cooperated in replacing the archaic structure of the old regime with new, vital institutions. To combat Spain's economic problems after the European recession of the early 1970's, Suárez, in October 1977, maneuvered the Moncloa Pact, an agreement between the government, opposition parties, and trade unions to institute austerity measures designed to reduce inflation, increase the growth rate, attain a balance of payments equilibrium, and build sizable foreign reserves. By 1978 the government had responded to the nagging problem of provincial separatist demands by granting limited autonomy to Catalonia, Galicia, Andalusia, and the Basque province. A liberal democratic Constitution became law in late December 1978, after passage by the Cortes and overwhelming approval by the voters in a referendum.

Meanwhile, in February 1978 Calvo Sotelo's flair for organization and negotiation had been called into play when Suárez appointed him to a newly created Cabinet ministry without portfolio to act as chief negotiator in Spain's efforts to join the European Economic Community. Although Spain had been excluded from the Common Market during the Franco regime for political reasons, the EEC member countries were Spain's major trading partners under a preferential agreement of 1970, and technocrats such as Calvo Sotelo had long

maintained that the country's economic future depended upon full EEC membership. In 1977, therefore, the Suárez government formally applied for entry. Calvo Sotelo's job was to work out necessary adjustments with government and business to satisfy Common Market conditions. The announcement by the EEC commission in April 1978 that Spain should be accorded full membership within a decade enhanced his reputation as a negotiator.

According to Meir Serfaty's analysis in Current History, Suárez' second period of leadership, which began with his reelection in March 1979, was characterized by "inertia, false starts, and a large dose of complacency." Although he surrounded himself with loyal men like Calvo Sotelo, who were willing to surrender responsibility to what Serfaty called Suárez' "Machiavellian style of leadership," the Prime Minister made little headway in solving such major problems as a stagnating economy, which by 1981 had brought the growth rate down to less than 1 percent, a $5 billion external trade deficit, and a 12 percent unemployment rate. The armed forces were badly in need of modernization to bring them into line with democratic institutions, and the future of provincial autonomy was not defined clearly enough to satisfy the separatist movements.

A wave of terrorism that was taking hundreds of lives, mostly of police and military personnel killed in clashes with the Basque separatist ETA, prompted the military to demand stringent antiterrorist action and to consider the prospect of intervention in the political process. In May 1980 Suárez barely escaped a Cortes censure motion on his handling of the economy and of a referendum on Andalusian autonomy. Reshuffling his Cabinet repeatedly in response to increasingly harsh criticism, Suárez saw his support, as indicated in public opinion polls, reduced from 76 percent in 1977 to 26 percent in early 1981.

When the fifth Suárez Cabinet was appointed in September 1980, Calvo Sotelo was called from negociations with the EEC to become Deputy Prime Minister in charge of economic affairs, a move that signified confidence in his economic skills. Although Calvo Sotelo thought at first that the post might lead to a dead end, as it turned out it placed him in a favorable position to become Suárez' successor. As the January 1981 party congress of the UCD approached, there appeared to be little prospect for Suárez to resolve the differences of ideology and political strategy that divided his uneasy coalition of Social Democrats, liberals, Christian Democrats, and moderate Francoists. Meanwhile, the Roman Catholic hierarchy attacked Suárez for permitting his Minister of Justice, Francisco Fernández Ordóñez, to draft legislation that would allow divorce on mutual consent. On January 29, 1981 Suárez abruptly resigned his Prime Ministership and castigated politicians and the press for "systematically irrational" criticism, but he failed to give specific reasons for his resignation.

On the following day, the thirty-five-member executive committee of the UCD assented to Suárez' nomination of Calvo Sotelo as Prime Minister. Seven right-wing members of the committee initially threatened to withhold support because, they maintained, under Suárez the UCD had drifted too far from its conservative roots. When the party's 1,800 delegates finally met in Mallorca for four days beginning on February 6, 1981, the congress endorsed Calvo Sotelo, but only after acrimonicus debate between its right wing and its left and center factions. Although the UCD's center forces, represented by Suárez, seemed to have won a victory with the endorsement of Calvo Sotelo, the latter indicated that he also wanted to reach an accommodation with the party's right wing.

Formally named Prime Minister-designate by the King on February 10, 1981, Calvo Sotelo outlined his government's policies in a vigorous address to the Cortes eight days later. He called for tight curbs on public spending, encouragement of the private sector by tax and social security payment reductions, new measures to reduce unemployment and strengthen Spain's nuclear energy program, and a speedup in reconversion of key industries. His government, he declared, would "choose the moment" of Spain's juncture with the North Atlantic Treaty Organization, and he heralded a "new epoch" for Spanish democracy.

Although Calvo Sotelo impressed the members of the Cortes with his considerable forensic skills during a three-day debate on his policies, he failed on February 20, 1981 to receive the absolute majority he needed to form a new government. The vote in his favor fell seven votes short of the necessary 176, and thus a second ballot had to be taken, this time requiring only a plurality. Hardly had the voting begun on February 23, when some 200 Civil Guards under the command of Lieutenant Colonel Antonio Tejero Molino, in what was later described as a "comic opera" coup attempt, burst into the chamber, fired automatic weapons at the ceiling, and took the 344 legislators hostage. Tejero, who in 1978 had tried unsuccessfully to overthrow Suárez and his Cabinet, announced his intention to establish a military government "until terrorism is defeated." Although Tejero had support from some senior officers, military leaders overwhelmingly stayed loyal to King Juan Carlos, who announced in a televised address on February 24 that he firmly rejected any actions "that aim at interrupting by force the democratic process." The collapse of the coup, eighteen hours after it began, was a moment of personal glory for the King. When voting resumed on February 25, the Cortes, as if shocked into unity, gave Calvo Sotelo the absolute majority it had refused him earlier, voting 186 to 158 in his favor.

With the very survival of Spanish democracy at stake, Calvo Sotelo pulled his government together cautiously, as if, in the words of a *Time* correspondent (March 16, 1981), "he were walking through a minefield." His streamlined Cabinet, announced on February 26, 1981, retained twelve holdovers from the Suárez regime and excluded members of the military, making it the first all-civilian Cabinet since 1939. The Prime Minister turned down the offer of the popular Socialist leader Felipe González to form a majority coalition in the Cortes, evidently fearing that a government that leaned too far to the left would touch off another military coup.

In the next few months, as Basque separatists stepped up their terrorism, Calvo Sotelo concentrated his efforts on combating the violence while keeping the armed forces in tow. Guided by the King's admonition to approach the military with "the greatest serenity and moderation," the Prime Minister was reluctant to take any drastic steps against the right for fear of provoking another coup. As a result of the Tejero affair, a number of high-ranking officers, including four generals, had been arrested. But after terrorists assassinated, among others, the police chief of Bilbao and grievously wounded Lieutenant General Joaquín Valenzuela, a military aide of King Juan Carlos, in a bomb attack, Calvo Sotelo was restrained from any further crackdown on the military. After meeting with his Cabinet in May, he announced new measures that included tougher legal procedures for dealing with terrorists, punishment for news organizations that condoned violent acts, and greater involvement of the military in the antiterrorist campaign in the north.

While Spain's democratic future hung in the balance, conditions seemed to some extent to favor the essential conservatism of Calvo Sotelo. Voters were reluctant after the coup to support Felipe González, despite his popularity, for fear of a military backlash. Furthermore, in view of the military's opposition to provincial autonomy, Calvo Sotelo could slow down progress in that direction. In addition, by publicly suggesting that the terrorism that took twenty-three lives in his first ten weeks in office may have been part of a conspiracy directed from abroad, possibly from the Soviet Union, the Prime Minister made a point for the rapid entry of Spain into NATO, a matter that he discussed with United States Secretary of State Alexander M. Haig Jr. during the latter's April 1981 visit to Madrid. Calvo Sotelo won his first major foreign policy victory on October 29, 1981, when the lower house of the Cortes approved by a vote of 186 to 146 the government's proposal to join NATO. With $3 billion in business investments in the Spanish economy and 10,000 American servicemen stationed on Spanish bases under a defense treaty, United States interests remained, in 1981, closely linked with the fate of Calvo Sotelo's government.

Prime Minister Leopoldo Calvo Sotelo is described as a bluff, dour man who keeps people at a distance. According to a correspondent for the *Economist* (February 28, 1981), he has "an unflappably solemn expression that reminds some Spaniards of the comedian Harold Lloyd." His dark, heavy-rimmed glasses and high forehead seem to reinforce that impression. But although he is aloof and "somehow Anglo-Saxon" in his manner, he enters public debate with what James Markham of the New York *Times* (February 21, 1981) described as a combination of "wit, literary allusions, and, occasionally, cool disdain to silence a foe." He is married to Pilar Ibáñez Martín Mellado, the daughter of a former Minister of Education. They have eight children and live in Somosaguas, an exclusive Madrid suburb, which Calvo Sotelo prefers to the official Moncloa residential complex, where the Prime Minister's office is located. He speaks French and English well, and he lists among his favorite reading the speeches of President Ronald Reagan and British Prime Minister Margaret Thatcher. Despite his long association with the world of business, Calvo Sotelo apparently has never harbored ambitions for enormous wealth or for personal aggrandizement in political office.

References: N Y Times A p7 F 12 '81 por; International Who's Who, 1980-81

Carlucci, Frank (Charles, 3d)

Oct. 18, 1930- United States Deputy Secretary of Defense. Address: b. The Pentagon, Washington, D.C. 20301

As second-in-command at the Pentagon, Frank Carlucci, the Deputy Secretary of Defense, has been granted considerable authority by his boss, Caspar W. Weinberger, the Secretary of Defense, in both military policy-making and in administering the vast bureaucracy of the Defense Department. His broad mandate stems from his excellent professional and personal relationship with Weinberger, for whom he worked in the early 1970's as the number two man in the Office of Management and Budget and in the Department of Health, Education, and Welfare. Weinberger insisted upon Carlucci's appointment despite the opposition of many conservatives who, while admiring his managerial ability, regarded with suspicion his long record of nonpartisan diplomatic and administrative service under both Republican and Democratic administrations. Carlucci is no ideologue of the right. "My own philosophy," he told a Senate committee during his confirmation hearing last January, "is that we all have to compromise. That's what it's all about."

The grandson of an Italian immigrant stonecutter, Frank Charles Carlucci 3d was born on October 18, 1930 in Scranton, Pennsylvania to Frank Charles Carlucci Jr., a successful insurance broker, and Roxanne (Bacon) Carlucci. (One source gives his birthplace as Bear Creek, a suburb of Wilkes-Barre, Pennsylvania.) After attending Wyoming Seminary College Preparatory School at Kingston, Pennsylvania, Carlucci enrolled at Princeton University, where he obtained his A.B. degree in 1952. For the next two years he served in the United States Navy as a gunnery officer on the *USS Rombach*. After his discharge with the rank of lieutenant junior grade, Carlucci entered the Harvard Graduate School of Business Administration but left after taking only one year of its two-year curriculum. He then worked briefly as a rental agent and as a salesman, before joining, in 1955, the firm of Jantzen Swimwear, Inc., in Portland, Oregon as a management trainee.

Dissatisfied with his business career, Carlucci joined the United States Foreign Service in July 1956. Beginning in a State Department management job, he received his first overseas assignment in 1957 as vice-consul and economic officer at the American Embassy in Johannesburg, South Africa. After returning to the United States for additional training, he was sent in March 1960 to the American Embassy at Leopoldville (now Kinshasa) in the former Belgian Congo (now Zaire), first as vice-consul and then as second secretary and political officer.

Because of the political instability and turmoil then wracking the newly independent Congo, Carlucci faced the most difficult assignment of his diplomatic career. Since in the prevailing circumstances physical agility and courage sometimes proved to be as important as diplomatic skills, he soon discovered that the athleticism that had served him well on the wrestling team at Princeton became an important asset in the Congo as well. On November 20, 1960, for example, he rescued a carload of Americans in Leopoldville from an angry mob after a traffic accident in which a Congolese was killed. In that incident, Carlucci was stabbed in the back of the neck and barely escaped with his life. As the "outrider" of the Embassy, he took monthly trips into hostile areas to make firsthand reports on daily developments. He became a friend of both Cyril Adoula, the future Congolese Premier, and of Patrice Lumumba, who once helped him to secure the release of some Belgian hostages.

On his return to Washington, in 1962, Carlucci was assigned to the Congo desk at the State Department. Two years later, he became consul general in Zanzibar, but in 1965 he was expelled by the government of Tanzania for alleged subversive activities, possibly in retaliation for American support of Moise Tshombe, then President of the Congo. From 1965 to 1969 Carlucci held administrative posts at the United States Embassy in Rio de Janeiro, Brazil, where he took part in a reorganization that sharply reduced its staff.

Notwithstanding his demonstrated capabilities, Carlucci might have been lost among a host of other equally talented persons at the State Department, had it not been for his Washington reunion with his former Princeton wrestling teammate, Donald Rumsfeld, the recently appointed director of the Office of Economic Opportunity. Carlucci was on his way to the Massachusetts Institute of Technology for a year of study when Rumsfeld persuaded him to take charge of the antipoverty agency's hundreds of community action programs as deputy director for operations. In that post, Carlucci earned a reputation as an attentive and sympathetic listener to the problems of his associates and as an administrator who could be counted on to stand by his decisions once they were made. Furthermore, his nonpartisan status seemed a genuine asset in an agency created by Democrats but operating under the Republican Administration of Richard Nixon.

When Rumsfeld became an adviser to Nixon in the fall of 1970, Carlucci was nominated to succeed him as the director of the Office of Economic Opportunity. Although Democrats in Congress feared that the Nixon Administration was trying to emasculate that agency by decentralizing its programs and giving local authorities ultimate control, they gave Carlucci high marks for his antipoverty performance. His confirmation was delayed by the Senate after he declined to override a veto by Ronald Reagan, then governor of Califor-

nia, of an OEO grant to a legal services program for that state's rural poor. Since, however, it was generally believed that Carlucci actually favored an override but had been instructed by the White House to work out a compromise, the Senate confirmed him in March 1971.

Early in 1971 Carlucci was also admired in some quarters for overriding a veto by the governor of Mississippi of a legal services project in that state. In their syndicated column in the Washington *Post* (March 1, 1971) Rowland Evans and Robert Novak wrote that although he was closing down many inefficient community programs, "Carlucci is committed to make the poverty program work, [while] Reagan leaves little doubt that he wants it plowed under." Yet it seemed somewhat paradoxical to some political observers that at the same time Carlucci implemented the Nixon Administration's decentralization program, arguing that it offered "new opportunities for community action agencies to influence the use of a broader range of resources, by participating in the expanded local decision-making."

In July 1971 President Nixon announced the appointment, to be effective on September 1, of Carlucci as associate director of the Office of Management and Budget, in charge of management functions. When, in July 1972, he was promoted to deputy director, he became number two man under Caspar W. Weinberger, at the Office of Management and Budget. Soon afterward, he had an opportunity to demonstrate his administrative ability in dramatic fashion when, on August 12, Nixon appointed him to coordinate the federal relief effort for flood victims of tropical storm Agnes in the Wilkes-Barre area of Pennsylvania. Arriving in Wilkes-Barre two days later, Carlucci drastically improved the previously disorganized relief programs within a few weeks. Working twelve hours a day, he held daily meetings with representatives from all the agencies involved in the flood to promote coordination; commandeered contractors for electric, heating, and plumbing repairs so that flood victims could return home before winter; and provided free legal services, health assistance, services to the elderly, and, perhaps of greatest importance, clearly written literature explaining how those services could be obtained.

Once again, Carlucci found himself number two man under Caspar W. Weinberger, when, in the summer of 1973, he became Under Secretary of Health, Education, and Welfare to his former boss, who had become Secretary of that department the previous fall. And once again, as at the Office of Economic Opportunity, he found himself administering one of Nixon's programs, this time a plan known as the New Federalism, to give states and localities greater control over federal social programs. In December 1973 he defended the

New Federalism in a speech that he delivered at the meeting of the Georgia chapter of the American Society of Public Administration, the burden of which was his contention that "the Federal grant has put too much decision-making in Washington." According to Carlucci, the New Federalism " seeks to dismantle the top-heavy power of Federal grantsmen and regulators.... and to reassemble that power and the capacity to use it at state and local levels" through "revenue-sharing, grant consolidation, and decentralizing HEW's decision-making machinery." But as a moderate given to compromise, Carlucci did not advocate total abandonment of traditional social programs. In August 1974, for example, he urged President Gerald R. Ford to make compromises on national health insurance opposed by the medical profession and the insurance industry. In particular, Carlucci urged the imposition of increased payroll taxes for catastrophic illness insurance.

With his appointment as United States Ambassador to Portugal in December 1974, Carlucci resumed his interrupted diplomatic career. His assignment resulted from Secretary of State Henry A. Kissinger's dissatisfaction with Stuart Nash Scott, Carlucci's predecessor. Kissinger believed that Scott's reports understated the growing Communist influence in Portugal's revolutionary government following the military coup d'etat in April 1974 that overthrew the nation's rightwing dictatorship. Carlucci, who arrived in Lisbon in January 1975, headed a minority of policymakers who favored working with the Portuguese government so long as a semblance of democracy remained, while Kissinger led the majority, which was convinced that Portugal was bound to go Communist and should not receive any American aid. After the Communists made a poor showing in Portugal's election for the constituent assembly on April 25, 1975, the majority adopted Carlucci's point of view.

After the Communist influence in the Portuguese government had been eliminated in 1976, State Department observers gave Carlucci much of the credit for having kept Portugal allied with the West by resisting Kissinger's inclination to write off that nation. In his New York *Times* column for March 13, 1976 C. L. Sulzberger also paid tribute to the "percipient" Ambassador, noting that "only a handful of diplomats, led by Carlucci, recognized the full weight of local factors."

Although President Jimmy Carter had hoped to appoint Carlucci as his Deputy Under Secretary of State for Management in 1977, he abandoned the plan when some Democrats in Congress complained that they had not been consulted and that the prospective nominee had served under Republican administrations. In January 1978 Carlucci obtained the post of CIA Deputy Director, second-in-command to the agency's Director, Admiral Stans-

field Turner. When he met with Turner before his appointment, Carlucci insisted on full authority, including complete access to intelligence evaluations previously received only by the Director. Conseqently, when Carlucci testified at his ratification hearing before the Senate Intelligence Committee on January 27, he was able to assert with some confidence that he anticipated being given an important role in much of the agency's decision-making.

As the Deputy Director of the CIA, Carlucci tried to restore some of the authority and prestige that the agency lost in the mid-1970's after some of its abuses of power became public knowledge. He has criticized the 1974 Freedom of Information Act, which provides access to government information on demand except for certain sensitive materials, and he informed a House Intelligence subcommittee in April 1979 that the CIA was losing important information because its domestic and foreign sources feared that their identities might be exposed under that law.

Favoring modification of the Freedom of Information Act to enhance the government's ability to protect its vital secrets, Carlucci also called for legislation to punish the unauthorized disclosure of names of American intelligence agents or sources, even if the disclosers deduced such identities from unclassified sources. In response to charges that his proposal violated the First Amendment to the Constitution, he told the Senate Judiciary Committee in September 1980: "Nothing could be more subversive of our constitutional system of government than to permit a disgruntled minority of citizens freely to thwart the will of the majority."

After President-elect Ronald Reagan chose Caspar W. Weinberger as his Secretary of Defense, Weinberger insisted that Carlucci, his colleague at the Office of Management and Budget and at the Department of Heath, Education, and Welfare, be his deputy again. Some conservatives on Capitol Hill and some of Reagan's advisers opposed the appointment, alleging that Carlucci had supported social revolution while director of the Office of Economic Opportunity, had backed Socialist Party leader Mario Soares as an alternative to the Communists while Ambassador to Portugal, and had closed down some covert operations while Deputy Director of the CIA. They also cited his nonpartisan service under the administrations of both the Democrat and Republican parties. But after Weinberger indicated that he refused to serve without his former associate, Carlucci was nominated for Deputy Secretary of Defense in early January 1981 and was confirmed by the Senate on February 4 by a vote of 91 to 6.

According to one colleague, Weinberger "has enormous trust in Frank, as a person and as a friend." Since Carlucci's relationship with the Defense Secretary is so close that Carlucci even claims to be able to anticipate

Weinberger's thinking, the Deputy Secretary was expected to exercise considerable power in the Pentagon. During the early months of the Reagan Administration, Weinberger informally made Carlucci the chief executive officer of the Defense Department, responsible for overseeing the Pentagon bureaucracy, but as Weinberger's alter ego, he was also free to delve into policy making. In the early spring of 1981 he issued a memo announcing a decentralization of authority within the Department to give the service secretaries and Joint Chiefs more responsibility. Its purpose, Carlucci indicated, was to allow him and Weinberger to concentrate on major policy decisions, on the definition of planning goals, and on the allocation of resources.

At his confirmation hearing, Carlucci registered his agreement with President Reagan's belief that American military strength is declining and that the Soviet Union is an imperialist power that can only be intimidated by a "determined and consistent foreign policy based on a strong military deterrent." Given the colossal military budget obtained by Reagan, Weinberger and Carlucci are expected to preside over one of the costliest and most extensive rearmament programs in American history. But they are also determined to cut costs, especially through Carlucci's efforts to synchronize strategic planning with the acquisition process more efficiently.

In his Defense Department post, Carlucci displays his customary diligence and managerial expertise, arriving at the Pentagon at eight in the morning, putting in a twelve-hour day, and taking work home with him. A government official who has followed Carlucci's career with ungrudging admiration has said that though many men come to Washington with brilliant ideas, "often they can't get the damn thing done. The problem is getting it to happen. Frank makes it happen." But more skeptical observers, noting Carlucci's relative lack of experience in military matters, question whether able management and efficient business methods alone will produce a sound defense policy.

Frank Carlucci is a soft-spoken, slightly built man whose dedication to work seems to allow him little time for the cultivation of outside interests. By his first marriage, to Jean Anthony in 1954, he has two children, Karen and Frank. In 1976 he married Marcia Myers. In 1962, for his work in the Congo, he received the State Department's superior service award, its highest foreign service citation, and in 1969 he was given its superior honor award, for his service in Brazil. He holds honorary degrees from Wilkes College and from Kings College, both of which were bestowed on him in 1973.

References: N Y Post p35 Ja 4 '71 por; N Y Times p24 D 31 '70 por; Wash Post A p3 Ja 14 '81 por; Who's Who in America, 1980-81

Caro, Anthony

Mar. 8, 1924- British sculptor. Address:
111 Frognal, Hampstead,
London, NW 3, England

In the opinion of no less an authority than Hilton Kramer, the New York Times's influential resident art critic, Anthony Caro is the first British sculptor since Henry Moore and Barbara Hepworth to produce a body of work of more than parochial interest. The catalyst of the "new sculpture" movement in England, Caro began creating large-scale, low-lying abstract sculptures in the early 1960's after working for several years as a more traditional figurative sculptor. In his open, floor-oriented pieces of welded, and occasionally brightly painted, steel, he explores the basics of form by pushing sculpture to its limits. "I suppose what I'm trying to show is what it's like to be alive," he said in a recent interview. "But that's what all art's to do with. . . . Some people say art changes people's lives. I think that in some way it can, but the way in which it does is a very subtle, gentle, touching way. I really like that about art—like a poem or something that gets you going somehow."

Anthony Alfred Caro was born in London, England on March 8, 1924, the son of Alfred Caro, a prosperous stockbroker turned gentleman farmer, and his wife, Mary. A self-described "dreamy kid" who sketched for pleasure, he began modeling figures in clay while he was a student at the Charterhouse School, a posh private school, which he attended from 1937 to 1941. At the insistence of his father, who disapproved of art as a suitable career, Caro dutifully studied engineering at Christ's College, Cambridge. After taking his degree, in 1944, he served with the Fleet Air Arm for the duration of World War II.

On his return to civilian life, Caro decided to attend art school despite continued family opposition to his plan. With the assistance of Sir Christopher 'Wheeler, who was then the president of the Royal Academy, Caro secured a place at the Regent Street Polytechnic in 1946, and the following year, he enrolled at the Royal Academy Schools, where he remained until 1952. In an interview with Dorothy Gallagher for the New York Times (May 18, 1975), Caro looked back on his years at the Royal Academy as a limiting experience. "We just did the figure every day . . . ," he said. "I couldn't believe that this was what it was all about. It wasn't until the end of my time at the Academy that I discovered Henry Moore existed. The Academy treated him as kind of a threatening joke."

Fascinated by Moore's monumental abstract sculptures, Caro visited the older artist at his home in Hertfordshire and asked him for a job. Six months later, in 1951, Moore took him on as a part-time assistant. Moore exposed his young apprentice to new concepts of form, space, and volume and freed him from the constraints of his traditional academic training. Caro worked with Moore for two years, then returned to London to discover his own style out from under the shadow of his influential mentor. Late in 1952 he accepted a job as a part-time instructor at the St. Martin's School of Art in London, where he taught sculpture on and off for the next twenty years. As a teacher, he has influenced—and in turn, been influenced by—some of Britain's finest young sculptors, including David Annesley, William Tucker, Phillip King, Michael Bolus, Tim Scott, and Isaac Witkin.

Throughout the mid-1950's, Caro concentrated on creating massive figurative bronzes, which Andrew Hudson, then art critic for the Washington Post, saw as "a kind of caricature of Moore's work." (Caro himself thought his distorted, swollen shapes were "rather Picassoesque.") He exhibited the tortured, brutish figures, such as Man Taking Off His Shirt, at a one-man show at the Galleria del Naviglio in Milan, Italy in 1956 and at several group shows in England and abroad over the next two years. Primitive, lumpish, and heavy, the sculptures met with generally negative and occasionally sarcastic reviews. One critic remarked caustically, as quoted in Time (July 22, 1966), "One almost wishes them back into clay." Increasingly dissatisfied with his work, Caro experimented with different materials and styles, but he failed to find a congenial method. "The things I was making were models," he told Dorothy Gallagher in the Times interview. "They weren't real enough. I began to think about what sculpture was, and I thought that it's something to do with experience, and I felt that what I was making were imitations of real experiences. They were a pretense, really."

The year 1959 proved to be the turning point in Caro's career. A conversation with Clement Greenberg, the highly respected art critic, prompted him to reexamine pure abstract art. Later that year, on a trip to the United States, he met David Smith, the American sculptor who had acquired an international reputation for his abstract sculptures made of welded industrial steel, and other American nonrepresentational artists, among them, the painters Kenneth Noland, Robert Motherwell, and Helen Frankenthaler. Caro commented on the impact of those encounters in his interview with Dorothy Gallagher: "I'd always said I wouldn't go into abstract sculpture because I thought abstraction was about ideas and not about feelings. And I think art should be about feelings. But I discovered that was quite a misinterpretation of the meaning of abstraction. I didn't have to represent, and I could still put my feelings into it."

Back in London, Caro took lessons in welding and, adopting Smith's technique of direct-metal construction, began to arrange scraps of preformed steel—a material he had chosen because it was "anonymous," "arbitrary," and "cheap"—into abstract sculptures. Once he was satisfied with his improvisational composition of rods, pipes, I-beams, and plates, he welded or bolted the pieces together, then painted them. It took him three months to complete his first sculpture, 24 Hours, a low-lying, free-standing form composed of a disk, a triangle, and a rectangle. Caro initially applied brown or black paint to his finished sculptures to protect and preserve the steel, but he soon abandoned those dark tones, which he associated with traditional sculpture, in favor of bright, vibrant colors—green, magenta, scarlet, yellow—that emphasized the newness of his finished pieces. He also used color to add dimension, express emotion, as in Deep Body Blue (1967), and give a sense of unity to the separate elements.

In creating such monumental pieces as Midday (1960) and Early One Morning (1962), a graceful, bright red construction of I-beams and steel rods that Hilton Kramer has since described as "possibly the finest thing" the artist has ever done, Caro reduced sculpture to its basic elements without making the traditional allusions to the human body, the landscape, or other physical forms. "I have been trying to eliminate references and make truly abstract sculptures, composing the parts of the pieces like notes in music," he explained to Amei Wallach in an interview for a Newsday (March 27, 1975) profile. "Like music, I would like my sculpture to be the expression of feeling in terms of the material, and like music, I don't want the entirety of the experience to be given all at once."

At traveling group shows in Great Britain and at individual exhibitions in London, New York City, and Washington, D.C. in the early 1960's, Caro's striking constructions attracted considerable public attention as well as favorable critical comment. In an *Art News* (December 1963) article analyzing the importance of Caro's work to the development of contemporary art, John Russell singled out as his major contribution his break with "all traditional connotations of sculpture—the plinth, the noble material, the advantageous site, the personal handling, the rhetorical or allegorical allusions." Yet, as Gene Baro noted in his review of a 1963 Caro exhibition at the Whitechapel Gallery in London for *Arts* magazine (November 1963), Caro "achieved with rigid and austere materials the warmth, sensuousness, spatial variety, romantic feeling and monumentality that are qualities of sculpture in stone and bronze."

Over the next few years, discerning gallery goers noticed a subtle change in Caro's style. Instead of relying almost entirely on large, heavy steel plates, he increasingly chose thinner, flat-surfaced components which gave his sculptures a delicate, lighter-than-air appearance. Typical of his work during that period are *Prairie* (1967), a sprawling, golden-yellow structure of horizontal pipes and sheet steel that suggests an endless field of ripening wheat; *Month of May* (1966), a handful of magenta, orange, and green aluminum rods seemingly flung at random over a supporting framework of chunky I-beams; and *Titan* (1964), a ground-hugging, electric blue welded steel construction composed of three separate and, at first glance, unrelated shapes. One of Caro's most frequently exhibited sculptures, *Titan* is one of approximately twenty pieces he created while he was a visiting instructor at Bennington College in Bennington, Vermont during the 1963-64 academic year and the spring semester of 1965.

Because of the way Caro's sculptures appear to spread and snake their way along the floor, several art critics, among them Hilton Kramer, have described Caro as "a kind of choreographer among sculptors." The choreographic element is especially evident in the graceful, rhythmic lines that characterize such works as *Red Splash* (1966), four uneven vertical tubes unexpectedly joined by two overlapping sections of chicken wire; *Carriage* (1966), two green mesh "walls" connected by a long, curving metal tube; and *Span* (1966), three semicircular cutouts in a dark red frame-shape. In those pieces, exhibited at the André Emmerich Gallery in New York City in 1966, Caro "moves the sculptural elements that make up his constructions across the space they occupy rather as dancers move," Kramer noted in a review written for the *New York Times* (November 26, 1966). "One does not take in such sculptures at a glance, but on the contrary, follows the course of its development from element to element. . . . A work like *Span* never really settles in the mind as a single image; one's memory of it is the memory of its unfolding before our eyes in a succession of images, no one of which completely contains the whole work."

Critics hailed Caro as the heir to the tradition and style of David Smith, although his work is persistently more open and has a stronger, more horizontal thrust than the older sculptor's. As Clement Greenberg once observed, Caro is "the first sculptor to digest Smith's ideas instead of merely borrow from them." Caro digested the ideas of artists in other media as well. Both John Russell and Hilton Kramer saw in Caro's rhythmically balanced, blade-like *Orangerie* traces of Matisse's cut-paper paintings. In a recent interview, Caro acknowledged his debt to Matisse and to other painters, including Cézanne, Monet, Titian, and Bellini, whose works he selected to accompany a special exhibit of *Orangerie* at the National Gallery in London in 1977. "Painters have influenced me enormously and in a great many ways," he said. "It was better to go to painting than to old sculpture, because painting gave one ideas of what to do but no direct instructions on how to do it."

According to James R. Mellow, each of the seven works that constituted a favorably reviewed 1971 Caro exhibition at the David Mirvish Gallery in Toronto, Canada "set up anew the terms of its own sculptural discourse, its own rules of the game." And in each piece, Mellow noticed Caro's typical "quality of restraint," his habit of "sustaining the tension by holding back just a bit." For instance, *After Summer,* four sets of pearl gray, wing-like shapes placed along the length of two long parallel beams, is "almost—but not quite—repetitive in its forms," and the squat, gunmetal gray *Nocturne,* a post-and-lintel structure of forged and tube steel, is "almost—but not quite—architectural in scale." "It is the command of the tactical and structural complexities involved that allows one to know that in confronting a Caro sculpture, one is securely in the presence of a master," Mellow concluded in his review of the show for the *New York Times* (July 18, 1971).

In the next few years, Caro gradually abandoned his use of color, shifted from a multiple-view orientation to a more frontal approach, and began working with large pieces of rusted and varnished factory steel and "found" scraps of weathered steel. The weighty, austere geometric abstractions of the so-called "Emma Lake" sculptures and other constructions made during the 1970's stand in sharp contrast to the delicate tracery of *Orangerie* and other earlier works. At the invitation of David Mirvish, Caro spent a number of months in the mid-1970's at York Steel Construction, Ltd. in Toronto, collaborating with Canadian sculpture students on a series of thirty-seven massive, rusted-steel constructions. Those dominating works, many of them well over six feet high, were on outdoor display at the Downsview campus of York University in Toronto in 1976. When some two dozen examples of the York sculptures were shown at the Christian Science Center in Boston, Massachusetts in 1980,

Theodore F. Wolff, the art critic for the *Christian Science Monitor*, appreciated Caro's attempt to show that his sculpture did not depend on illusion but on the spatial and visual relationships among the various components. Kenneth Baker, writing in *Art in America*, went so far as to suggest that the obvious heaviness of the materials was the underlying theme of the exhibit.

In 1975 the Museum of Modern Art in New York City mounted a major exhibition of Caro's work. The exhibit, which later traveled to Minneapolis, Houston, and Boston, was the museum's first full-scale retrospective honoring an English sculptor since its 1947 exhibition of the sculptures of Henry Moore. A representative selection of the 300-odd bronze and steel "table sculptures" that Caro had been making since the early 1960's were first publicly shown at the Acquavella Gallery in New York City in 1980. In the opinion of most critics, the small, graceful, delicately balanced pieces were pleasing to the eye, but superficial —the visual equivalent of listening to "a master musician doing scales," to use Hilton Kramer's phrase.

Anthony Caro is a short, compact man with what one reporter described as "the weathered look of a Hollywood English sailor." He and his wife, the former Sheila May Girling, who have been married since 1949, have two sons. The family lives in London, where Caro spends several hours a day in his studio in a converted piano factory. He usually listens to music, especially Mozart, while he works. "I love being in the studio," he told one interviewer. "I mess around and have a lot of fun. Sometimes there's a bit of agony, but it's more fun than anything else."

Caro's constructions have won him a number of honors, including the sculpture prize at the First Paris Biennale, in 1959; the David Bright Sculpture Prize at the Venice Biennale, in 1966; and the second-place sculpture prize at the Tenth Bienal de São Paulo, Brazil, in 1969. In 1969 he was created a Commander of the Order of the British Empire, and in 1976 he received the key to New York City. He is an honorary member of the American Academy and Institute of Arts and Letters, and he holds honorary D.Litt. degrees from the University of East Anglia and York University. Caro's works are in the permanent collections of a number of art galleries and museums, including the Tate Gallery in London, the Museum of Modern Art in New York City, Brandeis University in Waltham, Massachusetts, the Cleveland Museum of Art, and the Hirshhorn Museum and Sculpture Garden and the National Gallery of Art in Washington, D.C.

References: N Y Times II p21 My 17 '70, II p1+ My 18 '75 por; Newsday II p21+ Ap 27 '75 por; Time 88:68 Jl 22 '66 por, 105:58+ My 5 '75 por; Vogue 155:208+ My '70; Washington Post G p11 O 2 '66 por; Contemporary Artists (1977); Whelan, Richard. Anthony Caro (1974)

Carter, Hodding, 3rd

Apr. 7, 1935- Journalist. Address: b.
1 Lincoln Plaza, New York City, N.Y. 10023

As a crusading Mississippi newspaperman and Democratic party reformer during the 1960's and early 1970's, Hodding Carter 3d was a major contributor to the emergence of the "new South." The broad American public, however, was unaware of him until he became a fixture on the network evening news shows as the spokesman for the United States Department of State during the hostage crisis in Iran, in 1979 and 1980. In his press briefings as Assistant Secretary of State for Public Affairs, Carter gave a stunning demonstration of coolness under media pressure, fielding a barrage of questions with a combination of easy spontaneity and exquisite carefulness. Carter is the son of the late Hodding Carter Jr., who was known as "the conscience of the South" for his courageous early espousal of the cause of civil rights in his newspaper, the Greenville (Mississippi) *Delta Democrat-Times*. Succeeding his father, Hodding Carter 3d edited the *Delta Democrat-Times* before going to Washington, D.C. in 1977. Since May 1981 he has been the anchorman of *Inside Story*, the Public Broadcasting Service television series that looks critically at the performance of the news media.

William Hodding Carter 3d was born on April 7, 1935 in New Orleans, Louisiana, the hometown of his mother, Betty (Werlein) Carter, whose family owned a music company there advertising itself as "the original publishers of Dixie." He has a younger brother, Philip, the former publisher of two weekly newspapers in Louisiana. A third brother,

Tommy, the youngest of the Carter siblings, died in a Russian roulette incident in 1964. Hodding Carter Jr., the father, died in 1972. To distinguish one from the other, Hodding Carter Jr. and Hodding Carter 3d were known at home as "Big Hodding" and "Little Hodding," or "Big Hod" and "Little Hod," respectively. In 1932 Big Hod and his wife founded the Hammond (Louisiana) *Daily Courier,* which campaigned against the political machine of Huey Long. Before Senator Long was assassinated, his puppet government in Baton Rouge passed a law forbidding the printing of sheriff's auctions and other public notices in newspapers not approved by the state. The *Daily Courier* was the only paper not approved.

Deprived of an important source of income, the Carters moved in 1936 to Greenville, Mississippi, where they founded the *Delta Star* in competition with Greenville's already existing newspaper, the *Democrat-Times.* Two years later Big Hod bought out the rival *Democrat-Times* with financial backing from Will Percy, an uncle of the novelist Walker Percy, and other Greenville citizens who believed in his thorough, honest reportage. Thus was born the *Delta Democrat-Times.*

For his editorials endorsing racial moderation and justice at a time when such an attitude went against the grain of most Mississippi whites, Hodding Carter Jr. won a Pulitzer Prize in 1946. But he also attracted some local animosity and racist insults and threats. "There was a long period of life in which the knowledge that I was the son of 'the nigger lover' was inescapable, and what that carried with it was obvious," Hodding Carter 3d has said, as quoted in *People* (June 15, 1981). "He [Big Hod] had a great reputation for courage, which he deserved, and yet I never knew a time when he wasn't afraid of the consequences of what he was writing and doing. I learned from my father what courage was really about—it was being afraid but doing what you had to do."

Philip Carter denies, however, that he and his brother had a Gothic childhood. He told Louise Sweeney of the *Christian Science Monitor* (April 1, 1980): "No, it wasn't Gothic at all, it was a happy life, in a pleasant, small Southern city, with good friends. There were scary aspects to it from time to time. It was sometimes quite tense. But I don't think Hodding suffered from it. It was a remarkable kind of moral and intellectual crucible for him."

Carter attended Phillips Exeter Academy, the New Hampshire prep school, for two years. Because he wanted to be regarded in Greenville "as a local boy, not somebody who rode in from outside to tell them how to live," he completed his secondary education at Greenville High School, where he was class president and valedictorian and played tennis and basketball. After taking a B.A. degree in international affairs *summa cum laude* at Princeton University, in 1957, he served in the United States Marine Corps for two years.

Although Carter was contemplating a foreign service career, he returned to Greenville in 1959 because he and his wife "felt that we owed it to Dad and the paper to go back there and give it one year." The one year gradually grew into many, as Carter took on more and more responsibilities because of his father's failing eyesight and his depression over the death of his youngest son. Hodding 3d began writing most of the editorials (his forte) in 1960, became managing editor in 1962, and rose to the dual post of editor and associate publisher in 1965.

Going into the 1960's, Carter was, by his own description, "a moderate segregationist moving toward becoming a moderate integrationist." It was in his "moderate segregationist" persona that he wrote *The South Strikes Back* (Doubleday, 1960), an account of the formation and work of Mississippi's Citizens Councils in resistance to the United States Supreme Court's 1954 school desegregation decision.

Carter entered party politics in 1965 as a member of a biracial group that took control of the Mississippi Young Democrats. Three years later he cofounded the Loyal Democrats of Mississippi, a biracial party dedicated to challenging the state's regular Democratic party. At the 1968 Democratic National Convention he and the black civil rights leader Aaron Henry led the Loyal Democrats' delegation of twenty-two blacks and twenty-two whites in its successful fight to unseat the regular delegation.

Among the black or predominantly black groups that went into the formation of the Loyal Democrats were Fannie Lou Hamer's pioneering Freedom Democrats and the National Council of Churches' Delta Ministry. Owen Brooks, a leader of the Delta Ministry from Boston, remembers Carter, somewhat disparagingly, as an "operator," a power broker. "I like Hodding," Brooks told Gene Lyons when Lyons was preparing his article "The Other Carters" for the New York *Times Magazine* (September 18, 1977), "but I have seen white liberals like him before. Hodding has always prided himself on his ability to talk to what he would call both sides."

Carter told Lyons that, to a certain extent, he understands Brooks's criticism. He said that he is uncomfortable in the role of "liberal white crusader," but that critics such as Brooks are disingenuous about the compromise and trading-off inherent in all politics. "We had to make a symbolic statement in 1968 that we wanted an integrated party. After [Senator Robert F.] Kennedy was shot that year I didn't care one way or the other who got the nomination. All I cared about was getting seated. But those deals were all brokered, so to speak. At least a quarter of the battles I fought were with the left. We were arguing about image, and what it came down to was so many seats for the Freedom Democrats, so many for the NAACP, so many for the Loyalists, and so on."

In the years following the 1968 convention, Carter served on the committee on reforming the convention rules. He was vice-chairman of the credentials committee at the 1972 convention, which seated the Loyalist delegation from Mississippi, which he also chaired. Like other Southern liberals, he feared that the nomination of Senator George S. McGovern of South Dakota would further erode the already diminished Democratic strength in the South. Accordingly, at Miami Beach he placed the name of former Governor Terry Sanford of North Carolina in nomination for President. (Carter's own name was placed in nomination for Vice-President, but he withdrew it before the balloting.) But the day was carried by McGovern, who was easily defeated by Republican candidate Richard Nixon in November.

Early in the 1976 Presidential campaign, Jimmy Carter, the former governor of Georgia and a candidate for the Democratic nomination for President, visited Greenville and impressed Hodding Carter as a potential winner. After Terry Sanford withdrew from the race, Hodding Carter joined Jimmy Carter's campaign staff. At the polls in November 1976 Carter defeated President Gerald R. Ford by 40,827,394 votes to 39,145,977, or a little better than 51 percent.

When incoming President Carter named him Assistant Secretary of State for Public Affairs in January 1977, Hodding Carter turned over his duties at the *Delta Democrat-Times* to his brother, Philip, and moved to Washington. It did not take him long to establish an excellent rapport with the State Department press corps. "I've been here twenty years," William Beecher of the Boston *Globe* said, "and this is the best job I've seen from a foreign-policy spokesman." Others explained that they trusted Carter because of his candor, his self-deprecation, his refusal to speculate, and his willingness to give them as much information as official discretion permitted, on large policy matters as well as on details needed for rounding out a story. He did not inject his own philosophy into his answers, they pointed out, and he never misled them. If he did not know the answer to a question, he frankly confessed his ignorance; if he knew the answer but felt constrained from direct divulgence, he might suggest by a physical gesture or a nuance of voice whether they were on the right track or not.

Basically, the key to Carter's exceptionally good relationship with the reporters was the respect that he accorded them as professionals and that they returned to him. He conveyed a sense that he was one of them, a journalist temporarily channeled into another job. Characteristically, he would begin a briefing by saying something like, "I have an announcement or two before we get to the important part of this exercise, your questions." If the questions were antagonistic, he accepted the hostility as a legacy of Watergate. "If there weren't an adversary relationship between the government and the press," he explained, "I'd wonder what was wrong with the press."

Popular as he was with the Department of State press corps, Carter did not achieve celebrity status until the Iran hostage crisis, which began on November 4, 1979 with the seizure of the United States Embassy and its personnel in Teheran by militant student supporters of the Ayatollah Ruholla Khomeini, the leader of the revolutionary government in Iran. Excerpts from his daily hour-long press briefings, shown nightly on the television network news programs, made him the American public's chief official source of information on the crisis because the press conferences given by White House press secretary Jody Powell were closed to television cameras. Many close observers speculated that, because of Carter's equanimity under pressure, the White House preferred him as the chief government spokesman in an area where a misstatement could hurt the efforts for release of the hostages or even jeopardize the hostages themselves. As a man who in his personal life had learned to keep his hot temper in check, he was able to respond to grueling questions with carefully circumscribed and diplomatically worded statements and, at the same time, convey an impression of the Administration's frustration and seething anger.

By gentlemen's agreement, the press conferences were recorded in their entirety but only the serious portions, showing a deliberately deadpan Carter speaking in a flat monotone, were televised. Those segments revealing the playful side of Carter were never aired. In one such, hounded for an answer he could not give, he reached behind the podium and came up with a rubber chicken, which he hurled at the troublesome reporter.

During the hostage crisis, Carter saw Secretary of State Cyrus Vance early every morning and often several more times throughout the day. He described himself as "very comfortable" with Vance's policies, and he considered himself "lucky" to be working for "a guy who didn't once ask me to go out and play Joe Idiot." Like Vance, he intended to leave the Department of State after four years of Jimmy Carter's Presidency, regardless of the outcome of the November 1980 election. When Vance resigned as Secretary of State in April 1980 over the issue of the aborted United States rescue raid into Iran, Hodding Carter decided to expedite his own departure. "The whole Vance thing exhausted me emotionally," he explained. "We had a strong bond, a close relationship."

After he resigned his State Department post, on July 1, 1980, Carter did not return to Greenville. "All that stuff in the 1950's and 1960's was so distinct," he explained, "I would be at a loss as to what to do if I went back." (He, his mother, and his brother had sold the *Delta Democrat-Times* earlier in the year, for a reported $16,000,000.) Instead he went into two months of "decompression" at his vacation home in Camden, Maine and then began lecturing—at $5,000 an appearance—and working on a biography of his father. On May 7, 1981 Carter made his debut as anchorman, chief correspondent, and commentator of *Inside Story*, a Public Broadcasting Service half-hour weekly series examining how, and how well, the press covers the news. "The project is consistent with everything I have worked for . . . ," Carter explained to a reporter. "We are not out to 'get' the press, but to examine its performance with care. The press is an institution virtually all Americans depend on and it should be a subject for public scrutiny, as other institutions are."

Presented as a television new magazine, *Inside Story* consists of a feature, or cover story; a section called "Hits and Misses" giving examples of good and bad press coverage; a review of free-press issues called "First Amendment Alert"; comic relief provided by the satirical team of Bob Elliott and Ray Goulding; and a commentary by Carter. In addition to the commentary, Carter writes a lead-in and lead-out for each show. Early subjects included a New Jersey school newspaper's interview with a drug dealer, press coverage of the civil war in El Salvador, the shooting of President Ronald Reagan and his press secretary, James Brady, and the recent string of unsolved murders of black boys and young men in Atlanta, Georgia. In newspaper reviews the show was described as "genuinely important," "entertaining," and "enlightening," but the ratings were anemic.

Hodding Carter 3d is a tall man with glossy dark hair, blue-gray eyes, and a manner that can change from the courtly to the raucous when his sense of humor takes over. While aggressive, he has what Gene Lyons in his *New York Times Magazine* article referred to as "the genteel Southerner's preference for avoiding both open conflict and the appearance of effort." A close family friend told Lyons that Carter is just as "hard-driving" as his father was, but more politically oriented, "much more capable of compromise," and "even more committed to civil and human rights." Henry Truitt, a reporter for the Baltimore *Sun* and a fellow Southerner, was quoted by Louise Sweeney in her *Christian Science Monitor* profile as viewing Carter as "a well-raised Southern elitist who feels his responsibilities very strongly." Philip Carter told Louise Sweeney that his older brother is "fastidious" and "enormously kind," but capable of being "an implacable enemy." "He is in many respects less volatile than my father, and in his own way is even stronger . . . ," Philip said.

Once described by a friend as being "in the great tradition of the Delta—party-going and hard-drinking," Carter has in recent years restrained his gregariousness considerably, and in the *People* interview he said, "I dropped hard liquor for a year and now I usually stick to wine or beer." Also, he was a chain smoker of cigarettes until January 1, 1979, when he quit cold-turkey. His musical taste ranges from show tunes to Beethoven, and he reads widely.

Carter and Patricia Derian, a longtime Southern political ally of his, were married in December 1978, when she was serving alongside him in the State Department, as Assistant Secretary for Human Rights. Earlier that year Carter had been divorced from the former Margaret Ainsworth Wolfe, his wife of twenty-one years, by whom he has four children, Catherine Ainsworth, Elisabeth Fearn, William Hodding 4th, and Margaret Lorraine. When doing his television work, Carter commutes between his office in New York City and the three-story town house in which he lives with his wife in Alexandria, Virginia.

References: Chicago Tribune I p9+ Je 16 '80 por; Christian Sci Mon B p1+ Ap 1 '80 pors; N Y Times Mag p14+ S 18 '77 pors; People 15:60+ Je 15 '81 pors

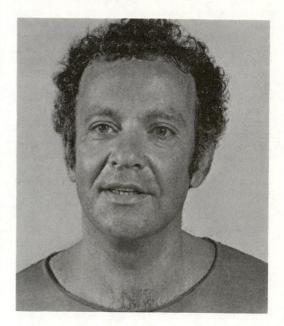

Chaikin, Joseph

Sept. 16, 1935- Theatrical director; actor. Address: b. c/o Performing Artservices, Inc., 325 Spring St., Room 347, New York City, N.Y. 10013

For nearly a decade Joseph Chaikin directed one of the most influential experimental theatre groups in the United States, the New York City-based Open Theater, which he founded in 1963 after working as an actor with the Living Theater of Judith Malina and Julian Beck. Under Chaikin's guidance the Open Theater devoted itself to the collaborative creation of drama that is imagistic rather than narrative and impressionistic rather than naturalistic.

Neither overtly didactic nor doctrinaire in content, its works are investigations of the essential problems of human existence. Although the Open Theater consciously avoided commercial popularity, it ultimately earned such a widespread reputation that Chaikin, fearing the constriction of the group's creative powers, disbanded it in 1973. Later Chaikin moved on to other innovative collaborations in the capacity of actor as well as director.

Joseph Chaikin was born on September 16, 1935 in Brooklyn, New York to Abraham and Leah Chaikin. His family, of Russian-Jewish background, includes his older sister, Shami, who was an actress with the Open Theater, two other sisters, Miriam and Fay, and his brother, Ben. During his childhood Joseph Chaikin suffered from rheumatic fever, and since his family was poor, he was sent to a charity institution, the National Children's Cardiac Home in Florida, for an extended period of convalescence. While he was re-cuperating his family moved to Des Moines, Iowa, where his father taught Hebrew and Russian. Chaikin spent his adolescence in Des Moines, graduating from North High School and then attending Drake University, where he studied philosophy and devoted himself to drama. Fascinated from his earliest childhood by the stage, he had acted in backyard theatre, grade-school plays, and high school presentations. At Drake, he performed in university productions of Shakespeare, classical Greek drama, and contemporary plays and formed his own theatrical troupe, the Harlequin Players, in which he practised his skills as actor and director.

After three years at Drake, Chaikin left the university in the mid-1950's without taking a degree and moved to New York City to pursue an acting career. He studied his craft first at the Herbert Berghof Studio and then with a number of individual teachers, including Bill Hickey, Nola Chilton, Mira Rostiva, Viola Spolin, and Peter Kass, all of whom taught psychological acting methods. Until he began to get steady acting jobs he had to support himself with part-time employment as an office worker and a waiter. Chaikin undertook his first professional role, as the hero's sidekick in No Time for Sergeants, at a summer stock theatre in Pennsylvania. He made his New York City debut in the role of Mr. Atkins in a spirited revival of Howard Richardson and William Berney's Dark of the Moon, which opened in February 1958 for a ten-week run at the Carnegie Hall Playhouse.

In 1959 Chaikin met Judith Malina and Julian Beck and joined their politically oriented avant-garde troupe, the Living Theater. His first performance for the Living Theater, in the summer of that year, was in the role of Ephron in The Cave at Macpelah, Paul Goodman's innovative verse drama derived from Old Testament tales of Abraham and his progeny. Depressed by his role as Leach in Jack Gelber's brutally naturalistic depiction of heroin addicts, The

Connection, Chaikin temporarily left the Living Theater in July 1960 to perform with the Theatre for the Swan in its brief run of a triple bill of plays by Michel De Ghelderode, W. B. Yeats, and e. e. cummings. When the Theatre for the Swan folded, he returned to the Living Theater and resumed his role in The Connection since there was nothing else open for him at the time. He felt more comfortable with roles in Living Theater productions of William Carlos Williams' Many Loves, Luigi Pirandello's Tonight We Improvise and Mountain Giants, and Bertolt Brecht's In the Jungle of Cities.

With his portrayal of Galy Gay, a mild-mannered Irish day laborer brainwashed into becoming a "human fighting machine," during the Living Theater's 1962-63 run of Brecht's 1953 version of Man Is Man, Chaikin seemed well on his way to becoming an established actor. His performance earned him a 1963 Obie Award. But the difficulties that Chaikin encountered in fleshing out his role in Brecht's didactic drama led him to question the applicability of psychological acting methods to other than naturalistic plays. Consequently he organized, within the Living Theater, a study group to investigate other acting styles.

Despite his deep sense of loyalty to Malina and Beck, Chaikin left the Living Theater for good after an October 1963 performance of Kenneth H. Brown's play The Brig, during which the theatre was raided by Internal Revenue agents and its directors were arrested for tax evasion. Chaikin, who had been jailed twice before because of Living Theater activities, chose to cast his lot with other theatre ensembles. He won his second Obie award for his performance as the Detective in Eugène Ionesco's Victims of Duty, presented by the Writers Stage Company in May and June 1964. His portrayal of the victimized Coolie in Brecht's parable The Exception and the Rule, presented at the Greenwich Mews Theater from May to September 1965, earned him his third Obie award. Other plays in which he appeared in 1964-65 included Ionesco's The New Tenant and Arthur Kopit's Sing to Me Through Open Windows.

Chaikin devoted most of his creative energy, however, to the formation of another group to study acting problems. Many of the workshop's original members had been students of Nola Chilton before she immigrated to Israel. In the early days of the Open Theater, as the group came to be called, its members paid monthly dues for the upkeep of a Soho loft in which they tried out innovative improvisational and ensemble exercises. From 1963 to 1966 they offered periodic public performances, at Ellen Stewart's La Mama Experimental Theatre Club or at the Sheridan Square Playhouse, of pieces written by its resident playwrights, such as Megan Terry's Calm Down Mother and Keep Tightly Closed in a Cool Dry Place and Jean-Claude van Itallie's The Odets Kitchen.

In 1966 the Open Theater ventured into commercial theatre with Off-Broadway productions of two pieces originally developed in its workshops. The first, *Viet Rock,* written and directed by Megan Terry and presented at the Martinique Theater in November and December, is a fluid series of abrasive vignettes condemning the Vietnam war; its production failed to win widespread critical approval. Stanley Kauffmann, who felt that the play was misunderstood by fellow critics, explained it, in a November 18, 1966 broadcast on New York City's Channel 13, as "a strong, free-moving theatrical composition on the persistent verities of war—using the Vietnam war as a basis." Much more popular was the Pocket Theater's presentation of Jean-Claude van Itallie's trio of satirical scenarios entitled *America Hurrah.* Chaikin directed one of them, *Interview,* and Jacques Levy directed the other two, *TV* and *Motel.* In August 1967 Levy and Chaikin took *America Hurrah* to London, where it was well received at the Royal Court Theatre despite some censorship problems. At the Pocket Theater *America Hurrah* continued to be performed by a replacement cast, closing in the spring of 1968 after racking up profits of about 300 percent.

After his work with *America Hurrah,* Chaikin vowed that the Open Theater would avoid further involvement with commercial theatre because, in his opinion, it unavoidably engendered a drive to earn money and critical approval that warred with the willingness to take creative risks. Henceforth, in the privacy of various Greenwich Village lofts, the troupe concentrated on the collaborative development of original theatre pieces centered on specific questions concerning aspects of human existence. The Open Theater managed to survive financially with the aid of grants and the proceeds of occasional benefit performances.

The first of the Open Theater's full-length ensemble works was *The Serpent: A Ceremony,* an exploration of personal reactions to the myths of the Book of Genesis. Using their bodies and voices as instruments for creating images, the actors presented a seamless sequence of vignettes about the creation of the world, the loss of Paradise, and the discovery of sex and of murder. Jean-Claude van Itallie gave a final shape to the spoken text, which the actors had essentially created during their workshop improvisations. The Open Theater first exhibited *The Serpent* to audiences in the spring of 1968, on a tour of Western Europe. In 1969 the troupe unveiled it in New York City during a two-week engagement at Joseph Papp's Public Theater and at free Wednesday evening performances in their loft. In October 1970 a taped and edited version was televised on Channel 13's *NET Playhouse. The Serpent* earned the Open Theater an Obie award in 1969 and a Brandeis University Creative Arts award in 1970. Chaikin and the Open Theater also won a 1969 Vernon Rice award for "outstanding contributions" to theatre. Otis L.

Guernsey Jr. included *The Serpent* in his *Best Plays of 1969-70.*

The Open Theater's second major collaborative work was *Terminal,* an investigation of the inevitable reality of death and the modern tendency to avoid confronting that reality. The company's aim in *Terminal,* as Chaikin explained in his book, *The Presence of the Actor* (Atheneum, 1972), was "to see ourselves, in the largest way, as part of the process of nature, and to see that dying is part of that process." Susan Yankowitz fashioned *Terminal*'s finished text, and Chaikin directed it with Roberta Sklar. After performing it in Western Europe, the Open Theater presented *Terminal* in repertory with *The Serpent* and Samuel Beckett's dark comedy *Endgame* at Harvard University and at the Washington Square Methodist Church in New York City in the spring of 1970. Later that year the Open Theater incorporated *Terminal* into *Opera,* an avant-garde musical composition by Luciano Berio, and performed it with the Santa Fe Opera. For the Open Theater's repertory production of the Beckett play, Roberta Sklar directed Chaikin in the role of Hamm. The only other acting project Chaikin undertook during that period was Robert Frank's film *Me and My Brother* (1968), in which he played a role derived from the life of Julius Orlovsky, a man who spent thirteen years in an insane asylum.

The Mutation Show, the Open Theater's third major collaborative work, unfolds the theme of human transformation through the format of a sideshow presentation of circus freaks. In 1971 and 1972 the group performed it together with *Terminal* at Harvard University and on tours of Algeria, Israel, Iran, the midwestern United States, and eastern Canada and in the spring of 1973 presented it alone at the Space for Innovative Development in New York City. As Mel Gussow explained its theme in the New York *Times* (March 29, 1973), "*The Mutation Show* is not just about the shock of civilization upon mutants, but, finally, about civilization itself, about mankind as mutants. As such, it is a revelation." *The Mutation Show* won the 1972 Obie award for the best theatre piece, and Chaikin's direction of it earned him a 1973 Drama Desk award.

The Open Theater's fourth and final full-length collaboration, *Nightwalk,* is about a journey taken by two creatures through the subconscious realms of human dream and nightmare. Jean-Claude van Itallie, Megan Terry, and Sam Shepard contributed to the creation of the text, which also includes poems by Wallace Stevens, Ted Hughes, and Bob Dylan. The Open Theater presented *Nightwalk* in 1973 in repertory with *Terminal* and *The Mutation Show* at St. Clement's Church in New York City and at the Roundhouse Theatre in London.

After a tour of the United States in the autumn of 1973, the Open Theater disbanded at the insistence of Chaikin, who feared that, because of the pressures of public acclaim, the group would become "institutionalized." As he explained to Michael White of the *Guardian* (June 6, 1973), "I feel our work is still alive and creative, but the work is so important to me I could not live in it atrophying." The members of the company moved on to form new groups, and Chaikin began work on his own, directing playwright Robert Montgomery's *Electra*, an adaptation of classical myth and drama, at St. Clement's Church in the spring of 1974. The austere new version involves only the three principal characters, Orestes, Electra, and Clytemnestra, and features a play within a play in which Orestes rehearses with Electra the murder of their guilty mother.

In 1975 Chaikin directed Jean-Claude van Itallie's new English-language rendition of Anton Chekhov's play *The Seagull* at the Manhattan Theater Club. Chaikin's deft handling of the classic work earned him widespread critical praise. Later that same year Chaikin directed *A Fable*, a collaborative work of music theatre with text written by van Itallie and music composed by Richard Peaslee, at the Westbeth Exchange Theater. The actors made use of the innovative performance techniques typical of the Open Theater to tell the story of a woman commanded by a king to free his land from a mysterious beast. That same year Chaikin collaborated with the Theatre of Latin America on *Chile, Chile,* their "staged documentary" about the 1973 military takeover of the Chilean government.

Chaikin returned to acting in 1976, when he joined the Shaliko Company's production of Georg Büchner's *Woyzeck* at Joseph Papp's Public Theater. Under Leonardo Shapiro's direction he played the title role in Mira Rafalowicz's newly translated and adapted version of the unfinished nineteenth-century text. He was acclaimed for the physical "eloquence" of his performance as the humble soldier driven to mad revolt against the cruelties of life. To shape his role, Chaikin put to use his theory, developed during his years with the Open Theater, that the actor must be empathetically involved in his role yet sufficiently distanced from it to be able to comment on the character, as he explained to Elenore Lester of the New York *Times* (March 7, 1976). With his controlled performance Chaikin intended to speak to the audience and for the audience.

In late 1977 Chaikin resumed his role as a director with his staging of a Public Theater production of *The Dybbuk*. Mira Rafalowicz translated and revised S. Ansky's Yiddish text to emphasize the social backdrop of the tale of a demon's passionate possession of his beloved on the day of her marriage to another man. As Chaikin told Eileen Blumenthal of the New York *Times* (January 1, 1978), he chose to work with the play because it represents a legacy from his own past (it was the first play of which he had ever heard) and from the religious and social past of the Hasidic culture. Chaikin later took the play to the Habimah Theater in Tel Aviv.

Chaikin continued his direction of experimental theatre with the Winter Project, a collaborative group founded in 1977 and made up mostly of former members of the Open Theater. In early 1979 the Winter Project offered its first public presentation of a theatre piece, *Re-Arrangements*, at La Mama Annex. With the help of techniques borrowed from vaudeville acting and modern dance, the players created a set of scenarios concerned with human longing for romance and fascination with death. In mid-1980 the Winter Project staged its second work, *Tourists and Refugees*, at La Mama Annex. The piece juxtaposes variations on the theme of homelessness, which can result from the torment of restless emotions as well as the persecution of despotic governments. Using the same theme and some of the same images with equal comedy and poignancy, the Winter Project developed *Tourists and Refugees No. 2*, presented in 1981 at La Mama Annex and at the International Festival in Caracas. Chaikin's recent directorial efforts also included a 1980 Manhattan Theater Club production of Samuel Beckett's *Endgame*, which he chose to present as "a comedy about suffering" and "entertainment at the border of despair," as he told Leah D. Frank of the New York *Times* (January 13, 1980).

In collaboration with playwright Sam Shepard, Chaikin developed the text for *Tongues*, a solo piece in which a variety of voices speak of death through the medium of a lone figure seated on a throne. Chaikin performed *Tongues* at the Magic Theatre in San Francisco in 1978. The following year he presented it at the Public Theater in New York on a double bill with *Savage/Love*, which Sam Shepard wrote for him. *Savage/Love* is, like *Tongues*, a solo piece that explores the limits of language's expressiveness, while it probes the pains and problems of love relationships. Chaikin performed the two pieces in 1980 on tours of Europe, the western United States, and Canada. In 1981, at the Public Theater in New York and at Riverside Studios in London, Chaikin performed the solo work *Texts*, which he adapted in collaboration with Steven Kent from Samuel Beckett's prose works *How It Is* and *Texts for Nothing*.

Joseph Chaikin is a commanding professional presence despite his youthful face, curly hair, and eyes that seem to make him look perpetually astonished. According to Ross Wetzsteon of the *Village Voice* (November 3, 1975), he "has the uncanny quality of conveying intensity through serenity, passion through silence. The thing his friends call most characteristic of him is . . . charisma." Although he has periodically undergone surgery for the heart trouble that began in childhood, he works tirelessly to perfect the craft he loves. Among his other distinctions, Chaikin has received Guggenheim fellowships in 1969 and 1975, an honorary Ph.D. degree from Drake

University in 1972, and the first Lifetime Achievement Obie Award in 1977. He makes his home in lower Manhattan.

References: Drama Review 20:18+ S '76; Guardian p12 Je 8 '73 por; N Y Times II p1+ D 25 '66 por, II p1+ Mr 29 '70; Chaikin, Joseph. The Presence of the Actor (1972); Notable Names in the American Theatre (1976); Who's Who in the Theatre (1977)

Chicago, Judy

July 20, 1939- Artist. Address: b. 1651B 18th St., Santa Monica, Calif. 90404; Through the Flower Corporation, P.O. Box 842, Benicia, Calif. 94510

The West Coast artist Judy Chicago, who has devoted her career to feminist as well as aesthetic achievements, began her campaign to encourage women to incorporate female imagery into their art work and to understand it in other women's creations after her own paintings and sculptures had been rejected by critics. For the benefit of women artists, she established educational programs and wrote an autobiography, Through the Flower, that offers them an example of fortitude and feminist awareness. She also spent five years creating The Dinner Party, a monumental ceramic and needlework project that seeks to convey the social history of women in the Western world and to broaden the base for art.

Judy Chicago was born Judy Cohen in Chicago, Illinois on July 20, 1939. Her father, Arthur M. Cohen, a union organizer, and her mother, May (Levenson) Cohen, a doctor's secretary, brought up their only daughter and their younger son Ben in Chicago. Encouraged by her parents, Judy began drawing at the age of three and longed to be an artist early in childhood. From 1947 to 1957 she attended Saturday classes at the Chicago Art Institute, and in 1957 she received a scholarship from her public high school to continue her art studies at the University of California at Los Angeles. She obtained her B.A. degree from UCLA in 1962 and her M.A. degree from there in 1964. During her undergraduate years, she spent some time teaching art in New York City.

Judy Chicago first experienced male chauvinist prejudice in graduate school when she had to accept a teaching assistantship in sculpture because the painting department did not award such positions to women. Moreover, she had to abandon the personal, content-oriented style of her art when the two painting instructors on her thesis committee threatened to withdraw their support of her work if she subjected them to any more "biomorphic" imagery. The offending pictures presented forms resembling "phalluses, vaginas, testicles, wombs, hearts, ovaries, and other body parts," as she later explained in her autobiography. She allowed her early paintings to be destroyed and, adopting the standards of California's male art community, learned to hide her ideas behind more abstract, minimalist images fashioned out of plexiglass and spray paint.

In 1965 she took a loft in Pasadena, California and devoted herself to making sculpture, which she exhibited under her married name, Judy Gerowitz. In early 1966 she made her professional debut in a solo show at Rolf Nelson Gallery in Los Angeles, where she exhibited a rearrangeable environment called Sunset Squares and a series of photos of a work entitled Rainbow Pickett (1965), a set of pastel-colored beams. That same year she sent sculpture to New York City for the Jewish Museum's show entitled "Primary Structures." In 1967 she exhibited in "Sculpture of the Sixties" at the Los Angeles County Museum of Art and the Philadelphia Museum of Art and, in 1968, in the show entitled "West Coast Now" at the Seattle Art Museum, the Portland Museum of Art, and the San Francisco Museum of Art.

In 1969 the Pasadena Museum of Art presented a solo show of Judy Chicago's work that featured an ambitious series of plexiglass dome structures, arranged in groups of three and consisting of transparent surfaces containing layers of softly colored plastic. As Judy Chicago later explained in her autobiography, the melting hues of the domes' interiors signify her own "multi-orgasmic sexuality"; moreover, the three elements in each grouping represent the basic family constellation of mother, father, and child. Peter Selz of Art in America (November 1969) showed some sensitivity to their meanings in noting that "the domes initially appear reductive and systematic, but soon prove lush, emotive and human."

Other critics failed to show equal perceptiveness when they evaluated the solo exhibition that she mounted the following year at the Art Gallery of California State College at Fullerton. In order to emphasize the feminine perspective of her exhibited work, she posted, outside the gallery entrance, an announcement of her legal change of name: "Judy Gerowitz hereby divests herself of all names imposed upon her through male social dominance and freely chooses her own name Judy Chicago." Thomas H. Garver of Artforum (January 1971) incorrectly assumed that she had adopted an alias and was exploiting the feminist movement to promote her own work. Critics compared the domes, which she included in the exhibit, to those of sculptor Craig Kauffman and dismissed Pasadena Lifesavers (1969), her first group of paintings to be shown since her graduate school days, as an uninspiring formal exercise.

The focus of Pasadena Lifesavers, however, is actually upon expression of personal emotion rather than upon experimentation with minimalist forms. It consists of three series of the same sequence of five pictures executed in different color schemes on sheet acrylic; each painting in the repeating sequence displays four vulviform shapes, and color schemes convey conflicting personal feelings. Judy Chicago later celebrated the emotional release that Pasadena Lifesavers afforded her by creating a series of "atmospheres," or colored smoke displays in outdoor environments, which she documented in photographs and films for her Fullerton show. Although critics applauded the atmospheres as "perceptual and spatial experiences of momentary nature but powerful impact," they failed to grasp their thematic implications.

After the Fullerton show Judy Chicago decided that her work could be better understood and accepted by a female art community. Having taken a teaching post at Fresno State College in 1970, she founded a women's art program there in which the participants developed self-confidence and self-reliance as well as technical expertise. Accompanied by some of her students, Judy Chicago moved the next year to the California Institute of the Arts in Valencia to join artist Miriam Shapiro in establishing their Feminist Art Program, with which she worked until early 1973. For its first project the class renovated a rundown mansion in Los Angeles and turned it into Womanhouse, an environment embodying feminine fantasies about domestic interiors in rooms ranging from a "Nurturant Kitchen" to a "Lipstick Bathroom." When it was opened to the public for a month in 1972, Womanhouse attracted almost 10,000 visitors.

During her two and a half years in the academic world, Judy Chicago produced art that was noteworthy for its increasingly overt feminist imagery. While at Fresno she created Fresno Fans (1970-71) and Flesh Gardens (1971), two series of large paintings on sheet acrylic.

The colors of each Fan radiate outwards from the center to the edges of the format in much the same way that a woman reaches out from her receptive center. The colors of each Flesh Garden oppose their soft vulnerability to the hard rigidity of its forms. While at Cal Arts she experimented with lithography, beginning with Red Flag (1971), a graphic image of a woman's hand holding a bloody tampon, and continuing with Through the Flower (1972), a series that expresses her longing to transcend the boundaries of the human condition. "To me, the flower in O'Keeffe stands for femininity," she told Lucy R. Lippard in an interview for Artforum (September 1974), "so moving through the flower is moving into some other place."

In 1972 Judy Chicago organized a nationwide Conference for Women Artists that took place at Cal Arts, a major result of which was the creation, in 1973, of Womanspace, an exhibition space and art gallery. When Womanspace presented a show based on the theme of female sexuality, she was invited to make a contribution. She executed a huge painting on canvas entitled Let It All Hang Out (1973). Because she was, for the first time, creating specifically for a female audience that would intuitively understand her imagery, she designed a forthright symbol of her concept of herself and produced a painting combining power and vulnerability.

In 1973 Judy Chicago launched yet another feminist art project: with art historian Arlene Raven and designer Sheila de Bretteville she founded in Los Angeles the Feminist Studio Workshop, an independent institution dedicated to perfecting the artmaking and leadership skills of its students. The Feminist Studio Workshop created a congenial environment for itself by opening the Woman's Building, a facility that leased space to feminist theatre groups, political organizations, and publishers in addition to providing galleries for Womanspace. The Woman's Building took its name from a historical example of cooperative artistic effort, namely, the pavilion at the 1893 World's Columbian Exposition whose architect, managers, and contributing artists were all women.

On November 28, 1973 the Woman's Building celebrated its opening, attended by 5,000 people, with special exhibitions in its several galleries. In Gallery Grandview One Judy Chicago mounted a solo show to unveil the Great Ladies (1972-73) and the Reincarnation Triptych (1973). The former series of canvases presents the personalities of particular historical queens through the use of undulating abstract imagery, vibrating colors, and the handwritten captions that Judy Chicago considers important as a means of clarifying the feminist content of her imagery. Melinda Terbell of Art News (February 1974) praised the Great Ladies for their "intense impact" but reserved her real accolades for the Reincarnation Triptych, a set of three canvases representing Mme. de

Staël, George Sand, and Virginia Woolf. According to the artist, the differences among the three paintings represent the growth of feminine consciousness throughout the past 200 years as well as the stages of her own development as a feminist artist.

Throughout the 1970's the work of Judy Chicago appeared in solo and group shows throughout the United States—at the Whitney Museum's exhibition "The Structure of Color" in New York City in 1971; the Jack Glenn Gallery of Corona del Mar, California and the University of Washington at Seattle in 1972; the University of North Dakota at Grand Forks and the de Saisset Museum at Santa Clara, California in 1973; the Kenmore Gallery of Philadelphia and Western Washington State College in Bellingham in 1974; Cerritos College of Newark, California in 1975; and the Quay Ceramics Gallery of San Francisco and the Ruth Schaffner Gallery of Los Angeles in 1976. Judy Chicago was also represented in Canada at the Winnipeg Art Gallery in 1975 and in England at the JPL Fine Arts Gallery in 1976. Her work in visual art and feminist education brought her *Mademoiselle* magazine's Women of Achievement award for 1973.

In 1975 Doubleday published Judy Chicago's autobiography, *Through the Flower: My Struggle as a Woman Artist,* which examines her past from a perspective attained through years of struggling alone in her studio. Replete with her observations about feminine imagery and ideas in art and literature, *Through the Flower* was well received by many book reviewers and became an important text for study in feminist programs. Even its most ardent admirers, however, questioned Judy Chicago's capability as a writer and deplored the slipshod editing of her book, while its detractors were quick to denounce its clichéd and ungrammatical style.

By the time *Through the Flower* had begun to generate its share of controversy, Judy Chicago was already absorbed by an ambitious project that combined feminist art and education. Because of her growing interest in china painting as an unappreciated women's artform, she originally planned to make a new series of *Great Ladies* paintings on porcelain plates to hang on gallery walls. To underscore her conviction that women of achievement are often swallowed up by history, she intended to call her plates *Twenty-Five Women Who Were Eaten Alive.* When she decided to incorporate them into the place settings of a banquet table for important mythic and historic women of Western civilization, the concept of *The Dinner Party* was born. To complete her project, Judy Chicago organized a collective workshop in her studio in Santa Monica, where 400 volunteers toiled under the direction of Diane Gelon, chief administrator and fundraiser; Leonard Skuro, technical adviser for ceramics; and Susan Hill, coordinator of needlework.

The finished art work, first presented to the general public at the San Francisco Museum of Modern Art on March 16, 1979, overwhelmed viewers with the immensity of its scale and the intricacy of its detail. The banquet table consists of three wings, each one measuring $46^{1}/_2$ feet in length and displaying, atop linen table cloths, thirteen place settings complete with plate, cup, knife, fork, spoon, napkin, and embroidered linen runner. Judy Chicago chose thirteen as a number that recalls both the number of guests at the Last Supper and of witches in a coven. Each plate represents the honored guest herself, and the corresponding linen runner depicts either scenes from her life or symbols of the society in which she lived. The first wing honors women from prehistoric through Greco-Roman times, the second, from the early Church era through the Reformation, and the third, from the seventeen through the twentieth centuries. The table rests upon the porcelain tiles of the Heritage Floor, which bears the names of 999 other women of achievement.

After the San Francisco showing ended in June 1979, *The Dinner Party* moved to a warehouse because both the Seattle Art Museum and the Memorial Art Gallery of Rochester had canceled their exhibition contracts. In March 1980 *The Dinner Party* resurfaced for a three-month show at the University of Houston at Clear Lake City, Texas. After that, it traveled to the Boston Center for the Arts for an Independence Day opening and finished the year by spending fall and winter at the Brooklyn Museum.

The Dinner Party elicited a divided response from the general public as well as from established art critics. Compelled by curiosity or by strongly held convictions of feminist ideology, crowds of viewers flocked from all over the country to its exhibition sites. Critics either hailed *The Dinner Party* as "the definitive feminist art work" or condemned it as "the ultimate in 1970's kitsch." Its detractors focused principally on the plates, deeming them inadequate representations of the women they ostensibly honor; on the other hand, the linen runners were universally admired for their beauty and the historical fidelity of their needlework. To many critics, the literalness of its ceramic imagery reduces the guests at *The Dinner Party* to sex objects, thereby reinforcing the traditional attitudes of Western men. Conceptual criticism focused on the exhibit's exploitation of the popularity of goddess worship among feminists in California or on its implicit suggestion of a lesbian eucharist ceremony.

To enhance the educational value of her monumental art exhibit, Judy Chicago wrote *The Dinner Party: A Symbol of Our Heritage* (Anchor Press/Doubleday, 1979) and *Embroidering Our Heritage: The Dinner Party Needlework* (Anchor Press/Doubleday, 1980). Besides documenting the painstaking technical processes involved in producing the plates and the runners, the two books provide biographical information and historical background concerning the 1,038 women honored in the exhibit. The five-year project is also documented in *Right Out of History: The Making of the Dinner Party* (Phoenix Films, 1980), a color film directed by Johanna Demetrakas.

The energetic and outspoken Judy Chicago lives in the San Francisco Bay area, where she has initiated a new project that will again deal with content relevant to women's lives in forms accessible to a wide audience. She is single: her marriage to Jerry Gerowitz lasted from 1961 to 1963, when he died in an auto accident, and her marriage to sculptor Lloyd Hamrol lasted from 1969 to 1979, when they were divorced. One of her ultimate goals is to house *The Dinner Party* in a permanent installation in California or Washington, D.C. Otherwise, she believes, her art, like that of countless women creators of the past, will disappear from history.

References: Art News 78:60+ Ja '79 pors; Artforum 13:60+ S '74; New York 13:50+ O 20 '80 por; Chicago, Judy. *The Dinner Party: A Symbol of Our Heritage* (1979), *Through the Flower: My Struggle as a Woman Artist* (1975); Who's Who in America, 1980-81; Who's Who in American Art (1980)

Christopher, Warren M(inor)

Oct. 27, 1925- Lawyer; former United States government official. Address: b. O'Melveny & Myers, 611 W. 6th St., Los Angeles, Calif. 90017

As the chief United States negotiator for the release of the fifty-two American hostages held in Iran, Warren M. Christopher figured more prominently in the news in the first weeks of 1981 than at any other time in his four years of service as the Deputy Secretary of State in the Carter Administration. The nation watched anxiously as Christopher and a team of aides worked feverishly in Algiers, Algeria to bring to a successful conclusion months of intense effort to rescue the captured Americans. "I am indebted to him and so is the nation," President Jimmy Carter said in the closing days of his Administration when he awarded Christopher, *in absentia*, the Medal of Freedom. The award's citation described the quiet Californian as having "the tact of a true diplomat, the tactical skills of a great soldier, the analytical ability of a fine lawyer and the selfless dedication of a citizen-statesman." With the end of the Carter Presidency, Christopher returned to the practice of law in Los Angeles, resuming a career that he had interrupted on several earlier occasions to serve in government posts, including that of Deputy Attorney General in the Department of Justice from 1967 to 1969.

Warren Minor Christopher was born on October 27, 1925 in the small farming community of Scranton, North Dakota, the fourth of five children of Ernest W. and Catharine Anna (Lemen) Christopher. His father, a banker, died while Warren was still young. During the Depression the Christopher family moved to the Los Angeles area, where Warren attended Hollywood High School. He enrolled at the University of Redlands in 1942, but transferred the following year to the University of Southern California, from which he graduated *magna cum laude* with a B.A. degree in 1945. On completing three years of service, from 1943 to 1946, as a lieutenant (j.g.) in the Naval Reserve, Christopher entered the Law School of Stanford University. He was elected president of the law review, was admitted to the Order of the Coif, and was awarded the LL.B. degree in 1949. His record caught the notice of Justice William O. Douglas of the United States Supreme Court, with whom he was invited to serve his clerkship in 1949-50.

After his year in Washington, D.C., Christopher returned to Los Angeles to join, in 1950, the prestigious and politically influential law firm of O'Melveny & Myers, of which he became a partner in 1958. As time passed, Christopher devoted increasing attention to public affairs. He served as special counsel in 1959 to Governor Edmund G. ("Pat") Brown of California, whose Democratic campaign he had supported; sat on the California Coordinating Council for Higher Education from 1960 to 1967 and was its president from 1963 to 1965; and served as a member of the state's board of bar examiners in 1966-67. Christopher was also the vice-chairman of an eight-person commission established by Governor Brown in 1965 to investigate the causes of the race riots in Watts, Los Angeles. On the federal level, from 1961 to 1965 Christopher was a consultant to Undersecretary of State George W. Ball on foreign economic problems. During his association with the State Department he played an important, but low-key, role in regulating the international textile trade. He was the chairman of the American delegations to the United States-Japan Cotton Textile Negotiations and to the Geneva Conference on Cotton Textiles, both of which took place in 1961, and he acted as the special representative of the Secretary of State to the Wool Textile Meetings in London, Rome, and Tokyo in 1964 and 1965.

Recalled to Washington by President Lyndon B. Johnson in June 1967 to become Deputy Attorney General, Christopher made his California experience a valuable asset to that Democratic Administration in its final years. When race riots erupted in Detroit in August 1967, Johnson dispatched Christopher and Deputy Secretary of Defense Cyrus R. Vance to assess the situation in the city. Likewise, when violence flared in Chicago after the assassination of Dr. Martin Luther King Jr. in April 1968, the President put Christopher in charge of coordinating efforts by the Army and local authorities to control the disturbances. After the inauguration of Richard Nixon in 1969, Christopher returned to the private practice of law in Los Angeles, where he remained on the periphery of the limelight. Early in the Watergate crisis Nixon offered to name him special prosecutor, but he declined the post, which eventually fell to Archibald Cox. During the Presidency of Gerald Ford, however, Christopher was chairman of the American Bar Association panel that reviewed the credentials of candidates to succeed his mentor, William O. Douglas, on the United States Supreme Court.

On December 13, 1976 President-elect Jimmy Carter announced that Warren Christopher would become his Deputy Secretary of State. According to political commentators, the selection reflected the wishes of Vance, the newly designated Secretary of State, who had hand-picked the Californian to be his second-in-command. Senator Jacob K. Javits, a liberal New York Republican, and William Safire, a conservative columnist, were among those protesting the choice. Drawing on testimony delivered before Senator Sam Ervin's constitutional rights subcommittee in 1971, they charged that Christopher, as Deputy Attorney General, had condoned illegal military surveillance of domestic dissidents. But Christopher, in hearings before the Senate Committee on Foreign Relations, denied prior knowledge of any wrongdoing, and the full Senate confirmed his nomination on February 24, 1977.

As Deputy Secretary of State, Christopher became one of the chief spokesmen for the human rights policy of the Carter Adminis-

tration. Speaking before the American Bar Association on August 9, 1977, he declared that "our underlying principles and values must be reflected in American foreign policy if that policy is to have the support of our people and if it is to be effective." In a speech before the Bar Association on February 13, 1978 he identified the principal areas of concern as "the right to be free from governmental violations of the integrity of the person; the right to fulfill one's vital needs such as food, shelter, health care and education; and civil and political rights." Moreover, it was Christopher who often applied the combination of quiet diplomacy, symbolic gestures, public statements, and economic sanctions needed to implement the human rights policy. He was particularly involved in denouncing in 1978 the Communists' slaughter of hundreds of thousands of people in Cambodia and in making known in 1979 the Administration's withdrawal of support from the repressive regime of Anastasio Somoza in Nicaragua.

President Carter came to rely on Christopher as an able troubleshooter in times of crisis. When, in late 1977 and early 1978, popular opposition mounted to the proposed Panama Canal treaties, Christopher effectively defended the pacts before Congress and citizens' groups. In March 1978, following Premier Bülent Ecevit's threat to withdraw Turkey from NATO, Christopher soothed feelings in Ankara by promising an end to the American arms embargo imposed on the country for its actions on Cyprus. Again, Christopher was the man assigned to work out a new framework for United States relations with Taiwan after America's decision to recognize the People's Republic of China made impossible the maintenance of formal ties with the Nationalist government after December 31, 1978. In a demonstration of hostility toward the United States angry students attacked the Deputy Secretary's car after his arrival in Taipei on December 27, 1978, but eventually he managed to establish acceptable agreements that guaranteed American support for Taiwan's security and continued trade and other relations through the mechanism of an unofficial American Institute on the island. Moreover, Christopher became a key Administration spokesman on the Soviet incursion into Afghanistan in December 1979. He spoke before the Senate Committee on Foreign Relations on January 28, 1980 on behalf of Carter's proposed boycott of the Moscow summer Olympics to protest Soviet aggression; visited Islamabad in February to coordinate American and Pakistani opposition to the invasion; and in March publicly denounced Soviet executions of Afghan political prisoners.

While handling an array of sensitive diplomatic assignments, Christopher shared in the ongoing work of bolstering America's relations with its Western European and Middle Eastern allies. He participated on several occasions in the ministerial meetings of the

North Atlantic Council and of the Organization for Economic Cooperation and Development. At such gatherings he emphasized the theme of economic interdependence and stressed the necessity for mutual support in facing the energy crisis, halting inflation, and aiding developing nations. For the most part, Christopher carried out his work unobtrusively. In May 1980, however, he stirred considerable controversy by asking the Public Broadcasting System to consider the offense it would offer a valued American ally by televising the docudrama *Death of a Princess,* which concerned the execution of a royal Saudi Arabian young women for adultery. An editorial in the New York *Times* accused Christopher of dallying with censorship, but he denied the charge, arguing that he had only asked the network to "give appropriate consideration to the sensitive religious and cultural issues involved and assure that viewers are given a full and balanced presentation."

Christopher was not a central figure in the initial stages of resolving the Iranian crisis, which began in November 1979 when militants in Teheran seized the United States Embassy. A change in his role resulted from the abortive military attempt of April 25, 1980 to free the hostages. He had approved the mission in the mistaken understanding that Secretary Vance had consented to it before leaving Washington for a vacation. Then, after Vance resigned to protest the use of force, Christopher was expected to succeed his friend in office, regardless of some officials who saw the Deputy Secretary as a legal technician lacking the breadth of vision and forceful personality needed for the Cabinet post. Political considerations, however, persuaded President Carter that the appointment of Senator Edmund S. Muskie would help his sagging fortunes in Congress. Bitterly disappointed, Christopher said that he would suggest that Muskie pick another deputy, but at the President's request and on Vance's advice, he agreed to stay. He later said of his choice, "I decided it was the right thing to do."

Although Deputy Secretary Christopher drafted a secret analysis of the Iranian situation, he did not become directly involved in negotiations over the hostages until September. Early that month Sadeqh Tabatabai, a relative of Iran's revolutionary religious leader, the Ayatollah Ruhollah Khomeini, and a former press attaché in Bonn under the government of Shah Mohammed Reza Pahlavi, told West German officials that he wanted to meet an American representative to discuss the release of the hostages. As a sign of his good faith, Tabatabai delivered advance notice of four prerequisites for negotiations that Khomeini would announce on September 12: return of the deposed Shah's wealth, cancellation of all United States claims against Iran, a guarantee of no American intervention in Iran, and the freeing of all Iranian investments. Upon receiving news of that development, Carter on

September 10 put Christopher in charge of a small team that would pursue the talks to their conclusion.

In the ensuing months Christopher had ample opportunity to practise his philosophy that negotiating "is a matter of identifying common interests rather than differences." He met with Tabatabai in Bonn on September 16 and 18 and sensed that an agreement was possible. The outbreak of the Iran-Iraq war on September 22, however, cut off Christopher's contact with Tabatabai and forced the American to seek new liaisons. In October he went to the United Nations and asked Secretary General Kurt Waldheim and the Algerian ambassador to arrange a meeting between him and the Iranian Prime Minister Mohammed Ali Rajai. The Prime Minister refused to confer with any Americans, but Christopher's initiative had the important effect of drawing Algeria, a revolutionary Islamic nation, into the negotiations to free the hostages.

On November 2, 1980 the Iranian Parliament, or Majlis, signaled its renewed willingness to negotiate by publicly endorsing Khomeini's four conditions and asking the Algerians to act as intermediaries. Eight days later Christopher flew to Algiers with the American response, promising to try to prevent the transfer overseas of the former Shah's wealth, to release $5.5 billion of frozen Iranian assets, and to discuss the return of an additional $4 billion against which claims existed. When Rajai complained that the American offer was "neither explicit nor clear," Christopher returned to Algiers where, on December 2 and 3, he elucidated Carter's position and advised the Iranians, through the Algerians, to act before recently elected Ronald Reagan entered the White House. On December 21 the Iranians instead demanded payment of $24 billion for the hostages' release. Christopher described the message as "rather stunning," but the Carter Administration chose to ignore it rather than end the talks.

The negotiations regained momentum after Christmas with an exchange of proposals that resulted in whittling down Iranian money demands. To be on hand to clarify American offers, on January 7, 1981 Christopher flew once more to Algiers, where he remained until the negotiations were completed. The two sides reached an important breakthrough on January 15, when the Iranians agreed to accept about $7.9 billion, of which a substantial portion would be used to repay outstanding loans. For the next few days Christopher and his aides, the Algerians, the Iranians, and a team of bankers and lawyers hammered out the final terms, which actually brought the Iranians a net of less than $3 billion.

Early in the morning of January 19, 1981 Christopher met with Algeria's Foreign Minister Mohamed Seddik Benyahia to sign two public agreements and a secret one. At the same time in Tehran, Iran's negotiator, Behzad Nabavi, signed another copy of the documents.

The ceremony completed, Christopher commented, "At last I can smile again." But word soon arrived that the director of Iran's Central Bank, Ali Reza Nobari, objected to provisions in the appendix to the agreements. In particular, he protested a stipulation that would have barred the Iranians from claiming bank deposits or interest that might be discovered at a future date. The mixup prevented the release of the hostages before President Carter left office, but round-the-clock negotiations resolved the matter by Tuesday morning, January 20, Reagan's inauguration day. That afternoon the hostages left Iran for Algiers, where Christopher greeted them on their arrival. The meeting was an emotional one, even for the usually reserved Christopher. "There were very few people with dry eyes," he later reported, "and I was not among them."

When the Republicans moved into top Washington posts in late January 1981, Christopher went home to resume practice with O'Melveny & Myers, declining attractive job offers elsewhere. According to *Time* (January 26, 1981), "One key reason: an agreement with the firm's partners that he will have time for considerable *pro bono publico* work (cases undertaken gratis for the good of the community)." In April 1981 Christopher and the law firm were engaged by three American gas-pipeline companies—the Consolidated Natural Gas Company, the Columbia Gas System Inc., and Southern Natural Resources Inc.—to negotiate with Algeria's petroleum enterprise, Sonatrach, for the renewal of contracts for shipment of liquified natural gas from Algeria.

Described as a "lawyer's lawyer," Christopher, according to an associate quoted in the New York *Daily News* (January 25, 1981), is "so discreet that even when he has explosive information, information that is so big you just have to tell somebody, just to get it out of your system, he won't even tell his wife." He blends somewhat contradictory characteristics of toughness, courtesy, diffidence, and self-confidence into an amalgam of strength and self-control. A lean, dapper appearance and a penchant for perfectly tailored suits enhance his image of professionalism. Christopher rarely reveals his emotions and is said to advise his colleagues, "Never get mad except on purpose." All told, the former Deputy Secretary is a natural diplomat who, in the words of one friend, "was an elder statesman when he was in diapers."

Small wonder, then, that colleagues in the legal profession regard Christopher as "the quintessential lawyer, with exquisite judgment and an uncanny sense of organization." Agreeing with that assessment, Jimmy Carter remarked, on awarding Christopher the Medal of Freedom, "He is indeed outstanding." According to *Time* (January 26, 1981), Carter privately expressed his regret on the same occasion that he did not appoint Christopher United States Attorney General in 1979, when Griffin B. Bell resigned.

Warren M. Christopher has been married since December 21, 1956 to Marie Josephine (Wyllis) Christopher. He has a daughter, Lynn, from his first marriage, which ended in divorce, and two sons and a daughter, Scott, Thomas, and Kristen, from his second. While in Washington, Christopher lived at a hectic pace. He rose at 5:30 A.M. to jog near his house, reached his office by 7:00 A.M., and usually did not return home before 7:30 P.M. In California he may have the leisure to enjoy his favorite pastimes, tennis and jazz.

References: N Y *Daily News* Ja 25 '81 por; N Y *Times* p3 D 22 '78 por, p14 Ap 29 '80 por; *Time* 117:19 Ja 26 '81, 117:37+ F 2 '81; *Congressional Directory, 1979;* Who's Who in America. 1980-81

Chun Doo Hwan

Jan. 18, 1931- President of the Republic of Korea. Address: b. Blue House, Seoul, Republic of Korea; h. 302-3 Yonhidong, Sodaemunku, Seoul, Republic of Korea

By his gradual but dramatic amassing of power during the months following the assassination of South Korea's President Park Chung Hee in October 1979, Chun Doo Hwan, an American-trained paratroop and infantry commander and a veteran of the Vietnam War, gained the Presidency in late August 1980 with the endorsement of a rubber-stamp electoral college. His use of martial law to suppress all political opposition, among similar stratagems, echoed the authoritarian measures of

Park, of whom he was a protégé. At his inauguration on September 1, 1980 President Chun proclaimed his "determination to build a democratic welfare state," with the qualification that it would be "a democracy suited to [the Korean] political climate." Although alarmed by intimations of dictatorial rule in South Korea, its military ally in the Far East, the United States, which has some 39,000 servicemen stationed there, declined to do more than exhort moderation, in view of the fact that Chun, who is dedicated to national security and inner stability, does serve as a powerful counterpoise to the elderly, erratic Premier Kim Il Sung in bordering North Korea.

An official biography released after the inauguration of Chun Doo Hwan recorded his birthdate as January 18, 1931. (Various other dates had appeared in the American press, and *International Who's Who, 1981-82* gives the birthday as January 23.) The sixth of nine children of a humble farming family, he was born to Chun Sang-Woo and his wife in the village of Naechonri in Kyongsang, southeastern Korea, a mountainous province known for its intense regionalism. His father was an herbal medicine man who also gave his time to Confucian studies and to tutoring his son in his preschool years. When Chun was old enough for formal education, the family moved to the city of Taegu, where he attended Heedoh Primary School until 1945 and afterward the five-year Technical High School.

At the time of Chun's graduation, in October 1951, the Korean War was in full swing. Patriotic zeal, as well as financial necessity, led him to enroll in the free Korean Military Academy in Chinhae rather than in a private university. His application had the support of Park Chung Hee, who was both a native of Kyongsang and a graduate of the academy. Although a conscientious student, Chun is said not to have excelled academically, but he distinguished himself as captain of the soccer team and cadet company commander. His was the celebrated "eleventh class" of the academy, the first to finish a full four-year course modeled on the West Point curriculum of the United States. Noted for their solidarity, its members came to view themselves as Korea's first genuine professionals and disdained their predecessors, who had completed a one-or-two-year academy program founded on Japanese methods. Upon his graduation in September 1955, Chun was commissioned a second lieutenant.

Chun Doo Hwan's twenty-five-year military service began with his assignment as a platoon commander in a frontline rifle company. In the rank of first lieutenant, he entered the four-month military English course at the Republic of Korea (ROK) Army Adjutant School in January 1959 to prepare for the psychological warfare course with the United States Special Forces, which he completed in November 1959. His advanced training, including six months of instruction at the United States Army Infantry

School, from July to December 1960, qualified him for the assignment of acting planning director of the ROK Army special warfare bureau in the spring of 1961.

The forced resignation in 1960 of Syngman Rhee, who had been President of the Republic of Korea since its formation under United Nations auspices in 1948, precipitated widespread internal unrest. As head of the ruling military junta, in 1961 General Park Chung Hee initiated a series of economic and social reforms to restore stability. During part of that crucial period of change, from September 1961 to August 1962, Captain Chun Doo Hwan served as domestic affairs secretary to Chairman Park of the Supreme Council for National Reconstruction, as the junta was called. He afterward held the key posts of chief of the personnel administration department of the Central Intelligence Agency, from January to August 1963, and deputy chief of staff for personnel at army headquarters, from September 1963 to August 1964.

Immediately following a year-long stint as executive officer of the 1st Airborne Special Forces Group, in August 1967 Lieutenant Colonel Chun became commander of the 30th battalion of the Capital Garrison Command. In that post he repulsed a platoon of North Korean suicide commandos in a raid on Ch'ong Wa Dae, the Presidential residence in Seoul, which had been occupied by Park Chung Hee since his election as President in 1963. Chun's next tour of duty, beginning in December 1969, was as senior aide to the Chief of Staff of the ROK Army.

A staunch supporter of United States intervention in the Vietnam conflict, President Park committed some 47,000 Korean troops to what he regarded as an anti-Communist effort. By the time that Chun went to fight in South Vietnam as regimental commander, in November 1970, he was a full colonel, the first in his academy graduating class of 1956 to attain that rank. For his service in the Vietnam War with the 9th ROK Infantry Division (the White Horse Division), he was decorated with the United States Bronze Star, as well as various Korean orders of military merit. Back in Korea, Chun returned as commander in November 1971 to the 1st Airborne Special Forces Group, which together with the Capital Garrison Command had the responsibility of guarding the capital under the direction of President Park. In the mid-1970's, according to a report of Henry Scott Stokes in the New York *Times* (December 18, 1979), Chun was chosen by the President's top bodyguard, Cha Chi Chul, to serve as senior staff officer under him in the Presidential security force. The post brought Chun again into close proximity to President Park, who reportedly treated him as a godson.

In January 1978 Chun Doo Hwan was transferred to the command of the South Korean Army's 1st Infantry Division, stationed in the strategic area between Seoul and the demilitarized zone separating North and South Korea. Here he earned his first general's star and a commendation from President Park when his men discovered an invasion tunnel dug by Communist North Koreans. Investing him with a second star, Park promoted General Chun in March 1979 to the post of commanding general of the Defense Security Command, in charge of the gathering and analysis of all military intelligence. "Thus," as his official biography stated, "he was in a position to fully utilize his knowledge of special warfare tactics in anticipating and countering North Korean provocations and infiltrations."

It was an attack, however, from a far different camp that propelled Chun Doo Hwan, who had been little known outside military circles, into the national limelight. On October 26, 1979 Kim Jae Kyu, the disaffected chief of the Korean Central Intelligence Agency, shot to death President Park, Cha Chi Chul, and four other bodyguards. As head of a military intelligence unit with the authority to question dissidents and to control the media, Chun had the means of exerting immense power in South Korea. He moved in quickly and decisively to take charge of the investigation into the assassinations, and seemingly on his own initiative, on December 12, 1979, he personally and forcibly, arrested his superior, South Korea's martial law commander and Army Chief of Staff, four-star General Chung Seung Hwa, on charges of complicity in the murders. To bolster his own troops in the ensuing gun battle, Chun boldly called in units of the 9th Division from United Nations forces headed by the American commander, General John A. Wickham Jr., whose permission he did not ask. The assault was necessary, Chun contended, to "restore discipline" in the armed forces, and in a conversation some months later with Robert Shaplen of the *New Yorker* (November 17, 1980), he referred to the action of December 12 as "a minor incident in the course of the investigation" into the assassinations. General Chun's takeover of military power, nevertheless, is seen by some Western observers as the outcome of political rivalry that had been developing at least since mid-November 1979 between older generals like Chung and those in Chun's group from the eleventh class, who opposed the modest steps toward liberalization that the government was beginning to take. After the removal of Chung, Chun forced the retirement of some forty high-ranking officers of the Old Guard and managed to place allies in several important Cabinet posts, including the defense and justice ministries.

Chun Doo Hwan further tightened his grip on South Korea's government when, on April 14, 1980, President Choi Kyu Hah, the ineffectual successor to Park, made him acting director of the Korean Central Intelligence Agency, a post vacant since December. The appointment of a military man, already the head of a military intelligence unit, to a civilian political intelligence operation was unprecedented. Within a month Chun reportedly replaced thirty-three of the organization's forty

top officials. In early May swelling student unrest over the authoritarian regime spawned massive street demonstrations that ceased only with the imposition of martial law throughout the land on May 18. As the power behind the government, Chun was believed responsible for the issuance of the martial law decree, which halted any progress toward democratic reform that President Choi had been attempting. Those arrested included former Premier Kim Jong Pil and Kim Dae Jung, both Presidential aspirants. The next day some 3,000 students in Kwangju began rioting and were joined by 50,000 citizens. Paratroopers who crushed the nine-day rebellion left an estimated 300 dead and many hundreds wounded.

With the Cabinet shunted aside and the National Assembly suspended, at the end of May the Seoul government announced the formation of a twenty-five member Special Committee for National Security Measures that included fifteen military officers. General Chun, who had resigned his KCIA post without any actual lessening of his powers, was named chairman of the thirty-member standing committee of the new military junta-like ruling council. On June 13 a "purification" drive was instituted as an official policy. According to press reports, at least 40,000 people were affected: more than 8,000 federal and state officials and employees were systematically purged for corruption or incompetence; media owners were ordered to fire 424 journalists, and 617 publishing firms and 172 periodicals were closed down; and more than 30,000 "hooligans" and other undesirables were jailed or sent to reeducation camps. Educational reforms included the abolition of college entrance examinations and all private tutoring; students were to be selected for the universities on a quota system.

An unofficial interview appearing in the Los Angeles *Times* on August 8, 1980 may have encouraged Chun Doo Hwan to accelerate his assumption of the Presidency, some political observers have speculated, perhaps six months earlier than he had originally intended. Correspondent Sam Jameson quoted an unnamed American official (known to be General Wickham) as affirming that the United States would support Chun—"provided that he comes to power legitimately and demonstrates, over time, a broad base of support from the Korean people and does not jeopardize the security situation [against Communist North Korea] here." (The United States State Department later maintained that Wickham had been quoted out of context.) In the chain of formalities that followed, "puppet" President Choi resigned on August 16, two days after the start of the trial of Kim Dae Jung for sedition charges that are said to be mostly fabricated, duly turning over the government to Acting Premier Park Choon Hoon. General Chun Doo Hwan, who had received his fourth star on August 6, resigned from the army on August 22 in compliance with the constitutional provision barring active-duty officers from the highest civilian office. The sole candidate for the office, Chun was "elected" on August 27 Korea's third President in two weeks (and the fourth in a year) by an electoral college of over 2,500 members known as the National Conference for Unification. As the "transitional" President, Chun promised that Presidential and legislative elections would be held within the first half of 1981.

In his inaugural address on September 1, 1980 the new chief executive stated that for Korea to establish a democracy "the political climate must first be improved" and that its system of democracy must, above all, "conform with [Korea's] long-lasting national traditions and cultural heritage." Chun's new constitution, which a New York Times editorial described as "South Korea's promissory note," was approved by a national referendum held under martial law on October 22, 1980. Less despotic than the 1972 Yushin constitution of the late President Park, which had allowed him unlimited reelection, it stipulated a single seven-year Presidential term and the direct election by the voters of two-thirds of a 330-member national assembly. In addition, the document guaranteed the right of habeas corpus for the first time although the Western view of human rights is not acknowledged in Korea. Despite a civilian facade, the army still runs South Korea's "new era" and orders the so-called "reforms" in politics, the economy, and the mass media. According to reports of foreign diplomats, about fifty civilians were drafted to sit in the current eighty-one-member Legislative Council only for the sake of appearance. On November 14, 1980 a government reorganization ended newscasts by all privately owned radio and television stations and merged the news agencies into a single agency.

With the apparent purpose of strengthening ties between the United States and South Korea, in late January 1981 Chun lifted martial law throughout his country, commuted to life imprisonment the death sentence imposed on his political opponent Kim Dae Jung, and scheduled a Presidential election for February 25, 1981. Relations between Washington and Seoul had been strained during the Carter Administration because of President Jimmy Carter's human rights policy. President Ronald Reagan, however, who took office on January 20, 1981, invited Chun to a top-level meeting in Washington on February 2, when he assured the Korean leader of military and economic support.

South Koreans voted on February 11, 1981 for a 5,278-member Presidential electoral college, which on February 25 cast 90 percent of its ballots in favor of reelecting President Chun, candidate of the Democratic Justice party, for a seven-year term. To celebrate his inauguration on March 4, Chun granted amnesty to a total of 5,221 people. In his inaugural address he repeated a proposal that he had made earlier for an exchange of visits with

North Korea's Kim Il Sung. Later in March in a nationwide parliamentary election Chun's Democratic Justice party won 151 of 276 seats.

Some South Koreans, as well as some outsiders, see the specter of the dictatorial Park, his mentor, in Chun and fear that he may become even more repressive. An American observer, Robert Shaplen, cautioned in the New Yorker: "Chun's fundamentalist manner and style, his almost Khomeini-like ardor and determination to rid the society of evils—he is said to be taking evangelical instruction from a Baptist preacher named Kim Chang ('Billy') Hwan—are somewhat scary over and above his passion for law and order." Although there is now apparent stability in South Korea, before his reelection Chun's popular support seemed uncertain. The centuries-old Confucian tradition of respect for authority was a sizable factor in his favor. And big business, ever wary of labor unrest, was believed to be allied with him.

Until mid-July 1980, steadfastly disclaiming interest in politics, Chun Doo Hwan had posed as a simple warrior who longed to go back to the barracks. In a biographical article in the Los Angeles Times (May 26, 1980) Sam Jameson perceived that Chun's aloofness from the general public was premeditated and that the image of him that emerged—"with blurred focus"—was "one of a frank, outspoken (in private), tough, incorruptible, uncompromising military professional who views himself as a patriot and who is unforgiving to those whom he regards as less than patriots." Concerning Chun's executive ability, General Wickham in the August interview disavowed by the United States State Department conceded that Chun was "terribly unsophisticated about the difficulties of running Korea in the 1980's." The sharp-eyed, five-foot six-inch former general has "a gleaming face, a shining pate, and a straight military back." One of his press interviewers, Linda Bridges of the National Review (October 17, 1980), found that her preconception of him as a "forbidding personage" needed to be amended: "He can be engaging when he wants to, and he spoke animatedly, indulging in a fair amount of give-and-take."

When Chun Doo Hwan was a cadet at the Korean Military Academy, he met Lee Soon Ja, daughter of Brigadier General Lee Kyu Dong, the academy's chief of staff. Chun and Lee Soon Ja were married in 1958 and have three sons, Jae Kook, Jae Yong, and Jae Mahn, and a daughter, Hyo Seon, whom they reared in their modest home in western Seoul. For recreation Chun enjoys tennis matches and teaches his youngest son the techniques of soccer.

References: Los Angeles Times p1+ My 26 '80 por, p1+ Ag 16 '80 por; N Y Times p5 D 18 '79 por, p3 My 20 '80, A p2 S 22 '80 por; N Y Times Mag p110+ O 19 '80 por; New Yorker 56:174+ N 17 '80; Newsweek 96:43+ Ag 25 '80 por; Time 115:32 My 26 '80, 116:36 S 8 '80 por; International Who's Who, 1981-82

Church, Sam(uel Morgan), Jr.

Sept. 20, 1936- Labor union official. Address: b. United Mine Workers Bldg., 900 15th St., NW, Washington, D.C. 20005

As president of the United Mine Workers of America, Sam Church Jr. has been trying to restore to that 160,000-member union the prestige and power it had enjoyed in earlier decades under John L. Lewis. He has also been promoting the use of coal as an answer to the world energy crisis. Between 1970 and 1981, the proportion of coal mined in the United States by members of the U.M.W.A., as compared with nonunion coal, declined from 70 to 44 percent, as a result of the opening of new fields in Western states, where highly desirable, low-sulphur coal could easily be taken from shallow strip mines. Operators there could afford to pay more than union scale, and Western mine workers resisted joining an organization with a long history of bitter strife.

Since becoming U.M.W.A. president late in 1979, Church has been trying to improve the union's image with a leadership style that represents a compromise between the democratic but not always effective ways of his predecessor, Arnold Miller, and the autocratic tactics of W. A. ("Tony") Boyle, who had been roundly defeated by Miller in 1972 in his bid for reelection to the union presidency. In the spring of 1981, after painstaking negotiations and a seventy-two-day strike, the U.M.W.A. and the Bituminous Coal Operators of America, representing Eastern and Midwestern coal producers, arrived at a mutually acceptable forty-month contract.

Samuel Morgan Church Jr. was born on September 20, 1936 in the coal company town of Matewan, West Virginia. Coal and the United Mine Workers have long played a major role in the life of his native region where, he remembers, "All the homes had three pictures on the wall—Jesus, Franklin D. Roosevelt, and John L. Lewis." Both of Church's grandfathers had been miners, as was his father. An on-the-job accident, however, crushed the elder Sam Church's foot and compelled him to turn to barbering to support his wife and eight children. When Sam Jr. was eight years old, the family moved to Appalachia, Virginia, where he learned his first lesson in labor relations. At thirteen, while working at a local bowling alley, he and fellow pinsetters used the threat of walking out one busy night to force the proprietor to raise their pay from five cents to seven cents a game. The next day they were all fired.

After graduating from Appalachia High School, Church enrolled at Berea College in Kentucky, but he dropped out in 1955, within less than two years of study. Since the era of cheap oil and the advent of the diesel locomotive had brought hard times to the coalfields, Church went to Baltimore, where he took a job as a maintenance mechanic in a Domino Sugar Company warehouse. He soon became active in the United Packing House Workers union, serving as a safety committeeman, a shop steward, and a reporter for his local's newspaper. In 1965 Church, by now married and the father of three children, finally found employment in the mines. He worked briefly for the Clinchfield Coal Company and then obtained a job as an electrician-mechanic with the Westmoreland Coal Company in southwestern Virginia.

In the coalfields, Church once again became engaged in union activities. He served as a mine committeeman and a safety committeeman, and then rose to financial secretary, and later president, of his U.M.W.A. local. In 1969 he supported the successful reelection campaign of union president Tony Boyle against Joseph A. "Jock" Yablonski. He also supported Boyle against Arnold Miller and the reform-minded Miners for Democracy in 1972. But when Boyle lost and was subsequently convicted of involvement in the murder of Yablonski, Church switched his allegiance to the new president.

Church made his first bid for statewide union office in 1973, just after he had been fired by the Westmoreland Coal Company for allegedly striking a foreman. He won election as a salaried field representative for U.M.W.A. District 28 and was later reinstated by the company. Church was victorious in over 70 percent of the arbitration cases he handled as field representative and won reelection in 1975 with Miller's support. Later that year the U.M.W.A. president asked Church to work at the union's national headquarters in Washington, D.C. Church served as a "troubleshooter" for Miller, with the title of international representative, until March 1976, when he became deputy director of the union's contract department. In October 1976 Miller, who had dismissed most of the young, college-educated staff of the union, named Church his executive assistant. About two months later the U.M.W.A. president, whose relations with many of his early allies had become badly strained, nominated Church to replace vice-president Mike Trbovich on his ticket for the union's June 1977 presidential election. Miller and Church won a narrow victory in the hard-fought campaign and were sworn in for five-year terms on December 22, 1977.

The U.M.W.A. faced difficult times as Miller's second term began. For the first three months of 1978 the union struggled through a 111-day strike, and twice during the stoppage the miners rejected pacts initially accepted by the leadership. Church blamed "Communists" for some of the dissension, but informed observers suggested that it resulted largely from the bargaining team's willingness to accept medical insurance provisions and other fringe benefits that many members found inadequate. As Miller, already chronically ill with black lung disease and arthritis, spent much of 1978 recuperating from two strokes and a heart attack, Church's responsibilities steadily increased. Although Miller was still making "the major decisions" and had no intention of resigning, Church and secretary-treasurer Bill Esselstyn ran the union on a day-to-day basis. If Miller chose not to seek reelection to the presidency in 1982, Church told Ann Bardach of the Village Voice (September 25, 1978), he would "certainly consider the opportunity" himself.

Although he claimed to have Miller's complete confidence, Church's relationship with the U.M.W.A. president gradually deteriorated. Late in October 1979 Miller accused Church of trying to oust him and vowed to remove him as vice-presidential candidate from his ticket for the 1982 election. Then, while on a hunting trip early in November, Miller suffered a heart attack and entered the hospital for the third time in two months. Under that stress, Miller acceded to calls for his resignation and received the title of president emeritus and the guarantee of his annual salary for the remaining years of his scheduled term.

On November 16, 1979 the U.M.W.A. executive board unanimously elevated Sam Church to the presidency. Accepting the post, Church praised Miller for having "given unselfishly of himself to this union," expressed the hope that all factions would "wipe the slate clean," and promised to confer with district leaders "to get their thoughts and feelings on how we can hold this union together." Most miners seemed willing to give Church a chance; they knew that the U.M.W.A. was almost bankrupt and that an epidemic of wildcat strikes under Miller had nearly ruined its credibility and capacity to recruit members. "The goddam union's about gone," said one miner, quoted in Forbes (December 24, 1979). "Going after Sam now is like shooting yourself in the foot."

Other union members, quoted in Business Week (December 3, 1979), asserted that Church was "more politically astute" than Miller and knew "how to make peace with his enemies," while spokesmen for industry commended him as a man who "can be talked to."

The forty-eighth constitutional convention of the U.M.W.A., which met in Denver for ten days beginning December 10, 1979, offered a quick and important test of Church's leadership. The new president's keynote address called for strength through unity. "We must once again be the mighty power we once were," Church told the delegates. "With your help, I will see to it that America and its leaders know we are strong, and above all united for the common good of the union. . . . Our heritage is that of strongwilled and determined workers. We shall endure, and our image will not suffer, not at the hands of politicians, coal operators, or any other opposition." Captivated by his address, the delegates gave Church a standing ovation that, in the words of one aide, put the president on "Cloud 9."

By all accounts, the convention was a triumph for the new leadership. In what many called "a referendum on Sam Church," the delegates, on December 11, 1979, agreed to enable the president to waive the constitutional mandate for an election and allowed him to appoint his vice-president. That maneuver spared the union political controversy and a campaign that would have cost $750,000. The next day, the delegates, on a voice-vote followed by a 1,181-to-912 roll-call tally, agreed to increase the union's monthly dues from $12 to $27, in accordance with Church's demands. Having staved off bankruptcy, the convention, on December 13, created a special strike fund to facilitate selective work actions against coal companies that might defect from the practice of industry-wide bargaining and thereby endanger the union's multi-employer pension plans. The fund, supported by a $25-a-week assessment on working miners, was aimed directly at the Consolidation Coal Company. A subsidiary of Conoco Oil, and the employer of ten percent of the U.M.W.A. membership, "Consol" had withdrawn from the Bituminous Coal Operators of America (BCOA) in May 1979.

After the Denver convention, Church hired a management survey team from the West Virginia University College of Business to recommend innovations in the operation of the U.M.W.A.'s antiquated business office. He stepped up the effort to organize nonunion mines both in the Eastern and the Western states, and he reduced the frequency of wildcat strikes, in part by sharpening his denunciations of unsafe conditions that had led to deaths in the mines. Moreover, the new president gained favorable publicity for the U.M.W.A. when the National Bank of Washington, in which the union owned a 76 percent interest, reduced its car loan rate by 1 percent for purchasers of American vehicles.

Church's actions won widespread approval. Leaders in the coal industry had been impressed by him since the 1978 negotiations, during which he seemed to show a better understanding of the issues than Miller. They praised the new U.M.W.A. president for "showing the kind of leadership we admire, whether or not we like the specifics." Assistant Secretary of Labor William P. Hobgood reported in early 1980 that Church was "going about things in a highly systematic fashion" and that his initial moves had been "sound and sensible." But there was opposition as well, especially among miners who wanted to preserve and extend the democratic reforms instituted under Miller. They accused Church, who was trying to live down a reputation as a brawler, of being dictatorial and prone to violence. "He's an old-time thug," one critic remarked, comparing him with Tony Boyle. "Things couldn't have come more full circle." The union suffered a setback when, in October 1980, the United States Comptroller of the Currency reacted to questionable loan practices at the National Bank of Washington by installing Deputy Secretary of Commerce Luther B. Hodges as the institution's chairman and by reducing U.M.W.A. representation on its board of directors to one-third. The government did not, however, directly accuse Church of any wrongdoing, and he denied charges that his union was interfering politically with the operations of the bank.

Sam Church's major goal for 1981 was to reach the first strike-free settlement with the BCOA in seventeen years. "I don't consider them the enemy," he has said of the mine operators. "Both the union and the industry have a job to do, and that is to promote coal." Church often sported a big "Why Not Coal?" button in his lapel, and in 1979 he and his wife recorded two country-style songs that hymned the virtues of coal. Referring to the threat of disaster that might result from the production of nuclear power, the lyrics to "Black Gold" advised: "America, take warning, there's something you should know,/There would be no Three Mile Island, if we were burning coal." With some foresight, Church set aside five cents from each $3 sale of the record for the U.M.W.A. strike relief fund.

Negotiations began on January 22, 1981 between bargaining teams led by Church and by Bobby R. Brown, president of Consolidation Coal, who had brought his company back into a leading position in the BCOA. The operators took a tough stance in the hope that they could make union mines more competitive with those that were nonunion and gain the upper hand before the expected coal boom of the 1980's. "Negotiations are meant to be a time of give and take," Church complained, as quoted in *Time* (March 30, 1981). "But the only thing I have seen from [the industry's] negotiators is take, take, take." After a week-long breakdown in the talks, Church emerged on March 23 with a tentative agreement. It

provided for a 36 percent wage increase over three years, introduced a pension for the widows of miners who died before 1974, abolished an unpopular arbitration review board, preserved the traditional ban on Sunday work, and maintained the principle of an industry-wide pension system. In view of the Union's long-standing practice of not working without a contract and its mandatory ten-day ratification process, the agreement came too late to avert the strike scheduled for 12:01 A. M. on March 27. Nevertheless, hopes ran high that the shutdown would be brief.

Church encountered considerable hostility on a five-day tour he made of Appalachian and Midwestern coalfields to explain the proposed pact to the miners. Critics objected in particular to clauses that allowed operators to sublease fields to nonunion contractors and permitted them to buy coal from nonunion operators for resale without paying a formerly required royalty to the union's pension fund, and many miners rejected Church's argument that court decisions forced the latter concession. "If the coal operators can pay less for non-union coal, they'll stop buying union," one West Virginia miner complained. "Before long, we'll be getting laid off and the union will be undermined." When the ballots were finally cast on March 31, 1981 miners in the Rocky Mountain and Great Plains states and those in Illinois, Indiana, and Tennessee voted to accept the contract. But opposition from Eastern miners was so strong that the overall vote was 69,937 to 32,299 against the new agreement. Consequently the strike continued for all but a few miners who worked for companies that were not among the 130 affiliated with the BCOA.

Stung by the rejection, Church admitted that he had "made a mistake" and was now aware that the rank and file was willing to endure a long strike in order to win a better contract. Negotiations resumed on April 14, 1981, but Brown accused the U.M.W.A. of a "serious leak of bargaining discipline" and broke off the talks three days later. Backed by a unanimous vote of confidence from the union's elected executive board, and supported by major segments of organized labor, Church publicly denounced Brown as "just a servant of the Continental Oil Company" but continued privately to urge him back to the table. The talks were resumed on May 7 and, after some tense moments, the two parties reached an accord on May 29. The U.M.W.A. regained the royalty for nonunion coal and obtained an agreement to the effect that the industry would not lease existing mine operations nor subcontract maintenance, construction, and coal hauling work when doing so would cause layoffs among union employees. The negotiators also agreed to extend the life of the contract to forty months from the usual thirty-six, bringing it beyond the summer vacation period of 1984. In return for relinquishing the bargaining advantage that the coincidence of the termination date of the contract and the start of the summer holidays would have given them, the miners gained a wage increase of thirty cents an hour for the extra four months of the contract.

On June 6, 1981 the miners voted by a two-to-one margin to accept the new pact. To encourage ratification the operators offered to the workers the option of receiving both their vacation pay and their regular wages if they would stay on the job through their scheduled 1981 breaks. In addition, miners who reported for their first regular shifts on June 8 gained $150 bonuses. Most of them returned at once, but sporadic picketing by mine construction workers kept about 43,000 U.M.W.A. members off the job until negotiations for their separate contract were completed in mid-June.

Some observers wondered whether the new contract was worth its cost to the union. The average miner lost about $6,000 in wages; the industry could still avoid paying the royalty for non-union coal by buying and selling through subsidiaries; and the guarantees of increased job protection seemed to be not especially effective. Furthermore, the U.M.W.A., which lost three representation elections during the strike, had suffered a serious setback in its prospects for organizing nonunion mines. Nevertheless, the overall gains that Church achieved for his union in the second contract were impressive, and it was with some pride that he called the agreement "probably the best that will be negotiated this year in any industry."

Portly Sam Church Jr. stands five feet nine inches tall and weighs 250 pounds. He favors vested suits, and his recently grown beard gives him an appearance somewhat resembling that of England's Henry VIII. The U.M.W.A. president chews Red Man tobacco and speaks with the drawl and the folk idiom of his native mountain country. He enjoys hunting, and he has spent many hours poring over Niccolò Machiavelli's The Prince, the classic sixteenth-century study on the use of power. Church's first wife, from whom he is divorced, lives with their three children in Baltimore. He and his second wife, Patti, a secretary with the U.M.W.A., were married on March 23, 1978 and spent their honeymoon in the West Virginia coalfields, where he was speaking in favor of ratification of a contract. The Churches live in suburban Springfield, Virginia with their son, who was born on May 29, 1981, the day on which the year's pact was concluded.

References: Bsns W p39+ D 3 '79 por; Industry Week p50+ Mr 9 '81 por; N Y Times A p18 N 19 '79 por, B p14 Mr 24 '81 por; Newsweek 95:67+ Ap 28 '80 por

---

Cimino, Michael (chi-mē′nō)

1940(?)- Motion picture writer-director. Address: b. c/o William Morris Agency, 151 El Camino Dr. S., Beverly Hills, Calif. 90212

The controversial three-hour Vietnam war epic The Deer Hunter, viewed in consensus as powerful but flawed and excoriated by its severest critics for "misinterpretation of history," swept the 1978 Academy Awards, garnering five Oscars, including the best director citation for Michael Cimino, one of the most exciting members of Hollywood's "new-boy network." "Bewildered" by the charges brought against The Deer Hunter, especially the charge of "racism," Cimino has described the film—which is about the American loss of innocence as symbolized in the harrowing of three Pennsylvania steelworkers in the Indochinese "heart of darkness"—as an ode to "what we once were and will be again." The way for Cimino's shockingly effective depiction of violence in The Deer Hunter was prepared in part by his experience on Magnum Force (1973), starring Clint Eastwood, which he co-wrote with John Milius, and his touching treatment of male camaraderie was presaged, in a lighter vein, in another Eastwood vehicle, Thunderbolt and Lightfoot (1974), which he wrote and directed. American critics panned his over-bud-

get, over-long Heaven's Gate (1980), an epic about immigrants settling the West, even in its pared-down version, which found some critical defenders in Europe.

According to his entry in Who's Who in America, 1980-81, Michael Cimino was born in

1943, but other sources suggest dates three or four years earlier. When Letitia Kent interviewed him for the New York Times (December 10, 1978), she had difficulty pinning down such personal statistics. "I have no personal life," Cimino told her, and she recounted that he "frequently parries a question with a question. For instance he is vague about how many siblings he has. But Mr. Cimino does reveal that he is the oldest son of a music publisher. And that while [he was] growing up in New York City [and Old Westbury, Long Island], his grandfather enchanted him with wonderful stories and his grandmother cast the final die for his current endeavors by taking him to the movies three times a week."

While attending the best private schools, Cimino was fascinated by tough characters from less advantaged backgrounds, as he recounted in an interview with Jean Vallely for Esquire (January 2, 1979): "I was always hanging around with kids my parents didn't approve of. Those guys were so alive. When I was fifteen I spent three weeks driving all over Brooklyn with a guy who was following his girlfriend. He was convinced she was cheating on him, and he had a gun, and if she was, he was going to kill her. There was such passion and intensity about their lives. When the rich kids got together, the most we ever did was cross against a red light."

Cimino matriculated at Yale University as a major in fine arts. "When I was at Yale," he told Vallely, "I used to walk by the drama school and think, 'That's where I belong,' but I didn't have the courage to make the change." While at Yale, he enlisted in the United States Army Reserve, in 1962. During his term of active duty, he was stationed for approximately six months at Fort Dix, New Jersey and had a month or so of medical training at Fort Sam Houston, Texas.

After receiving his master of fine arts degree at Yale in 1963, Cimino moved to New York City, where he studied acting and ballet and went to work for a small company that produced documentary and industrial films. "They taught me to use a Movieola," he recalled in the New York Times interview with Letitia Kent. "I operated the Movieola and swept the floors. I was hooked—I decided to become a filmmaker." In the late 1960's he was well known in New York as a director of television commercials.

In 1971 Cimino gave up his lucrative work in television commercials to seek his fortune in Hollywood. Renting a small house in Los Angeles, he approached filmmaking through screenwriting. His first credit was an assist to Deric Washburn on the script of the futuristic ecological sermon Silent Running (Universal, 1971), the first directorial effort of Douglas Trumbull, who had been responsible for the special effects in Stanley Kubrick's 2001. Silent Running, set in a time following the nuclear devastation of earth, starred Bruce Dern as a renegade, dedicated botanist-astro-

naut piloting through space a domed forest-garden representing all that remains of earth's plant heritage. Reviewers confessed to captivation by the film's visual pyrotechnics even when they were, in some cases, unhappy with its bathos and slow pace.

More substantial was Cimino's second writing job, as John Milius' collaborator on Magnum Force (Warner Brothers, 1973), directed by Ted Post, the second feature in Clint Eastwood's Harry Callahan series. The first had been Dirty Harry (Warner, 1971), based on an original screenplay by Harry Julian Fink and Rita M. Fink, with some additional writing by Dean Riesner, and directed by Don Siegel.

In Dirty Harry, the title character, a violence-prone San Francisco police inspector, takes private, savage revenge in bringing to justice a mad sniper released for lack of evidence. In Magnum Force the "pornography of violence," as one disapproving British critic called it, remained, but with a shift that was viewed as significant by many reviewers. This time, the villains were a band of avenger rogue patrolmen. As Paul D. Zimmerman observed in Newsweek (January 7, 1974), "It is a measure of how far the social barometer has swung that Dirty Harry—yes, the same Dirty Harry of 1972's law-and-order blockbuster—is the man who finally wipes out these fascistic vigilantes."

"The general shift in tone and philosophy produces a marked improvement," Gary Arnold wrote in his review of Magnum Force in the Washington Post (January 1, 1974). "The fact that Harry is in danger from other cops—and cops who assume that he is one of them—changes the emphasis significantly. Magnum Force benefits from having a plausible dramatic conflict, with ironic and suspenseful possibilities that weren't available the first time around. Some of the advantageous changes may [in part] reflect the contributions of a new screenwriter—Michael Cimino."

For Clint Eastwood's production company Cimino wrote and directed Thunderbolt and Lightfoot (United Artists, 1974), a rambling, picaresque melodrama about a pick-up gang of Montana bank robbers (Eastwood, Jeff Bridges, George Kennedy, and Geoffrey Lewis). With the egregious exception of Rex Reed, who dismissed Cimino as "a no-talent" (New York Daily News, May 31, 1974), the notices ran from fair through enthusiastic. Typical were the reviews of Jay Cocks in Time (June 10, 1974) and Betty Lee in the Toronto Globe and Mail (June 27, 1974). Cocks wrote: "He [Cimino] demonstrates a scrupulously controlled style that lends sinew even to such dreary scenes as the preparations for the robbery and the strategies for escape. In his feeling for the almost reflexive defenses of masculine camaraderie and for its excesses, with his eye and grudging affection for Western lowlife, Cimino has an obvious affinity for the work of Sam Peckinpah. What really animates

Thunderbolt and Lightfoot, though, and makes it distinctive are its shellbursts of lunatic comedy." Betty Lee observed: "It's difficult to know, of course, whether the spontaneity of *Thunderbolt and Lightfoot* resulted from Cimino's fresh directorial methods or whether the highly professional cast loosened up the director. Possibly both things happened."

Following the success of *Thunderbolt and Lightfoot,* Cimino received many directorial offers, all of which he turned down because he had decided he "would only get involved with projects [he] really wanted to do." He also worked on several screenplays, none of which reached production. "It was a terrible period of nothing," he recalled in an interview with Linda Christmas of the *Guardian* (February 17, 1979), "and I felt that everything was going downhill."

In her interview with Cimino, Letitia Kent asked him how "such an ambitious project" as *The Deer Hunter* (Universal, 1978) originated. He responded: "Not from intellectual notions. My characters are portraits of people whom I knew. During the years of controversy over the war, the people who fought the war, whose lives were immediately affected and damaged and changed by the war, they were disparaged and isolated by the press. But they were common people who had an uncommon amount of courage. . . . My film has nothing to do with whether the war should or should not have been. This film addresses itself to the question of the ordinary people of this country who journeyed from their homes to the heart of darkness and back. How do you survive that?"

In November 1976 Cimino took the idea of *The Deer Hunter* to executives of EMI, the British entertainment conglomerate. The idea, as it emerged, had to do with a trio of close steelworker friends, representative Middle American "ethnic" types, who go off to fight in Vietnam as a matter of patriotic course and what happens to their characters and their feelings for each other. EMI agreed to finance the production, and Cimino hired Deric Washburn to write the screenplay. For seven months before shooting began he worked out a script in collaboration with Washburn and traveled 150,000 miles while scouting locations in Thailand, the state of Washington, and the Ohio River Valley. With obsessive attention to detail, he and Robert De Niro—who had agreed to play the title character—visited towns throughout the valley, absorbing the atmosphere of the steel mills, the bars, and the VA hospitals and getting to know the people. All was grist for the script, which went through seven drafts.

The story as finally developed had the three Russian-American working-class pals, Michael (De Niro), Steven (John Savage), and Nick (Christopher Walken), captured by the Vietcong and forced to participate in grisly games of Russian roulette (spinning the cylinder of a revolver loaded with one bullet, pointing the muzzle at one's own head, and pulling the trigger). After their escape, Steven returns home

with both legs gone and Nick, deeply disturbed by his war experiences, goes A.W.O.L. in Saigon, where he ends up in the back room of a club playing Russian roulette for money. Michael goes home physically intact, but without Nick his life seems incomplete and he returns to Saigon to find his buddy just as the city is falling to the North Vietnamese. In the gambling den, he plays Russian roulette with Nick as the only way of getting through to him, and Nick, until now the "star" of the house, loses. Michael takes Nick's body back to Pennsylvania.

The shooting of *The Deer Hunter,* which began on June 27, 1977, was done entirely on location, in keeping with Cimino's belief that "encountering a real place changes the performance of actors in subtle ways, and changes the spiritual texture of the film." Sites in eight cities and towns in four states were used in addition to the steel-mill town of Clairton, Pennsylvania. Much of the home-town life of the characters—occupying the first hour of the movie—was shot in the Pittsburgh area, where, among other sequences, a prolonged wedding feast and dance was "acted" by real Russian Orthodox revelers whose joyous spirit comes through in the film; the wedding scene itself was shot in St. Theodosius (Russian Orthodox) Cathedral in Cleveland. The pre-Vietnam hunting sequences, filmed in the Cascade Range in Washington, featured Michael (De Niro) as a brooding hunter, most at home in the mountain wilds and so sure of his aim that he stalks deer with one bullet in his gun. The effect is heroic, establishing Michael in the tradition of Natty Bumppo (the frontier hero of James Fenimore Cooper's *The Deerslayer,* a white man raised by Indians and engaged in guerrilla warfare with Indians) and Ernest Hemingway's lonely, *macho* slayers of game.

From Washington State the crew flew to Bangkok, where, among other extravagances, Cimino rented Patpong Road, "the Street of 1,000 Pleasures," for two nights to recreate the seedy nightlife of wartime Saigon. Among the scenes shot there were some of the Russian roulette sequences, which act as a central metaphor for the absurdity of war. Many who were in Vietnam during the war, including correspondents Peter Arnett of the Associated Press and Tom Buckley of the New York *Times,* have raised their voices to protest that the important metaphor is an invention, or, in Arnett's words, "a bloody lie." Cimino has explained that he used the metaphor for "dramatic reasons," as a "shocking" device: "I wanted people to see what it was like to be there, to be in jeopardy every moment. How do you get people to pay attention, to sustain twenty minutes of war without doing a whole story about the war?"

From Bangkok, Cimino and his crew moved to the River Kwai, where realism in shooting almost resulted in tragedy on two occasions, including a helicopter rescue scene involving De Niro and Christopher Walken. Because of fears that the film might be confiscated by the Thai government (which was then facing a bloodless military coup), Cimino viewed no daily rushes in Thailand. "When I got back to L.A.," he recounted to Jean Vallely, "it took thirteen, fourteen hours a day for three months just to look at the footage we had shot." The final cost of production was approximately $15,000,000, far in excess of budget, and the film ran an extraordinary three hours and four minutes. Attempts by EMI and Universal (the distributor) to truncate it were stoutly and successfully fought by Cimino.

Nine reserved-seat showings in New York and Los Angeles in December 1978 made *The Deer Hunter* eligible for consideration for the 1978 Academy of Motion Picture Arts and Sciences awards. In addition to the best director Oscar, it won four Academy Awards, for best picture, best supporting actor, best sound, and best editing. It also was named best picture of the year by the New York Film Critics Circle, and Cimino was cited as best director by the Directors Guild of America.

On the night of the Academy Awards, April 25, 1979, police arrested thirteen members of the Vietnam Veterans Against the War who were protesting *The Deer Hunter*'s interpretation of history. At the same time, members of the *ad hoc* Hell No We Won't Go Away Committee handed out to the arriving members of the Academy press digests denouncing the film as "a racist attack on the Vietnamese people" and "a criminal violation of the truth." Linda Garrett, who formed the committee, explained: "We didn't want the film to be honored blindly. . . . Even my progressive friends seemed blinded by the power of the film, by the emotional impact. They felt it was a great film despite its racism, despite its misinterpretation of history."

Withdrawn from exhibition following the exclusive engagements in December 1978, *The Deer Hunter* had its national opening in February 1979. The controversy over artistic responsibility to historical truth aside, critics generally, like audiences, were powerfully moved by the film, and in the main they hailed it as a demanding but striking look at the effects of the Vietnam experience on the United States and as a true, if awkward, American epic rendered with original directorial vision. Even Peter Arnett, describing his initial reaction to the movie in the Los Angeles *Times,* was compelled to confess: "The sheer power of the film's photographic imagery, particularly the agonizing torture scenes, stunned me into mute acceptance of the divine right of the Hollywood dream-machine operators to drench us in fictional nightmares if they wish."

Arnett's colleague Tom Buckley was less relenting. In a long denunciation of *The Deer Hunter* in *Harper's* (April 1979), Buckley took issue with Cimino's argument that he should not be faulted for departures from realism when his aim was surrealistic: "He is wrong. His characters, their milieu, his version of the Vietnam war, all suffer from the same defect. They are neither real nor surreal—merely pretentious and false. It would be a remarkable conclusion if there were ironic intent, but there isn't. The political and moral issues of the Vietnam war, for ten years and more this country's overriding concern, are entirely ignored. By implication, at any rate, the truth is turned inside out. The North Vietnamese and the Vietcong became the murderers and torturers and the Americans their gallant victims. Cimino's ignorance of what the war was about, symbolically and actually, as reflected in *The Deer Hunter*, is incomplete and perverse to the point of being megalomaniacal. He had no technical adviser and no one who even served in Vietnam on his production staff. It is as though he believed that the power of his genius could radically alter the outlines of a real event in which millions of Americans took part and that is still fresh in the memory of the nation."

Among the positive assessments of *The Deer Hunter*, perhaps the most lucid was that of Philip French in the London *Observer* (March 4, 1979). After discussing the film's treatment of the "perennial American preoccupation" with male friendship and "the other side of that coin, loneliness," French wrote: *"The Deer Hunter* deals with an ethnic community largely untouched by the great social currents of the 1960's and is constructed quite deliberately to eliminate discussion of war aims and the larger issues involved in the Vietnam conflict. This is a grave weakness (some will think it an invalidating one), but it is what enables Cimino to attain something approaching the tragic grandeur of a popular epic."

Heaven's Gate (United Artists, 1980), written and directed by Cimino, was shot on the set of a Western town built on the shores of Two Medicine Lake in Glacier National Park. The film, starring Kris Kristofferson, Jeff Bridges, Christopher Walken, and Isabelle Huppert, is about a settlement of immigrant farmers in the West battling ranchers for survival on the range. In keeping with his insistence on authenticity, Cimino used eighty wagon teams in the picture—the largest number ever assembled for the screen—because, he pointed out, using fewer horses "would have been like trying to show Fifth Avenue with only ten taxicabs."

Dismissing *Heaven's Gate* as "something quite rare in movies these days, an unqualified disaster," Vincent Canby wrote in the New York *Times* (November 19, 1980): "The grandeur of vision [of *The Deer Hunter*] has turned pretentious. The feeling for character has vanished. Mr. Cimino's approach to his subject is so predictable that watching the film is like a forced, four-hour walking tour of one's own living room. . . . You thought the wedding feast that opened *The Deer Hunter* went on too long? Wait till you see *Heaven's Gate*." In the New York *Daily News* (November 20, 1980), Liz Smith reported that the audience at the screening she attended was "bewildered, bored, and stunned" by the "senseless plains epic," and she marveled that none of the executives who saw the rushes of *Heaven's Gate* "had the brass to tell Cimino to stop." "Where does Cimino go from here?" Miss Smith asked. "Want to bet that instead of down the drain, he will become the industry's new Robert Altman, allowed to range from one indulgence to another?"

In several months of editing, Cimino reduced the length of *Heaven's Gate* from three and three-quarter hours to a more bearable and more coherent two and a half hours. But most critics still withheld their approval. "The story now makes some sense," Richard Corliss wrote in *Time* (May 4, 1981). ". . . The film's coda no longer baffles; it only disappoints. But in his editing-room sauna Cimino has sweated away *Heaven's Gate*'s one strength: its brazen visual virtuosity."

The lesson of *Heaven's Gate* was clear to Corliss: "Cimino should . . . make a musical—a form that is all movement and no message, with the story told through the songs. As it happens, he is set to direct the film of *Evita*. So don't cry for Michael Cimino. Through the haze of his handsome failure beckons the ghosts of Eva Péron."

Michael Cimino is short (about five feet six), round-faced, and solidly built, with dark curly hair, sad brown eyes, and an intense, serious manner. His customary dress is casual, typified by jeans, boots, and open shirt, so that, according to Jean Vallely in *Esquire*, "he looks more like a garage mechanic than a director." In the Washington *Post* (September 2, 1979), Les Gapay described him on the set: "[He] usually operates very quietly, giving his orders through an assistant director. . . . Cimino demands formality. Crew members call him 'sir.' He is never seen making small talk, and even during breaks and lunch he continues working. Cimino rarely eats with the actors and crew at lunch tables and usually has his food brought to him on the set." Gapay added that the *auteur* usually speaks "in a near whisper" and that he notices any tiny detail that may be out of accord with the previous day's shooting. A bachelor, Cimino, who has been living in Los Angeles, has reportedly bought land for a new home in Montana.

References: *Esquire* p89+ Ja 2 '79 pors; *Guardian* p13 Feb 17 '79 por; *Harper's* 258:84+ Ap '79 por; *NY Times* II p15+ D 10 '78 por; *Washington Post* E p1+ S 2 '79 por

---

Clausen, A(lden) W(inship)

Feb. 17, 1923- Banker. Address: b. c/o International Bank for Reconstruction and Development, 1818 H St., NW, Washington, D.C. 20433

On July 1, 1981 A. W. Clausen inherited a host of problems when he relinquished his post as president and chief executive officer of the giant California-based BankAmerica Corporation and its wholly owned subsidiary, the Bank of America National Trust & Savings Association, to succeed Robert S. McNamara as president of the International Bank for Reconstruction and Development, or World Bank. The United States Congress had reduced the American commitment to the international lending agency; other countries, such as West Germany and Japan, with economic problems of their own, cut back their contributions; and the bank had been confronted with a dilemma facing lending institutions in an inflationary period: it must borrow money at higher interest rates and shorter terms of maturity while it is saddled with a backlog of long-term loans at low interest. At the same time, the need for such loans in developing Third-World countries is greater than ever.

A realist and a self-styled "stubborn" Norwegian-American, who earned a reputation as a hard-nosed businessman in his eleven years at the head of the Bank of America, Clausen was not intimidated by the challenges he faced.

"The World Bank has done a tremendous amount of good . . . and hopefully we'll continue the good and avoid inefficiencies and errors," he asserted at a news conference at World Bank headquarters in Washington, D.C., as quoted in the New York *Times* (June 30, 1981). "You can write that Clausen is going to make mistakes. . . . I may lose a battle here and there, but I am not going to lose the war."

Alden 'Winship ("Tom") Clausen, the second child of Morton and Elsie (Kroll) Clausen, was born on February 17, 1923 in the small Mississippi River town of Hamilton, Illinois, where his father published and edited the local weekly newspaper. Alden and his sister Jocelynn attended public schools in Hamilton and were brought up in a staunch Presbyterian and conservative Republican atmosphere. The family weathered the Depression years of the 1930's with relative ease.

Clausen acquired his nickname while playing the role of a boy named "Tom" in a high school play, and the name has remained with him ever since. After completing high school in 1940 and obtaining his B.A. degree from Carthage College in Illinois in 1944, he served in the United States Army Air Corps as a meteorological officer. Discharged in 1946, Clausen entered the law school of the University of Minnesota in Duluth, received his LL.B. degree in 1949, and was admitted to the Minnesota bar that same year.

His career plans were sidetracked, however, by romance. After graduation he went to Los Angeles in pursuit of Mary Margaret ("Peggy") Crassweller, the sister of a former classmate, who had moved to California. Clausen's plan was to marry her, then return to Minnesota, and practise law. "The only problem was that she said 'no'," Clausen recalled in an interview in the *AMBA Executive* (January 1978), the newsletter of the Association of Master of Business Administration Executives. "So I had to stick around Los Angeles to convince her that I wasn't all that bad. In the meantime I took a temporary job counting cash in Bank of America's cash vault and [went] to night school to study for the California Bar. Of course, I also found time to woo and pursue."

Up to that time, Clausen admits, he had never even heard of the Bank of America. It took him a year and a half, but he finally convinced Miss Crassweller that he was, indeed, marital timber. His part-time job as a cash counter, meanwhile, led to an offer to enter the bank's fledgling executive training program at a salary of $225 a month. Having passed the California bar examination in 1950, Clausen hoped to be invited into the bank's legal department as a step toward a career in corporation law. "I didn't get any offers so I had to make do with what I was doing," he has recalled. "Up to that point I had been progressing through the ranks of branch management. After four or five years, I realized that banking involved many different things and that maybe it was more interesting than practising law."

Clausen's rapid ascent through the corporate ranks of the Bank of America has been attributed by his colleagues to his high level of energy, capacity for hard work, attention to detail, prodigious memory, drive for perfection, and above all, dedication. On the day of his wedding, for example, he worked overtime two hours to track down a $10 error in bookkeeping. "Once I decided to stay with the bank," Clausen told the interviewer for the *AMBA Executive,* "I set out to be the very best at whatever I was doing. . . . But I had to start out at the bottom like a waterboy on a football team. . . . Later, I started to question and contribute. We've all got to learn how to walk before we can start to run. First thing I knew, I was running."

Assigned to the lending department of the Los Angeles branch, Clausen worked his way up to head its corporate finance department. His skill in dealing with such high-technology firms as Memorex and Teledyne that were beginning to flourish in Southern California impressed his superiors. "Tom was more than just decisive; he had an incredible appetite for making decisions," Joseph Pinola, a veteran Bank of America executive, observed, as quoted in *Forbes* (March 6, 1978). Clausen's career as a loan officer was, however, not without its setbacks. He can still remember to the penny the amount of his first major loan loss: $546,312.13. "I started to second guess myself and for a couple of weeks I lost a lot of sleep," he has recalled. "Then one of our senior officers said, 'You know you can only do your best, and if you've done your best, who could do better?' That made a lot of sense to me; it was what got me through a very tough period of self-doubt."

In 1961 Clausen became assistant vice-president for financial relationships in electronics. By 1963 he had acquired a reputation as one of the Bank of America's most promising young executives and was transferred from Southern California to the bank's world headquarters in San Francisco. In 1965 he became a senior vice-president, and the following year, after completing the advanced management program at the Harvard University Graduate School of Business Administration, he was moved into the office next to that of Rudolph A. Peterson, then the president of the Bank of America.

As executive vice-president, a position he occupied from June 1968 to May 1969, Clausen engineered one of the Bank of America's most important international transactions. That project involved its role as liaison for two international syndicates that raised $250,000,000 for the development of open-pit copper mines on the South Pacific island of Bougainville by a subsidiary of the Rio Tinto Zinc Corporation. Although the transaction appeared simple enough on the surface, it was complicated in its details because it demanded the marshaling of funds from a variety of international sources into a single unit. According to one associate involved in the negotiations, who was quoted in *Fortune* (January 1971), Clausen had a way "not just of seeing something that should be done, but working out the way it *can* be done."

When Rudolph A. Peterson announced his imminent retirement in 1969, Clausen, who had become vice-chairman of the board of directors in May of that year, was tapped for the bank's presidency, although he was only forty-six and relatively unknown. On January 1, 1970 he assumed the post of president and chief executive officer of the Bank of America and its parent company, the BankAmerica Corporation. Under the direction of Peterson, the Bank of America had undergone major changes. Until the late 1950's, it had been largely a regional institution that served farmers, homeowners, auto dealers, small businessmen, and some of the new high-technology firms, and its growth generally kept pace with that of California. Peterson foresaw, however, an inevitable slowdown in California's growth rate, and he expanded its international operations in competition with the major Eastern banks. At the time Clausen took over, the Bank of America still had its base of 948 home-state branches and was the largest private agricultural lender and home-mortgage holder in the country, but it also had branches in seventy-five countries around the world.

Taking the reins of the Bank of America after Peterson's period of international expansion, Clausen faced a challenge that was primarily internal. "People around here used to be very concerned about size and volume," Clausen told the reporter for Forbes. "Ask an officer, 'how's business?' and you'd immediately hear how many loans he'd made. I've tried to leave my stamp by making everyone aware of profit." To accomplish that goal, Clausen tightened controls. He developed a "building block" system of cost allocation that gauged return on assets based on operating function and geographical need. Each branch was looked upon as a profit center, and local managers based their pricing decisions on individual cost. The bottom line was the primary criterion.

During Clausen's eleven years as president of the Bank of America, its assets more than quadrupled, from about $25 billion to $111 billion. Under his direction, it became the most profitable commercial bank in the world and alternated with New York's Citicorp as the largest. Clausen also went a long way toward meeting his goal of decentralization of the bank's management, and he delegated as much responsibility as was feasible among the 83,000 employees that it numbered as of 1980 in its 1,100 California branches and its more than 500 offices in over 100 countries.

Imbued with a social conscience, Clausen has registered disagreement with economist Milton Friedman's dictum that corporations can fulfill their social responsibility only by making profits, and in the day-to-day operation of the Bank of America he showed himself to be attuned to social problems. Soon after he took office in 1970, student radicals burned down the Bank of America branch at Isla Vista near Santa Barbara. Clausen's strategy for handling the problem was typical of the man, although hardly what one might expect of a conservative banker. He instituted a series of talks with local protest groups and expanded Bank of America's social policy staff. Loans to minority group members were given priority, and a policy was introduced for hiring from among minorities at all levels of organization including the executive training programs. Clausen also won praise for a wide-ranging disclosure code that anticipated the Truth-in-Lending laws passed by Congress several years later. Internationally, Clausen had for some time championed the cause of the developing nations of the world, but his views on that subject did not always accord with official United States policy.

Such evidence of high principles caught the attention of Jimmy Carter. The two men met when, soon after the November 1976 election, the President-elect invited business leaders to his Georgia home. Carter's advisers had named Clausen as their first choice for the Cabinet post of Secretary of the Treasury. Among his supporters were DuPont chairman Irving Shapiro and Congressman (later Ambassador to the United Nations) Andrew Young, who had met Clausen in 1973 at an International Monetary Fund meeting in Nairobi, at which the Bank of America chief called for more aid to developing countries. But Clausen, who considered himself a conservative Republican, turned down the offer. "I know how to get things done in the corporate world," he was quoted in Forbes as saying, "but I'm not so sure about Washington."

When Robert S. McNamara told President Carter in June 1980 that he planned to retire as president of the International Bank for Reconstruction and Development when he turned sixty-five in mid-1981, the President remembered the California banker. Having obtained the approval of Republican candidate Ronald Reagan, he nominated Clausen for the post of president of the World Bank in late October 1980, shortly before the November Presidential election, to forestall a move among other member nations to name a non-American to the office. (It had been occupied by Americans ever since the bank's founding thirty-five years earlier.) Clausen agreed to take over as the 139-nation World Bank's sixth president after McNamara stepped down.

Before assuming his new office, Clausen immersed himself in a study of international business affairs and financial problems and undertook a ninety-day world tour to meet with political leaders, businessmen, and financiers and learn their views at first hand. Despite a sharp reduction in his personal income, from the $600,000 a year that he earned at the Bank of America to his $78,000 annual salary as president of the World Bank, Clausen considered his new post as a "step up in challenge." He saw his task primarily as that of a salesman who must convince the "have" nations that they must help the "have-not" nations as a matter of self-interest. Although he supports the Reagan Administration's efforts to reduce government spending, he feels that diminished United States funding for the World Bank would constitute a wrong approach to that goal. "I am disappointed that there is some reluctance in the Administration and in Congress to support the World Bank," he told Lewis M. Simons of *Smithsonian* magazine (June 1981). "It is absolutely essential that the United States continue to support the World Bank just as it has done in the past. Otherwise we are all in for some serious trouble."

Committed, like his predecessor, to the World Bank's battle against poverty, Clausen has had to contend with some Reagan Administration officials and members of Congress who objected to what they saw as the bank's "socialistic" or "redistributionist" goals. They have tried unsuccessfully to block fulfillment of the Carter Administration's commitment to the bank's "soft-loan" affiliate, the International Development Association, which grants long-term loans without interest to the world's poorest nations. At the same time, as a "private sector person," he hopes to extend the role of the International Finance Corporation, the World Bank's affiliate that encourages private investment in developing countries. "I don't believe in transferring wealth," he has said, "but I believe in helping those who want to help themselves."

In a press conference reported in the New York Times (June 30, 1981) the day before he took office as World Bank president, Clausen stressed the fact that one-third of all American exports are bought by developing countries. "If we can help the Third World countries expand their economies," he said, "ours will also expand, and there will be more jobs in the United States." He conceded that the challenge of running the World Bank just as he was about to put his "foot in the stirrup" looked much more formidable than it did in October 1980, when he accepted the appointment. "The horse is bucking a bit harder than I had anticipated, but my job is to get on it and try to ride it," he said, adding: "I want to develop people. I want to develop economies of nations. I want to be part of the solution, not part of the problem."

Among other organizational affiliations, Clausen has served as a director of the U.S.-U.S.S.R. Trade and Economic Council and of the National Council for United States-China Trade, co-chairman of the Japan-California Association, vice-chairman of the California Roundtable, and a trustee of the Brookings Institution. Distinctions that he has earned include several honorary degrees, the 1971 outstanding achievement award of the University of Minnesota, the 1972 alumni achievement award of the Harvard Business School Association, the 1977 international achievement award of the World Trade Club of San Francisco, and the 1978 California industrialist of the year award.

Married since February 11, 1950, A. W. Clausen and the former Mary Margaret Crassweller have two sons, Mark Winship and Eric David. In a profile in the Los Angeles *Times* (May 1, 1979), Clausen is variously described as "pleasant, bookish, perhaps even bland," or as "abrupt, tough, and feared by many in the middle management," and he is quoted as saying: "I am not paid to be liked." A private person, he shuns the limelight and avoids the social scene. "Being on page one of the newspaper isn't something I need to build my confidence," he has asserted. "I'm a listener, not a talker; that's the only way you learn anything."

Taking walks with his wife after dinner and adding to his huge wine cellar have been Clausen's chief diversions. On his rare vacations, he enjoys touring vineyards and wineries in different countries. According to one colleague, quoted in *U.S. News & World Report* (October 27, 1980), Clausen is a "workaholic" who "gives the job 100 percent plus." But, as Clausen said in 1978, "Work is not a sacrifice if you really enjoy doing it. My son who is a medical student doesn't understand why I work so hard. But to me it's not hard work. . . . I enjoy what I am doing, and I've not made any sacrifices."

References: Forbes 121:43+ Mr 6 '78 pors; Fortune p90+ Ja '71 pors; Los Angeles Times IV p1+ My 1 '79 por; N Y Times II p3 D 21 '69 por; Wall St J p14 D 17 '69 por; Who's Who in America, 1980-81

Clavell, James

Oct. 10, 1924- Novelist; motion picture scenarist; director; producer. Address: b. c/o Paul Reynolds Inc., 12 E. 41st St., New York City, N.Y. 10017

As he himself is wont to put it, the novelist and filmmaker James Clavell "purveys entertainment" on a grand scale. All of the sprawling novels in what he has come to call his "Asian Saga" are best sellers, and one of them, *Shōgun* (1975), a swashbuckling evocation of medieval Japan, was a publishing phenomenon, with sales exceeding 7,000,000. A television miniseries adapted from *Shōgun* in 1980 had an estimated audience of 130,000,000. Clavell's flair for storytelling was first evident on the motion picture screen, where his early scenarios included that for the science-fiction horror film *The Fly* (1958). Most of his later screen credits, including *To Sir With Love* (1967), were in his preferred triple capacity of producer-writer-director.

James duMaresq Clavell once described himself as a "half-Irish Englishman with Scots overtones, born in Australia, a citizen of the U.S.A., residing in England, California, and Canada or wherever." From the day of his birth—October 10, 1924—his life has had an international aura about it. His father, Richard Charles Clavell, was a captain in the British

James Clavell

Royal Navy whose duty carried the family to a succession of Commonwealth port cities, including Hong Kong. His mother was Eileen (Collis) Clavell. As a child, Clavell was regaled with swashbuckling sea tales by both his father and his grandfather, descendants in a military lineage reputedly dating back at least to Walterus de Claville, a Norman adventurer who landed at Hastings, England with William the Conquerer in 1066. He was also instilled with a pride in his origins, especially by his father. Never forgetting the paternal admonition, "Remember, you are blessed by being British," he still feels "a responsibility to [his] heritage."

In 1941 Clavell finished his secondary schooling in England and joined the British Royal Artillery. His service in World War II was cut short the following year, when he was captured in Java, and he spent the rest of the war in two Japanese prisoner-of-war camps, the second of which was the infamous Changi camp near Singapore, where only 10,000 of 150,000 POW's survived. "The Japanese tore the heart out of me when I was eighteen," he recounted in an interview with Bart Mills for the *Guardian* (October 4, 1975). "Changi was a school for survivors. It gave me a strength most people don't have. I have an awareness of life others lack. Changi was my university. . . . Those who were supposed to survive didn't. Changi is the rock [on] which I put my life. So long as I remember Changi, I know I'm living forty borrowed lifetimes. What else can they do to me?"

Shortly after his return to England as a captain in 1946, Clavell saw his seemingly inevitable military career terminated with a disability discharge, following a motorcycle acci-

dent that left him lame in one leg. Considering an alternative career in law or engineering, he attended Birmingham University in 1946-7. Destiny intervened, however, in the person of his wife, April Stride, then an aspiring British ballerina and actress. With Miss Stride, he paid his first visit to a movie set, where he "saw this nasty little man in a chair" and noticed that "whenever he spoke or got up a hush fell over the set and people rushed to do his bidding." As he recalled in an interview with Edwin McDowell for the New York *Times Book Review* (May 17, 1981), he asked his wife who the man was and she told him he was the director. "I didn't know what a director did, but I knew I wanted to be one."

Acting on the advice that the shortest route to directing was through production via distribution, Clavell found his way into film distribution and worked at it for several years before immigrating to the United States in 1953. After picking up some television production experience in New York City, he moved on to California, where he earned a living as a carpenter while making the rounds of the Hollywood studios. "Eventually somebody gave me a job as a screenwriter," he told Cynthia Gorney in an interview for the Washington *Post* (February 4, 1979). "I told everybody I was a brilliant writer. They'd say, 'What have you done?' and I'd mumble things that seemed reasonable. . . . They liked my accent, I suppose."

In his first Hollywood assignment, Clavell collaborated on the writing of a screenplay, "Far Alert," which was never produced. His first produced screenplay was *The Fly* (Twentieth Century-Fox, 1958), based on a story by George Langelaan about a scientist who exchanges heads with a fly in an atomic experiment gone awry. That generously budgeted, splendidly mounted film, an outstanding entry in the sci-fi shock genre, made $4,000,000 for its producers, drew praise for its imaginativeness even from critics who considered its premise bizarre and its continuity contrived, and spawned the inferior sequels *Return of the Fly* and *Curse of the Fly*.

Subsequently, Clavell wrote *Watusi* (MGM, 1959), an unexceptional remake of *King Solomon's Mines*, and he won a Screen Writers award for his collaboration on the screenplay for *The Great Escape* (United Artists, 1963), the box-office smash adapted from Paul Brickhill's account of Allied prisoners planning to escape from a German POW camp during World War II. He also co-wrote the screenplays for another World War II thriller, *633 Squadron* (United Artists, 1964) and for *The Satan Bug* (United Artists, 1965), based on Ian Stewart's science-fiction novel about the theft of a deadly virus from a top-secret military research station for use by a mad millionaire.

From the beginning, Clavell aimed at the triple role of writer, director, and producer because he knew that "if you're only a director or writer you have to explain things to the producer rather than say, 'Do it.'" He first turned the "hat trick" with *Five Gates to Hell* (Twentieth Century-Fox, 1959), a low-budget, high-box office melodrama about beleaguered medics in the French phase of the war in Indochina. In that instance, as Howard Thompson observed in the *New York Times* (July 2, 1959), Clavell made himself "a man to watch" by his moving treatment of material "that could easily have been outright trash."

As producer-director-writer, Clavell followed up *Five Gates to Hell* with *Walk Like a Dragon* (Paramount, 1960), an offbeat western, set on the frontier of the 1870's, about the violent rivalry between two men, one a white gunslinger and the other a Chinese immigrant, in love with a young Chinese woman. Later in the 1960's he displayed his triple talent with *Where's Jack?* (Paramount, 1968), a carefully realistic period piece about the legendary eighteenth-century British highwayman Jack Sheppard, and *To Sir With Love* (Columbia, 1967), based on E. R. Braithwaite's autobiographical novel about a teacher from British Guiana (Sidney Poitier) who wins the hearts of his problem students in a tough secondary school in London's East End.

Clavell and Poitier gambled on the financial success of *To Sir With Love,* contracting for percentages of the profits instead of large salaries. Their gamble paid off when the film, made for $625,000, returned $15,000,000—an unusual gross for "a positive story," as Clavell described the film. He carried off the exercise in Pollyanna sociology as perhaps only he could, with his writer's knowledge of the ways and means of handling sentiment candidly and his genius for casting colorful types and his confidence in directing them. As Archer Winsten suggested in his review of the film in the *New York Post* (June 15, 1967), "Clavell knew what he was doing every inch of the way to the pot of gold." Clavell again tripled with the lavish historical action picture *The Last Valley* (ABC Films, 1971), convincingly set in an idyllic Swiss village threatened during the Thirty Years War by an invading army that has lost touch with its purpose and its humanity. Despite pillage and carnage, the film impressed critics with its literacy and its haunting, dreamlike quality, and some saw in it a comment on America's military expedition in Vietnam.

Meanwhile, two chance factors had turned Clavell to novel writing. One was a Hollywood screenwriters' strike that left him with some free time in 1960. Another was a sudden, inexplicable impulse to talk about his Changi prison camp experience, previously "bottled up" inside him. At his wife's urging, he began writing a novel about the struggle for power and survival in Changi, using himself as the model for one of the two main characters, British Flight Lieutenant Peter Marshall, who has been educated to think that "trade" is reprehensible. The other, the title character, is Marshall's moral opposite, a pragmatic American corporal who is able and willing to wheel and deal. The unusual friendship that develops between the two men and the repercussions of that friendship constitute the core of the story.

Clavell finished his original version of *King Rat* in three months. At Little, Brown the manuscript fell into the hands of editor Herman Gollub, who blue-penciled vast sections of it (including all of the first page save the first sentence) as "pretentious, overwritten." Clavell spent many more months revising the book, in painstaking partnership with Gollub. "He really taught me how to write," Clavell acknowledged in an interview with Archer Winsten of the *New York Post* (May 17, 1971).

When Little, Brown finally published *King Rat* in a 406-page edition in 1962, reviewers took note of its power, sharp writing edge, tension of plot, fascinating narrative detail, and provocative analysis of right and wrong under stress. Some felt, however, that Clavell missed having created a true classic of the prison-camp genre by downplaying his own subjective experience and sensitivity in favor of a more marketable approach. Clavell sold the screen rights to Columbia Pictures in a contract that paid him $25,000 a year for five years. James Woolf produced and Bryan Forbes adapted and directed the motion picture version of *King Rat* (Columbia, 1965).

As Clavell explained to Edwin McDowell of the *New York Times* (May 17, 1981), the writing of *King Rat* was a catharsis that started him thinking again about Japan and its culture: "I started reading about Japan's history and characteristics, and then the way the Japanese treated me and my brothers became clearer to me." He particularly remembered one Japanese officer's taking offense when Clavell rejected his kind offer to lend him his hara-kiri kit. "They thought we were dishonored, because it's totally wrong in their culture to be captured, while we believe that by surviving we live to fight another day. I came to admire greatly certain characteristics of the Japanese."

In 1963 Clavell lived with his family in Hong Kong, soaking up atmosphere and history for his second novel, *Tai-Pan,* set in the British crown colony in 1841, the year the Chinese ceded the island to the British. *Tai-Pan* is the fictional story of Dirk Struan, the first of the tai-pans (merchant overlords) of Noble House, the oldest and most important trading house in Hong Kong. Undaunted by obtuse and apathetic politicians back in England and by multiple enemies in Hong Kong, in China, and on the high seas, Struan builds Noble House on barren Hong Kong with the zeal of a man with a prophetic vision—the vision of Hong Kong as a future base for British power in the Far East.

Clavell took *Tai-Pan* to Atheneum Publishers, because his editor, Herman Gollub, had moved there, and Atheneum published the book in 1966. Some restive critics wondered if readers would have the patience of Dirk Struan and his archenemy, Tyler Brock, who are obliged to wait from page one almost to page 590 for the settling of their scores, but the reviewer for *Time* (June 17, 1966) reflected the consensus in calling *Tai-Pan* "a belly-gutting, god-rotting typhoon of a book." The *Time* writer explained: "Its narrative pace is numbing, its style deafening, its language penny dreadful. . . . It isn't art and it isn't truth. But its very energy and scope command the eye." In the decade following its publication, *Tai-Pan* sold some 2,000,000 copies. Clavell sold the movie rights to Metro-Goldwyn-Mayer, but a film version of *Tai-Pan* is yet to be made.

The idea for *Shōgun* (Atheneum, 1975) came from a sentence Clavell spotted in his nine-year-old daughter's history text: "In 1600 an Englishman named Will Adams went to Japan and became a samurai." That miniscule suggestion triggered a year's research in the British Museum, visits to Japan, and three years in re-creating on paper a Japanese feudal culture encompassing all strata of society as well as such extraneous elements as British colonials, Portuguese traders, Jesuit missionaries, and competing Japanese warlords. Plainly, *Shōgun's* blond, blue-eyed hero, John Blackthorne, derived from Adams, the first English adventurer to navigate the Straits of Magellan and the tutor of the supreme warlord Tokugawa Ieyasu (called Toranaga in *Shōgun*), who established a Shōgunate power lasting for centuries. The reader witnesses in Blackthorne the gradual transformation of a lowly Christian "barbarian" captive into a true samurai, by Japanese standards a man of strength, honor, and courage. As in *Tai-Pan,* the story is told through numerous fast-moving plots, violent action, romance (between Blackthorne and Lady Mariko, his appointed tutor), and assorted hair-raising disasters.

The critical response to the 802-page *Shōgun* ranged from a description of it as "slick" and "ambitious" in the *New Yorker* (July 28, 1975) to a virtual rhapsody by Webster Schott in the *New York Times* (June 22, 1975). "Clavell has a gift," Schott wrote. "It may be something that cannot be taught or earned. He breathes narrative. . . . Yet [*Shōgun* is] not only something that you read—you live it. The imagination is possessed by Blackthorne, Toranaga, and medieval Japan . . . It's irresistible, maybe unforgettable. . . . Clavell's hero is not a person. It's a place and time: medieval Japan on the threshold of becoming a sea power."

In September 1980, capitalizing on *Shōgun's* huge popularity, NBC presented its five-part, twelve-hour television adaptation to a miniseries audience second only to that which saw *Roots* in 1977. Shot in Japan at a cost of $22,000,000, the miniseries was made by Shōgun Productions, written and produced by Eric Bercovici, and narrated by Orson Welles. As executive producer, Clavell received an estimated $1,000,000. In addition to the American actor Richard Chamberlain, who played Blackthorne, there were fifteen Europeans and twenty-eight Japanese in the cast. For the sake of authenticity, Japanese spoke in their native language, on Clavell's insistence. Tied in with the miniseries were two Dell paperbacks, a 2,500,000-copy edition of *Shōgun* and *The Making of James Clavell's Shōgun.* The Japan Society's *Learning from Shōgun* had been prepared before the miniseries. A two-and-a-half-hour theatrical version of *Shōgun,* filmed at the same time as the miniseries, was later released internationally.

"What isn't in this novel, about which only terms like colossal, gigantic, titanic, incredible, unbelievable, gargantuan, are properly descriptive?" Harrison Salisbury asked rhetorically about *Noble House* (Delacorte, 1981), the massive sequel to *Tai-Pan,* in a review in the *Chicago Tribune* (April 12, 1981). With its thirteen criss-crossing plots, teeming cast of characters, wealth of cultural details, and catalog of adventures and catastrophes, *Noble House* takes place in the short space of ten days in August 1963. Its hero, Ian Struan Dunross, the twelfth tai-pan in a direct line from Dirk Struan, battles to save the company, now threatened with financial collapse by the machinations of Quillan Gornt (descendant of Tyler Brock) and by two American big-business manipulators. Intertwined with that warp of international finance is a woof of world-wide political espionage. Even critics who faulted Clavell for flat characterization, an occasional slip to the comic-book level in dialogue, and arbitrary turns in plot, continued to admire his ability to limn the broad panorama of a foreign culture and to compel the reader to turn the page. (Clavell himself sees the latter knack—which he knows he has but does not understand—as the secret ingredient in his success.) "Plotting is where Clavell excels," Robert Smith wrote in the *Washington Post* (May 5, 1981.) "*Noble House* may not merit the term literature—Clavell will never win a Nobel Prize—but as storytelling done with dash and panache and as a rousing read it looms above most of the commercial pap published today."

Clavell, who became a naturalized American citizen in 1963, calls his novelette *The Children's Story* (Delacorte/Eleanor Friede, 1981) "a gift to my adopted land." The story originated almost twenty years ago, out of a conversation with his daughter Michaela, who was then six, in which it became clear that she did not understand the meaning of the Pledge of Allegiance she recited at school. Set in an America that has been conquered by an authoritarian enemy, it tells of a new teacher taking over a classroom and seducing the students from their allegiance to the flag, religion, and parents. When it first appeared, as a short story in *Ladies' Home Journal,* "The Children's Story" drew a barrage of angry letters from readers who misconstrued it to be propaganda against God and country. Delacorte Press announced the publication of the story in book form with a publicity campaign calculated to avert a repetition of that misunderstanding. In one stage of the campaign, James and April Clavell had dinner at the White

House with President and Mrs. Ronald Reagan and presented them with the first copies of the book.

James Clavell is a large man, over six feet tall, solidly built, with a thick chest and broad shoulders, ruddy complexion, soft eyes, and a healthy mane of graying hair. Interviewers have described him variously as exuding self-control and an almost "wheeler-dealer" self-assurance and as gentle-voiced and deferential, with "a warm, friendly face that lights up when he smiles, which is often." Jean Bernkopf, his editor at Delacorte on Noble House, has said he "was a dream to work with." Clavell regularly writes five pages a day, on a manual portable typewriter. He never finishes a day's work without "knowing what's going to happen tomorrow," leaving himself at least half a page for that purpose. In addition to his fiction and screenplays, he has written a play, Countdown

to Armageddon E-MC2, and he tries his hand at verse now and then.

James and April Clavell, who were married on February 20, 1951, are peripatetic householders, having over the years lived in homes in Hollywood, London, the English countryside, British Columbia, and the south of France, among other places. They have two daughters, Michaela and Holly, both married. The couple, who have long shared an interest in flying, recently moved on to helicopters, "the nearest thing to becoming a bird," as Clavell says.

References: Chicago Tribune VII p1+ Ap 12 '81; Guardian p8 O 4 '75 por; N Y Times C p2 Ag 28 '81; N Y Times Mag p46+ S 13 '81 por; Washington Post L p1+ F 4 '79 pors; Contemporary Authors 1st rev vols 25-28 (1977); Who's Who in America, 1980-81

Conway, Tim

Dec. 13, 1933- Comedian. Address: b. c/o CBS Inc., 51 W. 52nd St., New York City, N.Y. 10019

Carol Burnett is among the many who think that there is no one funnier than Tim Conway, a comedian who looks like a pained, confused, or naughty cherub, and who has an instinct for well-timed mugging and slow-motion verbal and visual gags. Conway's television career has been a seeming contradiction: on the one hand, he has been a repeated loser in the ratings wars, the star of so many short-lived series that his personalized auto license plate

reads "13 WKS," and, on the other, his inspired dead pan and low-keyed slapstick have kept him in demand on the networks since the early 1960's. As a "second banana," he first delighted TV audiences in the role of the bumbling Ensign Parker in the situation comedy McHale's Navy, from 1962 to 1966, and in the 1970's he won two Emmy awards for his inspired contributions to sketch comedy on the Carol Burnett Show.

On the Burnett show Conway created a gallery of characters that included a doddering codger, an aggrieved ethnic businessman, a blasé buffoon, and various oafs and schleppers. He has carried his most familiar characterization, the guileless bungler, to the motion picture screen in family-oriented feature films that have generally scored better at box offices in the boondocks than they have with metropolitan critics. Conway's eighth starring vehicle on television, the Tim Conway Show (his second series with that title), ran sporadically on the CBS network in 1980 and 1981.

An only child, Tim Conway was born Thomas Daniel Conway in Willoughby, Ohio on December 15, 1933. Growing up in Chagrin Falls, Ohio, outside Cleveland, he rode as a practice jockey for his father—a horse trainer who later became a tinsmith—and he was good at athletics, especially tumbling. He gave little early indication of his future career, as he told Tom Donnelly of the Washington Post (July 6, 1975): "As a kid I didn't do a great gallery of impressions. And in the privacy of my room I never thought, 'Ah hah! Here's a joke I'll tell when I get to the living room.'"

As a student at Chagrin Falls High School, Conway aspired to become a physical education teacher. Setting aside that ambition when he "saw that a career in radio or TV was even easier," he studied speech and dramatics at Bowling Green (Ohio) State University. After serving in the United States Army for two years and then joining a friend in trying out a nightclub act—not very successfully—Conway went to work at station KWY-TV in Cleveland.

At KWY-TV, Conway quickly moved up from the minor clerical job of answering mail to assignments as a writer, director, and occasional performer. His most important responsibility was *Ernie's Place,* a two-hour daily late-night program hosted by Ernie Anderson. "We had a movie and guests," Conway recounted in his Washington *Post* interview with Tom Donnelly, "but the guests never seemed to show up, so I began filling the holes. I mean I impersonated a whole slew of guests. . . . One day Rose Marie [the comedienne] passed through town, saw me cutting up on the TV screen, and said, 'You've got to be on the *Steve Allen Show!'* And pretty soon I was." It was reportedly at Steve Allen's suggestion that Conway changed his first name ("I just dotted the 'o' ") in order to avoid confusion with Tom Conway, the actor.

Conway made three appearances on the *Steve Allen Show,* on the ABC network, before it left the air in December 1961. *McHale's Navy* began its four-year run on ABC the following October, with Ernest Borgnine as Lieutenant Commander Quinton McHale, a blustery confidence man who, with the connivance of his undisciplined PT boat crew, turns a Pacific island into a gamblers' and drinkers' paradise during World War II. Conway played Ensign Charles Parker, an addlepated, feckless clod assigned to McHale's unit to keep Navy headquarters apprised of the rampant wheeling and dealing, and Joe Flynn played Captain Wallace B. Binghamton, the long-suffering superior officer, the nemesis of both the carousing McHale and the klutzy Parker. Borgnine, Conway, and Flynn carried their TV roles to the big screen in *McHale's Navy* (Universal, 1964), and Conway and Flynn also made the film *McHale's Navy Joins the Air Force* (Universal, 1965).

By the time *McHale's Navy* ended its run, the portrayal of inept innocence had become a Conway trademark, making the comedian a natural for the title role in *Rango.* The role was that of a Texas Ranger, the son of the chief Ranger, who is assigned to the quietest post in the state and manages, by dint of his ineptitude, to inspire outlawry and disorder where none had ever existed. Assisting him in his inadvertent promotion of crime is Pink Cloud (Guy Marks), an Indian corrupted by white ways, who runs the post's supply room. Frustrated by the whole situation is the post commander, Captain Horton (Norman Alden). Inserted into the ABC lineup in the middle of the 1966-67 season, *Rango* survived to the end of that season despite bad reviews but was canceled soon after the 1967-68 season began, after a total run of thirteen weeks. George Gent of the New York *Times* (January 17, 1967) spoke for many when he called *Rango* "a half-hour series grossly misrepresented as a spoof of TV westerns, starring Tim Conway [in a role] suspiciously like his previous role as the ensign on *McHale's Navy"* and added that "the shift to the wide open spaces has not expanded the humor of Mr. Conway's brand of double-take comedy."

Conway was the guest host of the first and only telecast of the ABC fiasco *Turn-On,* which was ballyhooed by its producers as a new, more daring *Laugh-In,* "a visual, comedic, sensory assault involving . . . animation, video tape, stop-action film, electronic distortion, computer graphics, even people." Following the airing of the comedy-variety half hour on February 5, 1969, the Bristol-Myers company withdrew its sponsorship and many ABC affiliates announced that they would carry no further telecasts of the program because of public protest against the show's blatant double-entendres, its depersonalization of human beings, and its general tastelessness. ABC immediately canceled the show.

The first *Tim Conway Show,* a situation comedy in which Conway and Joe Flynn played the hapless pilot and irascible owner, respectively, of a small-time charter airline, drew poor ratings on CBS during the last half of the 1969-70 season and was replaced with a comedy-variety hour, the *Tim Conway Hour,* the following September. Conway credited William S. Paley, the board chairman of CBS, with the change to a format which Conway found more comfortable, because it allowed him to give freer rein to his comedic instinct. "I'm told Paley saw me on the *Carol Burnett Show* and wondered why I was doing one guy in a situation comedy when I could be doing six or seven guys in a variety hour," he said.

Conway warmed up for his first stint as "top banana" of a variety series with a special that aired on CBS on March 19, 1970. The premiere of the *Tim Conway Comedy Hour,* on September 20, 1970, was presented as a Christmas show because, as Conway explained, he had "never had a show on the air that lasted till the holiday season" and "this time [he was] taking no chances." The sketches included a Kamikaze briefing session, a disastrous television cooking show, an amateur theatrical, and a drunken private detective bit. The most effective routine, perhaps, was the opening monologue, a gushing speech by Conway to which guests were seen reacting with undisguised boredom. In the premiere, Conway was joined by Dan Rowan and Lana Turner, among others, and guests on subsequent programs included MacLean Stevenson, Sally Struthers, Dick Martin, and Art Metrano. Drawing mixed reviews and low ratings, the *Tim Conway Comedy Hour* was canceled after its thirteenth telecast, on December 13, 1970.

Meanwhile, when Conway was not doing a series or special of his own he was appearing as a guest on other programs, including those hosted by John Gary, Red Skelton, Danny Kaye, Dean Martin, and Carol Burnett. An appearance on the *Carol Burnett Show* on the

CBS network in 1974 brought him a Golden Globe Award from the Hollywood Foreign Press Association. He became a regular on the show the following year, and he remained in the cast when the show moved to ABC for a brief final run in 1979. Thriving in the Burnett format of sophisticated comedy laced with slapstick, he won two Emmy awards as a supporting actor, the first in 1977 and the second in 1978. The characters he created on the show included Mr. Dudball, a businessman with a Scandinavian accent and askew toupee who strives in vain to introduce his gum-cracking secretary, Mrs. Wiggins (Carol Burnett), to the wonders of the intercom, and a dentist facing his first patient (Harvey Korman). The latter was one of his personal favorites, he has said: "I got novocain in my hand, my leg, my head, everywhere. I always end up laughing at that sketch because of Harvey—he was a total basket case. He was just standing there in tears, trying to continue with the sketch."

Two weeks after the new *Tim Conway Show* began its run on CBS, Marvin Kitman of *Newsday* (March 31, 1980) rated as "brilliant" Conway's spoof of a tacky company president doing his own commercial for a plastic food wrap, his claiming to have the dreaded "Schnauzer disease" (which makes the victim cough like a schnauzer), and his going into a Fred Astaire-style dance routine with his tap shoes glued to the floor. "What a master comic Tim Conway is," Kitman wrote. "What a face. What gestures. What a marvelously sleazy manner he can have when caught in some deception, like having Burt Reynolds as a live guest (when he is really on film and it's Conway doing the voice behind his hand)." Nevertheless, Kitman considered Conway "a prisoner" of Joe Hamilton, Carol Burnett's husband and producer. "Every time he [Hamilton] does a variety series for Tim or Harvey [Korman]," Kitman told his *Newsday* readers, "it's always 'The Carol Burnett Show Without Carol.'"

Nicholas Yanni of the New York *Post* (March 31, 1980) added no such qualification to his positive notice. Describing Conway as "sensationally funny," Yanni noted that the comedian had "surrounded himself with just the right mix of talented supporting players," and that "the show's pacing is perfect." When it was renewed for the 1980-81 season, the *Tim Conway Show* was cut from an hour to thirty minutes, and with that format it ran, with interruptions, on CBS from September 1980 through August 1981.

In addition to a made-for-television movie, *Roll, Freddy, Roll* (ABC, 1974), Conway has made a number of screen comedies aimed at family audiences, some of them costarring Don Knotts. He was featured in the following Walt Disney (Buena Vista) productions: *The World's Greatest Athlete* (1973), as one of the coaches of a Tarzan-like youth; *Gus* (1976), as one of the kidnappers of a mule

that kicks field goals for the New York Jets; and *The Apple Dumpling Gang* (1975) and *The Apple Dumpling Gang Rides Again* (1979), as a misfit western outlaw who tries to go straight and fails at that too.

Conway collaborated on the script for *The Billion Dollar Hobo* (International Picture Show, 1978), and he played the film's title role, Vernon Praiseworthy, who, as the sole heir of an eccentric transportation tycoon, must prove his resourcefulness by riding the rails (as the tycoon once had) before he can claim his fortune. Gary Arnold of the Washington *Post* (May 6, 1978), who regards Conway as "one of the most original and inventive funnymen of his generation," thought he was "wasted as a comic resource" in *The Billion Dollar Hobo*. Arnold recommended that Conway seek looser formats that would allow "his genius for physical comedy . . . and for spontaneous, deadpan verbal wit" to range beyond the "bland dumbbell personality that he's stuck with in *Hobo*," because "if he persists in impersonating nothing except a bewildered naif, he is doomed to cinematic dullness."

His second International Picture Show release was *They Went That-a-Way and That-a-Way* (1978), written by Conway and starring him and Chuck McCann as incompetent, Laurel-and-Hardy-style cops posing as prison inmates in order to learn the whereabouts of some stolen goods. "If the material was sharper, the casting might have been inspired," the reviewer for *Variety* (December 6, 1978) wrote, "since McCann and Conway play off each other extremely well."

Tim Conway is five feet eight inches tall, varies in weight from 160 to 185 pounds, depending upon his diet, has light brown hair (what there is of it), and grayish hazel eyes that look slightly crossed. To keep his smoking to a minumum, he does not buy cigarettes, but he has been known to cadge one on occasion. Among his recreations and hobbies are golf and furniture refinishing. On May 27, 1961 Conway married Mary Anne Dalton, a college friend who had been his godmother when he converted to Roman Catholicism three years earlier. After separating from his wife in 1980, Conway set up bachelor quarters in Encino, California, a mile away from her and their six children, Kelly Anne, Timothy, Patrick, Jaimie, Corey, and Sean. "I see the kids all the time," he told Robert MacKenzie in an interview for *TV Guide* (November 1, 1980). "They ride over on their bikes, stay overnight, or for a week at a time. We're very close."

Conway is not as slow-mannered as most of his characters, and he is as friendly as the gentlest of them. Miriam Flynn, a member of the troupe that does sketch comedy with him on the *Tim Conway Show,* has testified, "People love Tim. He just has that lovable quality, like that endearing little naughty boy in school." The comedian is philosophical about success, saying that he doesn't mind being second banana when required, and even on his own show he tries to design situations in which he will be "just one of the bunch" because it's "relaxing."

References: N Y Sunday News S p21+ Ja 8 '67 pors, III p9 Jl 6 '75 por; N Y Times II p15 Je 30 '63; TV Guide 15:15+ Je 17 '67 por, 28:29+ N 1 '80 por; Washington Post mag p2 S 27 '70 por, Washington Post H p1+ Jl 6 '75; Who's Who in America, 1980-81

Cossiga, Francesco (kō-sē′gə frän-chās′-kō)

July 26, 1928- Former Prime Minister of Italy; member of Parliament. Address: b. Camera dei Deputati, Rome, Italy; h. via G. Asproni 11, I-07 100 Sassari, Italy

In August 1979 Francesco Cossiga formed the thirty-eighth Italian government to come to power since the end of World War II. His accession to the office of Prime Minister resolved a six-month crisis during which several of the country's leading politicians had failed in their efforts to build a Cabinet capable of surviving a parliamentary vote of confidence. It also ended the political retirement Cossiga had imposed on himself when he resigned as Interior Minister after the assassination in 1978 of former Prime Minister Aldo Moro, his friend and fellow Christian Democrat. Cossiga's tenure as Prime Minister was marked by a drive against Italy's rampant political terrorism, a rapprochement with the Socialists, and a successful struggle to avoid impeachment on charges of political impropriety leveled

by Communists and neo-Fascists. But in September 1980 Cossiga was compelled to resign after being defeated by a single ballot in his effort to secure adoption of his program to shore up Italy's faltering economy. He was succeeded the following month by Arnaldo Forlani.

A member of a landowning family with a civil service tradition, Francesco Cossiga was born on July 26, 1928 in the city of Sassari, in the northern part of the island of Sardinia, to Giuseppe Cossiga, a bank director, and Maria (Zanfarino) Cossiga. His second cousin Enrico Berlinguer became one of his foremost political adversaries as secretary-general of Italy's Communist party. "Our grandfathers were brothers," Cossiga has recalled. "Mine was a Freemason and anticlerical and his was not. But I don't know which of us has been helped by this politically." Involved in Roman Catholic church activities since childhood, Cossiga joined the newly reconstituted Partito Democrazia Cristiana (DC) or Christian Democratic party, at the end of World War II, when he was sixteen.

Although little information has been made available about Cossiga's higher education or academic achievements, he is known to have acquired a doctor of laws degree and to have embarked on a career as a professor of constitutional law at the University of Sassari. Meanwhile he remained active in the Christian Democratic party, and from 1955 to 1958 he served as the organization's secretary for his home province. In 1958 he became a member of the Christian Democrats' national council and won election to Parliament as a deputy from Sassari. In the Chamber of Deputies, Cossiga became identified with the liberal wing of the Christian Democrats and began a gradual rise to prominence, eventually becoming chairman of the DC parliamentary group and a protégé of Antonio Segni, a fellow native of Sassari, who was President of the Republic from 1962 to 1964.

From 1966 to 1970 Cossiga occupied the post of undersecretary of defense. Then, in 1974, he achieved Cabinet status as Minister without Portfolio and was made responsible for organizing public administration, a job that entailed reforming the government's amazingly complex and inefficient bureaucracy. In February 1976, after former Minister of the Interior Luigi Gui asked to be excluded from a new government headed by Aldo Moro as a result of allegations that he had accepted bribes from the Lockheed Aircraft Corporation, Cossiga was appointed to succeed him in that post.

As Minister of the Interior, Cossiga inherited the Herculean task of curbing the epidemic of political terrorism that had ravaged Italy since the late 1960's. The pace of violence quickened during the spring of 1976 in anticipation of the elections set by Moro for mid-June. For example, Sandro Saccucci, a neo-Fascist member of Parliament, was arrested for the murder of a Communist youth, and leftist urban guerrillas assassinated Enrico Pedenovi, a prominent right-wing politician in Milan, and Francesco Coco, the public prosecutor of Genoa. But Cossiga remained firm in the face of such acts of terrorism. He refused to advise the postponement of the scheduled elections and vowed that the terrorists would not undermine the country's democratic institutions.

In the 1976 election the Christian Democrats retained their plurality in Parliament with only minimal losses, and the Socialists, the nation's third largest party, suffered only minor damage. The real winner, however, was the Communist party, which gained about fifty seats, mostly at the expense of the minor factions of Italy's left and right. As a result, the Socialists refused to take part in any government that did not include the Communists, but the Christian Democrats adamantly refused to share actual power with the latter, who comprised Italy's second largest political party. Compelled to build a ruling coalition without the Socialists' help, the Christian Democrats decided to allow Communists to take over the presidency of the Chamber of Deputies and the chairmanships of seven of the twenty-eight parliamentary committees. They also promised to consult the Communists more closely on matters of policy. In return, the Communists agreed to refrain from opposing the new minority Christian Democratic government led by Giulio Andreotti by abstaining from voting on key measures that they could not support.

Cossiga, whose decisive handling of rescue operations following the disastrous Friuli earthquake in May 1976 had earned him much praise, returned as Interior Minister in the Andreotti government, which was sworn in on July 30, 1976. The struggle against terrorism continued to consume much of his energies. Nevertheless, Cossiga shunned repressive tactics and instead pursued his goal of reforming and reorganizing Italy's police forces. He refused to be intimidated even after radicals bombed his office at the Interior Ministry on April 7, 1977. When demonstrators at the University of Rome shot a policeman to death two weeks later, Cossiga told journalists: "I don't want to be misunderstood. From now on let it be clear to those who attack the state with weapons that the state will respond in the same way." And, in an allusion to the comfortable bourgeois background of many of the ultraleftist urban guerrillas and student activists, and the predominantly humble origins of Italy's policemen, the Interior Minister commented: "I want to be even clearer. We will no longer allow the sons of the Roman middle class to kill the sons of southern peasants."

On January 16, 1978 the seventeen-month-old Andreotti government fell as the Communists, whose bid for inclusion in the Cabinet had been rejected, announced the withdrawal of their passive support. Italy suffered through almost eight weeks of crisis before Andreotti was able to fashion what became known as a "parliamentary programmatic majority." By March 11 the Communists, although still outside the Cabinet, had agreed to abstain from opposing a new Christian Democratic minority government that would include them in the decision-making process on critical issues. Then, on March 16—the day on which the Parliament was to ratify the new understanding for parliamentary cooperation among Christian Democrats, Communists, Socialists, Social Democrats, and Republicans—the Christian Democratic party president and former Prime Minister Aldo Moro, who deserved much of the credit for creating the new alliance, was kidnapped by Red Brigade terrorists. Fifty-four days later, on May 9, 1978, Moro was found murdered in central Rome.

Moro's kidnapping placed an awesome burden on Cossiga. The Interior Minister was officially put in charge of the search for his close friend, and Moro's family counted on him to save the Christian Democratic leader. On March 29 Cossiga received Moro's first letter from captivity, in which the former Prime Minister, apparently under duress, asked his old ally to exchange imprisoned terrorists for him. Cossiga, however, bore the responsibility for proclaiming the government's policy of rejecting all bargains with the kidnappers and organized police and army forces in a massive manhunt that has been described as the largest peacetime operation in the nation's history. On May 10, after Moro's body had been found, Cossiga resigned his post, taking on himself the "moral and political responsibility" for the government's actions. "From now on you must consider me politically dead," he told friends. Observers noted that Cossiga's decision was unprecedented, inasmuch as no Italian Cabinet minister had voluntarily resigned since the end of World War II, and the move earned him much respect among the populace.

Italy lurched through yet another political crisis in 1979. The second Andreotti government fell on January 31, after the Communists, who complained that they had not been adequately consulted on key issues, went into open opposition. For the first time since 1945 Italy faced the prospect of a Prime Minister from outside the ranks of the Christian Democrats. The country's aged Socialist President, Sandro Pertini, asked Ugo La Malfa in February to form a Cabinet, but the Republican leader proved unable to accomplish the task. Then, in March, Andreotti failed to win parliamentary approval for a government composed of Christian Democrats, Social Democrats, and Republicans, and the stage was set for new elections to be held on June 3. The results were inconclusive, however, except in showing an erosion of Communist strength. In the weeks that followed, Andreotti, the Socialist leader Bettino Craxi, and the Christian Democrat Filippo Maria Pandolfi all fell short in efforts to create governing coalitions. Finally, on August 2, the exasperated Pertini turned to Cossiga.

Departing from tradition, Cossiga organized a Cabinet that reflected his own point of view rather than the relative voting strength of the coalition's members. The new Cabinet included sixteen Christian Democrats, four Social Democrats, and two Liberals; the two remaining members were economic experts with close ties to the Socialist party, which agreed to refrain from opposing the new government, so long as it confined itself to "technical action" against inflation, unemployment, and terrorism. Sworn in on August 5, 1979, Cossiga promised that his administration, which many regarded as only a temporary "government of truce," would do all that was necessary "to face the needs of the country, to adhere to the constitution, and to fulfill the duty of those who chose to give it life." Although his coalition controlled only 291 votes—twenty-five short of a majority—in the 630-member Chamber of Deputies, Cossiga won two crucial votes of confidence, on August 11 and 12, with the Socialists abstaining and only the Communists, the Radicals, and the neo-Fascist Italian Social Movement registering their outright opposition.

Italians responded favorably to the new Prime Minister, who identified himself with the spirit of the late Aldo Moro, referring to him as "the politician, the friend, the Christian who is always in my mind." Cossiga won praise for his humility and his negotiating skills from the editors of the influential Milan newspaper *Corriere della Serra,* who called him "the right man at the right time." Even Cossiga's opponents spoke kindly of him, and one leftist deputy conceded that the Prime Minister was "a democrat" and "a civilized man."

In December 1979 Cossiga, who had promised that there would be "no truce with terrorism," put into immediate effect a series of stern security measures that the Chamber of Deputies, including Socialists and Communists, approved overwhelmingly in February 1980. The new laws condemned terrorists to life imprisonment, without the possibility of parole, for the murder of judges and policemen, and they doubled existing penalties for inflicting injuries. Officials were permitted to hold suspected terrorists incommunicado for as many as four days in some cases, and persons accused of political violence were classified as ineligible for bail. Furthermore, the legislation authorized police to search for terrorists not only in their suspected hideouts but also in nearby buildings, and it required banks to demand proof of identity from men and women depositing more than 20,000,000 lire.

Cossiga's economic policy emphasized, among other matters, Italy's need to solve its energy problems. The Prime Minister warned the people that they would have to make sacrifices, and he negotiated for the acquisition of Canadian nuclear reactors whose purchase had been opposed by environmentalists. At the same time the Prime Minister remained committed to the European Community. From January

through June 1980 it fell to Cossiga to take Italy's turn at the rotating presidency of the EC's Council of Ministers. In that post he helped to work out a plan to reduce Great Britain's contribution to the organization's budget, which British officials felt had placed an unwarranted burden on their country's flagging economy.

In his foreign policy, Cossiga took a distinctly pro-American stance. Against Communist opposition, he won parliamentary approval for the basing of Pershing II and Cruise missiles on Italian soil. In January 1980 he visited the United States, where he and President Jimmy Carter agreed in their White House talks to step up cooperation on economic, social, and foreign policy issues. Although he condemned Iran's recent seizure of hostages at the American Embassy in Teheran, Cossiga later expressed a desire to understand Iran's revolution and to protect Italy's interests in relation to that country. "But," he added, "there is the fullest solidarity with the people and government of the United States and the firmest determination to contribute, internationally, multilaterally, and bilaterally, towards the safety and liberation of the unjustly detained hostages."

Cossiga's accomplishments did not immunize his administration against the political troubles that had toppled its predecessors. Continuing terrorism, the highest inflation rate in Western Europe, a worsening balance of payments, and evidence of corruption caused national concern in late 1979 and early 1980. The Prime Minister suspended the chairman of Ente Nazionale Idrocarburi, the state energy group, after irregularities were uncovered in its dealings with Saudi Arabia. And in March 1980 revelations of improper loans made by Italcasse, the Central Institute of Savings Banks, resulted in the arrests of forty businessmen and bankers and forced the resignation of the Minister of Merchant Marine. A major blow to the Cossiga government was the Socialists' decision to withdraw their support from the coalition. After warning Cossiga of their plans in January 1980, they made the split official early in March, when the Christian Democratic party reaffirmed its policy of excluding Communists from the Cabinet and named Flaminio Piccoli, a member of the DC's right wing, as the party's general-secretary.

To forestall the prospect of defeat on a formal vote of confidence, Cossiga resigned as Prime Minister on March 19, 1980. Four days later, President Pertini once again asked him to form a government. Cossiga worked with an alacrity uncommon in Italian political crises; he abandoned his center-right alliance with the Social Democrats and Liberals for a center-left union with the Socialists and Republicans. In joining with the Christian Democrats, the Socialists seemed to violate the pledge of their own central committee not to be part of any government that excluded the Communists. But Socialist leader Bettino Craxi was apparently willing to tolerate such an inconsistency in return for a greater role in the formulation of key policies and a pledge from the Christian Democrats not to veto the appointment of a Socialist Prime Minister at some future date. From the Christian Democrats' viewpoint, Cossiga's shift in alliances was an example of the "change of horses" maneuver that had helped the party to maintain control of the government continuously since the end of World War II. The move also revived the Christian Democratic-Socialist combination that had guided Italy for more than a decade after 1962. With 340 of the 630 seats in the Chamber of Deputies, Cossiga's coalition now commanded an absolute majority, and for the first time in six years the government did not have to rely on abstentions to ensure the passage of key measures.

The new Cossiga Cabinet—Italy's thirty-ninth since World War II—took office on April 4, 1980 and survived votes of confidence in the Senate on April 17 and in the Chamber of Deputies three days later. But late in May, Roberto Sandalo, an imprisoned member of the Prima Linea (Front Line), a leftist guerrilla group, charged that, thanks to information provided by Cossiga, Carlo Donat-Cattin, a Christian Democratic party official, had been able to warn his leftist son of an impending police raid on his hideout. Communist leader Enrico Berlinguer, seeing an opportunity to stress his own party's anti-terrorist position, called for Cossiga's resignation, but the Prime Minister vehemently denied the charge and asked rhetorically: "Is it possible that anyone could accuse me of protecting terrorists?" On May 30 Cossiga testified about the affair before a parliamentary commission which, in a party-line vote of eleven to nine, decided on the next day that there was a "manifest lack of grounds" to pursue the inquiry. The governing coalition remained firmly behind the Prime Minister.

The affair seemed to have little effect on the regional elections held on June 8 and 9, 1980, in which the Christian Democrats and the Communists suffered slight losses while the Socialists made a gain of about 3 percent. When Cossiga acted as host to two major international summit conferences—of European Community leaders and of officials of the major industrial nations—that were held in succession in Venice that same month, his prestige remained intact. Nevertheless, radical groups on the left and right gathered enough signatures in Parliament to force an impeachment hearing before a joint session of the two houses. But on July 27, after four days of debate, the Parliament exonerated Cossiga and rejected a Communist motion calling for further investigations as well as a demand by the neo-Fascist Italian Social Movement for putting the Prime Minister on trial before Italy's Constitutional Court.

On September 27, 1980, ten minutes after his government had won a resounding vote of confidence, Cossiga was narrowly defeated, by a vote of 298 to 297, in his effort to secure adoption of an economic plan to support the value of the lira and to help Italy's sagging industries. The defeat, which resulted from the defection of some thirty members of the coalition parties in the secret balloting, forced Cossiga to surrender his post that same day. A new four-party coalition government—Italy's fortieth since World War II—was sworn in on October 18, 1980, with Christian Democratic party president Arnaldo Forlani as Prime Minister.

Francesco Cossiga is a tall, sandy-haired, bespectacled man who, according to a New York *Times* profile (August 13, 1979), "combines the reputation of a tough, practical politician with the benign and witty manner of a slightly distracted professor." His quiet dignity has won him the nickname "the Cardinal," and he is known for his wit and his self-effacing irony. The former Prime Minister remains a practising Roman Catholic. He has been married to Giuseppa Sigurani since September 24, 1960 and is the father of two daughters, Anna and Maria.

References: N Y Times A p11 Ag 13 '79 por; Britannica Book of the Year, 1980; International Who's Who, 1980-81; Who's Who in Europe, 1980-81

Cotrubas, Ileana (kō-troo-bäsh')

June 9, 1939- Romanian lyric soprano. Address: b. c/o Columbia Artists Management, Inc., 165 W. 57th St., New York City, N.Y. 10019

The touching and imaginative interpretations of the Romanian lyric soprano Ileana Cotrubas have helped to shatter the stereotype of the opera singer intent only on the production of sensuous sound at the expense of characterization and musicianship. Miss Cotrubas has risen to international prominence by carefully pacing her career and by making a series of judicious choices of the roles that she is willing to perform, under optimum conditions, in the major opera houses of the world. She is therefore respected and admired by the most exigent critics, but warily approached by some stage directors and colleagues who are less demanding of themselves and of others. Unwilling to appear in productions based exclusively on novelty or on what she regards as wrongheaded approaches, she insists on singing only when standards are conducive to an exciting and integrated operatic experience. "I have to be at my best level, surrounded by the best people, the best conductor," Miss Cotrubas once explained to Robert Jacobson in an interview for *Opera News* (March 28, 1981). "For me opera is teamwork. You have

Ileana Cotrubas

to be part of a group, and if you are in this beautiful team of good people, you are one of the best. This kind of opera is my ambition."

Born on June 9, 1939 to Vasile and Maria Cotrubas in Galati, Romania, an ethnically diverse industrial town on the lower Danube, Ileana Cotrubas grew up in a family in which music and the performing arts were part of everyday life. Her father, a civil servant in the ministry of agriculture, sang in the tenor section of an amateur chorus; her mother constantly sang around the house; and her sister eventually became a professional actress.

Inheriting from her illiterate mother "a good sense of life" and from her father an instinct for self-criticism and self-discipline, Ileana Cotrubas was fortunate enough to be a member of a warmly supportive and loving family, and as a result she remembers her childhood as being "wonderful," happy, and exciting. Even at the age of eight she showed signs of single-mindedness in pursuing a goal: intent on a film career after indulging in a steady diet of movie fan magazines, she and two of her girlfriends planned a clandestine escape by train and ship to the United States, with Hollywood as their eventual destination.

At nine years of age Ileana Cotrubas became a member of a children's radio chorus, which also performed when needed at the local opera house, and by the time she reached eleven, she was one of its leading soloists. Her first encounters with opera were therefore as a performer, as part of the chorus in Bizet's *Carmen*, Puccini's *La Bohème*, and Mussorgsky's *Boris Godunov*. After her family moved to Bucharest in 1952, she enrolled in the Scoala Speciala de Musica, for musically gifted children. Since its authorities considered her too

young, at thirteen, for full-time vocal study, she also conducted the school chorus, learned piano, violin, and accordion, and worked on such theatre disciplines as poetry recitation. Finally, at fifteen, she was allowed to embark on an ambitious program of vocal studies.

When, at eighteen, Ileana Cotrubas auditioned for the Ciprian Porumbescu Conservatory in Bucharest, she was turned down by its officials on the grounds that her voice was too "white," too small, and too childlike. Undaunted, she spent a year studying music theory, and in 1958, at the age of nineteen, again auditioned for the conservatory, this time successfully. There she studied first with Eugenia Elinescu and then, more importantly, with Constantin Stroescu, who forced her, through unremitting hard work, to change her voice from that of a child to that of an adult. In addition to the usual subjects of harmony, piano, and music history, she studied dance, gymnastics, and fencing, and, of course, languages, in which she displayed such facility that she is now fluent in French, German, English, and Italian.

While acting as an assistant in recital and oratorio classes at the Conservatory, Ileana Cotrubas made her solo operatic debut at the Bucharest Opera, in 1964, as the child Yniold in Debussy's *Pelléas et Mélisande*. The famous French music pedagogue Nadia Boulanger, who happened to be in Bucharest at the time for a Georges Enesco festival, congratulated her backstage on her mastery of French and correctly predicted that someday she would be a wonderful Mélisande. Her other early roles at the Bucharest Opera included the trouser parts of Siebel in *Faust*, Tebaldo in *Don Carlo*, and Oscar in *Un Ballo in Maschera*, as well as the more challenging assignments of Gilda in *Rigoletto* and Blondchen in *The Abduction from the Seraglio*.

International recognition came to Miss Cotrubas in a somewhat spectacular fashion in 1965, when she walked away from a singing competition in 's Hertogenbosch, Holland with first prizes in opera, lieder, and oratorio. That triumph led to a brief engagement at the Théâtre Royal de la Monnaie in Brussels in two Mozart roles: that of Pamina in *The Magic Flute* and of Constanze in *The Abduction from the Seraglio*. Another honor came her way in 1966, when she won the important Munich radio-television competition, an accolade that prompted the German conductor Wolfgang Sawallisch to hire her to sing one of the genii in *The Magic Flute* at that year's Salzburg Festival. Although it was admittedly a minor role, it served to introduce Ileana Cotrubas to an influential international audience.

During the next five years Ileana Cotrubas made a series of auspicious and well-planned debuts in most of the major opera houses of Europe. Although she signed a three-year contract with the Frankfurt Opera, its liberal management gave her the freedom to make guest appearances at other houses. She made her British debut at the Glyndebourne Festival in the summer of 1969 as Mélisande, under the direction of John Pritchard, who on hearing her audition for the role earlier in the year, had jumped to his feet and exclaimed, "You are my Mélisande!" In 1970 she made her debut at the Royal Opera House at Covent Garden in London as Tatyana in Tchaikovsky's *Eugene Onegin,* a role especially suited to the aura of frail vulnerability that she projects onstage. She has since become a special favorite of the British public. That same year she was offered a three-year contract with the Vienna State Opera, after making her debut at that illustrious house as Pamina. During her tenure there she ranged over a wide repertory: Susanna in *The Marriage of Figaro;* Zerlina in *Don Giovanni;* Gilda in *Rigoletto;* Violetta in *La Traviata;* Mimi in *La Bohème;* and Sophie in *Der Rosenkavalier.*

The British critic Alan Blythe has singled out Ileana Cotrubas' Violetta at the Vienna State Opera on Christmas Day, 1971, in a new production under Otto Schenk, as a new departure in her career, although she initially undertook the role with some misgivings. Traditionally the role demands the type of dramatic coloratura singing exemplified by a Maria Callas, Joan Sutherland, or Montserrat Caballé. In other words, it presupposes a weighty, yet agile voice that is capable of spectacular coloratura technique. Cotrubas has used that technique with expertise and facility, but she has never considered herself to be one of the coloraturas, to whom she has referred in interviews as mere "canaries." Characteristically, she approached the role of Violetta with caution, using her vocal technique to suggest the growth of character and an increasing vulnerability, instead of trying to dazzle the audience with prodigious vocal display.

American audiences belatedly heard Ileana Cotrubas in 1973 as Mimi, at the Chicago Lyric Opera, at the invitation of its impresario, Carol Fox. The following year she made her debut at the Paris Opéra in the title role of Massenet's *Manon,* at which time, according to the critics, she stood out from the lacklustre cast that surrounded her. The next major event in her career took place unexpectedly, on what she herself has described as the most exciting day in her life: her unscheduled debut at Milan's La Scala on January 7, 1975, replacing an indisposed Mirella Freni in *La Bohème.* Notified at her home in Sevenoaks in Kent on the same day of the performance, she rushed through adverse winter flying conditions from England to Italy and arrived at La Scala only fifteen minutes before curtain time. "Before I started," she has related of that appearance as Mimi to Luciano Pavarotti's Rodolfo, "there was such a silence . . . because everyone was curious to hear this new person. . . . After my aria it was an earthquake. I was shaking and trembling and starting to cry. . . . In the end they shouted and shouted."

It was in the same role of Mimi that Ileana Cotrubas made her debut at the Metropolitan Opera on March 23, 1977, in a cast that included José Carreras as Rodolfo and Renata Scotto as Musetta. Raymond Ericson's review in the New York *Times* (March 25, 1977) recapitulated the special distinctions already noted by European critics: "She is slim and dark, with a long oval face whose features are haunting, rather than pretty. They give her a vulnerable, pathetic look. She has a poise that suggests a stillness within her, giving depth to her acting. While somewhat light for Mimi, the voice is fresh and clear, soaring easily into the upper reaches. As the evening went on, the voice took on a small vibrato, adding warmth to the tone. Complete this list of attributes with sensitive and musical phrasing, and you have an unusually fine artist."

During the 1977-78 season Ileana Cotrubas returned to the Metropolitan Opera to star as Gilda in a new production of *Rigoletto* that was lambasted by critics not for its performers but for John Dexter's controversial staging. She was introduced to millions of American viewers when one of those performances of *Rigoletto* was televised on the "Live from Lincoln Center" series over PBS. During the 1980-81 season at the Metropolitan, much abbreviated because of a protracted musicians' strike, she appeared as Violetta opposite Placido Domingo's Alfredo in a new production of *La Traviata* that became one of the few undisputed triumphs of that troubled time. In the summer of 1981 she returned to one of the bucolic musical settings she loves best, to captivate Glyndebourne audiences with her Titania in Benjamin Britten's *A Midsummer Night's Dream.*

The dramatic and vocal integration that characterizes Ileana Cotrubas' performances holds true of her relationship to the opera production itself. She readily admits that she is demanding of both colleagues and directors because the questions that obsess her during the preparations for a production are: "Is this in the music? in the score? Is this my feeling, my emotion?" Her interest in the dramatic truth of opera, a hallmark of her work, stems from her early and continuing love of the theatre; she constantly tries to integrate body and facial movement with vocal technique into a unified and convincing portrayal. Her dedication to the music and words as written does not, however, exclude such vocal embellishment as inserted high notes and ornamentation, so long as she believes that it serves the overall purpose of the score.

As Miss Cotrubas once explained to Thomas Lanier in an interview for *Opera News* (December 3, 1977): "I'm unhappy if I have a bad conductor or my partner isn't so serious. I'm demanding a lot from other people, because I'm giving. I have to give, because I have some special qualities; like any artist, I have to transmit these feelings, and I can't do this without a good conductor, understanding colleagues, and a serious director. Today it is fashionable to bring in a director from the theatre with a big name to make new ways of expression, but this you must find in the music. If you don't know what the music says, it's a disaster for the theatre, the singers, the composer, for everyone."

One instance of Ileana Cotrubas' skirmishes with directors over divergent views of production values had to do with a new production, in 1973, of *Eugene Onegin* at the Vienna State Opera. At odds with what she felt were the autocratic and arbitrary ideas imposed by the German stage director Rudolf Nolte, she walked out during a rehearsal, creating the type of flurry that the media find so fascinating. Another much publicized contretemps took place in 1980 at the Metropolitan Opera, when she radically disagreed with the director John Dexter's interpretation of the character of Norina in *Don Pasquale*. Again she left the production in the rehearsal phase. Although she once again found herself at loggerheads with Dexter over their clashing views of the Met's new production of *La Traviata*, scheduled for 1981, a confrontation was avoided when he withdrew because of illness and was replaced by Colin Graham.

Inevitably, Ileana Cotrubas has often been compared to the Brazilian lyric soprano Bidu Sayão, who not only had a similar repertory but also radiated a dramatic intensity onstage and played upon the compassion of her audiences. Aware of those resemblances, Cotrubas insists that she deliberately avoids exposure to the work of Sayão and of other great artists who have left recorded legacies. She tries to define the role within her own personality rather than through the interpretations of other singers, even those of Teresa Stratas, the contemporary soprano whom she most admires. In trying to describe Cotrubas' distinctive voice, critics have rifled their lexicons for such adjectives as "lyric," "fresh," and "clear," although less adulatory reviewers have suggested that she lacks tonal variety and vocal color. As a recitalist, she has been mentioned as a possible successor to Elisabeth Schwarzkopf, especially in her interpretations of the lieder of Hugo Wolf.

Perhaps because of her own happy childhood, Ileana Cotrubas has often expressed to interviewers her dream of someday becoming part of an opera company based on excellence of ensemble and a family spirit. She would, she has said, be willing to give up her international career if she could find an opera house in Europe under the direction of one of her favorite conductors like Carlos Kleiber or Carlo Maria Giulini, in which major artists would be willing to tackle both stellar and minor roles. In what sounded almost like an entreaty, she told Robert Jacobson in her *Opera News* interview: "Let me be a star through stars, between stars, among stars, and not a star among stones. Just let me be the best among the best."

In 1972 Ileana Cotrubas married the German musician Manfred Ramin, who acts as her coach and manager. Because of the demands of their careers, they have decided to have no children. Cotrubas is a small, intense, and dark-haired woman, with dark-brown eyes, mobile features, and animated gestures, who impresses interviewers with her analytical intelligence and sometimes stinging wit. In spite of her cosmopolitan career, she still views herself as being fundamentally a simple and provincial person and seldom avails herself of the perquisites available to prima donnas. She deliberately limits herself to about forty performances a year (sixty is the average for most jet-set opera stars), to allow ample time for rest, recuperation, and musical preparation. With characteristic simplicity she has defined her career as her "life and raison d'être." She cannot conceive of existing without it.

One of a handful of international opera stars in constant demand by record companies, Ileana Cotrubas can be heard in both opera and solo recital on such labels as Argo/Decca, Philips, Columbia, Deutsche Grammofon, RCA Victor, and EMI/Angel. Her recorded operas include *Louise; Gianni Schicchi; Rinaldo; La Traviata; Carmen; Les Pêcheurs de Perles; The Marriage of Figaro;* and *Hansel and Gretel.*

References: Newsweek 47:105 Ap 6 '81 por; N Y Times II p23+ Ap 10 '77 por; Opera 27:428+ My '76 por; Opera N 40:38 S '75 pors, 45:16+ Mr 28 '81 pors; International Who's Who, 1981-82; Who's Who in Opera (1976)

Crosby, John (O'Hea)

July 12, 1926- Conductor; opera impresario; educational administrator. Address: b. P.O. Box 2408, Santa Fe, New Mexico 87501

When he launched the first two-month season of his Santa Fe Opera Company in the summer of 1957, John Crosby founded an innovative cultural institution that has since become one of the few genuinely international festivals in the United States and demonstrated his abiding faith in the power of regional support for opera at the grass-roots level. Now celebrating its twenty-fifth anniversary, the Santa Fe Opera is entitled to lay claim to some twenty-five American and world premieres, including the complete version of Alban Berg's *Lulu*, several of them conducted by such composers as Igor Stravinsky, Hans Werner Henze, and Paul Hindemith. Among its former apprentices who once sang in its justly famous chorus are such world-rank alumni as Sherrill Milnes, Judith Blegen, and Samuel Ramey.

Crosby is the man chiefly responsible for the success and enviable financial stability of what

John Crosby

has been called "the miracle in the desert" and "the Salzburg of the Southwest." A formidable planner and organizer, he clearly formulated his objectives from the very beginning and went on to realize them as general director, chief conductor, and the person in charge of overall administration and finances as well as of artistic policy. As he explained to Stephen E. Rubin in an interview for the New York *Times* (June 16, 1974): "What I was after was a festival, a distinguished series of events presented in a very special way and made possible by long advance and careful off-season planning, with adequate and proper provision for preparation, rehearsals, etc., all the way to costume fittings." By budgeting his time as adroitly as he does his festival's finances, Crosby has also managed to serve as president of the Opera America Association (since 1975) and as president of the Manhattan School of Music (since 1976).

John O'Hea Crosby was born on July 12, 1926 in New York City to Laurence Alden Crosby, a partner in the prestigious law firm of Sullivan & Cromwell, and the former Aileen O'Hea, an English-born musician and chemist. Although Laurence Crosby, a former Rhodes Scholar at Oxford, traced his ancestry on his mother's side to the Puritans of the Massachusetts Bay Colony, including John Alden, he professed Roman Catholicism. His son John Crosby, who dropped his middle initial "O" after he could no longer be confused with the American newspaper columnist of the same name, recalled in a *New Yorker* profile by Winthrop Sargeant (August 4, 1975) that he and his brother, James, learned from their gifted mother not only how to play the violin and piano but also how to read, paint, and

make pottery. Aileen Crosby even learned how to write with her left hand in order to be able to teach her left-handed son John. The Crosbys lived in suburban Bronxville, New York, where they often took advantage of the nearby bridle paths for horseback riding.

After attending the Pelham Day School, John Crosby entered the Hotchkiss School in Lakeville, Connecticut, but an asthmatic condition he developed there led his family to transfer him for a year to the Los Alamos Ranch School in New Mexico. There he fell in love for the first time with the beauty of the juniper-studded desert landscape in the foothills of the Jémez mountains and sensed some of the reverberations of the area's illustrious past, when D. H. Lawrence, Mabel Dodge Luhan, and Witter Bynner lived in the Indian and colonial Spanish countryside. Returning to New England to complete his prep school education, Crosby graduated from Hotchkiss in 1944.

Drafted into the United States Army that same year, Crosby found himself playing accordion, trombone, double bass, violin, and piano with his infantry regiment's dance band. After being mustered out with the rank of corporal, he and several other recently discharged G.I.'s formed a professional five-piece band of their own, an experiment that soon ended when he entered Yale University. His studies of musical composition with Paul Hindemith, then the most inspiring teacher in what Crosby considers to have been an otherwise ingrown department, and his continued work with piano and violin, led to a B.A. degree in music from Yale in 1950. Crosby's interest in musical comedy, dating from his New Haven days when he attended local Broadway tryouts and wrote orchestrations for undergraduate shows, prompted him to spend several months as an assistant to Broadway arrangers after graduation.

Within a year of his graduation from Yale, Crosby was back in the classroom, this time at Columbia University, where he studied conducting with Rudolph Thomas, the director of its opera workshop, and it was during his three-year association with Thomas that he began to gravitate towards opera. His fellow student John Kander, who went on from Columbia to write the scores for *Cabaret* and other Broadway musicals, remembers that Crosby could play the piano reduction of Richard Strauss's *Salomé* from memory. Under Thomas' tutelage, Crosby learned the scores of many operas that he practised conducting while Thomas played the piano score, and vice versa.

Meanwhile, Crosby spent much of his leisure time as a standee at the old house of the Metropolitan Opera at 39th and Broadway, standing down in front where he could observe the conducting as closely as possible. Unlike the present, the Met's roster of conductors during the 1950's included such luminaries as Fritz Reiner, whose conducting Crosby especially admired and whom he finally met through striking up an acquaintance with Mrs. Reiner. Some years later, when his Santa Fe venture was already underway, Crosby stopped off occasionally in Chicago for talks about conducting with Reiner, then the head of the Chicago Symphony Orchestra.

During his three years at Columbia University, John Crosby also accompanied singers, served as assistant director of its opera workshop, and began playing for the opera classes of Leopold Sachse, a well-known German opera stage director then working at the New York City Opera. Not surprisingly, Crosby credits Sachse, formerly of the Hamburg Staatsoper and the Met, as being the most important influence on his career, since it was from his talks with Sachse that the concept of the Santa Fe Opera eventually emerged. Meanwhile, he attended Pierre Monteux's summer conducting classes in Maine, where he finally made up his mind at the end of his Columbia studies that he wanted to become an opera conductor.

It was Leopold Sachse who eventually went to Crosby's father to broach the idea of the Santa Fe project. Although Laurence Crosby had not at first approved of his son's musical career, he contributed $200,000 to get the venture underway. With that money and the encouragement of William Primrose, among others, John Crosby bought the San Juan ranch adjoining the Tesuque Indian reservation about five miles north of Santa Fe in the foothills of the Sangre de Cristo mountains. There, during the winter of 1956-57, he constructed a wooden opera house with some 450 seats, which, when completed, was called by a *Time* magazine critic "one of the handsomest operatic settings in the Western Hemisphere." By the following summer, Crosby and his company of sixty-five members were ready to present their first six-week season featuring a repertory of seven operas: *Madame Butterfly*, *The Rake's Progress*, *Così Fan Tutte*, *The Barber of Seville*, *La Serva Padrona*, *Ariadne auf Naxos*, and Marvin David Levy's contemporary work, *The Tower*. That mix of the new, the old, and the neglected set the pattern for subsequent seasons of the Santa Fe Opera.

The first 1957 season yielded $40,000 in box office receipts in addition to $60,000 from the largely affluent local citizenry. In 1958 Crosby increased the seating capacity of his opera house to 700 and presented six works: the world premiere of Carlisle Floyd's *Wuthering Heights*, commissioned by Santa Fe, the American premiere of Richard Strauss's *Capriccio*, and *La Bohème*, *La Cenerentola*, *Falstaff*, and *Così Fan Tutte*. Beginning in 1959, Crosby limited himself to five productions during the July and August season so that his associates might enjoy the luxury of four weeks of rehearsal time.

One of the key factors in the continued success of the Santa Fe Opera has been its apprentice-artist program, under which about thirty young aspirants are chosen, after extensive auditions, to join the chorus for a limit of two seasons. As schooled in body movement and acting as they are in vocal training, they can dance as well as sing, and many of them go on to successful careers in Europe or the United States after their apprenticeship. Another asset is its relatively sophisticated audience, about one-half of which comes from outside New Mexico, sometimes traveling as far as 100 miles by car to attend a performance or arriving by train or plane from thousands of miles away. With some justification, those devotees feel superior to the average urban opera audience in the catholicity of their taste.

Their fealty is rewarded with performances that are rich in theatrical values and in superior ensemble, if somewhat impoverished in the presence of big names. Furthermore, the Santa Fe Opera has been fortunate in being able to call upon for financial help some of the many moneyed local inhabitants, who have been astute enough to realize that the prestige brought to the community by the opera house can mean increased patronage for the town's restaurants, hotels, boutiques, and other adjuncts of tourism. By the mid-1970's the personnel of the Santa Fe Opera had grown to include eighty musicians in the orchestra, forty-five members of the chorus, twenty-five soloists, six pianists, two solo dancers, ten members of the corps de ballet, and eighty-five members of the production staff.

With a repertory that was approximately twenty-five percent contemporary, the Santa Fe Opera could from time to time enlist the services of such twentieth-century giants as Stravinsky and Hindemith to conduct their own works, thus adding the magnetism of celebrity to its other attractions. During the 1960's, for example, the Santa Fe repertory interspersed with its standard fare such contemporary operas as Blitzstein's *Regina*, Moore's *The Ballad of Baby Doe*, Henze's *The Bassarids*, *The Stag King*, and *Boulevard Solitude*, Hindemith's *News of the Day*, Stravinsky's *Renard*, *Perséphone*, *Le Rossignol*, and *Oedipus Rex*, Berg's *Wozzeck*, Poulenc's *Dialogues of the Carmelites*, and Shostakovich's *The Nose*. And the American and world premieres have included works by Berio, Villa-Lobos, Britten, Schoenberg, Menotti, and Penderecki.

One typical John Crosby coup was the American premiere of Alban Berg's *Lulu* in its incomplete two-act version in the summer of 1963. That same year, Crosby made a deal with Universal Edition, Berg's European publisher, under the terms of which it was agreed that Crosby would be the first to present the complete work in the United States whenever it became available. After the death of Berg's widow, the three-act complete version was finally released, and *Lulu*, under the baton of Michael Tilson Thomas, was the major event of the 1979 summer season at Santa Fe, unanimously acclaimed by the major music critics of the United States.

Like most cultural institutions, the Santa Fe Opera has not been without its setbacks. After a decade of impressive accomplishment, the opera house suddenly caught fire and burned to the ground on July 27, 1967, following a performance of Hindemith's *Cardillac*. Even as Crosby and his backers watched their opera house go up in flames, they began plans to go through with the rest of the season and to build a new home for the Santa Fe Opera. Only two nights after the fire, the indomitable members of the company presented *The Barber of Seville* in the Sweeney gymnasium of the Santa Fe High School (the costumes had been saved by being at the drycleaners) and followed that up the next evening with an ingenious production of *La Bohème* in modern dress.

Turning to the same architects—McHugh and Kidder—and the same acoustical expert—Jack Purcell—who had collaborated on the first opera house, Crosby and his board of directors brought their characteristic drive and imagination to bear on their new project, aimed at a bigger, better, and more fireproof home for the Santa Fe Opera, at a cost budgeted at $1.8 million. In less than a year they were able to raise $1.5 million; the rest they obtained through a mortgage that was paid off in 1979. Recalling the financial and other stresses of 1967-68, Crosby remarked to Sarah Moore in an interview for *People* magazine (August 14, 1978): "That year my hair turned white." "I believe in losing money," Crosby added, "but lose it on things you want to lose it on. My approach is simple: understaff and work the hell out of everybody."

On July 3, 1968 the Santa Fe Opera Company began its twelfth season, under budget and ahead of schedule, in its new home of redwood, rose-colored adobe, and reinforced concrete, with *Madame Butterfly,* the same opera with which it opened its first season in 1957. Constructed in only 300 days, the new theatre featured a deep tapering stage opening of fifty-six feet, two feet wider than that of the Metropolitan Opera House. There is no proscenium, no curtain, and no place to fly scenery, but there are wooden flats to resist the sometimes overpowering wind. Open at the rear and at the sides, the house has about twelve middle rows that are exposed to the vagaries of the cold and wet summer climate, so that the Santa Fe inhabitants who usually occupy those seats are obliged to bring along blankets, hot water bottles, and an occasional consoling flask of bourbon. The open rear sometimes works to Crosby's advantage, as during the last act of *Madame Butterfly,* for example, when the twinkling lights of Los Alamos in the distance convey the illusion of being the lights of Nagasaki.

When the Santa Fe Opera Company celebrated its twentieth birthday in 1976, it showcased the same kind of repertory that had filled its house almost to capacity from the beginning: a new production of Virgil Thom-

son's *The Mother of Us All* and a revival of *L'Egisto,* the seldom performed opera by Pietro Francesco Cavalli, that dates back to 1643, along with *La Traviata, Salomé,* and *The Marriage of Figaro.* In the late 1970's some dissidents among music reviewers, including Thor Eckert Jr. of the *Christian Science Monitor,* began to hint that Crosby needed to appraise his entire endeavor, while such influential critics as Harold C. Schonberg of the New York *Times* and Paul Hume of the Washington *Post* felt that he should give up conducting to concentrate on overall direction of the Santa Fe Opera. Both men cited certain deficiencies in Crosby's conducting technique and in his occasional lack of control over the orchestra. But when the Santa Fe Opera Company opened its twenty-fifth anniversary season in July of 1981, with *La Bohème* as the only production left over from previous years, negative criticism seemed largely muted in the critical chorus of praise for *The Barber of Seville,* Strauss's *Daphne,* and Hindemith's *News of the Day.* The new production of *Daphne,* in particular, was an unqualified triumph.

Since 1975 John Crosby has been the president of Opera America, an association of American and Canadian opera companies that share information and pool their productions. As an adjunct, he became a member of the board of the American Arts Alliance, representing art museums, orchestras, and nonprofit professional theatres as well as opera and dance companies. In 1976 he became president of the Manhattan School of Music, the largest private conservatory in the United States, which had been suffering severe deficits for the six preceding years and drawing on cash reserves to cover expenses. During his tenure the conservatory's big deficit has been considerably reduced and its budget has been balanced, thanks to an efficiency study he ordered to find a way of reducing operating costs.

John Crosby, who is a bachelor, stands about five feet ten inches tall and weighs about 170 pounds. His blue eyes are framed by horn-rimmed glasses, and his wavy gray hair is receding. Interviewers and associates have described Crosby as an intense, idealistic, reserved, and compulsively neat perfectionist, with a memory like a computer and a legendary temper. According to Winthrop Sargeant, he "more closely resembles most people's idea of a well-brought-up, prosperous lawyer or stockbroker" than an opera impresario. Among his predominantly solitary leisure interests are swimming, calisthenics, horseback riding, gardening, carpentry, and the reading of biographies, often of Victorians. To clear his brain before conducting performances, he stands on his head, like many other practitioners of Yoga. Crosby divides his time between his Santa Fe ranch and his elegant five-story townhouse in the East Sixties of New York City that also serves as the winter headquarters of the Santa Fe Opera Company. He holds honorary degrees from the Cleveland Institute of Music, the College of Santa Fe, and the University of New Mexico. His club is the University Club in New York City, and his religion is Roman Catholicism.

References: Christian Sci Mon p15 Je 23 '69 por; N Y Times II p13+ Je 2 '68 por, II p21+ Je 16 '74 por, II p11+ Ja 1 '78 por; New Yorker 51:35+ Ag 4 '75 por; Opera News 35:12+ Je 12 '71 por; People 10:44+ Ag 14 '78 pors; Slonimsky, Nicholas. Baker's Biographical Dictionary of Musicians (1978); Who's Who in America, 1980-81; Who's Who in Opera, 1976; Who's Who in the West, 1980-81

Cruyff, Johan (krīf yō′hän)

Apr. 25, 1947- Soccer player. Address: b. c/o North American Soccer League, 1133 Ave. of the Americas, New York City, N.Y. 10036; Inter-Soccer Inc., 576 5th Ave., New York City, N.Y. 10036

Succeeding Pelé, who had retired the year before, the mercurial, aggressive Dutch midfielder and forward Johan Cruyff became the imported "savior" of North American soccer in 1979, when he joined the Los Angeles Aztecs. The electric presence of the "Flying Dutchman" doubled the Aztecs' gate, drawing huge crowds wherever he played, and his prowess inspired the team to rise from the North American Soccer League's basement and brought Cruyff himself the NASL's Most Valuable Player title. Before joining the Aztecs, Cruyff had led European teams to six league championships, three European titles, and one world club team championship. He was the Most Valuable Player in the 1974 World Cup finals, and he and Franz Beckenbauer are the only persons to have won the European Player of the Year award three times. In 1980 and 1981 he played with the now defunct Washington Diplomats. What he hopes to do, he has said, is to be instrumental in making soccer "a major sport from April to September" in North America. "Pelé brought American soccer to 60 percent of its potential. My job is to raise it to 75 percent."

Johan Cruyff was born in Amsterdam, the Netherlands, on April 25, 1947. After the death of his father, a grocer, his mother went to work as a charwoman at the nearby Ajax Stadium, the home of the Ajax, a professional soccer team that begins grooming its future players when they are in elementary school. Cruyff, who was bouncing and kicking soccer balls from the age of four, beat out 200 other young aspirants to win membership on the Ajax Juniors when he was ten. Rinus Michels— who was then coach of the Ajax and who would later coach Cruyff in Barcelona and Los Angeles—has recalled: "You could see that as a baby he was an exceptional player. The only obstacle was that he had no body. [At fifteen, Cruyff was five feet three inches tall and weighed 115 pounds.] He learned tricks to survive."

In 1965 the Ajax signed Cruyff to his first professional contract. As forward and midfielder with the previously lowly team, he led it to six league titles, four national cups, and three consecutive European championships. He was named Dutch Player of the Year in 1967, 1968, and 1969 and European player of the year in 1971 and 1973. His nine-year totals with the Ajax were 256 goals in 350 games. He led the Dutch National Team in scoring with thirty-three goals in 1966-67 and twenty-five in 1971-72. In 1974 (the year after he left the Ajax) he captained the national team to the World Cup final—which it lost to West Germany—and he was voted Most Valuable Player in that event. Midfielder Johan Neeskens, who played on the World Cup team with Cruyff, observed, "He knows everything. He sees things before other players do." Defender Wim Rijsbergen, another World Cup teammate, said, "He has everything as a soccer player, not only the legs but the head."

Meanwhile, in 1973 Cruyff was sold at his own request to El Club de Fútbol de Barcelona. Among his reasons for the move, as he later explained them, were the 80 percent income-tax bite in the Netherlands, "lots of problems" with "amateurs running the club" in Amsterdam, and the presence of his old coach, Rinus Michels, in Barcelona. The Barcelona club paid the Ajax a reported $2,250,000, the highest transfer sum in soccer history up to that time, and its contract with Cruyff specified a monthly salary of $10,000 in addition to bonuses. Cruyff also signed lucrative contracts with several Spanish companies to do commercials endorsing their products. It was not without reason that he quickly became known as "El Holandés de Oro" in Spain.

Cruyff's impact in Barcelona was immediate. At an exhibition match early in September 1973, his presence raised the gate by 25 percent, an enhancement that would be dwarfed by later increases in attendance figures. He made his debut with Barcelona in league competition on the last Sunday of the following month, when the team was fourth from the bottom of Spain's eighteen-club first-division league. Barcelona's victory in that game was the beginning of a streak that continued into the following year. The club went undefeated in more than five months of play, compiling twenty-six consecutive victories or ties and clinching the league championship seven weeks before the 1973-74 season was over. Cruyff's sixteen goals and dozens of assists made him the third highest scorer in Spain. "Johan revolutionized our team," his teammate Hugo Sotíl told a reporter. "He directed us on the field. . . . Cruyff is as good as, if not better than, Pelé at his peak."

Sparked by Cruyff, Barcelona won the Spanish League title in 1974 and was runner-up in 1976 and 1977. But the pressures that came with Cruyff's being what the Spanish call a "Sunday hero" became unbearable to him, as did the eleven-month European season. Press and public gave him no rest, making it impossible for him to walk down a street undisturbed, to go out to eat, or to lead a normal family life. "I had no free time," he recalled in an interview with David Hirshey for Sport (May 1980). "I had to give up my children. If I played bad, my oldest daughter would go to school and the other children would say, 'Your father's a disaster.' I wasn't enjoying it anymore. You play, play, play. If you don't get results, you get criticized, tortured by the press." Death threats and actual invasions of his home by enemies as well as fans made it necessary for him and his family to retreat to a guarded mountain compound forty-five minutes from Barcelona. In June 1978 he announced that he was retiring, not because he was tired of soccer but "because [he was] tired of professional soccer in Europe [and especially] in Spain, [where] even if you go to the toilet, somebody's marking you."

The New York Cosmos, who had lured Pelé out of retirement, tried the same with Cruyff. They succeeded only in signing him on August 3, 1978 for a series of exhibition games (for $500,000) and a commitment to play for them in regular season if he ever should come out of retirement. Two factors finally made him change his mind in favor of returning to professional competition. One was the failure of some of his business ventures in Europe. The other was the hiring of Rinus Michels to coach the Los Angeles Aztecs. Acceding to his wish to play under Michels, the Cosmos sold their rights to Cruyff to the Aztecs for $600,000. "We could have held onto him," the Cosmos' president, Ahmet Ertegun, said. "But I would rather have him playing somewhere in the league [the North American Soccer League] than not playing at all. And, looking at it from the league's standpoint, it's better to spread the stars out." In July 1979 the Aztecs signed Cruyff to a two-year contract worth more than $1,000,000 annually to him, with options for renewal on both sides.

"From the American spectators' viewpoint, I think that Cruyff has more to bring to the game than Pelé," Rinus Michels told a reporter on the occasion of Cruyff's signing with the Aztecs. "You must remember that Pelé came to the United States late in his career. He was great but not as great as he had been. But Johan is still at the top of his game; he can still demonstrate the skills that have made him the world's greatest player. We are mostly a new team that is still learning to play together. But Cruyff, because he makes better players of the people around him, will help us to mature faster than we ordinarily would. We are not the most skilled team at attacking and then finishing off our plays. But with Johan to lead us that will also change."

Washington Diplomat defender Robert Iarusci spoke in a similar vein to John Feinstein of the Washington Post (July 27, 1979) after playing against Cruyff: "Pelé was magic at thirty-five. But Cruyff, he is something else, something different. He's beyond belief. It's tempting when you're playing against him just to stand back and watch. Trying to have one man defend him is impossible. One on one with any defender in the world, he is virtually unstoppable."

Scoring thirteen goals (five of them game winners) and sixteen assists with the Aztecs, Cruyff was the NASL's Most Valuable Player in 1979. The Aztecs, who had been worst in the league in 1978, with a 9-21 record, began enjoying better press and attendance (up 25 to 50 percent) and they reached the NASL playoff semifinals. Cruyff was not entirely happy in Los Angeles, however, partly because of the Astroturf, the artificial playing surface used there, as in many NASL clubs. On many occasions he voiced his opinion that artificial turf must go, along with the thirty-five-yard offside rule (as opposed to the midfield offside rule standard in the rest of the world), if the NASL was to become competitive with Europe. On the other hand, he came out in favor of the league's "shootout" concept of breaking ties.

When Mexican interests bought the Aztecs, after the 1979 season, Cruyff went to the Washington Diplomats, who invested $1,500,000 in a three-year contract—in addition to an amount of the same magnitude paid to the Aztecs—in the hope of toppling the New York Cosmos as the NASL's premier gate attraction. Aside from the money, Cruyff said that he was happy to go to the Diplomats because "they have a nice field" and "it is important to have soccer on grass." With the Diplomats in 1980, he scored ten goals and had twenty assists and helped the team to draw an average attendance of more than 19,000. He had many disagreements with teammates and coach Gordon Bradley, however, chiefly having to do with his outbursts of temperament and perfectionistic scolding of teammates on the field.

In the Toronto *Globe and Mail* (March 14, 1980), Allen Abel described Cruyff in action with the Diplomats: "All eyes are on . . . Cruyff the improvisor, Cruyff the con man, standing still one moment, flying the next, never betraying his intentions with his dispassionate eyes. He takes the ball down the left wing as if it were attached to his feet by string and outruns two puffing Rogues and, without casting the slightest glance behind him, left-foots a thirty-yard pass."

Sonny Werblin and the Madison Square Garden organization (a subsidiary of Gulf and Western), then owners of the Diplomats, terminated their franchise in November 1980. Cruyff's contract reverted to the New York Cosmos, who placed him on waivers, and he ended up playing for the Levante club in Valencia, Spain in 1980-81. In May 1981 he suffered a groin injury for which he underwent surgery.

In 1981 the Diplomats returned to the NASL under a new owner, Jimmy Hill. On June 17, 1981 Hill and his son Duncan, the team's general manager, hoping to bolster the Diplomats for the stretch drive and improve attendance, negotiated a contract with Cruyff. The terms of the contract were not revealed, but Jimmy Hill said that the salary would be "a lot less money" than the $500,000 or $600,000 Cruyff reportedly made the season before.

Returning to action with the Diplomats against San Diego on July 1, 1981, Cruyff strained a muscle in his thigh trying to compensate for muscles weakened by his groin surgery. He resumed play briefly in mid-July and then went back on the disabled list. The team management said that it did not expect him to play again that season, but he reappeared in the lineup spectacularly in the Diplomats' final regular season home game, on August 16, 1981. On that occasion the Diplomats overpowered the Toronto Blizzard with a swarming offense and a sparkling defense led by defender Eddie Colquhoun and goalkeeper Jim Brown. The play that stunned the 9,226 spectators, however, was one of the most memorable goals ever seen in Robert F. Kennedy Stadium, a forty-yarder executed by Cruyff while being guarded by three defenders. The goal put the Diplomats in the lead, 2-0, and they went on to defeat the Blizzard 5-1.

For the last game of the season the Diplomats traveled to Montreal, where they lost in a "shootout," 1-0. The loss brought their season record to 15-17, putting them in sixteenth place in the league and thus cutting them out of the playoffs, for which only the top fifteen teams qualify. The team was disbanded after the end of the 1981 season. Cruyff's statistics for 1981, two goals and one assist in five games, brought his NASL career totals to twenty-five goals and thirty-seven assists in fifty-three games.

Although he usually starts at forward—where he plays a step ahead of the line—Cruyff is a master of all positions and can be shifted anywhere. He does not so much play as "conduct" a game, taking into consideration all action on the field, as if he had eyes in back of his head, imperiously directing his teammates into position, and constantly talking, if only to confuse the opposition. With grace and balance, he is able to elude the most obdurate of defenders, and he can dribble fluidly and pass softly in the heaviest of traffic. Although he is considered fast, he says that his major asset is not so much speed as acceleration. He is always anticipating, and thus he is always one step ahead of the opposition. On the field, with his hair flying and his arms and head (as well as his mouth) in constant motion, he seems to have limitless energy.

Deceptively frail-looking, Johan Cruyff is five feet eight and half inches tall and weighs between 150 and 155 pounds. Off the field as on, he is usually in constant motion, biting his nails, puffing on cigarettes, and playing practical jokes. He speaks near-perfect English in addition to Spanish, Italian, and his native Dutch. He and his wife, Danny, have three children, Susila, Chantal, and Jordi. Cruyff's marketing and promotion, including his endorsement of commercial products, is handled by Inter-Soccer Inc.

References: Newsday p54 Jl 30 '79 por; People 12:36+ Ag 20 '79 pors; Sports 80:72+ My '80 pors; Washington Post D p4 Mr 9 '80 pors, D p1+ Je 24 '80

Dale, Jim

Aug. 15, 1935- Actor; comedian. Address: b. c/o David Powers, 1501 Broadway, New York City, N.Y. 10036

To his Tony Award-winning performance as the flamboyant circus impresario Phineas T. Barnum in the razzle-dazzle Broadway musical *Barnum*, Jim Dale brought, as he says, "all the training that [he had] stored in the muscles and the old brainbox" in his more than thirty years in show business. Essentially a physical and visual comic, Dale began his career as a knockabout music-hall entertainer in his native England, and he went on to become a pop singer, television star, and one of the wild crew in the *Carry On* films. Coming to the United States with a National Theatre troupe in 1974, he made his first conquest of New York audiences and critics as the swashbuckling

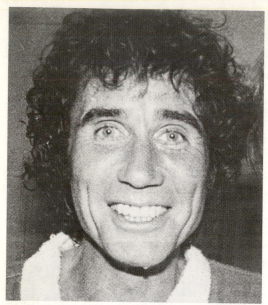

Jim Dale

title rogue in *Scapino*, an outrageous slapstick modernization of Molière's *commèdia dell'arte* farce. Dale carries off such strenuous, protean roles as Scapino and Barnum with an acrobat's coordination and balance, a dancer's grace, a pantomimist's mastery of movement and "shtick," a comic's sense of timing, and an athlete's stamina. As Dan Sullivan wrote in the Los Angeles Times (April 29, 1975), what distinguishes Jim Dale from the average comic actor is "a disciplined body and a generous spirit." After appearing for more than eleven months in the role of Barnum at the Saint James Theatre, Dale was replaced by Mike Burstyn in October 1981, when his contract expired.

Jim Dale changed his name from Jim Smith when he entered show business in order to avoid confusion with another British entertainer named Jim Smith. He was born in the industrial town of Rothwell, Northamptonshire, England to William Henry Smith, a foundry worker, and Miriam (Wells) Smith, a shoe factory employee, on August 15, 1935. Both parents are deceased. A younger brother, Michael, a welder and instructor in welding, still lives in Rothwell.

There were no theatres in Rothwell, not even a cinema, as Dale recalled in an interview with Leo Seligsohn of Newsday (May 18, 1980). "But when I was nine," he told Seligsohn, "I went to a show at the Victoria Palace in London and saw a comic named Lupino Lane. I was surrounded by 2,000 people and when I heard the roar of the laughter. . . . Do you know what a cat looks like when the hair goes up on its back? That was the way I felt."

Instantly stagestruck, Dale knew that what he wanted to do in life was "to make people laugh." He and his parents also knew that to become a stage comic he would have to learn movement. For six years, while other children were playing or fighting in the street, he spent most of his free time at a local dance school, learning ballet, tap, and the *outré* British art of "eccentric" dancing, which Dale has described as "learning to move the body as if it had no joints, like an India rubber doll." He also studied judo and tumbling.

At sixteen Dale dropped out of state school to go to work in a shoe factory—from which he was rescued by a traveling vaudeville troupe, Carroll Levis and his Discoverers. Entering the troupe's talent contest as an impressionist, he caught Levis' attention less by his impressions than by the spectacular accidental fall he took when running onstage. For two years he toured the music halls of England's Midlands with the troupe as a comic tumbler, somersaulting from a springboard onto the stage, falling on his face, and doing double somersaults down staircases. His neatest trick was to walk backward to the edge of the stage and stand there teetering on toes alone. If he was unlucky, he fell into the orchestra pit.

"Sometimes I could feel the blood running down my knees," he recounted to Michiko Kakutani in an interview for the New York Times (May 2, 1980). "It was sad perhaps, but when you're a kid all you want is a laugh, and I was so inexperienced then that I thought that was the only way to do it. I guess it's wanting to be loved, really—that's the answer any clown will give you—wanting to make people laugh or cry." His body still carries many scars acquired during his apprenticeship as a pratfalling variety comic.

As a conscript in the Royal Air Force, Dale was assigned to the equipment section, with time out for camp shows and some radio and television work. Following his discharge, in 1956, he returned to the variety stage—which was fast disappearing because of the growing competition of television—and then was a BBC disc jockey for six months.

In 1957 Dale's career took a sudden new turn when chance transformed him into a pop singer. The occasion arose when he was asked to do a warmup comic routine for Tommy Steele on the BBC's *6:05 Special*, the first, and most popular, rock 'n' roll show on British television. On an impulse, he picked up Steele's guitar and did some singing. Although he has a voice that he describes as "asthma set to music," he was an instantaneous sensation.

Dale remained on the *6:05 Special* for almost three years as a singer, not a comic, and the show led to a recording contract. The biggest hit among the sides he recorded was "Be My Girl." In 1959 he left the *6:05 Special* and returned to comedy with his own television program, the *Lunchtime Show* on Southern Television in Southampton. For two years he did that show three times a week, often writing as well as performing in the sketch comedy that it featured.

In the early 1960's Dale began appearing in *Carry On* films, the series of gross screen comedies that had begun with the 1958 army farce *Carry On Sergeant*. The typical *Carry On* movie was basically a string of smutty, sometimes scatological, jokes strung together on a farcical plot. Although critics often found them offensive, they became a British institution, on a par with fish and chips, and drew appreciative art house audiences in the United States as well.

In roles of varying weight, Dale was in some dozen *Carry On* films, including the following: *Carry On Cabby* (Governor, 1963), about rivalry and sabotage between cab companies; *Carry On Cleo* (Governor, 1964), a parody of the film *Cleopatra*; *Carry On Spying* (Governor, 1964), a spoof on spy movies of the James Bond type; *Carry On Screaming* (Anglo-Amalgamated, 1966), a horror movie takeoff; and *Carry On Doctor* (American-International, 1978). The critic for *Variety* (April 6, 1966) thought that *Carry On Cowboy* (Anglo-Amalgamated, 1966) was "a distinct cut above some that have clicked in the series" and that Dale, in the role of a sanitary engineer mistaken for a frontier marshal, proved himself "a likeable and inventive comedian."

Among Dale's other motion picture roles in the 1960's was that of one of the three lusty sailors in *Lock Up Your Daughters* (Columbia, 1969), a loose, bawdy adaptation of Henry Fielding's *Rape Upon Rape*. "The whole show," Archer Winsten wrote in the New York Post (October 16, 1969), "appears to be a bunch of English hams having a ball in glorious Technicolored costumes." Indulging what he calls his "hobby" of lyric writing, Dale wrote the words for the Oscar-nominated title song of *Georgy Girl* (Columbia, 1966) and contributed to the music for the films *Shalako* (Cinerama Releasing, 1968) and *Lola* (American-International, 1970), which was originally titled *Twinky*.

Dale made his West End debut in *The Wayward Way*, a musical version of *The Drunkard* in which he gave "the performance of the evening . . . leaping and moralizing" in the drunk's comic role, according to the reviewer for the London Times (November 17, 1965). When Frank Dunlop, the administrative director of the National Theatre, asked him to play the rogue Autolycus in a pop version of *The Winter's Tale* at the Edinburgh Festival in August 1966, he hesitated at first, fearful that as a vaudevillian who had never read Shakespeare he might not be equal to the task. "At first I asked myself, 'Who the hell are you to do Shakespeare?'" he later remarked. "But the laughter of a Shakespeare audience was just the same as the laughter in a music hall."

The following year Dale again performed at the Edinburgh Festival, as Bottom in a pop version of *A Midsummer Night's Dream*, and in 1969 he joined the National Theatre Company at the Old Vic. His first roles as a regular with the company were the two that he played in 1969 in Peter Nichols' sardonic comedy about socialized medicine in Britain, *The National Health, Or Nurse Norton's Affair*: the wisecracking narrator-orderly in a ward of dying men in a shabby London hospital, and a doctor in a soap-opera love story about doctors and nurses in a dream hospital. Critics applauded the deft way in which he held together the play's dark humor and its pathos. After a turn as Nicholas in *The Travails of Sancho Panza* (1969), Dale essayed Costard—his favorite among Shakespearean clowns—in *Love's Labour's Lost* (1970), and Launcelot Gobbo in *The Merchant of Venice* (1970).

Frank Dunlop established the National Theatre Company's Young Vic in 1970 to attract younger audiences with "irreverent" plays and nominal admission fees. At the Young Vic, Dale's first role was that of Scapin in the *The Cheats of Scapin* (1970), one of the milestones in the evolution of the National Theatre's adaptation of *Les Fourberies de Scapin*. The National Theatre had begun doing the Molière farce in 1967, with various actors contributing to the title role. "It's like a piece of clay," Dale once observed. "You just keep adding things to it. You start molding it and somebody throws another lump on, and various people start molding that."

His next Young Vic role was that of Petruchio in *The Taming of the Shrew* (1970). At the Old Vic, he broadened his tragicomic range in the role of the tearful, strident architect in Fernando Arrabal's avant-garde *The Architect and the Emperor of Assyria*; that of Mr. Lofty in Oliver Goldsmith's *The Good-Natured Man* (1971); and that of Kalle in Carl Zuckmayer's *The Captain of Köpenick* (1971). As Petruchio, he toured Europe with the Young Vic in 1972.

For six months beginning in July 1973 Dale starred as Denry Machin, the opportunistic hero of *The Card,* a musical based on Arnold Bennett's novel of the same name, at the Queen's Theatre in London. One London critic complained of Dale's "lack of voice" while granting him "a nimble pair of legs," and another noted his "shy, goofy charm." In a dispatch to the *Christian Science Monitor* (August 2, 1973), Harold Hobson wrote: "He is simply marvelous. I cannot remember having seen a performance so electrical, so exciting, so full of good humor, high spirits, and inspiration in a musical. . . . He radiates happiness."

In sabbaticals from the National Theatre, Dale made several films. One was *Adolf Hitler—My Part in His Downfall* (United Artists, 1972), an anarchic comedy based on Spike Milligan's memoirs of his army service in World War II, in which Dale played the manic Milligan. Another was *Digby, the Biggest Dog in the World* (Cinerama Releasing, 1974), a Disneyesque family comedy in which Dale was animal psychologist to a Brobdingnagian sheep dog. A third was *The National Health, Or Nurse Norton's Affair* (Columbia, 1973), in which he reprised for the screen the dual role he had created on the stage. In another departure from his stage work, he hosted *Sunday Night at the Palladium,* England's most popular television variety show, for a fifteen-week season in 1973-74.

Dale made his American debut as Petruchio when the National Theatre took its three-ring-circus version of *The Taming of the Shrew* to the Brooklyn (New York) Academy of Music in March 1974. While at the Brooklyn theatre the troupe also presented *Scapino.* From May to August 1974 the British company, with Americans added, presented its ever-more-refined adaptation of the Molière farce—a mixture of Italian *commèdia dell'arte,* British pantomime and music-hall comedy, Punch and Judy, and a touch of American vaudeville—at the Circle in the Square in Manhattan. As Scapino, a crafty but ingratiating scamp hoodwinking two miserly fathers in behalf of their lovelorn sons, Dale sang songs of his own composition to his own guitar accompaniment, fell off a balcony, and skittered about the stage doing all the bits of "business" he had developed over the years, including spinning plates of spaghetti without losing a single strand—all the while maintaining an extraordinary rapport with the audience.

The notices Dale garnered were among the most ecstactic for any New York performance in years. Critics placed him in the direct line of descent from such great physical clowns as Bobby Clark, Bert Lahr, W. C. Fields, Buster Keaton, Charlie Chaplin, and Harold Lloyd. Writing in *New York* (June 3, 1974), the fearsome John Simon rated Dale "one of the five or six funniest comedians" he had ever seen. "If I should be granted a dying wish," Simon said, "it would be for a command performance by him—so I could die laughing." His performance in *Scapino* brought Dale the Drama Desk Award, the Outer Critics Circle Award, and a nomination for a Tony.

While looking for a Broadway property to equal or top his tour de force as Scapino, Dale made three Walt Disney movies: the musical fantasy *Pete's Dragon* (Buena Vista, 1977), in which he portrayed the charlatan snake oil salesman Doc Terminus; the comic western *Hot Lead and Cold Feet* (Buena Vista, 1979), in which he had three roles, an eccentric 100-year-old man and his twin sons, one a gun-toting terror and the other a diffident do-gooder; and *Unidentified Flying Oddball* (Buena Vista, 1980), in which he played an American astronaut who is caught in a time warp and winds up in Arthurian England. All three received mixed reviews. Of *Pete's Dragon,* the most ambitious of the three, Janet Maslin wrote in the New York *Times* (November 4, 1977) that it was "the most energetic and enjoyable Disney movie in a long time . . . full of performers who nicely detract attention from each other's weaknesses."

In *Joseph Andrews* (Paramount, 1977), Tony Richardson's screen adaptation of Henry Field-ing's novel about mistaken identities and unknown parentage, starring Peter Firth and Ann-Margret, Dale played the wandering peddler who supplies some missing ancestral links. Although most reviewers exempted Dale from their criticism of the film's ludicrous vulgarity, he himself wondered what he "was doing in it."

Back on the stage, Dale was one of the auditioning comics in Trevor Griffith's *Comedians* at the Mark Taper Forum in Los Angeles in 1977, and he played a performer with a British special service unit in Malaysia in the American premiere of Peter Nichols' *Privates on Parade* at the Long Wharf Theatre in New Haven in 1979. In his notice in the New York *Times* (June 7, 1979) Mel Gussow described Nichols' revue-like comedy as "occasionally outrageous in its humor but also pertinent in its commentary on the hypocrisies of the military and the perils of colonialism. . . . At center stage is the irresistible Mr. Dale, impersonating everyone from Noel Coward to Carmen Miranda."

Dale found the ideal Broadway property he was scouting around for in *Barnum,* a musical about the life and times of the nineteenth-century American showman by Cy Coleman and Michael Stewart. In preparation for the title role, Dale trained in juggling, tightrope walking, trampoline, unicycle, and other such skills at the Big Apple Circus School in Manhattan. He also became an expert on Barnum, steeping himself in literature and memorabilia relating to the "Prince of Humbug" and coming to the conclusion that he "had a kind of elfin quality about him," that Barnum was "ten years old inside, rather like me." He decided that the side of Barnum that he would play up was "his gaiety."

Staged in a circus atmosphere, *Barnum* opened to one huge rave of critical acclaim at the Saint James Theatre on April 30, 1980. "The reviews are too much," Dale commented. "It's as if I'd written them myself." Again, even John Simon could summon not a hint of his dreaded bile. "The damned thing buoys your spirit, lifts up your heart, and *lives,*" Simon wrote of *Barnum* in *New York* (May 12, 1980). About Dale, he wondered how "even he can manage all that charm, wit, energy, multiplicity, Jimdalishness nonstop." Again facing the problem of what to do for an encore, Dale remarked, "The only thing that could top this would be a state funeral."

Dale gave his last performance in the Broadway production of *Barnum* on October 11, 1981, when his contract expired. According to reports in the press at the time, the producers of the show were trying to sign him to salvage their road company, which had disbanded because of poor business. The reports indicated that Dale was asking for an arrangement that would bring him $40,000 a week for starring in the musical in Los Angeles and San Francisco for about five months, beginning in December 1981.

Lean and bony, and with a weathered face, Jim Dale has mischievous aqua eyes, a warm, sunny disposition—and smile to match—and a range of voices to equal his physical agility. When he wishes, he can revert to his Midlands accent, which has been described as sounding like a man "talking with a mouthful of marbles." On March 23, 1981 Dale married Julie Schafler, the owner of a crafts gallery on Madison Avenue. He was previously married, in England, to Patricia Gardiner, by whom he has three sons, Murray, Adam, and Toby, and a married daughter, Belinda Stock.

Dale lives in a co-op apartment on Park Avenue in Manhattan that is decorated in the style of a turn-of-the-century nursery and contains his collection of puppets, dolls in bell jars, and other antique toys. He also has a predilection for fishing, although he seldom finds the opportunity to indulge it. In the *Newsday* interview with Leo Seligsohn he compared the challenge of winning an audience's attention to fishing: "When I say challenge, I'm not talking about dangerous things. It's more that when I'm up there [on the tightrope] I'm like a fisherman with 2,000 lines out. It's beautiful. It's the knowledge that each day, when the show begins, you and the audience are all, in a sense, starting from nothing." One of the reasons that his favorite audiences are children, he said, is that "kids know the most important thing, that you can only create magic from nothing." In common with P. T. Barnum, he wants "to give excitement and magic to as many people as possible."

References: *After Dark* 7:52+ D '74 pors, 13:28+ Jl '80 pors; *Guardian* p9 Mr 10 '70; N Y *Daily News* p97 My 30 '74 por; N Y *Post* p15 Je 1 '74 por; N Y *Times* p9 My 27 '74, C p3 My 2 '80 por; *New York* 13:45+ My 19 '80 por; *Newsday* II p3+ My 18 '80 po.

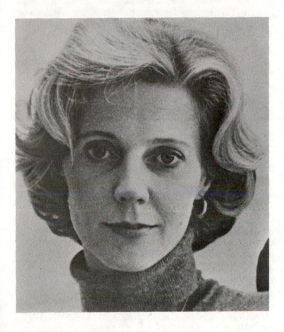

Danner, Blythe

1944(?)- Actress. Address: b. c/o Agency for the Performing Arts Inc., 120 W. 57th St., New York City, N.Y. 10019

Ever since she first captured their hearts as the flighty and sensuously delightful blonde in the hit Broadway comedy *Butterflies Are Free* in 1969, Blythe Danner has remained the darling of the critics. In the intervening years she has honed her craft in a wide range of roles, such as the psychotic Zelda in *F. Scott Fitzgerald and "The Last of the Belles"* and the long-suffering wife of an unfaithful husband in *Too Far to Go*, both on television, and the free-spirited earth mother in the movie *Lovin' Molly*. While she is a favorite with audiences, she has not become a popular idol, and John Simon, one of the most demanding of New York critics, expressed the view of several of his colleagues when he protested that she has been "the most underrated and underused major leading lady of our screen and stage." With her recent portrayals on the New York stage, including that of the cuckolding British sophisticate in Pinter's *Betrayal*, Miss Danner continues to secure her place among the elite of the American theatre.

Of largely German origin, Blythe Katharine Danner was born in Philadelphia, Pennsylvania about 1944, the youngest of three children of Harry Earl and Katharine Danner. She has declined to reveal her birthday because, reportedly, she wants to avoid the possibility of directors' casting her only in roles that match her own age. According to family accounts, she owes her name to her father, who anticipating her career, exclaimed, "Blythe Danner! I can see that name in lights!" At one time, before becoming a banking executive, he had sung with the Philadelphia Orchestra. One of Blythe Danner's brothers, William, heads a violin manufacturing company in Philadelphia, and her other brother, Harry, is an opera tenor. Mrs. Danner also loves music, having once sung professionally. It was to her mother's habit of singing around the house that Blythe Danner attributes some of her early interest in a show business career.

As a young girl, reared in a large house in a community on Philadelphia's Main Line, Blythe Danner conjured up a world of make-believe and peopled it with characters from Grimm's fairy tales whose roles she would act out. "Every childhood should be as filled with fun and fantasy as mine was," she told Mel Gussow, who interviewed her for the New York Times (October 23, 1969). Still, she grew up somewhat aloof from her peers, for while others her age devoured the latest rock 'n' roll hits, she preferred classical music, lieder, and show tunes.

Blythe Danner attended the George School, a coeducational Friends school in Bucks County, Pennsylvania, where she was captain of the swimming team. During a year as an exchange student in West Berlin, she performed in American musicals and on graduation from preparatory school enrolled in Bard College at Annandale-on-Hudson to major in drama. While a student there, she occasionally sang soprano with a jazz group at the Baggy Pants in Stowe, Vermont. After earning her B.A. degree in 1965, she sharpened her skills in regional theatre—at the Theater Company of Boston, where in the spring of 1966 she appeared in The Service of Joseph Axminster and the topical revue The Way Out of the Way In, among other productions, and at the Trinity Square Playhouse in Providence, Rhode Island, where the following spring she had the roles of Helena in A Midsummer Night's Dream and of Irena in The Three Sisters. "Repertory is the best experience I've ever had," Miss Danner said in an interview with Judy Klemesrud of the New York Times (December 7, 1969). "It's a lot better for young actors than Off Broadway is. Every week you're playing another role. I think I grew more in Boston than I ever did [elsewhere]."

One of the ventures of the Boston troupe, Andy and Dave Lewis' World War II drama, The Infantry, became the vehicle of Blythe Danner's New York City debut, which she made in the role of the German girl at Off Broadway's 81st Street Theater in November 1966. She hoped to return from Providence to the New York stage as Michele in David Merrick's Mata Hari, but that musical folded during its pre-Broadway tryout at the National Theater in Washington, D.C. in the autumn of 1967. In March 1968 she accumulated her first considerable batch of notices, all of them favorable, from New York critics, for her portrayal of the Girl in Ron Cowen's Summertime, presented by the Repertory Theater of Lincoln Center at the Forum Playhouse. The next month she played Sister Marthe in that company's production of Cyrano de Bergerac at the Vivian Beaumont Theater. For a later performance there with the Repertory Theater, as Elise in the May 1969 revival of The Miser, she received the Theatre World Award. Meanwhile, she had appeared in two short-lived Off-Broadway productions, the musical Up Eden at the Jan Hus Theater in late 1968 and Someone's Comin' Hungry at the Pocket Theater in March and April 1969. In the latter play, about a crisis in an interracial marriage, she played the pregnant wife of a black Vietnam War veteran.

Later in 1969, on October 21, Blythe Danner made what has been termed her "big league debut" on Broadway at the Booth Theater in Butterflies Are Free as Jill Tanner, the sexually liberated, kooky nineteen-year-old divorcée who soothes and strengthens a young blind man, played by Keir Dullea. Enhanced by Eileen Heckart's forceful performance as the blind youth's overly protective mother who tries to drive a wedge between the lovers, Leonard Gershe's comedy was the first Broadway hit of the season. Along with an Antoinette Perry (Tony) Award for best supporting actress and selection by Variety's poll of New York drama critics as the most promising new Broadway actress, Miss Danner earned many reviews of unalloyed praise.

Writing in Newsweek (November 3, 1969), Jack Kroll marveled at her command of "that female thing of being perceptibly consumed by an emotion while never losing her identity." He went on to observe, "Miss Danner uses everything, the pitch of her voice, the lines of her body, the intimate rhythms of human responsiveness, to turn a conventional part into a formal achievement." Brendan Gill paid homage in the New Yorker (November 1, 1969): "Obviously, she is this season's Girl for All Reviewers to Fall in Love With, but . . . she is a fine actress and will survive our adulation." Upon her entrance at the performance on the night following the Tony ceremonies, the audience gave her a standing ovation that almost cost Miss Danner her composure. "I was terrified," she admitted to Helen Dorsey in an interview for the New York Sunday News (May 12, 1974). "I just about didn't get through the first act because I thought those people came to see what they thought was a great performance. I kept thinking I was going to let them down!"

Butterflies Are Free ran until July 1972, but Blythe Danner left the cast at the end of August 1970, when her contract expired, a departure much in keeping with her eagerness to act in a variety of roles. She continued to perform, occasionally, on the stage, playing the title character in Major Barbara at the Mark Taper Forum in Los Angeles in August 1971, Viola in the Lincoln Center Repertory production of Twelfth Night in March-April 1972, and Nina in The Seagull at the Williamstown (Massachusetts) Theater Festival in July 1974, among other roles. Beginning in 1970, however, Miss Danner became increasingly familiar to viewers of television, on which she had first appeared in 1968 in a bit part in an episode of N.Y.P.D. (ABC). Other TV series on which she had guest shots included the popular murder mystery Colombo (NBC, September 1972) and the satirical M*A*S*H (CBS, February 1976). She also costarred with Ken Howard from September through December 1973 in her own series, Adam's Rib, in which she portrayed a spirited lawyer, Amanda Bonner, the role perfected by Katharine Hepburn in the 1949 film that inspired the TV comedy.

Some of the top-drawer actors that Blythe Danner played opposite in her early TV assignments were Lee J. Cobb in *To Confuse the Angel*, an offering of the Canadian-produced *On Stage* (NBC, March 1970); Joel Grey, who portrayed George M. Cohan in *George M!* (NBC, September 1970); and Bing Crosby in a made-for-TV horror movie *Dr. Cook's Garden* (ABC, January 1971). The presentations of dramatic anthologies produced for public television in which she performed included *The Scarecrow* (Hollywood Television Theatre, January 1972), *To Be Young, Gifted and Black* (NET Playhouse, October 1972), *The Seagull* (Theatre in America, January 1975), and *The Eccentricities of a Nightingale* (Theatre in America, June 1976), in which her interpretation of spinster Alma Winemiller, "the eccentric and the nightingale," impressed John Leonard of the New York *Times* (June 16, 1976) as "superb."

Portraying the mentally afflicted Zelda in ABC-TV's two-hour quasi-documentary *F. Scott Fitzgerald and "The Last of the Belles"* (January 1974), Blythe Danner similarly won the admiration of the television critic John Carmody, who wrote in the Washington *Post* (January 7, 1974) that she and her costar, Richard Chamberlain, played their roles "to perfection." As Alice Sycamore she was the lone normal member in a household of lovable oddballs in the television remake of the hilarious Moss Hart-George F. Kaufman play *You Can't Take It With You* (CBS, May 1979). In another contrasting role, that of the betrayed wife of Richard Maple in a play of disintegrating marriage adapted from a series of short stories by John Updike, *Too Far to Go*, Miss Danner shared the credit with Michael Moriarty for helping to make that drama a "landmark in television programming," as John O'Connor described it in the New York *Times* (March 12, 1979).

Blythe Danner had been interspersing her television work with performances in motion pictures since 1972, when she appeared with Alan Alda in *To Kill a Clown* (Twentieth Century-Fox) and Ken Howard in *1776* (Columbia). The latter is a screen version of the successful Sherman Edwards' stage musical about the quarrelsome Second Continental Congress and its effort to forge a new nation. As Martha Jefferson, the beautiful wife of the author of the Declaration of Independence, Miss Danner appeared just long enough to sing a suggestive song of her husband's lovemaking prowess, "He Plays the Violin." The film received mixed reviews.

Cast in the title role of *Lovin' Molly* (Columbia, 1974), her next movie, Blythe Danner portrayed a sexually accommodating woman in a shifting relationship with two Texas rustics, played by Anthony Perkins and Beau Bridges, over a forty-year period ending in 1965. Although critics again failed to agree on the merits of the film, which was adapted from Larry McMurtry's novel *Leaving Cheyenne* and

directed by Sidney Lumet, Miss Danner won general approval for her role, which required her to be seen briefly in the nude. She had avoided nudity up to that time, but, as she explained in an interview with Helen Dorsey for the New York *Sunday News* (May 12, 1974), "the character of Molly warranted it. . . . Once I realized it was critical to her character, I felt it was far more important than being self-conscious about my body."

In *Hearts of the West* (United Artists/MGM, 1975) Blythe Danner was Miss Trout, a good-hearted script girl who befriends a naïve would-be writer in Hollywood during the 1930's. She matched the strong showing of Jeff Bridges as the writer, of Alan Arkin as the pretentious director of B westerns, and of Andy Griffith as a washed-up actor who becomes a stunt man. Stanley Kauffmann, writing in the *New Republic* (October 25, 1975), singled out Miss Danner as the hit of the film. Several others agreed, even those who disliked the movie. As if in reply to one reviewer who felt that her performance was "too mannered," Frank Rich, then of the New York *Post* (October 3, 1975), contended, "Danner continues to be the most underrated comedienne in American movies right now."

Unenthusiastic notices befell Miss Danner for her part in *Futureworld* (American International Pictures, 1976), a sequel to the generally superior science fiction film *Westworld*. She played Tracy Ballard, a television news reporter who with her former lover and rival in the print media, Chuck Browning (Peter Fonda's role), uncovers a plot to take over the world by power-mad scientists operating a fantasy amusement park as a front for their plans to clone world leaders and program the clones to murder their originals. "Reasonably entertaining escapism" was about the highest praise any reviewer was able to dredge up. But John Simon, who disliked the film intensely, championed Miss Danner in *New York* (August 23, 1976): "One smashing performance, a splendidly understated and absolutely devastating takeoff on certain female TV factotums."

Miss Danner's recent film, *The Great Santini* (Warner Brothers/Orion, 1980), suffered at the box office principally because of public confusion over the title. It is not about a circus performer, magician, or carnival strongman, but rather is the "ripe, bursting story" of Bull Meecham, played by Robert Duvall, a Marine pilot who acquired the nickname of the title during World War II and who in 1962 finds his gung-ho, win-at-any-cost credo to be out of fashion. Miss Danner, as his wife, is torn between love for her husband and concern for their sensitive oldest son growing up under the crushing burden of his father's macho lifestyle and relentless insistence on victory in all things. Typical of the mostly favorable reviews was that of Vincent Canby in the New York *Times* (July 14, 1980), who noted that the three principal characters "play together with the kind of ease and self-assurance that, in a movie, is as exhilarating as it is rare."

"I would love doing some high comedy," Blythe Danner said when she was being interviewed in 1974 for the New York Sunday News. Three years later, in March 1977, she fulfilled that goal in sterling form on the stage with a leading role in Langdon Mitchell's 1906 social comedy, The New York Idea, which launched the semirepertory company of the Brooklyn Academy of Music. During the limited nineteen-day engagement her performance as Cynthia Karslake, a sportive, independent-minded divorcée who eventually reconciles with her husband (played by René Auberjonois), pleased most New York critics and elicited from Jack Kroll of Newsweek (April 11, 1977) this effusion: "Blythe Danner is simply one of the best American actresses: . . . with a face like truth, a golden intelligence and a superb stage voice, she is pure delight from the moment of her entrance."

On January 5, 1980 Miss Danner returned to Broadway in a new Harold Pinter play, Betrayal, an innovative treatment of marital infidelity and its corrosive effect on a marriage in which most of the play's nine scenes move the story line backward in time to unravel the plot. Heading a cast that included Raúl Julia and Roy Scheider, she played Emma, whose affair with her husband's best friend is disclosed in a wrenching scene made all the more tense by Pinter's characteristic pauses and stifled emotion. "With a barely expressed expression, a slight rift in her voice or posture, a hopeful gaze that breaks into smithereens," John Simon wrote in New York (January 21, 1980), "Miss Danner conveys more than most others with a steamer trunkful of Actors Studio tricks." Some reviewers who criticized the play for its chronological gimmickry or lack of substance found in her mastery of a difficult part the production's saving grace.

For its first presentation at the Vivian Beaumont Theater in the fall of 1980, the newly formed Lincoln Center Theater Company, of which Blythe Danner is a member, chose Philip Barry's comedy The Philadelphia Story. The many resources that critics had long recognized sustained Miss Danner in her portrayal of Tracy Lord and in inevitable comparison with Katharine Hepburn, who had created the role on Broadway in 1939 and on the screen in 1940. "If Danner's Tracy isn't at first as fiercely unconquerable—and at last as vulnerable—as Hepburn's, her interpretation is nevertheless a thoroughly satisfactory one," Brendan Gill concluded in the New Yorker (November 24, 1980). Although Frank Rich in the New York Times and John Simon in New York both missed a sufficient change in Tracy's character as the play unfolds, Douglas Watt wrote delightedly in the New York News of Blythe Danner's "radiant, quicksilver performance" on opening night (November 14), and Clive Barnes of the New York Post admired her "surpassing style."

Blythe Danner is favored with blue eyes, blond hair, a slim figure, and a height of slightly more than five feet seven inches. Her throaty voice is one of her assets as an actress. Although she has been described as a "vivacious talker," her few appearances on TV talk shows have proved to be uncomfortable experiences for her, and she is not eager to give press interviews. On December 14, 1969 she married Bruce W. Paltrow, a writer and producer who had cast her in Someone's Comin' Hungry. With their two children, Gwyneth Kate and Jake, they make their home in Santa Monica, California; they also have a Manhattan address. Blythe Danner enjoys cooking, along with various other domestic tasks, and skiing, and because of her interest in ecology, she takes part in the drive to decrease the nation's dependency on nuclear energy and promotes solar energy, recycling, and clean air.

References: N Y Post p15 Ap 13 '74 por; N Y Sunday News III p1 My 12 '74 por; N Y Times II p1+ D 7 '69 por; Newsday A p48 N 10 '69 por; People 11:108+ Mr 19 '79 por; Seventeen 32:38+ O '73 por; TV Guide 21:21+ O 27 '73 por; International Motion Picture Almanac, 1980; Who's Who of American Women, 1981-82

Dausset, Jean

Oct. 19, 1916- French medical scientist.
Address: b. Institut de Recherches sur les Maladies du Sang, Hôpital Saint-Louis, 2 Place du Docteur-Fournier, Paris 75475, France; h. 9 rue de Villersexel, Paris 75007, France

The 1980 Nobel Prize in Physiology or Medicine was shared by Jean Dausset, Baruj Benacerraf, and George B. Snell, immunogeneticists whose research in cellular structure has enhanced physicians' understanding of the body's immunological system and contributed to the increasing success of organ transplants. Drawing on the results of his colleagues' earlier experiments with animals, Dr. Dausset, a specialist in blood diseases, demonstrated, in the late 1950's, the existence in humans of a genetically controlled system of antigens—the histocompatibility complex—that determines the body's response to foreign tissue grafts. As the Karolinska Institute, which makes the Nobel award, explained in its accompanying citation, Dausset's contribution was "to dramatically blaze the trail" toward organ transplants by showing that a transplant between individuals having identical tissue types had the greatest chance of success. But the results of his studies have even more far-reaching implications because knowledge of the body's immune system makes it possible to explain the susceptibility of certain individuals to infections, diseases, and tumors. In 1977, after teaching for many

Jean Dausset

years as a professor at the University of Paris, Dausset was appointed professor of experimental medicine at the prestigious Collège de France.

Jean Baptiste Gabriel Joachim Dausset was born on October 19, 1916 in Toulouse, France, one of the three children of Henri Dausset, a well-known physician and radiologist, and his wife, the former Elisabeth Brullard. After attending the Lycée Michelet in Paris, Dausset enrolled, in the late 1930's, in the medical school of the University of Paris. Drafted by the French medical corps at the outbreak of World War II, he later volunteered to serve with the Free French in North Africa. Before leaving for Tunisia, Dausset gave his identity papers to a Jewish colleague at the Pasteur Institute to help him evade the Nazis. He returned to France in time to take part in the Normandy campaign.

Mustered out of the military service in 1945 with the rank of second lieutenant, Dausset received his M.D. degree from the University of Paris in 1945. He completed his internship and residency in internal medicine and hematology at the Hôtel-Dieu, St. Louis, Broussais, and St. Antoine municipal hospitals in Paris between the years 1946 and 1950. In 1946 he was appointed director of laboratories at the National Blood Transfusion Center, a position he retained until 1963. He took a leave of absence in 1948 to accept a fellowship in hematology at Harvard University Medical School, and he then stayed on an extra year as a fellow in immunohematology.

While working in the resuscitation service during World War II, Dausset became interested in the biological side of medicine, particularly the immunological aspects of blood

transfusions. Considerable progress was made in the study of blood types and blood-typing techniques in the years immediately after the war, discoveries that led to further developments in the field of hematology and, eventually, to advances in immunology, which has always largely depended on scientific contributions from related disciplines. Dausset began investigating blood replacement transfusion methods in the mid-1940's, and by the end of that decade he had published more than twenty papers on the subject. In one paper published in 1951 he outlined the adverse reactions to transfusions caused by strong immune anti-A antibodies in the plasma of universal donors and showed how the systematic testing of donor blood for those antibodies helped to prevent such accidents. Dr. Dausset also pioneered a method of exchange transfusion in adults suffering from kidney failure or from septicemia.

Another focus of Dausset's interest during that period, in addition to and consonant with blood replacement transfusion, was autoimmune hemolytic anemia. Using the serological characteristics of the corresponding autoantibodies as a base, he classified the various forms of that disorder, which is caused by the destruction of red blood cells and is often associated with the use of certain drugs. His research into the causes and treatment of agranulocytosis, an acute feverish illness, usually resulting from drug hypersensitivity, manifested as a severe reduction in the leukocyte, or white blood cell count, led him to a significant discovery that was to affect the course of his life's work. The startling results of that research were published, in 1952, in a paper entitled "Présence d'une leuco-agglutinine dans le sérum d'un cas d'agranulocytose" (Presence of a Leucoagglutinate in the Serum of a Case of Agranulocytosis). The paper, which he wrote with a colleague, described, for the first time, an immunological reaction in which antibodies reacted with white blood cells in the donor's blood, but not with their own leukocytes. Because blood transfusion is a form of tissue transplantation, Dausset's observations seemed to offer a possible solution to the problem of histocompatibility— the capacity to accept or reject a tissue graft. That phenomenon had been extensively investigated in experimental mice, but not in humans.

In research with congenic mice beginning in the mid-1930's, Peter Gorer and George Snell discovered that certain antigens—substances that induce an immune reaction—found on the surface of cells could determine whether or not a tissue graft from one animal would be accepted by another. Having determined that the occurrence of a particular antigen was genetically programmed, Gorer and Snell were able to pinpoint the locus of the "major histocompatibility complex" of closely linked genes on one of the chromosomes of the experimental mice.

Dausset extended their work from mice to men with his systematic study of a similar hypothesis in humans and, in 1958, proved the existence of antigens that denote a genetically based histocompatibility complex. He began by studying the antibodies produced by patients with serious blood diseases. Those patients, who had had many blood transfusions, and thus had been exposed to antigens from foreign tissues, made antibodies that reacted with antigens found on leukocytes from others, but not with those on their own cells. Several patients produced antibodies against the same alloleukocyte antigen, which Dausset called MAC, after the initials of three nonagglutinated donors. "This was the first serum to define an HLA [the designation for the human major histocompatibility complex] antigen and led in part to the definition of the histocompatibility system in man," Fritz Bach of the University of Minnesota Medical School said, as quoted in *Science* (November 7, 1980).

Further unraveling the human major histocompatibility complex became the focus of Dausset's work in the 1960's and 1970's. After a period of initial confusion, when various experiments by a large number of independent investigators brought to light an array of antigens whose relationships were unclear, the leading scientists in the field, among them Dr. Dausset, organized a series of international workshops on histocompatibility to compare notes and techniques. At the second of those workshops, held in 1965, Dausset and Pavol and Dagmar Ivanyi, who were then at the Czechoslovak National Academy, delivered a paper that helped to organize and clarify a mass of occasionally conflicting information. In their report the authors described a system of some ten antigens and suggested that the genetic region responsible for the coding of the system, which they designated Hu-1, included several subloci, each of which determined the appearance of a limited number of specific antigens on the surface of human cells. The name of the system was later changed to HLA (for Human Leucocyte, locus-A).

While immunologists conducted experiments to confirm that hypothesis, other researchers found that skin grafts and organ transplants were more likely to succeed if the donor and the recipient shared the same tissue antigens. Working in collaboration with Felix T. Rapaport, Dausset performed a number of skin grafts that showed that antigen incompatibility was harmful to the skin's survival. To obtain a precise analysis of the role of antigens in transplantation, the two doctors started a skin graft program that eventually attracted more than 500 individual volunteers and 200 families. Skin grafts, in various genetical situations, furnished statistical evidence of the importance of tissue compatibility and helped to establish the immunogenetic law of human transplantation. In an effort to persuade surgeons of the need for HLA donor screening in transplant operations, Dausset cochaired, in 1966, the International Tissue Transplantation Conference of the New York Academy of Sciences and helped to found the Transplantation Society, which he served as secretary from 1966 to 1970.

Meanwhile, collaborative serological studies of families made under the auspices of the third and fourth international histocompatibility workshops proved that differences in human tissue types were inherited. To discover whether the genetic concept, as established for Caucasians, was valid for all mankind, the fifth workshop, under the direction of Dr. Dausset, conducted a broad anthropological investigation of fifty-four populations throughout the world. "Disguising ourselves as explorers, we penetrated the thickest jungles, climbed the highest mountains, and sailed to the most forsaken islands to collect samples of blood," Dausset wrote later. "Thus we learned that the genetic laws we had worked out were true in all populations. Fortunately, the biological map of humanity was drawn before the modern mixture of populations, which will soon obscure all the differences."

In the late 1960's Dausset began studying the association between HLA antigens and disease. Although his investigation of a possible link between acute lymphocyte leukemia and HLA antigens produced a negative result, it encouraged other scientists to consider other possibilities and led to the discovery of connections between HLA antigens and juvenile diabetes, autoimmune disease, multiple sclerosis, rheumatoid arthritis, and other illnesses. Dausset discussed the significance and applications of those findings in *HLA and Disease* (Williams & Wilkins, 1977), which he coedited with Arne Svejgaard. Many immunological researchers believe that scores of diseases might be prevented by manipulating the body's natural immune responses to the histocompatibility antigens.

Dausset has written more than 300 articles describing the methods and results of his research for scientific and medical journals, and he has served on the editorial boards of such professional publications as *Vox Sanguinis, Nouvelle Revue Française d'Hématologie, Transfusion, Clinical and Experimental Immunology,* and *Blood.* He is the author of *Immunohématologie biologique et clinique* (Flammarion, 1956) and the coauthor, with George Snell and Stanley Nathenson, of *Histocompatibility* (Academic Press, 1976) and, with Felix Rapaport, of *A Modern Illustration of Experimental Medicine in Action* (Elsevier/North-Holland, 1980). In addition, he edited *Tissue Typing* (S. Karger, 1966) and coedited *Human Transplantation* (Grune & Stratton, 1968), *Advances in Transplantation* (Williams & Wilkins, 1968), *Tissue Typing Today* (Grune & Stratton, 1971), and *Histocompatibility Testing* (Williams & Wilkins, 1973).

Throughout his career Dr. Dausset has held research and teaching positions. He was chief biologist for the Paris municipal hospital system from 1963 to 1978, cochairman of the Institute for Research into Diseases of the Blood from 1963 to 1968 and, since 1968, director of research at the National Institute of Health and Medical Research. From 1968 to 1977 he taught immunohematology at the University of Paris. He has also been a visiting professor at New York University, in 1970-71, and at the University of Brussels and the University of Geneva, in 1977.

Standing about five feet eleven inches tall and weighing around 160 pounds, Jean Dausset has blue eyes and white hair that is combed straight back. Passionately interested in modern art, he was once part owner of Le Galerie du Dragon, a Parisian art gallery that specialized in Impressionistic painting. Hardworking and modest, he has always followed the credo "vouloir pour valoir." "It was a quote he used so often that it became our motto," Felix Rapaport, the director of the Transplantation Service at the State University of New York at Stony Brook and a longtime colleague of Dausset's, explained to a reporter for the New York Times (October 11, 1980). "It means, to achieve any worthy goal, you must wish it hard enough." Dausset married Rose Mayoral on March 17, 1962. The two share their apartment in Paris with their children, Henri and Irène.

An officer of the Legion of Honor and a commander of the National Order of Merit, Dausset has received more than a dozen awards, including the Grand Prix des Sciences Chimiques et Naturelles from the Academy of Sciences, the Grand Prix Scientifique de la Ville de Paris, the Stratton Lecture Award of the International Hematology Society, the Karl Landsteiner Award from the American Association of Blood Banks, and a prize from the Gairdner Foundation. He has served as president of the French societies of immunology, hematology, and transplantation and is a member of several other professional societies. In 1977 he was elected to the Academy of Sciences of the Institute of France and to the Academy of Medicine. Two years later, he was made a foreign honorary member of the American Academy of Arts and Sciences.

References: N Y Times p7 O 11 '80; Newsweek 96:66 O 20 '80 por; Science 118:244 O 18 '80 por; Time 116:57 O 20 '80 por; McGraw-Hill Modern Scientists and Engineers (1980); Who's Who in France, 1979-80

De Montebello, (Guy-) Philippe (Lannes)

May 16, 1936- Museum administrator. Address: b. Metropolitan Museum of Art, 82d St. at Fifth Ave., New York City, N.Y. 10028; h. 1150 Fifth Ave., New York City, N.Y. 10028

In the variety, range, and beauty of its holdings, at least a million and a half precious objects, the Metropolitan Museum of Art is matched by no other museum in the United States and by few throughout the world. The Metropolitan's eighth director since its founding in 1870, Philippe de Montebello supervises the curatorial and educational functions of the museum in a two-man administration that he shares with William B. Macomber Jr., the Metropolitan's president. When they took charge in the spring of 1978, the Metropolitan entered into a period of consolidating the many diversified gains that it had accumulated during the preceding decade of acquisition and feverish expansion under Thomas P. F. Hoving's dynamic leadership. Hoving groomed de Montebello to be his successor after the latter's return in 1974 to curatorial work at the Metropolitan from a four-year directorship at the Houston Museum of Fine Arts. With the intention of making the Metropolitan's own treasures more accessible to the public, de Montebello has favored curtailing the number of traveling blockbuster exhibitions, such as "Treasures of Tutankhamen," on loan from foreign countries. "What I would like to see,"

he told William H. Honan of the New York Times (July 7, 1979), "is the day when people no longer think of the Metropolitan as a place to visit only from event to event, but instead frequently and at will to discover and savor its own inexhaustible riches."

Born in Paris, France on May 16, 1936, Guy-Philippe Lannes de Montebello is a count by descent from Marshal Lannes, Prince de

Siévers, who received the title from Napoleon following his victorious battle in the Italian town of Montebello. Another ancestor, on his mother's side of the family, was the brother of the Marquis de Sade. Marie-Laure de Sade, de Montebello's grandmother, was Proust's model for the Duchesse de Guermantes in *Remembrance of Things Past.* From childhood he was surrounded by people steeped in the arts, as Grace Glueck explained in the New York *Times* (May 26, 1978). His father, Count Roger Lannes de Montebello, was a painter and art columnist; his mother, the former Germaine de Croisset, played the piano and had a literary salon. Her father, Francis de Croisset, wrote plays, and her half sister, the Viscountess Marie-Laure de Noailles, was a patroness of the arts and a friend of Picasso. Philippe de Montebello has three brothers, Georges, Alain, and Henry.

The de Montebello family left France about 1950 to settle in New York City, where Philippe enrolled in the Lycée Français. Later as a student at Harvard University, he majored in art history. He had been painting for some time in a style that he described to Grace Glueck as a "kind of cross between Cubism and Surrealism," but when his father told him, "You have talent but not genius," de Montebello accepted the criticism. In 1956, the year after he became a naturalized American citizen, he interrupted his study to serve in the artillery in the United States Army, where he eventually reached the rank of second lieutenant. Resuming his classes at Harvard in 1958, he wrote a thesis on Delacroix and obtained his B.A. degree *magna cum laude* in 1961.

As a Woodrow Wilson fellow in 1961-62, Philippe de Montebello concentrated on fifteenth- and sixteenth-century Flemish, Dutch, and French painting at New York University's Institute of Fine Arts. The subject of his Master of Arts thesis was the sixteenth-century French artist Jean Cousin. He had only one requirement, the German reading examination, to complete for his degree when, in 1963, Theodore Rousseau, then head of the European painting department of the Metropolitan Museum of Art, offered him the post of curatorial assistant. It was fifteen years before de Montebello found the time to take the German exam and claim his M.A. degree. At the Metropolitan he advanced to the position of associate curator of European paintings, centering much of his research on the artists of the sixteenth-century Fontainebleau School. He also wrote the monograph *Peter Paul Rubens,* which was published by McGraw-Hill in 1968. Aside from working at the Metropolitan, he arranged the Spingold Collection exhibition at Brandeis University in 1965, 1967, and 1968.

In 1969 Philippe de Montebello succeeded James Johnson Sweeney as director of the Museum of Fine Arts in Houston, leaving the Metropolitan with the encouragement of Thomas Hoving, who apparently recognized that he was too ambitious to remain as a subordinate in the European paintings department. As Lee Rosenbaum recounted in *Artnews* (September 1979), from the beginning he had a rather strained relationship with the Houston press, which took some exception to his opposition to using public and museum funds to buy contemporary art because he reasoned that the city's many collectors of contemporary art would probably be donors in time. De Montebello later defended his attitude as "highly logical in a town which hasn't got a single collector of old masters." Giving up his specialty in European painting to become a generalist, as his Houston position demanded, he capably filled the substantial gaps in the collection, acquiring more works for the museum in diverse cultures and periods during his four-year term, it was estimated, than had been acquired during the preceding forty years.

To provide for the expansion of the collection, de Montebello took a principal role in an effort that more than quintupled the museum's general fund, securing a $2,000,000 endowment for acquisitions. The first major purchase from the Agnes Cullen Arnold Endowment Fund, established in 1970, was *The Penitent Magdalen* (1648) by Philippe de Champaigne. Other distinguished works added to the collection were an early Claude Lorrain, a large Theodore Rousseau landscape, the museum's first group of old masters drawings, a Byzantine ivory from the tenth century, and a German reliquary monstrance of the Guelph Treasure from the early fifteenth century. De Montebello also enlarged the professional staff from one art historian to six, set up five curatorial departments and a thriving publications program, contributed to the museum's bulletin, and supervised the preparation of its first illustrated guidebook. He advanced, moreover, a building campaign that included a pavilion designed by Mies van der Rohe. While in Houston he served on the advisory board of the Alley Theatre, from 1970 to 1973, and on the board of trustees of the Chamber of Commerce, from 1969 to 1973.

In view of the planned retirement of Theodore Rousseau, shortly before his death in late 1973, Thomas Hoving recalled de Montebello from Houston to assume, in February 1974, the position of vice-director of curatorial affairs at the Metropolitan Museum of Art. Working side by side with Hoving in what the director called "a massive teaching exercise," de Montebello had charge of acquisition policies and the exhibitions and supervised the work of 125 curatorial employees in eighteen departments. Five months later he was given the added responsibilities for educational affairs when Hoving merged the curatorial and education departments to achieve parity in pay and benefits for the curators and teachers at the museum.

During his three years in his dual executive post, de Montebello participated in a long series of sensitive negotiations with foreign countries for exchange exhibitions in the visual arts. The first show from the Soviet Union, which opened at the Metropolitan in April 1975, was made up of Scythian gold and silver ornaments on loan from the Hermitage Museum in Leningrad and the Lawra Museum in Kiev. In 1976 the Spanish government lent a display of Goya paintings. Impressed by de Montebello's "decisiveness, forcefulness, character, honesty, and 'grand goût,'" as Lee Rosenbaum quoted him in *Artnews* as saying, Hoving placed de Montebello's name first on his three-person list of recommendations for his successor. When Hoving departed in July 1977, de Montebello was given the title of acting director, and less than one year later, on May 25, 1978, he was named permanent director of the Metropolitan Museum of Art.

Because of the Metropolitan's new administrative policy calling for a two-man leadership, de Montebello shares authority with the museum's first salaried president, William B. Macomber Jr., a retired State Department official, to whom he is subordinate. Macomber's responsibility for nonart affairs—such as operations money, the building program, labor problems, and security—frees the director to engage in strictly artistic matters, including work on exhibitions and publications and travel to acquire works of art and to attend conferences with foreign officials. Grace Glueck reported in the New York *Times* (April 8, 1979) that at the Metropolitan the president and the director "are referred to *sotto voce* as Cucumber and the Count of Monte Cristo." Clarifying for her their division of authority, de Montebello explained, "My job is to say, 'We should be doing x and y and z.' His is to say, 'We have money for x and y, and we'll see how we can find the differential for z.' But he can't allow me to be profligate—we review the priorities together." When it came to approving $300,000 to refurbish the stairway that Louis Sullivan had designed for the Chicago Stock Exchange and to install it in the courtyard of the American Bicentennial Wing, Macomber deferred to de Montebello's insistence on the aesthetic need for the authentic staircase.

The search committee of the Metropolitan's board of trustees had been especially impressed by Philippe de Montebello's ability to cooperate with foreign government and museum officials, since he speaks French and Spanish fluently and can converse in Russian and Italian. He had also proved to them to have an "excellent eye" for museum finds through his efforts to acquire the painting *Lavoisier and His Wife* by Jacques Louis David and a rare ninth-century plaque *St. John the Evangelist*. Significantly, about two thirds of the curatorial and education department heads polled by the trustees named de Montebello as their first choice out of some twenty candidates. Dissenters were skeptical about his academic qualifications, citing his lack of a Ph.D. degree and the paucity of his publications. According to press reports, however, de Montebello has proved to be an able, hard-working leader with a winning enthusiasm who is ready to learn from his curators in areas where he is not an expert. Dietrich von Bothmer, chairman of the Greek and Roman art department, described his superior to Lee Rosenbaum as "a very open, immensely accessible and very impartial man," and he noted that under his administration, in comparison to Hoving's dramatic, unpredictable regime, "things are on a more even keel."

Under Philippe de Montebello's guidance, Hoving's master reconstruction blueprint has been proceeding apace with the reinstallations of many collections that are expected to impart a new look to the interior of the museum and constitute major events in themselves for museumgoers. The Sackler Wing, opened in September 1978, contains the Dendur Temple, given to the United States by the Egyptian government, and the Michael C. Rockefeller Wing, unveiled in the spring of 1979, is devoted to primitive art works that originated in Oceania, Africa, and the two Americas. The first phase in the reinstallation of the Far Eastern collections was completed in the spring of 1981 with the dedication of the Astor Court and Ming Room and the Douglas Dillon galleries of Chinese paintings.

In the future, the director announced, there will be fewer costly acquisitions and a minimum of "educational extravaganzas," on which the museum had depended as a prime source of income. Some of those tremendously popular shows were "The Splendors of Dresden" from East Germany and "The Treasures of Tutankhamen," both in 1978, and "Monet's Years at Giverny: Beyond Impressionism," "Treasures from the Kremlin," and displays of ancient Greek art of the Aegean, all in 1979. De Montebello's loan in 1980 of one of the mighty bronze horses from St. Mark's in Venice, long counted among the wonders of the world, was considered "a coup of the first order." The same year museum visitors saw displays of Viking objects from the British Museum and bronze vessels and animals as well as life-size terra cotta figures in "The Great Bronze Age of China" exhibition.

International art exchange has enormous benefits, but, de Montebello asked in *Architectural Digest* (September 1979), "does it not also threaten the museum with a loss of its distinctly precious identity? Could it be that museums are starting to resemble centers for the performing arts?" Confronted with queues of thousands waiting to see a hit exhibition, art lovers are discouraged from visiting the museum to wander about enjoying a few favorite masterpieces in the permanent collection. With his low-key style of administration, de Montebello intends to place new emphasis on such behind-the-scenes functions as research and conservation and to give the curators more time for writing and more recognition.

As de Montebello further commented in *Architectural Digest,* exhibitions must become "smaller, more focused, more curatorial, which does not mean that they will be any less exciting or enriching." He proposed staging a series of "dramatic, yes, even 'romantic'" shows around the museum's permanent holdings similar to "The Arts Under Napoleon" in 1978, which by borrowing from various departments —sculpture, textiles, furniture, paintings, and metalwork—not only offered a comprehensive view of a significant historical period but also permitted the spectator to reexamine the objects in a fresh, broader context. To improve communications with the public, he contemplated the development of both "booklets with itineraries" and detailed monographs on some of the museum's magnificent treasures. In rethinking the educational role of the museum, de Montebello suggested that the Metropolitan should be "a model and resource for the nation in redirecting the focus of our museums," and he envisioned the day when the museum will again be perceived as "a place to visit repeatedly . . . and not simply when a new banner is hoisted on the facade."

Philippe de Montebello received New York University's Alumni Achievement Award in 1978 and an honorary LL.D. degree from Lafayette College in 1979. His club is the Knickerbocker. Grace Glueck described him as "forceful, articulate and poised, with a brisk self-confidence." He is also distinctly personable, a blue-eyed, black-haired man who stands six feet two inches tall and weighs 190 pounds. In his interview with Lee Rosenbaum de Montebello conceded that he sometimes gives the impression of being arrogant and reserved: "Perhaps [it's] because I'm more formal than others. . . . I'm not folksy, I don't slap people on the back, I don't swear, I don't walk around in shirt sleeves. But it's natural, it's me. I'm not putting on an act. . . . I have a certain formal European background, perhaps the tinge of an accent."

With his wife, the former Edith Bradford Myles, to whom he was married on June 24, 1961, and their three children—Marc, Laure, and Charles—de Montebello lives near his work on Fifth Avenue. He sometimes drops into neighboring museums on his way home in the evening. When asked by Malcolm N. Carter in an article for *Artnews* (November 1973) what he would buy, if he could, for his own art collection, de Montebello stressed diversity in adding to the figurines, old master drawings, and modern paintings he already has, selecting a Greek vase, a Chinese bronze, a Renaissance bronze, drawings by Picasso and Matisse, and paintings by Delacroix, Olitski, Frankenthaler, and Motherwell, among others. His recreations include listening to chamber music and playing chess.

References: Artnews 72:59 N '73, 77:82+ S '78 pors; N Y Times III p18 My 26 '78 por, II p1+ Ap 8 '79 por; Who's Who in America, 1980-81

Diamond, Neil

Jan. 24, 1941- Singer; songwriter. Address: b. c/o Management III, 9744 Wilshire Blvd., Suite 507, Beverly Hills, Calif. 90212

Perhaps because of its eclecticism, the music of the bass-baritone Neil Diamond, including his seemingly simple but often elusive pop ballads about loneliness, love, and the healing power of song, appeals to a broader audience than that of most entertainers. Diamond's mellow compositions, with their swelling diapasons and dramatic changes in tempo, began insinuating themselves into the American consciousness in the 1960's, with such songs as the "bubble gum" rocker "Cherry, Cherry," the upbeat country-folk song "Brother Love's Traveling Salvation Show," and the plaintive "Sweet Caroline." Since then Diamond has been represented on the charts by an unbroken string of hits, including "I Am, I Said," "You Don't Bring Me Flowers," "Song Sung Blue," and "Touching You, Touching Me." All of his albums, including that from the soundtrack of the 1980 motion picture *The Jazz Singer,* in which he starred, have passed the million-dollar mark in sales. Diamond has said, "I'm like the Will Rogers of pop. There isn't a musical form that I've heard that I haven't liked. . . . Rock 'n' roll was never substantial enough for me to devote my life to it."

The descendant of Polish and Russian Jews, Neil Leslie Diamond was born on January 24, 1941 in the Coney Island section of Brooklyn, New York to Kieve Diamond, a struggling dry goods store proprietor, and Rose Diamond. Growing up in a succession of Brooklyn neighborhoods as their father moved his business from place to place, Neil and his older brother spent much of their time in the care of Yiddish-speaking grandparents. Constantly changing schools, the introverted Diamond found it difficult to make and keep friends. In his loneliness (evoked in his song "Brooklyn Roads") he habitually indulged in flights of fantasy, which sometimes impeded his school work, and found comfort in an imaginary companion (the title character of his song "Shilo") as well as in music.

Even before he entered the first grade, Diamond was lip-synching operatic recordings, a diversion he picked up from his father, an amateur performer who was popular at parties, and among his earliest idols were the singing cowboys he saw at the movies. While working in his father's store after school, he listened to the top forty songs on the radio, and at home he played his parents' Latin dance records. At Erasmus Hall High School in Brooklyn, Diamond and another future singing star, Barbra Streisand, sang in the same mixed choral group, but they did not know each other at the time. Outside of school, he sang with a pick-up folk group.

As a schoolboy, Diamond discovered that he had "a knack for doing little rhymes," which he would address to girls to ease his shyness in broaching dates. The idea of writing a song did not occur to him until, at summer camp one year, some fellow campers played an original song for the visiting folksinger Pete Seeger. At sixteen, as soon as he learned his first chord progressions on a nine-dollar second-hand guitar he had received as a gift, he wrote his first song, a piece called "Hear Them Bells."

Diamond found songwriting to be "an outlet for a great deal of frustration." "I never had a great deal of self-esteem as a child," he has recounted. "I grew up in a family where everyone else seemed to be something special. A cousin was the smartest kid in school. My brother was an electronic genius, and so forth. I was sort of a black sheep. Writing songs finally gave me something of my own." As a senior in high school he picked up another specialty, fencing.

Also developing an interest in science, especially biology, Diamond thought he might become a physician, and with that in mind he entered New York University as a premed student on a fencing scholarship. But songwriting won out. "I began cutting classes and taking the train up to Tin Pan Alley, [trying] to get the songs heard," he told Ben Fong-Torres of Rolling Stone (September 23, 1976). "I never really chose songwriting. It just absorbed me and became more and more important in my life as the years passed."

In 1962 one of the Tin Pan Alley song-writing mills he had contacted, the Sunbeam Music Company, located in the Brill Building on Broadway, offered him a sixteen-week staff writing contract. Then in his senior year at NYU, Diamond unhesitatingly dropped out of school to accept the offer. He later described

his "apprenticeship" at Sunbeam Music: "You had to tailor your songs to particular artists, and you wrote whatever was in demand. They would post a notice, say, that Johnny Tillotson wanted an up-country song with a positive lyric, and I'd sit down and write it." In the cubicle adjoining his at Sunbeam Music were Jerry Bock and Sheldon Harnick, who later wrote the musical Fiddler on the Roof. Following their example, Diamond went out and bought that invaluable tool of the lyricist's craft, a thesaurus.

Unable to click as a custom tunesmith, Diamond was released by Sunbeam at the end of the sixteen weeks, and he was in and out of other such music publishing assembly lines for several years, until he decided to follow his own bent. In 1965 he rented an office above the Birdland Club, down the street from the Brill Building, and installed a used piano. "I worked there, I lived there, I slept there," he recalled in an interview with Jan Hodenfield of the New York Post (October 30, 1972), "and just began to write the songs I wanted to sing. For one entire year." During that year one of his songs, "Sunday and Me," recorded by Jay and the Americans, finally made the charts, reaching number eighteen in Billboard's "Hot 100" listings at the end of 1965.

Diamond began singing his songs at the Bitter End, a nightclub in Greenwich Village owned by Fred Weintraub, who was then his manager. Through the record production team of Jeff Barry and Ellie Greenwich, he was introduced to Jerry Wexler at Atlantic Records, who in turn introduced him to the late Bert Berns, a songwriter and Atlantic producer who was starting a new record label, Bang Records, with financial backing from Atlantic Records.

Out of his first recording session for Bang, in 1966, came three hit singles: the melancholy "Solitary Man," the up-tempo straight rocker "Cherry, Cherry," and "I Got the Feelin'." He made the charts the following year with "You Get to Me," "Girl, You'll Be a Woman Soon," "I Thank the Lord for the Night Time," and "Kentucky Woman" and in 1968 with "New Orleans" and "Red, Red Wine." In Cashbox magazine's poll of disc jockeys for 1967 he tied with Frank Sinatra for singer of the year.

In the meantime, Screen Gems, the television production company, asked Diamond to create, in his words, "a plain, happy, dumb" song that would move the Monkees—a rock group created expressly for the TV situation comedy of the same name—away from the Lennon-McCartney sound without commercial sacrifice. He succeeded beyond expectation with "I'm a Believer," which was number one in late 1966 and early 1967, and followed that up with "A Little Bit Me, A Little Bit You," with which the Monkees scored almost as well several months later.

At Bang Records, tension between Diamond and Berns came to a head in their bitter disagreement over "Shilo," the singer-songwriter's first attempt at an autobiographical song. Diamond has told how he kept asking to record "Shilo" and how Berns kept postponing such a radical departure from the safe formula of a "Cherry, Cherry" or "Kentucky Woman." (The song was finally recorded in 1967.) Adding heat to the discord was the rivalry between Fred Weintraub and Berns, who, according to Jerry Wexler, was "zealous and jealous about what he considered his equity."

Escaping what he regarded as an explosive situation, as well as his failed first marriage, Diamond moved to Los Angeles. There he signed with Uni Records, the record division of MCA's Universal Studios, for $250,000 after considering many other offers. The greater artistic freedom granted him by Uni paid off in instant musical growth, evident in the singles that represented him on Billboard's Top 100 chart between the spring of 1968 and the following winter: "Brooklyn Roads," "Two Bit Manchild," "Sunday Sun," and "Brother Love's Traveling Salvation Show." "Sweet Caroline" climbed to the number four spot soon after it entered the Billboard listings in June 1969, and "Holly Holy" rose to number six later in the year.

The Uni album Velvet Gloves and Spit (1968) was the first of Diamond's seven gold albums for Uni. The bearded jacket portrait and some of the lyrics of the Uni album Brother Love might suggest to some a socially involved Diamond, in tune with the "flower power" and protest movements of the late 1960's. But the suggestion would be false, he assured Ben Fong-Torres in the Rolling Stone interview. An essentially reclusive artist, he said that he "could never identify" with and "never did understand . . . this rebelliousness," and that he "could never relate . . . hanging out with people" to what he "was trying to do, which was essentially to try and be Alan Jay Lerner and George Gershwin." "I didn't have time to be hip and 'with it' and groovy."

Contributing to Diamond's status as the top-selling male vocalist of 1970 were the number-one single "Cracklin' Rosie" and the top-ten album Gold. His ambitious LP Tap Root Manuscript ranked sixteenth on the Billboard charts early in 1971, giving him four top-selling albums at once. A stunning example of Diamond's experimentation in pop crossbreeding, Tap Root Manuscript contained cuts ranging from the rock hit "He Ain't Heavy, He's My Brother" to "The African Trilogy," a tracing of the stages in individual human life and, rhythmically, an exploration of the African roots of gospel music. During 1971 his album Touching You, Touching Me appeared on the charts, as did "Stones" and the LP of the same title at the end of the year.

The most wrenchingly personal of Diamond's autobiographical songs was "I Am, I Said," the title of which comes from the line, "I am, I said to no one there/And no one heard at all, not even the chair" (Prophet Music Inc., 1971). It was inspired by his tryout for the title

role in the film version of Julian Barry's Lenny, based on the life and words of the late, controversial comedian Lenny Bruce, notorious for his obscene, scatological language. Diamond explained to Ben Fong-Torres in the Rolling Stone interview that "all the anger that was pent up" in him came out with the Brucian words he had to mouth, and he "couldn't deal" with it. "It was frightening because I had never been willing to admit this part of my personality." In addition, he said, he was depressed over the screen test, thinking he had done badly. Sitting in his dressing room afterward with his guitar, he "just came out" with the song, and he "went into therapy almost immediately after that." Apparently Diamond did not do as poorly in the screen test as he imagined, but the film production was postponed, he became involved in other projects, and Dustin Hoffman ended up in the title role of Lenny (United Artists, 1974).

In contrast with the palpable depression of "I Am, I Said" was the exhilaration in creativity expressed in "Play Me" and "Song Sung Blue," both of which were included in the 1972 album Moods. A performance by Diamond at the Greek Theatre in Hollywood was recorded live for Hot August Night, released later in the same year, the first double album ever to generate sales of over $2,000,000 worldwide.

On the concert circuit in 1972, Diamond was described by Grace Lichtenstein of the New York Times (October 1, 1972) as "a mod Jewish cowboy with dark brown hair flowing to his shoulders, electric guitar draped over a fringed buckskin suit" who was "totally in command, belting out tunes in a rich baritone." On October 5, 1972 Diamond became the first pop-rock star to headline on Broadway and the first solo artist since Al Jolson in the 1930's to be booked by the Shubert Organization at New York City's Winter Garden Theater. The heavily promoted twenty-show engagement was a success at the box office, but the reviews were mixed. While some critics were put off by his "posturing," Robert Christgau of the New York Daily News (October 6, 1972) could report, "For the most part, his singing combines rawness and control in a way that can please both rock fans like myself and the stylish young adults who were as proud as Neil himself to take over the Winter Garden."

Following his Winter Garden engagement, Diamond took himself off the road and went into temporary semi-retirement for several years in order to take stock of himself personally and professionally, to devote more time to his family, and to catch up on the study of music, especially the technical language of classical music. His few recordings during that sabbatical included the albums Rainbow (1973), Jonathan Livingston Seagull (1973), and Serenade (1974). Jonathan Livingston Seagull—which did even better commercially than Hot August Night—was from his original-score soundtrack for the film of the same title, for which he received a Grammy, a Golden Globe award, and an Oscar nomination. It was the first recording released under a $5,000,000, five-year contract with Columbia Records, to which he was signed by Clive Davis.

Resuming his concert work, Diamond toured New Zealand and Australia in January 1976, and the following July he was the opening attraction at the new Theatre for the Performing Arts at the Aladdin Hotel in Las Vegas, which paid him $500,000 for three performances. On the eve of the Aladdin engagement, a squad of Los Angeles policemen, acting on an anonymous tip that Diamond had a stash of cocaine, raided his home. They found a half ounce of marijuana but no cocaine, and after he joined a drug education program the marijuana charge against him was dropped.

For his concept album *Beautiful Noise* (1976), an affectionate backward look at the history of Tin Pan Alley, Diamond expanded his talent by obliging himself to write in virtually all of the pop forms in vogue over the previous seventy-five years. The recording was produced and arranged by Robbie Robertson, the lead guitarist of The Band, and among the many musicians backing up Diamond were saxophonist Tom Scott and organist Garth Hudson. Diamond climaxed the album, as Joan Downs observed in her review in *Time* (August 23, 1976), "with the lush strings and clouds of sound that he loves" in "If You Know What I Mean"—an ostentatious big-band production that had "the ring of yet more gold."

A return engagement at the Greek Theatre was the source of Diamond's album *Love at the Greek* (1977) and of his first television special, which had been put off for years partly because he preferred being a famous voice with an unknown face. He carried off the *Neil Diamond Special,* aired on NBC, with a low-key projection that was judged by the reviewer for *Variety* (February 23, 1977) to be "near perfect for the cool medium."

His second TV special, *I'm Glad You're Here With Me Tonight,* shown on NBC in November 1977, was reprised on his next album, with the same title. One of its selections, the wistful "You Don't Bring Me Flowers," whose lyrics Diamond wrote in collaboration with Alan and Marilyn Bergman, in turn became the Grammy-nominated title song—this time a duet with Barbra Streisand—of an album released in 1978. In 1978 Diamond was inactive for three months, recuperating from an operation for a tumor on his spinal cord.

Diamond was among the many guest performers seen in the concert film *The Last Waltz* (United Artists, 1978), Martin Scorsese's documentary of the final reunion of Bob Dylan and The Band. His first starring big-screen venture was the title role in *The Jazz Singer* (Associated Film Distributors, 1980), created by Al Jolson in 1927 and recreated by Danny Thomas in 1953. In the third version of *The Jazz Singer,* Yussel Rabinovitz (Diamond), the assistant to his cantor father (Laurence Olivier) in a Lower East Side synagogue, forsakes his roots and his marriage for a new life as a Los Angeles recording artist and a new *shiksha* love (Lucie Arnaz). As in the previous versions, there is a tearful reconciliation when he returns to Manhattan to sing the "Kol Nidre" in place of his ailing father at Yom Kippur. "There were so many connections between it and me," Diamond has said of the role. "I used my Jewish background, even to teaching Yiddish to Olivier." He sang both traditional Jewish melodies and his own originals, of which "Love on the Rocks" and "Hello, Again" zoomed to the top of the charts. The soundtrack album, which also includes "America," the movie's signature song, has grossed more than the film itself.

Jerry Leider, the producer of *The Jazz Singer,* was "surprised and devastated" when the movie's bad notices outnumbered the good ones four to one, but Diamond was philosophical. "We expected serious critics wouldn't like it," he told a reporter. "It is not an art movie. It is a modern-day Hollywood musical." In the Chicago Tribune (December 14, 1980) Larry Kart observed: "Even if one has a low tolerance for schmaltz, the film . . . has a core of authenticity to it, especially when Diamond is front and center. . . . Acting may not be the right word for what Diamond does on screen, but his ability to convey a sense of power-in-reserve, to delineate a character whose emotions are always simmering under the surface, is rare enough to suggest that he has a full-blown movie career ahead of him."

By the beginning of 1981, Diamond's total sales internationally were approaching the 50,000,000-record mark. With practice, his showmanship on stage has become as masterful as his perfectly formulated recordings, and his rapport with audiences extends to leading sing-alongs, hugging and kissing female fans, and posing for photographs even during his performance. But he is most at home artistically in his composing, which he views as his "shield." "It's like being invincible, like no one can hurt me." The process, he says, "basically begins with a feeling," which sometimes "expresses itself in a melody, and the melody writes the words."

Tall, dark brown-haired, and soft-spoken, Neil Diamond usually impresses interviewers as being vulnerable, open, and personable. Although better at verbalizing in interviews and less moody than before he underwent psychotherapy, he is still intense and often restless, with a large fund of nervous energy. A non-joiner who does not socialize easily, he winds down by playing chess, riding his motorcycle, going on movie binges, and, when in New York, going from the first act of one Broadway show to the second of another and finally to the third act of still another. His favorite charities include his parents, whom he staked to an early retirement, various drug rehabilitation programs, a camp for artistically gifted underprivileged children, the Robert F. Kennedy Memorial, and the Bedford Stuyvesant Restoration Corporation.

Diamond and his wife, the former Marcia Murphy, have two sons, Jesse and Micah. By an earlier marriage to a childhood sweetheart he has two daughters, Marjorie and Elyn. With his present wife and his two sons, Diamond lives in homes in Malibu and Beverly Hills. The singer-songwriter—whose psychotherapy consisted chiefly of probing the meaning of his own compositions—told Jan Hodenfield in the New York Post interview that the public too must look to his music more than to publicity if it wants to know and understand him. "I've only exposed myself through my music. I did do interviews when I first had hit records, but they were with teen magazines and after a year I decided I could not discuss what my favorite color was. So I didn't do interviews for three years. Then I realized you do need public relations . . . and I went through four or five PR firms and was totally uncooperative with all of them. Only devotees of my music know who I am, because my music says what I am. It speaks about what I feel as a person, what I dream about, what I hope to be, what I ache for, what I love, what I laugh at, what my weak moments are, what my strong moments are."

References: Biog News 1:268 Mr '74 por; Chicago Tribune mag p20+ D 14 '80; Nat Observer p16 S 2 '68 por; N Y Post p17 O 30 '72 pors; N Y Times II p1+ O 1 '72; People 11:52+ Ja 22 '79 pors; Rolling Stone p100+ S 23 '76 pors; O'Regan, Suzanne. Neil Diamond (1975)

Dickinson, Angie

Sept. 30, 1932- Actress. Address: b. c/o Blake Agency Ltd., 409 N. Camden Dr., Beverly Hills, Calif. 90212

Stardom eluded the grasp of Angie Dickinson as, for two decades, she played everyone's understanding wife or favorite girlfriend in motion pictures. Then, in 1974, with hesitation, Miss Dickinson accepted the lead in a television series, NBC's *Police Woman*. As the first hour-long dramatic action show built around a female character, glamorous but tough undercover cop Sergeant Suzanne ("Pepper") Anderson, *Police Woman* was a landmark, paving the way for such later entries as *Charlie's Angels*. The show became a hit and Angie Dickinson finally achieved stardom, with three Emmy nominations tendered her during its four-year run. Returning to the big screen, Miss Dickinson scored the greatest success of her career in Brian De Palma's controversial thriller *Dressed to Kill* (1980). But to long-term Dickinson fans, including David Thomson, her best film will probably always be the one in which she graduated from grade B to grade A— Howard Hawks' *Rio Bravo* (1959). In his *Biographical Dictionary of Film* (1976), Thomson wrote of Feathers, the frontier gambling hall hostess she portrays in *Rio Bravo*: "For all that the role seems restricted to *genre*, Feathers is one of the truest female characters in modern cinema. And it is characterized by Angie's ability to inhabit a man's world without asking for concessions and without needing to rock the conventions."

Angie Dickinson—who derives her current last name from her first marriage—was born Angeline Brown on September 30, 1932 in Kulm, North Dakota, where her parents published the Kulm weekly *Messenger*. With her sisters, Marylou and Janet, she grew up in Kulm, in Edgeley, North Dakota (where her parents published the Edgeley *Mail*), and in Glendale, California. The family was Roman Catholic, and Angie attended parochial schools before matriculating at Glendale College, where she met her first husband, a fellow student, Gene Dickinson, from whom she was divorced in 1959.

After graduating from Glendale College, Miss Dickinson worked as a secretary for an aircraft company. Her interest in a career in show business lay dormant until her girlfriends persuaded her to enter a local television beauty contest, just as a lark. Her winning the contest led to a place in the chorus line of the network television show *The Colgate Comedy*

Hour, starring Jimmy Durante—and to the awakening of her acting ambition. Being, as she once described herself, "of the practical sort," she held on to her livelihood as a secretary while looking for, and occasionally finding, bit parts in television dramatic shows produced in Burbank, California. At the same time, she attended Batami Schneider's acting workshop and took singing and dancing lessons.

Miss Dickinson made her motion picture debut delivering the single line "Happy birthday, Uncle Otis" in *Lucky Me* (Warner, 1954), starring Doris Day and Robert Cummings, and she had similarly minuscule roles in *Man With the Gun* (United Artists, 1955), *Tennessee's Partner* (RKO, 1955), and *Tension at Table Rock* (RKO, 1956). She moved up to weightier portrayals as the frontier woman who dies trying to save the bank-robber hero (James Arness) in *Gun the Man Down* (United Artists, 1957), as the half-caste ex-prostitute using her charms as anti-Communist weapons in Samuel Fuller's *China Gate* (Twentieth Century-Fox, 1957), about French Foreign Legionnaires in Indochina; and as gun moll to Rod Steiger in *Cry Terror* (MGM, 1958).

The director-producer Howard Hawks "discovered" Miss Dickinson not via the large screen, but the small. Alerted by Chris Nyby, then one of his assistants, Hawks watched her in an episode of *Perry Mason*. Impressed, he signed her to a seven-year contract and gave her the only substantial female role in the western *Rio Bravo* (Warner, 1959), starring John Wayne, Dean Martin, and Ricky Nelson. As Feathers, the girl with a past, she caught the eye of critics, especially the male reviewers. Not untypically, Philip K. Scheuer of the Los Angeles *Times* (March 19, 1959) wrote: "Miss Dickinson, a tall, shapely brunette with an irresistible Mona Lisa smile, plays it cool in much the same enigmatic but fascinating manner as Lauren Bacall in Hawks' memorable *To Have and Have Not*."

While not denying some sexual exploitation, Hawks himself thought he had helped Miss Dickinson "to get past the bathing beauty syndrome," as he told Digby Diehl of *TV Guide* (January 4, 1975): "I changed her acting style a little by making her slow down. She used to say her lines as though she were trying to get rid of them. . . . Of course, she does have great legs, and we made use of them, too."

David Thomson (who confesses that Miss Dickinson is his "favorite actress," although he realizes that "her virtues are probably not those of a leading actress") wrote in his entry on her in his cinematic dictionary: "It is significant that in her best film, *Rio Bravo*, she appeared very happy with Hawks' masculine code and ensemble playing. But equally, her Feathers in that film could be defended as a portrait of an intelligent, nervous, attractive woman that perfectly embodies the director's philosophy."

On the strength of her success in *Rio Bravo*, Hawks sold Miss Dickinson's contract to Warner Brothers, to her regret. "I had signed to be under contract to Howard, and I felt that under his guidance I had a good shot at stardom," she recalled in an interview with Ron Base for the Chicago *Tribune* (October 28, 1979). "But not at Warner's. They had stopped developing stars. They used me in parts nobody else wanted." Those parts were the following: the nurse who makes successful overtures to Richard Burton in *The Bramble Bush* (1960), a voyeuristic social drama in the *Peyton Place* tradition; wife to Danny Ocean (Frank Sinatra) in *Ocean's Eleven* (1960), a flippant story about a caper pulled off by a merry gang of criminals (Sinatra's real-life "Rat Pack") in Las Vegas; spouse of a politician (Don Ameche) who tries to bribe a judge in *A Fever in the Blood* (1961); the title role of the spinster missionary who bears an illegitimate child in *The Sins of Rachel Cade* (1961); and the femme fatale in *Rome Adventure* (1962). Her general attitude toward the Warner films was summed up, she said, by Richard Burton when he remarked, concerning *The Bramble Bush*, "I know we have no masterpiece on our hands, but we'll do our best." A common critical response was expressed by Irene Thirer of the New York *Post* (March 23, 1961) in her review of *The Sins of Rachel Cade*: "The talent of attractive Angie Dickinson is wasted on so trite and stagy a story."

On Broadway, Miss Dickinson starred with Gene Barry and Jan Sterling in *The Perfect Setup*, a comedy about a businessman with a wife in the country and a mistress in the city. The show closed after five performances at the Cort Theatre in October 1962. Venturing outside of her contract with Warners, she played the title role in *Jessica* (United Artists, 1962), about an American nurse who disturbs the peace of a small Sicilian village, setting the blood of the male population aboil and, consequently, drawing the ire of the female population. "As the unwitting temptress, Angie Dickinson is definitely a sight to behold," A. H. Weiler wrote in the New York *Times* (April 20, 1962). "The role . . . does not require much beyond physical attributes, and the honey-haired Miss Dickinson, in shorts or tight-fitting bodices, undulates through her assignment to perfection."

After extricating herself from her Warner Brothers contract, Miss Dickinson signed a seven-year pact with Universal, lured by the chance to star opposite Gregory Peck in the army hospital drama *Captain Newman, M.D.* The bait turned out to be less substantial than she had anticipated, as Richard L. Coe observed in the Washington *Post* (March 28, 1964): "On the edges of these [hospital] situations, Angie Dickinson is a sympathetic nurse, a role which asks for far less than this individualistic player could give."

"After *Captain Newman*, that was it," Miss Dickinson recalled in the Chicago *Tribune* interview with Ron Base. "Universal never followed it up with anything. I was dressed beautifully, but I didn't seem to fit into any of their categories. They didn't know what to do with me." They starred her in a remake of *The Killers* (1964), in which, as the unscrupulous Sheila Farr, she betrayed Johnny North (John Cassavetes) in accordance with the master criminal plan of her lover, Browning (Ronald Reagan). They then featured her (as an affianced American lady) with James Garner, Dick Van Dyke, and Elke Sommer in *The Art of Love* (1965), a comedy about an American artist (Van Dyke) in Paris.

As she had done previously at Warner Brothers, Miss Dickinson won release from her contract at Universal. Remaining in Paris after the shooting of *The Art of Love*, she was studying French with the idea of appearing in motion pictures in Europe, but two events intervened. One was her marriage to Burt Bacharach, the composer. The other was a call from producer Sam Spiegel, when she was visiting London, asking her to star with Marlon Brando, Jane Fonda, and Robert Redford in *The Chase* (Columbia, 1966), an opulent melodrama about terror in a Texas town. Her role in *The Chase*—as the loyal wife of a sheriff (Brando) protecting from an angry populace an escaped convict mistakenly suspected of murder—was, as various reviewers described it, "subdued," "plain," "comfortable," and "closer to normal" in a film that generally perished of "perverse giganticism."

In *Cast a Giant Shadow* (United Artists, 1966), Miss Dickinson played the spouse of Colonel David (Mickey) Marcus, the American lawyer-soldier who became a fanatic leader in the battle for the establishment of the state of Israel in 1947. "Miss Dickinson does a good job," the reviewer for *Variety* (March 30, 1966) observed, "in a role that calls for her to be a flip, sardonic chick, also an adoring wife."

Miss Dickinson was the saloon keeper in love with Marshal Dan Blain in Richard Thorpe's western *The Pistolero of Red River* (MGM, 1967), which was also distributed under the title *The Last Challenge*. In the violent *Point Blank* (MGM, 1967), she helped a double-crossed thief (Lee Marvin) to wreak vengeance on his betrayers and retrieve his loot. Martin Levine of the *Washington Post* (March 21, 1969) advised his readers that if going to see the comedy western *Sam Whiskey* (United Artists, 1969)—in which Burt Reynolds had the title role—was "better than a lot of other ways of killing two hours, the reason is Angie Dickinson." He elaborated: "She's been around for a long time, and although she lacks any reputation as an actress, here she's a sexy, classy, funny one."

Less successful was another, zanier comedy, *Some Kind of Nut* (United Artists, 1969), in which Miss Dickinson played one of the women in the life of a bank clerk (Dick Van Dyke) who grows a beard as an act of rebellion against conformity. She costarred with Robert

Mitchum and Burt Kennedy in *Young Billy Young* (United Artists, 1969), about corruption in a New Mexico town, and she was one of the principals in the science-fiction thriller *The Resurrection of Zachary Wheeler* (Vidtronics, 1971), the first American motion picture to use a videotape-to-film process. In Roger Vadim's *Pretty Maids All in a Row* (MGM, 1971) Vadim's first American film, a tasteless excursion in prurient gallows humor starring Rock Hudson as a murderously satyric high school athletic coach and guidance counselor, she played a nymphomanical teacher, and she was amusing as the less-than-bereaved wife of an assassinated Los Angeles crime syndicate chief in *The Outside Man* (United Artists, 1973). Nude scenes of Miss Dickinson and William Shatner from an unexpurgated print of *Big Bad Mama* (New World, 1974), a grade-C "girl gang" movie set in Texas in 1932, found their way into *Hustler*, the "skin" magazine, five years later.

Meanwhile, Miss Dickinson had been making occasional appearances in television dramas, but she was opposed to any extended work in television, such as a series, that would interfere with her personally raising Nikki, her daughter by Burt Bacharach. After she guest-starred as Sergeant Pepper Anderson in an episode of *Police Story* on NBC in 1973, she was asked to carry a spinoff in the Anderson role. On the iron-clad condition that work on the show be limited to a four-and-a-half day work week, with shooting ending at 6 P.M. each day, she accepted. She explained: "I've got a contract that supposedly will allow me to be in a series and still live like a human being."

Introduced into the NBC Friday evening line-up in September 1974, *Police Woman* presented Angie Dickinson as a member of a Los Angeles Police Department vice squad team who was called upon to pose each week as a gangster's girlfriend, a prostitute, a go-go dancer, and the like. In January 1975 the series became the top-rated show on television, and it remained in or near the top ten into 1977. Analyzing the success of *Police Woman* in the Washington *Post* (May 9, 1975), Tom Donnelly wrote: "[It] is an often listless and almost always hackneyed series. . . . It must have something. But what? The signature sequence that opens the show every week may provide a clue. There are closeups of the lushly pretty face of Angie Dickinson. Angie smiling. Angie grimacing in terror. Angie being mugged. Angie aiming a gun. Angie trying on brass knuckles. And, above all, closeups of Angie's torso swathed in a satin evening gown and of Angie's legs descending a staircase. . . . Maybe *Police Woman* is a big draw because Angie Dickinson is the nearest thing to an old-time Hollywood glamour queen the tube offers in a regular series." Aside from *Police Woman*, Miss Dickinson's most successful television venture was the title role of the adulterous Army wife in Pearl Harbor, 1941, in ABC's *Pearl*. Televised in November 1978, *Pearl* was the eighth most watched miniseries in history.

Miss Dickinson portrayed the title character in *The Suicide's Wife,* (CBS, 1979) a made-for-television movie about a university assistant professor seeking tenure who succumbs fatally to publish-or-perish pressure. In *Klondike Fever* (CFI, 1980), based on the adventures of Jack London in the Klondike gold rush and starring Rod Steiger and Jeff East, she was a saloon madam.

Brian De Palma explained why he cast Angie Dickinson as Kate Miller, a frustrated suburban matron with a wandering eye and violent fantasy life who becomes the victim of a razor-wielding transvestite sex maniac in *Dressed to Kill* (Filmways, 1980): "I wanted someone to convey an erotic sensibility, but not blatantly. Angie was the right combination." A box-office smash, *Dressed to Kill* was also a critical success, giving Miss Dickinson, as she said, "for the first time . . . this instantaneous reaction, the feeling that I'm a hot number."

Hailing *Dressed to Kill* as "the first great American movie of the eighties," David Denby of *New York* (July 18, 1980) wrote: "Violent, erotic, wickedly funny, *Dressed to Kill* is propelled forward by scenes so juicily sensational that they pass over into absurdity. . . . Angie Dickinson is so sad and sweet in this movie! She has the symmetrical bone structure of a classic beauty—the kind of bone structure that implies breeding and control and dignity in old age. Yet Kate is a woman churning around inside and falling into rapt fantasies, and De Palma, with his teenager's dirty-mindedness and entertainer's instinct working in tandem, can't help seeing her tremulous longings as funny." The reviewer for *People* (August 18, 1980) described Miss Dickinson as "looking indecently gorgeous at forty-eight" in what is, "except for the bloodbaths . . . the season's most dazzling, high-gloss chiller."

Dissenting criticism ranged from the academic charge that *Dressed to Kill* is "a total cheat" artistically, that it "represents pure exhibitionism" and "vulgar manipulation of the emotions for pure sensation" to angry indictment of a film that "perpetuates the ideology that brutality, pain, and humiliation are essential to women's sexuality." Miss Dickinson's response to the criticism, and especially to the protests by feminist groups, was quoted in *People* (September 15, 1980): "I suppose there are rapists and murderers walking around just waiting to be triggered, and this could do it. But so could an innocent billboard of a woman cutting a melon."

Angie Dickinson, who is five feet five inches tall, says she keeps her weight at approximately 115 pounds by exercise and "just not eating." Her once auburn hair is now dyed blond, but her mischievously dancing eyes and radiant dimpled smile have not changed. In his Chicago *Tribune* article Ron Base, who once observed her on location in British Columbia, wrote: "At five in the morning . . . , her hair in curlers, *sans* makeup, fantasy disintegrates with a thud, and she is a middle-aged woman. Carefully prepared, though, the old Hollywood alchemy still works, and she is once again the movie starlet, honey-blond and dazzling. And that 500-watt smile of hers can still reduce you to so much blubbering mush when she decides to turn it on full force."

Separated from Burt Bacharach since 1976, Miss Dickinson filed for divorce in November 1980. She lives in an eight-room house in Beverly Hills with her daughter, Nikki, and a housekeeper, and she occasionally socializes with such friends as Ben Gazzara, Peter Falk, the Kirk Douglases and Gregory Pecks, and agents Swifty Lazar and Sue Mengers. In the past, gossip columns used to buzz with stories linking her romantically to such men as Frank Sinatra, the late David Janssen, and even President John F. Kennedy.

"I've learned that you use what you've got to the best of your ability," the actress told Digby Diehl in the *TV Guide* interview. "It took me a while to realize that it's OK just to be there and glamorous. I'm not an actress in the same sense that Geraldine Page or Anne Bancroft is. . . . There are usually a lot of holes in motion-picture scripts and you have to fill them with personality, not acting. . . . Right now, I'm very happy being a sex symbol." Recently she amended that philosophy, saying, "But I will not embarrass myself by pretending to be thirty when I'm fifty. Life is going on, maybe alone, but at least up." Her proudest boast is her recognizability by her first name alone: "People only have to say 'Angie,' and they usually know who it is."

References: *Ladies Home J* 92:67+ Je '75 por; *N Y Mirror mag* p9 Mr 5 '61 por; *N Y Post* p42 Mr 22 '75 por; *People* 10:120+ N 27 '78 pors; *TV Guide* 23:23+ Ja 4 '75 por; *Washington Post* B p1+ My 9 '75 por

---

Doe, Samuel K(anyon)

May 6, 1951(?)- Head of state of Liberia. Address: Executive Mansion, Monrovia, Liberia

In the predawn hours of April 12, 1980 a band of soldiers under the leadership of twenty-eight-year-old Samuel K. Doe, a master sergeant of the National Guard, stormed the executive mansion in Monrovia and assassinated Liberian President William R. Tolbert Jr. and twenty-seven officials and guards. "The rampant corruption and continuous failure by the government to effectively handle the affairs of the Liberian people," Doe maintained, "left the enlisted men no alternative." After proclaiming himself head of state and commander-in-chief of the armed forces, he established a People's Redemption Council (PRC), composed

Samuel K. Doe

of noncommissioned officers, to run the government and appointed himself its chairman. The ousting of a civilian rule by a military junta surprised foreign diplomats and many Liberians themselves, because Liberia, a long-time United States ally, had been regarded as one of the most stable nations in Africa.

Among the probable underlying causes of Doe's coup, however, is a glaring, historic ethnic split in Liberia's population. The nation's ruling majority, of which Tolbert was representative, is made up of Americo-Liberians, descendants of the freed American slaves who founded the West African colony in 1822 and established it as a republic in 1847. The majority of the country's 1,800,000 inhabitants are indigenous Africans who retain cultural links to their tribal origins. Those so-called "country people," the group to which Doe belongs, have long resented the Americo-Liberians' favored political, economic, and social status.

Samuel Kanyon Doe was born on May 6, 1951 in Tuzon, Grand Gedeh County, in eastern Liberia, the son of Matthew G. K. and Anna Doe. His father, now seventy-eight, is, according to different accounts, a retired farmer, a former private in the Liberian army, or a former schoolmaster. His mother is forty-five years old. Doe is a member of the Krahn tribe, one of Liberia's sixteen major tribal groups, which to some extent still observe traditional African customs and have been less affected than Americo-Liberians by Western cultural influences.

Tuzon remained Doe's home until his graduation from elementary school in 1967. He then enrolled at the R. B. Richardson Baptist Junior High School in Zwedru, the capital of Grand Gedeh County, but dropped out of school in the eleventh grade for "economic reasons." The principal of Doe's high school, Amos Sawyer, is now dean of Liberia College in Monrovia and a close adviser to Doe. At the age of eighteen, on July 11, 1969—two years after leaving school—Doe enlisted in the Liberian armed forces and was sent, along with other new recruits, to the John H. Tubman Military Training Camp in Todee, in the coastal county of Montserrado.

After completion of the early phase of his training in 1970, Doe was transferred to Camp Schiefflen, also in Montserrado County, and shortly thereafter was assigned to the third battalion at Barclay Training Center in Monrovia. In the evenings he resumed his high school education, attending classes in the Barracks Union School at Barclay and in Marcus Garvey Memorial High School. Doe also enrolled in the Ministry of Defense Radio and Communication School in Monrovia, completed the course in 1971, and, according to an official biographical sketch, received his diploma "with honor." In 1973 Doe, still a private, was made acting first sergeant in command of 150 troops. Other assignments put him in charge of the Central Prison, the Post Stockade, and the Military Arsenal in Monrovia and, later, a detachment of soldiers stationed in Grand Cape Mount County.

In the military, Doe quickly earned a reputation "as a skilled sharpshooter and an agile hand-to-hand combat fighter," as reported in the New York Times (April 24, 1980). On August 19, 1975 Private Doe was promoted to corporal and, on the following day, to the rank of first sergeant. Because of his combat skill, he was selected in January 1979 to be among those trained at Camp Todee by the American Special Forces, better known as the Green Berets. Doe's official biography described that cadet training program as "several months of vigorous basic unit and advanced unit courses" including "combat and advanced individual (infantry) training." One senior American diplomat who visited the camp while training was in progress was particularly struck by Doe's performance and was later introduced to him.

When his Special Forces training ended, Doe was reassigned to the third battalion at Barclay Training Center as adjutant in charge of administration; and on October 11, 1979 he was promoted to master sergeant. Pranay B. Gupte in the New York Times (April 24, 1980) described Doe during that period as "career-oriented" and "apolitical," an ambitious young man who "always chafed at the thought that his own progress upward through the military might be hindered because the highest officer positions always went to . . . Americo-Liberians." Gupte based his characterization of Doe on reports given by his colleagues in the National Guard.

The dominant political party in Liberia since 1955, when President William V. S. Tubman proclaimed opposition parties illegal, had been the True Whig party, which was pledged to economic development and the integration of the country's two major cultural groups. After Tubman's death in 1971, ending his twenty-seven-year administration, Vice-President William R. Tolbert Jr. became head of state. In 1975 Tolbert was elected to a term that was to expire in 1983, in accordance with a new provision in Liberia's constitution limiting Presidents to a single eight-year term in office. His program of limited reforms included building new roads and improving educational and health facilities. He brought increased trade and foreign investments to Liberia and took a role in international relations, such as serving as chairman· of the Organization of African Unity, that heightened his country's prestige.

"As Tolbert's foreign stock rose, however," J. Gus Liebenow wrote in Current History (March 1981), "his domestic base became untenable because of the unbridled greed and corruption of the Americo-Liberian class and the centrality of his own immediate family in the mounting system of avarice." As an example of "public waste in behalf of Whig vanity," Liebenow pointed to the expenditure of more than $200,000,000 on the 1979 OAU meeting in Monrovia. By the late 1970's a serious challenge to True Whig rule had come from a newly recharged leftwing movement within the country, the two major elements of which were the Marxist Progressive Alliance of Liberia (PAL), led by Gabriel Bacchus Matthews, and Dr. Togbanah Tipoteh's Movement for Justice in Africa (MOJA), which sought the elimination of class and tribal differences through social restructuring.

On April 14, 1979 a protest against a proposed rice-price increase in Monrovia turned into a political riot in which $35,000,000 worth of property damage occurred and forty-one demonstrators were killed. President Tolbert believed that PAL, which had been involved in the riots, triggered the violence in an effort to foment civil unrest and opposition to the government. As a consequence, he arrested Matthews and several other PAL leaders and briefly imprisoned them. Nevertheless, in January 1980, to relieve tension, the Tolbert government accorded PAL legal status under the name of the People's Progressive party, or PPP. Shortly thereafter the PPP called for a general strike to overthrow the government, with the result that in March 1980 Tolbert again ordered the arrest and imprisonment of Matthews and his associates. Charged with sedition and treason, they were scheduled to go on trial before a military tribunal in mid-April. Meanwhile, the London-based human rights organization, Amnesty International, accused Tolbert of offering rewards for the capture of other PPP leaders.

Doe had close ties with the PPP and MOJA. In late 1979 several of his allies in the PPP asked Flight Lieutenant Jerry Rawlings, who had spearheaded the leftist military coup in Ghana in June of that year, to come to Liberia for an advisory briefing. Rawlings, however, declined the invitation. Little is definitely known about the planning of the Liberian coup, although it is supposed that details of the operation were probably put in final form during late-night poker games in the military barracks. According to Newsweek (May 5, 1980), some well-informed Liberians believed that "Doe was merely a stalking-horse for Matthews and Tipoteh." But Liebenow called attention in his Current History article to lack of evidence that "the coup was a product of military-civilian conspiracy" or, indeed, that "the coup was anything other than a sporadic decision on the part of Master Sergeant Doe and his fellow Krahn."

About 1 A.M. on the morning of April 12, 1980, President Tolbert returned from a Baptist conference and went to bed in the executive mansion. A short time later Doe and a seventeen-man assault team from the first brigade of the National Guard besieged the mansion, engaging in a short, sharp gun battle with Presidential guards. Shooting also occurred simultaneously at several military installations. Early reports indicated that Tolbert died as a result of three gunshot wounds to the head. But a secret pathology report later revealed mutilation indicative of the plotters' extreme enmity. The bodies of the twenty-eight persons who died in the coup were dumped into a pit that became their unmarked grave.

One of Doe's first official acts as head of state was to free the jailed leftists. He named Gabriel Bacchus Matthews Minister of Foreign Affairs and Togbanah Tipoteh Minister of the Economy in his Cabinet, which was formed shortly after the takeover and which included several of the PPP and MOJA followers, as well as military officers. As if to prove his contention that he opposed discrimination against the Americo-Liberians, Doe also gave Cabinet posts to a few Tolbert officials who were known to be advocates of reform.

Real power, however, was vested in the People's Redemption Council, or PRC, a committee of soldiers that continues to exercise effective political power in Liberia. Following the coup, high-ranking military officers lost their standing, and junior officers, primarily captains and lieutenants, were promoted to senior ranks. For a time, soldiers wandered the capital triumphantly, firing their guns in jubilation, looting, and commandeering private vehicles. Substantial civilian looting also occurred, and the homes of former government officials were ransacked. Some officials were stripped naked and paraded through the streets to the taunts of jeering crowds. Finally, in a successful attempt to curb the anarchy, a nighttime curfew was imposed and three soldiers and a civilian were executed by a firing squad as a harsh warning to would-be looters. United States military advisers counseled Doe on how to control the violence.

Two days after the coup Doe, dressed in green army fatigues, wearing sunglasses, carrying a hand grenade in his belt, and flanked by enlisted men holding rifles, made his first national televised appearance. In his speech he promised a government without discrimination, respect for property rights and free enterprise, openness to foreign investment, and increased emphasis on housing, transportation, and food. He also announced sharp pay hikes for military personnel and civil service workers. "Gone forever are the days of 'Who you know,' and 'Do you know who I am?' " Doe assured the people. "We now enter a time of 'What can you do?' " On excursions into the streets of the capital, he was greeted by cheering throngs, indicating undisputed popular support for his rule.

Fulfilling one of his early vows as head of state, Doe ordered his soldiers to round up and jail some ninety former officials of the Tolbert regime so that they could stand trial for "high treason, rampant corruption and gross violation of human rights." Thirteen of the most important officials were tried first, before a military tribunal and without benefit of defense counsel. When the court advised that only four of the officials be put to death, Doe overruled the tribunal and personally ordered that all thirteen be executed, despite pleas for clemency from foreign diplomats. On April 22, 1980 the condemned men were executed by firing squad before thousands of cheering onlookers on a seaside beach at the Barclay military installation in Monrovia. Among those killed were Frank Tolbert, the former President's brother; Foreign Minister Cecil Dennis, one of the continent's most highly regarded diplomats; the Chief Justice of the Liberian Supreme Court; the speaker of the House of Representatives; and the chairman of the True Whig party.

Other African nations quickly expressed their disapproval. In early May a meeting of the Organization of African Unity in Lagos, Nigeria refused to seat the Liberian representatives, even though the country held the chairmanship of the organization. On May 27 Doe was personally barred from a meeting of the Economic Community of West African States in Tago, where he reportedly arrived in combat gear and armed with pistols. After that, no further executions of former Tolbert officials took place, and in an effort to improve relations with other African states, Doe visited Ethiopia and Tanzania.

Although Doe faced no organized opposition at home to his overthrow of Tolbert, in late April 1980 he felt the need to legalize his control by a declaration of martial law that vested all power in the People's Redemption Council and suspended Liberia's constitution. He announced that elections and a return to civilian rule would not take place for a least three years. He later explained that he could not restore civilian government until he had eased Liberia's economic distress. Soon after seizing power, Doe discovered that Liberia had $5,-000,000 in the national bank and $700,000,000 in foreign debts. In August 1980 United States officials, fearful that Doe would turn to Communist countries for aid—as he threatened to do—increased assistance from $8,000,000 to $25,000,000 for the fiscal year, an increase Doe dismissed as "token." Later the Carter Administration promised to send $47,000,000 and 200 military trucks. Meanwhile, Doe's government staved off bankruptcy with emergency loans from the United States and other foreign sources. To promote stability in Liberia and strengthen pro-American leanings, the United States sent 100 Special Forces to Monrovia in April 1981 for joint exercises with Doe's military forces.

With exports of iron ore and rubber declining because of a worldwide recession, Doe sought to protect Liberia's other major source of revenue by announcing soon after the coup that the government would continue unchanged its system of registering foreign tankers and other ships—a practice that appeals to shipowners because of Liberia's relatively low registration fees and lenient safety requirements. The economic situation in Liberia was worsened under Doe's rule by military intimidation of Indian and Lebanese merchants and Americo-Liberians, driving both capital and skilled Liberians out of the country. An estimated $27,000,000 out of $130,000,000 in Liberian banks may have been transferred elsewhere. In November 1980 the unemployment rate stood at 50 percent. Late that year, in order to win an $85,000,000 assistance loan from the International Monetary Fund, Doe agreed to strict austerity measures, including reductions in government spending and a freeze on government hiring. Nevertheless, monthly government revenues eight months after the coup stood at $17,000,000, while expenditures were $30,-000,000.

Samuel K. Doe and his wife, Nancy, have two children. A man without ostentation when he came to power, Doe later exchanged his modest car for a Mercedes-Benz limousine and, instead of his military fatigues, sometimes donned well-tailored suits. He is slightly built and stands five feet ten inches tall, but boots make him appear taller. Associates have said that he is not gregarious and fraternizes mainly with a small circle of army friends. Swimming and running are his recreations. Doe has been described in the Western press as articulate and sincere, though ignorant of statesmanship. Amos Sawyer told newsmen that recent months of intensive decision-making have matured him and that he eagerly seeks guidance in his goal of giving Liberians a new constitution.

References: N Y Times A p9 Ap 24 '80 por, A p8 Ja 20 '81 por; Newsweek 95:50 Ap 28 '80 por, 97:49 Ja 12 '81 por; Time 115:34 Ap 28 '80 por, 116:56 S 15 '80 por, 118:47 S 14 '81 por; International Who's Who, 1981-82; International Year Book and Statesmen's Who's Who, 1981

Drabble, Margaret (drab′əl)

June 5, 1939- British writer. Address: b. c/o A. D. Peters and Co., 10 Buckingham St., London WC2N 6BU, England

Although her fiction relies on the conventions of the old-fashioned novel, the British writer Margaret Drabble has had few, if any, literary precedents to guide her in treating situations that women, and to a lesser extent men, are experiencing for the first time in history. Her early novels read somewhat like subtle self-analytical case histories of intelligent young women who themselves cannot make do with the old solutions. The inner world of her characters is still Miss Drabble's concern, but beginning with *The Realms of Gold* (1975) and continuing through *The Middle Years* (1980), she has shown an expansion of consciousness that led Phyllis Rose to comment in the New York *Times Book Review* (September 7, 1980), "She is becoming the chronicler of contemporary Britain, the novelist people will turn to a hundred years from now to find out how things were, the person who will have done for the late-20th-century London what Dickens did for Victorian London, what Balzac did for Paris." Her work has wide appeal not only because of the timeliness of her subject and her lively, lucid readability, but also because of her skill in writing on more than one level of meaning. Weidenfeld and Nicolson is Margaret Drabble's publisher in England. In the United States her first four novels were published by William Morrow & Company; since 1969 her novels have been published by Alfred A. Knopf.

London may be Margaret Drabble's principal territory, but she has a special feeling for the provinces that she owes to her roots in the North of England. She was born in Sheffield, Yorkshire on June 5, 1939 to John Frederick and Kathleen Marie (Bloor) Drabble. Her father is a retired circuit judge for Suffolk and Essex, and her mother was once a teacher of English. The fact that her maternal grandparents came from the Potteries region is for Margaret Drabble a point of affinity with the novelist Arnold Bennett, who had a similiar background. There were three other children in the family: an older sister, Antonia Susan, who, under the name A. S. Byatt, became a noted novelist and literary critic; a younger sister, Helen, now an art historian; and a younger brother, who followed the father's choice of law as a career. Interviewed for *People* magazine (October 13, 1980), Mrs. Drabble recalled that Margaret "was a fiery child with a hyperactive mind. She gave me many sleepless nights. In Christmas pantomines, Margaret was invariably a witch, dark and scowling."

The Drabble family shared an enjoyment of reading that made literature a part of Margaret Drabble's life from an early age. A book that deeply influenced her moral thinking as a very young girl was John Bunyan's *Pilgrim's Progress*. She was also strongly, but not repressively, affected in her religious values by her education at a Quaker boarding school, the Mount School in York. Once she had overcome a childhood stutter, her consciousness of right and wrong and her propensity toward arguing causes made her a persuasive debater. Like her older sister, with whom she engaged in continuous rivalry, she went from Mount School to Newnham College, Cambridge, to which she had won a major scholarship. There she concentrated on English literature and wrote a thesis on Arnold Bennett that contributed to her graduating with first-class honors in 1960.

At Cambridge, however, Miss Drabble did not become associated with any literary group. In an interview with Peter Firchow for *The Writer's Place* (1974), she said that the atmosphere at Cambridge, partly because of the exceedingly high standards of F. R. Leavis, had been forbidding to a person with creative aspirations. The circle in which she chose to move was theatrical. As a student she spent a lot of time on the stage, playing, for instance, opposite Derek Jacobi in *'Tis Pity She's a Whore*. Another of the plays in which she appeared was *Deutsches Haus,* presented in London in 1959. About the time of her graduation, in June 1960 she married the actor Clive Walter Swift, with whom she then spent a year as a member of the Royal Shakespeare Company at Stratford-on-Avon.

When she saw that assignments such as understudying Vanessa Redgrave in *Cymbeline* were leading nowhere, Margaret Drabble felt attracted to motherhood. Idle during pregnancy, she wrote her first three novels while she was expecting her three children. From the beginning, with one or two exceptions, she wrote about persons of her own age, because she best understood their points of view and because writing novels was a therapeutic means of sorting out her own immediate problems. During her last year at Cambridge she had discovered vast resources of literary material in Simone de Beauvoir's *The Second Sex*. In her early novels she wrote about what it means to be a woman in a man's world, to play the feminine role imposed by men. Commenting on her work in a statement for *Contemporary Novelists* (1976), Miss Drabble explained, however, "My books are I think mainly concerned with privilege, justice, and salvation. Equality and egalitarianism preoccupy me constantly, and not very hopefully. None of my books is about feminism, because my belief in the necessity of justice for women (which they don't get at the moment) is so basic that I never think of using it as a subject. It is part of a whole."

In a salute to Arnold Bennett, Margaret Drabble gave the name Sarah Bennett to the heroine of her first novel, *A Summer Bird-Cage* (1963). A recent Oxford graduate, Sarah has now to answer the question of what she will do with her life. The problem of choosing between marriage and a career is compounded, on the one hand, by her discouraging observations of the marriage-for-money of her older sister and, on the other, by her perception that despite her scholarly inclinations she cannot be a don. "You can't be a sexy don," she is convinced. "It's all right for men, being learned and attractive, but for a women it's a mistake."

The witty, vigorous style and attention to ordinary details of contemporary life that delighted reviewers of *A Summer Bird-Cage* also characterized *The Garrick Year* (1964), which Margaret Drabble based in part on her year with the Royal Shakespeare Company. Emma Evans, the principal figure, reluctantly leaves London, where she has an opportunity for a television career, to spend a season in Hereford with her two young children and her husband, an actor in a repertory company. Her ambivalent feelings about her sexuality affect both her relationship with her husband and her love affair with her husband's theatrical producer. But while her assent to marriage remains qualified, in a crucial incident in which her daughter is almost drowned, her maternal instincts are solidly confirmed. "Here is a writer of real intelligence," a reviewer of the London *Times Literary Supplement* (July 23, 1964) concluded, "using the English language with precision but without affectation, and shaping words and plot to a clear purpose. She has the cogency of an Iris Murdoch without the creamy symbolism."

When interviewed for the *Atlantic Monthly* (November 1980), Margaret Drabble replied to one of Diana Cooper-Clark's questions, "I see motherhood in such positive terms that I feel almost embarrassed to admit it. I think it's the greatest joy in the world." Because of that conviction, she was able to make what Bernard

Bergonzi in *Contemporary Novelists* thought was her "particular contribution to the contemporary novel." He pointed out that "for many novelists the emancipated woman and the mother are two sharply different types: Margaret Drabble has shown that in the modern world the two roles are often combined in the same person."

Rosamund Stacey, accordingly, in *The Millstone* (1965) is a bright Cambridge graduate student at work on a thesis on Elizabethan sonnets. When she unintentionally becomes pregnant, she amazes her scholarly friends by deciding to give birth to her illegitimate child, whom she then takes care of by herself while following through on her goal of becoming a university don. The experience proves to be a means of liberation and emotional growth for a young woman of puritanical views and constricted academic values. *The Millstone* was made into a 1969 motion picture, with the novelist's script, starring Sandy Dennis and titled *A Touch of Love* in England and *Thank You All Very Much* in the United States. (Also in 1969 Miss Drabble's play *Bird of Paradise* was produced in London. Her television play *Laura* had been produced by Granada Television in 1964.)

Switching from first-person narration to third person, Margaret Drabble nevertheless made *Jerusalem the Golden* (1967) probably the most openly autobiographical of her novels. She later acknowledged in her study of Arnold Bennett her indebtedness to his attitudes, which, anyway, were close to her own, certainly in such a "passion" as "the yearning of the provincial for the capital." As she comes of age, the youngest of Miss Drabble's heroines, Clara Maugham, is obsessed not by prospects of a husband and babies, but by escape to London from the industrial town of Northam and from a neurotic, joyless mother. Not all reviewers liked *Jerusalem the Golden*, but Ellen Cronan Rose appraised it in *The Novels of Margaret Drabble* (1980) as "Margaret Drabble's first wholly realized novel, economical in its construction, finely precise in its characterization of the heroine. In later novels she will be more profound, never will she be more completely in control of her material."

So satisfactorily did the traditional nineteenth-century form of the novel serve Margaret Drabble's desire for clarity that she felt no need for innovative narrative techniques. Although she has a high regard for Doris Lessing's boldly experimental novel *The Golden Notebook* (1962), she deplores avant-garde eccentricities that confuse the reader. In *The Waterfall* she departed from her usually prevailing single point of view to tell the story partially in the third person and partially in the first person—a device that underscores the divided self of her heroine, Jane Gray, a mother of two children, and a poet, who discovers in an extramarital affair her capacity for love. Her confrontation with her feminine sexual nature lends itself well to analysis in terms of the conflicts examined in Valerie Grosvenor Myer's study of Margaret Drabble's work, *Puritanism and Permissiveness* (1974).

Like the novelist herself, Rose Vassiliou, whose journey toward salvation unfolds in *The Needle's Eye* (1972), had been profoundly moved in childhood by her reading of John Bunyan. She is the divorced mother of three children who in her desire to do the right thing has given away her inheritance and lives in a shabby section of London. In a greater renunciation she comes to deny herself other forms of self-abnegation and returns to her husband. "Only a truly serious novelist can be funny," Joyce Carol Oates commented in the New York *Times Book Review* (June 11, 1972). ". . . The Needle's Eye, while addressing itself to a spiritual dilemma so profound that many readers—and writers—will not grasp it at all, is at the same time immensely humorous, readable, 'unserious,' in its depiction of total human beings." One of those human beings is Simon Camish, a self-doubting, unhappily married lawyer who loves Rose. In Bernard Bergonzi's opinion, he is Miss Drabble's "most successful portrayal of a male character."

In *The Realms of Gold* (1975) Margaret Drabble surprised her readers, who had come to expect, at best, an equivocal resolution of her heroines' conflicts, by providing a happy ending for Frances Wingate, a divorced mother of four children. She is a world-renowned archeologist whose realms of gold lie not so much in her excavations of ancient civilizations as in her discovery of a mother-figure in an eccentric, independent, recently deceased great-aunt. The web of subplots and prodigality of everyday detail in the rambling novel permit, despite the upbeat conclusion, abundant opportunity for condemnation of present-day social ills. Miss Drabble stops considerably short, however, of blaming patriarchal oppression for her heroine's frustrations. "I'm not at all keen on the feminist view that there's a male conspiracy to put women down," she said in the *Atlantic* interview.

Even more bleak is the state of the universe, as exemplified by England in the 1970's, in *The Ice Age* (1977), whose title refers to the freeze on wages and other aspects of commercial enterprise in an economic depression and also to spiritual stagnation. The predicament of the country is analyzed through the tribulations of a group of men and women with varied attitudes and backgrounds. Because of her absorption in the interior life of her characters and her care with nuances of sensibility, particularly in her early novels, Margaret Drabble has occasionally been compared to Virginia Woolf and Henry James. But in *The Ice Age*, she more nearly resembles George Eliot, whose social conscience and range of subject matter she greatly respects. Ellen Cronan Rose noted that *The Ice Age* is one of the books in which she demonstrates that, like George Eliot, "she can imaginatively appropriate and convincingly portray male experience."

Explaining why she had made her protagonist in *The Ice Age* a man, Margaret Drabble told Mel Gussow in an interview for the New York *Times Book Review* (October 9, 1977), "I was fed up with women—slightly." Similarly, the central figure of *The Middle Ground* (1980), Kate Armstrong, a divorced mother of three children and a popular journalist, is growing tired of many areas of her life, including women's issues as the chief subject of her reportage. Adrift between the past and the future, uncertain of purpose, she suffers through her middle-age crisis against a London backdrop of changing lifestyles and traditional values and intracultural collisions. In her conversation with Diana Cooper-Clark, Margaret Drabble pinpointed one aspect of her novel: "*The Middle Ground* is about one's children growing up. . . . I've dedicated it to my daughter, because I use quite a lot of copy from her. It's about being the mother of teenage children and knowing that the children are going to be gone any minute now."

Although *The Middle Ground* concludes with the heroine in "an attitude of indecision," it is a less dreary novel than *The Ice Age*. The reader's feeling of reassurance about prospects resembles Margaret Drabble's own reaction to the novels of Arnold Bennett: "He always leaves me with a sense that life is full of possibility." Her affection for Bennett, whom she believes has been underrated, had prompted her, in "an act of gratitude," to continue the research she had begun with her thesis at Cambridge. Between writing novels, she read hundreds of books by and about him in preparation for her *Arnold Bennett: A Biography* (McGraw-Hill Ryerson; Knopf, 1974). "The result," Dennis Potter observed in the *Guardian* (July 11, 1974), "is a warm and exhilarating book, extremely enjoyable, intelligent, partisan and at times combative when putting down the vulpine snobberies of . . . Bloomsbury."

The concern for "ordinary common human experiences" that Miss Drabble has said she admired in Bennett also drew her to William Wordsworth, on whom she wrote a short, straightforward critical study, *Wordsworth* (Evans, 1966; Arco, 1969). Wordsworth, moreover, keynotes *A Writers' Britain: Landscape in Literature* (Thames & Hudson; Knopf, 1979), Margaret Drabble's discussion of the interaction between British literature and the natural environment. Her compilation of literary passages has splendid photographs by Jorge Lewinski. Also notable for its fascinating illustrations is her thought-provoking book for teenage readers, *For Queen and Country: Britain in the Victorian Age* (Deutsch, 1978; Seabury Press, 1979).

In other literary undertakings aside from fiction Margaret Drabble edited the group novel *London Consequences* (Greater London Arts Association, 1972), in collaboration with B.S. Johnson; Jane Austen's *Lady Susan, The Watsons, Sanditon* (Penguin, 1974); and *The Genius of Thomas Hardy* (Weidenfeld, 1975; Knopf,

1976), a collection of critical essays on Hardy's life and work. At present she is engaged in the five-year (1979-1984) task of editing the revised *Oxford Companion to English Literature.* She also writes essays and book reviews for the London *Observer,* the New York *Times,* and the Washington *Post/Book World,* among other publications.

Along with Angus Wilson and two other British writers, Margaret Drabble lectured in Wales in the late 1960's as a member of the pioneer tour of the Arts Council. For some years she has been teaching a weekly class in literature at Morley College in London. Her books won the John Llewellyn Rhys Memorial Award in 1966, the James Tait Black Memorial Prize in 1968, and the E. M. Forster Award in 1973. She received an honorary D. Litt. degree from the University of Sheffield in 1976.

Margaret Drabble and Clive Swift were divorced in 1975. Their three children, Adam, Rebecca, and Joseph, have been living with their mother in a house near Hampstead Heath. So that she can concentrate on her writing without interruption for a few hours several days a week, she rents an office in Bloomsbury. A personable, unpretentious woman, "she has a wide, intelligent face, and cuts a neat, precise figure, scholarly rather than Bohemian," to quote Catherine Stott's impression of her in the London *Sunday Telegraph* (July 6, 1980). Pendennis wrote in the London *Observer* (May 25, 1969) of her "sharp, birdlike eyes and long brown hair." Besides lecturing and teaching, Margaret Drabble occasionally takes part in radio and television discussions and serves as deputy chairman of the National Book League. "The writers that I most admire," she said in the *Atlantic* interview, "are the people who strive to retain their links with the community and not indulge in their own consciousness to such a degree that they become very rarefied."

References: Contemporary Authors 1st rev vols 13-16 (1975); International Who's Who, 1980-81; Who's Who, 1980-81; World Authors: 1970-75 (1980)

Druckman, Jacob

June 26, 1928- Composer. Address: b. Yale University School of Music, New Haven, Conn. 06520

The demanding and complex music of Jacob Druckman, the much honored American composer who won the Pulitzer Prize for Music in 1972, often introduces haunting and tantalizing reminiscences of the tonal music of the past into twentieth century atonality.

Providing a theatrical as well as a musical experience, his work merges tape with live sounds and places as much of a premium on the histrionic and improvisatory ability of the performer as it does on his instrumental or vocal virtuosity. By emphasizing accessibility and communicability, Druckman is trying to bring back to audiences for contemporary music the affection they had for it earlier in the century, before the gap widened so greatly between composers and their alienated listeners. Druckman's music, rich in striking sonorities and intricate percussion effects, synthesizes the past and present so successfully that it is enlarging the audience for experimental music and breaking down the barriers that have existed between symphonic musicians and contemporary composers. Druckman is convinced that "music is moving in the direction of things mystical and romantic," serving as an "accurate barometer of the Zeitgeist."

Jacob Druckman was born in Philadelphia, Pennsylvania on June 26, 1928, the only son of Miriam (Golder) Druckman and Samuel Druckman, a manufacturer. Encouraged by his father, a fine amateur musician, he started piano when he was three but switched to violin three years later. His formative musical training began at the age of ten under Louis Gesensway of the Philadelphia Orchestra who, as Jacob Druckman later recalled to Raymond Ericson in an interview in the New York *Times* (November 4, 1977), provided "the kind of background that stays with you forever."

Louis Gesensway accepted Druckman for specialized training in composition only after the teenager had impressed him with an original woodwind quintet. "[Gesensway's] was really a very interesting and kind of a unique training," the composer told Walter Wager in an article in *ASCAP Today* (January 1974), "because it was a thorough and completely traditional conservatory discipline. I was not even allowed to utter the word 'chord' until I had written a five-voiced mass in 16th Century style." Of special appeal to Druckman were works by Debussy and Stravinsky that "seemed to strike nerves that were receptive to them" and that "coincided with puberty" and his "own awakenings."

During his adolescence Druckman alternated between playing the violin in string quartets and the trumpet in jazz ensembles, for especially during World War II he discovered that there was an enormous amount of work available for musicians. A brief stint as violinist with the Boston Symphony Orchestra at the Berkshire Music Festival at Tanglewood during the summer of 1948 made him feel as if he were "in a chain gang, with nobody caring how [he] felt about music." But private study with Aaron Copland during the following summer at Tanglewood finally persuaded him to pursue a career as a musician.

In the fall of 1949 Druckman therefore enrolled as a scholarship student at the Juilliard School of Music in New York City, where he studied composition under Bernard Wagenaar, Vincent Persichetti, and Peter Mennin, and obtained a B.S. degree in 1952 and an M.S. degree in 1954. He then spent the year of 1954-55 on a Fulbright grant at the Ecole Normale de Musique in Paris. There Tony Aubin piqued his curiosity about orchestration, Jacob Druckman told Raymond Ericson, "by posing the problem of how a certain chord might be scored by different composers." Shortly after his return to the United States, Druckman joined the faculty at Juilliard, where he remained until 1972, teaching courses in the literature and materials of music. From 1961 to 1967 he also taught part-time at Bard College, at Annandale-on-Hudson.

Druckman's early compositions include *Duo* for violin and piano (1949); *Divertimento* for clarinet, horn, harp, violin, viola, and cello (1950); *Laude* for baritone, alto flute, viola, and cello (1952); *The Seven Deadly Sins* for piano (1955); and *Four Madrigals* for unaccompanied mixed chorus (1958). Of particular note was *Dark Upon the Harp* for soprano, brass quintet, and percussion (1962), a richly inventive setting for six of the Old Testament's Psalms.

Like many composers of his generation, Druckman went through a twelve-tone phase, responding to the pressure of his coevals to examine the procedure thoroughly. The result was his String Quartet No. 2, commissioned by the music philanthropic group LADO and consisting of a single seventeen-minute movement distinguished by such technical feats as ricocheting bows and finger tapping. When first performed by the Juilliard Quartet at the Hunter College Assembly Hall on December 13, 1966, the work elicited mixed reviews.

Even while composing his String Quartet, Jacob Druckman was drifting away from the twelve-tone school in the direction of electronic music. He has described himself as a "kind of Johnny-come-lately" to the electronic studio, since his first exposure did not take place until 1965-66 at the Columbia-Princeton Electronic Music Center. "I couldn't wait to get in," he explained to Shirley Fleming in an interview for *High Fidelity* (August 1972). "I hung around for about year until Vladimir Ussachevsky finally admitted me. . . . I thought with electronic tape I can really do something. With a live string quartet you can write maybe five against seven, but with tape I can put thirty-six against thirty-seven if I want to. . . . So that was just what I did. And you know, I listened to it and was totally disenchanted. It was a rather shaking experience. And I realized that it's not the five against seven that means anything, it's hearing the human beings trying to *achieve* five against seven."

Druckman's interest "in people, in human participation" led him instead to involve singers and instrumentalists in the electronic process. He not only merged taped with live music but gave to the concert experience a theatrical impact by engaging performers dramatically as well as musically in a format outside the conventional operatic structure. His series of four chamber-scaled compositions entitled *Animus*, for example, focuses on "a particular area of human affections as well as a limited body of musical materials." *Animus I* for trombone and tape (1966) centers on the dilemma of man (the live trombone player) versus machine (the prerecorded tape of electronic sounds). The story-like framework around which the composer interspersed dramatic-theatrical elements includes the initial dialogue, the temporary "victory" of the tape, whose overwhelming sounds drive the instrumentalist offstage, the player's reappearance once the tape peters off, and the final tenuously balanced exchange. Critical response was divided.

In contrast, *Animus II* for soprano, percussion, and tape (1968) was generally well-received and remains perhaps the best known of Druckman's pieces that combine music and histrionics. As part of its built-in theatricality, the central figure, a mezzo-soprano, slowly proceeds up the aisle and both entices and challenges two percussionists. In the process, according to Harold C. Schonberg in the New York Times (June 1, 1973), she "dances a bit, has her own percussion to play with and moves through the post-*Lunaire* kind of vocal writing with a mean twinkle in her eye and a post-Westian shake of the hips." Thanks in part to the definitive performances of the mezzo-soprano Jan DeGaetani, *Animus II* has already become a classic of the contemporary music scene.

Animus III for clarinet and tape (1969) pits a live clarinetist against the prerecorded electronically-produced sounds of both his own "ephemeral virtuosity" and the "laughter, the banter, the irritation, the fatigue, the impatience" of the recording sessions. Opposing "the human and the inhuman, and man and his present-day sonic environment," it assures, according to the composer's own program notes, "a surreal, aloof arch-virtuosity which follows its whimsy through many states leading to an eventual decay into a mindless hysteria." Covering the New York premiere of *Animus III*, which the International Society for Contemporary Music (ISCM) presented at Carnegie Recital Hall in the fall of 1977 along with two other new works, Peter G. Davis observed in the New York *Times* (November 6, 1977): "Of the three, Mr. Druckman's piece seemed by far the most congenial for its madcap wit, inventive originality and sheer creative vitality as the clarinetist, Stanley Walden, jousted heroically against a veritable sonic hailstorm of electronic explosions."

Luciano Berio, the avant-garde Italian composer who is the electronic music director at the Institute for Research and Coordination of Acoustical Music in Paris, commissioned *Animus IV* for tenor, six instrumentalists, and tape (1977). Like its predecessors, *Animus IV* represents "an exaggeration of those things that are human." It revolves around the tenor protagonist who confronts himself on tape in sometimes humorous, sometimes melancholy fashion, using as his repertory two nineteenth-century songs—Chabrier's *La villanelle des petits canards* and Liszt's *Die drei Zigeuner*. Hitches in technical equipment resulted in its premiere in the Pompidou Center on September 29, 1977 as a straight concert item instead of an integral part of Berio's audio-visual spectacle about the history of electronic music, but *Animus III* nonetheless was greeted with a round of praise from international critics.

At the same time that he was gaining prominence as an electronic composer, Druckman proved himself a master at symphonic orchestration starting in the early 1970's, able, as Andrew Porter of the *New Yorker* (November 20, 1978) pointed out, to create "thin, luminous washes of sound" and "thick, rich impastos." A watershed in his career was *Windows*, a single-movement orchestral piece that captured the Pulitzer Prize for Music in 1972. In an interview with Robert Finn, music critic of the Cleveland *Plain Dealer* (October 13, 1974), Jacob Druckman recalled: "I was reaching for a kind of music that would have about it the perfume of memory, the kind of thing that is so old it sounds like songs your mother taught you, but it really isn't. . . . This is more than a stylistic trick. It is a reaction of 15 to 20 years of strictly controlled post-Webernian structuring, the kind of thing that has held music in a prison. It is also a reaction against the terrible alienation we used to hear about between composers and orchestras, the predictions of doom and the end of music and such."

Commissioned by the Serge Koussevitzky Music Foundation in the Library of Congress, *Windows* was composed expressly for the Italian conductor-composer Bruno Maderna, who had requested a Druckman composition for a guest appearance with the Chicago Symphony Orchestra in the spring of 1972. Large orchestral effects, notably from an enlarged percussion section, alternate with short sudden pauses or "windows," allowing listeners to hear brief melodies by solo instruments much like—the composer has explained—"thick clouds that would part, and one would catch a little glimpse of blue sky." Writing about the premiere of *Windows* on March 16, 1972 for the Chicago *Tribune* (March 17, 1972), Thomas Willis termed the composition an "intriguing admixture of alternately evocative and obscure musical gestures," in which the composer "fashioned planes, layers, and corners of sound" and "found some fascinating, translucent textures of extraordinary vitality."

Another symphonic composition, *Lamia* (1974), embodied Druckman's conviction about the need to "cast off the vanity of this orgy of intellectual approaches to music" and to re-establish the lines of communication between composer and audience. His inspiration for the work stemmed from mezzo-soprano Jan DeGaetani's "magical" performance of *Animus II* at the 1972 Aspen Music Festival when "everything that sounded and befell seemed to be the direct result of her will and her powers." For the "celebration of those powers" Druckman wrote a powerful score for large orchestra plus small ensemble. He chose neither to compose a symphonic portrait of Lamia, a sorceress and vampire in classical mythology, nor to provide musical settings for direct texts about her. Instead he chose quotations from several works of varying age, origin, and language that depicted involvement with the occult ranging from the damning of witches to folkloric dream conjurations.

Lamia was first performed at the Palace Theater in Albany, New York on April 20, 1974 by the Albany Symphony under conductors Juliu Hegyi and Robert Kogan with Miss DeGaetani as soloist. A revised version (1975) included a Malaysian magic spell described by Andrew Porter in a *New Yorker* review (November 3, 1975) as "a conjuration to call back a human soul that has darted from its body like a little bird." "Imaginative, dramatic in effect, cleverly orchestrated and often amusing" was Harriett Johnson's verdict in the New York *Post* (October 18, 1975) the day after the premiere of the revised version at Avery Fisher Hall on October 17, 1975 with Pierre Boulez and David Gilbert conducting the New York Philharmonic. Echoing her sentiments in the New York *Times* (October 18, 1975), Allen Hughes called Druckman "erudite, catholic in his tastes, and with an ear for sumptuous sound."

National recognition for Druckman as one of the leading younger composers in the United States came on the occasion of the country's 1976 bicentennial celebration, when he was awarded two out of the six commissions for an orchestral composition to be funded by the National Endowment for the Arts and to be given its premiere by a major American orchestra. Five other orchestras later performed the works on a round-robin basis over a three-year period. Both of Druckman's compositions—*Mirage* (introduced by the St. Louis Orchestra under Leonard Slatkin on March 4, 1976) and *Chiaroscuro* (given its premiere by the Cleveland Symphony Orchestra under Lorin Maazel on April 14, 1977)—documented his premise that musical ideas, rather than being developed in a preordained way from a stated theme, should gradually evolve out of shadowy beginnings and be enhanced by after-images. Vivid color, tonal subtleties, and "layers of consciousness," created in part by having twenty-four musicians play offstage initially, characterized *Mirage* and established its kinship with Debussy's *Sirènes*, "the musical progenitor of such layered illusion." As its title suggests, *Chiaroscuro* depicts the musical equivalents of *chiaro* (light) and *oscuro* (dark) in Italian Renaissance painting. In Druckman's articulate opinion, "the opening dense, dark sound slowly clarifies and reveals simpler sounds within it almost as a dark gem slowly turned will reveal each of its facets in turn." Significantly, reviewers have often resorted to terms borrowed from art criticism in evaluating Druckman's work.

The majority of critics employed incandescent phrases in assessing the two pieces—such as "a mosaic that makes the ear visualize as it listens" and "a post-Debussian exercise in magic sound which elucidated the continuing and growing mastery of means and ends of this fine American composer." A negative response came from a mere handful of critics, among whom was a disgruntled Harold C. Schonberg, who observed in the New York *Times* after the New York premiere of *Chiaroscuro* at Avery Fisher Hall on November 3, 1977: "Mr. Druckman is an experienced composer, and there can be no complaint about the professionalism of his organization and orchestration. On the other hand, the music echoes most of the clichés of the immediate past. It is athematic, dissonant, full of constant movement but with very little that grips the imagination. Basically it is academic modernism and, in this opinion, pretty much a bore."

On November 2, 1978 James Levine and the New York Philharmonic presented at Avery Fisher Hall the world premiere of Jacob Druckman's *Concerto for Viola and Orchestra,* commissioned by that orchestra as a showcase for its principal violist, Sol Greitzer. The single-movement work consists of seven sections in which the composer relied on basically orthodox techniques to portray the viola as "the aristocrat of the orchestra" and transform "the relationship between the soloist and the orchestra." Hostile confrontations and delicate exchanges ensue as the violist achieves his modus vivendi with what the composer terms "the terrible power of the full orchestra." Re-

porting in *New World* (November 5, 1978), Andrew DeRhen complimented Druckman for having cleverly responded to a challenging assignment, noting: "There is good cause to lament that composers such as Mozart and Beethoven were not offered similar incentives to write viola concertos in their time, for if they had performed as satisfactorily as Druckman has, the viola repertory would be a treasure chest."

More recently Jacob Druckman won acclaim for *Aureole* (1979), an orchestral piece evoking visual imagery in the compositional mode of *Mirage* and *Chiaroscuro* that Peter G. Davis of the New York *Times* (June 11, 1979) has called "virtually a textbook demonstration of how to achieve shimmering, vaporous, iridescent textures." Consisting of a monothematic melodic line based on the Kaddish tune from Leonard Bernstein's Third Symphony, *Aureole* was generally favorably received at its premiere at Avery Fisher Hall on June 9, 1979, although one critic wondered whether *Aureole* would ever be "anything more than a gorgeous bauble of sound."

Writing in *High Fidelity* (September 1980), Stephen Cera entertained a similar doubt about *Prism* for orchestra (1980), which the Baltimore Symphony Orchestra introduced on May 21, 1980. Although he questioned *Prism's* "substantiality," Cera nevertheless made laudatory observations about the "craftsmanship, resourcefulness, and sense of adventure" with which the composer had meshed the counterpoint, rhythms, and melodies of seventeenth- and eighteenth-century notables—"pert, buoyant Charpentier, haunting Cavalli, strong rhythmically supple Cherubini"—with modern-day dissonant harmonies and varying orchestral timbres. "To this pair of ears," he concluded, "Druckman casts the light of a lively intelligence on the past masters."

Jacob Druckman is especially well-known for his ballet scores, which include *Spell* (1951), *Interlude* (1953), *Suite* (1953), *Performance* (1960, for José Limon), and *Valentine* (1969), an extraordinary tour de force for solo bass that Gerald Arpino choreographed for a Joffrey City Center Ballet production. Several of the composer's works have been recorded on such labels as Nonesuch, Vox, Turnabout, and CRI. His earlier works were published by Merrymount and MCA music; since 1973 they have been exclusively published by Boosey & Hawkes, Inc.

Jacob Druckman directed Yale University's Electronic Music Center in 1971-72 and later held a similar position at Brooklyn College, where he also served as professor of music, between 1972 and 1976. He is currently professor of music, director of the electronic music studio, and coordinator of composition studies at the Yale University School of Music. Besides his Fulbright and Pulitzer Prize, he has received many awards, including two Guggenheim fellowships (1957 and 1968), the Society for the Publication of American Music award

(1967), a National Institute of Arts and Letters grant (1969), and the Brandeis University Creative Arts award (1975). Between 1975 and 1978 Druckman was a member of the Music Advisory Panel of the New York State Council on the Arts. He was appointed in April 1976 to the ASCAP board of directors and elected to the American Academy and Institute of Arts and Letters in 1978. Since 1980 he has been chairman of the Composer-Librettist Panel of the National Endowment of the Arts. He also serves as president of the Koussevitzky Music Foundation, Inc., and as chairman of the Koussevitzky Foundation in the Library of Congress.

Brown-eyed, curly-haired, and stockily built, Jacob Druckman looks, according to Shirley Fleming, "as if he might be employed in quite another line of work—maybe building houses, or raising livestock." His favorite recreations include sailboat racing and tennis. On June 6, 1954 he married Muriel Topaz, a dancer whom he had met in a sociology class at Juilliard and who is presently executive director of the Dance Notation Bureau. The Druckmans, who have two grown children, David and Karen, live in New York City in a large Upper West Side apartment where they are "surrounded by musicians, not necessarily by choice" and where the composer's "works in progress" often cover his studio as "temporary wallpaper."

References: ASCAP Today p16+ Ja '74 por; Boosey & Hawkes Newsletter, 1977-78; Hi Fi 22:MA4+ Ag '72 por; New Yorker 50:111+ F 10 '75; N Y Times C p31 N 4 '77; Baker's Biographical Dictionary of Musicians (1978); Dictionary of Contemporary Music (1974); International Cyclopedia of Music and Musicians (1975); Who's Who in America, 1980-81

Duarte (Fuentes), José Napoleón
(dōō-är′tä)

1926- President of El Salvador. Address: Casa Presidencial, San Salvador, El Salvador; c/o Partido Demócrata Cristiano, 17 Avenida Norte 131, San Salvador, El Salvador

The Republic of El Salvador, the smallest, most densely populated of the Central American states, has been embroiled since the late 1970's in a civil war that has claimed tens of thousands of lives and left its economy a shambles. At the root of the conflict stands the familiar Latin American phenomenon of social injustice and grossly unequal distribution of power and property. Since December 1980, José Napoleón Duarte, a founder of the reformist center-right Christian Democratic party and a former three-term mayor of the city of San Salvador, has stood at the helm of the government as President of an extra-constitutional civilian-military junta. Because he has only limited support and authority, he is regarded by some observers as too hemmed in by the right and left to be able to point El Salvador in the direction of stability and peace. Others, including spokesmen for the United States government, consider him the best hope for the establishment of an effective and enlightened non-Communist government in El Salvador.

José Napoleón Duarte Fuentes, the second of the three sons of José Jesús Duarte, was born in 1926 in San Salvador. His mother, before her marriage, had worked as a domestic servant, market vendor, and seamstress. His father, who grew up in rural poverty, began as a tailor and eventually became the proprietor of a thriving candy-manufacturing business. Duarte's older brother, Rolando, served as the government's Minister of Economy in the early 1960's; his younger brother, José Alejandro, is a Roman Catholic priest of progressive bent.

As a youngster in San Salvador, Duarte was a Boy Scout, and he has remained interested in the scouting movement and dedicated to its ideal of service to others. Aided by a scholarship, he received his secondary education at the Liceo Salvadoreño, a Roman Catholic school run by the Marist Brothers. In 1944, the year of his graduation, he served on a students' committee in the general strike that helped to topple the military regime of General Maximiliano Hernández Martínez, who had ruled El Salvador since 1931.

Following the seizure of power, in the fall of 1944, by Colonel Osmín Aguirre y Salinas, Duarte made two abortive efforts to join the government-in-exile headed by the popular civilian presidential hopeful Arturo Romero in neighboring Guatemala, but each time he was stopped at the frontier and returned to his father. Finally, to keep him from getting into further trouble, his father sent him to join his older brother at Notre Dame University in the United States.

Duarte has recalled that his stay at Notre Dame taught him, above all, "to have guts." Arriving at South Bend, Indiana without any knowledge of English, he supplemented his income from a scholarship he obtained through the Marists with work as a dishwasher and laundryman while carrying a full-time academic course load, often working as much as eighteen hours a day. He even tried out for the freshman football team although he had never played the game before. The Reverend Theodore M. Hesburgh, then an instructor, who later became Notre Dame's president, remembers his "strong character" and "sense of justice."

Following his graduation in 1948 with a degree in civil engineering and his return to El Salvador, Duarte married the daughter of a wealthy construction contractor who was also his godfather and his parents' long-time friend, and he joined his father-in-law as a partner in his prospering construction firm. In his spare time he taught engineering at the National University and the military academy and was active in such organizations as the Boy Scouts and the Red Cross. During those years he apparently displayed little interest in politics.

Following a period of relative stability in El Salvador, a coup by leftist officers overthrew the government of Lieutenant Colonel José María Lemus on October 26, 1960. His regime was followed by the somewhat progressive Junta de Gobierno, which was succeeded in January 1961 by the rightist Directorio Cívico-Militar. During that period of growing polarization between the impoverished rural masses and the powerful ruling oligarchy that controlled the government and the army, many observers felt that a violent revolt along Communist lines was almost inevitable. Troubled by that prospect, an influential segment of El Salvador's burgeoning middle class concluded that a national disaster could only be averted through a working democracy and genuine social and economic reform.

As early as 1958, small groups had been meeting to discuss the possibility of establishing a political movement on the model of Christian Democracy, a reformist, anti-Communist ideology that had won wide acceptance in Western Europe and Latin America. Duarte, who had not been involved in those study groups, accepted an invitation in 1960 to join the nascent movement. Years later he told Tom Buckley of the *New Yorker* (June 22, 1981): "I began comparing what was being said with what I believed and with what I saw around me. In this country, which then had a population of two and a half million, fewer than a

hundred thousand people had any privileges at all. . . . Until then, there had been no political solutions in El Salvador. There were no opposing parties—only coups d'état. We presented an electoral solution, and all the political intellectuals said we were crazy."

When the Partido Demócrata Cristiano (PDC) was formally founded in San Salvador on November 21, 1960, Duarte was elected to its eight-man organizing committee. Soon after he became head of the new party's organization branch, a post that gave him considerable authority yet enabled him to avoid factional infighting and ideological disputes. Those came to a head in May 1961 at the PDC's first national convention. Divided between the "cooperationists," who were willing to work with the ruling Directorate, and the "purists," who were not, the delegates were unable to choose between the two original candidates for party leader and instead elected Duarte as the PDC's first permanent secretary-general.

In April 1962 Colonel Julio Adalberto Rivera ascended unopposed to the Salvadoran Presidency. Although he was known as an authoritarian anti-Communist with ties to the military hardliners, he saw himself as a man of the people and was convinced that repression alone could not stave off a Marxist revolt for long. He hoped, by means of his newly founded Partido de Conciliación Nacional (PCN), also known as the *oficialistas*, to guide the country gradually to constitutional rule and social justice. Rivera's program engendered widespread optimism, enhanced by El Salvador's relative economic prosperity in the 1960's.

Under Duarte's leadership, the PDC moved rapidly to take advantage of the more liberal atmosphere. For the election of March 1964, the party decided to concentrate its efforts on the city and district of San Salvador. Duarte was nominated for mayor, the country's second-most visible political office. Although he was not expected to win, party leaders felt that his popularity would attract enough voters to enable the PDC to obtain several seats in the Legislative Assembly.

Pitted against an *oficialista* candidate and one representing the moderately rightist Partido Acción Renovadora, Duarte conducted an energetic and charismatic campaign. Contrary to expectations, and despite the circulation of rumors alleging that he was a Communist, he won the mayoralty by a small plurality. Nationwide, the PDC won fourteen seats in the fifty-two-member Assembly and gained control of thirty-seven municipalities, a striking victory that securely ensconced it in Salvadoran political life.

Reelected in 1966 and 1968 by increasing majorities, and backed by such conservative forces as the newspaper *El Diario de Hoy*, Duarte was one of the most dynamic and capable mayors in San Salvador's history. During his seven years in office he was responsible for a host of municipal projects, ranging from the construction of a new system of public markets to the streamlining and computerization of the city's recordkeeping and other operating procedures. Having inherited a huge municipal debt but lacking the legal power to levy new taxes, Duarte managed to raise substantial funds for the city by pressuring wealthy citizens who were in arrears. He also launched a campaign in the Assembly to obtain additional revenue-producing powers and plumbed new sources of funding, such as the Inter-American Development Bank, when that met with failure.

Partly to counteract the city's lack of money but also as a key step in implementing Christian Democratic social policy, Duarte decentralized the municipal council's authority and instituted a Communitarian Action program. Eventually as many as eighty self-help groups were organized to carry out such neighborhood civic projects as the construction or repair of schools, retaining walls, bridges, and parks. The groups also conducted relief and rescue operations after the earthquake of May 1965 and fielded a force of 20,000 men to patrol the streets during the "football" war with Honduras in 1969.

Duarte scored his most notable successes, however, in modernizing the overcrowded city's aging physical plant and improving its sagging ability to deliver basic services. As Stephen Webre noted in *José Napoleón Duarte and the Christian Democratic Party in Salvadoran Politics* (1979), "In the context of Latin American politics, where such transcendent issues as colonialism and underdevelopment tend to dominate the literature, it is easy to overlook the importance of something as mundane as street lighting or garbage collection. But in attacking these problems the [Duarte] administration concentrated its efforts upon the possible, and in achieving it accomplished improvements in city life that were both immediate and visible."

As Tom Buckley noted in the *New Yorker*, "Duarte turned out to be a mayor of a type more frequently encountered in the Middle West [of the United States] than in Central America: he was a booster, a backslapper, a businessman with a conscience." Although the *oficialistas* tried to take credit for many of his achievements, his mayoral performance enabled him to build up a sizable hardcore of devoted supporters. Just before the election of 1970, Duarte announced that he would not seek a fourth term, ostensibly to return to his engineering business but actually, according to Webre, to prepare for the Presidential election of 1972. Without his charismatic presence on the ballot, the PDC suffered some losses in 1970. In the aftermath a major internal dispute ensued, with some party leaders maintaining that the PDC program was too moderate and others criticizing the party's organizational structure. As in 1961, Duarte remained aloof from the conflict, resigning as secretary-general to avoid involvement.

For the national election of February 20, 1972 the PDC formed a coalition with two small leftist parties, the Union Democrática Nacionalista (UDN) and the Movimiento Nacional Revolucionario (MNR). The resulting Unión Nacional Opositora (UNO) nominated Duarte for President and Guillermo Manuel Ungo, head of the MNR, as his running-mate. The coalition's platform continued the PDC's emphasis on private property, electoral democracy, individual liberty, and communitarian activism but was more nationalistic, gave a higher priority to agrarian reform, and blamed "oligarchy and imperialism" for El Salvador's problems.

Duarte faced three other contenders for the Presidency: José Antonio Rodríguez Porth, a laissez-faire liberal, representing the Partido Popular Salvadoreño; the ultra-rightist General José Alberto Medrano of the Frente Unido Democrático Independiente; and the *oficialista* candidate, Colonel Arturo Armando Molina. Since the Salvadoran constitution permitted presidents to serve for only one five-year term, Molina was the hand-picked successor to the incumbent, Colonel Fidel Sánchez Hernández, who had been chosen by Rivera in 1969. The three-month campaign, one of the most strenuous in Salvadoran history, was marked by anti-UNO harassment, including anonymous charges that the coalition was Communist-dominated, aspersions on Duarte's honesty and competence, and the fatal shooting of one of Duarte's aides. Focusing mainly on his strongest adversary, the lacklustre Molina, Duarte visited over 200 towns, made more than 600 speeches, and repeatedly challenged the PCN candidate to a televised debate.

When the early election returns showed Duarte in the lead, the government imposed a news blackout and apparently began doctoring the tally. The official count the next morning showed Molina beating Duarte by about 22,000 votes, while the UNO's count indicated a victory for Duarte by some 9,500 votes. Since neither had a majority, because of the strong showing made by Porth and Medrano, the final decision, by law, was left to the PCN-dominated Assembly. Quickly convened on February 27, with many opposition members not present, it unanimously elected Molina President.

Political passions flared in the next few weeks, and on March 25, 1972 some of Duarte's supporters in the army attempted to overthrow the government. Duarte apparently had no advance knowledge of the coup, but later in the day he made a radio broadcast supporting the revolutionary junta. By then government troops had already regained control, and that night Duarte was arrested. Detained for three days and subjected to interrogation and physical abuse, he was charged with treason and, according to some observers, slated for court martial and execution. But on March 28, thanks to the intercession of the Venezuelan government, the Vatican, Notre Dame's president, Theodore M. Hesburgh, and others, he was released and flown to Guatemala City. Joined there by his family, he went to Miami and then to Caracas, Venezuela, where he settled down to life in exile, working as an engineer.

Over the next few years the political situation in El Salvador deteriorated rapidly, and by the late 1970's several armed guerrilla movements were engaged in a bloody civil war with government forces. On October 15, 1979 moderate army officers, backed by the PDC and the Democratic Revolutionary Front, a leftist coalition headed by Guillermo Manuel Ungo, Duarte's former running-mate, deposed General Carlos Humberto Romero, who had become President in February 1977, and set up a civilian-military ruling junta. Ten days after the coup Duarte returned to El Salvador, where he was greeted by cheering crowds. But because of attempts on his life, he remained aloof from politics for the time being.

The junta, standing between right and left and unable to restore order or to introduce effective reforms, became increasingly repressive. Losing the support of the Ungo faction and of some elements of the PDC, it collapsed at the end of 1979. A new five-man junta, supported mainly by the army and the now relatively weak PDC, was formed in January 1980. Criticized as an opportunist for backing it, Duarte responded: "Even if this new Government is not viable, it is our historic duty to seek a solution that is not death and violence." In March 1980, after one of the Christian Democratic members resigned, Duarte became a member of the junta.

Meanwhile, the junta, under mounting pressure from the left, initiated far-reaching economic reforms, including a sweeping land distribution program. The extreme right responded with an abortive coup attempt in May 1980, while right-wing "death squads" and paramilitary security forces vented their wrath against suspected leftists. Amid continuing violence, the junta underwent a complete restructuring in December 1980, aimed at restoring a semblance of constitutionalism, thus giving the government more authority in dealing with leftist guerrilla forces and enabling it to gain a degree of international respectability.

On December 13, 1980 Duarte was named President—becoming the first civilian to hold that office in nearly half a century. He was sworn in nine days later as head of the restructured junta. Meanwhile the United States restored aid, which had been cut off following the murders—apparently by right-wing forces—of four American Roman Catholic women missionaries earlier that month. Duarte, who is in effect the President of the junta, not of the country as a whole, was seen in some quarters as a tool of the oligarchy, while right-wing businessmen maintain that the reform measures he is pursuing are ruining the economy. Firmly backed by the United States under President Ronald Reagan, who regards Duarte as the best hope for the prevention of a Communist takeover, Duarte's government has received substantial military and economic aid. Duarte has insisted, however, that economic aid is more vital than military aid and has expressed concern that the Reagan Administration policy might strengthen the military at the expense of the civilians in the government.

Meanwhile, Duarte has scored some notable success in implementing the economic reforms begun in 1980, including an extensive multiphase agrarian program to distribute the land, often through cooperatives, to the peasants who have traditionally worked it. He has also taken steps toward the nationalization of the banks, the export industry, and other sectors of the economy, and he has begun preparations toward election of a constitutional assembly in March 1982. (The assembly elected at that time would frame a new constitution and select an interim government to hold power until the Presidential election scheduled for 1983.) In the words of Edward Schumacher in the New York *Times* (March 30, 1981), "The military remains the ultimate arbiter, but Mr. Duarte—bargaining, cajoling and sometimes even threatening—has propagated what for this impoverished country are revolutionary economic and political changes."

In September 1981 Duarte visited the United States for talks with President Reagan and other officials. Addressing the United Nations General Assembly, he affirmed his government's commitment to national elections, favored by the Reagan Administration, and he implicitly condemned French and Mexican government proposals that his government negotiate with the leftist Democratic Revolutionary Front as a "representative political force." He asserted that his government's policy excluded any "dialogue with organized armed sectors," but he invited any group that laid down its arms to take part in forthcoming elections.

José Napoleón Duarte and his wife, Inés Durán de Duarte, who was educated at a community college in New Jersey, have six children and several grandchildren. Protected by armed guards, barbed wire, and high walls, they live in a large house in San Benito, San Salvador's most exclusive suburb. Standing five feet ten inches tall and weighing 190 pounds, brown-eyed "Napo" Duarte has, according to Tom Buckley, "the build of a football player" and the thick black hair, copper-colored skin, and broad cheeks "indicative of the Indian inheritance of almost all Salvadorans." Since his exile in Venezuela, Duarte has enjoyed oil painting, often depicting scenes of peasant life. He keeps a marble bust of the late West German Chancellor Konrad Adenauer, a hero of the Christian Democratic movement, on his desk.

References: N Y Times A p16 D 19 '80 por; New Yorker 57:41+ Je 22 '81; Newsweek 97: 37 Mr 16 '81 por; International Who's Who, 1981-82; Webre, Stephen. José Napoleón Duarte and the Christian Democratic Party in Salvadoran Politics, 1960-1972 (1979)

Elizabeth, Queen Mother of Great Britain

Aug. 4, 1900- Dowager Queen. Address: Clarence House, St. James's, S.W.1, England; Royal Lodge, Windsor Great Park, Berkshire, England; Castle of Mey, Caithness-shire, Scotland

At a spirited eighty years of age, Her Majesty Queen Elizabeth, the Queen Mother, widow of King George VI and mother of Queen Elizabeth II of Great Britain, is one of the most popular of all royal figures. As Duchess of York she brought the warmth of her large, loving Scottish family and her own outgoing personality to her marriage with Prince Albert Frederick Arthur George, Duke of York. When Prince Albert became George VI, following the abdication of his elder brother, King Edward VIII, in 1936, Elizabeth, as Queen Consort, played a major role in restoring the monarchy to public favor. Since the premature death of King George VI in 1952 and the succession of their daugher, Queen Elizabeth II, to the throne, the Queen Mother has continued to be regarded as "a symbol of all that Britain wants to stand for."

The second-youngest of ten children, the Queen Mother, baptized Elizabeth Angela Marguerite Bowes-Lyon, was born on August 4, 1900 at St. Paul's Waldenbury, Hitchin, Hertfordshire. Through her mother, the former Nina Cecilia Cavendish-Bentinck, the daughter of the Rev. Charles W. Cavendish-Bentinck, she is related to the Duke of Portland. Her father, Claude George Bowes-Lyon, the fourteenth Earl of Strathmore and Kinghorne and the twenty-second Lord Glamis, was a direct descendant of Robert the Bruce through his grandson King Robert II of Scotland. The ancestral home of the Strathmores, Glamis Castle

in the Glen of Strathmore north of Dundee, Scotland, was, according to legend, the site of Macbeth's murder of King Duncan. It was there and at the family's country house at St. Paul's Waldenbury that Lady Elizabeth spent most of her childhood.

With her younger brother, David, Lady Elizabeth received her early education from her mother under a regimen that included daily chapel attendance, Bible study, music, dancing, and drawing. Later, her education continued at home under the direction of a governess. When, after the outbreak of World War I, Glamis Castle was turned into hospital for military convalescents, Lady Elizabeth helped attend to the patients.

In 1920 Lady Elizabeth was formally introduced to King George V's second son, Prince Albert, Duke of York (known to his intimates as Bertie), although the two are said to have met at a children's party in 1905. The King and Queen were fond of Lady Elizabeth, and King George reportedly wrote to his son: "You'll be a lucky fellow if she accepts you." She refused Prince Albert's first proposal, in the spring of 1921, but in January 1923 she agreed to the marriage. Preparations were made for a spectacular wedding, the first of a King's son to be held in Westminster Abbey in over 500 years. The marriage, which took place on April 26, 1923, was immensely popular with the public, and it greatly pleased King George, who began to show more warmth toward his son. The young Duke and Duchess moved in June 1923 into their own home, White Lodge, in Windsor Park, which had been the childhood home of Queen Mary, the Duke's mother.

The new Duchess of York was first introduced to international royal responsibility in October 1923, when she and the Duke acted as godparents to Crown Prince Peter of Yugoslavia and represented the British royal family at the wedding of Prince Paul of Serbia and Princess Olga of Greece. This was the Duchess' first meeting with many of the royal cousins of the large family of descendants of Queen Victoria and, as the Duke reported to his father, "They were all enchanted with Elizabeth."

In the course of her official duties, the Duchess of York assumed the national presidencies and patronage of such organizations as the Young Women's Christian Association and the Girl Guides and became involved in a variety of charitable works. She traveled all over England, visiting hospitals and children's homes, attending horse shows, opening regattas and flower shows, and laying cornerstones. Late in 1924, the King permitted the couple to visit East Africa and the Sudan, giving them an opportunity to experience the functioning of the Empire at first hand. On April 21, 1926 the Duchess of York gave birth by Caesarean section to a daughter at the London home of her parents. The new Princess of York, who was third in line of succession to the throne, after the Prince of Wales and the Duke of

York, was christened Elizabeth Alexandra Mary by the Archbishop of York on May 29, 1926 in the private chapel of Buckingham Palace.

The Duke of York took on his first major assignment as a representative of the Crown when he was chosen by the King to attend the opening of the Australian Parliament in May 1927. The Duke, who had been working hard to overcome his disabling stammer, carried out his many speaking assignments capably. For the Duchess the tour was also a great triumph, prompting John W. Wheeler-Bennett to comment in his biography *King George VI* (1958): "Indeed the vivid charm of the Duchess of York was a very real factor in the success of the tour. A more responsive personality than the Duke, she was able to complement his greater shyness with a radiance which carried all before it."

For the Duke and Duchess, who were by then living in their own London town house at 145 Piccadilly, the next few years were a period of tranquility, although the Duke's royal duties had increased somewhat because of the King's failing health. The Duchess gave birth to a second daughter, Margaret Rose, at Glamis Castle on August 21, 1930. Devoting herself to her children, the Duchess taught Elizabeth to read, instructed her in French, drawing, music, and dancing, and read Bible stories and children's classics to both the girls. The family spent their holidays in the Royal Lodge in Windsor Park, which the King made available to them in 1931

After the death, on January 20, 1936, of King George V, his oldest son, Edward, Prince of Wales—called David by the members of his family—became King Edward VIII. By the autumn of that year, the new King's attachment to the American divorcée Wallis Simpson had exploded into a public crisis. All efforts to dissuade the King from marrying Mrs. Simpson failed, and on December 11, 1936, the brief reign of Edward VIII ended with his abdication. On the same date, Albert Frederick Arthur George, Duke of York, became King George VI of Great Britain. The new Queen Elizabeth never overcame the antipathy she felt toward Mrs. Simpson, whom she held responsible for Edward VIII's dereliction of duty, and "Uncle David," who became the Duke of Windsor, was no longer favored in the Queen's household.

Shortly after his accession to the throne, the new King conferred upon his Queen the title of Lady of the Most Noble Order of the Garter. Preparations were begun in haste for the Coronation to be held on the date originally chosen for Edward VIII. This allowed only five months for the jewelers, robemakers, and others to prepare for the ceremony. But all was ready in time, and on May 12, 1937 in Westminster Abbey, after the Coronation of King George VI, the Archbishop of Canterbury placed upon Elizabeth's head the four-arched crown centered with the Koh-i-Noor diamond and put into her hands the sceptre and ivory rod with dove.

To help the British people regain confidence in the monarchy, special efforts were made to emphasize the family life of the new King, and the two young Princesses as well as the Queen were increasingly involved in public functions. As Queen Consort, Elizabeth had her own coat-of-arms, with the "canting or punning arms of the Bowes-Lyon family . . . impaled with the Royal Arms." At Buckingham Palace, where she lived with her family, she presided over a personal household of her own, including a lord chamberlain, a treasurer, a mistress of the robes, ladies-in-waiting, and pages. Following the Coronation and the traditional celebrations and trips to Wales, Scotland, and Northern Ireland, the round of royal duties resumed. Queen Elizabeth concerned herself particularly with better housing for the people and often made impromptu visits to the poorer sections of London. The Queen was still in mourning for her mother when she and the King went to Paris on July 19, 1938 on their first state visit. With the threat of war keeping the King tied to London, the Queen, in September 1938, launched the world's largest ocean liner, the *Queen Elizabeth*, which had been named for her, from a shipyard in Scotland. Meanwhile, although the Munich pact, concluded by Great Britain and France with the Axis powers on September 30, 1938, seemed, in the words of Prime Minister Neville Chamberlain, to secure "peace in our time" and gave rise to some feelings of optimism, the world moved one step closer to war.

In May 1939, the King and Queen embarked on a month-long visit to Canada and the United States, where they were greeted by cheering crowds and established a lasting relationship with President Franklin D. Roosevelt. But their usual summer holiday in Balmoral had to be cut short, for by September 3, 1939, all efforts to preserve peace had failed and a state of war was declared between Germany and Britain.

During the war, while the two Princesses stayed at Windsor for their protection, King George and Queen Elizabeth maintained their residence at Buckingham Palace, although they spent much of their time traveling around the country, visiting factories and hospitals and giving moral support to those who had suffered heavy losses in bombing raids. While the King was overseas visiting troops, the Queen assumed some of his duties as Counsellor of State. Buckingham Palace was attacked nine times in the course of the war, and the Queen commented after the first raid: "I'm glad we've been bombed. It makes me feel I can look the East End in the face." King George and Queen Elizabeth also sheltered royal refugees from occupied Europe. When the Allied victory in the European phase of the war was finally announced on May 8, 1945, huge crowds gathered at Buckingham Palace and cheered the King and Queen. According to one tribute, "During the full weight of the enemy attack on London, the Queen became the shining example of her sex. Wherever the bombs fell thickest, there she was to be found bringing comfort and encouragement to the homeless." After the war, Queen Elizabeth devoted much of her time to assisting families whose homes had been ravaged by the conflict.

Meanwhile, the Princesses were growing to maturity. In 1939, Princess Elizabeth met Prince Philip of Greece and Denmark, a distant cousin, with whom she corresponded during the war. She accepted his proposal in the fall of 1946, but King George insisted on secrecy and a waiting period at least until after the royal family's African tour, scheduled for the spring of 1947, was completed. The Prince, who had renounced his titles to become a British subject, became known as Lieutenant Philip Mountbatten, having taken his mother's family name. On November 20, 1947, the wedding in Westminster Abbey between Princess Elizabeth and Prince Philip, who had been created Duke of Edinburgh, was the first great gala public occasion in the austere postwar period. The following year, on April 26, 1948, King George VI and Queen Elizabeth celebrated their Silver Wedding anniversary with a special service conducted in St. Paul's Cathedral.

The King and Queen's first grandchild, christened Charles Philip Arthur George Windsor, was born on November 14, 1948 in Buckingham Palace, where Princess Elizabeth and the Duke of Edinburgh were living until bomb-damaged Clarence House could be repaired. But the joy of the occasion was tempered by concern for King George, who was suffering from a leg ailment that he had first noticed in 1947. Despite the King's illness, which forced him to cancel an important trip to Australia and New Zealand, the Queen carried on her public duties. In March 1949 an operation helped to improve the King's condition, but his activities were severely curtailed.

On August 4, 1950, the Queen's fiftieth birthday, the London *Times* paid tribute to the "serene and steady support" that she had rendered to the King and noted that she "sustained him in sickness and in health, at all times taking her full share in the burdens of royal service." (By that time, the royal physicians knew that King George had lung cancer, although they never told him.) To relieve the King of some of his public engagements, the Queen received King Haakon of Norway on his offical visit in June 1951 and, with Princess Margaret, went on a tour of Northern Ireland. After undergoing lung surgery, the King seemed strong enough for Princess Elizabeth and the Duke of Edinburgh to go on a planned Canadian tour in October 1951 and to embark on the postponed Australian trip in place of the King and Queen at the end of January 1952. But in the early morning hours of February 6, 1952, following a comfortable day at Sandringham with the Queen and Princess Margaret, King George VI died peacefully in his sleep.

Despite her loneliness and desolation, Queen Elizabeth resumed her public duties only three months after the death of King George. In May 1952, in mourning black, she flew to Fife, Scotland, to inspect the First Battalion of the Black Watch at Crail before it left for Korea. Although the Dowager Queen was no longer entitled to the special prerogatives of Queen Consort, the new Queen, Elizabeth II, through the Regency Act of 1953, made her eligible to serve as Counsellor of State. The Queen Mother received a substantial income from the Civil List and continued to maintain her own household. She was styled Her Majesty, Queen Elizabeth, the Queen Mother, to distinguish her from her daughter, the Queen.

In 1953, the Queen Mother acquired as a retreat the isolated Castle of Mey at the northern tip of Scotland. In London she kept her apartment in Buckingham Palace until Clarence House was ready for her and Princess Margaret. She also moved from Balmoral, the royal summer home, to the smaller Birkhall, about eight miles away, but she maintained the Royal Lodge as her London area country home.

In the years following the death of King George VI, no member of the Royal Family, with the exception of Prince Philip, was of greater help to the new Queen than her mother. From 1953 on, when she and Princess Margaret visited Rhodesia, official visits to North America, Western Europe, the Pacific, and elsewhere have been regularly on the itinerary of the cheerful and tireless Queen Mother. Her tour of the United States and Canada in 1954 was immensely popular. During her 1958 tour of New Zealand, a former Prime Minister praised her for "spreading happiness wherever she goes" and "strengthening . . . the bonds that tie us to the mother country." In addition to attending conferences, dedications of buildings, ceremonies at universities, openings of dams, and other projects during the grueling overseas tours, the Queen Mother fulfilled a variety of public duties at home, presiding over meetings, delivering speeches, and giving patronage to institutions as varied as the Aberdeen Angus Cattle Society, the Bar Musical Society, and St. Paul's Cathedral. Among many other functions, the Queen Mother has served as treasurer of the Middle Temple and as chancellor of the University of London. Two days before her seventy-ninth birthday, she was installed in Dover as 160th Lord Warden of the Cinque Ports, becoming the first woman to occupy that post in 900 years. In honor of her eightieth birthday a special commemorative stamp was issued.

Princess Margaret's expressed desire, in the early 1950's, to marry Group Captain Peter Townsend, the comptroller of the household at Clarence House and the former equerry to the King, caused some distress to the Queen Mother, who liked Townsend personally but could not approve the marriage of a Princess to a divorced man. The Church of England was emphatic in its disapproval, as was the government of Prime Minister Winston Churchhill. In October 1955, Margaret, mindful of her "duty to the Commonwealth," formally renounced the relationship. After the breakup of Margaret's romance with Townsend, the Queen Mother was relieved by the Princess' interest in Anthony Armstrong-Jones, the commoner son of a Welsh barrister. Armstrong-Jones, who was later created Earl of Snowdon, and Princess Margaret were married on May 6, 1960. The marriage ended in divorce in 1978.

The Queen Mother is considered to be a "super grandmother" by her six grandchildren. Besides Charles there are the Queen's daughter Anne, born in 1950, and the Queen's two younger sons—Andrew, born in 1960, and Edward, born in 1964—and Princess Margaret's son, David, born in 1961, and daughter, Sarah, born in 1964. Princess Anne, who married Mark Phillips in 1973, has given the Queen Mother two great-grandchildren. In February 1981 the Queen Mother welcomed into Clarence House Lady Diana Spencer, whose engagement to Prince Charles had just been announced. Lady Diana took up her new residence with the Queen Mother in order to receive instruction in the "strict code of royal conduct."

Photographs of the petite, blue-eyed Queen Mother, whose figure shows her fondness for sweets, have never done justice to her superb complexion and winning smile. She is happiest out-of-doors, especially when fishing for salmon in Scotland, often with her grandson Charles, or enjoying her gardens full of fragrant flowers. Other objects of her passion are her dogs, especially her beloved Welsh corgis, and her 350 race horses. Her human qualities have won over even so fierce an antimonarchist as the Scottish Member of Parliament William W. Hamilton, who has admitted that as a "public relations officer for the monarchy Her Majesty the Queen Mother has been superb."

References: Duff, David. Elizabeth of Glamis (1973); Donaldson, Frances. King George VI and Queen Elizabeth (1977); Lacey, Robert. Majesty (1977); Laird, Dorothy. Queen Elizabeth, the Queen Mother (1966); Longford, Elizabeth. The Queen Mother (1981)

Falwell, Jerry

Aug. 11, 1933- Clergyman; political lobbyist.
Address: b. Thomas Road Baptist Church,
701 Thomas Rd., Lynchburg, Va. 24514

The 1980 United States Presidential and Congressional campaigns were marked by the mushrooming involvement of the Christian evangelical movement in politics. The most visible group embodying that trend has been Moral Majority, Inc., a conservative political lobbying organization, with a membership estimated at 2,000,000, that was founded in June 1979 by the Rev. Jerry Falwell, an independent fundamentalist. Since 1956, Falwell has been pastor of the Thomas Road Baptist Church in Lynchburg, Virginia, with a congregation of some 17,000. A leading exponent of the so-called "electronic church," Falwell claims to reach as many as 18,000,000 souls a week with a Biblically based message of salvation through his Old-Time Gospel Hour, broadcast over some 400 radio and 390 television stations in the United States and abroad.

In his hortatory book Listen, America! (Doubleday, 1980), Falwell called for "a coalition of God-fearing moral Americans" to "reverse the politicization of immorality in our society." While criticized by liberals for allegedly trespassing on the principle of separaton of church and state, Falwell has asserted: "What we want is not control, it is influence." By registering millions of new voters, informing them of the voting records of their elected representatives, and mobilizing his supporters into a massive political action movement, Falwell is believed to have contributed substantially to the landslide victory of President-elect Ronald Reagan and the replacement of a number of liberal Senators and Congressmen in the November 1980 election.

Jerry Falwell, the son of Carey H. and Helen Falwell and, according to Mary Murphy of Esquire (October 10, 1978), "a bootlegger's grandson," was born on August 11, 1933 in Lynchburg, in Campbell County, Virginia. His father, a successful businessman who at one time or another operated a restaurant, a trucking company, and service stations, died in 1948, at the age of fifty-five, as a result of alcoholism. The family included Jerry's twin brother, Eugene, and an older brother, Lewis, who together manage the family's commercial enterprises, as well as an older sister, Virginia.

A diligent student, Jerry Falwell skipped the second grade at Mountain View Elementary School, where he was also something of a rowdy prankster. At Brookville High School he compiled a grade average of 98.6 percent and excelled in football, baseball, and basketball, but he was barred from giving the valedictorian's speech at graduation because auditors found out that he and other athletes had obtained free meals for a year by using counterfeit lunch tickets.

In the fall of 1950, when he was seventeen, Jerry Falwell enrolled in Lynchburg College with the intention of majoring in mechanical engineering and then transferring to Virginia Polytechnic Institute for his junior year. The superior grades he obtained in mathematics as a freshman—the highest in the college for that year—earned him a B.F. Goodrich citation. During his sophomore year, however, he became a "born again" Christian and decided to transfer to the Baptist Bible College in Springfield, Missouri. About the same time he turned down an offer to play baseball with the St. Louis Cardinals.

The foundation for Falwell's conversion was laid during his years of listening to the Old Fashioned Revival Hour, broadcast by Charles E. Fuller, one of the pioneers of radio evangelism, from the Long Beach Municipal Auditorium in Southern California. On Sunday mornings his mother used to switch on the program for the benefit of the family, aware that, as Falwell recalls, "we were too lazy to get out of bed and turn off the radio." That conditioning bore fruit when Jerry Falwell, who had been unaccustomed to attending church, decided to accompany some friends to a service conducted by the Rev. Paul Donnelson at the Park Avenue Baptist Church in Lynchburg on the evening of January 20, 1952. At the end of that service Falwell declared his acceptance of Christ. Apparently an important factor in his conversion was his first encounter, that same night, with the church's pianist Macel Pate, who later became his wife.

With the purchase of a Bible, a Bible dictionary, and James Strong's Exhaustive Concordance of the Bible the next day, Falwell began to study the Scriptures avidly. He soon became active in the church's youth department, and two months after his conversion he decided to make the ministry his life's profession. "I totally surrendered my life to God," Falwell has recalled, as quoted by Gerald Strober and Ruth Tomczak in Jerry Falwell: Aflame for God (Nelson, 1979). "There was no emotion. . . . It all happened quietly, inside my heart." While attending Baptist Bible College in his junior and senior years, Falwell taught Sunday school at a Springfield church.

He graduated, according to Strober and Tomczak, with a Th.G. degree in 1956. Later he was awarded an honorary D.D. degree by Tennessee Temple University in Chattanooga and an honorary Litt.D. by the California Graduate School of Theology in Glendale.

On his return to Lynchburg, Falwell founded an independent Baptist church with funds totaling $1,000 and an initial congregation of thirty-five adults and their families. From the first service, on June 24, 1956, in an abandoned building owned by the Donald Duck Bottling Company, Falwell labored to establish the Thomas Road Baptist Church. In addition to discharging his ministerial duties, he handled maintenance, carpentry work, and fund raising. He persuaded the owner to underwrite the church's purchase of the deteriorating structure and, aided by a city map and a file of names and addresses furnished by the Lynchburg city director, he embarked on an aggressive campaign of door-to-door evangelism. The church was only a week old when Falwell started a half-hour daily radio broadcast. Six months later, he presented his first religious television program, then, as now, called the Old-Time Gospel Hour. By the end of its first year the church counted 864 regular worshipers.

The physical facilities of the church steadily expanded, and by 1969 its membership neared 10,000. Meanwhile, Falwell had set up the Elim Home for Alcoholics on a 165-acre farm in 1959; the Lynchburg Christian Academy, a full-time day school, in 1964; a bus ministry for people lacking transportation to attend services, in 1969; and a free summer camp for children, a Bible institute, and a seminary. The church also undertook missionary and relief work, sending teams to Guatemala, Haiti, South Korea, Indochina, Australia, and other parts of the world.

In addition to obtaining financial support through tithing, Falwell's church derived much of its income through gifts from the loyal audience of the Old-Time Gospel Hour, which was broadcast from a studio until 1968. The decision was then made to televise the Sunday morning service in the sanctuary, and in 1971 the program began to be broadcast nationwide.

In the unchanging format of the Old-Time Gospel Hour through the years, television cameras record the services just as they are conducted, in contrast to the varyingly elaborate productions staged by such other religious programs as those presented by Billy Graham, Oral Roberts, or Rex Humbard. As Edward M. Berckman observed in Christian Century (March 29, 1978), Falwell's program is "neither a one-man show nor a cult of personality," and "on the whole, there is an upbeat thrust to the Old-Time Gospel Hour as it features pleasant faces, happy sounds, images of success, and messages of hope and redemption."

In July 1973 the Thomas Road Baptist Church was charged in a federal suit by the Securities and Exchange Commission with "fraud and deceit" and "gross insolvency" after selling $6,600,000 worth of bonds to finance the expansion of its educational facilities and other church enterprises. But a month later a United States District Court, having found "no evidence of any intentional wrongdoing," dropped the charges. An advisory board of five local businessmen was appointed to oversee the Thomas Road Baptist Church's financial operations, and within three years the church was again operating in the black.

Meanwhile, Lynchburg Baptist College—now known as Liberty Baptist College—which had been launched by Falwell in 1971 without a campus or facilities, had developed into an accredited four-year liberal arts institution offering B.S. degrees in business administration, religion, communications, education, natural science, and other fields. A new campus was built in 1977 on Candler's Mountain—renamed Liberty Mountain. In celebration of the American Bicentennial, during the 1975-76 academic year eighty-three of the college's 1,244 students toured 112 major cities with Jerry Falwell in the first of his "I Love America" rallies, aimed at bringing Americans "back to God." Now fully accredited, Liberty Baptist College had a student body of some 3,300 undergraduates in the fall of 1981.

Originally, Falwell had opposed political activism, and in a 1965 sermon entitled "Ministers and Marches" that was quoted in the Washington *Post* (May 2, 1979) he observed: "Nowhere are we commissioned to reform the externals; we are not told to wage war against bootleggers, liquor stores, gamblers, murderers, prostitutes, . . . or any other existing evil as such." But in the late 1970's Falwell made an about-face and began to affirm a religious leader's right to make his views known on such sensitive public issues as abortion, homosexuality, or pornography.

Convinced that the foundation of the family lies in God's creation of "Adam and Eve, not Adam and Steve," Falwell concentrated much of his fire on homosexuality. In 1977, for example, he helped singer Anita Bryant in her successful campaign to repeal an ordinance granting equal rights to homosexuals in housing, employment, and public accommodations in Dade County, Florida, and in 1978 he took a similar stand in California. He launched an extensive "Clean Up America" campaign in May 1978 and organized a second in April 1979, highlighted by a mass rally on the steps of the Capitol in Washington, D.C. Contending that gambling was "typical of a nation losing its moral values," Falwell also conducted a campaign that led to the defeat of a measure to legalize pari-mutuel betting in Virginia in October 1978.

In June 1979, acting "as a private citizen," Falwell founded Moral Majority, Inc., under the tutelage of political professionals. They included Paul M. Weyrich, a Roman Catholic who heads the Committee for the Survival of a Free Congress; Howard Phillips, a Jew who

organized the Conservative Caucus; Robert Billings, an unsuccessful Republican Congressional candidate from Indiana; and Ed McAteer, a marketing expert who set up the interdenominational Religious Round Table. A "political-moral organization," Moral Majority is Falwell's first purely secular enterprise. It comprises four separate units, dealing with education, lobbying, endorsement of candidates, and legal aid, and it espouses substantially the same causes Falwell promotes on the *Old-Time Gospel Hour* but is completely separate from his church. As implied by its name—originally suggested by Weyrich—the organization maintains that the vast majority of Americans subscribe to traditional moral values and believe the Ten Commandments remain valid for today.

In addition to condemning abortion on demand as "legalized murder," homosexuality as "a perversion, not an alternative lifestyle," pornography as "brainwashing the American people into accepting . . . what is abnormal," and the Equal Rights Amendment as striking "at the foundation of our social structure," Falwell, as spokesman for Moral Majority, advocates voluntary prayer in public schools, the work ethic, free enterprise, a balanced budget, and a "strengthening of the military fiber and fabric of this country." He considers the survival of Israel essential to American security, and although he has called the Jews "spiritually blind and desperately in need of their Messiah and Savior," he regards them as "God's people" and asserts that "in the world today Bible-believing Christians in America are the best friends the nation of Israel has." In November 1980 Falwell was among 100 Americans honored by Israeli Prime Minister Menachem Begin during his visit to New York City.

Primary election victories in the summer of 1980 underscored the escalating effect of Moral Majority and other religiously oriented conservative groups such as Christian Voice and Religious Round Table. Charles E. Grassley in Iowa, Admiral Jeremiah Denton in Alabama, and Don Nickles in Oklahoma were among successful Moral Majority favorites for the United States Senate. By means of a door-to-door campaign, Moral Majority members helped to defeat Alabama Representative John Buchanan, a moderate Republican and a Baptist minister, who had voted to extend the deadline for passage of the Equal Rights Amendment. In June, Alaska members of Moral Majority elected all of the state's nineteen delegates to the Republican National Convention.

At the July 1980 Republican National Convention in Detroit, Falwell reportedly warned Presidential nominee Ronald Reagan against choosing George Bush as a running mate, but without success. Nevertheless, the party adopted a platform that encompassed many of Moral Majority's views, including a historic turn away from the Equal Rights Amendment and a demand for a constitutional ban on abortion.

But although Falwell's efforts have been frequently identified with Reagan's Presidential campaign, he has denied being a "Reaganite" and has warned his supporters against committing themselves to a candidate or party. At a rally in Harrisburg, Pennsylvania that featured his audio-visual presentation *America, You're Too Young to Die,* Falwell insisted: "I am not a Republican, I am not a Democrat! I am a noisy Baptist!" In his book, *Listen, America!,* Falwell stressed the "imperative of moral involvement" and outlined a plan of action that went far beyond political parties and election campaigns. A Moral Majority project to "clean up" television programs was launched by Falwell in late 1980.

Evaluating the political phenomenon that Falwell has wrought, Dudley Clendinen wrote in the New York *Times* (August 20, 1980): "In organizing to arouse a particular electorate, to shape the ways it views issues, to register its members to vote . . . , to use it to influence law and policy at state and national levels, to raise funds to support certain candidates . . . , Falwell has created something very similar to a political party." Although some observers believe that Falwell's political clout has been exaggerated, his influence on the "sleeping giant" of American politics—as the evangelical movement, with its estimated 21,000,000 votes, has been called—causes liberals to view Falwell's success with some trepidation. Moral Majority's widely circulated yes-and-no questionnaires which, Falwell claims, place 95.8 percent of the respondents on the side of "righteousness," have been criticized as a simplistic approach to complex issues.

Defending his opposition to what he sees as the rapid growth of "secular humanism" in government, Falwell declares vigorously: "I believe in the separation of church and state but not in the separation of God and government." President Jimmy Carter's Secretary of Health and Human Services, Patricia Roberts Harris, has compared the "moral absolutism" of such politically militant groups as Moral Majority with the Ayatollah Ruhollah Khomeini's "religious zealots" in Iran. In late October 1980 television producer Norman Lear organized a counter-group called "People for the American Way," which presented five sixty-second television commercials that challenged the message of Moral Majority. Conservative columnist James J. Kilpatrick, although skeptical about some of Moral Majority's aims, characterized the liberal backlash as "a kind of bigotry" and demanded: "What is so wrong about the fundamentalists in politics and so right about the National Council of Churches in politics?" And a *New Republic* editorial (October 11, 1980) concluded: "To demand that any person suppress his or her political beliefs because they are based on religious values is to practice the same intolerance that supposedly is the threat."

Although Falwell did not directly take credit for Reagan's victory on November 4, 1980, he pointed out that Moral Majority had registered some 4,000,000 new voters, had urged another 10,000,000 to go to the polls. Elated with the results of the election, he called it "the greatest day for the cause of conservatism and American morality" in his adult life. He indicated that he would advise the Reagan Administration only if asked to do so, and then only in an unofficial capacity, but said that his organization would continue to function as watchdog and as a lobby for such measures as the proposed human life amendment and Senator Paul Laxalt's family protection bill.

Not all of those who consider themselves conservative have given their wholehearted support to Falwell's Moral Majority. The Rev. Billy Graham, for example, has criticized Falwell for his political sermonizing on "secular, nonmoral issues like the Panama Canal" and for his failure to deal with matters such as the armaments race and social injustice. And Senator Barry M. Goldwater castigated Falwell for his opposition to President Reagan's nomination, in July 1981, of Judge Sandra Day O'Connor to the United States Supreme Court on the ground that her position had not been consistently opposed to abortion.

In contrast to such hellfire-and-brimstone pulpiteers as the Rev. Billy James Hargis, Falwell suavely sermonizes on his Baptist religious doctrines and simultaneously disseminates right-wing politics "in a nonthreatening way," as Mary Murphy noted in *Esquire.* Usually dressed in a three-piece suit, his thumbs anchored in his vest pockets, the smiling, large-framed, blue-eyed leader of Moral Majority conveys an air of "untroubled and worldly self-satisfaction" according to Henry Fairlie of *New Republic* (August 2-9, 1980), who cautions, however, that "the poison is no less deadly because it is sweetened." To Joseph Sobran of the *National Review* (June 27, 1980), who observed that Falwell's method is "not to harangue but to marshal witnesses," he seemed "about as menacing as the corner grocer" and "as much a religious Lawrence Welk as a preacher."

Jerry Falwell and his wife, the former Macel Pate, whom he married on April 12, 1958, live with their three children, Jerry Jr., Jeannie, and Jonathan, in a twelve-room Southern-style mansion—equipped with a swimming pool and protected by a high wall and a Bible-quoting guard—that was made available to him by an affluent congregant. In addition to his salary, reported to be $42,500 in 1980, he enjoys the perquisites of an expense account, free life insurance, and a personal jet plane on which he travels some 200,000 miles a year. "I'll never retire," Falwell has said. "I want to drop dead at 100." At least once a year he intones into a tape recorder his recommendations for the church's goals, methods of financing, and media relations. Falwell's enterprises, which in 1980 employed some 950 people and took in about $1,000,000 a week, have been certified by the

Evangelical Council for Financial Accountability in Pasadena, California. "There's nothing wrong with religion being big business," Falwell asserts. "It ought to be the biggest business in the world." In 1979 he was named "Clergyman of the Year" by Religious Heritage of America.

References: Esquire 90:25+ O 10 '78 por; Los Angeles Times I p31 O 13 '79 por; N Y Times B p22 Ag 20 '80 por; New Yorker 57:53+ My 18 '81; Newsday L I p14+ Mr 22 '81 pors; Newsweek 80:76 Jl 24 '72 por, 96:28+ S 15 '80 pors; Time 114:62+ O 1 '79 por; Strober, Jerry and Tomczak, Ruth. Jerry Falwell: Aflame for God (1979)

Folon, Jean-Michel (fō-lōⁿ ')

Mar. 1, 1934- Belgian painter and illustrator. Address: b. c/o Lefebre Gallery, 47 E. 77th St., New York City, N.Y. 10021; h. Burcy, 77890 Beaumont-du-Gátinais, France

The graphic designs of Belgium's Jean-Michel Folon strike a familiar chord in viewers throughout the Western world. His bold posters, innovative illustrations, and delicate watercolors reflect and reshape the modern world in enduring images. Assessing the impact of Folon's work, his friend Milton Glaser, the American graphic artist, has said, "One of the ways we judge the quality of an artist's vision is the degree to which our vision is altered by his work. . . . Since knowing Folon I see the world differently." The admirers, many of them Europeans, for whom he speaks rate Folon among the significant artists of the avant-garde.

Jean-Michel Folon was born in Uccle, a suburb of Brussels, Belgium on March 1, 1934 to André Folon, a salesman, and Victoire (Coenen) Folon. His fascination with graphic art began early in life: "In my case, drawing had been almost a childhood disease," Folon once explained. He first sold his handiwork to the Belgian newspaper *Pan* when he was eighteen years old. His father, however, disapproved of his interest and recommended architecture as a preferable career. Accordingly, Folon studied for four years at the École Nationale Supérieur d'Architecture in Brussels before he finally decided to move to Paris and follow his own bent. Although he never worked as an architect, his training for that profession gave him a sensitivity to structure that informs his compositions.

From 1960 to 1965 Folon worked in relative obscurity except for a 1963 show at the Galerie du Palimugre in Paris. Recognition of his talent first came from Italy and the United States. In Italy he won grand prize at the third Triennale of Humor in Art in 1965, and in 1966 the Italian novelist and poet Giorgio Soavi commissioned Folon to design an advertising poster for Olivetti, the Milanese manufacturers of typewriters and business machines. The two artists became friends and collaborators, producing such pieces as the Olivetti publicity pamphlet entitled "Le Message" (1967). Its series of whimsical line drawings portrays a lone figure slinking down a city street to an office that houses a vast typewriter, performing strenuous gymnastics on its keys to type a larger-than-life letter, and launching the painstakingly folded message toward its destination. Working on a grander scale, Folon executed a painting, a mural aglow with 500 dots of light, on 110 square feet of polyester for the Milan Triennale of 1968.

One of Folon's first American assignments was another series of line drawings, published in *Horizon* magazine's Summer 1965 issue as "New York, Site Unseen." The images of fantasy that Folon sketched before his first visit to Manhattan feature anonymous herds of humans carrying newspapers as large as themselves and wandering through cityscapes of stern skyscrapers or forests of antennae. After actually seeing the metropolis, Folon depicted it with intensified clutter and confusion for a *New Yorker* cover of December 3, 1966. Amidst a background of smoggy sepia, signposts of civilization spring up side by side in stubborn contradiction of one another. The human figures in the foreground imitate the snarled signs by arguing absurdly about opposing directions.

Americans bestowed two honors on Folon in 1966: the Art Directors Club of New York awarded him a Certificate of Merit and *Fortune* magazine published a portfolio of seven of his pictures in its February issue. The collection, entitled "Laughter in the Labyrinth," displays the characteristic colors and motifs of Folon's early work; the world according to Folon is shaped with hot, pure hues into recurring images of modern malaise. The motif of the labyrinth appears both as walls of stairs leading nowhere and as a jumble of streets cowering in the urban canyons. Omnipresent arrows are a related motif. The world can become a puzzle, with little men industriously scrambling its pieces. The anonymous inhabitant of the puzzling maze of modern society is the Folon man, his body a large rectangular lump of trenchcoat and his face a few minimal features under a hat.

Folon's Everyman has aroused considerable critical commentary. "Folon's little man, enmeshed in all his arrows, is trying to find his way in an implacable universe," explained François Mathey in *Graphis* (1971-72); "he stands there lonely yet undismayed, wearing an unimaginative hat. Maybe he is lost and bewildered, but somewhere beyond the labyrinth and the ramparts of the impersonal city there is always some unexpected ray of hope. In his way, Folon is a prophet. He reminds man that his vocation is to spiritualize the world." Alexandre Alexandre discerned the same somber optimism, observing in *Gebrauchsgraphik* (May 1969) that Folon "feels that we must first live through a terrible catastrophe before we can hope for a 'golden age.'" For with man's fate firmly in mind, Folon keeps his hold on a strong sense of humor: as he himself has said, "Humor is the unwillingness to speak tragically of tragic things." While some critics have applauded his humor, others have focused on his wistful nostalgia, "not so much nostalgia for a lost past as nostalgia for lost man."

Once he had achieved recognition in Italy and the United States, Folon soon became popular in France, where in 1967 he joined others in audiovisual research for a Paris theatre company headed by André Perinetti and Jean-Marie Serreau. That year he also exhibited his work at the Paris Biennial and helped to produce two films, *Qui êtes-vous Polly Magoo?* with William Klein and *Le Cri* with Alain Resnais. In 1968 he made an animated cartoon for French television and saw his success celebrated by a critically acclaimed show at the prestigious Galerie de France.

The following year New York's Lefebre Gallery mounted Folon's first show in the United States. Although an occasional reviewer failed to appreciate his sense of humor, most agreed with John Canaday of the New York *Times* (May 3, 1969), who insisted that "Mr. Folon's serious joking is bright and affectionate." A critic for *Arts* magazine (Summer 1969) lauded the dexterity with which Folon expresses his metaphysical wit: "These are technically perfect drawings. The meticulous precision of linear detail, characteristic of his work, is further enhanced by delicate and subtle tonalities of colored ink-washes. The technique only takes second place to concept,

the vastness of which makes these small drawings seem monumental in scale."

Widening interest in Folon's work required him to travel during 1970 to several countries, including Japan, where four of his animated cartoons were shown in the Belgian pavilion of the World Exposition (Expo '70), which opened in Osaka in March. At the invitation of Olivetti and the publishing house Mainichi Shimbon, he also presented an exhibition in Tokyo. Moreover, he represented Belgium at the thirty-fifth Venice Biennale. His work appeared in Milan as well, at the Galleria Il Milione, on the occasion of his first one-man show in Italy. Folon finished the year in the United States with his second Lefebre show, which once again garnered critical approbation.

Back in Paris in 1971, Folon had his first retrospective, organized by the Louvre's Musée des Arts Décoratifs. The exhibition generated expressions of adulation for the artist. Ellen Schwartz of *Art International* (March 20, 1972) announced that henceforth Folon could be considered "not only as an illustrator of the highest rank, but as an artist of great merit and talent." Contradicting Pierre Martory of *Art News* (March 1972), who complained that "Folon's well-known cartoons lose their bite when transferred from the printed page to a museum wall," she asserted that Folon's collected works exerted greater impact than any isolated examples could: together they added up to "a revelation of modern society, executed with perspicacity and suggestive wit." After February 1972 the show traveled to Belgium, to the Palais des Beaux-Arts in Charleroi and the Musée d'Art Moderne in Brussels, and to Italy, to the Castèllo Sforzesco in Milan.

A smaller selection of Folon's work, originating at the Arts Club of Chicago, circulated during 1972 through the United States in tandem with pieces by Roland Topor. Folon also had a one-man exhibition at the Grand Palais in Paris. Moreover, his work began appearing in European playgrounds. On the ground the *Folonum*, an abstract life-size human figure, sprang up in legions of red, green, or blue reinforced polyester. In the air the *Flying Man*, a huge kite of nylon sailcloth supported by aluminum and plastic rods, carried on "conversations with the wind." As Folon explained, "I have made a giant kite which resembles a man so that he will come back and tell us what he has heard from the wind." Back in the galleries in 1973, Folon's work appeared in exhibitions in Brussels, Paris, Saõ Paulo (at the twelfth Bienal, where he won grand prize), and New York (at the Lefebre Gallery, where he again joined forces with Topor).

In 1973 Alice Editions of Geneva published *La mort d'un arbre (The Death of a Tree)*, a volume of twenty-four Folon watercolors prefaced with a new lithograph by Max Ernst.

In his revealing introduction Folon enumerates the diverse artists, including Ensor, Magritte, Klee, Ernst, Samuel Beckett, Lewis Carroll, and Buster Keaton, who have influenced his work; above all, Cartier-Bresson and Steinberg have educated his eye. Nevertheless, he emphasizes, life itself, "the only true influence," has provided his most compelling inspiration. Folon also explains the appeal of different media to the graphic artist. Magazine illustration offers the opportunity to communicate with millions of people; because its images exert only momentary impact, it demands a constant flow of new ideas. The poster is a similarly ephemeral means of instant mass communication. Watercolor, a more private medium in which images gradually emerge, allows "the most intense feeling of freedom. . . . The images are born before your eyes. And these realities become your reality." It is, he says, his favorite medium.

The images that bloom from Folon's brush in tints of extraordinary delicacy are imbued with a misty, mystical ambiance. *Sans poids* (Weightless) (1973) is a cosmic vision of the isolation and alienation of modern man. Tiny figures float in fetal positions within colored bubbles; like miniature planets, they stud the sky or alight upon the landscape. Earth and air are alike a pale luminous brown, but each little prisoner undoubtedly perceives them according to the colors of his own intervening bubble. *La faim* (Hunger) (1973) is an expression of alienated man's need for the beauty of nature. Overwhelmed by mechanization, man has himself become a machine, a figure made of factory pipes with a head that spurts steam in several directions as he kneels in supplication before a solitary rose. In his desperation, he opens his mouth with a voracious cry, as if he might devour with spiky steel teeth the flower that he grasps with incongruously gentle hands.

Another volume of Folon watercolors, with text and photographs by Giorgio Soavi, was published in 1974 as *Vue imprenable* (Impregnable View) (Editoriale Domus). In his poetic prose, Soavi explains the decision Folon made in 1970 to move to a farmhouse in Burcy, near the forest of Fontaineblue. In his photos, he shows Folon very much at home, creating his visions of urban chaos amidst rural tranquility. In 1975 yet another volume of watercolors appeared in a diminutive volume entitled *Lettres à Giorgio* (Alice Editions). The correspondence consists of postcards, complete with canceled stamps, that Folon painted and sent to Soavi. It constitutes a unique record of Folon's international wanderings.

During the mid-1970's Folon exhibited his work at several galleries new to him—including Galerie La Hune in Paris, Galerie Artel in Geneva, Galleria dell'Oca in Rome, Galerie Stufidre in Turin, and Studio Marconi in Milan—as well as returning to Lefebre in 1974 and 1976. More unusual environments for his work were provided by subway stations in

Brussels and London, for which he executed huge wall paintings. A second major retrospective was launched in 1975 at the Palais des Beaux-Arts in Brussels; in 1976 and 1977 it traveled to the Boymans-van Beuningen Museum in Rotterdam, the Deutsches Plakat Museum in Essen, and the Institute of Contemporary Art in London.

Milton Glaser, a designer whose style has influenced graphic art internationally, wrote the introduction to a 1978 volume of posters published simultaneously in France as *Folon Affiches* (Alice Editions) and in the United States as *Posters By Folon* (Harry N. Abrams). The collection includes various advertisements for cultural events that Folon created from 1969 to 1978. Moreover, as he explains in his brief text, "each poster represents a particular adventure, a meeting with someone who has persuaded me to do something that I never would have thought of doing myself." One of the most effective results of Folon's creative encounters is his commemoration of Amnesty International's Prisoners of Conscience Year (1977). "The idea of freedom," Folon believes, "can never be depicted too often." In his poignant poster, freedom is personified by a flying figure in striped blue prison garb whose wings take on the tints of the sunny red and gold atmosphere in which he soars.

The Eyewitness (Alice Editions, 1979; Abrams, 1980) is a collection of twenty-six watercolors, painted during the years from 1975 through 1978, that combine landscape and the human face in eerie, enigmatic compositions suggesting cosmic voyeurism. In some, for example *Le Regard* (The Look) (1975), the sun becomes nature's eye, gazing down upon man; in others, for example *Un Matin* (One Morning) (1975), a disembodied hand draws back a curtain that conceals the countryside, thereby making the viewer a voyeur gazing at nature. The dissonance of the pale, electric color schemes reinforces the prevailing surrealism.

In both 1978 and 1980 Folon returned to Lefebre to exhibit new works. The stylistic and thematic developments they revealed were explained by Ellen Schwartz in the exhibition catalogue for the 1978 show. She noticed a subtle shift in Folon's style: "His images have moved out of strictly defined limits to fill out the edges of his paper, just as his drawn contours have become furred and suggestive. Intense, eye-stopping hues have been replaced with earth tones more consistent with the growing humanism of his vision." She sensed a growing glimmer of optimism concerning man's spiritual fate: "Folon's little men, though obedient, show unmistakable signs of dissatisfaction. They identify something in themselves with nature, and seek release in the open countryside. In recent years, Folon has led them more and more frequently outside their regimented cities, seeking in green hills and moonlit skies that unidentifiable something they have lost."

Jean-Michel Folon continues to live in Burcy, visited occasionally by his teenage son François. He is separated from his wife, author and illustrator Colette Portal. Traveling abroad frequently in connection with his exhibitions, Folon also periodically leaves his rural haven to pursue his favorite hobby, which is film acting. He made a particularly favorable impression on film critics in the role of the phlegmatic journalist in Maurice Dugowson's *Lily Aime-Moi* (Camera One, 1975). Folon's friends call him Michelangelo Junior, but he resists any more specific labels. As he wrote in Lefebre's 1980 catalogue, "I want to escape from labels. In reality, I am neither a painter, a draughtsman, nor a poster-designer. I am neither an actor, a writer, nor an etcher. I am neither abstract nor figurative. I do not belong to any school....I have only tried to capture my dreams in the hope that others will link theirs with mine."

References: Esquire 89:70+ My 9 '78 por; *Gebrauchsgraphik* 40:2+ My '69 por; *Graphis* 23 no130:132+ '67 por, 27 no156:382+ '71-72 pors; Folon, Jean-Michel. *La mort d'un arbre* (1973); Soavi, Giorgio. *Vue imprenable* (1974); *Who's Who in France, 1979-80*

Foot, Michael (Mackintosh)

July 23, 1913- British political leader; former government official. Address: b. House of Commons, London, SW1A OAA

NOTE: This biography supersedes the article that appeared in *Current Biography* in 1950.

Since the death of Aneurin Bevan in 1960, Michael Foot, a Labour MP with more than thirty years' experience in Parliament, has been his party's social conscience. Having made his reputation as a writer and as editor of Bevan's leftist weekly, *Tribune*, Foot turned to parliamentary politics in 1945, and fifteen years later, succeeded Bevan as leader of Labour's left wing. He served as Opposition front bench spokesman on matters relating to the European Community, from 1970 to 1974, and as Secretary of State for Employment after Labour returned to office in 1974 under Prime Minister Harold Wilson. In November 1980 he was elected to the party's top leadership post. As an exponent of political ideas that are true to Labour's socialist tradition but out of tune with contemporary British attitudes, Foot is widely considered to be merely a caretaker whose main task is to hold the party together in the face of defections to a new centrist party and rebuild its former strength. Nevertheless, he has shown surprising strength among the voters, and a public opinion poll taken in November 1980 gave him a 44 percent to 39 percent edge over Margaret Thatcher, the Conservative Prime Minister.

Of English and Scottish descent, Michael Mackintosh Foot was born on July 23, 1913 in Plymouth, England, one of the seven children of Isaac and Eva (Mackintosh) Foot. His father, a solicitor, Methodist lay preacher, and noted bibliophile whose collection of 80,000 books was one of the largest private libraries in England, sat as a Liberal Member of Parliament in the House of Commons from 1922 to 1924 and from 1929 to 1935 and served as Secretary of Mines in the government of Prime Minister James Ramsay MacDonald. Two of Foot's four brothers have also been active in public affairs. Hugh Foot, now Lord Caradon, held a number of colonial government posts and was United Kingdom's Permanent Representative to the United Nations, from 1964 to 1970, in the Labour government headed by Harold Wilson, and Dingle Foot, a former Labour MP, served as Solicitor-General, from 1964 to 1967. (During the period when the brothers were all still in politics, London wags sometimes referred to them as "the three left Feet.")

Michael Foot received his early education at Forres School in Swanage and Leighton Park School, a Quaker boarding school in Reading, then went on to Wadham College, Oxford on a scholarship. Active in student political organizations, he was elected president of both the Liberal Club and the Oxford Union, the university's debating society. After graduating with honors in philosophy, politics, and economics, in 1934, he worked for a time in a shipping office in Liverpool. Moved by the suffering endured by the city's poor and unemployed during the Depression and inspired by Aneurin Bevan, the controversial and colorful leader of the radical wing of the Labour party, Foot abandoned his family's longstanding Liberal tradition and, in March 1935, joined the Labour party. Seven months later he ran as a Labour candidate for Monmouth, in southeast Wales, but was defeated.

In 1937 Foot accepted a job as assistant editor of *Tribune,* a radical weekly political journal founded by Aneurin Bevan. That marked the beginning of what was to be a long and fruitful association with Bevan, who became Foot's close friend as well as his political model and mentor. According to some observers of the British political scene, Foot's views are virtually indistinguishable from those expounded by Bevan in the 1930's. More or less at the same time, but at the opposite end of the political spectrum, Foot began a long friendship with Lord Beaverbrook, the pugnacious and tyrannical Conservative press magnate. In 1938 Foot left *Tribune* to accept a position as an editorial writer for Beaverbrook's right-wing *Evening Standard.* He spent a few months as a staff writer with the *Daily Express* in the early 1940's, then rejoined the *Evening Standard,* as its acting editor, in May 1942.

Foot's relationship with Lord Beaverbrook flourished during the early days of World War II, when the struggle for national survival necessarily muted political differences. The fact that both were asthmatic—a condition that disqualified Foot from military service—strengthened the bond between the two men, as did their deep-seated mutual respect and their intellectual rapport. Toward the end of the war, however, Foot found himself disagreeing more and more with Beaverbrook's political beliefs and with the *Standard's* jingoistic editorial position. Finally, in 1944, he resigned to become a political columnist for the *Daily Herald,* a post he retained until 1964. But despite their pronounced political differences, and despite the complaints of Foot's political colleagues, many of whom felt that his ongoing social relationship with Lord Beaverbrook amounted to ideological hypocrisy, the two men remained friends until the end of Beaverbrook's life.

By the time he began writing for the *Herald,* Foot was already the author of several widely read political pamphlets, among them *Guilty Men,* a condemnation of prewar Conservative politics, which he wrote with two likeminded colleagues under the joint pseudonym "Cato," *Armistice 1918-39,* and *The Trial of Mussolini,* which was published under the pseudonym "Cassius." Recognized as one of the foremost young intellectual spokesmen of the Labour party by the mid-1940's, Foot made a bid for the parliamentary seat for the Devonport Division of Plymouth on July 5, 1945. In the nationwide Labour landslide, he easily topped his opponent, former Secretary of State for War Leslie Hore-Belisha, by about 2,000 votes. That

same year, he rejoined the staff of *Tribune* as managing director, serving in that capacity until 1974. Concurrently, he acted as *Tribune's* editor, from 1948 to 1952 and from 1955 to 1960, and from 1964 to 1974, he was, as well, the literary critic for the London *Evening Standard.*

As a Labour backbencher in the House of Commons, Foot rapidly gained a reputation as an articulate, witty, and occasionally acerbic speaker. Closely associated with the Bevanite wing of the party, he was an outspoken advocate of policies that even many of his Labour colleagues considered to be extremist, such as nationalization of British industry and commerce, disengagement from the Cold War and from the traditional British alliance with the United States, nuclear disarmament, and nonparticipation in the developing European Economic Community. Although he served on Labour's national executive committee from 1948 to 1950, Foot declined a second term, preferring not to make the doctrinal compromises the job sometimes required.

Foot lost his parliamentary seat in the election of 1955, but through his writing, for *Tribune* and for other publications, he continued to play an important role in the Labour party. Among the political pamphlets he wrote in the 1950's were *Keep Left, Full Speed Ahead, Guilty Men, 1957,* and *Parliament in Danger!* He also completed work on *The Pen and the Sword* (MacGibbon & Kee, 1957), about one year in the life of Jonathan Swift. During that decade, he became one of British television's most familiar political personalities as a regular panelist on two public affairs programs, *Free Speech* and *In the News.* His reputation was further enhanced, although in a rather backhanded way, when he was deported from France, in 1958, after making, in public, a derogatory comment about President René Coty.

After Aneurin Bevan's death, in 1960, Foot succeeded his mentor both as a leader of the Labour party's radical faction and as an MP, for in the November election of that year, he won the parliamentary seat for the Welsh mining town of Ebbw Vale, the constituency which for several decades had regularly sent Bevan to the House of Commons. He has held the seat ever since. Foot's devotion to Bevan's memory was further revealed by his decision to write a definitive account of Bevan's life, a major project that took up much of his spare time for the next twelve years. MacGibbon & Key released, to mixed reviews, volume one, covering the years 1897 to 1945, of *Aneurin Bevan; a Biography* in 1962. The second volume, which dealt with the remainder of Bevan's life, was published in 1973.

On the floor of the House of Commons throughout the 1960's, Foot showed himself to be, in the eyes of some political observers, an uncompromising and doctrinaire ideologue more given to criticizing his moderate colleagues than to formulating a compromise program that could win elections and, at the same time, solve Britain's mushrooming economic problems. As British journalist Bernard Levin noted in an article for the New York Times Sunday Magazine (April 21, 1968), "Foot, for all his brilliance, represents with appalling faithfulness the inability of the left in the Labour party to recognize what the world is actually like. It is, for instance, quite clear that Foot, and the bulk of his left-wing followers, would rather the Labour party stayed out of office forever than get in and do good with its precious principles even slightly frayed at the edges."

Although his ideological rigidity ran contrary to the preferences of the majority of Britain's Labour voters, who began deserting the party by the end of the decade, Foot nonetheless was a power to be reckoned with because his ideas were true to the party's socialist heritage and, in addition, conformed to the views of the powerful trade unions, Labour's grassroots base and the principal source of its funds. Labour, which had not won an election since 1951, was returned to power in 1964, largely due to the widespread belief that it was time for a change. The moderate government of Prime Minister Harold Wilson immediately became a target for Foot's invective, but despite his frequent disagreements with Wilson, he persuaded disenchanted radicals to remain in the party. Offered a post in Wilson's Cabinet after the 1966 election, Foot turned down the invitation, citing as his reasons Labour's general economic policy as well as its support of American military involvement in Southeast Asia.

Following the Conservative victory in the 1970 election, the Labour Members of Parliament, now in Opposition, elected twelve of their number to the Shadow Cabinet headed by Wilson, the party's acknowledged leader. Foot, who had polled a respectable 124 votes in the party election, agreed to accept the post of Shadow Minister of Power, thus becoming one of the party's official spokesmen in parliamentary debates. Many Britons were puzzled by his willingness to move to the front bench, especially since it entailed restrictions on his freedom to criticize the party's leadership, and some of his colleagues even sensed a right-wing plot. According to Ian Aitken, a political reporter for the Guardian (July 17, 1970), several backbenchers had expressed "the unworthy thought that a proportion of Mr. Foot's large vote might be traceable to a desire among the subtler right-wingers to silence the most effective left-wing spokesman in the Commons." Foot seemed determined, however, to strive for party unity and, in 1971, he was elected, as well, to the Labour party's national executive committee, a post he continues to hold.

Battered by skyrocketing inflation and a worsening economy, British voters, in the 1974 election, turned out the Conservative government of Prime Minister Edward Heath in favor of a new Labour government. Much to the surprise of veteran political observers, Foot accepted the portfolio of Secretary of State for Employment in Wilson's Cabinet. The appointment was, in the words of journalist Ann Clwyd, a case of "set a thief to catch a thief." Miss Clwyd, writing in the Guardian (March 6, 1974), thought that Wilson displayed "intuitive brilliance in appointing a man with an impeccable trade union pedigree to sweeten any nasty pills that may have to be handed out to the unions."

In his maiden speech as Secretary of Employment, Foot denounced Heath's policy of wage controls to check inflation, but conceded that they would be retained until a voluntary agreement could be worked out with the Trades Union Congress (TUC). "There may very well be cases where it would be better to deal with such a cancerous growth with x-ray therapy rather than by surgical action," he said, as quoted in Newsweek (April 1, 1974), "particularly at a moment when somebody wants to jog your elbow." Convinced that there is a "convergence of interests" between socialist government and the unions, he negotiated a settlement of a crippling mineworkers' strike and helped to draft the so-called "social contract," under the terms of which the TUC agreed not to demand wage increases larger than the rise in the cost of living. The social contract virtually guaranteed a Labour victory in the general election of October 1974, but as a means of controlling inflation, it failed, and Foot's critics, charging that he had been too eager to agree to the unions' demands, dubbed him "the unions' poodle."

Foot's policies as Employment Minister may not have made a constructive contribution to Labour's larger program or to the national economy as a whole, but they verified his socialist credentials with the powerful TUC and with many key members of the parliamentary Labour party. Consequently, when Harold Wilson announced his retirement in 1976, Foot was one of the chief contenders in the election to choose a successor. As if to underscore his new status, he began appearing in Parliament in well-tailored suits instead of his customary rumpled corduroys. Foot led on the first ballot, but since no candidate received a majority, subsequent votes were taken, and on the deciding tally, he came in second, behind James Callaghan, Wilson's Foreign Secretary. His second-place position earned him the title of deputy party leader and the post of floor leader of the House of Commons. He also served as Lord President of the Privy Council. As leader, he sided with Prime Minister Callaghan in attempting to hold down pay raises to restrain inflation and thus helping to keep the minority Labour government in office.

Inflation, rising unemployment, and other economic and political problems, among them the financial drain imposed by Britain's continuing military presence in strife-torn Northern

Ireland, catapulted the Conservative party, headed by Margaret Thatcher, back into power in the general election of 1979. Labour's crushing defeat brought the party to the lowest ebb of its nearly century-long history. No longer able to claim the loyalty of the great majority of Britain's working-class voters, most of whom dismissed its program as irrelevant, Labour lost thousands of card-carrying members. By 1980 the membership had dropped to about 200,000, much less than it had been at any time since 1928, the first year for which a figure is available. Moreover, most of Labour's supporters were middle-aged or older, and the number of full-time local party representatives, or agents, had fallen to eighty, down from about 300 in the early 1960's. In addition, the party was plagued by ideological strife, with its right and left wings further apart than ever before.

Following Callaghan's resignation in October 1980, the parliamentary Labour party convened to choose a new leader. By a vote of 139 to 129, Foot was elected to the post on the second ballot, on November 10, 1980, defeating Denis Healey, the former Chancellor of the Exchequer and the head of the party's right-wing faction. Since public opinion polls had consistently shown Healey to be the preferred candidate of the Labour electorate, it was widely held that Foot was a centrist-left compromise caretaker who would step down after putting Labour's troubled house in order. Foot, however, immediately denied those rumors, and in a post-election press conference, announced his intention to "combine protection of my principles with effective action." Among other things, he reaffirmed his commitment to nuclear disarmament, which is, in his words, "essential to the salvation of the world," and promised to "unite" the party "on the matters of supreme importance to us—economic policy, domestic policy—and to attack the outrages and infamies which this government is inflicting on our people." In closing, he quoted Aneurin Bevan: "Never underestimate the passion for unity in the party, and never forget that it is the decent instinct of people who want to do something."

Determined to unify the squabbling Labour factions in opposition to the "blockheaded, blackhearted" Thatcher government, Foot named both left- and right-wing MPs to his Shadow Cabinet. He appointed Denis Healey Foreign Minister, but decided to oversee defense himself, although he asked Brynmor John, a moderate, to act as defense spokesman on the floor of the Commons. In his New Year's message for 1981, he identified as the party's "major task" the refutation of "the wicked lie that there is no alternative to chronic unemployment in Britain's present economic climate." But his "full, wide-ranging socialist program" for ending unemployment was sidetracked by a revision in the party's governing rules, which gave the trade unions and the local party organizations the dominant voice in the selection of party leader, and ultimately, Prime Minister. According to a report in *Time* (February 9, 1981), Foot, who took no part in the crucial debate leading to the controversial rules change, has committed himself to reversing the ruling.

Tony Benn, who recently supplanted Michael Foot as a leader of the Labour party's radical faction, and other left-wing MPs applauded the rules change as a kind of democratization, but some moderates, led by former Cabinet officers Shirley Williams, David Owen, Roy Jenkins, and William Rodgers, anticipating an increasing radicalization of Labour's platform, bolted from the party to form, in March 1981, the Social Democratic party. Foot immediately began taking steps to halt further defections to the new party. Among other things, he calmed nervous Labourites by stressing the importance of multilateralism in foreign affairs and by assuring them that he backed a mixed economy.

A large-boned man of average height, Michael Foot has been described as looking "like a mad scientist, with thick Coke-bottle glasses, rumpled clothing and untamed white hair which flops around alarmingly." He walks with a slight limp, the result of an automobile accident in the early 1960's in which he nearly lost his life. Although he still suffers from a variety of minor ailments, he is, by all accounts, stronger and healthier than he has been in years. Like his father, he is an avid reader and book collector. He included his favorite writer, William Hazlitt, the nineteenth-century English essayist and literary critic, in his most recent book, *Debts of Honour*, a study of heroes published in Great Britain in 1980 and in the United States by Harper and Row in 1981. Other recreations include swimming, walking, and playing chess, and he is an enthusiastic fan of the Plymouth Argyles football team.

A witty, literate, and charming conversationalist and a spellbinding public speaker whose rhetorical flights are adored even by his political adversaries, Foot is one of the best-liked men on the British political scene, though in many quarters his views are thought to be a bit eccentric. Foot was married on October 21, 1949 to Jill Craigie, a film producer and writer, whose credits include the documentaries *Blue Star* and *The Way We Live*, the screenplays for *Man with a Million* (1953) and *Windom's Way* (1957), and a book on the women's suffrage movement in Britain. The Foots live in a large, book-crammed Victorian house near Hampstead Heath, in London. They have no children.

References: Christian Sci Mon B p10 N 25 '80 por; London Observer p11 Mr 10 '74 por, p13 N 16 '80 por; Newsweek 96:78+ N 24 '80 por; Time 116:44 N 24 '80 por; Toronto Globe & Mail p7 N 14 '80 pors; International Year Book and Statesmen's Who's Who, 1981; Who's Who, 1980-81; Writers Directory, 1980-82

Foster, Jodie

Nov. 1962(?)- Actress. Address: b. c/o
Ufland Agency, Inc., 190 N. Canon Dr.,
Beverly Hills, Calif. 90210

At the age of thirteen Jodie Foster enjoyed the
tribute of seeing three of her films screened
at the 1976 Cannes Film Festival—*Taxi Driver*,
Bugsy Malone, and *The Little Girl Who Lives
Down the Lane*. Her portrayals, respectively,
of a preteen hustler, a slapstick speakeasy
singer, and a child murderer evidence the
steady professional growth of a decade from
adorable moppet on television commercials,
through wide-eyed Disney-type youngsters, to
older or more complex characters requiring
subtle and mature interpretation. In their reviews of *Bugsy Malone* Vincent Canby of the
New York *Times* predicted that Jodie Foster
was "on her way to becoming one of the
screen's great beauties" and Gary Arnold of
the Washington *Post* maintained, "Her pre-
cociousness is truly extraordinary, . . . this
may be a prodigious movie talent in the making." *Foxes* and *Carny*, her 1980 films, brought
her nearer to fulfilling those expectations and
confirmed her reputation, to quote *People*, as
at present "the most experienced and arguably
the best young actress in Hollywood."

Alicia Christian ("Jodie") Foster was born in
November 1962 in Los Angeles, California, the
youngest of the four children of Lucius Foster
3d, now a real estate agent in Los Angeles,
and Evelyn (Almond) ("Brandy") Foster. Jodie
has two sisters, Lucinda and Constance, and
a brother, Lucius 4th ("Buddy"), whose own
career as a child actor culminated in the television series *Mayberry, R.F.D.* (CBS, 1968-71),
in which he played Mike Jones.

Some months before Jodie's birth, her parents
were divorced. Having grown up under the
care only of her mother and having rarely seen
her father, Jodie Foster told Patrick Pacheco
in an interview for *After Dark* (July 1980), "I
feel lucky in a way that I never knew a
father, that there was never a marital conflict
in the house. I've always felt like a replacement . . . that I took the place of a husband,
roommate, or pal." To help meet the expenses
of bringing up four children, Mrs. Foster
worked for a time on publicity for the film
producer Arthur Jacobs, who had earlier been
a publicist. After her son Buddy began doing
television commercials at the age of eight, he
became the family breadwinner. Because Jodie
was too young to be left alone in the car,
Mrs. Foster took her along one day when
Buddy was auditioning for a tanning lotion
commercial. The admen in charge noticed
three-year-old Jodie in the studio and later
notified Mrs. Foster that her daughter had been
chosen to be the bare-bottom Coppertone child.

Mrs. Foster readily recognized and cultivated
her youngest daughter's talent. An obviously
gifted child, Jodie had begun talking at nine
months, was speaking in sentences at one year,
and taught herself to read at three. By age
five, she could understand commercial scripts
by herself. Having learned something of the
inner workings of Hollywood from her job as
a producer's publicist, Mrs. Foster managed
Jodie's career from the beginning. She set very
definite goals for her young client and kept
her career on track. A veteran of some forty-
five commercials, including Ken-L-Ration and
Oreos, eight-year-old Jodie was valuable advertising property when Mrs. Foster decided
that it was time for her to play dramatic parts.

Thus, on May 19, 1969, Jodie Foster made
her acting debut on an episode of her brother's
rural situation comedy, *Mayberry, R.F.D.* Over
the next five years she appeared on more than
a dozen television programs, including *The
Courtship of Eddie's Father* (ABC), *My Three
Sons* (NBC), *Gunsmoke* (CBS), *Julia* (NBC),
Ironside (NBC), *Bonanza* (NBC), *Ghost Story*
(NBC), *The Partridge Family* (ABC), *Kung Fu*
(ABC), *The New Adventures of Perry Mason*
(CBS), *Love Story* (NBC), and *Medical Center*
(CBS). During the fall of 1973 she was seen
regularly as Elizabeth Henderson, the daughter,
on *Bob & Carol & Ted & Alice* (ABC). She
also appeared in the 1974 made-for-television
movie *Smile, Jenny, You're Dead* (ABC) and in
three hour-long presentations for young people
of *ABC Afterschool Specials*: "Alexander"
(1973); the Emmy Award-winning "Rookie of
the Year" (1973), in which she had the starring
role; and "The Life of T.K. Dearing" (1975).
A television pilot *My Sister Hank*, with Jodie
Foster in the title role, failed to make it into
CBS' program lineup in 1972, but she did star
briefly during 1974 in her own series, *Paper
Moon* (ABC), in which she played Addie Pray,
a wisecracking orphan on the road with a fast-
talking conman, portrayed by Chris Connelly.

For television's *World of Disney* (NBC) Jodie Foster appeared, moreover, in "Menace on the Mountains" in 1970. Two years later she undertook at the Walt Disney studio her first film, *Napoleon and Samantha* (Buena Vista), a touching tale of a boy (Johnny Whitaker) who, aided by Samantha (Jodie Foster), struggles to keep his unusual pet, an aging circus lion, from the uncaring hands of authorities. While making her "appealing" debut as a motion picture actress, however, she encountered danger not seen on the screen, when Major the lion became overly playful one day and lifted Jodie by his jaws. The gentle mauling put her in the hospital for several days and left her with scars across her stomach. Two camels served as the animal attraction in her next Disney production, *One Little Indian* (Buena Vista, 1973), a tale of the Old West in which she had a small supporting role as the handsome widow's daughter.

In her first motion picture for adult audiences, *Kansas City Bomber* (MGM, 1972), Jodie Foster escaped critical notice as the neglected daughter of a roller derby queen (Raquel Welch). Returning to juvenile films in *Tom Sawyer* (United Artists/Reader's Digest, 1973), the musical adaptation of Mark Twain's novel, she drew mixed reviews (as did the film in general) for her portrayal of Becky Thatcher. Martin Levine of *Newsday* (March 16, 1973) commented that her "vocal intonations and facial expressions, especially, are charming—but it's the charm of someone two or three times her actual age of nine." After pointing out flaws in the scenario, acting, and direction, Richard Schickel concluded his review in *Time* (April 2, 1973): "Only Jodie Foster, as Becky, suggests that she somehow remembers what it is like to be a real person in a real world."

In a marked departure from her heretofore wholesome roles, Miss Foster portrayed a wine-drinking street urchin in *Alice Doesn't Live Here Anymore* (Warner Brothers, 1974), a "fine, moving, frequently hilarious" film that earned its star, Ellen Burstyn, an Academy Award for best actress of 1974. "Jodie Foster (who looks like a boy and talks like a man) is a match for Tatum O'Neal," Kathleen Carroll told readers of the New York *Daily News* (January 30, 1975). Although in her brief role she was almost overshadowed by the deft performance of Alfred Lutter as the boy she teaches to steal, her talent and responsiveness to guidance caught the eye of director Martin Scorsese, who cast her in an even grittier role in *Taxi Driver*.

An explosive film about the brutal consequences of emotional and psychological isolation among life's fringe elements, *Taxi Driver* (Columbia Pictures, 1976), starring Robert De Niro as the psychotic night cabbie Travis Bickle, generated much controversy, although most critics acknowledged its power. Martin Knelman of the Toronto *Globe and Mail* (March 6, 1976) praised it as "the most cathartic treatment of violence in America since *Bonnie*

and Clyde and . . . likely to emerge as one of the key social documents of its era." Miss Foster portrayed Iris, a twelve-year-old prostitute who rejects Bickle's attempts to reform her and thus pushes one of the buttons that sets him off toward the climactic orgy of violence near the end of the film. "I knew," she later admitted to columnist Liz Smith of the New York *Daily News* (September 20, 1976), "when the hustler part in *Taxi Driver* came up that I had to be really perfect or it would ruin my career. That role was really risqué for a child."

The possibility that the role would be harmful to such a young actress alarmed members of the Los Angeles Welfare Board, who subjected Jodie Foster to a battery of psychological tests before pronouncing her emotionally mature enough to handle the role. "I spent four hours with the shrink," she later complained to Rex Reed in an interview that appeared in the New York *Sunday News* (June 6, 1977), "to prove I was normal enough to play a hooker. Does that make sense? He asked me what kind of food I ate and would I like to get married. I said not at 13." Nominated for an Academy Award as best supporting actress for the role, she elicited from reviewers such descriptions as "an amazing blend of innocence and precocious sexuality" and "an unusually physical child actress." In an interview for *Working Woman* (May 1980) she spoke of her recognition of "depth" in the personality of Iris: "I didn't see myself as a baby hooker, but as a runaway, a sad character." *Taxi Driver*, which won the Cannes Film Festival's Golden Palm grand prize in 1976, proved to be a financial turning point in Miss Foster's career. She has since commanded $100,000 and higher for a film.

From *Taxi Driver*, Miss Foster turned to a parody of violence in the children's movie, *Bugsy Malone* (Paramount, 1976), a British-made innovative but "wildly uneven" musical satire of American gangster pictures. As the only veteran actress in an all-juvenile cast, she won high marks for her portrayal of Tallulah, a "tough, comic" speakeasy queen. She greatly impressed British director Alan Parker with her lightning memory for dialogue and her sophisticated professionalism. "My total direction of her," Parker said, "consisted of telling her I wanted a cross between Lauren Bacall and Mae West and she did all the rest." As some puzzled reviewers suggested, *Bugsy Malone*'s abundance of cinematic clichés, references to movie classics, dialogue of period genre, and other nostalgic delights were probably lost on young viewers for whom it seems to have been primarily intended. But the critics had no reservations about Jodie Foster, several of them comparing the effectiveness of her performance to her work in *Taxi Driver*.

Needing all her talent to cope with a difficult subject and trying script, in *Echoes of a Summer* (Cine Artists, 1976) Jodie Foster portrayed Deirdre Striden, a terminally ill daughter caught between her mother's (Lois Nettleton) never-ending and discomfiting quest for a cure and her father's (Richard Harris) attempts to accept the inevitable and make life as comfortable as possible. "In the eighth film of an increasingly promising career," the critic for *Variety* (February 4, 1976) observed, "[she] brings a fanciful spirit and gutsy depth to the part. Her precocious, almost androgynous quality is well suited to the task of playing a child forced to be 'old' at the age of 12."

Back at Disney studios in the offbeat comedy *Freaky Friday* (Buena Vista, 1976), Miss Foster portrayed Annabel Andrews, who exchanges identity with her mother (Barbara Harris) temporarily, so that each comes to respect the perspective of the other. The reviewers who accepted the film as fine children's entertainment thought that the cast itself was a good reason for adults also to sit through it. A similar appeal to both young and old could be claimed by the standard Disney comedy *Candleshoe* (Buena Vista, 1977), in which Jodie Foster, appearing with David Niven and Helen Hayes, played a juvenile delinquent from Los Angeles who is taken to England and passed off as the missing heiress to an estate.

The Little Girl Who Lives Down the Lane (American International, 1977) was the first nonjuvenile film to star Jodie Foster. As Rynn, an orphan who relies on her wits and a handy vial of poison to dispatch unwanted adults, including a loathsome child molester (Martin Sheen), she impressed Derek Malcolm of the *Guardian* (February 18, 1977) with her "icy aplomb" and "professionally adult" performance. Most critics agreed, while dismissing the plot as nonsensical. Although the script called for Miss Foster to appear briefly in the nude, she refused, believing the scene to be "tasteless and unnecessary." "I don't mind playing hookers," she explained in the interview with Rex Reed, referring to her role in *Taxi Driver*, "but I don't think people want to see a girl my age naked on the screen." The producers therefore hired her older sister Constance to disrobe in her place.

"In the midst of mediocrity," Louise Farr wrote in *Crawdaddy* (April 1978), "Jodie's presence is always felt. Her particular kind of quiet screen authority makes it seem as if she'll manage the transition from cute kid to adult after that stock-in-trade of child actors—childhood itself—is gone." Her two movies released in 1980 proved that she could confidently handle transitional roles. In *Foxes* (United Artists) she played the leader of a group of four tough but vulnerable high school girls in Southern California whose tribulations stem largely from their conflicts with their neurotic parents. As Donna in *Carny* (United Artists), of which Robbie Robertson was the producer and one of the stars, she conveyed the sensitivity, restlessness, and shrewdness of a lonely teenager who exchanges her boring job as a waitress for the grimy, wandering life of a carnival performer.

In June 1980 Jodie Foster graduated at the head of her class of thirty from the prestigious bilingual Lycée Français in Los Angeles and delivered the valedictory address in French. Although much in demand as an actress, she chose to continue her education, relegating acting assignments to summer vacations. Accepted by several Ivy League schools on the basis of her outstanding scholastic record and admissions test scores, she decided on Yale because of its proximity to New York City. She had looked forward to a normal student life in a college community, but during her freshman year at Yale she attracted unwelcomed attention on campus and in the national media when a fan, John W. Hinckley Jr., who allegedly tried to kill President Ronald Reagan on March 30, 1981, attributed his "historical deed" to a desire to impress her.

Throughout her career Jodie Foster never attended an acting class, relying in her work on what she calls "instinct." Although she made her stage debut at Yale on April 2, 1981 in the role of a prison inmate in a student production of *Getting Out,* she did not study drama there. A lover of reading, she preferred to concentrate on literature and creative writing. Among her favorite authors are André Malraux, whose books she reads in French, and Joan Didion. She collects contemporary art and has a taste for Thai cuisine. For exercise she enjoys water sports, tennis, skiing, horseback riding, and karate.

Jodie Foster is five feet four inches tall, has straight blond hair and blue eyes, and speaks in a soft, deep voice. In his *After Dark* article Patrick Pacheco noted that "she assiduously avoids the Hollywood party scene as boring. . . . Detachment is something she shares with all of her characters. Identifying herself as a 'closet romantic,' she remains aloof." Others who have interviewed her for the press have been delighted by her equanimity, articulateness, and lack of pretension.

References: Mlle 86:80+ Ag '80 pors; N Y Post p36 Mr 6 '76 por; N Y Sunday News III p7 Je 6 '76 por; N Y Times II p13 Mr 7 '76 por; Parade p8+ O 10 '76 pors; People 13:122+ My 19 '80 pors; TV Guide 22:27 N 16 '74 por; Working Woman 5:122+ My '80 por; Who's Who in America, 1980-81; Wilcox, Desmond. Americans (1978)

Francis, Dick

Oct. 31, 1920- British writer. Address: Penny Chase, Blewbury, Didcot, OX119NH, England

For almost twenty years, mystery buffs have eagerly awaited the annual publication of each new Dick Francis thriller. The author of a score of best-selling mysteries, which have

Dick Francis

been translated into nearly two dozen foreign languages, Francis is the winner of two prestigious literary awards: Britain's Silver Dagger, presented in 1965 for *For Kicks,* and the Edgar Allan Poe award, presented by the Mystery Writers of America in 1970 for *Forfeit.* A former professional steeplechase jockey who rode 350 winners in his illustrious ten-year career, Francis turned to writing mystery novels with a racing setting in the early 1960's. His most recent novel, *Reflex,* first appeared on the New York *Times Book Review*'s list of hardcover best sellers the week it was published, and it remained there for more than three months.

"If it is possible to inherit so vague a quality as a wish to be a jockey, I did so," Dick Francis once said. The son and grandson of horsemen, Francis was born to George Vincent and Catherine Mary (Thomas) Francis on October 31, 1920, near Tenby, a coastal town in southern Wales. His earliest memories are of his grandfather's farm, where he retreated to the stables at every opportunity. He learned to ride when he was just five years old. His first mount was a donkey, an animal he still considers to be an "excellent" choice for small children because of its "natural tendency to stay still."

When Dick Francis was seven, his father accepted a job as the manager of a famous hunting stable at Holyport, where many members of the royal family learned to ride, and for the next ten years Dick and his older brother, Douglas, who went on to become a noted horse trainer, rode "every possible sort of pony." George Francis, who bought, trained, and resold young horses, allowed the boys to work with the animals that were too young or too small for the regular riders. Neither boy ever

had a riding lesson, their father being a proponent of the trial and error method, but as Francis later recalled, he and his brother frequently listened in when the stable's riding master was teaching other children and "silently followed his advice." Like his father, who believed that "it was better for a boy to learn about riding than about arithmetic," Dick Francis thought school was "an intolerable interruption of the serious business of life." With his father's connivance, he attended classes only two or three days per week and spent the rest of his time at horse shows or on fox hunts.

In 1933, while he was recovering from a riding accident that had left him with two missing teeth and a broken palate, jaw, and nose, the twelve-year-old Francis eagerly accepted an offer to ride for Bertram Mills, a circus owner with a string of show horses. He rode Mr. Mills's horses in show after show throughout the summer of that year. His debut in hunter classes at horse shows came two years later when, at the last minute, he replaced his father, who had been stricken with sciatica. To the surprise of almost everyone, young Francis rode the spirited Ballymonis to victory.

Unable to bear the constraints of the classroom any longer, Francis dropped out of the Maidenhead County School when he was fifteen to devote himself to working toward his goal of becoming a professional jockey. He had by that time grown too tall and too heavy for flat racing, but he had always been more interested in steeplechasing anyway. "Jumping was the most beautiful thing in the world to me," he told Peter Gorner in an interview for the Chicago *Tribune* (April 15, 1981). "I wanted to jump." Unable to get an apprentice position in a steeplechasing stable, he spent the next few years as, in his words, "a sort of extension of Father," racing and training horses at Holyport, transporting and showing the animals to prospective buyers, and riding with the hounds to show what the hunters could do.

When George and Catherine Francis purchased their own stables near Wokingham in 1938, Dick Francis temporarily shelved his racing ambitions to help his parents make a success of their new enterprise. A year later, Britain was at war. Frustrated by red tape in his attempt to enlist in the cavalry, Francis joined the Royal Air Force instead in the hope of becoming a pilot. First assigned to aircraft maintenance, which he loathed, he bombarded headquarters with applications for pilot training. He eventually flew fighters as well as the cumbersome, troop-carrying gliders that ferried Allied forces across the Rhine. Toward the end of the war, he flew Wellington bombers on patrol duty over the North Sea and on diversionary raids over Germany.

Returning to civilian life, Francis worked for a time at his parents' stables, but the desire to be a jockey still gnawed at him, and after several months, he gratefully accepted a job as secretary to George Owen, a jockey turned farmer and horse trainer, who promised to let him ride horses whenever their owners "did not object to having an amateur on them." The chance came sooner than expected. Less than two weeks after assuming his new post, Francis made his riding debut as an amateur jockey at Woore on October 17, 1946, atop Russian Hero, an untried horse. Concentrating only on "finishing safely without disgracing ourselves," the novice rider guided his horse to a respectable fourth-place finish. Thirty-eight races later, on May 3, 1947, Francis achieved his first victory, at Banger-on-Dee aboard Wrenbury Tiger. He went on to win nine of the sixty-two races he entered that year. The following year, Francis, who retained his amateur status to gain experience, rode in 142 races.

Because they were not allowed to accept a fee, amateur riders were frequently employed by horse owners of modest means, who used what little extra cash they had to pay a trainer. In accordance with tacit custom, however, when Francis rode a horse to victory, he was the recipient of an under-the-table "gift" from the animal's owner. Francis turned professional in 1948, after the stewards of the National Hunt Committee, which oversees steeplechasing in Britain, declared that by riding gratis so often he was taking rides away from professional jockeys who depended on fees for their livelihood. Later that year, he began a long and fruitful association with Lord Bicester, whose horses, considered by many racing aficionados to be the best in England, regularly competed in some of the most important races in the country. Over the next few years, Francis perfected his already considerable skills atop such horses as Silver Fame, Lochroe, Crudwell, and his favorite mount, Finnure, a big chestnut with "an accelerator like a Chrysler," to use his words.

At the peak of his career, Francis rode in 300 to 400 races a year. During the 1953-54 racing season he rode seventy-six horses to victory in 331 races to win the title of champion jockey. The next season, he began riding for Queen Elizabeth, the Queen Mother. He won several races for the Queen Mother before becoming, in 1956, the central player in what a reporter for the Liverpool *Daily Post* called "the greatest tragedy in the history of sport"—the failure of the heavily favored Devon Loch, who was owned by the Queen Mother, to win the Grand National of Steeplechasing.

Held annually at Aintree racecourse, the Grand National is a grueling test of both horse and rider. Since 1839, of the more than 3,000 horses that have been entered in the race, less than 1,000 have finished. The course, a four-and-one-half-mile "law unto itself," according to Francis, has been the scene of many an odd mishap, but none so bizarre as that which befell Devon Loch near the finish line. One of twenty-nine starters, the front-running Devon Loch cleared fences and hurdles with astonishing ease, and, at one point, even changed directions in midair to avoid landing on a fallen horse. As the crowd of 250,000 cheered, Devon Loch sailed over the last fence and pulled even further away from his closest challenger. Then, some fifty yards from the wire, the horse suddenly stiffened, fell on all fours, and slid on his stomach to an inglorious halt. Francis is convinced that the animal, frightened by the wave of noise from the huge crowd, convulsively threw himself away from the deafening sound, thereby collapsing in mid-stride.

Although he was bitterly disappointed by that loss, Francis was back in the saddle three days later, and before the season was over, he had placed first in eight additional races. The following year, after a horse fell with him, kicked him in the stomach, and broke his wrist, he yielded to pressure to retire from horse racing while he was still at the top of his profession, having ranked among England's top half dozen steeplechase jockeys every year of his ten-year professional career. "You're only good for about ten years," he told one interviewer. "That's about all your bones will stand in the way of spills."

Within months of his retirement, Francis was hired as a racing correspondent by the London *Sunday Express,* a job he held for sixteen years. At about the same time, he began work on his autobiography. His literary agent recommended a ghost writer, but as Francis told Jack Newcombe in an interview for *Life* magazine (June 6, 1969), "When this chap came around and suggested that he move in with us I wanted none of that." Instead, he wrote the book himself. The polished prose of *The Sport of Queens* (M. Joseph, 1957; Harper, 1969), a breezy, chatty personal history, took reviewers by surprise. Allen J. Hubin echoed the sentiments of many critics when he wrote in the New York *Times Book Review* (March 10, 1969), "One might (as an American non-horselover) appreciate less attention to the impersonal geography of steeplechases. But the story of Dick Francis is here, as alive as those blowing stallions he rode to victory."

Francis turned to writing mystery novels because, as he put it, "the carpets were wearing thin, the house needed painting, and my two boys needed educating." His first effort, *Dead Cert* (M. Joseph, 1962; Holt, 1962), a tightly constructed story about a steeplecase jockey who penetrates an organized crime racket in pursuit of a murderer, was well-received by critics and readers alike. He has produced a book a year ever since, and, in the process, acquired a worldwide following and earned a reputation as a master of the mystery genre. Francis' novels are both predictable and surprising: they are guaranteed to be about horses and horse racing, but within that framework Francis has found countless plot twists. For example, a prize thoroughbred stallion is hijacked in *Blood Sport* (M. Joseph, 1967; Harper, 1967); a jockey is barred from racing after he is falsely accused of throwing a race in *Enquiry* (M. Joseph, 1969; Harper, 1969); a journalist probing a doping scandal is murdered in *For Kicks* (M. Joseph, 1965;

Harper, 1965); a private plane carrying a famous jockey explodes in mid-air in *Rat Race* (M. Joseph, 1970; Harper, 1971); a jockey vanishes, presumably with the racetrack's gate receipts, in *Slayride* (M. Joseph, 1973; Harper, 1974); and several top race horses are stricken with a deadly swine disease in *Whip Hand* (M. Joseph, 1979; Harper, 1980).

Franciscan heroes are not devilishly attractive supermen in the James Bond mold. On the contrary, almost all of them are rather ordinary, introspective, middle-aged loners. If they have anything in common beyond a love of horse racing it is a stoic ability to endure brutal physical punishment, pain being a subject that Francis perhaps understands better than most of his rivals in the mystery field. During his riding career he sustained ten concussions, fractured his skull and his wrist, and broke each collarbone six times, his nose five times, and, in his words, "no end of ribs."

Many of Francis' central characters have to contend against some personal physical or emotional handicap as well as against assorted villains. For example, Sid Halley, the brooding hero of *Odds Against* (M. Joseph, 1965; Harper, 1965) and *Whip Hand* who lost his hand in a racing accident, is paralyzed by fear when the malicious Trevor Deansgate threatens to shatter his remaining hand. "Whatever anyone said, I intimately knew about fear," Halley thinks in *Whip Hand*. "Not fear of any horse, or of racing or falling, or of ordinary physical pain. But of humiliation and rejection and helplessness and failure... all of those. All the fear I'd ever felt in all my life was as nothing compared with the liquefying, mind-shattering disintegration of that appalling minute. It broke me in pieces.... And instinctively, hopelessly, I tried not to let it show." In his review of *Whip Hand* for *New York* magazine (April 21, 1980), J. I. M. Stewart observed, "At times, indeed, [Sid Halley] is the almost Conrad-like character who feels deeply in his soul that he has irrevocably lost his honor by flinching before one test or another. This theme, although not labored, lends a little depth to an expert and fast-moving yarn."

Reviewers have often commended the "poise" and "economy" of Francis' spare, first-person narrative. As might be expected, he is at his best when he is describing the tension and excitement of a horse race. "I could still feel the way I'd moved with the horse, the ripple of muscle through both the striving bodies, uniting in one," Halley says in *Whip Hand*. "I could still feel the irons round my feet, the calves of my legs gripping, the balance, the nearness to my head of the stretching brown neck, the mane blowing in my mouth, my hands on the reins...."

The racing scenes in *Reflex* (M. Joseph, 1980; Putnam, 1981) are "as good as anything Mr. Francis has done," Julian Symons, the mystery writer, commented in the New York *Times Book Review* (March 29, 1981), and Symons found the characterizations in *Reflex* to be "more interesting" than previous Francis creations. In Philip Nore, the disillusioned, aging jockey and amateur photographer who stumbles into a blackmailing scheme, Francis has created his most complex and perhaps his most appealing hero. Over the years, critics have occasionally complained about gratuitous "sado-masochistic" violence, "loose" plotting, and "too stagey" villains, but most would agree with Symons that, "in the end, action is the name of the Dick Francis game," and "in writing scenes of action, not all of them violent, and blending them into a mystery adventure, he is now a long way ahead of the rest of the field."

A careful writer, Francis admits that he has to "think every word." "It's far harder than riding a horse," he once said, as quoted in *Forbes* magazine (April 15, 1970). "As a jockey, there was a certain amount of worry: Did I please everyone? But now I spend hours looking at that blank piece of paper." He writes only one draft of each novel, in longhand on school notebooks. His wife, Mary, a former publisher's reader, corrects the grammar and spelling before he turns the manuscript over to his publishers. To meet his contractual obligations, Francis usually begins writing a new novel in January, finishing it by May. He spends the remainder of the year researching story ideas. As he told the New York *Times*'s Judy Klemesrud, in an interview for a profile published on June 1, 1980, he gets his ideas "by going to the races two days a week, mixing with the racing world, reading other books, and keeping [his] eyes and ears open."

Because he refuses to write about a place he has not seen at firsthand, Francis and his wife have circled the globe, stopping for extended stays in Moscow, the locale of *Trial Run* (M. Joseph, 1978; Harper, 1979); South Africa, the site of *Smokescreen* (M. Joseph, 1972; Harper, 1972); and Australia, the setting of *In the Frame* (M. Joseph, 1976; Harper, 1977). Before writing *Blood Sport*, which takes place in the United States, Francis traveled the length and breadth of the country by Greyhound bus. For *Flying Finish* (M. Joseph, 1966; Harper, 1967), which involves the international air transport of race horses and brood mares, Dick Francis became a partner in a charter airplane cargo service, and Mary Francis earned a pilot's license.

Dead Cert, the only Francis adventure to date to be made into a theatrical motion picture, fared poorly at the box office, but episodes of *The Racing Game*, which were broadcast as part of the PBS series *Mystery* during the 1979-80 television season, drew a surprisingly large audience. Based on the exploits of Sid Halley, the series was so popular with viewers that it was renewed for the 1980-81 season. In addition to the aforementioned works, Francis is the author of *Nerve* (1964), *Forfeit* (1968; 1969), *Bonecrack* (1971), *Knockdown* (1974; 1975), *High Stakes* (1975), and *Risk* (1977). All were published by M. Joseph in Great Britain and by Harper & Row in the United States. Francis also edited *Best Racing and Chasing Stories* (Faber, 1966) and *Best Racing and Chasing Stories 2* (Faber, 1969), and he has contributed articles to *Horseman's Year, In Praise of Hunting, Stud and Stable,* and other periodicals.

Dick Francis is five feet eight inches tall and weighs 155 pounds, about fifteen pounds over his racing weight. In his tongue-in-cheek profile for the *Guardian* (July 28, 1973), John Hall described the writer as "a lightweight pug gone heavy." "He still looked kind of a tough nut," Hall wrote, "with rawhide cheeks, beat down eyebrows, and a nose as crooked as a cripple's shoehorn." When he is working on a book, Francis rises early, jogs, swims, or rides horseback, then writes for five or six hours.

Despite his rather rigorous schedule, he claims that he "never" lets writing interfere with his social life. Francis and his wife, the former Mary Margaret Brenchley, whom he married on June 21, 1947, live in Blewbury, Oxfordshire, and they spend their winters in Fort Lauderdale, Florida. They have two sons, Merrick, a horse trainer, and Felix, a physics teacher.

References: *Chicago Tribune* I p19+ Ap 15 '81 por; *Life* 66:81+ Je 6 '69 pors; *N Y Times Bk R* p42 Je 1 '80 por; *Newsweek* 97:98+ Ap 6 '81 pors; *Sport Illus* 28:76+ Mr 25 '68 pors; *Pub W* 193:27+ Ja 8 '68 por; *Contemporary Authors* 1st rev vols 5-8 (1969); *Who's Who,* 1981-82

Gajdusek, D(aniel) Carleton (gotʻə-chek)

Sept. 9, 1923- Biomedical scientist. Address: b. National Institutes of Health, Bethesda, Md. 20205

Slow virus infection, first known in animals, was unknown in human medicine when Dr. D. Carleton Gajdusek in the late 1950's began his elucidation of the etiology and epidemiology of kuru, a strange brain disease that was decimating an isolated population in New Guinea. In the 1960's Gajdusek and his associates demonstrated that kuru was transmissible, with incubation periods measured in years and a progressive accumulative pathology leading always to death. They thus showed that slow virus infections in humans can produce chronic degenerative disease with apparent heredofamilial patterns of occurrence and with

none of the inflammatory responses associated with conventional virus infections. They went on to extend their demonstration to a range of worldwide degenerative neurological diseases, beginning with Creutzfeldt-Jakob disease, with incalculable implications for all of medicine, especially as it applies to the basic processes of degeneration and aging. Perhaps more important than their neurological accomplishments was their biological discovery of an entirely new group of unconventional viruses, apparently pieces of genetically active nucleic acid bound to fragments of plasma membrane. For "a major breakthrough" that has "revolutionized thinking" in microbiology as well as neurology, Gajdusek was corecipient of the Nobel Prize in Physiology/Medicine in 1976. Since 1958 he has been with the National Institutes of Health, in Bethesda, Maryland, where he heads the Laboratory of Central Nervous System Studies.

The older of two boys, Daniel Carleton Gajdusek was born on September 9, 1923 in Yonkers, New York to Karl Gajdusek, a butcher of Slovakian birth, and Ottilia (Dobrozscky) Gajdusek, whose parents had emigrated from Hungary. "On my father's side," Gajdusek wrote in his autobiographical contribution to *Les Prix Nobel en 1976* (Norstedt and Söner, 1976), published under the auspices of the Nobel Foundation, "we were a family of farmers and tradesmen, vocations which never interested my brother or myself, but my father's temperament for laughter and ribald fun, lust for life in work and play, music, song, dance, and food, and, above all, conversation, affected us strongly. On my mother's side were the more somber academic and aesthetic aspirations of four university educated first-generation American siblings."

Among those maternal siblings was his aunt Irene Dobrozscky, an entomologist at the Boyce Thompson Institute for Plant Research in Yonkers. With his aunt he often visited the laboratories and greenhouses of the institute, where he came under the tutelage of the mathematician and chemist Dr. William J. Youden.

She also took him on insect-collecting excursions in nearby fields and woods, and through her he became a precocious habitué of New York City's museums, including the Metropolitan Museum of Art, where he attended courses in Egyptology on schoolday afternoons after his fifth-grade classes, and the Museum of Natural History, where he attended evening and weekend lectures on entomology, geology, and botany. "Before I was ten years old," he wrote in his autobiographical Nobel piece, "I knew that I wanted to be a scientist like my aunt and my quiet mathematician tutor. I rejected completely, as did my younger brother, Robert, who is now a poet and critic, the interests of our father and maternal grandfather in business, which made our life style possible."

Before they learned to read, Gajdusek and his brother listened to their mother reading from Homer, Virgil, and Plutarch. Among the early books Gajdusek read on his own were works by Henrik Ibsen and Sigrid Undset, and those that had the most profound effect on him were René Vallery-Radot's biography of Louis Pasteur, Eve Curie's biography of her mother, Madame Marie Curie, and Paul de Kruif's *Microbe Hunters*. He stenciled the names of the twelve microbiologists who were the subjects of de Kruif's book on the steps leading to his attic chemistry laboratory. "At about this time, when I was ten years old," he relates in his contribution to *Les Prix Nobel en 1976*, "I wrote an essay on why I planned to concentrate on chemistry, physics, and mathematics rather than classical biology, in preparation for a career in medicine. Dr. Youden had succeeded in making it clear to me that education in mathematics, physics, and chemistry was the basis for the biology of the future."

During the summers of his thirteenth to sixteenth years, Gajdusek worked at the Boyce Thompson Institute under Dr. John Arthur, synthesizing a series of halogenated aryloxyacetic acids, including 2,4-dichlorophenoxyacetic acid, the commercial weed killer. He graduated from high school at sixteen, in 1939; from the University of Rochester with a B.S. degree *summa cum laude* in biophysics at nineteen, in 1943; and from Harvard University Medical School three years later.

"Fascinated" by children and "captivated" by clinical pediatrics, Gajdusek lived and worked within the walls of Children's Hospital, Boston, through much of medical school. Following his internship and residencies in pediatrics, he served on a pediatric mission in postwar Germany, and in 1948-49 he was a senior fellow in physical chemistry at the California Institute of Technology. From 1949 to 1952 he did virus research in Dr. John F. Enders' laboratory at Harvard on a fellowship from the National Foundation for Infantile Paralysis, and during most of the same period he continued his postgraduate specialty training in clinical pediatrics at Children's Hospital, Boston.

In a tour of military service at the Walter Reed Army Institute of Research in Washington, D.C. in 1952 and 1953, Gajdusek studied viral and rickettsial diseases under Dr. Joseph Smadel, who recognized his brilliance and tried to bring his diffuse energy into focus. "I found that he [Smadel] responded to my over-ambitious projects and outlandish schemes with severity and meted encouragement," Gajdusek recounts, "teaching me more about the methods of pursuing laboratory and field research and presenting scientific results than [about a] theoretical superstructure, which he assumed I already possessed."

From Smadel and from Marcel Baltazard of the Institut Pasteur in Teheran, Iran—where he worked in 1954-55 on rabies, plague, arbovirus infections, scurvy, and other epidemic diseases of Iran, Afghanistan, and Turkey—Gajdusek learned "of the excitement and challenge offered by urgent opportunistic investigations of epidemological problems in exotic and isolated populations." Such investigations, he realized, could throw light not only on the diseases in question but on the development of the nervous system and associated learning and behavioral patterns.

His quest for medical problems in primitive population isolates took Gajdusek to the valleys of the Hindu Kush, the jungles of South America, the coast and inland ranges of New Britain, and the islands of Micronesia and Melanesia, among other exotic spots on the globe. In 1955 he went to Australia as a visiting investigator in virus genetics and immunology with Sir MacFarlane Burnet at the Hall Institute of Medical Research in Melbourne. Between periods of bench work in Melbourne, he launched studies in child development and disease patterns among Australian aboriginal and New Guinean populations. Among those studies was his historic investigation of kuru, begun in 1957 and continued after he joined the National Institutes of Health in 1958. His original NIH title was, rather cumbersomely, Director of the Study of Child Growth and Development and Disease Patterns in Primitive Cultures and of the Laboratory of Slow, Latent, and Temperate Virus Infections, National Institute of Neurological and Communicative Disorders and Stroke.

During one of his field trips out of Melbourne Gajdusek met Dr. Vincent Zigas, a territorial health officer who had just returned from a tour of a remote, isolated area in the eastern highlands of New Guinea, the home of the Fore, a tribe of some 35,000 people living in 160 villages. It was, Zigas reported, a tribe with a stone age culture, still practising ritual funeral cannibalism and afflicted with a bizarre fatal degenerative disease of the central nervous system called kuru, the native word for shakes or tremors. Traveling to the tribal site with Zigas, Gajdusek concurred in his opinion that here was indeed a disease previously unknown to medical science. He remained for almost a year, getting to know, and love, the Fore people, acquainting himself with their culture, and trying to understand the disease. During that time, more than 200 persons died of kuru, and a number of communities were near extinction because of its high incidence among women and children. Over the following years the total number of known victims of the disease—counted from the time of its discovery—rose to more than 2,500, most of them women and children.

The cause of the disease was difficult to ascertain. Neuropathologically, however, kuru was easily described by Gajdusek and Zigas. The symptoms of the neurological disorder progressed from the initial shivering to cerebellar signs of ataxia and incoordination and increasing motor weakness. Walking became difficult, then impossible; soon the victim could not stand; and finally he or she could not even sit up. Dementia was followed by death, about a year after the tremors began. In their pathological examination of the brains of victims, Gajdusek and his associates found gray matter lesions characterized by vacuolization and dropping out of neurons, astrocytic hypertrophy and proliferation, degeneration of Purkinje cell axons and dendrites, and presence of amyloid plaques. They therefore classified the disorder as a spongioform encephalopathy.

At first Gajdusek looked for an inherited etiology, perhaps a defect in the isolated tribe's gene pool, because there were none of the usual indications of infection, such as inflammation, fever, or a detectable production of antibodies. In addition, attempts to grow the disease in animal and human tissue cultures in the laboratory proved unsuccessful, as were efforts to transmit it to animals by the conventional short-term virus inoculation technique.

When Gajdusek and Zigas published a professional report on kuru in 1959, Dr. William Hadlow, a veterinary neuropathologist at the NIH's Rocky Mountain Laboratory in Hamilton, Montana, called attention to pathologic similarities between kuru and scrapie, a transmissible disease of sheep and goats with a very long incubation period. In confirming the transmissibility of scrapie in 1954, the Icelandic veterinarian Björn Sigurdsson had introduced the concept of the slow virus infection to veterinary science.

Fitting in with Hadlow's suggestion was the high incidence of kuru among women and children, that portion of the Fore population chiefly involved in the ritual cannibalism, the eating of the kuru victim's brain and visceral tissue and the smearing of it over face and body. Acting on the suggestion, Gajdusek and his colleague Dr. Clarence J. Gibbs Jr. inoculated subhuman primates with brain suspensions from natives who had died of kuru and then observed the animals for extended periods of time. Finally, two chimpanzees inoculated in 1963 began to show symptoms of the disease in 1965. A second pair of chimps, inoculated with brain sus-

pensions from the first victims, also contracted the malady, and by 1967 the disease had been passed from chimp to chimp three times, in the classic laboratory test of infection.

Soon afterward, several other progressive degenerative diseases of the brain were shown to be slow virus infections. They included delayed and slow measles encephalitis (also known as subacute sclerosing panencephalitis), progressive multifocal leukoencephalopathy, and transmissible virus dementias, usually of the Creutzfeldt-Jakob disease (CJD) type. Gajdusek and Gibbs's success in the Creutzfeldt-Jakob experiments demonstrated for the first time that a degenerative human brain disease occurring worldwide—and not geographically limited to a primitive population—could result from a slow virus infection.

The work of Gajdusek and his associates has led to a more exciting frontier in microbiology than merely the demonstration of new mechanisms of pathenogenesis of infectious disease. That frontier, as Gajdusek pointed out in the Nobel acceptance speech he delivered in December 1976, is the recognition of a new group of viruses that possess unconventional physical and chemical properties and biological behavior far different from those of any other group of microorganisms.

In the Nobel speech, Gajdusek summed up with admirable succinctness his findings thus far and the future prospects. "The group [of atypical agents] consists of viruses causing four known natural diseases: two of man, kuru and CJD; and two of animals, scrapie in sheep and goats, and transmissible mink encephalopathy. . . . For neurology, specifically, we have considerable new insights into the whole range of presenile dementias and, in particular, the large problems of Alzheimer's disease and the senile dementias. The implications of vertical transmission of slow virus infections, and of host genetic control of disease expression for all genetic diseases, and the relationship of these slow virus infectious processes to those that may lead to neoplastic transformation, are obvious." He went on to say that, although the major problems among the degenerative diseases known as multiple sclerosis, amyotrophic lateral sclerosis, and parkinsonism remain unsolved, there are "tantalizing laboratory and epidemiological data" pointing to the possible role of virus-like agents in those diseases. "For a now disappearing disease in a small primitive population to have brought us this far," he said, "is ample reason for pursuing intensely [in other small population enclaves] the challenges offered by the still inexplicable high incidence and peculiar profusion of different neurological syndromes, pathologically distinct yet somehow related to each other."

An indefatigable worker, Gajdusek usually rests in two-hour catnaps, snatched any time of day or night, and his laboratories are cluttered and humming with the activity of visiting Public Health Fellows in addition to the regular staff. He continues to spend about six months each year in the field, in the South Pacific or elsewhere. In addition to his home in Bethesda, Maryland, he retains the family homestead in Yonkers. A bachelor, he has adopted many New Guinean boys over the years. Some fifteen boys are now living with him in the United States, and fifteen educated here have returned to New Guinea. As one of his associates has observed, "Carleton is helping to create the educated class in those countries."

Dr. D. Carleton Gajdusek is a scientist for all seasons, a neo-Renaissance man whose interests stretch far beyond virology. He is widely recognized as a comparative child behaviorist, and he is, in fact if not in name, an anthropologist. He has continued to broaden his reading in world literature, especially the classics, and he speaks German, French, Spanish, Russian, Slovak, and Neo-Melanesian, has a limited knowledge of Persian, Bahasa Indonesian, and Dutch, and has some knowledge of several languages of New Guinea and other areas in Melanesia and Micronesia. Most of his collection of primitive art and artifacts has been given to the Salem Peabody Museum in Massachusetts, where it is on public exhibition. In *Nature* (October 28, 1976) Sir Cedric Mims noted the "insight, patience, and persistence" that Gajdusek brought to his work with kuru and related diseases, and he went on to say: "His encyclopaedic memory, his familiarity with strange places and primitive peoples have generated many legends. He is the sort of man one might have expected to win a Nobel prize and at the same time it is both a surprise and a pleasure to find such a gentle and likeable man behind the legends."

References: Archives of Neurology 34:205+ Ap '77; Nature 263:716+ O '76 por; N Y Times p1+ O 13 '76 por, IV p6 O 17 '76 por; Science 194:928+ N 26 '76 por; Science 81 II:544+ S '81 pors; Time 79:70 Mr 6 '72, 108:66 N 1 '76; US News 81:38 N 1 '76 por; Washington Post A p6 O 15 '76

Garth, David

1930(?)- Political consultant. Address: b. Garth Associates, Inc., 745 Fifth Ave., New York City, N.Y. 10022

Since the decline of the party bosses in the 1960's, media-oriented campaign consultants have gradually assumed many of the functions of traditional political organizations. One of the most sought-after of those modern behind-the-scenes power brokers is David Garth, a shrewd, aggressive public relations expert and a fiercely competitive veteran of twenty years of political warfare. Among those who hold public office at least partly by virtue of his highly successful television offensives are Thomas Bradley and Edward I. Koch, the mayors of Los Angeles and New York City, Governors Hugh L. Carey of New York and Brendan T. Byrne of New Jersey, and United States Senators Jennings Randolph of West Virginia and H. John Heinz 3d of Pennsylvania. With victories in about 75 percent of the contests he has managed, Garth has come to be regarded as "a certified miracle worker whose very presence on a campaign is believed to start the coffers filling," as Carey Winfrey, a political reporter for the New York *Times,* once observed. Nevertheless, Garth's wizardry has occasionally failed, most recently in John B. Anderson's 1980 independent Presidential campaign. "I have never told a candidate I could elect him to anything," Garth said, as quoted in the New York *Times* (September 15, 1977). "That's madness. If I have a talent, it is the ability to look at a candidate and perceive something before other people perceive it."

David Garth was born in 1930 in Hewlett, New York, the son of Leo and Beulah Garth. His father, a Russian immigrant who had begun his career as a tailor, was a well-to-do manufacturer, and his mother, a onetime national vice-president of the American Jewish Congress, was active in local Democratic politics in their upper middle-class, predominantly Republican Long Island community. Bedridden for five years by bouts of mastoiditis and rheumatic fever, David Garth suffered agonizing pain as a child. Listening to the radio was virtually his only diversion. He regularly tuned in the commentaries of H. V. Kaltenborn and Edward R. Murrow, and he heard, among other things, Haile Selassie's dramatic plea to the League of Nations in 1936 and some of Adolf Hitler's speeches, which his mother translated. Like his parents, the boy became intensely interested in politics and world affairs. "The biggest arguments over our dinner table were always about Walter Lippmann's latest column," he said, as quoted in *New Times* (October 30, 1978). "You either talked or perished."

Determined to disprove his doctor's dismal prognosis, Garth devised grueling leg-strengthening exercises, which he performed by the hour, and dreamed of playing football and taking long walks through the leaves. By his midteens, he was strong and healthy. It was, he said, "like letting out a caged animal." Neglecting his schoolwork, he played baseball and basketball eighteen hours a day. "When you go through something like that, you try to live twice as much," he explained to Robert Sam Anson for the *New Times* profile. "If you survive something like that, you achieve a realization of what is pain and what is trouble. You become terribly competitive. You are always testing your own existence. . . . You have the ability to push yourself when other people say they're tired."

During his freshman year in college, Garth was more interested in boxing and karate than in his studies. Eager for action, he dropped out of school to fight in the Israeli War of Independence in the late 1940's. "I loved their passion, their intensity," he once said of his companions in the border kibbutz. "They were living on the edge, every day. It was all on the line. . . . Life and death, the whole shot." Several months after the end of the war, Garth returned to the United States to complete his college education. Following his graduation from college in the early 1950's, he spent three years with the United States Army Security Agency, where he learned communication techniques and acquired what he has called an "empirical approach to knowledge." Having decided on a career in clinical psychology, he enrolled in the graduate school at Columbia University in about 1954. After undergoing three years of Freudian analysis, he left the program because he felt a job in that field would be "too sedentary" and boring for his taste, but as he explained to Jane Perlez, the three years of analysis helped him to understand himself and others. "It is the single most important thing I have ever done," he told Miss Perlez in an interview for the New York *Daily News* (June 15, 1980). "The most critical thing is that you understand yourself before helping other people. Running campaigns—50 percent of that is handling people."

In the late 1950's Garth bluffed his way into the office of a nonaffiliated New York tele-vision station with a plan to telecast local high school football games. Enthusiastic broadcast executives signed the persuasive young man to produce the programs even before he secured the schools' cooperation for the project. Within months, he was producing public affairs programs as well as sports broadcasts. Garth's professional political involvement began in 1960. A longtime admirer of Adlai E. Stevenson, the liberal Democrat who had been his party's Presidential nominee in 1952 and 1956, Garth, along with a few like-minded friends, set up a "Draft Stevenson" committee in preparation for the upcoming 1960 Democratic National Convention. After talking Eleanor Roosevelt, the former First Lady, into acting as his co-chairman, he began circulating petitions and soliciting campaign contributions. When the convention opened in Los Angeles, California in July 1960, Stevenson was still an undeclared candidate, although he had indicated that he would be willing to accept a draft. In a last-minute attempt to stampede the delegates into the Stevenson camp, Garth skillfully stage-managed a prolonged and emotional "spontaneous" floor demonstration that Theodore H. White, the political journalist, described as "the greatest and most authentic demonstration of emotion since the galleries of Philadelphia had overwhelmed the Republican delegates of 1940 with their chant of WE WANT WILLKIE." John F. Kennedy's first-ballot nomination did little to dampen Garth's enthusiasm for politics. Years later, he told one reporter he had "felt tremendous" during the boisterous demonstration. "It was an aura," he added, as quoted in the *Los Angeles Times* (February 21, 1978). "I had a taste." He subsequently produced a television program in which Stevenson reported on his activities as the United States Representative to the United Nations.

Garth helped marshall support for President Lyndon B. Johnson in thirty-six states in the 1964 national election, but his growing reputation as a media specialist stemmed mainly from the 1965 New York City mayoral campaign of John V. Lindsay. Acting as an unpaid television adviser to the candidate, Garth filmed the photogenic Lindsay walking the streets of New York with his sleeves rolled up, his tie loosened, and his coat slung casually over his shoulders. Those cinéma vérité television commercials, which Garth has since described as being "halfway between a Ford ad and a news clip," revolutionized political advertising, and they were so widely copied that the image of the youthful Kennedyesque candidate quickly became a cliché. At the time, however, the novelty helped Lindsay overthrow the entrenched Democratic political machine to win election on both the Republican and Liberal lines.

After Lindsay's election, Garth mounted a high-visibility promotional blitz to boost the mayor's popularity with the public. At first successful, the plan eventually backfired because the media created an unrealistic impression of invincibility. In 1968 Garth took time out from New York City politics to work in Senator Eugene McCarthy's Presidential campaign. Back in New York the following year to direct the advertising campaign in Lindsay's reelection bid, he risked political suicide by having the then unpopular mayor publicly acknowledge his mistakes. The unprecedented stratagem worked. After losing the Republican primary, Lindsay, running as a Liberal and an Independent, was reelected to a second term without the support of a major party.

Garth used exactly the same tactic in 1977, when he was hired to revive the flagging reelection effort of New Jersey Governor Brendan T. Byrne, who had angered the voters by approving a state income tax after promising them, in his 1973 campaign, that he would not call for such a tax. Garth advised the skeptical candidate to admit his error to the public in a television commercial, and Byrne's forthright apology resulted in his reelection by an overwhelming margin. One incredulous local reporter called Byrne's victory "the most remarkable comeback since Lazarus rose from the dead."

In the 1970 off-year election campaign, David Garth's political commercials successfuly sold to the voters three telegenic Democrats: John J. Gilligan, who won the Governorship of Ohio, and Adlai E. Stevenson 3d and John Tunney, who were elected to the United States Senate from Illinois and California, respectively. Sidney Blumenthal, the political historian, views Tunney as something of a transitional figure in Garth's shift from what he calls "the age of charisma" to "the age of toughness." Tunney's slogan—"The Big Boys Have Enough Friends. You Need a Fighter in Your Corner"—epitomized the tough, no-nonsense approach Garth's candidates projected in the early 1970's. According to some observers, New York Representative Richard L. Ottinger's expensive 1970 run for the United States Senate failed primarily because of the striking contradiction between the thoughtful, shy candidate and the tough image Garth had created for him. Another Garth-hewn image toppled in 1976, when Dan Walker, the outspoken, antiorganization populist who had been elected Governor of Illinois in 1972 with the help of Garth's hard-hitting promotional spots, attained the dubious distinction of being the first Illinois gubernatorial incumbent in the twentieth century to lose his own party's primary.

One of Garth's most successful political advertising campaigns in the early 1970's was designed for Thomas Bradley, a black candidate for mayor of Los Angeles, a sprawling city with a predominantly white population and an incumbent mayor, Sam Yorty, who often resorted to blatantly racist campaign tactics. In his television advertisements for Bradley, Garth met the racial issue head on and turned it into an asset. To counter Yorty's contention that Bradley was a dangerous radical, Garth stressed his candidate's modera-

tion and reasonableness and his tough record against crime as a former police officer. When the ballots were counted in May 1973, Bradley won by nearly 100,000 votes.

The following year, Garth transformed Hugh Carey from a portly, lackluster Congressman to a trim, dynamic leader in a "come-from-behind" effort that ended in Carey's landslide victory as the first Democratic Governor of New York in sixteen years. But none of Garth's triumphs was deemed more unlikely than the election of New York Representative Edward I. Koch as mayor of New York City. Garth himself initially entreated Koch, a "forty-to-one shot" in his estimation, not to run, but the Congressman was adamant, and Garth finally agreed to manage his ad campaign. Realizing that his rather colorless client needed a new look, Garth ordered him to spruce up his wardrobe and to lose some weight. He also helped the candidate plot campaign strategy and define dominant issues. To solve Koch's identity problem, he bombarded the airwaves with thousands of radio and television spots that played up the candidate's reputation for honesty and hard-working efficiency. "After eight years of charisma, and four years of the clubhouse," one commercial asked, "why not try competence?" Koch survived a hotly contested seven-man Democratic primary and, in November 1977, won the election by 125,000 votes.

Garth's characteristic thirty- and sixty-second television spots play up his candidate's strengths rather than the opponent's weaknesses. Straightforward and informative, with a string of facts and figures racing across the bottom third of the screen, the commercials concentrate on substance rather than mood. "Our commercials are designed for the long haul," Garth explained to Robert Sam Anson. "We know that people are going to be seeing them ten or twelve times during a campaign, and we want to keep them interested. We want to leave them with a little bit more of the message every time they see it, so, by the end of the campaign, they will have taken in a lot of facts backing up one impression."

Garth sees his television ads as an adjunct of the local news operation. Sidney Blumenthal, writing in his book The Permanent Campaign (1980), agreed: "David Garth's television spots imagine politics so well that they become politics. They're not the message; they're the process. The spots allude to issues and candidates in a campaign and are a hidden issue themselves, straddling the chasm between truth and illusion. Everything Garth reports is true, but is it the truth?" Blumenthal theorized that Garth "may have more impact on politics than his candidates" because he is concerned not with the working details of government, but with "the grand outlines of power."

Garth was briefly associated with John Lindsay's short-lived Presidential bid in 1972, but his first major involvement in a national Presidential campaign came in 1980, when he agreed to help John B. Anderson, the Republican

Congressman who announced his decision to run as an independent candidate on April 24, 1980. "Our job is to position Anderson where he can get heard, and then see what happens," Garth said after accepting the Anderson media account. In an effort to obtain more national press exposure for his little-known candidate, Garth replaced the so-called "Doonesbury Kids," the amateurs who had steered Anderson's crusade through the early Republican primaries, with a highly trained professional staff. But because so much money was devoted to the effort to place Anderson's name on the ballot in every state, there was little left over for vital television advertising.

As they watched their candidate's standing in the polls drop steadily, some of Anderson's advisers complained that Garth's fact-packed commercials were not as eye-catching or thought-provoking as those produced by Bob Sann, the advertising strategist who had developed the theme "The Anderson Difference" for the Republican primary campaign. Others questioned the wisdom of advising Anderson not to discuss issues before the Democratic and Republican parties announced their platforms. When Anderson, hoping to turn his faltering effort around, named Garth campaign director with "full control" on August 28, 1980, several of his top aides resigned in protest. During the closing months of the Presidential race, Anderson's independent candidacy was, in the words of Kevin Philips, the political columnist, "drowning . . . [in] its own futility." In the general election on November 4, Anderson garnered 5,581,379 votes, 7 percent of the total cast.

Working out of his Fifth Avenue headquarters in New York City, Garth directs a relatively large professional staff of about two dozen, including four partners. The campaign architect gives his high-priced advice—in 1978, his base fee was reportedly $15,000 per month, plus 15 percent for broadcast placement—to those liberal politicians he finds compatible, regardless of party affiliation. For example, he helped elect two Pennsylvania Republicans, H. John Heinz 3d, in 1976, and Arlen Specter, in 1980, to the United States Senate, but declined a lucrative offer from Daniel P. Moynihan, the New York Democratic Senatorial nominee in 1976, because of his neoconservative politics. Garth also managed the campaign of Luis Herrera Campíns, the standard-bearer of the moderate Social Christian Party in the 1978 Venezuelan Presidential election. The other major candidates also hired professional campaign experts from the United States, but Garth was once again successful. In addition to planning media campaigns, Garth offers his clients expertise in all aspects of electioneering, from polling and scheduling to speech-writing, fund raising, and top-level staffing. Between elections, Garth's firm handles public relations for such corporate clients as Pepsico, the New York Jets, Warner Communications, and the New York Stock Exchange.

Supposedly the inspiration for the hard-bitten political consultant in Robert Redford's 1972 film The Candidate, David Garth resented actor Allen Garfield's portrayal of the character as a cynical "hack." In his off-hours, Garth is "the nicest guy you'd ever want to be with," according to Jeff Newfield, a political reporter who has known Garth for years. "[He's] charming, funny, literate, bright, incredibly bright," Newfield said, as quoted in the New Times article. "But in a campaign, he's an animal. Brutal. He just has no sense of limits." A stockily built man of five feet eight inches in height, Garth has a round face and brown eyes. To keep in shape for his frequent eighteen-hour workdays, he plays tennis and jogs daily with his Yorkshire terrier, Bismarck. A voracious reader, he generally chooses nonfiction because, as he puts it, "very few fiction books are more interesting than my life is today." During business meetings and interviews he chain-smokes hand-rolled Brazilian cigars.

Once divorced, and now separated from his second wife, Garth lives alone in an apartment on Manhattan's Upper West Side. Although he once tried "to live the dual life," he has since totally immersed himself in his all-consuming job. "I think it's important to live, to be involved in the game," he explained to Myra MacPherson, who interviewed him for the Washington Post (September 19, 1980). "There are two kinds of people. The 'smart' people ... who sit around the table and kind of examine life. And then there are other people—who run for public office, and some of the idiots like myself who are just in there fighting. I'm much more comfortable being an activist."

References: N Y Times p30 Ap 10 '72, B p22 S 15 '77; New Times 11:18+ O 30 '78 pors; Time 110:19+ N 21 '77 por, 112:35 O 30 '78 por; Washington Post E p1+ S 19 '80 por; Blumenthal, Sidney. The Permanent Campaign (1980)

Gibb, Barry

Sept. 1, 1946- Recording artist. Address: b. Robert Stigwood Organization Inc., 1775 Broadway, New York City, N.Y. 10019

In the late 1960's Barry, Robin, and Maurice Gibb, better known as the Bee Gees, came out of Australia by way of England singing sentimental ballads of their own creation in recordings marked by lush vocal harmonies and elaborate melodic structures. The uneducated ear often mistook the Bee Gees for the Beatles, but they had their own large following and their own share of records on the best-seller charts, including "Massachusetts." After several years of decline, the three brothers

Barry Gibb

better known as Berri, the youngest. Leslie is a dog breeder, and Berri, a teenager, has a propensity for singing.

In Barry, Robin, and Maurice Gibb's *The Illustrated Bee Gees* (Delilah Communications, 1979)—an "authorized" hybrid biography-autobiography, written in the third person—their mother remembered Leslie talking to the baby twins "like a little lady," and "poor old Barry" feeling stranded as the middle child and being "a little bit introverted at the beginning." She added that his introversion was exacerbated by a near-fatal childhood accident, which left him scarred for life: "He was about a year and a half old when he poured a boiling pot of tea all over himself. He was seriously ill for about three months, and he didn't talk until he was nearly three because of this."

The Gibb family, originally from Manchester, England, returned there in 1955. Barry, Robin, and Maurice were harmonizing together from the time they could talk, under the encouragement of their father, who "had the Mills Brothers in mind," according to Maurice. They won a local amateur talent contest in 1956, and during the following year they entertained between shows at a Manchester cinema, lip-synching records by such pop singers as Paul Anka and Tommy Steele. One day the sound man dropped and broke the record they were to mime to, and they were on their own. "We had a natural harmony," Barry recalls, "and we got through it."

In 1958 the Gibbs immigrated to Australia, where they lived first in Brisbane and later in Sydney. Early on, Barry, Robin, and Maurice dropped out of school to pursue their careers in show business, and their father quit band-leading to manage them. In their first Australian engagement, in 1959, they entertained between auto races at Redcliffe Speedway in Brisbane. The following year, when television arrived in Brisbane, they began to get TV exposure. Eventually they came to the attention of Col Joye, then the leading singer on the Australian pop scene, and soon afterward Kevin Jacobsen, Col Joye's brother, became their agent.

An appearance by the Gibb brothers at a Chubby Checker concert in Sydney in 1962 led to a contract with Festival Records. In 1963 their single "Three Kisses of Love" made the top twenty in Australia and "Timber" made the top ten. The following year "Peace of Mind" and "Claustrophobia" made the national top ten, and later "Wine and Women" and "I Was a Lover and a Leader of Men" hit the number one spot on the national charts. But their success was insubstantial until, in 1966, one of their fans, Ossie Byrne, offered them the use of his private recording studio in the Sydney suburb of Hurtsville. Unable to read or write music, the Gibbs needed "noodling" time when recording, especially if they were to create their own songs. In Byrne's studio they had all the time for experimentation they

shifted in the mid-1970's in the direction of rhythm-and-blues-flavored dance music, a modified disco, adding an urgency to their bass line and a falsetto height to their sweet whine without abandoning their sumptuous, middle-of-the-road, romantic sound. The result was one of the most surprising comebacks in pop rock history, one in which the trio became the dominant pop group, pervading the air waves as the Big Bands had in the 1930's and 1940's and the Beatles had in the 1960's. Their two-record *Saturday Night Fever* soundtrack smashed every mark in the music business, and they sold 50,000,000 records in the three years 1976-79 alone. In "writing for the present," the Bee Gees admit they are "almost totally commercial," but what comes through in all their best work and raises it above the level of its often trite material is, as Albert Goldman has observed, "a peculiar vocal tone and spiritual stance that stabs straight to the heart of contemporary sensibility." The Bee Gees record on the RSO Records label.

Barry Gibb, the Bee Gees' rhythm guitarist, chief songwriter, and falsetto singer (behind lead singer Robin) is the second of the six children of Hugh Gibb, a former band leader, and Barbara (Pass) Gibb, a former singer and, according to one press release, a psychic. He was born on September 1, 1946 in Douglas on the Isle of Man, a British crown possession in the Irish Sea, where Hugh Gibb and his thirteen-piece orchestra were regularly performing at a hotel. In 1949 Barry's fraternal twin brothers Robin and Maurice (the Bee Gees' bassist) were born, and Andy (who has a solo singing career) was born nine years later. The Gibb brothers have two sisters, Leslie, the oldest of the siblings, and Bernice,

needed, a luxury not permitted them at the Festival facilities. The difference became evident in the quality of the album they recorded in Byrne's studio, *Monday's Rain,* and their smash hit single from that album, "Spicks and Specks."

Meanwhile the Gibb brothers had made two major decisions. One was to get rid of their suits and ties and Brylcream and, in Barry's words, "dress up like Elvis [Presley] and comb our hair like the Beatles." The other was to return to England, in order to reach wider markets at a time in Britain and the United States when Beatlemania was at its height and "heavy metal" rock (incipient in Jimi Hendrix and the groups Jefferson Airplane and Cream) was dawning. Before leaving Australia in January 1967, they sent their album *Monday's Rain* to English talent management companies, including NEMS, owned by the late Brian Epstein, the manager of the Beatles, and managed by Robert Stigwood, Cream's mentor.

When the Gibbs arrived back in England, Robert Stigwood was waiting for them, contract in hand. With a spectacular party at a London discothèque and a publicity campaign costing in the upper registers of four figures, Stigwood announced the emergence of "the new Beatles" in April 1967. As their mother predicted, within a year the Bee Gees were international pop celebrities, with stellar television and concert exposure in Britain and the United States and an unbroken string of chart-busters on both sides of the Atlantic. Their plaintive "New York Mining Disaster 1941" made the top-twenty record charts in England and America and reached number ten in Germany. The emotional "To Love Somebody" became their first standard, covered by Frank Sinatra, Janis Joplin, and others. "Massachusetts" was their first mammoth single, scoring number one in Britain and Germany and eleven in the United States and selling 5,000,000 copies worldwide. As the year 1967 ended, "World" was in the top ten in England and in the number-two spot in Germany, and at the beginning of 1968 "Words" was among the top twenty in England and the United States.

Other hits recorded by the Bee Gees in what Robert Stigwood calls "round one" of their career included "In My Own Time," "Holiday," "I Can't See Nobody," "First of May," and "I've Got a Message for You." Their albums in the same period were *The Bee Gees' First* (1967), *Horizontal* (1967), and the less successful *Odessa* (1968). Their ballads—always more attentive to lyrics than the songs of the harder rock groups—were often described by critics as an extension of the soft, McCartneyesque side of the Beatles, with a touch perhaps of Simon and Garfunkel added. The harder rock songs essayed by the brothers in the late 1960's were rejected by the Robert Stigwood Organization, which wanted their neat, nasal, three-part harmonies applied only to the kind of ballads consistent with their well-scrubbed image as holdovers from a more innocent age, ostensibly inimical to the drug-oriented counterculture. Their success in projecting that image was reflected in the impression made on an American critic that "there are no sound effects in their music" and "they take no drugs, drink no alcohol, and smoke no cigarettes." He was right about the cigarettes.

Under the pressure of sudden success, disagreement over the direction their career should take, and various sibling rivalries, Barry, Robin, and Maurice began to "do silly things," as Barry's wife once put it. Maurice, who confesses that he was "getting to be a real alky," relates in *The Illustrated Bee Gees:* "I was the goof-off, Barry was the pothead, and Robin the pillhead. It was instability. . . . Everything was going so fast." Barry points to their problems as the cause of their breakup: "It was really showing its damage on Robin. Robin suffered a lot. I managed to realize what it was doing, and I stopped. He went into his own world, became a recluse. And we split."

After a separation of eighteen months, the Bee Gees regrouped in the fall of 1970. At the beginning of "round two," as Stigwood calls it, they had several hits, including "Lonely Days," "How Can You Mend a Broken Heart?," "My World," "Run to Me," and "Alive." But they did not become revitalized as a group until the mid-1970's, when the Bee Gees moved to the United States and Stigwood put them in touch with Atlantic Records' producer Arif Mardin, the Florida rhythm-and-blues specialist whose credits included hits with Aretha Franklin and the Average White Band. Under Mardin's guidance, Barry Gibb developed his falsetto in playful accompaniment to Robin's deeper, quavery lead vocals and the Bee Gees for the first time attempted contemporary "soul," à la Stevie Wonder. Without abandoning the wafting harmonies that had long been their trademark, they began to master dance rhythms, and the result, as one wag noted, was "born-again bubblegum." More seriously, Maurice said of Mardin: "He showed us the right track. This was the track leading to R&B and hits."

Despite such fine pieces as "Dogs," "Charades," and the title song, *Mr. Natural* (1974), the first Bee Gees album produced by Mardin, was a commercial failure and, in general, an artistic false step, too close to their old style. The harbinger of the group's transformation was its second collaboration with Mardin, *Main Course* (1975), its first platinum album, with sales of more than 1,000,000 copies and three cuts that became monster hit singles: "Jive Talkin'" (featuring Barry's whisper), "Nights on Broadway" (featuring his falsetto), and "Fanny."

After Stigwood broke off his RSO from Atlantic Records, Mardin was no longer able to produce for the Bee Gees, but they admirably managed to continue on the course set for them by Mardin under two new producers, Karl Richardson, who had engineered *Main Course*, and Albhy Galuten. *Children of the World* (1976) was, if anything, even more affirmative of their changed style than *Main Course* had been. It became their second platinum album, and it spawned the disco hits "You Should Be Dancing" and "Love So Right." *Here At Last . . . Live* (1977), a greatest-hits concert package, was on the charts well into 1978. The Bee Gees' "How Deep Is Your Love" won a Grammy in 1978.

Nothing contributed more to the opening of the floodgates for disco music's inundation of American pop currents than the Stigwood-produced motion picture *Saturday Night Fever* (Paramount, 1977) and the music created and performed by the Bee Gees that dominated that film. The soundtrack album topped the *Billboard* LP chart for twenty-three weeks, sold 23,000,000 copies worldwide, and grossed $235,-000,000. Among the cuts from the album, "Stayin' Alive" and "Night Fever" and the less frenetic "How Deep Is Your Love" headed the singles charts for months, and by February 1978 an incredible half of the top-ten hits on the charts belonged to the Bee Gees.

Writing in the New York Times (March 19, 1978), John Rockwell described the soundtrack of *Saturday Night Fever* as "rich and full-textured yet never murky" and the Gibbs's "husky, plaintive vibrato" as "both telling and instantly identifiable amidst the other disco pap one encounters on the radio." In his assessment in *Esquire* (April 11, 1978), Albert Goldman marveled at "the chameleon-like versatility that enables these classic products of the 1960's to pop up again as the acme of the latest thing. . . . In their latest avatar, as heroes of the boogie-down disco scene, the Bee Gees have evinced all their accustomed cleverness and abstractive ability to condense the familiar gimmicks of the black-inspired beat for the feet."

"Grease" was written by Barry Gibb as the title song for the screen adaptation of the musical of the same name, produced by Robert Stigwood and Allan Carr and released by Paramount Pictures in 1978. The song became a single hit for Frankie Valli, whose voice was on the soundtrack. In another Stigwood enterprise, the motion-picture musical fantasy *Sgt. Pepper's Lonely Hearts Club Band* (Universal, 1978), inspired by the Beatles' album of the same title, the Bee Gees co-starred with Peter Frampton, providing the right touch of harmony to thirty-two Lennon-McCartney songs. The film was a commercial and critical failure, but the Bee Gees emerged relatively unscathed, with a soundtrack that had sales of more than 3,000,000 copies and that brought them the Grammy awards for best album of the year, best producer, best pop vocal performance, and best arrangement for voices. Aside from the Average White Band and Peter

Brown, the Bee Gees were the only white act listed on black charts in the summer of 1978. Barry, Robin, and Maurice backed up their brother Andy on his "Shadow Dancing," the best-selling single record of 1978.

After they finished filming *Sgt. Pepper's Lonely Hearts Club Band,* the Bee Gees put ten months into the making of their album *Spirits Having Flown* because, as Maurice explained to a reporter, they knew they "had one hell of an album to follow" and "didn't know what to do." Released early in 1979, *Spirits Having Flown* made its debut in the top five in countries all over Europe, including Denmark, where it immediately hit number one. The first single hit to spin off the album was "Too Much Heaven." The second was "Tragedy," the biggest advance seller in history for an international release in Japan. When "Tragedy" reached number one on *Billboard's* singles chart in the middle of March 1979, it made the Bee Gees the only rock group to have eight number-one singles on that chart in the 1970's.

The International Year of the Child was officially launched on January 10, 1979 with the television concert "Music for UNICEF," a ninety-minute special headlined by the Bee Gees on NBC. Again on NBC, a ninety-minute semi-documentary on the Bee Gees, their music, and their career was presented on November 21, 1979. Also in 1979, the Bee Gees made a thirty-eight-city concert tour of the United States and Canada. Barry Gibb co-produced and, with some help from Robin, wrote the material for Barbra Streisand's 1980 hit album *Guilty,* and he sang a duet with Miss Streisand on the title track. That venture brought him nominations for best record, best song, and best album at the 1981 Grammy Awards, and he and Miss Streisand took the prize for best pop vocal performance by a duo or group.

Barry Gibb produces and writes for his brother Andy, and he has written or produced for other acts, sometimes with the help of Robin and Maurice and co-producers Albhy Galuten and Karl Richardson. Among those for whom he has created hits are Samantha Sang, Conway Twitty, Rare Earth, and Tavares. Bee Gees' songs have been covered by Susie Allison, Candi Staton, Olivia Newton-John, Carol Douglas, Melba Moore, and Moulin Rouge, among other recording artists. Unhappy with the way he and his brothers were handled in *Sgt. Pepper's Lonely Hearts Club Band* but looking forward to making more movies, Barry Gibb has hired the William Morris agency to represent him in the solo movie career he plans.

Barry Gibb lives in a mansion overlooking Biscayne Bay in Miami Beach, Florida with his second wife, the former Lynda Gray, who was Miss Scotland 1967, and their two sons, Stephen and Ashley. Maurice lives nearby, and Robin, Andy, and the Gibbs's parents visit frequently.

The brothers do most of their recording at the Criteria Studios in Miami. Barry used to own a string of expensive cars, but now he invests his money in real estate and confines his driving to a speedboat. Barry is "irritated" by so much current pop music that is "just noise." His listening preferences run from classical to country, which has had the greatest influence on him since childhood. "The emotion was what attracted me," he explained to Lynn Van Matre in an interview for the Chicago Tribune. He told Miss Van Matre: "We've been lucky, because we've had success twice. The first time, it just about destroyed us. . . . Now, with the second success story, we know what we're doing. We have more control. We've had the lesson."

References: Chicago Tribune VI p14 Mr 1 '81 pors; N Y Daily News mag p14+ Ag 26 '79 pors; N Y Post p27 S 4 '79 pors; N Y Times II p24+ N 28 '76 por; People 9:74+ F 6 '78 pors; Rolling Stone p42+ Jl 14 '77 pors; Time 111:88 Ap 3 '78 por; Us 2:22+ Ag 8 '78 pors; Gibb, Barry, Robin, and Maurice. The Illustrated Bee Gees (1979)

Gilder, George

Nov. 29, 1939- Writer; economist. Address: b. c/o Basic Books, 10 E. 53d St., New York City, N.Y. 10022; h. "Sky Hill Farm," Tyringham, Mass. 01264

The largely self-taught economist and social philosopher George Gilder has emerged as the most widely read of the American "supply-side" economists and appears to be well on his way toward becoming to the Administration of President Ronald Reagan what John Maynard Keynes and John Kenneth Galbraith were to those of Franklin D. Roosevelt and John F. Kennedy. A controversial writer, whose earlier works on social theory—such as *Sexual Suicide* (1973)—provoked the wrath of feminists and others, Gilder presents in his best-selling book *Wealth and Poverty* (1981) what he calls a "theology for capitalism" that provides moral arguments in support of substantial reductions in taxation, federal spending, and government intervention in the nation's economic life. David Stockman, President Reagan's budget director, has called *Wealth and Poverty* "Promethean in its intellectual power and insight" and "the best thing written on economic growth in about fifteen years."

The scion of a distinguished American literary family that included Richard Watson Gilder (1844-1909), the newspaperman and poet, and Rosamond Gilder, the editor of *Theatre Arts Monthly*, George Gilder was born on November 29, 1939 to Richard Watson Gilder and the former Anne Alsop. His father, a namesake of their literary ancestor, was a politically ambitious graduate of Harvard University and a grandson of Louis Comfort Tiffany, the famous painter and artist in stained glass. After her husband was killed in World War II at the age of twenty-eight, when George was three, Anne Gilder rented rooms in her Manhattan townhouse and gave music lessons. Growing up in a household headed by a woman left a lasting impression on Gilder, and another important influence was that of Father Divine, the charismatic black religious leader, whose followers included some of the servants in his mother's house. On one occasion he accompanied them to Harlem, where he heard Father Divine preach on salvation through hard work, a theme on which he eventually expatiated in his writings.

Later, George Gilder's mother married Gilder Palmer, a cousin of his father, and moved with her husband and son to her family's farm in Tyringham, Massachusetts. "I was a fatherless child during my earliest years, and . . . ascribed a lot of my emotional turbulence to the absence of a father," Gilder has recalled, as quoted in *People* (May 18, 1981). "Then my stepfather came along and taught me how to work. I saw the contributions a father can make." His character was also molded by David Rockefeller, his father's roommate at Harvard, who remained a close friend of the family and helped to finance his education. From him Gilder learned how a man who "has no need for further material wealth . . . nonetheless submits to arduous discipline and firm moral values."

Gilder failed, however, to emulate his mentor's self-discipline. At preparatory school in Exeter, New Hampshire, he occupied last place in his graduating class, and later, at Harvard University, he was placed on probation so often that he never realized his ambition to become a member of the track team. Finally, after flunking out of Harvard in 1958, he joined the Marine Corps Reserve with the hope of getting "beaten into shape," and he believes that the discipline he received as a Marine "worked pretty well."

While remaining on inactive duty with the Marine Corps Reserve, Gilder returned to Harvard in 1959. There he and Bruce Chapman collaborated in founding the liberal Republican magazine *Advance* and served as its co-editors in 1961-62. After obtaining his B.A. degree from Harvard in 1962 he went to Washington, D.C., where he served as an assistant and speechwriter for several moderate Republicans, including Jacob K. Javits and Nelson A. Rockefeller. In 1964-65 he was a junior fellow with the Council on Foreign Relations, and in 1965 he became associate editor of the *New Leader* magazine.

In keeping with his liberal Republican views of that period, Gilder sharply criticized the 1964 Presidential campaign of conservative Republican candidate Barry M. Goldwater in his first book, *The Party That Lost Its Head* (Knopf, 1966), on which he collaborated with Bruce Chapman. The authors decried Goldwater Republicanism as a vehicle for reaction rather than traditional conservatism and accused the party of negativism and contempt for new ideas. They particularly denounced the campaign's "Southern strategy," which aligned the Republicans with the forces of segregation. The book, which received generally favorable reviews, outlined a program of "constructive alternatives" and urged progressive Republicans to unify and revitalize the G.O.P. by transforming it into a responsible and effective party of moderation.

Gilder served as speechwriter for Michigan Governor George Romney in 1967 and for Richard M. Nixon in 1968. He held a fellowship with the Kennedy Institute of Politics at Harvard University in 1970-71, and during that same period served as editor of the liberal Republican *Ripon Forum*. Meanwhile, his earlier liberalism was gradually giving way to a more conservative outlook, inspired in part by William F. Buckley, whom he admired. Other influences included the writings of Milton Friedman, Ayn Rand, and Friedrich von Hayek. His social views, as they developed at that time, were influenced by what he considered the excesses of some feminists. He aroused the ire of members of the women's movement when he wrote an editorial in the *Ripon Forum* in 1971 supporting President Richard Nixon's veto of a bill to establish day care centers for economically disadvantaged children, which the President opposed in part because of its "family weakening implications."

Feminists designated Gilder "the nation's leading male chauvinist pig" after publication of his book *Sexual Suicide* (Quadrangle/The N.Y. Times Bk. Co., 1973), in which he argued that men are biologically and symbiotically dependent on women and that sex differences are "the single most important fact of human society." Denial or minimization of those differences, he warned, would result in the death of civilization by sexual suicide. He condemned feminism, gay liberation, open marriage, and other aspects of contemporary society that in his view contributed to sexual suicide in that they tend to deny to the sexes their proper biological roles and thereby undermine the traditional family structure. J. A. Hennessee, in his review in the New York *Times* (December 9, 1973), reflected the views of many of Gilder's critics when he wrote: "One reads this elaborate, Freud-haunted apology for patriarchy with a depressing sense of *déjà vu*. . . . It is Gilder's theory that sexism is inevitable in a civilized society and that women should just relax and enjoy it." And David Gutman accurately predicted the feminist response to the book when he wrote in *Commentary* (December 1973): "Gilder's praise of women as a civilizing force will be seen as a piece of Victorian hypocrisy designed to flatter women into loving their chains."

Some of the ideas and arguments in *Sexual Suicide* were reformulated and further developed by Gilder in *Naked Nomads: Unmarried Men in America* (Quadrangle/The N.Y. Times Bk. Co., 1974), which seemed to reflect his dissatisfaction with his own disordered bachelor life. Convinced that bachelorhood is detrimental to a man's physical and psychic being, Gilder turned the feminist argument around by describing single men as an oppressed and brutalized faction in society and maintained that family life was the necessary condition for masculine stability.

Gilder's major argument for marriage was that unmarried men constituted the foremost social problem in present-day society. He presented statistical evidence that single males earn less than their married counterparts, commit twice as many crimes, tend to develop physical and emotional illnesses, and are likely to die well before their time. In Gilder's view, as a bachelor, a man has no clear-cut sexual identity; he needs women for his survival and well-being. Marriage transforms antisocial and self-destructive bachelors into stable citizens because it ties men to a purposeful future.

The evidence given in *Naked Nomads* concerning the destructive potential of the single male in American society was continued and expanded by Gilder in *Visible Man; A True Story of Post-Racist America* (Basic Bks., 1978), a "nonfiction novel" based on an accidental encounter the author had with Sam, a young black man, that led him to a two-year study of the ghetto, the "welfare syndrome," and the breakdown of families. A product of hundreds of interviews with poor people in Albany, New York and Greenville, South Carolina, the book profiles Sam, who is single, fatherless, and prone to violence, showing him in his life in the streets, during his trial for rape, and finally in search of his relatives. Sam's adult life is one of idleness and alcoholism, consorting with prostitutes, and taking money from welfare mothers. The existing welfare system, in Gilder's view, perpetuates the ghettos and the life-style of men like Sam since it offers them rewards for inactivity. Despite some favorable reviews, *Visible Man* did not receive wide circulation and sold only slightly over 500 copies.

In addition to writing books, Gilder began in the early 1970's to contribute articles to such publications as *Harper's, Commentary*, the *National Review*, the New York *Times*, and *Playboy*. Reviewing the NBC television special *Of Men and Women*, hosted by Barbara Walters and Tom Snyder, in the New York *Times* (January 19, 1975), Gilder accused the network of exhibiting three hours of "slickly produced but ineptly researched propaganda for a sexual revolution that has yet to take place, and in all likelihood never will." When attacked by the National Organization of Women a few weeks later in the New York *Times* for his assertion that sex bias was no longer a significant cause of low earnings for females, he replied, "I would find it most astonishing if women and men in the same job categories earned the same amounts. This can happen, I maintain, only when employers begin discriminating heavily against male aggressiveness, leadership and competitiveness—the characteristics that in every human society known to anthropology have led to male dominance."

After only a few years of systematic study of economics, during which time he seemed to have read virtually everything written in the field since Adam Smith, Gilder published the book that for the first time brought him wide recognition, *Wealth and Poverty* (Basic Books, 1981). He completed it over a two-year period while staying with friends in the state of Washington. Edited by Midge Decter, the work was described in *Time* (February 9, 1981) as "a bible for supply-siders" and as "a 306-page ode to the economic and moral benefits of unfettered capitalism." Convinced that the most critical problem for contemporary society is "how to increase wealth and curtail poverty," Gilder tries to strip away what he considers erroneous economic theories and cultural attitudes and argues for the abolition of antipoverty campaigns, environmental regulations, and antidiscrimination laws, maintaining that they serve only to impede capital formation and stultify economic development in the United States.

Much of *Wealth and Poverty* is based on assumptions carried over from Gilder's earlier books: that men are by nature more aggressive than women and therefore constitute the backbone of the capitalist system and spirit; that "the first priority of any serious program against poverty is to strengthen the male role in poor families;" and that reductions in social spending provide incentives for the poor to work harder. "The capitalist system gives rewards precisely to those people who will forgo immediate gratification in pursuit of larger goals and who succeed in making their risky ventures correspond with general needs," he has observed. In contrast to the "demand" economics of Keynes and Galbraith, Gilder's "supply-side" economics asserts that "the very conscience of capitalism is the awareness that one must give in order to get, supply in order to demand." The highest service to society that a man can perform is, according to Gilder, to accumulate wealth by providing desired goods and services; that wealth is then invested in new business ventures and assures further economic growth and prosperity.

Gilder maintains that the capitalist, far from being rapacious and reprehensible for ignoring the social good, is moved by faith, the courage to take risks, and the altruism of giving without assured return. Enterprising men who take risks are, in his view, the ones who promote economic growth. The demand-oriented politics of the liberals only serve to increase unemployment and to create administrative bureaucracies that result in overtaxed businesses and subsequent industrial decline. A really effective tax policy would leave suppliers with enough capital for creative investments. The consequent production of new wealth would then benefit all people, the poor included.

As economic and social ideas much at variance with contemporary liberal policies and practices, Gilder's supply-side economics, antifeminism, and justification of "benign neglect" for the poor and minorities have provoked much hostile criticism. With the publication of *Wealth and Poverty* he was termed a "crackpot" whose aim is the "defense of established privilege." Andrew Klavan wrote scathingly in the *Saturday Review* (January 1981) that *"Wealth and Poverty* is rendered nonsensical not by its methodical defense of . . . supply-side economics, but by the moral hogwash on which that defense is based. . . . At a time when a reasonable reevaluation of conservative economics is certainly in order, it's a pity to waste time with Gilder's rosy images of Horatio Algers, beneficent millionaires, and nonexistent bigots. . . . Gildering the lily won't make it gold." Irving Kristol, a spokesman for neoconservatism, called *Wealth and Poverty* a "pseudo-anthropological analysis" and observed that Gilder's endorsement of a market economy could "provide us with economic growth and individual liberty" but not "consolation amidst disaster [or] reassurance as to the meaningfulness of life when our bourgeois virtues do not avail us."

On the other hand, Joseph Sobran of the *National Review* (February 6, 1981), echoing the views of other right-wing commentators, called *Wealth and Poverty* a "masterly book" that "sings the theme of the eighties—the anthem of American renewal." Even so hostile a critic as Michael Kinsley of the *New Republic* (February 7, 1981) found Gilder to be "obviously a bright and sincere man" who "writes with flash and often with eloquence" and whose "attempt at a grand synthesis of ascendant conservative thinking cannot be laughed off just because much of it is ridiculous." *Wealth and Poverty* has been cited as one of President Reagan's favorite books, and William J. Casey, the director of the Central Intelligence Agency, has said that it would "serve as an inspiration and guide" for the Administration. Originally published without high expectations on the part of either its author or its publisher, *Wealth and Poverty* had a first printing of only 8,000 copies, but the Reagan Administration's warm endorsement was apparently responsible for the book's skyrocketing popularity. As of the spring of 1981 there were 135,000 copies in print, and the book was firmly established as a best seller.

As a speechwriter, Gilder seems to have met with somewhat less success than he has with his books. In 1976 Senator Robert J. Dole of Kansas, then the Vice-Presidential running mate of President Gerald R. Ford, expressed dissatisfaction with a campaign speech that Gilder had written for him. Early in 1981 Gilder helped to write President Reagan's economic message to Congress, but some of the President's top aides thought it "overwrought" and decided against using his contribution. Such minor setbacks do not, however, appear to have diminished his new-found fame, and he is much in demand as a speaker. Jeffrey Bell, a past political director of the American Conservative Union and a former aide to Ronald Reagan, read *Wealth and Poverty* in manuscript form and was so impressed that he hired Gilder for $50,000 a year to spend two days a week in New York City as program director of the International Center for Economic Policy Studies, a nonprofit organization dedicated to promoting conservative economic ideas. Gilder is also chairman of the Economic Roundtable at the Lehrman Institute in New York City.

George Gilder's disorganized bachelor existence ended in 1976, when he married Cornelia ("Nini") Brooke, a graduate of Vassar College and a part-time consultant on historical preservation projects, who had been one of his mother's music pupils. They live in the family's nineteenth-century farmhouse in Tyringham, Massachusetts, with their daughters Louisa and Mary Ellen ("Mellie") and their Norwegian elkhound Laffer, named after the

economist Arthur Laffer, who was one of the originators of the theory of supply-side economics. Under his wife's influence, Gilder has become a practising Episcopalian. The Gilders, who do not own a television set, enjoy spending their evenings reading to each other from such literary classics as *War and Peace* or *Madame Bovary*. Gilder is an enthusiast for track and field and a long-distance runner. He has invested $30,000 in the Single Brook record company, of which he is chairman and for which his half-brother Walter Palmer records as the lead singer with a country-and-western group, the Cobble Mountain Band. According to his early collaborator and friend Bruce Chapman, writing in the *National Review* (April 17, 1981), "George Gilder has always been a kindly man. . . . He is wrongly imagined by some critics as an unbending and cruel Puritan. . . . But to see him changing the baby's diapers, washing the dishes, taking the brood off to the church he used to ignore, even to hear him argue gently with a foe, is to see a man at peace with himself."

References: N Y Times III p9 Ap 26 '81 por; N Y Times Bk R p18 My 24 '81 por; Nat R 33:412+ Ap 17 '81; Newsweek 97:64+ F 16 '81 por; People 15:92+ My 18 '81 pors; Time 117:71 F 9 '81 por; Contemporary Authors 1st rev vols 17-20 (1976)

Glass, Philip

Jan. 31, 1937- Composer; musician. Address: b. c/o Performing Artservices, 325 Spring St., New York City, N.Y. 10013; h. 231 2d Ave., New York City, N.Y. 10003

One of the most innovative of contemporary American composers, Philip Glass has fashioned what he has described as a "new language" that attracts a large and diverse audience from the worlds of classical music, disco, progressive rock, and jazz. His "fusion" or "crossover" music, distinguished by repetition, modular form, and extended duration, takes from classical music its conventional notation and recognizable keys; it borrows from popular music its use of amplification, electronic organs, and huge sound mixers. A series of four retrospective concerts that was held at New York City's Town Hall in February 1981 measured the distance that Glass has traveled from his original minimalism and reaffirmed the importance of his audacious work in the American musical scene.

In the late 1960's Glass broke with the classical music pattern for which his training at the Peabody Conservatory and Juilliard and with such private teachers as Nadia Boulanger had groomed him. Instead, he pro-

Philip Glass

gressed from monophonic pieces based on additive rhythmic modules to complex avant-garde compositions encompassing changes in harmony, color, and density. National recognition for Philip Glass and the ensemble that he had formed in 1968 came so slowly that his major debuts at Town Hall and Carnegie Hall in New York City did not take place until 1974 and 1978, respectively. Even *Einstein on the Beach,* the opera on which he collaborated with playwright and director Robert Wilson, failed to arouse substantial interest or bring him foundation support, though it received warm praise from the critics when it was introduced to a packed and enthusiastic house at the Metropolitan Opera in 1976. Widely honored and admired in Europe, Glass created a critical sensation in October 1980, when his second opera, *Satyagraha,* had its premiere in Rotterdam with the Netherlands Opera.

Philip Glass was born in Baltimore, Maryland, on January 31, 1937, to Benjamin and Ida (Gouline) Glass. As a boy, he frequented his father's record store. "I hauled records around from as early as I can remember," he told Charles Michener in an interview for *Newsweek* (May 26, 1975). "We sold mostly top-40 stuff and, though I knew it all, I thought it was pretty much junk. We took home the records we *didn't* sell and a lot of it was chamber music. That's what I really listened to."

The precocious Glass began studying the flute at the age of eight at the Peabody Conservatory in Baltimore. Several years later he took up the piccolo and played both instruments in local orchestras. After passing his college entrance examinations at fourteen, he enrolled in 1952 at the University of Chicago,

where he studied mathematics and philosophy and obtained his B.A. degree in 1956. During that formative period Glass became drawn to the music of Charles Ives. When he first scrutinized an Ives score, he was astonished, for, as he recounted to Michener, he could not "believe anyone could write all that." His own fledgling compositions, mainly atonal chamber music, were influenced by such twentieth-century composers as Arnold Schoenberg, Alban Berg, and Anton Webern.

Determined to study composition, at twenty Philip Glass entered the Juilliard School of Music in New York City, where he learned his craft with Vincent Persichetti and William Bergsma. Although he collected such prizes as the Broadcast Music Industry Award (1960), the Lado Prize (1961), and the Benjamin Award (1961 and 1962), he discovered that his success could not compensate for his dissatisfaction with the direction of his career and with what he has described as his "traditionally American-classical, Coplandesque" musical output. "I didn't really have anything of my own to say," he later recalled to Michener. "I was so busy imitating academic music that I'd never really mastered the fundamentals." Eventually he realized that his own preference lay neither with classical nor popular music. "I found 12-tone music ugly and didactic, and I didn't care for French or German or any other kind of 'school,' " he told Robert Jones, who interviewed him for *Cue* (May 27, 1978). Instead of being purely theoretical, music, in his opinion, had to be more accessible and possess "a sense of community."

After receiving his M.S. degree from Juilliard in 1962, Glass spent two years in Pittsburgh on a Ford Foundation grant, composing overtures for high school bands as part of a training program for promising young composers. In 1964 his increasing frustration and restlessness led him to move to Paris, where he studied harmony and counterpoint on a Fulbright grant under the renowned Nadia Boulanger. There, in the winter of 1965-66, Philip Glass met Ravi Shankar, the Indian sitar master whose music Glass was notating for a film soundtrack.

Based upon premises vastly different from those of the West, Shankar's highly evolved music had a decisive impact upon Glass's compositional development. In particular, as he explained to Robert Jones in an interview for the New York *Daily News* (May 1, 1977), its additive rhythmical structure turned out to be "a revelation." "In Western music, we take a large unit and divide it, whole notes into half notes, then into quarter notes, and so on," Glass pointed out. "In Eastern music, they begin with small units and add them together. We divide, they add. It's a different point of view."

While hitchhiking across Spain to North Africa, the Middle East, and finally Asia, Philip Glass analyzed the intricate rhythmic pattern of Eastern music. "I didn't understand it all," he admitted to Jones, "and I made mistakes, but often my mistakes were more interesting than my successes." In 1967 he returned to New York City, determined to create a new "world music" that he perceived as a pure medium of sound unencumbered by dramatic structure. "Ravi, not drugs, was my acid trip," the composer has said. "It was like totally clearing all my decks, and overnight I began writing a completely different kind of music."

Having jettisoned such traditional Western musical principles as climax, harmonic movement, and sonata form, Glass at first concentrated on monophonic material, including solo or ensemble compositions played in unison and fashioned with successive modules that either added to or subtracted from the basic unit. He tried to reduce his music to a rhythmic structure with a minimum of notes and a maximum of rhythmic ingenuity.

The formation of the Philip Glass Ensemble in 1968—a unique amplified instrumental line-up of electric keyboards, winds, and electronic devices—provided the composer with a vehicle to perform the lengthier scores that he had categorically refused to publish. Over the years the group has included such exacting and dedicated musicians as Jon Gibson and Richard Landry on flute and soprano saxophone; Richard Peck Jr. on alto saxophone; Michael Riesman (and Glass himself) on electric organ; Kurt Munkacsi on the sound mixing board; and Irene Hirsky and Joan La Barbara as vocalists. At first the ensemble appeared as an "underground phenomenon" in the lofts of Greenwich Village. On April 13, 1968 it performed two works, In and Out Again for Jon Gibson and Strung Out, at Queens College and repeated Strung Out a month later at the New School for Social Research. Broader acceptance came only in 1969, when the works of Philip Glass, together with those of several other young composers including Steve Reich, Terry Riley, and La Monte Young, became cult items among the minimalist avant-garde of the New York art world who shared a similar fascination with sparse understatement and a precisely defined process of composition. As Glass explained to John Rockwell in an article in the New York Times (January 3, 1973): "Artists aren't very intellectual, and my music is very accessible. It has a physical presence people can respond to. Artists are very eager to get art out from under the academy."

Decidedly at a far remove from the academy, on May 19, 1969 two of Glass's compositions, How Now and Two Pages, were included in the Whitney Museum's Anti-Illusion Show, a forum for a developing school of multimedia conceptual artists, among them Glass, Reich, and the sculptor Richard Serra. Another New York program at the Guggenheim Museum in mid-January 1970 featured his Music in Eight Parts, Music in Similar Motion, and Music in Fifths. (The last-named work is a personal tribute to Nadia Boulanger that consists of an unbroken chain of parallel fifths.) During the early 1970's Music with Changing Parts and Music for Voices, performed at La Mama Theatre Club, New York University's Loeb Student Center, and Yale University, among other places, served as harbingers of his restlessly evolving style. During those lean years Glass supplemented the limited support he received from foundations and private individuals by working as a mover, cab-driver, plumber, and as the musical director of the Off-Off-Broadway Mabou Mines experimental theatre group.

Although Philip Glass attracted wildly enthusiastic fans who were mesmerized by his hypnotic devices of the drone and his syncopated swinging rhythms, the musical establishment in general pointedly ignored him. His marked lack of interest in harmony, tempo, and melody, combined with his emphasis on repetitive and simplistic structure, alienated most concertgoers, and the majority of contemporary composers ostracized him for deviating from 12-tone or atonal music. "I didn't accept the Schoenberg, Boulez, Stockhausen tradition," Glass remarked to Annalyn Swan in an interview for Time (June 19, 1978), "and that's threatening to them." Even the usually open-minded New York critics remained somewhat aloof, except for a few dissenters like the Village Voice's Tom Johnson, the New York Times's John Rockwell, and New York magazine's Alan Rich. After a June 1972 outdoor concert at Hammarskjold Plaza, Rich reported in New York (June 12, 1972): "Phil Glass's unnamed piece pleased me very much, although it is difficult to define by any specific musical standards."

On June 1, 1974 Philip Glass began to receive wider recognition when he made his first major New York debut, at Town Hall. His performance, which began at six p.m. and ended at midnight, with a ninety-minute Bayreuth-style dinner break, featured for the first time in its entirety the marathon Music in Twelve Parts. For that series of a dozen pieces, each of which concentrated on one musical aspect, the composer requested of his hearers "another mode of listening—one in which neither memory nor anticipation . . . has a place in sustaining the texture, quality, or reality of the musical experience." Glass's augmented use of chromatic harmonies, ornamentation, and sustained note improvisation, and especially the dreamlike unprepared modulations and counterpointed materials of Parts Eleven and Twelve respectively, provided a culmination to his development as a composer since 1967 and foreshadowed future trends. In covering for the New York Times (June 3, 1974) the innovative endurance contest that attracted an audience of some seven hundred, John Rockwell registered his pleased surprise. "What [Glass] proved Saturday was that, given an intuitive appreciation for the idiom, his work can sustain attention for extended periods of time, and sound continually full of incident, interest and emotional resonance," Rockwell wrote. "What was most refreshing about Saturday's performance was that it seemed short, in a way that all intense artistic experiences do."

Another Look at Harmony, whose first two sections were performed at Town Hall on May 6, 1975, built progressively on the intricately shifting rhythmic activity of Part Ten, the modulations of Part Eleven, and the cadential features of Part Twelve of *Music in Twelve Parts.* As Charles Michener noted in his review for *Newsweek* (May 26, 1975), the work revealed "an accumulative power that is at once sensuous and religious in feeling." Glass soon incorporated those two sections into his new opera *Einstein on the Beach,* a project that combined his renewed interest both in harmonic movement and in theatrical elements.

A collaboration in which Glass provided the music and lyrics and Robert Wilson the direction and decor, *Einstein on the Beach* was inspired both by the novel and the film *On the Beach* as an apocalyptical study of civilization in a nuclear age. Its four acts and five entr'actes, lasting nearly five hours without an intermission, dealt with three disparate and impressionistic visual, aural, and musical "images" loosely related to the life and times of Albert Einstein: a steam engine train, a courtroom, and a spaceship. The libretto consisted of sung or spoken numerals and solfège syllables. "It's abstract, like a Balanchine ballet," Robert Wilson once explained. "Operas should not require stories any more than ballets do. Go to *Einstein* and enjoy the sights and sounds, feel the feelings they evoke. Listen to the pictures."

Einstein on the Beach had its world premiere at the Avignon Festival in France on July 25, 1976 and was performed in Venice, Belgrade, Brussels, Paris, Hamburg, Rotterdam, and Amsterdam before it was brought to the United States for two sold-out Sunday evening performances at the Metropolitan Opera House on November 21 and 28 of that same year. Underwritten by the Byrd Hoffman Foundation in cooperation with the Met, it proved to be one of the sensations of the fall music season. Discriminating listeners and critics alike noted with interest Glass's changing instrumental textures, including his dramatic motives for character descriptions and short but memorable melodies. Writing in the *Guardian* (September 5, 1976), Daniel Caux observed: "It is true that classic Western harmony, which we thought we knew so well, 'resounds' here in a strange, unaccustomed way, reminiscent of old clothes turned inside out which suddenly appear brand new." When he reviewed the release of the complete *Einstein on the Beach* on the Tomato label, Don Heckman commented in *High Fidelity* (July 1979): "[Glass] understands the powerful dramatic impact that can be produced by sudden changes of rhythm and melody. These are qualities we would expect in Verdi or Puccini; to find them in a contemporary composer identified with the avant-garde is, to say the least, refreshing."

Glass's Carnegie Hall debut on June 1, 1978 featured the American premiere of *Another Look at Harmony, Parts III and IV.* Part III, based on music he had composed earlier for a Mabou Mines' production of Samuel Beckett's *Cascando,* consisted of a solo organ piece; Part IV, performed by the Gregg Smith Singers, was a choral work originally commissioned for the 1977 Holland Festival. Among the critics who voiced approval was Annalyn Swan, who noted in *Time* magazine (June 19, 1978) that Part IV in particular had "an airy quality new to Glass's work" and was "spacious and oddly religious, like a new form of Gregorian chant."

With Lucinda Childs, the choreographer who had played a crucial role in *Einstein on the Beach,* and Sol LeWitt, the artist, the composer collaborated on *Dance,* a suite of five solo and ensemble dance numbers, which Miss Childs described as adhering to "definite geometric patterns, with simple movements, a spatial format." *Dance* had its premiere on October 19, 1979 in Amsterdam and was first presented in the United States at the Brooklyn Academy of Music on November 29 of that year. Reflecting on Glass's involvement in *Dance,* Arlene Croce suggested in the *New Yorker* (June 30, 1980): "Perhaps the reason he is attracted to dance is that dance is a present-tense art form, with no precise way of recalling or predicting itself. Glass's hammering beat seems to drive dancers ever onward into the outer space of unanticipated movement."

In the late 1970's Philip Glass developed a repertory that he could perform on the organ independently of his ensemble. Among the dozen or so solo recitals he now gives annually was a benefit performance given in June 1980 at New York's Plymouth Church of the Pilgrims. Reviewing the event for the *New Yorker* (June 23, 1980), Andrew Porter had some reservations about that program, which featured the American premiere of *Fourth Series, Part 4:* "Given out thick and loud on a big church organ with no changes of registration in the long sections, stripped of its glittering, sensuous surface—the play of saxophones and other winds and of voices upon the crisp sparkle of electric keyboards—his music loses some of its instant appeal." But Robert Palmer of the *New York Times* (June 10, 1980) speculated optimistically about Glass's future: "One left feeling that the composer had found a compelling new mode of presentation for his music and that solo performance will prove more and more fruitful for him."

Although he is not without honor in his own country, as was attested by a Rockefeller Foundation grant of $90,000 he received in February 1981, Philip Glass has increasingly concentrated on Europe, where he has been greatly admired as representing a vital trend in contemporary American music ever since his first overwhelmingly successful Continental tour in 1969. His second opera, *Satyagraha,* commissioned by the city of Rotterdam for the Netherlands Opera, had its premiere there on September 5, 1980. Sung in Sanskrit with a libretto adapted from the *Bhagavad-Gita*, the three-hour work depicted incidents in the early life of Mahatma Gandhi. For *Satyagraha* Glass employed a chorus of forty and an orchestra of about sixty pieces, forces much more conventional than those he deployed for *Einstein on the Beach*. Enthusiastically received, *Satyagraha* struck one critic as being "reminiscent in mood" of Wagner's *Parsifal* and seemed to provide encouragement for Glass's hope, once expressed to Robert Jones, that his music will not die when he dies.

When *Satyagraha* was presented for the first time in the United States at Artpark in Lewiston, New York on July 29, 1981, with most of the cast that had taken part in the Rotterdam world premiere, it received a standing ovation. Opening on November 6, 1981, it ran for five performances at the Brooklyn Academy of Music, with Christopher Keene conducting the Brooklyn Philharmonia and the Artpark Opera Chorus.

Dennis Russell Davies, the music director of the Stuttgart Opera, not only plans to mount his own production of *Satyagraha* in that city in 1981 but has commissioned Glass's third opera, *Akhenaton and Dedalus*, based on similarities between the Akhenaton and Dedalus myths as set forth in a book by Immanuel Velikovsky. Supported by funds from the Rockefeller Foundation, the opera is scheduled for an American production in 1983. Davies was quoted in *Quest/80* (November 1980) as saying, "In the end, you've got to judge composers by whether they challenge or merely satisfy themselves and the public. Popular or not, Glass sets out to challenge." The most recent example of that challenge, Glass's "madrigal opera," *The Panther*, was given its world premiere at the Houston Grand Opera in May 1981 and fulfilled a limited engagement at the Café La Mama Annex in New York in the following month. Its music was praised, but the arcane abstractions of the play by Manuel Lutgenhorst, inspired by Rainer Maria Rilke's poem "The Panther," baffled and eluded some critics.

That challenge has also appealed to rock, jazz, and even disco enthusiasts, especially in Europe, where his music has influenced such rock groups as Tangerine Dream and Kraftwerk and such rock celebrities as David Bowie and Brian Eno. The latter has been fascinated by Glass's structural concepts ever since 1970, when he attended a Philip Glass Ensemble performance at London's Royal College of Art. "I'm attracted to the textural density of his music," Eno has explained. "Either you can hear it as slow music with rapid ornaments or as fast music with slow underpinnings." In turn, Glass finds the rock world intriguing, tapping pop musicians for their expertise in recording and marketing techniques and even performing himself at such rock venues as New York's Bottom Line and Hurrah's. His tentative explorations of the progressive rock market have included the album *North Star*, a series of short pieces drawn from his score for a documentary film about sculptor Mark di Suvero and released in 1977 by the British rock label Virgin. In an interview with Wayne Robins for *Newsday* (April 29, 1977) Glass admitted: "I don't write music for a market, like Eno, Pink Floyd, or Bowie. I don't imagine people buying my stuff. I mean, I'd like to sell records, but I'll go on making music whether they sell or not. I'm not trying to be a rock star." And shortly after helping to produce an RCA album by a New York art rock band called Polyrock, he told John Rockwell (*New York Times*, June 6, 1980): "This was a good opportunity to get involved with [pop music] without really getting my hands dirty. I like Polyrock's music; it's a lot of fun. But this is not my career; I'd rather write operas."

Philip Glass, whom one critic has described as having "a craggily engaging face," was formerly married to the Off-Off-Broadway actress and theatrical director Jo Anne Akalaitis, by whom he has two children, Juliet and Zachary. In October 1980 he married Luba Burtyk, an internist. The composer lives modestly in a four-room walk-up apartment on Manhattan's Lower East Side and dresses casually. A shy and reticent person, he finds fanfare, applause, and the groupie phenomenon embarrassing. "I love it when people cheer, but I never know what to do," he once told Annalyn Swan. "I don't want to kowtow to popular culture—break my instruments onstage." To Robert Jones he stressed his desire for privacy. "I will not exploit my life for publicity, and I refuse to discuss my personal philosophies and beliefs," Glass said. "My music is so very odd already, I see no need to make myself any odder."

References: *Christian Sci Mon* p18 Mr 4 '81; *Hi Fi* 29:MA 4+ Ap '79 por; *Horizon* 23:38+ Mr '80 pors; *N Y Times* p48 Ja 3 '73 por, II p11+ My 26 '74 por, C p1+ N 19 '76, II p13 My 28 '78; *N Y Times Mag* p69+ O 25 '81 pors; *Opera N* 46:17+ Jl '81 por; *People* 14:76+ O 6 '80 pors; *Quest/80* 4:32+ N '80 pors; *Time* 111:62 Je 19 '75 por; *Contemporary American Composers* (1976); *Harvard Concise Dictionary of Music* (1979)

Gordon, Mary

Dec. 8, 1949- Author. Address: b. c/o Peter Matson, 32 W. 40th St., New York City, N.Y. 10018

When Mary Gordon's first novel, *Final Payments*, an anguished meditation in the guise of a *bildungsroman*, or old-fashioned realistic

Mary Gordon

quite crazy. He was an absolutely enchanting father, but in some ways I'm lucky that he died when I was so young because I don't think that he could have coped with my adolescence. He was a magical father for me."

The father, a Harvard-educated convert from Judaism who romanticized working-class Catholicism, was a member of the American expatriate community in Paris in the 1920's. "Slowly he became, like Ezra Pound, disgusted with modern culture," Miss Gordon told Edmund White in an interview for the Washington Post's *Book Week* (April 9, 1978). Deciding "that he wanted to make some money, he came back to the States and, believe it or not, started a girlie magazine . . . called *Hot Dog.*" Sympathy with "the embarrassing side" in the Spanish Civil War led him to convert to Catholicism. "He gave up the girlie magazine and started one right-wing Catholic periodical after another. They all folded after a few issues. And he married my mother, his romantic ideal: a working-class Irish Catholic girl. Although he died when I was seven, he managed to start teaching me French, Greek, philosophy; in a way he was not sexist at all. I was to be his intellectual heir. When he died, there I was, a morose, plain child who read all the time." He died of a heart attack at the New York Public Library, while doing research for a biography of Paul Claudel.

Miss Gordon grew up in Valley Stream, Long Island, where she attended Holy Name of Mary parochial school. It "never occurred to [her] that [she] wouldn't write," she has said, even when, as a schoolgirl, she aspired to become a nun. "I thought I'd write poetry in my habit and lead a very disciplined life." For practice, she wrote pious tracts, such as "'What Is Prayer?' by Mary Gordon, age 8." She "read the lives of the saints over and over" and "loved the virgin martyrs," she told Nan Robertson of the New York *Times* (May 31, 1978), but "the minute [she] hit puberty" her "thing with religion went right out the window." She was, she said, "a very docile child and a very rebellious teenager."

After graduating from the Mary Louis Academy, an all-girl Catholic high school in Jamaica, Queens, New York, Miss Gordon went on scholarship to Barnard College at Columbia University in New York City. "That changed my life, especially when I took creative writing from Elizabeth Hardwick," she recounted in the Washington *Post Book Week* interview with Edmund White. "I think she's the greatest prose stylist in America now. At that time I was writing nothing but poetry, but Lizzie kept telling me, 'You're a prose writer, honey.' . . . She was also a wonderful role model for me; until I met her I had no idea how to be a woman writer."

Miss Gordon received her B.A. degree at Barnard in 1971. After taking her M.A. in the Writing Program at Syracuse University, in 1973, she continued on for a Ph.D. for several years, until the work on her doctoral

story of a character's moral development, appeared in 1978, the author was widely acclaimed as her generation's foremost novelist of Roman Catholic manners and mores, and that judgment was reinforced with the appearance of her second novel, *The Company of Women* (1981). But as Wilfrid Sheed has pointed out, Miss Gordon is much more than a Catholic novelist in the usual narrow sense, seeing the Roman Catholic Church as she does, in Sheed's words, "not as a good or bad place, with batteries of lawyers to prove both at once, but as a multilayered poem or vision which dominates your life equally whether you believe it or not; which doesn't even need your belief once it has made its point."

"The metaphors of Catholicism, the Catholic way of looking at the world," are, as Miss Gordon acknowledges, "in [her] bones." The only child of David and Anna (Gagliano) Gordon, Mary Catherine Gordon was born by Caesarian section in Far Rockaway, New York on December 8, the Feast of the Immaculate Conception, 1949. The date, according to Miss Gordon, was carefully chosen by her mother, a devoutly religious woman, the daughter of Irish and Italian immigrants. "My mother is so strong-willed that I think she would have held off labor until then [the feast day] if she had had vaginal delivery," Miss Gordon told Barbara Kantrowitz in an interview for the Chicago *Tribune* (April 19, 1981). "She would have bitten a bullet or jumped around the table if she had to."

Her mother, she said, supported the family as a legal secretary while her father, "besotted with [her], his only child," stayed home and took care of her. "He was wonderful," she told Barbara Kantrowitz. "He also was

dissertation conflicted with her professional writing. Her first novel was preceded by years of practice in other literary forms, firstly and chiefly poetry, which she has never published. The writing of poetry has given her, she has said, a sensitivity to the sound and rhythm of language and to pacing in writing. "Perhaps more than anything else, poetry has given me a sense of metaphor as being centrally important. Metaphor and simile do some of the work of explanation in a more efficient and profound way than other narrative techniques," she has said. "I include them when something needs to be made more concrete, more physical." She explained to Edmund White in the *Book Week* interview how she began writing short stories: "I think I was afraid of the length of fiction. But finally a woman friend took me in hand. She gave me a bluebook and told me it was like an exam; I had an hour to write a story. So I filled up the book—and I've been going ever since."

From the beginning, Miss Gordon tended to be more autobiographical in her short stories than in her novels. Among her early published stories were "Now I Am Married" (*Virginia Quarterly Review*, Summer 1975), "The Other Woman" (*Redbook*, August 1976), and "The Thorn" (*Ms.*, January 1977). "The Thorn," a poignant reclamation of the death of her father and a revelation of the burden of parental love, was anthologized in *Fine Lines: The Best of Ms. Fiction* (Charles Scribner's Sons, 1981). In the opinion of some critics, Miss Gordon is preeminently a meditative storyteller better at writing short fiction than sustaining long plots, and such critics tend to view her novels as assembled vignettes. The other common criticism of her work is the two-dimensionality of her male characters once she moves beyond the father-figures and heroic celibates—a criticism to which she accedes, as she confessed to Diana Cooper-Clark in an interview for *Commonweal* (May 9, 1980): "I'm not very good at young men who have a sexual identity. . . . Flannery O'Connor says that everything that is important to a writer she learns before the age of eight, and I was brought up in a very female-centric world. . . . I find men so incomprehensible that I can't write about them very well."

The seed of her first novel, *Final Payments*, was "the idea that among [her] mother's friends there were a lot of women who'd given up their lives to care for someone," Miss Gordon told Richard R. Lingeman, the columnist for the New York *Times Book Review* (April 30, 1978). "For someone in my own generation to undergo that imprisonment would be highly peculiar." She wanted to examine "what would happen if someone in [her] generation performed this kind of sacrifice."

The "someone" she created for that purpose was Isabel Moore, the intelligent, caustically witty protagonist of *Final Payments*, a once devout but now disillusioned daughter in a working-class Irish-Catholic Queens home. Regarded as a self-mortifying saint by those around her, Isabel is within herself struggling painfully to come to terms with the strict ethos of self-denial in which she has been bred as well as the more universal question of balancing one's own rights against the responsibility of caring for others. Partly out of feelings of guilt, she selflessly nurses her beloved but difficult paralytic father—a domineering reactionary, consumed with fanatic hatred for all things liberal and non-Catholic—for eleven years. After his death, she finds herself, at age thirty, facing the necessity of inventing an independent life for herself. She moves up the Hudson, takes a social-service job interviewing old people in foster homes (one of the more light-hearted stretches in the book), and has two adulterous affairs, one of which, with a brutish male chauvinist, nearly destroys her. In expiation for what she considers her "self-indulgence," she afflicts herself with the onerous task of looking after a woman she despises—her father's former housekeeper, Margaret Casey, a crazy, most unpleasant ingrate—until she realizes that such self-sacrifice is really self-indulgence. The book ends with her retreat to the redemptive company of her two oldest women friends to gather strength before giving the world another try.

"What was very important to me," Miss Gordon told Diana Cooper-Clark in the *Commonweal* interview, "was to make the distinction between genuine sacrifice, motivated not only by love but by affection—which seems to me to be of immense importance in life—and the kind of sacrifice that Isabel practiced in relation to Margaret [which] is a kind of theft, sacrifice for its own sake, without any movement of the heart. Sacrifice as an abstraction is hateful unless you really want to [practice it]. Certainly there would be points when the [beloved] person is physically appalling to you. . . . But unless you have a memory of a stirring in the heart, I think you have no right to sacrifice."

Final Payments, which Miss Gordon began to write in 1975, when she was teaching freshman English at Dutchess Community College in Poughkeepsie, New York, had two endings and went through three drafts before completion. Miss Gordon told Edmund White in the *Book Week* interview how it came to be published: "I was in London for a year with my [first] husband. He's an anthropologist and we were there for his sabbatical. I was very lonely. One day I saw Margaret Drabble on television, and I liked her so much I wrote her a letter. She phoned me the next day and invited me to dinner—extraordinarily generous of her. We became friends and later I showed her *Final Payments*, which I was just finishing. She put me in touch with her American agent [Peter Matson], who took me on as a client."

When Peter Matson took *Final Payments* to Viking Press and Alfred A. Knopf Inc., it was written in the third person, so as to give it "a sense of detachment," because Miss Gordon had been persuaded in graduate school to believe that women must beware of writing too personally. Convinced by Elizabeth Hardwick and Anne Freedgood (an editor at Random House) that such a notion was prejudiced nonsense, she converted the entire manuscript into the first person, and in that form it was accepted by Random House and published in the spring of 1978.

After the rave notices and spectacular sales reports on *Final Payments* came in, Mary Gordon said that what surprised her most was that a novel about "sacrifice and old age" had "such widespread appeal." Using the conceit of Frankenstein and his laboratory to explain the writer's creative power, Madora McKenzie in her review of *Final Payments* in the *Christian Science Monitor* (May 25, 1978) wrote: *"Final Payments* is a painful, powerful, transforming book. It is the monster we have all been waiting for. . . . With *Final Payments* Mary Gordon has . . . dethroned the mythical nobility of suffering, of choosing to be self-seen as victim. The world needs Samaritans more than it needs martyrs." The "genuine achievement" of *Final Payments,* as Maureen Howard pointed out in the New York *Times Book Review* (April 16, 1978), is that "we are made to care about Isabel Moore's arrested emotional development and her agony of guilt and pain."

Other critics found *Final Payments,* with its careful, knowledgeable documentation of Catholic mores, at once fascinating and moving. Many remarked Miss Gordon's stylistic elegance, her assurance in the use of metaphor, her verbal skill in giving her heroine complex but precise emotional and intellectual attitudes, her sharp eye for social and physical detail, and the subtle combination of humor and compassion with which she handled intensely serious moral perplexities. Many placed her in the tradition of Jane Austen—whom she indeed emulates—and some, like Richard Locke in the New York *Times Book Review* (May 21, 1981) found that "after a run of would-be Dostoyevskys, it's a refreshing change to read a young novelist who works in the line of Chekhov, who would rather be Jane Austen than Charlotte Brontë."

Although she was gratified by the critical response in general, Miss Gordon told Diana Cooper-Clark that "only the [Wilfrid] Sheed review was instructive" to her. In his review in the New York *Review of Books* (June 1, 1978), Sheed wrote: "Mary Gordon's *Final Payments* is much more than the latest thing in Catholic novels . . . but it does show brilliantly the effects of the new [post-Vatican Council II] dispensation on American Catholic fiction. It gives a picture of certain Catholic lives . . . more ambiguous than anything either a loyalist or a heretic would have had a mind to produce a few years ago."

Sheed made a parallel between Isabel tending her father and a nun presiding over the last days of the pre-Vatican Council II church. "Like such a nun, she doesn't regret a minute of it. . . . Astonishingly he [the father] emerges as the most impressive and attractive character in the book. . . . After him the outside world would seem trashy and pointless. The religious vocation has been made incarnate. Which means that Isabel cannot begin to explain it to her friends. Her father the Church dies at last, and she finds them waiting for an explanation. . . . The novel is an exploration of whether the years with God were wasted." The comic mode was an appropriate, seemingly inevitable choice for that sad exploration, Sheed asserted, a "marking of danger with jokes," in the way that priests and nuns used to hide their tumultuous feelings with sardonicism and wry wit. "If God really has died as a presence to many Christians in this century, even as a grouchy, demanding presence, this still seems like the best way to talk about it."

After four years at Dutchess Community College, Miss Gordon joined the faculty of Amherst (Massachusetts) College in 1979 as a teacher of courses on the religious novel and the writing of fiction. While teaching at Amherst she wrote her second novel, *The Company of Women* (Random House, 1981), the story of Felicitas Taylor (who is fourteen when the novel begins, in 1963), Felicitas' widowed mother, Charlotte, and three of the mother's childless women friends. The older women are united in their devotion to Father Cyprian, a charismatic, fiercely conservative Paracletist priest whose special vocation is the giving of retreats for working women. After the priest leaves his monastic order in disgust over the liberal post-Vatican II policies, the women spend their summer vacations visiting him at his homestead in Orano, a small town in upstate New York where he maintains the "traditionalist" ways, including the Latin Mass. As the only child in the priest-dominated group, Felicitas is, as Cyprian tells the women, its spiritual daughter, its hope for the future. In the late 1960's Felicitas rebels against the religiosity and joins the hippie-style harem of a New-Left professor at Columbia University, but after her lover abandons her she returns, pregnant, to the "company of women." The whole group moves to Orano, building homes near Father Cyprian's farm and caring for the aging priest and Felicitas' baby, Linda, who in her turn becomes the hope of the group. In their closing soliloquies, the dying Father Cyprian feels that he has failed in his vocation; Felicitas grudgingly accepts "the ordinary life" of a wife (she is about to marry a hardware merchant primarily for Linda's sake) and mother and consoles herself with the thought that she does "less harm than good"; Linda, in a counterpoint to the moribund Father Cyprian, closes the book with the affirmation, "We are not dying."

Critics varied widely in assessing *The Company of Women* in relation to *Final Payments,* some seeing it as a variation on the themes of the first, to lesser effect, others crediting it with deepening and widening the reader's view of Miss Gordon's exquisitely detailed, deliberately circumscribed landscape, and still others delivering notices somewhere in between. "Given the scope, depth, and perfection of its lyrical passages," Barbara Grizzuti Harrison wrote in the *Saturday Review* (February 1981), "it is fair to call this a brilliant novel." Robert Towers in the New York *Review of Books* (March 19, 1981), enumerating the multitude of themes explored (reconciliation, the need for charity toward self as well as others, the role of women in relation to male authority and to the church, the rhythms of submission and rebellion, love as entrapment, and the conflicting needs of shelter and escape), called *The Company of Women* "this most *thoughtful* [his italics] of recent novels," but he felt the thematic abundance was more successfully realized in short episodes than in any prolonged dramatic sweep. In her review in the New York *Times Book Review* (February 15, 1981) Francine Du Plessix Gray described the book as "a novel of marvelous parts rather than a marvelous novel," explaining that if she was harsh with it, it was because of her "enormous admiration" for Miss Gordon's first novel and "for the purity, ambition, and grandeur of vision offered in both her books."

Mary Gordon, a dark-haired woman with large eyes, lives in New Paltz, New York with her husband since 1979, Arthur Cash, the chairman of the English Dept. at the State University of New York at New Paltz, and their daughter, Anna. She was previously married to, and divorced from, James Brain. One of her favorite recreations is "show business," by which she means a wide range of musical theatre, from musical comedies to the Radio City Music Hall Rockettes.

In between her novels, Miss Gordon regularly publishes short nonfiction, usually critical essays, in addition to short stories. Having what she calls "a fetish about [her] writing tools," she composes not at a typewriter but in longhand, with a pen in bound, narrow-ruled notebooks from England. In her reading of fiction, she is attracted to writers with a "depth of understanding of their characters combined with a poetic use of language," including Virginia Woolf, Ford Madox Ford, and Georges Bernanos. In nonfiction, she prefers theology and such writers as Simone Weil. Still a practising Catholic, she is torn between a liberal feminist frustration with the church's policies on such matters as women priests and a conservative nostalgia for a church that took sin and sacrifice more seriously. Like her fictional protagonists, she seems to think it is unfortunate that when rebels return to the church they left, they find it gone. Among her liberal attitudes is her positive position on any "passionate attachment": as she explains, "Even 'warped' love is some-

how life-giving and in the end it will probably come out okay."

References: Commonweal 107:270+ My 9 '80; London Observer p35 N 19 '78 por; N Y Times Bk R p55 Ap 30 '78, p26+ F 15 '78; Pub W 219:274+ F 6 '81 por; Contemporary Authors vol 102 (1981)

Graves, Nancy (Stevenson)

Dec. 23, 1940- Artist. Address: b. c/o M. Knoedler & Co., Inc., 19 E. 70th St., New York City, N.Y. 10021

Diversity and complexity are the hallmarks of the work of Nancy Graves, who has made a reputation over the past decade as sculptor, painter, and filmmaker. The subject matter that lends representational imagery to her abstract studies ranges from Bactrian camels to bathymetric maps, and from primitive totems to lunar landscapes, but the primary concern of much of her recent work is the creative process itself. No matter how diverse they may be in medium or in meaning, all her works of art are conceived with imaginative power and executed with impeccable technical expertise.

Nancy Stevenson Graves was born on December 23, 1940 in Pittsfield, Massachusetts, the daughter of Walter L. Graves, an assistant to the director of the Berkshire Museum of Art and Natural History, and Mary B. Graves, a secretary and volunteer worker. Together with her sister, Judith, Nancy grew up in Pittsfield; she attended Miss Hall's School in Pittsfield and the Northfield School for Girls. Because of her father's position, Nancy spent considerable time among the works of art and natural artifacts of the Berkshire Museum. "I came to think of art and natural history as one, in a way that never would have happened in a bigger town," she has said. "When I was growing up those stuffed animals were Michelangelo and Bernini rolled into one." Unlike her parents, who pursued art as an avocation (her father carved wood and painted and her mother practised flower arrangement), Nancy decided to make art her career by the time she reached the age of twelve. After graduating from secondary school in 1957, she entered Vassar College with the intention of studying applied arts, but when she discovered that its art curriculum focused on history, she changed her major to English literature. She obtained a B.A. degree in 1961.

To acquire formal training, Nancy Graves next enrolled at Yale University's School of Art and Architecture, where her work was particularly influenced by the paintings of Matisse, the sculptures of Brancusi, the tenets of abstract expressionism and Pop Art, and the teaching of the painter Josef Albers. After she earned her B.F.A. and M.F.A. degrees in 1964, a Fulbright-Hayes Fellowship enabled her to spend 1965 in Paris. There her study of old masters made her aware of her greater affinity for such contemporary sculptors as David Smith, Claes Oldenburg, and Bruce Nauman. In 1966 she continued her aesthetic investigations in Florence, where she discovered, at the Museum of Natural History, the wax casts of Clemente Susini, an eighteenth-century Italian anatomist who fashioned life-size studies of human beings and animals. His fine craftsmanship and naturalistic subject matter ignited her imagination; "I felt as if I were seeing a body of my own work in the future," she later explained.

Inspired by Susini, Nancy Graves used subject matter from the animal kingdom for the exploration of her aesthetic concerns from 1966 to 1971, creating anatomical studies of the Bactrian, or two-humped, camel. While still in Florence, she modeled her first camel, a life-size polyurethane sculpture supported by a wooden framework and covered by painted animal skins. At the end of 1966 she moved to New York City, where she soon made two more animal sculptures. Her first New York solo show, at the Graham Gallery in the spring of 1968, featured the three sculptures, which were laden with burlap sacks and bridled with lead ropes to enhance their "formal, austere presence" as beasts of burden. Nancy Graves then crafted four more camels, three of which appeared at a second solo show that took place in the spring of 1969 at the Whitney Museum of American Art. The second Bactrian grouping was presented without any extraneous props.

The exhibitions of Nancy Graves's sculptures aroused considerable critical clamor. Most reviewers assumed that in creating the camels her purpose was to surpass the achievements of taxidermy; thus they either applauded or disparaged the works on the basis of representational accuracy. One writer suggested that the sculptures were "an ingenious put-on" mocking the tenets of abstract expressionism; another asserted that they were a revolutionary statement defying the established art world. But Nancy Graves's objective was, in the words of Brenda Richardson in Arts magazine (April 1972), to meld "figuration and abstraction," which have traditionally been considered as "antithetical" by American artists, or in the words of Marcia Tucker, curator of the Whitney show, to establish "sustained tension . . . between the viewer's reaction to the 'real' subject matter and his aesthetic awareness of the camels as sculptural objects." Nancy Graves intended her camels to be the products of a combination of personal imagination and natural observation.

In her next sculptural work Nancy Graves treated the camel as "a prehistoric form from North America," as she explained to Emily Wasserman in an interview for Artforum (October 1970). Using wax molded over steel rods and colored with acrylic paint and marble dust, she fashioned forms resembling the bones of ancient camels. Whether scattering them about the floor, as in Fossils (1970), placing them within pieces of skin, as in Inside-Outside (1970), or standing them upright in ranks, as in Variability of Similar Forms (1970), Nancy Graves positioned her bone forms into disparate groupings that cannot be assimilated visually into unified entities but instead remain variegated patterns that shift as viewers move around them. In further sculptural experiments, Nancy Graves fragmented her bones and skins and hung them on wires or poles as totemic arrangements reminiscent of early North American religious artifacts. Critics considered the most complicated of the totemic pieces, Variability and Repetition of Variable Forms (1970), to be more like an environment than a single sculpture, a forest of fantastical forms that invites viewers into its depths.

In 1970 and 1971 Nancy Graves also used camels as the subject of three short motion pictures, which, like her camel bone structures, focus on the effects of motion on the human perception for forms. Her first cinematic effort, an eight-minute film entitled 200 Stills at 60 Frames (1970), creates the illusion of motion by flashing a new still image every two and a half seconds. Her other two movies, shot in Morocco, are color films with sound tracks. Goulimine (1970), eight minutes long, captures the patterns of movement made by a hobbled herd at a camel market. Izy Boukir (1971), twenty minutes long, shows camels running, drinking, urinating, and nursing. Like Nancy Graves's camel sculptures, the films, as Brenda Richardson observed in the Arts magazine article, combine simultaneous figuration and abstraction. "Carefully directed shots and angles [reveal] patterns of abstraction without obviating the viewer's ability comfortably to recognize and respond to the camel itself," she wrote.

In 1971 Nancy Graves exhibited her bone and totem sculptures and sometimes her films in solo shows at Reese Palley's New York and San Francisco galleries, the National Gallery of Canada in Ottawa, Vassar College Art Gallery, and the Neue Galerie der Stadt in Aachen, West Germany. The Museum of Modern Art featured her as the fifth artist in its series of solo exhibitions entitled "Projects," and that same year she received a fellowship from Vassar and a grant from the Paris Biennale, which were supplemented in 1972 by a grant from the National Endowment for the Arts.

Nancy Graves's exhibition at the Museum of Modern Art also included a series of paintings on which she began work in 1971. Turning her attention from camels to camouflage, she created, with small, shimmering brushstrokes, paintings depicting snakes, insects, and fish that blend in with their environments. From one vantage point, the dots resolve into recognizable animals; from another, figures and background blend into an abstract continuum. Reviewers displayed a wide range of reactions to their first encounter with Nancy Graves's painting style. Some identified the brushwork with post-impressionist pointillism, while others perceived it as a form of "distinctly controlled, ascetic gesturalism." Although some found the paintings to be "big disappointments," others considered them examples of original conception and refined technique. As a spokesman for the latter point of view, Barbara Rose wrote in New York magazine (January 17, 1972): "Because she does not resort to the regressive spatial convention of the various 'returns' to the figure in representational terms, but combines figuration with abstract space and forms, Graves is a remarkable painter."

In her second series of paintings, which she executed in 1972, Nancy Graves used the underwater environment of her camouflaged fish as her subject but changed her scale of vision. Employing carefully controlled patterns of dots, she traced whole sections of ocean floor in the manner of bathymetric maps. That same year she made another set of paintings inspired by maps, a series based on satellite photographs of lunar topography, in which, to simulate the grainy quality of her source materials, she again used stippled brushstrokes. The most ambitious of her lunar paintings, entitled Nearside of the Moon 20° N-S x 70° E-W, is the largest of all her existing canvases. The pictorial elements arranged across its four panels allude to several different types of twentieth-century mapping of the moon. In 1973 she made another four-panel map painting using the planet Mars as her subject.

For her next series of paintings based on satellite photographs, which she worked on in 1973 and 1974, Nancy Graves used canvas panels in a different way. She took long, slender rectangles and laid them side by side on a slant, leaving space between them to indicate transmission gaps in her source materials. The original photographs from which she worked were Nimbus 4 satellite studies of cloud formations. In the shaped paintings Nancy Graves allows her brushwork, so carefully modulated in her earlier paintings, to burst forth in a profusion of bold strokes. Shortly thereafter she made a final series of paintings based directly on satellite photographs, in which the brushwork takes over to an even greater degree. Although their subject is ostensibly Antarctica, the paintings, as Richard Channin pointed out in Arts magazine (October 1975), "seem to bear less upon topography as shape and pattern and tell more about the manual procedures and physical materials of making." Nancy Graves's map paintings appeared in several solo shows throughout the United States, including those at Cleveland's New Gallery in 1972; her hometown's Berkshire Museum, La Jolla's Museum of Contemporary Art, and Corpus Christi's Art Museum of South Texas in 1973; New York City's André Emmerich Gallery in 1974; and Houston's Janie C. Lee Gallery in 1972, 1973, 1974, and 1975. In 1974 she received a Creative Artist Public Service grant.

Her map paintings elicited a more favorable response than the one that had greeted her camouflage paintings. Critics praised their compositional complexity and painterly refinement and hailed them as examples of a resurgence in landscape painting. Richard Channin defined Nancy Graves's style of landscape painting more specifically by observing, in an article for Art International (November 15, 1974), that she takes cartography, a scientifically rendered record of the perception of an environment, and further abstracts it into a work of art.

As an adjunct to her paintings, Nancy Graves made two films. In 1973 she began Aves: Magnificent Frigate Bird, Great Flamingo, a twenty-three minute color film depicting the flight patterns of migratory birds, which took two years to complete. Filming the frigate birds at the Marquesa Keys in Florida and the flamingos at Lake Nakuru in Kenya, she succeeded in capturing the motion of both the gracefully gliding black forms of the frigate birds and the awkwardly flapping pink forms of the flamingos that defines the shape of the space through which they fly. In her thirty-three minute black and white film called Reflections on the Moon (1974) the camera itself does the moving, scanning about 200 still photographs taken by the Lunar Orbiter. The goal of that film, Nancy Graves wrote during its production, is "to overwhelm the viewer with the presence of the moon." Together with her earlier camel films, Aves and Reflections resemble Nancy Graves's paintings in that "they are fundamentally abstract even though the images are 'representational,'" according to Lucy R. Lippard in Art in America (November/December 1975).

From 1976 onwards Nancy Graves abstracted her imagery one step further from the direct depiction of landscape when she began to create paintings that allude to her earlier paintings and concern themselves primarily with facture. In pastels such as *Bish* (1976) and the *Yot K. Series* (1976), she freed her brushwork to play across the surface of the paper without any obligation to imitate cartographic information. In later works on paper she stroked watercolor onto wet sheets, creating even softer, looser lines and forms. In the *Moonwater Series* (1977), for example, the colors both recorded the painter's gestures and interacted of their own volition after she removed her brush. With similar freedom of gesture, Nancy Graves created oil paintings, such as *Defacta* (1977) and *Zitla* (1977), composed of dense, complicated layers of brushstrokes. Her oils refer back to her earlier sculptures as well as her earlier paintings. Works such as *Lam* (1978) and *Calipers, Legs, Lines* (1979), for example, employ forms from her camels and camel bone pieces.

In 1976 Nancy Graves also began making bronze sculpture that alludes to her earlier sculpture when she received a museum commission, from Doctor Peter Ludwig of Cologne, West Germany, to create a more permanent version of a camel bone piece. Working with the Tallix Foundry in New York, she cast bronze bone forms from wax models and made the huge outdoor piece *Ceridwen* (1969-77), which she exhibited at the Hammarskjold Plaza Sculpture Garden in New York City in the spring of 1978 before sending it off to West Germany. In addition to creating other bronzes, such as *Column* (1979), that echo earlier camel bone sculptures, Nancy Graves embarked on a group of polychrome sculptures colored with paints and patinas. Those innovative works translate into three dimensions a variety of two-dimensional forms from her map paintings and films as well as from archeological drawings she sketched at the Academy of Rome in 1977. Her lyric polychrome pieces include *Bathymet-Topograph* (1978-79), *Archeologue* (1979), *Aves* (1979), and *Trace* (1980).

Nancy Graves exhibited her most recent paintings and occasionally also her sculptures at André Emmerich's New York and Zurich galleries and the Galerie im Schloss in Munich in 1977; at the Gallery Diane Gilson in Seattle in 1978; at the Janie C. Lee Gallery in Houston in 1977 and 1978; and at M. Knoedler & Co. in New York in 1978, 1979, 1980, and 1981. At Getler/Paul Gallery in New York in 1977 she exhibited a series of prints.

Reviewers, with few exceptions, greeted the paintings enthusiastically, citing their "energy," beauty, "airy luminosity," and "carefully considered" brushwork. Susan Heinemann, in an article for *Arts* magazine (March 1977), called the pictures studies in motion and rhythm, which offer a complex impression that the viewer gathers with the passing of time rather than a single static image that he perceives instantly. Reviewers who saw the sculptures liked them in general even more than the paintings, calling them "brilliant," "overpowering," and "courageous" in their challenge to sculptural traditions. Together with a comprehensive selection of her earlier work, the latter-day paintings and sculptures were presented by the Albright-Knox Art Gallery of Buffalo as a retrospective exhibition that opened in the spring of 1980 and then traveled for the next year to museums in Akron, Houston, Memphis, Purchase, Des Moines, and Minneapolis.

Energetic, articulate, and dedicated to her art, Nancy Graves has been called "the Renaissance woman for the eighties." She was married to the sculptor Richard Serra from 1965 to 1970, and for the past several years she has lived alone in a loft in lower Manhattan. Her work can be found in three of the major museums of her adopted city, the Metropolitan, the Whitney, and the Museum of Modern Art, as well as in a dozen other institutions throughout the United States, Europe, and Canada, including the Albright-Knox, the Chicago Art Institute, the Houston Museum of Fine Arts, the Yale University Art Gallery, and the National Gallery of Canada in Ottawa.

References: Cathcart, Linda L. Nancy Graves: A Survey 1969/1980 (1980); *N Y Times* C p16 Ja 26 '79; *Vogue* 170:202+ Je '80 por; *Who's Who in America, 1980-81; Who's Who in American Art* (1980)

Guinness, Alec

Apr. 2, 1914- British actor. Address: b. c/o London Management, 235/241 Regent St., London WIA 2JT, England; h. "Kettlebrook Meadows," Steep Marsh, Petersfield, Hampshire, England

NOTE: This biography supersedes the article that appeared in *Current Biography* in 1950.

On both stage and screen Sir Alec Guinness is admired as "an actor who makes you forget that he is acting." His achievement may be attributable, at least in part, to the exquisite economy of his technique. As New York *Times* television critic John J. O'Connor (September 29, 1980) noted in a review of *Tinker, Tailor, Soldier, Spy*, the TV miniseries in which Guinness recently starred, "Sir Alec . . . can say more with a slight pursing of his lips than most actors can communicate while shouting from the rafters." Famed, moreover, for his versatility, he has triumphed in the theatre in roles as startlingly dissimilar as the urbane psychiatrist in T. S. Eliot's *The Cocktail Party* and the drink-sodden, womanizing Welsh poet

Alec Guinness

in Sidney Michaels' biographical drama *Dylan*. In motion pictures his finely detailed characterizations have ranged from a tour-de-force delineation of eight members of an eccentric English clan in *Kind Hearts and Coronets* to an Oscar-winning portrayal of military priggishness in *The Bridge on the River Kwai*. Over the years it has become impossible to predict in what guise the protean Guinness will turn up next; in 1977 astonished critics found him cast as a whiskery wizard in the sci-fi spectacular *Star Wars*. But his is such a prodigious talent that, as the *Oxford Companion to the Theatre* put it, "whatever he does is worth watching."

For a long time Alec Guinness was close-mouthed about his origins, except to reveal the place and date of his birth—London on April 2, 1914. Lately he has grown less protective of his privacy. According to *Notable Names in the American Theatre*, his parents were Andrew and Agnes (Cuffe) Geddes. In September 1980 the *Dial*, a publication of New York's Public Broadcasting channel, contained an article by Auberon Waugh that divulged that the actor "was conceived in the summer of 1913 on the Isle of Wight," that a Scottish banker named Andrew is "reported" to have been his father, and that his mother later wed a Scottish Army officer, Captain Skiven, "who detested young Alec and tormented him in various ways." When, three years after the marriage, Captain Skiven was posted to New Zealand, he expected his wife and stepson to follow in due course, but they did not.

From 1922 to 1927 Guinness attended a boarding school in Southborne called Pembroke Lodge, whose headmaster thwarted his desire to participate in student theatricals by declaring, "You're not the acting type." As an outlet for his dramatic imagination, Guinness turned to telling stories in the dormitory at night after the lights had been extinguished. At Roxborough, in Eastbourne, where he finished his formal education in 1932, he was given his first chance to act. Assigned the role of a breathless messenger in *Macbeth*, he achieved verisimilitude by running around the nearby playing field six times before his entrance.

At the age of eighteen Guinness went to work for a London advertising agency as an apprentice copywriter. A year and a half later, having been designated a layout man, he found himself so poorly suited to the work that he decided to prepare for a career in the theatre and arranged to study with Martita Hunt. After his first session with her, she informed him that he had "no talent at all," but Guinness insisted that he continue. Her coaching quickly bore fruit; he was awarded a two-year scholarship to the Fay Compton Studio of Dramatic Art. But unable to meet even exceedingly modest living expenses, he left drama school at the end of seven months to seek employment. In 1934 he landed the wordless role of a junior counselor in the courtroom drama *Libel!* Then, at the Piccadilly Theatre, in a lurid shipboard thriller called *Queer Cargo*, he essayed three small parts: a Chinese cook, a French pirate, and a British sailor. What Guinness regards as his big break came in November 1934 when John Gielgud cast him as both Osric and the Third Player in *Hamlet*.

After appearing—again in support of Gielgud—as a wolf in French dramatist André Obey's *Noah*, Guinness doubled as Sampson and the Apothecary in the now legendary revival of *Romeo and Juliet*, which Gielgud directed and which, with Laurence Olivier and Peggy Ashcroft in the title roles and Gielgud himself as Mercutio, opened at the New Theatre in October 1935. Guinness then portrayed Yakov the laborer in a presentation of *The Sea Gull* enlighteningly staged by Theodore Komisarjevsky, who for the first time made English audiences aware that the constricted world of Chekhov's characters could be funny as well as sad. Between September 1936 and April 1937 Guinness acted in an all-Shakespeare season at the Old Vic. In addition to being seen as Boyet in *Love's Labour's Lost*, Sir Andrew Aguecheek in *Twelfth Night*, and Exeter in *Henry V*, he understudied Laurence Olivier as the melancholy Dane in Tyrone Guthrie's *Hamlet*. When the troupe traveled to Elsinore in June 1937 to inaugurate an annual festival performance of *Hamlet* in the Castle of Kronborg, Guinness assumed the roles of Osric, Reynaldo, and the Player Queen.

In the fall of 1937 Guinness joined Gielgud's London company and, with the "great simplicity and pathos" of his Aumerle in *Richard II* and the "magically poetic quality" of his Lorenzo in *The Merchant of Venice*, established himself as one of England's most promising young actors. At Guthrie's urging he returned to the Old Vic late in 1938 to play the lead in an uncut, modern-dress version of *Hamlet;* it is remembered as "a remarkably sincere, straightforward performance which had in it some unforgettable moments." During the remainder of the season he played Arthur Gower in *Trelawny of the 'Wells'* and Bob Acres in *The Rivals.* For an old Vic tour of the Continent and Egypt in 1939, he added the role of Michael Ransom in *The Ascent of F.6* to his repertoire.

Testing the theory of several critics who, on the strength of his lyrical Lorenzo, had prophesied a future for him in romantic parts, Guinness attempted Shakespeare's Romeo at the Scottish Theatre Festival in Perth in July 1939. Later that year he portrayed Herbert Pocket on the London stage in his own adaptation of Dickens' *Great Expectations.* During 1940 he divided his time between the commercial theatre, where his vehicles were *Cousin Muriel* and a touring edition of Robert Ardrey's *Thunder Rock,* and the Old Vic, where he was Ferdinand in *The Tempest.*

As World War II raged, Guinness enlisted in the Royal Navy in 1941 as an ordinary seaman; commissioned a lieutenant the following year, he served on an escort vessel in the Mediterranean. In New York in 1942, while awaiting repairs to his ship, Guinness obtained leave so that he could make his Broadway debut on December 23 as an outwardly courageous but secretly terrified flyer in Terence Rattigan's paean to the RAF, *Flare Path,* which ran a scant ten days. His only other acting before his discharge from the Navy was in London in the spring of 1945, when he impersonated Lord Horatio Nelson in the Pageant *Hearts of Oak.*

In postwar London, Guinness resumed his stage career as Mitya in his own dramatization of the Dostoevsky novel *The Brothers Karamazov,* which Peter Brook directed. Although an artistic success, it fared poorly at the box office. Immediately thereafter, with Brook again at the helm, Guinness played in *Vicious Circle,* the first English-language production of *Huis clos,* existentialist Jean-Paul Sartre's harrowing vision of hell. Early in 1947 Guinness portrayed the Dauphin in George Bernard Shaw's *Saint Joan.* When, in April, he tackled the title role in Shakespeare's *Richard II,* the critic for the London *Sunday Express* wrote, "Mr. Guinness is slight, with an interesting angular face and a clear, flexible voice. He has dignity, but no majesty; he has range and control, but no surprises. He is intensely good without being great—yet. His future may bring that."

Back under the Old Vic banner for a season, Guinness contributed an "outstanding" Fool to *King Lear* and a "definitive" Abel Drugger to *The Alchemist,* as well as a portrayal of Hlestakov in the Gogol satire *The Government Inspector.* In 1948 he directed but did not act in a production of *Twelfth Night* that was intriguing for the unusual importance it attached to Feste, the servant-clown. At the Edinburgh Festival in 1949 Guinness created the role of Sir Henry Harcourt-Reilly, the seemingly omniscient psychiatrist, in T. S. Eliot's poetic allegory *The Cocktail Party.* When he repeated it on Broadway from January to June 1950 at Henry Miller's Theatre, he was voted best actor in *Variety's* annual poll of New York drama critics.

On the London stage in 1951 Guinness played Shakespeare's Prince of Denmark again, this time in Elizabethan dress in a production that he himself directed. To help launch Canada's Shakespearean Festival in Stratford, Ontario in the summer of 1953, Guinness appeared in the title role of *Richard III* and as the King of France in *All's Well that Ends Well.* London critics unanimously applauded his sensitive interpretation in 1954 of a beleaguered Roman Catholic cardinal in *The Prisoner,* Bridget Boland's terse study of the psychologically insidious methods of interrogation employed by a police state. After playing a would-be adulterer in Feydeau's *Hotel Paradiso,* in 1956, he was not seen on the stage until 1960, when he had the title role in *Ross,* Terence Rattigan's dramatic portrait of the enigmatic T. E. Lawrence. "Sir Alec is at his subtle, suggestive best," a critic for *Time* (May 23, 1960) reported, and the London *Evening Standard* conferred on him its annual Best Actor award. Absurdist playwright Eugène Ionesco's *Exit the King* was Guinness' vehicle in 1963, first at the Edinburgh Festival and then at London's Royal Court Theatre; as Berenger the First, a ruler as desiccated as his domain, he gave "a dazzling bravura performance."

Prodded by director Peter Glenville, in 1964 Guinness hazarded the difficult title role in the Broadway production of *Dylan,* the anecdotal drama dealing with the last few months in the life of Dylan Thomas. In a representative review Walter Kerr of the New York *Herald Tribune* (January 20, 1964) termed his performance "mesmerizing." "There is a still center in the actor, a coal in the ashes," Kerr wrote, "that defies us to will our eyes away." The play's eight-month run was a virtual sellout, and by season's end Guinness had picked up Tony, Page One, and Aegis Theatre Club awards. In January 1966 Guinness and Anthony Quayle were the principals in the London replica of Arthur Miller's *Incident at Vichy,* a play set in occupied France in 1942. The melodrama drew decidedly mixed notices, but critics lavishly praised Guinness as the Christian with a conscience. "For him," Philip Hope-Wallace told his readers in the *Guardian* (January 27, 1966), "the evening is worth while." Obversely, during the 1966-67 season at the Royal Court Theatre, Guinness could not redeem a Brechtian revival of *Macbeth* that, according to one reviewer, "appeared to be set in a sandpit." A frequently unintelligible Simone Signoret as Lady Macbeth compounded the artistic felony. A much happier experience was Simon Gray's black comedy *Wise Child.*

As the older of a pair of on-the-lam thieves who dresses as a woman and palms himself off as the mother of his confederate, Guinness entered gleefully into the spirit of the romp. At the Chichester Festival in the summer of 1968 he re-created the role of Sir Henry Harcourt-Reilly in *The Cocktail Party*, which then moved to London's West End for a stand of nearly twenty weeks.

Of the plays that Guinness elected to do in the 1970's, the majority were substantial hits. Bridget Brophy's *Time Out of Mind*, a bizarrely plotted denouncement of nuclear proliferation, was the only unqualified disaster. *A Voyage Round My Father* by John Mortimer, with Guinness portraying the irascible parent, a sightless solicitor who never permitted his disability to get the better of him, proved to be an extremely popular attraction. So did Alan Bennett's rueful frolic *Habeas Corpus*, which provided him with a splendid starring role as Arthur Wicksteed, a world-weary general practitioner. He enriched Julian Mitchell's stage adaptation of the Ivy Compton-Burnett novel *A Family and a Fortune*, with a fine performance in the role of Dudley, an Edwardian gentleman whose impeccable exterior masked a cruel heart. In the autumn of 1976 he acted in *Yahoo*, a four-character entertainment that he and director Alan Strachan had derived from the writings of Jonathan Swift. A year later, in *The Old Country*, Guinness enjoyed what Mollie Panter-Downes referred to in the *New Yorker* (November 14, 1977) as a "smash success." The comedy drama by Alan Bennett managed, in her opinion, "to be extremely funny, as well as laceratingly melancholy," and Guinness was "magnificent" in the part of a British Foreign Office veteran who had defected to the Soviet Union and was now reduced to "fretting his brains out in a purgatory of loneliness."

Alec Guinness made his movie debut as an extra in *Evensong* in 1934. To him, it was "a horrible experience" and he resolved "never to work in a crowd again." His first real screen role was Herbert Pocket in *Great Expectations* (1947), a highly praised Universal-International release that owed an unacknowledged debt to Guinness' 1939 stage version of the classic novel. But it was *Kind Hearts and Coronets* in 1949 that brought Guinness the status of movie character actor par excellence. His feat in Eagle-Lion's elegantly satiric period piece was impersonating eight doomed members of the fictional d'Ascoyne family so deftly that his cameos dominated the action. Press and public were awestruck, with "simply miraculous" the joint consensus. Guinness had major parts in three other films shown in the United States during 1950: he was the meek gardening editor of a London newspaper entrusted with the chaperonage of a pair of visiting Welsh coalminers in Universal-International's *A Run for Your Money*; in *Last Holiday*, an Associated British Picture Corporation release, he portrayed a farm machinery salesman who,

under the erroneous impression that he has just a short while left to live, opts to spend it as a do-gooding guest at a posh resort hotel; and in *The Mudlark*, Twentieth Century-Fox's "beguiling combination of stately pomp and impudent fantasy," he played Disraeli.

Because of charges brought by some Jewish groups that Guinness' characterization of Fagin was anti-Semitic, the 1948 David Lean-directed screen translation of *Oliver Twist* was not booked into American movie theatres until the summer of 1951. Even then United Artists had to allow a certain amount of "judicious" trimming, which, however, reviewers insisted had not impaired the quality of the Dickens adaptation. One critic extolled Guinness for leavening Fagin's wickedness "with streaks of humanity and humor that are oddly magnetic and warm." Later in 1951 he and Stanley Holloway won plaudits for being "deliciously adroit" in their roles as, respectively, a bowler-hatted, bespectacled bank clerk and his elderly accomplice, who smuggle a hoard of gold bullion out of England, in Universal-International's droll comedy *The Lavender Hill Mob*.

Two more sprightly spoofs that starred Guinness were distributed by Universal-International the following year: *The Man in the White Suit*, in which he was cast as a chemist monomaniacally intent on his quest for a wear-and-soil-resistant fabric; and *The Promoter*, in which he appeared as a morally imperturbable fellow bamboozling his way from the grimy bottom to the immaculate top of England's social ladder. In *The Captain's Paradise* (Lopert, 1953) Guinness had yet another choice comedy role: that of a ferryboat skipper who fulfills a favorite male dream by commuting between wives as well as ports. Less appealing to audiences was his comparatively straight part of a love-smitten aviator in *The Malta Story*, a 1954 United Artists release. They preferred his representation of G. K. Chesterton's ecclesiastical sleuth Father Brown in *The Detective* (Columbia), which Alton Cook of the New York *World-Telegram and Sun* (November 2, 1954) hailed as "a film of grace and charm" with "an undertone of sly, quiet mirth."

After a dispiriting bout with lackluster material in *To Paris with Love* (Continental, 1955), Guinness changed pace drastically in Columbia's movie version of *The Prisoner*, the play in which he had scored a huge hit on the London stage, with his marrow-freezing portrait of a churchman coerced by his Iron Curtain-country jailers into admitting to crimes he did not commit. Reviewers marveled at Guinness' ability to transmit emotional frenzy without rolling his eyes or raising his voice or flailing his arms, and one of them rated *The Prisoner* "the most searching indictment of communism the screen has given us." Reverting to lightweight escapist fare in 1956, Guinness enacted the ugly leader of a gang of robbers in the macabre farce *The Ladykillers* (Continental) and suavely courted Grace Kelly in MGM's remake of Ferenc Molnar's *The Swan*.

In *The Bridge on the River Kwai* Guinness personified a fascinating paradox: as Colonel Nicholson, a British officer interned in a Japanese prisoner-of-war camp, he portrayed a man whose strict adherence to an antiquated code of military ethics was both his salvation and his scourge. The New York Film Critics cited the movie, his performance, and David Lean's direction as 1957's best; the Academy of Motion Picture Arts and Sciences concurred and, in addition, awarded Oscars to the Columbia release for best screenplay, cinematography, editing, and musical scoring. By contrast, MGM's mildly diverting *All at Sea*, in which Guinness appeared as the *mal de mer*-prone descendant of a long line of naval heroes, seemed insignificant.

Vastly different from Guinness' other characters was Gulley Jimson in *The Horse's Mouth*, an aging rogue of a painter so obsessed by his art that he has no patience with people who impinge on his creativity. The story of his shenanigans was, as John Beaufort pointed out in the *Christian Science Monitor* (December 2, 1958), "not merely a tale of eccentricity in extremis. . . . A Swiftian kind of satire underlies the lampoonery." Guinness had also supplied the script of the United Artists release, distilling it from Joyce Carey's novel and earning himself an Oscar nomination for best screenplay based on material from another medium.

Guinness disappointed his fans in his 1959 depiction of a decadent French count and a colorless English schoolteacher who improbably swap identities in MGM's plodding mystery melodrama *The Scapegoat*. But he regained their allegiance the following year with two masterful characterizations: as a vacuum cleaner salesman recruited to spy for the British secret service in Columbia's *Our Man in Havana* and as a hard-drinking, fiery-haired, up-from-the-ranks officer forced to relinquish his command of a famous Scottish regiment to a colonel with more traditional credentials in the Lopert release *Tunes of Glory*.

As a Japanese industrialist and a Jewish widow from Brooklyn who fall in love, Guinness and Rosalind Russell were flagrantly miscast in the Warner Brothers 1962 movie version of Leonard Spigelgass' play *A Majority of One*. Guinness was much more at home that year in the uniform of a stalwart ship's captain in the Columbia sea saga *Damn the Defiant*, and he brought immense conviction to the part of Prince Feisal in the same studio's refreshingly literate epic *Lawrence of Arabia*. Although he continued to collect excellent personal notices, the films that followed were not unalloyed hits: *The Fall of the Roman Empire* (Paramount, 1964), *Situation Hopeless, But Not Serious* (Paramount, 1965), *Doctor Zhivago* (MGM, 1965), *Hotel Paradiso* (MGM, 1966), and *The Quiller Memorandum* (National General, 1966). A sluggish subplot involving Richard Burton and Elizabeth Taylor

as illicit lovers detracted from the effectiveness of *The Comedians* (MGM, 1967), in which Guinness had a gem of a role, as a foxy gun smuggler. Similarly, the actor's intelligent performance as King Charles I in *Cromwell* (Columbia, 1970) was inadequate compensation, some reviewers thought, in a tedious costume drama.

Neither National General's *Scrooge* (1970) nor Paramount's *Brother Sun, Sister Moon* (1973) reversed the downward trend of Guinness's cinematic fortunes. The saccharine musical mutation of *A Christmas Carol*, to which he contributed a delightfully campy cameo as Marley's Ghost, was spurned, in the words of one reviewer, as "a curdled cup of holiday cheer." In Franco Zeffirelli's effete, quasi-fictional biography of Francis of Assisi, Guinness had only a brief, though relatively lively, scene as Pope Innocent III. Paramount's *Hitler: the Last Ten Days* with Guinness in the title role sounded promising but in the final analysis was, according to *Sight and Sound* (Summer, 1973), "hard to stomach, and more of a hindrance than a help to historical comprehension."

In *Murder by Death* (Columbia, 1976), Neil Simon's commercially successful burlesque of old-fashioned detective stories, Guinness easily stole the show in the part of a wildly incompetent but resolutely unflappable blind butler named Bensonmum. No flesh-and-blood actor could have stolen the show from the special effects in *Star Wars*, writer-director George Lucas' homage to the sci-fi cliff-hangers of his youth, but by playing a space-age sage with dignity and no hint of condescension, Guinness supplied the 1977 Twentieth Century-Fox release with a touch of class it might otherwise have lacked. Guinness also had a brief role as a surviving crew member in Lew Grade's disappointing $35,000,000 *Raise the Titanic* (Associated Film Distribution, 1980).

Until recently Alec Guinness had been something of a hold-out where television was concerned. Before the 1980-81 season his appearances on the tube had been limited to *The Wicked Scheme of Jebal Deeks* (NBC, 1959), an entry in the short-lived *Startime* series, and a stint on the *Ed Sullivan Show* over CBS on June 7, 1964, when he performed an excerpt from *Dylan*, the play that he was then doing on Broadway. Since September 29, 1980, however, with the Public Television System's airing of the first segment of the six-part series based on John le Carré's novel *Tinker, Tailor, Soldier, Spy*, Guinness has had advantageous exposure on the small screen in the United States. His understated characterization of George Smiley, the middle-aged and spiritually forlorn secret agent, impressed reviewers as "uncommonly brilliant" and prompted Martin Mayer to predict in *American Film* (November 1980) that no watcher of *Tinker, Tailor, Soldier, Spy* would "ever be able to read anything le Carré writes about George Smiley without seeing Guinness." Coproduced by Paramount and the BBC, the series has spawned a sequel titled *Smiley's People*, in which the actor will again star.

Just how potent his brand of underplaying can be Guinness again demonstrated in the CBS-TV movie version of Frances Hodgson Burnett's *Little Lord Fauntleroy* (November 1980), which today's viewers might have been expected to find cloying. But Guinness—abetted by ten-year-old Ricky Schroder and an exemplary supporting cast—applied so unerringly delicate a touch to his portrait of the castle-dwelling Earl of Dorincourt, whose icy reserve slowly melts under the influence of his sweet-natured grandson, that, as O'Connor of the *New York Times* (November 25, 1980) affirmed, the story, for all its "simple-minded ingredients," still managed to "weave a magic spell."

The blue-eyed, bald actor, who is of average height, was once described by an interviewer as being "supremely dignified and excruciatingly shy." Guinness has been quoted as saying that he believes he possesses "an unfortunate chameleon quality" that has been an asset to him as an actor "but not as a person." In approaching a part, he told Joan Crosby of the New York *World-Telegram and Sun* (August 8, 1964), he invariably starts with the feet. "Until I have decided how the character walks," he explained, "nothing happens."

Married since June 20, 1938 to Merula Salaman, whom he met when they were both appearing as animals in Gielgud's production of *Noah,* Guinness admits to having stipulated at the time that she abandon her career. Matthew, the couple's only child, who was born during World War II, is also an actor. Sir Alec and his wife are converts to the Roman Catholic faith. They reside in an unpretentious house that they had built many years ago in the county of Hampshire in southern England. His hobby is fishing.

Star Wars now ranks as the biggest-grossing motion picture of all time, and its 1980 sequel, *The Empire Strikes Back,* in which, without billing, Guinness makes a token appearance, has amassed comparable earnings. From the percent of profits due him under the terms of his contract with Fox for the two films, Guinness would become a very rich man if it were not for Britain's tax rate. He is assuredly rich in honors, having been created a Commander of the British Empire in 1955 and a knight in 1959 and having had honorary degrees bestowed on him by Boston College in 1962 and by Oxford University in 1977. At the Academy Award ceremonies in 1979, when he was presented with a special Oscar to commemorate his many splendid performances on the screen, he delivered an acceptance speech that was a model of brevity, wit, and graciousness.

References: Dial I:54+ S '80; N Y Times II:19+ S 10 '72 por; Show 4:28+ D '64 por; Oxford Companion to the Theatre (1967); Who's Who in the World, 1978-79

Habib, Philip C(harles)

Feb. 25, 1920- United States foreign service officer. Address: h. 1606 Courtland Rd., Belmont, Calif. 94002

In May 1981 Philip C. Habib came out of retirement at the request of President Ronald Reagan to act as a special envoy in an attempt to extinguish the smoldering Lebanese civil war before it ignited a wider conflict between Syria and Israel. Habib, who played a major behind-the-scenes role in the formulation of American foreign policy during his three decades in the diplomatic corps, first came to public prominence in 1969, when he was named acting head of the United States delegation to the Paris peace talks that officially ended American involvement in the Vietnam war. An expert in Asian affairs, he turned his attention to the Middle East in 1977, after President Jimmy Carter asked him to help arrange the meetings between President Anwar Sadat and Prime Minister Menahem Begin that eventually resulted in the Camp David peace agreement ending hostilities between Egypt and Israel. At the time of his retirement in 1978, Habib was Undersecretary of State for Political Affairs, the highest position attainable by a career foreign service officer.

Of Lebanese descent, Philip Charles Habib was born in New York City, New York on February 25, 1920. The son of Alexander Habib, a grocer, and Mary (Spiridon) Habib, he grew up in the Bensonhurst section of Brooklyn and worked for a time as a shipping clerk in a local sheet metal factory before enrolling at the University of Idaho. After taking his B.S. degree, in 1942, he enlisted in the United States Army, which he left as a captain in 1946.

Returning to civilian life, Habib was admitted to the doctoral program at the University of California at Berkeley. While completing his course work in economics, he also taught undergraduate classes at the university and worked as a research assistant. He earned his Ph.D. degree in 1952, upon the submission of his dissertation on the economics of the lumber industry. By that time, he had already begun his career in the foreign service. From 1949 through 1951, he was the third secretary at the United States embassy in Canada, and he served as second secretary at the American embassy in New Zealand from 1952 to 1954. The next year he was transferred to the State Department in Washington, D.C., where he was a research specialist. Three years later, in 1958, he was named United States consul general to Trinidad, a post he held until 1960.

Back in Washington by the end of that year, Habib served as a foreign affairs officer at the State Department until he was sent, in 1962, to South Korea as the new counselor for political affairs. He remained in Seoul for three years, then, when the war in Vietnam began to escalate in the mid-1960's, he moved on to Saigon to bolster the American diplomatic presence there. Promoted to the rank of minister in 1966, he became Ambassador Henry Cabot Lodge's chief political adviser. Widely considered to be the State Department's most knowledgeable Southeast Asian expert, he was chosen, in July of the following year, to head an interdepartmental task force assigned to study the political situation in Vietnam and suggest possible courses of action. According to Paul Hofmann of the New York Times, Habib's position papers and briefs significantly contributed to President Lyndon B. Johnson's decision to restrict American bombing of North Vietnam beginning on April 1, 1968 and to take part in bilateral negotiations toward a cease-fire.

Habib, who had recently been elevated to the position of deputy assistant secretary of state for East Asian affairs, was an obvious choice for the American negotiating team. The leaders of the delegation, W. Averell Harriman and Cyrus R. Vance, relied heavily on Habib, who was at the center of both the public and private negotiations. During the crucial talks leading to the bombing halt on November 1, 1968, Habib, the highest-ranking career diplomat in the delegation, worked virtually around the clock. After the election of Richard Nixon as President of the United States in November 1968, Harriman and Vance were succeeded by Nixon appointees Henry Cabot Lodge and Lawrence E. Walsh, but Habib stayed on. Over the next few months, he sat in for Lodge, who was, in the eyes of many observers, temperamentally unsuited for the role of negotiator, at several critical sessions. At one such meeting, on August 21, 1969, he bluntly told the North Vietnamese delegation, "There can be no negotiated settlement to the war unless you are prepared to withdraw all

North Vietnamese troops and elements from South Vietnam, Laos, and Cambodia back to North Vietnam."

Although the four-way talks among the United States, North and South Vietnam, and the Viet Cong bogged down soon after the initial meeting in January 1969, Habib never lost faith in the negotiating process. When Lodge and Walsh, disappointed by their lack of progress, resigned in November 1969, President Nixon named the diplomat acting head of the American delegation. But despite his acknowledged expertise, few political analysts expected Habib's presence on the negotiating team to end the long deadlock. Because Habib did not have "a direct line to the White House," Marilyn Berger, Newsday's diplomatic correspondent, feared that his efforts would not be taken seriously by the North Vietnamese. As Miss Berger and others had predicted, the North Vietnamese charged that in choosing Habib, whom they described as a representative of "unelevated rank," to lead its delegation, the United States had "deliberately lowered the level of the Paris Conference and [was] seeking deliberately to sabotage it."

Taking a slightly more conciliatory approach in the negotiations than his predecessors had done, Habib stressed "mutual withdrawal" as the ideal basis for a lasting settlement in Vietnam, but North Vietnam and its allies continued to insist on unilateral withdrawal by the United States. Undeterred by his counterparts' intransigence, in January 1970 Habib proposed private sessions as "a way of ending sterile debate" and beginning "serious discussions." The North Vietnamese rejected that and other suggestions as "perfidious" maneuvers to downgrade the Paris talks. After "living, breathing, reading, talking, and even sleeping Vietnam," to use his words, for months, Habib was finally relieved by David K. E. Bruce, whom President Nixon had chosen as chief delegate on July 1, 1970. On leaving Paris, Habib advised the North Vietnamese that the bargaining sessions would be successful only if they were "not misused for propaganda purposes but rather [dealt] with the fundamental issues on the basis of genuine and relevant negotiation."

On July 28, 1971 Habib was nominated to succeed William J. Porter as Ambassador to the Republic of Korea. He took office shortly after he was confirmed by the United States Senate on the following September 29 and remained in that post until 1974, when he was designated assistant secretary of state for East Asian and Pacific affairs. For the most part, Habib's new assignment kept him in Washington, D.C., although in June 1975 he spent several days in Indochina trying to develop economic and political ties with the Communist regime in Laos. During the first half of that year, he concentrated mainly on trying to procure military and economic aid for war-torn Cambodia. "Only through this can that nation survive, can the Khmer Communists be convinced that military victory is impossible, and can a compromise solution through negotiation be reached," he testified at a Senate hearing. Habib blamed the deteriorating situation in Cambodia on Congress' decision to halt American bombing of the area in 1973. According to Habib, as quoted in the New York Times (March 6, 1975), "Once the bombings stopped, the Communist-led insurgents had little incentive to pursue negotiations."

Habib was also questioned by a House International Relations subcommittee in June 1975 regarding American support of repressive regimes in the Philippines and South Korea. While he condemned alleged human rights violations in both countries, he argued that those nations were vital to American "security interests." In his statements, Habib went further than any other senior government official in criticizing President Ferdinand E. Marcos' imposition of martial law in the Philippines and South Korean President Park Chung Hee's adoption of restrictive "emergency measures," but he nonetheless maintained that "the nation's security in the face of [an] external threat [is] of overriding importance and must weigh heavily in the balance."

When, in May 1976, President Gerald R. Ford made him Undersecretary of State for Political Affairs, Habib shifted his focus of attention from Asia to the Middle East. Retained in that post by President Jimmy Carter, who took office in January 1977, Habib played a major role in what was perhaps the Carter Administration's finest achievement: the Camp David peace accords. Late in 1977 Egyptian President Anwar Sadat agreed to meet with Menahem Begin, the Prime Minister of Israel, at Camp David, Maryland, to discuss with President Carter a settlement of the Arab-Israeli dispute. Habib, who was influential in arranging that historic meeting, discussed the wide-ranging implications of the negotiations on CBS-TV's public affairs program Face the Nation in November 1977. Acknowledging the United States government's role as a "middle man," Habib expressed hope that the summit meeting would help reduce tension in that volatile area of the world. A month later, he asked Soviet leaders to support Arab forces of moderation and to urge Syria to break with the hardliners who were attempting to block the peace initiative. Always a workaholic, Habib overtaxed himself in his search for a new political realignment in the Middle East, and early in 1978, he suffered a massive heart attack—his second in six years. After a long period of recuperation, he retired from the foreign service. Habib remained politically inactive until the spring of 1981, when President Ronald Reagan called on him to help defuse an explosive situation in Lebanon that threatened to touch off an all-out war in the Middle East.

In April 1981 Israeli jets intervened for the first time in the fighting between Syrians and Christian Phalangists in Lebanon. Israel, contending that it could not allow the Lebanese Christians "to be annihilated," shot down two helicopters taking part in a Syrian offensive in the Beirut-Zahle area of Lebanon. Syria responded by deploying Soviet-made surface-to-air missiles in the Bekaa Valley in eastern Lebanon. In an attempt to avert a military confrontation between Syria and Israel, President Reagan sent Habib to the Middle East on May 6 to discuss the dispute with government officials and political leaders in Beirut, Damascus, Jerusalem, and Riyadh.

Habib reportedly proposed a compromise peace plan that called for, among other things, Syria to withdraw its missiles from Lebanon and end its siege of the Lebanese Christian village of Zahle in exchange for an Israeli pledge to restrict its reconnaissance flights over Lebanon. But after an Israeli drone plane was shot down by Syrian missiles, Begin announced additional conditions for ending the dispute. Convinced that a peaceful solution was, in his word, "achievable," Habib returned to Washington on May 27 to confer with President Reagan.

Although some political analysts thought that Habib's shuttle diplomacy mission had been fruitless, others contended that his efforts had clearly eased the tensions in the Middle East. According to an editorial in the Christian Science Monitor (May 22, 1981), his "patient on-the-spot diplomacy has won a welcome from both sides and fostered an environment in which steps toward settlement can be taken. . . . Both parties, as well as Mr. Habib's home government, seem willing to allow him time for his conciliatory labors as long as hope remains. The fact that hope does remain is reason enough for gratitude to Mr. Habib. We note that his very name conveys in Arabic such ideas as love and appreciation—apt ingredients in anyone's search for peace."

While Habib was in Washington, Israeli war planes destroyed the Osirak nuclear reactor near Baghdad, Iraq. The surprise attack, which was almost universally condemned by the international community, further undermined Habib's quest for stability in the Middle East. Amid reports that Syria's position had noticeably hardened because of the Israeli attack on its neighbor, the diplomat returned to the Mideast on June 9 for a second round of talks. His weeks of mediation finally paid off on July 24, 1981, when he announced a ceasefire across the Israeli-Lebanese border. "The progress achieved so far must not be lost," he told newsmen after reporting to President Reagan in Washington on July 27. "Everyone involved must exercise the greatest care and caution. The end of armed attack which has been achieved could be a first, important step on the road to greater calm and security in the area."

A man of medium height, Philip C. Habib has dark eyes, always shielded by horn-rimmed spectacles, and a swarthy complexion. An intensely private person, he dislikes publicity and avoids representatives from the news media whenever possible. According to his colleague Helmut Sonnenfeldt, a former aide to Dr. Henry A. Kissinger, the former Secretary of State, Habib is "not stuffy at all" and has "a good sense of humor, which he sometimes turns on himself." He enjoys golfing, and he is an expert poker player. Habib and his wife, the former Marjorie W. Slightam, were married on August 27, 1942. They have two grown daughters, Phyllis A. and Susan W. Habib's colleagues in the foreign service elected him president of the Foreign Service Association in 1968. The following year he was the recipient of the Rockefeller Public Service Award, and in 1970 he was honored by the National Civil Service League. He was given the President's Award for distinguished federal service in 1979.

References: Christian Sci Mon p5 Je 9 '81 por; N Y Post p55 D 10 '69 por; N Y Times p2 D 26 '68 por; People 16:32+ Ag 10 '81 pors; International Who's Who, 1981-82; State Department Biographic Register, 1974-75; Who's Who in America, 1980-81

Hardwick, Elizabeth

July 27, 1916- Writer. Address: h. 15 W. 67th St., New York City, N.Y. 10023

In New York's elitist literary circles few writers and critics have attained the influence and respect that belong to the essayist and novelist Elizabeth Hardwick. As a founder and the advisory editor of the New York Review

of Books, to which she also contributes reviews and essays, she has helped since 1963 to shape that cultural biweekly into what Philip Nobile described in Intellectual Skywriting as "the premier literary-intellectual journal in the English-speaking world." In that achievement, as in her books, the latest of which is her semiautobiographical novel, Sleepless Nights (1979), she has been credited with an elegant and epigrammatic style and a fine, discriminating intelligence that resists the trendy and the cliché. Susan Sontag recently named Elizabeth Hardwick—along with E. L. Doctorow, Donald Barthelme, and only two or three others—among the contemporary American writers who, in her judgment, are "playing for the real stakes" and are "involved in the enterprise of literature."

Elizabeth Hardwick was born on July 27, 1916 in Lexington, Kentucky to Eugene Allen Hardwick, a businessman of modest means, and Mary (Ramsey) Hardwick. In an affectionate recollection of her native city in Harper's Magazine (July 1969), she wrote of Lexington, "This was, is, truly home to me, not just a birthplace." To the question that she has apparently often been asked, "How can you be from there, and think like you do?" she responded, "What can I answer except to say that I have been, according to my limits, always skeptical, and that I have, always, since my first breath, 'been from Kentucky.' "

Like the narrator of Sleepless Nights, who was one of nine children, Elizabeth Hardwick came from a large family. She grew up with many brothers and sisters in Lexington's North End, where different races and social classes lived side by side. Main Street fascinated her, and so did reading. She attended Lexington Junior High School and Henry Clay High School before pursuing her love for literature at the University of Kentucky, which awarded her the B.A. degree in 1938 and the M.A. degree in 1939.

"When I was in college," Elizabeth Hardwick recalled in an interview with Richard Locke for the New York Times Book Review (April 29, 1979), ". . . my aim was to be a New York Jewish intellectual. I say 'Jewish' because of their tradition of rational skepticism; and also a certain deracination appeals to me—and their openness to European culture . . . the questioning of the arrangements of society, sometimes called radicalism." In 1939 she left Lexington for New York City and enrolled at Columbia University to work for her doctorate in English literature. Soon becoming aware that a Ph.D. degree might not be very useful to a woman, because few of them at that time landed top teaching positions, she withdrew from Columbia in 1941 and devoted herself to writing fiction.

Presumably autobiographical in some aspects of its theme and in many of its descriptive details, Miss Hardwick's first novel, The Ghostly Lover (Harcourt, 1945), studies the entangled relationships and difficulties of communication within a middleclass Kentucky family. The story unfolds, sensitively and subtly, from the perspective of a daughter thwarted in her efforts toward self-realization. Most critics felt that the novelist's promises, such as the freshness of her perceptions, far outweighed her flaws; and Diana Trilling, the book reviewer at that time for the *Nation,* compared her moments of "imaginative intensity" with those achieved by Eudora Welty and D. H. Lawrence.

The action of Elizabeth Hardwick's second novel, *The Simple Truth* (Harcourt, 1955), centers on the trial of a penniless student of an Iowa college, Rudy Peck, who is accused of murdering his rich sweetheart. Disclosures during the trial are seen through the eyes of two observers from the academic community whose reactions contrast with those of the jury, made up of townspeople. Some reviewers seemed to be puzzled about Miss Hardwick's purpose, but Thomas Fitzsimmons asserted in the *Sewanee Review* (Spring 1955), "The author's statement comes to this: simple or sophisticated, neither the collective nor the single mind is equipped to distinguish reality from appearance; to pretend otherwise is absurd." Although disappointed in the way Miss Hardwick worked out her theme, Fitzsimmons liked much about the novel—"the kinds of things that make for a good short story."

During the decade between her two novels, Elizabeth Hardwick had, in fact, written many superb short stories. One of her early stories, "People on a Roller Coaster," was selected for *O. Henry Memorial Award Prize Stories of 1945,* and "What We Have Missed" was similarly honored the following year. "The Golden Stallion," which she contributed to the January 1946 issue of *Sewanee Review,* was reprinted in both *The Best American Short Stories of 1947* and *The Best World Short Stories: 1947* and was anthologized also by Thomas Blair in *Fifty Modern Stories* (Row, Peterson, 1960).

"The Classless Society," another of Miss Hardwick's anthologized stories, exposes with keen-edged irony the social and intellectual snobbery, along with various tactics of self-deception and self-preservation, that infect a small dinner party at which a University of Chicago professor and his wife entertain his colleague and her relative, a woman, like herself, from a prominent family of vanished wealth. The story first appeared in the *New Yorker* (January 19, 1957) and won the distinction of being included in *Stories from the New Yorker: 1950-1960* and *How We Live, Contemporary Life in Contemporary Fiction* (1968). Among her several other *New Yorker* stories are "The Purchase," reprinted in *The Best American Short Stories: 1960* and "The Faithful," reprinted in *The Best American Short Stories: 1980.* The latter, a witty tale of the gallantries of an aging Dutch doctor, is a chapter from *Sleepless Nights.*

Fairly early in her development as a writer, while she was earning critical regard for her first novel and short stories, as well as a Guggenheim fellowship in fiction for 1948, Elizabeth Hardwick discovered her congeniality with another literary form. Her concern about political and social, along with cultural, matters led her "inevitably to the essay," as she wrote in an autobiographical sketch for *World Authors: 1950-1970* (1975). "I have great affection for the form," she explained, "and have given to it everything and more than would be required of fiction, that is, everything I possibly could. Indeed I have always written essays as if they were examples of imaginative writing, as I believe them to be."

An opportunity to prove herself as an essayist came soon after the publication of *The Ghostly Lover,* when Elizabeth Hardwick received a phone call from Philip Rahv, a founder in 1933 of *Partisan Review.* With his coeditor, William Phillips, in 1946 Rahv summed up the politics of his monthly periodical as "a kind of independent and critical Marxism." *Partisan Review* attracted many bright young contributors, including Elizabeth Hardwick, who had been a devotee of that literary journal while still in Lexington and who recalled in her *World Authors* sketch that writing for *Partisan Review* was "the very peak of [her] ambition" when she arrived in New York.

In her conversation with Richard Locke, Miss Hardwick, referring to her first contact with Rahv, recounted, "Thus was a lowly reviewer born. I say 'lowly' because it took me a number of years to get anything like a voice in my critical writing." Besides book reviews and other essays, she contributed short stories to *Partisan Review.* She also wrote articles for other periodicals, among them, the *Reporter, Mademoiselle, New Republic, New York Times Book Review,* and *Harper's Magazine.* Seventeen of her essays make up *A View of My Own; Essays in Literature and Society* (Farrar, Straus, 1962), a much-praised collection that suggested to Charles Poore of the New York *Times* (August 23, 1962) that Miss Hardwick shared "Mary McCarthy's brilliance, Margaret Fuller's [the nineteenth-century New England writer and feminist leader] masterly range of ideas and Virginia Woolf's aloof felicities of style."

David Riesman and the vocabulary of sociology, Bernard Berenson and the lifestyle of American expatriates in Italy, and the husband of George Eliot were among the subjects of Miss Hardwick's essays. Another was the New England philosopher William James, whom she found to be so interesting that she edited and wrote the introduction to *The Selected Letters of William James* (Farrar, Straus, 1961). When she was working on James's letters, Elizabeth Hardwick was living in Boston, on Marlborough Street, with her husband, the poet Robert Lowell. About that time she also wrote an essay that has been called an "autopsy"—

"Boston: the Lost Ideal," which was published first in *Harper's* (December 1959) and then included in *A View of My Own*. According to Steven Gould Axelrod in *Robert Lowell; Life and Art (1978)*, it was to that essay, together with one of her edited letters of William James, that Lowell owed the "genesis" of some of the poetic drafting of one of his major works, *For the Union Dead*.

In another of her essays for *Harper's*, "The Decline of Book Reviewing," which appeared in the October and November 1959 issues, Elizabeth Hardwick lamented, "A book is born into a puddle of treacle; the brine of hostile criticism is only a memory." Deploring the blandness and banality of American book reviewing, she made clear the need for a literary journal that would seek out "the unusual, the difficult, the lengthy, the intransigent, and, above all, the *interesting*." The 114-day New York City newspaper strike, which began in late 1962 and blacked out book reviews and book advertising along with the news, provided whatever further impetus was required for Miss Hardwick and her like-minded friends and acquaintances among the intelligentsia to launch the *New York Review of Books*.

Having moved in 1960 from Boston to New York, Robert and Elizabeth Hardwick Lowell were living on Manhattan's Upper West Side at the time of the newspaper strike. As recounted by Susan Edmiston and Linda D. Cirino in *Literary New York* (1976), the *New York Review of Books* "was conceived" one evening when the Lowells were having dinner at the apartment of their neighbors Jason and Barbara Epstein, and "the first issue was dummied up on the dining room table of the Lowell-Hardwick apartment." With Jason Epstein serving as acting publisher and Barbara Epstein sharing the editorship with Robert B. Silvers, the *New York Review of Books* appeared in February 1963, informing its readers that it presented "reviews of some of the more important books published this winter," but spent neither time nor space "on books which are trivial in their intentions or venal in their effects, except occasionally to reduce a temporarily inflated reputation or call attention to a fraud." After quoting that "editorial credo," as he called it, in his *Intellectual Skywriting: Literary Politics & The New York Review of Books* (1974), Philip Nobile observed, "What style. What class. What brass."

Although it has been condemned as well as admired for its highbrow appeal, by 1980 the *New York Review of Books* was filling the need of some 100,000 subscribers for intelligent discussion of political, social, and cultural issues by writers with recognizable names. Besides serving as its editorial adviser, over the years Elizabeth Hardwick has upheld its standards with many contributions of her own. The essays on the theatre that she wrote for the *New York Review of Books* made her the first woman to win the $4,000 George Jean Nathan Award, which was presented to her

in December 1967. Although she had contributed "Theatre Chronicle: Disgust and Disenchantment: New British and American Plays" to *Partisan Review* (Spring 1958) and had covered the theatre for *Vogue* during the year 1964, she said on the occasion of winning the award that she did not consider herself a drama reviewer. She was, rather, a literary critic, "a person whose interest in the drama is principally literary" and who sees and writes about only those plays she chooses.

Several of Miss Hardwick's essays on literature for the *New York Review of Books* were collected, in somewhat altered form, in *Seduction and Betrayal: Women and Literature* (Random, 1974), studies of women writers and fictional women in which she glides back and forth between the real and the imagined, life and art, biography and literature. Her subjects include the Brontës, Virginia Woolf (whose *The Common Reader* she has said influenced her own criticism), and Sylvia Plath; the "amateurs" Dorothy Wordsworth and Jane Carlyle; Ibsen's women; and Tess D'Urberville and other luckless female protagonists of the novel.

"Hardwick's personal involvement with women writers is the genesis of this new collection; it dictates the style and constitutes the true subject matter of the book," R. P. Solomon wrote of *Seduction and Betrayal* in the New York *Times Book Review* (May 5, 1974). Although her book is factually informative and well researched, Elizabeth Hardwick takes a nonacademic approach to literature that favors her fluid style. In her review for the New York *Post* (May 20, 1974) Doris Grumbach tried to pinpoint Miss Hardwick's "strength as a literary critic": "She is an eye-opener, a revealer of truths not contained, often, in the scholarship on a writer. She is a reader of fierce insights."

Interviewed for a profile in the New York *Post* in late 1967, Elizabeth Hardwick told Bryna Taubman, "I've had no desire to write fiction for more than ten years. I don't think I can now." Her proposed solutions to the problems she encountered on her return to the novel form some years later were incorporated into a draft of the first chapter of a novel in progress, "Writing a Novel," which she published in 1973. The short, plotless novel that emerged in 1979, *Sleepless Nights* (Random), fuses fiction and autobiography in what its narrator, Elizabeth, describes as a "work of transformed and even distorted memory." Francine du Plessix Gray, in *Vogue* (June 1979), pointed to an affinity between Peter Handke's *A Sorrow Beyond Dreams* and *Sleepless Nights*: the two authors share "a Socialist concern for the victims of middle-class morality, a boldly collagist, modernist handling of autobiographical fact which breaks through stilted definitions of 'novel' or 'memoir' and forges the vitality of a new genre." Like Elizabeth Hardwick's other novels and many of her short stories, *Sleepless Nights* conveys the elusive, mystifying nature of human experience.

The character of Elizabeth of *Sleepless Nights* is developed indirectly through what she happens to remember about persons and places. Desultory memories call to mind fragments of her reading of Pasternak, Goethe, Borges, and others—again in a blending of life and literature. Miss Hardwick's incisive, condensed style accommodates a range and variety of experience that is ordinarily the burden of a full-length novel. The perception by some reviewers of style as the unifying force of the episodic *Sleepless Nights* may have been gratifying to Elizabeth Hardwick, a practitioner of a "high style" that she defined in her talk with Francine du Plessix Gray as "a text that can be interpreted on many different levels of meaning, a text that is very much *written*, and this doesn't necessarily mean Nabokovian baroqueness. When I talk to students, they think I mean writing with a lot of adjectives, but the sparsest of styles can be the highest."

The students to which Elizabeth Hardwick referred were very likely those in her creative writing courses at Barnard College, where she began teaching as adjunct professor of English in 1964. She gave three lectures for the Christian Gauss Seminar in Criticism at Princeton University, including those that appear as essays on Dorothy Wordsworth and Jane Carlyle in *Seduction and Betrayal*. At Vassar College in 1972, moreover, she read the concluding, title chapter of that collection of essays. Miss Hardwick was chosen a member of the advisory committee for the National Book Awards in 1963. She holds an honorary degree from Smith College, awarded in 1973. Since 1976 she has been a member of the American Academy and Institute of Arts and Letters.

Elizabeth Hardwick and Robert Lowell were married on July 28, 1949 and had one daughter, Harriet Winslow Lowell, born on January 4, 1957. The marriage was at times a tormenting one, as Lowell disclosed in some of his poems to his wife that were published in *Notebook* (1970). The couple divorced in 1972, and Lowell remarried but returned to Elizabeth Hardwick before his death in September 1977. Their Manhattan home, where she still lives, is one of the duplex apartments on West 67th Street that Lowell described as "the last gasp of true Nineteenth-Century Capitalistic Gothic." Elizabeth Hardwick is a tall woman with reddish hair, a well-proportioned figure, and, in the words of Francine du Plessix Gray, "a rich, warm gracious voice still faintly honeyed with a Kentucky drawl."

"In some ways, the mysterious and somnambulistic 'difference' of being a woman has been, over 35 years, Elizabeth Hardwick's great subject," Joan Didion proposed in the New York *Times Book Review* (April 29, 1979). That consciousness has pervaded her three novels and many of her essays. In reply to a question of Richard Locke, she affirmed, "Yes, I call myself a feminist in that I believe there are cultural, social and economic boundaries set for women which are immoral and unnecessary and which should be resisted publicly and privately."

References: N Y Post D 13 '67 por, p35 Je 15 '74 por; N Y Times Bk R p1+ Ap 29 '79 por; Time 113:94+ My 7 '79; Vogue 169:202+ Ja '79 por; American Women Writers vol 2 (1980); Contemporary Authors 1st rev ed vols 5-8 (1969); World Authors: 1950-1970 (1975)

Harry, Debbie

1946(?)- Singer; actress. Address: b. c/o Alive Entertainments Inc., 8600 Melrose Ave., Los Angeles, Calif. 90069

Among the bands of the "punk" or "new wave" genre trying to put the primal energy back into rock 'n' roll in the 1970's and the early 1980's, the one that first crossed over to a mass audience and maintained hegemony there was Blondie, an antic "sleaze rock" group named for its bleached-blonde lead singer and main attraction, Debbie Harry, the self-mocking pinup of punk. Miss Harry's pretty come-hither-and-drop-dead face, accented by its painted pout, became the most photographed in the rock music world, while such Blondie albums as *Parallel Lines* and *Eat to the Beat* sold in the millions worldwide, along with such singles by the group as "Heart of Glass" (its breakthrough), "Call Me," "The Tide Is High," and "Rapture."

Miss Harry's forte as a singer is that of an actress, the dramatic "selling of a song," as she puts it. With a view to trying out "other characters, other roles," especially in motion pictures, she has struck out on her own, making her emergence as a solo performer—who wears her hair naturally dark brown or dyed or wigged in various colors (from pink to green) as occasion demands—with the 1981 solo LP *KooKoo*. "Blondie is just on vacation . . . getting a tan," she has assured her fans. "I can bring her back any time I want."

Deborah Ann Harry, who avoids discussion of her age, was born in Miami, Florida in or about 1945 or 1946. When she was three months old she was adopted by Richard and Catherine Harry of Hawthorne, New Jersey. Richard Harry was at that time a salesman who commuted to Manhattan; he and his wife now run a gift shop in Cooperstown, New York.

The Harrys raised Deborah—along with a younger daughter, Martha, and a nephew they took in, William—in Hawthorne, where the family lived in a quiet middle-class neighborhood and attended the local Episcopal church. Mrs. Harry told Jamie James in an interview for *Rolling Stone* (June 28, 1979) that Debbie was a shy child with a "pixie sense of humor" and very family-oriented—"the one who got homesick at camp." Debbie made her singing debut in a sixth-grade stage show, and at Hawthorne High School she was a baton twirler and a member of the fencing club, the student council, and the yearbook staff as well as a participant in the annual variety show. Her only obvious aberrations seem to have been a partiality for black clothing and a propensity for experimenting with makeup and hair dyes. She was, as she has said, "destined to be an artist even then," although she was quoted in the 1963 high-school yearbook as being "undecided" about a career.

After graduating from high school, Miss Harry matriculated at Centenary College in Hackettstown, New Jersey. "I really didn't want to go," she recounted to Joanne Kalter in an interview for *After Dark* (October 1977), "but my parents thought it was a good idea [and] I wasn't ever rebellious enough to just take off. . . . I stuck it out until I legally could go off on my own and then I did. I came to St. Mark's Place and got an apartment."

St. Mark's Place, a connecting strip between New York City's East Village and Greenwich Village, was at the time Debbie Harry arrived there the Mecca of the psychedelic "hippie" counterculture. In the center of the block between Second and Third Avenues was the Dom (later the Electric Circus) nightclub, host to such rock groups as the neo-decadent Velvet Underground. Featuring the female lead singer Nico (an actress protégée of Andy Warhol) and Lou Reed's songs about perversion, drugs, and death, the Velvet Underground was probably the preeminent precursor of the Blondie style of punk rock, at least in some of its elements.

Trying to find her artistic niche in New York's bohemia, Miss Harry dabbled in painting, writing, acting, and singing while earning a living at various jobs, including beautician, Playboy bunny, and waitress at Max's Kansas City restaurant, a hangout of the Warhol crowd a few blocks north of St. Mark's Place. She hung out with the Fugs, another pre-punk group, more politically oriented (antiwar and pro-marijuana) than the Velvet Underground, and in 1968 she became a backup singer with the short-lived folk group Wind in the Willows. She flirted dangerously with drugs until she "felt [her]self going under" and decided she did not want to suffer the fate of Janis Joplin, the rock-blues singer who died of an overdose of a combination of drugs and alcohol in 1970. She retreated from the New York City music scene until she "felt strong enough to do the things [she] wanted to do without being some kind of victim."

By the time Miss Harry returned to the rock world, the scene there had changed to "glitter," typified by the New York Dolls, a male transvestite group, and the Theatre of the Ridiculous, a "camp" company staging such shows as *Vain Victory*, starring the "drag" actor Holly Woodlawn and including Miss Harry as Juicy Lucy, a "chorus girl." With Elda Stilletto and Rosie Ross, Miss Harry formed the Stillettoes, a self-described "tacky" trio that sang such songs as "Dracula, What Did You Do With My Mother?" at Club 82, on East Fourth Street in the East Village, an old transvestite nightclub given a new lease on life by the glitter rock phenomenon.

Eric Emerson, who was dating Elda Stilletto, took his roommate, the Brooklyn-born guitarist Chris Stein, to see a performance by the Stillettoes. "When I saw her [Miss Harry] in that smoke-filled room," Stein said later, "it was love at first sight." Stein joined the Stillettoes' backup band, and after the Stillettoes broke up, in 1974 he and Miss Harry formed the group that evolved into Blondie. Debbie Harris and Chris Stein have been partners, in private as well as professional life, ever since that time.

The evolution of Blondie began with Angel and the Snakes, which soon became Blondie and the Banzai Babies, a trio mixing campy glitter rock and top-forty music and featuring Miss Harry flanked by Tish and Snooky Bellomo, who did more dancing than singing. Performing at White's Pub, a bar on Wall Street where Debbie Harry worked as a barmaid, Blondie and the Banzai Babies did many of the songs that would later appear on Blondie's first album, including "Little Girl Lies," "Man Overboard," and "Giant Bats From Space" (which became "Attack of the Giant Ants"). The act sometimes included an audience-participation conga line, and the costumes would typically be big, puffy party dresses, removed to reveal bathing suits in the finale ("Fun Fun Fun").

By the beginning of 1976 Blondie was a viable band, with, in addition to Stein and Miss Harry, Clem Burke on drums, Gary Valentine on bass, and Jimmy Destri on keyboard. It became a regular act at CBGB's, the shabby, cavernous nightclub on the Bowery that is chief claimant to the title of birthplace of punk rock. There—and later at the Mudd Club—they vied with such other groups as the Ramones, the Patti Smith Group, the Dead Boys, Richard Hell and the Voidoids, the Talking Heads, Television, and other raucous new groups trying to jar alive the blasé ears of rock audiences with blasts of decadent romanticism. From the beginning, Chris Stein described Blondie's music as "loud, hard, fast, aggressive rock 'n' roll." In contrast with the heat of her backup, Debbie Harry, in keeping with the prevalent in-joke of playing dumb, often assumed the zombie pose of a narco-chanteuse in the Nico tradition. Her antique, rummage-sale clothing, including zebra-stripe miniskirts and mesh stockings, fit in with her style, which she characterized as "trash, flash, and freak chic." From the beginning, the group functioned as an artistic collective, with each of the members writing, individually or collaboratively, many of the songs they performed.

A demo recorded by Blondie in 1976 included three cuts that have since been bootlegged: "Platinum Blonde," "Out in the Streets," and "The Disco Song," the original version of "Heart of Glass." Later in 1976, through the instrumentality of the record producer Richard Gottehrer, Private Stock Records issued Blondie's first commercial recording, the single "X Offender" (with the X substituting for "sex" to avoid radio censorship problems), which, partly because of Gottehrer's influence, received an amount of air play relatively large for a punk song at the time.

Toward the end of 1976 Blondie's first album, *Blondie,* produced by Gottehrer, was released on the Private Stock label. Gottehrer's handling of such golden oldies as "My Boyfriend's Back," which he himself had written and produced years before for the Crystals, gave a fine touch to the music of that LP, much of which echoed, with the irony of deadpan nihilism, the surfing and girl-group sounds of the 1950's and 1960's. Among the tracks was "In the Flesh," one of Miss Harry's favorites among her early compositions. It became Blondie's first hit as a single, going gold in Australia. The other tracks included "Rip Her to Shreds," about women backbiting each other ("Red eyeshadow/green mascara/yecch/she's too much"), the sharply satiric "Kung Fu Girl," and takeoffs on kitsch from comic books, urban sleaze, Japanese sci-fi, and so forth.

Critics generally assess the first Blondie album as cruder and more primitive than its successors, but freer and more "fun." "The songs were outrageous, . . . with a sense of humor and the fun of it all," Lester Bangs writes in his book *Blondie* (1980). "The interesting thing is the first album's a bit out of tune, and just the way it goes together makes an interesting noise, an interesting sound. That's what I think the charm of it is, too. It's almost like listening to the early Bob Dylan records when he first went electric. You know, those overtones are as important as the notes people are playing."

The first album was also refreshing because of the temporal context in which it emerged. To Bangs, as to many other observers, rock 'n' roll seemed to be moribund in 1976: "With all the things that had previously stood us through, like Heavy Metal and Southern boogie, having been reduced to formulas, it seemed like the only things left were disco (an airlock), Peter Frampton, and 'Year of the Cat': Adult Oriented Rock, which of course is just Middle of the Road in ram's clothing. Things were pretty miserable everywhere, and suddenly along came this album, as lighthearted as if from another age yet not at all another dead slice of Sixties nostalgia. . . . Within the next twelve months the New Wave floodgates opened and [in] roared a riptide of new vitality previously unmatched in the 1970's."

In the spring of 1977 Blondie opened for Iggy Pop in a tour of the United States that included a performance at New York's Palladium described by Joanne Kalter in her article in *After Dark:* "Debbie Harry . . . is wearing a single-strapped black knit minidress, cropped in a vee at the crotch, black stockings, black ankle-length boots with razor-sharp toes, and mean, dark shades. The look is both menacing and surreal. But as they slide into their opening song, the cold funereal glaze is shattered: it's an old, top-forty favorite, 'Palisades Park.' And as Debbie begins to move, the stage warms to a sizzle. She whips off her shades, and bucks and twists and writhes, belting out the songs with . . . range and power. . . . Her voice goes from soothingly sexy to strong, from playful sixties pop to heavy, hard-edged melodrama."

The promotional strategy of Peter Leeds, then the band's manager, emphasized foreign tours, and that strategy paid off in early recognition abroad, with Debbie Harry's face appearing on magazine covers in England, other European countries, Australia, Japan, and elsewhere in the Orient before Blondie broke in America. Europeans especially appreciated such cosmopolitan touches as the insertion of a French verse in Blondie's cover of the old Randy and the Rainbows song "Denis," the first of Blondie's hits worldwide (not counting the United States). "Denis" was one of the tracks on the group's second album, *Plastic Letters,* released by Private Stock in 1977. Among the other tracks were the sexually ambiguous "Love at the Pier," the police-blotter song "Youth Nabbed as Sniper," the international-intrigue sendup "Contact in Red Square," and "Touched by Your Presence, Dear." The last mentioned, written by Gary Valentine, was Valentine's farewell gift to the group. By the time *Plastic Letters* was cut, he had already left. He was replaced on bass by Frank Infante, who moved to guitar when Nigel Harrison joined Blondie.

Under Peter Leeds's management, Blondie bought out of its contract with Private Stock and Richard Gottehrer and moved to Chrysalis Records, Terry Ellis' independent, adventurous label, and to producer Mike Chapman, the "bubblegum music" wizard, known for his success in capturing the teenage audience. Much slicker than anything the group had previously done, Blondie's third album, *Parallel Lines*, produced by Chapman and released by Chrysalis Records in 1978, was a platinum blockbuster, selling 7,000,000 units worldwide within two years. Among the more successful cuts on *Parallel Lines* were "11:59," with its staccato refrain "still alive, still alive," and "One Way or Another," with Miss Harry snarling menacingly, "I'm gonna getcha getcha getcha getcha getcha." The most successful track was "Heart of Glass," a Stein-Harry love song at once cynical and scorchingly sensuous. Recorded with pulsating Kraftwerk-like synthesizer effects by James Destri, it proved as popular with the mainstream disco set as with new-wave fans. Released as a single in 1979, it quickly soared to number one on the charts.

Reviewing a Blondie performance at the Greek Theatre in Los Angeles for the *Los Angeles Times* (August 17, 1979), Robert Hilburn observed that the group seemed to be more "sluggish" than in its early days. In its most effective moments, the early Blondie was "as hard to resist as a carnival fun zone," Hilburn recalled. But "a cartoonish approach is difficult to maintain," he went on, and Blondie's move "beyond the teen audience" to "a harder, more contemporary sound," has "not been a smooth transition." With "Heart of Glass," however, the set finally caught fire, according to Hilburn. The song "not only stirred the audience" but "gave Harry spark," so that "she was as electric as her photos." On the strength of "Heart of Glass," Blondie headlined an all-disco network NBC television program in the *Midnight Special* series.

Blondie's fourth album, *Eat to the Beat,* was released in September 1979, just after Shep Gordon replaced Peter Leeds as the group's manager. In February 1980 Blondie was featured on the cover of *Cash Box,* which reported that *Eat to the Beat* was fourteenth on the publication's album chart, that *Parallel Lines* was still on the chart after seventy-two weeks, and that "Dreaming," the first single from *Eat to the Beat,* was in the Top Twenty. Later in the year another single from *Eat to the Beat,* "Atomic," made the charts, as did "Call Me," produced by disco master Giorgio Maroder, the theme song done by Blondie for the soundtrack of the motion picture *American Gigolo.* In its own identity, Blondie appeared and performed in the motion picture *Roadie,* an acting vehicle for the rock singer Meatloaf, who was temporarily sidelined from his singing career with severely strained vocal chords.

Many critics pounced on Blondie for going "arty" on the *Autoamerican,* the album released by Chrysalis early in 1981, but most were harder on Chris Stein than on Debbie Harry. In his review in *Rolling Stone* (February 19, 1981), Tom Carson described Stein as "living out his fantasies of himself as a deep thinker" in the album. "*Autoamerican* is his [Stein's] LP all the way . . . ," Carson wrote, "an anthology of intellectual onanism." He saw as Stein's "largest mistake" his "willingness to short-change Blondie's biggest asset," Miss Harry. "Her voice is all wrong for the tunes. . . . It is denied any chance to utilize that peculiar metallic urgency characteristically found in her finest vocals. . . . And when she does try to show some sass and spunk—in the rap that (all too typically) gives 'Rapture' its title— she's sunk by the leaden schematic lyrics." Carson's opinion notwithstanding, "Rapture" became an outsized hit. Played over and over by radio disc jockeys, it was the record that brought to a mass audience the new sound in music known as "the rap." Rap music—long, cadenced "jive" orations, heavy on rhyme, sung/talked to a quick disco beat—had been brought from the streets of Harlem into recording studios by such disc jockeys as Kurtis (né Walker) Blow. "I have mixed feelings about the success of Blondie's 'Rapture,'" Blow told a reporter. "But it helped more than it hurt. They had the No. 1 record for eight weeks. Do you know what that does for my record sales?"

Wanting to prove that "the little blond chickie has her own identity," Miss Harry began branching out into solo projects as the 1970's came to an end. In 1980 she signed a three-year contract to do television commercials for a line of designer jeans, and in the same year Kinesis Productions, a small independent company, released the low-budget feature film *Union City,* in which, as a frustrated suburban housewife, Miss Harry displayed an ability for serious acting that surprised some critics, even though she had always pointed out that her performing with Blondie was essentially acting. On television she did some skit comedy in an appearance on *Saturday Night Live* and she was a featured guest on *The Muppet Show.*

In another independent move, Miss Harry made promotional video tapes with the Swiss futuristic fantasy artist H. R. Giger, who did the cover for her first solo album, *KooKoo* (Chrysalis, 1981), a picture of her with her natural dark brown hair pulled taut and with four skewers piercing her head. Collaborating on *KooKoo,* in addition to Chris Stein, were Nile Rodgers and Bernard Edwards from the group Chic, producers of modish black dance music. Outstanding among the cuts on *KooKoo* was the ballad "Now I Know that You Know."

As Stein predicted, some of the reviews of *KooKoo* might have been headlined, "Blondie Tries to be Black and Fails." Some critics who had found a surfeit of styles in *Auto-*

american complained that here, in contrast, there was a paucity. "Her [Miss Harry's] glossy aloofness makes every song sound like Blondie," Jim Miller observed in *Newsweek* (August 24, 1981), and in the Washington *Post* (August 30, 1981), Richard Harrington wrote: "Harry was never blessed with a facile [vocal] instrument, but her unschooled voice was well-suited to Blondie's gutsy, beat-heavy pop. She also used to display a puckish humor and sense of style. . . . On *KooKoo* though, Harry's voice—at once strident and lifeless—dominates the mix." Among the positive notices was that of Hugh Wyatt in the New York *Daily News* (August 21, 1981): "Once listeners get past her still squeaky voice and the album cover . . . they will find that Harry's singing is no longer confined to catchy phrases. She appears, for the first time, to understand the physiology of singing, which encompasses punk, reggae, Oriental, and jazz. . . . The result of this new association with Chic has given her even more appeal, manifested by a resounding pulsation and drive that is unusual for rock singers."

Debbie Harry, who shares a Manhattan penthouse apartment with Chris Stein, is five feet three inches tall and in private life has a street-accented style of speech. She neither drinks nor smokes and is reputed to be a much quieter, simpler, warmer person than her Blondie persona would suggest. She still goes home to spend Christmas with her adoptive parents, and her mother says that she is still "sort of retiring" and has a "pixie" sense of humor. In an interview with Liz Derringer for the New York *Daily News* (September 13, 1981), Miss Harry said, "Blondie's appeal, in a way, was for a very young audience. We didn't really intend that; it just happened. This way [in her new solo career], I get to grow up." When Miss Derringer asked her if she had been quoted correctly as saying that her father's being a salesman gave her a good background in "understanding the marketing of sex . . . that sex sells," she replied, "When you're singing a song, you're selling a song. That's what I was talking about." The interview ended with Miss Harry saying, "Here I am, just mouthing off—and I think that celebrities are not the people to listen to."

References: After Dark 10:38+ O '77 por; N Y Daily News L p3+ S 13 '81 pors; N Y Times Mag p18+ Ag 26 '79 pors; Newsweek 98:76+ Ag 24 '81 pors; People 11:81+ My 21 '79 pors, 15:88+ Mr 16 '81 pors; Rolling Stone p60+ Je 28 '79 pors; Vogue 170:134+ Jl '80 pors; Bangs, Lester. Blondie (1980)

Hartman, David

*May 19, 1935- Television personality; actor.
Address: b. c/o Trascott Alyson & Craig, Inc.,
222 Cedar Lane, Teaneck, N.J. 07666*

When, in May 1979, *Good Morning, America* finally edged out the *Today* show as the most watched early-morning television program, jubilant ABC executives gave the lion's share of the credit to David Hartman, the congenial ex-actor who has anchored that mélange of news, weather, interviews, and features since its inception in November 1975. Saluted by television critics as "perhaps the most successful chatsman since Dave Garroway," the original host of the *Today* show, Hartman came to *Good Morning, America* via the Broadway musical theatre, three reasonably successful television series, and several unheralded made-for-television movies. Distinguished by down-home sincerity and insatiable curiosity, Hartman describes his role on the show as that of a "conduit" or "communicator." As he explained in a recent interview, "When people get up in the morning, they have little time. Mostly, they're listening, not looking. We want to get usable information to them . . . , but we want to do it with a sense of individuality. In my mind I don't see a mass of people, I see one person."

Of Dutch, Swiss, English, and German descent, David Downs Hartman was born in

Pawtucket, Rhode Island on May 19, 1935, the second son of Fannie Rodman (Downs) Hartman and Cyril Baldwin Hartman, a Methodist minister turned advertising executive. Hartman remembers his parents as "tremendously exciting" individuals. They were "swinger-of-the-week people, loose, groovy," he told Arnold Hano in an interview for a *TV Guide* profile

(June 7, 1969). "My folks' attitude was, 'C'mon, it's a new day. Let's get going.'" Brought up to believe that he could, in his words, "do anything, literally," Hartman excelled in music and in sports. He began playing the violin when he was six, and over the next eight years, he learned to play half a dozen other instruments, including clarinet, saxophone, and flute. Taught by his older brother Cy to play baseball "before I could even walk," as he put it, Hartman eventually earned seven letters—two in baseball, two in football, two in basketball, and one in soccer—at the Mount Hermon School, a college preparatory school in Mount Hermon, Massachusetts.

Upon his graduation from Mt. Hermon, Hartman rejected professional baseball contracts tendered by the Philadelphia Phillies and the then Boston Braves and enrolled at Duke University in Durham, North Carolina. An economics major, he maintained a straight "A" average and still found time to play on the varsity baseball team, work as an announcer for both campus and local radio and television stations, and serve as president of Sigma Chi fraternity and the men's glee club. He was also a cadet commander in the United States Air Force ROTC program. After taking his B.A. degree, with honors, in 1957, he turned down job offers from nearly three dozen major firms to join the Air Force as a second lieutenant. During his three-year hitch in the service as a specialist in computer operations, he also played semiprofessional baseball and appeared in strawhat productions of the musical comedies *Showboat* and *Oklahoma!*

Convinced that he had found his niche, Hartman enrolled in classes at the American Academy of Dramatic Arts in New York City after his military discharge in 1959. To pay for his courses in opera and ballet, he worked nights as an NBC page and tour guide. He graduated from the Academy two years later and, following an apprenticeship in Off-Broadway musicals and summer-stock productions, landed a job with the Harry Belafonte Singers. He spent most of 1961 on an eighty-city tour with that group, then signed on with the national touring company of *My Fair Lady*. Returning to New York City in the spring of 1963, he appeared in the Off-Broadway revival of the 1941 musical *Best Foot Forward*. His "big break" came later that year when he was signed to play Rudolph, the officious German headwaiter, in the original Broadway company of *Hello Dolly!* Two years and 800-odd performances later, he left that long-running musical to join the Broadway cast of *The Yearling*, a lackluster musical drama based on Marjorie Kinnan Rawlings' novel. The play closed after three performances, but most reviewers commended Hartman for his effective portrayal of Oliver Hutto, a romantic sailor.

Setting his sights on Hollywood, Hartman sent the tape of a television commercial with a Western flavor to Universal City Studios, Inc. Universal executive Frank Price, who saw in the lanky actor "a nice quality, a likeability," immediately signed him for a feature role in *I Love a Mystery,* a made-for-television movie starring Ida Lupino and Les Crane. Hartman subsequently appeared in supporting roles in two theatrical releases for Universal Pictures: *The Ballad of Josie* (1968), a whimsical Doris Day vehicle, and the comedy *Nobody's Perfect* (1968). His television assignments in the late 1960's included an episode of *Ironside,* a police drama, and a guest appearance on *The Virginian,* which he parlayed into a regular spot during the series' 1968-69 season on NBC-TV. In *The Virginian,* a popular, ninety-minute adult Western, he played the role of David Sutton, a medical school dropout hired as a greenhorn ranch hand by the enigmatic title character.

Hartman's popularity with the viewing public led to a feature role in *The New Doctors,* one of three rotating segments in NBC's innovative dramatic series *The Bold Ones.* (Other elements in the umbrella series dealt with crusading lawyers and politicians.) *The New Doctors* starred E. G. Marshall as Dr. David Craig, the founder and chief administrator of the fictional David Craig Institute of New Medicine, John Saxon as Dr. Ted Stuart, the Institute's chief of surgery, and Hartman as Dr. Paul Hunter, its director of medical research. From the program's first telecast, on September 14, 1969, until its cancellation at the end of the 1972-73 season, Hartman immersed himself in his role. He visited many of the country's leading teaching and research hospitals, developed ideas for episodes, addressed medical gatherings, and spearheaded medical fund-raising drives. During *The New Doctors'* four-year run, he took time out to appear in single episodes of *Marcus Welby, M.D., The Name of the Game,* and *Owen Marshall, Counselor at Law,* in the television movies *San Francisco International Airport* (1970), *The Feminist and the Fuzz* (1971), *You'll Never See Me Again* (1973), and *Miracle on 34th Street* (1973), a remake of the 1947 motion picture fantasy, and in *The Island at the Top of the World* (Walt Disney, 1974), an old-fashioned adventure about four turn-of-the-century polar explorers who discover a lost land inhabited by Vikings.

No sooner was *The New Doctors* canceled than Hartman was signed to play the title role in *Lucas Tanner,* a dramatic series about a former baseball player and sportswriter who turned to high school English teaching after his wife and son were killed in an automobile accident. Episodes of the program, which had its premiere on September 11, 1974, focused primarily on student-teacher relationships and on the conflicts between the idealistic Tanner and his tradition-bound colleagues. Hartman identified strongly with the warm and understanding Tanner, telling one interviewer, "I think I'd be like Tanner if I were a teacher." Television critics generally agreed that the role suited him, but despite its favorable reviews, the show was axed after one season.

As he had been with *The New Doctors*, Hartman was deeply involved in the conception and production of *Lucas Tanner*, and he takes pride in the fact that episodes of both series have been used for educational purposes. When asked by one reporter to name his stellar achievement, however, he pointed to *Of Birth and Babies*, a documentary in which he was involved as host, narrator, and producer. The project grew out of Hartman's observation that "network television had never shown the birth of a baby." As he explained to an interviewer for *Good Housekeeping* (May 1977), "You could show violence of any kind, murder, rape—you name it. But this was the first view of an actual birth." He was also intent on exploiting the "teaching potential" of television. "The point of the show," he said, as quoted in the New York *Post* (March 20, 1974), "is to demonstrate what a couple can do to help insure a healthy baby. . . . It's designed to relieve anxiety." Broadcast by ABC-TV in a late-night time slot on March 20, 1974, the ninety-minute documentary was unanimously praised by television reviewers as "useful" and "optimistic."

Of Birth and Babies brought Hartman together with Bob Shanks, the ABC vice-president who was packaging a successor to *A.M. America*, ABC's first attempt to cash in on the lucrative early-morning news market. Recognizing in Hartman's "rare ability not to be intimidated" the makings of a topnotch interviewer, Shanks selected the actor to anchor *Good Morning, America*, a lively, two-hour potpourri of news headlines, soft features, consumer information, household hints, and entertainment designed to lure viewers away from NBC's durable *Today* show, the long-time ratings leader among America's wake-up programs. Shanks's choice of Hartman raised some eyebrows, especially among news department executives, many of whom felt that the coveted job should have gone to a professional broadcast journalist, but George Merlis, the new show's executive producer, wholeheartedly endorsed the decision. "David's strength is that he's not afraid to ask the naïve question that newspersons wouldn't deign to ask," Merlis explained to Doug Bauer in an interview for *TV Guide* (August 12, 1978). "He's the catalyst for this show, and in the sense that what the show does is 'consumer journalism,' he's the consumer, asking and learning, trying to figure out how to cope right along with the rest of us."

When *Good Morning, America* made its debut on the morning of November 3, 1975, most television reviewers thought that Hartman, with his penetrating curiosity, warmth, and pleasant, relaxed manner, was its greatest asset. Reactions toward the other regulars—cohost Nancy Dussault; Steve Bell and Margaret Osmer, the Washington-based news readers; humorist Erma Bombeck; Jack Anderson, the political commentator; Jonathan Winters, the tongue-in-cheek movie critic—

and to the show as a whole were mixed. In the opinion of John J. O'Connor of the New York *Times*, *Good Morning, America* was a "corny and, worse, rather dull . . . assortment of plastic features held together with Silly Putty." John H. Corcoran Jr., writing in the *National Observer*, complained that "too much" of the program, especially the "gossip and name-dropping people-in-the-news fluff," was just "visual cholesterol." Still, he added, the show provided "an alternative, not an echo, to the *Today* and *CBS Morning News* efforts. It is hardly art, but you can always read your paper during the insufferable parts."

Within weeks, however, *Good Morning, America* began to win over many of its detractors, among them, the *Christian Science Monitor*'s Arthur Unger, who had "shrugged off the whole show" at first, but was soon "leaving the house feeling jolly and well-informed," as if he had spent "a couple of hours with friends." Viewers apparently concurred. By the end of its first full year, *Good Morning, America* had doubled its audience. The growing number of regular watchers induced many ABC affiliate stations to pick up the program, and in May 1979, *Good Morning, America* took over the ratings lead from the *Today* show by a slim margin. According to industry reports, *Good Morning, America*'s gains have not been made at the expense of *Today*, which has also increased its audience. Rather, the network's new entry attracted thousands of people who had never before watched early morning television. As Squire Rushnell, an ABC-TV vice-president, explained to one reporter, those new viewers apparently found in *Good Morning, America*'s "human interest" approach a welcome change from the more news-oriented NBC and CBS morning offerings. Although *Good Morning, America* no longer dominates *Today* in the weekly ratings charts, the two programs are rarely separated by more than a fraction of a point.

Unlike the *Today* show and the *CBS Morning News*, which are products of their respective news departments, *Good Morning, America* is a coproduction of ABC's news and entertainment divisions—a distinction David Hartman applauds. "We have a capacity in television to present information, sure, but the trick is to do it in an interesting way," he told Arthur Unger in an interview for the *Christian Science Monitor* (June 20, 1980). "There's no reason why something with substance has to be boring. The only thing that stands in the way of combining the two is imagination. That's the barrier we are trying to break through on *Good Morning, America*. And succeeding at it, too."

Despite its "featurish" approach, *Good Morning, America* competes vigorously with the other early-morning news shows for headline-making guests. Over the years, Hartman has interviewed, by his count, nearly 5,000 people, including President Jimmy Carter, Margaret Mead, and Raquel Welch. At first criticized for being "too soft," he has since perfected his interviewing technique, although he still insists that his gently probing questions are not as important as "the quality of information in the answers." "I don't perceive my job is to prove to everybody how much I know, how smart I am," he explained to Arthur Unger. "The key is: Do I elicit from our guests the kind of information that people can apply in their own lives? Because that's why we have guests on, to let the audience know what is going on in a broad range of subjects."

Good Morning, America has continued to prosper despite several changes in personnel. Hartman's original cohost, Nancy Dussault, who left the show in 1977 to concentrate on her acting career, was succeeded by Sandy Hill. After three years in Hartman's shadow, Miss Hill was made a special roving correspondent for the show. Joan Lunden is Hartman's current video companion. Hartman himself has become so involved in the production of *Good Morning, America* that he monitors the commercials and vetoes the broadcast of any he deems too "scary," "violent," or otherwise "objectionable." Convinced that he has, in his words, "the best job in the world," he seems to thrive on a grueling fifteen-hour workday that begins at 4:00 A.M. He even finds time to tackle additional assignments, such as serving as host for the ABC-TV special *David Hartman . . . The Shooters*, a survey of the life and work of five top photojournalists that was telecast on June 25, 1980.

David Hartman, who has described himself as "giraffelike," stands a towering six feet five inches tall and weighs about 200 pounds. He has a craggy face, pale blue eyes, and dark blond hair. Married since June 8, 1974, he and his wife, the former Maureen Downey, a television producer, have three children, Sean, Brian, and Bridget. An intensely private person, Hartman rarely gives interviews, and he refuses to discuss his politics, salary, or other aspects of his personal life. Although his schedule allows little time for recreation, he occasionally works out with a local professional baseball team. He also enjoys listening to music, photographing sporting events, reading, and watching old movies on television. Because of his hours, he cannot—to his disappointment—take advantage of New York City's cultural attractions. "We don't have much of a social life, Maureen and I," he admitted to one interviewer, "but we've always liked each other's company." David Hartman and his family live in Westchester County, New York.

References: Christian Sci Mon p19 Je 20 '80 por; Good H 186:66+ My '77 por; Horizon 21:80+ Jl '78 pors; Newsday II p39A Jl 25 '74 por; Sat Eve Post 249:45+ S '77 pors; TV Guide 17:18+ Je 7 '69 por, 26:19+ Ag 12 '78 por; International Motion Picture Almanac, 1981; Who's Who in America, 1980-81; Who's Who in Hollywood, 1900-1976 (1976)

Haughey, Charles J(ames) (hô′ē)

Sept. 16, 1925- Irish politician. Address: Abbeville, Kinsaley, County Malahide, Dublin, Ireland

The election of Charles J. Haughey as Taoiseach, or Prime Minister, of the Republic of Ireland on December 11, 1979 capped one of the most remarkable political comebacks in recent history. Just a decade earlier, Haughey, then the Minister for Finance, was arrested and tried on charges of gunrunning for the Provisional Irish Republican Army. Although he was acquitted of all charges, he spent several years in political limbo; then, in 1973, by skillfully employing his particular brand of charisma, imagination, and dogged determination, he won reelection to Parliament from the Dublin Artane Constituency. Rapidly regaining his prominent position within the Fianna Fáil party, he served as Minister for Health and Social Welfare from 1977 until his election to the party leadership post and the prime ministership.

Living up to his reputation as a man who "gets things done," Haughey passed his first crucial leadership test in November 1980 when Clement Coughlan, the Fianna Fáil candidate for whom he had campaigned vigorously, won a hotly contested by-election in County Donegal, which borders on Northern Ireland. With the country's economy still in turmoil and with a feasible solution of the problem of Northern Ireland yet to be devised, Haughey called, in May 1981, a parliamentary election in an effort to win a "clear and definite mandate" for a negotiated settlement in Ulster. But Haughey's party failed to maintain its majority in parliament, and on June 30, 1981, he was ousted as Prime Minister by Garret FitzGerald, the leader of the Fine Gael party, by a vote of 81 to 78.

Charles James Haughey was born on September 16, 1925 in Castlebar, County Mayo, where his Roman Catholic parents, Seán and Sarah [McWilliams] Haughey, had taken refuge after Protestant raiders burned the family farm in the northern county of Derry. Commandant Seán Haughey, an officer in the original Irish Republican Army and the new Free State's army, died at a young age, leaving his family poor. Financial hardship notwithstanding, Charles Haughey, a bright, ambitious lad, attended Scoil Mhuire in Marino, Dublin and St. Joseph's Christian Brothers' School in Fairview, Dublin, then enrolled, successively, at University College, Dublin and King's Inns, Dublin, where he studied accounting and law.

After leaving college, Haughey worked as an accountant and dabbled in real estate, ultimately amassing a fortune from land transactions. He also served as a commissioned officer in An Fórsa Cosanta Áitiúil, the local defense force, from 1947 to 1957, and as a member of Dublin Corporation, from 1953 to 1955. Following in the political footsteps of his father-in-law, Seán F. Lemass, who served as Prime Minister of Ireland from 1959 to 1966, Haughey joined the Fianna Fáil party. A few years later, in 1957, he was elected to the Dáil, Ireland's house of representatives. Following a four-year apprenticeship, which culminated in a one-year term as parliamentary secretary to the Minister for Justice, Haughey was himself named to that post in 1961. During his tenure as Minister of Justice, he infuriated diehard republicans by ordering the arrest and imprisonment of IRA agents and by publicly deploring the sporadic outbreaks of violence along the border between the Republic of Ireland and Northern Ireland. "The partition of our country has been deeply resented by the great majority of Irishmen," he said, as quoted in the *Christian Science Monitor* (February 27, 1962), "but the foolish resort to violence by a few of them has been repeatedly condemned by all responsible people as conducive to the perpetuation instead of the abolition of the border."

A shrewd administrator, Haughey was appointed Minister for Agriculture and Fisheries in 1964, allegedly because, in the words of Anne McHardy, a political correspondent for the *Guardian,* Prime Minister Lemass thought that he had "a speedy way with departmental briefs." In a Cabinet shuffle two years later, he was made Minister of Finance, a post he held until 1970. Dedicated to preserving and strengthening what he has called "a separate, distinctive, lively Irish culture," he formulated a comprehensive financial policy for the support of the arts, and perhaps more importantly, introduced legislation giving tax-free concessions to writers, artists, and composers living and working in Ireland.

Cynics pointed out that Haughey's tax bill, which was announced shortly before a general election, was primarily a ploy to ensure victory for his Fianna Fáil party. As expected, the party was returned to power and, within days of the election, the measure sailed through the Dáil, touching off a wave of favorable international publicity for Haughey. The prevailing local attitude was summed up by a member of Ireland's Arts Council, who told a reporter for the New York *Times* (September 19, 1969), "This fellow is determined to make his mark, and thank goodness it's in this line of country instead of horsebreeding or something."

Haughey's promising political career suffered a severe setback in May 1970 when he was implicated in a plot to smuggle weapons from abroad and ship them across the border to the dissident Catholic minority in strife-torn Northern Ireland. According to Liam Cosgrave, then the leader of the Opposition party, Fine Gael, Haughey had arranged for a consignment of small arms and ammunition, worth approximately $192,000, to be imported into Ireland from continental Europe without the normal customs inspection. The resulting scandal shook the government of Prime Minister John Lynch. Outraged, Lynch dismissed Haughey and Neil T. Blaney, the Minister for Agriculture, who was also incriminated in the gunrunning scheme, from his Cabinet on May 5. Three weeks later, both men were arrested and charged with conspiracy to smuggle arms. The case against Blaney was eventually dismissed for lack of evidence, but Haughey and three others were brought before a judge later that year in what New York *Times* columnist Anthony Lewis called "the most important political trial [in Ireland] in a generation." After an abortive first trial, Haughey and his codefendants were acquitted of all charges. The favorable verdict sparked a spontaneous demonstration in which all four men were carried from the courthouse on the shoulders of their jubilant supporters.

Buoyed by the court's decision, Haughey began to pick up the pieces of his political career. He made no secret of his desire to replace Lynch as leader of the Fianna Fáil party, and he publicly scorned the Prime Minister's stubborn refusal to press for the reunification of Ireland. Commenting on the situation for the New York *Times* (October 25, 1970), Anthony Lewis observed: "[Haughey's] acquittal and the resulting emotional support for him are seen here as giving new strength and credibility to the doctrine of reunification by any means—whether or not Mr. Haughey achieves his ambition of becoming Prime Minister."

For the next few years, Haughey maintained a relatively low profile, although he occasionally outlined his philosophy of government to interested foreign correspondents, among them Desmond Rushe. Writing in the New York *Times* (August 2, 1971), Rushe hailed Haughey as Ireland's "great hope of the future." Impressed by the former Cabinet minister's "proven interest" in the arts and the environment, Rushe singled out for special praise his enlightened attitude toward cultural development and his imaginative efforts to attract expatriated artists and writers to Ireland. "Let the young artists of today make their own special Irish contribution and let them make it from Ireland," he told Rushe. "Let them absorb and assimilate from abroad, but only to enrich what is their own. If we do this we will be providing something that is not alone satisfying from our own point of view in improving the quality of Irish life, but we will be making a significant contribution to a better world culture." "If ever Ireland is to have a Camelot situation," Rushe concluded, "[Haughey] will create it."

Haughey took the first step toward political rehabilitation in March 1973, when he won a seat in the Dáil, a personal victory made all the more remarkable by the fact that the Fianna Fáil party fared badly nationwide, losing control of parliament for the first time in sixteen years. Yielding to pressure from within the party, Lynch restored Haughey to Fianna Fáil's leadership group in 1975 as Opposition spokesman on health, and when the party regained control of the Dáil by an overwhelming majority in 1977, he promoted the resurrected politician to Minister for Health and Social Welfare. Making the most of his new assignment, Haughey immediately initiated a massive public health campaign by ceremoniously giving up smoking and by severely limiting his consumption of alcohol. He even took the Irish Medical Association jogging, much to the delight of the press, but he carefully tiptoed around such delicate issues as contraception and abortion.

Buffeted by runaway inflation, a huge balance of payments deficit, a series of crippling strikes, and growing dissatisfaction with Lynch's conciliatory approach toward Britain's policy on Northern Ireland, Ireland's political climate began to change in the late 1970's. Concerned about repeated poor showings in recent by-elections, Fianna Fáil backbenchers sought new leadership "to save our jobs," as one disgruntled party member put it. In a hastily called election on December 7, 1979, just two days after Lynch's surprise resignation, Haughey defeated his long-time rival, George Colley, the Minister for Finance, 44-38, to become party leader. His narrow victory was engineered primarily by Fianna Fáil's rank and file; he was supported by only three of his twenty-one fellow Cabinet members. He was formally elected Prime Minister one week later.

Dismayed by Haughey's ascendancy to the leadership of his party and nation, the new Prime Minister's political enemies unleashed a barrage of invective almost unprecedented in Irish politics. John Kelly, the stunned deputy opposition leader, spoke for many of his colleagues when he expressed his displeasure in the words of Edmund Burke, the eighteenth-century Irish statesman: "An event has happened upon which it is difficult to speak and impossible to stay silent." Dr. Garret Fitz-

Gerald, the leader of the Fine Gael party, called Haughey a man of "flawed pedigree," and Frank Cluskey, the head of the Labour party, denounced him for being one of "a breed of people dominated by the principle that the end justifies the means." The preponderant British point of view was represented by Dr. Conor Cruise O'Brien, the editor of the London Observer, who solemnly warned his readers: "With Mr. Haughey in office, Ulster Protestant hatred and suspicion of Dublin, and of Catholic neighbors in Northern Ireland, are likely to rise to new heights. The drift toward civil war accelerates."

Prime Minister Haughey's staunch nationalism and his alleged republican sympathies dominated the headlines in the days following his election, but in a news conference on December 7, 1979, Haughey managed to disarm some of his more outspoken critics by publicly condemning the violent tactics of the Irish Republican Army and by pledging to cooperate with the British on antiterrorist measures along the Irish-Ulster border. Although he dismissed Britain's latest proposals to end the bloodshed as "inadequate," he continued to insist that "the peaceful unification of the people of Ireland" was his "primary political priority."

To the dismay of his republican supporters, most of whom had expected him to take a hard-line anti-partition stand, Haughey's approach to reunification has been restrained and conciliatory. In a major policy speech before the annual convention of the Fianna Fáil party on February 16, 1980, Haughey urged the British to withdraw voluntarily from Northern Ireland. "The time has surely come for the two sovereign governments to work together to find a formula and lift the situation onto a new plane that will bring permanent peace and stability to the people of these islands," he said. "In my view a declaration by the British Government of their interest in encouraging the unity of Ireland, by agreement and in peace, would open the way towards an entirely new situation in which peace—real, lasting peace—would become an attainable reality."

In a meeting with British Prime Minister Margaret Thatcher on May 21, 1980, Haughey took another step in what Mary Holland, a political columnist for the New Statesman, described as "a brilliantly orchestrated campaign to kill off the popular British media image of the erstwhile gunrunner and replace it with that of the reasonable statesmanlike politician." After reaffirming his commitment to reunification, he conceded that any change in the status of Northern Ireland could come about only with the agreement and consent of the Protestant majority. "We don't wish to dominate anybody," he stressed to Mrs. Thatcher. "We don't wish to take anybody over. We have no idea to impose our will or our way of life or our political beliefs." Perhaps as a demonstration of his sincerity, Haughey, in a public statement in July 1980, condemned two United States-based organizations—the

Irish Northern Aid Committee and the Irish National Caucus—for actively assisting the provisional wing of the IRA in its campaign of violence in Northern Ireland and asked Irish-Americans to cut off all "financial or moral" support to "those whose actions serve only to delay Irish unity."

Amidst heightened tension because of a hunger strike in two Northern Ireland jails by prisoners on both sides of the conflict, Prime Ministers Haughey and Thatcher met for a second time at Dublin Castle on December 8, 1980. Following a five-hour meeting, they issued a joint communiqué acknowledging "the unique relationship" between Ireland and Great Britain and pledging their two leaders to "special consideration of the totality of relationships within these islands." Most observers of the Irish political scene interpreted that formal statement as a sign that some progress, however slight, toward a solution had been made.

According to William Borders, the New York Times's London correspondent, Haughey's strategy was to induce Mrs. Thatcher to help persuade the Ulster Protestants that reunification, or some other form of federation with the Irish Republic, would be preferable to what Haughey called the present "steadily deteriorating and increasingly intolerable situation" that

"benefits nobody." "It should be clear to all that a center of instability on this island, which occupies such a key geographical position, is not in the best interests of the people of any part of Ireland, Britain, or indeed the Western world as a whole," he explained, as quoted in the New York Times (June 19, 1980). In holding out his olive branch, Haughey offered to revise the Irish Constitution in the event of reunification to allow a different legal code for the North that would, for example, permit divorce.

A short, sturdily built man, Charles J. Haughey keeps in trim by swimming and riding horses. His preferred indoor recreations are reading and listening to music. The Prime Minister, whose net worth is said to be about $6,600,000, and his wife, Maureen (Lemass) Haughey, divide their time between a Georgian manor house on a 280-acre estate north of Dublin, where they breed thoroughbreds, and an island retreat off the southwest coast. Married since September 1951, they have one daughter and three sons.

References: Commonweal 107:388+ Jl 4 '80; Guardian p19 D 16 '79 por; N Y Times A p3 D 14 '79 por; Newsweek 94:65 D 17 '79; Time 114:49 D 17 '79 por; International Who's Who, 1980-81

Heinz, (Henry) John, (3d)

Oct. 23, 1938- United States Senator from Pennsylvania. Address: b. 443 Russell Office Building, Washington, D.C. 20510; h. 1950 Squaw Run Rd., Pittsburgh, Pa. 15238

Senator John Heinz of Pennsylvania is one of the rising young stars of the renascent Republican party. The heir to the H. J. Heinz Company fortune, he served five years in the United States House of Representatives before winning election to the Upper House in 1976. A moderate liberal in an increasingly conservative party, he was nonetheless chosen over Senator Orrin G. Hatch, a conservative, to chair the Republican Senatorial Campaign Committee in 1979. The following year, he had the astute political sense to ride with the conservative surge that delivered the Presidency to Ronald Reagan and the good fortune to be in a campaign leadership position when the Republicans regained control of the Senate for the first time since 1953. As the nineteenth-ranking member of the Senate's majority party, Heinz ought to enjoy sharply increased influence in his two key assignments to the Finance and the Banking, Housing, and Urban Affairs committees. That bodes well for the Senator, who is said to be looking past his 1982 reelection bid to eventual higher political office.

John Heinz, as he prefers to be known, was born Henry John Heinz 3d on October 23, 1938 in Pittsburgh, Pennsylvania, the only child of Henry John Heinz 2d and his first wife, Joan (Diehl) Heinz. His father is chairman of the H. J. Heinz Company, the Pittsburgh-based food processing business founded by the Senator's great-grandfather in 1869. After his parents' divorce, John Heinz divided his time between his father's house in Fox Chapel Boro, Pennsylvania and San Francisco, California, where his mother and stepfather, Monte McCauley, who was then a captain in the United States Navy, made their home. Heinz attended Phillips Exeter Academy, an exclusive private prep school in Exeter, New Hampshire. After his graduation in 1956, he enrolled at Yale University, where he majored in history. He received a B.A. degree from Yale in 1960 and, three years later, an M.B.A. from the Harvard Graduate School of Business Administration. His education completed, Heinz enlisted as an airman in the United States Air Force and served a tour of duty with the 911th Troop Carrier Group. He was honorably discharged from the Air Force Reserve in 1969 with the rank of staff sergeant.

In keeping with the family tradition of "roughing it," Heinz took summer jobs as a factory hand at a Heinz plant in Michigan and as a sales representative for International Harvester, Inc., in Sydney, Australia, then worked for a time as a banker in Geneva, Switzerland before officially joining the family firm in 1965. From an entry-level position as an analyst in the controller's office, Heinz moved up to associate manager, in 1966, and general manager, in 1968, of the grocery product marketing division. Under his direction, the company introduced nearly fifty new food items. During the academic year 1970-71, he also served as a lecturer on the faculty of Carnegie-Mellon University's Graduate School of Industrial Administration in Pittsburgh.

Convinced that "almost all the real vital decisions affecting our lives [were] being made in the public sector," to use his words, Heinz was active in local Republican politics throughout the latter half of the 1960's. He worked as a campaign aide in Senator Hugh Scott's successful reelection bid in 1964, attended the 1968 Republican National Convention as a delegate pledged to Nelson A. Rockefeller, New York's liberal governor, and chaired Pennsylvania's Republican party platform committee in 1970.

The vacancy created by the death, in April 1971, of Robert J. Corbett, the Republican Representative from Pennsylvania's Eighteenth Congressional District, spurred Heinz to pursue elective office himself. He easily secured the Republican nomination for the seat, and then squared off against Democrat John E. Connelly, a wealthy businessman, in a hard-fought, seven-month campaign. In their stump speeches, both candidates emphasized the declining economy. Heinz generally supported President Richard Nixon's wage-price freeze, although he urged even stronger measures. In his platform, he called for, among other things, the withdrawal of American forces from Vietnam, a 5 percent cut in federal income taxes for families earning less than $12,000 annually, federal assumption of welfare costs, and increased

federal aid to education. With registered Democrats in the district outnumbering Republicans by 16,000, Connelly enjoyed a built-in edge, but in the special election on November 2, 1971 Heinz demonstrated his ability to appeal across party lines by winning in a landslide, garnering 103,543 votes to Connelly's 49,269.

The youngest member of the Ninety-second Congress, Heinz quickly established a voting record that was moderate by general standards but decidedly liberal by Republican ones in both foreign and domestic affairs. On the House floor, he continued to demand an early end to American military involvement in Southeast Asia, urged President Nixon to normalize relations with Cuba, and frequently criticized the White House for using the threat of deploying new weapons as a tactic in arms limitations talks with the Soviet Union. On the domestic front, Heinz supported a number of progressive social programs in education, human welfare, health care, housing, and mass transportation, and he regularly approved environmental protection legislation. During his first year in office, he voted against the majority of his Republican colleagues as frequently as he voted with them, earning a 63 percent rating from the liberal Americans for Democratic Action and just 9 percent from its conservative counterpart, Americans for Constitutional Action.

Returned to Congress by overwhelming majorities of 73 and 72 percent in, respectively, 1972 and 1974, Heinz was so well liked by his constituents that he even took 25 percent of the votes as a write-in candidate in the 1974 Democratic primary. Heinz's popularity among Democrats was such that Jimmy Carter, in the early days of his quest for the Presidency, mistakenly identified the Pennsylvania Republican, whom he described as "one of the finest Congressmen in the nation," as a member of his own party. In the Ninety-third and Ninety-fourth Congresses, Heinz's voting record reflected his frequent disagreements with the conservative wing of the party. In 1975 and 1976, for example, he sided with his fellow Republicans on 31 percent of the roll call votes and opposed them on 44 percent.

On the House floor, Heinz persisted in his support of some of the most liberal social legislation of the decade. He asked regulatory boards to consider the "special needs" of the elderly and the handicapped in devising product safety standards, proposed a federally funded ethnic heritage studies program, and cosponsored a bill asking the federal government to assume responsibility for the medical insurance of unemployed workers, but he also turned down a measure authorizing federally-funded abortions for the poor and voted to ban busing to achieve racial desegregation, except to the nearest neighborhood school. Continuing his strong stand on environmental issues, he approved strict federal standards for strip mining and mandatory automobile emission controls, among other things.

Outraged by the spiraling costs of energy, Congressman Heinz called for a price ceiling on domestic crude oil, arguing that OPEC should not be allowed "to control the price Americans will pay for American oil." To conserve dwindling fuel supplies, he recommended increased appropriations to upgrade existing mass transit systems and suggested hiring 50,000 persons to repair the nation's railroad beds. As chairman of the House Republican Task Force on Antitrust and Monopoly Problems, Heinz strongly supported the Antitrust Procedures and Penalties Act of 1974, which strengthened the government's ability to monitor and block large corporate mergers. He also spearheaded the task force's investigations of various industries. Its first targets were the food industry and farm cooperatives.

In the inauspicious post-Watergate atmosphere, Heinz passed up the opportunity to challenge the 1974 reelection bid of Milton J. Shapp, Pennsylvania's popular Democratic governor, but on December 11, 1975 he declared his candidacy for the United States Senate seat soon to be vacated by Republican Hugh Scott, who was retiring after eighteen years in office. Long touted as a potential successor to Scott, Heinz immediately emerged as the favorite in the April 27 primary election that pitted him against Arlen Specter, a onetime Philadelphia district attorney, and George R. Packard, the former managing editor of the Philadelphia *Bulletin*. But the Congressman's foes found his Achilles' heel in his admission, early in the campaign, that he had accepted illegal contributions of $6,000 from the Gulf Oil Corporation in 1971 and 1972. Despite Heinz's assurances that there had been "no intent to deceive" and that he had subsequently returned the money, support for his candidacy declined, and for the first time in his political career, he experienced fund-raising problems. Consequently, the race turned out to be much closer than originally expected. Heinz won the nomination with 38 percent of the votes, while Specter took 35 percent and Packard 17 percent.

Heinz's Democratic opponent in the November general election was Philadelphia Congressman William J. Green 3d. Because the two young candidates were so similar in philosophy and appeal, most political observers predicted a tight race marked by the traditional east-west division in Pennsylvania state politics. Heinz benefited, however, from a timely United States Supreme Court decision declaring unconstitutional the $35,000 limit imposed on the personal expenditures of Senatorial candidates by the Federal Election Campaign Amendments of 1974. Freed from the constraints of the financing law, which, ironically, he had supported, Heinz gave or loaned his own campaign $2,466,910. The Pittsburgh Congressman, who repeatedly called attention to Green's close association with the powerful Philadelphia Democratic machine, defended the lavish use of his own money by insisting that

it allowed him "to get [his] message across to the people, without ties to the power brokers." Heinz raised a total of $3,016,731, the largest amount collected by any Senate candidate in 1976, and he outspent his opponent by better than three to one. Much of the money went for television commercials that portrayed the well-heeled Republican as a friend of labor and ethnic minorities—groups traditionally thought to be in the Democratic camp. In the opinion of many political commentators, Heinz's media blitz was the determining factor in the outcome of the election, in which he received 2,381,891 votes to his opponent's 2,126,977.

As a freshman Senator, Heinz has yet to make his mark as an originator of major pieces of legislation, but he has won praise as an effective floor manager of a variety of bills. "All of a sudden I'm making a difference," he told Bernard Weinraub in an interview for the New York *Times* (March 8, 1977). "You have more say, more of an input. You're more intimately involved with the executive branch. Your vote, you feel, counts for much more." His only quarrel is with the Senate's "badly organized," "fragmented," and "absolutely medieval" administration.

A specialist in economic affairs, Heinz has taken a strongly nationalistic stance on money matters. As a member of the Senate Banking Committee, he has frequently spoken out against the rapidly increasing number of takeovers of American banks by foreign investors and institutions. In an article published in the New York *Times* on July 22, 1979, Heinz warned that it would be hard to regulate foreign-controlled banks, which might resist carrying out monetary policies and investment practices supportive of American needs, but contrary to the interests of their alien owners. In November 1979 Heinz appended to a bank deregulation bill an amendment calling for a six-month moratorium on foreign purchases of American commercial banks, but the parent measure never became law. One of the Senate's leading "fair traders," he fought later that same year for tougher antidumping provisions in the legislation passed to implement the agreements made in the Tokyo round of the Multilateral Trade Negotiations. "If we don't make sure that our international trading partners play by the rules," the Senator noted, "then our country is going to continue its massive trade deficits and loss of jobs."

Senator Heinz's protectionist views extend to the particular interests of his economically hard-pressed state and region. Although he is one of the most outspoken environmentalists on Capitol Hill, he urged the Environmental Protection Agency to make minor changes in its regulations to encourage the use of the clean-burning anthracite coal that is abundantly available in eastern Pennsylvania, and he submitted several unsuccessful amendments that would have required electric power plants and factories to switch from oil and natural gas to coal. In an attempt to save hundreds of local jobs, he asked the Pentagon to weigh the potential economic impact before making a final decision on the proposed closing of military bases in the area. He was usually backed up in his efforts by his regional colleagues, but his suggestion that the federal government allocate public works projects for the unemployed on the basis of the total number of jobless persons in each state rather than on its per capita unemployment rate provoked sharp criticism from some of his erstwhile supporters. His opponents, among them New York Senator Daniel Patrick Moynihan, flatly rejected his argument that the Northeast, because it had suffered from sectionally biased government spending in the past, must discourage all specially weighted programs.

As he had done in the House, Heinz continued to support far-reaching social programs, energy conservation, meaningful tax reform, including the so-called Kemp-Roth across-the-board income tax reduction bill, and civil rights measures, such as the one extending the ratification deadline for the Equal Rights Amendment. Troubled by the plight of many Vietnam veterans, he cosponsored, in 1979, legislation giving the veterans broader assistance in health care, employment, and education. "The war may have been over years ago, but for the veteran, the struggle to survive continues," he said in defense of the measure on the Senate floor, "and it is a battle many of them are losing." More recently, he sought relief for veterans harmed by exposure to Agent Orange, a toxic chemical defoliant.

Senator Heinz has long advocated a greater role for Congress in the conduct of foreign affairs. For example, he voted to make United States policy toward South Korea a joint decision of the executive and legislative branches. He endorsed the Panama Canal Treaties, turned down the sale of weapons to Egypt and Saudi Arabia, and approved the prohibition of foreign aid to countries that aided and abetted international terrorism. In the occasionally acrimonious debate on the development of the neutron bomb, Heinz, speaking against the bill, asked his fellow Senators, "Is deterrence better achieved if the other side thinks we're more likely to go to war, but with less destructive weapons, or if it thinks we are less likely to go to war, but with more destructive weapons?" In keeping with his moderately liberal voting record, Heinz has usually scored well with ADA, who rated him as high as 60 percent, in 1978, as compared to 18 percent from the ACA. His most recent evaluation, however, reflects a slight shift toward the center: for the year 1979, the ADA marked him at 42 percent, the ACA at 44 percent.

Looking even younger than his years, John Heinz has been described as being "handsome in the male model way." A natural athlete with a fondness for competitive sports, he jogs two miles daily and swims and plays

tennis regularly. He particularly enjoys skiing and is an expert downhill racer. Married since 1966 to the former Maria Teresa Thierstein Simoes-Ferreira, he has three children, Henry John 4th, André, and Christopher. While in Washington, the Heinzes live in the fashionable Georgetown section in a house that was once the Russian embassy. Their Pennsylvania residence is the white-pillared farmhouse built by the Senator's grandfather in Fox Chapel Boro, a suburb of Pittsburgh.

Senator Heinz takes an active role in the civic affairs of his hometown. He is the chairman of the H. J. Heinz 2d Charitable and Family Trust, a fellow of the Carnegie Institute Museum of Art, a member of the board of the Children's Hospital of Pittsburgh, and a co-founder of the Pittsburgh Penguins professional hockey team. He also sits on the boards of visitors of Harvard University's Graduate School of Business Administration and the Graduate Schools of Public Health and Public and International Affairs at the University of Pittsburgh. He is the recipient of an honorary doctor of laws degree from Temple University, Man of the Year awards from the Pittsburgh Jaycees and the Southwestern Pennsylvania Building Trades Council, and the National Americanism Award from the Anti-Defamation League of B'nai B'rith as well as several awards for his contributions to mental health and medical research. Heinz is probably the richest man in the Senate. According to data released by his office in May 1979, his assets range between $11,200,000 and $19,700,-000 and his liabilities from $1,300,000 to $2,-800,000. His reported income for 1979 was $302,180.34.

References: Washington Post B p1+ N 17 '71 por; Almanac of American Politics, 1980; Congressional Directory, 1979; Who's Who in America, 1980-81; Who's Who in American Politics, 1979-80

Hoffman, Abbie

Nov. 30, 1936- Social activist; writer. Address: b. c/o G. P. Putnam's Sons, 200 Madison Ave., New York City, N.Y. 10016

When he surrendered to federal authorities in order to face narcotics charges on September 4, 1980, the radical activist and writer Abbie Hoffman embarked on a new life, having already, at forty-four, lived more disparate existences than most people ever do. A former pharmaceuticals salesman and fairly staid husband, he became an antiwar activist and self-styled revolutionary, whose antic behavior made him a media celebrity and best-selling author. As a founder of the Youth International Party or Yippies, and as the instigator of flam-

Abbie Hoffman

boyant pranks with a political message, Hoffman came to be for many young people the leading ideologue of the 1960's. It was they who bought his books, such as *Revolution for the Hell of It* (1968) and *Steal This Book* (1971), which facetiously advocated measures ranging from the overthrow of the government and experimenting with LSD to "ripping off" the telephone company.

But Hoffman's much publicized career came to a halt in 1974, when, facing a life sentence on charges of selling cocaine to undercover agents, he jumped bail and went underground. In 1980 he surfaced to plead guilty to lesser charges and, characteristically, to promote a new book, having lived in recent years as a successful community organizer and ecological activist in upstate New York, under the alias of "Barry Freed."

Abbie Hoffman was born Abbott Hoffman on November 30, 1936 in Worcester, Massachusetts, the oldest of three children of John Hoffman and the former Florence Schanberg. John Hoffman was a pharmacist who worked in his brother's drugstore until it closed after World War II; he then founded the Worcester Medical Supply Company, which sold supplies to doctors. The firm is now run by Abbie Hoffman's younger brother Jack. By his own description a troublemaker from the start, Abbie was expelled from Classical High School after a fight with his English teacher and finally graduated from Worcester Academy, a private school. He then attended Brandeis University in Waltham, Massachusetts, where he was influenced by the radical social views of Herbert Marcuse and the humanistic psychology of Abraham Maslow. In 1959 he graduated from Brandeis with a B.A. degree in psychology.

After spending a year at the University of California at Berkeley, during which he obtained an M.A. degree in psychology and received his baptism in activist politics, Hoffman returned to his hometown of Worcester. In 1963 he took a job as a traveling salesman of pharmaceuticals, but during the three years that he held the job, he devoted most of his energy to a growing passion—political organizing, particularly in the burgeoning civil rights movement. In 1964 he journeyed to the South to take part in the Freedom Summer in Mississippi, where he was arrested, and in 1965 he returned to Mississippi and Georgia.

In 1966 Hoffman moved to New York City and founded a store, Liberty House, that sold crafts made by poor people's co-ops in Mississippi, but since the civil rights movement was being split by the rise of "Black Power" militancy, in the following year he left Liberty House and addressed his political energies to opposing the Vietnam War. Hoffman found his natural constituency among the hippies who had thronged to New York's East Village, where he lived, and he easily identified with those restless, rebellious children of the middle class, who appealed to the anarchic, puckish side of his personality. But as he wrote in his autobiography, *Soon to be a Major Motion Picture*, (G. P. Putnam's Sons, 1980), "Personally, I always held my flower in a clenched fist. A semi-structure freak among the love children, I was determined to bring the hippie movement into a broader protest."

The result of that determination was a seemingly endless series of Hoffman-inspired "happenings" that combined prankishness, mischief, and politics. The first event that attracted the attention of the mass media was staged in April 1967, when Hoffman and a group of his cohorts threw dollar bills from the visitors' gallery onto the floor of the New York Stock Exchange, provoking pandemonium as the traders rushed to pick up the money. In October of that same year, during a massive antiwar demonstration in Washington, D.C., Hoffman's Till Eulenspiegel style was evident in an effort to surround the Pentagon and levitate it by mental force, thus exorcising its evil spirits. In 1967 he helped to organize "be-ins" in Central Park, sent 3,000 marijuana cigarettes, with directions on how to smoke them, to people randomly selected from the telephone book, and took part in countless newsworthy demonstrations and acts of vandalism against symbolic "Establishment" targets.

For Hoffman, those antics represented a theory of political change and an understanding of the American power structure perhaps more profound than that of any other youth leader of the 1960's. Influenced by the writings of the media guru, Marshall McLuhan, Hoffman regarded the communications industry, especially television, as the central factor in modern American life. "A modern revolutionary group heads for the television station, not for the factory," he has written. "It concentrates its energy on infiltrating and changing the image system." To that end, Hoffman wanted to create a "guerrilla theater" in the streets that would engage in a "war of symbols" carefully calculated to communicate forcefully on the evening news.

On New York's Day, 1968 Hoffman and several cronies coined the word "Yippie" for themselves and their followers. That soon led to the founding of the Youth International Party (YIP), a group that boasted that it had "no leaders, no members, and no organization." It was a misleading allegation since, in actuality, Hoffman and his close friend Jerry Rubin led the YIP, using it as a rallying-point to stage ever more ambitious street dramas. Not yet a well-known personality, Hoffman often used aliases, and when his first book, *Revolution for the Hell of It* (Dial Press, 1968), appeared, the author's name was given only as "Free." The book is a mélange of anecdotes, reminiscence, aphorisms, political musings, exhortations, photos, and drawings, all calculated to incite a youthful audience to bring about a rather ill-defined revolution. Although it sold well, reviewers were perplexed. Jack Newfield, writing in the New York *Times Book Review* (December 29, 1968), remarked that the book "is clever, fun, and should be read. Perhaps its pages should even be smoked. But if one is still serious about redeeming the American dream, then he should read some of those linear, over-30 squares, like I. F. Stone, Norman Mailer and Howard Zinn."

The Yippies' Armageddon came in August 1968, when they converged on Chicago to protest the Democratic Presidential convention that would nominate Hubert H. Humphrey. A series of violent confrontations between the demonstrators and authorities culminated on August 28, when the police savagely attacked a peaceful protest march down Michigan Avenue, in an action that a government report would later term a "police riot." Television viewers watched in horror as the coverage of Humphrey's nomination was intercut with scenes of the donnybrook taking place outside the convention hall. Hoffman was arrested that day for appearing in public with an obscene word written on his forehead. Since the Chicago confrontations made him a well-known activist and a target for police attention, Hoffman was arrested eight more times in the next eight months.

From one of those cases developed the most spectacular piece of guerrilla theatre that Hoffman ever helped to produce—the Chicago conspiracy trial. In March 1969 a federal grand jury indicted him and seven others on charges of conspiracy and crossing state lines to incite a riot. From the beginning the defendants intended to conduct a political defense that would put the judicial system itself on trial, and as they had done during the Democratic convention, they succeeded by provoking the authorities into a repressive overreaction that made them appear villainous. During the twenty weeks of testimony that lasted from September 1969 until February 1970, Judge Julius J. Hoffman was outraged by the refusal of the defendants and their lawyers to observe what he considered to be proper courtroom decorum. In October he ordered the Black Panther leader Bobby Seale bound and gagged. He then separated Seale's case from the others and sentenced him to four years in jail for contempt of court. The judge also favored the prosecution in his procedural rulings.

The "Chicago Seven," as the defendants came to be called after Seale's case was separated, responded with raucous and sometimes zany protests. One day Hoffman and Rubin wore judicial robes as a mockery of the judge, and during the battle over Seale's shackling they refused to stand when the judge entered the courtroom. At another point, enraged at one of Judge Hoffman's rulings, Abbie called the judge "a disgrace to the Jews" (both men are Jewish). The defendants not only flouted accepted courtroom behavior but also called dozens of witnesses, many of them well-known political figures, writers, and entertainers, who introduced into their testimony the underlying political issues, particularly the Vietnam war. The jury eventually acquitted the defendants of conspiracy but found five of them, including Hoffman, guilty of crossing state lines to incite a riot. For his part, Judge Hoffman convicted the Chicago Seven of 175 charges of contempt and sentenced them to jail, with Abbie Hoffman receiving an eight-month term. Nevertheless the trial was viewed by many observers as a huge victory for the defendants in the "war of symbols."

The Chicago trial made Abbie Hoffman a certified celebrity. Released on bail pending appeal, he found himself in demand as a speaker, writer, and guest on television talk shows. His second book, *Woodstock Nation: A Talk-Rock Album* (Random House) had appeared in 1969, the year the trial began. It sold well, leading Hoffman to remark, "It's embarrassing. You try to overthrow the government, and you end up on the best-seller list." Like his first, the book was a pastiche, with its central theme the "cultural revolution" symbolized by the Woodstock festival.

Through the turbulent years of 1970 and 1971 Hoffman crisscrossed the country as a full-time agitator, speaking in opposition to the Vietnam war at dozens of colleges, and visiting Canada, Britain, Northern Ireland, and Europe. He loved his mission, but the frantic pace and the notoriety wore him down, and he was harassed constantly by the FBI and local police. The antiwar movement itself began to sour, beset by bickering factionalism and frustrated by its inability to end the war. In May 1971 Hoffman's nose was badly broken by Washington, D.C. police during a demonstration, and discouraged and exhausted, he began to withdraw from activism.

One of the disillusioning experiences of 1971 involved Hoffman's third book, *Steal This Book* (Pirate Editions, 1971). A how-to manual for the counterculture, it includes detailed advice, drawings, and even wiring diagrams on a multitude of subjects for the alienated, including shoplifting, explosives, false identification, hitchhiking, self-defense, and legal problems. It also reveals how to get a wide array of goods and services for nothing, including long-distance telephone calls and transportation. Random House, Hoffman's previous publisher, refused to publish *Steal This Book* on the ground that much of what it advocated was illegal, and thirty other publishers followed suit. Hoffman finally raised the money to publish the book himself, and Grove Press agreed to distribute it.

But Hoffman's headaches with *Steal This Book* were just beginning. Not a single radio station, and only one mainstream newspaper in the country, accepted advertising for the work, most bookstores refused to sell it, and no reviews appeared until the New York *Times Book Review* printed a favorable one by Dotson Rader on July 18, 1971. After his review the boycott slackened, and by November, 260,000 copies had been sold. But Hoffman and Grove Press began to squabble about the distribution agreement. When he finally closed down Pirate Editions and declared the book out of print, he had earned about $26,000 on *Steal This Book*.

In 1972, after spending several months of restful anonymity in the Virgin Islands, Hoffman campaigned for the Presidential election of Senator George McGovern and wrote a paperback with Jerry Rubin and Ed Sanders on the Presidential conventions in Miami, titled *Vote!* (Warner, 1972). In November a federal appeals court unanimously overturned the convictions of the Chicago Seven on both the riot and contempt charges, citing innumerable serious errors by Judge Hoffman. Abbie was eventually re-tried on reduced contempt charges, convicted, and released without a jail term.

But on August 28, 1973, in New York, Abbie Hoffman was arrested for participation in the sale of three pounds of cocaine to undercover agents. What actually occurred has never been fully clarified, though Hoffman admits in his autobiography that he "helped bring people together." After spending six weeks in prison he raised bail, but he faced a mandatory life sentence with no possibility of parole before fifteen years. In late February 1974, before the trial began, he vanished.

If Hoffman is evasive about his years underground, it is partly to protect those who aided him. Not long after disappearing he underwent plastic surgery to alter his appearance, particularly his prominent nose, and he changed his walk, gestures, and style of speech. He lived for awhile in Mexico and Canada, worked in a variety of jobs, and used at least two dozen aliases. Those years of insecure secrecy proved to be extremely hard on Hoffman, and he suffered two serious nervous breakdowns, but, somewhat miraculously, he was not captured. Ever playful, he gave occasional interviews, including one that caused an uproar because a television production company and the magazine *New Times* paid $3,000 and some television equipment to obtain it. In 1976 a book of his correspondence with his second wife, Anita, was published, called *To america with Love: Letters from the Underground* (Stonehill Press). The "america" of the title is Abbie and Anita's son, who was born in 1971.

During his self-imposed exile in Mexico, Hoffman met Johanna Lawrenson, who traveled with him during much of his surreptitious odyssey, and eventually they moved to her hometown of Fineview, New York, on Wellesley Island in the St. Lawrence River, where Hoffman lived for about four years as "Barry Freed," a free-lance writer. At first, Hoffman and Lawrenson kept to themselves, but when the United States Army Corps of Engineers announced plans to dredge the St. Lawrence to permit winter navigation, Hoffman helped to organize the Save the River Committee, which battled successfully to stop the project for environmental reasons. "Barry Freed" often appeared on local television and radio, befriended reporters, and once, in 1979, testified before a Senate panel and was photographed with Senator Daniel Patrick Moynihan, Democrat of New York.

Finally deciding to surface, Hoffman appeared on national television over ABC with Barbara Walters on September 3, 1980. On the next day he surrendered in New York City. He insisted that he chose that moment because he faced imminent exposure in Fineview and because the passions of the 1960's had cooled down enough for him to expect relatively lenient treatment. (In fact, in January 1981 he pleaded guilty to reduced charges.) But observers were skeptical, since Hoffman's appearance exactly coincided with the publication of a new book, his autobiography. *Soon to be a Major Motion Picture* is essentially an apologia, although as wisecracking and self-congratulatory as ever, in which he stresses that he was not simply a mischievous exhibitionist but also a serious organizer. The strong feelings he still arouses were reflected in the *ad hominem* reviews, which focused less on the book than on Hoffman's role in the 1960's.

Despite pleas for leniency in letters from celebrated friends and supporters of Abbie Hoffman, on April 7, 1981, in the New York State Supreme Court, acting justice Brenda Soloff sentenced the activist to up to three years in prison for taking part in selling $36,000 worth of cocaine to undercover police officers in 1973 and for jumping bail before trial in 1974. Hoffman, who has acknowledged his complicity as a "crime of stupidity" and as an "act of insanity," had to serve for at least a year before becoming eligible for parole.

Abbie Hoffman is a solidly built man, voluble, high-strung, and with an expressive face that one writer has described as "Semitic." His long, unruly hair was both a trademark and a political statement in the 1960's; today he is somewhat bald, and as "Barry Freed" kept his hair cut conventionally. He jokes about his oversized ego in a letter published in *To america with Love*: "I'm such an egomaniac I figure if I'm an egomaniac then it's a good quality!!" Hoffman was first married in 1960 and divorced in 1966. In 1967 he married Anita Kushner, who shared in most of his exploits but chose not to accompany him underground. Besides his son america, Hoffman has two children, Andy and Amy, from his first marriage. His future is somewhat clouded, since he has been sentenced to a jail term on the drug charges. But he still commands a lecture fee that ranges from $3,000 to $5,000, may earn as much as $50,000 as a consultant to Universal Pictures on a movie that has been scheduled to be made of his life, and certainly can count on having his work accepted as a writer. His current ambition, he says, is "to start a school for organizers, especially young people in the environmental field."

References: N Y Daily News p25 O 5 '80 pors; New Times p21+ My 30 '75; Newsday W p3+ N 6 '71 pors; People 14:40+ S 22 '80 pors; Washington Monthly p261+ Je '76; Who's Who in America, 1976-77

Holmes, Larry

Nov. 3, 1949- Boxer. Address: b. c/o World Boxing Council, Apartado 75-254, Mexico City, 14 D.F. Mexico

With some justification, Larry Holmes calls himself "the world's baddest heavyweight." The irony in Holmes's struggle for recognition and respect in the post-Ali era in boxing is that he is so proficient he makes most of his opponents look like mediocrities. In his twelve title defenses since he won the World Boxing Council championship by defeating Ken Norton in June 1978, Holmes has stopped all his opponents save one, Trevor Berbick, by knockout or technical knockout. His professional career record is 39-0, with twenty-nine KO's or TKO's.

The seventh of twelve children in a family of sharecroppers, Larry Holmes was born in Cuthbert, Georgia on November 3, 1949 to John and Flossie Holmes. In 1954 the family moved north, to Easton, Pennsylvania, where the father hoped to find work. When he did not, he moved on alone, and the mother went on welfare. Larry "wasn't a bad boy," although "out on the streets he was mean," his mother recounted in an interview with Pat Putnam when Putnam was preparing a profile of Holmes for *Sports Illustrated* (November 6, 1980). "He called himself a street fighter. Larry was a good boy. He just would take no guff from anybody. He was stubborn."

Holmes himself told Putnam, "I was no angel. I know how it feels to get in trouble with the police. I know how it feels to drink and get drunk. I know how it feels to smoke grass and get high. I've done it all. You can't tell me about it. But I worked for a living. I worked from the time I was a little boy. A lot of the guys I ran with didn't want to do that. They wanted to hustle and to pimp. Some got killed; some are in jail. I've always felt that you had to work for anything you got."

Dropping out of school in the seventh grade, when he was thirteen, Holmes went to work in a succession of menial jobs, in a car wash, a rug mill, an artillery shell factory, a paint factory, and a quarry. His second home during adolescence was the St. Francis Youth Center in Easton, where he learned to box and where he was entrusted with locking up at night. On Saturday nights he, his brother Lee, and some friends did exhibition boxing in bars in and around Easton.

Among the persons exerting a strong positive influence on the young Holmes were Father Francis Barbato, the founder of the St. Francis Youth Center, John DiVietro, the car-wash owner and social worker *manqué* who gave Holmes his first job; Charles Spaziani, the former district attorney of Northampton County, Pennsylvania, who came to Holmes's rescue when he was arrested mistakenly in a police sweep of the streets when race riots broke out in Easton in 1968; and Earnee Butler, a former welterweight who was running a small record shop and shoeshine parlor in Easton. When Holmes decided at age nineteen that, given his negligible educational credentials and his bleak employment prospects, he "might as well" make boxing his career, Butler became his manager and trainer, and later, when he turned pro, Spaziani became his legal counselor.

Supporting himself by driving a dump truck between bouts, Holmes fought as an amateur for three years, beginning in 1970. Out of twenty-two amateur fights, he won nineteen, including the New Jersey A.A.U. championship and the Eastern Olympic championship. In his first professional fight, in March 1973, Holmes, still under Butler's tutelage, defeated Rodell Dupree.

Butler remained Holmes's trainer and manager for a few more fights, until Don King, the fight promoter, who promised to hasten the pace of Holmes's professional career, took over as his manager. As trainer, King brought in Richie Giachetti, his Cleveland associate, a former welterweight with local political as well as pugilistic connections. As Holmes's career progressed and King moved into the big time as a promoter, King and Giachetti dissolved their formal business relationship and Giachetti turned over his auto-body business to his brother in order to devote himself to managing as well as training Holmes.

During his early, lean years as a pro, Holmes honed his pugilistic skills as a sparring partner for Earnie Shavers, Joe Frazier, and Jimmy Young, and above all Muhammad Ali, whose style he tried to emulate. By the time he confronted Roy Williams, in April 1973, he had a record of twenty-two straight victories, seventeen by knockout, and he had gained a reputation for his quick hands, lightning jab, peerless hook, and flashing footwork. *Ring* magazine ranked him eighth among heavyweights.

In boxing Williams warily, by "point" work done well out of range, Holmes was successful, but drew from critics the charge that he lacked "heart." Actually, the ten-round decision was quite impressive, considering the fact that Holmes finished the fight with a broken right thumb, which would keep him out of competition for nine months. Even after the thumb healed, Holmes continued to favor it through four fights, until March 25, 1978, when he came up against Earnie Shavers, the first opponent of indisputable international stature who dared to face him. In winning a decision over Shavers, Holmes fearlessly took shots and returned two-fisted barrages, proving both by heart and hand that he was worthy of challenging Ken Norton, the then reigning World Boxing Council champion. Norton had acquired the championship without a title fight in March 1977, after the WBC withdrew its recognition of Leon Spinks as champion on a legal technicality. The WBC handed the championship to Norton because he was the ranking challenger at the time.

The encounter with Norton, in Caesar's Palace in Las Vegas, Nevada on June 10, 1978, was Holmes's first bout scheduled for more than twelve rounds. It was rated by many seasoned observers as the most memorable heavyweight title fight since the "Thrilla in Manila" in which Muhammad Ali and Joe Frazier had all but destroyed each other. Holmes had the edge until the sixth round, when a blow to his left shoulder re-injured a muscle that he had torn in training. He fought the rest of the fight virtually one-handed, without his invaluable left jab, the punch he was in the habit of using as the set-up for his climactic right. Despite that disadvantage, he entered the fifteenth round even with Norton on all three judges' cards. In that final round he gave many staggering blows, and the judges awarded him the round, and thus the fight and the championship.

In his first title defense, Holmes knocked out Alfredo Evangelista in the seventh round of a scheduled fifteen-round fight in Las Vegas on November 10, 1978. His second fight as champion was again a seventh-round knockout, of Ossie Ocasio, in Las Vegas on March 23, 1979, and in his third, an otherwise lackluster performance, he knocked out Mike Weaver in the twelfth round in Madison Square Garden in New York City on June 22, 1979.

In a return match with Earnie Shavers in Las Vegas on September 28, 1979, Holmes sustained the second knock-down of his professional career in the seventh round, when Shavers connected with one of his lethal roundhouse rights. Holmes managed to rise at the count of five, and then, as referee Davey Pearl continued on to the mandatory count of nine, he jumped up and down. "An ordinary fighter would have stood there dazed and helpless, waiting to get knocked down again," Pearl later observed, "but as stunned as he must have been, he reacted the way a smart, seasoned fighter should. The jumping up and down cleared away the cobwebs." Shavers had exhausted his resources with his one mighty blow, and Holmes dominated the following rounds. Pearl stopped the fight two minutes into the eleventh round because, as he explained, although Shavers was never off his feet, he was in "a trance," having taken too many punches to the head.

Easily coping with the flicking left jab of Lorenzo Zanon, the former European champion from Italy, in Las Vegas on February 4, 1980, Holmes floored him twice in the fourth round and decked him for the count in the sixth. After a long rest, Holmes's own stinging jab was conspicuously reactivated on March 31, 1980, when the champion fought Leroy Jones in Las Vegas. Referee Richard Green stopped that fight at 2:56 of the eighth round, after Holmes had forced Jones into his own corner and peppered him with twenty-one unanswered punches. In Bloomington, Minnesota the following July, the fiercely competitive Scott LeDoux angrily objected when referee Davey Pearl stopped the LeDoux-Holmes bout in the seventh round because it appeared to him that LeDoux was blinded by a cut over his left eye. "I never saw a cut like that," Pearl later remarked, "and I've been in this game for more than twenty years."

Even more one-sided than Holmes's victories over Jones and LeDoux was his defeat of Muhammad Ali, when the former three-time champion made an attempt to regain the title in Las Vegas on October 2, 1980. A vestige of his former self, "the Greatest" seemed flat-footed, fighting from a crouch, dancing away, resorting to "rope-a-dope." By round seven, his face was a puffy mass, and blood was trickling from one nostril. When he was unable to answer the bell for the eleventh round, referee Richard Green ruled a technical knockout.

Tears filled Holmes's eyes as he left the ring after putting the first KO loss on the record of his former employer and model and thus destroying a legend. "Why did he have to come back?" he rhetorically asked reporters afterward. "Why did he have to do this? He has a new family and a new little girl. When is he going to learn that the important things in life are his children and his wife? I pray to God that Ali learns the true values of life."

Close observers felt certain that Holmes had mercifully pulled some punches in the closing rounds of the fight with Ali. A week later Ali blamed his poor performance on an overdose of thyroid medicine and asserted, "I can beat Holmes. I shall return." An angry Holmes announced that he did not want to fight Ali again, but if he was forced to do so he would "knock him out cold [so that] he won't come back making excuses about how he lost."

Early in 1981 Holmes fired Richie Giachetti, the manager and trainer who had come up through the ranks with him, because he believed that Giachetti was "exploiting" him. Holmes explained to a reporter that Giachetti had made damaging statements about him to a grand jury investigating boxing. When Holmes went before the grand jury, he recounted, he heard a tape that Giachetti had placed in testimony. "It proved he had been leading me down the trail. I gave $1,500,000 to Giachetti and he still led me down the trail." Eddie Futch was brought in as Holmes's new trainer. Among those remaining on Holmes's staff were the veteran second Freddie Brown, Holmes's brother Jake, who takes care of security, and Eddie Sutton, a childhood friend who serves as a jack-of-all-work.

The only challenger to go the distance against Holmes in a title fight was Trevor Berbick, whom Holmes defeated by unanimous decision in a fifteen-rounder in Las Vegas on April 11, 1981. When he faced Leon Spinks in Detroit on June 12, 1981, Holmes felt free to experiment, to change his tactics from round to round, to "demonstrate all [his] talents" because, as he later explained, he "knew from the start" that "the fight wouldn't last too long," that he was "too big and too fast and . . . stronger than Leon Spinks." He began defen-

sively, dancing and parrying as Spinks rushed him ferociously, but to no avail. In the second round he became angry over a disputed early bell, twenty-five seconds before the end of the round, because while he heard that bell and stopped fighting, Spinks did not hear it and kept swinging away. With the opening bell of the third round, he moved purposefully to the center of the ring, prepared for the kill. After taking the wind out of Spinks with a left hook to the belly, he staggered him with a right to the jaw, and then, following him to his corner, decked him with a hard right followed by a combination to head and body. The groggy challenger rose at the count of nine only to be pummeled by a barrage that made a punching bag of his head. After Spinks's cornermen began screaming for an end to the slaughter, referee Richard Steele intervened, declaring a technical knockout two minutes and thirty-four seconds into the round.

Following the victory over Spinks, Holmes was interviewed by television newsmen at ringside. As the interview was ending, Jerry Cooney, the ranking heavyweight contender, approached because he had been asked by the American Broadcasting Company to contribute some comments on the fight. The presence of Cooney infuriated Holmes, because Cooney had been quoted in the press as making disparaging remarks about him. Angry words flew, with Holmes shouting, "White hope for the white dopes!" and Cooney responding, "You have no class." Lunging for Cooney, Holmes was restrained by aides, and in the process his right elbow inadvertently caught sports commentator Howard Cosell on the lower lip, splitting it on the inside.

The day after the Spinks fight, Holmes discussed the remaining prospective challengers with a reporter. "I won't fight [Mike] Dokes because he's managed by Carl King [the son of Don King, Holmes's promoter]," he said. "That would cause a scandal. Mike is going to have to wait until I retire. [Greg] Page is getting real good, but he ain't ready for me yet. And [Jerry] Cooney won't fight me."

Cooney had a different story: he could not fight Holmes because he had a prior commitment to fight Mike Weaver, whom Holmes had KO'd two years before and who was now recognized as champion by the World Boxing Association, the other world championship sanctioning body. The plot of the story was changed at the end of June 1981, when the WBA threatened to strip Weaver of his title if he did not fight James ("Quick") Tillis, the number-three-ranked WBA contender, before taking on the number-one-ranked Cooney. WBA officials explained that at the time they were choosing the "best available" next challenger, Tillis was that man, because Cooney had forfeited his number-one position for the "mandatory" WBA bout by signing to fight Ken Norton.

As soon as Holmes heard about the demolition of the Cooney-Weaver bout, he called

Don King to tell him, "Make the Cooney fight right now. . . . Don't let money get in the way. Just make it fair to both sides. I'm the champion. I deserve more. If I'm not getting it, don't tell me." Dick Young, who reported the phone conversation in his column in the New York Daily News (July 1, 1981), observed, "A man can't get more sincere than that. He doesn't want his pride bruised publicly, but he wants even less to have his shot at Cooney fizzle out because of an extra $500,000, after taxes, that he doesn't need." Young pointed out that "there is so much money to be made on Cooney-Holmes, each fighter can take a $5,000,000 guarantee, gamble on a percentage option, and come out with $10,000,000 each, maybe more." Two and half months later Cooney finally signed to fight Holmes in Caesar's Palace in Las Vegas, Nevada in March 1982. The contract assured each fighter of $10,000,000.

While waiting for the Cooney match, Holmes was booked to fight with Renaldo Snipes, on November 6, 1981. The fight against Snipes went as easily as expected until the seventh round, when Holmes walked into a wild punch that sent him sprawling to the count of nine. He managed to hold off Snipes for the remainder of the round, regained control of the fight in the eighth round, and survived a shakey moment in the tenth to win a TKO sixty-five seconds into the eleventh round.

Larry Holmes is six feet three inches tall, weighs about 213 pounds, and, in contrast with his ring persona, is gentle in speech and manner. Although he enjoys the glitter of Las Vegas, he is most at home in Easton, Pennsylvania, where he has built a mansion for himself and his family, including his mother, where he owns Round One, a restaurant and night club, and where he is honorary chairman of the Easton Boys Club. He is also the chairman of the recruiting committee of the National Association for the Advancement of Colored People.

On December 23, 1979 Holmes married Diane Robinson, by whom he has daughter, Kandy. He also has two older daughters by a woman he never married. For a long time, Holmes resented being in Muhammad Ali's shadow and not getting the respect he deserved, but he now seems content to know that whether people recognize him in the street or not, they will in the record books. And he is proud of the fact that, unlike many other boxers, he has husbanded his prizefight earnings wisely. When he recently stated that he intends to quit fighting after "one more year, at the most," he was asked what he would be doing at thirty-eight, Muhammad Ali's age at the time of the Ali-Holmes match. "I'll be washing cars," he said, "but this time they'll be mine."

References: Ebony 34:112+ F '79 pors; People 13:88+ S 29 '80 pors; Sport 71:40+ Jl '80 pors; Sports Illus 49:46+ N 6 '78 pors, 53:75+ S 22 '80 pors

Holt, John (Caldwell)

Apr. 14, 1923- Educator; writer; musician. Address: b. Holt Associates, Inc., 308 Boylston St., Boston, Mass. 02116

Convinced that schools teach children to be "stupid," the educational reformer John Holt has argued in his books, lectures, and articles that the best way for parents to educate their children is to undertake the job themselves. Holt first broached his radical ideas in two books, How Children Fail (Pitman, 1964) and How Children Learn (Pitman, 1967), which he based on the diaries and letters he wrote during his fourteen years of teaching in elementary schools. His observations led him to conclude that the natural propensity of children to learn is often suppressed by teachers and educational institutions. Young people learn more effectively, Holt argued, when they are aided to pursue their own interests, unthreatened by such repressive appurtenances of conventional schools as tests, drills, and homework. His controversial views became enormously influential, and along with those of other educational reformers, helped to spark a widespread movement for "alternative" schools and methods.

By the mid-1970's, however, that movement had largely lost its momentum, and Holt lost hope that schools could be reformed from within. In his later books, such as Instead of Education (Dutton, 1974), he urged parents to protect their children from irrevocable harm by keeping them out of schools altogether. "Two things are wrong with the very notion of education," Holt once wrote. "First, it is seen as a process separate from all the rest of life; secondly, it is a process whereby one group of people do things to other groups of people, supposedly for their own good, and without getting their consent."

John Caldwell Holt was born in New York City on April 14, 1923, the son of Henry Holt, a wealthy insurance broker, and Elizabeth (Crocker) Holt. When John was a boy the family moved to the exclusive exurban preserve of New Canaan, Connecticut. Although he attended elite private schools—first Le Rosey in Switzerland and then Phillips Exeter, which he entered in 1936—education for him proved to be the discouraging experience that he believes it is for many children. He had taught himself to read when he was four or five years old, and by the usual definition, was a good student. "Well, I knew how to 'play the game,' so I never had any difficulty with school," he told an interviewer for the *Mother Earth News* (July/August 1980). "But I got bored with it as I got older, and by the time I reached high school I wouldn't read a book unless it had been assigned."

After graduating from Yale University with a degree in industrial engineering in 1943, Holt entered the United States Navy and served on the submarine *U.S.S. Barbero*. In his semi-autobiographical *Never Too Late; My Musical Life Story* (Delacorte, 1978) he has described his experiences on that submarine during World War II as the best learning community to which he has ever belonged. "I had a very unusual captain," Holt explained, "who believed in giving his youngest and most inexperienced officers—like me—a lot of responsibility right off the bat. . . . That was the first time anyone had ever put some real trust in me, and it was a very powerful educational experience."

When World War II ended, Holt moved to New York City. From 1946 until 1952 he worked for World Federalists, U.S.A., a group that advocated world government as the best way to prevent nuclear war, lecturing to Federalist chapters throughout New York State. In 1952 he spent a *Wanderjahr* in Europe and on his return found work at the newly established Colorado Rocky Mountain School in Carbondale, Colorado. At first he worked as a cook in exchange for his room and board, but eventually he was given a teaching job. Between 1953 and 1957 he taught English, French, and mathematics and coached soccer and baseball.

These early years of teaching profoundly influenced John Holt. For *Mother Earth News* he recalled: "On the whole, I was a perfectly conventional schoolmaster . . . who gave the high-school-aged students lots of tests and flunked my pupils right and left. The only difference between me and the average teacher was that—because I hadn't taken any education courses—I didn't know all the alibis that conventionally trained instructors use . . . excuses which imply that something's wrong with *students* who don't learn. I thought, if you can imagine such a simple-minded idea,

that if my pupils weren't grasping their lessons, it was my responsibility to figure out a way to explain the subject so that they *would* understand it!"

John Holt eventually concluded that "an awful lot of the youngsters did poorly in school because they *expected* to do poorly." With that in mind he moved to Cambridge, Massachusetts and began teaching in the fifth grade of the Shady Hill School, a select private school. There he discovered that even highly intelligent children acted "dumb" in class and were unable to perform simple math problems that had caused them no difficulty in the first or second grade. His unconventional methods of helping such children understand mathematics, rather than performing the usual drills, led Shady Hill to dismiss him in 1959. He then went to the Lesley Ellis School in Cambridge, where he taught fifth grade, developed mathematics curricula for grades one through six, and finally worked with beginning readers in the first and second grades.

Drawing upon letters he wrote during that period, and upon journal entries he recorded between 1958 and 1961, Holt, at the suggestion of a friend, wrote *How Children Fail*, which appeared in 1964. The experiences recounted in the book support Holt's contention that for children and young people, much of what goes on in school is boring, frightening, humiliating, confusing, and therefore oppressive, and that they quite naturally react by becoming poor students. Even when they do not, what they are really doing is "playing the game"—that is, learning how to give the answer the teacher wants, in order to win rewards, avoid punishment, and progress towards a "successful" future. According to Holt, the natural process of learning, which involves inquisitiveness and the challenging of established views, is crushed.

Not unexpectedly, reactions to *How Children Fail* were mixed. Most reviewers praised Holt's sensitivity, powers of observation, and description of the learning process, but some felt that his underlying prescription for radical changes in educational methods was exaggerated, if not totally misguided. "It is utopian, as Holt realizes," remarked Ronald Gross in *Book Week* (February 7, 1965). "But Holt's ideal school would hardly be desirable, even if it were practical. It is one thing to rule out adult pressure, but quite another to rule out adult direction and experience as well. . . . In what seems an excessive reaction against theories that didn't work, Holt overlooks the fact that some ideas and methods have an intellectual potency that children must master to appreciate." In his *Commonweal* review (June 11, 1965) Nat Hentoff also praised Holt's criticism of schools but objected to his "surprisingly cursory analysis of what can be done to arrest and reverse the mis-education of children."

From 1965 to 1967 Holt taught high school English at the Commonwealth School in Boston, and in 1967 he published his second book, *How Children Learn*. Like the earlier volume it consisted largely of stories about children, but this time it focused less on school than on the broad range of children's activities—their games, sports, conversations, problem-solving, reading, and so on. And the point Holt made was positive rather than negative, since the stories provided evidence that children, when left to their own devices, learn eagerly, efficiently, and happily. In Holt's view, children actively want to learn what is necessary for them to operate in the world, and their judgment about what to learn should be respected, for, by and large, "the things we most need to learn are the things we most want to learn." Adults can be most helpful by being patient and trusting, by opening new possibilities for the child, and by acting as a resource person when the child poses questions.

Although some reviewers again charged Holt with naïveté, the general response to *How Children Learn* was overwhelmingly favorable, and the book, like his first, sold well. Writing in the *Nation* (March 11, 1968), Chandler Brossard said the book "should be made required reading for every teacher in America (but of course it won't). . . . *How Children Learn*, like all first-rate books, is really about a great deal more than its stated subject. It is a calm, penetrating and extremely revealing examination of American mores, from top to bottom." In the *New York Review of Books* (January 18, 1968), the educator Herbert Kohl wrote: "*How Children Learn* is an important book. Not the least of the reasons for this is that it shows children learning without teachers. People accustomed to functioning in institutions where what is taught is of more concern than whether or how it is learned cannot conceive of this possibility."

By the late 1960's John Holt was being cited as a leading member of a movement of educational reformers with similar ideas, including such men as Jonathan Kozol, Herbert Kohl, Edgar Z. Friedenberg, Paul Goodman, and James Herndon. Their ideas suited the anti-authoritarian mood of the turbulent 1960's, and the counterculture adopted alternative schools and teaching methods as part of its political and cultural agenda.

With the success of *How Children Learn*, Holt found himself much in demand as a lecturer at schools and colleges throughout the United States, as well as in Canada, Mexico, and Europe. He served as visiting lecturer at the Harvard Graduate School of Education in the fall term of 1968, and as visiting lecturer at the University of California at Berkeley during the winter term of 1969. After the latter experience, he wrote an article for the New York *Times Magazine* (February 22, 1970) that sympathized with a student strike at Berkeley and called for open admissions at universities, among other reforms. The article brought a torrent of angry letters to the editor. Other articles by Holt have appeared in *Redbook*,

the *PTA Magazine, Harper's, Look, Life*, the *Atlantic Monthly*, and other publications. In 1969 some of his articles were brought together in a book, *The Underachieving School* (Pitman), and in the following year Dutton published the favorably reviewed *What Do I Do Monday?*, which reviewed the state of the school reform movement and demonstrated the abundance of resources available to teachers who wished to put Holt's theories into practice.

In 1969 John Holt made the first of several visits to the Intercultural Center of Documentation, Ivan Illich's controversial educational institute and discussion center on contemporary Latin American life and thought in Cuernavaca, Mexico. There, along with other intellectuals of all political persuasions from all over the world, he came under the influence of Illich's revolutionary stance on the "institutionalization" of society—his conviction that modern man has become too dependent on his large, centralized institutions.

That new direction in his thinking was reflected in Holt's next book, *Freedom and Beyond*, the first half of which consists of an analysis of freedom, authority, and choice. Then Holt goes on to envision a "de-schooled society," in which "nobody would be compelled to go to school, either by the law or by the threat of joblessness, poverty, discrimination, and exclusion from society, all of which are in force today. . . . It would be a society in which there were many paths to learning and advancement, instead of one school path as we have now—a path too narrow for everyone, and one too easily and too often blocked off from the poor." Among the added aids to learning would be more libraries, storefront reading centers, and the widespread use of cassette tapes.

Partly in order to pursue his passionate interest in playing the cello, Holt decided in 1973 to trim down his intensive schedule to no more than two lectures a week and resolved never to stay away from his home in Boston for more than two days at a time. One factor in his retrenchment may also have been his growing disillusionment with school reform, for with the subsiding of the social ferment of the 1960's, the movement for alternative schools began to fade and Holt was losing his enthusiasm for it. He told Richard Flaske in an interview for the New York *Times* (April 16, 1976) that for the most part the reform movement was "nonsense, foolishness," based on the mistaken belief, which he himself had shared, that the schools actually wanted to reform. Holt observed that in the United States "not two percent of the students were ever really touched by it—the schools didn't change an inch." Now, he went on, his advice to parents was to keep their children out of school: "Let all those escape it who can, anyway they can."

The valedictory book that according to Holt would be his last about schools was *Instead of Education; Ways to Help People to Do*

Things Better (Dutton, 1976), in which Holt declared that "Education, with its supporting system of compulsory and competitive schooling, all its carrots and sticks, its grades, diplomas, and credentials, now seems to me perhaps the most authoritarian and dangerous of all the social inventions of mankind." The brief and somewhat random essays in Instead of Education attacked conventional methods of schooling, proposed alternative methods based on home instruction and community-based learning centers, and advised parents on how to go about removing their children from school. Some reviews were negative, including that of Joseph Featherstone, who wrote in the New York Times Book Review (November 21, 1976) that "in its fervent simplicities, its sentimentality about children, its scorn for adults and ordinary teachers . . . and its exaggerated conception of the baleful capacity of education to tyrannize and enslave people [the book] reads like a caricature. Holt is a gifted observer of children's learning. Why has he wasted his time on this cranky tract?"

As a battle-hardened veteran of such controversy, Holt professed unconcern at hostile criticism and devoted himself to promoting what he calls the "home schooling" movement. Not long after the appearance of Instead of Education he began to publish a newsletter called Growing Without Schools, which, as he told the interviewer from the Mother Earth News, "describes materials and ideas that are useful to home schoolers, reports on the experiences of people who are already teaching their children at home, and provides a directory of others who can be contacted for advice." Growing Without Schools also reports on legal developments in cases involving the compulsory schooling laws that are in effect in most states.

In a kind of reconciliation of his two major interests, John Holt published Never Too Late; My Musical Life Story (Delacorte, 1978), in which he uses his lifelong passion for music and his joys and discouragements in playing various instruments to document his ideas about learning. Holt shows how fear of mistakes prevents us from learning, demonstrates how those fears are exacerbated by inept teachers, and points out that the fact that he took up the cello at the age of forty illustrates his conviction that, contrary to the popular maxim, "old dogs can learn new tricks." Among the reviewers who responded favorably to the warmth and candor of Never Too Late was A. J. Sherman, who recommended in Library Journal (September 15, 1978) that it be "required reading for parents who contemplate embarking upon or abandoning their child's musical education."

A bachelor, John Holt is a shy man with a somewhat pixyish face and a retreating hairline. He has taken up other skills besides the cello in his middle years: downhill skiing at thirty-one, water skiing at forty-seven, and strenuous horseback riding at forty-eight. In-terested in the ecology movement, especially as it relates to the development of natural and renewable forms of energy, he lists among his several works in progress in Contemporary Authors a book about space colonies. Holt, who is also the author of Escape from Childhood (Dutton, 1974), about the way American adults mistreat children as beings without rights, important desires, or serious opinions, has had his books published in many countries, including Great Britain, some nations in Western Europe, and Japan. In 1970 he was awarded an honorary degree from Wesleyan University but refused it on the ground that he is completely opposed to any form of academic degree and wishes that he could get rid of the ones he already has.

References: Mother Earth News p11+ Jl/Ag '80; N Y Times p54 Mr 25 '68; Time 90:37 S 1 '67 por; Contemporary Authors vols 69-72 (1978)

Hughes, Barnard

July 16, 1915- Actor. Address: h. 250 W. 94th St., New York City, N.Y. 10025

After nearly half a century of steady, dependable, fine work as a character actor on stage, screen, and television, Barnard Hughes reached the high point of his career as the cantankerous but lovable old Irish rascal who is the central character in Da, a portrayal that brought him a Tony Award as best actor on Broadway in the 1977-78 season. Hughes's other credits, which now total more than 400, range from the pathetic, whining aging homosexual brutalized by Joe Buck (Jon Voight) in one of the most memorable scenes of the motion picture *Midnight Cowboy* (1969) to many roles in New York Shakespeare Festival productions, including a highly acclaimed Dogberry in *Much Ado About Nothing* in 1972, and an Emmy-winning guest performance on *Lou Grant* in the 1977-78 television season. On October 7, 1981 he began to star as Max Merlin, a 1,600-year-old sorcerer, in the situation comedy *Mr. Merlin* on the CBS television network.

Barnard Hughes, the sixth of seven children, was born on July 16, 1915 on an estate in Bedford Hills, New York, where his father (who died when Hughes was fourteen) worked as a chauffeur. His parents, Owen and Madge (Kiernan) Hughes, had immigrated to the United States from Ireland. "I've always had a great feeling for Ireland and I have a lot of relatives over there," Hughes told Robert Berkvist of the New York *Times* (June 11, 1978). "God knows I'm no Irishman, but I do feel close to my family and traditions. It takes a long time to get the bog out of your system, I guess."

Hughes grew up in New York City, where he attended Our Lady of Good Counsel parochial school, LaSalle Academy, and Manhattan College (for one year). Inheriting a love of the theatre from his mother, he was a regular theatregoer from childhood. When he was nineteen a friend mischievously submitted his name for an audition after Hughes boasted that he would "give up acting" if he "couldn't do better" than a performance they had just seen. In response, Hughes received a note from director Frank Lee Short, who was putting together a traveling repertory company called the Shakespeare Fellowship, inviting him to appear for an audition, prepared to recite a memorized passage. Hughes went, recited Alexander Pope's poem "The Dying Christian to His Soul," and was hired. He made his stage debut in October 1934 as the haberdasher in *The Taming of the Shrew*.

The Shakespeare Fellowship toured schools, church basements, community centers, and country clubs in the New York area. "We worked with prompt books that Booth and Barrett had used," Hughes recounted in an interview with Jennifer Dunning for the New York *Times* (July 25, 1979). "Short expected the men to know all the men's parts, and the women all the women's, and we played them all on consecutive nights if the old man was in a bad mood. We learned to ad lib in rhymed couplets." During his two years with the Shakespeare Fellowship, Hughes supplemented his salary as an actor (two dollars a performance) by working as proofreader for a law office. After leaving the Shakespeare Fellowship, Hughes continued his theatrical apprenticeship by working in summer stock and touring with other repertory companies. "I never had any formal acting lessons, but I

[was] lucky enough to work with some very good people," he commented to Robert Berkvist in the New York *Times* interview. "And I was always able to apply what I'd learned right away, for the next audience."

Hughes made his Broadway debut in a bit part in *The Cat and the Canary* at the Majestic Theatre on June 14, 1937, and he returned to Broadway two seasons later in the role of Joe in *Please, Mrs. Garibaldi* at the Belmont Theatre. In November 1939 he appeared in the pre-Broadway tryout of *Herself, Mrs. Patrick Crowley* in Wilmington, Delaware. After service in the United States Army in World War II, he toured military hospitals in a show called *Laugh That Off*. In New York, he played Martin in *The Ivy Green* at the Lyceum Theatre in 1949 and Clancy in *Dinosaur Wharf* at the National in 1951. Between 1949 and 1954 he had a variety of roles in numerous productions at the Tenthouse Theatre in Highland Park, Illinois.

With his characteristic wry humor, Hughes has remarked that there was a period when he was in his forties when a large proportion of his roles could have been played "without pants." "I was always sitting behind something like a desk. I was a judge, or a businessman, or a lawyer, or a doctor," he recalled in the New York *Times* interview with Robert Berkvist. "Nobody ever saw my bottom half." From 1954 to 1956 he toured as Captain McLean in the national company of the Broadway hit *Teahouse of the August Moon*. His stage credits in the years following included Major Jappolo in *A Bell for Adano*, T. J. in *Home of the Brave*, Lantry in *The Will and the Way*, Doctor Genoni in *Enrico*, Peter Mortensgaard in *Rosmersholm* and Nils Krogstad in *A Doll's House*. On Broadway, he was Inspector Norcross in *A Majority of One* at the Sam S. Shubert Theatre in 1959, Senator Tom August in *Advise and Consent* at the Cort in 1960, the Governor in *The Advocate* at the ANTA in 1963, Bert Howell in *Nobody Loves an Albatross* at the Lyceum in 1963, both Marcellus and the Priest in John Gielgud's production of *Hamlet* at the Lunt-Fontanne in 1964, and Father Frank Feeley in *I Was Dancing* at the Lyceum in 1964.

In his vigorous portrayal of Father Stanislaus Coyne, a Brooklyn parish priest in *Hogan's Goat*, a hit of the 1965-66 Off-Broadway season, Hughes made "Catholic morality a force and a benediction," as Norman Nadel of the New York *World-Telegram and Sun* (November 12, 1965) noted. During the run of *Hogan's Goat*, Hughes understudied Henry Fonda as Jim Bolton in *Generation* on Broadway, and in August 1966 he replaced Robert Young in the role of Bolton on tour. Back on Broadway, he was Senator McFetridge in the musical comedy *How Now, Dow Jones* at the Lunt-Fontanne Theatre in 1967, Judge Belknap in *The Wrong Way Light Bulb* at the Golden in 1969, and General Fitzhugh in *Sheep on the Runway* at the Helen Hayes in 1970.

At the Theatre de Lys in Greenwich Village in February 1971 Hughes played the husband, Arnall, in *Line*. At the Brooks Atkinson Theatre later in the same year he was, in the judgment of Brendan Gill of the *New Yorker* (March 20, 1971), "splendid" as the sadistically vengeful Fulbert in *Abelard and Heloise*. He appeared as Alexander Serebryakov in *Uncle Vanya* at the Circle in the Square-Joseph E. Levine Theatre in 1972 and he played several roles in *Older People* at the Public and Anspacher theatres in 1972 and in *The Good Doctor* at the Eugene O'Neill in 1973.

In the early 1970's Hughes had roles in several productions of Joseph Papp's New York Shakespeare Festival, including those of Falstaff in *The Merry Wives of Windsor* and Gower in *Pericles, Prince of Tyre*. Allan Wallach of *Newsday* (June 30, 1972) was among the critics who found him "enormously funny" when he played Polonius to Stacy Keach's Hamlet in a festival production of *Hamlet* in 1972. His most acclaimed festival performance was as the buffoon Chief Constable Dogberry in director A. J. Antoon's celebrated imaginative updating of *Much Ado About Nothing*, a production that opened at the open-air Delacorte Theatre in Central Park in August 1972, moved to the Winter Garden on Broadway in November, and was filmed for presentation on the CBS television network in 1973. For his portrayal of Dogberry, Hughes won the Clair Bayfield Award and was nominated for a Tony Award.

In other stage roles in the 1970's, Hughes was the Voice in *Edgar Allan Poe* at Alice Tully Hall in 1973, Dr. Lionel Morris in *All Over Town* at the Booth Theatre in 1974, and Jeeter Lester in a summer stock production of *Tobacco Road* in Chicago in 1977. As Parson Anderson in a production of George Bernard Shaw's *The Devil's Disciple* at the Brooklyn Academy of Music in February 1978, he was, according to Clive Barnes of the New York *Post* (February 9, 1978) "miscast," but he "made the bluff best of it." Edith Oliver, writing in the *New Yorker* (February 20, 1978), described his performance as "quietly solid," making "credible the metamorphosis from clergyman to rebel soldier." Hughes himself confessed that the role of Anderson "didn't sit as well on [his] shoulders as some others [he had] played."

Among Hughes's early motion picture credits was a role in *Play Girl* (RKO, 1941), and he was Dr. Kent O'Donnell in *The Young Doctors* (United Artists, 1961), starring Frederic March and Ben Gazzara. In *Midnight Cowboy* (United Artists, 1969), he played the homosexual tourist robbed and beaten by the hustling title character (Jon Voight), and he portrayed Dr. Procter, the frantic local physician, in *Cold Turkey* (United Artists, 1971), a farce about a greedy town trying to quit smoking *en masse* in order to win $25,000,000. He portrayed the berserk patient Drummond in the cynically satirical *The Hospital* (United Artists, 1971),

and he had supporting roles in *Where's Poppa?* (United Artists, 1970), *Rage* (Warner Brothers, 1972), and *Sisters* (American International, 1973).

Hughes first appeared on television as Bob Cratchit in a production of *A Christmas Carol* in 1946. He subsequently had roles in dramatic presentations or episodes of *Robert Montgomery Presents* (NBC), *The Defenders* (CBS), *Naked City* (ABC), *U.S. Steel Hour* (ABC), *The Trials of O'Brien* (CBS), *The Catholic Hour* (NBC), *You Are There* (CBS), *NET Playhouse* (NET), *The Bob Newhart Show* (CBS), *Playhouse 90* (CBS), and the *CBS Playhouse* (CBS). In addition, he appeared in the dramatic specials *All the Way Home* (CBS, 1971), *The Thanksgiving Treasure* (CBS, 1973), *The Borrowers* (NBC, 1973), and he had several regular daytime serial roles, including that of Dr. Bruce Banning on *The Guiding Light* (CBS). In the 1971-72 and 1972-73 seasons he made several appearances on the situation comedy *All in the Family* (CBS) as Father Majeski, an "ethnic" foil for the bigoted Archie Bunker. Among his made-for-TV movie credits were *The UFO Incident* (ABC, 1975) and *Sanctuary of Fear* (NBC, 1979). The latter film, in which he starred, was based on G. K. Chesterton's Father Brown detective stories and was the pilot for a prospective series that never materialized. In September 1978 the Academy of Television Arts and Sciences awarded Hughes an Emmy for outstanding lead actor for a single appearance in a drama series, for his role as a judge in *Lou Grant* (CBS).

Hughes's major sustained television role was the title part in *Doc*, a situation comedy about a kindly, old-fashioned physician practising medicine in New York City that aired on CBS from August 1975 to October 1976. Of *Doc*, Hughes told Robert Christiansen in the Chicago *Tribune* interview: "I was absolutely delighted with it, and we were a modest hit in the ratings. Then Fred Silverman [the programming executive], who had been my friend in court, left CBS for ABC; and the next season they tried to widen the spectrum of viewers by killing off my wife in the series, moving my seven children out of town and out of the show, and putting me into a storefront clinic. So in trying for a larger audience, we lost all the people from thirty-eight to sixty-five who had been loyal viewers."

During a hiatus in the taping of *Doc*, Hughes, visiting his agent's office in New York City, for the first time saw the script of *Da*, a play representing a young Irishman's confrontation and eventual reconciliation with the ghost of his dead father and the shades of his own past. Actually, the play is about Hugh Leonard's own father and, in Leonard's words, is "an attempt to know him better and also to be a modest memorial to a man who, by the world's standards, was so insignificant that even the date on his gravestone was incorrect." The play, set in Ireland, was based in part on events in the elder Leonard's life.

As soon as Hughes read *Da,* he knew that it was "gold" and that it was for him. He took an option on it (an unusual step for him), and when his other commitments were out of the way, he turned his attention to it. With him in the title role (which he played with an authentic-sounding Dublin accent and not the soft brogue of his own parents) *Da* opened Off Broadway, at the Hudson Guild Theatre, early in 1978. The Hudson Guild production was planned as a brief month-long showcase only, but the critics embraced it, and *Da* moved to Broadway in May 1978.

Typical of the plaudits bestowed on *Da* was that of Mel Gussow in the New York *Times* (May 2, 1978). Of the play, Gussow wrote: "Warmly but unsentimentally, it concerns itself with paternity, adolescence, the varieties of familial love and the tricks and distortions of memory. In a class with the best of Sean O'Casey, it is steeped in Irish language, laughter and atmosphere." And of Hughes's performance he observed: "He takes a most ordinary man—who, issuing platitudes, blithely accepts the limits of his life—and makes him lovable to his sardonic son and to the audience. Mr. Hughes' success is complete: his Da is endearing." Hugh Leonard himself wrote that it was not until he saw Hughes in *Da* that he "realized what not one critic has ever said and which is on the stage for all—including myself—to see: that in his entire life, my 'da' never had one egotistical or self-serving thought."

The New York Drama Critics Circle and the Outer Critics Circle both named *Da* the best play of the 1977-78 season, and the Outer Critics Circle also honored Hughes for his performance. *Da* also won the Antoinette Perry (Tony) Award for best play, and three other Tony awards as well, including one for Hughes as best actor. After playing in *Da* in New York City for more than a year, Hughes turned the Broadway role over to Brian Keith and headed a new company in a year-long national tour in 1979-80.

Hughes had another choice Irish role in Brian Friel's *Translations* at the Manhattan Theater Club in April 1981. The theme of that play, set in the Irish hamlet of Baile Beag in 1833, was linguistic imperialism. As Frank Rich observed in the New York *Times* (April 15, 1981), Hughes's portrayal of a rustic schoolmaster was "no retread of the cuddly Irish patriarch" in *Da.* "Wearing a moth-eaten frock coat and pants that seem to be woven of peat moss . . . he wanders dazedly about quoting the classics, stealing swigs from a flask and vainly trying to accommodate himself to the 'inevitabilities' of his country's future. Funny as he is, Mr. Hughes always turns his eyes sadly downward, as if he's surveying the defeated landscape of his own soul."

Mr. Merlin had its premiere on CBS-TV on October 7, 1981. Marvin Kitman, writing in *Newsday* on the same date, expressed his dis-like of the show ("It gives wholesomeness a bad name"), but he gave Hughes a backhanded compliment in observing that the "distinguished comedic actor" played the latter-day sorcerer-with-an-apprentice "without his usual quiet, creaky gusto." That gusto was evident, however, in Hughes's sprightly supporting portrayal of the Chief Justice of the Supreme Court in the film version of Jerome Lawrence and Robert E. Lee's comedy *First Monday in October* (Paramount, 1981).

Barnard Hughes and Helen Stenborg, an actress who has shared the stage with him in some hundred productions over the years, were married on April 19, 1950. They have two children, Douglas, a theatrical director, and Laura, an actress. With his wife and their dog, Flicka, Hughes lives in a co-op apartment in an unfashionable neighborhood on Manhattan's Upper West Side, and he usually commutes to the theater by subway.

To be an actor, Hughes has said, you must have "some intelligence" and "good coordination" and you "have to believe in the make-believe." It also helps to have "a point of view, not only about the part, but also about something personal and important to the actor." In his approach to acting, Hughes describes himself as a "feeler" rather than a "thinker," although lately he has "come to appreciate second and third thoughts" about a role. His advice to aspiring actors includes the admonitions to keep a role "down to bare essentials" and to have a healthy respect for props, which can come to the rescue in a crisis. Above all, he advises a concentration on craft. "Today, a lot of youngsters go into it for the life-style. . . . I never cared about the life-style. It's the work, only the work."

Out of costume, Hughes is an amiable, chatty man with bright, bespectacled gray-blue eyes under mobile eyebrows, a bald pate, and a slight paunch. According to his wife, he "reads cookbooks like novels," and he helped in the raising of the children more than might have been expected from a man of his generation. A pretzel bought from a street vendor always hangs above the mirror in his dressing room, because the Hugheses give each other pretzels on opening nights in the same way the Barrymores used to give each other apples. Although he claims he is not superstitious, Hughes goes through a precise routine before every performance. The routine begins with the recitation of a favorite "childish prayer" of his in the dressing room and ends with his touching two ladders in the wings. "Two. Not one," he has pointed out. "And then I go out."

References: Chicago Tribune VI p10+ N 18 '77 pors; N Y Times II p1+ Je 11 '78 por; People 9:39+ Je 26 '78 pors; Kalter, Joanmarie. *Actors on Acting* (1979); *Notable Names in the American Theatre* (1976); *Who's Who in America, 1980-81; Who's Who in the Theatre* (1977)

Huppert, Isabelle (up-âr')

Mar. 16, 1955- Actress. Address: b.
17 Hoche Ave., Paris, France 75008

By the time she was twenty-five years old, Isabelle Huppert had made more than two dozen films, but she did not attract public attention until the release, in 1977, of *La dentellière* (*The Lacemaker*), her seventeenth screen credit. Since then, her markedly personal interpretations of a variety of roles ranging from ingenues to prostitutes have won her critical acclaim and a worldwide following. Her portrayal of the self-possessed Violette Nozière in Claude Chabrol's chilling motion picture of the same name earned her a share in the best actress award at the 1978 Cannes Film Festival and the César Prize. David Denby, the critic, ascribes her special appeal to the peculiarly French ideal of "woman as beautiful, mysterious object—a still life with a haughty soul."

Isabelle Anne Huppert was born on March 16, 1955 in Paris, France, the youngest of the four children of middle-class Hungarian emigrés. Her father, Raymond Huppert, was a manufacturer of safes; her mother, Annick (Beau) Huppert, an English teacher. She was reared in Ville-d'Avray on the outskirts of Paris with her three older sisters, Carol, Jacqueline, and Élisabeth. Élisabeth Huppert, a writer and actress, is the author of the novels *L'homme-chewinggum et la femme ventre* (1976) and *La terrasse; ou, Le temps d'une chute* (1973).

After graduating from the Lycée de St. Cloud, Isabelle Huppert enrolled in a Russian studies program at a university in Paris. While a student there, she occasionally took bit parts in televised dramatic productions. She eventually became so interested in the craft of acting that, with her parents' approval, she transferred to the prestigious Conservatoire National d'Art Dramatique in Paris. In 1971 she landed a small part in *Faustine et le bel été* (*Faustine and the Beautiful Summer*), a sentimental film about a teenager's first love that was written and directed by Nina Companeez. The following year she appeared in Claude Sautet's romantic *César et Rosalie* (*César and Rosalie*), which starred Romy Schneider and Yves Montand, and in 1973, she had a small part in Rachel Weinberg's *L'Ampelopède*. "I never had to audition or screen-test much," she told Stephen Harvey in an interview for the New York *Times* (November 16, 1980). "Once you're working and they know you and your work, other things follow."

Miss Huppert's next motion picture, *Les valseuses* (*Going Places*), which was released in 1974, proved to be one of the most popular and controversial films of the year in both France and the United States. Directed by Bertrand Blier and starring Gérard Depardieu and Patrick Dewaere as a pair of brutish nihilists, *Les valseuses* spoke to and for an alienated younger generation. Miss Huppert played Jacqueline, an impressionable teenager who deserts her parents during a family vacation to take to the road with two young vagabonds. Some American critics, including Rex Reed and Judith Crist, objected to what they saw as the film's sadistic amorality; others, among them Stanley Kauffmann and Gary Arnold, thought that it was as seminal and influential as Jean-Luc Godard's classic *A bout de souffle* (*Breathless*).

Several films followed in quick succession: *Aloïse*, directed by Liliane de Kermadec, *DuPont la joie*, *Sérieux comme le plaisir* (As Serious as Pleasure), *Le grand délire* (The Big Delirium), *Docteur Françoise Gaillard* (No Time For Breakfast), *Je suis Pierre Rivière* (I Am Pierre Rivière), *Le petit Marcel* (Little Marcel), Bertrand Tavernier's *Le juge et l'assassin* (The Judge and the Assassin), and Otto Preminger's well-made but lethargic melodrama *Rosebud* (United Artists, 1975). Although most of those films were only moderately successful at the box office, Miss Huppert's accomplished performances won her the admiration of film makers and audiences alike.

Claude Goretta's *La dentellière* (The Lacemaker), the touching story of an inarticulate and withdrawn young girl who is shattered by a disastrous love affair, was a perfect vehicle for Miss Huppert. An untutored hairdresser's assistant, Béatrice, or "Pomme," falls in love with an intellectual university student from an upper-class family. Pomme's whole life revolves around François, and when the young man, inevitably exasperated by her ignorance and passivity, finally leaves her, she suffers a nervous breakdown and is institutionalized.

Before stepping in front of the camera, Miss Huppert, as is her custom, came up with what she has called a "visual key" to her character —in the case of Pomme, her small, flat shoes. "I try to give a different physical appearance to each character from the ones I did before," she explained to Stephen Harvey in an interview for the New York *Times* (November 16, 1980). "You look for an image . . . to express the psychology of the part. Fifty percent of your work is done when you can begin with this—the way she wears her hair, the way she moves and walks. . . . I start by thinking about what might have happened to the character before the story began, and this preparation helps you to work on what's underneath—the unseen part which has to be very much built into your mind."

Most American critics, like their European counterparts, were moved by Isabelle Huppert's reticent and understated portrayal of the doomed girl. In his review for the New York *Times* (October 6, 1977), Vincent Canby observed, "Miss Huppert is all too believable as a figure of idealized innocence who would drive any ordinary man out of his mind with boredom and then, in a final irony, leave him feeling guilty for not having sufficiently appreciated the rare gift that briefly had been his." Although she agreed that Isabelle Huppert was "extraordinarily expressive" within the "mute and painterly perfection of her role," Molly Haskell felt that she had been "manipulated" by the director. Pomme "is like a china doll who has been placed, quite consciously, on the edge of a mantelpiece so that the slightest breeze will bring her tumbling, crashing down," Miss Haskell wrote in her review of the *La dentellière* for *New York* magazine (November 7, 1977). "When the crackup comes, it has been too carefully engineered to touch us deeply." For her performance in *The Lacemaker*, Miss Huppert was awarded the Suzanne Blanchetti Prize in France, and she was voted the "Most Promising Newcomer" of the year by the British Academy of Motion Pictures.

From *La dentellière*, Isabelle Huppert turned briefly to the stage, appearing in a production of the play *On ne badine pas avec l'amour* (You Don't Fool Around With Love) in June 1977. Her next screen credit was a small role in *Les indiens sont encore loin* (The Indians Are Still Far Away), which was directed by Patricia Moraz. For her second starring role, she chose *Violette Nozière*, Claude Chabrol's meticulous re-creation of a notorious 1933 French murder case. Leading a double life, eighteen-year-old Violette is an innocent school-girl during the day, a street-hardened prostitute at night. When she contracts syphilis, she persuades her gullible parents that the disease is hereditary and prevails upon them to take some medicine, which is actually poison. Her mother, who survives the murder attempt, presses charges, but in the end forgives her daughter.

Isabelle Huppert invested Violette with a lowering intensity that suggested, in the words of *Time* critic John Skow, "endlessly watchable depths." "I'm fascinated by the sort of person who offers a certain appearance and behind it there hides something contradictory," the actress told Dan Yakir in an interview for an *After Dark* profile (October 1980). "Modern passions are invisible. You may see their expression in crime, but the feelings remain hidden." Critics greeted the film's 1978 American release, under the abbreviated title *Violette*, with mixed reviews, but for Miss Huppert there was unreserved praise.

Firmly established as a box-office draw in France, Miss Huppert went on to make *Retour à la bien aimée* (Return to the Beloved), directed by Jean François Adam, and André Techine's *Les soeurs Brontë* (The Brontë Sisters), in which she costarred with Isabelle Adjani and Marie-France Pisier. Despite its high-powered cast, *Les soeurs Brontë* fared so poorly in Europe that it has not yet been released in the United States. Isabelle Huppert has attributed the film's disappointing showing to Techine's "cerebral" style. "It's a fault of many French directors maybe to be more theoretical than pragmatic," she told one reporter.

After seeing just ten minutes of *Violette*, Michael Cimino, the Oscar-winning director of *The Deer Hunter*, decided to offer Isabelle Huppert the part of Ella, the French immigrant bordello keeper, in his new film *Heaven's Gate*, an overproduced western based on the Johnson County (Wyoming) war of the early 1890's, in which wealthy cattlemen drove immigrant farmers from the territory. Miss Huppert described her character as a "strong" and "matter-of-fact" woman, a "survivor" who understands and accepts the ambiguity of her relationship with the two heroes, played by Kris Kristofferson and Christopher Walken.

When *Heaven's Gate* (United Artists) was released to a fanfare of publicity in 1980, it was condemned by the critics as "an unqualified disaster." Stunned by damning reviews, Cimino withdrew the film for recutting, but the shorter, tighter version, released in April 1981, did no better at the box office. In several interviews, Miss Huppert has defended Cimino's work. "[Heaven's Gate] operates always on three levels, the historical, the political, and the psychological," she explained to Stephen Harvey. "It's a kind of denunciation of certain Western values—the importance of power and money—followed by the rise of other, more feminine values—more human and concrete. A film is alway political in a sense," she went on, "because politics really means the way people live together and relate to each other. Films are never abstracted from this, as long as they deal with human beings in a real way. But *Heaven's Gate* deals with this in a more conscious way."

As Isabelle Huppert's first American motion picture, *Heaven's Gate* represented "a kind of parenthesis" in her career, to quote her. Her other releases in 1980—*Loulou* and *Sauve* qui peut la vie (Every Man For Himself)—were considerably more successful. In *Loulou*, Maurice Pialat examines "the difficulty of passing from one universe to another," to use Miss Huppert's words. She played Nelly, a bored, upper-class housewife who leaves her humorless husband for a lovable scoundrel, portrayed by Gérard Depardieu. While some critics thought that *Loulou* lacked substance, most agreed that the film was unusually entertaining to watch, mainly because of the "magnetic" personalities of the two stars. Miss Huppert was singled out by several reviewers for her uncommon ability to "be ordinary without being lifeless."

In *Sauve qui peut la vie*, Jean-Luc Godard's long-awaited return to commercial film-making, Miss Huppert took the part of Isabelle, a proud country girl turned city prostitute. She eventually becomes involved with a restless television producer named Godard (Jacques Dutronc) and his disgruntled mistress, Denise Rimbaud (Nathalie Baye). Caught in a world of sexual fantasy, alienation, and male domination, she remains cooly aloof and thus achieves a kind of heroic stature. "Godard told me he wanted my character to be the image of suffering . . . ," Miss Huppert told Dan Yakir in the *After Dark* interview. "It's about what he has always said in his films, that love is impossible and that all relationships are based on violence, sex, money, and power. There's a note of despair in his belief that one has to react but can't really do much. I personally think of my character as being in the tradition of Anna Karina in *Vivre sa vie* and Macha Méril in *A Married Woman*. These characters remain very innocent and almost indifferent amidst incredibly difficult situations."

For Vincent Canby, *Sauve qui peut la vie* turned out to be "a process of discovery." In his enthusiastic review for the New York *Times* (October 8, 1980), Canby spoke for the majority of his colleagues: "The actors are so much a part of the texture of the film that they can't be easily separated as performers' performances. [The film] is a single seamless endeavor, a stunning original work about which there is still a lot to say, but there's time. I trust it will outlive us all."

Throughout her career, Miss Huppert has been especially attracted by roles that allow her to express "the ambiguity" of feminity. "I would like to project both things on the screen—the mystery of woman and the real, practical side, the ability to handle all situations," she said in her interview with Harvey for the New York *Times*. Miss Huppert's most recent films have afforded her that opportunity. She played the title role of the consumptive courtesan in an Italian production based on *La dame aux camélias* and a surrogate mother in Marta Meszaros' bleak tale about life in Hungary during World War II, and she co-starred with Dominique Sanda in a film adaptation of Henry James's novel *The Wings of the Dove*.

Isabelle Huppert is a slender, diminutive woman with long red hair, green eyes, and the freckled face of "a shrewd but innocent French country girl," to use the words of John Simon, the critic. For relaxation she reads, listens to music, or goes to the movies. Passionately interested in her chosen field, she animatedly discusses cinema history with interviewers. Her crowded schedule leaves little time for socializing. "Sometimes I feel I don't have enough time to just live," she admitted to Dan Yakir. "There must be a reason why I chose acting, but I also feel a need to stop, to take a vacation, do something 'normal.' I'm always being productive. I haven't stopped in two years, and maybe I capitalize too much on my person." Miss Huppert makes her home in Paris.

References: After Dark 13:44+ O '80 pors; N Y Times II p15 N 16 '80 por; New York 13:31+ O 6 '80 por; Katz, Ephraim. The Film Encyclopedia (1979); Who's Who in France, 1980-81

Hussein, Saddam (al-Tikriti)

Apr. 28, 1937- President of Iraq. Address: b. Revolutionary Command Council, Baghdad, Iraq

A leading candidate for the position once occupied by the late Gamal Abdel Nasser as the dominant political personality in the Middle East, Iraqi President Saddam Hussein arrived at his present power through the route of student activism, exile, and imprisonment. As the second in command in the government of President Ahmed Hassan al-Bakr, who took office in 1968, Hussein from the beginning held the reins of power, and his position was formalized when he took over the Presidency in July 1979. While heading his rigidly repressive regime, Hussein managed to apply Iraq's vast petroleum wealth to leading his country of some 13,000,000 people out of the morass of poverty. At the same time he tried to establish it as a formidable member of the family of nations. A Rand Corporation report published shortly after Hussein launched Iraq's military attack on Iran, and quoted in *Newsweek* (October 6, 1980), concluded that Iraq under Hussein sought nothing less than "hegemony in the Persian Gulf and perhaps throughout the Middle East, inevitably at the expense of both superpowers."

The son of peasants, Saddam Hussein al-Tikriti (transliterated from the Arabic, his family name is sometimes given as Hossein, Husain, or Husayn) was born on April 28, 1937 in a village adjacent to the town of Tikrit (or Takrit)—the birthplace of the famed twelfth-century sultan Saladin—on the banks of the Tigris, some 100 miles north of Baghdad. A number of his future political associates in the drive toward pan-Arab unity and socialism came from his native region and have been termed the "Tikriti Mafia." Orphaned at an early age, Hussein spent much of his boyhood in the pastoral environment of a melon farm owned by an uncle who was a devout member of the Sunni branch of the Muslim faith. At the age of nine he entered primary school in Tikrit.

Isolated from the mainstream of world events, Hussein nevertheless became aware at an early age of the effects of British domination of Iraq in the decades after World War I. The economic depression suffered by Tikrit when its native textiles and leather goods industry was supplanted by British imports helped to turn that town into a hotbed of political and intellectual ferment. Hussein's maternal uncle Khairallah Talfah, an army officer, took part in the ill-fated 1941 uprising led by Rashid Ali al-Gailani against Iraq's British-controlled monarchy. Talfah's dismissal from the military and his arrest after the failure of the coup added to the family's grievances against the British and helped to motivate Hussein to take part in nationalist activities aimed at eliminating foreign influences from the Arab world.

In the fall of 1955 Hussein left Tikrit and went to Baghdad to continue his studies at the al-Karkh secondary school, one of the incubators of student nationalist activity. While there he became involved in the Arab Baath Socialist party, and in late 1956 he took part in a coup attempt against King Faisal II and Prime Minister Nuri as-Said that, although abortive, was a landmark in the party's drive to power. In 1957 Hussein formally became a member of the Baath party. After the Iraqi monarchy was overthrown and King Faisal killed in July 1958

in a coup headed by military strongman Abdul Karim Kassem, the Baath party fared no better than it had under the old regime. To keep the pan-Arab nationalists of the Baath movement in check, Kassem allied himself with their bitter rivals, the Moscow-oriented Communists.

Hussein was one of ten young men chosen by the Baath leadership to assassinate Kassem, who as Iraq's Prime Minister exercised virtually absolute control. In October 1959 Hussein and his comrades ambushed Kassem's station wagon, killing the driver and an aide, but missing the dictator. Most of the participants in the attempt were caught, but Hussein, although suffering a leg wound, managed to escape, cutting out the bullet with a pen-knife. Sentenced to death in absentia, Hussein fled Iraq in disguise by way of his hometown and made his way to Syria by riding a donkey across the desert. His arrival at the Syrian frontier came to the attention of Egyptian President Gamal Abdel Nasser, who had heard of his role in the plot against Kassem and arranged for his passage to Cairo. Settling in the community of exiles from Arab countries, Hussein was profoundly influenced by the revolutionary rhetoric of Nasser, whose aim was the creation of an independent Arab realm from "the Atlantic to the Gulf," free from all Western control. Continuing his education with the help of an Egyptian government stipend, Hussein graduated from al-Qasr al-Aini secondary school in Cairo in 1961. He joined the leadership of the Cairo unit of the Baath party in the following year and entered the University of Cairo law school in the fall of 1962.

Following the overthrow and execution of Kassem in February 1963 and the formation of a new government under Baath party leadership, Hussein returned to Baghdad and became actively involved in the party's affairs, taking part in its fourth regional and sixth national congress that year. He also resumed his education with the study of law at Baghdad's al-Mustansiriyah University. When the Baath regime was overthrown later in 1963, Hussein went underground for a year, and sometime during 1964 he was in Syria as a member of the party's seventh national congress. Tracked down by the authorities in November 1964, he tried to fight them off until his ammunition ran out, then spent two years in prison, where he continued his law studies. In 1965, while still in prison, Hussein was elected to the leadership of the Baath party's eighth national congress, and in 1966 he became deputy secretary of the party's regional leadership. After his escape from imprisonment, he went underground once more, concentrating his efforts on a thorough reorganization of the Baath party into an effective revolutionary tool and writing propaganda tracts that helped to establish an ideological basis for the revolution.

It was the party militia organized by Hussein that played the major role in bringing the Baath party into undisputed power in a bloodless coup in July 1968. Although the elder statesman and head of the party's military wing, Major General Ahmed Hassan al-Bakr, formally headed the state as President and chairman of the ruling five-member Revolutionary Command Council, the real power seems to have resided from the beginning in his second in command, Hussein, a distant relative from his hometown, who was his secretary and the acting deputy chairman of the Revolutionary Command Council. Hussein became deputy chairman in 1969.

The two leaders of the new regime complemented each other, with Bakr overseeing the fundamentals of government and Hussein concentrating on its details. To enhance his academic stature, Hussein continued his law studies in Baghdad even after coming to power, but his attainment of academic honors appears to have been of dubious validity. According to Patrick Seale of the London *Observer* (September 28, 1980), "In 1969 he added a law degree to his other honors by the simple expedient of turning up in the examination hall with a pistol in his belt and accompanied by four armed bodyguards. The examiners got the point." While stressing the civilian nature of the regime to a population that on the basis of past experiences distrusted military authoritarianism, Hussein tried at the same time to improve his standing with the armed forces by taking on military honors. In 1973 he received the rank of lieutenant general and was awarded Iraq's highest military decoration, the Rafidain Order in the first category. Three years later he persuaded Bakr to make him a full general, retroactive to 1973, thus giving him seniority over all other generals. Also in 1976, Hussein was decorated with the military staff signal and obtained an honorary M.S. degree in military sciences.

In view of the considerable opposition to the Bakr-Hussein regime, the rulers from the beginning maintained a strict authoritarianism. Although Hussein asserted that the ultimate aim of the government, in line with Baath party philosophy, was the eventual establishment of democratic rule, he insisted that progress must first be made in economic and social development and the attainment of some measure of Arab unity. Periodically faced with subversion and coup attempts—culminating in an abortive effort by the internal security chief, Colonel Nazem Kazzar, in June 1973, to assassinate Bakr and Hussein and seize the government—the leaders responded with mass executions and other repressive measures that caused Amnesty International to classify Iraq among the worst violators of human rights.

Meanwhile, the government took strong measures to revitalize Iraq's stagnant economy and to make the country more self-sufficient. A five-year economic development plan initiated in 1970 aimed at freeing Iraq from dependence on foreign oil interests and projected a substantial growth in the gross national product and per capita income. In 1972 Hussein began the nationalization of the Iraq Petroleum Company, a consortium of American, British, Dutch, and French firms that produced about 10 percent of Mideastern oil. With increased production that made Iraq the second-largest oil producer in the Middle East by the mid-1970's—exceeded only by Saudi Arabia—Hussein was able to launch ambitious social and educational programs and to invest heavily in such projects as agricultural modernization, rural electrification, water purification, and the construction of highways, housing, and hospitals, as well as steel, cement, petrochemical, and printing plants. A massive compulsory literacy program was started in 1978, and higher education aimed at the creation of a "new technological Arab generation."

On the international level, Iraq under Bakr and Hussein wavered between East and West. Although anxious to benefit from Western technology, it was more closely related ideologically to the Soviet bloc. Khalid Kishtainy, who translated some of Hussein's writings and speeches, referred to him in 1979 as a Marxist who is "obsessed with the dynamic change of society and dialectical appreciation of history" but who makes no reference to Marx or to Marxist terminology. In February 1972 Hussein made a visit to Moscow that paved the way to the conclusion of a fifteen-year treaty of friendship and cooperation between Iraq and the U.S.S.R., and in the years that followed, the Soviet Union was Iraq's chief supplier of armaments. Furthermore, Iraq's pro-Soviet Communist party was included with the Baath party in the country's National Progressive Front coalition established in the summer of 1973. Nevertheless, friction arose between the two nations on a number of issues and reached its height when Hussein in May 1978 ordered the execution of twenty-one Communist members of the armed forces on charges of subversion.

One of the most militant of the so-called "rejectionist" states, Iraq steadfastly opposed accommodation with Israel, and following the 1967 six-day war it had no diplomatic relations with the United States because of American support for the Jewish state. In October 1973 the Iraqi government sent 18,000 troops to the Syrian front in the Arab war against Israel and nationalized the properties of two American oil companies, Exxon and Mobil, on Iraqi soil. Nevertheless, trade between the United States and Iraq steadily increased during the 1970's, and Hussein indicated on several occasions a desire to normalize relations.

Largely as a result of Hussein's diplomatic efforts, Iraq reached accommodation in the mid-1970's with its conservative neighbors, notably Saudi Arabia, Kuwait, and the Gulf Emirates. Its long-standing conflict with neighboring Iran was temporarily defused in the spring of 1975, when Hussein and Shah Mohammed Riza Pahlevi signed a treaty of reconciliation eliminating matters of dispute between the two nations. Under its provisions, Iraq renounced claims to exclusive control of the Shatt-al-Arab river, the confluence of the Tigris and Euphrates, forming the boundary between the two countries just north of the Persian Gulf. Iran, on the other hand, agreed to end its support of autonomy-seeking Kurdish rebels in northern Iraq, thus ending a civil war that claimed some 60,000 Iraqi casualties during 1974-75. It was at the Shah's insistence that Hussein arranged for the expulsion of the Ayatollah Ruholla Khomeini from his exile in Iraq in October 1978. The move prompted the Iranian religious leader to go to France, paving the way for his triumphant return to Teheran in early 1979, after the departure of the Shah.

On July 16, 1979 President Bakr, citing ill health, relinquished the Presidency to Hussein, who at the same time became head of state, chairman of the Revolutionary Command Council, Prime Minister, commander of the armed forces, and secretary general of the Baath party. Some observers suggested that rivalry had developed between the two men or that Hussein had grown impatient with Bakr's slow-moving style, but in fact the change merely ratified the position of power that Hussein had been occupying for more than a decade. Shortly after taking office, Hussein claimed to have uncovered a plot against him, allegedly instigated by the Syrian government, and ordered the arrests of scores of Cabinet ministers, bureaucrats, and political leaders, including five high-ranking members of the Baath party. Twenty-one men were executed by firing squad on August 8, 1979.

In the months that followed his accession to the Presidency, Hussein became the subject of a carefully orchestrated personality cult. Portraits of him appeared everywhere, and his populist image was enhanced by his almost nightly appearances on television, in which he helped farmers with their harvest or distributed candy to children, to the accompaniment of soft music. His virtues were extolled in popular songs, poems, stories, and films. A private telephone line was made available to citizens who wished to chat with him about their problems. Meanwhile, Iraq's prosperity under the impact of its oil wealth continued, consumer goods abounded, high-rise office buildings, hotels, and housing projects proliferated, higher education and medical care were made available free of charge to the masses, and Iraq contributed generously to the poorer nations of the world.

By June 1980 Hussein felt secure enough to permit election of a new 250-member National Assembly, and 200 foreign journalists were invited to witness the balloting. But no real opposition was tolerated, and all legislation had to be ratified by the Revolutionary Command Council, which had the power to dissolve the parliament at will. Despite such advances as the emancipation of women and the virtual elimination of poverty, the country remained under the strict control of the Baath party, with the main power residing in Hussein, his two half-brothers Barzan Ibrahim al-Tikriti and Sabawi Ibrahim al-Tikriti, and his brother-in-law Adnan Khairallah Talfah. Freedom of expression was circumscribed, most Western news media were banned, and no one was permitted to own a typewriter without a special license.

Meanwhile, the long-standing conflict between Iraq and Iran flared up anew following the departure of the Shah and the rise of the Ayatollah Khomeini to power in early 1979. As leader of the fundamentalist Shiite Muslims, the Ayatollah called on his coreligionists in Iraq to rise up against the "infidel Baathist regime," dominated by the rival Sunni Muslim sect of which Hussein was a member, and to join his Islamic revolution. In response, Hussein expelled some 40,000 Shiites to Iran, arrested thousands more, and reportedly ordered the execution of some, including the Ayatollah Mohammed al-Bakr Sadr, a close ally of Khomeini.

Hussein's main concern about Iran, however, seems to have been the prospect that the instability of the Khomeini regime might bring about intervention of the United States and possibly the Soviet Union, thus posing a threat to his plans for hegemony over the Persian Gulf region. An attack on Iran, he hoped, would bring about a more stable regime that would be more accommodating to Iraq. On September 17, 1980 Hussein summoned the National Assembly to proclaim his unilateral abrogation of the 1975 treaty with Iran, which he claimed Iraq had signed under duress. Five days later he launched an air attack to pave the way for an invasion of Iran's Khuzestan province. But although Iraqi forces scored some initial territorial gains, the Iranian army proved stronger than had been expected, and the war was stalemated for many months.

In June 1981, while Iraq was still in the midst of its war with Iran, Israel launched an air strike destroying a nearly completed French-built nuclear reactor, which the Israelis claimed posed a threat of nuclear attack against them. In response, Hussein, while insisting that the reactor had been built strictly for peaceful purposes, called on "all peace-loving nations" to help Arabs to acquire nuclear arms to balance what he called Israel's nuclear capability. He declared, however, that he would "leave for the future" any decision regarding retaliation against Israel. Hussein won a partial victory when the United Nations Security Council in a unanimous resolution condemned Israel for the attack.

Married since 1963 to his first cousin Sajida Khairallah Talfah, a primary school teacher, Saddam Hussein has two sons and two daughters to whom he is devoted. A stocky man, slightly under six feet tall, with close-cropped hair, a moustache, and penetrating eyes, Hussein "speaks with the language of the poet," according to the Iraqi writer Jabra Ibrahim Jabra, and has a shrewd, methodical mind. He reads history and political theory and has published some of his speeches and essays in English translation in *Saddam Hussein on Current Events in Iraq* (Longman, 1977), *One Common Trench, or Two Opposite Ones?* (published in Milan, Italy by Grafis in 1977) and *Social and Foreign Affairs in Iraq* (published in London, England by Croom Helm in 1979). Hussein has a luxury yacht that was built for him in a Danish shipyard, and his wardrobe is said to contain over 200 business suits, military uniforms, and tribal costumes. The inconsistency between his benign image and his brutally repressive actions can be explained, according to a profile in the *Wall Street Journal* (June 13, 1980), by his "Jekyll-and-Hyde" personality.

References: *Asian Recorder* p15053+ Ag 27-S 2 '79; *Forbes* 126:37 Ag 18 '80 por;. *Guardian Weekly* 123:14 O 12 '80; *London Observer* p14 S 28 '80 por; *London Sunday Times* p13 S 28 '80 por; *N Y Times A* p12 S 24 '80 por; *N Y Times Mag* p43+ O 26 '80 por; *Newsweek* 97:37 Je 29 '81 por; *People* 14:49+ O 20 '80 pors; *International Who's Who, 1981-82*; Khadduri, Majid. *Socialist Iraq* (1978); *Middle East and North Africa, 1980-81*

Huston, John

Aug. 5, 1906- Motion picture director; writer. Address: b. c/o Jess S. Morgan and Company, 6420 Wilshire Blvd., Los Angeles, Calif. 90048

NOTE: This biography supersedes the article that appeared in *Current Biography* in 1949.

John Huston, an American-born Irish citizen who now resides in Mexico, is the international cinema's most traveled cosmopolite. As impulsive and unpredictable in his ways as he is efficient in his craft, he is also the cinema's grand old maverick, with thirty-odd distinctive films behind him and more in prospect. Huston went to Hollywood as a writer at the dawn of the talkie era and made his directorial debut a decade later with *The Maltese Falcon* (1941), a "textbook" film, considered by many to be the best detective melodrama ever made. Among the subsequent motion pictures he directed under the old studio system were the classic study in self-destructive greed, *The Treasure of the Sierra Madre* (1948), and that prototype among crime "caper" movies, *The Asphalt Jungle* (1950). Such pictures as *The Red Badge of Courage* (1951) gained due recognition only with the passing of the years, but *The African Queen* (1952), Huston's first step into international filmmaking, was an immediate favorite.

Following a slump in artistic reputation and popularity, Huston found his touch again with *Fat City* (1972)—his first American film in twenty years—and retained it with *The Man Who Would Be King* (1975) and *Wise Blood* (1980). David Thomson, the author of *A Biographical Dictionary of Film* (1976) and one of Huston's severest critics, describes him as a "tame cynic" surveying "a crazy world," and others see his primary theme as the stubbornness and resourcefulness of human nature set against difficult patterns of survival in a largely masculine world or as the universal experience of pointlessness and failure. Huston himself, who always retains at least a hint of amusement regardless of his theme, has said that he fails to see any continuity in his work from picture to picture, that "what's remarkable is how different the pictures are, one from another."

John Huston was born on August 5, 1906 in Nevada, Missouri to Walter Huston, the actor, and Reah (Gore) Huston, a journalist. Walter, who had temporarily retired from acting, was at that time the chief engineer with the power, light, and water company in the town of Nevada, and during the following three years his engineering jobs took the family to Indianapolis, Indiana and Weatherford, Texas. In 1909 Walter returned to New York to resume his acting career; three years later Walter and Reah were divorced, and John spent the rest of his childhood shuttling between his parents' homes. Having a larger than average heart and suffering from Bright's disease, John at age eleven went with his mother to live in Arizona, in the hope that the climate there would benefit his health; his condition improved after a doctor in Arizona insisted that he eat and exercise the way any normal boy would.

From his mother, who used to take him with her to racetracks, Huston says he learned "that money's for spending, and to hell with the odds." For several years he lived with her in Los Angeles, where he learned to box at Lincoln High School. Dropping out of school at fifteen, he became one of the top-ranking amateur lightweights in California, but he decided not to pursue boxing as a profession. Turning at first to painting, he studied with Stanton MacDonald-Wright at the Art Students League of Los Angeles until 1924, when he moved to New York and did some acting with the Provincetown Players.

While recuperating from a mastoid operation in 1925, Huston spent a long vacation in Mexico, where his adventures included riding as an honorary member of the Mexican cavalry. After returning to the United States, he published a short story, "Fool," in H. L. Mencken's *American Mercury* and worked as a reporter for the New York *Daily Graphic*, where his mother was then employed. He had eight lines in the two-reeler *Two Americans* (Paramount Famous Lasky Corporation, 1929), in which his father played both Abraham Lincoln and Ulysses S. Grant.

On the strength of his directing of the 1930-31 Broadway hit *Grand Hotel*, Huston's friend Herman Shulin was called to Hollywood to produce and direct for Sam Goldwyn. Through Shulin, Huston became a contract writer for the Goldwyn studio. Nothing worked out between Shulin and Goldwyn, however, and after several months of salaried idleness, Shulin and Huston were granted release from their contracts. Shulin returned to New York and the theatre and Huston went over to Universal Pictures, where he collaborated on the writing of two films starring Walter Huston, *A House Divided* (1931) and *Law and Order* (1932), as well as *Murders in the Rue Morgue* (1932), starring Bela Lugosi. He also wrote a screenplay based on Oliver La Farge's book about the Navajos, *Laughing Boy*, but production was repeatedly delayed until Universal finally sold the property to Metro-Goldwyn-Mayer, which made what Huston considers a "wretched, vulgar picture" out of it in 1934. At Universal, he became a close friend of William Wyler, the director of *A House Divided*.

Huston's reputation as a hard-drinking, lusty roustabout developed early in his Hollywood career. In his autobiography, *An Open Book* (Knopf, 1980), he remembers his life in the early 1930's as "a shambles," a "series of misadventures and disappointments," including the loss of his first wife to alcoholism. A fatal automobile accident in which he was the driver brought his "whole miserable existence to a head" and he "wanted nothing so much as to get away." Following a fruitless stint as a writer for Gaumont-British Studios in London, he lived from hand to mouth in London and Paris for a brief time. Returning to the United States, he worked for the short-lived picture magazine *Mid-Week Pictorial* in

1934 and played a reincarnated Abraham Lincoln in Howard Koch's *The Lonely Man* at the WPA Theatre in Chicago in 1935.

After the run of *The Lonely Man*, Huston renewed his contact with Hollywood with the sale of a story to Warner Brothers that was later filmed as *Three Strangers* (1946), with screenplay by him and Howard Koch. As a contract writer for Warners, Huston came to the aid of William Wyler on the script of *Jezebel* (1938), and he worked on *Juárez* (1939), *The Amazing Dr. Clitterhouse* (1938), and *Dr. Ehrlich's Magic Bullet* (1940). After directing his father on Broadway in *A Passenger to Bali* (which closed after a few performances in 1940), he returned to Warners to work on *Sergeant York* (1941) and *High Sierra* (1941).

In accordance with a stipulation in his contract, Huston came due for a chance to direct in 1941. For his first directorial effort he chose (and wrote the screen adaptation of) *The Maltese Falcon*, one of Dashiell Hammett's novels about Sam Spade, private detective. The film, which starred Humphrey Bogart, Mary Astor, Peter Lorre, and Sydney Greenstreet, scored an immediate popular and critical success when it was released in 1941. "The trick which Mr. Huston has pulled," Bosley Crowther wrote in the New York *Times*, "is a combination of American ruggedness with the suavity of the English crime school—a blend of mind and muscle—plus a slight touch of pathos." Twenty-seven years later Pauline Kael would describe the film as "a work of entertainment that is yet so skillfully constructed that after many years and viewings it has the same brittle explosiveness—and some of the same surprise—that it had in 1941."

Huston had directed his second Warner Brothers film, *In This Our Life* (1942), and was in the process of directing his third, *Across the Pacific* (1942), when he was called up to duty in the United States Army Signal Corps. As a World War II officer, Huston made three documentaries. The first was *Report from the Aleutians* (1943), showing the men at an Alaskan air base coping with boredom as they prepared for combat. The second was *The Battle of San Pietro* (1944), consisting of coverage of fighting in Italy so brutally honest that the War Department, viewing it as "an antiwar film," kept it on the shelf until General George C. Marshall decreed that, with deletions, it be used as a training film.

His last documentary film for the army was *Let There Be Light* (1945), about the treatment of combat neuroses at Mason General Hospital in Brentwood, Long Island, the photographing of which he has described as "practically a religious experience": "These men came in from the boats in batches of seventy-five and 100, mute, shaking with amnesia, blind, with paralysis, as a result of warfare. Many were healed. The original idea was that the film be shown to those who would be able to give employment in industry. . . . When the brass in the Pentagon saw the film, the reaction was strongly against releasing it for general viewing." *Let There Be Light* remained suppressed until December 1980. Reviewing its theatrical premiere the following month, Vincent Canby wrote in the New York *Times* (January 16, 1981): "With its voice-over narration (provided by Walter Huston), its use of wipes and dissolves, and its full-orchestra soundtrack music, *Let There Be Light* is an amazingly elegant movie."

After his service in the army, which he entered as a lieutenant and left as a major, Huston directed Jean-Paul Sartre's *No Exit* on Broadway, in 1946, and then returned to Warner Brothers, where he made two final motion pictures. The first was *The Treasure of the Sierra Madre* (1948), a bitter action fable about three gold prospectors (Humphrey Bogart, Walter Huston, and Tim Holt) done in by greed. That film brought Huston two Academy Awards, for writing and directing, and his father the Oscar for best supporting actor. It drew extraordinary critical acclaim for its brilliant characterization and graphic use of Mexican settings and stylized facial close-ups to convey a compelling impression of human nature reduced to raw nerves in an ominous atmosphere.

With Richard Brooks, Huston wrote the screenplay for the last picture he directed at Warners, *Key Largo* (1948), about a returning World War II veteran (Humphrey Bogart) combating gangsters in the Florida keys. Outside of his Warners contract, Huston worked with Tony Veiller on two screenplays, *The Killers* (Universal, 1946) and *The Stranger* (RKO, 1946), and he directed James Stewart and Henry Fonda in an episode of *On Our Merry Way* (United Artists, 1948). In all three instances he was uncredited.

When Huston left Warner Brothers to become an independent director, he first teamed up with producer Sam Spiegel to form Horizon Pictures, which produced *We Were Strangers* (Columbia, 1949), a prophetic story about a revolution against a corrupt dictatorship in Cuba, and *The African Queen* (United Artists, 1952). The latter, written by James Agee and shot in color on location, recounts the unlikely romance and adventures of a grizzled, gin-drinking trader (Humphrey Bogart) and a prim spinster missionary (Katharine Hepburn) aboard the trader's leaky Congo riverboat. Bogart won his first Academy Award for his portrayal of Charlie Allnut, and critics hailed the film's endearing character portraits and splendid mixing of gentle comedy and offbeat love interest.

Meanwhile, Huston made two final movies under the old studio system for Metro-Goldwyn-Mayer. One was *The Asphalt Jungle* (1950), about a jewelry store heist masterminded by an elderly crook (Huston's old friend Sam Jaffe), a film that inspired a long stream of crime-seen-from-the-inside pictures. (Although her part was too small to be mentioned in the credits, it was in *The Asphalt Jungle* that Marilyn Monroe made the appearance that first caught the attention of moviegoers.) The other was *The Red Badge of Courage* (1951), a bold adaptation of Stephan Crane's Civil War novel about the turbulent emotions felt by a raw recruit in his first battle experience, a film especially memorable for its magnificently staged battle scenes (the filming of which is chronicled by Lillian Ross in her account of the making of the movie, *Picture,* published in 1952).

During the House Un-American Activities Committee's investigation of Communism in Hollywood in the late 1940's, Huston went to Washington to protest the "witch hunt" as a member of a Hollywood group called the Committee for the First Amendment. As the anti-Communist hysteria grew, he found the "moral rot" it promoted in the entertainment industries intolerable and moved to Ireland in 1952. Twelve years later he became an Irish citizen.

After severing his connection with Horizon, Huston made *Moulin Rouge* (United Artists, 1952), based on Pierre La Mure's sentimentalized biography of Henri de Toulouse-Lautrec and starring José Ferrer as the artist. Perhaps the most striking aspect of the film was the Oscar-winning color photography of Oswald Morris, which captured Toulouse-Lautrec's palette in evoking nineteenth-century Montmartre. *Beat the Devil* (United Artists, 1954), a spoof of *The Maltese Falcon* and its like, was, as Huston himself has observed, "ahead of its time," with "off-the-wall humor" that "left viewers bewildered and confused." The first audiences to see *Moby Dick* (Warner Brothers, 1956), preconditioned by John Barrymore's 1930 interpretation of Ahab as a raving lunatic, also found it difficult to appreciate the quiet intensity of Gregory Peck's Ahab in his quarrel with God. *Moby Dick* was shot in sepia.

Huston next directed three films for Twentieth Century-Fox: *Heaven Knows, Mr. Allison* (1957), the tender, tastefully done story of a nun (Deborah Kerr) and a Marine (Robert Mitchum) marooned on a South Pacific island during World War II; *The Barbarian and the Geisha* (1958), starring John Wayne as the first American diplomat sent to Japan following Commodore Perry's visit in 1853; and *The Roots of Heaven* (1958), the saga of an eccentric idealist (Trevor Howard) who leads a guerrilla campaign against the slaughter of elephants in French Equatorial Africa. Huston was so appalled at scenes re-shot for *The Barbarian and the Geisha* after it left his hands that he considered having his name removed from the credits, and he felt that because of flaws and limitations caused by production problems *The Roots of Heaven* "was never what it might have been." Of all his films, the worst, in his opinion, was *The Unforgiven* (United Artists, 1960). Huston wanted the discovery of the Indian origins of the adopted girl (Audrey Hepburn) in *The Unforgiven* to be a study of racial intolerance, but the producers insisted that he create a more conventional Western melodrama.

The ill-starred film *The Misfits* (United Artists, 1961), written by Arthur Miller as a serious vehicle for Marilyn Monroe (then his wife), starred Miss Monroe as a divorcee in Reno who becomes involved with a latter-day cowboy (Clark Gable) and persuades him of the callousness of rounding up wild mustangs to be slaughtered for dog food. Many critics faulted that Huston film for what they considered its vague sentimentality and self-conscious straining for symbolism.

According to Huston, the post-production cutting of *Freud* (Universal, 1962), starring Montgomery Clift, removed "vital links" from a delicately plotted "intellectual suspense story." On the other hand, he was "surprised" that the mystery-thriller *The List of Adrian Messenger* (Universal, 1963), a tour de force in "protean change of faces," was "not better received than it was." He went on to score a major success with his adaptation of Tennessee Williams' tragicomic play *The Night of the Iguana* (MGM, 1964), about erratic Anglo types (Richard Burton *et al*) in Puerto Vallarta, Mexico. The biggest money-maker of his career was producer Dino De Laurentiis' *The Bible . . . In the Beginning* (Twentieth Century-Fox, 1966), among whose spectacular scenes was one in which Noah (Huston himself) leads the animals into the Ark. Huston directed the opening segment of another box-office smash, *Casino Royale* (Columbia, 1967), the wackiest of the James Bond spy stories and thus a parody of a parody. Despite its mixed reception, Huston considers *Reflections in a Golden Eye* (Warner Brothers, 1967), starring Marlon Brando as the homicidal latent homosexual Major Pendleton, one of his best films. Like *Moulin Rouge* and *Moby Dick,* it was experimental in its use of color.

Five films Huston made over the next five years, *Sinful Davey* (United Artists, 1969), *A Walk With Love and Death* (Twentieth Century-Fox, 1969), *The Kremlin Letter* (Twentieth Century-Fox, 1970), *The Life and Times of Judge Roy Bean* (National General, 1973), and *The Mackintosh Man* (Warner Brothers, 1973) were considered failures. "There is no doubt about the meaning of the word 'failure' in the motion picture industry," he comments in his autobiography. "The industry operates for profit, and a failure is a film that doesn't make money."

Fat City (Columbia, 1972) was also a commercial failure, but critics applauded it for its expert encapsulation of the gritty ambience of the world of small-time boxing, in which they detected a commentary on American speech and a metaphor for life and its disappointments. Also well received by critics— and, in this instance, the public as well—was the rousing adventure film *The Man Who Would Be King* (Columbia, 1975), Huston's masterful adaptation of Kipling's tale.

After recovering from heart surgery in 1977, Huston made the quirkiest motion picture of his career, a grimly faithful and therefore grotesque adaptation of *Wise Blood,* Flannery O'Connor's American Gothic novel about do-it-yourself religion in the South. On location in Macon, Georgia, Huston recreated the intense, Christ-haunted world through which Hazel Motes (Brad Dourif), the fanatic yokel preacher of a "Church without Christ," stumbles in his futile quest to escape his fundamentalist rearing. Produced by Michael and Kathy Fitzgerald, *Wise Blood* was first shown at the New York Film Festival in 1979 and given general release the following year. Reviewers generally agreed that Huston's "straightforward," "sardonic" direction reinforced the "compact," "unusually literate" screenplay by Benedict Fitzgerald, and the result was a "perfectly stylized" movie. "*The Man Who Would Be King* showed him at the peak of his powers," David Ansen wrote in *Newsweek* (March 17, 1980). "*Wise Blood* is further confirmation that Huston is still in his prime."

Huston does not consider *Phobia* (Spiegel-Bergman Films, 1980), a Canadian-made murder mystery for which he was recruited after production began, to be a "true John Huston film." As 1981 began, he was doing the final cutting of "Escape to Victory," a World War II story about Allied POW's in a German camp, and he was preparing to begin filming his thirty-seventh picture, "Annie," a movie version of the Broadway musical hit about the comic strip character Little Orphan Annie.

As an actor, Huston had roles in *The Cardinal* (Gamma, 1964), *Candy* (Cinerama, 1968), *De Sade* (American International, 1969), *Myra Breckinridge* (Twentieth Century-Fox, 1970), *The Bridge in the Jungle* (a Mexican release, by Pancho Kohner, 1979), *The Deserter* (Paramount, 1971), *Man in the Wilderness* (Warner Brothers, 1971), *Battle for the Planet of the Apes* (Twentieth Century-Fox, 1973), *Chinatown,* (Paramount, 1974), *Breakout* (Columbia, 1975), *The Wind and the Lion* (United Artists, 1975), *Tentacles* (American International, 1977), and *Winter Kills* (Avco-Embassy, 1979). In addition, he often appears in his own films.

Throughout the years Huston has led a highly publicized extracurricular life as painter, horseman, hunter, gambler, and lover. He has been married five times: to Dorothy Harvey in the late 1920's and early 1930's, to Lesley Black in the late 1930's and early 1940's, to Evelyn Keyes from 1946 to 1950, to Enrica Soma from 1950 to 1969, and to Celeste Shane from 1972 to 1975. All of Huston's marriages ended in divorce except for that to Enrica Soma, who died in 1969 after a ten-year separation from her husband. By Enrica Soma he has two children, Tony and Anjelica. His other children are Danny, his son by Zoë Sallis, and Pablo and Allegra, whom he adopted.

Huston lives at "Las Caletas,'" an oceanside villa south of Puerto Vallarta, Mexico. He is a very tall, slightly stooped man, described by Gerald Pratley as "unfailingly courteous" despite an abstracted air that "always conveys the impression that he is somewhere else."

References: Sat R 8:12+ Ja '81 pors; Washington Post B p1+ O 5 '71 pors; Huston, John. An Open Book (1980); Kaminsky, Stuart. John Huston: Maker of Magic (1978); Katz, Ephraim. The Film Encyclopedia (1979); Nolan, William F. John Huston: King Rebel (1965); Pratley, Gerald. The Cinema of John Huston (1977); Who's Who in America, 1980-81

Ivory, James

June 7, 1928- Motion picture director. Address: b. Merchant Ivory Productions, 655 Madison Ave., New York City, N.Y. 10021; h. 400 E. 52nd St., New York City, N.Y. 10022

The international success of The Europeans (1979) and Quartet (1981) has enhanced the reputation of James Ivory as a film director of impeccable taste, quiet wit, and gentle craft. Ivory, who moves between continents and cultures with grace and humanitarian empathy, began his career with the exquisite one-man art documentaries Venice: Theme and Variations (1957) and The Sword and the Flute (1959), and he is best known as the American half of Merchant Ivory Productions. He began making modestly budgeted feature films in India with the Indian producer Ismail Merchant in 1963, with The Householder, and in 1972 Merchant Ivory Productions released its first American-based feature, Savages.

Over the past seventeen years the staunchly independent producer-director team of Merchant and Ivory has given worldwide cinema and television audiences a total of seventeen highly original motion pictures, including Autobiography of a Princess (1975), made in India and London, and Roseland (1977), which represented a major thrust beyond festivals and art houses toward commercial success. Most of the screenplays were written by the novelist Ruth Prawer Jhabvala, whose marriage to an Indian profoundly influenced her career. Each of the films is marked by Ivory's idiosyncratic sensibility, his loving attention to color, texture, and light, his interest in the subtleties and foibles of human emotion, and his fascination with the ways of an outsider in an alien culture and that culture's receptiveness to outside influence—the meeting of two worlds. But his dimension of operation is always the small, the personal, away from grand themes and pontifical social commentary.

James Ivory was born on June 7, 1928 in Berkeley, California and grew up in Klamath Falls, Oregon, where his father ran a sawmill. In an interview with Joyce Egginton for the London Observer (July 9, 1978), Ivory described his mother as "a Southern lady with lots of memories of Louisiana and a strong desire to go back there and escape from the cold," a woman who "hated the wind whistling round the corners of the house and the long winters and the strange plants that barely put out a blossom before they shrivelled up." As a child, he recalled, he had "this interest in buildings and interiors" and "wanted to be a set designer." At the University of Oregon, where he majored in fine arts, his interest shifted from set design to filmmaking, and after taking his bachelor's degree he enrolled in the film department of the University of Southern California.

As his master's thesis at USC, Ivory made the twenty-four-minute color documentary Venice: Theme and Variations (1957), described by him as "a portrait of the city in a historical context [using] paintings to get a sense of the social life of Venice in the past." "The reason I chose Venice," he has explained, "—and I think this is typical of my whole career, in a way—is simply that I was attracted to the place, and making the film was an excuse to go there." Shown at the 1957 Edinburgh Film Festival, Venice: Theme and Variations made the New York Times's list of the ten best documentary films of the year.

In his search for material for Venice: Theme and Variations, Ivory, visiting the shop of a San Francisco art dealer one day, became fascinated by a collection of Rajput and Moghul miniatures—those exquisitely detailed, vividly colored paintings of the life of the maharajahs, princesses, and warriors of the golden age of royal India. Deciding to use those works of art to tell their own story, he filmed all the miniatures he could find in California collections and then went to New

York City to film more there. The result, the twenty-four-minute color documentary *The Sword and the Flute* (1959), so impressed the Asia Society of New York that it commissioned Ivory to make a documentary about Delhi, India. In *The Delhi Way* (1964), a forty-five-minute color film, he again used a mixture of works of art, old photographs, and contemporary footage to give a portrait of a city across a period of time.

While making *The Delhi Way*, Ivory met the American-educated Indian motion picture producer Ismail Merchant. Even before Ivory had finished the Delhi film he and Merchant, along with cinematographer Subrata Mitra, began making the black-and-white feature *The Householder* (1963), adapted by Ruth Prawer Jhabvala from her novel of the same title. That book tells the humorous story of a young teacher in Delhi, his marital problems, and his frustration with a bemused, unwittingly patronizing American friend. "You [Indians] grow souls," the American says in one interchange. The protagonist replies, "Our steel output is also increasing."

"*The Householder* is an entertainment rarity: a comedy from India, a country whose film exports to us so far have generally been on the grim, gloomy, and/or dramatic side," Jesse Zunzser wrote in *Cue* (October 10, 1963). "Stranger still, for a film made in Delhi, the entire cast speaks English." Ivory and Merchant made two versions of *The Householder*, one in English for world export and the other in Hindi for most of India as well as the Hindi-speaking populations in Southeast Asia, South Africa, and the West Indies.

Columbia Pictures bought the world distribution rights to *The Householder* with rupees which, because of currency regulations, could not be taken out of India. With the money, the equivalent of $85,000, Ivory and Merchant made a second black-and-white feature, the already classic *Shakespeare Wallah* (1965), the story, written by Ivory and Mrs. Jhabvala, of an English theatrical troupe in India, left over from colonial days and still performing Shakespeare's plays before indifferent and ever-diminishing audiences. "It was set at the time of declining British influence in India," Ivory explained to Joyce Egginton in the *Observer* interview. "It was interpreted in Britain as being about the fading out of the Raj. But it is also about the disappearance of classical European culture in India."

Thanks partly to distribution by Walter Read in the United States, *Shakespeare Wallah* was the first of the Merchant-Ivory films to become a commercial success, grossing four times the cost of production. It was also an artistic success, winning a prize at the Berlin Film Festival and praise from critics for its elegance, subtlety, masterful technique, and depth of feeling. Joan Fox of the Toronto *Globe and Mail* (October 9, 1967) was impressed by its "Chekhovian evocativeness" as well as "its pure truth in setting, presentation of character and conflict of cultures, and its tender humanity."

After a contract with Paramount Pictures came to naught, Ivory and Merchant returned to India to make their third feature, *The Guru* (1969), on a commission from Twentieth Century-Fox. That subtle comedy, written with understatement by Mrs. Jhabvala and Ivory and filmed in muted pastel-like color by Subrata Mitra, starred Michael York as an egocentric British rock star who goes to India to study the sitar under a fashionable guru—to their mutual disenchantment. *The Guru* ran well over its $660,000 budget (in blocked rupees) and flopped at the box office, but its wit, the richness of its insights, and the sweetness and candor with which it exposed the kinks and quirks of universal human nature did not escape the majority of critics. "The style of the film is its content," Scott Mac-Donough wrote in *Show* (March 1970), "and the style—a skillfully woven tapestry of verbal and visual nuances—is exquisite."

The international real-estate entrepreneur Joseph Saleh put up the initial funds for Ivory and Merchant's fourth feature, *Bombay Talkie* (1969), a flashily parodic drama about an American writer (Jennifer Kendall) who becomes involved with an Indian movie star (Shashi Kapoor). Later, when the production went into the red, United Artists took an option on it in blocked rupees, which covered the cost overrun. To audiences unfamiliar with the escapist celluloid dreams that are ground out for home consumption by the Bombay film industry, the melodrama and lavish musical production numbers of *Bombay Talkie* seemed "overwrought" (the adjective used by *Time*'s critic). "I liked it a lot," Ivory later said of *Bombay Talkie*, "but it was absolutely detested by the press. We were supposed to have reached our nadir with that. But now it is appreciated and plays in revival houses."

In 1970 the BBC commissioned *Adventures of a Brown Man in Search of Civilization*, an hour-long profile of the octogenarian Bengali sage Nirad Chaudhari. Produced by Merchant in association with Anthony Korner, written and directed by Ivory, and photographed by Walter Lassally, the film followed Chaudhari as he made his way around Oxford University, oblivious of traffic and other pedestrians as he inveighed, with a disarmingly sweet manner, against the failings of both India and the West. The BBC televised the film in two screenings.

The short *Helen, Queen of the Nautch Girls* (1973) was written by Ivory, produced by Merchant, directed by Anthony Korner, and photographed by Subrata Mitra. That film is mainly a montage of production numbers from some of the 500 movies of the Bombay cinema's most popular musical star, along with an interview with her in her dressing room. The film is a heady, whirlwind introduction to the commercial Indian cinema, where the action of mythological sagas and conventionalized melodramas always stops for fantastic song and dance. Ismail Merchant made his first essay in direction with the short film *Mahatma and the Mad Boy* (1972). Filmed on Juhu Beach in Bombay, it is a parable about a poor, hungry beach boy whose practical needs are ignored by an outdoor gathering of white-garbed speechmakers idealistically mouthing Gandhian principles.

Ivory was inspired with the idea for Merchant Ivory's first non-Indian feature when he visited Beechwood House, a sprawling Victorian mansion owned by Dudley Schoales in Scarborough, near Ossining on the Hudson, in upstate New York. George Trow and Michael O'Donoghue turned the idea into a screenplay, an allegorical comedy-drama about a group of savages, without tools, language, or other cultural accouterments, who emerge from the wilderness to find the mansion and come under the civilizing influence of what they find in it. Ultimately, however, they decide to return to their savage state.

Among the actors in the title roles of *Savages* (1972) were Salome Jens, Ultra Violet, and Sam Waterston. The picture was shot by Walter Lassally under Ivory's direction on location in Beechwood House at a total cost of $325,000 (including $75,000 from Saleh and an advance of $125,000 from Walter Reade), one-tenth the budget normal for a film of such technical gloss and quality. In Europe *Savages* impressed critics and did well commercially, but it flopped on both counts in the United States. "I know Ismail doesn't like me to say this," Ivory told Judith Trojan in an interview for *Take One* (January/February 1974), "but it [*Savages*] was really something of a joke and was not ever really meant to be taken all that seriously. And in this country it was taken too seriously, which is a pity. In Europe, people know how to sit through something like that without becoming bored or outraged." Merchant interjected a comment about "the snob appeal of American critics," explaining: "If it had been done by Buñuel or some other European director, they would've gone and licked the boots of it and said, 'Ah, what a great masterpiece has come our way.'"

Ivory was outraged over what American International Pictures, the distributor, did to his second American-based color feature, *The Wild Party* (1974), starring James Coco and Raquel Welch. Walter Marks's screenplay was loosely based on a long narrative poem published by Joseph Moncure March in 1926 about vaudeville types at a Greenwich Village party that ends tragically. March's fictitious party had some parallels with the Fatty Arbuckle scandal of the same era, involving the death of an under-aged girl at a sordid Hollywood party. "The wreck that is being made of my work," Ivory wrote to the film critic Derek Malcolm, "is the distributor's cheap attempt to exploit everything exploitable, with discarded sex scenes piled on top of one another, with poor sequences dropped by me stuck back in the hope of some easy laughs, with flashbacks and flashforwards thrust into the middle of perfectly workable scenes, with dialogue scenes either shortened or eliminated entirely, and, most important of all, with the central relationship between the star and his mistress thrown off-center in an attempt to make him more likeable."

After the debacle of *The Wild Party*, Ivory returned to his best directorial form with *Autobiography of a Princess* (1975), an hour-long color film made for National Educational Television. "*Autobiography of a Princess* is a very inexact title," Ivory explained in the *Take One* interview with Judith Trojan, "because the film is not an autobiography in any sense. It's really about maharajahs and court life. We used a lot of footage made by maharajahs in the twenties, thirties, and forties. . . . It's about other things too. It's about English people in India, what happens to them. The whole thing is really just two characters. Most of it was shot in London. A good deal of it was shot in India, too, but without actors."

The two characters in *Autobiography of a Princess* are the Princess (Madhur Jaffrey) and Cyril Sahib (James Mason), who had been her father the Maharajah's tutor and secretary. The two present strikingly different attitudes toward the passing of royal India as the Princess runs off some old home movies and reminisces in her London flat with the visiting Sahib. Remembering only her flamboyant father's joyfulness and charm, she is filled with unclouded nostalgia; the tutor, recalling as well the Maharajah's mindless cruelty and selfish, sybaritic ways, looks with remorse to a wasted past and with fear to an empty future. "Ruth Prawer Jhabvala's screenplay is tactful but resonant," Derek Malcolm wrote in the *Guardian* (March 4, 1976), "full of irony yet without a hint of malice. And Ivory, with the help of Walter Lassally's unobtrusive camera work, points it perfectly."

The team of Merchant, Ivory, and Jhabvala reached its largest popular audience with *Roseland*, shot in color on location in New York City's landmark dance hall by Ernest Vincze and released by Common Shares in 1977. The film comprised three warm-hearted, imaginative episodes about denizens of the ballroom: "The Waltz," a funny, touching story about opposites (Theresa Wright and Lou Jacobi) who are attracted to each other; "The Hustle," about a young gigolo (Christopher Walken); and "The Peabody," starring Lilia Skala as an aged *grande dame*.

In her review of *Roseland*, Pauline Kael of the *New Yorker* (December 5, 1977), perhaps Ivory's severest critic, was predictably merciless ("James Ivory has now made eight feature films without jeopardizing his amateur standing"), but she was a glaring exception. Most reviewers had nothing but praise for *Roseland*'s capturing of details of character, dialogue, and an ambiance combining tinsel and tackiness. In the opinion of Judith Crist, the distinction of the film lay above all in "a carefully selected cast capable, under Ivory's light directorial hand, of adding brilliant facets to a polished ensemble performance." Writing in the New York *Post* (October 1, 1977), Miss Crist added: "Further, the film is marked by an affection for maturity, a compassion for older and unbeautiful people that is untouched by the patronage and sentimentality to which moviemakers are prone."

Hullabaloo over Georgie and Bonnie's Pictures, made in color for the British ITV network, was televised by ITV in two segments in July 1978. Written by Mrs. Jhabvala and photographed by Walter Lassally, it was, in Ivory's own description, "sort of a comedy" about attempts by a group of British, American, and Indian collectors to pry some prize miniatures from a maharajah. British television critics singled out for special praise Peggy Ashcroft's portrayal of a crusty British aristocrat insisting on her imperial right to native treasures.

Ivory, who feels a strong kinship with Henry James, fulfilled a long-held ambition when the National Film Finance Corporation of Britain provided the financial backing for him to film Mrs. Jhabvala's screen adaptation of James's novel *The Europeans* (1979). That story of two worldly, impoverished Britons, a brother (Tim Woodward) and sister (Lee Remick), visiting their rich, unsophisticated American cousins, was photographed in and around authentic colonial mansions in New England. Except for de-emphasizing the greed motive and changing the time of the visit from spring to autumn —which allowed cinematographer Walter Pizer to take advantage of the glorious fall colors— the screenplay was unswervingly faithful to the James novel. The sumptuousness of the photography was admired even by those few critics who considered the film a "lackluster" production, and most acknowledged Lee Remick's brilliance in the demanding role of Eugenia, the British baroness whose estrangement from her husband has left her destitute and without social prospects. Writing in the London *Observer* (July 1, 1979), Philip French ranked *The Europeans* "a film of great distinction," and in the Washington *Post* (December 21, 1979) Judith Martin wrote: "It is an enormous pleasure for a devoted Henry James admirer to rejoice in the beauty of James Ivory's film of *The Europeans*."

Mrs. Jhabvala's screenplay for Merchant-Ivory's *Jane Austen in Manhattan* (1980) was a story within a story, about an Off-Off Broadway troupe attempting to produce a recently discovered play by Jane Austen. Commissioned by ITV in England, it has not yet been released in the United States. The Ivory-Merchant-Jhabvala movie *Quartet*, based on a novel by Jean Rhys and starring Maggie Smith, Alan Bates, and Isabel Adjani, had its premiere at the Cannes Film Festival in May 1981. With some exceptions, including *The Wild Party* and *Roseland*, Merchant Ivory productions are available in 16mm. as well as 35mm. The

16mm. distribution is handled by Contemporary Films. A festival of Merchant-Ivory films was held at the Art Theatre in New York City in October and November 1981. The retrospective included Ivory's nonmutilated version of *The Wild Party*.

James Ivory is a silver-haired, aquiline-featured man of medium height and slender build. In contrast with the bustling, outspoken Merchant, a born promoter, Ivory is quiet and serious in temperament, weighing his words carefully and possessing a detached urbanity that befits an outside observer of the personal minutiae involved in a post-Empire India attempting to come to terms with Western ways. When they are not making films abroad, the two men share an apartment on Manhattan's East Side.

References: *Filmmakers Newsletter* p22+ Ja '78 por; *Guardian* p8 F 5 '73 por; *N Y Times* II p1+O 5 '80; *Take One* p14+ Ja/F '74; *Oxford Companion to Film* (1976)

Jacobi, Derek (jak′ō-bē)

Oct. 22, 1938- British actor. Address: 22 Grafton St., London W1, England

With England's most illustrious actors, John Gielgud and Laurence Olivier, now in their seventies, debate as to who will someday "fill the shoes of the aging masters" has become a popular pastime in British theatrical circles. One name sure to crop up in any discussion of the heir apparent is that of Derek Jacobi. Although he is best known in the United States through his performances on public television as star of the Masterpiece Theatre miniseries *I, Claudius* and delineator of the title roles in the BBC-produced Shakespeare plays *Richard II* and *Hamlet,* Jacobi has long been regarded in his native land as a consummate stage actor. And, on the occasion of his Broadway debut in *The Suicide* in the fall of 1980, New York's drama critics exuberantly concurred: his portrayal of a Russian Everyman was described as "dazzling."

Born on October 22, 1938 in the East London suburb of Leytonstone, Derek George Jacobi is the son of Alfred George and Daisy Gertrude (Masters) Jacobi. His father, who had emigrated from Germany, managed a small department store; his mother worked as a secretary. An only child, Derek fell under the spell of the theatre as a mere tot when his doting parents took him to see a traditional English pantomime. He knew then that he wanted to be an actor and shortly thereafter, at the age of six, ambitiously essayed the twin title roles in a local library-based drama group's presentation of *The Prince and the Swineherd.* "Most people pass out of that make-believe stage," he told a team of interviewers from *People* (November 10, 1980). "I'm still in it. Most actors have one foot in the cradle."

Apparently, the single dark patch in a childhood that Jacobi recalls as having been very happy was an attack of rheumatic fever that he suffered when he was ten and that left his legs paralyzed for a brief period. When he was able to walk again, he embarked on a strenuous regimen of swimming, cycling, and tennis to regain his strength. (That may explain why, as an adult, the form of exercise he says he favors is "thinking about using [his] rowing machine.") Upon completion of his studies at Leyton County High School—where, besides excelling academically, he had succeeded in shedding his cockney accent—Jacobi scored what, for a youth of his distinctly middle-class background, was an unusual coup: he was awarded a full scholarship to St. John's College at Cambridge.

Though history was Jacobi's major at the university, an acting career was always his primary goal. Earlier, he had appeared with England's National Youth Theatre, most notably as Hamlet at the Edinburgh Festival in 1955. Cambridge, with its century-old A.D.C. (Amateur Dramatic Club) famed as a funnel for recruits to the professional stage, afforded ample opportunity for further training. He found another outlet in the Marlowe Society, which had been established in 1908 and which made its annual production, usually of an Elizabethan or Jacobean play, an important event on the school's theatrical calendar. In fact, it was as a result of having been seen in the title role of Christopher Marlowe's *Edward II* that, immediately following his graduation from Cambridge, Jacobi was offered a job in the resident company at the prestigious Birmingham Repertory Theatre.

Typical of the eclectic fare that its founder, Barry Jackson, had advocated from the beginning was *One Way Pendulum,* a surrealist comedy by N. F. Simpson that on September 20, 1960 marked Jacobi's bow with the Birmingham troupe. In Simpson's farrago about a young murderer who spends his spare time teaching weighing machines to sing Handel's Hallelujah Chorus, Jacobi portrayed Stanley Honeybone, the first of hundreds of parts that he played in the course of an engagement ultimately encompassing several seasons. An invaluable asset in coping with the arduous repertory schedule was Jacobi's photographic memory; learning new lines posed no problem for him. He also had a dream to sustain him: many years before Laurence Olivier, the idol of many young actors, had served his apprenticeship on the same stage.

By coincidence, Olivier turned out to be the instrument of Jacobi's delivery from comparative oblivion in the provinces to London renown. As Jacobi himself rather breathlessly recounted the circumstances to Jerry Tallmer of the New York *Post* (October 23, 1980): "One Wednesday matinee I was playing or *attempting* to play Shakespeare's *Henry VIII,* and Olivier came round and we all fainted and he said he enjoyed it." A few days later a note from Sir Laurence arrived, proposing that Jacobi act in two of his productions at the Chichester Festival Theatre that summer. Sensing that the momentous break he had been hoping for was at hand, Jacobi submitted his resignation to the management of the Birmingham Rep.

Brother Martin in Shaw's *Saint Joan* and P. C. Liversedge in *The Workhouse Donkey,* a Brechtian drama about political chicanery by John Arden, were the roles assigned to Jacobi at Chichester in the summer of 1963. His acting brought him Olivier's invitation to join the National Theatre Company, which was then in the final phase of organization, almost ready to launch its inaugural season at the Old Vic. Thus, through an accident of timing, Derek Jacobi made his London stage debut in the National's opening production, playing Laertes to Peter O'Toole's Hamlet, on October 22, 1963—his twenty-fifth birthday.

During the eight years that Jacobi remained with the National, he was cast in a rich variety of parts: as the maddeningly irresolute yet rather pathetic Prosorov in Chekhov's *The Three Sisters;* as Cassio, the innocent tool of Iago's malevolence, in *Othello;* as Simon Bliss, the brash young son of a celebrated actress, in Noël Coward's *Hay Fever;* as Adam, the quintessential progenitor, in the rarely produced Shavian fantasy *Back to Methuselah;* as Ferdinand, the endearingly naïve king of Navarre, in *Love's Labour's Lost;* as vengeful Count Lodovico in John Webster's blood-drenched tragedy *The White Devil;* and as evil Don John, whose slander of the blameless Hero dissipates the prevailingly joyful atmosphere in *Much Ado about Nothing.*

Jacobi also figured prominently in the National's stylish resuscitations of two Restoration comedies by George Farquhar, *The Recruiting Officer* and *The Beaux' Stratagem*, and contributed a "cuttingly humorous" Touchstone to director Clifford Williams' unorthodox all-male staging of *As You Like It*, wherein Anthony Hopkins appeared opposite him as Audrey, the cynical clown's rustic sweetheart. Jacobi and Hopkins were also seen together in an effective revival of Thomas Heywood's drama of domestic strife *A Woman Killed with Kindness*, in which Joan Plowright played the title role. Later, Jacobi was among the company stalwarts who fleetingly supported Miss Plowright in *The Advertisement*, a near-monologue for an actress written by Natalia Ginzburg.

More rewarding for Jacobi were his roles in *The Royal Hunt of the Sun* and *Black Comedy*, two vastly differing plays by Peter Shaffer—the former an epic about Pizarro's savage conquest of the Incas, the latter a one-act frolic that drew its inspiration from the Chinese mime theatre—which had their world premieres at the National. While the least enviable task allotted Jacobi was probably his substitution for an indisposed Olivier in the troupe's much-praised rendering of the Congreve classic *Love for Love*, his obscurest assignment may have been a leading role in John Maddison Morton's *A Most Unwarrantable Intrusion*. That little-known nineteenth-century farce was presented in 1968 at the Old Vic as part of a triple bill that included *The Covent Garden Tragedy* by Henry Fielding and a dramatization of the 1965 John Lennon book *A Spaniard in the Works*.

"Highly accomplished" typified the praise that reviewers habitually heaped on Jacobi—until the National's catastrophic mounting of *The Idiot* in 1970 prompted them to express certain reservations concerning the scope of his talent. "Derek Jacobi's Myshkin shows a sweet nature and some fine epileptic contortions," Irving Wardle wrote in the New York Times (July 11, 1970), "but he does not project the character's invincible power of goodness." "He simmers," another critic complained, "but never burns." Blame for the failure of the production was not laid at the actor's door alone: what Simon Gray had performed in adapting the Dostoevsky novel to the stage was deemed a saddening feat of "butchery" and Anthony Quayle, who had directed, was charged with having employed "a heavy melodramatic emphasis and a sexual coarseness quite foreign to the spirit of the book."

That the overwhelmingly negative response to *The Idiot* should have had a bearing on Jacobi's decision to leave the National in 1971 seems a reasonable conclusion. As if determined to refute the imputations of inadequacy that had greeted his Myshkin, he scored a huge hit for the Birmingham Rep in May 1972 in the difficult double bill in which Laurence Olivier had created a sensation twenty-five years before at the Old Vic, playing the tormented king who blinds himself in *Oedipus Rex* by Sophocles and the coxcombical Mr. Puff in Sheridan's exceedingly broad comedy *The Critic*. Since then, Jacobi's reputation in England as a skilled and sensitive actor has been secure. Far from suffering any more reverses, it has been enhanced during the past decade through his intermittent involvement with the predominantly tour-oriented Prospect Theatre Company.

Electra by Sophocles, *The Royal Hunt of the Sun*, Shakespeare's *Twelfth Night* and *Pericles, Prince of Tyre*, Christopher Fry's *The Lady's Not for Burning*, and Chekhov's *Ivanov* are among the plays in which Jacobi has acted under the Prospect banner, customarily combining short stands in London with trail-blazing treks to foreign countries. None of them has generated greater excitement in audiences than *Hamlet*. In November 1979, in the wake of precedent-shattering engagements in Peking and Shanghai, where no other British drama group had ventured since the Communist takeover in 1949, Jacobi's physical and vocal pyrotechnics as the Dane were reported to have "alternately disconcerted and exhilarated the Chinese."

When *The Suicide*, the anti-Stalinist satire by Nikolai Erdman in which Jacobi made his Broadway debut, opened at the ANTA Theater on October 9, 1980, reviewers hailed it as "a prodigious work that bursts with dark surrealistic wit" and "an evening of pure theatrical enchantment." In the pivotal role of Semyon, a jobless man who dwells with his wife and mother-in-law in a depressing Moscow tenement and who seriously contemplates ending his futile life, Jacobi earned unanimous raves. John Simon credited him in *New York* (October 17, 1980) with possessing "a face that can hurtle from nondescript to tragic, from nonplussed to exultant, in a matter of fractions of a second"; Jack Kroll of *Newsweek* (October 20, 1980) commended him for imbuing a potential dolt with "humane modesty and yearning pathos"; and in *Time* (November 3, 1980) T. E. Kalem rated his multifaceted characterization "a thumping virtuosic triumph."

Ticket sales, however, could not keep pace with the steep weekly operating costs of the production. The exceedingly imaginative director Jonas Jurasas, himself an emigré from the Soviet Union, had seen fit to augment the sizable complement of actors that the script called for with a tightly choreographed Gypsy chorus, thereby heightening the phantasmagoric aura of the Erdman tale but also causing the payroll to mushroom. Santo Loquasto had devised an imposing yet mobile set so staggeringly intricate in design that extra stagehands had to be hired to manipulate it. A *succès d'estime*, *The Suicide* was forced to close after twenty previews and sixty regular performances, on November 29, 1980. Ironically, for a star whose vehicle was a commercial flop, Jacobi had almost invariably received a

"Bravo!"-punctuated standing ovation at the final curtain.

Television began to loom significantly as a factor in what the media might refer to as Jacobi's "visibility quotient," when, following the severance of his ties with the National Theatre Company, he periodically abandoned the boards to act in such long-format series as *The Strauss Family*, which ABC-TV introduced into its prime-time schedule in the spring of 1973. For American consumption, that biography of Vienna's famous father-and-son waltz composers, which had been produced in England by Sir Lew Grade, was divided into seven episodes. In the subsidiary role of Josef Lanner, Jacobi acquitted himself admirably. Next, in *The Pallisers*, the BBC's grandiose dramatization of half a dozen related political novels by Anthony Trollope, he appeared to formidable advantage, portraying an inept fortune hunter whose pursuit of a wealthy and worldly widow named Madame Max Goesler supplied comic relief.

Originally aired in the United States from November 1975 to April 1976 as a programming ploy of Home Box Office, Time-Life's entry in the pay-TV arena of cable television, *The Pallisers* resurfaced in 1977 under the auspices of the Public Broadcasting System. To loyal PBS viewers of *The Forsyte Saga* and *Upstairs, Downstairs*, the twenty-two episodes of *The Pallisers*, which traced the fortunes of an aristocratic British family through two decades, proved equally addictive. Derek Jacobi's face was therefore familiar to fans of the Trollope-derived chronicle when, later that year, they tuned in to the Masterpiece Theatre presentation of *I, Claudius*.

For readers of the New York Times (November 3, 1977), television critic John J. O'Connor summed up *I, Claudius*, the thirteen-episode series that scriptwriter Jack Pulman had adapted from a brace of novels by Robert Graves, as "a fiendishly sophisticated concoction of Roman history, political intrigues, murderous ambitions and consuming passions" that "set new standards for superb quality in popular entertainment." As Claudius, whose shambling gait and stammer-strewn speech masked a keen mind and an infallible instinct for survival, Jacobi proved himself to be, in O'Connor's words, "incredibly good." Regarding his challenging part, the actor has been quoted as saying that, although he "loved it to death," his fear afterward was that he "wouldn't get any other work because everyone would think all [he] could play was ancient Roman emperors." A bid from the BBC to tackle the meaty title role in a production of *Richard II* soon allayed his anxiety about being typed.

In the American press Jacobi's portrayal of the last of the Plantagenet kings was termed "glorious." "There is," Howard Rosenberg of the Los Angeles Times (March 28, 1979) declared, "a sense of decadence, a stench of rotting foundations that Jacobi captures in

Richard, as well as the instability—the heights and brooding depths—and ambivalence of the man." The fourth offering in a projected six-season survey of Shakespeare's oeuvre that the BBC and Time-Life had contracted to co-produce for viewing on public TV, *Richard II* was cited in *The Television Annual, 1978-79* as "the most admirable and eloquent" of the series to date. Jacobi's performance as the deposed monarch was, in the opinion of that yearbook's editor, Steven H. Scheuer, "peerless."

If the role of Richard II represented a radical change of pace for Jacobi, the part of Soviet spy Guy Burgess, which Granada Television enlisted him to play in its ninety-minute docudrama *Philby, Burgess and MacLean*, required a still more startling transformation. How masterfully he had managed it was confirmed by O'Connor, who wrote in his New York *Times* (July 21, 1980) review of the "fascinating" program that he had not recognized "the actor doing marvelous things with the effete, mincing, ostensibly weak but ominously threatening character of Burgess." Upon learning that he had been Derek Jacobi, O'Connor dubbed him "remarkably versatile."

Mindful of the assertion by several English theatre critics that Jacobi would be remembered as *the* stage Hamlet of his generation, the BBC signed him to portray the procrastinating prince in its production of the tragedy for television. When it was transmitted in the United States in the fall of 1980 as the initial offering in the Public Broadcasting System's second season of Shakespeare plays, *Hamlet* brought Jacobi a lapful of fresh laurels. "A fantastic performance" was the accolade of Marvin Kittman in *Newsday* (November 10, 1980), who ranked him as "one of the top five TV actors of the year, . . . the others being John Hurt, Tom Conti, Alec Guinness and Toshiro Mifune." In the New York *Times* (November 10, 1980) O'Connor echoed Kittman's enthusiasm, finding it "a Hamlet that demands attention and acclaim."

Derek Jacobi made his movie debut in the 1966 screen version of *Othello*. But, as some reviewers noted, the Warner Brothers release was flagrantly uncinematic, amounting to little more than a photographed record of the Shakespeare tragedy as it had been done on the London stage by the National Theatre Company. Olivier's bold interpretation of the title role remained mesmerizing to a degree but, it was suggested, should have been scaled down to accommodate the merciless scrutiny of the camera. As for Jacobi, he was the victim of a critical shellacking that bordered on the snide: one acidulous critic protested that his callowness precluded belief in Othello's acceptance of him as a rival for Desdemona's love, while another carped that his Cassio came across as "a fop that no commander would have put in charge of the regimental Dixie-cups."

In his next film, Universal's quasi-documentary *The Day of the Jackal* (1973), Jacobi portrayed a young police detective who helps his supercop boss, played by Michel Lonsdale, to foil a plot to assassinate French President Charles de Gaulle. Although based on the best-selling novel by Frederick Forsyth and meticulously directed by Fred Zinnemann, it elicited only mixed reviews: William Wolf of *Cue* (May 19, 1973) dismissed it as "a mild divertissement," but Judith Crist in *New York* (May 28, 1973) proclaimed it "a brilliant fact-fiction suspense thriller" and "a model for the genre."

Derived, like *The Day of the Jackal,* from a widely read novel by Forsyth, Columbia's *The Odessa File* (1974) became, in the opinion of Russell Davies of the London *Observer* (October 24, 1974), "a paltry chase-and-vengeance narrative." In it, Jacobi had the not insignificant part of Klaus Wenzer, a printshop proprietor on whose premises the journalist hero, played by Jon Voight, has an extremely tense, but not his last, confrontation with the ex-Nazi villains of the piece. Another 1974 release in which Jacobi appeared as a featured player was the starkly contrasting *The Three Sisters.* The Olivier-directed transfer to film of Chekhov's poignant drama, in which Jacobi repeated his splendid stage portrayal of the weakling brother, impressed Vincent Canby of the New York *Times* (March 12, 1974) as "something quite rare." It demonstrated, as *Othello* had not, that a National Theatre Company production could undergo the cinematizing process and emerge not only unscathed but with every delicate nuance intact. The picture's audience consisted solely of subscribers to the American Film Theatre series before it became available to commercial TV channels and on videocassette.

As a publisher named Townley, Derek Jacobi had a meager role in *The Medusa Touch* (1978), which starred Richard Burton, Lee Remick, and Lino Ventura. The anonymous author of a capsule review in the British publication *Sight and Sound* (Summer 1978) conceded that the Warner Brothers release got off to a promisingly spooky start, but argued that the psychic horror story then devolved into "a preposterous series of catastrophes." In *The Human Factor* (MGM, 1980), Otto Preminger's scrupulously faithful screen adaptation of the Graham Greene novel, Jacobi had the small but showy part of Davis, a minor employee of England's espionage establishment whose soulless bosses, wrongly suspecting that he is a double agent, efficiently engineer his demise. Commenting on the film in the *Saturday Review* (March 29, 1980), Arthur Schlesinger Jr. pronounced it "one of the very best of spy movies" and Preminger's "finest in twenty years." In his first starring role in a motion picture Jacobi embodied the character of Martin Beck, familiar to readers of crime fiction as the police lieutenant protagonist in a series of novels by Maj Sjowall and Per Wahloo, in *The Man Who Went Up in Smoke (Mannen Som Gick Upp I Roek).* The Swedish-West German-Hungarian coproduction, which was shot on location in Stockholm and Budapest, had its world premiere in Sweden in early 1981.

Russet-haired, blue-eyed Derek Jacobi is six feet four inches tall and has a solid build and a roundness of cheek that once led a theatre critic to call him "moon-faced." Douglas Watt, in his review of *The Suicide* for the New York *Daily News* (October 10, 1980), remarked that the pale-complexioned actor looked "as though he'd been fashioned out of modeling clay." A bachelor, Jacobi keeps open house for his many friends in the theatre at his Victorian residence in the Stockwell section of London, a neighborhood as unpretentious as the one in which he grew up. In an indirect reference to his plans for the future he once reflected, as quoted in *People,* "Movies make you rich, TV makes you known, but theatre is what it's really all about." The roles that he looks forward to playing are classics of the stage—Rostand's Cyrano de Bergerac, Ibsen's Peer Gynt, and Shakespeare's Macbeth, Coriolanus, and King Lear.

References: Dial 1:25+ N '80 pors; International Herald Tribune p14 N 21 '79 por; N Y Post p30 O 23 '80 por; N Y Times II p35 Je 10 '79 por; New York 13:20 S 22 '80 por; People 14:148+ N 10 '80 pors; International Who's Who, 1980-81; Who's Who in the Theatre (1977)

John, Tommy

May 22, 1943- Baseball pitcher. Address: b. New York Yankees, Yankee Stadium, E. 161st St. and River Ave., Bronx, N.Y. 10451

The New York Yankees' ace sinkerball southpaw Tommy John is baseball's bionic marvel, a thirty-eight-year-old finesse pitcher with an eight-year-old arm that seems only to improve with wear. John began his major league career with the Cleveland Indians (American League) in 1963. After stints with Cleveland and with the Chicago White Sox (American League), he achieved superstar status with the Los Angeles Dodgers (National League) in the early 1970's. In the mid-1970's he injured his pitching elbow so seriously and underwent a surgical reconstruction of that left elbow so precarious that he was not expected to pitch again. Making medical as well as sports history, he came back stronger than ever, reaching the twenty mark in wins for the first time in 1977. Moving to the New York Yankees (American League) as a free agent after the 1978 season, he became baseball's winningest pitcher in his first two years in New York, with a 43-18 record. As of the end of the 1981 season, his American League career totals were a record of 136 wins and 117 losses and a 3.03 earned-run average.

Tommy John

His National League totals had been 87-42 and 2.97.

Unostentatiously but unequivocally, Thomas Edward John Jr. attributes his unflappability, his strength in adversity, and his "eternal optimism" to a Christian faith that his parents were instrumental in planting. "The very fact that I can even move my hand and fingers today is testimony to the power of prayer," he said in a press conference, the transcript of which was appended to *The Tommy John Story* (Revell, 1978), by Tommy John and his wife, Sally, as told to Joe Musser. "Forget about my being able to pitch—just moving my hand is an answer to the prayers of many people [including] my folks." John was born in Terre Haute, Indiana on May 22, 1943 to Thomas Edward John Sr., an employee of the Indiana Public Service Company, and Ruth John. He has an older sister, Marilyn. His father, a former semi-pro infielder, encouraged but "didn't push" his athletic bent, John told Bill Benner when Benner was preparing an article on him for the *Saturday Evening Post* (October 1978). "He was my only coach until high school. We played catch, shot baskets, golfed, bowled . . . whatever normal Midwestern fathers and sons do."

Growing up, John was a superior all-around athlete, but pitching seems always to have been his preference. He idolized Robin Roberts of the Philadelphia Phillies, a pitcher who finessed rather than "flamed" his way to the Hall of Fame, and Whitey Ford of the New York Yankees, who, John says, "threw a lot like I wish I could throw." His vade mecum was Bob Feller's *How to Pitch*, the first acquisition in his collection of baseball instruction books. He practised pitching on a mound he improvised in his backyard, throwing balls at a narrow strike zone defined by two parallel vertical poles connected by two horizontal strings.

John began to pitch in the Spencer Park Recreational League in Terre Haute when he was eight. He joined a Little League team coached by his father when he was ten, and later he pitched American Legion ball. With the Gerstmeyer High School baseball team in Terre Haute he had a record of twenty-eight wins and two losses, and his combined American Legion-high school average was sixteen strikeouts per twenty-one-out game. Although his obvious strengths at that time were a curve and plain fastball, his high school coach, Howard Sharpe, told Bill Benner in the *Saturday Evening Post* interview that he could not use John in batting practice because "he had that darn sinker" even then. "It was natural. The ball would duck right over the plate, just like it does now. All my kids could do was hit the ball into the ground, right into the dirt."

Sharpe also coached the school's basketball team, on which John played forward and set the Vigo County single-game scoring record of forty-seven points, which stood for ten years. John's athletic laurels were obviously not won at the expense of his academic work, for he was a straight-A student, the valedictorian of his class. "I hated English," he has recalled, "but I loved math and science. My favorite class was trig. It was fun, like a puzzle. You had to be logical. Baseball's logic, too."

By the time he graduated from high school, John had received thirty-five athletic scholarship offers from colleges that wanted him to play basketball, but he knew that if he "expected to do anything in sports [he] was going to have to do it in baseball." His love for baseball aside, his height of six feet four inches "would have hurt" him in basketball, the sport of giants, as he explained to Bill Benner. "Even at that time, a 6-4 forward was marginal, and I couldn't have played guard."

Among the major-league baseball teams that had been scouting John, the Cleveland Indians made him the best offer. Signed by the Indians for a $40,000 bonus, he was assigned to the Dubuque (Iowa) Packers, Cleveland's affiliate in what was then the Class D Midwest League. Pitching for Dubuque in 1961, he won ten games and lost four, but he was accomplishing his wins with an undue, unrelenting intensity until a wise Dubuque pitching coach advised him to stop trying to strike out every batter. "Think of pitching this way," the coach said. "Say to the hitter: 'Here's the ball. Hit it.'" John has recalled: "The next day I threw a shutout, and I don't think I struck out more than two or three men. It was easy. That's my formula today. 'Here's the ball. Hit it.' Every ball I throw, I think it will be hit."

In 1962 and 1963 John shuttled between Charleston, West Virginia in the Eastern League and Jacksonville, Florida in the International League, accruing along the way twenty-three wins and twenty losses. In the off-season 1962-63 he attended Indiana University, with the abortive intention of majoring in mathematics in a bachelor's degree program. Called up to the majors toward the end of the 1963 season, John appeared in six games with Cleveland, losing two and winning none. While playing winter-league ball in Puerto Rico later in the year, he had a bout with tendonitis that left him with a chronically aching left elbow. "I can pitch up to pain," he told a reporter. "After a while it becomes bearable. Either it goes away or you stop noticing it."

Back in Cleveland at the beginning of 1964, John learned to throw a slider under the tutelage of pitching coach Early Wynn. In the process he lost confidence in his fastball, and the lack of self-assurance was reflected in a 2-9 record. He finished the season with Portland in the Pacific Coast League, pitching 6-6.

In a five-player trade, John went to the Chicago White Sox in January 1965. The testimony of his high school coach notwithstanding, John did not really master the sinking fastball until he came under the tutelage in Chicago of manager Al Lopez and pitching coach Ray Berres, both of whom had been catchers. "Until then I didn't know why a ball sank," John told Dave Anderson of the New York *Times* (May 11, 1980). "But then Al Lopez and Ray Berres taught me that the pitching motion is like a golf swing. In golf, you pop the ball at the club. As a pitcher, you pop the ball at the plate. Some people just can't get the ball to sink, but I can." Using the same analogy, John explained to Malcolm Moran in an interview for *Sport* (September 1980): "The way I pitch is a lot like the way Gene Littler hits a golf ball. You see his easy swing and you say he can't hit it that far, but he's out there with them. You don't have to grunt to crank out a long drive. The art of pitching is making the hitter think you're throwing the ball harder than you are, or slower than you are."

With Chicago in 1965, John won fourteen and lost seven. From Eddie Stanky, who replaced Al Lopez as manager of the White Sox after the 1965 season, John picked up one of the important points in his philosophy of pitching. He has recalled, "He [Stanky] always said if you lost your composure, you lost your 'science' for playing baseball and lost the point of what you were supposed to do on the field, which is win. Your mind controls your actions."

To fulfill his military obligation without interrupting his career, John enlisted in the Indiana Air National Guard three days before he would have been drafted in 1966. Three seasons in a row, from 1966 through 1968, he was among the leaders in earned-run average in the American League, with tallies of 2.62, 2.48, and 1.98. Over the same period, his win-loss record was 34-29. In July 1968 he made his first appearance in an All-Star game, pitching to one batter and giving up one hit. A month after the All-Star game, on August 22, 1968, John, hurling against the Detroit Tigers, uncocked a wild pitch over the head of Dick McAuliffe. The latter, interpreting the throw to be an intended "bean ball," charged the mound in a fit of anger. John, seeking to avoid fisticuffs by tackling McAuliffe and wrestling him to the ground, met him head on. On impact, McAuliffe's knee rammed John's left shoulder, tearing two ligaments and consigning John to the bench for the final six weeks of the season.

In his last three seasons with the White Sox, John won only thirty-four games, as against forty-four losses, and his control wavered, especially in 1969, when he walked ninety batters, and 1970, when he gave up 101 bases-on-balls. On December 2, 1971, in a trade for Richie Allen, John left the American League and, along with Steve Huntz, joined the Los Angeles Dodgers, in the National League. The following month he completed his tour of duty in the Indiana Air National Guard.

With the Dodgers in 1972, John had an 11-5 record, and he was leading when taken out of seven additional, no-decision games. Sliding into home plate in a game against the San Francisco Giants on September 22, 1972, he jammed his left elbow, causing a bone fragment to be knocked into the ulnar nerve, or "funny bone." The success of the surgery for removal of the fragment was obvious the following year, when, with a 16-7 record, he had the best winning percentage in the National League.

With a 13-3 record and a 2.58 ERA, John was again leading the league when, on July 17, 1974, he suffered two setbacks. The first was the news, which came to him during the day, that he had not been selected for the National League's All-Star team. That disappointment probably contributed to the second setback, at least subconsciously, because when he went to the mound to face the Montreal Expos that evening his morale seemed unusually low and he appeared unusually tense. He has referred to that evening as "the night [he] broke [his] arm with The Pitch." Attempting to throw a sinker to Montreal's Hal Breedon, he felt "a pop" and "tearing sensation" in his left elbow. Despite the frightening experience, he unleashed the ball again, and this time he knew he had done something "bad, very bad" to his arm, which felt as if it had been "somehow ripped from its socket." The feeling was not far from the medical fact, for he had ruptured the medial collateral ligament of the left elbow, the function of which, as the team physician, Dr. Frank Jobe, explained to him, "is to keep the elbow from flying apart." Nothing was holding the elbow together except an elongated and bruised ulnar nerve and skin.

Assuring John that his chances of pitching again would be slim even with surgery, but without it they would be nil, Dr. Jobe decided on an experimental operation, tried with polio victims but never before done on a pitcher's arm: the fashioning of a transplanted tendon into a new ligament to hold the elbow together. At Centinela Hospital in Inglewood, California on September 25, 1974 a team of surgeons headed by Jobe removed the six-inch palmaris longus tendon from John's right forearm, laced it through holes drilled in the contiguous bones in his left elbow, and fashioned it into a new ligament to hold those bones together. "Only 75 percent of people have this tendon," Jobe explained, as quoted in *The Tommy John Story*. "He's one of the lucky ones."

In the weeks following the operation, John's right forearm was immobile and scar tissue began to block the ulnar nerve in his left elbow, crimping it as one might a garden hose. The arm went numb from the elbow down, and the fingers of his left hand curled to form a claw. In a second, even riskier operation, in December 1974, Dr. Jobe scraped away the scar tissue and repositioned the inflamed ulnar nerve, rerouting it from behind the elbow to the front. While the nerve was regenerating, growing about an inch a month, the left arm was crippled. "I couldn't use it at all," John has recalled. "I couldn't open a car door. I couldn't hold a newspaper. . . . My wife had to cut my food and feed me. It looked like the arm of a skeleton." All the while, John and his wife never lost their sanguinity, believing as they did that "with God nothing shall be impossible" and that "because God delays does not mean He denies." They finally came to see the protracted convalescence as "a gift from God," because otherwise John might have aggravated the condition of his elbow in his haste to pitch again.

After months of therapy and exercises, feeling began to return to the fingers of John's left hand in July 1975. In the autumn of that year he returned to the mound, testing his arm in the Arizona Instructional League, where he won three games and lost one. By the time he showed up for spring training in 1976, he had regained complete use of his hand and arm, but it took him half of the 1976 season to relearn his skills. Starting in thirty-one games with the Dodgers, he won ten of twenty decisions. The *Sporting News* named him National League Comeback Player of the Year, and he received the Fred Hutchinson Award for Outstanding Character and Courage.

For the first time in his big-league career, John was a twenty-game winner in 1977. In the league playoffs he pitched the winning game against the Philadelphia Phillies, and in the World Series he pitched a losing game against the New York Yankees, the victors in the series. He came in second in the Cy Young Award voting for the league's outstanding pitcher.

In 1978 John's record was 17-10. John was selected for, but did not appear in, the 1978 All-Star game. In the National League playoffs the Dodgers again defeated the Philadelphia Phillies, with John contributing one of the three games Los Angeles won. He won the opening game of the World Series against the New York Yankees, but the Yankees went on to win the world championship again.

When John's contract with Los Angeles expired, he played out his option and asked for a new three-year contract, but the Dodgers' front office, fearing that he was too old, by pro baseball standards, and too vulnerable, refused to promise him more than two years' security. As a free agent, he then signed with the New York Yankees. The Yankee contract, signed on November 22, 1978, was a package deal estimated to be worth somewhere between $1,400,000 and $2,500,000. It reportedly called for a signing bonus of $300,000, a yearly salary of $200,000 for three years (with an option for a fourth year), an insurance policy, and a sinecure of $20,000 a year for some twenty post-playing years. During those years John will remain on the team's staff with the title of special assignment scout.

In his first season with the Yankees, John finished second in the American League in wins (twenty-one), ERA (2.96), innings pitched (276.1) and Cy Young Award voting. He was again selected for the American League All-Star team but again did not play in the All-Star game.

Another banner year for John was 1980, when his twenty-two wins represented a career high, and he led the league in shutouts, with six. Named an All-Star for the fourth time, he pitched 2.1 innings for the American League in the All-Star game, which the National League won. He pitched 6.1 innings for the Yankees in the American League championship series, which Kansas City won. His major-league career totals as of the end of the 1980 season were a 214-151 record, a 3.02 ERA, 523 games pitched, 3,345 innings pitched, 918 walks, and 1,800 strikeouts.

Opening the bifurcated 1981 season for the Yankees on April 9, 1981, John beat the Texas Rangers 10-3, and he hurled four more wins, as against four losses, during the following six weeks. Sidelined with a back problem, he faced no batters between May 22 and June 12, when the players in both major leagues went out on strike. As the strike began, the Yankees were in first place in American League standings and John had an ERA of 2.78. When the strike finally ended, on August 10, 1981, John reopened the season for the Yankees with a 2-0 victory over the Texas Rangers. Compiling three additional wins, as against four losses, he finished the year with a 9-8 record and a 2.63 ERA.

In the American League East playoffs, the Yankees defeated the Milwaukee Brewers, the first-place team in the division in the second half of the season. They went on to trounce Oakland, the victor in the league's western division, and in the World Series they lost to the National League titleholders, the Los Angeles Dodgers. In the series, the Yankees won the first two games and then lost four straight.

Pitching seven shutout innings, John was credited with their second win. He continued his shutout streak through two relief innings in the fourth game and the first three innings of the sixth and last game, on October 28, 1981. After the Dodgers tied the score, 1-1, in the first half of the fourth inning of that sixth game, Bob Lemon, the Yankee manager, sent a pinch hitter to bat for John in the Yankee half of the inning, thereby eliminating him from the game. George Frazier replaced John on the mound in the fifth inning, when the Dodgers began the rally that gave them a 9-2 victory. After the series, Bob Cohn, John's lawyer, told the press that George Steinbrenner was planning not only to pick up John's option but to sign him for at least two more playing years.

The Yankees are a congenial team for John for several reasons. One is the layout of Yankee Stadium, which gives lefthanded pitchers an advantage. Another is New York's cracker-jack infield, because, with his sinking fastball, which breaks down over the corner of the plate at the last moment, John is a good infielder's dream, inducing batters to ground out as he does. A third is the natural grass of Yankee Stadium and the American League in general; the astro-turf favored in the National League makes grounders treacherous. In addition to his sinking fastball and his curve, John throws an occasional changeup, and he has been perfecting a split-fingered fastball and working on a screwball, with a view to extending his career and keeping him, as he puts it, "one step ahead of the guy down the road."

Tommy John is six feet four inches tall and weighs about 189 pounds. To keep in shape, he runs and jogs longer distances than most pitchers, adding a thirty-minute sprint to his forty-five-minute jog the day after he pitches—usually every fifth day. He is conservative in his outlook, and his grooming and wardrobe might be described as small-town neat. In the foreword to *The Tommy John Story*, Tom Lasorda, who managed John in Los Angeles, writes that he is "every manager's dream . . . a man who gives of himself at all times, an unselfish pitcher who ignores his own individual achievements and is solely concerned with team effort." Others who work with him likewise attest to his congeniality, adjustability, sense of humor, and unfailing courtesy. Despite a slight stammer, John is pleasantly garrulous. His recreations include reading, taking in Broadway shows and other Manhattan cultural events, and playing golf. In 1977 he started his own charity golf tournament, the Tommy John Celebrity Tournament, to raise money for the Cystic Fibrosis Foundation. He spends much of his free time making civic and charity appearances and giving Christian testimony talks.

John and Sally Simmons, who met at Indiana State University, were married on July 13, 1970. With their three children—Tamara Marie, born in 1974, Tommy John 3d, born in 1977, and Travis, born in 1978—they live in a cedar and stone home with swimming pool that they own in Franklin Lakes, New Jersey. On August 13, 1981 their son Travis suffered a severe cranial injury when he fell from the third floor of their rented beachfront vacation home in Bay Head, New Jersey. After two weeks in a coma, the child made a rapid recovery and was released from New York University Medical Center in September.

Tommy John and his wife are members of the Evangelical Free Church, which he describes as "a Bible-teaching church that is very fundamentalist," and John is among the more active members of the Fellowship of Christian Athletes. "A lot of people are confused about my praying," he has said. "They think I pray to win every time I get on the mound. It's not so. I pray that God will help me do my best with the talent He gave me, that's all."

References: Christian Sci Mon p11 Jl 5 '74 por; N Y Times V p7 My 11 '80 por; Newsday S p10+ My 27 '79 por; Philadelphia Inquirer C p1 Ag 17 '78; Sport p55+ S '80 pors, 60:66+ Mr '75 por; Sporting News 187:3+ Je 30 '79 por; Burchard, S. H. Sports Star: Tommy John (1981); John, Tommy and Sally, and Musser, Joe. The Tommy John Story (1978)

Jones, James R(obert)

May 5, 1939- United States Representative from Oklahoma. Address: b. 203 Cannon House Office Bldg., Washington, D.C. 20515

A Congressman from Oklahoma, James R. Jones wields a great deal of power on fiscal issues in the House of Representatives as chairman of its Budget Committee and as a member of its Ways and Means Committee. In the late 1970's the moderately conservative Representative rose to eminence in only his third term as American public opinion began to favor middle-class tax relief and encouragement of investment capital accumulation. Skilled in the arts of bargaining and compromise, the assiduous Jones helped to secure a tax cut on capital gains in 1978 and subsequently rallied considerable backing for tax reductions on business. After he was elected head of the Budget panel in December 1980 over the opposition of more liberal House Democratic leadership, he led his party's efforts to modify White House budget proposals in the early months of the Reagan Administration.

James Robert Jones was born in Muskogee, Oklahoma on May 5, 1939 to a father who was a postman and a mother who was a telephone operator. He grew up in Muskogee's black ghetto because his family, having fallen deeply

James R. Jones

repudiated Great Society liberalism. He told a reporter for *Time* (June 4, 1979): "We created a lot of cynicism, both for those supposedly being helped and those footing the bill. Our ideas far surpassed our ability to make them work."

Returning to Oklahoma in 1969, Jones practised law in Tulsa. In 1970 he ran for Congress from Oklahoma's first district as the Democratic challenger to long-time incumbent Page Belcher, and although he lost, he waged an aggressive campaign and received a creditable 44 percent of the vote in that predominantly Republican district. When Belcher retired in 1972, Jones ran again that year against the Mayor of Tulsa, winning with 55 percent of the vote.

The first Congressional district, consisting of Tulsa and its immediate environs, was highly conservative, for as regional center of the oil industry with a booming economy, Tulsa was an affluent city with a decidedly pro-business outlook. As an Oklahoma political observer told Seth S. King of the New York *Times* (July 29, 1978): "In a district like his, it's kind of an honor to be in league with a big oil company." Although in 1976 Jones pleaded guilty to a misdemeanor for not reporting a 1972 campaign contribution from Gulf Oil and paid a $200 fine, he did not experience any significant political fallout. As an incumbent, he received substantial corporate campaign contributions from oil companies and other types of businesses.

In Congress, Jones's voting record harmonized with the views of his constituents. Not an extreme right-winger, he joined with liberal colleagues to support the Equal Rights Amendment, a Panama Canal Treaty, and President Jimmy Carter's labor law reform bill. Nevertheless, since he entered Congress in 1973, his rating from the liberal Americans for Democratic Action (ADA) has not surprisingly hovered around 30 percent or below, since he opposed a Consumer Protection Agency, strip mining regulation, financing of abortions, and the CETA public jobs program, while backing the antiballistic missile system, the B-1 bomber, the deregulation of natural gas, and oil company stances in general.

A relatively obscure rank-and-file Congressman for five years, Jones stepped to the fore in 1978 as a member of the tax-writing Ways and Means Committee when the Carter Administration failed to gather majority support in the House for a tax cut bill aimed at providing substantial reductions for low- and middle-income groups. Taking advantage of a burgeoning middle-class tax revolt accompanied by growing public support for investment incentives as a means of improving economic productivity, Jones secured House backing for a more conservative measure. His bill shifted the bulk of individual reductions to the $15,000-to-$40,000 brackets and included a controversial tax cut on capital gains. To win support

into debt during the Depression, could not afford to live anywhere else. But by the age of twelve, James R. Jones was working as a volunteer on the campaign staff of local Democratic Congressman Ed Edmondson. "I was just fascinated by it," Jones told Steven V. Roberts of the New York *Times* (April 7, 1981). "I enjoyed competition, being where the action was. And I enjoyed the pressure. You always had more to get done than could get done." While an undergraduate at the University of Oklahoma, where he majored in journalism and government, Jones became further involved in politics. As a campus correspondent for several Oklahoma newspapers to help defray his college expenses, he met Democratic party leaders, including Representative Ed Edmondson. After graduating from the University of Oklahoma in 1961, Jones became Edmondson's administrative assistant in Washington. Concurrently, he attended the Georgetown University Law Center, which granted him an LL.B. degree in 1964, the year in which he was admitted to the Oklahoma bar.

In 1964 and 1965 Jones was a captain in the United States Army counterintelligence and successfully sought an assignment as a special military aide to President Lyndon B. Johnson. He joined the White House staff as a civilian in 1965, serving as a deputy to chief of staff Marvin Watson, and after the latter left early in 1968, Jones directed its staff for the remainder of the Johnson Administration, as one of a small number of staffers in close contact with the President, who became his political mentor. From Lyndon B. Johnson, the future Congressman learned the fine art of passing legislation through compromise, coalition-building, and astute timing, but he subsequently

from moderate and conservative Democrats for his capital gains tax reductions, he altered a Republican proposal for cutting the maximum rate from 49.1 percent to 25 percent; he reduced it instead to 35 percent. Jones's bill for the first time indexed capital gains to eliminate taxation of gains stemming from inflation. Although the Carter Administration had denounced Jones's capital gains tax cut as a "windfall for millionaires," the bill signed by the President contained all of the basic provisions of the Oklahoman's proposal.

Jones was a comparatively new member of the lower chamber, but his success with the 1978 tax bill helped to make him a major leader of the conservative Democratic-Republican bloc in the House, particularly on the fiscal issues that came before the Ways and Means Committee. His standing was further enhanced with the retirement of Democratic Representative Joe D. Waggoner Jr. of Louisiana at the end of 1978. A member of the Ways and Means Committee, Waggoner had often united the panel's conservative Democrats and Republicans into a majority, and now, with Waggoner gone, Jones moved in to perform that junction. In January 1979 his influence on fiscal matters became even greater when he won his fight for a seat on the House Budget Committee. The Democratic Steering Committee selected more liberal members to fill vacancies on the panel, but Jones successfully appealed his case to the House Democratic Caucus with the argument that in the era of Proposition 13, the party should place some fiscal conservatives on the Budget Committee.

Capitol Hill observers attributed Jones's sudden rise in large part to his early and astute perception of the movement of power from the Frost Belt to the Sun Belt, from unionized blue-collar workers to middle-class, white-collar suburbanites, and from the New Deal coalition to a new configuration more critical of big government and less hostile to big business. But equally important were the qualities that made Jones a master at forging majority coalitions in the House. A tireless worker, he scrupulously read mail from his constituents and listened carefully to witnesses at committee hearings to get a sense of the type of consensus that would receive grass-roots backing. Far from intransigent, and ready for give-and-take, he not only excelled at the art of persuasion but was willing to listen to the views of his colleagues in the House. "One reason we like to work with him is that he consults us," Republican Representative Bill Frenzel of Minnesota told Ward Sinclair of the Washington *Post* (December 6, 1979). "He's not hidebound. He is very reasonable; he is willing to work things; he offends no one. You can put his word in the bank." A quiet, low-keyed person who is hardly a commanding figure in public, Jones achieved his influence through his skill at compromise.

In 1979 Jones watered down a windfall profits tax on the oil industry, a tax aimed at guaranteeing the government a portion of the higher profits resulting from the oil price decontrol that had begun that year. The Ways and Means Committee proposed a 70 percent tax on profits attributable to decontrol and rejected a Jones amendment exempting newly discovered oil from the tax, but after talking with his Democratic colleagues on the panel one-by-one, he secured Committee passage of a formula that almost guaranteed the exemption of new oil from the tax. Then, on the House floor, Jones and Republican W. Henson Moore of Louisiana secured adoption of a substitute proposal that applied that formula to "tertiary" oil—residue extracted from existing wells using costly techniques. Their measure also reduced the basic rate to 60 percent, cut the tax on marginal wells with low production, and phased out the tax in 1990. Altogether, Jones helped to save the oil industry billions of dollars.

Regarding the 1978 capital gains tax cut as merely the first part of a program to promote capital formation, late in 1979 Jones cosponsored legislation to speed up depreciation deductions for productive assets. That proposal, known as the Capital Cost Recovery Act, offered business tens of billions of dollars in tax relief for the 1980's. The bill severed the link between the time span of depreciation deductions and the useful life of the asset and authorized writeoffs for buildings over ten years, for equipment over a five-year-period, and for light trucks and automobiles over three years. With Jones marshaling the business community behind the measure, enthusiasm in and out of Congress for the 10-5-3 formula grew during the final months of 1979, but in the absence of a general tax cut in 1980, passage of a business tax reduction was politically impossible. Believing that reduced federal budget deficits were essential for reducing the high interest rates that retarded business growth, Jones toward the end of 1979 also gained considerable backing for a proposal to limit the size of the annual budget to 20 percent of the Gross National Product. But in 1980 the bill was blocked by House Rules Committee chairman Richard Bolling of Missouri.

With the retirement of Budget Committee chairman Robert Giaimo of Connecticut, Jones went before the House Democratic Caucus in December 1980 as a candidate for the post. Although the House Democratic leaders, most of them more liberal than Jones, did not embrace him as one of their own, and Speaker Thomas P. ("Tip") O'Neill backed Wisconsin liberal David R. Obey, Jones defeated Obey by five votes on the third ballot. He interpreted his victory as a response to the conservative tide of the 1980 election, which put Republican Ronald Reagan in the White House, gave the Republicans control of the Senate, and narrowed the Democratic majority in the House.

Some observers felt that Jones's personality also played an important role, noting that he had a reputation of being more conciliatory and congenial than Obey.

As chairman of the Budget Committee, which was responsible for setting spending limits, and as a member of the Ways and Means Committee, Jones is the most influential Democrat in the House on economic issues, and like President Reagan, he is a fiscal conservative. Their basic economic goals—cuts in federal spending and in taxes for individuals and businesses—are fundamentally the same. But because of differences in emphasis and the necessity for Jones, as Budget chairman, to work with the liberals of his party, the Oklahoma Democrat and the White House clashed over the budget resolution for fiscal 1982.

The fiscal 1982 budget proposed by President Reagan in the winter of 1981 offered $48.6 billion in cuts from the package that President Carter had offered, but Jones was critical of its projected $45 million deficit stemming from Administration acceptance of the Kemp-Roth 10 percent income tax cut for each of three successive years. Martin Tolchin of the New York Times (April 29, 1981) quoted him as saying that "Interest rates and inflation will come down more if we reduce the deficit than if we borrow money to finance the tax cut." He also criticized the White House budget for slashing social programs. In April, reconciling those apparently contradictory objections, he drew up an alternative Democratic budget that adopted 75 percent of Reagan's cuts but restored funds to many social programs and assumed a smaller tax cut than Kemp-Roth. The result was a somewhat higher spending level and a reduced deficit of $25.6 billion.

Despite his unimpeachable conservative record over the years and the sharp spending reductions included in his budget proposal, Jones came under right-wing attack for his opposition to President Reagan's plan, and when he returned to his district during Easter recess, he found himself under attack by Tulsa businessmen and the local news media. At about the same time, the influential National Conservative Political Action Committee (NCPAC) announced that it had targeted him for defeat in 1982.

James R. Jones's wife, the former Olivia Barclay, whom he married in 1968, is a graduate of the Harvard Law School who belongs to the prestigious Washington, D.C. law firm of Hogan & Hartson. Jones tries to see as much of his two young sons, Geoffrey and Adam, as possible, observing that "I've heard too many men in politics here, including Lyndon Johnson, say they always regretted not knowing their kids better when they were growing up." Quiet but affable, he is a slightly built, professional-looking man with a receding hairline and rimless glasses. Jones does some jogging and bicycle riding, but his favorite pastime is listening to music while sitting in

a rocking chair and reading biographies of men who, like Winston Churchill and Douglas MacArthur, "craved power and knew how to use it." He appended his credo to his biographical entry in Who's Who in America, 1980-81: "In essence I try to follow the admonition of Thomas Aquinas, 'To work as if everything depends upon you, and pray as if everything depends upon God.' By attempting to pursue a daily course of excellence in all responsibilities, I hope that when my earthly work is completed, they will say of me, 'that I gave it my all.' "

References: Chicago Tribune I p17 Mr 22 '81; N Y Times B p8 Apr 7 '81 por; Time 113:41 Je 4 '79 por; Who's Who in America, 1980-81

Kania, Stanisław

Mar. 8, 1927- Former First Secretary of the Polish United Workers' Party. Address: b. c/o The Polish United Workers Party, 6 Nowy Świat, 00-497 Warsaw, Poland

When he succeeded Edward Gierek as First Secretary of the Polish Communist party on September 6, 1980, Stanisław Kania inherited responsibility for the most perilous set of problems to confront any Polish chief of state since World War II. A widespread workers' revolt that began in a shipyard in Gdansk in August of that year not only toppled Gierek, but also forced a reluctant Communist government to permit the founding of an independent trade union known as Solidarity. Kania thus faced the difficult task of responding to the sweeping political and economic demands of an angry and disaffected populace while maintaining enough control over the process of democratic reform to prevent a possible Soviet invasion.

A career bureaucrat, Kania held a number of provincial party posts and, in the late 1970's, directed internal security operations, but he was almost completely unknown both at home and abroad. Informed Western analysts speculated that Kania had been elevated to the position of First Secretary at least partly because his reputation as a hard-line, orthodox Communist would reassure nervous Russian leaders, but he is above all a pragmatic politician. After taking power, he repeatedly insisted that the reforms mandated by the so-called Gdansk agreeemnts were "irreversible." At the same time, however, he came down hard on the "antisocialist" agitators that he believed responsible for much of the turmoil. Kania survived several early challenges to his leadership, but on October 18, 1981 he resigned in the face of deteriorating economic conditions and mounting criticism by his political opponents that he was too conciliatory in dealing with Solidarity. He was succeeded by General Wojciech Jaruzelski, who also holds the posts of Prime Minister and Minister of Defense.

Stanisław Kania was born into a peasant family on March 8, 1927 in Wrocanka, a small rural community in the southeastern province of Rzeszów, Poland. Apprenticed to the village blacksmith during most of World War II, he joined the resistance to the German occupation in 1944 and eventually fought in the peasants' battalion. After the liberation the following year, he signed up with the Polish Workers' party, as the Communist party was then called. Rising rapidly in the hierarchy of the party's youth organization, largely in posts relating to agriculture, he was cofounder and chairman of the Youth Combat Union in his district and, later, head of the Union's rural youth division for the province and vice-chairman of the Polish Youth Union's province board. When, in 1948, the Polish Workers' party merged with the Polish Socialist party to form the Polish United Workers' party (PUWP), the effective ruling body of the nation, Kania was a delegate to the unification congress, and he subsequently served as a member of the executive of the PUWP Province Committee in Rzeszów.

After completing a training program at a party school in Warsaw, in 1952, Kania was named director of the PUWP's Rural Youth Department and, at about the same time, he was appointed to the presidium of the main administration of the Polish Youth Union in the capital. Six years later, he was chosen to head the agricultural division of the PUWP's Warsaw Province Committee. He eventually was promoted to the post of vice-secretary of the committee. Since his original appointment in the early 1950's, he has spent his

entire career in similar administrative jobs in Warsaw, where he operated almost entirely behind the scenes, attracting little public attention.

Named a deputy member of the Central Committee of the PUWP in 1964, Kania attained a more powerful position after intraparty squabbling led to a major organizational shakeup in 1968. At the Fifth Party Congress in November of that year, the delegates elected a new Central Committee of 115 members, among them, Stanisław Kania. Kania was also tapped to direct the Central Committee's administration department, a position he held for three years. During that time, he studied economics at the Higher School of Social Sciences of the Central Committee of the PUWP in Warsaw.

Infuriated by the drastic consumer price hikes announced by the government of First Secretary Władysław Gomułka on December 13, 1970, Polish workers and housewives staged a massive protest. Within a few days, riots broke out in the Baltic seaport of Gdansk and in other northern shipbuilding cities. Gomułka crushed the strike, killing scores of workers. With much of the country virtually under martial law, the Central Committee, in an emergency meeting on December 20, forced Gomułka to resign and elected as his successor Edward Gierek, an economic expert with little interest in ideology.

As part of the political maneuvering that brought Gierek to power, General Mieczysław Moczar, a xenophobic hard-liner who headed a conservative, ultranationalistic faction of the PUWP, was named to the ruling Politburo. A few months later, however, as Gierek moved to consolidate his position by purging rivals, Moczar was ousted from the Politburo and from his post of Interior Minister. Kania replaced him in the Central Committee Secretariat and as a deputy member of the Politburo, thereby becoming a member of the party's select inner circle. More important, he took over Moczar's post as chief of the country's internal security forces: the army, the militia, the police, and the secret police. In 1972 he was elected to the Sejm, the unicameral national assembly, in which he has served ever since.

Throughout the 1970's, Kania was in charge of maintaining law and order in Poland. He also acted as the government's liaison with the powerful and politically active Roman Catholic Church. Although he kept a close watch on such potential sources of trouble as the Roman Catholic Church, dissident groups, and the press, he refrained from instituting draconian restraints. As a writer for the *Guardian* observed in an analysis of Kania's career published on September 14, 1980, "It would be foolish indeed to suggest that Mr. Kania is, in any commonly understood sense, a 'liberal.' And yet compared, say, with next door Czechoslovakia or East Germany, Mr. Kania has run a relatively tolerant ship. He permitted a degree of freedom and debate in the official press. He obstructed, rather that suppressed, underground publications. Harassed and intimidated, the dissidents were nonetheless allowed to exist. The Church, always a special case in Poland, was able to arrive at something approaching a *modus vivendi* with the authorities."

The newly installed Gierek regime made some economic gains during the early 1970's. Industrial production soared, largely on the strength of massive loans from Western banks, but agricultural output continued to decline. In an effort to cut consumer demand, the government, on June 24, 1976, increased the prices of many foodstuffs by as much as 100 percent. The directive provoked such violent demonstrations and strikes that Gierek rescinded it the next day. Kania's handling of the protests was typical of his tenure as security chief. Under his orders, the police used tear gas and water cannons to disperse the demonstrators, many of whom were arrested and jailed. According to the Workers' Defense Committee (WDC), which was organized by about a dozen dissident intellectuals to provide financial and legal aid to the prisoners, more than 100 people were beaten by the police during the demonstrations. All those convicted and sentenced for their participation in the protests were released from prison within a few months.

Nevertheless, political tensions in Poland remained at a high level. Emboldened by its success, the WDC grew more aggressive and, changing its name to the Committee for Social Self-Defense (KOR), expanded its activities to combat all political repression. Kania responded with periodic raids on the dissenters' homes, confiscations of underground publications and printing equipment, and arrests of dissident intellectuals. KOR reported several incidents of alleged police brutality. As a warning to dissidents not to exploit the upcoming visit of Pope John Paul II, who had been a determined enemy of Communism and a champion of human rights while he was a Cardinal in Poland, Kania arrested Jacek Kuroń and Adam Michnik, the leaders of KOR, in April 1979 and held them for over a month.

Many knowledgeable observers believe that the Pope's return to his homeland, in June 1979, was the catalyst for the dramatic events of the summer of 1980. As John Darnton, the New York *Times*'s Warsaw bureau chief, observed in an article for the *Times Magazine* (November 9, 1980), the Pope's nine-day visit "unleashed a flood of national and religious pride and cut through the cocoon of anesthetized indifference that had surrounded the workers." Instead of sullenly accepting another sharp increase in meat prices, which had been ordered by the Gierek regime on July 1, 1980, angry Warsaw workers immediately demanded corresponding pay raises. Within days, the protests and the accompanying wildcat strikes spread to other cities. The unrest peaked on

August 14, when striking workers took over the Lenin Shipyard in Gdansk. At first, their demands were strictly economic, but they eventually submitted a long list of specific political demands as well. One of their major demands was the right to form independent trade unions.

Some members of the ruling Politburo wanted to use military force to put down the workers' rebellion. Others, among them Stanisław Kania, argued in favor of a political solution. After talking to strikers in Gdansk, Kania bluntly told party officials, as quoted by the New York *Times* (October 4, 1980), "This is a mass protest by workers which cannot be resolved by force. We must understand the roots of the crisis." Convinced by Kania's persuasive arguments, Gierek sent a government committee headed by Deputy Prime Minister Mieczysław Jagielski to negotiate with Lech Wałesa, the leader of the strike committee. Finally, on August 31, Jagielski and Wałesa signed an agreement unprecedented in a Communist state. The government not only granted workers the legal right to form an independent union and to strike, but also agreed to increase wages and benefits, relax press censorship, release imprisoned dissidents, and allow the Church and the union access to the state-controlled mass media. For its part, the union promised not to form a political party and to recognize the supremacy of the Communist party in Poland.

Despite the government's major concessions to the workers, labor disruptions broke out in the Silesian coal mining region and in other areas throughout the country. For his failure to settle the labor disputes to the satisfaction of his Communist party colleagues, Gierek was eased out of office. According to some reports, Kania was a key figure in the behind-the-scenes maneuvering to replace the discredited party leader. In an emergency session on September 6, 1980, the Central Committee unanimously elected Kania First Secretary to succeed Gierek, who was officially reported to have been hospitalized for treatment of "serious" heart trouble.

In his first speech as party leader, delivered just a few hours after his election, Kania adopted a decidedly conciliatory tone. Acknowledging that the striking workers had been protesting "not against the principles of socialism but against the mistakes of the party," he pledged to honor the Gdansk agreements, but he warned "antisocialist elements" not to exploit the situation and reaffirmed Poland's ties to the Soviet Union, which were, in his words, of "paramount importance for the security and economic wealth of the country." His most important task was "to restore the confidence of the working class and all working people" in the Communist party, he said, adding that he was "deeply convinced that after the implementation of all these principles, the workers shall again say, 'Our Party.' "

To demonstrate the government's good intentions to the workers and to gain their support, Kania traveled extensively throughout the country, but his personal diplomacy yielded only modest results. The Solidarity movement had released social forces that had been bottled up for decades, and with the government demoralized and the Communist party in disarray, Poles were determined to press for such liberal reforms as higher pay, shorter hours, political and religious freedom, and the dismissal of corrupt and autocratic officials. Although he was receptive to many of their demands, Kania realized that he must walk what Tad Szulc, writing in the New York Times (October 4, 1980), called an "exquisitely delicate political line" in trying to democratize socialism without provoking a Soviet invasion like the one that ended the liberalization efforts of the so-called "Prague Spring" in Czechoslovakia in 1968.

In late October Kania traveled to Moscow, where he won at least temporary approval for his conciliatory policies from Leonid I. Brezhnev, the head of the Soviet Communist party. In mid-November he discussed with Lech Wałesa the role Solidarity could play in Poland's economic development, and later that month the union leader, who was equally alarmed by the deteriorating situation, declared a six-week moratorium on wildcat strikes. The continuing labor unrest had brought Poland to "the brink of economic and moral destruction," Kania told his countrymen in a speech to the Central Committee on December 1, 1980. "It is high time to sober up and understand that the basic condition for a successful national destiny is an immediate end to activities that imbalance and weaken the functioning of the people's state and, what is more, threaten the destabilization of peaceful order in Europe," he said. With the Soviet Union and other Eastern bloc nations threatening intervention if he could not restore order, Kania attended a hastily convened meeting of Warsaw Pact leaders in Moscow a week later. After the tense, closed-door session, Poland's allies expressed guarded confidence in Kania's regime and, in effect, granted the Polish leader more time.

On the home front, Kania maneuvered to consolidate his position within the Communist party, which was riven by factional conflicts. Contending that Gierek and his associates had accumulated "too much power" and that they had ignored "opinions and ideas originating outside the circle of rule," Kania expelled a number of hard-liners from the Central Committee in October and, the following month, he dismissed several leading provincial PUWP officials. By the end of December he had replaced all of Gierek's supporters in the Politburo, putting his own moderate group firmly in command. Among those elevated to the Politburo was the charismatic General Mieczysław Moczar, apparently in a bid for his political support.

To revive Poland's devastated economy, Kania obtained a $1.3 billion loan from the Soviet Union, appealed to Western nations for assistance in the form of credits, curtailed government spending, imposed a food rationing system, and increased aid to individual peasant farms by 80 percent. Those stopgap measures were designed to buy him time to work on the more fundamental problems of renegotiating Poland's crushing foreign debt, estimated at well over $20 billion, and reorganizing its old-fashioned productive structure. The new leadership is known to favor substantial economic liberalization, including decentralized decision-making and the restoration of market forces in some sectors.

Kania had scarcely begun working on those long-term goals when scattered work stoppages erupted again, in January 1981, amid worrisome indications that Solidarity's membership, then numbered at about 8,000,000, was no longer inclined to heed Lech Wałesa's appeals for moderation. Farmers, workers, students, and professionals presented for consideration a dizzying list of demands, ranging from a five-day work week to revisions in university curricula to state recognition of a farmers' union. Warning that he was prepared to use force, "if necessary," to "defeat the enemies of socialism," Kania threatened to crack down on the protesters, then ordered negotiations, in which the government eventually gave ground. Among other things, the government granted workers three Saturdays off per month, fired local and provincial officials whom workers had accused of corruption, gave students the right to form an independent student union, and approved the establishment of a "Rural Solidarity" organization. Perhaps infected by what one Solidarity strategist called the "democratic plague" that has swept across Poland, increasingly restless rank-and-file Communists, looking forward to a scheduled national party congress, drafted a detailed program of extraordinary reforms, including elections to party posts by secret ballots and membership controls over the leadership. To fortify the government's authority as it attempted to deal with those problems, Kania appointed General Wojciech Jaruzelski, another tough-minded pragmatist, Prime Minister in February 1981.

Stanisław Kania is a short, heavyset man, with neatly trimmed, graying hair. He usually appears in public wearing the rather shapeless dark suits and overcoats favored by many Eastern European leaders. Often dismissed by Western correspondents as a "colorless" bureaucrat, he displayed a surprisingly popular touch during a tour of Poland shortly after he came to power, shaking hands and making folksy, off-the-cuff speeches in a style that one Newsweek reported likened to "an American politician running hard for election." In 1977 Kania was awarded the Order of Builders of People's Poland, the nation's highest decoration. He is also the recipient of the Order of the Banner of Labor, the Knight's Cross and Officer's Cross, and the Order of Polonia Restituta.

References: Guardian p6 S 14 '80 por; N Y Times A p14 O 19 '81 por; Newsweek 96:46+ S 15 '80 por; Macleans 93:34+ S 15 '80 por; Time 116:32+ S 15 '80 por; International Who's Who, 1980-81; Who's Who in the Socialist Countries, 1978

Karmal, Babrak

1929- President of Afghanistan. Address: b. Office of the President, Revolutionary Council, Da Khalkoo Koor, Kabul, Afghanistan

In December 1979 a Russian-backed military coup in Kabul, Afghanistan overthrew the Marxist regime of President Hafizullah Amin and installed in Amin's place Babrak Karmal, a former Afghan government official and the leader of the pro-Soviet Parcham wing of the People's Democratic party of Afghanistan. In the West, the coup—the third in the country in less than two years—and the subsequent Soviet military occupation were widely viewed as examples of Russian aggression, possibly aimed at establishing a base from which to seize control of the Mideast oil fields. Denying that charge, both Moscow and Kabul insisted that the Russian invasion was carried out at the request of the Karmal government. Since his accession to power, Karmal has made several major changes in governmental policy and in his party's stance toward revolutionary change. Generally speaking, he has played down the emphasis on Marxist social and economic change that had caused the Moslem villagers and tribesmen, whose support for Islam and opposition to both Marxism and the Soviet Union are deeply entrenched, to rebel against their Communist rulers. Nevertheless, the widespread guerrilla war, which began in 1978, has continued, despite Soviet attempts to crush the insurgents. According to most Western political analysts, the Karmal regime enjoys the support of no more than 10 percent of the population and would almost certainly collapse if the Kremlin withdrew its troops from the country.

The son of a well-to-do Afghan army general, Babrak Karmal was born in 1929. He attended a German-language high school in Kabul, the capital city of Afghanistan, then enrolled at Kabul University, where he studied law and political science and became involved in Marxist politics. When he was twenty years old, he was arrested and jailed for his left-wing political activities. Upon his release five years later, he returned to school to complete work on a law degree. Following his college graduation, he served for one year in the Afghan army. From 1957 to 1965 he worked as an official in the Ministry of Planning under the constitutional monarchy of King Mohammad Zahir Khan.

In 1965 Karmal was elected to the lower house of Afghanistan's bicameral National Assembly, where he soon gained a reputation as a forceful and hot-tempered speaker. During one acrimonious debate, he reportedly slugged a rival politician. Reelected in 1969, he served in the assembly until 1973, when that body was abolished. Karmal had been a leading member of the pro-Communist People's Democratic party of Afghanistan (PDPA) since its founding in 1965 as the Khalq ("Masses") party, but he frequently clashed with Nur Mohammad Taraki, the party's founder, and his closest associate, Hafizullah Amin. Their differences, which at that time were primarily ideological in nature, came to a head in the early 1970's, when the party split into two rival factions: the Maoist Khalq wing, under the leadership of Taraki and Amin, and the pro-Soviet Parcham ("Banner") group, which was headed by Karmal. Most Western observers considered the broadly based Khalq faction to be the more extreme of the two.

Throughout that period, dwindling financial resources, recurrent famine, and lack of support from intellectuals and the educated middle class undermined King Zahir's government. Impatient with the ineffective civilian leadership, the military, in 1973, overthrew King Zahir, proclaimed Afghanistan a republic, and installed Prince Sardar Mohammad Daoud, the former Prime Minister, as President. Karmal's Parcham wing was the only Marxist group in the country that actively supported the coup.

When, four years later, Daoud abolished the legislature and outlawed all opposition political parties, the rival wings of the PDPA put aside their philosophical differences to join forces underground, where they began recruiting key members of the armed forces. On April 26, 1978 Taraki, Karmal, and Amin spearheaded an antigovernment demonstration to protest the assassination of a PDPA official. Daoud promptly arrested them. The following day, presumably in response to the imprisonment of the three Marxist leaders, a military junta, led by Colonel Abdul Khadir, seized power and executed Daoud and his aides. According to Robert G. Neumann, the former United States ambassador to Afghanistan and Morocco, the Soviets were "directly involved" in the coup. "Karmal, in particular, always prided himself (in conversations with me) on his good relations with both Moscow and the Soviet Embassy in Kabul," Neumann wrote in an article for the Los Angeles Times (January 6, 1980). "It would have been inconceivable for him not to inform Moscow of his intentions beforehand."

On April 30, 1978 the governing National Revolutionary Council announced the establishment of the Democratic Republic of Afghanistan, named Taraki President and Prime Minister, and appointed both Karmal and Amin to the posts of Vice-President and Deputy Prime Minister. Within weeks, however, the expedient partnership between the Khalq and Parcham wings of the PDPA collapsed, and Taraki and Amin began a systematic purge of their Parcham rivals, including Karmal, who was dismissed from the Cabinet on July 10, 1978 and reassigned as ambassador to Czechoslovakia. Two months later, Karmal was stripped of his Afghan citizenship and, along with other Parcham ambassadors, ordered to return to Kabul, presumably to face arrest, trial, and possible execution on charges of plotting to overthrow the Taraki regime. Karmal refused to obey the order and sought asylum in Eastern Europe. He spent more than a year in exile, probably in Czechoslovakia and East Germany.

Resentful of the radical social and political reforms instituted by Taraki, Afghan villagers, most of whom are devoted Sunni Moslems, rebelled. Soon a bloody guerrilla war raged between the rebels, known as the *mujahidin,* or "holy warriors," and the government. Taraki and Amin, who had been promoted to the post of Prime Minister in March 1979, used military force to put down the revolt, but their repressive tactics only served to strengthen opposition to the Communist regime. By July 1979 the rebels controlled most of the countryside; only Kabul and two other major cities remained in government hands. In an effort to shore up the tottering Taraki regime, the Soviet Union urged a more conciliatory policy toward the insurgents and, according to some reports, backed a proposed attempt to oust Amin, whose brutal ironhanded rule alienated all classes of Afghan society. The plan backfired when Amin himself overthrew Taraki in a coup on September 16, 1979.

A Soviet-supported countercoup, launched with an airlift of about 5,000 Russian combat troops, ostensibly sent to help Amin suppress the Moslem rebellion, began on December 25, 1979. The troops quickly took control of Kabul, then fanned out through the countryside. Within forty-eight hours, Amin had been arrested, tried by a revolutionary court, and executed for "crimes against the state," and Babrak Karmal had been installed as President. Karmal was also named Prime Minister, secretary general of the PDPA's central committee, and commander in chief of the Afghan armed forces. (He resigned the post of Prime Minister in June 1981, giving the job to a close political ally.) The United States, Great Britain, West Germany, the People's Republic of China, and other countries protested the Soviet Union's military intervention in the internal affairs of Afghanistan, but the Kremlin, backed up by President Karmal, insisted that it had acted in accordance with the United Nations Charter, which gives any country the right to provide military assistance to a member state that has asked for such aid.

In a radio speech to the nation shortly after taking office, Karmal said that he was "deeply grateful" to the Soviet Union for its assistance in freeing his "long-suffering countrymen" from "the machine of tortures of Amin and his henchmen, wild butchers, usurpers, and murderers." To correct the "harmful mistakes" made by his "adventurist and criminal" predecessor, Karmal pledged to wage "a holy war for genuine democratic justice, for the respect for the sacred Islamic religion, for the respect of our family and national tradition." He went on to outline a program of moderate economic and social reforms to eliminate poverty, disease, ignorance, unemployment, and inequality, among other things, and to spur economic development and raise living standards. "While it is not our immediate task, under contemporary conditions, to introduce socialism," he explained, as reported by Tass, the Soviet press agency, "the new democratic government dooms it its historic mission to strengthen and develop the progressive social and political foundations of the Democratic Republic of Afghanistan."

To achieve his ambitious economic goals, Karmal turned to the Soviet Union for financial and technological assistance. (In the wake of the coup, most Western countries had suspended foreign aid to Afghanistan.) During the first few months of Karmal's Presidency, the Russian government invested so much money in Afghanistan that Karmal was able to announce, in March 1980, a balanced budget for the upcoming fiscal year, financed largely through Russian loans and grants of about $200,000,000, or roughly 30 percent of the country's projected revenues. According to U. S. News & World Report (February 4, 1980), the total Soviet investment was expected to be about $3.6 billion, or more than three times what it had been in the past. The Russians also promised to give technical aid in the development of copper, coal, oil, and natural gas deposits and to string electricity transmission lines into the country from Soviet Central Asia.

In an effort to rally domestic support and to broaden his political base, Karmal appointed military leaders and non-Communists as well as Parcham party regulars to his twenty-member "national unity" Cabinet, and he publicly appealed to the Afghan people to "come together and support our glorious revolution." Calling for an end to fratricide, he asked those Afghans who had fled to neighboring Pakistan to return home. "The question of those who have taken up arms against the government will be settled by political means," he promised the refugees, as quoted in the New York Times (January 1, 1980). To demonstrate his good faith, he abolished the hated KAM security police, which he claimed Amin had used for "his own criminal ends," replacing it with a new force modeled on the Soviet intelligence agency. He also ordered the release, under a "general amnesty," of about 2,000 political prisoners, most of them Parchamists jailed under previous administrations. At the same time, however, he reportedly rounded up and incarcerated as many as 1,700 Khalqi sympathizers.

Openly courting the fundamentalist Moslems, Karmal removed political portraits and slogans from public buildings, asked radio and television stations to broadcast passages from the Koran regularly, and redesigned the country's all-red flag, a color which many associated with Communism, to include green, which is symbolic of Islam. In a televised address in late January 1980, President Karmal guaranteed "freedom for all religions, sects, national customs, and traditions" and threatened to prosecute those who "oppose the sacred religion of Islam." He also made overtures of friendship to the Ayatollah Ruhollah Khomeini, the Iranian religious leader, in which he promised that his government would "never allow anybody to use our soil as a base against Islamic revolution in Iran."

Despite such conciliatory moves, Karmal's popular support remained at about 10 percent, according to Western estimates. His life was in constant danger, several members of his government and their relatives were assassinated, and even his closely guarded palace was set afire. "The people question his legitimacy and view him as an atheist who has sold himself completely to the Soviet Union," one senior Western diplomat explained to a reporter for Time magazine (January 28, 1980). "Karmal's number one problem is to get some political support from the people, by whatever means." Other diplomats commented on escalating Soviet troop strength and increased Kremlin involvement in the day-to-day running of the government. A political representative from an unnamed Third World country maintained, as quoted in the New York Times (January 8, 1980), that Karmal "[saw] the Russians constantly" and that "they [were] in

every ministry," but no one knew "just who [gave] the orders and who [took] them." Angered by those widely circulated reports, which he claimed were exaggerated by the "propagandistic liar machinery" of the United States, the Afghan President expelled Western journalists in late January.

Over the next six months, the Moslem rebels, their numbers swelled by disaffected Khalq party members and defectors from the Afghan armed forces, continued to stage hit-and-run guerrilla raids against the Soviet troops and Afghan government units that patrolled the towns and major highways, and in the capital, the insurgents and their student supporters clashed repeatedly with police in violent anti-Soviet demonstrations. The protesters distributed leaflets denouncing Karmal as an "obedient slave of the Russians" who "should be cursed for using heavy guns, tanks, and machine guns against our daughters and sons who had no weapons other than handkerchiefs, books, and pens." Karmal responded by issuing several draft calls to replenish his depleted armed forces.

Hoping to increase public acceptance of his government, Karmal began a purge of Khalqi loyalists in July 1980, replacing them with nonpartisan figures. He also moved to eliminate bureaucratic inefficiency and, at the same time, consolidate his power by setting up what Kabul radio, in its broadcast of July 20, described as a "general presidency for guidance" to oversee provincial and municipal administration. Instead of raising his government's credibility, Karmal's reorganization plan sparked more defections and mutinies by soldiers loyal to the Khalq faction. In mid-July, Soviet troops reportedly quelled an attempted coup against Karmal, planned by Afghan forces at a base near Kabul.

Mindful of the upcoming United Nations debate on Afghanistan, scheduled for November 1980, Soviet President Leonid I. Brezhnev invited Karmal to Moscow for a series of high-level talks aimed at establishing the legitimacy of the Afghan regime in the eyes of the world. On October 19, three days after Karmal arrived in Moscow, the two leaders issued a joint communiqué expressing their "profound satisfaction" with the results of their meetings. The public announcement stressed their "full identity of views on all issues discussed" and maintained that new bilateral agreements would "strengthen" and "deepen" the ties between the two countries. Rejecting any solution to Afghanistan's civil strife that disregarded President Karmal's "legitimate government," the two men further agreed that Soviet troops would remain in Afghanistan until "an end is ultimately put to the aggression against Afghanistan and guarantees are given of nonresumption of subversive activities from abroad against the Afghan people and its government." Karmal was supposed to be in Moscow for just five days, but he remained in the Soviet Union for several weeks, reportedly undergoing unspecified medical treatment.

On his return to Kabul, Karmal gave a homecoming speech in which he contended, as quoted in the New York Times (November 7, 1980), that his reception in Moscow "proved to the whole world that Afghanistan was an independent and truly free country and that the Soviet Union was the true and sincere friend of Afghanistan." In what many veteran Kabul-watchers saw as an attempt to demonstrate to the Soviets his control over the government, Karmal criticized some party regulars and public employees for inefficiency, political infighting, bribe-taking, and other abuses of authority. He ordered government officials to recognize the "people's basic rights" and "revolutionary legality" and reminded them that the PDPA had taken power in 1978 "not for the purpose of enhancing personal glory and the creation of a rich new bureaucratic stratum," but to advance the welfare of the people. The new yardstick for professional advancement would be "the pursuance of

eternal friendship and solidarity with the Leninist Communist Party of the USSR," he said, as reported in the Christian Science Monitor (December 3, 1980).

A stocky man with thick black hair and dark eyes, Babrak Karmal has been described by journalist Robert Fisk as "a philosophical Marxist of considerable intelligence and even charm." He speaks English and German as well as Pushtu and Dari, the official languages of Afghanistan. While in exile in Eastern Europe, Karmal was rumored to have married Anahita Ratebzad, his longtime companion and Afghanistan's former ambassador to Yugoslavia. Miss Ratebzad, who serves as Minister of Education in Karmal's Cabinet, was reportedly shot to death by an unknown assailant in July 1980, but subsequent dispatches indicated that those reports were in error.

References: Los Angeles Times I p11 D 28 '79 por; N Y Times A p12 D 28 '79; Newsweek 95:22 Ja 7 '80; Time 115:73 Ja 7 '80 por; International Who's Who, 1980-81

Kaufman, Henry

1927- Economist; investment counselor.
Address: b. Salomon Brothers,
1 New York Plaza,
New York City, N.Y. 10004

Among Wall Street pundits, the best record for forecasting the direction of the United States economy is currently held by Henry Kaufman, the pragmatic non-ideologue who with grim steadfastness defied a general

optimism to predict the pivotal downturns in the bond market in 1970 and 1974 and the rise of the prime interest rate to 20 percent in the spring of 1980. Kaufman is the chief economist with the investment banking house of Salomon Brothers, a premier trader in bonds and other fixed-income obligations as well as stocks, with an annual turnover exceeding $600 billion and annual underwritings approximating $10 billion. His judgments are issued privately, for the benefit of Salomon Brothers and its clients—among whom number some of the largest corporations—but word of them invariably spreads quickly through the financial community, affecting the market to the extent that at least one official in a rival investment firm has wondered "if some of the prophecies aren't self-fulfilling." Kaufman responds to such criticism with the argument that his market impact is temporary unless he has perceived a trend correctly: "No one can buck a trend indefinitely. I'm never able to tell ahead of time whether a speech or memorandum will have a market impact. My role, as I see it, is to tell which way events will go, rather than which way they should go. That's quite different from a national policy maker who influences the events themselves."

The son of a Jewish meat merchant, Henry Kaufman was born in Wennings, Germany in 1927. Among his earliest memories are the stories his parents told of the frightful runaway inflation in Germany in the early 1920's, when the price of dessert in a restaurant might rise even as one was eating the entrée. The poverty into which much of the population slipped before the government succeeded in bringing the economy under control and in stabilizing the currency contributed to the discontent that made possible the national acceptance of Adolf Hitler and his persecution of the Jews.

"All of that had an influence on me in many ways," Kaufman told Stanley H. Brown in an interview for *Quest* (January/February 1981). "It made me very sensitive to the destruction of values that occurred, to the uprooting of society that was all part of it, and to the problems of political failure." Another important early influence was the idea imbued in him by his parents and grandparents that, as he has worded it, "you have the obligation and responsibility to make a contribution to some human endeavor."

In 1936, when Henry was nine years old, the Kaufmans, fleeing the Nazi holocaust, immigrated to the United States, where they settled in New York City. Kaufman at first aspired to become a physician, but he had trouble with chemistry, a premed prerequisite, and found himself more at home in economics. After taking his B.A., M.A., and Ph.D. degrees in banking and economics at New York University, he served an apprenticeship in commercial banking, taught at N.Y.U., and worked as an economist and assistant chief of research at the Federal Reserve Bank of New York. In 1962 he joined Salomon Brothers, where Sidney Homer, the widely respected author of the definitive *The History of Interest Rates* (1963), was then the chief economist. Under Homer, Kaufman had responsibility for Salomon's cash-flow analysis. He was named a general partner of the firm in 1967 and was appointed to the executive committee five years later, after Homer's retirement.

Many an economic prognosticator was made to look foolish by the Johnson Administration's reluctance to face up realistically to the cost of the Vietnam war, and Kaufman did not entirely escape such a fate. He made one of the few major errors of his career in the summer of 1968, when the Administration finally pushed through Congress legislation for a tax increase, and the Federal Reserve Board began to ease interest rates. It looked to Kaufman as if there was going to be a significant rally in the bond market, and he said so for two months. "But then, by September, I had the apprehension that monetary policy hadn't really eased that much," he recounted to Douglas Bauer when Bauer was preparing a profile of him for the New York *Times Magazine* (May 27, 1979). "And what was really going to happen was that the economy was going to heat up again. And by fall, that's what was happening. It was an agonizing period. But I learned something from it. I learned that what the Administration intends to do is not always what really happens. And I learned that it was best to re-evaluate quickly, admit you were wrong as soon as you knew it. If I hadn't, I'd have been in serious trouble."

Redeeming himself, Kaufman was remarkably on target in calling the interest-rate scourges of 1970 and 1974. In a speech in 1971 he blamed the 1970 debacle on the compromises with inflation contained in Phase II of President Richard Nixon's economic policy. Those compromises included an end to the wage-price freeze of Phase I and the establishment of targets of 3 percent and 2 percent inflation over a period of years. In the struggle against "destructive and impoverishing" inflation, he asserted, Americans wanted "not compromise and not long federal involvement in the private economy," but rather action that would be "quick," "decisive," and "unyielding regardless of the claims of the different economic participants." Instead, they were given a program with "baffling dimensions" that caused uneasiness among investors.

Some of Kaufman's rivals gloated over what they interpreted to be the bullish position on long-term bonds he took in his December 30, 1976 *Comments on Credit* newsletter to Salomon clients. As it turned out, the bond market declined 3.1 points over the next month. "I just said that for the immediate future I thought there weren't many obstacles ahead—for the next two or three weeks," he later explained. "It had nothing to do with my basic view of the direction of interest rates, although it was [thus] misinterpreted by some." When, in late 1977, Kaufman predicted significantly higher interest rates and some squeezing out of the credit markets for 1978, many of his peers thought he was being unduly pessimistic. Just as he predicted, by the end of May 1978 short-term interest rates had risen to 8½ percent and long-term rates for high-grade utility bonds had risen to 9 percent.

In testimony before the Joint Economic Committee of Congress in June 1978, Kaufman described the escalation in the rate of inflation as "ominous." The behavior of the credit markets during the summer of 1978 seemed encouraging to many, but not to Kaufman. In October of that year he told a convention of the American Bankers Association in Honolulu that the markets were "about to experience the most dramatic increase in interest rates since the cyclical rise began in 1976." He also predicted that interest rates would continue to rise through mid-1979 and "perhaps quite a bit later," and that they would reach 12 percent or more. As soon as reports of his speech reached Wall Street, the market dropped ten points.

In the March 1979 edition of Salomon's *Memorandum to Portfolio Managers*, Kaufman dealt with the implications of trends in household credit activities, of accommodations to inflation in the financial markets, and of the public's perception of the government's unwillingness to take the measures necessary for braking inflation. He summed up by expressing his belief that our economic and financial system has "slipped from the moorings" that in the past "kept our behavior within reasonable limits." The loss of those moorings, he warned, "poses grave risk and danger to us all."

Among the moorings we have lost, in Kaufman's view, have been the mechanisms for keeping the small investor from operating beyond his means. The sum effect of that loss has been "to create huge debt in this country and to make it easier and easier to create more debt," as he told Douglas Bauer in the New York *Times Magazine* interview. Other lost moorings specified by him have been bankruptcy as a punishment for mismanagement and the distinction between money and credit. But perhaps the most fundamental mooring of all, he said, has been more psychological than structural. "There has always been the perception in this country that whenever inflation got too high the government would step in and break its back. Today that perception is gone. Americans have lost confidence in their government. They assume inflation will continue, so they're spending more and more, buying now because it will cost more tomorrow. Reserves in conventional savings accounts have dropped to almost four percent of income. Incredibly low! And very dangerous, because it only fuels inflation more and more. People are saving in very unconventional ways, as hedges. They're buying land, gold, and art. That is a European attitude toward investment. It is a European *disease*."

Bauer observed that as Kaufman talked one heard him describing an economy that has "not only assumed shape and speed outside the old, fundamental definitions, but one that has disappointed his far more personal ethic; an economy granting temporary reward for too little effort; an economy escaping the old instructive punishments, moving lazily and, so far, getting away with it; an economy, in short, performing with no redeeming discipline, succeeding, but not on merit."

In testifying before Congressional committees in 1979, Kaufman advised "slow growth of federal expenditures," "tax incentives to reduce inflation," and "the great need to liberalize the capital gains tax instead of tightening it." Above all, he reiterated his warning that a halfhearted, gradualistic governmental anti-inflation policy would serve only to entrench further the national inflationary psychology.

As much as Kaufman feared the absence of an effective governmental policy, he personally seemed to think it was more important for a person like himself to remain in the private sector, as he indicated in the New York *Times Magazine* interview. "People have the wrong perceptions about Washington's role," he said. "There are no goods and services produced in Washington. There are just a lot of people. There's always talk about the great sense of reward one feels in helping to run this Big Machine, but I'm not sure the Big Machine is run from Washington." Nevertheless, a Salomon partner observed of Kaufman, "He's never said so, but I'm sure he'd like to be running the Federal Reserve." Kaufman's attitude toward government was perhaps best conveyed in one of his 1980 speeches: "Some say that the spectacular advance in interest rates during the past thirty years was the result of excessive fiscal and monetary stimulation, thus placing the blame on government and monetary officials. . . . Governments, however, do not act in isolation, particularly in a democratic society. Rather, they reflect in their actions the behavioral qualities and the will or the laxity of their people."

In an address at the annual convention of the American Bankers Association in Los Angeles, California on February 21, 1980, Kaufman proposed that the government declare a "national economic emergency." To stem an inflation that was "running wild," he recommended steps that would include even the temporary imposition of wage and price controls. On the impact of his words, the Dow Jones Industrial Average fell 18.34 points and bond prices, which rise or fall in inverse ratio to the expected direction of interest rates, lost $20 for each $1,000 of face value. When President Jimmy Carter announced his new anti-inflation program in March 1980, Kaufman criticized the Carter strategy for relying too much on monetary restraints and paying too little attention to government expenditure. He said that the federal budget would continue to run a deficit because the "balanced" budget proposed by Carter was "based on economic assumptions that won't materialize."

Early in the spring of 1980 Kaufman correctly predicted that the prime interest rate would reach 20 percent. In a telephone conference with the Salomon portfolio managers on April 16, 1980, he said that it was "likely that money rates have reached their cyclical peaks and will decline irregularly," and that the recession other analysts had been predicting prematurely year after year was now unavoidable. As word of the conference quickly spread, the industrials lost 12.11 points because of the fear that a recession would erode corporate profits. On the other hand, the bond market had a one-day price rally of $50 for each $1,000 of face value.

In statements made in the following weeks, Kaufman said that, barring an unforeseen major external challenge or domestic failure, such as the collapse of a giant corporation like Chrysler, the recession would be a "mild" one in which real growth would constrict more than the 2.6 percent average of the previous five economic downturns and less than the 5 percent drop in the 1973-75 recession. It would not, however, be the slight dip prefacing a return to sustained vigor that the Carter Administration envisioned. "To believe that a small recession is all that is necessary to bring us out of our dilemma is contrary to all the powerful forces in place today," he explained. To begin with, business balance sheets were in such bad shape that plant and equipment expenditures would be delayed, and the household sector was "in need of a tremendous amount of financial rehabilitation," he said. Defense spending would help, but "that never comes on stream very quickly" and would "not be meaningful until 1981." As Kaufman predicted, the prime rate fell below 15 percent during the summer of 1980, but it rose to 21.50 in December 1980 and remained at 20 going into 1981. Kaufman repeatedly pointed out that inflation was so ingrained in the economy that the problem was not about to go away completely. He estimated that the underlying rate of inflation would continue to be "at least 8 to 10 percent" for several years under the best of circumstances. As uncertainty over the direction of interest rates restrained buying on Wall Street at the end of June 1981, Kaufman forecast a brief decline in short-term rates to be followed by a soaring of rates over the following twelve months or so. He revised that forecast on October 30, 1981, predicting a continued decline in short-term and long-term interest rates because "a sluggish economy will make further monetary accommodation probable."

Kaufman usually arrives at his office forty-one stories above Wall Street at 7:30 in the morning. Although he sees himself as a "participant" who is "on the side of business," as opposed to an academic economist, he differs from his sixty-four partners at Salomon Brothers—who virtually live in the markets—in that he does not become involved in daily trading decisions. There is interaction between him and the other executives, who do not hesitate to disagree with him when they think he is wrong, but he has the special function of being the firm's thinker. His huge research staff constantly gathers statistics on the performance of the economy, but Kaufman's greatest advantage over his rivals in maintaining surveillance over the economy and keeping in touch with the minute-by-minute mood of the market is the Salomon trading room, just a few steps down the hall from his office.

When Kaufman walks into the trading room, as he does several times a day, he is standing at the world's financial crossroads. "I'm in a fortunate position," he told David Eisner of the Chicago *Tribune* (May 8, 1980). "We are a primary source of market information. All I have to do is walk into our trading room to see what is going on. We have relationships with central banks and governments. I don't have to pick up a book to see what a particular figure is." The grist for his economic judgments also includes long rounds of telephone conversation; prodigious reading; habitual personal observation, even of such matters as the business his favorite restaurant is doing and the number of cars parked in the local shopping center; a shrewd knowledge of human nature; and, of course, the catalyst of intuition.

Much of Kaufman's time is spent on the road, addressing Salomon Brothers' clients—all of whom are institutions—and such organizations as the World Bank and the Council on Foreign Relations on such subjects as yield curves; financing and monetary policy; credit flow; governmental, industrial, and individual debt financing; and other aspects of the economy

relating to the business and financial community and especially to the credit markets. He speaks without notes, but beforehand he writes the speech out completely. "The process isolates me and forces me to reflect," he explained to Douglas Bauer. "I find it a thorough, rigorous discipline." Articulate and pithy but not glib, he speaks in a calm, unhurried manner, using plain English instead of economic jargon and often displaying an understated wit and punctuating his remarks with a rolling, staccato laugh. "When Henry starts talking about interest rates," George T. Rowe, a manager of fixed income assets for T. Rowe Price, has testified, "you almost get the feeling it's the devil speaking. A strange mood comes over the crowd."

Henry Kaufman, who is short and round-faced, lives in a suburb of New York City with his wife and three children. He personally almost never buys anything on credit. "The notion of debt bothers me very much," he explained in the New York *Times Magazine* interview. "It's just a function of my upbringing. I have a very hard time buying something and not paying earned cash." In that 1979 interview, he was quoted as saying, after pointing out that his politics, like his economics, are unaffiliated: "With that stipulation, let me say that as I look around I see some bleak times ahead, and it makes me worry about things on a very personal basis. I'm worried about my country, about the place where I live, about the future of the firm and of business in this country. I'm worried because I'm afraid Washington does not recognize the severity of the problems, and I can see nothing in place that can effectively deal with them." Kaufman's "great pride" is Leonard Baskin's bronze of the Biblical Abraham, which overlooks the desk in his office. "I didn't purchase the Baskin as an investment," he has explained. "I purchased it because I love it. . . . What I get from the sculpture is a feeling of patience and great strength. He [Abraham] was tested, he had faith, and he endured."

References: Chicago Tribune VI p3 My 8 '80 por; Institutional Investor 14:45+ My '80 pors; N Y Times Mag p24+ My 27 '79 pors; Quest 5:15+ Ja/F '81 pors

---

King, Stephen (Edwin)

Sept. 21, 1947- Writer. Address: h. RFD 2 Kansas Road, Bridgton, Me. 04009

Beginning with *Carrie* in 1974, Stephen King's seemingly inexhaustible imagination has produced seven novels of heart-stopping terror in as many years. Each of his macabre novels has been a best seller, and at one point in 1980, he became the only American writer ever to

Stephen King

have three different books—*Firestarter*, *The Dead Zone*, and *The Shining*—on the lists at the same time. Following the pattern of its predecessors, King's most recent novel, *Cujo*, leaped to the top of the New York *Times*'s best-seller list within days of its publication in August 1981.

By 1981 there were considerably more than 22,000,000 copies of Stephen King's nine books in print, most of them in paperback. Two of them, *Carrie* and *The Shining*, have been filmed; two more, *The Stand* and *The Dead Zone*, have been scheduled for motion picture production in the near future; and his *'Salem's Lot* became a successful miniseries on CBS-TV in 1979. In his autobiographical *Danse Macabre* (Everest House, 1981), King tried to account for the vogue of the horror genre: "We make up horrors to help us cope with the real ones." As he elaborated, "The dream of horror is in itself an outletting and a lancing . . . and it may well be that the mass-media dream of horror can sometimes become a nationwide analyst's couch."

Stephen Edwin King was born in Portland, Maine on September 21, 1947, the son of Donald and Nellie Ruth (Pillsbury) King. His father, a merchant seaman, deserted the family in about 1950. Consequently, he and his older brother, David, saw little of their mother, who took a succession of low-paying odd jobs to support her children. A lonely, rather introverted child, King invented a more outgoing alter ego—Cannonball Cannon, a daredevil who "did good deeds"—and derived other vicarious thrills from listening to tales of horror on the radio, reading such spine-tingling comic books as *Weird Science*, *Tales from the Crypt*, and *Tales from the Vault*, and going to see science

fiction and monster movies. When in October 1957 the local theatre manager interrupted a Saturday matinee screening of *Earth vs. the Flying Saucers* to announce the Soviet Union's launching of Sputnik, the first artificial earth satellite, King sensed for the first time "a useful connection between the world of fantasy and that of what *My Weekly Reader* used to call Current Events," as he wrote in *Danse Macabre*. Countless viewings over the years of such classic horror films as *The Invasion of the Body Snatchers*, *The Creature from the Black Lagoon*, *The Thing*, and *It Came From Outer Space* eventually convinced him that the horror movie's chief value is "its ability to form a liaison between our fantasy fears and our real fears."

The fortuitous discovery of his father's paperback collection of fantasy-horror fiction, including several stories by H. P. Lovecraft, a twentieth-century master of macabre gothic tales, gave King, in his words, a "taste of a world that went deeper than the B-pictures . . . or the boys' fiction of Carl Carmer and Roy Rockwell." The boy was surprised to find that his long-absent father had shared his interest in the genre, but even more surprised to learn that Donald King wrote several horror stories and submitted them, without success, to *Bluebook*, *Argosy*, and other magazines. Determined to make his own mark as a writer, Stephen King tried his hand at composing offbeat short stories while still a student at the local high school. Although he failed to sell a single one, he did win first prize in an essay competition sponsored by a scholastic magazine. He took time off from his studies to play tackle on the varsity football team, and he was for several years the rhythm guitarist in an amateur rock 'n' roll band called the MoonSpinners.

Following his graduation from high school, King attended the University of Maine at Orono on a scholarship. Majoring in English, he took creative writing courses and contributed a weekly column called "The Garbage Truck" to the campus newspaper. By the time he obtained his B.S. degree in 1970, he had sold two stories—"The Glass Floor" and "The Reaper's Image"—to *Startling Mystery Stories* for $35 each. Over the next few years, he published short stories in *Cavalier*, *Gent*, *Penthouse*, and *Cosmopolitan*, but he earned so little money as an author that he was forced to add to his income by working at such jobs as janitor, library aide, gas station attendant, and presser in an industrial laundry.

From 1971 to 1973 King taught English at the Hampden Academy, a private coeducationl secondary school in Hampden, Maine. Closeted in the school's boiler room with a child's desk propped against his knees, he continued to write short stories in his spare time. He also tried his hand at longer works, turning out what he has since called "a big novel on a race riot" and another that his literary agent later compared to the political thriller *The Parallax View.*

Discouraged and dejected by his mounting pile of rejection slips, King almost scrapped the manuscript of what was to become his first published novel, *Carrie.* Luckily, his wife retrieved the discarded pages from the trash and encouraged him to complete the book and submit it to Bill Thompson, an editor at Doubleday & Company, Inc., who had shown an interest in his work in the past. Impressed by King's riveting narrative, Doubleday handed him a $2,500 advance and, in 1974, published *Carrie.*

Carrie tells the story of Carrie White, the tormented teenage daughter of an overbearing religious fanatic who uses her telekinetic powers to take revenge on her persecutors. After she is publicly humiliated at a high school prom, Carrie retaliates by liquidating her enemies and by virtually destroying the entire town. "The book tries to deal with the loneliness of one girl, her desperate effort to become a part of the peer society in which she must exist, and how her effort fails," King explained in *Danse Macabre.* "If it had any thesis to offer, this deliberate updating of *High School Confidential,* it was that high school is a place of almost bottomless conservatism and bigotry." He sees Carrie's coldblooded incineration of the packed gymnasium-turned-dance hall and her destructive walk home as "a dream revolution of the socially downtrodden."

Most critics dismissed *Carrie* as gory and overdone, but horror buffs snapped it up. Boosted by the publication of a paperback movie tie-in edition, total sales of the book eventually topped the 4,000,000 mark, and the film version, directed by Brian De Palma and starring Sissy Spacek in the title role, overcame generally unfavorable reviews to become one of the top-grossing films of 1976. King cheerfully admits that "the movie made the book and the book made me."

Over the next several years, Doubleday published four more books of bone-chilling horror by Stephen King: *'Salem's Lot* (1975), in which vampires take over a small town in Maine; *The Shining* (1977), which King has called "a very nasty, dark book" about a haunted hotel and a little boy with extrasensory perception; *Night Shift* (1978), a collection of bizarre short stories; and *The Stand* (1978), a Doomsday encounter between the forces of good and evil.

After disputing with Doubleday over softcover rights, King negotiated a $3,000,000, three-book contract with New American Library, a publishing house that specializes in paperbacks. Under an agreement with NAL, Viking began publishing the hardcover editions of King's novels in 1979 with *The Dead Zone,* the story of a young man who awakens from a four-year coma with second sight—a gift that carries with it the awesome responsibility of preventing a nuclear war. *The Dead Zone* was succeeded in the national hardcover best-seller list by *Firestarter* (1980), a complicated tale involving a paranormal child and a ruthless, top-secret government agency known as "The Shop," which wants to turn the little girl's pyrokinetic ability into a secret weapon. King's most recent novel is *Cujo* (1981), which New York *Times* reviewer Christopher Lehmann-Haupt called his "cruelest, most disturbing" book to date. In *Cujo,* a formerly gentle St. Bernard dog terrorizes a small New England town after he has been bitten by a rabid bat, the implication being that he is possessed by the ghost of a mass murderer.

Danse Macabre (Everest House, 1981), which King has described as "an informal overview" of the horror genre in radio, television, film, and popular fiction from 1950 to 1980, was the outgrowth of a course in supernatural literature that he taught at his alma mater while he was a writer-in-residence there during the 1978-79 academic year. According to King, "the work of horror . . . is a dance—a moving rhythmic search . . . [for] the place where you, the viewer or the reader, live at your most primitive level." Universal human fears, or "phobic pressure points," which are, in his opinion, often political, economic, and psychological rather than supernatural, "give the best work of horror a pleasing allegorical feel." In essence, horror is therapeutic as well as enthralling. "Beneath its fangs and fright wig," the horror tale is really "as conservative as an Illinois Republican in a three-piece pinstriped suit," King maintained in his introduction to *Night Shift.* "Its main purpose is to reaffirm the virtues of the norm by showing us what awful things happen to people who venture into taboo lands. Within the framework of most horror tales we find a moral code so strong it would make a Puritan smile." King agrees that the horror story can be seen as a "rehearsal for death," but he insists that, because of its "strict moralities," it is also "a reaffirmation of life and good will and simple imagination—just one more pipeline to the infinite."

King finds the inspiration for his stories in a variety of ways. For instance, while teaching his Hampden Academy students Bram Stoker's *Dracula,* he began to speculate about the problems vampires would face in the contemporary United States—speculations that eventually led to *'Salem's Lot. The Shining* was prompted by the uneasy feeling he had as one of the few guests at a fashionable Colorado resort on the last day of the tourist season. King has readily admitted to interviewers that he was "actually scared" while he was writing it. In *The Shining,* Jack Torrance, a hot-tempered would-be writer, his wife, and their young son, who has the ability to "shine," or see things others cannot, are the winter caretakers of the isolated and seemingly unoccupied Overlook Hotel in the Colorado mountains. The sinister hotel harbors in its rooms so many ghostly guests that one reviewer called it "a Grand Guignol *Room*

Service." Stanley Kubrick's long-awaited cinematic version of *The Shining* (Warner Brothers, 1980), which was widely advertised as "the ultimate horror movie," was more Kubrick than King and was generally considered to be less effective than the novel.

In his review of the novel *The Shining* for the *New York Times* (March 1, 1977), Richard R. Lingeman complained that because the evil was so "slapdash" and "unfocused," it became "eventually preposterous." King is "a natural," he acknowledged, "but he lacks control; he simply rears back and lets fly with the fireball, and a lot of wild pitches result." According to Lingeman's colleagues, the "wild pitches" include prolixity, muddled syntax, "pseudoscientific hokum," "inelegant" and "heavyhanded" style, and unintentional humor.

But even those critics who, like Walter Kendrick, think King cannot write have confessed to being mesmerized by his masterful storytelling. "There's unmistakable genius in Stephen King," Kendrick grudgingly conceded in the *Village Voice* (April 29, 1981), "and though it's genius of a trivial kind . . . still it's inimitable. [He writes] with such fierce conviction, such blind and brutal power, that no matter how hard you fight . . . he's irresistible." Others have applauded his careful attention to realistic detail, the "inexorable force" of his plots, his nail-biting climaxes, and his gift for characterization. "He manages to create characters who, while never convincing, nonetheless interest and move us," John Podhoretz observed in the *Wall Street Journal* (September 3, 1980). "The fun of Mr. King's novels rests in the ability to read them with delight and then put them aside without a thought."

In his foreword to *Night Shift*, King himself maintained that if the story kept the reader spellbound "all else can be forgiven." As he explained to William Wilson in an interview for a *New York Times Magazine* (May 11, 1980) profile, "Talent is cheap. It lies inside you like crude ore. What's really interesting are those depth charges, the ones that, when the talent begins to get refined, swing it toward a particular way of looking at things. . . . For me, the idea of writing always came after the idea of creating an event. Love of the word wasn't first, it was second." When he is working on a book, King spends about eight-to-ten hours a day in an office in his home, batting out with two fingers some 1,500 words a day to the accompaniment of rock music. He does not consider himself to be "a great artist." Writing what he has called "fearsomes" is, for him, a compulsion. "If I weren't writing, I might be like that guy in the Texas tower," he told a reporter for *People* magazine (May 18, 1981). "Writing is what God put me on earth to do."

A towering, bear-like man, Stephen King stands six feet three inches tall and weighs 225 pounds. He has squinty blue eyes, always shielded by tortoiseshell eyeglasses, and thick black hair, and he usually sports a bushy black beard. Affable and easygoing, he cares little for the trappings of fame and fortune. His few extravagances include a videotape recorder and a library of hardcover books. Bowling, swimming, cross-country skiing, poker, and an occasional beer binge are among his simple pleasures. Describing himself as "more Big Mac than Chateaubriand," King is a rather reluctant celebrity, and on his rare business trips to New York City, he prefers the come-as-you-are anonymity of a neighborhood fast-food emporium to the elegant surroundings of the expense-account restaurants favored by the literary elite.

King lives quietly with his wife, the former Tabitha Jane Spruce, whom he married on January 2, 1971, and their three children, Naomi, Joe Hill, and Owen, in a rambling Victorian house in Bangor, Maine. In 1981 Mrs. King embarked on a writing career of her own with the publication of her first book, *Small World* (Macmillan), a fantasy about a mad scientist and his "minimizer." Stephen King's next venture is the five-segment, low-budget motion picture *Creepshow*, which he wrote in collaboration with George Romero, the director of *Night of the Living Dead* and *Knightriders*, in which King played a bit part. The idea of *Creepshow*, as King outlined it to a reporter in a recent interview, is "simply to put people in movie theatres and see if we can scare hell out of them. I want people crawling under the seats with popcorn and jujubes in their hair."

References: *Film Comment* 17:60+ My/Je '81; *Horizon* 21:87 F '78; *N Y Daily News* p7+ S 23 '79 por; *N Y Times Mag* p42+ My 11 '80 por; *People* 14:53+ D 29 '80, 15:81+ My 18 '81; *Pub W* 211:12+ Ja 17 '77 por; *Take One* p33+ Ja '79 por; *Writers Digest* 57:26+ Je '77 por; Ashley, Mike. *Who's Who in Horror and Fantasy Fiction* (1978); *Contemporary Authors* new rev vol 1 (1980); *Who's Who in America*, 1980-81

Kirkpatrick, Jeane (Duane) J(ordan)

Nov. 19, 1926- United States Permanent Representative to the United Nations; political scientist. Address: b. 799 United Nations Plaza, New York City, N.Y. 10017

The political scientist Jeane J. Kirkpatrick was appointed United States Permanent Representative to the United Nations by President-elect Ronald Reagan in December 1980 because of her forthright advocacy of a hard-line policy toward the Soviet Union. Self-described as a "Humphrey-Jackson Democrat," Mrs. Kirkpatrick drew the attention of Republican Presidential aspirant Reagan through her article in

Jeane J. Kirkpatrick

the November 1979 issue of *Commentary* magazine, in which she denounced President Jimmy Carter's diplomacy for allegedly undermining pro-American right-wing autocracies while ignoring the threat posed by pro-Soviet dictatorships. A former professor of political science at Georgetown University and the author of scholarly works, Mrs. Kirkpatrick is widely respected as an academician, but her critics contend that she lacks flexibility and that her single-minded anti-Communism tends to weaken the United States in its relations with the strategically important Third World countries.

Mrs. Kirkpatrick was born Jeane Duane Jordan in Duncan, Oklahoma on November 19, 1926, the daughter of Welcher F. and Leona (Kile) Jordan. Her father, an oil wildcatter, whose dreams of making a major strike failed to materialize, moved his family to a succession of small towns in Oklahoma and Illinois. Jeane Jordan received an A.A. degree from Stephens College in Columbia, Missouri in 1946, a B.A. from Barnard College in New York City in 1948, and an M.A. in political science from Columbia University in 1950. After working as a research analyst with the office of intelligence research of the United States Department of State, she did postgraduate work during 1952-53 at the Institut de Science Politique of the University of Paris under a French government fellowship. She served as assistant to the director of the Economic Cooperation Administration history project under the Governmental Affairs Institute in 1953-54 and then worked as a research associate with the Human Resources Research Office of George Washington University in Washington, D.C. from 1954 to 1956.

Having married Dr. Evron M. Kirkpatrick, a fellow political scientist, in 1955, Jeane Kirkpatrick delayed her full-time academic career for a few years to minister to the needs of her growing family, but she took time out between 1956 and 1962 to work as a research associate with the "Communism in government" project of the liberal-oriented Fund for the Republic. In 1962 she became an assistant professor of political science at Trinity College in Washington, D.C., and five years later she was appointed associate professor of political science at Georgetown University. On completing her dissertation, "Peronist Politics in Argentina," she obtained her Ph.D. degree from Columbia University in 1968. Mrs. Kirkpatrick was appointed a full professor at Georgetown in 1973 and became Leavey Professor in the Foundations of American Freedom there in 1978. Intermittently, between 1955 and 1972, she also served as a consultant to the American Council of Learned Societies and to the Departments of State, Defense, and Health, Education, and Welfare.

A prolific writer and scholar, Mrs. Kirkpatrick contributed to *Commentary*, the *New Republic*, the *American Political Science Review*, and other publications. She edited the volume *The Strategy of Deception: A Study in World-Wide Communist Tactics* (Farrar, Straus, 1963), which critics found to be useful and timely, although some thought that it dwelled too much on the no longer valid concept of Communism as a monolithic movement. Among her early monographs are *Foreign Students in the United States: A National Survey* (1966) and *Mass Behavior in Battle and Captivity* (1968). Her *Leader and Vanguard in Mass Society: A Study of Peronist Argentina*, based on her doctoral dissertation, was published by MIT Press in 1971.

With the publication of her *Political Woman* (Basic Books, 1974), Mrs. Kirkpatrick's work began to attract a more general readership. Having interviewed fifty women state legislators in 1972, she concluded that, like their male counterparts, they were generally upwardly mobile, highly educated, and active in their communities, that they had strong egos and a need for achievement, and that they tended to be analytic and pragmatic. One significant difference was that the women often began their political careers late, after they had raised their families. Furthermore, since many of the women were not dependent on political office for a living and did not entertain hopes for higher office, they tended to be more public-spirited, more issue-oriented, and more reform-minded than many of their male colleagues.

In *The New Presidential Elite: Men and Women in National Politics* (Russell Sage Foundation, 1976), Jeane Kirkpatrick, with the help of Warren E. Miller and others, examined the delegates to the 1972 Democratic and Republican conventions—in her words, "a cross section of the effective elite of the Presidential parties"—through 1,300 interviews and responses to mailed questionnaires. Among her important findings was that on most major policy issues women delegates held virtually the same views as men. She also found that the supporters of the candidacy of South Dakota Senator George S. McGovern constituted a "new breed" of delegates who had "a vested interest in the intellectual and moral aspects of politics" because of their skills in analyzing and moralizing. In her view, under the aegis of such ideologically oriented leaders, there would be a continuing deterioration of political parties, since those individuals were committed to causes rather than organizations.

In her brief study *Dismantling the Parties: Reflections on Party Reform and Party Decomposition* (American Enterprise Institute for Public Policy Research, 1978) and in an interview in *U.S. News & World Report* (September 18, 1978), Mrs. Kirkpatrick expressed her concern over the declining strength of party organization, which she attributed to such factors as the growing importance of primaries, the increased role of television, public financing of candidates instead of parties, and the weakening of intergenerational ties. In her view, stable democratic government depended on the parties' abilities to form coalitions from diverse interest groups. Without strong parties, she asserted, the political system was fracturing into a multitude of single-issue organizations, which, because of their uncompromising nature, were incapable of uniting into governing coalitions.

A lifelong Democrat, Mrs. Kirkpatrick was spurred to political activism by her disaffection with the rise of the counterculture and the antiwar movement in the 1960's. Those forces, she felt, were fundamentally antagonistic to American culture and institutions, since they perceived the United States as a sick society surfeited by materialism and technology and advocated what she viewed as unrealistic, utopian reforms. She regarded the McGovern-for-President movement in 1972 as the embodiment of that tendency, and in May of that year she ran unsuccessfully in the Maryland primary on a slate of delegates committed to former Vice-President Hubert H. Humphrey.

Although the nomination of McGovern by the Democrats represented for Mrs. Kirkpatrick the triumph of the countercultural and antiwar movement within the party, she remained a Democrat because she supported the welfare state and organized labor. Futhermore, the Republicans, she asserted in *Commonsense* magazine (Fall 1979), were so preoccupied with private concerns, such as profits and taxes, that they had failed to articulate "any inclusive vision of the public good that reflects concern for the well-being of the whole community."

To reduce the influence of the McGovernites in the Democratic party, Mrs. Kirkpatrick and her like-minded party colleagues formed the Coalition for a Democratic Majority in 1972. Its members, most of them writers and scholars, who became known as "neoconservatives," were, like Mrs. Kirkpatrick, generally liberal on domestic issues, but rejected the reform program of the McGovern supporters as too radical. In foreign policy, they opposed the "dovish" stance of the McGovern Democrats, advocating instead a hard-line posture toward the Soviet Union. Mrs. Kirkpatrick was quoted in the *New York Times* (December 23, 1980) as saying that the goal of the CDM was to reclaim the Democratic party from the "antiwar, antigrowth, antibusiness, antilabor activists."

Within the party, Mrs. Kirkpatrick was active as a member of the Democratic National Committee and as vice-chairman of the committee's vice-presidential selection commission, from 1972 to 1974. She sat on the Democratic National Convention's national commission on party structure and presidential nomination from 1975 to 1978, and she served on the credentials committee that prepared for the 1976 Democratic National Convention.

Mrs. Kirkpatrick at first backed Senator Henry M. Jackson of Washington, a leading advocate of a strengthened military establishment, for the 1976 Presidential nomination. After Jackson's effort failed, she switched to Jimmy Carter. In 1977 she became a resident scholar at the American Enterprise Institute for Public Policy, a conservative think tank in Washington, where her hard-line views on defense and foreign policy issues were welcomed. Meanwhile, she was becoming increasingly critical of the Carter Administration's foreign policy, which she felt reflected the Democrats' guilt-ridden and irresolute approach to the use of American power in the post-Vietnam era.

In her article in *Commentary* (November 1979) entitled "Dictatorships and Double Standards," Mrs. Kirkpatrick asserted that the failure of the Carter Administration's foreign policy was now "clear to everyone except its architects." Citing as an example the United States's role in the destablization of friendly governments in Nicaragua and Iran, she criticized the Carter Administration for condemning and undermining pro-American right-wing autocracies while taking a relatively benign view of totalitarian revolutionary movements and governments although, she contended, the latter were less friendly and more repressive than the right-wing regimes. The Carter Administration was applying not only a double standard on human rights, she said, but a double standard that operated against the United States's strategic and economic interests. Its roots, Mrs. Kirkpatrick believed, lay in the Carter Administration's mistaken conviction that the United States in the past had stood in the way of a supposedly inexorable process of modernization in the Third World, and to atone for that alleged sin, Carter and his advisers encouraged movements for change even when Soviet-aided Marxist revolutionaries played a major role in them.

While admitting that "traditional autocrats . . . favor the affluent few and maintain masses in poverty," Mrs. Kirkpatrick suggested in her article that "because the miseries of traditional life are familiar, they are bearable to ordinary people." She argued that, in fact, the pro-American traditional dictatorships of the Third World were more amenable to liberalization and democratization than totalitarian regimes of the left and that the United States could best promote both its interests and those of the Third World by backing its friends against Soviet subversion. "Liberal idealism," she concluded, "need not be identical with masochism, and need not be incompatible with the defense of freedom and the national interest."

Along with other neoconservative Democrats, Mrs. Kirkpatrick met with President Carter in January 1980 to urge him to adopt a stronger anti-Soviet policy, but failed to persuade him. Soon afterward, Richard V. Allen, the chief foreign policy adviser to Republican Presidential aspirant Ronald Reagan, showed her Commentary article to the candidate. Reagan wrote to Mrs. Kirkpatrick that it was the best article he had ever read on the subject, and after talking with him, she decided to back his candidacy. In an article in the Washington Star (November 2, 1980), Mrs. Kirkpatrick asserted that Reagan, in contrast to Carter, was "a very skilled politician who . . . has demonstrated his ability to unite in back of him a political coalition as diverse as that which followed Franklin Roosevelt." She felt that "he might just be able to restore the consensus and confidence that has been missing in this country for more than a decade." In the months preceding the election, Mrs. Kirkpatrick was active on one of Reagan's advisory committees and coached him for the campaign debates. After Reagan's election victory she became a member of his interim foreign policy advisory board.

Mrs. Kirkpatrick became the first Democratic appointee to a Cabinet-rank position in the Reagan Administration when the President-elect named her, on December 22, 1980, to succeed Donald F. McHenry as United States Permanent Representative to the United Nations. She told Bernard Nossiter of the New York Times (January 12, 1981) that although she hoped to have some influence at Cabinet meetings, she took a "very strict constructionist view" of her role as an ambassador and that she did "not expect to be making policy," adding that she was not a professional diplomat. She promised that she would resign if she did not feel in good conscience that she could represent the policies of the Reagan Administration.

In response to descriptions of her as a "hawkish" conservative, Mrs. Kirkpatrick pointed out that one of her intellectual mentors at Columbia was the late Professor Charles Frankel, a decided liberal, who resigned from a high State Department post in 1967 in protest against President Lyndon

B. Johnson's Vietnam war policies. To an interviewer for Time (January 5, 1981) she remarked: "By habit and temperament, I am rather low-key in my jobs. I do not come in swinging or making pronouncements." After she assured members of the Senate Foreign Relations Committee that she would present Administration policy at the U.N. "with neither bluster nor self-abasement," her appointment as Permanent Representative to the U.N. was confirmed by unanimous vote of the United States Senate on January 29, 1981.

Taking office as United States Ambassador to the U.N. soon after Reagan's inauguration, Mrs. Kirkpatrick defended the Administration's policy of granting arms assistance to El Salvador's military junta, which was under attack by Cuban-backed Marxist guerrillas. In a February 26 debate with the Carter Administration's Ambassador to El Salvador, Robert E. White, sponsored by the Members of Congress for Peace Through Law and reported by the New York Times (March 8, 1981), she asserted that the alternatives were "whether we do anything at all, or whether we leave the government unsupplied while the Cubans or the Soviet Union supply the guerrillas." She added: "Nobody is worried that we are about to put our foot down on that slippery slope that led to Vietnam. . . . To use American power in selected circumstances and in an economical fashion does not risk [that] kind of wholesale commitment." In an interview for U.S. News & World Report (March 2, 1981), Mrs. Kirkpatrick insisted that the Reagan Administration would be concerned with human rights, but that the Carter Administration's human rights policy "was utopian, because it was conducted outside of the political and historical context."

Mrs. Kirkpatrick's meeting in New York City on March 13, 1981 with the chief of intelligence and four other senior military officers of South Africa caused a minor uproar as well as speculation concerning the Reagan Administration's South African policy. The Congressional Black Caucus called for her dismissal, and spokesmen for black African nations expressed concern that the meeting signaled a friendlier policy toward white supremacist South Africa. Mrs. Kirkpatrick insisted that she had not known the status of the South Africans, that the meeting represented her policy of "being open to people and being willing to listen to almost any point of view," and that in any case her action was technically not a violation, since the Reagan Administration had not yet decided whether to continue the policy, in force since 1962, of avoiding official contact with high-ranking South African military officials. She asserted that President Reagan "abhors" apartheid, but in a shift of emphasis from Carter Administration policy considers the threat of Communism in southern Africa of primary importance. In the Security Council debates in April on the independence of South West Africa, or Namibia, from South African rule, Mrs. Kirkpatrick spoke out against imposing economic sanctions on South Africa and called, instead, for unspecified "practical alternatives."

In June 1981 Mrs. Kirkpatrick won some praise for her role in helping to draft a compromise resolution—unanimously passed by the Security Council—condemning Israel for its air strike that destroyed a nuclear reactor in Iraq but stopping short of imposing sanctions as demanded by militant Arab nations. "Nothing in the resolution will affect my government's commitment to Israel's security," she asserted after the voting.

During a Latin American tour in early August, Mrs. Kirkpatrick defended the Reagan Administration's efforts to improve relations with the military regimes of Argentina, Uruguay, Chile, and Brazil. While visiting India later that month she maintained that military aid to Pakistan would "introduce an element of stability rather than instability" to the region.

The former Jeane Duane Jordan was married on February 20, 1955 to Dr. Evron M. Kirkpatrick, a fellow Democrat and a past president of the American Political Science Association. They have three sons, Douglas Jordan and John Evron, who are attending Georgetown University Law School, and Stuart Alan, who is at Kenyon College. The Kirkpatricks have moved from Bethesda, Maryland to an apartment in New York City's Waldorf Towers reserved for the Permanent Representative to the U.N. Fluent in French and Spanish, Mrs. Kirkpatrick also has some familiarity with Italian and Portuguese. An excellent cook known especially for her French cuisine, she often gives intimate dinner parties. She enjoys listening to Baroque music, especially Bach.

References: N Y Times A p13 D 23 '80 por; New York 14:36+ Jl 20 '81 pors; Newsweek 97:18 Ja 5 '81 por; Time 117:61+ Ja 5 '81 por; Washington Post A p4 D 23 '80 por; Who's Who in America, 1980-81

Kuralt, Charles

Sept. 10, 1934- Broadcast journalist; writer. Address: b. CBS News, 524 W. 57th St., New York City, N.Y. 10019

For thirteen years Charles Kuralt's homespun "On the Road" essays lent charm, humor, and grace to the *CBS Evening News* and, along the way, picked up virtually every major award for television journalism. An affable and insatiably curious former foreign correspondent, Kuralt finally gave up his footloose wandering in

October 1980 to become the anchorman of CBS's morning news broadcast. It is generally acknowledged by critics to be the best of the three network wake-up programs, although it has consistently lagged behind NBC's *Today* show and ABC's *Good Morning, America* in the ratings. Thanks to Kuralt's personal warmth and considerable journalistic skills, the ratings for *Morning With Charles Kuralt* jumped 40 percent in the first two weeks alone. Kuralt also anchors the imaginative and critically acclaimed *CBS News Sunday Morning*. For his "wit and wisdom" on the morning news shows, he was recently awarded the 1981 George Polk Memorial Award for national television reporting.

Charles Bishop Kuralt was born in Wilmington, North Carolina on September 10, 1934, the son of Wallace Hamilton Kuralt, a social worker, and Ina (Bishop) Kuralt, who was a teacher. Raised in nearby Jacksonville, he spent much of his childhood at his grandparents' tobacco farm. He remembers his youth as a "very happy" time. "I liked the routine of farming," he told Diane Casselberry Manuel in an interview for the *Christian Science Monitor* (December 12, 1979), "and I fancied I was helping out . . . [but] mostly, I loved to read, and what there was in the house to read was *National Geographic,* and the complete works of Dickens and O. Henry, ordered one at a time by mail."

While he was a high school student, Kuralt won the American Legion "Voice of Democracy" essay contest. His prize was a trip to Washington, D.C. and a meeting with President Harry S. Truman, but hearing Edward R. Murrow, his boyhood idol, read his prize-winning piece over the CBS radio network proved to be even more exciting. Upon his high school graduation, Kuralt enrolled at the University of North Carolina in Chapel Hill, where he edited the campus newspaper, the *Daily Tar Heel*. After he received his B.A. degree in history, in 1955, he joined the staff of the Charlotte (North Carolina) *News* as a reporter. His off-beat human-interest stories for that newspaper's daily "People" column earned him the 1956 Ernie Pyle Memorial Award.

Recruited for CBS by Sig Mickelson, who was then trying to build up the network's news operations, Kuralt spent a few months in 1957 rewriting wires and cables from overseas correspondents for radio newscasts, then moved up to the position of writer for the televised national evening news broadcast, *Douglas Edwards With the News*. The following year he advanced to the news assignment desk. Because the news department was still understaffed, Kuralt often covered fast-breaking stories himself. Impressed by the reporter's journalistic know-how and by his self-possession on the air, Mickelson touted his find as "the next Ed Murrow," a comparison Kuralt dismissed as "ridiculous."

Shortly after he was made a full-fledged correspondent in 1959, Kuralt was chosen, over Walter Cronkite, to host *Eyewitness to History*, CBS's new weekly public affairs program. Four months later, he was replaced by Cronkite, reportedly at the insistence of James T. Aubrey Jr., who had recently taken over as president of the CBS television network. Back on general assignment, Kuralt covered, among other things, the 1960 Presidential campaigns and political unrest in Latin America. His inside report from Havana for the CBS News special *What Can We Do About Cuba?* so impressed top management that he was named to head CBS's newly established Latin American bureau, a post he held until 1963, when he returned to the United States to become chief West Coast correspondent.

During the mid-1960's Kuralt spent a considerable amount of time overseas, reporting from, as he once put it, virtually all the "tropical trouble spots," "Middle Eastern sinks," and "hell holes of Asia," including four tours of duty in Vietnam. He also prepared a number of pieces for the documentary series *CBS Reports* and anchored such public affairs specials as *Christmas in Appalachia, FDR Remembered*, and *16 in Webster Groves*, a disturbing and controversial view of teenagers in an affluent Midwestern suburb, and its follow-up, *Webster Groves Revisted*. In 1967 he accompanied the Plaisted polar expedition team on its unsuccessful attempt to follow the route of Admiral Robert E. Peary across the Arctic wasteland to the North Pole, an adventure he described in the CBS news special *Destination: North Pole* and in his book *To the Top of the World* (Holt, 1968).

Although considered by his peers to be among the best network correspondents, Kuralt eventually came to the conclusion that he was, in his words, "by temperament and physique

. . . just not suited for hard news." "I was always worried that some NBC man was sneaking around behind my back getting better stories," he explained to Arthur Unger of the *Christian Science Monitor* (July 24, 1974). Tired of the cutthroat rivalry of daily reporting, he came up with a plan for regular reports celebrating America's unsung heroes and enduring values. "I got the idea . . . one night in an airplane as I looked down at the lights in the countryside and wondered . . . what was going on down there," he said several years later. "There are a lot of Americans who don't live in cities and don't make headlines. I was interested in finding out about them." At first, the news department turned him down, but when, in 1967, he resubmitted his suggestion, he won the support of Richard S. Salant, then the president of CBS News, and Ernie Lester, the executive producer of the *CBS Evening News*, who decided to give his "On the Road" segments a three-month trial.

Accompanied by a three-man technical crew, Kuralt set off on his backroads odyssey in a refitted, second-hand camper in October 1967. Following no fixed itinerary, he wandered aimlessly in search of what he called the "unimportant," "irrelevant," and "even resolutely insignificant" story. When he filed his first piece, a paean to New England's brilliant autumn foliage, on October 26, public response to his unabashedly sentimental appreciation of the beauty of nature was immediately and overwhelmingly favorable. His later pieces encountered a similar reception, and even Walter Cronkite, the anchorman of the *CBS Evening News*, was impressed. "In a way, with so much vital news to report, Charlie's stories might seem a waste of time," Cronkite said, as quoted in *TV Guide* (May 15, 1968). "But I believe there's a moral point to them: they remind people that all is *not* lost, that life goes on much the same for a lot of people."

Over the next few years Kuralt added more pieces to "the jigsaw puzzle that this country is." He visited a school for unicyclists, stopped in at Pinkstaff's Gas Station and Poem Factory, followed wild mustangs running free in Montana, floated down Wisconsin's Apple River on an inner tube, and learned the art of horse-trading, among other things. He talked to lumberjacks, gandy dancers, beer can collectors, and wilderness philosophers—the "little people with the big ideas," as he put it. Because of his reassuring manner, Kuralt almost always managed to discover the "real character in real characters," to use the words of Arthur Unger. Among the strangers who have opened up to Kuralt are Wahoo McDaniel, a Cherokee Indian wrestler; a 104-year-old woman who entertained at nursing homes to earn a little extra money for her retirement; an Iowa farmer who constructed a fifty-eight-foot yacht behind his corn crib; an elderly brickmaker who painstakingly produced six bricks at a time on a mule-powered mud mill; and Tiger Olson, a nonagenarian who spent his days carving wooden carousel horses "slowly with basswood and chisel—and patience."

To produce an average of thirty-five four-to-five-minute vignettes a year, Kuralt and his crew put in three to four weeks a month on the road, logging up to 50,000 miles annually. Kuralt stumbled upon some of his best stories by serendipity, but he also relied on a state-by-state file of newspaper clippings from small towns, letters from viewers, and, occasionally, suggestions from public relations firms and local chambers of commerce. When, from time to time, he came across a legitimate news story, he immediately notified the nearest CBS News bureau.

Carefully matching words and visuals, Kuralt wrote his copy and then sent the film and the script to network headquarters in New York City, where an editor followed the reporter's suggestions in putting together the final piece. He never knew when one of his informal essays would be broadcast. As he explained to Arthur Unger in the interview for the *Christian Science Monitor's* profile, it would have been "irresponsible" to televise "On the Road" segments "every night when such big things are happening in the news." Nevertheless, he added, "I have come to believe that it is useful to just once in a while acknowledge that the whole country is not in flames and that everything going on in America is not represented by those big black headlines on page one. . . . 'On the Road' is an occasional acknowledgement of that."

By the mid-1970's "On the Road" had earned a special place in the affections of viewers and critics, many of whom welcomed Kuralt's neighborly reports as a temporary respite from the daily barrage of wars, riots, crime, and terrorism. Its success can be measured by its collection of prestigious broadcasting awards, including two Emmys and three George Foster Peabody Awards, and by the number of imitations it has spawned, such as the Milwaukee station WITI-TV's "Wandering Wisconsin." Even Kuralt's own weekly "Dateline: America" series for CBS Radio, first broadcast in 1972, is a kind of spin-off from "On the Road." Some of those beguiling essays, on such subjects as the behavior of mules, the shortage of bottled ink, and the untrustworthiness of the "tidy dresser," were published in his *Dateline America* (Harcourt, 1979).

Kuralt occasionally took time out from crisscrossing America to anchor documentaries or to preside over public affairs specials, among them, *But What If the Dream Comes True,* a profile of an upwardly mobile Midwestern suburban family; *Open Classroom,* a 1972 documentary that one critic hailed as the "best look on the homescreen yet at [that] style of education"; *You and the Commercial,* an exposé of television hucksterism; *Kids!—53 Things to Know About Health, Sex and Growing Up,* an open and honest discussion of the problems of adolescence; *Inside Public Television;* and *A Day in the Life of the United States,* which

Kuralt described as "a portrait of all of us—millions of people going separate ways and yet all hanging together"—on July 20, 1969, the day men first landed on the moon. Kuralt also created several specials that were derived from his "On the Road" reports. One of the most memorable was *On the Road With Charles Kuralt: the Individualists,* a collection of profiles about six men, including a crusading small-town newspaper editor, a homesteader in Alaska, and a traditional small-business man, whose lives epitomize traditional American values.

Recognizing Kuralt's appeal, network news executives seriously considered, in the early 1970's, assigning him to the anchor desk of the revamped *CBS Morning News* or to the staff of *60 Minutes,* the award-winning news magazine, but the reporter was reluctant to leave "On the Road." He did agree, however, to serve as cohost, with Sylvia Chase, of *Magazine,* an afternoon news and features program aimed at housewives that made its debut in May 1974, and to contribute pieces to the short-lived *Who's Who,* a prime time, hour-long news magazine that emphasized people.

Never one to mince words, Kuralt has publicly chastised broadcast executives for "hiring hair instead of brains" to man the anchor desks of local and network news programs. Anchormen should be experienced reporters "with a lively and curious intelligence, and with a calm and disciplined mind," not "highly paid poseurs," he said in a speech at the 1975 convention of the Radio and Television News Directors Association. "I am ashamed . . . that twenty-five years into the television age, so many anchormen haven't any basis on which to make a news judgment, can't edit, can't write, and can't cover a story."

Kuralt put some of his ideas about broadcast journalism into practice when he took the helm of *CBS News Sunday Morning,* the network's new, ninety-minute news magazine, which had its premiere in the 9:00 to 10:30 A.M. time slot on January 28, 1979. Leisurely and low-key, the program opens with a survey of headline news and a "cover" story and then moves on to special reports on such subjects as law, science, health, education, and religion, "back-of-the-book" cultural features, and a silent "visual essay." Kuralt saw the show as "a natural extension" of "On the Road." "We didn't really set out to do that, but it has turned out to be mostly an extended many-faceted essay on America," he explained to Arthur Unger. "Almost all of the stories illuminate some small corner of the United States, covering aspects you wouldn't expect to find on the evening news." Largely because of Kuralt's articulate writing and engaging delivery, *CBS News Sunday Morning* was an immediate critical success. In its short history, the program has won a handful of awards, including the 1979 George Foster Peabody Award and the Odyssey Institute's Third Annual Media Award.

For eighteen months Kuralt combined his *Sunday Morning* chores with his ongoing "On the Road" assignment. His years of wandering finally came to a halt in October 1980, when he became anchorman of the weekday editions of the CBS morning news broadcasts. He ended "On the Road" as he had begun it—from the leaf-strewn autumnal countryside of New England. "For the last thirteen years, I have been a kind of maple leaf, carried along by the current of America, exploring the swirls and eddies, seeking the main stream," he told viewers. "We have found a lot to be confident and reassured about, in the course of wandering many times to every state. We have found it a much more neighborly country than you would think from just reading the papers, a much more beautiful one, a stronger and much more enduring one. That's what we've learned. . . . Maple leaves don't float forever," he said in closing. "Sooner or later, they wash up on the shore."

Morning With Charles Kuralt began on Monday, October 27, 1980. Perennially last in the early-morning ratings sweepstakes, CBS's entry has always been information-oriented, relying on the reporting and writing skills of its correspondents rather than homey sets and electronic wizardry. Maintaining that "there's something to be said for plainness," Kuralt, perched atop a high stool, delivers the news in a straightforward, no-nonsense manner. He writes his own opening and closing remarks and "as much of the middle as [he] can." Although he is committed to the notion of "a real news program," Kuralt has occasionally lamented the "necessary preoccupation" with national and international political affairs. He and his senior executive producer, Robert Northshield, extended *Morning*'s regular coverage to education, the arts, science, and other neglected areas of life when the news program expanded to ninety minutes in September 1981.

Plump, round-faced, and slightly rumpled, Charles Kuralt looks "less like an anchorman than your average TV repairman," according to one *Time* interviewer. He takes issue with those who invariably describe him as "avuncular." "I'm fat and bald, but I don't think of myself as avuncular," he said recently. "It's too bad. I'd rather look like [CBS's evening news anchorman Dan] Rather. Of course, wouldn't anybody?" A genuinely friendly man who exudes down-home warmth, he often sends small gifts to some of the people he has interviewed for "On the Road."

Because of his demanding schedule, Kuralt leads what he has called "a very strict, disciplined life." He usually goes to bed at about 6:00 P.M., arises in time to hear the 2:00 A.M. newscast, then takes a taxi to the CBS studio to prepare *Morning*. In his spare time, he enjoys fishing and renovating old typewriters. Contending that "newsmen ought not to go about aggrandizing themselves," Kuralt seldom grants interviews. He lives rather quietly with his second wife, the former Suzanna Folsom

Baird, whom he married on June 1, 1962, in a New York City home filled with souvenirs from his travels. He has two daughters, Lisa Catherine Bowers and Susan Guthery Bowers, from an earlier marriage.

References: New York 14:24+ *Je* 1 '81 *pors Newsweek* 71:54 *Ja* 1 '68, 81:73 *My* 7 '73; *Quest/81* 5:14+ *pors Time* 91:44+ *Ja* 9 '68 *por*, 116:79 *S* 22 '80; *TV Guide* 16:20+ *My* 15 '68 *por; Wall St J* p1+ *D* 11 '73; *Washington Post B* p1+ *Ap* 28 '81 *pors; Who's Who in America*, 1980-81

Land, Edwin H(erbert)

May 7, 1909- Inventor; former business executive. Address: b. Polaroid Corp., 730 Main St., Cambridge, Mass. 02139; h. 163 Brattle St., Cambridge, Mass. 02138

NOTE: This biography supersedes the article that appeared in *Current Biography* in 1953.

Of the 525, or more, patents that Edwin H. Land holds, the ones to which he owes his international renown are those that made possible his development of instant, one-step Polaroid photography, a process that he has steadily improved since its inception in the late 1940's. Many of his other inventions, including polarized sunglasses that cut the glare of sunlight, derive from his original contributions to optics, which he began to make when he was an undergraduate at Harvard University. While still a teenager, Land had begun the experiments that resulted in the first synthetic sheet polarizer, a major achievement in the field of polarized light that has been widely applied in science and industry. More recently he has also conducted experiments that led him to propose a new theory of color vision.

Combining his scientific talent with unusual business acumen, until March 1980 Land was chief executive officer of the Polaroid Corporation, which he had founded in 1937. Polaroid, one of Wall Street's "glamour" issues for many years, faltered in the mid-1970's when its Polavision system for home movies failed to ignite public enthusiasm. But Land, who once told his stockholders that "the bottom line is in heaven," is currently giving much of his attention to basic research, the rewards of which have in the past repeatedly contributed to moving Polaroid ahead of competing companies.

Edwin Herbert Land was born in Bridgeport, Connecticut on May 7, 1909, the son of Harry M. Land, a merchant, and Martha F. Land. Photography was one of his childhood interests, as he recalled in an interview with Philip Taubman of *Time* (June 26, 1972), in which he talked about the values of photography. "To a child," he said, "a photograph gives a permanent thing that is both outside himself and part of himself." The first picture that he developed as a child was of the family's French poodle, which was constantly running away. But the photograph made a difference: "There I had him. He couldn't get away." At Norwich Academy in Norwich, Connecticut he achieved an almost perfect academic record, showing a special aptitude for physics, and was a member of the debating team and the track team. Graduating from the academy in 1926, he entered Harvard University, where he continued the research and experiments, begun in his home laboratory, on polarization phenomena that led to his contributions to optics and his first inventions.

When Land began his experiments, the only available light polarizers were fragile and expensive crystals, despite widespread recognition that a synthetic polarizer would have many and various scientific applications. Inspired by contemporary interest in a "plane polarizer"—a substance that would transmit light waves in a straight line instead of around all the planes of an axis—Land took a leave of absence from Harvard to pursue his research. He formulated a possible solution—orienting many small crystals of iodoquinine sulfate in a synthetic sheet—and set out to solve the associated problems while living in New York City, where he had access to a small physics laboratory at Columbia University. "In my then youthful innocence," he has recalled in a discussion of his work, "it seemed to me that these problems could be solved in a rather short time, perhaps in a few months." A year and a half later Land returned to Harvard, and after further work in a laboratory there, presented his ideas in a paper, "A New Polarizer for Light in the Form of an Extensive Synthetic Sheet," at a colloquium of the physics department in 1932.

Instead of remaining at Harvard to graduate, Land joined George Wheelwright 3d, a Harvard physics instructor, in setting up the Land-Wheelwright Laboratories in Boston in 1932. At first their partnership was a consulting firm not exclusively concerned with Land's polarizer, but by 1934 the company was manufacturing the Polaroid J-sheet, as the first polarizer was called, for commercial uses. Land also developed other sheet polarizers, which introduced substances besides crystals and which quickly became useful in colloid chemistry and other fields of science. They also had commercial applications: Eastman Kodak began using polarized filters in its cameras in 1935, and the American Optical Company began marketing polarized sunglasses in 1936. Polarizers for automobile headlights, to reduce glare and make night driving safer, had been one of Land's early objectives in his research. But auto manufacturers declined to make use of them, because, according to *Time* (June 26, 1972), "polarizing sheets deteriorated when exposed to heat."

The Polaroid Corporation was founded by Land in Cambridge, Massachusetts in 1937, with the financial backing of a number of Wall Street businessmen, including W. Averell Harriman and Lewis Strauss. Although the hoped-for application of headlight polarizers did not materialize, Polaroid prospered during World War II. Together with his research associates, Land invented a number of weapons improvements, including optical elements for use in infrared night-vision instruments and an infinity optical ring sight. He served as a consultant to the Navy on guided missiles and to the National Defense Research Council and participated in a project to create computerized thermal homing heads for 1,000-pound bombs. The Polaroid Corporation produced filters for goggles, gunsights, periscopes, range finders, aerial cameras, and the Norden bombsight.

Unlike many companies bound to wartime contracts, Polaroid did not suffer a prolonged decline with the end of hostilities. The return of peace encouraged Land to carry to fruition an idea that had preoccupied him since 1943. On vacation in New Mexico that year he took a picture of his three-year-old daughter, who then asked him why she could not see the picture right away. Pondering her question as he walked around Santa Fe for an hour, he designed the camera and film that would produce an immediate photograph. Many years later he referred to that event when explaining "cumulative creativity" in an interview for *Life* (October 27, 1972): "All that we at Polaroid had learned about making polarizers and plastics, and the properties of viscous liquids, and the preparation of microscopic crystals . . . was preparation for that day in which I suddenly knew how to make a one-step photographic process."

In February 1947 Land demonstrated his revolutionary process with a working model of his camera at the American Optical Society. Polaroid's product first reached the market at Christmas in 1948—Model 95, which weighed about four pounds and made sepia-toned prints. Although the Polaroid Land Camera, as it was called, has undergone many refinements since its inception, its main principles continued for some time to remain the same. The photosensitive element used was a silver halide emulsion. A full-size negative was exposed when the picture was snapped, and it was brought into contact with a positive print sheet. Rollers through which the sheet was drawn ruptured a pod of developing reagent and spread it evenly across the surface. The jellied compound developed the negative and positive prints simultaneously, and the photo was finished—a minute afterward in the early models, a few seconds in later ones. The first Land camera, in addition to making the first practical use of "dry" processing, incorporated an "exposure value system" that simplified the calculation of aperture and shutter speed to the single adjustment of a dial and has since become a standard feature on almost all cameras.

An immediate commercial success that brought sales of about $5,000,000 in its first year, the Land Camera, as a writer for *American Photography* commented in March 1949, "has certainly opened up new opportunities for photographers which many of them have not been slow to embrace." Although some professional photographers were said to dismiss the new camera as a high-priced toy, it soon found many applications in science, industry, the military, and medicine. It was adapted to X-rays, and improved and sophisticated models became available for use in aerial photography, real estate photography, and commercial and press photography. Black and white film replaced the sepia prints in 1950, and faster developing film was introduced in 1955.

Another idea of Land's, the vectograph, became especially lucrative for Polaroid in the early 1950's, with the sudden and immense popularity of "3-D" movies. The vectograph, which Land and the Czechoslovakian scientist Joseph Mahler had conceived of during the 1930's, is an image rendered in terms of the percentage of polarization, rather than in dyes. In collaboration with Mahler, who joined the Polaroid laboratories in 1940, Land implemented the vectograph in the older process of stereoscopic pictures to obtain a three-dimensional image. Vectographs were used during the war and later in X-ray work, and during the 3-D movie fad Polaroid manufactured about 100,000,000 of the special polarized glasses for viewing such movies. Land also developed a projector specifically for 3-D, but movie companies preferred to use two projectors, which, however, were difficult to keep in synchronization.

With the introduction, in 1963, of color film for Land cameras, the inventor achieved a goal toward which he had been working for many years. Also important was the related outcome of Land's extensive experiments in color perception, which led him to challenge the classical theory of color vision—that the color perceived depends on the relative amounts of blue, green, and red light reaching the eye. He proposed, ultimately, what he called the "retinex" theory. The experiments, carried out by Land and his collaborators during the 1950's, were described in Land's article in the May 1959 issue of *Scientific American*. He demonstrated what he believed were inconsistencies in the generally accepted theory, coming to the conclusion that color perception cannot be described in terms of an analysis of wavelengths of light.

To explain how a person sees the same colors or hues under different conditions of illumination, Land suggested that several hypothetical retinal-cortical mechanisms ("retinexes") interpret color through their comparative interaction. Although not all scientists agreed that Land's theory was preferable, the experiments themselves were striking in conception. "Land's major contribution," Joseph J. Sheppard Jr. wrote in his *Human Color Perception* (1968), "has been to demonstrate the astonishing extent to which the human visual system is able to make adjustments in order to perceive object colors of all hues, even though the visual system receives incomplete color information."

Until recent years the continual improvement of the Land camera, together with the introduction of less expensive models, assured Polaroid's commercial appeal under Land's direction. The low-priced Swinger took small black-and-white instant photographs and retailed for about $20 when introduced in 1965. It was an immediate success that brought Polaroid into competition with the Instamatic of Eastman Kodak. Other models soon followed, and in 1969 an inexpensive camera that took color prints, the Colorpack II, also sold well.

Polaroid's exceedingly sophisticated SX-70 camera, which went on sale in late 1972, required almost a decade to develop because of the technological innovations incorporated into its elaborate design. In previous Polaroid cameras a layer of paper had to be peeled away from the picture, but in the "no-garbage" SX-70, seventeen layers of chemical compounds were built into the single sheet that became the finished photo. The self-developing print was ejected from the camera instantly after exposure and was gradually processed within minutes as an "opacifier" shielded the chemicals from light. The twenty-six-ounce, four-by-seven-inch SX-70 was so small that Land had to equip it with an optical system using a series of precision mirrors. The battery that powered the camera was built into the film pack rather than into the camera.

Five new plants to manufacture and assemble the components of the SX-70 cost Polaroid $250,000,000 out of the $500,000,000 spent on the entire project. Previously the company had bought its film and camera components of its design from other firms. Although Polaroid invested $20,000,000 in advertising, it sold only about 700,000 SX-70 cameras during the first year they were marketed, instead of the several million it expected to sell. Land later said in an interview for *Forbes* (June 1, 1975) that several small problems for the customer, one of them with focusing, affected the sales and that in introducing the SX-70, the company "did underestimate how infinitely important a small amount of instruction is." Even though its initial low sales disturbed Polaroid's hitherto virtually unqualified record of success, the SX-70 eventually became a best seller and is today a standard.

Another of Land's long-cherished objectives, an instant-movie-camera system, which he introduced in 1977, has yet to prove itself in the marketplace. Polavision consisted of a hand-held camera and a viewer, which together had a list price of $675, and a two-minute-forty-second film cartridge, costing $9.95. It provided no sound. An unfavorable market for home movies and competition from videotape cameras forced Polaroid to write off its entire Polavision inventory as of September 1979. The technology of Polavision, however, may be adapted to teaching devices, medical endoscopy, and instant color slides. Peter W. Bernstein pointed out in *Fortune* (April 7, 1980) that despite a decline in earnings, "Polaroid remains financially strong" and that the manufacturing facilities that it had set up for the production of the SX-70 "can serve as the basis for future diversification."

In early March 1980 Land, who had retired as his company's president in May 1975, announced that he would step aside as chief executive officer, turning that position over to William J. McCune Jr., his successor as president. Remaining as chairman, Land also continued to advance Polaroid's research program as its consulting director. He was expected to devote most of his time to scientific experiments at his newly established nonprofit center for basic research in Cambridge. Under his administration the Polaroid Corporation had become a model company in terms of fair hiring practices, employee relations, and community involvement.

Edwin H. Land is a recipient of the National Medal of Science and of the Presidential Medal of Freedom. Among his thirty or so other medals and awards are the Frederick Ives Medal of the Optical Society of America and the Cresson and Potts Medals of the Franklin Institute. He holds honorary doctoral degrees from Harvard, Yale, Columbia, and about a dozen other universities and colleges. Elected to the National Inventors Hall of Fame in 1977, Land also belongs to the Optical Society of America, the American Academy of Arts and Sciences, of which he was once president, and many other learned societies. Since 1956 he has been a fellow and visiting institute professor at the Massachusetts Institute of Technology. Land has also taught at Harvard, where he was William James lecturer in Psychology in 1966-67 and Morris Loeb lecturer in physics in 1974.

Married in 1929, Land and his wife, the former Helen ("Terre") Maislen of Hartford, have two daughters, Jennifer and Valerie. Land shies from personal publicity and is reported to be reclusive, although he belongs to many clubs, and to be sometimes diffident in conversation, but he is nevertheless capable of dynamic presentation of his ideas and aspirations. In *Time* he was described as looking "every inch the scientific genius," but when the *Forbes* interviewer asked him how he saw himself, Land replied, "I suppose that I am first of all an artistic person. I'm interested in love and affection and sharing and making beauty part of everyday life. And if I'm lucky enough to be able to earn my living by contributing to a warmer and richer world, then I feel that it is awfully good luck. And if I use all of my scientific, professional abilities in doing that, I think that makes for a good life." One of his recreations is music.

References: Forbes 103:34+ Je 15 '69 pors, 115:48+ Je 1 '75 por; Fortune 101:66+ Ap 7 '80 pors; N Y Times p57 Ap 26 '72 por; Time 99:80+ Je 26 '72 por; American Men and Women of Science (1979); Heyn, Ernest V. Fire of Genius (1976); McGraw-Hill Modern Men of Science (1966); Who's Who, 1980-81; Who's Who in America, 1980-81

Lansing, Sherry (Lee)

July 31, 1944- Motion picture company executive. *Address:* b. Twentieth Century-Fox Productions, 10201 W. Pico Blvd., W. Los Angeles, Calif. 90064; h. 10575 Santa Monica Blvd., W. Los Angeles, Calif. 90025

A changing Hollywood in the 1980's faces the challenge of supplying a variety of new electronic markets at a time of insecurity engendered by an aggregation of stars, directors, and writers who are not tethered by the long-term contracts of past eras. As Budd Schulberg explained in his article, "What Makes Hollywood Run Now?" in the New York *Times Magazine* (April 27, 1980), those factors, which call for a new type of executive equipped to handle the current individual approach to filmmaking, have paved the way, with the help of the women's movement, for the advancement of able women to positions of power in the film business. The first woman to be put in charge of production at a major film studio

Sherry Lansing

is Sherry Lansing, named president of production at Twentieth-Century Fox on January 2, 1980. Now among the top-salaried women executives in any industry, Miss Lansing, a former mathematics teacher, model, and actress, began her third career in 1970 as a script reader. She joined Metro-Goldwyn-Mayer in 1975 as executive story editor, rising to vice-president of creative affairs in March 1977. Her reputation soared when, in the position of senior vice-president of production at Columbia Pictures, she was responsible for guiding two of 1979's critical and commercial blockbusters, *The China Syndrome* and *Kramer vs. Kramer*. Referring to the sensation her appointment to the highest creative berth at Twentieth-Century Fox caused in the press, Sherry Lansing protested, "I just hope this is maybe the last time a woman holding a position such as this will be newsworthy. It should be natural."

Born in Chicago, Illinois on July 31, 1944, Sherry Lee Lansing is the daughter of Margo Heimann, a Jewish woman who fled to the United States from Nazi Germany. Upon her father's early death, her mother worked as a realtor to support herself, Sherry, and another daughter, Andrea. She later married Norton Lansing, a furniture manufacturer, and had two more children, Richard Lansing and Judy Lansing. A determined achiever early in life, Sherry Lansing graduated from the University of Chicago Laboratory High School, a special school for gifted children, in 1962. Four years later she earned a B.S. degree *summa cum laude* from the department of theatre at Northwestern University. "I have been an incredibly hard worker," she recalled in an interview with Charles Schreger of the Los Angeles *Times* (January 4, 1980). "I got all A's in col-

lege not because I'm so bright, but because I studied all the time." Her explanation confirms Budd Schulberg's observation that her success is attributable not to "superficial appearances" but to "a deeply imbued Jewish-intellectual work ethic."

Only about a year after the devastating 1965 riots in Watts, Sherry Lansing went to that Los Angeles black ghetto to teach mathematics in the public high school. She gave up teaching in 1969 because, by her own account, she had "lost passion" and was becoming the sort of "repetitive teacher" she had disliked as a student. Turning to a career as a model, which would give her plenty of free time, she appeared in television commercials in 1969-70 for the Max Factor Company and Alberto-Culver Company. Between modeling assignments she was able to take on small roles in two films: Susan, a "chic sexpot," in the George Segal-Eva Marie Saint vehicle *Loving* (Columbia, 1970) and the victimized and disfigured Amelita in the John Wayne western of the Civil War era, *Rio Lobo* (National General, 1970), produced and directed by Howard Hawks. She was also associated with the national company of the 1970 Pulitzer Prize-winning play, *No Place to be Somebody*.

"I was a terrible actress. I found it so difficult and painful to do," Sherry Lansing admitted a decade later, soon after she became studio head, in an address before a group of film industry aspirants. But as she looked around the movie set, she was fascinated by the production process and wondered what all the technicians and others were doing. To find out, she enrolled in film courses in the University of California at Los Angeles and the University of Southern California. When she was not in class, she was likely to be at the movies.

One of the films in which Miss Lansing appeared, *Loving*, had Raymond Wagner as its executive producer. She began reading scripts in 1970 at $5 an hour for his small production company, Wagner International, and within two years she was working with writers and developing screenplays as executive story editor. From time to time Daniel Melnick, then head of feature-film production at Metro-Goldwyn-Mayer, and Wagner, who had become an MGM vice-president, kept offering her a job. In 1975 she accepted the position of executive story editor with MGM, at that time the ultimate nonacting job a woman could attain at a major studio. In March 1977 she advanced to vice-president of creative affairs, the second-ranking production post and her first vice-presidency title.

Ready for even more direct involvement with production, in November 1977 Sherry Lansing switched studios when Daniel Melnick, who had taken over the helm of production at Columbia Pictures, lured her to that company with a job overseeing projects from their very beginning. First named vice-president for production, in September 1978 she stepped up to the senior vice-presidency. Although she had seen attitudes toward women in management changing during her climb upward, Sherry Lansing declared in an interview in *Working Woman* (August 1979): "People were suspicious of me. A woman couldn't make a mistake without everyone's wondering how she got the job." While acknowledging her professional advancement, she nonetheless expressed doubt, as quoted in *Life* (April 1979), that "in [her] working lifetime, [she would] see a woman as president of a movie company."

In general, the sector of the film industry in which women had been working most prominently since the mid-1970's was development, or preproduction. As outlined by Roz Kramer in *Working Woman,* their duties included guiding properties in book or idea form through the stages of script completion and packaging in cooperation with a producer, director, cast, and any additional writers. Serving as liaison between the production company and the artistic staff, a development executive may be concerned with any one or all facets of production. During her first two years at Columbia, Sherry Lansing steered to completion the prestigious 1979 films *The China Syndrome* and *Kramer vs. Kramer.*

A $6,000,000 technological thriller, *The China Syndrome* was a timely and prophetic film about a near accident and attempted coverup at a nuclear power plant. It owed its effectiveness to the collaborative effort of the cadre including Michael Gray, who wrote the first draft in 1974; T. S. Cook, who polished it; Michael Douglas, who brought it to Columbia, produced, and costarred in it; and James Bridges, who rewrote and directed the final script. Executive producer Bruce Gilbert and others on the project at first regarded the new Columbia vice-president assigned to the movie, the beautiful ex-actress Sherry Lansing, as "window dressing," or, worse, "studio interference incarnate," but before long, they were won over by her technical expertise and emotional support. To Michael Douglas, who informed Schulberg that he was amazed by the way she pinpointed problems and then broached useful solutions, Sherry Lansing was "a great sounding board . . . never afraid to voice her own opinions." In another interview, with Aljean Harmetz of the New York Times (February 7, 1980), he said, "Sherry is one of the few studio executives I'm comfortable with. When I talk to her, I don't feel like I'm going into the principal's office." Sherry Lansing's first suggestion was to sustain tension by cutting out a subplot, and with her assistance in editing, the running time of the film was reduced to 122 minutes. Her imprint also appears in the shaping of Jane Fonda's role so that audiences would react more sympathetically to Kimberly Wells, the television newswoman who is valued more for her looks than her competence.

As attacks from the nuclear industry grew, *The China Syndrome* opened in New York City on March 16, 1979, to mainly rave reviews. (The title was explained as scientific jargon for a nuclear reactor meltdown that might burn downward through the foundation, through the earth, and all the way to China, just as an American child imagines himself digging a hole deep enough to reach China.) In a representative review Vincent Canby analyzed the film in the New York Times (March 18, 1979) as "good and clever enough to work on several levels simultaneously—1) as first-rate melodrama . . . , 2) as a satire of big business, including the television news industry in which the people who present the news become more important than the news itself, and 3) as an ageless morality play about greed and vanity." Twelve days after the premiere, an actual accident occurred at Three Mile Island in Harrisburg, Pennsylvania, the meeting of art and life being less coincidental, in James Bridges' view, than inevitable. The news stunned Sherry Lansing. "I thought it was good to have this movie out. This time they would have to pay attention," she told Aaron Latham, the author of the article "Hollywood vs. Harrisburg," which appeared in *Esquire* (May 22, 1979). "But I never thought it [the public debate over the safety of nuclear energy] would mushroom the way it has." The film garnered Academy Award nominations for its screenplay, art direction, and its stars, Jane Fonda and Jack Lemmon, who played the distraught engineer with a conscience.

Sherry Lansing's second project, the sensitive, intelligent treatment of a child custody battle and "a document of marriage in the '70's," *Kramer vs. Kramer,* was released in December 1979. The following April it walked off with the Oscar race: awards for Best Picture of 1979, Best Actor (Dustin Hoffman), Best Supporting Actress (Meryl Streep), Best Director and Best Screenplay (Robert Benton), and nominations for Best Supporting Actor and Cinematography. Summing up her contribution, Benton called Sherry Lansing "a good friend to my movie." As he related to Budd Schulberg in the New York Times Magazine article, "After 16 drafts I was exhausted, ready to quit. That's when Sherry's enthusiasm and creative energy and support came in. She helped me go on to the 17th, the 18th." Contributing directly to the editing and casting of the film, Sherry Lansing was concerned, she said, with "reordering sequences to increase the likeability" of the male protagonist, whose wife walks out on him. She held out for Dustin Hoffmann as the husband even after he had twice rejected the role and fought for the casting of Meryl Streep, then a relative unknown, as the wife. In story conferences she discussed with Benton the possible reasons behind a woman's abandonment of her child, with the result that the wife's speech about her need to find herself "outside of being somebody's daughter, somebody's wife or mother" generated understanding of her motivation and made the character more appealing.

When her contract at Columbia expired in November 1979, Sherry Lansing spent several weeks considering other opportunities, such as the possibility of producing her own movies or becoming an anthropologist to satisfy her love of travel. On January 2, 1980, in the wake of the executive exodus from Twentieth-Century Fox that began with the resignation of president Alan Ladd Jr. in mid-1979, the new vice-chairman of the board, Alan Hirschfield, appointed Sherry Lansing president of the company's feature-film division. She succeeded Sandy Lieberson, who had replaced Ladd for about six months. Her three-year contract stipulated an annual salary of $300,000 plus bonuses. Setting the news media agog by her invasion of a male-dominated bailiwick, Sherry Lansing was widely publicized as "the most powerful woman in the film industry." Hirschfield commented on his landmark decision: "Why not a woman? I did a lot of looking and Sherry's qualifications were as good as anyone's." He felt that her youth would help her to attract and relate to the young, creative filmmakers and extolled her "finely-honed sense of the marketplace for movies." To contradict innuendoes that her authority would be limited, he declared, "She'll be completely responsible for investing the hundreds of millions of dollars needed for the projects she chooses."

Those projects are expected not necessarily to be films about women's concerns. Sherry Lansing's goal is "to make movies that stir up your emotions; movies where you root for the people." She explained to Aljean Harmetz, "When I was growing up, I loved *The Pawnbroker, A Thousand Clowns, Petulia*—all movies that came out of somebody's passion." In the process of production at Twentieth-Century Fox before Sherry Lansing took over were *The Empire Strikes Back: Star Wars II* and the Robert Redford vehicle *Brubaker*. She welcomed as "a nice gift" the fact that the filming of *Nine to Five* had been scheduled to begin in mid-January 1980. That office comedy with touches of farce, feminism, and fantasy, starring Jane Fonda, Lily Tomlin, and Dolly Parton, failed to meet critical approval, although delighted audiences flocked to the box office. Sherry Lansing's own decisions have included giving the green light to the thriller "The Ninja."

In "What Makes Hollywood Run Now?" Budd Schulberg quoted the New York advertising agent Steve Frankfurt's evaluation of Sherry Lansing: "Her special talent is for creating an atmosphere in which talented people want to work. In the middle of civil war, she's creating a garden out there." She customarily reads two or three scripts a night, as well as several over the weekend, and does not rest until she has phoned the writer or sent a note. According to her secretary, every one of some 200 daily calls is returned. "Don't mistake her enthusiasm and genuine niceness for lack of strength," her former mentor,

Daniel Melnick, has warned. "I think she is descended from a long line of tracer bullets." Aware that she must surmount the image of not being aggressive, Sherry Lansing distinguished between strength and toughness in one of the many interviews she gave when her appointment was announced: "I would like to think of myself as being a strong woman. But I'm not a tough woman. I don't understand why human decency, kindness, respect for people, have to be mutually exclusive from strength."

With her long, dark-brown hair, wide-set blue eyes, and high cheekbones, Sherry Lansing has been likened to Sophia Loren, Rita Hayworth, and Jacqueline Onassis for her striking beauty. She is five feet ten inches in height and weighs 120 pounds. One of the ways that she keeps in trim is by swimming at a health club before going to work in the morning. She does not have her own pool, or a maid, at her relatively modest home in an area west of Beverly Hills. Although she tends to keep her personal relationships private, it was reported in the press that her early marriage to a doctor, contracted in accordance with her parents' expectations, ended in divorce ten years ago. An inveterate moviegoer, Sherry Lansing guesses that she has probably seen every film made in the last decade. Except for unedited cuts, as Schulberg reported, she prefers to view movies in a theatre rather than in studio screening rooms: "I like to stand on line, buy my popcorn and see a picture with the people. There's something sterile about seeing pictures in private homes after dinner. All the in remarks. I miss the people."

References: *Chicago Tribune* XII p1+ My 11 '80 por; *Financial World* 149:57 Ja 15 '80 por; *Los Angeles Herald Examiner* B p1+ Ja 4 '80 por; *N Y Times Mag* p52+ Ap 27 '80 pors; *Newsweek* 95:69+ Ja 14 '80 por; *Time* 115:61 Ja 14 '80 por; *Wall St J* p23 Ja 3 '80; *Working Woman* 4:35+ Ag '79 por; *International Motion Picture Almanac* (1981); *Who's Who in America,* 1980-81

Leonard, Sugar Ray

May 17, 1956- Boxer. Address. b. c/o World Boxing Council, Apartado 75-254, Mexico City, 14 D.F. Mexico

World champion Sugar Ray Leonard, the most celebrated young fighter since Muhammad Ali and boxing's most marketable current commodity, has restored to the welterweight class (147 pound limit) the razzle dazzle it had in the heyday of his namesake, Sugar Ray Robinson. America fell in love with the lithe, photogenic Leonard, who is as cleancut and charming outside the ring as he is cunning

Sugar Ray Leonard

and lethal within it, when it saw him, via television, win the gold medal at the 1976 Olympics in Montreal. Boosted by TV sports commentator Howard Cosell, he was a network attraction from the very beginning of his professional career; his purses soon exceeded even those of most heavyweight contenders and are now approaching eight figures. With a record of twenty-five pro victories and no defeats behind him, Leonard took the World Boxing Council's welterweight title from Wilfredo Benitez in 1979. He lost the title to Roberto Durán in June 1980 and regained it in a rematch with Duran five months later, and he unified the title by taking the World Boxing Association championship from Thomas Hearns in September 1981. The defeat of Hearns was Leonard's thirty-first victory in thirty-two starts and his twenty-second by knockout. Leonard, who regards himself not as a brutal gladiator but as an artist in a sport of precision, is known for his fast, flashy foot and hand work as he registers his left hooks and jabs and right uppercuts or crosses—or swift and accurate combinations of the same—and then moves out of retaliatory range.

Born in Wilmington, North Carolina on May 17, 1956, Ray Charles Leonard is the fifth of seven children (four sons and three daughters) of Cicero and Getha Leonard. Before they were incapacitated by illness, his father was a truck loader at a produce market and his mother was a nursing assistant in a convalescent home. Taking care of his parents was a major factor in Leonard's decision to enter professional boxing.

Leonard grew up in Wilmington, North Carolina, in Washington, D.C., and in Palmer Park, Maryland, a racially mixed lower-middle-class suburb of Baltimore. Although his father and grandfather had been amateur boxing champions, he was not immediately attracted to the ring, preferring at first tumbling and basketball. "I wanted Ray to be a singer," his mother told Phil Berger in an interview for an article in the New York Times Magazine (June 24, 1979). "I named him after [rhythm and blues singer] Ray Charles. As a boy, he was a little shy guy. I never had to go to school because of problems with him. Ray was good. He sang with two of my daughters in church, and people said he sounded like [the late rock 'n' roll singer] Sam Cooke. He sang until he was fourteen and a half. Then his older brother Roger turned him over to boxing. And like Ray used to tell me, 'Mama, I put the singing into swinging.'"

Cicero Leonard remembers his famous son as being "a funny sort of kid," as he told Thomas Boswell of the Washington Post (August 28, 1977): "He never gave us one bit of trouble, not at home or in school, but he always hung back, you know? It used to worry me. All my other boys were always into something, but Ray . . . not until boxing. I didn't believe it until I saw him fight the first time. I still can hardly believe it."

Aside from his brother, Leonard's first pugilistic mentors were two volunteer boxing coaches at the Oakcrest Community Center in Palmer Park, Dave Jacobs, who remained Leonard's trainer until 1979, and Janks Morton, who is still his cornerman as well as his closest friend and adviser. Jacobs and Morton demanded of their charges not only dedication in the ring but discipline in scholarship and comportment outside the ring. "We tried to set examples," Morton told Pete Axthelm of Newsweek (June 23, 1980). "I know that Ray never heard me say a bad word until he was twenty." (What provoked the blue outburst, he explained, was the lack of commercial demand for Leonard following his Olympic victory: "The American public . . . didn't seem to believe that a black athlete could eat Wheaties too.")

"When I first started," Leonard has reminisced, "I used to fight like Joe Frazier. I would come in low, bob and weave, and I knocked out many guys like that. I straightened up when I saw Ali, when I started studying Sugar Ray Robinson." As an amateur, Leonard won 145 bouts (seventy-five by knockouts) and lost five (four by disputed decision and one by disqualification). His trophies included a National Golden Gloves title and two international championships at 132 pounds and the light-welterweight (139 pounds) gold medals at the 1975 Pan-American games and the 1976 Olympics in Montreal. The televising of the climactic bout in Montreal, in which Leonard ignored intense pain in his two badly injured hands (still a chronic problem with him) to win by a decision over Andrés Aldama of Cuba, brought him instant celebrity. Angelo Dundee, then the trainer of Muhammad Ali and now Leonard's manager, has recalled watching Leonard on television on the occasion: "He was pretty as a picture. He shined. He lit my living room. I could see everything he did because he throws from the outside. And he was throwing every punch in the book."

While he enjoyed the "gentlemanly" art of amateur boxing (as he refers back to it, fondly), Leonard had no desire for professional competition, knowing as he did the physical, mental, spiritual, and moral toll it too often takes on those who dare to run its gauntlet. Partly as an example to young people, he planned to quit boxing after reaching the amateur heights and enter the University of Maryland. "This is my last fight," he announced when he won the gold medal in Montreal. "My decision is final. My journey is ended, my dream fulfilled." Later he said, "In my heart all I ever wanted was this gold medal and the chance at a straight life. I wanted to set an example and I have."

His decision to quit the ring rested partly on the assumption that lucrative endorsement offers would be pouring his way. Instead, Leonard returned home to sensationalized news stories about Juanita Wilkinson, the mother of his son (and now his wife), filing a paternity suit against him. (All she had actually done, apparently, was apply for food stamps; the suit against Leonard was standard bureaucratic "non-support" procedure.) "It killed every commercial he could have gotten after the Olympics," Janks Morton has claimed. "Bruce Jenner puts his face on a cereal box. Mark Spitz, who can't even talk on camera, holds up an after-shave bottle. All he has to do is drop it. Ray, who's a natural actor, has to work four more years after the Olympics to start getting major offers. It's better not to think about it too hard. Ray doesn't. I've seen him come from a dollar to a million with a smile."

Meanwhile, Leonard's mother had suffered a heart attack and his father had been hospitalized with spinal meningitis. With three generations of Leonards in financial need, he thought of a statement his Olympic coach had made: "Ray would go through the pros like a dose of salt." He also knew that boxing was what he did best and decided he might as well go on to prove professionally that he was the best at it for his size in the world. "Ten years from now," he explained just before he turned pro, "people are going to look at me and say, 'He won the gold medal and then quit. I wonder why?'"

Michael G. Trainer, an attorney friend of Janks Morton, became Leonard's business manager. Wisely eschewing the usual indenture to venal promoters—the trap into which most novice prizefighters fall, to their career-long regret—Trainer rounded up twenty-four friends and associates who loaned Leonard a total of $21,000, to be paid back at 8 percent interest within four years. (As it turned out, the debt was paid after Leonard's first professional fight.) He then incorporated Leonard, signing over all the shares in Sugar Ray Leonard Inc. to the boxer himself. To bypass boxing's promotional demimonde, he turned Leonard into a made-for-television commodity, signing him to a contract with the ABC network that was nonexclusive, leaving him free for engagements on NBC, CBS, and Home Box Office as well.

To complement Trainer's business know-how, Angelo Dundee was brought in for his expertise in the pro boxing world. Given the nominal title of "manager," Dundee was actually hired as teacher-matchmaker, to be paid approximately 15 percent of each purse (as against the 30 percent or more exacted by proprietary managers). His job was to screen possible opponents, choosing in each instance an adversary calculated to advance Leonard a grade higher in pugilistic skill without overmatching him; to join Leonard's camp as supervisor of training a few days before each bout; to address the boxer between rounds of the fight; and to act as a quotable source for the press.

Accustomed to three-round fights as an amateur, Leonard began his professional career with six-rounders and advanced gradually to fifteen-rounders. In his first pro fight, on February 6, 1977, he defeated Luis Vega by a decision, and three months later he scored a similar victory over Willie Rodriguez. In four subsequent bouts in 1977, he beat Vinnie DeBarros by a technical knockout, and he knocked out Frank Santore, Augustine Estrada, and Hector Diaz.

Leonard's victories in 1978 were over Rocky Ramon (decision), Art McNight (TKO), Javier Huntz (KO), Bobby Hayman (TKO), Randy Milton (TKO), Rafael Rodriguez (decision), Dick Eklund (decision), Floyd Mayweather (TKO), Randy Shields (decision), Bernado Prada (decision), and Armando Muñiz. Between January and September 1979 he beat Johnny Gant (TKO), Fernand Marcotte (TKO), Daniel Gonzales (KO), Adolfo Viruet (decision), Marcos Geraldo (decision), Tony Chiavarini (TKO), Pete Ranzany (TKO), and Andy Price (KO).

Former champ Sugar Ray Robinson, who was in Las Vegas to witness the Leonard-Ranzany fight, confounded the boxing buffs who gagged at the "arrogance" of Leonard's borrowing Robinson's nickname by disagreeing with them. Robinson told a reporter: "I'm gratified he's using my name. I think it's great when kids think enough of you to use your name." Robinson went on to say, "Leonard has great possibilities. He's fast and puts combinations together. He's learning every time he fights."

With his television-inflated purses, Leonard accrued unprecedented earnings for a boxer of his weight on the road to the championship —an estimated $2.5 to $3 million. On the strength of his saleability on the tube, he successfully insisted on $1,000,000 for challenging

Wilfredo Benitez, then the World Boxing Council's welterweight champion, in Las Vegas on November 30, 1979. In deference to tradition, Benitez, as the defending champion, had to be given a greater amount ($1,200,000), and he thus joined Leonard in passing the million-dollar mark for the first time in welterweight history. The fight itself reached the fifteenth round, in the final seconds of which, with the scorecards in doubt, Leonard took the decision away from the judges by a technical knockout. The TKO began with a short left hook that dropped the champion. Benitez bounced back up almost immediately, but with six seconds remaining there was no hope now of his winning. With a look into Benitez's dreamily smiling visage, referee Carlos Padilla Jr. made a split-second decision—that the seconds remaining would mean jeopardy to Benitez.

"Against Benitez," Leonard said shortly after the fight in Las Vegas, "people didn't see me, just a shadow. In the future, I'll be a better craftsman, and more artistic too. [Muhammad] Ali called me the night before the Benitez fight and told me not to do anything flashy because the judges would resent me hotdogging against a world champion. I was a basic boxer that night, and very cautious. Now I can go back to fighting my way because I'm the champ."

In his first defense of his title, on April 1, 1980, Leonard ended the fight in the fourth round by knocking out Davey "Boy" Green from England with a left hook so powerful that Leonard himself became numb with fear for the recovery of his vanquished foe. "It might have been the hardest punch I've ever thrown," he told reporters following the fight, "and I was actually afraid . . . hoping he was going to make it." (Finally Green had arisen and walked with unsure step to his locker room.)

In his first fight with Roberto ("Stone Hands") Durán, a brutal infighter, Leonard unwisely abandoned his fluid style because he wanted to prove that he was not afraid to slug it out with the Panamanian challenger toe-to-toe. In that confrontation, in Montreal on June 20, 1980, fans expected to see an agile Leonard throwing jabs and dancing out of reach of a stalking Durán. Instead, they saw him meeting Durán's whirlwind charges head on, absorbing staggering punches (the worst of which was a blow to the head in the second round) as well as returning some of his own. The savagery reached its peak in the thirteenth round, when both men forsook defense to engage in a mutual onslaught that would have buckled average fighters. At the end of fifteen rounds, the three judges unanimously gave Durán the edge, scoring him 148, 145, and 145 while giving Leonard 147, 144, and 144 points.

"The fight in Montreal was not a boxing match," Leonard told the press shortly before his rematch with Durán, in New Orleans on November 26, 1980. "It was a street brawl. What took place there is something I can cor-rect here in New Orleans. I didn't utilize my skills there. I was determined to stand my ground and fight Durán his way. I've conquered my stubbornness. I don't like Durán's way. He walks around like he owns the world, and I want to do something about it."

True to his word, Leonard outboxed Durán the second time around (except in the fifth round), feinting to keep him off balance, pivoting and dancing this way and that to prevent him from mounting a sustained attack. At the same time, Leonard made a weapon of his jab, countered with his hook when Durán tried to move inside, and delivered sharp uppercuts when Durán succeeded in so moving. His worst humiliation of Durán came in the seventh round, when he wound up his right hand, as if to throw a bolo, and then surprised Durán with a left jab to the face. But Leonard's victory by TKO in the eighth round was controversial because Durán did not appear to be very seriously hurt when he threw up his hands and quit, complaining of a stomachache. On March 29, 1981 Leonard scored a tenth-round technical knockout over Larry Bonds. His victory over Thomas Hearns for the WBA welterweight crown on September 16, 1981 was by a TKO in the fourteenth round.

When in training at his camp-gymnasium in New Carrollton, Maryland, Leonard rises at daybreak and runs four miles. He runs one of the miles backward, shadowboxing as he does so, and the last mile he runs in less than five minutes. Later in the morning he spars for fifty-five minutes, and the afternoon he studies videotapes of fights of his opponent as well as some of his own past bouts. He usually sleeps ten hours a night. "I tend to showboat in the ring, and that takes energy," he explained to Dolly Langdon of *People* (December 3, 1979).

Unlike most fighters, Leonard does not hesitate to admit that fear grips him before a fight. "They say the look in my eye changes as the fight approaches," he told Thomas Boswell in the Washington *Post* interview. "My friends say, 'Ray, it's scary.' But I still never feel anything until five minutes before the fight. Then it hits me. It's like somebody's scraping your insides out. You can't even catch your breath." Before leaving the locker room, he spars with his reflection in the mirror.

When he enters the ring, Leonard bows and blows kisses to the crowd from all four sides of the ring. His modest, gentle manner disappears and he develops a strut in his walk; in the fight itself, he occasionally goes into an Ali-like shuffle. "In the ring everything's all right," he told Thomas Boswell. "Your fists are like snakes that strike before you even tell them to." In the *People* interview with Dolly Langdon he said: "Most of the time I look my opponents in the eye, but not because I like them. Mostly I'm looking for bruises, scar tissue—things I can work on. In the ring I can feel that halo over my head turn into those two little horns."

Sugar Ray Leonard is five feet nine and a half inches tall and weighs 147 pounds. His handsome, miraculously unscarred face is more often than not creased by his famous smile, and his manner of speaking and acting contributes to a disarming presence, or what is described in some of the less literate quarters of the fight world as "composture" (a combination of composure and posture). Those who know him say he is "decent," "generous," and "family-oriented." With his wife Juanita (whom he finally married on January 19, 1980) and his son, Ray Jr., he lives in a $700,000 house (which includes a gym and a swimming pool, among other facilities) in Glen Dale, Maryland. His mother (who lives with his father in a house Leonard bought for them in Lanham, Maryland) still cooks chitterlings for him, but he says he now prefers caviar.

Leonard also provides his close relatives with automobiles, and he himself has a Mercedes and a van. His biggest indulgences, however, are wardrobe and jewelry. He invests much of his income (some of which comes from endorsements for a soft drink and other commercial products and from sports commentary for Home Box Office) in real estate. The champion regularly lectures boys clubs and civic groups on such subjects as "Good Sportsmanship," "Brotherhood," and "The Importance of Staying in School," and his patience with autograph seekers is unusual. It has been said that he is unlike Muhammad Ali in being as content in privacy as in the limelight. Asked to compare Leonard to Ali, Angelo Dundee once said: "He's got the same charm, the same excitement about him. But Ray's easier to teach. You can show him his mistakes. With Muhammad you had to talk round and round —until Muhammad thought he'd got the idea on his own."

Reference: Ebony 35:66+ Mr '80 pors; Mr '80 pors; N Y Times Mag p14 Je 24 '79 pors; Newsday S p10+ Je 17 '79 pors; Newsweek 95:49+ Je 23 '80 pors; Time 118:68+ S 28 '81 pors; Washington Post K p4 S 23 '79 por; International Who's Who, 1981-82

Limann, Hilla (li-män' hi'lä)

1934(?)- President of Ghana. Address: b. Office of the President, State House, Accra, Ghana

The inauguration, on September 24, 1979, of Dr. Hilla Limann, a pragmatist and political moderate, as the civilian President of Ghana's third republic, following more than seven years of military rule, parallels a trend toward democratization in a number of other African countries. Nigeria has experienced a similar transition from military to civilian government, and Uganda, Equatorial Guinea, and the Central African Republic have rid themselves of oppressive dictatorships. A former schoolteacher, Limann was virtually unknown, even in his own country, when he was chosen as the Presidential candidate of the People's National party. That political movement represents the heritage of the late Dr. Kwame Nkrumah, under whose leadership Ghana was the first black African nation to gain independence from colonial rule.

Once relatively prosperous, Ghana was one of the most influential countries of the Third World, but the West African nation of some 11,700,000 people has suffered a steady decline since gaining independence. By the time Limann took office it was burdened with rampant inflation, unemployment, and corruption, a staggering foreign debt, declining agricultural and industrial production, and political chaos. Since he became President, Limann has made slow progress in solving Ghana's problems, but his astuteness and skill have earned him considerable respect at home and abroad. "For the moment, Dr. Limann's government constitutes the best hope for the future of Ghana," Marcel Berlins wrote in the London Times (September 24, 1980): "It has behaved both responsibly and democratically so far, and it has a coherent economic policy which . . . has a chance of working. Ghana, after two years of civilian rule, will be a very interesting country indeed."

Hilla Limann, whose native dialect is that of the Sissala tribal group, was born in Gwollu (or Gwellu), a country village in the isolated and underdeveloped upper region of Ghana, then the British colony of the Gold Coast. He is a nephew of Imoru Egala, who served as a minister in the government of Kwame Nkrumah and later was a founder of the People's National party. Current sources, including government publications, give the year of Limann's birth as 1934, but earlier reference works give his birthday as December 12, 1929. Although his family, like most people of his native region, were humble peasants, Limann's ambition to excel prompted him to seek the best education available to him, financed by his earnings as a hunter and later by scholarships.

Limann obtained his early education at a primary boarding school in Lawra, on the Gold Coast's northern frontier, and then attended a secondary boarding school at Tamale, in the country's north central region. In 1949 he entered teacher training college in Tamale, and after qualifying for "certification B" in education in 1952, served for three years as a teacher. While still a student, Limann supported the independence efforts of Kwame Nkrumah, who became Prime Minister of the new nation of Ghana in 1957 and was chosen its President when the country became a constitutional republic within the British Commonwealth in 1960. Elected a member of the Tumu district council in his native region in 1952, Limann served from 1953 to 1955 as its chairman and ran as an independent candidate in the parliamentary elections held under British auspices in 1954.

In 1956 Limann entered Westminster College in London. On obtaining his "A" level general certificate of education in 1957 he enrolled in the London School of Economics and Political Science, which granted him a B.Sc. degree in economics in 1960. He then enrolled at the Sorbonne in Paris, where he obtained an advanced degree in French language at its School of French Civilization in 1962. Entering the Faculty of Law and Economics at the University of Paris that same year, he qualified as a docteur en droit in political science and constitutional law in 1965. Concurrently with his studies in Paris, Limann was an external student of history at the University of London, which granted him a B.A. degree with honors in 1964.

Returning to Ghana in 1965, Limann joined the Ministry of Foreign Affairs in Accra as a foreign service officer. In addition, from 1967 on he served under the auspices of the West African Examinations Council as an examiner administering tests to candidates for civil service employment or promotion. As a constitutional lawyer, he was also a member of the constitutional commission, organized in 1967, that drafted a constitution for Ghana's second republic, which in 1969 replaced the military regime that had ousted the Nkrumah government three years earlier.

From 1969 to 1971 Limann was at Lomé, the capital of the neighboring Republic of Togo, as head of chancery and official secretary at the Ghana Embassy. While there, he attended the regular meetings of the Cocoa Producers Alliance, promoting Ghana's most important agricultural product. After serving from 1971 to 1975 as counselor to Ghana's Permanent Mission to the United Nations in Geneva, Switzerland, Limann returned to the Ministry of Foreign Affairs in Accra, remaining there as a foreign service officer until January 1979. In the course of his diplomatic career, Limann served as a delegate to a number of international assemblies, including conferences of nonaligned nations and meetings of the Organization of African Unity, the International Labor Organization, the World Health Organization, and the International Atomic Energy Agency. He took part in the International Conference on Cocoa Agreement in 1972 and the first review conference on the Nuclear Nonproliferation Treaty in 1975. In addition, he was a member of government delegations that negotiated for the formal opening of Ghana's borders with the Ivory Coast and Upper Volta, and he traveled to France to recruit qualified Ghanaians in residence there into his country's foreign service.

Meanwhile, Ghana's steady economic and political decline had been aggravated by the regime of Colonel (later General) Ignatius Kutu Acheampong, who overthrew the second republic in January 1972. Acheampong tried to tighten his hold on Ghana by suspending the constitution, banning political parties, and dissolving the National Assembly and Supreme Court. Although he was eventually willing, under pressure, to permit a partial return to civilian rule, Acheampong was ousted in July 1978 by medium-rank officers who charged that he was running a "one-man show," and was replaced as head of state by Lieutenant General Frederick W. K. Akuffo, his deputy. The Akuffo regime removed officers closely linked with Acheampong, took drastic but futile measures to stabilize the economy, and pledged a return to civilian rule by mid-1979. It appointed a constitutional commission that drafted proposals for a new basic law providing for a popularly elected executive President, a unicameral National Assembly, and such checks and balances as an advisory Council of State, an electoral commission, a press commission, an ombudsman, regional councils, and an independent judiciary.

The Akuffo regime's legalization of political parties in January 1979 prompted Limann to resign his diplomatic post in order to join the People's National party (PNP) then being organized by his uncle Imoru Egala and other former members of the late President Nkrumah's Convention People's party. Although the founders of the PNP recognized Nkrumah as its spiritual father, they emphasized parliamentary democracy rather than one-party rule and made it clear in their manifesto that they intended to pursue progressive policies rather than doctrinaire socialism. Admitting that under Nkrumah some mistakes had been made, they advocated a pragmatic approach to Ghana's problems. Dissatisfied with what they saw as a conservative form of Nkrumahism, some doctrinaire followers of Nkrumah formed the more radical People's Revolutionary party, but eventually merged their organization with the PNP.

When Egala, the interim party chairman, was disqualified by the military from competing for the Presidency because of his alleged involvement in financial irregularities, he named as Presidential candidate his virtually unknown nephew, Hilla Limann, who became the first major party leader from the north. Although some leading party members opposed the nomination, it was eventually approved by a conference of delegates, who believed that Limann's lack of previous political involvement would prove an advantage in his campaign since, unlike many of the more experienced politicians, he was untainted by charges of corruption. Capitalizing on the Nkrumah heritage, the PNP soon acquired a formidable political organization that derived substantial support from Ghanaians in all parts of the country.

On June 4, 1979, two weeks before the scheduled parliamentary and Presidential elections, the Akuffo regime was overthrown by an Armed Forces Revolutionary Council of junior officers and enlisted men headed by Flight Lieutenant J. J. ("Jerry") Rawlings, who believed that senior military officers and others who had plundered Ghana might go scot-free. (They had failed in a similar attempt at a coup d'état three weeks earlier, in May.) In a surge of moral fervor, the Armed Forces Revolutionary Council launched a "housecleaning" campaign against allegedly corrupt elements in Ghana. In the weeks following the coup, a number of senior military officers, including Acheampong and Akuffo, were found guilty of corruption by a revolutionary court and executed. The new regime's actions seemed to have the approval of millions of Ghanaians, who even considered Rawlings something of a hero, but the executions set off a wave of international protest and a threatened Nigerian oil embargo.

The Armed Forces Revolutionary Council allowed the Presidential and parliamentary elections to proceed as scheduled, although the transition from military to civilian rule was postponed for three months to give the army enough time to complete its purge of corrupt elements. Only about 35 percent of Ghana's 5,000,000 registered voters went to the polls on June 18, 1979 to elect the 140 members of the National Assembly and to choose a President from among ten candidates—six representatives of political parties and four independents. The PNP emerged from the elections with seventy-one seats, a narrow majority, and it was the only party to win representation in every region of Ghana. Like Limann, most of the elected representatives had little or no political experience.

In the Presidential race, Limann won a plurality of 35.3 percent against 29.9 percent obtained by his nearest rival, Victor Owusu of the right-of-center Popular Front party, who had served as foreign minister in Ghana's second republic. On July 9, 1979 a runoff contest was held between the two leading candidates, in which Limann obtained a majority in 105 of the 140 districts, winning the Presidency with 1,118,405 votes, or 62 percent of the total, against 686,132 cast for Owusu. Two days later, after Owusu conceded defeat, Limann promised in a radio speech to continue the "housecleaning" begun by the Armed Forces Revolutionary Council and to pay much more attention to Ghana's growing food shortage. Declaring that the election results showed the PNP to be a genuinely national party, he promised that his government would reflect all shades of opinion in the country. To ensure a smooth transition from military to civilian government, a joint AFRC-PNP commission was established, and a special tribunal was set up to carry on the "housecleaning" measures inaugurated by the Rawlings regime. As one of its last gestures before relinquishing power, the Armed Forces Revolutionary Council granted amnesty to a number of prisoners, including those convicted of political offenses by previous regimes.

The return of Ghana to civilian rule on September 24, 1979—a week ahead of schedule—was marked by celebrations, military parades in Accra, and an address by visiting President Sekou Touré of Guinea, who called on Ghanaians to shun tribal disunity and to reoccupy their place in the "African liberation struggle." According to a report in the London *Daily Telegraph* (September 24, 1979), the event evoked enthusiasm among leaders throughout black Africa, who regarded it as the beginning of "a crucial and potentially promising period of postcolonial history."

In his inaugural address after being sworn in as President for a four-year term, Limann thanked the Armed Forces Revolutionary Council for its "selfless devotion and sincerity of purpose" and spoke of the "dawn of a new era of peace and hope for progress and stability." He paid tribute to the memory of Nkrumah and pledged, "without promising the moon," to maintain an "honest government" that would "wage relentless war on poverty and corruption." He declared that he would try to "ensure regional balance and national unity without sacrificing talent, experience, and competence." On handing over the scroll of office to the new President, Rawlings promised that all members of the Armed Forces Revolutionary Council would "return to the barracks" but indicated that the new regime would be closely watched. Limann's sixteen-member Cabinet consisted largely of politically untried professionals and technocrats and for the most part excluded members of the "old guard" associated with Nkrumah. At the time the Cabinet was organized, a "tactical alliance" was formed between the PNP and the United National Convention—which occupied thirteen seats in the National Assembly and one ministry in the government. But the coalition was dissolved a year later because the leaders of the United National Convention were dissatisfied with the government's performance.

When Limann took office, Ghana was, by his own admission, in a state of "virtual bankruptcy." Its foreign debt stood at about $1.3 billion, external reserves were rapidly running out, cocoa production was at a twenty-year low, industrial production was down to about 25 percent of capacity because of the breakdown of machinery and lack of spare parts, consumer goods were virtually nonexistent, and its communications and transportation systems were on the verge of collapse. Because of high inflation combined with unemployment and food shortages, there were widespread hunger and malnutrition, and the country was plagued by lawlessness and industrial unrest. The military continued to be a thorn in the side of the civilian government, and although Rawlings was forced to retire from the armed forces on November 27, 1979, he remained a vociferous critic of the Limann government. With reference to the apparent lack of progress in the government's efforts to deal with the country's crisis during its early months in power, one diplomatic observer commented, as quoted in the Chicago Tribune (May 4, 1980): "Limann still seems awed by the fact that he is President. You don't see the kind of hard political manager that a head of state has to be. He is still too much of a gentleman. . . . He doesn't quite understand the political game he's in."

Nevertheless, the Limann government took some effective measures during its first year in power. As his first priority, the President launched a two-year agricultural development program to make Ghana more self-sufficient in food production. Although he continued to resist demands for devaluation of the nation's currency, which international experts judged essential for recovery, he was able through strict austerity measures to pay enough of Ghana's foreign debt by mid-1980 to reestablish the country's credit abroad and attract much-needed foreign aid. Politically, Limann succeeded during 1980 in undercutting the power of the "old guard" bosses in the PNP and emerged as the dominant figure in his party. On his periodic visits to the remote areas of Ghana he met with farmers, workers, military men, students, and tribal chiefs.

On the international front, the Limann government strengthened its ties with the Organization of African Unity (OAU) and the Economic Community of West African States (ECOWAS), and the President made "bridge-building" trips to such nearby states as Togo, Sierra Leone, Ivory Coast, Nigeria, and Upper Volta. Although Ghana remains firmly within the bloc of nonaligned nations, the Limann government has looked more to the Western nations—notably Great Britain, Canada, the United States, and West Germany—than to the Soviet Union and China for aid. A visit to Ghana by Pope John Paul II in the spring of 1980 helped considerably to enhance the international prestige of the Limann government. In June 1981 Limann met with Prime Minister Margaret Thatcher and British business leaders in London to discuss means of improving Ghana's economic prospects. On the whole, Ghana appeared by 1981 to have regained much of the goodwill that had been lost in the preceding decades.

President Hilla Limann, who has been married since 1968 to Dora Yaro and has five children, is described in the London Times as a "short, greying man" with a "brisk and confident" manner, who sometimes gives "the impression of arrogance" but also has a lively sense of humor. Although said to lack charisma, he is credited with "strength of character and ability" and inspires "respect, rather than love and devotion," among his people. An intellectual who prides himself on his knowledge of English literature, European and African history, economics, and international affairs, he nevertheless remains close to the common people and the rural environment from which he came. Alluding to the fact that he had once been a sprinter, Limann told an interviewer for Africa magazine (March 1980): "The public at large will soon find out that they have to work extremely hard in order to cope with the pace I want to set for our economic recovery and growth. But we have first to take a hard, sober, and realistic look at our problems."

References: Cur World Leaders 23:10+ Ja '80 por; Ghana News Bulletin I:1 O '79; London Times Special Report p1+ S 24 '80; N Y Times A p2 S 4 '80 por; Africa South of the Sahara, 1980-81; Africa Yearbook and Who's Who, 1977; Britannica Book of the Year, 1980; International Who's Who, 1980-81; Who's Who in the United Nations (1975); Who's Who in the World, 1980-81

Loquasto, Santo

1944(?)- Theatrical designer. Address: b. c/o United Scenic Artists, 1540 Broadway, New York City, N.Y. 10036

Because of his distinctive scenic and costume designs for plays of regional theatres and the New York stage, especially Joseph Papp's New York Shakespeare Festival complex, and for ballet, opera, and, recently, for films, Santo Loquasto has come to be regarded as "almost ubiquitous" in the performing arts. His sets for an inclusive range of plays, from The Bacchae

Santo Loquasto

in 1969 to *The Suicide* in 1980, have been applauded for being as integral a part of the production as are the script and actors. When both *American Buffalo* and *The Cherry Orchard* opened in New York during the same week in 1977, the contrast between the heaped-up, realistically detailed set of the one and the suggestive scenery of the other impressively pointed up Loquasto's skill in adapting his style to the play itself. As he explained in an interview for the New York *Times* (April 14, 1977), he believes that scenery should not merely decorate, but should "aid [in] revealing the point of view of the play and the production. The way that furniture and spaces are put together can create tensions that illuminate what the actors are doing. Sometimes it's done subliminally—a table that's too small, a painting that's crooked, or a room that's all right angles, with enough exceptions around so it looks real. When it's done right, the effect can add a whole new dimension to the play."

Santo Loquasto was born about 1944 in Wilkes-Barre, Pennsylvania, the younger son of an Italian-American salesman of cooking utensils. His brother is thirteen years older than he. In his kindergarten class Santo seems to have been an art prodigy. "I was drawing in perspective before anyone else," he has recounted, as quoted in *Newsweek* (March 21, 1977). "While other kids were doing stick figures, I was drawing breasts on women. I was asked to leave kindergarten for being contrary." At the age of fifteen he painted a group of nude murals for a cocktail lounge that his mother, Ruth Loquasto, owned and operated. When his parents were divorced in 1959, he remained with his mother, who en-

couraged his fascination with interior decoration by helping him rearrange the furniture in their home and on weekends by making the rounds with him of houses for sale to look at the decoration. "More and more, I wanted the rooms my way," he recalled in an interview with Barbara Rowes for *People* (November 17, 1980).

Attending a theatre class for children had stimulated another early interest of Santo Loquasto, the stage. Later, during summer vacations from Moravian Preparatory School in Bethlehem, Pennsylvania, he acted in summer stock at the Ross Common Playhouse in the Poconos. As his enthusiasm for the theatre began to focus on scenery, he created his first sets there, when he was sixteen, for productions of *Picnic* and *Gigi*. While attending King's College in Wilkes-Barre, he neglected his more academic studies to work on plays. At the age of twenty-one he produced his first professional set designs, for plays by Brecht, Ibsen, and Chekhov, at the Williamstown Theater in Williamstown, Massachusetts.

New England regional theatre became the proving ground of Loquasto's apprenticeship. During 1968 he designed sets for productions of *Tiny Alice* at the Long Wharf Theater in New Haven, of *The Hostage* and *The Rose Tattoo* at the Hartford Stage Company, and of *Narrow Road to the Deep North* at the Charles Playhouse in Boston. With the Hartford company the following year, he created the scenery for *The Waltz Invention* and *The Homecoming* and the scenery and costumes for *A Delicate Balance* and *The Farce of Scapin*. Meanwhile, he had enrolled in the Yale School of Drama to major in stage design, just about the time that newly appointed Dean Robert Brustein was reorganizing and reinvigorating the school's faculty and course of study. After earning his M.F.A. in 1969, Loquasto remained at Yale as resident designer.

For the School of Drama Repertory Theatre's presentation of Euripides' *The Bacchae* in March 1969, Loquasto designed an evocative set that Jack Kroll of *Newsweek* (March 24, 1969) credited with "catalyzing the entire production." Kroll went on to observe, "Obviously inspired by Julian Beck's wonderful design for the Living Theatre's 'Frankenstein,' Loquasto achieves his own success with his beautiful oval cage that structures the entire stage into levels, grades and heights that become the public places of Athens, the sequestrations of the Dionysiac forests and the hidden groins and shadows of the mind." Furthermore, as Julius Novick pointed out in the New York *Times* (March 23, 1969), Loquasto devised "a wonderfully usable playing area," with a curved floor, platforms, and poles that facilitate sliding, rolling, climbing, and jumping.

During 1970 Loquasto worked on scenic problems for the Yale Repertory's adaptation of *Three Philip Roth Stories* and *Cops and Horrors* and designed sets and costumes for *The Story Theater: Gimpel the Fool, Saint*

Julian the Hospitaler and *Olympian Games* and sets for *The Revenger's Tragedy*. Still associated with the Hartford Stage Company, he was responsible for the scenery of *A Day in the Death of Joe Egg, The Trial of A. Lincoln,* and *Ring Round the Moon* and for both the sets and costumes of *Misalliance, Anything Goes,* and *Rosencrantz and Guildenstern Are Dead.* Over the next year or so, besides returning to Yale and Hartford, Loquasto began to use his artistic resources in productions of regional theatres outside New England. Among his sets for Washington, D.C.'s Arena Stage were those for *Pantagleize* and *The House of Blue Leaves,* as well as the American premieres of Ionesco's *Wipe-Out Games* and Günter Grass's *Uptight.* He also handled the stage designs for the production by the Mark Taper Forum in Los Angeles of Pinter's *Old Times.*

Santo Loquasto had made his Off-Broadway debut at the Astor Place Theater on April 1, 1970, when he provided the scenery for a program of two one-act plays by Sam Shepard, *The Unseen Hand* and *Forensic and the Navigators.* He owes his passage to Broadway to Joseph Papp, the venturesome producer and director and founder of the New York Shakespeare Festival Theater, who while teaching at the Yale School of Drama had liked Loquasto's work and a few years later engaged him to design the setting for *Sticks and Bones.* David Rabe's shattering drama of a blinded Vietnam veteran's return to an uncaring, TV-bewitched Middle-American family opened Off Broadway on November 7, 1971, at the Public/Anspacher Theater. Despite the controversy provoked by the harshness of its indictment of middle-class attitudes, *Sticks and Bones* received so many glowing reviews that on March 1, 1972 it moved to Broadway's John Golden Theater. Among the play's assets was Loquasto's setting, which Clive Barnes described in the New York Times (November 8, 1971) as "an American dream-house of nightmarish furnishing mediocrity, with just the right shaggy, tufty carpet in just the correct bilious shade of green, the hard and uncharitable davenport, the easy chair that is anything but, and the cocktail cabinet that looks all ready for a Pinteresque weasel to crouch under it." That living room won Loquasto a Drama Desk award for scenic design in 1972.

Like *Sticks and Bones,* Jason Miller's hard-hitting *That Championship Season,* the next Papp production on which Loquasto worked, was transferred uptown from Off Broadway. On September 14, 1972 it continued at the Booth Theater the run that had begun at the Newman/Public Theater in May. Loquasto's painstakingly detailed, atmospheric setting—with its sturdy staircase, heavy upholstered chairs, antimacassars and tassels, coat hooks, gun rack, colored glass transom—was another living room, that of a high school basketball coach, the host of a discomfiting reunion of a former championship team. "The set is a powerful example of Loquasto's ability to de-

sign an environment that's solid and real and yet emanates an unaccountable aura of disruption and portent," Jack Kroll wrote in *Newsweek* (March 21, 1977). Kroll also quoted Loquasto's explanation of his objective in designing the scene, which placed first on the 1972 *Variety* poll of New York drama critics for best set: "I wanted to say something about the kind of American who built this kind of house. It looks real, but it's theatrical, bigger than life. As the audience listens to the play, I want them to be drawn in, to respond subliminally to the mystery of the house."

While *That Championship Season* was still playing, Broadway audiences saw another of Loquasto's scenic designs in Paul Zindel's *The Secret Affairs of Mildred Wild,* starring Maureen Stapleton as a madcap obsessed with the movies, which began its run at the Ambassador Theater in mid-November 1972. Loquasto's agglomeration of thousands of fan magazines, kewpie dolls, and baubles jammed into a shabby apartment "expressively displayed muddle on a rampage," as Clive Barnes wrote in his review. Also in late 1972 Loquasto's scenes of early nineteenth-century Jewish Russia graced a production of Isaac Babel's *Sunset* by the Chelsea Theater Center of Brooklyn.

Except for supplying the scenery for the American premiere, on January 31, 1973, of Max Frisch's *A Public Prosecutor Is Sick of It All* at the Arena Stage in Washington, Santo Loquasto was occupied throughout 1973 with presentations at Papp's Public Theater. Early in the year he designed sets for Dennis R. Reardon's grim family drama, *Siamese Connections,* and David Rabe's first failure, *The Orphan,* a free adaptation in a modern American context of the *Oresteia* triology of Aeschylus. During the summer, at the 2,300-seat open-air Delacorte in Central Park, he executed backgrounds for *As You Like It* and *King Lear.* The latter, with James Earl Jones in the lead, was televised. When the Shakespeare Festival was invited uptown to take over the Vivian Beaumont Theater and Forum (renamed the Mitzi E. Newhouse Theater) as the resident theatre company of the Lincoln Center for the Performing Arts, Papp made Loquasto his principal designer.

Loquasto began to meet the challenge of designing for the cavernous Vivian Beaumont, a theatre serving the dual purpose of both a proscenium and a thrust stage, with the Shakespeare Festival's production of David Rabe's *Boom Boom Room* (originally and later called *In the Boom Boom Room*), which opened on November 18, 1973. There, the basic tawdry bed-sitting room set was encircled by gracefully contoured cages for gyrating go-go girls who function as a Greek chorus. Ron Milner's drama of black ghetto life, *What the Wine-Sellers Buy,* which brought Loquasto another Tony nomination, followed in 1974, as did August Strindberg's *The Dance of Death,* with its dramatic circular staircase in the vast, fan-shaped room of a stone fortress, and Anne Burr's *Mert and Phil*, with its dispiriting, run-down apartment set. For a stark *Hamlet*, in 1975 Loquasto offered an immense, tilted disk of polished oak as a platform stage. His first assignment for the Beaumont's small companion theatre, the Mitzi E. Newhouse, which has steep, three-quarter round seating, was *The Tempest* (1974). The summer Shakespeare plays for which he was designer at the larger Delacorte included *Pericles* and *The Merry Wives of Windsor*, as well as *The Comedy of Errors*, which took an Obie award for both sets and costumes in 1975. Clive Barnes described the setting as "adorable—a scenic Valentine from Sicily, a building that revolves with continuing interest," and further remarked, "It was the kind of theatrical setting that Baedeker would have said is worthy of a detour."

On Broadway, Loquasto was engaged in setting such diverse vehicles as Robert Patrick's *Kennedy's Children*, an incisive "wail for the sixties" (1975), Bob Barry's comedy thriller, *Murder Among Friends* (1975), and Samuel Taylor's comedy western, *Legend* (1976). Abundantly supplied with hundreds of wine and liquor bottles and festooned with dozens of Off-Broadway posters, the Lower East Side saloon of *Kennedy's Children* was a forerunner of the extraordinary glut of trash in the Chicago junk shop of *American Buffalo* (1977), David Mamet's study of three thieves who merely talk about robbing a man of his coin collection. For "that sight to make sore eyes much sorer," as Otis L. Guernsey Jr. referred to the set in *The Best Plays of 1976-77*, Loquasto earned a Tony nomination, a Drama Desk Award, and a Joseph Maharam Foundation Award. He also won a Maharam award for his costumes in Andrei Serban's production of *Agamemnon*, another 1977 presentation of the Shakespeare Festival.

In an antithetical style, after weeks of discussions with director Andrei Serban and the building of countless models and scenes that were never used, Loquasto created a breathtaking, evocative set for the Shakespeare Festival's *The Cherry Orchard* (1977), achieving, as he explained, "a refined poetic space in which Chekhov's images live." Walter Kerr described it in the New York *Times* (February 27, 1977) as "a larger, airier, freer and at the same time more ominous landscape" than is customary for that drama. The exquisite, almost barren set featured a great white carpet, a hint of white walls at the sides, and a scrim at the rear that revealed the full cherry orchard to audiences after the opening of the first act—"row upon row of feathered May trees, not quite released from the winter's cold but iridescent with on-coming life. . . . Death and life at once." "Surpassing even himself," in Clive Barnes's opinion, Loquasto nonetheless lost the Tony to the designer of *Annie*, although he won for his costumes for *The Cherry Orchard*.

Other plays of 1977 for which Loquasto designed sets were John Guare's *Landscape of the Body*, William Gibson's *Golda*, and Robert Athayde's *Miss Margarida's Way*. He found appropriate clothes for characters in the last two by making shopping expeditions to the Lower East Side. The most active designer of 1978-79, Loquasto produced sets for *The Mighty Gents*, *The Goodbye People*, *Curse of the Starving Class*, and the musicals *Daddy Goodness*, *King of Hearts*, *Stop the World I Want to Get Off*, and *Sarava*, as well as costumes for the last two. His sets for *Bent* (1979), a play about the Holocaust and homosexuality, and *The Suicide* (1980), a farce by Nikolai Erdman banned in Russia since 1932, greatly intensified the dramatic impact. The latter stunned audiences at the ANTA Theater with the intricacies of its staircases, swinging doors, moving platforms, paintings transmuted to peepholes, and oscillating banquet table. During the late 1970's Loquasto added *Awake and Sing*, *The Glass Menagerie*, *Heartbreak House*, *The Caucasian Chalk Circle*, *The Lower Depths*, and *The Play's the Thing* to his long list of regional theatre credits.

At the same time that he met a growing demand for his scenic designs on the New York stage, Loquasto increased his contributions to other forms of the performing arts, reflecting that "all these things feed into each other." He created the sets and costumes for the New York Pro Musica's chamber opera *La Dafne*, which was performed at the Spoleto Festival of Two Worlds in Italy in 1973, and has designed for the San Diego Opera, the San Francisco Spring Opera, and the Opera Society of Washington, D.C. For the American Ballet Theatre he designed costumes for *Concerto* (1967) and Twyla Tharp's *Push Comes to Shove* (1967) and costumes and sets for the nineteenth-century Russian classic *Don Quixote, or Kitri's Wedding* (1978) and *Raymonda* (1980-81). When Eliot Feld revived the *Sephardic Song* ballet in 1974, Loquasto provided "a beautiful environmental setting of ragged nets." Collaborating since 1975 on presentations of the Twyla Tharp Dance Foundation, he created the chic costumes of *Short Stories* and *Baker's Dozen*, performed in 1981 at the Los Angeles Music Center. He has also worked with Robert Joffrey's ballet company. Costumes by Loquasto may also be seen in several recent films—Woody Allen's *Stardust Memories* (1980); Marshall Brickman's *Simon*; *The Fan*, which stars Lauren Bacall; and Andrew Bergman's comedy *So Fine* (Warner Brothers, 1981), for which he came up with a pair of snug-fitting, blue denium jeans with see-through plastic windows, in a spoof of the current designer jeans fad.

The bearded, boyish-looking, casually dressed designer lives in a roomy Manhattan apartment on Riverside Drive, with plenty of space for his pack-rat collections of props, like old afghans and lace tablecloths. Santo Loquasto believes in decorating his own home gradually:

"A room should develop layers." To achieve the "authentic ambience" of his stage designs he scrounges around New York and vicinity for furnishings, upholstery fabrics, lamps, and just the right drawers pulls, looking for bargains in antique, thrift, or junk shops. In supermarkets and subways he studies and sketches the kinds of clothes people wear. He takes pleasure in decorating even the offstage rooms that audiences of a play only glimpse occasionally. Very self-critical, Loquasto disclosed to Robert Berkvist of the New York Times (September 16, 1977), "You try not to become typed, but of course you *are* typed. Finally, you begin to act as your own devil's advocate; you torment yourself into examining your work and tearing it apart." Less seriously he went on, "On second thought, maybe it's just my Catholic upbringing that makes me reject anything that comes too easily; I immediately decide it has to be terrible." Totally dedicated to his work, he has expressed some regret for the ephemeral nature of an art that does not survive the run of a play, except perhaps in book form, as is the case with the designs of Gordon Craig.

References: Cue 46:14+ Ap 2-15 '77 por; N Y Times C p1+ Ap 14 '77 por, C p2 S 16 '77 por; Newsday A p4+ My 22 '73 por; Newsweek 89:84 Mr 21 '77 por; People 14:127+ N 17 '80 pors; Notable Names in the American Theatre (1976); Who's Who in the Theatre (1977)

McColough, C(harles) Peter (mə-kul'ə)

Aug. 1, 1922- Corporation executive. Address: Xerox Corporation, 800 Long Ridge Rd., Stamford, Conn. 06904

C. Peter McColough, the chairman and chief executive officer of the Xerox Corporation, joined the firm in 1954 when it was known as the Haloid Company, a Rochester, New York manufacturer of industrial photographic products. Five years later the firm introduced the first office copying machine, the 914, which employed an electrostatic copying process invented in 1938 by Chester F. Carlson. With its dominance established in a fantastically lucrative growth market, Xerox's annual revenues jumped from $40 million in 1960 to almost $3 billion in the early 1970's.

After taking over the presidency of Xerox in 1966, McColough drastically altered the corporation's goals and transformed its self-image. Jacob E. Goldman, Xerox's chief scientist, explained McColough's impact on the firm to a writer for Forbes (July 7, 1980): "In the late 1960's, Peter McColough redefined our company. It's the old question of whether you consider yourself as providing a function or a product. We're not a copiermaker. We're an information company that got into the business via copiers." By 1979 McColough had built up the Xerox revenues to $7 billion a year and its annual earnings to $563 million.

Charles Peter McColough was born in Halifax, Nova Scotia on August 1, 1922 to Reginald W. McColough, a Deputy Minister of Public Works, and Barbara Theresa (Martin) McColough. After receiving his primary and secondary education in the Halifax school system, McColough served as an airman with the British Royal Navy during World War II. On his return to Canada in 1945 he studied for one year at the Osgoode Hall Law School in Toronto and then enrolled at Dalhousie University in Halifax, where he received his LL.B. degree in 1947. Although he was admitted to the Canadian bar in that same year, McColough chose to follow his bent for business and industry rather than embark on a legal career. He enrolled in the Harvard Graduate School of Business Administration, which granted him his M.B.A. degree in 1949.

From 1951 to 1954 McColough worked for the Lehigh Navigation Coal Sales Company in Philadelphia as vice-president in charge of sales. Before long he negotiated an interview with the vice-president of marketing at the Haloid Company in Rochester, New York. After recovering from his initial shock over the dilapidated condition of the company's offices, he accepted the job because of his interest in Haloid's development of copier technology. He later was substantially responsible for Haloid's successful marketing strategies of its 914 copier.

During the 1950's and 1960's McColough moved through the ranks of the Xerox Corporation rapidly. He was appointed general sales manager of the first reproduction service center in Chicago in 1954; assistant to the vice-president in charge of sales in Rochester in 1956; manager of marketing in 1957; general sales manager in 1959; and vice-president in charge of sales in 1960. In 1961 he was elected to the board of directors and appointed a member of the executive committee. Two years later he became Xerox's executive vice-president of operations.

While in that post, in 1965, McColough explained to a group of security analysts Xerox's reason for making a thrust into the area of educational materials. He was later quoted by *Newsweek* (September 30, 1968) as having said at the time that "'publish or perish,' is a phrase sometimes heard in universities. In industry, it will become 'educate or erode.'" The diversification McColough was discussing led in the mid-1960's to the purchase of Ginn and Company, the textbook publishing firm in Boston, for $120 million in Xerox common stock. That acquisition was the largest ever made by Xerox up until that time.

In 1966 C. Peter McColough became president of Xerox. In an interview granted a year later he expressed his conviction that Xerox needed to diversify and redirect the focus of its efforts. "These are changing times," McColough said. "For us, it means a change in the way we're organized and a change in the fields we're interested in." In September 1968, four months after he became chief executive officer of Xerox, McColough began to act on his belief by entering negotiations with the CIT Financial Corporation aimed at a merger of the two firms, since he was convinced that the acquisition would enable Xerox to move into such fields as graphic communications systems and information systems and services. Although observers at the time noted that Xerox's plans to expand into the computer technology field would have been enhanced by acquiring the financial resources of CIT, negotiations were broken off without explanatory comment by the two firms on November 13, 1968.

In the following year, however, Xerox paid $1 billion worth of its stock to acquire the El Segundo, California firm known as Scientific Data Systems. That acquisition endowed Xerox with computer capability in the areas of data storage and transmissions systems, a technology the corporation had not been able to develop on its own. The diversification into computers was a project initiated solely by McColough. Some years later he explained his decision to a writer for *Forbes* (August 15, 1972): "Our objective in acquiring SDS was to offer broader-based information systems. We feel that to really seize the opportunities around the world for supplying information, we had to broaden out from graphics." Among other changes instituted by McColough were

the hiring of upper-echelon executives with no previous experience at Xerox, the moving of the company headquarters to Stamford, Connecticut, and the decentralizing of company decision-making. In an effort to propitiate nationalist elements in countries in which Xerox operated, foreign nationals were taken in as partners.

At a stockholders meeting on May 20, 1971 McColough described current company endeavors and future plans. He announced the start of business negotiations with the Republic of China and Xerox's preeminent position in the field of telephone facsimile transceivers. Full-scale production of the new 4000 copier, designed to print copies on both sides of the paper, would begin in 1971, according to McColough, who also mentioned plans to develop a telecopying machine using the Xerographic process and a non-Xerographic color imaging system using a process known as photoelectrophoresis. At the end of the stockholders meeting he was appointed chairman of the executive committee by the board of directors.

Seven months later, McColough became the chairman of Xerox. The gloomy economic climate that prevailed at the time, characterized by recession and a decline in government spending, adversely affected Xerox's developing computer business, with SDS (renamed Xerox Data Systems) alone losing $100 million before taxes. Some months later McColough discussed the problems of Xerox Data Systems with a reporter for *Forbes* (August 15, 1972): "I didn't anticipate losing money. We bought a growing company that was profitable when we bought it. . . . In hindsight, I certainly would have preferred to wait because I would have paid less; but the basic decision was the right one. The thing that made me the most nervous was that I saw no options."

Despite its losses with Xerox data systems, McColough continued to expand into computers with the purchase of Diablo Systems, a producer of peripheral computer equipment, in April 1972. Xerox paid $29 million in stock to buy that company, which produced disc-drive storage units and high-speed printers. Inevitably, Xerox began to face competition with IBM, the giant in the computer field. McColough explained his attitude towards the challenges Xerox would have to face in its development of the new technology to the writer for *Forbes* (August 15, 1972): "If we ever get to be afraid to stick our necks out, we'll be just another big corporation."

In 1974 Xerox introduced the 800 electronic typing system, its first entry in the word-processing field, and the model 9200 copier, a high-speed, high-volume duplicator that churned out two copies per second, in an effort to compete with the small offset printing presses used in corporate and government printing offices. The advantage of the 9200, which leased for between $22,000 and $23,000 per month, was that it printed from the original document instead of from a master copy. Xerox, which hired 1,000 employees in Dallas, Texas to build the copier, eventually spent over $300 million for its production. That staggering outlay led a New York *Times* reporter (December 1, 1974) to refer to it as one of "the most ambitious products ever conceived by American industry," putting it in a class with duPont nylon and the Boeing 747.

Xerox needed the new market created by the 9200 because of the decline in growth of the copier business, which dropped from 15 percent to 8 percent per year in the 1970's, and because, as the dominant force in the copier industry, it was coming under increasing attack with antitrust suits filed by competitors challenging the corporation's marketing and pricing systems. In the period between 1964 and 1974 Xerox's earnings gains were approximately 22 percent yearly. In 1974, however, the figure stood at 10 percent because of recession, inflation, and the cost of producing the 9200. Added to Xerox's woes was its lack of a strong management team, because many executives had left in protest when McColough brought in outside talent.

By 1975, after six years of struggle, Xerox had lost $264 million in its computer business and had therefore decided to stop computer production and sales by mid-1976. In the second quarter of 1975 Xerox wrote off $84 million to cover its losses from the computer shutdown and its profits dropped drastically. "The mainframe [computer] is not at the heart of what we want to do," McColough assured a reporter for *Business Week* (August 4, 1975). "If it were, we would have had to stomach our losses." What Xerox gained from its venture was a sound base in electronics and, especially, in digital technology, which could be used in the long run for more advanced office copier systems. A first step in that direction was the establishment of a micro-electronics center in El Segundo, California.

"For years Wall Street thought Xerox could do no wrong, make no mistakes, walk on water," McColough quipped at a news conference covered by the New York *Times* (January 8, 1976). "In the last year the pendulum has swung the other way; we can do no right." But in spite of what McColough viewed as an overreaction to Xerox's difficulties by observers on Wall Street, the corporation still seemed to be in a decline.

McColough had counted on a price-cut early in 1976 to halt the inroads into the copier business by Xerox's many competitors. While Xerox was concentrating on the high-volume end of the business, the Japanese, in 1974, introduced inexpensive plain-paper copiers and firms such as IBM, Pitney-Bowes, Saxon Industries, Inc., Savin, and Eastman Kodak had either already introduced new low-volume machines or were about to do so. Yielding to pressure applied through many suits, Xerox signed a consent agreement with the Federal Trade Commission in 1975, which required that the corporation share its technology with its competitors by providing licenses for access to its information.

Besides making price-cutting attempts to deal with competitors and refocusing on making advancements in electronics equipment for offices of the future, McColough initiated cost-cutting programs to alleviate Xerox's financial problems. He introduced plans to cut marketing and servicing costs, laid off some workers, consolidated some rebuilding plants, shelved the plan to build a new headquarters building in Stamford, and eliminated a purchasing office in Rochester. He also instituted a new pricing structure called the Xerox Contract Pricing (XCP) plan, which altered the manner in which machines were leased in order to make Xerox more competitive in the copier market.

In 1975 Xerox had established the Business Product and Development Group to make future plans and oversee acquisitions. The firms purchased by Xerox during that period were Versatec, a manufacturer of electrostatic printers and plotters, and Daconics, a producer of computerized word-processing systems. Another sector in which McColough hoped to see progress made was that of foreign operations. With foreign business accounting for 45 percent of Xerox's earnings and sales in the mid-1970's, he hoped for even further growth in Latin America, Indonesia, and China.

Under McColough's direction, enormous strides towards the revitalization of Xerox were made during the latter part of the 1970's. Between 1976 and 1979 Xerox introduced the 2300 and 2600 copiers in the low-volume range, the 3100 in the low-to-middle-volume range, and the 9700, a two-copy per second laser-printing copier. As a new marketing technique, Xerox introduced retail stores into its sales framework. The corporation also made a number of acquisitions, including Shugart Associates, producers of floppy-disc drives, in 1977, and, in 1979, Century Data Systems, producers of rigid-disc drives. With the settlement, in the late 1970's, of the many suits and countersuits between Xerox and IBM, Xerox gained access to IBM patents in the areas of office copiers, information handling, and data processing and received $25 million.

Among the more spectacular innovations introduced by Xerox was the development of the XTEN domestic satellite telecommunications network, geared to transmit electronic mail. While IBM's counterpart, the Satellite Business Systems, was designed for use in larger companies, Xerox directed its network to use in smaller firms. To expand the XTEN system internationally, Xerox bought Western Union International for $200 million worth of Xerox stock.

In 1978 Xerox introduced the 850 word processor and, in December 1979, a work station containing word processors and electronic data bases and files. That same month Xerox also introduced its Ethernet system, a local-area communications network that interconnects offices in either a single building or in a complex of buildings. The Ethernet system was eventually installed with great success in the White House and in the Congressional buildings. In May 1980 Xerox announced that it was working on common standards and specifications with the Digital Equipment Corporation and Intel, a manufacturer of microprocessors. As as result of such standardization, any of the three companies' equipment could be installed in the Ethernet system, thereby lowering research and development costs for Xerox. With all those achievements, by 1980 McColough's plan to revitalize Xerox, especially through the development of office-of-the-future technology, was obviously well on its way.

McColough views an upper-echelon executive's role as being ceremonial in nature. He explained his viewpoint to a reporter for *Business Week* (May 4, 1974) by pointing out that "a company's reputation, good or bad, is made not only by the quality of its products and services but also by its people, especially its top people." McColough accomplishes his public relations function by spending half of his time visiting Xerox facilities in the United States and abroad and by dealing with concerns of a political and public service nature. Although he has decentralized the decision-making process at Xerox, he takes an active role in making critical decisions and has no qualms about bypassing executives in seeking information and opinions from lower-level employees.

McColough is a director of Rank Xerox Ltd., Fuji-Xerox Co., Ltd., and Citicorp. He is a member of the Council on Foreign Relations, the Business Council, the Business Roundtable, and the Steering Committee of the National Commission for Full Employment. He is also chairman of the President's Commission on Pension Policy. In 1973 and 1974 McColough served as the treasurer of the Democratic National Committee, in 1974 he was the campaign chairman for the National Urban League, and he is currently the chairman of the President's Commission on Pension Policy. He holds an honorary doctor of laws degree from his alma mater, Dalhousie University, conferred on him in 1970.

On April 25, 1953 C. Peter McColough married Mary Virginia White. Interviewers for business periodicals have characterized him as an energetic, restless, and amiable man, who tends to become impatient with the letters, memos, and reports that make up the daily routine of corporate enterprise. He likes to spend what little time he has left over from the claims of his career in sailing and skiing. He is a Roman Catholic and (since 1956) a naturalized citizen of the United States.

References: Bsns W p43 My 4 '74 por, p60 Ap 5 '76; Forbes 110:40+ Ag 15 '72; International Who's Who, 1981-82; Who's Who in America, 1980-81

Mason, Marsha

Apr. 3, 1942- Actress. Address: b. c/o William Morris Agency, 151 El Camino Dr., Beverly Hills, Calif. 90212

Marsha Mason's long apprenticeship in drama classes, repertory and regional theatre, and Off-Broadway productions to develop her acting talent tends to bear out the contention of her husband, playwright Neil Simon, as recently quoted in *Cue:* "The thing that is different about Marsha is that she wants to be a good actress and most of the people in this business are content to be movie and TV stars." She has apparently, however, found the screen more advantageous to her career than the stage, having won two Golden Globe Awards and three nominations for an Academy Award. Moviegoers and critics have been as much impressed by her facility for comedy, in the *Goodbye Girl* and *Chapter Two*, as for drama, in *Cinderella Liberty, Promises in the Dark*, and *Only When I Laugh.*

The daughter of strict Roman Catholics, Marsha Mason was born in St. Louis, Missouri on April 3, 1942 to James Mason, a printer who became an employee of the Department of Motor Vehicles, and Jacqueline (Rakowski) Mason. Her parents named her after the actress Marsha Hunt. "My father was a curly haired Irishman, with some English in him, judging from the name 'Mason,' while my mother was a Russian-German blonde with a patrician nose," Miss Mason told Bernard Drew of *Today* (January 10, 1980), adding, "My sister and I both desperately wanted our mother's nose but we got our father's." Her sister, younger than Marsha, is now Melinda Candido, a wife and mother.

Movie-struck as a young girl, Marsha Mason kept scrapbooks of Joan Crawford, Bette Davis, and her other favorite stars. Recalling that her father used to refer to her as "Sarah Bernhardt," she told Lloyd Shearer, who interviewed her for *Parade* (January 13, 1978), "I always liked acting. I found it stimulating, exciting. It always seemed to make me feel good." After she had graduated from the parochial Nerinx Hall High School, she was awarded a four-year drama scholarship to Webster College, a Roman Catholic college for women in St. Louis.

Equipped with a B.A. degree in speech and drama, Marsha Mason arrived in New York in 1964 and began to pursue an acting career. In September of that year, when her roommates sent her to borrow a vacuum cleaner from a neighbor, she met actor Gary Campbell. They were married five months later. In an interview with Rex Reed of the New York *Daily News* (November 20, 1977), Miss Mason attributed the marriage to "a need to feel an attachment to somebody—we were both scared and lonely." The marriage ended amicably after five years.

To improve her chances of securing a role in a Broadway play, Miss Mason studied drama with three coaches. In 1967 she made her Off-Broadway debut at the Theater de Lys in *The Deer Park*, Norman Mailer's adaptation of his own novel about a Hollywood mogul whose sleazy world is intended to serve as a microcosm of contemporary society. The mixed reviews it elicited largely ignored Miss Mason in the small role of Bobby. She fared better a year later when she was cast in another Off-Broadway production, *It's Called the Sugar Plum*, the first of two one-act plays by Israel Horovitz under the umbrella title *The Indian Wants the Bronx*. Miss Mason played Joanna Dibble, a woman who confronts—and is seduced by—a man who has killed her fiancé with his car. Although some critics felt she was miscast, her performance was described as "just right" by Edith Oliver in the *New Yorker* (January 27, 1968) and "unfailingly believable" by Richard Watts in the New York *Post* (January 18, 1968). Beginning in September 1968 on a national tour of ninety-five cities of *Cactus Flower*, she played Toni, the dentist's zany mistress, a role for which she had been an understudy in the Broadway production that opened in late 1965.

Like many struggling young actors, Miss Mason occasionally had to support herself by taking a series of part-time jobs that she remembers gave her migraine headaches and by hawking home products on television commercials. Her first steady work as an actress was an eight-month stint playing the role of a reporter on the CBS-TV soap opera *Love of Life*, but she later confided to Bernard Drew, "The rhythms of the soap opera just drove me crazy, and I desperately sought and finally obtained television commercials to take the financial crunch off me." TV viewers saw her in pitches for products such as Micron mouthwash, Blue Bonnet Margarine, and Manufacturers Hanover Trust.

A variety of parts in plays produced by the Eugene O'Neill Theater Center: Playwrights Conference in Waterford, Connecticut helped to prepare Miss Mason for her Broadway debut opposite Kevin McCarthy in a dramatization of Kurt Vonnegut's satiric comedy *Happy Birthday, Wanda June*, which opened at the Theater de Lys in October 1970 and moved uptown to the Edison Theater in November. In the antiwar play based on the Ulysses myth, Miss Mason portrayed Penelope Ryan, who is preoccupied with two suitors when her boisterous, Hemingway-like husband returns home after being lost in the jungle for eight years. Although critics pointed out flaws in the play, Stanley Kauffmann of the *New Republic* calling it "a disaster," most agreed with Marilyn Stasio of *Cue* (October 17, 1970) that Miss Mason's performance was "first-rate." Walter Kerr, who found much of Vonnegut's humor "exhilarating" and "irresistible," described her in the New York *Times* (October 18, 1970) as "a Shirley Temple doll, in tight auburn curls, improved by a lascivious lower lip and occasional bass tones in her voice."

For her portrayal of Penelope, Miss Mason earned a nomination as the most promising new Off-Broadway actress for the 1970-71 season in a poll of drama critics conducted by *Variety*. Mark Robson, the director, intended to cast her in his film version of *Happy Birthday, Wanda June*, but was overruled by studio executives. During the summer of 1971 she returned to Connecticut to perform at the Eugene O'Neill Theater Center in the world premieres of *Body and Soul*, as Masha, *Respects*, as Marion, *Bruce*, as Marjorie Bruce, and *Ishtar*, as Joya.

A part in the San Francisco-based American Conservatory Theater (ACT) production in early 1972 of Noël Coward's *Private Lives*, directed by Francis Ford Coppola, led to a small but significant role opposite George Segal in Paul Mazursky's film *Blume in Love* (Warner Brothers, 1973). As Arlene, the woman to whom the despondent Blume turns after his wife divorces him, Miss Mason was, according to Judith Crist of *New York* magazine (June 18, 1973), "more interesting than her role." Stanley Kauffmann thought her "appealing," and in his review for *Newsweek* (June 25, 1973) Paul D. Zimmerman named her among the "secondary figures who give the film most of its life."

Again in San Francisco, in 1972-73, Marsha Mason polished her skills in leading roles in the ACT productions of *A Doll's House, Cyrano de Bergerac, You Can't Take it With You, The Merchant of Venice*, and *The Crucible*. During that "happy, rewarding year," as she once described it, she established herself as a major film star by portraying Maggie, a bar-room-hustling prostitute with an illegitimate mulatto son in director Mark Rydell's bittersweet *Cinderella Liberty* (Twentieth Century-Fox,

1973). Miss Mason and her costar James Caan —playing a sailor who loves the masochistic Maggie—elicited critical raves: Judith Crist observed in *New York* (December 24, 1973) that Miss Mason emerges as "an off-beat screen enchantress" and went on to say that she "is that rare creature who not only makes being over 25 seem something less than senility but also makes her whore-with-heart-of-gold role perfectly acceptable." Jay Cocks of *Time* (January 7, 1974), however, found Miss Mason's interpretation more complex: "The whore (well acted by Marsha Mason) does not, at least, have a heart of gold. What she does have is a consuming pathology that the sailor finds irresistibly attractive." In addition to earning an Academy Award nomination, Miss Mason received the Golden Globe Award from the Hollywood Foreign Press Association as the year's best dramatic actress.

"If you play a down-and-out loser part, they send you down-and-out loser parts," Miss Mason once complained in reference to the movie scripts she was sent after *Cinderella Liberty*. She therefore went to New York to audition for *The Good Doctor*, Neil Simon's adaptation of nine Anton Chekhov short stories. She got the part almost immediately—reportedly at Simon's insistence—and met the playwright in early October 1973, the first day of rehearsals. Their whirlwind romance, which culminated in marriage three weeks later, on October 25, was, Miss Mason told Rex Reed, "just one of those extraordinary chemical things. . . . We were all sitting around this table reading the script aloud. We took a coffee break. He came around, put his hand on my shoulder, and I remember patting his hand with my hand like we were old friends." The marriage surprised many people, not only because of the briefness of the courtship, but because Simon's wife of twenty years, dancer Joan Baim, had died only three months earlier, leaving him with two daughters, Ellen, then sixteen, and Nancy, ten.

The Good Doctor, which ran on Broadway from November 27, 1973 to May 26, 1974, was not one of Neil Simon's more successful plays. Critic John Simon of *New York* (December 17, 1973) called it a "mediocre, nontheatrical hodge-podge," but the five-person cast in a variety of roles was lauded by Tom Donnelly of the Washington *Post* (December 23, 1973) as "splendidly accomplished," and Clive Barnes wrote in the New York *Times* (November 28, 1973) that Miss Mason was "sweetly virtuoso in her versatility." During the run of *The Good Doctor*, on February 6, Miss Mason was seen on television as Roxanne in PBS's presentation of an earlier taped ACT production of *Cyrano de Bergerac*.

Shortly thereafter, Marsha Mason's career went into eclipse. When asked by Neil Simon to choose either her career or him, she chose him. She later explained to Richard Ballad of *Cue* (February 15, 1980), "After we got married we both got scared. Particularly Neil. If I were not with him, he'd get this terrible feeling of abandonment. Why not? It isn't just kids who feel abandoned when a wife and mother dies." She had approached instant parenthood with her customary exuberance. "I never thought of, or worried about, being a stepmother [to Simon's daughters]," she told an interviewer. "I knew I'd deal with it as best I could. It was right for all of us. I liked the girls immediately, and taking them through their adolescence has fulfilled me as a woman." Soon after their marriage the Simons moved to California.

Three years later Miss Mason returned to work in a shaky vehicle, an almost universally panned film directed by Robert Wise called *Audrey Rose* (United Artists, 1977), in which she was the mother of a reincarnated child. Critic Vincent Canby declared in the New York *Times* (April 7, 1977) that Miss Mason's talents had been wasted. Others echoed his opinion, and some reviewers were less kind, Joy Gould Boyum, for instance, protesting in the *Wall Street Journal* (April 18, 1977), "Marsha Mason plays Ivy's mother on the same hysterical grating note throughout."

The *Audrey Rose* debacle was quickly forgotten, however, with the appearance of *The Goodbye Girl* (Warner Brothers), one of the biggest hits of 1977. Belying his request that his wife shelve her career, Neil Simon had begun writing movies with roles for her. The first, "Bogart Slept Here," which was to star Robert De Niro as a philandering actor, never went into production. De Niro was replaced by Richard Dreyfuss, who is shorter and younger than Miss Mason, prompting Simon to rework the script completely. The result was *The Goodbye Girl*, the funny-sad story of Paula McFadden, an emotionally bruised, divorced former chorus dancer whose actor-lover deserts her and sublets their apartment to another actor, played by Dreyfuss, who arrives in the middle of the night ready to evict Paula and her ten-year-old daughter.

Although a few critics railed at the film's hate-turning-to-love predictability, *The Goodbye Girl* was one of Marsha Mason's most rewarding vehicles. Lavish in her praise, Judith Crist commented in the New York *Post* (December 1, 1977), "Mason, brilliant as the hooker in *Cinderella Liberty* but given little to do but gush tears as the housewife in *Audrey Rose*, paints a subtle portrait of a used woman conditioned to losing." Stanley Kauffmann, in the *New Republic* (December 17, 1977), admired the way Miss Mason and Dreyfuss worked together: "They have the energy and precision of circus sharpshooters, knocking off the points and the quick emotions like bottles thrown in the air, never missing, firing over their shoulders, wheeling and smacking. Nothing is real, nothing is phony." The stars received Golden Globe awards as best actor and actress in a comedy or musical category. Miss Mason won her second Oscar nomination and Dreyfuss, an Oscar itself.

Neil Simon included a role for his wife in his next screenplay, *The Cheap Detective* (Columbia, 1978), a star-studded parody of Humphrey Bogart films. Marsha Mason played the type of character that Gladys George made memorable in *The Maltese Falcon*. "One of those maniacal, desperate, supportive women who never get the guy," Miss Mason explained in regard to her takeoff. "I wear a blonde floozie wig, long eyelashes and look wonderfully cheap and trashy."

Assigned a contrasting role in *Promises in the Dark* (Orion Pictures/Warner Brothers, 1979), Marsha Mason portrayed a doctor trying to relieve the physical and emotional suffering of a seventeen-year-old terminal cancer victim, played by Kathleen Beller. To one reviewer the film seemed to be a "tearjerker" and to another a "medical soap opera," but John Skow defended it in *Time* (November 2, 1979): "*Promises* is clear, direct and honest, and free of both cant and sentimentality." Andrew Sarris, moreover, told his readers in the *Village Voice* (November 5, 1979), "Mason and Beller ignite their scenes together with an affecting grace under pressure. They have done their homework on the subject, and they never strike a false note." Miss Mason herself has said that she especially liked the role of Dr. Alexandra Kendall and welcomed the challenges offered by what she called her "least emotionally gregarious character."

In Neil Simon's semiautobiographical comedy, *Chapter Two*, a widowed writer marries a divorced actress soon after his first wife's death and then must deal with his resultant guilt and self-doubts. The play opened for a long run on Broadway on December 4, 1977 with Anita Gillette and Judd Hirsch as Jennie and George, characters for which Marsha Mason and Neil Simon, respectively, were in part prototypes. At that time Simon insisted it would be "bizarre" for Marsha to play herself unless he played the male protagonist. But when he adapted *Chapter Two* (Columbia, 1979) for the screen, Miss Mason was cast as Jennie opposite James Caan. She later acknowledged in an interview with Tom Buckley of the *New York Times* (December 31, 1979), "I always wanted to do the movie version of *Chapter Two*. I thought enough time would have gone by by then so that I could approach it as an acting role. . . . What I wanted to do was to illuminate in a way that people could understand what the Jennie role is really about. That is, about the importance and necessity of taking risks."

As on several earlier occasions when Marsha Mason received better notices than her film, critics were generally more enthusiastic about her acting than about the script of *Chapter Two*, which, like *Promises in the Dark*, had Robert Moore as its director. One fairly representative review, Janet Maslin's in the New York *Times* (December 14, 1979), summed up her performance: "Miss Mason, who has been acting more confidently and looking prettier with each successive movie, is this time every bit as sunny and intelligently appealing as Mr. Simon's screenplay means her to be; the material rests the weight of the movie upon her shoulders, and she carries it ably." The movie brought Miss Mason her third Oscar nomination. In *Only When I Laugh* (Columbia Pictures, 1981), Neil Simon's totally rewritten screen version of his 1970 play, *The Gingerbread Lady*, Marsha Mason gave a consummate delineation, some reviewers thought, of one of the most complex characters her husband ever created, Georgia Hines, a divorced actress struggling to overcome alcoholism, behave as a mother to her teenage daughter, and make a comeback on the stage.

Marsha Mason is five feet six inches tall and has a slim figure, dark hair, and hazel eyes. One of her distinctive features is an upturned nose. Leo Seligsohn of *Newsday* (February 5, 1974) wrote of her "warm and unassuming manner and an easy smile that looks as though it wants to—and often does—turn into a delighted laugh." She impressed Tom Buckley as "a deft and witty conversationalist." With Neil Simon and Nancy, she lives in a hilltop Bel Air estate. (Simon's other daughter, Ellen, is married to John Leland.) Besides spending several years in psychoanalysis attempting to come to grips with her feelings of insecurity, Miss Mason has turned to transcendental meditation. She speaks glowingly of her Indian guru, Swami Muktananda, whom she met in New York in 1975 and some years later visited in India. At her urging, meditation is practised in the Simon household. Interested also in various liberal social causes, she supports the Equal Rights Amendment, handgun control, the Gray Panthers, and a project launched by Aldous Huxley's widow that provides day-care centers staffed by older people.

References: Cue 49:21+ F 15 '80 pors; Family Weekly p4 Ja 13 '80 pors; N Y Daily News III p3+ N 20 '77 por; N Y Times p34 Ja 3 '78 por; Newsday A p3+ F 5 '74 pors; Parade p4+ Ja 13 '78 pors; Notable Names in the American Theatre (1976); Who's Who in America, 1980-81

Meese, Edwin, 3d

1931(?)- Counselor to the President. Address: b. The White House, 1600 Pennsylvania Ave., NW, Washington, D.C. 20500

Although his name is not a household word to the average American, knowledgeable observers of the White House call Edwin Meese 3d the man "in charge of the man who's in charge." Since 1967, when he became an aide to Ronald Reagan, then the Governor of California, Meese has earned Reagan's respect for

Edwin Meese 3d

as a "law-and-order man" who "preferred sketching military reserve organization charts to outlining contracts and torts." His legal studies were interrupted by two years of army service, during part of which he served as a lieutenant in military intelligence. In 1958 he obtained his LL.B. degree.

For the first eight years of his career, Meese worked as a deputy district attorney in his native Alameda County. Making his mark as an administrator rather than as a trial lawyer, he took part in the development of a drug-abuse testing program, acted as a liaison to the grand jury, and lobbied before the legislature in behalf of the state district attorneys' association. Greatly interested in police work, which he has described as a fascinating laboratory for the "study of how management decisions are made in nonroutine situations," Meese spent much of his free time riding with patrol officers. His most publicized action as a deputy district attorney was his supervision, in December 1964, of the arrests of over 700 participants in disturbances associated with the "Free Speech Movement" at the University of California at Berkeley. He also helped to put down anti-draft protests in Oakland and Berkeley in the mid-1960's by pinpointing the ringleaders and removing them from the scene.

The political connections and the reputation that Meese developed during his years in the district attorney's office brought him to the attention of Ronald Reagan. Shortly after the former actor won the California gubernatorial election in November 1966, he named Meese—who shared his view of capital punishment as an effective deterrent to crime—as his secretary on clemency and extradition. Meese was Reagan's representative on the scene when violence erupted in 1969 at San Francisco State College and at the University of California at Berkeley. At the former institution Meese took charge from the college's president, S. I. Hayakawa—who later became Republican United States Senator from California—and ordered the arrest of the leaders of the demonstrations. Meese's evaluation of the disturbances at Berkeley, where protesters were demanding that a tract of land be turned into a "people's park," led Reagan to declare a state of emergency there.

In Meese's view the campus uprisings of the 1960's constituted "the greatest threat to academic freedom." He blamed the troubles on a handful of agitators and has asserted that his concern was for "the individuals who wanted to study and who were interfered with by people who sought to impose their views on all of the people." Meese also has expressed the view that the disturbances impeded the American effort in Vietnam. He reported in August 1966 to the Un-American Activities Committee of the United States House of Representatives on the activities of antiwar students and testified in favor of a bill to make the aiding of Communist forces in Vietnam a crime. "Basically, those demonstrations pro-

his "sheer ability and brainpower" and has gained a general reputation as "the kind of guy who makes government work." As Counselor to the President he coordinates the business of the Cabinet, plays an important role in the formulation of both domestic and foreign policy, and acts as a key spokesman for the Administration. In the opinion of 1,439 leading citizens who responded to a poll by U.S. News & World Report (May 18, 1981), those responsibilities gave Meese an influence in national affairs second only to that of President Reagan himself.

Edwin Meese 3d was born about 1931 in Oakland, California, the oldest of the four sons of Edwin Meese Jr. and his wife, Leone. The family has been in California as long as the state has been in the Union and has a tradition of public service. Edwin Meese 3d's great-grandfather emigrated from Germany and settled in San Francisco during the Gold Rush; his grandfather served as Oakland's treasurer and as a member of its city council; and his father was for a quarter of a century the treasurer and tax collector for Alameda County. The Meese family is staunchly Lutheran, patriotic, and Republican. Within its fold Edwin enjoyed a normal, active childhood that included membership in the Boy Scouts and the publication, with his brothers, of a mimeographed weekly neighborhood newspaper. After graduating from Oakland High School, Meese went to Yale University on a scholarship. He obtained his B.A. degree in 1953, worked briefly in an iron foundry, and then entered the Boalt Law School of the University of California at Berkeley. According to a profile by Martin Schram in the Washington Post (March 15, 1981), Meese earned a reputation in law school

longed the war and cost a lot of American lives," he has said. "The demonstrations encouraged them [the North Vietnamese] to go on, and prevented our elected officials from taking the steps necessary to win the war."

During Reagan's second term in Sacramento, Meese served as his executive assistant and chief of staff and took over so many responsibilities, including the selection of judges, that he was, according to some commentators, in effect the state's "deputy governor." When Reagan left office, Meese temporarily withdrew from the public sector. After serving from January 1975 to May 1976 as vice-president for administration at Rohr Industries, an aerospace firm based in Chula Vista, California, he entered private law practice in La Mesa, California. In 1977, at the University of San Diego Law School, Meese founded and became the director of the Center for Criminal Justice Policy and Management, whose aim is to help bridge the gap between legal theory and practice. In 1978 Meese became a professor at the University of San Diego Law School, specializing in criminal justice.

After Ronald Reagan began his campaign for the 1980 Republican Presidential nomination he asked Meese to join his staff as an adviser on key political issues. Meese soon found himself in a power struggle with the candidate's campaign manager, John P. Sears 3d, who feared that Reagan's California aides were undermining his control and giving the candidate too conservative an image. Sears persuaded Reagan to dismiss Lyn Nofziger and Michael K. Deaver, but his complaint that Meese and his aides were not adequately briefing the candidate on the substance of the issues apparently backfired. Reagan was already upset by the unexpected loss he suffered in the Iowa caucuses in January 1980 after Sears had persuaded him to broaden his support by moderating his conservative image, and he reportedly became infuriated with his campaign manager. On February 26, 1980, the day he won a resounding victory in the New Hampshire primary after reemerging as a "tough, straight-talking conservative," he dismissed Sears along with three other aides and replaced him as campaign manager with William J. Casey. For the key post of chief of staff of the campaign Reagan turned to his "alter ego," Meese, whom he had often described as the one man on whom he would rely in a crisis. Meese called back Nofziger and Deaver and with them set the course for the remainder of the race, stressing incumbent President Jimmy Carter's "lack of leadership" as a major theme of the campaign.

After the Republicans swept to victory in November 1980, Meese became director of Reagan's transition team and played an important role in the selection of Cabinet officers and other top officials. The President-elect decided, however, not to name Meese chief of staff for the new Administration. Some of Reagan's other advisers had apparently come to believe that Meese, despite his flair for analysis of issues, lacked the necessary decisiveness and organizational skill for the post. "If a problem gets in Ed's briefcase," one critic quipped, "it never sees the light of day again." On election day Reagan informed Meese that James A. Baker 3d, who had worked in the primaries for George Bush, would become chief of staff at the White House. He then asked Meese, who has denied that he felt slighted by the decision, to take the new policy-making post of Counselor to the President. Meese accepted the offer, after receiving from the President-elect the promise of Cabinet rank, authority to coordinate Cabinet policy, and control over the staffs of the National Security Council and of the newly established Office of Policy Development, which concentrates on domestic issues. Reagan formally announced the appointment on November 14, 1980. Meese was already on leave of absence from the faculty of the University of San Diego Law School and his post at the Center for Criminal Justice Policy and Management.

In the early months of the Reagan Administration, Presidential Counselor Meese, chief of staff Baker, and deputy chief of staff Deaver became known around Washington as the "big three," or "troika." They were the only persons authorized to enter the Oval Office without an appointment and they controlled the President's access to others. Although their functions at times overlapped, each had his own area of responsibility. Meese handled policy issues, Baker dealt with the broad scope of White House operations, and Deaver was concerned with the personal needs and schedule of the President. The three, who considered each other as equals, met at least twice a day to share information and to collaborate on matters of overlapping concern. Explaining the high level of cooperation among them, E. Pendleton James, the chief White House personnel officer, has observed: "You have three people who are mature enough not to be awed by power or ambitious for more. Each one is sufficiently happy with his life and the area he's focusing on that he doesn't feel any animosity, jealousy or infringement. They complement each other."

Within the "big three," Meese is considered "the first among equals." He is the only one with Cabinet rank, and his major assets are his knowledge of Reagan's mind and the ease with which he deals with the President. Those attributes make Meese the ideal conduit between the Oval Office and the rest of the executive branch. Meese has denied, however, that he has become Reagan's second in command or that he has assumed the role of "surrogate president" or "prime minister," as some observers have described him. "You look at any large, successful corporation," he says, "and you'll find that the man at the top does delegate a great deal of responsibility. Ronald Reagan follows that pattern. Anything I do is only in line with what he has directed."

Meese's approach to his responsibilities is managerial rather than creative. At meetings of the Cabinet, the National Security Council, and the Office of Policy Development he seeks to promote broad discussion and avoids taking sides. After the various viewpoints have been aired, Meese exercises his special talent for synthesizing arguments and proposing alternatives to the participants and to the President. "With Reagan, he's the best I've ever seen," one former rival of Meese has admitted. "Ed presents the issue in concise, accurate form with a terribly fair and balanced view of the conflicting arguments and parties; then he presents the options, A, B, C, and then lays out the ramifications of the decisions without favoring either viewpoint. He's brilliant at it."

The first test of the influence exerted by Meese and his associates came within a few weeks of the inauguration. At Meese's suggestion, President Reagan tentatively approved in late February a plan for placing Vice-President George Bush in charge of the Administration's crisis management committee. Meese hoped that giving control to a person whose constitutional rank exceeded that of a Cabinet officer would enable Reagan to avoid a serious problem encountered by his predecessor. Under President Jimmy Carter, National Security Adviser Zbigniew Brzezinski had vied with Secretary of State Cyrus Vance for that authority. Meese's proposal, however, displeased Reagan's Secretary of State, Alexander M. Haig, whose own plan called for him to have the central role. Haig's public protests to the announcement of the new arrangement confirmed the "big three" in their suspicion that Haig intended to dominate the Administration. In a showdown, they won the President's reaffirmation of the plan, but at the same time they tried to placate Haig. After the Secretary of State proclaimed himself "in control" following the attempt on Reagan's life on March 30, 1981, Meese and Baker went on television to put the most favorable interpretation on Haig's apparent misunderstanding of the constitutional order of succession.

How effectively Meese, Baker, and Deaver established their control became evident in the hours and days after the assassination attempt. The three rushed to George Washington University Hospital immediately after the shooting. They quickly set up the White House "situation room" to track potential crises, informed the Cabinet and designated Haig as its "contact point," and called Vice-President Bush back from a visit to Texas. They also ascertained from the doctors that the President was not so seriously hurt as to require the Cabinet, under the Twenty-fifth Amendment, to transfer formally the reins of government to the Vice-President. The three maintained a command post in the hospital from which Baker handled the press and matters pertaining directly to the President, Deaver responded to the needs of the Reagan family, and Meese, in his own words, "helped to coordinate the en-tire operation, particularly in the area of continuity of government," and to "see to it that the various governmental functions were prepared for any contingency that might occur."

In his White House post, Meese lost the anonymity in which he formerly preferred to operate. He emerged as the leading spokesman on policy for the Administration, and his close ties with the President have given his words added weight. For the most part, Meese's pronouncements have been noncontroversial and reassuring. He predicted, for example, that Reagan's spending and tax cut proposals would substantially improve the economy; advocated the compensation of crime victims by the Justice Department; indicated that the door remained open for negotiations on nuclear arms limitation with the U.S.S.R., depending on Soviet conduct; and asserted that "all the merits are not on one side of the issue" regarding Israel's bombing raid, in June, on a nuclear reactor project in Iraq. After accompanying Reagan to the economic conference at Ottawa in July 1981, he expressed satisfaction that the meeting went smoothly despite divergent views among its participants. He has reaffirmed Reagan's opposition to a peacetime draft and has asserted that the President would not allow the Central Intelligence Agency to engage in domestic surveillance.

But some comments by Meese, especially on matters relating to "law and order," have provoked controversy. In a speech before the California Peace Officers Association in May 1981 Meese attacked the American Civil Liberties Union as part of a nationwide "criminals' lobby." He has also decried the use of the insanity defense, justified preventive detention, complained of the exclusion of illegally gathered evidence from trials, and defended President Reagan's pardon of two F.B.I. officials convicted of unauthorized breakins. Meese favors abolition of the federal Legal Services Corporation, contending that its function of providing legal services for the poor was better fulfilled by local bar associations.

Edwin Meese 3d married his high school sweetheart, Ursula Herrick, in about 1958 after what she has jokingly called "a whirlwind courtship of eleven years." Mrs. Meese, who formerly worked as a probation officer, describes her husband as "ambitious for projects, but never for himself," and says that he is perfectly in tune with the President's thinking, although he is probably more liberal than Reagan on some issues, such as abortion. The Meeses have three children: Scott, who remained in California when the family moved to Washington, in order to complete high school; Dana Lyn, who accompanied her parents to the nation's capital; and Michael, who graduated in the spring of 1981 from the United States Military Academy. Mrs. Meese, whose father was a West Pointer, was raised on army bases and is used to moving. But she misses the large house in La Mesa, California and is concerned about the financial loss the family suffered when Meese accepted his present $69,630-a-year post. The Meeses make their home in a four-bedroom Tudor-style house in a newly developed area of McLean, Virginia.

Ed Meese stands just under six feet tall and carries a little more than 190 pounds on his stocky frame. He has closely cut sandy hair, blue eyes, and a round, jowly face. Described as confident, easygoing, unflappable, and unpretentious, he is noted for his wry sense of humor and congenial manner. A conservative dresser, he favors blue blazers and gray flannel slacks. Meese is vice-president of the First Lutheran Church in El Cajon and occasionally returns to California for its meetings. Recently retired as a lieutenant colonel in the Army

Reserve, Meese maintains a strong affection for the military and for the police. One of his few hobbies in California was listening to police calls on a home radio set. He also collects small model squad cars and statuettes of pigs, the uncomplimentary animal symbol assigned to law officers by the angry radicals of the 1960's.

References: Christian Sci Mon p5 D 31 '80 por; N Y Times A p14 N 7 '80 por; N Y Times Mag p14+ Ap 18 '81 pors; New Repub 185:21+ O 7 '81; Newsday p4 Mr 1 '81 por; Newsweek 47:27+ Ap 20 '81 pors; People 14:65+ N 24 '80 pors; Washington Post A p1+ Mr 15 '81 pors; International Who's Who, 1981-82

Mengistu Haile Mariam

1937- Head of State of Ethiopia. Address: c/o Provisional Military Administrative Council, Addis Ababa, Ethiopia

When Ethiopian Emperor Haile Selassie fell from power in 1974 after a reign of more than four decades, the resulting power vacuum was filled by Mengistu Haile Mariam, a young, unknown army officer who is both a Marxist and a fierce nationalist. Ruthless, cunning, and a consummate politician, Mengistu assumed the formal titles of head of state and chairman of the Provisional Military Administrative Council in 1977 and has since remained in control by brutally purging his opponents. But despite natural disasters and a series of armed conflicts with domestic and foreign guerrillas, Mengistu has made a good start on reforming

Ethiopia's feudalistic economic system and bringing its people into the twentieth century.

Described in the New York Times (March 1, 1977) as "an obscure figure whose age and birthplace can only be guessed," Mengistu Haile Mariam was reportedly born in 1937 in the Wollamo area in southwestern Ethiopia, about 120 miles from the Sudan border. His family were Christians belonging to the Ethiopian Orthodox Church, and he is believed to be a half-caste, partly of the Galla people, Ethiopia's largest single ethnic group. Some sources indicate that he came from a southern minority tribe scorned by the ruling Amharas as "Shankalas" or "Barias"—terms denoting slaves—and he is said to have developed a marked antagonism toward the Amhara aristocracy. He obtained his early education through wealthy landowners in the Harar region by whom his family was employed.

After joining the army, Mengistu served on Emperor Haile Selassie's palace staff as a baggage handler and logistics coordinator. He obtained his officer training at Holeta Military College, which had a reputation for turning out officers of inferior status to those produced by the more elitist Harar Military Academy. Most of the young officers who later comprised the military junta that removed Emperor Haile Selassie from power were trained at Holeta. Mengistu was sent to Fort Leavenworth, Kansas for additional military training and was said to have been embittered by the racial discrimination that he encountered during his stay in the United States.

Stationed as an ordnance officer with the Ethiopian army's "Eastern Lion" Third Division near the Somalian border, Mengistu attained the rank of major, an unusual distinction for a young man from a poor family. At the time, most Ethiopian army officers were called from the nobility surrounding Haile Selassie, a fact not lost on the ambitious Mengistu, who, according to Henry S. Haywood of the Christian Science Monitor (December 23, 1974), "became disgruntled with the corruption and favoritism existing in the military system" and, marked as a radical leftist by older officers, became "a rallying point for other young dissidents in the armed forces."

The nearly bloodless "creeping coup" that resulted in the ouster of the imperial regime began in February 1974, when soldiers mutinied for higher pay and better conditions, then gradually broadened the popular base of their revolt. About 200 of Haile Selassie's closest advisers were arrested on charges of embezzlement, corruption, and maladministration. Mengistu reportedly served as chairman of the new regime's coordinating committee for the armed forces, police, and territorial army. In September, after the junta overthrew Emperor Haile Selassie himself, placing the aged "Lion of Judah" under house arrest, Mengistu became the first of the two vice-chairmen of the newly established Provisional Military Administrative Committee (PMAC). Popularly known as the "Dergue"—meaning "shadow" in Amharic—the PMAC was composed of 120 men ranking from private to major. It was not until November 1974 that the Ethiopian press, praising him as "a profoundly patriotic and courageous officer," identified Mengistu as the "true moving force" behind the coup. "We owe a great deal to Mengistu," one Ethiopian soldier told a foreign diplomat, as quoted in the New York Times (December 10, 1974). "He put it all together."

In the beginning, Ethiopians reveled in their new-found freedoms. The promise of democracy flickered only briefly, however, and infant liberties—freedom of speech, press, and assembly—were abruptly quashed as the revolutionaries moved to solidify their shaky power base. On November 24, 1974 sixty aristocrats and former government officials—considered by many to be the cream of the old nobility and officialdom—were quickly rounded up and executed. Mengistu himself reportedly played a key role in a fierce gun battle at that time that resulted in the death of Lieutenant General Aman Michael Andom, chairman of the Dergue and acting chief of state. A popular war hero, Aman had taken a conciliatory approach on such volatile issues as student dissent and the fate of the Ethiopian nobility. More important, he had advocated a negotiated settlement with Eritrean guerrillas, who had been mounting violent raids ever since predominantly Christian Ethiopia annexed the largely Moslem former Italian colony of Eritrea in 1952. Aman's death established the little known, vehemently nationalistic Mengistu as Ethiopia's strongman, even though the formal position of chairman of the Dergue and acting head of state was assumed by Brigadier General Tafari Banti. Adopting a policy of "Ethiopia first"—involving the elimination of selfishness and a dedication to hard work, discipline, and heroism—Mengistu suppressed student demonstrations and, at the same time, bolstered Ethiopian forces in Eritrea, adding fuel to what some political and military analysts considered an unwinnable conflict.

With his political opposition in disarray, Mengistu issued his first major policy statement on December 20, 1974. Identifying himself as a socialist, he pledged to turn Ethiopia into a one-party state with direct government control of the economy, the establishment of collective farms on government land, and the takeover of all indigenous and foreign business interests. The ambitious reform movement remained a secondary concern, however, while Mengistu's nascent regime struggled for survival. A correspondent for Time (January 13, 1975) observed that the Dergue "is at least as unpopular as the Emperor was." Students and labor leaders who had been closely allied to the military in the ouster of Haile Selassie came into open conflict with the Dergue. High schools, universities, and labor union headquarters were shut down, and almost anyone viewed as a threat to the new government's authority was arrested. An opposition party, the Ethiopian Democratic Union, founded in early 1975, dedicated itself to the overthrow of the "tyrannical and terroristic" Dergue and called for a settlement of the fratricidal war in Eritrea.

Mengistu remained adamant in his refusal to negotiate with the Eritrean secessionists, claiming that any concessions might portend the dissolution of the Ethiopian empire. In February 1975, with the conflict threatening to erupt into a full-scale war, Mengistu reportedly journeyed to the Eritrean city of Asmara to take personal command of military operations. Later that month, addressing more than 5,000 army veterans at a rally, Mengistu declared that Ethiopia had more than 6,000,000 volunteer militiamen prepared to sacrifice themselves to prevent the "dismantling of Ethiopia." Meanwhile, the government's drive for a new socialist order intensified. In January 1975 banks, insurance companies, and many other private concerns were nationalized. In March the monarchy was formally abolished, and with it vanished the system of feudal landownership. All rural land was declared to be the collective property of the people, individual landholdings were limited to twenty-five acres, and teams of students were sent to rural areas to explain the new order to the peasants.

Although Mengistu was reported in December 1975 to have been stripped of power, he reemerged in April 1976, when he delivered a nationwide address coinciding with a government announcement of a political program that called for the eventual establishment of a "people's democratic republic" based on "scientific socialism." But on September 22, 1976, Mengistu was caught in a hail of submachine-gun fire, escaping with a slight leg injury. He retaliated by cracking down on the Ethiopian People's Revolutionary party, a group of dissident Marxist students, teachers, and trade unionists dedicated to the return of civilian rule. Soon, assassinations and executions in the streets of Addis Ababa became commonplace, spurring members of the Dergue to take steps to limit Mengistu's powers. On January 7, 1977 Brigadier General Tafari Banti, the Dergue's figurehead chairman, was given expanded powers, while Mengistu was named to the lesser post of council of ministers. The new order lasted for less than a month. On February 3, 1977 Tafari and several of his supporters were shot to death, reportedly on orders of Mengistu. Eight days later, Mengistu was named head of state by the surviving members of the Dergue. "The amazing part is that Mengistu got all of his enemies together in one room," one political analyst observed. "There are reports that suggest that they came together because they thought they were going to get rid of him." In addition to becoming head of state and chairman of the Dergue, which formalized his already dominant role in the government, Mengistu, now a lieutenant colonel, became chairman of the Dergue's three governing committees, as well as chairman of the civilian council of ministers and of the defense and security council, and commander of the armed forces.

Determined to root out all challengers, Mengistu launched what has been described as a "red terror" campaign of arrests, brutal interrogations, and executions that, according to a correspondent for *Time* (May 9, 1977), "rivaled Ugandan Field Marshal Idi Amin's considerable efforts in this area." Bodies of political prisoners who had been tortured to death were displayed in public places and on the state-run television network.

Now no longer a shadowy figure, Mengistu appeared in public with increasing frequency, sometimes leading crowds in shouting, "Down with Yankee imperialism." In a speech in Addis Ababa's Revolution Square in April 1977, he raised his hand in a clenched fist salute, then smashed to the ground six bottles filled with bloodlike dye to show how he would crush all enemies of his rule. After the Administration of President Jimmy Carter, citing human rights violations, withdrew $6,000,000 in military assistance earmarked for Ethiopia in February 1977, Mengistu expelled all American advisers, communications experts, and information officials, asserting that the United States—the principal supplier of military equipment and aid to Ethiopia under the imperial regime—had helped Emperor Haile Selassie in his efforts to "suppress the liberation struggle of the oppressed masses."

Despite continuing turmoil, there were some signs, by early 1977, that reforms begun by the revolutionaries in 1975 were yielding results. Land reforms, which relieved peasants of the burden of paying a large proportion of their income to feudal landlords, had resulted in increased agricultural production. Nationalized businesses appeared to be prospering. Urban dwellers' associations, known as *kebeles*, organized by Mengistu to provide paramilitary training, administer housing, and settle local disputes, allowed for some participation by the public in local government.

During a visit by the Ethiopian chief of state to the Soviet Union in May 1977, several pacts were signed, including a treaty of friendship and cooperation and a protocol providing for economic aid, to supplement the Soviet Union's agreement, in December 1976, to provide Ethiopia with $100,000,000 worth of vitally needed armaments. Meanwhile, as the Mengistu regime was steadily losing ground in its struggle with the secessionist Eritrean Liberation Front, it became embroiled in another conflict. By the summer of 1977 Ethiopia was at war with Somalia, its neighbor to the south and east, which was supporting a separatist movement in Ethiopia's Ogaden region. Somali guerrillas soon overran vast areas of Ogaden, easily routing poorly prepared and dispirited Ethiopian troops, and by September the Somalis had gained control of the strategically located Ogaden city of Jijiga.

Besieged on two fronts while trying to quell internal unrest, Mengistu stepped up his attacks on the United States, accusing the American government of giving political and military support to Somalia. Concerned that Mengistu would carry out his threats to sever diplomatic relations with the United States, Great Britain, and West Germany, President Carter dispatched a high-level delegation to Addis Ababa in mid-February 1978. A huge influx of Soviet materials and Cuban soldiers had in the meantime turned the tide of the Ethiopian-Somali war, and the American delegation sought—and received—Mengistu's assurance that Ethiopians would not pursue retreating Somali troops across their frontiers.

The armed conflict with Somalia subsided in March 1978 when, following Ethiopia's recapture of Jijiga, Somalia agreed to withdraw its forces from Ogaden. The settlement came after weeks of quiet diplomacy initiated by the United States to bring an end to the fighting and improve Soviet-American relations, which had deteriorated partly as a result of massive Soviet military aid to Ethiopia.

In anticipation of a renewed drive against Eritrean rebels, Mengistu moved to cement his alliances with the Soviet Union and Cuba and visited both countries in April 1978. The long-expected counteroffensive was launched in mid-May, when some 20,000 Ethiopian troops broke through rebel lines and surrounded Asmara, the capital of Eritrea. In November 1978 Ethiopian forces overran Keren, the principal garrison of the Eritrean People's Liberation Front. A decisive victory over the rebels remained elusive, however, and guerrilla activity continued unabated. One Ethiopian government defector explained, as quoted in the New York *Times* (December 1, 1978): "The Ethiopians will never defeat the Eritreans. They seem to have chased them from large pockets and into the countryside, but the Eritrean cause is backed by the entire population. It is a genuine popular movement."

Despite continued Eritrean and Somali guerrilla activity, Mengistu was able, by the beginning of 1979, to focus on domestic concerns and adopt measures to alleviate the effects of a nationwide drought as well as critical food shortages in Ethiopia's densely populated Wallo province. The nightly carnage in the streets of Addis Ababa had ended, and a more secure Mengistu now reportedly dealt with political rivals by moving them out of the capital and into governorships in the provinces. The Dergue, which once numbered 120 men, had by early 1979 shrunk to one-third that size, and by mid-1980 the council had, for all practical purposes, been dissolved, leaving Mengistu unchallenged as Ethiopia's leader. Ethiopia has been virtually the only Marxist state without an official Communist party, but in 1980 Mengistu created a Commission for Organizing the Party of the Working People of Ethiopia (COPWE) and ordered it to begin the process of establishing a "vanguard" political organization.

Ethiopia under Mengistu remains one of the poorest countries in the world, with an annual per capita income of only about $105. Nearly half of its children die before attaining adulthood, and two-thirds of the population lives more than a day's walk from the closest road. According to 1980 reports from human rights organizations, arbitrary arrests, torture, and summary executions continue in Ethiopia, and the flow of refugees from the country is unabated. Nevertheless, the Mengistu regime succeeded in reducing the country's illiteracy rate from 93 to about 80 percent between 1977 and 1980. United Nations and Red Cross officials acknowledge that peasants are better nourished, and correspondent Robin Wright observed in *Maclean's* (September 1980): "The average Ethiopian is probably better off under the Marxism of Mengistu than with the totalitarianism of Selassie."

A short, stocky man, five feet four inches tall, with a "sharklike grin," Lieutenant Colonel Mengistu Haile Mariam is the object of a personality cult that combines his Marxist ideology with the trappings of monarchy. His portrait hangs in public buildings, and thousands flock to hear him speak. He reviews his troops from a throne that once belonged to Haile Selassie, and he drives a scarlet Ford convertible. Among the distinctions he has received is Cuba's highest honor, the Plaza Girón medal. Aside from the fact that he is married and has children, little is known about his personal life. Mengistu's associates claim that the chairman dreams of extending his influence throughout the continent, hoping to become, in effect, the Fidel Castro of Africa.

References: Christian Sci Mon p4 D 23 '74; Los Angeles Times B p1 My 16 '79 por; Macleans 93:37+ S 29 '80 por; N Y Times p1+ Mr 1 '77 por, A p2 Jl 3 '80 por; N Y Times Mag p16+ Ja 8 '78; New Repub 180:16+ F 24 '79; Newsweek 98:46+ Jl 6 '81 por; Time 109:45+ My 23 '77; Africa Contemporary Record, 1974-75; International Who's Who, 1980-81

c. 1980 Thomas Victor

Merrill, James

Mar. 3, 1926- Poet. Address: h. 107 Water St., Stonington, Conn. 06378

Since the 1940's, the poet James Merrill has enchanted and enriched his readers with his fondness for puns, hyperbole, and word games and fascinated them with his metrical and structural ingenuity. His finely crafted poetry is noted for its ornate diction, labyrinthine syntax, and eccentric punctuation. But beyond such stylistic flourishes, Merrill's readers can find in his work a deep and abiding interest in love, the evocation of memory, and a concern with the relationships between reality and appearance and between life and art. As William Meredith observed in a review in the New York Times (May 3, 1959), "It is clear that from behind a mask of wit and urbanity speaks a serious philosopher, perhaps even a moralist. The verbal elegance, and the Jamesian or Proustian world he draws his people and images from, are neither frivolous nor precious. They parallel and support grave statements about human experience." Although he is identified with the New York school of poetry, Merrill has generally remained aloof from movements and from New York literary life. But the esteem in which he is held by the literary establishment is attested to by the fact that he was the recipient of the 1977 Pulitzer Prize, two National Book Awards, the Bollingen Prize in Poetry, and a variety of other honors.

James Ingram Merrill, who was born in New York City on March 3, 1926, belongs to the generation of poets that includes John Ashbery, Philip Levine, Adrienne Rich, and Galway Kinnell. His father, Charles Edward Merrill, who had two children from an earlier marriage, was a founder and senior partner of the Wall Street brokerage firm now known as Merrill, Lynch, Pierce, Fenner, and Smith. His mother, the former Hellen Ingram, who like his father had come from the South, published a small newspaper of her own. Merrill, whose boyhood home was a Greenwich Village town house, grew up among Manhattan's illustrious and elite.

But although Merrill attended the finest schools and spent winters in Florida and summers on Long Island, there is ample evidence in his poems to suggest that his childhood was not without pain and disappointment. In "The Broken Home," Merrill's persona remembers with bitterness a father too busy to care: "Too late now, I make out in his blue gaze/(Through the smoked glass of being thirty-six)/The soul eclipsed by twin black pupils, sex/And business; time was money in those days." The poem, which is in his 1966 volume *Nights and Days,* is one of many that recall Merrill's youthful dreams, hopes, and fears. As David Kalstone points out in *Five Temperaments* (Oxford Univ. Press, 1977), "a continuing access to childhood memories and insights nourishes Merrill's verse."

When Merrill was eleven and living with his mother in New York City after his parents' divorce, he discovered opera "and the sense of a feeling that could be expressed without any particular attention to words." This love of music was to serve as an occasional stimulus for composition and is evident in the carefully orchestrated rhythms present in all his poems. "Whenever I reach an impasse, working on a poem," Merrill told an interviewer for *Contemporary Literature* in 1968, "I try to imagine an analogy with musical form; it usually helps."

In the same interview, Merrill revealed: "I cared about music long before I cared about literature." In fact, he admitted to Eve Ottenberg in the *Village Voice* (February 25, 1980), he was at the time "perfectly ignorant of any contemporary literature," although this ignorance did not discourage him from writing poetry. "At fifteen," he recalled, "I knew, or thought I did, how verse was supposed to sound, and wrote reams of it. Both form and content were virtually automatic: sonnets and quatrains and dramatic monologues on the one hand; love, time, beauty, death, etc. on the other—as an adolescent I knew *all* about those." His friend, the future novelist Frederick Buechner, whom Merrill met in 1940 at the Lawrenceville School in New Jersey, remembered that "there was much competition between us as writers" and maintained that this competition influenced "the way that we came to write" and the reasons why "we kept on writing." While still in school, Merrill privately published a volume entitled *Jim's Book: A Collection of Poems and Short Stories* (1942).

After graduating from Lawrenceville, Merrill enrolled at Amherst College, where his career,

although interrupted in 1944-45 by a year as an infantry private in the United States Army, was successful and promising. He was elected to Phi Beta Kappa, had poems published by *Poetry* and the *Kenyon Review,* acted the title role in Cocteau's *Orphée,* and wrote a thesis on metaphor in the works of Marcel Proust, whose influence, as David Kalstone has observed, is tangible "everywhere in . . . [Merrill's] poems about the continuing presence of childhood memories." His volume of verse *The Black Swan* was published by Icarus in Athens in 1946. Merrill graduated from Amherst *summa cum laude* with a B.A. degree in 1947. Some years later, he taught at Amherst—because "it was the thing to do . . . for a poet in America"—but after a year he quit to devote himself full time to writing.

The 1950's were a period of self-discovery for Merrill. After Amherst, he returned to New York but felt, as he told Eve Ottenberg, that "there was just too much going on there, too much art, too much life," and that he "couldn't write or live hemmed in by all that." He reacted to his feelings of unrest by traveling to "many of the most looked-at places in Europe and the Orient" and by moving, in 1954, to the house in Stonington, Connecticut that he shares with David Jackson. The move later served as the occasion for the poems collected in Merrill's 1963 volume *Water Street* and "is inseparable," according to David Kalstone, "from the desire to stabilize memory, to draw poetry closer to autobiography, to explore his life, writing out of 'the dull need to make some kind of house/Out of the life lived, out of the love spent.' " After acquiring a similar house in Athens, Greece in the mid-1960's, Merrill and Jackson divided their time between the two residences.

In the 1950's, Merrill, whose early verse earned him such honors as the Oscar Blumenthal Prize in 1947, *Poetry* magazine's Levinson Prize in 1949, and the Harriet Monroe Memorial Prize in 1951, went through a period of artistic growth and experimentation. His volume *First Poems* (Knopf, 1951) received mixed reviews. Anthony Harrigan, writing in *Poetry* (July 1951), praised the book because it "allows the reader to enter into the most elegant existence in the republic . . . through the medium of the highest type of American sensibility," but in her review for the *New Yorker* (June 9, 1951), Louise Bogan, while finding the poems "impeccably written," insisted that they were "frigid and dry as diagrams." The central weakness in the book, Richard Howard asserted in *Alone with America* (Atheneum, 1980), was that Merrill "indulges the finite, or anyway the finished. Hence a good number of emblem poems . . . in which everything is given from the start, nothing allowed to happen or become."

Perhaps Merrill himself was aware of this weakness when he diverted his attention from poetry to prose and wrote two plays and a novel. Produced in collaboration with the

Artists' Theatre, Merrill's plays received some favorable notice. The first, *The Bait,* a one-act play presented Off-Broadway in 1953, is about a brother and sister seeking to avoid all emotional involvement with other people. The second play, *The Immortal Husband,* presented at the Theatre de Lys in Greenwich Village in February 1955, retold the ancient Greek myth of Tithonus and the goddess of dawn. Garrison P. Sherwood wrote in *Best Plays of 1954-1955* that there was "much to recommend this play," but he "found it pretty confusing." Although Merrill derived some satisfaction from his work for the stage, he found the theatre too much of a collaborative experience to suit him.

Merrill's novel *The Seraglio* (Knopf, 1957), about an aging semi-invalid American businessman surrounded by a bevy of admiring but predatory women, was described by a reviewer for the San Francisco *Chronicle* (May 5, 1957) as "a beautifully orchestrated comedy of manners." Although they admired its evocative imagery, its "light and bright" style, and its wry humor, other critics thought that the characters were shallow and that the story lacked substance. Merrill vowed some years later that he would never write another play or novel, yet he does not deny learning from his experiences outside the realm of poetry how, among other things, to speak in voices other than his own.

The hiatus in Merrill's writing of books of poetry ended with the publication of *The Country of a Thousand Years of Peace* (Knopf, 1959), including nine of the ten poems contained in his semi-privately published *Short Stories* (1954). According to a number of critics —May Swenson, Anthony Hecht, and Louis L. Martz among them—*The Country of a Thousand Years of Peace* is Merrill's first important volume. "It is in this metropolitan book," Richard Howard wrote, "that Merrill is able, to a degree because of . . . technical innovations . . . and to a degree because of a larger confidence in his own powers as a *persona* in the poem, the latter the fruit of travel . . . , to shift from history and myth, through dream, to an unmediated confrontation with his own life, his own voice." Reviewing the book in the San Francisco *Chronicle* (May 10, 1959), a critic called Merrill a "fiercely fine and frightening talent," while P. H. Davidson, writing in the *Atlantic* (July 1959), described the poems as "brilliant, neurotic, subtly made, and extremely intelligent."

In *Water Street* (Atheneum, 1963) Merrill had, as X. J. Kennedy wrote in the New York *Times Book Review* (November 25, 1962), "a deeper compassion, a kind of humility," and "a capacity for bitter amusement at his own expense," thus becoming "one of the American poets most worth reading." Peter Davison, who reviewed the book for the *Atlantic* (December 1963), found Merrill to be an "intensely visual poet" whose "visual sensations come from trick mirrors, colored glass, moving pictures, all the artifices of optics."

Merrill's novel *The (Diblos) Notebook* (Atheneum, 1965), which deals with a Greek-American's return to his ancestral homeland in search of his roots and contains "a novel within a novel," was described by Wilfrid Sheed in the New York *Times Book Review* (March 21, 1965) as the kind of book "it is a pleasure to take seriously, a disciplined, adventurous performance in the best tradition of fictional development." His publications of the early and mid-1960's also include the volume *Selected Poems* (Chatto, 1961) and the individually published poems *The Thousand and Second Night* (1963) and *Violent Pastoral* (1965). His poem "From the Cupola," which earned him the Morton Dauwen Zabel Memorial Prize in 1965, is included, with "The Summer People," in *Two Poems* (Chatto, 1972).

In his next volume of verse, *Nights and Days* (Atheneum, 1966), described by Gene Baro in the New York *Times Book Review* (June 26, 1966) as a "bridge between lyrical and philosophical poetry," Merrill continued his effort to attain his aesthetic ideal—"to render, transform, purify personal experience and make it relevant to others." That effort is exemplified in his humorous and sensitive description of the Greek maid who takes care of the house in Athens: "Her legs hurt. She wore brown, was fat, past fifty,/And looked like a Palmyra matron/Copied in lard and horsehair. How she loved/You, me, loved us all, the bird, the cat!/I think now she *was* love. She sighed and glistened/All day with it, or pain, or both." Howard Nemerov, who once sarcastically dismissed Merrill's *First Poems,* served with W. H. Auden and James Dickey on a panel that unanimously selected *Nights and Days* to receive the 1967 National Book Award. In 1968 Amherst College awarded Merrill an honorary Litt. D. degree.

Although designated by Richard Howard as a "transitional volume," Merrill's *The Fire Screen* (Atheneum, 1969) was described by a reviewer for *Harper's* as "an extraordinarily beautiful book in its total organization, as well as in its individual poems." Following his election in 1971 to the National Institute of Arts and Letters, Merrill published *Braving the Elements* (Atheneum, 1972), which in the view of some critics reaffirmed his status as one of America's foremost poets. In the New York *Times Book Review* (September 24, 1972), Helen Vendler wrote enthusiastically: "Merrill has found a use, finally, for all his many talents. His surreptitious fondness for narrative . . . has now found a clear medium in his wonderful short narrative lyrics; his almost unnaturally exquisite gift for euphony has become unobtrusive but no less exquisite . . . ; his single best subject—love—has found a way of expressing itself masked and unmasked at once." Merrill was awarded the 1973 Bollingen Prize in Poetry for his "wit and delight in language, his exceptional craft, his ability to enter into personalities other than his own, and his sustained vitality."

To questions about where Merrill would go from *Braving the Elements* his response was a trilogy of complex and cosmic poems composed on an epic scale with the guidance of a Ouija board. The first part, "The Book of Ephraim," comprises two thirds of the volume *Divine Comedies* (Atheneum, 1976), for which Merrill won a Pulitzer Prize in April 1977. A reviewer for *Library Journal* (March 1, 1976) commented on its "sumptuous, allusive, and exquisitely wrought" style, "in the manner of Auden, Yeats, and Marianne Moore," and noted that "Turkish, Greek, and Oriental motifs run through the book like a bright filigree." In the second part of the trilogy, *Mirabell: Book of Number* (Atheneum, 1978), which earned him his second National Book Award, Merrill explores the theme of human evolution and, in the words of R. B. Shaw, who reviewed the work for the *New York Times Book Review* (April 29, 1979), vacillates "between two thematic levels—the cosmic and the personal." The third and final portion, *Scripts for the Pageant* (Atheneum, 1980), was, in the view of Charles Molesworth of the *New Republic* (July 26, 1980), "the clearest and best of the three parts of this cosmological probe" and begged comparison with the work of "Yeats and Blake, if not Milton and Dante."

Throughout the three books, Merrill and David Jackson ponder the perplexities of existence and exchange tidbits of celestial gossip with departed friends, such as W. H. Auden, as well as with prophets, angels, the nine muses, and a host of deities of varying ranks and dispositions. As Charles Molesworth observed, Merrill "has written a poem that includes everything, everything he feels and has felt, but also everything he's dreamed and feared. He has made his world, . . . a way out of himself, but also the grandest act of self-assertion."

James Merrill has "made his world," but his world, he believes, has also made him. "I can't imagine my own life without poetry," he admits. "It created me." Once described by Richard Howard as "the most decorative and glamor-clogged poet that America has ever produced," Merrill is, according to Eve Ottenberg, "cagey, sophisticated, reticent, masked, someone who delights in doing the unexpected . . . , wary of contemporary literature and eager to ally himself with the past." He appears at poetry readings "in a suit, dark purple shirt and rust tie, the diamond flashing from his ring, a large leatherbound tome in hand . . . [looking] 'like a magician.'" Financially independent as heir to the Merrill Lynch fortune, he is not motivated in his creative work by the prospect of economic success. In addition to their homes in Connecticut and Greece, he and David Jackson also own a house in Key West, Florida. Once a believer in "art for art's sake," Merrill now adheres to the credo "art for life's sake." His artistic objective is "to try to match the intensity of experience life has given me with an intensity and complexity of language."

References: N Y Times p30 Ja 8 '73 por, C p28 Ap 22 '77 por; Village Voice p31+ F 25 '80 por; Contemporary Authors 1st rev ed vols 13-16 (1975); Contemporary Poets (1975); Who's Who in America, 1980-81; World Authors, 1950-1970 (1975)

Michals, Duane (Steven)

Feb. 18, 1932- Photographer. Address: b. c/o Sidney Janis Gallery, 110 W. 57th St., New York City, N.Y. 10019; h. 109 E. 19th St., New York City, N.Y. 10003

Duane Michals believes that photography is a medium whose mission is the expression of ideas rather than the exhibition of technique. Spurred by his own introspection to investigate the emotional and spiritual dimensions of human existence, Michals creates photographs about the relationships between man and woman and man and the Infinite, about the deceptiveness of surface reality, and about the mystery of death. His overwhelming desire to suggest what he calls the "interior landscape" rather than to record the "social landscape" that preoccupies most photographers has compelled Michals to use such stylistic innovations as the photographic sequence, the captioned photo, and the painted photo. They serve as means to achieve his artistic goal, which is "to photograph what is essentially unphotographable."

Duane Steven Michals was born on February 18, 1932 in McKeesport, Pennsylvania to John Ambrose Michals, a steelworker, and Margaret Cecilia (Matik) Michals, a housemaid. Shortly before his birth his father, of Czechoslovakian ancestry, had anglicized the family's surname from Mihal to Michals. His first name, Duane, was that of the scion of the wealthy family for whom his mother worked. During his childhood Duane Michals was intrigued by the original Duane but never got to know him because the older boy committed suicide during his freshman year of college. With his younger brother, Timothy, Duane Michals grew up in McKeesport, where he was reared first by his grandmother for five years, while his mother lived with her employers, and then by his parents. He held part-time jobs and devoted the rest of his spare time after school to drawing and painting. At the age of fourteen he won a scholarship that enabled him to attend Saturday watercolor classes at Pittsburgh's Carnegie Institute.

With the aid of another art scholarship and the funds earned from part-time jobs, Michals attended the University of Denver, graduating with a B.A. degree in 1953. "For me going to college wasn't so much a matter of getting an education as it was learning to stand on my own two feet," he explained in Ronald H. Bailey's book *The Photographic Illusion: Duane Michals* (1975). "If I'd stayed home, I would've become an emotional basket case." During his college years Michals stopped doing his art work but remained fascinated by modern painters, especially the surrealists Magritte, Balthus, and de Chirico, who would eventually influence his photography.

In 1956, following a three-year stint in the United States Army, Michals moved to New York City, where he spent a year taking courses at Parsons School of Design and then found a job as assistant art director of *Dance* magazine. In 1958, after moving to Time Incorporated to do graphic design for their promotional department, Michals decided to travel to Russia for three weeks. Before his departure he borrowed an old Argus C3 camera, which he used to photograph Russian schoolchildren and sailors. The subjects of Michals' first portraits seem to have stopped momentarily in the midst of their daily lives to confront the eager American, and their spirit seems to shine through their earnest, earthy faces. Ostensibly casual, the pictures nevertheless reveal a craftsman's sensitivity to delicate lighting and balanced composition. Upon his return to New York, Michals went to work for a small design studio that folded six months later. Instead of looking for another job involving graphic art, he chose to turn his recently-discovered avocation into a career.

After mastering the basic techniques of making photographs with the help of the commercial photographer Daniel Entin, Michals set to work with an assignment to take publicity portraits for the *The Fantasticks*, the musical that was then opening off Broadway. Within a few months he found himself employed by such magazines as *Show, Mademoiselle,* and *Esquire.* Later the list came to include *Vogue,* the New York *Times,* and *Horizon.* From the world of advertising he attracted such clients as Revlon, Elizabeth Arden, Eli Lilly Company, and the magazine *Scientific American.*

Michals' most widely acclaimed commercial work is his portraiture, which focuses especially on figures from the worlds of the visual and dramatic arts. Limiting his portrait sittings to half an hour, he prefers to hold them in his subjects' favorite or characteristic environments. If necessary, for example, he uses the hotel habitations of traveling celebrities as effectively enigmatic backdrops. Concerning the purpose of his portraits, Michals told Carol Stevens of *Print* magazine (September 1975), "I think it's important not to deal with appearances but with what people are. It's what people represent in your life that means something, not what they look like today or yesterday."

Michals' professional portrait work indirectly inspired the first phase of his private photography. While waiting in restaurants and hotel lobbies for his subjects to keep their appointments, he became interested in the character of empty rooms. From 1964 to 1966 he took pictures of the empty interiors of places normally filled with a constant flow of people—photographs of barber shops, laundromats, diners, subways, and theatres. He taught himself to shoot through the plate glass windows of buildings locked in their Sunday morning solitude. With their stark, symmetrical compositions, the photographs demonstrate a deliberate ordering of the chaotic transience of life into the serene stasis of art. Those empty environments, Michals discovered, bear the indelible mark of absent humanity. "Places are just extensions of people," he has said. "They leave a residue."

Michals' environmental photographs indirectly inspired the second phase of his private photography. Those empty rooms began to look like stage sets to him, and in 1966 he decided to people them with actors from his own imagination. Hence he developed the sequence, a series of six staged photos that, like a haiku, creates a moment or an atmosphere. Because they represented a new departure in photography, the sequences left art critics bemused after they appeared in exhibitions in 1968 at the Underground Gallery of New York City, which had shown Michals' work in 1963 and 1965, and at the Art Institute of Chicago.

Reviewers insisted that the sequences imitated the work of various predecessors or contemporaries, although Michals never draws his inspiration from other photographers, and judged the sequences according to standards appropriate for "decisive moment" photography, although Michals considers his work to be of an entirely different order. His photographs, as he wrote in *Camera* magazine (July 1969), "are based on very specific ideas and feelings and are premeditated illustrations of these feelings. They are based on past remembrances and new intuitive awarenesses. There are no accidents. They are the drama of the interior world, which may ultimately be more real than the exterior world. I illustrate myself."

The art world's eventual acceptance of Michals' sequences on his terms was demonstrated by the Museum of Modern Art's decision to mount "Stories," a one-man exhibition of his work, in 1970. That same year Doubleday published pieces from the show as a witty and profound book entitled *Sequences*, which includes such works as *Paradise Regained* (1968), in which a man and woman gradually lose their clothing and material possessions while plants spring up around them, until they return to the innocence of total nudity amid a primeval jungle; and *The Young Girl's Dream* (1969), in which a naked girl dreams of a naked man who touches her breast and awakens her from innocence. In one poignant sequence in the show, *Death Comes to the Old Lady,* Death takes the form of a businessman.

In 1971 Michals completed an ambitious sequence, inspired by the Tibetan Book of the Dead, of twenty-six photos dealing with resurrection and reincarnation. *The Journey of the Spirit After Death* appeared as a book published by Winter House and as an exhibition offered at George Eastman House of Rochester, New York. With the aid of blurs, double exposures, and negative sandwiches, Michals creates eerie photos that suggest the intangible presence of a disembodied spirit wandering among the people and places from which he has been recently separated. Because he lacks the purity to become one with the Infinite, the ghost reenters the tangible world as an infant. Thus the sequence ends with a new beginning.

In the early 1970's Michals showed his sequences in exhibitions at the School of Visual Arts in New York City, the San Francisco Art Institute, and the Museum of New Mexico (1972); at the Galerie Delpire in Paris, the Centre Culturel International of Anvers, and the Kölnischer Kunstverein of Cologne (1973); and the Frankfurter Kunstverein in Frankfurt, the Galleria 291 in Milan, and the Documenta of Turin (1974). He published them in volumes entitled *Things Are Queer* and *Chance Meeting* (A. & J. Wilde, 1973). In 1974 he began a third phase of his private work when he added a new visual and narrative element to his sequences by scrawling on the white borders of the photos captions in spiky black script. Michals first presented the captioned sequences to the public at New York City's Light Gallery in 1974, once again disconcerting art critics, who worried about the "literary implications" of his innovation. Michals' rebuttal, as quoted by Julia Scully of *Modern Photography* (March 1976), is that with his captioned pictures he intends "to create a new expression that has nothing to do with photography or writing necessarily."

Gradually Michals experimented with longer sequences of twelve and fifteen captioned photographs, such as *The Pleasures of the Glove* (1974) and *The Enormous Mistake* (1976), whose surrealistic story lines suggest garment fetishism and autoeroticism. At the same time he worked with the single image, into which, with the aid of a lengthy caption, he condensed the emotional impact of an entire sequence. One of the most powerful of those pictures is *A Letter From My Father* (1975). The photo, taken in 1960, shows Michals' brother and parents. The moody profile of the defiant adolescent dominates the foreground, and the stolid figure of the disapproving father, with his wife obscured in the shadows at his side, fills the background. The image evokes a sense of enduring alienation that intensifies the poignancy of the accompanying text, which explains that the father promised to send Duane a "special letter" whose contents were never divulged. Michals explains in the caption: "I know what I hoped would be in the letter. I wanted him to tell me where he had hidden his affections. But then he died, and the letter never did arrive. And I never found that place where he had hidden his love."

Michals' work received wide exposure in 1976, when exhibitions appeared at Cincinnati's Contemporary Arts Center, Kansas City's Douglas Drake Gallery, Dallas' Texas Center for Photographic Studies, New York City's Light Gallery, Paris' Galerie Jacques Bosser, and Vienna's Galerie Die Brücke. Moreover, Sidney Janis presented, at his Manhattan gallery, a major retrospective that Douglas Davis of *Newsweek* (October 18, 1976) proclaimed "a watershed event, both for Michals and the medium in which he works." Critical attention focused on Michals' most radical piece, which consists of a caption written in where the photographic image should be. Entitled *A Failed Attempt to Photograph Reality* (1976), the picture proclaims, "How foolish of me to have believed that it would be that easy. I had confused the appearances of trees and automobiles and people with reality itself and believed a photograph of these appearances to be a photograph of it. It is a melancholy truth that I will never be able to photograph it and can only fail. I am a reflection photographing other reflections within a reflection. To photograph reality is to photograph nothing." Nevertheless, Michals insists that photography is a legitimate tool with which to investigate the truths lurking beneath reality's surface; "I believe in the imagination," he declared in his handwritten introduction to *Real Dreams* (Addison House, 1976), his manifesto of artistic freedom. "What I cannot see is infinitely more important than what I can see." *Real Dreams* incorporates a wide-ranging selection of pictures drawn from a decade of private work.

In 1976 Light Impressions Incorporated distributed another book of Michals' entitled *Take One and See Mt. Fujiyama*. The small volume, with one photograph reproduced on each page, offers an ideal format for the presentation of four erotic sequences with captions. With considerable irony, the cover proclaims it "A Stefan Mihal Book," for Michal's fictitious alter ego would violently disapprove of the contents. Stefan Mihal, whose name is a Slovak version of Duane Steven Michals, is, according to Michals' imagination, a hairy working-class hulk with a wife, three children, and a row house in McKeesport. "He is the man I never became," Michals says of Stefan in the introduction to *Real Dreams*. "We are complete opposites, although we were born at the same moment. If we should meet, we would explode. We are like matter and antimatter. He is my shadow. I saved myself from him." Stefan serves as the subject of several of Duane's photographs.

In the late 1970's Michals continued to exhibit his photographs at galleries throughout the United States and Europe. His work appeared at the Galerie Breiting in Berlin and the Galerie Paul Maenz in Cologne (1977); and at the Camera Obscura in Stockholm, the 24 Collection in Miami, the Douglas Drake Gallery in Kansas City, and the Focus Gallery in San Francisco (1978). In 1978 and 1980 Sidney Janis Gallery presented major shows of Michals' new photographs.

Exhibition material came, in part, from the two books published for Michals in 1978. Addison House unveiled *Homage to Cavafy*, a series of ten photographs about the passing of time and the hunger of love that complements a series of ten poems by Constantine Cavafy. In his brief preface, Michals offers his book as a tribute to the Greek poet's exemplary courage in revealing his homosexual passions through his art. The French publishers Filipachi-Denoël released *Merveilles d'Égypte*, a book of photographs that Michals took during a trip for which they paid. Most of those pictures are single images of ancient temples and monuments, although some are candid street shots of Cairo and some are components of staged sequences. In his soft, glowing studies of the forms and textures of the remnants of antique Egypt, Michals seeks to define his own relationship to its timeless past.

Recent exhibition material also included examples of the latest phase of Michals' private work, which consists of oil painting atop photographic images. Michals has created a magical, mysterious mode of self-expression in his combination of bright, soft pigments and black and white prints. Some of the pieces resemble classic twentieth-century collage, with painted areas and untouched areas functioning as separate pictorial elements, while others offer shadowy photographic images nearly obscured by clouds of paint. Two principal concerns of the new works are portraiture and the history of painting, which intertwine in *Andy Warhol as a Demoiselle d'Avignon* (1980), in which Warhol's photographed face is wedged between two painted images quoted from Picasso's seminal work.

All Michals' photos, commercial and private, early and recent, reveal an enduring fascination with light. He loves the natural light of dawn and dusk and the indirect light that filters in through windows and rebounds off mirrors. Michals works with bright light, too, when he wants to suggest spiritual transcendence. In his sequence *The Human Condition* (1970), for example, a young man changes into a sphere of pure light, which in turn becomes a galaxy in a starry sky. He draws his notion of the human quest for illumination through union with the Infinite from his study of Eastern religions, which he has pursued since rejecting the Catholicism of his childhood.

Michals, a trim bachelor, lives and works in New York City. In his spare time he reads, cooks, gardens, and cultivates his sense of humor. He wrote in *Real Dreams*, "It is essential for me to be silly. If one is serious, one must also be foolish, to survive." Several major museums prefer to think of Michals as serious. His photographs can be found in the permanent collections of institutions throughout the United States and Europe, including the Metropolitan Museum and the Museum of Modern Art in New York City, the Art Institute of Chicago, the Boston Museum of Fine Arts, the Museum of the Rhode Island School of Design, the Nelson Gallery-Atkins Museum in Kansas City, the Folkwang Museum in Essen, and the Bibliothèque Nationale in Paris.

References: Bailey, Ronald H. The Photographic Illusion: Duane Michals (1975); Who's Who in America, 1980-81

Michel, Robert H(enry) (mī'kəl)

Mar. 2, 1923- United States Representative from Illinois. Address: b. Rm. 2112, Rayburn House Office Building, Washington, D.C. 20515

Elected Minority Leader of the House of Representatives in December 1980, Republican Representative Robert H. Michel of Illinois is in a position to play a pivotal role in the enactment of President Ronald Reagan's legislative program. Although the Democrats control the House, a potential alliance of Republicans and conservative Democrats could form a working majority. In his twenty-five years in the House, Michel has invariably taken the orthodox conservative side, but because he is a recognized master of legislative bargaining and compromise, most political analysts think that he is the man best able to put together such a coalition. The ranking minority member of the Appropriations Committee's Labor, Health, Education, and Welfare subcommittee from 1969 through 1980, Michel, who was a staunch advocate of cuts in social programs, often negotiated with Committee Democrats to

Robert H. Michel

obtain compromise reductions. "He isn't primarily a partisan," Missouri Congressman Richard Bolling, a Democrat, said in a recent interview. "He's primarily a legislator with a partisan point of view."

Robert Henry Michel was born in Peoria, Illinois on March 2, 1923, the son of Charles Michel, a French immigrant factory worker, and Anna (Baer) Michel. Following his graduation from the Peoria public school system, he enlisted in the United States Army, in 1942, and served as a combat infantryman in England, France, Belgium, and Germany. Severely wounded by machine-gun fire, he was given a disability discharge in 1946. During his four years in the service he earned two Bronze Stars, the Purple Heart, and four battle stars. Returning to civilian life, Michel attended Bradley University in Peoria, graduating in 1948 with a B.S. degree in business administration.

The following year Michel began his political career as an administrative assistant to Harold H. Velde, who represented Illinois' Eighteenth Congressional District in the United States House of Representatives. A rabid anti-Communist, Velde was chairman of the powerful House Committee on Un-American Activities during the witch-hunting days of the early 1950's. When Congressman Velde announced, in January 1956, that he would not seek reelection, Michel entered the Republican primary for his House seat. He edged out the candidate of the local party establishment to win the Republican nomination, then went on to defeat the Democratic nominee in the November general election by taking 58.8 percent of the vote. Since that time, he has been regularly returned to office by substantial majorities. The closest contest of his political

career to date was in the nationwide Democratic landslide in 1964, when he won reelection with 54 percent of the ballots cast.

During his first few years in office, the new Congressman took a decidedly conservative stand on both domestic and foreign affairs issues. For example, he submitted, in 1957, amendments to cut funding for the Food and Drug Administration, the Office of Education, and the federal employee unemployment compensation program while, at the same time, he sought to increase defense expenditures. According to the *Congressional Quarterly Almanac*, from 1959 through 1961 Michel voted with the conservative coalition of Southern Democrats and Republicans 100 percent of the time. Later in the 1960's he was a staunch supporter of United States military involvement in the escalating war in Southeast Asia, but he disagreed with most of President Lyndon B. Johnson's Great Society programs, voting against Medicare, antipoverty funding, federal aid to depressed areas in Appalachia, and the model cities program, among other things.

Representative Michel assumed an active role in the Republican party, too. In 1957 he was elected president of the Eighty-fifth Club, the organization formed by the twenty-two Republican freshmen members of the Eighty-fifth Congress. Five years later, he headed a group of fifteen House Republicans who, as the so-called "Paul Revere Panels," toured the Eastern seaboard giving talks in behalf of the party. In 1964 he campaigned tirelessly for Barry M. Goldwater, the conservative Senator from Arizona, in his Presidential primary races against New York Governor Nelson A. Rockefeller, and later that same year, he and Senator Carl T. Curtis of Nebraska cochaired the Republican party's "Truth Squad," which traveled the country throughout the campaign to rebut the Democrats. On the House floor, he took on additional party responsibilities when he became, in 1966, an assistant minority whip for the Midwest.

The ranking Republican on the Departments of Labor and Health, Education, and Welfare and Related Agencies subcommittee of the House Appropriations Committee since 1969, Michel frequently led his conservative colleagues in their repeated attempts to halt the expansion of increasingly expensive social programs. In committee and on the Democrat-controlled House floor, he often relied on his considerable skill as a negotiator to work out compromise budget cuts. For example, to break a deadlock in February 1970, he induced the other members of the Appropriations panel to adopt, by the narrow vote of 24 to 20, an amendment to the 1969-70 education bill giving President Richard Nixon permission to withhold the appropriated funds if he deemed it necessary. He achieved the compromise despite the opposition of the Committee's chairman, Democratic Representative George H. Mahon of Texas. On another occasion, he persuaded his fellow committee members to revise the fiscal 1971 Labor-HEW appropriations bill, which President Nixon had vetoed because of its expense, then narrowly lost, 189 to 205, a bid on the floor for further cuts.

Recognizing Michel's abilities as a peacemaker, President Nixon asked the legislator to head the White House Congressional liaison office in 1972. Michel was tempted, but after Melvin Laird, the Secretary of Defense and a former House colleague, warned him that Nixon Administration officials had to be yesmen, Michel turned down the job and so avoided complicity in the Watergate crisis, a potentially disastrous blow to his career. Michel was forced to deal with the ripple effect of that political scandal when he was named chairman of the National Republican Congressional Campaign Committee in March 1973. Serving in that post through the 1974 national elections, Michel tried to increase the size of the Republican House contingent by doling out money and technical assistance and by providing an effective theme to the party's Congressional candidates across the country. The growing impact of Watergate, however, undermined his efforts. "I just have to agonize over the fate of those who are counting on me and our committee to do the things that would normally be expected to get them reelected," Michel told Christopher Lydon in an interview for the New York Times (May 12, 1974). "It's a unique year for us. If this thing goes on and on . . . , we're looking at the prospect of this whole thing being uppermost in people's minds when they trek to the polls. It might all resolve itself down to no other issue but just: How did you vote on impeachment?"

House Republicans generally held Watergate, rather than Michel's chairmanship, responsible for the severe losses suffered by their party in the 1974 elections and, in December 1974, elected the Congressman to succeed Representative Leslie C. Arends of Illinois as minority whip, the second-ranking House Republican leadership post. In the final tally for that party election, he received 75 votes to 38 for Jerry L. Pettis of California and 22 for Illinois Congressman John N. Berlenborn. With the assistance of four regional whips and twelve assistant regional whips, Michel kept track of his fellow Republicans, took head counts on major bills, and tried to persuade potential defectors to support the party's position. "We try to build a feeling that the tough votes have to be spread around," he informed Richard L. Lyons of the Washington Post (July 2, 1975). "If I have to, I go to a member and say 'Look, we've had six tough votes and you haven't been with us once. You want to be part of the team or not?'" He and Minority Leader John J. Rhodes of Arizona decided, as Michel put it, which members "shouldn't be put through the wringer" and which should be pressured because they had been "playing games." When the Republicans controlled the

White House, Michel, as a last resort, occasionally asked the President to call a wavering Representative. Paying tribute to his colleague's leadership abilities, Republican Representative Barber B. Conable of New York told Charles Mohr in an interview for a New York Times (December 10, 1980) profile that Michel had "remained popular even in the essentially unsympathetic role of the party whip in which he has tried to keep in line people who don't want to be in line."

As the senior Republican member of the Labor-HEW appropriations subcommittee, Michel continued to lead House criticism of costly social programs. Realizing that his Congressional colleagues had received thousands of letters and telephone calls from concerned constituents who opposed President Gerald R. Ford's proposed cuts in programs for crippled children, alcoholics, victims of multiple sclerosis, and other disabled citizens, he acknowledged that "it [was] difficult in the face of these appeals to stand up here today to ask for cuts," but he argued that "budgets are getting bigger and bigger" and that "all of us need an adjustment in our thinking about the programs." In Michel's opinion, the liberal social welfare programs of the 1960's were largely responsible for the runaway inflation of the 1970's. "We keep pulling more and more Americans under the welfare umbrella and every time we do, we sap that much more energy from the economy, just that much more responsibility from individual citizens," he said on the House floor in defense of President Ford's 1975 veto of a $2.7 billion expansion of the federal school lunch and child nutrition programs. He was the only Congressman to approve the President's action.

During the mid- and late 1970's, however, Michel scored some significant successes in his attempts to cut federal social programs. In 1975, for example, he and Senator James L. Buckley, the conservative Republican from New York, proposed a measure to eliminate from the food stamp program, which Michel decried as a "middle-class rip-off," up to 50 percent of the nearly 19,000,000 recipients. Their bill limited eligibility to those below the poverty line and barred students and strikers from participating in the plan. Just a few months later, the Ford Administration submitted to Congress a revised food stamp program that was strikingly similar to the Michel-Buckley bill and led to significant cuts in the eligibility rolls. In June 1978 the House passed, by a vote of 290 to 87, a Michel amendment to the fiscal 1979 Labor-HEW appropriations bill that required the Department of Health, Education, and Welfare to reduce spending by $1 billion by eliminating waste, fraud, and abuse. The following year he successfully offered a similar amendment that slashed the Department's budget an additional $500,000,000.

After House Minority Leader Rhodes announced, in December 1979, that he would not seek reelection to that post, Michel and Michigan Representative Guy Vander Jagt vied to succeed him as the Republicans' floor leader. Both men had solidly conservative voting records, but there was a sharp contrast in their political styles. A congenial man on good terms with party moderates, Michel was a parliamentary technician and a skillful practitioner of the art of compromise who preferred quiet, diligent work to fiery partisan rhetoric. Vander Jagt, the chairman of the National Republican Congressional Campaign Committee, was more aggressively partisan and more inclined to stress the differences between Republicans and Democrats.

With the Republicans in control of the White House and the Senate after the 1980 election, the House became the chief obstacle to the enactment of President Ronald Reagan's programs, but because a surprising thirty-three-seat Republican gain had cut the Democrats' majority to fifty-one, a Republican-conservative Democrat coalition could conceivably control the House. Many House Republicans thought that Michel's conciliatory approach was more likely to achieve that end than Vander Jagt's partisan rhetoric. In a secret ballot on December 8, 1980, Republican Representatives chose Michel over Vander Jagt by a vote of 103 to 87. Writing in the *Congressional Quarterly Weekly Report* (December 20, 1980), one professional political analyst observed, "In choosing Michel, Republicans evidently decided that the unglamorous arts of parliamentary tactics and personal rapport were their best hope of fashioning themselves a functional majority in the last bastion of nominal Democratic control."

In his victory speech, Michel told his Republican colleagues, "We've got to be affirmative, forward-looking. The bottom line is enacting the Reagan program." A fiscal conservative, Michel himself had long called for the kinds of cuts in social programs that President Reagan favored. For instance, he vigorously opposed the creation of new entitlement programs, and he supported the controversial proposal to modify automatic cost-of-living increases in social security benefits. He also backed Reagan's plans for substantial cuts in personal income taxes and for a hike in the defense budget, but he realized that Republican officeholders would be in serious political trouble if the Administration's supply-side economic policies failed. At a breakfast meeting of House Republicans on December 15, 1980, he advised conservative freshmen who had emphasized moral issues during their campaigns to delay deliberation of the so-called "Moral Majority agenda" until Reagan's economic program was adopted.

During the first few months of 1981 Michel devoted himself to securing Congressional passage of the Reagan economic package. To assure approval from moderate Republicans and to attract the support of a sufficient number of conservative Democrats, he joined other Congressional leaders in urging the President to retain the basic "safety net" programs that sustained the poor. The Administration followed that advice in drawing up its proposed budget cuts. Although he occasionally used the legislative achievements of the Republican-controlled Senate as a lever in the House, the Minority Leader was also prepared to compromise on details to achieve his primary goal. "There will be plenty of time for confrontation," he said, as quoted in the New York *Times* (March 16, 1981). "But the bottom line is moving the Reagan program. We've always got to keep our eye fixed on that goal."

Described by one interviewer as "normally a man of great good humor, with the all-American manner of his hometown of Peoria," Robert H. Michel is five feet eleven inches tall and weighs about 220 pounds. He has little time for recreation, but over the years, he has earned a reputation among his colleagues as the best softball pitcher in Congress. On December 26, 1948 Michel married the former Corinne Woodruff, whom he had met at Bradley University. They have four grown children —Scott, Bruce, Laurie, and Robin. Michel is a member of the American Legion, Cosmopolitan International, Rotary International, the Orpheus Club, and several other social and philanthropic organizations. In 1961 he received the distinguished alumnus award from his alma mater.

References: N Y Times B p8 D 10 '80 por, p8 S 26 '81 por; Almanac of American Politics, 1980; Congressional Directory, 1979; Who's Who in America, 1980-81; Who's Who in American Politics, 1979-80

Mifune, Toshiro (mi-foo′na to-shir′o)

Apr. 1, 1920- Japanese actor; producer.
Address: b. Mifune Productions Co. Ltd., 9-30-7 Seijyo, Setagayaku, Tokyo, Japan

Best known for his portrayals of legendary sword-wielding warriors in countless samurai epics—the Oriental equivalent of Hollywood westerns—Toshiro Mifune is the first Japanese actor to win international recognition since the late Sessue Hayakawa rose to prominence in American silent films. The most memorable of Mifune's more than 100 films are made with the master director Akira Kurosawa, among them such classics as *Seven Samurai, Throne of Blood, The Bad Sleep Well, Yojimbo,* and the haunting *Rashomon.* Widely praised by motion picture critics for his naturalistic acting, Mifune dominates the screen with his flamboyant heroics in period films and with his exquisitely restrained performances in contemporary works. With his acting career in high gear, he turned to motion picture production in 1963, with the establishment of his own com-

Toshiro Mifune

pany, Mifune Productions. Since then, he has appeared in several international films, including *Grand Prix* and *Midway,* and he has starred in the Japanese television series *A Samurai in the Wilds* and in the American television miniseries *Shōgun.*

Toshiro Mifune was born in Japanese-occupied Tsingtao, China on April 1, 1920, the son of Tokuzo and Sen Mifune. Mifune's father, whose family included a number of doctors, was probably a physician, although some sources say he was a photographer. Raised in the Methodist faith, the boy attended schools in China and graduated from Port Arthur High School. When war broke out between China and Japan in the 1930's, the family returned to their native land, and Toshiro Mifune joined the Japanese army. During his seven-year hitch, from 1939 through 1945, he studied aerial photography at an air force training center in Manchuria and, later, served ceremonial libations of sake to departing kamikaze pilots.

After the end of World War II, Mifune found work at the Toho Film Company, Japan's largest and most successful motion picture studio. In an attempt to boost falling box-office receipts, Toho had launched a nation-wide "new faces" contest. Mifune, who had been applying for a position as a cameraman, was mistaken for one of the 4,000-plus "new faces" entrants. "As I recall those days, I don't think that I really wanted to be an actor . . . ," he told Kiyo S. Mourakami in an interview for the *Christian Science Monitor* (December 17, 1971). "I was sort of forced to take 'new face' tests. . . . It happened beyond my control—because my personal history was somehow slipped into a pile of those of the

young men who had applied for the tests to become actors."

Impressed by Mifune's undeniable talent, Kajiro Yamamoto, a veteran Toho director, helped him land a small role in *These Foolish Times* (1946), directed by Senkichi Taniguchi. The following year, he was given the lead in the gangster film *Snow Trail* (1947), possibly because location shooting in the mountains made the role too risky for any of Toho's established stars. During that period, he also studied acting for about a year at Toho's drama school. After seeing *Snow Trail,* Akira Kurosawa, who was then one of Toho's most promising directors, asked Mifune to play a leading role in his next film, *Drunken Angel* (1948), thus initiating a fruitful collaboration that was to last nearly twenty years, for although Mifune made scores of motion pictures with other directors, Kurosawa, from 1948 until the late 1960's, made only one—*To Live!* (1952) —without Mifune.

In order to accommodate Mifune's remarkable vitality, Kurosawa substantially altered his original concept for the neorealistic *Drunken Angel.* "[Mifune's] reactions are extraordinarily swift," he explained, as quoted by David Shipman in his *The Great Movie Stars: The International Years* (1972). "If I say one thing, he understands ten. He reacts very quickly to the director's intentions. Most Japanese actors are the opposite of this and so I wanted Mifune to cultivate this gift." In *Drunken Angel,* Mifune played Matsunaga, a sullen young hoodlum with tuberculosis, whose life an alcoholic slum doctor tries valiantly to save. The film won Japan's highest motion picture award, the "Best One" prize, in the year of its release and established Mifune as a top box-office draw.

In the next two years, Mifune starred in nine films: Taniguchi's *Jakoman and Tetsu* (1949); Yamamoto's *Escape From Prison* (1949); *Engagement Ring* (1950); *Conduct Report on Professor Ishinaka* (1950); *Pirates* (1950), which was directed by Hiroshi Inagaki, whom many film historians consider to be second only to Akira Kurosawa among Mifune's regular directors; and Kurosawa's *The Quiet Duel* (1949), *Stray Dog* (1949), *Scandal* (1949), and *Rashomon* (1950). By far the biggest triumph was *Rashomon,* a penetrating study of human personality and the nature of truth. Set in feudal Japan, the story recounts the murder of a nobleman and the rape of his wife from the widely differing viewpoints of four witnesses: the wife, the ghost of the nobleman, the bandit who committed the rape, and a woodcutter who happened to see the incident. In his review of the film for the *New York Times* (December 27, 1951), Bosley Crowther wrote that the "aptly provocative" acting of the four principals contributed to the film's "hypnotic power." He singled out for special praise Mifune's compelling portrayal of the bandit for its "terrifying wildness and hot brutality." *Rashomon* won the Grand Prize at the Venice International Film Festival in 1951 and, later that same year, an honorary Academy Award for best foreign language film.

Kurosawa and Mifune collaborated again on *The Idiot* (1951), a contemporary retelling of Feodor Dostoievsky's classic novel, in which Mifune took the part of the Rogozhin character. Japanese and foreign critics alike pounced on Mifune and the other actors for their exaggerated histrionics and on the film itself for its gothic excesses. Over the next few years, Mifune made more than a dozen films, the most notable being *Sword For Hire* (1952), a samurai adventure film; *The Life of Oharu* (1952), which was based on a seventeenth-century Japanese novel; *Eagle of the Pacific* (1953), a World War II epic; and *The Last Embrace* (1953), in which he played a dual role.

Kurosawa's *Seven Samurai* (1954), a visually stunning tragedy about a group of itinerant mercenaries hired to defend a farming village against bandits in sixteenth-century Japan, elicited from enthusiastic American reviewers almost as many superlatives as *Rashomon*, especially for Mifune's broadly humorous portrayal of a boasting, swaggering peasant posing as a warrior. *Seven Samurai*, which was itself heavily influenced by John Ford's westerns, was to have a far-reaching impact on world cinema, serving as the model for many films, including the American-made western *The Magnificent Seven* (1960) and countless "spaghetti" westerns. Reprising his role as a swashbuckling samurai for Hiroshi Inagaki, Mifune starred in that director's acclaimed samurai trilogy: *Samurai* (1955), *Duel at Ichijoji Temple* (1955), and *Musashi and Kojiro* (1956). The first film in the series won a special Oscar as the best foreign film of the year in 1955.

As at home in modern dress as he is in period costume, Mifune played a cantankerous wealthy businessman who, fearing a nuclear holocaust, wants to relocate his family in South America in *I Live in Fear* (1955). Although the film was generally dismissed as one of Kurosawa's weakest, Mifune's sensitive interpretation won widespread approval from the critics. "Through Mifune's perceptive portrait," Judith Crist wrote in the New York *World Journal Tribune* (January 26, 1967), "we see a strong man crumble before our eyes, we see the transition from fear to terror, the concern extend beyond household and family to all of humanity." Like many of Mifune's Japanese pictures, *I Live in Fear* was not released in the United States for many years, its first showing coming in New York City in 1967. Other contemporary films from that period include *The Underworld*, a detective thriller, *Downtown*, in which he took the part of a truck driver who falls in love with a widow, and *Holiday in Tokyo*.

For his *Throne of Blood* (1957), Kurosawa transplanted Shakespeare's *Macbeth* to medieval Japan and infused that tragedy with elements of traditional Noh dance-drama. Adapting easily to the unusual theatrical requirements of the role, Mifune played his Macbeth as "a sweat-simple soldier, as physical as his horse," according to a reviewer for *Time* magazine (December 1, 1961), who was perhaps most impressed by Mifune's prodigious energy. The London *Times* critic, as quoted by David Shipman, agreed that the actor brought to the part "a combination of physical strength and irresolution that is in the best *Macbeth* tradition," but he argued that Mifune's "greatest asset" was "an expressiveness in face and eyes that mirrors every mood of the film."

Turning once again to a European classic for his inspiration and to Mifune for his star, Kurosawa directed, in 1957, *The Lower Depths,* a picaresque adaptation of Maxim Gorki's tragedy about slum life. While most reviewers complained about the film's somber tone and "monotonous" dialogue, they generally approved Mifune's powerful interpretation of a petty thief charged with murder. In the last installment of Kurosawa's period film trilogy, *The Hidden Fortress* (1958), a comic medieval adventure that reminded some knowledgeable viewers of French *chansons de geste*, Mifune played the part of the knight-errant—in that instance, a defeated warlord—with gusto. According to Melvin Maddocks of the *Christian Science Monitor* (February 6, 1963), Kurosawa demanded from his actors "near-monastic dedication," but despite the personal sacrifices involved, Mifune held the director in high regard. "I have never as an actor done anything that I am proud of other than with him," Mifune told one interviewer.

Mifune displayed his exceptional versatility in a wide variety of roles in the late 1950's and early 1960's. Among his many film credits during those years are *Secret Scrolls* (1957), Inagaki's version of the legend about a samurai with magic powers, and its sequel, *Ninjutsu* (1958); the sentimental *The Rickshaw Man* (1958); *The Big Boss* (1959); *Samurai Saga* (1959), a droll retelling of *Cyrano de Bergerac;* *Saga of the Vagabonds* (1959); Kurosawa's *The Bad Sleep Well* (1959), in which he played the vengeful bastard son of a murdered businessman; *The Three Treasures* (1959); *The Last Gunfight* (1960); *Man Against Man* (1960); and *I Bombed Pearl Harbor* (1960), an account of the life of Admiral Isoroku Yamamoto.

Mifune also appeared in *Animas Trujano* (1961), a Mexican production in which he took the part of a poor Zapotec Indian; *The Loyal 47 Ronin* (1962), a Kabuki play about eighteenth-century court life; *High and Low* (1963), Kurosawa's taut thriller about a prosperous industrialist victimized by a kidnapper; and in a handful of undistinguished samurai films. He earned critical approval as an amoral samurai warrior in *Yojimbo* (1961), a bloody satire of American westerns, and its lighter sequel, *Sanjuro* (1962). In both films, Mifune was, in the words of Frank Morris of the *Toronto Globe and Mail* (November 22, 1970), "a kind of rough-hewn Douglas Fairbanks Sr., vaulting his way through scenes of derring-do with fierce and vindictive thoroughness." For his performance in Yojimbo, he won the award for best actor at the 1961 Venice Film Festival.

With the Japanese film industry in decline, Mifune decided, in 1963, to set up his own Tokyo-based production company, Mifune Productions. The company's first film, shot on location in the Philippines, was The Legacy of the 500,000 (1963), an adventure about the search for a cache of gold hidden during World War II. In addition to acting the leading role, Mifune produced and directed the motion picture. A box-office flop, it is his only directorial effort to date. "It was just too difficult," he explained to Howard Thompson in an interview for the New York Times (April 11, 1965), "and a case of directing because the ones I wanted weren't available." He was more successful with Samurai Pirate, a routine swashbuckler which was purchased by American International Pictures, who substituted an English soundtrack and released it as The Lost World of Sinbad in 1964.

The following year Mifune appeared in only one film, The Whirlwind, primarily because he was hard at work on Kurosawa's long and ambitious Red Beard (1965), which was two years in the making. The film—his last for Kurosawa —concerned the attempts of a senior physician (Mifune) and his young assistant to fight poverty, disease, and ignorance in nineteenth-century Tokyo. In his review for the Guardian (September 8, 1965) Ian Wright gave Mifune the credit for "holding the film together." "Not only has this actor a great cinematic presence," he wrote, "but his Doctor Niide . . . is the believable embodiment of that strength and virtue beloved of Kurosawa." At the twenty-sixth annual Venice Film Festival in 1965, Mifune received the Volpi Cup as best actor of the year for his restrained and moving performance. After the completion of Red Beard, Mifune and Kurosawa parted company. The specific nature of the disagreement between the two men has never been revealed.

Mifune's first English-language film was Grand Prix (MGM, 1966), John Frankenheimer's clichéd motor-racing drama in which the actors took a back seat to the dizzyingly photographed racing sequences. Mifune, who does not speak English, learned the lines for his part as a shrewd and aggressive businessman phonetically, with the aid of a voice coach and a tape recorder. His next feature in English was Hell In the Pacific (Cinerama, 1968), John Boorman's tale about the wearing series of confrontations between a Japanese soldier (Mifune) and his American counterpart (Lee Marvin) marooned on an isolated Pacific island during World War II. The two enemies stalk and alternately capture and torture one another, eventually achieving a private peace.

Over the next few years Mifune Productions turned out a number of motion pictures, many of them starring Mifune himself. Among the above-average samurai adventures in which he appeared were Red Lion (1969); Samurai Banners (1969), an absorbing drama about the uni-fication of Japan in the sixteenth century told from the viewpoint of a crippled warrior; Band of Assassins (1969), an especially violent film that is, in the eyes of some film critics, the best film Mifune ever made without Kurosawa; and Rebellion (1967), in which he leads an ill-fated revolt against a tyrannical overlord. Mifune also portrayed the Japanese minister of war in The Emperor and the General (1967), the title character in Admiral Yamamoto (1968), and a construction engineer in Tunnel to the Sun (1963), which he coproduced with the actor Yujiro Ishiwara.

Mifune continued to appear in international productions as well, among them the large-scale World War II battle drama Midway (Universal, 1976), in which he again took the part of Admiral Yamamoto; the French-produced Red Sun (1971), a rather contrived western involving a pair of outlaws, a Japanese diplomat, and his samurai bodyguard that also starred Charles Bronson and Alain Delon; and Paper Tiger (Maclean and Co., 1975), a plodding British comedy about an aging English tutor (David Niven) to the son of a Japanese ambassador (Mifune) stationed in Kuala Lumpur, Malaysia. In addition, he played the minor role of a faithful family retainer in the thriller Winter Kills (Avco Embassy, 1979) and Commander Mitamura in 1941 (Universal, 1979), Steven Spielberg's comic treatment of the invasion hysteria that gripped California after the Japanese attack on Pearl Harbor.

Because motion picture exhibitors in the United States, except in the art houses of large cities, generally shied away from Japanese films, most Americans made their first acquaintance with Mifune in September 1980, when he starred in the blockbuster television miniseries Shōgun. Based on James Clavell's bestseller of the same title, Shōgun told the story of the conflict between John Blackthorne (Richard Chamberlain), a supercilious British sea captain shipwrecked in feudal Japan, and the wily Lord Toranaga (Mifune), the most powerful of the several warlords vying for the title of shōgun, the supreme military ruler of the country.

Although it was an enormous ratings hit for NBC, Shōgun did not fare as well with television reviewers. Most critics conceded that the series was extravagantly produced and beautifully photographed, but a substantial number of them carped at its "excessive, unwarranted length," its "inscrutabilities of exposition," and its occasionally baffling sections of untranslated Japanese dialogue. Virtually all of them, however, applauded Mifune, whom they found both "imposing" and "grand" as Toranaga. As Tom Shales observed in his review of the production for the Washington Post (September 14, 1980), "[Mifune] is the absolute soul of dignity and a magnetic figure on the screen."

Tall for a Japanese of his generation, Toshiro Mifune is five feet nine inches in height and weighs about 160 pounds. He has black hair, dark eyes, and what one interviewer described as a "forbiddingly handsome face" with fine features. His hobbies include flying, horseback riding, fishing, hunting, and yachting. A reticent, rather introspective man, he lives quietly on the outskirts of Tokyo, Japan with his wife, the former Takeshi Shiro, whom he married in 1950. The couple has two grown sons.

References: Christian Sci Mon p15 D 17 '71 pors; N Y Times II p7 Ap 11 '65 por; Show 3:80 My '63 pors; International Who's Who, 1979-80; Shipman, David. The Great Movie Stars: The International Years (1972); Thomson, David. A Biographical Dictionary of Film (1976); Who's Who in the World, 1978-79

c. 1980 Thomas Victor

Miłosz, Czesław (mē'wôsh ches'wäf)

June 30, 1911- Writer. Address: Department of Slavic Languages and Literatures, 5416 Dwinelle Hall, University of California, Berkeley, Calif. 94720; h. 978 Grizzly Peak Blvd., Berkeley, Calif. 94708

When, as a Nobel laureate, Czesław Miłosz delivered his lecture in Stockholm in 1980, he told his audience that contemporary poetry, including his own, "was not prepared to cope with those catastrophes" of the twentieth century that "by their death-bearing range surpassed all natural disasters known to us." Probably more than any other aspect of his work, however, it was his articulation of his experience of World War II—the devastation of Warsaw and the Holocaust—among other historic events, that won him the 1978 Neustadt

International Prize for Literature and the 1980 Nobel Prize for Literature, which has a present monetary value of $212,000. Miłosz is a Lithuanian-born poet, novelist, essayist, translator, critic, and literary scholar who writes in Polish. In voluntary exile from Poland since 1951, he is now an American citizen and a professor of Slavic languages and literatures at the University of California in Berkeley.

The Nobel citation described Miłosz' writing as "many-voiced and dramatic, insistent and provocative." Other terms applied to his work were "difficult," "erudite," "challenging," "captivating," and "arresting." The citation pointed up his significance with the observation: "In both an outward and an inward sense he is an exiled writer, a stranger for whom physical exile is really a reflection of a metaphysical— or even religious—spiritual exile applying to humanity in general."

Czesław Miłosz' native Lithuania is an ethnic and linguistic amalgam that has lost its sovereignty to neighboring states at intervals in its history and happened at the time of his birth to be under Russian control. He was born into an old and distinguished Polish-speaking family on June 30, 1911 in Seteiniai, on the River Niewiaza and near the town of Kedainiai. His parents, Aleksander and Weronika (Kunat) Miłosz, were members of the intelligentisa, but not wealthy. Part of his early life was spent in Czarist Russia, traveling with his father, who worked on the Yenisey River in Siberia in 1913 as a civil engineer and near battle zone areas during World War I as a military engineer in the Russian army.

Much of the distinctive imagery of Miłosz' poetry derives from his boyhood experience of the countryside of Lithuania, whose beautiful landscape and diversified cultural entanglements, such as remnants of ancient pagan ritual in Christian practices, impressed him indelibly. The growing up of a boy, Thomas, in rural Lithuania is the subject of his autobiographical novel, *Dolina Issy* (Institut Littéraire, Paris, 1955; *The Issa Valley*, Farrar, 1981), which in some respects may be read as a celebration of his Eastern European heritage.

"If I were asked to say where my poetry comes from, I would say that its roots are in my childhood, in Christmas carols, in the liturgy of Marian and vesper offices, and in the Bible," Miłosz wrote in one of his philosophical essays. But in high school in Lithuania's capital city of Wilno (Vilnius), which had been incorporated into Poland by the time he became a student there in 1921, he objected to compulsory religious education, specifically the teaching of Roman Catholicism.

Recalling other factors in his development as a poet, Miłosz paid tribute to his high school teachers in his brief speech accepting the Neustadt International Prize for Literature: "Particularly I was shaped by seven years of Latin and by exercises in translating Latin poetry in class." Additional enduring influences of his high school and university years are meditatively detailed in his autobiography, *Rodzinna Europa* (Institut Littéraire, 1958; *Native Realm: A Search for Self-Definition,* Doubleday, 1968), a study of much sociological value in which he explains what it means to be "a typical Eastern European."

In 1929 Miłosz enrolled in the University of Wilno, where, hesitant to declare his literary aspirations, he studied law. He published his first poems the following year, however, in the university journal *Alma Mater Vilnensis* and soon afterward helped to found a literary group of leftists called Zagary, which put out a periodical of the same name. Because of their foreboding of a cosmic disaster, they became known as the Catastrophist School. While remaining skeptical of Russian Communism, Miłosz was attracted to Marxism, which seemed to him "vital and bracing," although he objected to its dogmatism. His experimental and prophetic poetry of social protest, published in *Poemat o czasie zastygłym* (Poem on Time Frozen, Wilno, 1933), stemmed in part from his disgust with conditions in Poland in the period between the two world wars. His work was well received, especially among avant-garde writers. But looking back on it in *Native Realm,* he admitted, "[It] had no connection with the living springs of art; it was journalism, which I wrote to redeem myself for not taking part in the workers' clashes with the police."

At about the same time that he obtained his Master of Law degree, in 1934, Miłosz won a state scholarship to study literature in Paris. During his year there he often visited his older relative, Oscar Vladislas de Lubicz Miłosz, a diplomat at the Lithuanian legation and a poet who wrote in French. Besides encouraging the young poet in disciplined exercise in writing, Oscar Miłosz deflated his awe of contemporary French literary movements and directed him toward more spiritual sources of inspiration.

Trzy zimy (Three Winters, Wilno/Warsaw, 1936), Miłosz' second book of poems, continued his exploration of cataclysmic themes. His mood tended to be despairing and melancholic and his symbolism often enigmatic, despite the precision of his visual imagery. After his return to Wilno from Paris, he worked as a program assistant at the local Polish Radio station, but was dismissed in 1937, when he came under attack from a rightist group because of his liberalism. A sympathetic Polish Radio director at the head office hired him for a programming job in Warsaw, however, so that he was in that city at the time of the invasion of Poland in 1939 by German and Soviet forces. Remaining in Warsaw throughout the Nazi occupation of World War II, he worked as a writer for the underground resistance and edited an anthology of anti-Nazi poetry.

One of the first books to be published in the Polish People's Republic, Miłosz' collection of poems *Ocalenie* (Rescue; Cracow, 1945) placed him among the country's most important writers. Formally, his wartime poems showed an increased inclination toward the classicism that had begun to emerge in *Trzy zimy* and that eventually prevailed in his poetry. Stylistic developments in *Ocalenie* and later writing may be attributed in part to the influence of T. S. Eliot, whose work Miłosz read during the war, when he learned the English language and studied its literature.

While much of his wartime and postwar poetry witnessed the sorrows and horrors of the tragedy, Miłosz had discovered salvation in what he called in one of his poems the "salutary aim" of good poetry. As Louis Iribarne observed in a paper on Miłosz published in *World Literature Today* (Summer 1978), the poems appearing after the war "are both a statement of loss and a shoring up of light against the darkness that would envelop what has survived." An article in the New York Times (October 10, 1980) by the Russian poet-in-exile Joseph Brodsky pointed to another aspect of Miłosz' reaction to the war: "Out of the scattered ashes emerged poetry which did not so much sing of outrage and grief as whisper of the guilt of the survivor."

Despite the fact that he was not a member of the Communist party, People's Poland welcomed Miłosz into its diplomatic service in 1946 as second secretary at the Polish embassy in Washington, D.C. By the end of his four and a half years in that post he had reluctantly made up his mind to break with the Warsaw government. He began his exile from Poland in 1951 in Paris, where he was serving as cultural attaché. To some degree his defection grew out of his resolution in 1943 to achieve a fusion of individual and historical elements in his poetry and to write neither "pure poetry" nor the propagandistic poetry of Russian socialist realism. His decision not to return to Warsaw had been preceded by agonizing efforts to understand his obligations as a writer when confronted with government demands for concessions that he insisted were not repressions of aesthetic expression but of truth.

The turmoil that Miłosz suffered is reflected in the poems collected in *Swiatło dzienne* (Daylight, 1955) and in the poem *Traktat poetycki* (Poetic Treatise, 1957), both published by the Institut Littéraire in Paris. The sociopolitical essays of his earlier *Zniewolony umysł* (Institut Littéraire, 1953; *The Captive Mind,* Knopf, 1953) examine more directly the relationship between culture and politics. In that work, which Stephen Spender regards as a masterpiece, he analyzed the lure of the doctrine of "historical necessity" and the suffocating impact of Communism on four imaginary writers, whom he named Alpha, Beta, Gamma, and Delta.

Although Miłosz feared that his absence from Poland, where his work became officially banned, would mean "sterility and inaction," as he wrote in *The Captive Mind,* his years in exile proved highly productive. He could have attracted a large audience by writing in French or English, but he preferred Polish because he believed that poetry must be written in the language of one's childhood. To the international attention that *The Captive Mind* aroused during a period of Cold War tension, he added the prestige of winning the Prix Littéraire Européen with another book of 1953, *Zdobycie władzy*, published in Paris in both Polish and French, in the United States as *Seizure of Power* (Criterion, 1955), and in England as *The Usurpers* (Faber, 1955). In that novel, which, like *The Captive Mind*, is considered an important historical document, he drew on his experiences in Poland during and after World War II to give still another form to issues involved in the relationship of intellectuals and creative individuals to Communism.

While in France, Miłosz contributed to several European periodicals, including *Kultura*, the Polish-language émigré monthly. He also edited and translated into Polish the selected works of the French writer Simone Weil, who, he has said, had a profound influence on his thinking, primarily because of her preoccupation with the question of evil. The "propensity for Manichaeanism" that he admitted in *Native Realm* accounts for the grimmer elements in much of his poetry and perhaps for the emphasis he puts on the need for the poet to overcome despair. Even in his evocation of an idyllic childhood in *The Issa Valley*, Manichaean dualism darkens his view of "Nature."

Since 1960 Miłosz has been a resident of the United States and since 1970 a naturalized citizen. After teaching Polish literature for a year at the University of California at Berkeley as visiting lecturer, in 1961 he accepted an offer of tenure and an appointment as professor of Slavic languages and literatures. The academic community at Berkeley evidently stimulated his capacity for scholarship, although he regards his undertakings in that area as the "least enticing" of his literary interests. Other scholars have praised his endeavor to make Polish writing more available and understandable to American readers through *Postwar Polish Poetry* (Doubleday, 1965), an anthology of ninety poems, some of them his own, that he selected and translated, and *The History of Polish Literature* (Macmillan, 1970). Studies on Polish writers are also among the scholarly essays collected in *Emperor of the Earth: Modes of Eccentric Vision* (Univ. of California Press, 1977).

Miłosz has said that of the several facets of his work translating into Polish is for him second only in importance to writing poetry. Among the writers in English whose books he has translated are Shakespeare, Milton, Eliot, Whitman, Sandburg, Robinson Jeffers, and Daniel Bell. He has also translated from Spanish, Yiddish, and Hebrew, as well as from French. Currently he is translating the Bible from Hebrew into Polish, after having recently published translations of the Book of Ecclesiastes, the Gospel According to St. Mark, and the Psalms.

Significantly, geographic titles abound in Miłosz' oeuvre, such as *Widzenia nad Zatoka San Francisco* (Views from San Francisco Bay, Institut Littéraire, 1969), in which he uses California locale and social behavior and diverse cultural encounters as springboards for metaphysical contemplation. That collection of essays has not yet been translated into English. Nor have two more recent prose publications, *Prywatne obowiazki* (Private Obligations, Institut Littéraire, 1972), a book of literary criticism, and *Ziemia Ulro* (The Land of Ulro, Institut Littéraire, 1977), a study on the continuity of the romantic tradition, which takes the Ulro of its title from William Blake's World of Ulro, or nothingness.

At Berkeley poetry continued to be Miłosz' foremost concern. Between 1962 and 1974 the Institut Littéraire published four volumes of his poems: *Król Popiel i inne wiersze* (King Popiel and Other Poems), *Gucio zaczarowany* (Bobo's Metamorphosis), *Miasto bez imienia* (City Without a Name), and *Gdzie wschodzi słonce i kedy zapada* (From Where the Sun Rises to Where It Sets). Very few of his poems were available in English translation, however, before the publication in 1973 of *Selected Poems* (Seabury; revised edition, Ecco, 1981), which includes some of the poetry that he wrote in Poland, but gives greater space to his work from 1960 to 1973. Another collection, *Bells in Winter* (Ecco), appeared in 1978.

When Joseph Brodsky presented Miłosz for the Neustadt award in 1978, he told the jury, "I have no hesitation whatsoever in stating that Czesław Miłosz is one of the greatest poets of our time, perhaps the greatest." In his acceptance remarks Miłosz said that his "poems do not translate well because of many cultural-linguistic allusions in their very texture." Other factors, however, also bear on his inaccessibility to the general reader. The "I" of much of his poetry is not the poet, but a character of his creation with whom he may agree or disagree in varying measures of intensity—an exchange likely to be confusing to new readers of his poems. Jan Błonski of the University of Cracow, explaining Miłosz' predilection for dialogue or polyphonic speech, pointed out, "It reveals doubt, division; the motive behind the dialogue is the pressing search for an ever-retreating truth." The experience, moreover, of that truth, or reality, is inexplicable.

Regardless of the difficulties that Miłosz' poetry presents both in its original language and in translation, he has been revered, at least among other writers, in Poland, where his work has circulated in underground editions. When, for the first time in thirty years, he returned in June 1981 to a changing, more liberal Poland to receive an honorary doctorate from the Catholic University of Lublin, he was overwhelmingly welcomed as a national hero.

Czesław and Janina (Dluska) Miłosz, who were married on January 1, 1944, have two sons, Anthony and John Peter. With his graying dark hair, bushy eyebrows, and wide, blue eyes, Miłosz has been described as "an imposing figure" on the Berkeley campus. James Atlas in the New York Times (October 10, 1980) quoted one of his colleagues as saying, "He is awesome in front of a class. His students tend to perceive him as one of those polymathical Europeans whose intellect is so compelling that you just have to listen. He is a stunning lecturer." Public recognition has never motivated him, and in his poem "The Accuser" he wrote wryly of his survival as "an item in the fourteenth volume of an en-cyclopedia/Next to a hundred Millers and Mickey Mouse." Reacting to the celebrity that accompanied his winning the Nobel Prize, he told newsmen that he was by nature a private and solitary person and that he hoped "not to fall into the pitfalls of fame."

References: N Y Rev of Books 28:29+ Je 25 '81 por; N Y Times A p10 O 10 '80 por; N Y Times Bk R p3 F 1 '81 por, p7 Je 26 '81 por; New Repub 184:28+ My 23 '81; World Lit Today 52:197+ Spring '78, 52:357+ Summer '78 pors; Contemporary Authors vols 81-84 (1979); Miłosz, Czesław. Native Realm (1968); Who's Who in America, 1980-81; World Authors 1950-1970 (1975)

Morrison, Philip

Nov. 7, 1915- Theoretical astrophysicist; educator. Address: b. Department of Physics, Massachusetts Institute of Technology, Cambridge, Mass. 02139

In the words of one admiring colleague of many years, Philip Morrison represents "an attitude, a way of life, a symbol for . . . the 'joy of insight' or 'lust for knowledge.' Nobody else has better demonstrated . . . what it means to the human soul to perceive or recognize a new scientific discovery or a new theoretical insight." Dr. Morrison, a professor of physics at the Massachusetts Institute of Technology since 1964, is known among his peers for his "intellectual long-distance runs." He was originally a nuclear physicist, but since the publication, in 1959, of what was widely considered as the first scientifically valid paper on possible methods of communication with extraterrestrial life forms, he has concentrated on questions of astrophysics and cosmology.

Philip Morrison was born in Somerville, New Jersey on November 7, 1915. He received his elementary and secondary education in the public schools in Pittsburgh, Pennsylvania, then enrolled in the Carnegie Institute of Technology there. After taking his B. S. degree in 1936, he continued his studies at the University of California at Berkeley, where he conducted his research in atomic electrodynamics under the guidance of J. Robert Oppenheimer, the brilliant nuclear physicist who was later to serve as the director of the atomic energy research project at Los Alamos, New Mexico. Upon submission of his doctoral dissertation on the behavior of gamma rays and energy fluctuations in the electromagnetic field, Morrison was awarded a Ph.D. degree in theoretical physics in 1940.

After having taught undergraduate physics courses at San Francisco State College and the University of Illinois, Morrison began, in 1942, what he has called "a long and intense tour of duty" with the so-called Manhattan Project, which was responsible for the development of the atomic bomb. First assigned to work at the Metallurgical Laboratory at the University of Chicago, he was eventually transferred to the atomic research facility at Los Alamos. As a group leader of the Manhattan District, he supervised and monitored testing procedures. For the bomb's first full-scale test in 1945, he rode from the Los Alamos laboratory to the remote desert testing site with the bomb's plutonium core resting beside him on the back seat of an automobile. A few weeks after that successful test, he went to Tinian Island in the Marianas chain to help assemble the atomic bomb that was to be dropped on Nagasaki, Japan.

Following the Japanese surrender on August 14, 1945, Morrison accompanied a team of scientists sent by the United States government to survey the damage caused by atomic weapons. As he passed over Hiroshima in a low-flying observation plane, he was appalled by the magnitude of the destruction. "There was just one enormous, flat, rust-red scar, and no green or gray," as there would have been had conventional bombs been used, "because there were no roofs or vegetation left," he said later, as quoted in the *New Yorker* (June 8, 1946). "I was pretty sure then that nothing I was going to see later would give me as much of a jolt. The rest would be just a matter of details. . . . Most of us who hadn't dropped out of this atom project during the last two or three years had developed our own private justifications for staying with it. I know I had done so."

Not long after he returned to the United States, Morrison began speaking out in favor of some kind of international control of atomic research. As he explained in an article for the *New Republic* (February 11, 1946), the atomic bomb was "not merely a new weapon," but "a revolution in war." "Destruction has now changed qualitatively with this new energy," he wrote. "War can now destroy not cities, but nations." Like many of his Los Alamos colleagues, he was, in his words, "completely convinced that another war cannot be allowed." With international control of atomic research based on "functioning, material agreements among the great and smaller powers," he argued, "we have a chance to build a working peace on the novelty and terror of the atomic bomb."

In July 1946, on the eve of the first anniversary of the first atomic explosion, Morrison met with a group of like-minded scientists and skeptical public officials in Washington, D.C. to discuss world control of atomic energy. Repeating his opposition to military involvement in atomic research, which he felt could be misinterpreted by other countries as an intention to wage "a new and more frightful war," he insisted that the "almost limitless" peacetime benefits of atomic energy could be realized only through international cooperation and civilian control. He once illustrated his point by asking his listeners to assume that an entire electrical system had been set up merely to produce current for an electric chair. "If, then," he said, to complete his analogy, "production of electricity were halted so that people could not go around electrocuting each other, that would be in minor proportion comparable to the major disaster if the world does not utilize atomic power for fear of the atomic bomb."

In 1946 Morrison joined the faculty of Cornell University in Ithaca, New York as an associate professor of physics and nuclear studies. When not teaching classes, he was in his laboratory or office working on such disparate subjects as the origin of cosmic rays, nuclear structure theory, the nature of information transfer in cells, and the radiogenic origin of the helium isotopes in rock. Except for a four-month sabbatical leave in 1953, during which time he was a visiting professor at MIT, he remained on the Cornell University faculty until 1964.

A passionate advocate of academic and intellectual freedom, Morrison publicly came to the support of Alexander Trachtenberg, the head of International Publishers, who was convicted, in January 1953, of conspiring to teach and advocate the forcible overthrow of the government by publishing such works as *Toward a Soviet America*. Dr. Morrison argued, as quoted in the New York *World Telegraph Sun* (February 23, 1952), that Trachtenberg's indictment involved "still greater dangers to the welfare and security" of the United States because it made the free exchange of ideas a crime. Partly because of his defense of Trachtenberg, Morrison was called to testify before the United States Senate internal security subcommittee in May 1953, at the height of the Red-baiting McCarthy era. Like other intellectuals of his generation, he had flirted briefly with Communism during the 1930's, but as he told reporters at a news conference following the hearing, he had not been affiliated with the party "since [he] was a young man."

Both awed and stimulated by groundbreaking discoveries in virtually every scientific discipline in the 1950's, Morrison was especially intrigued by the implications of new experiments in physics that apparently contradicted what had been thought to be universal laws. As he explained at the annual meeting of the American Physical Society in New York City in January 1958, there could be exceptions to, say, the laws of conservation and momentum, possibly in some other part of the universe.

Over the next few years, Dr. Morrison became more and more involved in theoretical astrophysics. Estimating that there may be several billion planets in the universe capable of sustaining advanced life forms, he and fellow physicist Giuseppe Cocconi proposed beginning "a discriminating search" for radio signals from intelligent extraterrestrial beings. "The presence of interstellar signals is entirely consistent with all we know and . . . if signals are present the means of detecting them is now at hand," the two men wrote in "Searching for Interstellar Communication," which was published by the prestigious British scientific journal *Nature* on September 19, 1959. "Few will deny the profound importance, practical and philosophical, which the detection of interstellar communications would have," they continued. "The probability of success is difficult to estimate, but if we never search, the chance of success is zero."

Conceding that such a quest was a formidable undertaking, Morrison and Cocconi outlined several ways to improve, however slightly, the astronomical odds against a fruitful search. They began by assuming that any advanced technical civilization bent on contacting another would make the detection of its signals as easy as possible. Therefore, the professors suggested limiting the search to the "most favored radio region" of relatively low atmospheric noise. Within that "window," at 1,420 MHz, is the hydrogen emission line—the constant background hiss that is the most common naturally occurring radio emission in the universe—and, at 1,662 MHz, the emission line of the hydroxol ion. Between the two is the quietest part of the radio spectrum. Because a hydrogen atom joined to a hydroxol ion forms a water molecule, that frequency band is generally known as "the water hole." The channel was, in the words of one radio astronomer, "the foreordained interstellar communication band" for "water-based life."

Taken by the theory, Dr. Frank Drake, an associate scientist at the National Radio Astronomy Observatory in Green Bank, West Virginia, initiated, in 1960, Project Ozma, the first deliberate attempt to receive radio signals from "suitable" nearby stars, in this case, Tau Ceti and Epsilon Eridani. Although the results of that project and of its successors have been discouraging to date, Morrison remains undaunted. "If there is life out there, sooner or later we are going to find it, or it will find us," he said at the symposium "Life Beyond Earth and the Mind of Man," which was held at Boston University on November 25, 1972. In Morrison's view, the single most important message we would receive from the inhabitants of another world would be "a description . . . of how these beings were able to fashion a world in which they could live, persevere, and maintain something of worth and beauty for a long period of time." But, he added, "if after considerable search we do not find that our counterparts exist somewhere else, I cannot think that would be wrong either, because that would give us even a heavier responsibility to represent intelligence in this extraordinarily large and diverse universe."

Over the years, Dr. Morrison has worked tirelessly to foster a continued interest in the search for extraterrestrial life. To that end, he has contributed dozens of articles to scientific journals and popular magazines, given countless lectures, and attended many international conferences and symposia on the subject. In 1976 the National Aeronautics and Space Administration appointed Morrison chairman of a group of scientists directed to investigate the feasibility of conducting a systematic search for interstellar messages. After a two-year study, the group concluded that such a search, using existing radio telescopes and data processing equipment, was timely, feasible, and relatively inexpensive. Morrison coedited the report, *The Search for Extraterrestrial Intelligence*, which was published by Dover in 1979.

In 1964 Morrison went to MIT as the Francis L. Friedman Lecturer and Visiting Professor of Physics. The following year he accepted a permanent faculty appointment there and, in 1973, he became Institute Professor. During his tenure at MIT, he has attempted to resolve some of the mysteries of supernovae, cosmic x-rays, neutrinos, quasars, black holes, and other baffling cosmological puzzles. For example, in the May 1968 issue of *Astrophysical Journal,* he suggested that the recently discovered quasi-stellar radio sources, or quasars, were really mammoth pulsars—the rapidly spinning, compacted relics of galaxies. His ten-year investigation of supernovae persuaded him that those awesome thermonuclear explosions of massive stars produced from 100 to 1,000 times more energy than is detected on earth. Moreover, supernovae "probably" create many chemical elements, including lead, uranium, deuterium, and gold. "Thus," he noted wryly in *Technology Review* (May 1975), "between bullets and printers' type, gold and nuclear weapons, all our troubles seem to come from supernovae."

An intense and communicative speaker, Morrison often lectures in halls filled to overflowing with spellbound students. Determined to get physics out of the laboratory and "into the corridor," he has devised special undergraduate seminars for intelligent laymen interested in the natural sciences, and he has tried also to improve scientific education at the elementary school level. In collaboration with Joe Griffith, the principal of the Thoreau School in Concord, Massachusetts, he developed prepackaged kits designed to demonstrate to young children the fundamental concepts of science, which in his view "represent anchors in a world of change." A prolific writer of scientific articles for the general reader, he has contributed pieces to such periodicals as the *New Yorker,* the *Saturday Evening Post, Life, Saturday Review,* the *Nation,* and the *New Republic.* He is the coauthor of *My Father's Watch: Aspects of the Physical World* (Prentice-Hall, 1969) and, with Hans Bethe, of *Elementary Nuclear Theory* (Wiley, 1956) and coeditor of *Charles Babbage and His Calculating Engines* (Dover, 1961).

Throughout his career, Morrison has been concerned about the relationship of science to society. To encourage others to discuss that issue, he helped found, in 1948, the Federation of American Scientists and served as its chairman from 1973 to 1976. In his opinion, science has become a "villain" and "scapegoat" because it "tends to . . . put power in the hands of the powerful." But as he observed in "Science: the Master and Servant," a syndicated newspaper article he wrote in 1974, "science cannot and ought not to take the blame." "The weapons in the dark silos are cruel and deadly; they arise not from science but from nationalism . . . ," he said. "It is the work of national fears based on class divisions gaining power from science. To blame science is . . . to avoid joining the battle for an equitable, worldwide social order."

Since the end of World War II, Morrison has refused to engage in weapons research, and he has continued to oppose the nuclear arms race, which he has described as a "stability of terror." In *The Price of Defense: A New Strategy for Military Spending* (Times Books, 1979), he and several colleagues set forth a detailed alternative defense posture for the United States that included, among other things, a 42 percent reduction in defense spending, sharp cuts in the number of "unnecessary, provocative, and destabilizing" strategic weapons, and a shift from vulnerable land-based missiles and bombers to missile-carrying submarines as the primary deterrent force. The authors maintained that their plan assured the security of the United States, even without reciprocal cutbacks by the Soviet Union. On the other hand, an unrestrained arms race could "induce a lack of reason in the apprehensive opposition, who may become frightened and lose control," Morrison pointed out to Suzanne Fairclough in an interview for *Technology Review* (November 1979). "The history of previous wars . . . shows very clearly: to induce fear is the worst possible way of averting conflict."

Energetic and congenial, Philip Morrison looks at least a decade younger than his chronological age. He is a voracious reader and, as the regular book editor for *Scientific American*, writes six to ten informative reviews each month on a wide variety of scientific subjects. His wife, Phylis, whom he married in 1965, collaborates with him on an annual appraisal of science books for children, which is published in the December issue of Scientific American. The Morrisons, who have one son, make their home in Cambridge, Massachusetts.

Dr. Morrison has lectured at the Imperial College of Science in London, England, the Tata Institute of Fundamental Research in Bombay, India, the University of Kyoto, Japan, the University of Ife, Nigeria, and many Canadian and American universities. He is the recipient of the Pregel Prize of the New York Academy of Science, the American Association for the Advancement of Science-Westinghouse Science Writing Prize, the American Association of Physics Teachers' Oersted Medal, and the Babson Prize from the Gravity Foundation and has several honorary degrees.

References: Newsweek 26:37 D 17 '45; Physics Today 24:88 Ag '71; Science 132:1823 D 16 '60; Sci Am 194:22 Ja '56; American Men and Women of Science (1979)

Mudd, Roger (Harrison)

Feb. 9, 1928- Broadcast journalist. Address: b. NBC News, 4001 Nebraska Ave, NW, Washington, D.C. 20016

"The premier broadcast journalist in Washington" was the accolade bestowed on Roger Mudd by his former colleague William J. Small, the president of NBC News, when Small announced on July 1, 1980 that Mudd was defecting to NBC from CBS. Small himself, a former CBS News Washington bureau chief, had made the same move ten months earlier. During his nineteen years at CBS, fifteen of them as Congressional correspondent and the last four as national affairs correspondent, the erudite Mudd became known to viewers for his wry, dispassionate style, which sharply contrasted with the benign warmth of Walter Cronkite. As Cronkite's backup, Mudd had been led to believe that he would succeed him as anchorman and editor of the *CBS Evening News;* instead Dan Rather was named Cronkite's successor, effective with Cronkite's retirement in 1981. Kept uninformed of Rather's selection until the day of its announcement, February 14, 1980, an "extremely disappointed" Mudd took a leave of absence for the last nine months of his CBS contract. During that prolonged hiatus he considered offers from ABC News as well as NBC News, finally opting for the latter partly because NBC would allow him to continue working in his native Washington, D.C. He began appearing as chief Washington correspondent—a position created especially for him—on the *NBC Nightly News* on November 17, 1980. NBC announced that Mudd would frequently substitute for John Chancellor on the *Nightly News*. He is scheduled to be coanchorman with Tom Brokaw on that program after Chancellor becomes network commentator in the spring of 1982.

Roger Harrison Mudd was born in Washington, D.C. on February 9, 1928 to Kostka Mudd, an engineer and cartographer, and Irma Iris (Harrison) Mudd. "I wasn't as responsible as I might have been," he told Edith Efron regarding his early school years. "My grades were not good." Miss Efron, who interviewed him for *TV Guide* (December 26, 1970), found Mudd to be exasperatingly laconic, providing her with no more personal information than she could pack into six modest paragraphs (one of them a mere sentence long). "It took a few hours to get it out of him . . . ," she wrote. "He's one of the worst interviewees we've ever encountered."

After graduating from Woodrow Wilson High School in Washington, D.C., Mudd entered United States Army service in 1945, just as World War II was ending. He obtained a B.A. degree at Washington and Lee University in Lexington, Virginia in 1950 and an M.A. in American history and literature from the University of North Carolina in 1951. His master's thesis dealt with intellectuals in government, a subject that he chose because of his fascination with President Franklin D. Roosevelt's "Brain Trust."

In the academic year 1951-52 Mudd taught history and English and coached football at the Darlington School, a preparatory school in Rome, Georgia, and he spent the following year as a research assistant for a Congressional committee in Washington. He intended at that time to return to his university studies and obtain a Ph.D. in contemporary history, with the focus on the relationship between the press and intellectuals in power. "I thought that before I did this," he has explained, "I had better work for a newspaper, to learn more than Frank Luther Mott told me in our journalism textbook." Accordingly, he joined the staff of the Richmond, Virginia News Leader as a reporter—and never returned to school.

Leaving the News Leader after several months, Mudd became news director of radio station WRNL in Richmond, where he remained for three years. In 1956 he moved to Washington, D.C. as a reporter for WTOP, the CBS radio and television affiliate in the nation's capital. Howard K. Smith of CBS News hired him to cover Congress for the network in 1961. Capitol Hill quickly proved to be a congenial base for the droll, cynical Mudd, who was able to use his poker-faced sense of humor to excellent effect in goading legislators from the sidelines. "I really like . . . covering Congress," he said on one occasion, "400-500 individuals all with different personalities, all in their way trying to do some good for the country, not usually succeeding."

Mudd's most memorable performance in his early years as Congressional correspondent was his marathon coverage of the Senate filibuster that delayed passage of the Civil Rights Act of 1964 for sixty-seven days. As John Horn of the Washington Post (May 4, 1964) pointed out, "His continued presence at the scene of Washington inaction has personalized and dramatized the halting process of our government to the average viewer in a way no amount of words or secondary reports could have."

Also in 1964, in August, Fred W. Friendly, who had recently taken over the presidency of CBS News, named Mudd and veteran newsman Robert Trout to anchor the Democratic National Convention, in place of Walter Cronkite. At that time the political conventions were the premier showcases of the networks' news divisions, and Cronkite himself conceded that CBS had taken a statistical "clobbering" in its coverage of the Republican National Convention two weeks earlier. The Trout-Mudd team failed to lure the majority of viewers away from Chet Huntley and David Brinkley on NBC but exhibited, as John Horn observed in the New York Herald Tribune of August 18, 1964, "an easy, understated, cooperative tandem manner that was ingratiating." In the New York Times (August 24, 1964), Jack Gould wrote: "Mr. Mudd is the new CBS star, and a most attractive one at that. His manner of speaking makes for very easy listening; he is unhurried yet not given to hesitation. He has a particularly agreeable smile and also quite obviously a good sense of humor. Probably comparisons with Mr. Brinkley will be inevitable, but last night Mr. Mudd was an individual in his own right. Moreover, he never tried for effect. He could wear well indeed."

Among Mudd's other assignments outside of Washington in the 1960's was the Presidential nomination campaign of Senator Robert F. Kennedy in the 1968 Democratic primaries. He was at the Ambassador Hotel in Los Angeles when Kennedy was assassinated in a kitchen passageway of the hotel in June 1968. As Ethel Kennedy, the Senator's widow, later reminisced: "It was because of Roger, who led me through the crowd, that Bobby and I got to say goodbye to each other."

In the 1970's Mudd narrated many of the installments of the hard-hitting documentary series CBS Reports, including The New Violence in the South (1971), Busing (1972), and The Issue of Busing (1972). Far and away, the blockbuster among the documentaries was the controversial The Selling of the Pentagon (1971), an indignant, muckraking departure from the networks' "balanced truth" policy in the post-Edward R. Murrow era. The scathing indictment of the Defense Department's $190,-000,000 public relations program was thorough, ranging in coverage from red-carpet military junkets for big businessmen, industrialists, and other influential citizens to the cooperation of the TV medium itself in the Pentagon's hustle. "On this broadcast," Mudd concluded, "we have seen violence made glamorous, expensive weapons advertised as if they were automobiles, biased opinions presented as straight facts. . . . Pentagon propaganda insists on America's role as the cop on every beat in the world. Not only the public but the press as well has been beguiled, including, at times, ourselves at CBS News. This propaganda barrage is the creation of a runaway bureaucracy that frustrates attempts to control it."

The reviewer for Variety (March 3, 1971) called The Selling of the Pentagon "a near-perfect example of television as a journalistic force," a "journalistic job ... so astounding that the most frequent question asked by the industry and the plain viewers is, 'How did it get on the air?'" He went on to observe, "CBS has come a long way from [last] December, when Roger Mudd ... told his alma mater Washington and Lee that the tube was no good for hard information, [that] one had to go to print to find out what's going on. In point of fact, only Senator Fulbright in his book on Pentagon propaganda has come close to the exposure this show gave to the military's picking of the public pocket and mind."

The Selling of the Pentagon," Fred W. Friendly (who had left television for academia) wrote in *Harper's* (June 1971), "may have been the most penetrating documentary since David Lowe's *Harvest of Shame* and the most explosive and condemned since the Murrow-McCarthy broadcast of 1954." Most of the condemnation came from the Pentagon, which might have ignored a low-audience television or radio slap but was not about to let a prime-time assault go unanswered. The Defense Department's objections were not addressed to the documentary's main arguments but to some marginal errors of fact, some oversimplifications, and, above all, what it called some "doctoring" of interviews. In response, CBS set up new rules for the editing of news presentations, including the stipulation that the viewer be advised if words from interview answers or excerpts from speeches or statements have been taken out of sequence.

The Selling of the Pentagon received the George Polk Memorial Award for outstanding achievement in journalism, and Mudd won Academy of Television Arts and Sciences' Emmys for his reportage of the shooting of Alabama Governor George Wallace in 1973 and the resignation of Vice-President Spiro T. Agnew in 1974. As the Nixon Administration's Watergate scandal unfolded, he won additional Emmys for his narration of the CBS special reports *The Senate and the Watergate Affair* (1973) and *Watergate: The White House Transcript* (1974). When he and Dan Rather shared commentary on President Richard Nixon's resignation in August 1974, Rather was much the kinder of the two in his remarks, partly perhaps because he was still trying to make amends for a heated interchange between him and Nixon in a televised news conference five months before. In the opinion of some observers, Mudd's relative lack of magnanimity toward Nixon in his hour of shame probably played an early, almost subliminal part in his decline—and Rather's rise—as heir apparent to Walter Cronkite as anchor for the *CBS Evening News.*

In covering the campaigns of Gerald R. Ford and Jimmy Carter in 1976, Mudd referred to the Presidential race as "vapid and egocentric," condemned to an "issueless status" by Carter's emphasis on personal integrity and trust. When Mudd was named national affairs correspondent of CBS News in January 1977, Wil-

liam J. Small, who was then a CBS senior vice-president, observed, "Much of today's news spans many beats and disciplines, and Roger is ideally equipped and trained to bridge those gaps."

In the fall of 1980, shortly before Senator Edward M. Kennedy declared for the Democratic Presidential nomination, Kennedy submitted to a full-scale prime-time interview with Mudd, hoping to dispel some of the public questions about his morality and his stability under pressure by confronting them head on. The interview, *Teddy,* broadcast on November 4, 1980 as a program in the *CBS Reports* series, backfired, marking what many observers regarded as the beginning of the end of Kennedy's 1980 candidacy. After inviting Mudd to ask him any question, Kennedy became visibly uncomfortable and irritated when the reporter zeroed in on such sensitive subjects as the tragedy at Chappaquiddick, Kennedy's troubled marriage, and his alleged infidelities. Far from coming across as a calm, decisive leader, Kennedy appeared vague, nervous, and inarticulate, often answering questions with platitudes and incomplete sentences. Conceding that his behavior at Chappaquiddick was "inexplicable," he was at a loss for words with which to answer Mudd's rejoinder: "But what guarantee does a citizen have or what assurance does a citizen have that in the future you would not act, as you said, irresponsibly or inexplicably when your own career came in conflict with the public's right to know?"

CBS Reports: Teddy was ranked in *Time* (July 14, 1980) as "the most important work of political journalism of the entire campaign," and it brought Mudd the 1979 George Foster Peabody Award for meritorious service to broadcasting. In his Peabody acceptance speech, he replied to those who accused him of focusing too intently on the Senator's personal life, pointing out that the interview had been "conceived and undertaken by honorable men and women," with "no tricks, no deceits, no contrivances." He concluded: "The editing was generous. We were not afraid to let the man be heard. We have nothing to apologize for."

Nevertheless, the Kennedy interview almost certainly made some contribution to Dan Rather's winning out finally over Roger Mudd as successor to Walter Cronkite. Rather had come from far behind in overtaking Mudd: for years, in the late 1960's and into the 1970's, the feeling that he was being left out of consideration in the Cronkite succession reportedly rankled him. "I suddenly found myself in a very competitive race, not of my making," Rather has said, as quoted in *Time* (February 25, 1980). "But If I am in this race, I intend to win it." According to the *Time* writer, Rather's 1977 autobiography, *The Camera Never Blinks,* written with Mickey Herskowitz, "amounted to effective lobbying over the heads of the network brass and toward the public at large." While Rather was energetically competing, Mudd remained complacently in the number one position in Cronkite's shadow, so sure of his future that at one point early in the 1979-80 season he refused to fill in for the venerable anchorman during a week he had set aside for a skiing vacation.

The CBS management swung definitely to Rather (who had gained stature with his investigative reporting on the CBS television magazine *60 Minutes*) as the other two networks were hotly courting him in the middle of the 1979-80 season. On February 14, 1980 the network announced that the *CBS Evening News with Dan Rather* would replace the *CBS Evening News with Walter Cronkite* effective with Cronkite's retirement in 1981. Mudd, who was not informed of the choice until an hour so before the announcement was made, issued a curt statement to the press: "The management of CBS and CBS News has made its decision on Walter Cronkite's successor according to its current values and standards. From the beginning, I have regarded myself as a news reporter, not as a newsmaker or a celebrity." The second sentence was an allusion to Rather's having what some regarded as more "star quality" than he. "One of the problems with broadcast journalists," Mudd pointed out, as quoted in *Time* (July 14, 1980), "is that we have been convinced, sometimes against our better judgment, that we are not reporters but show-business people. I've tried not to live my life that way." *Time*'s reporter commented, "To his many admirers, Mudd's special brand of urbane restraint and humor makes him a star whether he likes it or not."

After signing with NBC News, Mudd told Ron Alridge of the Chicago *Tribune* (August 13, 1980) that he was "not bitter" over his experience at CBS, as some reports described him as being, just "disappointed." "Every time he [Cronkite] coughed," Mudd said sarcastically, "I was called up and told to be available. . . . I had given nineteen years of my professional life to the company and brought them honor and credit. . . . I thought the way they handled it was very disappointing." Regarding John Chancellor's anchor position on the *NBC Nightly News*, he said, "I read a lot about it opening up [but] I don't have faith in promises anymore." Earlier, in his prepared statement on the occasion of his signing with NBC News, Mudd said, "To become part of NBC News is at once exciting and reassuring. It means that we share certain principles of journalism—that the news should be paramount, that nothing and no one should get in the way of the news, and that the news should not be trifled with."

Mudd's defection, while expected, was a blow to CBS News, which for competitive reasons refused to release him from his contract (originally scheduled to have run through December 1980) until after the November elections. Mudd reacted to his forced idleness philosophically: "It's given me an opportunity to enjoy a lot of things I normally don't enjoy, to get reacquainted with my family," he told

Ron Alridge in the Chicago *Tribune* interview. "I suppose if you had to pick an election year to sit out, this would be the one to sit out."

An imposing figure, Roger Mudd is six feet two inches tall, weighs a little over 200 pounds, and has blue eyes and brown hair. He and the former Emma Jeanne Spears were married in 1957 and have four children, Daniel, Maria, Jonathan, and Matthew. The imperturbability that Mudd projects in his broadcasts correctly suggests a man who stands outside the mold of the intense, competitive journalistic workaholic. Trying to keep his work in balance with his personal life, he has been willing to make professional sacrifices here and there as the price for steadfastly maintaining his base in Washington, close to his family and his home in McLean, Virginia.

References: Chicago Tribune I p18 Ag 13 '80; N Y Times II p11 Ag 23 '64; Newsweek 69:74 Je 22 '64 por; TV Guide 18:10+ D 26 '70 por; Who's Who in America, 1980-81

Obote, (Apollo) Milton (ō-bōt′ā)

1925(?)- President of Uganda. Address: Office of the President, Kampala, Uganda

After spending nine years in exile, Dr. Milton Obote returned to his native Uganda from neighboring Tanzania in 1980 to resume the leadership of his country of some 13,000,000 people from which he had been ousted in 1971 in a coup led by army commander Idi Amin. One of the architects of Ugandan independence in the 1960's, Obote served as his country's

Prime Minister and then as its President but failed in his efforts to forge unity in the strife-torn nation. After his reelection to the Presidency in December 1980, Obote proceeded with characteristic optimism to undertake the formidable task of repairing the devastation inflicted on his country by Amin's reign of terror. "The pearl of Africa will rise and shine again," Obote has predicted, borrowing a metaphor once applied to Uganda by Winston Churchill.

Apollo (or Apolo) Milton Obote was born about 1925 (some sources give the year as 1924 or 1926) in the village of Akokoro on Lake Kwania in Lango district, in what was then the British protectorate of Uganda. He was the third of the nine children of Stanley Opeto, a farmer and minor chieftain of the Lango tribe. His mother, Pulisikira, was one of his father's four wives. "I was born of a ruling family," Obote told Edward R. F. Sheehan, as quoted in the New York Times Magazine (January 22, 1967). "My grandfather, great-grandfather, and great-great-grandfather were all rulers." While tending his father's flocks of sheep, goats, and cattle, Obote would fantasize that they were human beings. "I tried to talk to them and to pretend that I was myself a chief governing men," he has recalled.

After a spear wound that he suffered at the age of twelve ended his career as a herd boy, Obote entered a local primary school. In the early 1940's he attended the Lira Protestant mission school and Gulu high school, both in northern Uganda, and from 1945 to 1947 he was at Busoga College, a breeding ground for African nationalism, at Mwiri, in the eastern part of the country. Although he did not distinguish himself as a student, former schoolmates remember him as being strong-willed and independent. In 1948 Obote entered Makerere University College in Kampala, where he studied political science, economics, and English but dropped out after two years. Bent on a career in law or politics, he obtained a scholarship to study law in the United States, but his plans were rejected by the British authorities in Uganda on the ground that American law would be of little use in his country. After his efforts to study in London or at Gordon College in Khartoum were also turned down, Obote completed his formal education with a number of correspondence courses.

Determined to enter public service through the trade union movement, Obote went to neighboring Kenya soon after leaving Makerere and took a menial job as a laborer in the sugar works near Kisumu. Later he worked for a construction company and took jobs as a clerk and as a salesman. At the same time he became increasingly active as a labor organizer, to the dismay of the British colonial authorities.

Obote started in politics as a member of elder statesman Jomo Kenyatta's Kenya National Union. It was banned in 1952 because of its alleged links with the terrorist Mau Mau, but there was no evidence that Obote was involved in its activities. During his stay in Kenya, Obote helped the lawyer and politician Argwings Kodhek to found the African District Congress and worked with Tom Mboya in the Peoples' Convention party. After political parties were banned in Kenya he helped organize so-called "social clubs" that conducted clandestine political meetings.

Returning to Uganda in the mid-1950's, Obote organized the Lango branch of the Uganda National Congress (UNC), one of the pre-independence political parties, of which he had been a member since 1952. In 1957 he was named by the Lango district council to represent his district in the pre-independence Uganda Legislative Council, where he was noted for his outspokenness with colonial authorities and, in the words of Edward R. F. Sheehan, "soon became a skillful craftsman in the black Byzantium of Ugandan tribal politics." He was returned to the Uganda Legislative Council as a member of the UNC in Uganda's first popular elections, held in October 1958. After a factional dispute in 1959 split the UNC, Obote led his followers into a merger with the Uganda People's Union to form the Uganda People's Congress (UPC) in 1960, with himself as president-general.

As British rule in Uganda neared its end, a major obstacle to national unity was the rivalry between the new nationalist parties, as exemplified by Obote's UPC, and the hereditary rulers of Uganda's four traditional tribal kingdoms, who resisted independence. The strongest and most advanced of these kingdoms was Buganda, whose Kabaka, or king, was Sir Edward Frederick Mutesa II, popularly called "King Freddie." A boycott of the March 1961 general election by Buganda enabled the predominantly Roman Catholic Democratic party under Benedicto Kiwanuka to form a government, while the UPC was relegated to second place and Obote became leader of the opposition.

During the months that followed, Obote shrewdly negotiated with the leaders of Buganda and of the other three kingdoms, Bunyoro, Toro, and Ankole, eventually winning them over to the cause of national independence by promising them federal autonomy. In September 1961 Obote's UPC concluded an alliance with the newly established Kabaka Yekka ("King Only") party of Buganda. The national election of April 25, 1962 brought the UPC forty-three seats and the Kabaka Yekka twenty-four, giving the governing coalition under the new Prime Minister, Obote, a solid majority in the ninety-one member unicameral National Assembly. At the constitutional conference held at Marlborough House in London in June, Obote played a major role in drafting the new compromise constitution, which made due allowances for the separatist aspirations of the kingdoms.

Amid festivities, on October 9, 1962 Uganda ended sixty-eight years as a British protectorate, as the black, yellow, and red Ugandan flag replaced the Union Jack. In a news conference that same day, Obote declared that his country was ready to take its place in the British Commonwealth and the United Nations, determined to remain neutral between East and West, and prepared to support all African nationalist movements while emphatically rejecting the white supremacist regimes of South Africa, Rhodesia, and the Portuguese colonies. He announced amnesty for thousands of political prisoners and praised the contributions of Uganda's white and Asian minorities, assuring them that they had nothing to fear from the African majority.

The alliance between nationalism and traditionalism in Uganda formally took effect in October 1963, after a year of independence, when the Kabaka of Buganda was installed in the ceremonial office of President, an arrangement that Obote had persuaded his reluctant party colleagues to accept in the interest of national unity. Meanwhile, Obote at first managed to maintain the precarious balance of forces within his country. In the spring of 1963 he succeeded in suppressing a separatist movement in Uganda's western province, and early in 1964 he enlisted British aid in quelling a mutiny in the army. Despite his stated preference for a socialist one-party state and his efforts to establish cordial relations with Moscow and Peking, he encouraged private investment and development aid from the United States and other Western nations. In May 1963 he joined thirty other African heads of government in signing the original charter of the Organization of African Unity. His government's $250,000,000 economic development plan, announced in July 1963, was based on a program drafted by a World Bank mission. In addition to the Prime Ministership, Obote assumed responsibility for the ministries of defense and foreign affairs from 1963 to 1965.

The uneasy alliance between the UPC and Buganda's Kabaka Yekka party broke up in August 1964 over the long-standing "lost counties" issue, which involved the return of territory taken by the British from the kingdom of Bunyoro and given to Buganda in the late nineteenth century. The transfer of the lands in question, following a popular referendum, fueled Buganda's opposition to the central government. Meanwhile, defections from the other parties during 1964 and 1965 gave the UPC a substantial majority in the National Assembly, ostensibly moving Uganda toward the status of a one-party state. At the same time, however, the unity of the UPC was increasingly threatened by tribal, ideological, and religious divisions.

The Obote government underwent a major crisis in early 1966 when an opposition spokesman charged the Prime Minister, along with deputy army commander Idi Amin and others, with having misappropriated some $350,000 in proceeds from gold and ivory captured during the 1964-65 revolt in the former Belgian Congo. Denouncing the charges as a frameup, Obote accused his opponents of plotting with foreign nations against him. On February 22, 1966 he assumed all powers of government and ordered the arrest of five members of his Cabinet who had supported the allegations. To forestall a move by the opposition to unseat him, he suspended the 1962 constitution two days later.

On April 15, 1966 Obote was installed in the office of executive President for a five-year term under a new constitution that greatly expanded the powers of the central government. The Kabaka of Buganda called the Prime Minister's seizure of the government illegal and ordered the Obote government in Kampala out of Bugandan territory. In May 1966 Obote surrounded the Kabaka's palace on Kampala's Mengo Hill with government troops under Idi Amin, who was now the army commander. After much bloody fighting, Bugandan forces were subdued, the Kabaka was forced into exile in London, and emergency regulations were imposed in Buganda. On September 8, 1967 Uganda formally became a republic after the National Assembly officially adopted the new constitution, which abolished the four hereditary kingdoms and concentrated powers over state, government, and armed forces in the Presidency. By August 1968 the parliamentary opposition had dwindled to six out of eighty-nine National Assembly seats.

Under Obote's virtual one-man rule, Uganda for a time experienced relative political stability and economic prosperity. In mid-1966 his government launched a new five-year economic development plan to diversify agricultural production and expand industry. Although he resorted to repression when he thought it necessary, he encouraged communication between the government and the people and devoted much effort to reconciling tribal and religious differences. In December 1967 he led his country into an East African Economic Community with Kenya and Tanzania. Obote enhanced his international prestige by serving as a mediator in the Nigerian civil war of 1968-69 and by acting as host to Pope Paul VI, whose trip to Uganda in the summer of 1969 made him the first pontiff to visit an African nation.

A "move to the left" was launched by Obote in October 1969, when he introduced a "Common Man's Charter" aimed at "creating a new political culture and . . . way of life," with the means of production in the hands of "the people as a whole." On December 19, 1969, at the close of a UPC conference that unanimously approved the charter, an attempt was made on the life of Obote, who suffered facial wounds. A state of national emergency was declared, and six persons were arrested for their part in the assassination plot, allegedly instigated by a member of the Bugandan royal family.

Once recovered from his wounds, Obote went ahead with his plans for socialization and "Ugandanization" of the economy during 1970. In January his government imposed restrictions on merchants who were non-citizens.

On May Day he announced that most of the country's import and export trade would be nationalized and that the government would acquire a 60 percent interest in manufacturing and other industries. In July 1970 Obote introduced new electoral laws aimed at eliminating voting along tribal lines, and in August the UPC passed a resolution that the party president would also be the President of Uganda, thus ensuring that Obote would be returned to office without opposition. But Obote's centralization and modernization efforts failed to take root in the essentially pluralist and traditionalist Ugandan society, and discontent was mounting on all levels.

Although Obote had at first maintained harmonious relations with Idi Amin, whom he promoted to major general in 1968, he soon regarded the army commander as a potential rival. The President steadily built up the strength of his own special corps of loyal Langi troops, and while Amin was visiting Cairo in September 1970, he moved to consolidate his control over the Army. But Amin, on his return, took advantage of the discontent with Obote's rule and took steps to ensure the support of the key elements of the army and police for himself.

On January 25, 1971, while Obote was attending a Commonwealth Prime Ministers' conference in Singapore, Amin staged a coup and installed a military regime in Kampala. At first the overthrow of Obote was welcomed by many Ugandans, after Amin assured them that he had no personal political ambitions. But before long, Amin seized absolute power and launched an eight-year reign of terror seldom equaled in world history, during which thousands were massacred, executed, or driven into exile. The steady deterioration of the economy was aggravated by Amin's expulsion of noncitizen Asians, who had dominated Ugandan commerce and industry, and Uganda's formerly friendly relations with Great Britain, the United States, and Israel were in a shambles.

Meanwhile, Obote, who still considered himself President of Uganda, had been granted asylum in Tanzania by President Julius Nyerere, along with some political supporters and about 1,000 loyal soldiers. While living quietly with his family in a beach house near Dar es Salaam, he kept abreast of events in Uganda, hoping for an opportunity to topple the Amin regime. In September 1972, following a year of tension between Uganda and Tanzania, Obote's exile forces, with the approval of Nyerere, launched an unsuccessful attack on Uganda. Breaking an eighteen-month silence, in May 1973 he sent a letter addressed to African heads of state, in which he accused the Amin regime of killing tens of thousands of Ugandans. Little was heard from him again until January 1979, when he denounced "the fascist dictator" Amin, who, he contended, had transformed Uganda into "a human slaughterhouse."

Renewed border clashes between Uganda and Tanzania prompted Nyerere, urged on by Obote and his supporters, to invade Uganda with Tanzanian and exile troops in February 1979. On April 12 Kampala fell to the invaders, and Amin fled to Libya. Obote had been regarded as the most likely successor to Amin, but there was considerable opposition to him among the political parties that had been formed in exile. The most important was the Uganda National Liberation Front (UNLF), a broad-based coalition, whose leaders felt that an early return to Uganda by Obote might promote disunity. Following Amin's downfall, the UNLF installed Dr. Yusuf K. Lule, a nonpolitical academician, as provisional President, and when he proved unable to cope with the problems of the ravaged country, he was replaced in June 1979 by the lawyer Godfrey Binaisa.

In May 1980, following the ouster of Binaisa by a six-member military commission, whose chairman, Paulo Muwanga, was a close ally of Obote, the former President returned to Uganda after a nine-year absence and launched his campaign for the Presidency under the banner of his own UPC. In the months that followed, he campaigned throughout the country, promising to promote peace and prosperity and to weed out poverty, corruption, and tribalism, while playing down his earlier socialist views.

In the midst of the campaign, on September 17, 1980, the ruling military commission expelled all non-UPC members from the twenty-eight member Cabinet. Obote was further aided in his campaign by the military, which made its planes, vehicles, and security troops available to him. His position was also enhanced by the fact that electoral districts were drawn up in such a way as to give a clear advantage to the northern region from which he drew his strength. Futhermore, in seventeen districts opposition candidates were disqualified, permitting UPC members to be elected unopposed in those constituencies.

Surrounded by chaos and maladministration, on December 9, 1980 Ugandans went to the polls for the first time in eighteen years. When it appeared that the rival Democratic party, led by Paul Ssemogerere, might be winning, the military commission chairman Muwanga personally took charge of the vote-counting. The election results, announced on December 13, gave the UPC a clear majority in the 126-member Parliament. A sixty-member Commonwealth observer team conceded that the elections had been fair, although some of its members expressed skepticism. As the leader of the winning party, Obote was sworn in as President for a five-year term on December 15, 1980 and promised a government of national conciliation in which his opponents would be invited to join.

During the first few months after his return to the Presidency, Obote tried to bring Uganda gradually back to normalcy by cementing relations with other African countries, seeking aid from the International Monetary Fund and the United Nations Development Program, devaluing the currency, and curbing the power of the military. But by the spring of 1981 Uganda seemed to be once more on the road to chaos, largely because of the actions of such dissident groups as the Popular Resistance Army and the Uganda Freedom movement, which attacked police and army installations, wrecked communications, and sabotaged the country's vital coffee crop.

The disorder was exacerbated by tribal unrest, economic instability, crime, the lack of discipline in the armed forces, and the exodus of the 10,000 Tanzanian peace-keeping troops that had remained in Uganda after the downfall of Idi Amin. The Obote government responded by reactivating the dreaded State Research Bureau, which had been Amin's chief agency of repression, by arresting and executing the opponents of the regime, and by closing down the newspapers of the opposition.

Dr. Apollo Milton Obote—who once quipped, "I'd rather have Milton's brains than Apollo's good looks"—has several children by three marriages. His third marriage, to Miria Kalule, a Buganda tribeswoman and a former secre-

tary at Uganda's U.N. mission, took place on November 9, 1963. Obote's doctorate is an honorary LL.D. awarded to him in 1963 by Long Island University in New York, apparently by arrangement with the United States State Department. He also holds an honorary degree from New Delhi University in India. Little is known of Obote's personal life, except that he is a voracious reader, and that he sometimes goes for days without food as a form of self-discipline. His church is the Uganda Anglican. Obote "oscillates between congeniality and belligerency" and sometimes "rages at his ministers as if they were schoolboys," according to Edward R. F. Sheehan, who also described him in the New York Times Magazine as "a pure political animal" with "an almost mystical understanding of the mechanics and sources of power."

References: African Index 3:39+ Je 25 '80; N Y Times Mag p36+ Ja 22 '67 pors; Africa Yearbook and Who's Who, 1977; Daggs, Eliza. All Africa (1970); Gingyera-Pinycwa, A.G.G. Apollo Milton Obote and His Times (1978); International Who's Who, 1981-82; Mittelman, James H. Ideology and Politics in Uganda (1975); Who's Who in Africa (1973)

Packwood, Bob

Sept. 11, 1932- United States Senator from Oregon. Address: b. 13221 Dirksen Senate Office Building, Washington, D.C. 20510

In 1968 Bob Packwood, a young and relatively unknown state legislator and lawyer, scored one of the major political upsets of that year when he unseated the venerable four-term incumbent Wayne Morse to become Oregon's junior member of the United States Senate. Since then, Packwood has been an outspoken proponent of such progressive policies as environmental protection, Congressional reform, population control, and family planning. He is probably the most persistent and eloquent defender of federal abortion funding in the Senate. Drawing his support from a broad-based coalition of environmentalists, women's groups, businessmen, and organized labor, he has won reelection to three consecutive terms, most recently in 1980.

A moderate-liberal Republican, Packwood has repeatedly chastised party regulars for failing to develop practical alternatives to Democratic party programs, particularly in social welfare legislation. To establish a national Republican consensus, formulate feasible policies, and dispel the public's perception of the party as a stronghold of "ingrained negativism," to use David S. Broder's phrase, he instituted, in the mid-1960's, annual brainstorming conferences for selected party leaders. Packwood's influence in the party increased substantially in 1979, when he defeated Senator James A. McClure, a conservative, for the chairmanship of the Senate's Republican Conference Committee, an important secondary leadership post. In January 1981 Packwood took over as chairman of the influential Commerce, Science and Transportation Committee, which oversees, among other things, consumer product safety, interstate commerce, railroad, airline, and bus transportation, gas pipelines, oil spills, commercial fishing, and economic development.

A great-grandson of William H. Packwood, an early settler of Oregon and a delegate to the Oregon Constitutional Convention in 1857, Robert William Packwood was born on September 11, 1932 in Portland, Oregon to Frederick William and Gladys (Taft) Packwood. His father, a professional lobbyist, represented the interests of Oregon Associated Industries in the state legislature. Frederick Packwood, who was interested in political science, instilled in his son a sense of the importance of public service. Following his graduation from Portland's Grant High School in 1950, Bob Packwood enrolled at Willamette University in Salem, Oregon. There he majored in political science and took an active part in campus politics, serving as president of Beta Theta Pi, his social fraternity, and of the local Young Republicans chapter. After obtaining his B.A. degree in 1954, he studied law at New York University on a Root Tilden scholarship. During his years there, he was elected president of the law school's student body.

Immediately after receiving his LL.B. degree in 1957, Packwood accepted a year's appointment as law clerk to former Oregon Supreme Court Justice Harold W. Warner. Following that assignment, he joined the Portland law office of Koerner, Young, McCulloch and Defendorf, where he remained until 1963, when he signed on with Mize, Kriesien, Fewless and Douglas, another local legal firm. In 1965 Packwood and several of his associates formed their own firm—Packwood, McMurray and Stearns—to specialize in the practice of labor law. Throughout that period, Packwood took part in local Republican politics. Among other responsibilities, he served as national committeeman of the Oregon Young Republicans, in 1957, and as chairman of the Multnomah County Republican Central Committee, in 1960.

In 1962 Packwood decided to run for the Oregon state legislature. Relying heavily on volunteer workers, mainly door-to-door canvassers, he racked up an easy victory with the widespread support of middle-class voters of both parties, who responded favorably to his brand of liberal Republicanism. State Republican leaders were so impressed by Packwood's organizational abilities and by his skill as a campaigner that they prevailed upon him to coach potential party candidates. Two years later, six of his nine protégés bucked the nationwide Democratic tide to win election to state offices. Packwood himself was reelected to the state legislature by comfortable margins in 1964 and 1966.

Dissatisfied with the lackadaisical Oregon Republican organization, Packwood convened, in 1965, the first of several annual unofficial party conferences to discuss the problems and assess the future of the Republican party in the state. Out of those informal meetings of about 300 Republicans grew a nucleus of staunch Packwood supporters known as the EPS (Elect Packwood Somehow) Committee. With the enthusiastic backing of that group, Packwood set his sights on national office and, in 1968, announced that he was a candidate for the United States Senate chair held since 1945 by Wayne Morse, an outspoken independent Democrat.

Packwood easily turned aside a challenge by John Boyd in the Republican primary, taking 88 percent of the votes, but Morse proved to be a more formidable opponent. Capitalizing on his Senate seniority, the canny campaign veteran belittled his opponent's inexperience, but Packwood, turning Morse's ridicule to his advantage, played up his youth, vigor, and fresh approach in a campaign schedule that took him to virtually every town in the state. In his standard stump speech he outlined his moderate political platform and then zeroed in on the incumbent's ultraliberal voting record. Aided by an army of some 30,000 well-organized volunteers, Packwood trailed badly in the early days of the campaign, but he gradually gained ground, and on election day in November, he won by the slim margin of 3,445 votes. After a recount, Morse finally conceded defeat on December 30, 1968. The official vote tally gave Packwood 408,645 votes to Morse's 405,382.

Even as the youngest member of the Senate, Packwood had considerable impact in Congress. Shortly after taking his seat in January 1969, he launched an attack on the entrenched and, in his opinion, undemocratic seniority system. "In a nation dedicated to democratic ideals, it is an anomaly for the Senate to elevate men to key positions of leadership without regard to any qualification except length of service," he declared in a speech on the Senate floor on August 24, 1970. "Even the law of the jungle operates on the principle of survival of the fittest. Congress operates only on the principle of survival. . . . Long service does not necessarily produce expertise. Natural ability, devoted interest, and detailed study do." During his first few years in office, the junior Senator submitted several bills calling for the election of committee chairmen rather than automatic promotion based on longevity, and he also suggested other reforms, such as the elimination of the filibuster and the adoption of the so-called "rule of germaneness" that would restrict amendments to the scope of the bill.

Determined to avoid the charges of neglect of his constituents that had occasionally been leveled at his controversial predecessor, Packwood kept in close contact with Oregon public officials and made frequent visits to his home state. He paid particular attention to the concerns of the lumber and fishing industries, on which Oregon's economy largely depends, but it was as an environmentalist that he perhaps best represented the interests of his state. Before the end of his first term, Packwood proposed or cosponsored more than two dozen environmental protection bills, including measures to preserve natural wilderness areas, protect whales and other endangered species, control air and water pollution, and fund conservation projects. He was especially distressed by the wholesale destruction of the natural environment in the frantic search for oil and coal. "We are at a place in the history of this great nation when we cannot bargain away our few remaining natural treasures to meet short-range needs without giving full consideration to alternative means with far less environmental impact," he explained to an interviewer for Ralph Nader's Congress Project. "Indeed we cannot afford this extravagance." He urged the development of safe, clean, and inexhaustible sources of energy, such as solar and geothermal power, instead of the current American dependence on nonrenewable fossil fuels.

Recognizing that unchecked population growth imposes an inordinate strain on the earth's natural resources, Senator Packwood repeatedly spoke out in favor of family planning programs, federally funded contraceptive research, and legalized abortion. "No state has the right to tell a woman she cannot have an abortion any more than it has the right to tell her she must have one," he said in an August 1970 newsletter to his constituents. "The decision to terminate a pregnancy must properly be left to the woman and her private conscience." His conviction that restrictive abortion laws violate an individual's Constitutional right to privacy led him to introduce on April 23, 1970 a bill to legalize abortion and thus end "compulsory pregnancy."

Packwood also sponsored the Family Planning Services and Research Act of 1970, a Senate resolution affirming a national commitment to achieving population stabilization by voluntary means, and legislation limiting to two the number of children a taxpayer can claim as dependents for federal income tax purposes. "This legislation encourages families, but it encourages smaller families," Packwood said, as quoted by George Douth in his *Leaders in Profile* (1975). "And that is what this country needs and must have if we are going to regain our composure. With smaller families, we have a chance to save our environment; without them, we are lost."

In the face of stepped-up opposition from antiabortion groups, Packwood continued his crusade. He endorsed federally funded abortions for the poor, arguing that the government had a "moral obligation" to help those women, and resisted a proposed Constitutional amendment banning abortion. His unreserved public support of reproductive freedom earned him the Margaret Sanger Award from the Planned Parenthood Federation of America, the Blessings of Freedom Award from Religious Leaders for a Free Choice, and several awards from the National Abortion Rights League.

Congressional Quarterly measured Packwood's overall support of the first-term programs and policies of President Richard Nixon at 63 percent. He most consistently backed the President in foreign affairs, including his handling of the Vietnam war, but as the war in Southeast Asia escalated, he became increasingly skeptical. Troubled by the "isolationist pall" the conflict cast over the country, he voted in favor of a number of end-the-war bills, including the 1970 Cooper-Church amendment barring American combat operations in Cambodia. The Senator's growing disenchantment with the Republican President was reflected in his voting record, for his approval of Nixon Administration programs slumped from a high of 76 percent in 1969 to 37 percent in 1974.

The Watergate revelations were, in Packwood's words, a "dagger in the heart" of the Republican party, and he was among the first members of Congress to call for the appointment of a special prosecutor to investigate possible White House complicity in the scandals. Nevertheless he, like many of his colleagues, suffered from his association with the disgraced party. In the off-year election of 1974, as voters turned their backs on dozens of Republicans, the Senator successfully staved off a determined challenge by Democratic State Senator Betty Roberts. Six years later, in 1980, he took 52 percent of the vote to overcome a well-financed assault by a coalition of antiabortionists and conservatives and win reelection to a third term.

In the wake of Watergate, Packwood renewed his efforts to clean up election campaigns. To replace what he called the "mishmash of Presidential extravaganzas," he proposed five regional primaries and the direct election of the President and Vice-President. In other domestic affairs, he called for tax reform to eliminate discrimination against unmarried taxpayers, tax credits for private school tuition, credit allocation to help control inflation, and the passage of the Kemp-Roth across-the-board tax-cut bill. Although he turned down a measure to contain spiraling hospital costs, he came out in favor of an insurance plan for catastrophic illness, primarily because it might help to squelch demands for a "British-style, or Kennedy-style national health service," as he called it.

As a fervent believer in the free enterprise system, the Senator approved the deregulation of the trucking industry and the telephone communications industry, turned down a federal bail-out of the failing Chrysler Corporation, and recommended the breaking up of commercial monopolies, like the major oil companies, so that, as he put it, "we might return to the numerous small- and medium-size competitive industries that made this country grow and continue to be needed to keep this country great." Over the years, he consistently supported an aggressive, well-defined foreign policy. In this regard, he was especially critical of

President Jimmy Carter, who was, in his view, largely responsible for the decrease in American military preparedness and the decline of American influence abroad. In 1981 he was a leader in the Senate floor fight against the controversial proposed sale of A'WACS radar surveillance planes to Saudi Arabia. "Selling military equipment, including AWACS, to Saudi Arabia will not lead to peace in the Middle East," he explained, as quoted in the Chicago Tribune (October 4, 1981).

Throughout his public career Packwood has generally shared the traditional Republican distrust of big government. "When I came here, maybe I came with the same kind of feeling that others come here with, that somehow there is a magic in Washington, that we have some superior knowledge, that God has spoken to us and only us, and we will translate what God says to the states and the local governments," he said on the Senate floor on January 29, 1976. "I no longer share that view. I have come to the conclusion that we cannot run this country well from Washington, D.C." He contended that local officials know more about their social welfare needs than "some middle-echelon, pettifogging bureaucrat in the bowels of HEW," and he vigorously defended expanded revenue-sharing plans and other proposals to return more decision-making authority to state and local governments. As an alternative to the ambitious Great Society social programs of the 1960's, which had fallen "woefully short" of their objectives, Packwood suggested turning over service programs, including day care, legal assistance, income security, home loans, health care, and even advanced education, to the private sector through a combination of labor-management agreements and tax credits.

To help the demoralized Republican party prepare for the 1980 election, Packwood invited about fifty Republican officeholders to attend the first annual Tidewater Conference in Easton, Maryland in March 1978. "You have to show cohesion among your Congressional and statewide Republic officials to have credibility as a party," he explained, as quoted in David S. Broder's book Changing of the Guard (1980). "I'm trying to find those issues upon which we agree and the elected Democrats disagree. And then make those our Republican platform."

Bob Packwood is an athletic six-footer with green eyes and sandy brown hair, who keeps his weight at about 180 pounds by swimming and by pitching for his Senate staff's softball team. After an arduous day on Capitol Hill, he often listens to classical music to relax. He and his wife, the former Georgia Ann Oberteuffer, whom he married on November 25, 1964, live in a red-brick, colonial-style house in Bethesda, Maryland with their two children, William Henderson and Shyla. Packwood has received awards from the Oregon Environmental Council, Greenpeace of Oregon, and the Omaha Woodmen Life Insurance Society, among others, for his contribution to environmental protection, and from the National Association of Blue Shield Plans, the National Health Federation, and the Ontario Podiatry Association for his health care efforts.

References: Biog N p1437 D '74 por; Broadcasting 92:56 Mr 28 '77 por; Nat Observer p1+ O 21 '68 por; Nation 208:205+ F 17 '69; N Y Times A p24 O 6 '81 por; Time 92:15 N 22 '68, 101:19 Ja 15 '73; Douth, George. *Leaders in Profile* (1975); Who's Who in American Politics, 1979-80

Pérez Esquivel, Adolfo (pã'rãs ãs-kē-vel')

Nov. 26, 1931- Argentine human rights activist. Address: b. c/o Servicio Paz y Justicia, Mexico 479, (1097) Buenos Aires, Argentina

The surprise winner of the 1980 Nobel Peace Prize was Adolfo Pérez Esquivel, the devout Roman Catholic Argentine human rights activist, who at the time was almost unknown even to the public in his own country. Nominated for the peace prize by its 1976 winners, Mairead Corrigan and Betty Williams of Ulster, Pérez Esquivel was chosen from a record number of candidates. In honoring him, the Nobel committee cited him for having "shone a light in the darkness" of strife-torn Argentina, and for having "devoted his life to the struggle for human rights since 1974," the year in which he became general coordinator of the Service for Peace and Justice, a church-based network of organizations working for social justice in Latin America by nonviolent means.

Before dedicating himself to the battle for human rights in his native Argentina, Pérez Esquivel was a sculptor and professor of architecture. Since the armed forces took power in Argentina in 1976, he has concentrated his efforts in behalf of the tens of thousands of Argentines imprisoned and tortured by the military regime—especially the so-called *desaparecidos* or "disappeared ones," who have vanished without a trace—with the result that he was himself jailed without trial and held for more than a year. On the day he learned that he had been awarded the Nobel Peace Prize he told Edward Schumacher of the New York *Times* (October 14, 1980): "I accept this prize in the name of Latin America and its workers, in the name of its *campesinos,* and its priests who are working diligently for the peace and rights of all."

Because of Pérez Esquivel's ingrown reticence and the scant amount of public attention he attracted before winning the Nobel Peace Prize, Edward Schumacher described him in his article as "a backrooms man, a committee organizer, not a charismatic public leader." It is therefore not surprising that relatively little is known about his background. He was born on November 26, 1931 to a Spanish fisherman who had immigrated to Argentina and his wife, who died when Adolfo was very young. The boy spent very little time with his father, who became a commercial representative for coffee firms. Although the family was poor, Adolfo attended private schools, where he acquired the habit of voracious reading. Prowling through the second-hand bookstalls of Buenos Aires, he found himself especially attracted to religious subjects, even as a teenager. In an interview with Carla Hall of the Washington *Post* (November 20, 1980) he recalled: "I read Gandhi's autobiography, where he says nonviolence is not just for saints. I read Thomas Merton, a Catholic monk. I was very impressed by his spiritualness. I read St. Augustine." He began to meet with other Argentines in small groups that combined prayer and reflection with social welfare concerns.

After graduating from his private secondary school, Pérez Esquivel enrolled at the National School of Fine Arts of Buenos Aires and La Plata. For the next fifteen years following his graduation from that institution on October 11, 1956, he pursued a successful and politically detached career as a sculptor and professor of art at the Manuel Belgrano National School of Fine Arts in Buenos Aires and at other art schools in or near the capital. When his sculptures were widely exhibited in Argentina, he won several prizes, including the important Premio La Nación de Escultura. His work is in the collections of the Buenos Aires Museum of Modern Art, the Museum of Fine Arts in Córdoba, and the fine Arts Museum of Rosario.

During the earlier years of his career as a sculptor, Pérez Esquivel explored themes from Latin American art and history. His 1966 terra cotta work *Templo del Sol* (Temple of the Sun), for example, employs rough architectural forms and a primitive standing figure reminiscent of pre-Columbian clay figurines. In a pamphlet that was published by the Argentine Ecumenical Movement for Human Rights while Pérez Esquivel was in prison, he is quoted as having said, "While all the contributions of different cultures and artistic movements combine in our epoch into a universal language that reflects today's problems, I feel the need to find in our American roots the means of expression in symbols and signs that can fuse with today's concerns. For that reason I'm interested in deeper knowledge of Pre-Columbian cultures." Another theme often found in Pérez Esquivel's work is that of motherhood. His *Monumento a la Madre* (Monument to Mothers) stands in the Argentine city of Azúl, and another with the same subject can be seen in Bernal. But by the late 1960's the social and religious ideas that were increasingly important to Pérez Esquivel came to dominate his sculpture.

Those later years of Pérez Esquivel's artistic career were difficult ones for his country, for Argentina had never recovered from the bitter class antagonisms exploited by Juan Domingo Perón, the populist dictator overthrown by the military in 1955. The urban industrial class, organized into strong unions, and the lower-middle classes remained passionately committed to Peronism, but the military was determined not to let the exiled dictator or his followers return to power. The result was a long and ultimately catastrophic political stalemate. Repression by a succession of military governments led many young Peronists and leftists to go underground and to organize urban guerrilla armies. By the early 1970's they were carrying out acts of terrorism that invited even more severe response from the armed forces.

The progressive unraveling of Argentina's political fabric, and the wretched conditions in which much of its population still lived, led Pérez Esquivel to turn from the absorptions of his artistic and academic career to political activism. In 1968 he attended a conference in Montevideo, Uruguay, where representatives of church, labor, student, intellectual, and community groups discussed means of achieving "change and development . . . through a process of nonviolent liberation," as Pérez Esquivel later described it. That conference was only one manifestation of a trend then developing throughout Latin America: the growing involvement of clergymen and deeply committed lay activists in social issues in behalf of the poor. At the 1968 meeting in Montevideo the "basic structure" of the Service for Justice and Peace (its full name in Spanish is the Servicio de Paz y Justicia en América Latina, Orientación No-Violenta) was created. At a second conference, held in Costa Rica in 1971, the Servicio was formally founded.

That same year Pérez Esquivel joined an Argentine group dedicated to Gandhian principles of "militant nonviolence," and one of his first projects was to organize weaving, carpentry, and ironworking workshops in urban neighborhoods to achieve the Gandhian goal of self-support through craft industry. In 1972 he carried out a hunger strike to protest the violence perpetrated both by terrorists and by police forces in Argentina; in 1973 he founded a monthly magazine, *Paz y Justicia* (Peace and Justice) that was later adopted as the official publication of the Service; and in 1974, at a conference in Medellín, Colombia, he was named general coordinator of the service, whose headquarters were officially established in Buenos Aires during that year.

From its inception, the Service for Peace and Justice has been a loosely structured, ecumenical network of disparate organizations pledged to maintain close contact and support each other's efforts. Its basic outlook was best enunciated by Pérez Esquivel in an interview with Larry Rohter of *Newsweek* (October 27, 1980). "Unjust structures must be changed," he said. "But only through nonviolence can those structures be transformed to build a more just and humane society." Such a commitment to pacifism, however, was not a common stance in Latin America, and for the first years of its existence the major task of the Service for Peace and Justice was simply to bring isolated groups in distant countries into touch with each other. To that end, Pérez Esquivel resigned his teaching positions and traveled tirelessly throughout South and Central America. In 1974 he launched a campaign in behalf of Indians in Ecuador whose attempts to acquire land were being repressed, and in the following year he visited Paraguay to help organize protests against the government's attacks on the church-organized Agrarian Leagues. During a trip to Brazil in 1975 he was briefly jailed, and he was arrested again in Ecuador in 1976, a year in which he also traveled to the United States and Europe.

Meanwhile, in Argentina matters were moving from bad to worse. Péron's return and his election to the presidency in 1973 had little calming effect, and after Perón's death in 1974, his widow and successor, Isabel Perón, proved incapable of halting the slide into chaos. Raging inflation, pervasive official corruption, terrorism in the cities and guerrilla warfare in the countryside finally led the armed forces to seize power on March 24, 1976 and install as president the army commander in chief, General Jorge Rafael Videla, who with the junta set out to crush the Argentine left with extraordinary brutality. In 1976 and 1977 tens of thousands of Argentines were jailed and tortured without charges or trial, and countless others fled into exile. Anyone suspected of the least sympathy or connection with leftist or Peronist activities was vulnerable. Many of the victims were kidnapped and murdered by right-wing paramilitary death squads apparently operating with the sanction of the government.

In the face of that wave of terror, and similar repression by neighboring military regimes in Chile, Bolivia, Paraguay, Brazil, and Uruguay, the Service for Peace and Justice concentrated its efforts on the defense of human rights. Pérez Esquivel led a campaign to publicize and press for enforcement of the Universal Declaration on Human Rights of the United Nations. Within Argentina, he helped found the Ecumenical Movement for Human Rights and served as president of the Permanent Assembly for Human Rights. His public denunciations of government atrocities did not endear him to the authorities, and in 1976, while he was traveling abroad, his headquarters of the Service for Peace and Justice in Buenos Aires were occupied and ransacked by security forces. On April 4, 1977, when Pérez Esquivel went to a local police station on a routine matter, he was arrested without warning and jailed.

During the fifteen months of Pérez Esquivel's imprisonment he was never formally charged, although the government let it be known that he was being held as a "subversive." He was severely tortured, an experience he refuses to discuss in detail, but constant prayer and the performance of yoga exercises whenever possible helped him resist the attempt to break his morale. Of the ordeal of torture, he said in a 1980 interview, "When you experience this extreme situation of being between life and death, you try to understand what Christ said on the cross: 'Father, forgive them, for they don't know what they are doing.' But I thought that, yes, these people *did* know what they were doing. This was very contradictory for me, and I tried to understand more deeply.... what was it that Christ was trying to say to us in this supreme moment? ... What I discovered, little by little, was that what [the torturers] did not know was that they were persons, and that we were persons. They had lost their identities."

Almost from the moment of his arrest, an international campaign took shape to demand Pérez Esquivel's release. While he was still in prison, important religious leaders called for his release, Mairead Corrigan and Betty Williams nominated him for the Nobel Peace Prize, Amnesty International adopted him as a prisoner of conscience, and the Carter Administration interceded with the Argentine government. The Argentine government finally released Pérez Esquivel in June 1978, but for nine more months he was kept under house arrest. Resuming his work, in 1980 he made another tour through Europe, by which time repression in Argentina had eased somewhat, largely because the junta had won its "war" on the left. But Pérez Esquivel insisted that Argentines be informed of the fate of the estimated 10,000 to 20,000 *desaparecidos,* and he began working closely with the women known as "Las Locas de Mayo" (the madwomen of May Square), who meet each week in a central plaza of Buenos Aires to protest and demand information about their missing relatives.

The award of the Nobel Peace Prize to Pérez Esquivel on October 13, 1980, after the committee had considered a record number of fifty-seven individual and seventeen organizational candidates, was clearly intended to aid his efforts in behalf of Argentine political prisoners. The citation stated that "Pérez Esquivel is among those Argentines who have shown a light in the darkness. He champions a solution of Argentina's grievous problems that dispenses with the use of violence, and is the spokesman of a revival of respect for human rights. ... The prizewinner is an Argentinian, but the views he represents carry a vital message to many other countries, not the least in Latin America, where social and political problems as yet unresolved have resulted in an escalation of the use of violence." Shocked and angered by the flurry of international publicity that accompanied the award, the Argentine government at first maintained a stony silence, while the tightly controlled media tried to play down the significance of the story. Some days later the government issued a statement that defended its jailing of Pérez Esquivel on the grounds that he had "contributed to the cause of those who promote terrorism in the nation." Meanwhile, congratulations poured in from all over the world, from such personages as Willy Brandt, Edward M. Kennedy, and Joan Baez.

Shortly after winning the Nobel Peace Prize, Pérez Esquivel traveled to the United States for a one-week tour that took him to New York City, Philadelphia, Washington, and Phoenix, where he addressed the annual convention of the Associated Press Managing Editors Association. He met with U.N. Secretary General Kurt Waldheim, with members of Congress, and with Rosalynn Carter and was awarded an honorary Doctorate of Humanities from St. Joseph's University in Philadelphia. Throughout his brief visit he stressed the theme that human rights issues are inextricably linked to economic ones. As he told Larry Rohter, "You cannot talk solely of human rights in terms of torture and imprisonment and killing. True, this is the gravest aspect. But we must also look at the case of the peasant who has no land and is dying of hunger." On December 10, 1980 he received the Nobel Prize in Oslo, Norway, where he attacked "the old, well-known, and dilapidated structure of injustice" in his acceptance speech. He added: "The rules of this play, which have been laid down by the big powers and have been inflicted upon the rest of the world, also permit the biggest crime of our time, the arms race." The Argentine ambassador was conspicuously absent from the ceremony.

Adolfo Pérez Esquivel is a slim man with thinning dark hair, usually disheveled, and the intense, austere appearance that one associates with a religious activist. He is usually described as being modest, soft-spoken and patient. His shabby, almost bare office in the Buenos Aires headquarters of the Service for Peace and Justice has pictures of Pope John Paul II and of Gandhi tacked on the wall. Pérez Esquivel married his wife, Amanda, in 1956; they have three sons, the oldest of whom, Leonardo, is a staff member of the Service for Peace and Justice and helped to run the organization while his father was in prison. The family lives in a modest house designed by Pérez Esquivel himself in the upper-class Buenos Aires neighborhood of San Isidro. Besides the Nobel Prize, Pérez Esquivel has been awarded the Pope John XXIII Prize in 1977 by the international Catholic organization Pax Christi. Certainly the greatest irony about his Nobel Peace Prize is that the Argentine government passed a law in 1977 providing that any Argentine who won a Nobel Prize would be awarded a lifetime stipend equal to the salary of a Supreme Court Justice—currently about $5,000 a month. Pérez Esquivel finally was granted the lifetime pension in September 1981, ending a five-month delay. His son Leonardo said that the funds will be used to further the work of the Service for Peace and Justice.

References: Fellowship O/N '80 p21+ por; N Y Times A p2 Jl 28 '81 por; Time 116:75 O 27 '80 por

Rambert, Marie

Feb. 20, 1888- Ballet company director. Address: b. Mercury Theatre Trust Ltd., 94 Chiswick High Road, London, W.4, England

Recognized as one of the most important forces in the creation of English ballet, Marie Rambert, the Polish-born founder of the Ballet Rambert, started her professional career in the corps de ballet of Diaghilev's Ballets Russes. Because she began her classical training too late in life to become a top-ranking ballerina herself, she turned to teaching in 1920. From her tiny studio in London came many of the world's greatest dancers, including Alicia Markova, Hugh Laing, Sally Gilmour, Lucette Aldous, and Celia Franca, and the future directors of the Royal Ballet, the National Ballet of Canada, the Australian Ballet, and the Royal Swedish Ballet. But it is her extraordinary flair for identifying and developing choreographic talent that has brought Marie Rambert her greatest distinction.

Of the eight twentieth-century choreographers acknowledged to be "indisputably great" by veteran dance critic Clive Barnes, two—Frederick Ashton and Antony Tudor—were trained and nurtured by Marie Rambert. Among the dozens of lesser-known choreographers who benefited from her artistic vision and indomitable spirit were Agnes DeMille, Andrée Howard, Walter Gore, and Norman Morrice. In

Marie Rambert

her fifty-year career as artistic director of the Ballet Rambert, she oversaw the production of more than 200 works, most of them original efforts by company dancer-choreographers. Although Madame Rambert relinquished the day-to-day management of the company to her co-directors, John Chesworth and Christopher Bruce, in the mid-1970's, hers is still the dominant voice in company policy. Robert North, a former associate director of the London Contemporary Dance Theatre, took over as artistic director in April 1981. Madame Rambert has received the Légion d'Honneur, the Queen Elizabeth II Coronation Award, and the Gold Medal, Order of Merit of the Polish People's Republic. In 1962 she was named Dame Commander of the Order of the British Empire.

The youngest of the three daughters of Yakov Ramberg, a bookseller, and his wife, Yevguenia Alapina, Marie Rambert was born Cyvia Rambam on February 20, 1888 in Warsaw, Poland. Her father and her paternal uncles each adopted a different version of the original family surname, presumably for political reasons, and Madame Rambert herself was known as Myriam Ramberg. She took the name Marie Rambert when she decided to become a professional performer. A lively child with an inquiring mind and an inexhaustible supply of nervous energy, she often improvised dances to short pieces of music or to poems that she recited herself, but she showed little interest in classical ballet because, as she explained to a reporter years later, "there was nothing human about it."

Throughout her childhood and adolescence, Madame Rambert attended a state-run school for girls in Warsaw, where she excelled in languages, history, mathematics, and Russian literature. She also took ballet and social dance classes, although her dancing was undistinguished. After graduating from school in 1904, Madame Rambert became involved in the revolutionary movement against Tzarist domination in Poland, and, fearing for his daughter's safety, Yakov Ramberg sent her to Paris in 1905 to study medicine. Since she was too young to enroll in a medical college, she decided instead to work toward a Certificat d'Etudes Françaises at the Sorbonne. In her spare time she visited art galleries and museums and attended scores of parties. At one costume ball, she dazzled the other guests, among them Raymond Duncan, the brother of the legendary modern dancer Isadora Duncan, with her exuberant performance of a mazurka. Recognizing in her emotional response to the music a natural talent for the dance, Duncan encouraged her to create her own solos, which she subsequently performed at private parties.

On a visit home, Madame Rambert attended a modern dance recital by Isadora Duncan, and profoundly moved by her ecstatic performance, resolved to become a professional dancer. Returning to France, she studied classical ballet with Madame Rat at the Paris Opéra Ballet School, and over the course of several months, prepared a program of Duncan-inspired dances for public presentation. In the summer of 1910 she went to Geneva, Switzerland to take an extensive two-week course at Emile Jaques-Dalcroze's Institute for Applied Rhythm. Jaques-Dalcroze, a Swiss music teacher and theoretician, had developed an organized method of analyzing music by translating rhythm into bodily movements. Fascinated by eurhythmics, as the technique was called, she stayed at the school for more than two years and eventually became a teacher. After observing one of Madame Rambert's classes in movement instruction, Serge Diaghilev, the director of the Ballets Russes, hired her to help Vaslav Nijinsky apply the eurhythmic method to the complicated rhythms of Stravinsky's *Le Sacre du Printemps.*

Joining the Ballets Russes in December 1912, Madame Rambert spent six months helping bewildered dancers to memorize their parts in Nijinsky's daring, unconventional *Sacre* by patiently counting each phrase over and over. After rehearsals she worked on the score with Nijinsky, disentangling the rhythms while he translated every beat into movement. Madame Rambert herself was onstage as a member of the corps de ballet when *Sacre* opened in Paris on May 29, 1913. Because of the almost unanimous public contempt for Nijinsky's strange, angular choreography and for Stravinsky's score, *Le Sacre du Printemps* was performed only six times. Madame Rambert, however, has always insisted that it is a "truly epic ballet," and over the years, she has campaigned tirelessly in behalf of Nijinsky's groundbreaking efforts as a choreographer of the Ballets Russes.

During her tenure with the Ballets Russes, Madame Rambert appeared as a bacchante in *Cléopâtre*, a wili in *Giselle*, a Polovtsian maiden in *Prince Igor*, one of the Shah's wives in *Schéhérazade*, and in corps parts in *Thamar*, *Firebird*, and *Swan Lake*. At the end of the company's extended South American tour in 1913, Diaghilev refused to renew her contract, probably because of her close association with Nijinsky, who had been dismissed following his marriage to a member of the corps de ballet.

Back in Paris, Madame Rambert returned to her ballet classes with Madame Rat and gave occasional performances of original dances at the Théâtre Imperial and in private homes. Late in 1914 she fled to London to escape World War I. There she supported herself by teaching at the London School of Eurhythmics and by giving private dancing lessons to the children of aristocrats. In her spare time she studied classical technique with Serafina Astafieva, a former ballerina with the famed Maryinsky Ballet, and devised ballets with her friend Vera Donnet. Their first effort, *La Pomme d'Or*, which symbolized the awakening of the medieval world to humanism, was produced by the Stage Society at the Garrick Theatre on February 25, 1917.

Following a whirlwind courtship, Marie Rambert married Ashley Dukes, the playwright and drama critic, on March 7, 1918. When Dukes returned to the warfront a few days later, his bride sought distraction and solace in her work. In addition to teaching, she appeared occasionally in music hall revues and collaborated with Vera Donnet on two more ballets, *Fêtes Galantes* and *Les Elégantes*, for the Stage Society. She also took the part of the saucy French maid in the Society's production of the Restoration comedy *The Provok'd Wife*, much to the delight of London's drama critics. Throughout that period she continued to study classical ballet, first with Enrico Cecchetti, the redoubtable former ballet master of the Ballets Russes, then with Margaret Craske.

In 1920 Madame Rambert opened her own ballet studio in Bedford Gardens, London. From the beginning, she selected her professional students with care, looking not only at a prospective pupil's build, physical proportions, hands and feet, but also at his eyes. "It is in the eyes that the soul is reflected," she explained in her autobiography *Quicksilver* (Macmillan, 1972). "They are the criterion by which one can judge an artistic temperament." In class she was a demanding taskmaster, stressing adherence to the geometrically precise classical line above all else. Throughout her long teaching career, Madame Rambert practised along with her students, even while she was pregnant with her two daughters, Angela, who was born in 1920, and Helen, born three years later, and she invariably ended each class with three cartwheels. Determined to turn out well-rounded theatrical artists as well as disciplined dancers, she also commented

regularly on the performances of visiting ballet troupes and frequently discussed art, literature, and music with her students.

As interested in the work of production as she was in the sheer technique of movement, Madame Rambert taught her pupils excerpts from ballets in Diaghilev's repertory and encouraged them to compose their own dances. Under her watchful eye, Frederick Ashton created his first ballet, *A Tragedy of Fashion, or The Scarlet Scissors*, a frothy confection about a dressmaker who commits suicide when a wealthy customer rejects his designs. Madame Rambert danced the role of Orchidée, the couturier's cigar-smoking partner, at the ballet's premiere in Nigel Playfair's revue *Riverside Nights* at the Lyric Theatre, Hammersmith on June 15, 1926.

In 1927 Ashley Dukes purchased a disused parish hall in Notting Hill Gate, London and converted it into the Mercury Theatre. Madame Rambert immediately moved her ballet school into the adjoining building and, from time to time, used the theatre to present productions of her students' ballets. In February 1930 Ashton persuaded her to put on a public matinée of several of his works, including the delightful *Capriol Suite*, his first fully successful ballet. The Marie Rambert Dancers, as the students were collectively known, were so warmly received that Nigel Playfair, the manager of the Lyric Theatre, engaged them for a two-week summer season and for three weeks at Christmas. With the incomparable Tamara Karsavina and Leon Woizikovsky, one of Diaghilev's outstanding character dancers, as her guest artists, Madame Rambert presented, in addition to short ballets by Ashton, Fokine's *Les Sylphides*, *Le Spectre de la Rose*, and *Le Carnaval*. Balletomanes and dance critics, many of whom saw in the fledgling company a probable successor to the great Russian touring companies, were impressed by the surprisingly accomplished performances of the young dancers and by the inventiveness of the apprentice choreographers.

To "preserve the art of ballet in England by forming a permanent company of dancers with a theatre of its own," as they noted in a promotional brochure sent to distinguished members of society and the arts, Madame Rambert and Ashley Dukes established the Ballet Club in late 1930. For the remainder of the decade, Madame Rambert and her dancers, most of whom earned their livings by appearing in films, revues, and musical comedies during the week, gave regular Sunday evening performances in the Mercury Theatre, a 150-seat shoe box with a tiny stage just eighteen feet square. The lilliputian dimensions of the stage and a woefully inadequate budget taxed the ingenuity, imagination, resourcefulness, and patience of performers, choreographers, and designers, all of whom often doubled as scene painters, prop makers, seamstresses, and stagehands. According to A. V. Coton, the British dance historian, it was because of the limitations of the Mercury Theatre stage that Rambert-trained choreographers developed a choreographic and dancing style that demanded, in Coton's words, "precision of timing, great finesse of acting, simplicity of dance images, and a fine standard of costuming, decor, and lighting" rather than " 'broad effects,' 'stage cheating,' and large corps de ballet."

Among the ballets produced by Madame Rambert at the Mercury and at short seasons in the West End during the 1930's were Ashton's *Foyer de Danse*, *Les Masques*, and *Mephisto Valse*; Andrée Howard's *Little Mermaid*, *Lady Into Fox*, and *Death and the Maiden*; Ninette de Valois' *Bar aux Folies-Bergère*; and Walter Gore's *Valse Finale* and *Paris-Soir*. Antony Tudor, a student of hers since the late 1920's, contributed, among other works, two acknowledged masterpieces, *Jardin aux Lilas*, a brilliantly realized melodrama, and *Dark Elegies*, a compelling dance of lamentation set to the Mahler song cycle *Kindertodtenlieder*.

Madame Rambert has described her role in relation to her choreographers as that of "a midwife." "I felt something that can be born is going to be born, and that I helped them to bring it into the world," she explained to Peter Williams in an interview for *50 Years of Ballet Rambert* (1976). "I knew them very well. I knew their characters, and . . . when I felt that they had something creative in them, I think that I then launched them." Largely because of her gift for recognizing and molding the talents of untested choreographers, the Ballet Rambert—the name formally adopted by the company in 1934 at the suggestion of a theatrical booking agent—was, by the end of the decade, firmly established in the minds of British ballet-goers as the wellspring of contemporary English ballet.

When World War II broke out, Madame Rambert temporarily suspended performances, but she was soon back in business, giving up to five performances a day at the Arts Theatre Club in London even at the height of the Blitz. Because of a legal dispute with the manager of the Arts Theatre Club, the company dissolved in September 1941, but it reformed eighteen months later under the auspices of the Council for the Encouragement of Music and the Arts (CEMA), later the Arts Council of Great Britain, to tour wartime training camps, hostels, and factories, and to dance for civilian audiences in the provinces, often on makeshift stages in the open air.

With the financial and moral support of CEMA, Madame Rambert recruited more dancers and annexed to the repertory productions of such classics as the second act of *Swan Lake* and, in 1946, the full-length *Giselle*, both of which demand a sizable corps de ballet. Dissatisfied with contemporary productions of *Giselle*, she had for years longed to produce a recreation of that mid-nineteenth-century classic that mirrored as closely as possible the spirit of Gautier's haunting tale.

At the London premiere on July 11, 1946, critics marveled at the story-book staging and at the extraordinarily emotional performances Madame Rambert had coaxed from her three young principals.

Despite the overwhelmingly favorable critical response to *Giselle* and to *The Sailor's Return*, Andrée Howard's new full-length work, the Ballet Rambert ended its 1947 London season in a precarious financial position. Hoping to add to the company's coffers, Madame Rambert gladly accepted a lucrative offer for a six-month tour of Australia and New Zealand. The six months stretched into eighteen as the Ballet Rambert played night after night to wildly enthusiastic standing-room-only houses in both countries. Although she was then in her sixties, the indefatigable Madame Rambert took all company classes and rehearsals herself and gave as many as ten private professional lessons a week. The transoceanic tour, the first ever undertaken by an English company, was a major triumph. Nevertheless, when the Ballet Rambert returned to London in mid-1949, it was depleted in finances, resources, and numbers. Most of the profits had been eaten up by traveling expenses and by the cost of replacing the sets and costumes lost en route. It was less easy to replace the dancers. Five of the company's principals had remained behind in Australia, and two more had defected to a rival troupe. As optimistic as ever, Madame Rambert, who had been losing promising dancers and choreographers to the Sadler's Wells Ballet, American Ballet Theatre, and other companies for years, patiently rebuilt her company. It took her nearly ten years to bring the troupe back to the status it had enjoyed before the tour to the Antipodes.

Squeezed out of London theatres by the larger, heavily subsidized companies, the Ballet Rambert, which depended for its existence on small grants from the Arts Council and on even smaller private donations, spent most of the 1950's and the early 1960's on the road in Great Britain, Europe, the northeastern United States and, in 1957, the People's Republic of China. To guarantee respectable box-office revenues on tour, Madame Rambert mounted new productions of such crowd-pleasers as *La Sylphide*, *Coppélia*, and *Don Quixote*. The company collected rave notices both at home and abroad, but as Madame Rambert told Clive Barnes in an interview for the New York *Times* (October 30, 1966), the troupe's creative energy was "drained away" by the "dreary succession" of classical ballets. Moreover, without a permanent London base, it was virtually impossible for the company's resident dancer-choreographers to create and rehearse new ballets.

Faced with the prospect of losing the financial support of the Arts Council, Madame Rambert and company choreographer Norman Morrice, whom she named associate director in 1966, reconstituted the Ballet Rambert as a small experimental troupe of eighteen equally-ranking soloists that emphasized choreography and choreographers rather than lavish productions. "We are returning to our very first traditions of being a small highly creative company," Madame Rambert told reporters. In its London debut season at the Jeannetta Cochrane Theatre in the winter of 1966-67, the Ballet Rambert presented new ballets by company principals John Chesworth, Jonathan Taylor, and Amanda Knotts, commissioned works by Pierre Lacotte and Rudi van Dantzig, and revivals of such Rambert staples as *Dark Elegies* and *Jardin aux Lilas*. From 1966 to 1976 the company produced ninety-six new works, most of them created by company members.

Marie Rambert is a tiny, frail woman with sharp, birdlike features, bright, dark eyes, and a mobile mouth. She stopped turning her celebrated cartwheels about twenty years ago, but as recently as 1976, she was doing her daily barre exercises to keep supple. Fluent in five languages, she put her knowledge of Russian to good use in 1962 when she translated M. I. Sizova's *Ulanova: Her Childhood and Schooldays* (A. & C. Black, Ltd.) into English. Having suffered from insomnia since childhood, she often reads late into the night, and she is still passionately fond of the great Russian literary masters. Since the death of her husband in 1959, Madame Rambert has continued to live in the house in Campden Hill Gardens, London that has been her home since the 1920's.

References: Dance 23:9+ O '49 pors, 29:26+ Ag '55 pors, 37:42+ Mr '63 pors, 47:44+ F '73 pors; Dance and Dancers 17:8+ N '66; Guardian p11 F 11 '78 pors; N Y Times II p10 Jl 5 '59; London Sunday Times mag p53+ Je 6 '76 pors; Clarke, Mary. Dancers of Mercury (1962); International Who's Who, 1980-81; Who's Who, 1980-81

Ramey, Samuel

Mar. 28, 1942- Opera singer. Address: b. c/o New York City Opera, Lincoln Center for the Performing Arts, 140 W. 65th St., New York City, N.Y. 10023; c/o Columbia Artists Management Inc., 165 W. 57th St., New York City, N.Y. 10019

As one of the New York City Opera's exemplary success stories, Samuel Ramey, the young basso cantante, is a paradigm of the small-town boy from Middle America who has achieved an international musical reputation through hard work, perseverance, and the unforced but steadily unfolding development of his considerable talents. After working his way through music studies at Wichita State University in Kansas, taking voice lessons in New York City, appearing in regional companies throughout the United States, and weathering the usual series of grueling auditions, Ramey made, in 1973, his debut with the New York City Opera, where he has been a rising star ever since. Meanwhile, his international reputation has escalated with his increasing appearances at such major opera houses as Glyndebourne, the Hamburg Staatsoper, the Vienna Staatsoper, the Paris Opéra, and La Scala in Milan. Endowed with a commanding stage presence and as much at ease in bel canto as he is in the heavier dramatic roles of the later nineteenth century, Ramey is also obtaining more and more worldwide recognition for his recordings with the Angel, Philips, and RCA/Erato labels, and for his appearances in the *Live from Lincoln Center* television series of the Public Broadcasting Service.

A self-described small-town boy from northwestern Kansas, Samuel Ramey was born on March 28, 1942 in Colby, Kansas to Guy Ramey, a meat cutter, and Grace Ramey, who eventually became a county treasurer. His brothers, Leonard and Joe, and his sister, Darlene, are considerably older than he. When he was a child, the Rameys lived for a time in Winona and in Quinter, where he began singing in elementary school. Sam Ramey made his solo debut in a memorable Christmas program at a church in Winona, when he sang one verse of "We Three Kings of Orient Are." After moving to Quinter, he embarked on voice lessons, took part in school music festivals, and found himself in demand as a soloist before he graduated from high school.

Returning to Colby with his family in the middle of his freshman year, Ramey sang in the glee club, boys octet, and mixed chorus at Colby High School. But music was only one of his many extracurricular interests. He played high school basketball and was first baseman on the American Legion youth team until he broke an ankle while trying to slide into second base. Although that accident put a quietus on his high school athletic career, he was still free to write a column for the school paper on the top ten song hits of the month, serve as classes editor of the yearbook, the *Golden Eagle,* and appear in the junior and senior plays. His classmates still treasure memories of his notable performance as the scarecrow in the senior production of *The Wizard of Oz.*

During those formative years an operatic career was far from Ramey's mind, and since the Metropolitan Opera did not deign to tour in northwestern Kansas, he neither saw nor heard an entire opera. During an interview with Gary Lipton for *Opera News* (May 1978), he recalled: "When Ed Sullivan had an opera singer on, I'd think, 'Yecch.' " Singers such as Pat Boone (in emulation of whom he bought a pair of white bucks) and Elvis Presley were Ramey's idols at that time, and he also considered becoming an engineer like his successful brother and brother-in-law.

Instead, after graduating from Colby High School in 1960, Ramey enrolled at Kansas State University with the intention of becoming a teacher of choral music but had to drop out for a year to work at Bernard's clothing store, a haberdashery in his hometown, because of the financial reverses his family suffered after the death of his father. When he returned to college, he transferred to Wichita State University, where he had the good fortune to work with the voice teacher Arthur Newman, who for twenty years had been a charter member of the New York City Opera. One day Ramey happened to hear a recording of Ezio Pinza that was to prove a decisive influence on his career. "I was thrilled with the sound of Pinza's voice," Ramey told Gary Lipton. "It provided my first serious contact with opera." As if in unconscious anticipation of what was to become his lifework, in addition to taking voice studies with Newman, Ramey learned the mastery of body movement in ballet classes and in university dramatic productions.

While still an undergraduate in Wichita, Ramey learned that the Central City Opera in Colorado hired young singers for its chorus on an apprenticeship basis. After submitting a tape recording, he was hired to sing in the chorus for productions of *Don Giovanni* and *Il Trovatore* in the summer of 1963. That provided him with his firsthand introduction to opera, and from his strategic position in the chorus of *Don Giovanni* he heard Norman Treigle perform the role of the legendary Spanish womanizer, an experience that helped him to decide that his life's ambition was to become an opera singer. As one of his later idols, Treigle exerted a marked influence on Ramey's professional career.

Returning from the Rockies of Colorado to the plains of south central Kansas in the fall of 1963, Ramey continued his studies at Wichita State University, where he appeared in such university operatic productions as Carl Orff's *Der Mond.* He worked his way through school slowly, supporting himself with such jobs as driving a delivery truck and selling shoes. Finally, in 1968, Ramey graduated from Wichita State University with a bachelor of music degree.

Following his graduation from Wichita State University, Ramey joined the Grass Roots Opera Company, a small repertory group based in Raleigh, North Carolina, with which he toured the southeastern United States in such bel canto operas as *Don Pasquale* and *The Italian Girl in Algiers.* After an arduous year of performing in cramped quarters, he packed all his belongings in cardboard boxes and in June 1969 left Kansas for New York City, where he found a steady nine-to-five job as a copywriter for a textbook publishing company and continued his vocal lessons with a teacher recommended by Kansas friends. Luckily for Ramey, his supervisor turned out to be an opera buff, who was generous enough to allow him time off for auditions. He found, however, after several months of discouragement, that he was making little progress with his vocal training and had to make the agonizing decision to find a new teacher. Having read about Armen Boyajian in a published interview with Paul Plishka, a bass whom he much admires, Ramey auditioned with Boyajian and was accepted. Boyajian's showcase opera company in Paterson, New Jersey gave Ramey the opportunity to perform such roles as Don Giovanni, Henry VIII in Donizetti's *Anna Bolena,* and Mephistopheles in Gounoud's *Faust.* Meanwhile, he held on to the financial security afforded him by his publishing job, augmented by fees derived from singing in churches and synagogues in the New York City area.

Important recognition came for Ramey in 1972, when he became a finalist in the Metropolitan Opera National Council auditions. That same year he also tried out for the New York City Opera under their policy of open auditions—which he has described as "the cattle calls that anybody who writes them a letter can go to"—in the basement of the New York State Theater, at Lincoln Center. After six suspenseful months, the management asked him back for an on-stage audition, but although Julius Rudel, then the company's director, immediately recognized Ramey's exhilarating voice, dramatic intensity, powerful stage presence, and musicianship, it was not until a year later that the young basso was asked to sign a contract. Finally, in the spring of 1973, Ramey made his debut with the New York City Opera, singing the role of the

Spanish lieutenant Zuniga in *Carmen*. He has been on its roster ever since.

Originally established in 1943 as the City Center Opera Company, the New York City Opera has been housed since 1966 in the New York State Theater. Since it stresses an ensemble approach rather than a star system, encourages younger singers (especially Americans), and concentrates on a venturesome repertoire, the company complements the more august and conservative Metropolitan Opera across from it on Lincoln Center plaza. In his interview with Gary Lipton, Ramey said: "The City Opera has been a fabulous place to work. It is striking proof of the superb performing opportunities available to artists in this country."

Within a year of his debut Ramey was busily engaged with the New York City Opera during its 1974 season, singing Creon in *Medea*, Basilio in *The Barber of Seville*, Henry VIII in *Anna Bolena*, Collino in *La Bohème* and roles of varying importance in *L'Incoronazione di Poppea*, *A Village Romeo and Juliet*, *Don Giovanni*, and *Turandot*. Venturing further afield, he sang in *La Gioconda* at the Opera Theater of New Jersey, to the admiration of S. A. Desick of *Opera News* (March 30, 1974), who reported that "Samuel Ramey brought authoritative voice and presence to Alvise."

Similar critical acclaim was not long in coming. After seeing Ramey's sinuous performance of the four villains in *The Tales of Hoffmann*—roles that he inherited from his idol Norman Treigle—John Rockwell wrote in the New York *Times* (September 13, 1975): "Mr. Ramey is a fine young singer, and he did his best to emulate Mr. Treigle's inimitable mannerisms. More lyric than his model and less catlike in his movements, Mr. Ramey would no doubt appear to better advantage in a production tailored to his talents." He apparently found that production when the Opera Company of Philadelphia presented *Anna Bolena* on December 16, 1975, for his portrayal of the Tudor king led Max de Schauensee to single him out for special praise in his review for *Opera News* (February 28, 1976). "Worthy of admiration was the Henry VIII of Samuel Ramey, possessor of a superb basso cantante," de Schauensee observed. "This is a voice with a future."

Samuel Ramey was introduced to British audiences in the title role of *The Marriage of Figaro* at the Glyndebourne Festival in the summer of 1976, and to the French as Don Giovanni at the Grand Théâtre in Bordeaux in January 1977. During that same season of 1976-77 he sang Don Basilio in a somewhat controversial production of *The Barber of Seville* that was both staged and conducted by Sarah Caldwell at the New York City Opera. Although the production itself garnered only mixed reviews, Ramey was garlanded with praise by the critics, even though he was a much younger Basilio than usual. A reviewer for *New York* magazine found him "a Basilio to cherish," and a critic for the New York

Times pointed out that "Samuel Ramey as a beanpole of a Basilio belongs to an extended line of notable basses who have managed to sing the music beautifully and be funny at the same time." When that production was televised nationally over PBS as part of its *Live from Lincoln Center* series, Ramey again sang Don Basilio, and when the Beverly Sills *Manon* was telecast over the same network, Ramey performed the role of the Count des Grieux.

But it was in the diabolical roles that operatic composers like to relegate to basses that Ramey really hit his stride. When the New York City Opera revived its spectacular production of Boito's *Mefistofele* on March 20, 1977, it was Ramey who was chosen to play the title role that the late Norman Treigle seemed to have patented for himself. Far from making invidious comparisons, the critics showered him with praise. Writing in *Opera News* (May 1977), Robert Jacobson commented: "In the title role the company had not only a successor to Norman Treigle (all who follow him have to meet his measure) but a bass of surpassing opulence, power, richness, and expression. Samuel Ramey's assumption of the role ended in a complete triumph, fulfilling all the promise he has shown in other parts, his noble, black sound beautifully focused, riding the crest of the music." And in the New York *Times* (April 1, 1977) Robert Berkvist conferred the ultimate accolade: "For Mr. Ramey, the occasion was a double triumph. Not only had he performed one of opera's more demanding roles to his own and the critics' satisfaction, but he had also made his own light shine through Mr. Treigle's shadow."

In the summer of 1977 Ramey returned to Glyndebourne, again in demonic guise, as Nick Shadow in Stravinsky's *The Rake's Progress*. "It's natural I'd get some of these roles," he once explained, "as composers tend to write devilish roles for basses. They can't make tenors sound evil, I suppose. But I enjoy singing these roles. You might even say I have a devil of a time."

By the late 1970's Samuel Ramey had joined the growing ranks of young American singers in great demand at the major European opera houses. In 1978 he made his debut at the Netherlands Opera as the four villains in *The Tales of Hoffmann* and at the Hamburg State Opera as King Arkel in *Pelléas and Mélisande*. At the Aix-en-Provence festival in the summer of 1981 he had the honor of singing with Montserrat Caballé and Marilyn Horne in a wildly acclaimed production of Rossini's *Semiramide*. His hectic schedule for 1981 included commitments for his debut at La Scala in May as Mozart's Figaro in a production staged by Giorgio Strehler and conducted by Riccardo Muti; an appearance early in June at the Hamburg State Opera as Raimondo, the chaplain, in *Lucia di Lammermoor*; and another debut, this time as Escamillo, the toreador, in a Vienna State Opera production of *Carmen* late that same month. All in all, his jet-propelled career was keeping him away from home for more than half the year.

Meanwhile, in an impressive tour de force, Ramey was demonstrating his versatility on home ground by alternating with Justino Diaz in the roles of Don Giovanni and Leporello, his man servant, at the New York City Opera in the fall of 1980. His Leporello was judged best in the cast by John Rockwell of the New York Times (October 5, 1980), who found his work "almost worth the price of admission." And the critical response to his Don Giovanni was perhaps best summed up by Annalyn Swan of Newsweek (March 17, 1980): "Tall and sinuous, with a smooth, resounding bass voice, Ramey is perfect as a sensual, swashbuckling rake. His is not a dark, dangerous Don. But . . . he makes a devilishly sexy one."

When, at the behest of High Fidelity magazine (January 1981), Bridget Paolucci surveyed recording executives, managers, and agents in an attempt to determine who might become the classical recording stars of the 1980's, she cited Samuel Ramey as "one of the most exciting, thoroughly musical new performers on the operatic stage." For the Philips label he has recorded Lucia di Lammermoor, Verdi's I due Foscari, Tosca, Otello, Handel's Ariodante, Haydn's Amida, and Bach's Mass in B Minor. After hearing Ramey on a recent Angel recording of Rigoletto, John Freeman wrote in Opera News (January 1980): "The doubling of Monterone and Sparafucile by the same singer is an appropriate Lulu-like touch, consolidating Rigoletto's inspirational demons, especially when a bass of the rich-voiced authority of Samuel Ramey is available." For a new RCA recording of Rossini's The Italian Girl in Algiers, released in 1981, Ramey counterpoised his own vocal acrobatics against the pyrotechnics of Marilyn Horne in a dazzling demonstration of a fact too often forgotten by music lovers: that the term "coloratura" in the age of bel canto befitted mezzos and basses as well as sopranos.

Six feet tall, slim, and wiry, Samuel Ramey sports longish wavy brown hair, and, often, a trim beard for his diabolical roles. In 1970 he married Carrie Tenante, who formerly worked for RCA Records. The Rameys live in an apartment on New York's Central Park West when they are not on the road together. Maintaining the athleticism of his boyhood, Ramey plays on the City Opera's softball team, jogs in Central Park, and goes camping and hiking with his wife in the mountains of upstate New York. His more passive recreations include watching football games and attending Broadway shows. Perhaps because he returns to his roots in Kansas when his schedule permits, Ramey remains unpretentious and unspoiled by success. One of his classmates at Colby High School, Tom Thompson, said recently: "Sam Ramey hasn't been changed by his success or by living in the big city. He's still the laughing, fun-loving person I knew in high school. You know, when I think of Sam, I think of him laughing and singing."

References: Newsday II p19 Mr 20 '77 por; Newsweek 95:107 Mr 17 '80 por; N Y Times II p21 S 18 '77 por; Opera N 42:30+ My '78 por; 46:8+ Jl '81 pors; Vogue 171:255+ Mr '81 por; Who's Who in Opera, 1976

Reddy, N(eelam) Sanjiva

May 13, 1913- President of India. Address: b. Office of the President, Rashtrapati Bhavan, New Delhi, India

Throughout his political career of nearly half a century N. Sanjiva Reddy has tried to follow Mohandas Gandhi's tenets of tolerance and compassion while mastering the skill in party maneuvering that in 1977 helped to secure for him the Presidency of a country that he often refers to as "the largest democracy in the world." Becoming an important figure in the national government of India after the death of Jawaharlal Nehru in 1964, he held two Cabinet posts during the 1960's, and he has twice served as speaker of the influential lower house of Parliament. In his first bid for the Presidency, in 1969, he was defeated by a candidate who had the backing of his political opponent Prime Minister Indira Gandhi, on whose advice he now exercises his executive power.

The son of a farmer, Neelam Sanjiva Reddy was born on May 13, 1913 in the village of Illure in the Anantapur district of the coastal state of Andhra Pradesh (then part of Madras) in southeast India. He was the oldest son in a large, much-respected family that he described as being "middle-class peasant." One of his brothers, Rajasekhar, also became active in politics, once running against Sanjiva for office as a Communist party candidate. Their father, Chinnappa Reddy, was so persuasive in his advocacy of abstinence from alcohol that residents of his village and some surrounding villages practised voluntary prohibition. For his secondary school education Sanjiva Reddy attended the Theosophical Movement School at Adyar, Madras. His sport there was field hockey. He later enrolled in college in Anantapur, but left after one year, in 1932, to join Mohandas Gandhi's freedom movement.

In an interview in *India Today* (August 1-15, 1977) Reddy spoke of the impact of Gandhi's personality on his decision to enter politics: "The first time I met the Mahatma was in 1929 as a student when he was auctioning some small things given to him at a meeting. I purchased a casket, a painting and a shawl. When I went to receive the things I had purchased from him, I felt ashamed that I was not wearing khadi [hand-woven Indian clothing]. It was on that day that I began wearing *khaddar* as a student of the tenth class." Before long, his eagerness to take part in the struggle for India's independence from British rule overrode his desire for a formal education. Reddy's own experience, moreover, of life in rural India, of working in the fields, also attracted him to Gandhi, whom years later he quoted as saying, "India lives in the villages and our strength as a nation depends upon the welfare of our rural population."

Inspired, as he also later acknowledged, by "the sense of purpose" that Gandhi gave to India's youth, Reddy used his gift as a public speaker to rise quickly in local politics. In 1936 he was named secretary of the Andhra Pradesh committee of the Indian National Congress party, of which Gandhi was the leader. Like Gandhi and many of his followers in the Satyagraha, as his civil disobedience movement was called, Reddy was frequently in and out of jail until 1945, when the British began to adopt a softer line toward Indian nationalism. By choice, he established his electoral base in Madras, where in 1946 he was made a member and secretary of the state legislative assembly. The following year he was named to represent Madras in the Indian Constituent Assembly (parliament). After India won its independence within the British Commonwealth in August 1947, he returned to Madras to serve, from 1949 to 1951, in the state Cabinet as minister for housing, forests, and prohibition (he himself is a teetotaler).

Within the Congress party Reddy advanced to the presidency of the Andhra Pradesh committee for 195152. In the 1952 state elections, however, he lost his assembly seat when the ruling Congress party won only 40 percent of the vote in southern India. The loss was generally interpreted as the result of dissatisfaction with prohibition and, more importantly, of the desire for an Andhra state separate from greater Madras. After the new state of Andhra was established in the following year, he was elected to the state assembly and became the government's deputy chief minister. In 1956 he advanced to the office of chief minister of the reorganized and enlarged state of Andhra Pradesh.

At a convention of the Indian National Congress in early 1959, Reddy had his first clash with Indira Gandhi, who would long remain his principal political adversary. A founder and member of a group of old-guard party stalwarts known as the Syndicate, he joined in promoting their candidate for Congress president. Mrs. Gandhi, however, who was running for that office with the advantage of being the daughter of Prime Minister Jawaharlal Nehru, a former party president, defeated the Syndicate's contender. Thereafter Reddy was considered to be in the anti-Indira Gandhi camp.

Reddy became chief minister of Andhra Pradesh for a second time in 1962. Two years later, in February 1964, his career suffered a temporary setback because the Indian Supreme Court quashed his proposal to nationalize the bus line in the state's Kurnool district, on the grounds that the move was primarily a means of punishing one of Reddy's political rivals. The decision of the court, that he had been "motivated by bias and ill will," did not make resignation mandatory, but he decided to leave the post "in order to establish high standards in public life." He then went back to his native village and began to plant a lemon grove. A few months afterward, however, a dramatic change in his fortunes returned him to New Delhi. Prime Minister Nehru died in May 1964 and was replaced the following month by Lal Bahadar Shastri, who appointed Reddy to his first national Cabinet post, Minister of Steel and Mines.

The death of Shastri in January 1966 ignited a power struggle for the office of Prime Minister between Indira Gandhi and Reddy's friend Morarji Desai. After Mrs. Gandhi became Prime Minister later in the month, she transferred Reddy to the comparatively minor post of Minister of Transport, Aviation, Tourism and Shipping. In the 1967 election several of the leading members of the Congress party with whom he was allied lost their seats in Parliament. Their defeat strengthened the hand of Prime Minister Gandhi, who in March 1967 dropped him from her Cabinet altogether. Successful, however, in his own legislative race in 1967, Reddy had won election to the Lok Sabha, the lower chamber of Parliament, to which he moved from the Rajya Sabha, the indirectly elected upper chamber, where he had served in 1952-53 and since 1964. Presumably as a sop to the old guard, after having deprived him of his Cabinet post, Mrs. Gandhi backed his bid for speaker of the Lok Sabha, a position to which he was elected by 278 votes to 207.

A contest for India's Presidency brought Reddy and Mrs. Gandhi again into open conflict and intensified the long-simmering fight within the Congress party. When President Zakin Husain died in May 1969, Reddy offered himself as a successor, and at a convention of the All India Congress Committee in Bangalore in July he was nominated as the party's official candidate. Soon afterward acting President V. V. Giri entered the race as an independent candidate. A few days before the election Mrs. Gandhi brushed aside the facade of party unity and threw her support publicly to Giri. During a bitter campaign Reddy's followers charged that Giri and Mrs. Gandhi were allied with Communist and radical forces, while his detractors contended that he was being used by the wealthy Indian elite. Anonymous campaign literature, reportedly from Mrs. Gandhi's faction, branded Reddy as "a debauchee," warning that "no woman is safe in his presence." The disparagement seemed to Reddy and his associates unworthy of response. At the Bangalore meeting some weeks earlier Mrs. Gandhi had persuaded party leaders to adopt a resolution nationalizing the country's fourteen largest banks. Partly as a result of that popular move, in August 1969 Giri narrowly won the election for President by 420,077 votes to 405,427.

Following his defeat Reddy joined the conservative Syndicate members in splitting formally with Indira Gandhi's allies in the Congress party. In the 1971 elections, which gave Mrs. Gandhi a landslide victory, he failed to win a parliamentary seat. He therefore returned home to his lemon grove and occupied himself in farming. Ironically, the elections that deprived Reddy of a government post became indirectly responsible for his resumption of political activity. Mrs. Gandhi's conviction in 1975 on charges of fraud in winning her parliamentary seat in the elections of 1971 precipitated a declaration of a state of nationwide emergency. In the guarded manner that was necessary to avoid imprisonment, Reddy criticized her suspension of civil liberties, her mandatory vasectomy campaign, and the urban renewal program of her son, Sanjai Gandhi, for the slums of New Delhi. When Mrs. Gandhi called for elections in 1977, Reddy redoubled his efforts, openly allying himself with leaders of the Janata party, a coalition, which he had helped to organize, of political groups opposing Mrs. Gandhi. In the March elections for the lower house of Parliament, Reddy was the only Janata party candidate to win in the state of Andhra Pradesh, but elsewhere Congress candidates were not so successful. Mrs. Gandhi resigned in the wake of her party's surprise defeat, leaving the office of Prime Minister to Morarji Desai, who had been chosen head of the triumphant Janata party.

A popular speaker, for the second time, of the Lok Sobha and a close associate of Prime Minister Desai, Reddy emerged as a natural choice for the Janata party's candidate in a Presidential election held in July 1977 to provide a successor to President Fakhruddin Ali Ahmed, who had died in February 1977. Since the Congress party was not strong enough to propose its own candidate, Reddy was elected unanimously to a five-year Presidential term on July 21 by an electoral college made up of members of the national Parliament and state legislatures. In his inaugural address President Reddy tried to strike a conciliatory note in contrast to the bitterness and repression of the emergency period and declared: "One of my main tasks during my term of office will be to provide the harmonizing touch that is required for healing the old wounds, promoting better understanding and removing the lingering fears and suspicions."

As if taking up the purpose of Mahatma Gandhi "to wipe every tear from every eye," on August 15, 1977 President Reddy devoted much of his Independence Day message to a plea for attention to the grievances of the great masses of Indian people, many living below subsistence level. He warned his affluent and politically powerful listeners of the need to "prevent the volcano of discontent and frustration from blowing its top." To set a moral example and to help cut government expenses, he announced that he intended to move out of Rashtrapati Bhavan, the elegant 340-room Presidential palace, and to return 70 percent of his salary and to request that the remainder no longer be tax exempt. As President he generally avoided taking positions on highly controversial issues, but in support of a birth-control program he suggested the imposition of "some sort of penalties or disincentives for having more than two or three children."

Although largely ceremonial, the Indian Presidency has constitutional powers that enabled Reddy to use his office as the steadying force in his country's politics when, during 1979, the ruling Janata party disintegrated as a result of rivalry among its principal leaders: Prime Minister Morarji Desai, Finance Minister Chavan Singh, and Defense Minister Jagjivan Ram. The crisis began in June when a parliamentary supporter of Singh stated that he would no longer vote for Desai, who he believed was being manipulated by a Hindu nationalist faction. Other defections followed, and on July 15 Desai resigned as Prime Minister. Reddy then appointed Singh to be Prime Minister, asking him to form a new parliamentary majority. But Singh failed to do so and resigned on August 20.

The resignation confronted Reddy with having to make the most difficult decision of his Presidency: whether to call for new elections, which would probably benefit former Prime Minister Indira Gandhi, or to offer the new head of the Janata party, Jagjivan Ram, a chance to form a government. From a legal standpoint, the Indian President was expected to follow the advice of the Prime Minister and Singh, who remained as acting Prime Minister, favored new elections. Some politicians and lawyers argued, however, that because Singh had never formed a parliamentary majority himself and had served as Prime Minister for only twenty-four days, Reddy could ignore his recommendations. The problem was further complicated by the fact that since Ram was an untouchable Reddy would be leaving himself open to charges of discrimination if he rejected Ram's claim. Regardless of that possibility, after several days of intensive consultations, Reddy decided to dissolve Parliament and to call for new elections.

Opinion concerning the wisdom and legality of Reddy's decision was divided. The *Hindustan Times* found it unwise on the grounds that the Indian President "had an obligation to prove beyond the shadow of a doubt" that Ram had no chance to win. On the other hand, the Indian newspaper the *Statesman* supported Reddy, arguing that Ram could have mustered a majority only with the help of defectors from other political parties who would have demanded political payoffs. Regarding the decision's legality, the former Indian Ambassador to the United States, Nani Palkhivala, one of the experts whom Reddy had consulted, called the decision "unjustified to the point of constitutional impropriety." By contrast, an authority on the Indian constitution and former vice-chancellor of Bombay University, T. K. Tope, held that the President, like the British sovereign, was free to use his own discretion both in appointing a Prime Minister and in dissolving Parliament after the resignation of a Prime Minister.

In deciding in favor of new elections, Reddy paradoxically accommodated his old political adversary, Indira Gandhi. By its overwhelming victory in January 1980, her party swept Reddy's former associates out of office and took command of the Lok Sabha. On January 10 the President asked Mrs. Gandhi to form a new government. After her resumption of power both appeared to recognize the importance of rapprochement. In the interests of political stability the Prime Minister, who had a clear mandate from the voters, and the President, who represented national unity, were discouraged from attacking each other. When Reddy left India for a state visit to the Soviet Union in September 1980, Mrs. Gandhi was among the officials at the airport who gave him a warm send-off.

N. Sanjiva Reddy is married to Nagaratnamma Reddy and has four children—three married daughters and a son who is a doctor in Anantapur. The President stands five feet ten inches tall and weighs 150 pounds. His attire in public usually includes a Gandhi cap and a long homespun jacket or coat with a Nehru collar. A heavy smoker, he was treated in 1977 in the United States for a lung cancer discovered soon after he became President. In a profile in the New York *Times* (November 13, 1969) Reddy's bluntness was singled out as being "the personality trait most people associate with him" and one of his friends was quoted as saying, "If you go to him, you'll know in a minute how you stand with him." Reddy holds an honorary D.Litt. degree awarded by Sri Venkateswara University in Tiruapti.

References: India Today p13+ Ag 1-15 '77 por; *N Y Times* p17 N 13 '69, A p3 Jl 8 '77, A p3 Jl 20 '79; *International Yearbook and Statesmen's Who's Who,* 1980; *International Who's Who,* 1980-81

Regan, Donald T(homas) (rē'gən)

Dec. 21, 1918- Secretary of the Treasury. Address: b. Department of the Treasury, 15th St. and Pennsylvania Ave., NW, Washington, D.C. 20220

The passage in July 1981 of President Ronald Reagan's proposed tax-cut legislation to stimulate investment not only signaled a triumph for advocates of supply-side economics but also confirmed Secretary of the Treasury Donald T. Regan, a late convert to supply-side thinking, as the President's chief economic spokesman. Regan received credit from many quarters for the skillful way in which the tax-cut package was maneuvered through Congress. White House aides called him "a class act" and "a rising star," and a Senator described him as "one of the hardest working men the President has." The highest praise came from Reagan himself: "I had some outstanding help from a number of people, but particularly from a very fine salesman named Don Regan."

A political unknown when he arrived in Washington to join the new Republican Cabinet on January 22, 1981, Regan had spent his entire life with the Wall Street firm now named Merrill Lynch & Company. In ten years as chairman and chief executive officer, he diversified the interests of that giant brokerage house, which has a thousand offices throughout the world, to include securities and banking, economic consulting, real estate, and other services.

Donald Thomas Regan was born to William F. and Kathleen (Ahern) Regan in Cambridge, Massachusetts on December 21, 1918. His father worked for the now defunct New Haven Railroad. It is a minor irony that his chief antagonist in the tax-fight was Thomas ("Tip") O'Neill, the Democratic Speaker of the House, who has long represented the Congressional district in which Regan grew up. He attended the Cambridge Latin School and then Harvard University, where he was a classmate of John F. Kennedy. On a scholarship at Harvard, he showed early signs of his considerable enterprise by organizing a dozen other students into a guide service to take tourists around Boston. Besides meeting expenses, he had saved a nest egg of $2,000 by the time that he graduated with a B.A. degree in English in 1940.

In preparation for a career in law, Regan enrolled in Harvard Law School, but as the United States' entry into World War II became imminent, he cut short his studies after less than a year to enlist in the Marine Corps as an officer candidate. 'While rising to the rank of major, he saw action in the Pacific campaigns at New Georgia, Bougainville, Guam, and Okinawa before he retired in 1946 as a reserve lieutenant colonel. As he told Hugh Sidey of *Time* (March 23, 1981), he had "no training for anything except fighting," but he could not afford to resume his law studies. He therefore canvassed businesses that offered educational programs and chose Merrill Lynch's course for stockbrokers as the most promising. A graduate of the company's second trainee class in 1946, he began a steady advancement to the top.

During the postwar years Merrill Lynch, Pierce, Fenner & Smith Inc. helped to spark a small-investor boom that increased the number of investors on Wall Street from 2,000,000 in 1946 to 26,000,000 in 1969 and that made Merrill Lynch the biggest brokerage firm in the country. Throughout those years, Regan was carefully groomed by the Merrill Lynch management, which moved him from job to job until he had experience in virtually every aspect of the securities business. His first assignment was as an account executive in Washington, D.C. Soon afterward transferred to New York City, he worked in the sales promotion department until 1952, when he was made the manager of Merrill Lynch's over-the-counter sales. He became a general partner in 1954, and from 1955 to 1960 he ran the company's

Philadelphia office. In 1960 he was reassigned to New York City as director of the Merrill Lynch administrative division.

One of Regan's achievements as head of the administrative division was the establishment of a long-term planning office for Merrill Lynch. In the mid-1960's the company began an extraordinary program of expansion and diversification that owed much of its success, according to Regan, to long-term planning. "It has enabled us to keep an even course during a turbulent decade on Wall Street," he explained in an interview for *Nation's Business* (April 1972). "Knowing which way we wanted to go has enabled us to diversify ahead of most of our competitors." Meanwhile, Regan's own rise continued with his election as executive vice-president in 1964 and as president in 1968, when he became the youngest man ever to hold that post. In January 1971 he advanced to chairman and chief executive officer, positions that he also assumed in the holding company, Merrill Lynch & Company Inc., formed by Merrill Lynch, Pierce, Fenner & Smith Inc. in May 1973.

As the investment boom of the 1960's ended, many brokerage houses staggered, but Merrill Lynch, its diversification program underway, kept growing and expanding. In 1970 Merrill Lynch agreed to make $15,000,000 available to Goodbody & Company, the fifth largest brokerage house on the New York Stock Exchange, to enable it to comply with the exchange's net capital rules, in preparation for absorbing that firm. Regan drove a hard bargain with the other members of the exchange, who put up $30,000,000 to indemnify the Merrill-Lynch takeover. Spared the possible disastrous consequences to capital markets of a Goodbody collapse, the other firms watched as their indemnity helped Merrill Lynch, the giant of their industry, grow by 25 percent with the merger.

In the following years, under Regan's guidance, what Richard Phalon of the New York *Times* (January 18, 1976) called Merrill Lynch's "single-minded effort to diversify" began to pay off. By 1976 Merrill Lynch was not only the number-one retail broker in the country but also first in mutual funds, commodity trading, municipal bonds, and investment banking; was forging ahead in international finance, money market funds, economic consulting, mortgage insurance, and precious metals; and had more than four times the assets and capital of its closest competitors. The company slogan —"We're bullish on America"—was being made a household phrase by a multimillion dollar advertising compaign.

Throughout the shaky brokerage industry Regan became known as an outspoken advocate of free-market practice and as something of a maverick in the clubby world of Wall Street. He set his sights, for example, on eliminating the fixed minimum commission, a stock exchange rule that kept brokers' commissions artificially high and prevented brokerage firms from competing vigorously with each other. Most stock exchange executives favored the fixed commissions, and many argued that Merrill Lynch could easily forgo the protection of fixed rates since its great size assured that it would win any competitive battle. "Wall Street is hiding behind a protective pricing system while it preaches free competition and free markets," Regan charged in a speech before the Rotary Club of Dallas in December 1970. "That is like catching Carrie Nation tippling in the basement." After fixed commissions were eliminated in 1975, a number of Wall Street firms did go under and were taken over by larger companies. Merrill Lynch itself acquired the old-line international banking house White, Weld & Company in 1978 for $50,000,000.

When Regan left Merrill Lynch in 1980, his firm was competing aggressively with banks. It sponsored a credit card, offered demand checking on its investor accounts, and earned the largest part of its income from interest, not from brokerage commissions. David Rockefeller of Chase Manhattan Bank regarded Merrill Lynch as "a bank in disguise." Having initiated the computerization of Merrill Lynch with a view to future needs, however, Regan believed that the traditional distinction between banks and investment companies would soon be academic. "When you talk about banking," he told Gary Putka of the New York Times (April 27, 1980), "you can't think in terms of 1979 but towards a day when the consumer looks up his bank balance with the same machine he uses to call his broker and pay for stock."

On December 11, 1980 President-elect Ronald Reagan nominated Donald T. Regan as the sixty-sixth Secretary of the Treasury. Although a lifelong Republican, he was strongly opposed by some of the President's most conservative supporters, having reportedly committed such apostasies as contributing to Democratic candidates and backing the price-wage controls of the Nixon Administration. Regan was pushed forward for the key Cabinet post by 'William J. Casey, the President's campaign manager and now Central Intelligence Agency director, who as president of the Securities and Exchange Commission had become acquainted with Regan in the early 1970's. Political observers generally assumed that the new Secretary would espouse orthodox Republican views to serve as ballast in an Administration that was already buoyant with supply-side thinkers.

At first Regan was content to stay in the background while David Stockman, the director of the Office of Management and Budget, garnered headlines with his program of budget cuts. According to press accounts, the Irish temper for which Regan was known at Merrill Lynch flashed only once, when Stockman trespassed in the area of tax policy, which Regan considered to be the Treasury Department's preserve. "This is where you'll hear administration tax thinking," he barked at reporters, as quoted in the New York Times (June 24, 1981).

"If you hear something different someplace else, then it's wrong."

To counter expected resistance to tax-cut proposals, Regan became more visible, selling the President's program to Congress and articulating what that program would mean for the country. It was soon clear that instead of advocating traditional Republican economic views, he had wedded his free-market faith to the supply-side idea that a massive tax cut could revitalize American industry. "The tax program cannot wait until budget outlays are reduced," he told the Senate Appropriations Committee in early 1981. "We must not make the mistake of assigning a higher priority to balancing the budget than to revitalizing the economy."

Although Regan disagreed with Reagan Administration officials who insisted that tax reduction and cuts in federal spending be linked in a single package, he predicted that the federal budget would be balanced by 1984 because the tax cuts would stimulate a "tremendous expansion" in American industry and hence in federal revenues. To hold down inflation during that expansionary period, Regan asserted in December 1980, the strict control of the nation's money supply by the Federal Reserve Board was "the only game in town." (Several months later, however, he conceded that a cautious easing of the present tight-money policy would help the economy over its current "flat period.") In an interview with U.S. News & World Report (March 9, 1981) he forecast that the economy would grow by about 50 percent between 1981 and 1985 if the President's program were enacted. "The more I examine supply-side economics," he said in the same interview, "the more I find I've always been on this side. But I thought it was just old-fashioned conservatism."

Backing away from its initial goal of a 30 percent reduction in federal income taxes in three years, the Reagan Administration eventually settled for a 25 percent cut over the same period. Regan was a tough, determined negotiator in lobbying for the program. He helped to persuade the President that changes in the tax proposal were necessary to ease it through Congress, and he served as "the point man" for the package in Congress itself. Although Regan quickly mastered the political complexities that had seemed overwhelming in his early days in office, it was not an easy adjustment. At Merrill Lynch he had been a strictly nine-to-five man, but in Washington he found himself working fourteen-hour days and eighty-hour weeks. A millionaire whose 1980 income exceeded $700,000, Regan admitted, as quoted in the Washington Post (March 17, 1981), that he was "surprised at the hours people work [in government] for the recompense they get. . . . It really shocks a guy coming from Wall Street."

The functions of the Department of the Treasury that Regan administers include various law enforcement responsibilities, such as those of the Bureau of Alcohol, Tobacco, and Firearms; manufacturing coins and currency; collecting taxes; and paying government bills. As the country's chief financial officer and a principal adviser to the President, he serves as chairman *pro tempore* of the Cabinet Council on Economic Affairs and chairman of the Cabinet-level Economics Policy Group and works with the President's Economic Policy Advisory Board, which is made up of non-governmental economists. In March 1981 he became chairman of the Depository Institutions Deregulation Committee, which Congress created the preceding year to phase out ceilings on interest rates for deposits in banks and savings and loan associations. Secretary Regan is also United States governor of the International Monetary Fund, the International Bank for Reconstruction and Development, the Inter-American Development Bank, the Asian Development Bank, and the African Development Fund.

Regan is an undeviating champion of free enterprise, deregulation, and competition in American industry. "If you're going to be a capitalist, you have to believe in a free-market economy," he said in an interview for *Newsweek* (December 22, 1980) soon after his nomination. "Some firms are going to fail in this environment—so be it." He believes, however, that most firms will thrive, given the Reagan program. But even after the thumping victory for the tax-cut package, the stock and bond markets continued to limp along, hurt by high interest rates and fearful that the tax cut would prove inflationary. His former colleagues in the investment community were one group that Regan had yet to convince. In a speech before the Chamber of Commerce of the United States in March 1981, he underscored the importance of cooperation from the business community: "We can get the bills through Congress and we can get the President to sign them. But then, business has to take over, and it's American business that's going to make our program succeed or fail."

From 1972 to 1975 Regan served as vice-chairman of the board of directors of the New York Stock Exchange. He is an avid reader, especially of history, and his own book, *A View From the Street,* which was published in 1972 by the New American Library, is a history of the crisis years of 1969 and 1970 on Wall Street. He was a member of the policy committee of Business Roundtable, a trustee of the Committee for Economic Development, and a member of the Council on Foreign Relations. Since 1978 he has been a life trustee of the University of Pennsylvania, one of several universities from which he holds honorary doctorates.

Hugh Sidey observed "the trace of a fighter in the face of Donald Regan, . . . the wary eyes, the cleft chin, the crooked nose." To Peter Grier of the *Christian Science Monitor* (January 8, 1981) he seemed "a businessman's businessman: prosperous, well tailored and an articu-

late defender of corporate enterprise." Regan is an enthusiastic golfer who shoots in the low 90's and belongs to the Baltusrol Golf and Burning Tree clubs. Known during his years at Merrill Lynch as a private, family-oriented man, he has been married since July 11, 1942 to Ann Gordon (Buchanan) Regan and has four children, Donna, Donald, Richard, and Diane. A few years ago he and his wife acquired their present residence, at that time intended for their retirement, a renovated carriage house on a Mount Vernon, Virginia estate that overlooks the Potomac and was once the property of George Washington.

References: Cong Q p3609+ D 20 '80 por; N Y Times A p28 D 12 '80 por; Newsweek 96:15+ D 22 '80 pors; Time 116:11 D 22 '80 por, 117:14 Mr 23 '81 por; US News 40:13 Ap 27 '81 por; Washington Post A p2 Mr 17 '81 por; Congressional Directory, 1981; International Who's Who, 1981-82; Who's Who in America, 1980-81

Rexroth, Kenneth

Dec. 22, 1905- Poet; critic; painter. Address: h. 1401 E. Pepper Lane, Santa Barbara, Calif. 93108

Although he might reject the title, the anarchist writer and literary arbiter Kenneth Rexroth is regarded by many as the greatest living populist poet in the United States. The patriarchal Rexroth, who lives on the West Coast, has been called "the last of the great Bohemians" and "the uncaged lion of American letters." He came of age during the so-called second Chicago Renaissance, following World

War I, and he served as the godfather of the Beat Generation when it was baptized in the San Francisco Renaissance of the late 1950's. "I've never understood why I'm a member of the avant-garde," Rexroth once said. "I write more or less as Allen Tate thinks he writes— like the great Greeks and Romans and Chinese. . . . I try to say, as simply as I can, the simplest and most profound experiences of my life, which I think will be of significance to others on a similar level—that is, which will touch them in significant regions of their experience."

The only child of Charles Marion Rexroth, a wholesale druggist, and Delia (Reed) Rexroth, Kenneth Rexroth was born in South Bend, Indiana on December 22, 1905. Except for English and Irish forebears in his mother's maternal line and "a few French, Indians, and Negroes way back," Rexroth traces his lineage through old German-American stock, predominantly Pennsylvania Dutch. Among his ancestors were Mennonites, Brethren, Schwenckfelders, Abolitionists, and early suffragists and socialists, and his great-grandparents were pioneers on the advancing frontiers of the old Northwest.

In his chronicle of his first twenty-one years, *An Autobiographical Novel* (Doubleday, 1966; Ross-Erickson, 1978), Rexroth speaks of a sense of *noblesse oblige* that came with his background, not a nationalistic spirit but a sense of social and cultural responsibility that "produces radical critics, rebels, reformers, eccentrics." The result was a "personality that has proved highly resistant to digestion by the mass culture" and yet "conservative of the characteristic values of American life."

In childhood Rexroth formed an omnivorous reading habit, devouring the literary classics and standard works in history, the sciences, and philosophy as well as eccentric reading lists in comparative mythology, the occult, mysticism, and religion. He liked French and Russian literature, but "American fiction, even Hawthorne, even Melville, to his day seems to [him] to be absolute trash."

Orphaned in early adolescence, Rexroth went to live with an aunt in Chicago, in the South Side neighborhood that became the setting for James T. Farrell's *Studs Lonigan*, a novel in which Rexroth appears as Kenny, the "blue-eyed, dizzy-faced" drugstore clerk with a "nervous original walk." In real life, as a matter of fact, Rexroth worked after school as a pharmacy apprentice and soda jerk at Vause's Drug Store, and summers he worked at his father's old wholesale pharmaceutical house, Kinsolving & Granisson. He "managed a couple of years" at Englewood High School, he recounts, "but left in a row over military training."

Rexroth found a potential patron in one of the owners of Kinsolving & Granisson, who offered to buy him into the business as he grew older, so that he would be sure to become one of the company's top executives. After engaging in long debates with himself,

Rexroth rejected the opportunity offered him in the wholesale drug business and decided to pursue his bents for art and writing. In childhood, the former inclination was more pronounced. "All my young days, it seems to me now, I took myself more seriously as an artist than as a writer," he has recalled. "It seems to me that I started off practically in infancy as an abstract artist because the first pictures that had made an impression on me, and that I tried to imitate, looked pretty abstract to me even if they weren't." Jay Hambridge's *Dynamic Symmetry: The Greek Vase* made him "a compass-and-ruler constructivist or suprematist painter" when he was "still in short pants and completely unaware that there was anybody else like that in the world."

Other early influences were the cubist and post-impressionist collections (then considered esoteric) of Arthur Jerome Eddy, a friend of his father's, and *Futurist Color Schemes*, a pamphlet published by the Chicago Art Institute. He attended classes at the institute, and, during a sojourn in New York City, at the Arts Students League, and he did his own testing of pigments, bristles, and other art materials before he could find any adequate books on the subject in English or French.

Emboldened by an inheritance from his maternal grandmother, Rexroth moved out on his own, first to Chicago's West Side and then to the Near North Side, in time to take part in the explosion of poetry, jazz, art, little theatre, and political radicalism in the early 1920's known as the second Chicago Renaissance. As an habitué of "Bughouse Square" and other forums for the "lunatic fringe," of the Radical Bookshop, and of such Bohemian proto-speakeasies as the Dill Pickle Club, the Wind Blew Inn, and the Green Mask Tea Room, he met and rubbed shoulders with a wide range of unusual people, from underworld and carnival types to jazz musicians and singers like Jimmy Yancey and Alberta Hunter, political activists like Eugene V. Debs, and writers like Maxwell Bodenheim, Ben Hecht, and Sherwood Anderson. At the Green Mask, where Rexroth and others read poetry to jazz, Hecht and Anderson were among the chairmen of the readings. At what he describes as "the great Chicago salon of those days—the incredible house of Jake Loeb, a more important Middle Western cultural institution in 1923 than the University of Chicago, the Art Institute, the Symphony, and the Chicago *Tribune* put together," the guests included such Chicago celebrities as Clarence Darrow, Carl Sandburg, Vachel Lindsay, and Frank Lloyd Wright, and such visitors as G. K. Chesterton and Bertrand Russell.

For several years Rexroth hoboed around the country, speaking from soapboxes for the International Workers of the World and working at a wide variety of jobs, including horsewrangler, sheep-herder, forest ranger, harvest hand, packer, fruit picker, mental hospital attendant, short-order cook, pitchman, and pass-the-hat poetry reader. In his autobiography he laments the co-opting, in the service of "the Social Lie," of the folk culture with which he was then in touch. "In the early twenties it was still at its sources," Rexroth wrote, "and I feel that the contact with folk culture through my grandparents and the old men I met working in the West and the South has been one of the most important factors in the shaping not only of my speech and literary style but of practically all my fundamental life attitudes."

Rexroth worked his way west to Seattle and from there down to San Francisco, where he settled in 1927. There he became active in the John Reed Club and other movements that were dependent on the collaboration of ex-members of the I.W.W. By the time of the San Francisco general strike in the 1930's, he was involved only in the regular trade unions. Since then he has been what he has described as "consistently anti-political—an anarchist and war resister." During World War II, although too old to be drafted, he was a conscientious objector, working as an attendant in a San Francisco psychopathic hospital.

The best preparations for his own work were his translations—seen by him as "poetic exercises in contact with the noblest minds"— of poetry from foreign languages, especially Greek, Chinese, and Japanese. "The first translation from the Greek I ever did," he recalled in his introduction to his Poems from the Greek Anthology (University of Michigan Press, 1962), "was the 'Apple Orchard' of Sappho, in my fifteenth year. It left me so excited with accomplishment that I couldn't sleep well for nights. Since that time . . . the Anthology and the lyric poets of Greece have been my constant companions. They, and the Chinese, have shaped me for better or worse as a poet, and they have given me whatever philosophy of life I have."

Rexroth's own early poems, many of them reflecting the influence of the imagist movement of the first two decades of the century and the experimental forms in vogue in the 1920's and early 1930's, were first published in Blues, Poetry, Pagany, New Masses, Fantasy, and Accent, among other magazines. Critics detected in some of those poems traces of surrealism and Dada, but Rexroth tended to classify himself rather as a literary cubist, an imagist, or an objectivist. A sampling of his early work appeared in Louis Zukofsky's An Objectivists Anthology (Humphries, 1932), but otherwise Rexroth withheld his early poems from permanent publication "until the time which produced them was no longer an element in the judgment of their value." When that publication finally took place, with The Art of Worldly Wisdom (Decker Press, 1949), Rexroth's sharp eye and ear, artistic control, humanistic fire, and wit shone through, notwithstanding the passage of years.

In What Hours (Macmillan, 1940), contained poetic recollections ranging from the author's emotional response to the execution of Sacco and Vanzetti and the Spanish civil war to his quiet enjoyment of flowers, meadows, mountains, and star-filled skies. The Phoenix and the Tortoise (New Directions, 1944) is a long meditative poem that has been compared to Wordsworth's autobiographical Prelude in its joining of personal, imagist lyric to philosophic didacticism. More elegiac were the contents of The Signature of All Things (New Directions, 1950), especially the title poem, a communing with nature in the spirit of Jakob Böhme, the seventeenth-century German mystic.

On a 1948 Guggenheim fellowship, Rexroth toured Wales, England, France, and Italy. Out of that trip came his major poem The Dragon and the Unicorn (New Directions, 1952), a discursive journal in unrhymed, enjambed verse in which his anecdotes and adventures are interspersed with tirades against contemporary capitalist society and its consumerism. Commenting on Rexroth's statement that "most poets resemble Whitman in one regard—they write only one book and that is an interior biography," James Atlas wrote in London Magazine (April/May 1974): "This has become even more true since Rexroth's poem [The Dragon and the Unicorn], since [William Carlos Williams'] Paterson, since [Pound's] Pisan Cantos, where the speaker stands immersed in some larger history. . . . The elements of American poetry in the last decade are to be found in these earlier poems, which prefigured the local democratic mode that was to follow."

What he prefigured most immediately was the Beat Generation, for which Rexroth served as a role model both because of his lifestyle and because of the plain-spoken, breath-controlled, run-on style he had developed as a poet. Most important, perhaps, was his serving as the impresario of the San Francisco Renaissance, in which the Beat Generation writers, the most famous of whom actually came from the East Coast, made their debut as a group. As the late novelist Jack Kerouac recounted, "The San Francisco Renaissance happened one night in 1955. We all went out and got drunk." What Kerouac was referring to was a poetry reading at the Six Gallery in San Francisco, where Rexroth was master of ceremonies and where the readers included Philip Lamantia, Philip Whalen, Michael McClure, Gary Snyder, and Allen Ginsberg. During the heyday of the Beats, in the late 1950's, Rexroth gave poetry readings to jazz accompaniment in clubs in San Francisco and Greenwich Village, New York City, and with the help of Lawrence Ferlinghetti and Allen Ginsberg he founded the Poetry Center at San Francisco State University. His association with the Beat movement, short lived because he never felt really comfortable with its artistic excesses and lack of rigor, was memorialized by Jack Kerouac in the character Reinhold Cacoethes, the anarchist leader of the San Francisco literary community depicted in The Dharma Bums (1958).

Always at his best in connecting personal desire with philosophical quest, observation of nature, and cosmic consciousness, Rexroth was never better at that task than in *The Heart's Garden, The Garden's Heart* (Pym-Randall Press, 1968), consisting of his reflections on the vastness of life on his sixtieth birthday, which he celebrated during a visit to Kyoto, Japan. All of Rexroth's shorter poems, including those in *In Defense of the Earth* (New Directions, 1956), and *Natural Numbers* (New Directions, 1963), were brought together in *The Collected Shorter Poems* (New Directions, 1967). *The Collected Longer Poems* (New Directions, 1969) comprised "The Homestead Called Damascus," written in the early 1920's; "A Prolegomenon to a Theodicy," perhaps his most difficult work, written in the late 1920's; "The Phoenix and the Tortoise"; "The Dragon and the Unicorn"; and "The Heart's Garden, The Garden's Heart." Reviewing *The Collected Longer Poems*, Laurence Lieberman in *Poetry* (April 1969) spoke of Rexroth's "crystalline, ingratiating style," and George Woodcock wrote in the *New Leader* (February 17, 1969): "Among American poets Rexroth is remarkable for his absorption . . . of a variety of European influences, from Guillaume Apollinaire to the English poets of the 1930's. He has overlaid these early plunderings with the gleanings of a middle age largely spent in studying the poetry and philosophy of the Far East. Rexroth nevertheless obstinately remains an American phenomenon."

His subsequent books include three slim volumes of poetry: *New Poems* (New Directions, 1974), *The Silver Swan* (Copper Canyon, 1976), and *The Morning Star* (New Directions, 1979). Among Rexroth's books of translations are *One Hundred Poems from the Japanese* (New Directions, 1955), *One Hundred Poems from the Chinese* (New Directions, 1956), *Thirty Spanish Poems of Love and Exile* (City Lights, 1956), *Love and the Turning Year; One Hundred More Poems from the Chinese* (New Directions, 1970), and *One Hundred Poems from the French* (Pym-Randall, 1972). Four verse plays by Rexroth based on Greek tragedies but modeled in form on Japanese Noh plays were published in *Beyond the Mountains* (New Directions, 1951), the title play of which was performed Off Broadway in 1951. He edited *New British Poets; An Anthology* (New Directions, 1949) and *The Buddhist Writings of Lafcadio Hearn* (Ross-Erikson, 1977).

Aside from his autobiography, Rexroth's most important sustained works of prose are *American Poetry in the Twentieth Century* (Herder, 1971), a book of history and criticism, and *Communalism: From Its Origins to the Twentieth Century* (Seabury Press, 1974), a history of communes from "the Neolithic to 1900." Rexroth as opinionated curmudgeon of acerbic wit and wide-ranging curiosity is nowhere more in evidence than in his essays, which have been compared to those of H. L. Mencken. In the essays collected in *Bird in the Bush* (New Directions, 1959), *Assays* (New Directions, 1961), *The Elastic Retort* (Sea-

bury Press, 1973), *The Alternative Society* (Herder, 1971), and *With Eye and Ear* (Herder, 1971), he challenges conventional wisdom on a wide variety of literary and other subjects, including technocracy, the ecological crisis, and the imminent collapse of the "dominant society" in our civilization.

From San Francisco, where he conducted a weekly radio show devoted to literary criticism and wrote a column for the *Examiner*, Rexroth moved in 1968 to Santa Barbara, California, where he was a special lecturer at the University of California until 1974. He continues to live in Santa Barbara, where he and his fourth wife, Carol Tinker, a painter, own a two-bedroom house filled with books and paintings. Rexroth was previously married to Myrtle Schaeffer (who as a painter used the name Andreé Dutcher), from 1927 until her death in 1940; to Marie Kass, from 1940 until their divorce in 1948; and to Marthe Larsen, from whom he is divorced and by whom he has two grown daughters.

Kenneth Rexroth, who was the model for the lusty, plain-spoken, debunking "proletarian poet" in Mary McCarthy's *Groves of Academe* (1952), is a medium-sized man with white hair, a towering forehead, twinkling blue eyes, an easy smile, and a voice that often rises in mid-syllable from a whisper to a roar or breaks into a staccato, monotone laugh. His wardrobe combines tweedy jackets, string ties, and jeans. He finds his recreation in pastel painting and walking in the mountains, especially the High Sierra, the setting for many of his poems. During his lifetime Rexroth has experimented with several religions, including Anglo and Roman Catholicism and Buddhism. In his mature years, he says, he has lost interest in politics and is "only interested in mystical experience."

References: Los Angeles Times p3 Ag 3 '80 por; N Y Times Bk Rev p8 Jl 8 '67 por; New Yorker 34:29+ My 3 '58; Washington Post L p4+ D 19 '76; Contemporary Authors 1st rev vols 5-8 (1969); Rexroth, Kenneth. An Autobiographical Novel (1966; 1978); Twentieth Century Authors, First Supplement (1955); Who's Who in America, 1980-81

Riley, Bridget (Louise)

Apr. 24, 1931- British painter. Address: b. c/o Rowan Gallery, 31A Bruton Place, London, WIX 7AB, England; h. 7 Royal Crescent, London W 11, England

By coincidence Bridget Riley and op art came into international prominence at about the same time, during the mid-1960's, when one of her paintings was chosen for the catalogue cover of New York's historic "The Responsive

Bridget Riley

Eye" show. Although her pictures, which have been described as "equivalents of states of mind," have none of the vacuous and faddist visual gymnastics that characterized many experiments in optical illusion, only with the winning of the 1968 Venice Biennale award was she able to free her reputation from association with the more limited aspects of op art and claim recognition as one of England's best painters. Working with serial form-units, such as black-on-white geometric shapes or straight or wavy stripes that carry color, she draws from nature, which for her is "not landscape, but the dynamism of visual forces," so that surfaces seem to ripple and buckle and colors to float in front of the canvas. Her early black and white pictures were metaphors of emotional crises, but in her color paintings of the 1970's, as Bryan Robertson pointed out in *Art in America,* the mood "is consistently tonic, optimistic, and radiant."

Of English descent, regardless of the Irish name that her mother gave her, Bridget Louise Riley was born in South London, England on April 24, 1931 to John Fisher Riley, a commercial printer, and Bessie Louise (Gladstone) Riley. Her maternal grandfather, a relative of the Victorian Prime Minister, worked with Thomas Alva Edison on the development of the electric light bulb. Another of her forebears, a great-uncle, helped to found the socialist Fabian Society. During World War II, when her father was serving in the Far East and London was being bombed, Bridget Riley and her younger sister, now a lawyer, lived in a cottage near Padstow in Cornwall with their mother and Aunt Bertha.

In his monograph *Bridget Riley* (1970), published some months after his death, the painter

and art teacher Maurice de Sausmarez noted that she acquired "an intensive visual education" as a child, although her schooling in Cornwall was spasmodic and fragmentary. "I had an enormous affinity for my mother," Miss Riley told John Gruen in an interview for *Artnews* (September 1978). ". . . She adored beauty. She was very sensitive to the beautiful in all kinds of situations. So we shared this great pleasure." Her early desire to draw and paint was stimulated by her aunt, who had attended Goldsmith's College School of Art in London. After the war Bridget's lack of instruction in such academic subjects as mathematics and French was remedied at Cheltenham Ladies' College, a posh boarding school in Gloucestershire. At her own suggestion, however, she spent most of her three years there, from 1946 through 1948, in the art department, drawing and studying the classical traditions of painting under the direction of Colin Hayes.

For another three years, beginning in 1949, Bridget Riley studied at Goldsmith's College School of Art, where her principal teacher, Sam Rabin, stressed the importance of draftsmanship. Exhibitions in London of the works of Picasso, Matisse, and other modernists introduced her to a world of art that was inconceivable in terms of her conventional training and impressed her enormously. In 1952 she enrolled in the painting school of the Royal College of Art in London, but her classes gave her no sense of purpose, and she left in 1955, before the end of her four-year course, to look after her father during his lengthy recuperation from injuries sustained in an automobile accident.

The ordeal of nursing her father, together with her failure to find an aesthetic direction, contributed to Bridget Riley's physical and psychological breakdown at the age of twenty-four. "I struggled with the business of what to paint, how to paint, how, in fact, to solve the whole problem of trying to be an artist," she explained in the interview with Gruen. "I suffered great distress and anguish over that and it lasted a very, very long time." While undergoing therapy at the Middlesex Hospital in 1956-57, she supported herself for a time by selling glass in a London shop. Another job, of teaching art to children during 1957-58 at the Convent of the Sacred Heart in London, helped her to regain self-confidence by sharpening her awareness of possibilities. "I used to tell the kids to take three colours and eight spots and make a picture," she has recalled, as quoted in the London *Observer* (August 1, 1971), "and they'd come up with *hundreds* of combinations." The insistently repetitive patterns that are the hallmark of her painting probably derive in some measure from the exercises in simple principles of art that she set for her students.

Also responsible for the breakthrough from her artistic dilemma had been an exhibition at the Tate Gallery of American abstract expressionist painting in 1956, when for the first time Miss Riley saw the energized, rhythmic, centerless canvases of Jackson Pollock—an experience that she has described as "shattering." Attending some classes of the several summer schools in modern art that Harry Thubron conducted in the North of England also proved to be a liberating and revelatory experience. At one of them, in 1959, she met Maurice de Sausmarez, with whom she fell in love. He encouraged her to pursue an idiom of her own, and together they toured southern Europe, visiting museums and examining architectural masterpieces. The work she saw in Italy of Futurist painters, expressive of dynamic energy, especially attracted her, as did Romanesque architecture, such as the buildings of Pisa whose decorative black and white bands pull against the structural design.

One afternoon in Venice when looking down from her hotel window on the black-and-white patterned piazza below, Bridget Riley watched the configuration dissolve as a violent rainstorm swept across the square. Her reaction to that incident, as Robert Hughes recounted in *Time* (May 12, 1975), was, "Could this breakup not be given an equivalent as painting?" Hughes went on to say, "It could; and that sense of disturbed equilibrium within what looks like a rigid serial structure was to be the essential 'subject' of Riley's work from then on."

Threatened disintegration of an established pattern is the optical effect that Miss Riley achieved in the oil painting *Pink Landscape* (1960), which conveys her perception of the shimmering haze above the plain south of Siena on an exceedingly hot day. In style the landscape was inspired by the French pointillist Georges Seurat, of whose *Le pont de Courbevoie* she had earlier made a full-sized copy, point by point, to understand better its pictorial structure and Seurat's application of the theories of Michel Chevreul regarding the interaction of colors.

Back in England in the fall of 1960, Bridget Riley resumed a part-time post she had accepted in 1959 as lecturer at Loughborough Art School in Leicestershire and began another part-time assignment as lecturer at Hornsey College of Art in London, where de Sausmarez was the director of the department of fine art. From 1962 to 1964 she lectured part time at Croydon College of Art in Surrey. Simultaneously, from 1961 to 1964, she worked part time for the J. Walter Thompson advertising agency in London on illustrations and designs for bookjackets and packaging.

Meanwhile, after completing several exercises in field painting, of which *The Kiss* (1960), with its vibrating massed energy, is an example, Bridget Riley arrived in more subtle black and white compositions at the medium through which she could develop her individual talent. She has occasionally had her name linked with that of Victor Vasarely as among the foremost practitioners of op art, and some

critics have suggested that her work was affected by his. When she first saw Vasarely's pictures, however, she had already begun her experiments in optical phenomena. Although she credits him with affirming her own ideas, she denies that he influenced them.

Bridget Riley's advancement toward the definition of her art is evident in the contrast between her Bonnard-like canvases in the group show at the Wildenstein Galleries in London in the late 1950's and the nine paintings in her first solo exhibition, at Gallery One in London in 1962. The confrontations of her geometric forms in *Movement in Squares*, *Horizontal Vibrations*, *Black to White Discs*, and other works produce a dynamism that, as de Sausmarez observed in his catalogue for the show, "is neither the description of movement nor the record of actual physical movement. . . . These works are not to be explained as demonstrations of a theory of perception; in addition to their teasing ambiguities, they have a lyricism, a structural strength, an immaculate and vibrating freshness that is the clearest evidence of a creative sensibility, an acutely refined judgment." Because of the aggressive patterning of her predominately circular forms in *Blaze I*, *Uneasy Centre*, *Interrupted Circle*, and other paintings of her second Gallery One show, in 1963, her work was associated, if only temporarily, with violence and distress, with retinal-punishing assaults that induce nausea.

So fashionable did the Riley "eye-ticklers" become that manufacturers plagiarized her designs for their fabrics and various other commercial products in England and the United States. Her work had been shown throughout both countries, as well as in France, West Germany, and Japan, by the time that her two paintings, *Current* and *Hesitate*, created a furore at the op art show "The Responsive Eye," which opened at the New York Museum of Modern Art in February 1965. Later in that month she had a solo show at the Richard Feigen Gallery in New York, where on the first day all sixteen of her canvases were sold.

Celebrated in newspapers and magazines as Queen of Op, Miss Riley tried to dispel in statements to the press some misunderstandings about her art. In one interview she explained that she was painting "a kind of tension" and that the "optical" aspect hardly mattered. Her dismay at the trivialization of her painting through increased commercial exploitation gained the sympathy of John Canaday, who argued in the New York *Times* (March 14, 1965) that the unauthorized use of her designs for dress fabrics was all the more offensive because her illusionary effect depended upon a flat surface of specific scale. He found the application of the Riley image to textile patterns "only a degree less obviously a perversion" than reproducing a Rembrandt on a wastebasket.

After her return to London, Bridget Riley protested in an article for *Artnews* (October

1965) that the hullabaloo surrounding "The Responsive Eye" show had prevented her work from being viewed with insight or considered judgment. To set the record straight she denied that she was a student of mathematics or optics, that she made use of scientific data, or intended to be illustrative. In language as precise as her paintings she spelled out carefully that in each picture "a particular situation is stated. Certain elements within that situation remain constant. Others precipitate the destruction of themselves by themselves. Recurrently, as a result of the cyclic movement of repose, disturbance and repose, the original situation is re-stated." The disturbances arise naturally and inevitably from qualities in the formal units she uses, such as dots, triangles, and swirling lines, somewhat like the disruptions in society and the human psyche that stem from intrinsic causes. What she referred to as the "event" in her paintings ideally evokes a certain recognition so that the viewer simultaneously confronts the known along with the unknown. "Other polarities which find an echo in the depths of our psychic being are those of static and active, or fast and slow," she wrote in regard to additional elements of her art. "Repetition, contrast, calculated reversal and counterpoint also parallel the basis of our emotional structure."

By the time of her shows in New York the black-on-white marks of Bridget Riley's pictures had begun sometimes to shade into a midway gray, as in *Burn* (1964), which allowed greater control of changes in visual tempo. The warm and cold tones of gray in paintings like *Drift* (1966) and *Deny II* (1967) added, moreover, another polarity to her work. Since the early 1960's she had been quietly making studies in color and for some time had worked with so-called "disembodied colors" that emerged in her black and white pictures. But it was not until after her introduction of gray and her explorations in warm and cold contrasts that she found a way unhesitatingly to extend her use of color—or, as de Sausmarez explained, "to replace a tonal scale by a graded color scale." Among her early paintings in color were the *Cataract* and *Chant* series, which develop their energies through bands, or stripes, of red and turquoise. One of her finest works, *Late Morning* (1967), now in the Tate Gallery collection, juxtaposes red and white bands with green-blue bands of graded scale.

Miss Riley's color paintings were shown for the first time in 1968 at the thirty-fourth Venice Biennale, where she was awarded the international prize for painting. The only other British artist to win a Venice grand prix was Henry Moore, who twenty years earlier had received the international prize in sculpture. For Bridget Riley, the prestigious award vindicated an effort that had once been dismissed as "gimmickry." With renewed confidence she explored more fully a phenonemon known as color spread, or color irradiation, which had appeared in some of her earlier color paintings. The orange, green, and violet horizontal bands of *Rise I* (1968) and elongated triangular bands of *Orient I* (1969), for instance, affect not only the identity of the three colors but spread color into the white areas of the painting.

"I take for example three colours, say Magenta, Ochre and Turquoise plus black and white, a situation which then triggers off airy irridescent bursts of colour," Bridget Riley wrote in a statement for *Contemporary Artists* (1977) describing what happens in her pictures. "I choose a form and a structure in which to repeat these colour clouds, to accumulate them, to mass them until each painted unit is submerged in a visual rhythm which, in turn, collectively generates a shimmering coloured haze. This luminous substance is completely meshed with the actual coloured surface and together they provide the experience of the painting."

From straight-line stripe paintings, like the magnificent *Apprehend* (1970), that have been compared with those of the American artist Kenneth Noland, Bridget Riley had turned by the mid-1970's to curvilinear color streams in such paintings as *Entice II* (1974), *Shih-Li* (1975), *Rill* (1976), and *Orphean Elegy I* (1978) whose undulating rhythm is somewhat reminiscent of the *Cataract, Drift,* and *Arrest* series of the preceding decade. Comparing her more recent color paintings with her black and white work of the early 1960's, John Russell observed in the New York *Times* (May 18, 1975), "The basic unit of her expression remains the same: the dichotomy between what is and what seems to be." But, he pointed out, the character of the feeling implicit in the paintings had changed: "What she has to show us [now] is nearer to the sight of a peach tree in a desert than to the case histories of the distracted mind."

Because of her explorations of the effect of the proximity of one color to another on the canvas, Bridget Riley believes that her work is closer to the impressionists than to any other group of painters. "But they put down what they see in front of them," she said in an interview for the *Guardian* (April 12, 1973). "I start from the colour itself." For her, painting is "a process of discovery," in which she reaches decisions intuitively in many experimental studies, painstakingly developed over a period that may be as long as two years. For her much-admired *Burn*, as an example, she made twelve preparatory sketches and four preliminary paintings. Her working studies, sometimes included in her exhibitions, often contain notations to her assistants, who under her supervision execute the precisely structured final paintings. Many of them are exceedingly large; *Shih-Li*, for instance, measures 140 inches in width.

In her own country Bridget Riley's work is reportedly in as great demand as the sculpture of Henry Moore and the paintings of Ben Nicolson. Major museum shows of her art have been held in several European countries, and in 1971 she had an important retrospective of 227 paintings and drawings at the Hayward Gallery in London. Her only solo show in New York City since her second Feigen Gallery show in 1967-68 was at the Sidney Janis Gallery in 1975. A retrospective, which opened at the Albright-Knox Art Gallery in Buffalo, New York in September 1978 and later at the Museum of Fine Arts in Dallas, traveled to New Zealand, Australia, and Japan. Several critics bemoaned its limited American tour, including John Russell, who maintained in *Art in America* (November/December 1978), "The experience of Riley's career as a whole is one of the most rewarding that living art has to offer."

Among Bridget Riley's tributes is an honorary LL.D degree from Manchester University, awarded in 1976. She is a slender, distinctly attractive woman, with blue eyes and dark hair. Her home is a five-storied Victorian house in Holland Park, London, which has studios on its first four floors. She also has studios in Cornwall and southern France. As a founding member and former director of S.P.A.C.E. Ltd., she has worked for several years on its program of providing studios for young artists. In pursuit of such causes, according to the London *Observer* (August 1, 1971), "she has been called a bulldozer, and rude with it. . . . At first encounters, strangers are apt to find her unfriendly. But she quickly calms down and shows the amiability her friends are aware of, and the consideration she always has for her helpers in the studio."

References: Artnews 77:80+ S '78 pors; Art in Am 55:98+ My '67 por, 63:69+ Mr '75; London Observer p2 Ag 1 '71, p26 Jl 25 '71; N Y Times II p25 D 29 '68 por; Time 96:82+ N 16 '70 por, 105:52+ My 12 '75 por; Contemporary Artists (1977); de Sausmarez, Maurice. Bridget Riley (1970); International Who's Who, 1980-81; Who's Who, 1980-81; Who's Who in the World, 1974-75

Rogers, Kenny

1939(?)- Singer. Address: b. Management Three, 9744 Wilshire Blvd., Beverly Hills, Calif. 90212

Kenny Rogers, who in 1979 reached his apogee of popularity on the country-western scene, is a product of the so-called "crossover" phenomenon—an entertainer who has changed from one musical genre to another. But while most singers cross over from country to pop, Rogers has done the opposite. As lead singer for a rock group in the late 1960's and early 1970's he enjoyed some success with such hits as "Just Dropped In" and "Ruby." It was not until he went on his own as a country solo artist, however, that Rogers really hit his stride. "Lucille," the first of his country hits, went "gold" (earned $1,000,000) in 1977. His greatest success to date came with the 1979 album *The Gambler,* which went "triple-platinum" (sold more than 3,000,000 copies) and racked up higher first-day sales figures than any other album of the 1970's. As of late 1979 Rogers' recordings have grossed more than $100,000,000. His honors include a half-dozen Academy of Country Music and Country Music Association awards and two Grammies. Rogers has set attendance records at personal concert appearances across the United States, and he has also begun to make his mark as a nonsinging star of television specials. "I've never felt I'm a particularly good singer," Rogers told Alanna Nash in an interview for *Stereo Review* (April 1980), "but I've always felt that I have a very *commercial* voice."

Kenneth Ray Rogers was born in a federal housing project in Houston, Texas about 1939, one of the eight children of Edward Floyd Rogers, a shipyard worker who died in 1976, and Lucille (Hester) Rogers. "We were very poor," Rogers told Norma McLain Stoop of *After Dark* (November 1972), "but I was just a kid with nothing to compare it to, so I thought everybody lived like that, and those were really some of the happiest times of my life." Despite his problem with alcoholism, Rogers' father, an amateur fiddle player, had an affectionate relationship with his children and taught them to love music. As a boy,

Rogers accompanied his family on trips to his grandfather's farm in Apple Springs, Texas, where relatives gathered from miles around for music-centered family reunions. At thirteen, while sick in bed with the measles, he taught himself to play the guitar.

An A student at Houston's Jefferson Davis High School, Rogers sang in the glee club and in his church choir and played guitar in a band that he had organized, called the Scholars. His most important musical influences at that time were Ray Charles and Sam Cooke. About 1957 Rogers and his band produced the hit single "Crazy Feeling," which sold a million copies. The Scholars appeared on *American Bandstand* (ABC-TV, 1957) and cut several additional singles that failed, however, to measure up to "Crazy Feeling." In an effort to sustain their sudden popularity the group even recorded "Kangewah," a song written by Hollywood gossip columnist Louella Parsons. "We figured she'd plug our record in her column," Rogers told *People* interviewer Sue Reilly (December 10, 1979). "It was a great idea but had no relationship to reality. We came home broke." According to Kenny Rogers' brother Leland, quoted by Peter H. Brown in *Parade* (February 17, 1980), "Kenny really thought he was 'it' then. He got all duded up like Elvis Presley and took his 'star role' to heart. He came back to Houston and told me: 'One thing I'm not gonna do is sign all those autographs. I haven't got the time for that stuff.' Well, brother, it was ten years before Kenny got another taste of success, and he's been signing autographs ever since."

The first member of his family ever to complete high school, Rogers wanted to become a professional musician but, in compliance with his parents' wishes, enrolled at the University of Houston after graduation from Jefferson Davis to major in commercial art. In 1960, however, after less than a year in college, he dropped out and joined the Bobby Doyle Trio, an avant-garde jazz band. He remained with the group for about six years, playing bass fiddle, and was for a time also a member of an outfit known as the Kirby Stone Four.

Aware of the continuing popularity of folk music, Rogers joined the New Christy Minstrels in 1966. He told Norma McLain Stoop: "I . . . went with the New Christy Minstrels because, though it was a monetary step down, I felt it was a professional step up and would do something towards my future career." Again, sensing the shift away from folk music to folk-rock, Rogers and several other members of the Christy Minstrels tried to change the group's approach. "A few of us in the group worked in nine songs Mike Settle had written, in hopes the Christy Minstrels would record them," Rogers explained in the *After Dark* interview, "but their opinion was that they had a successful image and they didn't want to gamble with it."

In 1967 Rogers and three other members of the New Christy Minstrels—Mike Settle, Terry Williams, and Thelma Camacho—left the group to form the folk-rock band the First Edition. From the beginning, Rogers—who at that time sported skin-tight suits, a beard, and a gold earring—tried to make the group's music and image appeal to the widest possible audience. The band made its debut at Ledbetters, a nightclub in Los Angeles owned by Randy Sparks, the founder of the New Christy Minstrels. Its first hit, "Just Dropped In (To See What Condition My Condition Was In)," written by Rogers' high school friend Mickey Newbury to cash in on the psychedelic or acid-rock craze, hit the *Billboard* "Top 100" in February 1968 and remained on the chart for ten weeks.

During the nine years of its existence, the group, formally called Kenny Rogers and the First Edition, recorded four gold albums and nine gold singles. Among its LP's were *The First Edition* and *The Ballad of Calico*—a concept album about a ghost-town near Barstow, California. Its hit singles included "But You Know I Love You," Mel Tillis' "Ruby (Don't Take Your Love To Town)," "Tell It All, Brother," "Heed the Call," Mac Davis' "Something's Burning," and Alex Harvey's "Reuben James" (not to be confused with Woody Guthrie's World War II song of the same title). After recording for five years under the Warner/Reprise label the band switched to MGM Records in the summer of 1972, primarily because Rogers managed to persuade the president of the latter company, Mike Curb (who later became Lieutenant Governor of California), to offer the band a million-dollar advance guarantee—the largest in recording history. In the *After Dark* interview Rogers candidly acknowledged: "I've tried to approach the [music] business as a business—just that."

The First Edition also toured the United States, Canada, England, Scotland, and New Zealand and was featured on seventeen television network variety shows. In the fall of 1972 it became the first pop group to headline at the Persian Room of New York's Plaza Hotel and broke house attendance records. The band also sang the songs for the soundtrack of the movie *Fools* (Cinerama, 1970) and in 1971-72 starred in its own syndicated musical television series *Rollin' On the River* (known from the fall of 1972 on as *Rollin' With Kenny Rogers and the First Edition*), which was set on board a Mississippi riverboat. The show was telecast over 192 stations in the United States and Canada in the course of its two-year run. The personnel of the First Edition changed several times, and only Rogers and guitarist Terry Williams remained with the group for the full nine years. Other members have included Mary Arnold, Gene Lorenzo, Mickey Jones, Kin Vassy, and Jimmy Hassell.

Not completely comfortable in the folk-rock idiom, Rogers maintains that he had always been a country singer and that much of the music performed by the First Edition had its roots in the country-western tradition. "When you look at most of our big hits, they were really country records," he told Alanna Nash of *Stereo Review* (April 1980). "But Warner Brothers . . . did not *have* a country-music department, so they merchandised us as a pop act, or a rock act." Miss Nash backed up that assessment, noting that "the songs of the First Edition did not fit neatly into any one category. Ostensibly a Top-40 rock group, the band built most of its fame with several country-flavored numbers. . . . In retrospect, it appears that the First Edition played a not-too-small but largely unheralded role in helping bridge the gap between country and rock."

Eventually, the band's records failed to sell. "We reached a point of what I call creative stagnancy," Rogers explained to Alanna Nash. "We had done about everything there was, and there was just no fresh input." But he has also said: "I loved the First Edition. There never was one minute I didn't feel proud of its success." Perceiving an upsurge of interest in country music, Rogers switched his label to United Artists in 1976 and moved to Nashville to try his luck as a solo artist. With the help of producer Larry Butler and manager Ken Kragen, he worked out a unique new musical style analyzed by Alanna Nash as "a little contemporary folk, a little pasteurized country, a little half-baked rock-and-roll, a few string-swathed love songs and ballads, and lots of good-natured congeniality."

Four of Rogers' singles in his new musical vein made the country-music charts almost immediately: "Love Lifted Me," "Homemade Love," "Laura," and "While the Feeling's Good." His popularity with audiences received a further boost from an appearance on the *Tonight Show* and a headline engagement at the Golden Nugget casino in Las Vegas. But Rogers' reputation as a country singer was not firmly established until 1977, with the release of "Lucille," a ballad by Roger Bowling and Hal Bynum about the woes of a man deserted by his wife. "Lucille" went "gold," became the nation's number one country hit, and brought Rogers a Grammy from the National Academy of Recording Arts and Sciences for the year's best male country vocal performance at the twentieth annual awards ceremony. It won the Academy of Country Music's best single and best song awards and earned Rogers its best male vocalist award for 1977. In addition, the Country Music Association designated "Lucille" its song of the year.

After "Lucille," Rogers and the popular female country vocalist Dottie West collaborated on the album *Every Time Two Fools Collide*, which included the hit song "All I Ever Need Is You." The pair became a popular singing team and made frequent concert appearances together. "Dottie is a very good friend of mine," Rogers has said, "and the thing I enjoyed most about doing the album is that it was all so genuine. It was done for the right reason; we really enjoy singing together."

Rogers' recent country-western recordings include the albums *Daytime Friends, Kenny Rogers, Love or Something Like It,* and *Ten Years of Gold.* Among his hit singles are "I Wish That I Could Hurt That Way Again," "Heart to Heart," "Morgana," "You Decorated My Life," "She Believes in Me," "Coward of the County," and Alex Harvey's "Making Music for Money"—a lampoon of commercialism in the music business. But his most successful recording by far is the 1979 album *The Gambler,* which elevated Rogers to the status of the leading male country vocalist in the United States. The title song, written by Don Schlitz, had previously been recorded by a dozen different artists, including Johnny Cash and Bobby Bare, but it took Rogers' distinctive voice and style to make the song a hit. By the end of 1979 the album had sold more than 3,000,000 copies. In February 1980 it earned Rogers a second Grammy for best male country vocal performance. *The Gambler* was dislodged from the top of the charts only when it was superseded by Rogers' next album, *Kenny,* which eventually went platinum. In January 1980 *Variety* listed *Kenny* fifth among the best-selling albums in the United States. Rogers' *Gideon,* a concept album relating the life story of a cowboy, written by the former New Christy Minstrels singers Kim Carnes and Dave Ellingson, was released in the fall of 1980.

Taking a hardheaded view of his future prospects, Rogers often tells interviewers that he does not expect his popularity to last. As he explained to Alanna Nash: "I'm on a hot spell right now, and I figure I've got two and a half years left on it. The rule of thumb is about three years, because the record-buying public changes on that three-year cycle." He has therefore expanded the range of his activities. In December 1979 he hosted the CBS-TV special *Kenny Rogers and the American Cowboy,* which included a Rogers outdoor concert in Los Angeles as well as footage of the life of modern-day cowboys in Nevada and Oregon. A reviewer for *Variety* (December 5, 1979) called it "a very professional and appealing product." Rogers made his acting debut in the made-for-television movie *Kenny Rogers as The Gambler,* a western adventure drama, based on his hit song, that was presented on CBS-TV in April 1980.

In *Kenny Rogers' America,* a special shown on CBS-TV in November 1980, Rogers performed his songs against a background of both rural and urban American scenes. During 1981 his single "Lady" and his album *Greatest Hits* made the lists of best-selling records, and his newest album, *Share Your Love,* on which he collaborated with Lionel B. Ritchie Jr. of the pop-soul group the Commodores, made its first appearance in the record shops.

Rogers views the so-called "bastardization" of country music—its fusion with rock, folk, and other elements—as a salutary thing. "It's brought a lot of people into the fold that wouldn't have listened to country music otherwise," he told Lynn Van Matre of the Chicago Tribune (August 12, 1979). "It used to be you either liked country music or you didn't, because it all sounded alike. Now it's no longer one-dimensional, and I think that's great." To aid aspiring musicians, Rogers collaborated on the book *Making It With Music* (Harper, 1978) with Len Epand. "The book heavily stresses what one should do to get started in the business," Rogers was quoted in *Contemporary Authors* as saying. "It's not designed to make a star out of someone who is not capable of or interested in becoming a star. It's designed to help a person with an average amount of talent who just wants to make a decent living in a very lucrative business."

Rogers' income was estimated in 1979 to be about $7,000,000 a year, and he is prudent in his handling of it. He owns a $4,000,000 mansion in the Bel Air section of Los Angeles, a 2 percent share in the Golden Nugget casino in Las Vegas, a $600,000 yacht, two private jets, two office buildings in Nashville and one in Los Angeles, and a fleet of cars, including a yellow Rolls-Royce. His honors for 1979 include the Academy of Country Music's best male vocalist and entertainer of the year awards and the Country Music Association's awards for duo of the year (with Dottie West), album of the year (for *The Gambler*), and male vocalist of the year. Rogers also holds *Billboard* magazine's 1977 "crossover artist of the year" award, as well as three awards from the trade association for juke box operators and a British Country Music Association award. President Jimmy Carter invited Rogers to entertain at the White House in 1979 on the occasion of the signing of the Israeli-Egyptian peace treaty by Prime Minister Menahem Begin and President Anwar Sadat.

Although Rogers occasionally writes his own songs, such as "Sweet Music Man," most of the songs he performs are written by others. "I think I have an excellent ear for hit songs," he said in the *Stereo Review* interview. "I try to find songs that have a hook, that have something to say, that touch people, and then I do that song the way I think it should be done." Rogers' producer, Larry Butler, regularly sifts through an enormous number of songs for suitability. After Butler narrows the number to about thirty, Rogers listens to them, makes the final selections, and usually records the songs that same night. "I've found that by doing that, there's a certain spontaneity that happens," he has explained. "I probably sing it better later, but I don't think it does the song as much good." William Carlton of the New York *Daily News* (March 26, 1979) wrote that Rogers "sings in a warm, supple, romantic, tender voice with a surprisingly wide range. His story songs are always fresh, tasteful, honest and intelligent, well-crafted and interesting. The man and his music are as welcome as old friends and family."

Kenny Rogers and Marianne Gordon, a former model and star of the country-western television comedy show *Hee Haw*, were married on October 2, 1977. Two of his previous marriages lasted a total of four and a half years and a third endured twelve years—until 1976. He admitted to Sue Reilly of *People* magazine (December 10, 1979) that his preoccupation with his musical career plays a large part in his "inability to sustain relationships." Rogers has a grown daughter, Carole Lynne, by his first wife, and a teenage son, Kenneth Ray Jr., by his third. The bearded, grizzled singer stands six-feet one inch tall and weighs 203 pounds. He enjoys golf, tennis, softball, and poker, and does not smoke or drink. With his tour band, Bloodline, Rogers maintains a rigorous concert schedule. In 1979 he sang before a total of some 2,000,000 people, and his engagements included a concert at Carnegie Hall. But despite the many demands of his profession, Rogers assured Alanna Nash: "I love what I'm doing. I would do it for a lot less money."

References: After Dark 5:30+ N '72 por; People 9:64+ Ja 9 '78 pors, 94:122+ D 10 '79 pors; Stereo R 44:68+ Ap '80 por; TV Guide 28:18+ Ap 5 '80 por; Contemporary Authors vols 85-88 (1980); Encyclopedia of Pop, Rock and Soul (1974); Who's Who in America, 1980-81

Russell, Mark

Aug. 23, 1932- Comedian. Address: b. 2828 Wisconsin Ave., Washington, D.C. 20007

Among durable Washington, D.C. institutions must be listed the topical stand-up humorist Mark Russell, the resident political satirist of the Shoreham-Americana Hotel in the nation's capital. As a young cocktail lounge piano player back in the Eisenhower era, Russell found his métier when he began inserting original song parodies and political wisecracks into his performances. Ever since, he has been entertaining Capitol Hill insiders and tourists with his brisk, jaunty routines, as fresh as the afternoon headlines, and for six seasons now he has reached a nationwide audience with his one-man comedy specials televised by the Public Broadcasting Service. In addition to doing five thirty-minute PBS specials each year, Russell tapes a daily ninety-second humorous commentary on politics and current events for the NBC radio network, writes a newspaper column (consisting mostly of his one-liners) that is syndicated by the Los Angeles *Times*, and has been a regular on the NBC television show *Real People*. In recent years he has reduced his annual stay at the Shoreham's Marquee Lounge to some sixteen weeks, or approximately 160 performances, in order to

Mark Russell

respond to an increased demand for personal appearances elsewhere, especially in colleges.

The first impression one gets of Mark Russell, as one member of the Capitol Hill press corps has observed, is "not show biz boffo, but Congressional." As Russell strolls onto the stage in his monochromatic three-piece suit and dark-rimmed glasses, he might be a Senator or Representative from Middle America, introducing in a resonant baritone voice a bill resolving that George Bush "be retired to a home for the chronically preppy" or remembering where he first saw Ronald Reagan— "in the picture frame department at Woolworth's, between Gale Storm and Walter Pidgeon." Russell's gleeful puncturing of political pomposity is nonpartisan, extending to Democrats and liberals as well as Republicans and conservatives; he used to compare President Jimmy Carter's promise to streamline the government, for example, to "putting racing stripes on an arthritic camel," and one of "Russell's Laws of School Transportation" reads, "The length of a politician's speech praising the virtues of busing is on a sliding scale with the number of children he has in private school." His fast-paced patter is interspersed with musical lampoons of his own invention— such as his nuclear industry "folk" song "This Uranium Is Your Uranium," to the tune of "This Land Is Your Land"—self-accompanied standing up at the piano. As a reviewer of Russell's book of humor *Presenting Mark Russell* (Everest House, 1980) wrote in *Publisher's Weekly* (October 10, 1980), "One misses the musical accompaniment to the ditties that are part of his routine; minus the piano and Russell's pixyish grin, they lose some of their verve."

Mark Russell was born Mark Ruslander in Buffalo, New York on August 23, 1932, the elder son of Marcus Joseph and Marie Elizabeth (Perry) Ruslander. His brother is Dan Ruskin, a cocktail lounge pianist who is, Russell acknowledges, a much better player than he. "He's a very traditional guy," Dan has said, remembering that Mark's childhood heroes were Abraham Lincoln and the United States Marines. Mark collected Lincolniana and followed every Marine battle in World War II, "fighting the war from a tabletop."

"My father worked in a Mobil gas station in Buffalo when I was born," Russell recounts in one of the autobiographical sections of *Presenting Mark Russell*. "He later advanced to a white-collar job with Mobil, which was then the Socony-Vacuum Oil Company.... My brother Dan and I worked for my father in his gas station, and that was the beginning of our present energy crisis. We were both inept. My shoes and socks were constantly drenched with gasoline, since I was totally incapable of filling anyone's tank without running at least thirty cents' worth onto the ground. In those days, thirty cents' worth could drench your shoes and socks."

As pianists and singers, Mark and Dan Ruslander (as they were known before they took their stage names) regularly performed at family get-togethers, and their father implanted show-business ambitions in both of them. "I come from a funny family," Russell told Richard Lee in an interview for the Washington *Post's Potomac Magazine* (June 27, 1976). "There was a kind of competitiveness, as far back as I can remember. We were always putting each other on. My father was a very funny man, a life-of-the-party type."

The Ruslander brothers made their first public appearance as an act when their father put them on an overnight boat to Detroit to visit an uncle and told the purser they would put on a free show. Mark was twelve at the time, and Dan was eight. Two years later Mark formed an orchestra and earned his first money as a professional entertainer—ten dollars for a New Year's Eve engagement in an Italian restaurant in Buffalo. He told Joseph B. Treaster in an interview for *Quest* (January 1980) that his dream was to become a jazz musician but that he "couldn't cut it."

Russell found his first great vocational model during a visit to New York City with his father when he was seventeen. In the Village Room of the Hotel Taft they caught the piano act of Charlie Drew, singing his "songs that mother never taught you," such double entendre-laden ditties as "Someone Kissed My Fanny in Miami." The effect on Russell of "that wonderful gentle man sitting there and singing those forbidden words" was, as he later described it, "like walking on the moon." A similar effect was made on him a few years later by another humorous songwriter-pianist, the irreverent social satirist Tom Lehrer. Another later influence was comedian Mort Sahl.

Reared in the Roman Catholic faith, Russell attended parochial grammar school and Canisius High School, an all-male Jesuit institution in Buffalo. The Ruslanders moved to Florida, where Mark spent three months at the University of Miami, and then to Washington, D.C., where he studied at George Washington University for twenty-eight days before enlisting in the Marines. He began playing the piano in nearby bars when he was stationed at the Marine Corps base in Quantico, Virginia, and after his discharge he worked in the Merryland Club and other strip-tease rooms in Washington, D.C. Sidney Yudain, the publisher of the Capitol Hill weekly newspaper *Roll Call*, heard him at the Merryland Club one night in 1958 and recommended him to his friend Tom Heslop, manager of the Carroll Arms Hotel, across the street from the new Senate Office Building.

When Russell arrived at the cocktail lounge of the Carroll Arms, he had a borrowed repertoire in which the humor was represented by the risqué routines of Charlie Drew and the brash parodies of Tom Lehrer. The turning point in the development of his act came in February 1959, with "Lucky Young Son," a parody of "Lucky Old Sun" written by Yudain about a Congressman from Iowa then making headlines for carrying an absentee teenaged son on his payroll at a high salary. Sung by Russell in his act one day after the news of the nepotism broke, the song convulsed his audience and inspired him to try his own hand at topical spoofs. The first was "Won't You Come Home, Coya Knutson?" (to the tune of "Won't You Come Home, Bill Bailey?"), inspired by a press conference held by the husband of Representative Coya Knutson of Iowa to announce that his wife was needed at home and he would support her opponent in the coming election if she did not voluntarily retire. Thereafter, Russell turned out a new parody every week or so, and he came up with new gags every day about current events to round out the patter between songs.

Russell's act made the Carroll Arms an "in" Capitol Hill hangout, as a reporter for *Variety* (June 8, 1960) observed: "It is an offbeat act in an offbeat place, [delivered] to a very 'beat' audience of politicos and their underlings, lobbyists, and political writers. The bright young men of Capitol Hill keep coming back so regularly that the Carroll Arms doesn't even need a cover charge or a minimum."

In 1961 Russell moved to the more prestigious Marquee Lounge of the Shoreham Hotel (now the Shoreham-Americana), which has remained his base, on and off, ever since. Attempts to transplant his humor outside of Washington failed for many years, most conspicuously in 1968, when a daytime television show he co-hosted with Clay Cole in Cleveland, Ohio was canceled after ten months, but a local Washington show he co-hosted in the mid-1960's, the *Mark and Inga Show*, proved more successful. In the early 1970's

he sank into what he has described as "a professional lethargy," a feeling that his act "had run its course." "The adrenalin started flowing" again temporarily during Watergate, when, in his words, he would "just rip and read" his material right off the ticker of the wire services. "My line was," he told Louise Sweeney when she interviewed him for the *Christian Science Monitor* (April 15, 1980), "that after he [President Richard Nixon] resigned, I had to go back to writing my own material." His Watergate act at the Shoreham —including such quips as "Bail to the Chief" and "Nixon has a staff infection"—was recorded live for the album *Mark Russell's Wild, Weird, Wired World of Watergate* (Deep Six Records, 1973).

During his period of professional crisis, Russell was also trying to save his first marriage. He and his first wife, Becky, who had become followers of the late clairvoyant healer Edgar Cayce, bought a small farm in Virginia, Beach, Virginia, where the Edgar Cayce Foundation and the Association for Research and Enlightenment are located. "I got into the meditation," he recounted in the *Potomac Magazine* interview with Richard Lee, "and still hung on to the inherent Catholicism—in fact embraced it in a very enveloping way, and this probably gave me a little more sustenance as far as the job was concerned."

In 1975, when his first marriage ended, Russell had what he has described as a "nervous breakdown," for which he was hospitalized for two weeks and because of which he took four months leave from the Shoreham. "When I left the hotel, it was with the idea of not coming back . . . ," he explained to Richard Lee. "And if it weren't for the [television] specials, I probably wouldn't have come back. . . . They're very lucrative—I can earn as much from doing five specials as I earn in a whole year at the Shoreham. But, technically, I would suffer if I left the Shoreham hotel. You need that day-to-day exposure to an audience. You can find out in two minutes if the stuff is working. I've gotten enormous support from people here [telling me] how much they missed having this [his Shoreham act], where they could bring their relatives, and even from out-of-towners. . . . So I thought, 'Yeah, I really need to go back there.'" Presciently, at a "Roast Mark Russell Night" attended by 720 notables at the National Press Club more than a year earlier, the UPI White House correspondent Helen Thomas, in her turn to tease Russell, had said: "Mark Russell plays the piano like Truman and the yo-yo like Nixon. He's been around a little longer than Nixon, but they do have one thing in common—despite popular demand, they won't quit."

During the Administration of Gerald R. Ford, Russell's Presidential barbs included the following: "The President says the Defense budget is not sacrosanct. That means they are laying off six waiters at the Army-Navy country club. . . . Gerald Ford reminds me of the guy who answers the meat buzzer at the A&P. . . . You know, Jerry is trying to deroyalize the Presidency. They're changing the name of the song to 'Hi to the Chief.'" When Ford granted amnesty to Vietnam war resisters, Russell visualized the Berrigan brothers, the prominent antiwar activists, "laying a wreath at the tomb of the Unknown Deserter." Other targets of his in the mid-1970's included Senator Edward M. Kennedy ("Not a candidate? If you believe Teddy Kennedy is not a candidate you also believe the Happy Hooker is a virgin and Strom Thurmond has rhythm"), John Connally as a Presidential candidate ("Peace Through Height") and Chief Justice Burger ("Burger Chief"). When a sex scandal toppled Representative Wayne Hays from Congressional eminence, Russell wrote the ditty, "The Reign of Wayne Seems Plainly Down the Drain," and when Senators Jacob Javits and Claiborne Pell returned from a reconciliatory mission to Cuba, he was reminded of Neville Chamberlain getting off the plane from Munich ("I expected the Senators to say, 'We will have Cuban cigars in our time.'") He likened détente with the Soviet Union to "going to a wife-swapping party and coming home alone," and after tax-slashing Proposition 13 became a fact of fiscal austerity in California he imagined that "you might drive into a little town and see a mom-and-pop morgue, or Ernie's hospital, or Frank and Irene's police department." He outlined how government contracts are awarded: "Step one, assemble the sealed bids in a military manner; step two, award the contract; step three, open the bids."

To the suggestion that the Carter Administration was overloaded with Georgians, Russell responded with the example of President Carter's foreign policy adviser, Zbigniew Brzezinski: "The rumor is that Brzezinski is actually Carter's cousin from Macon . . . Jethro Gump. . . . If you wake Zbigniew Brzezinski up in the middle of the night, he talks just like Billy Carter." In retrospect, he finds it difficult to laugh at Carter, as he told Francis X. Clines in an interview for the New York Times (January 19, 1981): "Ah, the poor guy, he was what we needed for the time, an antidote, that's all he could be. . . . I've been forgetting Carter for some time, this transition seems so long. I feel Ronald Reagan has been President for a long, long time and will always be kind of a figurehead." He said he had already tested some material for the Reagan Presidency, including a fantasy about Bambi and Rocky Raccoon forlornly leading other American woodland creatures up into Canada for refuge from Reagan's environmental views and from officials whose "idea of communing with nature is a cookout in a strip mine." According to Clines, he was making his stage entrances in a formal cutaway outfit (de rigueur at the Reagan inauguration), describing it as "a Republican leisure suit," and he had a new skit on Republican tourists at the Washington Zoo asking directions to "where they keep the liberals."

With his television work and his increased bookings around the country, Russell has advanced well into six figures in income. If he were not so "easygoing" about money and fame, according to his friend Stephan Schwartz, he could have even greater popular success. "Middle-class people just love him," Schwartz assured Richard Lee in the Potomac Magazine interview. "He has the ability to project Middle America's perception of political sophistication. If Middle America has a sense of humor about politics, that's what he projects." That sense of humor is basically "kind," Representative Morris K. Udall has pointed out. "I think he [Russell] really likes politicians. Political humor can be pretty mean at times. And his isn't. He's just as welcome at a Republican fundraiser as at a Democratic fundraiser, although basically, I think, he's a Democrat and a liberal." On the other hand, Russell says he is often criticized for being "too soft": "Nick von Hoffman is always telling me, 'You're too easy on those sons of bitches.' He's probably right."

By his first wife, Russell has three children, Monica, Matthew, and John. In 1980 he married Alison Kaplan, the advertising and promotion manager at WKYS, the NBC radio affiliate in Washington. With his second wife, he lives in a red-brick Colonial-style condominium in northwest Washington, and he maintains a room at the Shoreham-Americana Hotel to which he retreats between his early and late evening shows. In gathering the grist for his humor, he keeps constantly abreast of news and current events as reported in both broadcast and print media, including the Congressional Record. "You give me an hour with the Congressional Record," he told Joseph B. Treaster in the Quest interview, "and I'll find something I can use." He takes notes whenever an idea hits him, but his customary working place is a second-floor bedroom in his home. His writing is usually done with a ball-point pen in a spiral notebook.

Mark Russell has often been described as looking a little like Steve Allen, although he is shorter and more square-shouldered. He has neatly barbered glossy dark hair that is flecked with gray, a barking laugh, a mischievous smile, and a conservative taste that is evident in his casual as well as his working wardrobe. Unlike those comedians who exude a tragic sense of life when their comedy chores are done, he carries his sense of humor over into private life, albeit quietly. Those close to him say that he is "buoyant" in a "low-keyed" way, "gentle," and "disciplined." "His greatest gift, outside of his humor, is his memory," his brother, Dan Ruskin, told Louise Sweeney in the Christian Science Monitor interview. "He remembers everything, can quote whole passages from state and city amendments, tell you what happened on such and such a day in 1946, never forgets a name." Of himself, Mark Russell says, "I'm a performer. The thing I do best is get up there and perform live. Anything else is less. The radio is less, the TV is less, the writing is less."

References: Christian Sci Mon B p8+ Ap 15 '80 por; N Y Times A p20 Ja 19 '81 por; N Y Times Mag p113+ N 9 '69 pors; Newsweek 88: 58 Jl 19 '76 por; Quest 4:35+ Ja '80 pors; Washington Post mag p6+ Je 27 '76 pors; Russell, Mark. Presenting Mark Russell (1980)

Sanders, Marlene

Jan. 10, 1931- Broadcast journalist. Address: b. CBS News, 524 W. 57th St., New York City, N.Y. 10019

The barriers that Marlene Sanders has crossed during her twenty-five years in radio and television, where her work has included writing, producing, and appearing on-camera, link her name with those of Pauline Frederick and Barbara Walters for pioneering achievements in enlarging the role of women in broadcast journalism. Before joining CBS News as a correspondent and producer in 1978, she set several precedents at ABC News, having become the first woman to anchor a network evening newscast, as a substitute in 1964, and a Saturday evening news show, on a three-month assignment in 1971. The post of vice-president and director of TV documentaries for ABC News, to which she was appointed in 1976, was the highest executive office held by a woman in any network news division. Documentaries are her forte, as she proved with such award winners as Children in Peril and The Right to Die.

Marlene Sanders was born in Cleveland, Ohio on January 10, 1931 to Mac and Evelyn Ruth (Menitoff) Sanders. Her parents were divorced when Marlene was about a year old. Her mother later married Sol Fisher, whom she assisted in operating a beauty shop. Her father, a retailer of women's wear, also remarried. Altogether Marlene Sanders has three half brothers. She grew up in middle-class neighborhoods in Cleveland, until, at the age of thirteen, she moved with the Fishers to the affluent suburb of Shaker Heights. She attended Shaker Heights High School, where she compensated for lack of funds in a moneyed neighborhood by excelling in both academic and extracurricular activities. In an interview for Seventeen (September 1973) she recalled, "I was an achiever. The trouble is, I didn't stop. When I became gung-ho in all different directions, [my mother] said, 'Now, dear, remember boys don't like girls who are too smart.' All this time I'd been getting the message, do well, then suddenly, oh, oh, oh, hold it. ... That made me so angry I couldn't stand it! I knew that the traditional role was not going to be enough for me.... I was going to be a great something—that something kept changing." Casting about for a suitable role model, and not wishing to follow the usual career paths for women, such as teaching or nursing, she turned to the theatre with the determination of becoming an actress.

Accordingly, upon graduating from high school in 1948, Marlene Sanders enrolled in Ohio State University to major in speech. When tuition money ran out, after one year, she left college, earned enough money to take a trip to Europe, and studied at the Sorbonne in the summer of 1950. During the 1949-50 season she had been an apprentice at the Cleveland Play House and later studied acting at the Hedgerow Theatre, just outside of Philadelphia, where she worked in the theatre without pay. Then for three years in New York she took on a series of temporary jobs while she made the casting rounds. She did appear in one Off-Broadway theatre called Originals Only, but the name of the play, she has said, "mercifully escapes" her. Increasingly doubtful about a career on the stage, she began to consider seeking a full-time job in another field.

While she was working as assistant to the producer at a summer theatre in Matunuck, Rhode Island in 1955, Miss Sanders met the broadcast journalist Mike Wallace, who had gone to Matunuck as producer of a comedy having a pre-Broadway tryout there. He was responsible for her getting her first television position, in the fall of 1955, as a production assistant on his newscast, which was just starting on WABD-TV (later WNEW-TV) in New York City. In October 1956 Wallace and producer Ted Yates Jr., who had hired Marlene Sanders, launched an innovative week-nightly interview program that proved to be a huge hit. With its aggressive interrogation of notable personalities, *Night Beat,* as the show was called, stirred up enormous viewer excitement. Having been promoted to associate producer, Miss Sanders took on the responsibility for scheduling, booking guests, greeting them as they arrived, and bolstering their confidence if they were nervous. She also wrote several scripts for *Night Beat.*

When, in 1957, Mike Wallace moved to ABC-TV, Marlene Sanders remained at WNEW-TV, becoming coproducer of *Night Beat,* which had John Wingate in the spot Mike Wallace had created. In 1958, after that show had ended, she produced a successor titled *Probe,* with a subject, rather than person, orientation. During the following year she produced two interview programs, one starring Monty Hall, who a few years later won the hearts of audiences as master of ceremonies of *Let's Make a Deal,* and the other, called *I Speak for Myself,* starring the writer Marya Mannes. She also produced *Newsreel 5,* a weekly fifteen-minute review of the main stories of the week.

Again teamed with Mike Wallace, beginning in January 1961 Miss Sanders helped with the writing and production of the *PM East* segment of *PM East—PM West,* a Westinghouse Broadcasting Company program that included both news and entertainment. After that show folded in 1962, she switched media to take the post of assistant director of news and public affairs at WNEW-Radio. Besides writing and producing a half-hour documentary weekly, *News Closeup,* over the next two years she gradually assumed broadcasting responsibilities. She was the only woman broadcaster then at the station, regularly covering news stories around the city, as well as writing material in the studio. For her poignant documentary *The Battle of the Warsaw Ghetto,* she won her first Writers Guild of America Award, in 1964.

In the fall of 1964 ABC News vice-president, Jesse Zousmer, hired Miss Sanders as the network's second woman correspondent. Later in the year, when the other correspondent, Lisa Howard, left ABC, Marlene Sanders replaced her on the daily TV show *News with the Woman's Touch,* a five-minute newscast. Soon after she began that daytime assignment, she had the opportunity to set an important precedent for women: Ron Cochran, anchorman of the fifteen-minute nightly news, lost his voice, and Marlene Sanders was asked to replace him. Jack Gould, TV critic of the New York Times, in his column of December 3, 1964, commented, "The courageous young woman with a Vassar smile was crisp and business-like, and obviously the sort who wouldn't put up with any nonsense from anyone." Referring years later to that particular "first," Miss Sanders said, "It was to ABC's credit that they broke the ice in 1964 and showed it could be done. No one else followed suit for many years."

At the height of the war, in 1966, Zousmer assigned Marlene Sanders to a three-week stint in Vietnam. Several American women newspaper correspondents and photographers had been sent to report on the war, but she was the only woman in broadcasting. "I flew with the First Airborne Cavalry," she recounted in an interview for the Cleveland *Press* (April 20, 1966). "I visited medical hospitals in the Central Highlands, refugee villages and orphanages near Saigon. I learned how our military camps are set up and how they function." While covering Buddhist student demonstrations in Da Nang, she was exposed to the tear gas that authorities used to dispel the crowd. Her film reports were shown on her own afternoon show and on Peter Jennings' evening news report.

With the termination of *News with the Woman's Touch* in early 1968, Marlene Sanders turned her attention more fully to her work as a correspondent, covering such major stories for ABC as Eugene J. McCarthy's campaign for the Presidential nomination, the assassination of Robert Kennedy, the Republican and Democratic national conventions, student demonstrations at Columbia University, and a West Virginia mine disaster. Among the historic events on which she later reported was the visit in 1969 of Israeli Prime Minister Golda Meir to the United States.

Much concerned about the outlook for women in broadcasting, in the fall of 1970 Marlene Sanders took part in a panel discussion, with other distinguished women in the industry, at a meeting of the New York chapter of American Women in Radio and Television. "A woman still has more obstacles than a man," she said at that gathering. "One of the areas where women have not made it at all is as anchormen for evening news shows." Miss Sanders got her chance to score another breakthrough for women in television when, in April 1971, she was chosen to substitute for the regular anchorman on ABC's late Saturday evening news show. For three months she replaced Sam Donaldson, who was on a temporary assignment in Vietnam. As she herself has pointed out, "No other woman had done an evening job on the television network."

In 1972 Marlene Sanders was named a full-time documentary producer at ABC, a position for which she had become well qualified through her work on several earlier documentaries. They included the 1970 programs *Women's Liberation* and *We Have Met the Enemy and He Is Us,* a half-hour study of the population explosion, and the 1971 program *Strangers in Their Own Land: The Blacks,* a news special focusing on "black power, black pride, and black self-help programs," which she also wrote and for which she served as on-camera correspondent. When another documentary that Miss Sanders wrote, produced, and narrated, *Children in Peril,* was run as an ABC news special in March 1972, John J.

O'Connor praised it in the New York Times as a program that "directly tackled the unpleasant subject of child abuse . . . and proved to be remarkably valuable on a difficult [topic]."

For her documentary special ABC News Inquiry: The Hand that Rocks the Ballot Box, aired in July 1972, Marlene Sanders was honored by the New York chapter of the National Organization for Women (NOW) as the writer, producer, and correspondent of "an outstanding program documenting the emergence of women as a political power." Enjoying the challenge of working on touchy subjects, she wrote and produced Population: Boom or Doom, presented on ABC-TV in January 1973, which reviewed the arguments for and against some of the controversial recommendations made by the President's Commission on Population Growth and the American Future. Later in that year, in September, ABC-TV presented Marlene Sanders' Woman's Place, the first documentary to examine questions regarding sex roles for both men and women. As the program's narrator, Bess Myerson, phrased its theme, "How much of our own lives have we been able to choose for ourselves, and how much has been chosen for us by society, with biological typecasting."

The Right to Die, which examined ethical and legal issues confronting doctors, patients, and families of the terminally ill, was the fourth of ABC News Close-Up programs, a bold investigative series that Av Westin initiated after he became head of the network's documentary unit in May 1973. When The Right to Die was shown on January 5, 1974, Alan M. Kriegsman of the Washington Post commended Marlene Sanders, its writer-producer, and her collaborators for approaching "a subject of universal concern—once considered taboo and still regarded as delicate by the mass media —with sympathy, interest and honest curiosity." Enthusiastic about her handling of that sensitive topic, Westin assigned Marlene Sanders another "potential hot potato," Prime Time TV: The Decision Makers, a revealing, behind-the-scenes examination of the process of choosing the programs to be seen on each of the three commercial networks during the top viewing hours, from 8 to 11 P.M. Also for the Close-Up series, she focused on the legal profession in Lawyers: Guilty as Charged? in 1975 and on the life-threatening problems, such as breast cancer, that trouble women in Women's Health: A Question of Survival in early 1976.

During the nearly three years that Av Westin worked with Marlene Sanders, he found her to be "a very well-organized and professional journalist who has all the skills it takes," as he was quoted in Broadcasting (November 8, 1976) as saying. When he resigned from his ABC post in January 1976, she was named to replace him as head of the Close-Up documentary unit, with the title of vice-president and director of television documentaries, a promotion that made her the first woman vice-president of a news division in network history. The ABC News documentaries produced under her administration included Justice on Trial, Nuclear Power—Pro and Con, ERA—The War Between the Women, and The Class That Went to War.

The appointment of Roone Arledge, head of the sports division, to the additional post of president of ABC News in the spring of 1977 brought about several important personnel changes, including the move of Marlene Sanders from ABC News to CBS News, where in February 1979 she became producer and correspondent concentrating on documentaries. Explaining her resignation to Les Brown of the New York Times (January 5, 1978), she said that after two years of administrative work she looked forward to writing and producing her own documentaries again. She also told Brown that she had come to feel at ABC that her "interests may not be the same as those of the new management."

Among Marlene Sanders' early CBS assignments were several segments for multipart CBS Reports programs, including "Taiwan Dilemma" in June 1978 and the segment "Whatever Happened to Civil Defense?" for 60 Minutes in September 1978. For CBS Reports she also wrote, produced, and anchored the hour-long documentary How Much for the Handicapped?, shown in April 1979, which dealt with the conflict between moral obligation and the cost of making public facilities available to the handicapped. Again for CBS Reports she was writer and correspondent for the hour-long documentary What Shall We Do About Mother?, shown in July 1980, which explored the problem of caring for ailing, elderly parents. She has also anchored CBS-TV's Newsbreak on Friday evenings, has contributed regularly to CBS News Sunday Morning and Magazine on television, and from time to time has broadcast the news on CBS radio.

In her twenty-five years in broadcasting Marlene Sanders has won twenty-five or more awards. American Women in Radio and Television presented her with its Broadcast Woman of the Year Award in 1975, its certificate of commendation for Women's Health in 1976, and its Silver Satellite Award for overall contributions to the industry in 1977. For The Right to Die she won her second Writers Guild of America Award, in 1975, and an Emmy nomination, among other tributes. She also won the Christopher Award twice, for Children in Peril in 1972 and How Much for the Handicapped? in 1980.

Marlene Sanders taught radio and television news techniques as an adjunct professor at Columbia University in the mid-1970's. On the lecture circuit since 1967 she has mostly addressed college audiences and women's groups, talking about the impact of the news media and women's issues. A charter member of NOW, she has continued to show a vigorous interest in the women's movement, aside from her documentaries. Once when she was asked what her major contribution to women has been, she replied, "It was just being there, being visibly on television and serving as a role model." Although she was careful to maintain political detachment in her work, she participated in the Women's Action Committee at ABC and has said that management learned much from meetings with group members.

A noticeably attractive woman, Marlene Sanders has blue eyes and strawberry blond hair, stands slightly over five feet four inches tall, and weighs about 125 pounds. During the "struggling young actress" phase of her life, she was married to Samuel Kahn. The marriage began in June 1952 and ended in the fall of 1955 in divorce. On May 27, 1958 she married Jerome Toobin, now the director of news and public affairs at WNET-TV in New York. Their older son, Jeff, born in 1960, is a student at Harvard; his brother, Mark, born in 1967, is mentally retarded and does not live with the family. Home life is important to Marlene Sanders, who enjoys gardening and entertaining and is said to manage smoothly running households in both Manhattan and Sherman, Connecticut. For fun and exercise she swims and plays tennis.

References: Broadcasting 91:105 N '76 por; Danbury (Connecticut) News-Times p26+ Ag 19 '80 por; Ms 4:19 F '76; N Y Times C p18 Ja 5 '77 por; Seattle Times E p10 Ap 10 '80 por; Seventeen 32:48 S '73 por; Contemporary Authors vols 65-68 (1977); Who's Who in America, 1980-81

Sanger, Frederick

Aug. 13, 1918- British molecular biologist. Address: b. Medical Research Council Laboratory of Molecular Biology, Hills Road, Cambridge CB2 2QH, England; h. 252 Hills Road, Cambridge CB2 2QE, England

Among the handful of scientists ever to be awarded the Nobel Prize twice is the British biochemist Frederick Sanger, who has made seminally important contributions to molecular biology, that branch of science which, since its ascendancy in the 1930's, has led to a revolution in our understanding of the most fundamental life processes. Dr. Sanger has devoted most of his forty-year career to unraveling the molecular structures of proteins and of RNA and DNA, the nucleic acids that guide protein synthesis. His identification of the complete chemical structure of the insulin molecule won him his first Nobel Prize for Chemistry in 1958; his second prize, in the same category, came in 1980, for his contributions to the development of a method for determining the base sequences in nucleic acids. He shared the 1980 prize with Walter Gilbert, who had also developed a method for sequencing DNA, and with Paul Berg, whose field of study is recombinant DNA.

In his innovative search for solutions to seemingly intractable problems, Sanger often employed the classical techniques of organic chemistry to map the structure of the most complex molecule, eventually reconstructing the whole from an examination of its fragments. Preferring experimental research to administration, Sanger has spent his entire professional life at Cambridge University, where he has been a professor of molecular biology for twenty years. He also serves as director of the division of protein and nucleic acid chemistry at the Medical Research Council Laboratory of Molecular Biology in Cambridge, a post he has held since 1962.

Frederick Sanger was born in Rendcomb, Gloucestershire, England on August 13, 1918, the son and namesake of a prosperous general medical practitioner, Frederick Sanger, and his wife, Cicely (Crewdson) Sanger. Although he was, by his own admission, only an average student at the Bryanston School in Blandford, Dorset, which he attended from 1932 to 1936, he went on to St. John's College, Cambridge after receiving his school certificate. "I would not have got in with those qualifications today," he acknowledged to Bryan Silcock in an interview for the London *Sunday Times* (October 19, 1980). Sanger had intended to study medicine, but after a few months, he decided to switch his major to natural science, even though he doubted his ability to do the required research. His overall academic record at St. John's was generally undistinguished, but he did earn a first in biochemistry.

After taking his B.A. degree, in 1939, Sanger was accepted as a research student in the biochemistry department at Cambridge. A conscientious objector, he continued his studies at the university during World War II, receiving his Ph.D., in 1943, for investigating the metabolism of lysine, an amino acid. A year later, he was awarded the Beit Memorial Fellowship for medical research, which he held until 1951. It was during that period that Sanger, working in collaboration with the influential protein chemist Albert C. Chibnall, undertook his first series of experiments in the molecular structure of proteins.

The importance of proteins, the building blocks of all living matter, had been recognized since the nineteenth century. Experiments by Emil Fischer and others in the early years of this century demonstrated that proteins were highly complex chemical structures composed of amino acids. By the mid-1940's, research chemists, drawing on those experiments, had proved that the amino acids in a protein molecule were linked together by peptide bonds into polypeptide chains. Moreover, they had discovered that those chains could be broken by the chemical action of acids or enzymes into fragments small enough to identify. Reasoning that at least some of those peptide fragments would contain parts of the same amino acid sequences, Sanger set out, in 1944, to determine the order of the amino acids in the protein insulin.

Dr. Sanger chose to analyze the composition of insulin because it was one of the few proteins readily available in a reasonably pure form and because its individual atomic components were known. Using samples of bovine insulin, Sanger began by chemically breaking up the comparatively simple insulin molecule into more manageable fragments. Taking advantage of recent technical advances, he used the reagent 2,4-dinitro-1-fluorobenzene, later called Sanger's reagent, to label terminal amino acid groups. Then, adopting a recently developed technique called paper chromatography, he painstakingly identified the various amino acid groups by the stains they left when percolated through a sheet of filter paper. Having discovered through those methods that insulin has two separate chains of amino acids—one of twenty-one acid units and the other of thirty—joined together by disulphide "bridges," Sanger and Hans Tuppy, a longtime colleague, deciphered, in 1950, the exact sequence of the larger chain. Decoding the shorter chain proved to be more difficult because there were fewer amino acids that occurred only once, but by 1954 Sanger had worked out the complete structure of both the chains as well as their disulphide links. Sanger went on to analyze the structure of insulin from four other animal species. Because all insulins show the same activity, Sanger maintained that any differences in molecular structure might indicate that the particular section was not necessary for physiological activity.

In recognition of his groundbreaking work in isolating and labeling the components of the insulin molecule, Sanger was awarded the 1958 Nobel Prize for chemistry. In making its recommendation, the Royal Swedish Academy of Sciences noted, "Many hormones, all enzymes so far known, viruses, toxins which cause disease and antibodies which give immunity to disease, are all proteins. In all tissues of the body, in muscle, nerve, and skin, proteins form an essential functional constituent. Sanger's methods and results have opened a road to the determination of their detailed structure and thus one of chemistry's greatest problems has found its solution in principle." After learning that he had won the prestigious prize, Sanger himself said modestly, as quoted in the New York Times (October 29, 1958), "At the moment, my work is useful mainly in analyzing other proteins, but since proteins are the most important substances in the human body, understanding them is, in the long run, a step forward in fighting diseases which attack the body."

The successful sequencing of insulin presaged the possibility for analyzing larger and more complex proteins, but perhaps even more important were the implications that it held for the remarkable discoveries in genetics. As Jacques Monod, the Nobel prize-winning molecular biologist, told Horace Freeland Judson in an interview for The Eighth Day of Creation (1979), Sanger's sequencing "was absolutely essential" to molecular biology. "One could not even have begun to think seriously about a genetic code until it had been revealed, to begin with, that a protein is beyond the shadow of a doubt a polypeptide in which the amino-acid residues really are arranged in a definite, constant, genetically determined sequence—and yet a sequence with no rule by which it determined itself. So that therefore it had to have a code."

Although he was not trained in genetics, Sanger became intensely interested in that field in the 1950's, largely because of his friendship with Francis Crick, who discovered, with James Watson, the "double helix" structure of the DNA molecule. Crick, a colleague of Sanger's at Cambridge, closely followed the work on protein sequencing. As the relationship between protein sequencing and genetic research became clear, he and several of his associates even gave Sanger and his co-workers "little lectures on elementary genetics."

Increasingly bored by protein sequencing because, as he put it, the "methods were becoming too standardized," Sanger began, in about 1960, to explore the composition of the nucleic acids RNA and DNA. He began with an analysis of the chemistry of RNA, or ribonucleic acid, the substance basic to protein synthesis. Scientists had for years striven to understand the way in which the RNA molecule "read" and interpreted the sequence of paired bases that encodes the genetic information contained in the DNA molecule and specifies the particular amino-acid sequence that determines a protein. Biochemists had spent so much time attempting to crack the genetic code that they had compiled a virtual molecular "dictionary," but they had yet to learn where the coded message began. Working with Kjeld Marcker, Sanger discovered, in 1964, the chemical modification in a transfer-RNA molecule that required a particular amino acid (methionine) to take its place at the head of a polypeptide chain.

In his subsequent RNA research, Sanger dealt with sequencing problems similar in kind but greater in magnitude than those he had encountered while working on the sequencing of proteins. By 1965 Robert W. Holley, a biochemist at Cornell University, had deciphered the base sequence of a small (80-base) transfer-RNA molecule. Impressed by that achievement, Sanger decided to work on the problem of sequencing the longer and more complex messenger-RNA molecules. As he had done for his molecular analysis of insulin, Sanger developed new, faster sequencing techniques, such as using radioactive phosphorus to label the fragments. His reconstruction of the sequence of the RNA molecule of a bacteriophage called R17, which is made up of about 3,300 bases, provided important, if expected, proof that the genetic code that had been deduced from synthetic proteins also held for living organisms.

During the 1970's Sanger and his Cambridge associates further refined the sequencing techniques and applied them to the analysis of DNA molecules as well. In particular, Dr. Sanger was responsible for developing what has come to be known as the "plus-minus" method of rapidly reading the base sequences of DNA. In that ingenious procedure, the double strands of a DNA molecule to be sequenced are separated, thus exposing its structural units, or nucleotides, which always interlock in the same way. Segments of other samples of DNA, which have been nested together according to length and have been chemically marked for their terminal nucleotides, are then annealed to a separated strand. Incubated to stimulate growth, the nucleotides eventually begin to reproduce the double strand. If growth is stopped and fragments of the chain are incubated again with one of the four required nucleotides missing, the matching nucleotide can be located. As complex as it appears to be, the method provides relatively rapid analysis of long sequences of DNA. Sanger himself used it, in 1975, to decode the DNA of Phi X174 virus, an extremely primitive form of life which has only 5,375 nucleotides, and to plot its complete genetic structure.

Since that date, Sanger has worked indefatigably to perfect the procedure and to increase tenfold the speed of DNA analysis.

Most experts agree that the rapid determination of DNA structure is a key factor in the artificial manufacture of genes for the production of any protein, including human insulin or human interferon, the natural antivirus substance. The procedure also makes it possible to identify the faults that may cause congenital defects or such hereditary diseases as sickle cell anemia and hemophilia. "I hope our work can be of use in medical research," Sanger said recently, as quoted in the Chicago Tribune (October 15, 1980). "There are a lot of diseases that are probably due to mistakes in DNA, genetic mistakes."

Dr. Sanger is the recipient of many honors in addition to the Nobel Prize. He was made a Commander of the Order of the British Empire in 1963, and he has received both the Royal Medal and the Copley Medal from the Royal Society. His other awards include the Gairdner Foundation Annual Award, the University of Chicago's G. W. Wheland Award, the Alfred Benzon Prize, the Corday-Morgan Medal and Prize, the Hanbury Memorial Medal, and the Albert Lasker Basic Medical Research Award. He is a fellow of the Royal Society and of King's College, Cambridge and since 1954 has been a foreign member of the American Academy of Arts and Sciences. He is also an honorary member of the American Society of Biological Chemists and the Japanese Biochemical Society, a corresponding member of the Asociación Química de Argentina, a member of the Academy of Science of Argentina and Brazil and of the World Academy of Arts and Science, and a foreign associate of the National Academy of Sciences of the United States. He has honorary degrees from the University of Leicester, the University of Strasbourg, and Oxford University.

In spite of the magnitude of his achievements and the number of his awards and honors, Frederick Sanger remains modest, unassuming, even shy. "If you talk to Sanger and do not know who he is, you would think he is the lab caretaker," one colleague remarked recently, as quoted in Science (November 1980). "If you allow him to, he will melt into the woodwork." Sanger is, by his own account, a "strongly self-motivated" man who regularly puts in seven-day work weeks in his Cambridge laboratory. The reward for his efforts, he has said, is "recognition by one's peers that you are doing something important." Little is known about his private life. He lives rather quietly with his wife, the former Joan Howe, whom he married in 1940, in Cambridge. They have three children, Robin, Peter Frederick, and Sally Joan. He usually spends his holidays gardening or sailing with his family.

References: N Y Times p10 O 29 '58, A p16 O 15 '80; Science 210:887+ N 21 '80; International Who's Who, 1980; McGraw-Hill Modern Men of Science (1966); McGraw-Hill Modern Scientists and Engineers (1980)

Schrader, Paul

*1946- Motion picture director, writer. Address:
c/o Columbia Pictures, Colgems Square,
Burbank, Calif. 91505*

Among the young film makers forging new
trends in the movie industry with their graphi-
cally realistic, occasionally sensational treatments of the frustrations of modern urban life
as well as their personal visions of morality is
Paul Schrader. A former movie critic and the
author of the screenplays for such films as
Taxi Driver, Rolling Thunder, Blue Collar—
which marked his directorial debut—and most
recently, *Raging Bull*, Schrader has shown,
from the beginning of his career, a penchant
for depicting the more unsavory aspects of
human behavior. Because of his apparent obsession with depravity and violence, Schrader
has won a place in the ranks of the so-called
brutalist directors, including Martin Scorsese,
Walter Hill, Michael Cimino, and Brian De
Palma. Schrader makes no apologies for his
frequently blood-drenched offerings. "I don't
feel troubled by my reputation for violence,"
he said in one recent interview. "It's just something I have to live with. That was simply a
phase, and a valid one. That desire to wipe
out characters in movies has been satiated
anyhow, as future films will show. The common thread that runs through all my films
is redemption, a belief in God, a belief that
something must be sacrificed."

Paul Schrader was born in 1946 in Grand
Rapids, Michigan to Dutch Calvinist parents,
who hoped that their son would grow up to
become a minister of the Christian Reformed
Church. "I was raised in a restricted, bedrock
way, with mind control," Schrader said in

one recent interview. He vividly remembers
"pleading in one case to see [Walt] Disney's
Living Desert" and, on another occasion, "getting on [his] knees and crying to see *King
Creole."* When he was seventeen years old,
he finally sneaked into the neighborhood
theatre to see his first movie, Disney's *The
Absent-Minded Professor.* "It was the beginning of a legitimate form of rebellion, and one
with an artistic mantle to boot," he told Wayne
Warga in an interview for the Los Angeles
Times (March 12, 1978). "It was to me the ideal
way to be valuable. I came to the movies as
an adult, but I saw them as a child." Having tasted and enjoyed the forbidden fruit,
Schrader devoured movies at the rate of
several a day for the next four years.

While he was a student at Calvin College,
a local church-affiliated school, Schrader contributed articles about film to the campus
newspaper, but after the church synod condemned movies for their "worldliness," he was
abruptly dismissed as coeditor. He spent the
summer before his senior year in New York
City, taking all the film courses offered by
Columbia University. Such motion pictures as
Ingmar Bergman's *The Seventh Seal* and Federico Fellini's *La Strada* persuaded the youth
that film could become, as he put it, "a bridge
between my religious training and the forbidden world." "The church no longer had all
the answers, but that zealotry, that desire to
proselytize—'go ye unto all the corners of the
earth'—was still there," he explained to John
Morthland in an interview for a *Newsday*
profile (February 12, 1978). "It was only logical
that I chose a medium that would allow me
the most immediate effect. Film was the
medium of my generation, and so I merely
directed my intense zealotry into that area."
A chance meeting with Pauline Kael, the influential film critic, proved crucial to his future
career. Upon graduating from Calvin in 1968,
he turned his back on Grand Rapids and the
ministry, and with Miss Kael's assistance, won
admission to UCLA's film school, one of the
best in the country, even though he had, by
his own estimation, "no real credentials whatsoever."

A diligent, dedicated student, Schrader still
found time to write film criticism for the Los
Angeles *Free Press,* and he occasionally free-
lanced for radio station KPFK, the Los Angeles
Times Calendar supplement, and *Coast* magazine. After taking his master's degree in cinema,
he joined the first group of research fellows
selected by the American Film Institute for its
Center for Advanced Film Study at Greystone
Mansion in Beverly Hills, California. It was
during this period that Schrader began to make
a name for himself as a film critic and historian. Named editor of *Cinema* in 1970, he
turned that slick fan magazine into a respected,
scholarly journal of film criticism in just three
years. Further contributing to his growing
reputation was the publication, in 1972, by the
University of California Press of his master's

thesis, *Transcendental Style in Film: Ozu, Bresson, Dreyer*, which one reviewer described as "almost incomprehensibly opaque in its high seriousness." At about that time, he declined Pauline Kael's offer of a recommendation for a full-time job as a newspaper movie critic to try his hand at writing film scripts.

A self-described "quick study," Schrader picked up pointers in the art of "punching up" a script from Alex Jacobs, a writer with a fondness for violence. In his first efforts, Schrader dutifully employed the classic triangular dramatic structure, and he even tried to emulate the transcendental style he had described in his book. Repeatedly frustrated in his attempts to finance the production of his screenplay "Pipeliner," the semiautobiographical story of a dying man who returns to his Michigan home in search of sympathy, Schrader learned the ins and outs of the business side of film making the hard way. His failure to find financial backing for his project and his subsequent bankruptcy, coupled with the collapse of his marriage, contributed to his growing depression. Physically and emotionally exhausted, he took to drinking heavily, and he haunted the Los Angeles pornography district.

While hospitalized in 1972 for the treatment of an ulcer, Schrader came up with the idea for *Taxi Driver*. "I was looking for something like the metaphor of the cab driver to express the loneliness and the agony I was feeling," he explained, as quoted in the Washington *Post* (February 10, 1976). Harry Chapin's affecting song "Taxi" and the attempted assassination of George Wallace by a crazed loner helped to crystallize the story line in his mind. Writing feverishly, Schrader completed the script for *Taxi Driver* in about fifteen days, then gave it to his agent to peddle to the studios. Columbia Pictures agreed to produce the film almost immediately, but Schrader preferred to wait until Martin Scorsese, the director of *Mean Streets*, which he greatly admired, and Robert De Niro, the actor, were available.

Meanwhile, Schrader, in an admitted attempt to raise some quick cash, wrote a blood-and-guts screenplay based on stories about the *yakuza*, or Japanese gangsters, that were supplied by his older brother, Leonard, who was then a teacher in Japan. He sold the script, in which he introduced the theme of redemption through self-destruction that characterizes all his films, to Warner Brothers for $300,000. In *The Yakuza* (1975), a hardbitten American detective goes to Tokyo to rescue a friend's daughter, who has been kidnapped by a *yakuza* boss. Schrader had intended to make, in his words, "a violent, underworld film about blood, duty, and obligation," but the producers, hoping to attract a wider audience, hired Robert Towne to soften the character of the detective, played by Robert Mitchum, and emphasize the romantic subplot. Under Sidney Pollack's direction, what was to have been an examination of honor and obligation became instead "a sort of rich, transcultural film," as Schrader put it.

He was so incensed by the unauthorized changes in his script that he tried, to no avail, to have his name removed from the credits.

In 1976 Columbia released *Taxi Driver*, Schrader's compelling study of a repressed, sociopathic Manhattan cabbie—Travis Bickle—who is driven by loneliness to "cleanse" himself in an orgiastic bloodbath. Both Scorsese, who directed the picture, and De Niro, who took the title role, identified with the alienated protagonist. Because of its psychological rather than sociological approach, *Taxi Driver* forces the viewer to see life through the eyes of a psychotic. Schrader has insisted that this unusual vantage point is a rarity in American films, but he has readily acknowledged his debt to such motion pictures as Robert Bresson's *Pickpocket* and to Robert Aldrich's *Kiss Me Deadly* and Scorsese's own *Mean Streets*, with their "random brutality all around."

The climactic shootout, in which Bickle coldbloodedly murders the pimp and the customers of the teenage prostitute he is trying to reform, unnerved critics and viewers alike, even though Scorsese had deliberately desaturated the color to avoid an X rating. "I would have loved to see sheets of blood, literally flowing down the walls . . . ," Schrader wrote in *Film Comment* (July/August 1978). "Throw realism aside. The room should be bathed in blood, because that's what was happening in the character's mind."

When some reviewers denounced *Taxi Driver* as an amoral glorification of brutality, Schrader defended the picture as a serious statement about sin and redemption. "The most unthinking specators may cheer the violence in the theatre, but there is an emotional awareness that they are seeing something wrong—wrong in them and in their society," he explained to David Sterritt in an interview for the *Christian Science Monitor* (January 18, 1979). "They have glimpses of what the film means on a deeper level, and when they get home, something positive is working in their minds."

"Brilliant," "stunning," "powerful," "exhilarating," and "remarkable"—these were among the adjectives film critics used to described *Taxi Driver*. The "nastiest masterpiece in years," it was, in David Sterritt's opinion, "a paradoxically humane movie." Seconding his colleague's appraisal, the New York *Post's* Frank Rich added, "The movie explodes with awful but genuine human truth, and at the end, it offers up a devastatingly and sadly accurate view of the ambiguous role violence plays in our national life." At the opposite pole, Stanley Kauffmann, writing in the *New Republic* (March 6, 1976), deplored *Taxi Driver's* "fakery," "hollowness," and "ultimate insignificance." David Henninger of the *National Observer* and *Newsday's* John Cashman, who deemed it "a monumental cinematic shell game" that "reflects contempt," were both numbed with disbelief, and the New York *Times's* Vincent Canby, who was admittedly "disoriented" by the film's impact, complained, "We have to hunt around to find some expression of moral outrage within *Taxi Driver*. Eventually we have to supply it ourselves." *Taxi Driver* was a smash hit at the 1976 Cannes Film Festival, where it won the Golden Palm grand prize, and it was nominated for an Academy Award as Best Picture of the year. It was so popular at the box office that Schrader earned almost $1,000,000 from his percentage of the profits.

Schrader's next film credit was his screenplay for *Obsession* (Columbia, 1976), a romantic suspense drama inspired by Alfred Hitchcock's classic *Vertigo*. This tale of a man's monomaniacal guilt feelings and his bizarre struggle for redemption and rebirth was directed and substantially altered, much to Schrader's displeasure, by Brian De Palma. His script for *Rolling Thunder* (American International Pictures, 1977) is notorious for its scenes of "twisted violence" in the name of vengeance. But as Gary Arnold observed in his review of the film for the Washington *Post* (October 29, 1977), the violence is "never mitigated by the kind of character exploration and ambiguity that strengthened *Taxi Driver*." Schrader claimed later that because of the heavy rewriting of his original script, what had been "an anti-racist movie became a racist movie."

To retain artistic control of his scripts, Schrader decided, in the late 1970's, to direct his own films. He made his impressive directorial debut with *Blue Collar* (Universal, 1978), which won that year's first prize at the Paris Film Festival. Schrader found directing to be "unrelentingly unpleasant," primarily because he had to keep assuaging the competitive egos of Richard Pryor, Yaphet Kotto, and Harvey Keitel, who starred as frustrated automobile assembly line workers plotting to blackmail their union local. "The director works in a world of fear: 'How can I get this?'" he told John Morthland. "The writer can see it all as a whole. Writing is like running a mile, where you can feel the earth under your feet and see houses go by so you know when you're out of rhythm. The director doesn't know when he's out of rhythm. He shoots the film, puts it together, and doesn't have a sense of completion until the end, by which time he's sick of it anyhow." Despite his misgivings, Schrader's actors in *Blue Collar* had nothing but praise for his "creative sensitivity" as a director. As Yaphet Kotto put it, "Paul was able to keep a balance and emotional level that kept us going forward. . . . He was not only in control of himself, he had control of what he wanted to do."

Schrader, who had coauthored the screenplay for *Blue Collar* with his brother, Leonard, used the automobile industry as a metaphor for what he saw as the widespread injustice of an industrial society. Although the film was only moderately successful at the box office, most critics appreciated Schrader's sure handling of such downbeat material. Perceiving a new honesty in Schrader's work, Stanley Kauffmann was particularly taken by the "raunchily real" dialogue and the drab "dailiness dramatized as most documentaries cannot do it."

But after seeing *Hardcore* (Columbia, 1978), Schrader's next venture as a writer-director, Kauffmann changed his mind, complaining in the *New Republic* (March 3, 1979), "Now his honesty has slipped again." *Hardcore,* whose plot and style owe much to the classic John Ford western *The Searchers,* follows the odyssey of a devout Midwestern father, ably portrayed by George C. Scott, searching for his runaway daughter, who has become involved in pornographic film making on the West Coast. Several critics, among them, Ivor Davis of the Toronto *Globe and Mail* (July 31, 1978), questioned Schrader's purpose: "Do we have the condemnation of sin coupled with delight in the depiction of it? . . . Will *Hardcore,* in painting a sleazy despairing world of porn, make titillation respectable?" Denying any exploitative motive, Schrader insisted that Scott's character was "a heroic figure" patterned after his own father: "His beliefs are tested but not broken. This is a story about pornography versus classic moral values, and the moral values win," he told one interviewer. There were other critical complaints as well, among them, the incredibility of the plot, the shallow or stereotypical characterizations, and the lack of preparation for the violent ending. In a devastating review in the *New Yorker* (February 19, 1979), Pauline Kael lambasted her erstwhile protégé: "There may never have been another American director as lacking in spontaneity as Paul Schrader."

After serving as executive producer for Joan Tewkesbury's psychodrama *Old Boyfriends* (Avco-Embassy, 1979), which he had written in collaboration with his brother, Schrader went on to direct his third screenplay, *American Gigolo* (Paramount, 1980). Despite a dismal critical reception, the film rang up impressive numbers at the box office because of its frank treatment of a formerly taboo subject—male prostitution—and because its young star, Richard Gere, performed one scene nude. As he had been faulted for failing to give the character of the gigolo "discernible dramatic substance," to use Washington *Post* film critic Gary Arnold's words, so he was chastised for creating, in his screenplay for Scorsese's *Raging Bull* (Paramount, 1980), the life story of boxer Jake La Motta, a film without a soul. Schrader's script, which depicted with unrelenting honesty and, as Andrew Sarris noted, "remorseless pessimism" La Motta's brutality in the home as well as in the ring, was brilliantly interpreted by Robert De Niro, who won an Oscar for his forceful portrayal of the aging boxer.

Before *Raging Bull*, Schrader wrote only original screenplays, eschewing adaptations and rewrites. Unlike most of his colleagues, who usually begin by devising a plot, he first decides on a theme. Only after developing a metaphor for his theme does he contrive his plot. He teaches this rather unorthodox method in a script writing workshop through personal problem-solving discussions. By his own account, Schrader writes "very elliptically, concisely," with a minimum of dialogue—"enough for a director and an actor to make a scene out of." "If I were less lazy, I would be . . . a serious writer, not a screenwriter," he admitted in his article for *Film Comment*. But because a screenwriter is, in his opinion, not a writer, but "half a film maker," he chose to become a director and, thus, a whole film maker.

Paul Schrader has been variously described as "meek and soft-spoken" and "churlish and excitedly talkative." On meeting him for the first time, some reporters were struck by his "subdued melancholy air." Occasionally reticent about his private life, he talks animatedly about his work, often slurring his speech in what one interviewer called "a Brando-esque near whisper." A longtime chain smoker, he is said to be suffering from emphysema. At about the time he wrote *Taxi Driver*, he underwent Freudian psychoanalysis. When asked to explain the character of Travis Bickle, he responded, as quoted in *Film Comment* (March/ April 1976): "It is me without any brains. It's the same need to escape, to break through, that drives a script in my case—a real need to triumph over the system. Now I live pretty much the way I want, get paid for it, work when I want, get a certain amount of respect, and so I have beaten the system. If I was everybody's pawn, if I was Travis Bickle, the triumph would have to take another course, probably a violent one." Schrader's marriage to Jeannine Oppewall, a designer, ended in divorce in the early 1970's.

References: Film Comment 12:6+ Mr/Ap '76 por, 14:45+ Jl/Ag '78 por, 16:49+ Mr/Ap '80 por; N Y Sunday News III p9 F 22 '76 por; N Y Times II p15+ F 5 '78; Newsday II p4+ F 12 '78 por; Brady, John. The Craft of the Screenwriter (1981); International Motion Picture Almanac (1981); Katz, Ephraim. The Film Encyclopedia (1977)

Schreyer, Edward Richard

Dec. 21, 1935- Governor-General of Canada. Address: Rideau Hall, Ottawa, Ont. K1A 0A1, Canada

The Right Honorable Edward Schreyer, who in January 1979 succeeded Jules Léger to become the twenty-second Governor-General of Canada, is the youngest person to occupy that post since the 1830's. A former Premier of Manitoba and leader of that province's New Democratic party, he is also the first Governor-General who is of neither British nor French background, as well as the first native of Western Canada and the first member of an avowedly socialist party to serve as the British monarch's representative in North America. As Governor-General, Schreyer serves as Canada's formal head of state and commander-in-chief of its armed forces, acts as host to visiting dignitaries, presides over the opening and closing of Parliament, and gives final assent to laws. Since, according to precedent, the Governor-General acts only on the advice of the elected Prime Minister, his position is basically nonpartisan and ceremonial. For Schreyer, however, it appears to be an opportunity to work for Canadian unity and to act, in the words of one Manitoba observer, as the "nation's social conscience."

Edward Richard Schreyer was born on December 21, 1935 on a prosperous farm near Beauséjour, Manitoba, about forty miles northeast of Winnipeg. A third-generation Canadian of Austro-German ancestry, he was the youngest of five sons born to John James and Elizabeth (Gottfried) Schreyer, members of a pioneer family in the district. He attended the one-room Cromwell Public School near his home and obtained his secondary education at Beauséjour Collegiate. Although his mother, a devout Roman Catholic, hoped that he would become a priest, Schreyer's early ambition was to be a member of the Canadian Mounted Police. For a time he considered accepting a minor league baseball contract proffered by the St. Louis Cardinals, but eventually he decided to study at the University of Manitoba in preparation for a teaching career.

Scholarship, teaching, and political activity as a member of the Cooperative Commonwealth Federation (CCF)—a moderately socialist forerunner of the New Democratic party (NDP)—became intertwined in Schreyer's young adulthood. From 1954 to 1956, while at the university, he was a member of the Canadian Officers Training Corps, achieving the rank of second lieutenant in the Royal Canadian Armored Corps. In 1957 he managed the successful campaign of Jake Schulz for the federal Parliament. Later that year the CCF tapped him to become the candidate for the provincial riding (or electoral district) of Brokenhead in the Manitoba legislative assembly. When Schreyer accepted the challenge, he lost his contract to teach at Beauséjour in the upcoming year. Elected in 1958 and reelected in 1959 and 1962, Schreyer continued his education between assembly sessions, studying at United College and St. John's College of the University of Manitoba. Eventually he obtained four degrees, a Bachelor of Pedagogy in 1959, a B.A. in 1960, a B. Ed. in 1962, and an M.A. in international relations and economics in 1963. From 1962 to 1965 Schreyer was a professor of political science and international relations at St. Paul's College of the University of Manitoba.

In the long run, politics exerted a stronger attraction than teaching on Schreyer, who was moved by the idea that "government can solve many social and economic problems of maldistribution, social discrimination and lack of opportunity." In 1965 he won election to the federal House of Commons from the Manitoba riding of Springfield, and three years later, after redistricting, he was reelected, this time from the riding of Selkirk. He did not feel at home in Ottawa, however, and returned to Manitoba in mid-1969 when the province's Conservative Premier, Walter Weir, in a moment of optimism called for a general election a year and a half ahead of schedule. At the New Democratic party convention in June, Schreyer defeated the incumbent, Sidney Green, for the party leadership post by a vote of 506 to 177, thus becoming eligible for the Premiership in an NDP administration.

Having in the meantime resigned his federal House of Commons seat, Schreyer plunged into the whirlwind, eighteen-day campaign that preceded the provincial election of June 25, 1969. Billed as the "Man for All Reasons," because, as one of his associates explained, his qualifications for the Premiership made his election "the most natural thing in the world," Schreyer was returned to the Manitoba legislative assembly, this time as the candidate for the Rossmere riding, and swept his party into power. The NDP proved strong among voters of non-British ethnic background, who comprised some 55 percent of Manitoba's population, and in the urban constituencies, which had recently gained nine additional seats through reapportionment. The party also won favor in the province's northern district, where it swayed residents with promises of economic development, and in the depressed region between Lake Winnipeg and Lake Manitoba.

Schreyer's emergence as Premier of Manitoba at the age of thirty-three marked a series of departures for his province and for Canada. He was the first Roman Catholic to lead Manitoba, and the Cabinet he headed had an unprecedented number of members of ethnic minorities, including three Jews, two Ukrainians, a Pole, a French-Canadian, and an Icelander. His victory was the first on a provincial level for the NDP, which had been organized nationally in 1961, and it gave Manitoba its first socialist government, as well as the only one then existing in North America. During his tenure as Premier of Manitoba, from 1969 to 1977, Schreyer also held the provincial offices of President of the Council and Minister of Dominion-Provincial Relations. In addition, he served as Minister of Industry and Commerce from July to December 1969 and as Minister of Finance from 1972 to 1976.

To the dismay of some leftist NDP members and the relief of Manitoba's conservatives, Schreyer's socialism proved to be remarkably flexible. The Premier summarily dismissed Karl Marx for "being as passé and out-of-date philosophically as Adam Smith" and identified with the social democrats of Scandinavia and with such American Midwestern Democrats as Hubert H. Humphrey and George S. McGovern. He promised "to work untiringly toward a greater equality of the human condition" but at the same time expressed no ideological opposition to private enterprise. "We feel obligated to use the instrumentality of government," he said, "only where we think that private enterprise is not interested in developing a particular industry or a particular region, or where for some reason private enterprise, in a specific business, was not serving the community."

During Schreyer's first 500 days in office his government obtained passage of some 200 pieces of legislation, including a Human Rights Act that banned various discriminatory practices. In his most controversial move, the Premier in April 1970 called for the establishment of an economical, government-sponsored, "no-fault" automobile insurance program. As many as 10,000 demonstrators paraded in Winnipeg to denounce "Ed the Red," the Manitoba Bar Association condemned the proposed "Bill 56," and the Insurance Board of Canada spent $500,000 to defeat the measure. In the end, however, Schreyer prevailed, because he agreed to grant to independent agents some compensation for damages done to them by "Autopac," as the new government-sponsored insurance agency was called.

Schreyer's other innovations generated less emotionalism. Under his administration, Manitoba abolished premiums for government health insurance, introduced government financing for nursing home care and medications for senior citizens, raised welfare payments and minimum wage rates, inaugurated tax reforms to benefit those of modest means, and overhauled Winnipeg's unwieldy municipal government. The legislature also increased public housing expenditures substantially, provided for the hiring of seasonally unemployed craftsmen to repair pensioners' homes, and increased economic opportunities in depressed areas as part of an effort to keep rural Manitobans from deserting the country.

Premier Schreyer's first term had its dark moments as well. In 1971 he had to force the resignation of the Minister of Highways, Joe Borowski, a maverick politician who among other matters refused to temper his crusade against legalized abortion to conform with Cabinet consensus. The following year, the NDP's refusal to support Schreyer's plan for giving more aid to parochial and private schools led him to threaten resignation. But the Churchill Forest Industries project, which had been put in motion by the Conservative government of Duff Roblin in the mid-1960s, undoubtedly caused him the biggest headache. During the 1969 campaign Schreyer had called the conclusion of that deal "the blackest moment in Manitoba's economic history," but his reluctance to frighten business interests and disrupt existing contractual arrangements prevented him from putting CFI into receivership for more than a year and a half after he took office. By that time it had been revealed that a lavish loan to finance construction of a pulp mill, a paper mill, a saw mill, and a paper machines plant at the western Manitoba lumbering town of The Pas had cost taxpayers some $96,000,000, and the chief developer had allegedly pocketed $29,000,000 in profits.

In 1973 Schreyer confidently offered himself and his government for reelection. In response to Conservative attacks on Autopac and allegations of mismanagement of the government-sponsored Manitoba Development Corporation, the Premier boasted that Manitoba had the lowest unemployment rate in Canada and called attention to a monthly increase of almost 500 jobs in the province. Even the editor of the *Communicator*, the organ of the Manitoba Chambers of Commerce, warned his readers not to be fooled by the antisocialist diatribes being launched against Schreyer from the Conservative and Liberal camps. Schreyer's last-minute implied threat of reprisals against communities that elected "malicious" legislators, and his description of the Liberals' Jewish leader, Israel ("Izzy") Asper, as a "shyster lawyer" may have cost him votes. Nevertheless, in the June 28, 1973 election the NDP obtained 42 percent of the popular vote as compared with the 38 percent it had received four years earlier. Of the fifty-seven seats in the legislature the NDP had thirty-one, the Conservatives twenty-one, and the Liberals five.

Schreyer spent much of his second term concentrating on the problems of Canada's western provinces. In July 1973 he and the premiers of Saskatchewan, Alberta, and British Columbia met with Prime Minister Pierre Trudeau at the Western Economic Opportunities Conference in Calgary and demanded, among other things, the reform of discriminatory railroad freight rates and the authority to establish regional banks that might prove more liberal in providing loans for local development. Back in Manitoba, Schreyer put increasing pressure on mining companies to establish smelting and refining operations near their excavation sites rather than in central Canada, and he called for higher taxes on the industries that extracted nonrenewable energy sources from the province's land. The Premier argued that the revenues should be used to develop new sources of energy.

The energy crisis of the mid-1970's convinced Schreyer that the Canadian standard of living, which depended on the profligate use of fossil fuels, had reached its peak. In August 1975, at the sixteenth annual conference of Canada's ten premiers, at St. John's, Newfoundland, he called on the federal and provincial governments to establish a permanent planning body to formulate long-term economic policy. Schreyer's increasingly articulate advocacy of mandatory allocation of Canada's energy resources and support of Prime Minister Trudeau's effort to bring wages and prices under control gave rise to speculation during 1976 and 1977 that he might join the Liberal government in Ottawa, perhaps as chairman of the National Energy Board, but nothing came of the rumors.

Although he could legally have waited until 1978, Schreyer called for a general election a year earlier to conform with political tradition in Manitoba, which had become accustomed to provincial elections every four years. The province had weathered the recession of the mid-1970's thanks, in part, to its relative independence of the United States economy and to Schreyer's careful fiscal policies. But some voters were tired of rising taxes; labor objected to the Premier's resistance to demands for inflationary wage increases; and conservatives were shocked by Schreyer's proposal that no boss should receive more than two and one-half times the earnings of his lowest-paid employee. Under the new leadership of Sterling Lyon the Conservatives promised to lower taxes while maintaining popular NDP social programs. The Conservatives, who had cut Schreyer's margin of victory in Rossmere from 2,200 in 1969 to 600 in 1973, again pitted a strong candidate against the Premier to force him to concentrate his attention on his own race. In the election, on October 11, 1977, the Conservatives won ten additional seats to bring their total to thirty-three, the NDP's share fell to twenty-three places, and the Liberals retained only one seat.

Schreyer remained fairly quiet during his first year as the leader of the Opposition in the Manitoba legislature, but after the NDP in November 1978 unanimously reaffirmed him as its chief, the ex-Premier seemed ready to resume battle against those he called "the boys with the bucks." A short time later, Prime Minister Trudeau asked Schreyer to become Governor-General upon the impending retirement of Jules Léger. "I asked myself whether it was credible that I, of all people, should be asked," Schreyer later recalled. "How could I not accept it?" On December 7, 1978, after informing Queen Elizabeth II of his choice, Trudeau announced publicly in London that the leader of Manitoba's NDP would serve for the next five years as the monarch's personal representative in Canada.

The surprising elevation of Schreyer to a position traditionally reserved for senior diplomats or bluebloods was generally well-received by Canadians. Trudeau, who had confided in only a few people before making the choice, pointed out that the Manitoban had the virtues of being "young, dynamic, not from Central Canada, not from the establishment." Commentators noted that Schreyer was one of the few Western politicians who shared Trudeau's commitment to a strong central government and to the policy of bilingualism. Some Conservatives worried that the Prime Minister was insuring against the day when he might have to seek the Governor-General's permission to form a government based on a Liberal minority augmented by NDP support. Other observers argued more broadly that the sympathy between the two men would enable Trudeau to push ahead with his plan to give the Governor-General a substantive as well as ceremonial role in Canadian affairs.

Schreyer was installed as Canada's twenty-second Governor-General in an elaborate ceremony in Ottawa on January 22, 1979. In his inaugural address, written by himself and delivered mainly in English and French with smaller portions in German, Polish, and Ukrainian, he offered a plea for Canadian unity and a rebuff to separatism. He called attention to his own identity as "third-generation Canadian from the wheatfields of the West" and compared the nation's ethnic groups to diverse but valuable building materials that could be joined without losing their individual integrity. Schreyer predicted with confidence—more than a year before Quebec's voters rejected a pro-separatist referendum—that a "blessedly overwhelming majority in every province of Canada will provide, with the help of providence, a yearning for the preservation of one Canada that will not be frustrated, a wisdom that will not be denied."

Since Schreyer's work as Governor-General consisted largely of such ceremonial tasks as opening the Quebec Winter Carnival or declaring "O Canada" as the nation's official anthem, he showed growing signs of frustration with his position, especially after the victory of the Progressive Conservatives in the May 1979 elections and the accession of Joe Clark as Prime Minister seemed to indicate that his role would remain restricted. His prospects for a wider role improved, however, when the Clark government fell and Pierre Trudeau returned as Prime Minister in March 1980.

The Canadian Governor-General is a member of the Canadian Association of University Teachers and a former member of the Inter-Parliamentary Union and the Commonwealth Parliamentary Association. In 1979 he was named ex officio chancellor and principal companion of the Order of Canada as well as chancellor and commander of the Order of Military Merit. Schreyer holds the 1975 Vanier Award as the outstanding young Canadian of the year.

Edward Richard Schreyer is about six feet tall and broadshouldered, with steel-blue eyes and dark, wavy hair. The Governor-General, who is a chain-smoker, enjoys reading and listening to classical and country music, likes baseball, canoeing, curling, squash, hockey, and golf, and has a taste for such Eastern European delicacies as pirogi and golubchi. Since June 30, 1960 Schreyer has been married to the former Lilly Schulz, the daughter of the CCF candidate whose campaign he managed in 1957 and, according to some observers, "the best first lady ever." The Schreyers have four children: Lisa, Karmel, Jason, and Toban. In Manitoba the family lived in northeastern Winnipeg in a rambling home they called "The Cabbage Patch." In Ottawa the Schreyers make their home at Rideau Hall, the official residence of the Governor-General.

References: Toronto Globe and Mail p9 D 8 '78 por, Globe Mag p4+ O 25 '69 pors; Macleans 91:18+ D 18 '78 pors; Americana Annual, 1980; Britannica Book of the Year, 1980; Who's Who, 1980-81; Who's Who in America, 1980-81; Who's Who in Canada, 1977-78

Seaga, Edward (Phillip George) (sē-ä'gə)

May 28, 1930- Prime Minister of Jamaica. Address: b. Prime Minister's Office, Kingston, Jamaica; h. 19 Temple Meads, Kingston 6, Jamaica

On October 30, 1980, in an election with implications for the entire Caribbean region, the people of Jamaica decisively rejected the programs and policies of two-term Prime Minister Michael N. Manley's socialistic, pro-Cuban People's National Party in favor of Edward Seaga's moderate, pro-Western Jamaica Labour Party. The new Prime Minister, the fifth since Jamaican independence in 1962, has been a leader in his party for more than twenty years. A banker by profession, Seaga put his financial skills to work in ministerial posts in two pre-Manley Labour governments. Since taking office on November 1, 1980, Seaga, who also serves

Edward Seaga

as his country's Minister of Finance, has devoted himself to repairing Jamaica's battered economy by advocating a greater reliance on private enterprise and free market economics. "If we can get working capital," he said, as quoted in *Newsweek* (December 15, 1980), "you'll be looking at an entirely new Jamaica in three years."

Of Scottish and Lebanese ancestry, Edward Phillip George Seaga was born in a Salvation Army Hospital in Boston, Massachusetts on May 28, 1930, while his Jamaican parents, Phillip George Seaga, a prosperous travel agent, and his wife, Erna Aleta (Maxwell) Seaga, were vacationing in the United States. In the late 1940's Edward Seaga enrolled at Harvard University on a scholarship, intending to study physics, but he soon switched his major to sociology and anthropology. He also found time to study poetry with Archibald MacLeish. After receiving his B.A. degree in 1952, he returned to Jamaica and spent the next three years in the outback studying child development and revivalist cults. As he later explained to John Huey of the *Wall Street Journal* (August 11, 1980), his knowledge of the devastating effects of poverty did not "come from the middle-class point of view," but from "sleeping five across the bed" during his years in the Jamaican countryside. After completing his sociological research, he settled in Kingston, where he worked as a banker and financial consultant.

In the mid-1950's Seaga gave up his United States citizenship and became active in island politics. He was naturally attracted to the Jamaica Labour Party (JLP), the more conservative of the country's two major parties. Founded in 1943 by Sir Alexander Bustamante, the JLP espoused private enterprise and advocated economic expansion. Drawing its partisans from both business and labor groups, it was especially strong in the countryside. The rival People's National Party (PNP), which was organized in 1938 by Norman W. Manley, appealed mainly to city dwellers and middle-class intellectuals with its program of "democratic socialism." Impressed by Seaga's fiery speeches, Bustamante, in 1959, invited the young party worker to serve in the Upper House of the Jamaican legislature. The appointment made him the youngest member in the history of the Legislative Council.

Seaga soon achieved national recognition with his widely quoted "haves and have nots" speech in behalf of Jamaica's poor. When Jamaica was granted independence from Great Britain in 1962, it was a foregone conclusion that he would be among those chosen to draft the new nation's constitution. In April of that same year he was elected to a seat in the House of Representatives from Western Kingston, an impoverished urban district that has since returned him to Parliament with unfailing regularity. Bustamante, who was elected Prime Minister in the JLP's sweeping victory, named Seaga Minister of Development and Welfare. One of his most notable accomplishments in that post was the construction of Tivoli Gardens, a completely planned community that replaced Back-O-Wall, one of Kingston's worst slums. Seaga also encouraged the expansion of cottage industries and promoted the growth of Jamaican cultural pride by fostering interest in indigenous dance and music, in folk art, and in native crafts.

In the 1967 general election campaign, Seaga's opponent was Dudley Thompson, a fifty-year-old pistol-packing attorney of African slave descent. No incumbent legislator had ever been reelected to Western Kingston's parliamentary seat, but with the help of a tightly knit organization of some 4,000 volunteers, known as "Seaga's private army," Seaga won reelection to the House of Representatives by an overwhelming majority. Donald Sangster, who succeeded the ailing Bustamante as Prime Minister, immediately appointed Seaga to the newly created Cabinet position of Minister of Finance and Planning, which he held until the JLP was defeated in the 1972 election.

Seaga earned his reputation for fiscal expertise in that post. Determined to restore Jamaica to solvency, he established several important local financial institutions, among them the Jamaica Development Bank, the Jamaica Mortgage Bank, the Jamaica Unit Trust, and the Jamaica Stock Exchange, introduced a tax reform plan to strengthen local industry, and oversaw the transfer of many foreign-owned companies to Jamaican hands. To provide adequate housing and create thousands of jobs, he organized the Urban Development Corporation, which transformed the derelict waterfronts of Kingston, Ocho Rios, and Montego Bay into planned urban communities. For rural Jamaicans, he created the One Hundred Village program, in which total community development was brought to 100 hamlets annually. In an effort to reinforce a growing sense of national identity, he founded several museums, initiated a national heritage week, and established the National Heroes' Award. Perhaps most importantly, he negotiated the return to Jamaica of the remains of Marcus Garvey, the black nationalist.

On the international scene, Seaga represented Jamaica as a governor of the World Bank and as a delegate to the Inter-American Development Bank, the Caribbean Development Bank, and the International Monetary Fund. When the World Bank, then under the direction of Robert S. McNamara, decided, in 1968, to increase its aid to Third World countries, Seaga suggested that the Bank subsidize the interest rates for economic development loans. He proposed giving long-term credits at 3 percent interest to middle-level countries, that is, underdeveloped ones not poor enough to qualify for most international assistance programs. With that "3 percent window," he argued, the Bank could "meet the realities of the newer areas of emphasis." Equally interested in preserving the cultures of emerging nations, he helped to establish the International Fund for the Promotion of Culture, which operates within the framework of UNESCO.

Seaga lost his cabinet post in 1972, when the People's National Party, under the leadership of Michael N. Manley, the son of the party's founder, swept the Labour government out of office. Seaga was one of the few in his party to retain his seat in Parliament. Stunned by the PNP's upset victory, he seriously considered leaving politics, but he eventually decided against retirement and, in 1974, succeeded former Prime Minister Hugh Shearer as leader of the Opposition. Two years later he challenged Manley for the Prime Ministership.

Shortly after taking office in 1972, Manley had instituted an ambitious program of social and economic reforms designed to improve the country's standard of living. The enormous cost of his wide-ranging plan, coupled with the effects of a worldwide recession in the mid-1970's, had pushed Jamaica to the brink of financial collapse. To quell sporadic outbreaks of violence, which he contended were part of a conservative "destabilization" campaign against his regime, Manley declared a nationwide state of emergency in June 1976 and, a few months later, imposed direct censorship of the mass media.

In his stump speeches, Seaga charged that Manley had manufactured the national emergency in an attempt to turn Jamaica into a Cuban-style Communist state that would become part of a Caribbean "Red axis." Promising to turn back "Cubanism in Jamaica," he called for a renewed commitment to private ownership to restore business confidence and "balanced relations" with all countries. Manley countered with verbal attacks on his opponent's program of "capitalism warmed over" and election-eve announcements of a tax cut, government-funded food subsidies, increases in unemployment benefits, and salary raises for nurses and teachers. In what amounted to a convincing popular endorsement of Manley's policies, the PNP defeated the JLP by a landslide in the general election of December 15, winning forty-eight House seats to the JLP's twelve. In the local elections three months later, the PNP, which took 237 town council seats to the JLP's thirty-one, won control of all thirteen of the island's parishes. Many Caribbean political analysts interpreted the results of the local elections as a personal repudiation of Seaga, who was widely expected to be replaced as Opposition leader.

Over the next few years, however, Seaga gradually consolidated his leadership position as the Jamaican economy continued its downward slide. By the spring of 1980, more than 200,000 middle-class managers, technicians, and skilled workers, distressed by the chronic shortages of consumer goods, double-digit inflation, and an unemployment rate that hovered around 30 percent, had fled the country. A massive foreign debt had drained off precious currency and, to make matters worse, Prime Minister Manley had alienated the International Monetary Fund, on which Jamaica depended heavily for credit, by refusing to institute the austerity measures the Fund had demanded as a precondition for further financial aid. The rapidly deteriorating economic situation eventually forced Manley to call an election for October 1980, a full year ahead of schedule.

In the course of the grueling, nine-month campaign Seaga toured the entire island, from the slums of Kingston to remote rural villages to plush North shore tourist resorts, hammering away at Manley's "radicalism," his economic mismanagement, and his alleged ties to Fidel Castro. "A government that can't find work and can't find food has failed," he told the voters, as quoted in the New York Times Magazine (October 26, 1980). "They muck it up, and we have to come and pick it up." Seaga said that he would "restore Jamaica to a path of growth by operating on a market system that will reward individual initiative and enterprise." Reassuring those who feared he would dismantle Jamaica's elaborate social welfare system, which he described as being "very necessary in a small democratic country," he promised that the programs originated by Prime Minister Manley would be retained, but on a sounder foundation of "economic buoyancy."

As the day of the election drew near, the political violence that has always accompanied Jamaican campaigns increased. Armed thugs from both camps repeatedly disrupted rival political rallies, viciously attacking speakers and supporters, and both Seaga and Manley were reportedly the targets of assassination attempts. In one twenty-four-day period in the summer, 114 persons lost their lives in politically motivated killings. Estimates of the death toll for the entire campaign ranged from 600 to 725 persons. Appalled by the bloodshed, Seaga and Manley, on July 18, issued a joint public statement condemning the violence. Still rankled by Manley's 1976 declaration of an emergency, which he viewed as a blatant attempt to silence the JLP, Seaga had first extracted from his opponent a promise not to impose similar restrictions in 1980.

An unprecedented 80 percent of the Jamaican electorate went to the polls on October 30, 1980, despite scattered incidents of violence. In what Seaga called "a hard blow for Communism in the Caribbean," the JLP was returned to power by an overwhelming margin of 13 percent. More importantly, Labourites took control of Parliament, winning fifty-one of the sixty seats. In a victory speech to his cheering supporters, Seaga vowed to bring Jamaicans together to "build a nation." His first priority, he said, would be to restore the country's "almost battle-torn, war-torn economy . . . to health."

Seaga was sworn in as Prime Minister at the Governor General's residence in New Kingston on November 1, 1980. Because of the country's "desperate financial situation," to use his words, he also assumed the portfolio of the Minister of Finance. He immediately arranged short-term financing to keep his new government afloat, then took a series of positive steps to shore up the staggering economy. Among other things, he asked American- and Canadian-based mining companies to pay their bauxite taxes ahead of schedule, obtained $50,000,000 in credits against oil purchases from Venezuela, Jamaica's main petroleum supplier, and reopened negotiations with the International Monetary Fund that in April 1981 led to a $698,000,000 agreement. He eased currency restrictions on "unfounded" imports, discussed potential private investments with a delegation of corporate executives from the United States, and beefed up law enforcement to encourage tourists to return. "We must rebuild confidence in our system at home and abroad," he said, as quoted in U. S. News & World Report (November 17, 1980). "We need rapid investment to close the gap between our income and our debts, and we are confident that we can find the financing in the banking community, international groups, and from other governments." Renewed foreign and domestic confidence seemed to have a quick impact on the Jamaican economy. Within five weeks of the election, violence in Kingston had declined by half and hotel bookings were up 17 percent.

In his inaugural address, Seaga had charted an independent course for Jamaica as a nonaligned, "middle of the road" Third World country. To underscore his determination in that regard, he asked for a recall of Ulises Estrada, the Cuban ambassador to Jamaica, who was, in his words, "objectionable." Cuban foreign aid programs were gradually "phased down," too, but as he explained to Jim Lehrer on the January 28, 1981 edition of the MacNeil/Lehrer Report over PBS, he maintained diplomatic relations with Cuba because "we feel that there is still room for a government-to-government basis of operation . . . , but not one which involves the political systems of the two countries."

Seaga went on to propose a comprehensive economic assistance program that Robert MacNeil described as "a kind of Marshall Plan for the Caribbean and Central America." The proposal calls for an influx of financial aid from countries within and without the region to "take the economic development strategy to a point of better standards of living" and, at the same time, encourage and support political moderation. Although he insisted that Jamaica was "not one of those nonaligned countries that are tied to the coattails of any great power," he advocated a closer relationship with the United States because, as he told MacNeil and Lehrer, "it means . . . closer ties with the world's richest market for the purpose of developing greater financial and trading flows for the benefit of our country." After two days of talks with President Ronald Reagan, Seaga announced, on January 29, 1981, the formation of a high-level, private working group of Jamaicans and Americans to seek the development of joint economic projects in Jamaica.

Slim and "ascetic-looking," Edward Seaga has been described by Jo Thomas as "a thoughtful man whose introspection is often mistaken, even by his friends, as coldness." In the opinion of most Western reporters, he is a less charismatic figure than Manley, more at home in the boardrooms of corporate executives and international financiers than on the hustings, but as John Huey noted, he "slips easily from colonial English to native patois when on the stump." On August 22, 1965 Seaga married Marie Elizabeth ("Mitsy") Constantine, the former Miss Jamaica of 1964. They have three children: Christopher, Annabella, and Andrew-Marc, one of whom they found abandoned as a baby in Back-O-Wall and adopted. Among Seaga's recreations are music, reading, and skeet shooting.

References: Chicago Tribune II p1+ Ag 2 '81 por; Cur World Leaders 24:10 Ja '81 por; Forbes 127:35+ F 2 '81 por; Macleans 93:35 O 27 '80 por, 93:45+ N 10 '80 pors; N Y Times p3 N 1 '80; N Y Times Mag p48+ O 26 '80; Newsweek 96:72 N 10 '80 por, 96:86+ D 15 '80 por; Toronto Globe & Mail p7 N 6 '80 por; US News 89:15 N 10 '80 por, 89:80+ N 17 '80 por; Wall St J p17 Ag 11 '80 por; Washington Post A p3 Ja 29 '81 por; International Who's Who, 1980-81; International Year Book and Statesmen's Who's Who, 1981

Selye, Hans (Hugo Bruno) (sel'yā)

Jan. 26, 1907- Medical researcher; endocrinologist; physician Address: b. International Institute of Stress, 29000 Edouard Montpetit Blvd., Montreal, Quebec, H3C 3J7, Canada; h. 659 Milton St., Montreal, Quebec, H2X 1W6, Canada

NOTE: This biography supersedes the article that appeared in Current Biography in 1953.

Among the pioneers of twentieth-century medicine, Hans Selye led the way through his formulations concerning stress and endocrine-related diseases to the discovery of how the hormonal system contributes to a variety of degenerative illnesses, such as arteriosclerosis, arthritis, and ulcers. His theory of stress, which he defines as "the nonspecific response of the body to any demand," has induced new approaches to the treatment of disease, has helped to change popular thinking about the ecology of the human body and its vulnerability to illness, and has spawned an enormous amount of research in psychology, neurology, and other fields, as well as in endocrinology proper. He himself is the author of about forty books and 1,700 technical articles. In 1956 at the World Congress of Medical Psychology, which honored Selye, Frank Engel described his work as "breathtaking in its scope" and went on to maintain, "It has permeated medical thinking and influenced medical research in every land, probably more rapidly and more intensely than any other theory of disease ever proposed."

When Selye set forth his stress theory and "general adaptation syndrome" in the 1930's, however, his concepts suffered initial rejec-

tion by the scientific community. His 1,000-page 1950 monograph, Stress, among other publications, ignited further controversy. But although some medical researchers have continued to call for revision of certain components of the stress theory, the results of much research by Selye and others and new discoveries in endocrinology have made his basic formulation about the relationship between stress and a variety of diseases one of the cornerstones of contemporary medicine. In recent years Selye has devoted himself to exploring the social and psychological aspects of stress and has devised a code of behavior based on the widest implications of his theory.

Hans Hugo Bruno Selye was born on January 26, 1907 in Vienna, Austria, which was then the center of the Austro-Hungarian Empire. The family, in which he was the only child, lived in a Hungarian town that became part of Czechoslovakia after the collapse of Austria-Hungary at the end of World War I. His father, Hugo Selye, was a Hungarian national, a Hussar, and a well-regarded surgeon whose own father and grandfather were also physicians; his mother, Maria Felicitas (Langbank) Selye, was of a wealthy Viennese family. After acquiring his elementary education from French and English governesses, he attended secondary school from 1916 to 1924 at the College of the Benedictine Fathers in Komárom, Czechoslovakia. Certain about a career in medicine, he enrolled in medical school at the German University of Prague in 1924 and the following year went abroad to study first at the University of Paris, in 1925-26, and then at the University of Rome, in 1926-27. He returned to the German University of Prague to complete work for his M.D. degree, awarded in 1929, and to qualify for a Ph.D degree in organic chemistry in 1931.

Drawn from the start of his career to research and experimental medicine rather than to clinical practice, Selye held a position as assistant in experimental pathology at the university in Prague while meeting requirements for his doctorate. In 1931, having been appointed a Rockefeller research fellow, he spent a year working in the department of biochemical hygiene at Johns Hopkins University in the United States. He had his fellowship renewed for 1932-33 to carry out research in the department of biochemistry at McGill University in Montreal, Canada, where he was appointed lecturer in biochemistry in 1933 and assistant professor in 1934.

While Selye was experimenting with sex hormones in 1936, he first recognized a distinct group of endocrine-related changes that led, eventually, to his theory of stress. Using laboratory rats as subjects, he injected them with ovarian and placental extracts, and when he noticed a regularly occurring triad of tissue changes—enlarged adrenal cortex, shrinkage of the lymphatic structures, and stomach ulcers—he thought for a time that he may have identified a new hormone. Selye soon realized that those changes, however, far from isolating a new hormone, could be produced by the administration of virtually any toxic substance. His disappointment turned to elation as he became aware that his results suggested something more dramatic: that the body, executive of the hormonal system, produced a "syndrome of response to injury as such"; that is, the same group of effects were caused by various and sundry agents.

In his account of his discovery in *The Stress of Life* (McGraw-Hill, 1956, 1976) Selye wrote that he had wondered as early as 1925, while still a student, why no attention was paid to clusters of symptoms common to a variey of illnesses. "Could it be," he asked, "that this syndrome in man (the feeling of being ill, the diffuse pains in joints and muscles, the intestinal disturbances with loss of appetite, the loss of weight) were in some manner clinical equivalents of the experimental syndrome . . . that I had produced with such a variety of toxic substances in the rat?" By giving the concept of nonspecificity in bodily reactions due consideration at a point in the history of medicine when specific diagnostic concepts were ascendant, and also by conducting ingenious experiments that could be repeated and confirmed by others, Selye approached a major scientific breakthrough.

Selye's first report concerning the stress syndrome was a brief note that appeared in the July 4, 1936 issue of *Nature,* "A Syndrome Produced by Diverse Nocuous Agents." The initial response of the scientific community was not encouraging to Selye, who had to endure the disapproval of, among others, Walter B. Cannon, an influential teacher and physiologist who had pioneered the concept of homeostasis. But with the help of Sir Frederick Banting, the Nobel laureate who had discovered insulin, Selye secured modest financial support to continue his research. He was promoted to the rank of assistant professor of histology at McGill University in 1937 and four years later attained an associate professorship there.

To characterize the triad of changes that he had observed in his experimental animals, Selye suggested the term "alarm reaction." In *Stress of Life* he recalled, "I thought that this syndrome probably represented the bodily expression of a generalized call to arms of the defensive forces of the organism." Further observations led him to recognize a "stage of resistance," which signaled an adaptive reaction under continued stress, and a third "stage of exhaustion," which if sustained would lead eventually to death. Those three stages, together with their characteristic patterns of response, Selye named the " general adaptation syndrome" (G.A.S.), a concept that suggested a new, defensive order of action for the hormonal system.

At the time of Selye's basic research into the adaptational function of what came to be called the "adrenal-pituitary axis" (signifying the hormonal feedback system responsible for the stress reaction), researchers engaged in the general study of the endocrine system were on the brink of discovering the corticoids (secreted by the adrenal gland). Their investigations culminated in the discovery and clinical use of cortisone, now used pharmacologically for a wide variety of illnesses. Selye's own further research contributed both to the mainstream of endocrine function research—he identified a number of corticoids—and also to the advance of his theory of stress and the G.A.S. In particular, he suggested that a great number of "civilized" disorders deserve to be called "diseases of adaptation" due to stress.

Hypothesizing that the overproduction of certain hormones was attendant on stress engendered by psychological or physical causes, Selye demonstrated in a variety of experimental situations that stress could cause or contribute to kidney and cardiovascular diseases, arthritic and rheumatoid conditions, inflammatory tissue diseases, some infectious diseases, and allergic reactions—among many others. Although many of his experiments yielded findings that today are widely accepted—such as that heart attacks are partly caused by stressful living—at the time of their appearance they often challenged either the germ theory of disease or other physiological explanations. "When Selye formulated his stress theory," Félix Martí-Ibáñez wrote in "A Footnote to Medical History" (*International Record of Medicine*, 1955), "he crystallized a new historical current and anticipated the newest tendencies in medicine which were just then being adumbrated."

McGill University awarded Selye a D.Sc. degree in medical research in 1942. The following year the Montreal firm of A.W.T. Franks published the first section of his *Encyclopedia of Endocrinology* in four volumes; two further volumes appeared in 1946, published by Bond & Wright of Montreal. By that time Selye, having left the faculty of McGill University in 1945, was serving as director of the Institute of Experimental Medicine and Surgery at the University of Montreal, where since 1945 he also had the rank of professor. In 1947 he accepted the additional post of expert consultant to the Surgeon General of the United States Army, which he retained until 1957.

The publication in 1950 of Selye's long, comprehensive research monograph, *Stress* (Acta Medica), marked a turning point toward more general acceptance of the new theory. Although the nature of the theory—a specific syndrome with no particular cause—militated against its unqualified support in the medical community, continued pragmatic results as well as experimental findings lent it increasing credibility. Beginning in 1951 he gave the accumulating data on his theory exposure and synthesis by publishing annual reports on stress.

As new methodological research tools allowed for more precise measurements of hormones released by the endocrine system, the conclusions that Seyle had reached with older methods were in general confirmed.

During the 1950's and 1960's Selye published a vast amount of research on a variety of specialized topics related to stress. His studies on cardiovascular disease include *The Chemical Prevention of Cardiac Necroses* (Ronald, 1958), *The Pluricausal Cardiopathies* (Thomas, 1961), and *Experimental Cardiovascular Diseases* (Springer-Verlag, 1970). He is also author of *The Mast Cells* (Butterworth, 1965), *Thrombohemorrhagic Phenomena* (Thomas, 1966), *Anaphylactoid Edema* (Green, 1968), and *Hormones and Resistance* (Springer-Verlag, 1971). Selye applied the general principles of his research and theoretical reasoning to biology in a series of lectures published as *In Vivo* (Liveright, 1967), in which he made a plea for supramolecular biology as a unifying corrective to the discoveries of molecular biology.

For the lay audience Selye wrote *The Story of the Adaptation Syndrome* (Acta, 1952) and provided a wide-ranging synthesis of his work in *The Stress of Life*, which Ashley Montagu, commenting in the *Nation* (February 9, 1957), found to be "an extremely intense and personal book in which the personality of the writer is ever-present—a most unusual style for a book written by a scientist, and all the more welcome for that reason." Selye's *From Dream to Discovery* (McGraw-Hill, 1964) is a book of notes and ruminations on the research scientist's career, and *The Stress of My Life* (McClellan and Stewart, 1977, 1979) is his full-scale autobiography, which won the Canadian Authors Association Literary Award for nonfiction in 1977.

Since his retirement in 1977 as director of the University of Montreal's Institute of Experimental Medicine and Surgery, Dr. Selye has been free to spend more of his time on his work as president of the International Institute of Stress, which he had established in 1976. He also took over, in 1979, the presidency of the newly formed Hans Selye Foundation. Those organizations explore the psychosocial implications and the medical and psychological applications of Selye's concept; serve as a clearinghouse for the field of stress research and record its worldwide developments; seek to increase public awareness of the nature of stress; and in other ways contribute to the advancement of stress theory. Selye's own writings, some of which have been translated into thirty-four languages, are among the 150,000 books and other reference items comprising the institute's documentation center, the largest of its kind in the world. He serves also as editorial director of *Stress*, inaugurated in 1980 as the official journal of the International Institute of Stress and its affiliates.

During the past decade Selye's activities have focused increasingly on developing a code of ethics based on universal and everlasting laws of nature, such as "mechanisms that maintain homeostasis in cells, people, and entire societies." His basic guidelines, presented in his highly readable *Stress Without Distress* (Lippincott, 1974) and in articles and lectures, recommend that people find their own natural stress level in pursuit of goals that are chosen by themselves and not imposed by society; that they practise "altruistic egoism" by channeling self-interest through outlets that are useful to others; and that they thereby follow the maxim, "Earn thy neighbor's love." He points out that stress may be caused by excessive joy as well as by excessive pain, that one can learn to cope with stress or minimize its effects, but that one cannot avoid it totally because an organism without stress would die. "It is not what happens to you that matters," Selye teaches, "but how you take it."

The international scope of the work of Selye, who speaks ten languages, is evident in his extensive travels to fulfill lecture engagements; his service as a member of the editorial boards of professional periodicals in the United States, Europe, and India, as well as Canada; and in his affiliation with over sixty scientific societies throughout the world, many of which have conferred medals and other honors on him. He holds, moreover, at least twenty honorary degrees from universities in Canada and abroad. Among his other Canadian tributes are his fellowship in the Royal Society of Canada, the Starr Medal (the Canadian Medical Association's highest distinction), the Killam Scholarship (the Canada Council's highest award), the Prix de l'Oeuvre Scientifique (the highest award of the Canadian Association of French-speaking Physicians), and the Companion of the Order of Canada (his country's top decoration). He belongs to the Richelieu club in Montreal. His faith is the Roman Catholic.

Hans Selye was married on December 5, 1936 to Frances Rebecca Love and by that marriage is the father of a daughter, Catherine. By his second marriage, to Gabrielle Grant on February 17, 1949, he has four children, Michel, Jean, Marie, and André. His present wife is the former Louise Drevet, whom he married on October 5, 1978. Dr. Selye is a trim, energetic, self-assured man who stands five feet ten inches tall and has pale blue eyes and gray hair. "Yet," Joan Wixen found when she interviewed him for *Modern Maturity* (October-November 1978), "there is no human being more alive today." According to recent reports, he still enjoys swimming, bicycling, weightlifting, and, especially, working.

References: N Y Post p35 D 18 '75 por; *Psych Today* 11:64 Mr '78 por; *Toronto Globe and Mail mag* p6+ N 23 '74 por; *American Men and Women of Science* 14th ed (1979); *Canadian Who's Who,* 1980; *Contemporary Authors* 1st rev ed vols 5-8 (1969)

Sharon, Ariel (shä-ron')

1928- Minister of Defense of Israel. Address:
b. Ministry of Defense, Jerusalem, Israel

One of Israel's most colorful and controversial
figures, Ariel ("Arik") Sharon capped a lifelong career in the service of his country with
his appointment, in August 1981, as Minister of
Defense in Prime Minister Menahem Begin's
Cabinet. A bold and flamboyant battlefield
commander in the tradition of General George
S. Patton, Sharon planned and carried out decisive military operations in all of Israel's
wars, earning from his inspired troops the
appellation "Lion of the Desert." In the early
1970's he took that same unwavering determination and dedication to the political arena,
when he helped to found the right-wing coalition Likud party, which, in 1977, unseated the
governing Labor party for the first time in the
history of the Jewish state. A hard-line Zionist,
Sharon is the most outspoken advocate of his
government's aggressive program of Jewish settlement in occupied Arab territories as a
precondition to Palestinian autonomy talks. As
New York Times correspondent David K. Shipler recently observed, Sharon acts as "a kind
of militant conscience, adamant and relentless
in the face of any move that strikes him as
a betrayal of either the past or the future of
the Jewish people." In the eyes of many Israeli political observers, he is Begin's most
trusted adviser and his most likely successor
as leader of the Likud party.

Ariel Sharon, the son of Shmuel and Devorah
Sharon, was born in 1928 at Kfar Maalal in
the Sharon Valley, one of the first cooperative
Jewish farming settlements in Palestine. (The
family's original European surname was Schein-

erman). His parents, ardent Zionists who
had emigrated from Russia after the end of
World War I, frequently had to defend their
property from attacks by marauding Bedouin
tribes or raiding parties from neighboring Arab
villages. When anti-Jewish rioting spread
throughout Palestine in the early 1930's, the
Sharons joined other settlers to form defensive
units, and Shmuel Sharon taught his young
son armed combat and survival techniques. By
the time he was fourteen, Ariel Sharon was a
full-fledged member of GADNA, a paramilitary
youth battalion.

After completing his elementary education
at a regional school not far from his home,
Sharon attended high school in nearby Tel
Aviv, where he studied agriculture, politics,
and military affairs. During those years, he
joined the Hagganah, the underground Jewish
defense force. Upon his graduation from high
school in 1945, Sharon enrolled in an officers'
training course. Two years later he became
an instructor of the Hagganah police units
assigned to protect the farming settlements.
Promoted to platoon commander of the Al-
exandroni Brigade at the beginning of Israel's
war for independence in 1948, he was badly
wounded in the stomach during one especially
fierce battle in his native Sharon Valley. It
was while he was hospitalized that he came
to believe that victory depended, in a large
part, on esprit de corps and on the example
an officer set for his men. Idolized by his
troops, Sharon always went into battle at the
head of his unit, often in an armored car
stocked with caviar and vodka. "I believe to
control a battle you must be with the forward
units," he explained to Charles Mohr in an
interview for the New York Times (November
12, 1973). "One minute you are a general and
another minute a soldier shooting a machine
gun at Arabs and throwing grenades and
climbing on bulldozers to convince men they
can work under shellfire."

After an armistice was signed between Israel
and her Arab neighbors in 1949, Sharon enlisted
as a military intelligence officer in the Israeli
army. Assigned to the Northern Command,
he gathered information on Arab guerrillas in
Syria and Lebanon and performed various administrative functions. In 1952 he took a leave
of absence from the army to study Middle
Eastern history at the Hebrew University of
Jerusalem. In the following year the district
commander in Jerusalem recruited him to lead
commando raids into Jordanian territory in
retaliation for attacks against Israeli settlements.

When his first raid on a Jordanian village
was repulsed rather easily by well-armed
townspeople and Jordanian soldiers, Sharon
proposed the formation of a small mobile unit
of crack soldiers specifically trained to launch
surprise attacks. Mordechai Makleff, the chief
of staff, and Moshe Dayan, then the head of
operations, approved the project and appointed
Sharon to head the elite group, known as

Commando Unit 101. In his zeal, Sharon sometimes overstepped his orders. For example, in 1953, he was instructed to blow up ten homes in the Jordanian border village of Quibya in retaliation for a raid on an Israeli settlement that had resulted in three deaths. Instead, his men demolished thirty-nine houses and a school and killed sixty-nine Jordanians. The incident earned Sharon a worldwide reputation for ruthlessness and provoked such an outcry in the international diplomatic community that Prime Minister David Ben-Gurion was forced to apologize publicly.

Border disputes and bloody reprisals continued throughout the 1950's. Provoked by repeated Arab threats of invasion, Israel mounted a preemptive strike on Egyptian territory in October 1956. Sharon's troops captured the strategic Mitla Pass in the Sinai Peninsula in a gory battle that some of his superior officers, including Army Chief of Staff Dayan, thought was unnecessary. Sharon has always insisted that the solution to Israel's persistent security problem is a stronger, more self-confident army. "We have to prove that we can strike hardest and best," he explained to Matti Shavitt in an interview for Shavitt's book *On the Wings of Eagles; the Story of Arik Sharon* (Olive Books, 1972). "To do this we must be trained and able. And if we can strike secretly and efficiently, without employing large forces, we'll . . . have taught the Arabs a thing or two about our power. . . . If we succeed, our own mood will change for the better, and we will have reinstated the self-confidence that is so necessary to an army like ours."

After the war, Sharon studied military theory at Staff College in Camberley, England. Advanced to the rank of Colonel on his return to Israel in 1958, he spent the next three years as a senior administrative officer in the training division of the General Staff, where he headed the Infantry School. He was named Brigade Commander of the armored corps in 1962 and, two years later, Chief of Staff of the Southern Command headquarters on the Egyptian front. During that period he also studied law at Tel Aviv University, but although he received his law degree in 1966, he has never practised that profession. He was appointed head of the training division of the General Staff that same year and eventually promoted to the rank of Major General in February 1967.

In June 1967, in response to Egyptian President Gamal Abdel Nasser's blockade of the Israeli port of Elat, Israel attacked Egypt, Jordan, and Syria. As commander of the Egyptian front, Sharon directed a battle that has since become a classic in military textbooks. In a lightning assault conducted at night, his division overran the strongly fortified Egyptian encampment at Abu-Ageila, then went on to recapture the Mitla Pass and the vital corridor to the Suez Canal. According to some reports from the scene, Sharon and his men deliberately slaughtered Egyptian prisoners of war, but although Sharon admitted, as quoted in the *London Observer* (November 4, 1973), that he had made "no special effort to take prisoners," the charges were never confirmed.

In the late 1960's Israeli occupation of Arab territory—the Gaza Strip, the Sinai Desert, the West Bank of the Jordan, and the Golan Heights—taken during the Six-Day War removed heavily populated Jewish areas from the range of Arab artillery, but sporadic border skirmishes continued, and Arab guerrillas stepped up their incursions. During that so-called "War of Attrition," Sharon traded his desk job with the General Staff for a field position as Brigadier General of the Southern Command at the Suez Canal. While supervising internal security in the Gaza Strip, he was once again accused of brutality for his alleged mistreatment of suspected Arab terrorists, but he was exonerated after a government investigation.

At about the same time Sharon became embroiled in a dispute with other members of the high command over the proposed construction of extensive fortifications along the banks of the Suez Canal to protect Israeli positions there from possible Egyptian attacks. Contending that a permanent garrison would be little more than a stationary target for Egyptian artillery, he suggested the creation of a mobile defense force, spearheaded by tanks, but he was overruled, and the earthwork—the so-called "Bar-Lev Line"—was built. Sharon's outspoken opposition to the project further alienated the high command and the Labor government.

Apparently because of his impulsiveness, dogmatism, and fierce independence, Sharon failed to win the expected promotion to Chief of Staff. Frustrated by the rebuff, he resigned from the army to seek a seat in the Knesset, Israel's Parliament, as a member of Gahal, a right-wing coalition party led by Menahem Begin. Gahal advocated the annexation of the Arab lands taken in the Six-Day War to ensure Israel's continuing security and rejected the ruling Labor government's willingness to make territorial compromises in the event of a peace settlement. To broaden Gahal's political base and provide a viable alternative to the Labor party in the upcoming national election, Sharon helped negotiate, in September 1973, a right-center alliance known as Likud (Unity), which included Gahal, the Independent Liberals, and the Free Center. The parties kept their independent organizational structures but agreed to nominate a joint slate of candidates.

The Egyptian-Syrian surprise attack on Israel on October 6, 1973, the Jewish high holy day of Yom Kippur, interrupted Sharon's promising political career. Taking over as leader of the Southern Command, at the head of an army reserve division composed of three armored brigades, he smashed through the Egyptian lines and established an Israeli bridgehead at Ismailia on the western side of the Suez Canal. To secure that advantageous behind-the-lines position, he called for immediate reinforcements, but before committing additional troops, the high command ordered him to construct and defend bridges across the Canal. In Sharon's opinion, the delay cost Israel a decisive victory in strategic territory before the United Nations-sponsored ceasefire went into effect in late October. A few months later, largely through the mediation efforts of United States Secretary of State Henry A. Kissinger, formal disengagement agreements were signed.

Outraged by the hesitation that resulted in an "undecided war," to use his term, Sharon turned Israel's lack of military preparedness into a political issue. "We defeated the Egyptians, but we didn't finish the war," he told Joseph Kraft in an interview for the *New Yorker* (February 11, 1974). "I know we have a strong country and a lot of energetic and ingenious people . . . , but for twenty-five years, we had a posture of deterrence—a posture that deterred the Arabs from attacking us. Now we've lost it." Sharon's candid public criticism of Israeli strategy was disputed by other senior army officers, some of whom deplored his statements as self-serving and "biased."

In December 1973 Sharon was elected to the Knesset on the Likud ticket. Taking his fight to the floor of the Knesset, he demanded the resignation of the Labor government on the grounds that its mismanagement of the Yom Kippur war and its early acceptance of a ceasefire had deprived the Israeli army of an imminent victory over the Egyptians. A commission of inquiry appointed by Prime Minister Golda Meir absolved her government of any wrongdoing, but in April 1974, under continuing pressure from the Likud bloc, Mrs. Meir stepped down and was succeeded by Yitzhak Rabin. Fearful that Israel might become involved in another war, Sharon resigned from the Knesset in December 1974 to accept a senior emergency position in the reserves, where he could "contribute to the security effort," as he put it. Six months later Prime Minister Rabin chose Sharon to be his defense adviser, even though they frequently disagreed on defense policy. Sharon was totally committed to continued Israeli occupation of Arab territory taken in the Six-Day War and believed that Rabin might make too many territorial concessions in exchange for secure borders.

In 1976 Sharon left the government to form the Shlomzion (Peace-Zion) party, which was founded on the premise that lasting peace would come only if Israel permanently annexed and settled the lands captured in 1967. Despite its obvious appeal to the more nationalistic segments of the population, the party won just two seats in the Knesset in the June 1977 election. It was eventually absorbed by the larger, more powerful Likud group. "People trusted [Ariel Sharon] as a soldier," an Israeli poll taker explained, as quoted in *Newsweek* (Sep-

tember 19, 1977), "but as a politician, he sounded too reckless."

In the 1977 election the Likud party scored a historic victory over the Labor party, winning forty-four seats in the Knesset to Labor's thirty-three. The new coalition government, under the leadership of Prime Minister Menahem Begin, included Ariel Sharon, who had been appointed Minister of Agriculture. Sharon greatly expanded the role of the Ministry, which had previously restricted itself to such purely agricultural problems as land distribution, to include programs for establishing permanent Jewish colonies in the occupied territories. Shortly after taking office, he announced his own "master plan" to settle 2,000,000 Jews in the West Bank and Gaza Strip during the next two decades to prevent the establishment of a Palestinian state, which, he fervently believed, would threaten the security of Israel. "You're wrong if you think that peace will come if Israel remains a nation of 3,000,000 Jews," Sharon explained to Milan J. Kubic in an interview for *Newsweek* (September 19, 1977). "Peace will come, but our first problem is to [ensure] that Israel will exist forever. To that end, we have to have a population of 6,000,000 to 8,000,000 Jews within the next twenty to fifty years, and we have to settle them. I don't believe that my plan blocks any diplomatic solutions, because we've made it perfectly clear that we'll never leave the West Bank," he continued. "I believe that if we establish these settlements, we will feel sufficiently secure to accept risks for the sake of peace."

Sharon opposed his government's acceptance of the Camp David peace accords hammered out in 1978 by President Jimmy Carter, Anwar el-Sadat, the President of Egypt, and Prime Minister Begin because, in his opinion, the guidelines for future talks on Palestinian autonomy were not clearly defined. As a member of the six-man Israeli negotiation team that met with Egyptian and American officials in May 1979 to discuss that question, Sharon ruled out any concessions and reaffirmed his commitment to an intensive Jewish settlement effort. Without additional settlements, he said, as quoted in the New York *Times* (May 31, 1979), "we might as well proclaim a Palestinian state and withdraw to the coastal plains, permitting the breakup of everything we have created in thirty years of wars and 100 years of constructive efforts." To underscore his determination, he openly supported the attempts of Gush Emunim, a right-wing nationalist group that had set up several settlements in the Biblical lands of Judea and Samaria, the modern-day West Bank. More recently, he approved a controversial government plan to build seven settlements on state-owned land in the West Bank.

Since taking over as Minister of Defense in August 1981, Sharon has issued revised liberal guidelines for the administration of the occupied Arab territories. The new policy, which was confirmed by the defense ministry on September 23, 1981, was formulated to create the political and social conditions conductive to limited autonomy under civilian authority. Under Sharon's plan, the civilian government would be headed by Israelis but would also include Palestinians in a number of "senior positions."

Once described as "a large man who vaguely resembles a teddy bear but talks like a bulldozer," Ariel Sharon is short and solidly built, with a lined, weather-beaten face, fiery blue-gray eyes, and thick white hair. Although he is not given to socializing, he enjoys good food and wine and an occasional cigar, which he usually wields "like a field marshal's baton." His critics say he is arrogant, aggressive, and authoritarian, but interviewers, including David K. Shipler, have found him to be a man of "abundant charm." Sharon and his second wife,

Lili, a painter, divide their time between a 1,000-acre farm near Beersheba, in the Negev Desert, where they raise wheat and cotton, and a small apartment in a suburb of Tel Aviv. His first wife, Lili Sharon's sister, was killed in an automobile accident in 1961. He has two sons.

References: Guardian p5 N 17 '73 por; London Observer p13 N 4 '73 por; N Y Times p1+ N 9 '73 por, A p6 Ag 5 '81 por; N Y Times Mag p41+ O 18 '81 por; Nat Observer p1+ F 2 '74 pors; New Yorker 49:102+ F 11 '74; Newsday p17 N 11 '73 por; Newsweek 40:65 S 19 '77 por; Time 102:40 N 26 '73 por, 118:22+ S 7 '81 por; Washington Post A p22 N 6 '73 por; International Who's Who, 1980-81; Schiff, Zeev. A History of the Israeli Army (1974); Shavitt, Matti. On the Wings of Eagles (1972); Who's Who in Israel, 1978

Sheed, Frank (Joseph)

Mar. 20, 1897- Publisher; writer. Address: h. 85 Van Reypen St., Jersey City, N.J. 07306

BULLETIN: Frank Sheed died on November 20, 1981. Obituary: N Y Times p19 N 21 '81.

The Roman Catholic lay theologian Frank Sheed, with his wife, Maisie Ward, in 1926 founded Sheed & Ward, publishers of books of biography, history, philosophy, theology, and belles lettres widely respected in the secular as well as the religious world. Sheed, a precise thinker and a peerless platform speaker with a talent for explaining theology in simple,

fresh, commonsense terms, carried his lucid street-corner expository style over into the writing of such books as Theology and Sanity (1947) and Society and Sanity (1953). By post-Vatican Council II standards, his brand of theology may seem tame, but many of the leading lights of contemporary Catholicism have acknowledged their debt to him. In the 1940's and 1950's he was considered a flaming radical, as his son, Wilfrid, the novelist, has observed, "if only for daring to poach this clerical game preserve and assert the layman's right to think." Sheed & Ward is now an imprint of Andrews & McMeel, a subsidiary of the Universal Press Syndicate.

The older of two sons of a draftsman, Francis Joseph Sheed was born into a religiously divided family in Sydney, Australia on March 20, 1897. His steadfast Catholicism, as well as his love of reading, came from his self-educated mother, Mary (Maloney) Sheed, who had immigrated by herself from Ireland to Australia when she was fourteen. Although Sheed's father dropped religion early in favor of Marxism, his paternal grandparents, and still more his paternal aunts, were Scotch Presbyterians "of the type who dream of the Pope and wake up in a cold sweat screaming, 'Rome!'," as he writes in The Church and I (Doubleday, 1974), the closest of his books to an autobiography. "As far back as my memory goes, I was aware that my young brother [who died at sixteen] and I were being fought over.... The occasional questioner who tells me I believe as I do because I had been brainwashed in childhood hasn't a notion of the variety of washings—Methodism three times every Sunday, Marxism at breakfast and dinner every day, confession to Father Rohan in his study [at a local Sacred Heart Fathers mission] on one Saturday morning in the month, daily Mass and Communion during the two weeks of my father's annual vacation."

As "a little Catholic who didn't want to be there," Sheed took no part in the praying or singing at Methodist services, but nothing escaped his attention. To this day, he says, he knows "more of the hymns [he] never sang than lots of Methodists, and [he] sing[s] them now as [he] did not then." Also, "few Catholic boys were getting as much Scripture as [he] got, partly by listening to the readings, partly by dipping about in the Bible during sermons." The result was "a growing affection for Methodists and a devotion to John Wesley."

In Sheed's six years of attendance at Methodist services, he recalls, he "never heard a word against the Catholic Church." On the other hand, when he visited his paternal grandparents and aunts he was assaulted with anti-Catholic writings "of virulence hard to credit." The "No Popery" propaganda succeeded only in hardening his Roman Catholic faith.

Except for two weeks he spent in a school run by Sacred Heart nuns when he was eight, Sheed attended public schools. When he was in his senior year at Sydney High School, his English teacher gave him two books by authors previously unknown to him with the remark, "These will suit you." One of the books was Hilaire Belloc's *Danton;* the other was G. K. Chesterton's *Heretics.* For him, as for many other young English-speaking Catholics of his generation, Belloc and Chesterton represented the dawning of a "Catholic intellectual revival" marking the end of the siege mentality prevalent in Roman Catholicism for four centuries, beginning with the Council of Trent's reaction to the Protestant Reformation. As yet, however, although "fervently Catholic," he had "no interest in theology." "Given the course my religious thinking has taken since," he reremarks in *The Church and I,* "I cannot make any sense of my late teens and early twenties."

Midway through his law studies at Sydney University, Sheed decided to go to Europe "for a year." (The one year would grow into four, and after a return to Australia to complete the work for his law degree, into long-term residence in England.) He had only "the vaguest of reasons for going" and in fact "no longer remember[s] what they were." One of the reasons had to do with Ireland, where he "had an idea" he might study Gaelic. On his first visit to Dublin, at age twenty-five, Sheed, who until then had thought of himself as Irish-Australian, "with the accent on the Irish," realized his "full Australianness." He had "at last met the Irish-Irish, delighted in them but knew they were different."

In an interview with Jerry Tallmer in the New York *Post* (January 21, 1978), Wilfrid Sheed gave a different version of his father's first visit to Ireland: "He left to go to Ireland and fight the English, but arrived there in 1922 to find the English gone home and the Irish already fighting one another. After the 1922 thing he realized the English ruling class was just as mean to its own people as to everybody else."

Meanwhile, in London, Frank Sheed had joined the Catholic Evidence Guild, a society of street-speaking Roman Catholic catechists, and met Maisie Ward, a charter member of the guild. Miss Ward was a scion of English Catholic literary aristocracy, the daughter of Wilfrid Ward, the biographer of John Henry Cardinal Newman, and Josephine Mary (Hope) Ward, the novelist. Her grandparents had been prominent in the Oxford Movement, the migration of Anglican intellectuals to Roman Catholicism in the nineteenth century. Sheed and Miss Ward were married on April 27, 1926.

The original emphasis of the Catholic Evidence Guild in its soapbox explanations of the Roman Catholic faith was sectarian. Frank Sheed was the person chiefly responsible for redirecting the program to argue the proposition that "God matters." Together, he and Maisie Ward edited training outlines for guild speakers, and for the better part of half a century they prominently participated in guild activities, including platform appearances in Hyde Park in London, Times Square in New York City, and the Domain in Sydney.

In response to Maisie Ward's mother's suggestion that there was a genuine need for a Roman Catholic publishing house as much concerned with literary and intellectual excellence as with piety, Frank Sheed and Maisie Ward founded Sheed & Ward in London in October 1926 with a capital investment of £2,000, using packing crates until they could afford office furniture. Hilaire Belloc wrote them long letters of advice, but Frank Sheed says that he imbibed most of his knowledge of publishing from Stanley Unwin's *The Truth About Publishing.* From the beginning, Sheed was the company's president and Maisie Ward was vice-president. Sheed, a prodigy at arithmetic and accounting, handled all the business work, at one point doing a whole year's accounts in one night when the adding machine broke down.

G.K. Chesterton helped to launch the new company with a book of poems, and he later contributed *The Thing,* his apologia as a Roman Catholic convert. Belloc, who was then waging his war against H.G. Wells, gave the Sheeds *A Companion to Wells' Outline of History.* Christopher Dawson, the cultural historian, and Edward I. Watkin, the philosopher, both converts from Anglicanism, became mainstays of the company, both as writers and advisers. "From this provincial view of the Faith and of Europe [espoused by Belloc] Christopher Dawson saved us," Maisie Ward wrote in the first volume of her autobiography, *Unfinished Business* (1964). Dawson himself said, "Sheed and Ward have attempted to bring Catholic thought out of the cloister and the lecture-room into the world of everyday life.... They have been rewarded by the discovery ... that other people besides the clergy wish to read about theology. Even more important is the work that they are beginning to do as interpreters of the Catholic mind to that vast amorphous world outside."

Other English Catholic Revival authors published by Sheed & Ward included Christopher Hollis, Vincent McNabb, Ronald Knox, C. C. Martindale, and Caryll Houslander. Early on, the firm published translations of books by the Continental authors Paul Claudel, Jacques Maritain, François Mauriac, Nicholas Berdyaev, Léon Bloy, and Gertrud von le Fort. Among the other authors on the company's list over the years were the American Catholic social activists Dorothy Day and Catherine de Hueck and the progressive French theologian Henri de Lubac, the German revolutionary theologian Hans Küng, the British radical theologian Charles Davis, and the French worker-priests Henri Godin and Yves Daniel.

In 1933 the New York branch of Sheed & Ward was founded and Frank Sheed began traveling thrice yearly across the Atlantic, a commutation congenial to his temperamental wanderlust and restless energy. "Frank would be in two places at once if there was a night train," his mother-in-law once remarked. Jean Stafford, the poet, who worked for him briefly, has remembered him lying on top of his desk, with his dinner jacket in a shopping bag nearby, stealing a nap before some speaking engagement or other. In an article on his parents in the New York Times Book Review (April 2, 1972), Wilfrid Sheed summoned a childhood memory of his father as "the man who wore his hat funny (brim down all the way round) and looked like an amused stranger who'd just landed from somewhere at family functions." Wilfrid also remembered "the unexpectedness of their [his parents'] corner of the literary life—unexplained little men from the Continent turning up to play croquet, comic priests in black dickeys bellowing songs round the piano (my father played as if his pants were on fire), and always plenty of gossip steaming hot from the Vatican or chancery."

According to Wilfrid, a fluid, improvisational style ("squat where you land") characterized the Sheeds' personal life as well as their publishing venture: "One week you found a butler laying out your clothes and sneering at the underwear, the next you were cursing because the toilet wouldn't flush and you'd just stepped on a roach. It made absolutely no difference to my parents, and it had better not to junior either." In an interview with Diana Newell Rowan for the Christian Science Monitor (August 2, 1979), Wilfrid recalled that his father had two ways of dealing with him when he made grammatical mistakes as a child: "He would either put his head in his hands and groan hideously or he would look terribly embarrassed for both of us, as if it were really his fault. As a result, I was even afraid to write him a letter until I was past thirty."

For many years most of Frank Sheed's contributions to the Sheed & Ward's catalog were translations and compilations. The latter included the biographical collections The Irish Way (1932), Saints Are Not Sad (1949), and Born Catholics (1954). The translations included The Thundering Abbot (1930), Henri Brémond's biography of Armand de Rancé, reformer of La Trappe, Jacques Maritain's Theonas (1933), Stanislas Fumet's Joan The Saint (1937), Étienne Gilson's The Philosophy of St. Bonaventure (1938), The Confessions (1942) of St. Augustine, Orestes Ferrara's The Borgia Pope, Alexander the Sixth (1942), and numerous lives of the saints by Henri Gheon, beginning with The Secret of the Curé d'Ars (1929).

Sheed's own books grew out of his street-corner speaking. The first was Nullity of Marriage (1931), prompted by a widespread view of annulment, even among Catholics, as Roman Rota-style divorce, available to the rich. In the book he compared the English law of nullity with the Roman, showing that the concept of nullification, or the judgment that a marriage contract never really existed (as opposed to divorce, or the decision to end a contracted marriage) is respected in civil as well as church law. He brought out a new edition of Nullity of Marriage in 1959, adding a comparison with the matrimonial law of New York State.

His second book was A Map of Life (1933), a work of popular asceticism, and his third was the slim volume Ground Plan for Catholic Reading (1937). Sheed's Communism and Man (1938) was generally received by secular as well as religious reviewers as an eminently balanced and fair study, at least in its first half, an analysis of Marxism that was used in some Communist party study groups.

In the New York Post interview Jerry Tallmer asked Wilfrid Sheed if his father, like the father in Wilfrid's novel Transatlantic Blues, did some intelligence work for the British in the United States during World War II. "The only truth about that," Wilfrid answered, "is that my father was asked by MI-5 if he could do anything about this Father Coughlin feller. And I think he may have, in the sense of showing you could be Irish and Catholic and yet support the English war effort."

The Sheed family moved to the United States in 1940, settling in Jersey City, New Jersey, within reach of Sheed & Ward's offices in Manhattan. Frank Sheed continued to commute to London, despite the difficulties and hazards of wartime travel, making one crossing on a banana boat and another in the bomb rack of a B-24. After Sheed & Ward's English offices were wiped out by a German bomb, his sojourns in London were devoted in large measure to helping maintain the morale of the skeleton staff there.

In his platform speaking in the 1930's and 1940's, Sheed became "obsessed" with one theme—sanity, in the sense of "seeing what's there." That theme, he says, "has been the key to all [his] lecturing." "If a man starts seeing things which are evidently not there we call him insane and do what we can for him," he would explain to his audience. "But a man may fail to see the greater part of reality and cause no comment at all. He may live his life in un-awareness of God, of the spiritual order, of the unnumbered millions of the dead, and no-body thinks of him as needing help. . . . [To see] God in all things [is] not a high level of sanc-tity but . . . a first level of sanity." One of his favorite analogies was that of a coat hanging on a wall, hiding the hook from which it hangs. "If a man is not aware of the hook, then he is wrong about the nature of coats, of walls, or gravity. He is not living in the real world. But everything is held in existence by God: not to be aware of him damages sanity more than overlooking a hook."

In *Theology and Sanity* (1947) Sheed eluci-dated his thesis that if we and our universe are part of a greater reality and a greater purpose, we cannot hope to live sanely with-out knowing our place in that reality and our part in that purpose. The book was described by Leo J. Trese in *Commonweal* (February 7, 1947) as "an invitation to think" and by Granger Ryan in the New York *Times* (September 21, 1947) as the answer for "the thoughtful reader who wants to know what the Christian syn-thesis is like and what foundation it offers for the perplexities of modern life and society."

In an equally acute and penetrating compan-ion volume, *Society and Sanity* (1953), Sheed applied the principles set forth in *Theology and Sanity* to marriage, the family, society, and the state. His subsequent works included *Theology for Beginners* (1957), *To Know Christ Jesus* (1962), *God and The Human Condi-tion* (1966), and *Genesis Regained* (1969). His thoughts on the traumatic renewal of the Ro-man Catholic Church wrought by Vatican Council II were distilled in *Is It the Same Church?* (1968). Regarding the future of the Church, he recently wrote: "Given that we did not guess what would happen in the last six-teen years, why should we think we can know what will happen in the next sixteen—to say nothing of the next sixty? Only the innocent would prophesy. The one thing I know is that those who expect Mass and the sacraments will not find the Church disappointing them."

James F. Andrews, a former Sheed & Ward editor, founded the Universal Press Syndicate with John T. McMeel in 1970. Three years la-ter the Universal Press Syndicate bought Sheed & Ward and the name of the firm was changed, first to Sheed, Andrews & McMeel and finally to Andrews & McMeel. The im-print Sheed & Ward is now used by Andrews & McMeel for its reissues of "Sheed & Ward classics." The Universal Syndicate offices are in Fairway, Kansas.

Maisie Ward died in 1975. Asked by Our Sunday Visitor Inc., to write a book about her, Frank Sheed instead wrote the memoir "One Particular Heart," which became the first chapter of *The Instructed Heart* (OSV, 1979). Chapter Two, a consideration of the concept in Scripture of "heart" as "the organ not only of love but of all our willed activities, hate in-cluded," was a revision of a paper Sheed had read at Paray-le-Monial, France on the three-hundredth anniversary of the "revelations of the Sacred Heart" made to St. Margaret Mary Alacoque.

In the years following the sale of Sheed & Ward, Sheed devoted most of his time to lec-turing at universities and filling other speak-ing engagements. Following a recent heart at-tack, he curtailed his speaking itinerary, but when he does take the platform or the podium he is reportedly as sharp of tongue and vigor-ous of mind as ever. He continues to return fre-quently to Britain and Australia. "If he had his way," Wilfrid Sheed wrote in his New York *Times Book Review* piece on his parents, "he'd simply follow the cricket season around the world."

In addition to his son, Wilfrid, Sheed has a daughter, Rosemary (Mrs. Neil Middleton). "I am grateful for my husband's laughter and my children's," Maisie Ward wrote in the second volume of her autobiography, *To and Fro on the Earth* (1973). In his *Times Book Review* article, Wilfrid Sheed described his father as an "incurably cheerful" man. "[He] figures that if the pendulum comes back just a couple of inches, he's sitting pretty. If it doesn't, if it isn't a pendulum at all but a clock-hand moving away, he won't be heartbroken. This I sup-pose is the quality that most astounds me in both [parents]. They never expected it [pub-lishing venture] to last forever. 'We did what needed doing at the time,' Frank says. 'And we had a lot of fun doing it'."

References: Christian Sci Mon p18 Ag 2 '79; N Y Post p30 Ja 21 '78; N Y Times Bk Rev p2+ Ap 2 '72 por; Redfern, Martin. F. J. Sheed (1972); Sheed, Frank. The Church and I (1974); Ward, Maisie. Unfinished Business (1964), To and Fro on the Earth (1973)

Sheed, Wilfrid

Dec. 27, 1930- Novelist; critic. Address: h. Sag Harbor, New York 11963

"Probably the best living American novelist" is Anthony Burgess' assessment of Wilfrid Sheed, who has drawn on his experience as a British-born American to develop one of the most distinctive, polished, and urbane prose styles on either side of the Atlantic. Sheed's bi-cultural experience has also served him thematically, very autobiographically in his

Wilfrid Sheed

first novel, *A Middle Class Education* (1960), less so in the vigorous political novel *People Will Always Be Kind* (1973), and much less so in the straight farce *Transatlantic Blues* (1978). He reached his maturity as a novelist with *Office Politics* (1966), and John Leonard ranked his *Max Jamison* (1970) "the wittiest American novel since Randall Jarrell's *Pictures from an Institution.*" As a satirist of manners who brings even flippancy to the level of the moralist's art and whose wit masks an intuition of complex human motivation, Sheed has also been compared to the late Evelyn Waugh, with whom he shares a refined Roman Catholic sensibility. Outside of his fiction, Sheed is known as a literary and cultural critic, but he thinks of himself rather as an essayist, approaching reviewing as "the last refuge of the light essayist." In his essays as in his fiction, he is usually as serious in his message as he is entertaining in his wording of it.

Wilfrid John Joseph Sheed was born in London, England on December 27, 1930, the second of two children of the Roman Catholic writers, publishers, and activists Frank Sheed and Maisie Ward. He has one sister, Rosemary. The aristocratic Wards were Anglican converts to Roman Catholicism, prominent in England's Oxford Movement and, later, in the intellectual circle that included Hilaire Belloc, Gilbert Keith Chesterton, and Baron Friedrich von Hügel. Frank Sheed's family was nonliterary Australian of Scottish and Irish ancestry. Wilfrid Sheed has characterized his parents' professional style with the words "movement, improvisation, squat where you land," and he has said that that style carried over into the family's domestic life: "One week you found a butler laying out your clothes and

sneering at the underwear, the next you were cursing because the toilet wouldn't flush and you'd just stepped on a cockroach."

Frank Sheed and Maisie Ward established the avant-garde Catholic publishing house of Sheed & Ward in London in 1926 and opened an American branch in New York City in 1933. Wilfrid Sheed's transatlantic upbringing made "a chronic foreigner" out of him from the age of nine, as he has observed. His early education was divided between Downside Abbey, the famous Benedictine school in England, and schools in New Jersey, where the family settled in the United States, and Pennsylvania.

Regarding his compulsive drollery, in conversation as in writing, Sheed told Diana Newell Rowan in an interview for the *Christian Science Monitor* (August 2, 1979): "It seems second nature. I never wrote anything but funny pieces, parodies, when I was a teenager. I got this impression from my parents . . . that anything serious I wrote then would look pretty ridiculous in a few years' time." He went on to say that his father had two ways of dealing with him when he made grammatical mistakes. "He would either put his head in his hands and groan hideously . . . or he would look terribly embarrassed for both of us, as if it were really his fault. As a result, I was even afraid to write him a letter until I was past thirty."

When Sheed was fourteen an attack of polio cut short his wonted participation in athletics, turned his interest to books (which he had previously read under protest), and marked the beginning of the development of what he calls his "taste for English prose." "Since the first phase of my infatuation coincided with a dislike for postwar England," he recounted in his entry in *World Authors, 1950-70* (1975), "I tended to look to America for the basic sound. And although I have since admired, and scavenged, various English mandarins, I believe the undercoat is still American." Ernest Hemingway, Ring Lardner, James Thurber, E. B. White, E. M. Forster, and P. G. Wodehouse were among the formative influences on the Sheedian style, which he described as a "Thurber undercoat with a Wodehouse veneer." "But it could be Lardner and Forster," he added. "American prose is always on the bottom, though—my first love."

Sheed took his B.A. degree in history at Lincoln College, Oxford University in 1954 and received his M.A. degree at Oxford three years later. One year of his studies was spent at Columbia University. By his own account, he did no writing beyond the mandatory in college and university. Afterward, he went to live with his relatives in Australia with the idea of becoming a newsman there. He had "the shortest job on record with the Australian Broadcasting Company, taking shark-sighting reports," as he recounted in his *Christian Science Monitor* interview with Diana Newell Rowan, before finally choosing the United

States to live and work in because "it just seemed the center of the universe." "When I finally settled down here, I wrote advertising copy, promotion, bits and pieces of everything."

As a free-lance journalist, Sheed contributed to the New York Times Magazine and to Life, among other magazines. Regarding the reviews he wrote as a movie critic for the Catholic magazine Jubilee (1959-61) and for Esquire (1967-69), he told Barbara Bannon in an interview for Publishers Weekly (February 6, 1978): "Some of the movie reviews . . . come back to haunt me. You continue to have a reputation as a boy gunman long after you've left this kind of review." He also did drama criticism for Commonweal, the Catholic journal of opinion, during the 1960's, and he was associate editor of Jubilee from 1959 to 1966. Later, in the 1970's, he wrote a column that he called "The Good Word" for the New York Times Book Review.

A Middle Class Education (Houghton, 1960) is a satirical account of the Oxford education and scholarship year in America of John Choate, a Rhodes Scholar who publicly plays the happy-go-lucky wastrel while privately making sure that he is not burning any academic bridges. The reviews were a mixture of complaints that the long, sprawling novel was "untidy," with insufficient focus to its satire, and, on the other hand, of recognition that it was "full of life" and marked the debut of a novelist possessing "comic gifts of a high order." Also mixed were the reviews for The Hack (Macmillan, 1963), Sheed's second novel, about Bert Flax, a writer of inspirational prose and verse for the American Catholic lay press who undergoes a crisis of faith and professional self-respect that culminates in a nervous breakdown. Some reviewers felt that Sheed's comic thrusts at the sentimental and crass in American Catholicism in The Hack clashed with the moving, pathetic characterization of a man fighting to save his very soul, and others felt that the latter characterization did not reach the limits of Sheed's potential. "Mr. Sheed is ambitious to join the ranks of those who carry on the great tradition of the English comic novel," William Esty wrote in Commonweal (November 22, 1963). "Now that The Hack is off his chest, perhaps he will keep his characters on less tight a rein."

Like The Hack, Square's Progress (Farrar, Straus, 1965) is set in the deadly dull New Jersey commuting town of Bloodbury. That third novel focuses on two friends and neighbors of Bert Flax, Fred and Allison Cope, whose marriage is temporarily broken by boredom. Allison goes home to Mother and Dad only to realize that even life with Fred is preferable to being among the "real people" of rural Pennsylvania; Fred investigates the bohemian life, in Greenwich Village and an expatriate community in Spain, only to learn that "hip" is the obverse face of square—that vice can be as banal as virtue. Here again, some

reviewers found Sheed to be at odds with himself. One such was Sal Maloof, who wrote in the New York Herald Tribune's Book Week (September 5, 1965): "Two novels lie alongside one another—the comedy of manners, where Sheed is master; and the darker comedy of the heart's darkness and the will's paralysis, which Sheed has caught in The Hack and glimpsed here—and turned away from."

With its brilliant dissection of intellectual vanity, its fully realized central characters, its classical structure and style, and the gentleness, grace, and clarity with which it achieves its satiric intent, Office Politics (Farrar, Straus, 1966) marked Sheed's transition from apprentice novelist to master craftsman. Set in the run-down New York office of The Outsider, a small but prestigious liberal weekly journal of opinion, that novel, a virtual moral tale, chronicles the war of succession that takes place among the staff of the magazine when sudden illness forces its famous English editor to retire. Office Politics was nominated for a National Book Award, and critics received it enthusiastically. Noting that its characters "emerge in something (for this genre) uncommonly like depth," Norman Shrapnel wrote in The Guardian (February 10, 1967) that he could not recall "a better novel about journalism."

The dark emotion that Sheed can tap when he enters the milieu of childhood and adolescence first became evident in the two stories brought together in The Blacking Factory & Pennsylvania Gothic (Farrar, Straus, 1968). In the novella "The Blacking Factory," fifteen-year-old prep-school student James Bannister 3d invents in his mind a mythic country that is a refuge from the flux of a life in which his mother is mentally ill and his tycoon father spiritually abandons him and perversely sends him off to school in England for no ostensible reason. "Pennsylvania Gothic" is a long short story, a Gothic tale, or psychological ghost story, about twelve-year-old Charles Trimble, who discovers the seeds of suicidal violence in himself, as if by geographical infection, after his family moves to an eerie little town just outside Philadelphia. Some critics thought that the novella was more successful than the short story in evoking horror and psychological violence.

In Max Jamison (Farrar, Straus, 1970), most of the story is told through the interior monologue of its title character, a man done in by his own skillful intellect. The irascible Maximilan P. Jamison is a Broadway theatre critic for a national news weekly who cannot keep his obsessive, acerbic critical faculty from examining, and corroding, his personal life. Jamison nearly goes mad with despair as his self-criticism eats into his two marriages, his extramarital affairs, and his relationship with his children, whom he dearly wants to love uncritically but cannot. Jamison's dilemma applies also to his work as critic, but here Sheed's irony precludes pathos, for no one but Jamison notices how shabby, how cliché-ridden, his reviews are becoming.

Despite the mockery and rollicking fun, the moral vision in *Max Jamison* never fades, and the profile of Jamison is delineated with complexity and consistency, emerging as funny and sad, hurting and deeply caring, detestable and decent. "He [Jamison] is really too good for this world, even though he knows it himself," Richard Freedman observed in *Book World* (April 26, 1970). "The decent hero taking arms against a sea of clichés has always been a Sheed specialty, which accounts for his failure to produce a blockbusting novel, since clichés are the lifeblood of best sellers. But the even larger view of this new, triumphantly intelligent novel is that criticism is not a mask or a pose, a way for egomaniacs to vent their hostilities or for failed artists to make a buck. It is a deep-dyed view of life, a creatively aggressive attitude toward the world rather than a mindlessly passive one."

The title of *People Will Always Be Kind* (Farrar, Straus, 1973) is an allusion to a World War I poem by Siegfried Sassoon ("Does it matter?—losing your legs . . ."). The novel consists of two segments, divided by twenty years in the life of Brian Casey, an Irish-Catholic New Yorker. In the first, narrated by the protagonist himself, Casey is stricken at age sixteen with polio that cripples his legs, so that he cannot thereafter walk without braces and crutches. When he gives up hope for a cure, the hope is replaced by cynical fortitude. In the second segment, United States Senator Brian Casey, a contender for the Democratic Presidential nomination, is at once an idealistic peace candidate and pragmatic manipulator who will "use anything," including his handicap, in the pursuit of his political ends. Sam Perkins, a speechwriter for Casey and the narrator of the segment, finally drops out of the campaign, disillusioned and bewildered.

In an interview with Martha MacGregor for her column in the New York *Post* (May 12, 1973), Sheed denied the widespread speculation that *People Will Always Be Kind* was a *roman á clef* relating directly to his own work in the Democratic Presidential nomination campaign of Senator Eugene McCarthy in 1972. Pointing out that that work had been "very, very much on the fringes," he said, "I wrote one speech, and that was not for the candidate. I learned more about campaigning in 1970, when Joe Duffy was running in Connecticut against Senator [Thomas J.] Dodd. I suppose any cynicism in the book came from that." Writing in *Newsweek* (April 16, 1973), Walter Clemons called *People Will Always Be Kind* "a political novel that makes most others look like amateur night." Among the reviewers who remarked on Sheed's ability to be sensitive without losing his narrative pace or sense of humor was George Stade, who, writing in the New York *Times Book Review* (April 8, 1973), referred to "a certain quality of moral intelligence" in *People Will Always Be Kind*, "one graced by an unflappable and chastened sanity, a charity precise and unsentimental." The novel brought Sheed his second National Book Award nomination.

After Henry Robbins, Sheed's editor at Farrar, Straus and Giroux, moved to E. P. Dutton, Roger W. Straus Jr. saw the wisdom of allowing Sheed to follow Robbins to Dutton with *Transatlantic Blues*, which was published by Dutton as a Henry Robbins Book in 1978. *Transatlantic Blues* is the fictional autobiography of Monty Chatworth, an internationally famous television talk-show host who plays the Oxford-educated Englishman before American audiences and becomes a caricature of a rough, rude American when he is back in his native Britain. The autobiography is a comic tour-de-force, a desperate confession to "Father Sony," as Chatworth calls his tape recorder, by a culturally schizophrenic media fraud suffering pangs of Roman Catholic guilt. As the confession spills out, Chatworth draws a self-portrait of an "emotional whore" who personifies the sad results of toadying to the most superficial aspects of two cultures. Disagreeing with those critics who thought that Sheed was trivializing familiar ground in *Transatlantic Blues* were Julian Moynahan, in the New York *Times Book Review* (January 15, 1978), and Walter Clemons, in *Newsweek* (January 16, 1978). Moynahan saw beneath the humor a "wealth of insight into the two societies during and since World War II," especially when Sheed is dealing with the "fundamental dislocation and uprooting" of the members of the Chatworth family. Clemons wrote, "Oxonian clarity joins with American lowdown colloquial. Chatworth's confessional prose is rawer and speedier, edgier and more combative than anything we have heard from Sheed before."

Among Sheed's books of nonfiction are *Muhammad Ali* (Crowell, 1975), a portrait of the former world heavyweight boxing champion, and *Three Mobs: Labor, Church, and Mafia* (Sheed, 1974), a slim volume containing three previously published pieces in which he studied "American character collectively, as men-in-groups." Book, movie, and theatre reviews and essays on sports, politics, and other subjects originally published in the New York *Times Book Review, Sports Illustrated*, the *New York Review of Books*, and other publications were brought together in the collections *The Morning After* (Farrar, Straus, 1971) and *The Good Word and Other Words* (Dutton, 1978). Among the reviewers of the former who noted the serious, unfashionable morality and idiosyncratic taste hidden beneath Sheed's brilliant, self-debunking style was William McPherson, who asked in the Washington *Post* (November 6, 1971), "Is there anyone else who would work G. K. Chesterton, a favored Sheed touchstone, into an essay on Norman Mailer, lumping them together as 'these two dazzling, slovenly mystics'?" Reviewing *The Good Word and Other Words* in New York

(January 29, 1979), David Denby described Sheed the critic as a "witty and utterly serious" literary moralist "without a trace of self-righteousness" and with "a terse informal style, wised-up yet surprisingly gracious."

Wilfrid Sheed was a visiting lecturer at Princeton University in 1970-71, and he has been a judge and member of the editorial board of the Book of the Month Club since 1972. The bespectacled, cigar-smoking Sheed, who walks with the aid of a cane, was described by Jerry Tallmer, who interviewed him for the New York Post (January 21, 1978), as "agreeably acerbic." Sheed and his wife, Miriam Ungerer, a food writer, live with their children in a late-Victorian house with stained glass windows and veranda in Sag Harbor, Long Island, New York. A self-confessed "sports nut," the author plays pool, goes to ball games at Shea Stadium, and frequents the race track. Sheed told Diana Newell Rowan in the

Christian Science Monitor interview that he is not concerned about literary immortality because someone who lives by the pen has "so insecure a stake in the future" that "it's a waste of time" worrying about it. "What will be considered a masterpiece in the future depends on whether language stands still for it. . . . I have three very intelligent kids, and naturally I predict the future from them; that might be misleading, because they don't watch television, they love books, love to read. It probably gives me more hope than it should [about] what's going to become of the language."

References: Christian Sci Mon p18 Ag 2 '79 por; N Y Post p30 Ja 21 '78 por; N Y Times Bk R p9+ Ja 21 '79 por; Pub W 215:10 F 6 '78 por; Contemporary Authors vols 65-68 (1977); Who's Who in America, 1979-80; World Authors, 1950-1970 (1975)

Sidney, Sylvia

Aug. 8, 1910- Actress. Address: b. c/o John Springer, 667 Madison Ave., New York City, N.Y. 10021

Shortly after her seventy-first birthday, Sylvia Sidney opened to rave reviews in a revival of Light Up the Sky, Moss Hart's farce about show business, at the John Drew Theater in East Hampton, New York. She had made her Broadway stage debut nearly fifty-five years earlier, then moved to Hollywood, where she became one of Paramount's five top female stars (the others were Marlene Dietrich, Carole Lombard, Miriam Hopkins, and Claudette Colbert) in the 1930's. Best-known for her proletarian "victim" roles in such motion pictures as Street Scene, An American Tragedy, Fury, and Dead End, she was, in the words of film historian Ephraim Katz, "the perfect screen heroine" of the Depression years—"intense, vulnerable, [and] waiflike." Because she was hardly ever given the opportunity to demonstrate her versatility as an actress on the screen, she returned to the stage in about 1940. Since that time, she has made only a handful of films, but she has performed leading roles in dozens of plays on Broadway and in stock productions throughout the country, and she has frequently appeared in television dramas and, more recently, in made-for-television movies. In 1978 Miss Sidney won the Festival of the Americas Life Achievement Award, and in 1979 she was honored by the Chicago Art Institute for her long and distinguished career.

Of Russian ancestry, Sylvia Sidney was born Sophia Kosow on August 8, 1910 in the Bronx, New York, to Victor and Rebecca (Saperstein) Kosow. (Some sources give August 10 as her day of birth.) After her parents divorced, she was legally adopted by her mother's second husband, Dr. Sigmund Sidney, a dental surgeon. A shy, rather nervous child, Sylvia Sidney, at her mother's insistence, began taking elocution and dancing lessons when she was ten years old. A few years later, while she was a student at Washington Irving High School, she enrolled in acting classes at the Theatre Guild's school in Manhattan.

Miss Sidney made her stage debut in the title role of Prunella, the school's graduation play, on June 15, 1926. In his review of that performance, a New York Times drama critic noted that the young actress "had very definitely the qualities of charm and wistfulness, and endowed her Prunella with them in the proper proportions." Encouraged, Miss Sidney decided to pursue a stage career. After making the rounds of the theatrical producers' offices, she finally landed a supporting role in The Challenge of Youth, a shocking tale of small-town mores, which opened in Washington, D.C. in October 1926. She made her first Broadway appearance three months later when she replaced Grace Durkin as Anita in Jean Bart's drama The Squall. Over the next two years, Miss Sidney appeared in several Broadway productions, including Crime, a melodrama in which she portrayed an ingenuous young woman held hostage by a gang of bank robbers, and Gods of the Lightning, a courtroom drama written by Maxwell Anderson and Harold Hickerson. Her convincing portrayal in that production won her the small but important part of the murderess in Thru Different Eyes (Fox Film Corp., 1929). Although Miss Sidney earned good notices for her performance, she received no other film offers and, in 1929, she returned to the stage with George Cukor's stock company in Rochester, New York.

By June 1929 Miss Sidney was back on Broadway, as Elizabeth Girard in the short-lived romantic comedy Nice Women. She followed that up with leading roles in Cross Roads, a study of contemporary college life, and in the tearjerker Many a Slip, then scored a major dramatic success as the young wife in Viña Delmar's tale of marital life, Bad Girl, a daring venture, considering the moral climate of the time. Taken by her performance, B. P. Schulberg, the managing director of Paramount, chose her for the female lead in the film version of Dreiser's An American Tragedy. When that production was postponed, Miss Sidney was assigned the role—originally intended for Clara Bow—of Nan, the daughter of a small-time racketeer who is imprisoned for a murder she did not commit, in Rouben Mamoulian's City Streets (1931). Critical reaction was overwhelmingly enthusiastic. As the reviewer for Variety observed, "[The] picture is lifted from mediocrity through the intelligent acting and appeal of Sylvia Sidney. . . . From a histrionic standpoint she's the whole works."

Signed as a contract player by Paramount, Miss Sidney was subsequently cast as an unwed mother in Confessions of a Coed (1931) and as the trusting Roberta Alden in Josef von Sternberg's austere, detached version of An American Tragedy (1931). That same year, she won viewers' hearts with her touchingly credible characterization of a young woman trapped by her slum environment in King Vidor's Street Scene (United Artists). Her Paramount credits over the next few years included roles as an innocent prisoner in Ladies of the Big House (1932), a reformed crook in the remake of The Miracle Man (1932), an ex-convict in Pick Up (1933), and a hard-luck chorus girl in Good Dame (1934). She also played Cho-Cho-San, the Japanese geisha, in a nonoperatic version of David

Belasco's Madame Butterfly (1932), the title role in another Dreiser novel, Jennie Gerhardt (1933), and the Indian wife of a wealthy socialite in Behold My Wife (1935). Although she was invariably cast as a vulnerable, long-suffering working girl, Miss Sidney relished her roles in such comedies as Merrily We Go to Hell (1932), Thirty-Day Princess (1934), and Accent on Youth (1935), but as she told Arthur Bell in an interview for the New York Times (December 17, 1972), "Those were the days when they used to pay me by the teardrop, and since I needed the money, I compromised and played the tragic heroine in a few duds."

When her contract with Paramount expired in 1935, Miss Sidney signed a four-year agreement with Walter Wanger, an independent producer who proposed to cast her in opulent productions of such literary classics as Wuthering Heights, Ivanhoe, and Tess of the D'Urbervilles. Her first film for Wanger, however, was yet another formula melodrama—Mary Burns, Fugitive (Paramount, 1935)—in which she played yet another victimized working girl. She fared only slightly better in The Trail of the Lonesome Pine (Paramount, 1936), a rather hokey backwoods melodrama, but as the hero's worried girlfriend in Fury (MGM, 1936), Fritz Lang's indictment of mob violence, she held her own opposite Spencer Tracy's powerhouse performance.

In an attempt to change her image, Miss Sidney traveled to England to play the central role in Alfred Hitchcock's melodramatic motion picture A Woman Alone (Gaumont-British, 1936). In that brooding tale of revenge, she cold-bloodedly murders her husband, a saboteur, after he has unwittingly killed her younger brother. Back in Hollywood, she was reunited with Fritz Lang for You Only Live Once (United Artists, 1937), a powerful condemnation of social injustice in which she and Henry Fonda play petty criminals hounded to their deaths. In reviewing the film for the New York Herald Tribune, Howard Barnes praised Miss Sidney for the "splendid understanding" and "emotional depth" she brought to her role. "The portrait is stamped with tragedy almost from the first, but it is human and always in character," he wrote. "Her stout-hearted secretary, who gradually loses her faith in justice, gives the needed note of poignancy to a stark chronicle."

Miss Sidney was top-billed in Dead End (United Artists, 1937), William Wyler's investigation of slum life on New York's East Side, but her pat performance of the earnest, ambitious working girl was overshadowed by Humphrey Bogart's portrayal of the hardened killer Baby Face Martin and by the irresistible "Dead End kids." Discouraged by years of typecasting, she eagerly accepted when the Theatre Guild asked her to star in a Broadway production of Ben Hecht's new play, To Quito and Back, a rather pretentious and garrulous message drama. The play, which opened to unfavorable reviews at the Guild

Theatre on October 6, 1937, closed after forty-six performances. Although the playwright and the director bore the brunt of the criticism, Miss Sidney was rebuked for failing to give depth to her character. "Sylvia Sidney is a talented young women within her sphere," Burns Mantle wrote in his opening-night notice for the New York *Daily News*, "but when she tries to take on emotional stature she has little to work with except a frown and a suggestion of hurt pride. I can't believe she could be one to inspire a moody idealist of the Hecht breed."

During the heyday of her Hollywood career, Miss Sidney earned a reputation for her fiery temper. Her well-publicized tantrums were often "better than [her] emotional scenes on film," she admitted to Robert Wahls of the New York *Daily News* (April 10, 1977). "It was too much fame, too much stardom too soon." After completing work on Fritz Lang's *You and Me* (Paramount, 1938), a box-office flop, she decided to return to the stage. Over the next five years, Miss Sidney made only two motion pictures: the contrived *One-Third of a Nation* (Paramount, 1939) and *The Wagons Roll at Night* (Warner Brothers, 1941), a Humphrey Bogart vehicle. "I didn't leave Hollywood because of anybody but myself," she said in one recent interview. "I just got disgusted with myself. I didn't know who I was, as an actress or a person."

Miss Sidney spent the summer of 1938 playing Eliza Doolittle in summer stock productions of Shaw's *Pygmalion*, then joined a stellar cast, including Sam Jaffe, Franchot Tone, Karl Malden, Lee J. Cobb, Elia Kazan, and Martin Ritt, in rehearsals for the Group Theatre's production of *The Gentle People,* a drama by Irwin Shaw, which began a six-month run at the Belasco Theatre on January 5, 1939. After touring for several months on the road as Linda Brown in *Accent on Youth,* Miss Sidney triumphed as Bella Manningham in *Angel Street*, the Victorian thriller that was the surprise dramatic hit of the 1941-42 Broadway season. She subsequently appeared in the pageant *We Will Never Die* at New York City's Madison Square Garden and in touring productions of *Pygmalion* and *Jane Eyre*.

In the mid-1940's Miss Sidney returned briefly to Hollywood to play a Eurasian siren in *Blood on the Sun* (United Artists, 1945), a fast-paced adventure starring James Cagney. Other screen assignments followed. In *The Searching Wind* (Paramount, 1946), Lillian Hellman's examination of the generation that blundered into World War II, she played a foreign correspondent in love with an American diplomat. Later that year, United Artists released the inconsequential *Mr. Ace,* in which she played an unscrupulous politician seeking a governorship. The low-budget remake of *Love From a Stranger* (Eagle Lion, 1947), a suspenseful period melodrama, teamed Miss Sidney with John Hodiak, who was hopelessly miscast as an insane wife killer.

Returning to the stage, Miss Sidney toured the United States for the next few years, appearing in *Joan of Lorraine, Kind Lady, O Mistress Mine, The Two Mrs. Carrolls, Pygmalion, Goodbye, My Fancy, Anne of the Thousand Days,* and *The Innocents*. Late in 1951 she took over Flora Robson's role of Alicia Christie in a road production of *Black Chiffon,* a psychoanalytic drama about a well-bred woman turned shoplifter. Other congenial roles were Agnes in *The Fourposter*, the homey, two-character marital comedy; Anna in *A Very Special Baby,* a family drama that closed after just five performances on Broadway; and the title role in *Auntie Mame*.

Taking advantage of the opportunities offered by the drama anthology series that dominated television schedules throughout the 1950's, Miss Sidney was a frequent performer on such programs as the *Ford Theatre,* the *Kraft Theatre, Broadway TV Theatre,* the *Philco Playhouse,* and *Playhouse 90*. More often than not, she was cast as a troubled, occasionally neurotic mother, a role she played to perfection in "The Helen Morgan Story" on *Playhouse 90* and in Paddy Chayefsky's "Catch My Boy on Sunday" on the *Philco Playouse.* During those years, she also made three motion pictures, portraying Fantine in a remake of *Les Misérables* (Twentieth Century-Fox, 1952), a dowdy, kleptomaniac librarian in *Violent Saturday* (Twentieth Century-Fox, 1955), and the disabled wife of a corrupt prison warden in *Behind the High Walls* (Universal, 1956).

Over the years, Miss Sidney continued to find suitable, if small, character roles in television productions and in films. "There isn't a role that I wouldn't accept, provided it's good and has something to say," she assured George Maksian when he interviewed her for the New York *Sunday News* (September 7, 1975). "I have no regrets about the roles I have played. I don't think in those terms. If the roles weren't offered to me, then what's the sense? If you can't afford the finest champagne, then drink the best you can afford."

On television, Miss Sidney appeared in episodes of such series as *Route 66, The Nurses, My Three Sons, Ryan's Hope,* and more recently, in the pilot for the popular situation comedy *WKRP in Cincinnati*. In 1962 she was nominated for an Emmy for her affecting performance as the distraught mother of a criminally insane man in "Madman," a segment of *The Defenders*. Among her most recent screen credits are *Summer Wishes, Winter Dreams* (Columbia, 1973), *I Never Promised You a Rose Garden* (New World, 1977), *Damien-Omen II* (Twentieth Century-Fox, 1978), and several made-for television movies, including *Do Not Fold, Spindle or Mutilate, The Lovers in 3-B, Raid on Entebbe, The Gossip Columnist,* and *The Shadow Box*. Her performance as Joanne Woodward's hard-bitten mother in *Summer Wishes, Winter Dreams* won her the 1974 National Board of

Review's best supporting actress award and an Academy Award nomination in the same category.

A frequent performer with the traveling National Repertory Company in the 1960's, Miss Sidney played Mrs. Malaprop in *The Rivals*, Constance, the Madwoman of Passy in *The Madwoman of Chaillot*, and Mrs. Hardcastle in *She Stoops to Conquer*. Her long list of stock and touring production roles also includes Cora Flood in *The Dark at the Top of the Stairs*, Regina in *The Little Foxes*, Lady Bracknell in *The Importance of Being Earnest*, Mrs. Baker in *Come Blow Your Horn*, Fraülein Schneider in *Cabaret*, Mrs. Venable in *Suddenly, Last Summer*, Mrs. Baker in *Butterflies Are Free*, and Matty Seaton in *A Family and a Fortune*.

On Broadway, Sylvia Sidney created the character of Mrs. Kolowitz, a stereotypical Jewish mother, in Carl Reiner's 1963 comedy hit *Enter Laughing*, and four years later, she succeeded Ilka Chase as Mrs. Banks in Neil Simon's long-running *Barefoot in the Park*. She scored a personal triumph when, in 1964, she took over from Miriam Hopkins the leading roles in "Damn You, Scarlett O'Hara" and "All My Pretty Little Ones," which were presented together in an Off-Broadway double bill called *Riverside Drive*. Her most recent Broadway venture was Tennessee Williams' haunting *Vieux Carré*. The play itself received mixed notices and closed one week after it opened in May 1977, but Miss Sidney earned the critics' admiration for her resourceful portrayal of Mrs. Wire, a tough and abusive landlady.

In the mid-1960's Miss Sidney, who had taken up needlepoint years before as a "tranquilizer," began to reap profits from her long-time hobby when a New York City craft shop offered to sell her completed projects. Within months, a needlework manufacturer agreed to package her original designs in kits, and in 1968 she published the *Sylvia Sidney Needlepoint Book* (Reinhold Book Corp.), in which she describes her own introduction to needlepoint and gives illustrations of various stitches and diagrams and instructions for reproducing her imaginative designs. Her second volume on the subject, *Question and Answer Book on Needlepoint* (Van Nostrand, Reinhold), followed in 1974.

A petite, silver-haired woman with a heart-shaped face and large, sad blue-green eyes, Sylvia Sidney weighs ninety-eight pounds. She has for years refused to reveal her height because, in her words, "you cannot be a leading lady unless you're tall." Her distinctive low, raspy voice, which one interviewer described as being "suggestive of velvet sandpaper," is partly the result of years of chain-smoking. In addition to needlepoint, her leisure activities include gardening, painting, reading, and raising and showing Pug dogs. She steadfastly refuses to consider retiring. "I wouldn't know what to do with myself if I retired," she told George Maksian. "I'm an actress, and I'll take any part they give me. I have to work."

Miss Sidney's first marriage, to publisher Bennett Cerf in 1935, was dissolved eight months later. On August 15, 1938 she married Luther Adler, the actor, by whom she has one son, Jacob ("Jody"). The couple was divorced in 1946. A third marriage, to Carlton Alsop, the publicist, in 1947, also ended in divorce. Since her son contracted amyotrophic lateral sclerosis, popularly known as "Lou Gehrig's disease," in the mid-1970's, she has been a dedicated volunteer for the National ALS Foundation, and in 1981, she assembled the star-studded honorary committee for Byron Janis' ALS benefit concert at Carnegie Hall. The actress lives alone in a century-old house in the Connecticut countryside.

References: N Y Post p44 My 7 '77 por; N Y Sunday News III p7 N 11 '73 por; N Y Times II p3 D 17 '72 por; Notable Names in the American Theatre (1976); Parish, James Robert. The Paramount Pretties (1972); Shipman, David. The Great Movie Stars (1970); Thomson, David. A Biographical Dictionary of Film (1976); Who's Who in America, 1980-81; Who's Who in the Theatre (1978)

Soames, (Arthur) Christopher (John), Baron of Fletching

Oct. 12, 1920- British statesman; diplomat. Address: House of Lords, London SW1A OAA, England

Christopher Soames—known as Lord Soames, Baron of Fletching, since 1978, when he was created a life peer—is one of Great Britain's favorite diplomatic troubleshooters. A son-in-law and protégé of the late Sir Winston Churchill, Soames served with distinction in the British Army during World War II and occupied key government posts in the postwar era. As Minister of Agriculture, from 1960 to 1964, and as Ambassador to France, from 1968 to 1972, Soames, a staunch European, played a major role in the entry of Great Britain into the European Economic Community. Then, from 1973 to 1976, he was vice-president of the EEC commission, with responsibility for foreign affairs. In the winter of 1979-80, while serving as Leader of the House of Lords and Lord President of the Council in the Conservative government of Margaret Thatcher, Soames was Governor of Rhodesia for the period of transition that culminated in the transformation of that former British colony into the independent Republic of Zimbabwe. In his role as Lord President of the Council with responsibility for the Civil Service Department, Soames was engaged, in 1980-81, in implementing Prime Minister Thatcher's economy mea-

Lord Soames

sures while trying to placate the unions representing civil service workers. He was replaced as Leader of the House of Lords and Lord President of the Council in a reorganization of the government in September 1981.

A member of a well-to-do brewing and land-owning family, Arthur Christopher John Soames was born on October 12, 1920 at Penn, Buckinghamshire to Arthur and Hope (Parish) Soames. He was slated from birth for the military, and according to one account, on the day he was born his father, a former captain of the Coldstream Guards who already had two daughters, sent a telegram to the colonel of that regiment, announcing the arrival of a son. Exposed to politics at an early age, Christopher Soames remembers as a boy campaigning for his father in an unsuccessful bid for a Conservative seat in the House of Commons. After completing his preparatory schooling at Eton, Soames attended the Royal Military College at Sandhurst.

Commissioned in 1939 as a second lieutenant in the Coldstream Guards, Soames saw World War II service with his regiment in North Africa as a liaison officer to Free French forces under General Pierre Koenig and General Jean de Lattre de Tassigny. He earned the French Croix de Guerre, and in 1942 he rose to the rank of captain. After recovering from the severe leg wounds he suffered in the explosion of a land mine near El Alamein, Soames served with military intelligence in Egypt, Italy, and France. At the end of the war, he was appointed assistant military attaché to the British Embassy in Paris. While there, he met Prime Minister Winston Churchill's youngest daughter, Mary Spencer Churchill, whom he married in 1947 in a wedding ceremony that was a major London social event.

After being invalided out of the army that same year, Soames served for a time as manager of the farms on Churchill's Chartwell estate in Kent. Mary Soames recalled in her biography of her mother, Clementine Churchill, that her father and her husband "took to each other" from their first meeting and developed "a warm, moving relationship, which grew in affection and trust." With Churchill's encouragement, Soames made his first bid for political office, becoming the Conservative candidate for the House of Commons seat for Bedfordshire, northeast of London, in August 1949. Campaigning with his wife by his side and emphasizing the need for a minimum of government, Soames won the seat in the February 1950 general election despite efforts by the incumbent Labour party candidate, T. C. Skeffington-Lodge, to defeat him with such slogans as: "For full employment, health and homes,/ Stick to Skeff and turn down Soames."

As a Member of Parliament, Soames acted as a link between Churchill and a younger generation of politicians in the House of Commons. While serving as parliamentary private secretary to the Prime Minister from 1952 to 1955, he was Churchill's right-hand man, but a widely circulated account that he actually took charge of the government during a three-week period in 1953, while his father-in-law was recovering from a stroke, seems to have been exaggerated. Under Prime Minister Anthony Eden, Soames became, in December 1955, parliamentary undersecretary of state with the Air Ministry, and when Harold Macmillan took office as Prime Minister in January 1957, he was appointed parliamentary and financial secretary to the Admiralty. A year later, Soames was made a privy counsellor and named by Macmillan to succeed John Hugh Hare in the ministerial post of Secretary of State for War, under Minister of Defense Duncan Sandys, who was also Churchill's son-in-law. As Secretary of State for War, Soames defended the government's reliance on an anti-Soviet nuclear deterrent and the installation of rocket bases in Great Britain in debate with members of the opposition Labour party and, among other actions, presided over the reorganization and streamlining of the British Territorial Army.

In a revised Macmillan Cabinet in July 1960, Soames was elevated to full Cabinet rank as Minister of Agriculture, Fisheries, and Food, and he retained that post when Sir Alec Douglas-Home succeeded Macmillan as Prime Minister in October 1963. A staunch advocate of European unity, Soames played a leading role, along with the chief British negotiator, Edward Heath, in talks held at Brussels in 1961 and 1962 to facilitate admission of Great Britain into the European Economic Community (EEC), or Common Market. But his demands for concessions aimed at taking into consideration Britain's unique position, particularly in relation to the Commonwealth, met with determined resistance from spokesmen for France and other EEC countries. When French President Charles de Gaulle vetoed British entry into the Common Market in January 1963, Soames reportedly broke down and wept.

Soames's actions as Minister of Agriculture, Fisheries, and Food also included efforts to alleviate the harm done to the British fishing industry by trawlers from Iceland and other nations operating in British coastal waters; restrictions on the use of environmentally harmful pesticides; and promotion of the establishment of a marketing organization for home-grown cereals. To stabilize prices in the face of the mounting costs of government subsidies to farmers, Soames announced, in May 1963, the imposition of controls on the quantity and price of imported meats, grains, and other food products.

Following the defeat of the Conservatives in the November 1964 election and the formation of a Labour party government under Prime Minister Harold Wilson, Soames became front-bench Opposition spokesman for agriculture and then for defense in the House of Commons. After Edward Heath succeeded Home as Tory party leader in August 1965, Soames, as foreign affairs spokesman in the new "shadow" Cabinet, revived earlier demands for the admission of Great Britain into the Common Market. But in the national election of March 1966, Soames was defeated in his bid for re-election to the House of Commons, apparently, as some observers noted, because he was not enough of a "constituency man," preferring to concentrate on broader international issues. Unable to persuade party leaders to select him for another candidacy, he devoted himself to his business interests. From 1966 to 1968 he was executive director of Decca Ltd., having served for two years previously on its board of directors. He was also, from 1964 to 1968, a director of the brewery firm of James Hole and Company Ltd., in which his family had a controlling interest.

Meanwhile, the Labour government of Harold Wilson decided to renew Great Britain's bid for membership in the EEC. When de Gaulle vetoed it a second time in November 1967, Soames, appearing on BBC's *Panorama,* described the French President in uncomplimentary terms as "an old man of seventy-seven" who flouted the wishes of the British people and of most Europeans. Nevertheless, when Wilson decided the following year to try once more to bring Britain into the Common Market, he appointed Soames Ambassador to France, regarding him as the man best qualified to help attain that goal. In the words of Foreign Affairs Minister George Brown, who recommended Soames for the post, the British Embassy in Paris needed "a man with imagination, a knowledge and a feel of France, with a particular social flair, and . . . with some money." Although Soames had some second thoughts about representing Wilson's Labour government in Paris, he was, as he said at the time

of his appointment, "prompted to accept by the manifest sincerity and determination" of those responsible for Britain's European policy. Pledging his best efforts to bring Britain and France closer together within a European framework, Soames presented his credentials to President de Gaulle in Paris on September 21, 1968.

According to the London *Observer* (February 23, 1969), "Soames soon made himself felt, rustling up the press and beating the British drum in the provinces." As Stephen Aris noted in the London *Sunday Times* (December 9, 1979), the new Ambassador "did not fiddle about running the Embassy," but demonstrated his "instinctive ability to go to the heart of the matter" by concentrating on his main task: "to open the door for Britain to Europe." His efforts suffered a temporary setback, however, as a result of the so-called "L'Affaire Soames."

On February 4, 1969, de Gaulle invited Soames to a private meeting. During their forty-five-minute discussion, the French President pointed out that British membership in the EEC would necessitate substantial changes in its nature. He reportedly proposed that the Common Market be supplanted by a larger and more loosely organized free trade organization under an inner council, or "directorate," consisting of representatives from France, Britain, West Germany, and Italy, and that the new organization be independent of NATO and the United States. After checking his minutes of the conversation with the French Foreign Ministry, Soames conveyed the de Gaulle proposals to Prime Minister Wilson, who leaked them to the West German government, apparently with the aim of weakening the Franco-German *entente* in Europe. The French were incensed at what they regarded as an effort on the part of the British to discredit them with their EEC partners by dramatizing and distorting de Gaulle's proposals. Although for a time there was talk of Soames's impending resignation, in the end the Ambassador was held to be blameless, and the crisis engendered by "L'Affaire Soames" subsided.

Following President de Gaulle's resignation in April 1969, Soames diligently carried on the Common Market negotiations with his successor, Georges Pompidou, and he continued in his ambassadorial post after the Conservatives regained power in Great Britain in June 1970, under Prime Minister Edward Heath. Insisting that Great Britain was willing to accept the basic Common Market rules and that any special arrangements could be settled later by compromise, Soames eventually convinced the French that his country was "European" enough to merit inclusion in the EEC. Although others, such as Great Britain's chief Common Market negotiator, Geoffrey Rippon, were more visible in the talks, it was Soames who was credited with the key role in bringing about the agreement, signed in January 1972, that provided for British entry into the EEC a year later.

On October 7, 1972, Sir Christopher Soames, who had attained knighthood earlier that year, was named by Prime Minister Heath, along with the Labour Member of Parliament George Thomson, to the EEC's thirteen-member commission for a four-year term effective the following New Year's Day. Departing from the Paris Embassy, he assumed his new post in Brussels as a member of the executive of the expanded Common Market, which now included Great Britain, Ireland, and Denmark, along with its original members—France, Italy, West Germany, Belgium, the Netherlands, and Luxembourg. As Great Britain was in the midst of its "Fanfare for Europe" festival celebrating entry into the Common Market, Soames took his "oath of impartiality" on January 9, 1973, pledging to perform his duties "in the general interests of the community" and to refrain from accepting "instructions from any government." As one of the commission's four vice-presidents, Soames was assigned the portfolio for external relations, with responsibility for trade relations with other industrialized countries, including those in Eastern Europe, as well as with developing nations in Asia and Latin America.

As EEC vice-president for external relations, Soames played a leading role in the eighty-three-nation trade liberalization talks held in Tokyo in September 1973 under the General Agreement on Tariffs and Trade (GATT). In addition, he made several visits to the United States to strengthen European-American trade relations, which had been deteriorating; tried to forge unity among the Common Market countries in the face of the 1973 Arab oil embargo; promoted a system of controls that aimed at preventing stoppage in the flow of vital raw materials; approved increased benefits for developing countries taking part in the EEC's generalized trade preference system; and called for liberalized international trade as a means of averting depression. After visiting Peking in May 1975, he announced that China had agreed to enter negotiations to establish official relations with the EEC.

Returning to private life on the expiration of his tenure with the EEC commission at the end of 1976, Soames considered becoming once more a candidate for Parliament, but he was unable to do so for health reasons, having recently undergone heart bypass surgery. In 1977 he accepted the respectable but unchallenging position of non-executive director of N. M. Rothschild and Sons, which he held until 1979. He also served, in 1978-79, as a member of the board of the National Westminster Bank Ltd. On March 20, 1978 Sir Christopher Soames was created a life peer by Queen Elizabeth II, becoming Baron Soames of Fletching in the County of East Sussex. No longer able to be a candidate for the House of Commons, he was now eligible to enter the House of Lords, where he became Opposition spokesman for foreign and Commonwealth affairs later that year.

When the Labour government of James Callaghan was defeated in the May 1979 election and the Conservatives returned to power under Prime Minister Margaret Thatcher, Lord Soames became leader of the House of Lords and was elevated to Cabinet rank as Lord President of the Council, a position that placed him at the head of the Civil Service Department. "I'm simply revelling at being back between the shafts," he told an interviewer for the London Sunday Times Magazine (April 27, 1980), "even if they do rub a bit." He became a close adviser to Prime Minister Thatcher, served on a number of key Cabinet committees, and, in conformity with the new government's economy measures, phased out tens of thousands of jobs for civil service workers.

On December 7, 1979 Queen Elizabeth II named Lord Soames to serve as Governor of Rhodesia to launch that beleaguered former British colony in Africa on the road to independence under black majority rule. Although Soames had not had any particular experience in African affairs, he was considered eminently qualified for the task on the strength of his diplomatic skills. His arrival in Salisbury on December 12 marked the restoration of British sovereignty in Rhodesia fourteen years after Ian Smith had unilaterally declared its independence and launched his white supremacist regime. Aided by a five-nation, 1,300-man Commonwealth peacekeeping force, Soames was charged with the task of implementing a cease-fire agreement, signed in London on December 21, that was to end seven years of guerrilla warfare, and supervising the free elections that were to precede independence.

Despite continuing turmoil, Soames stood firm in his refusal to extend the deadline for the guerrillas of the Patriotic Front to lay down their arms at designated cease-fire camps, or to delay the elections, which were scheduled for late February 1980. Although Soames's relations with the militantly Marxist Patriotic Front leader Robert Mugabe were strained at first, after several private meetings the two men developed a relationship of mutual trust and respect. When the election resulted in a landslide victory for Mugabe, facilitating the smooth formation of a government, Soames was surprised and pleased, and Prime Minister Thatcher sent him congratulations for an "outstanding achievement." On March 4, Soames invited Mugabe to become Prime Minister-designate and form a Cabinet, and on the night of April 17-18, 1980, he accompanied Prince Charles to the independence ceremonies of the new nation of Zimbabwe, which became the 153rd member of the U.N. and the fiftieth member of the Organization of African Unity.

In a reshuffle aimed at replacing moderates in her government with officials more in agreement with her stringent monetarist views, Prime Minister Thatcher removed Lord Soames as Leader of the House of Lords and Lord President of the Council on September 14, 1981. Others replaced at the same time were Deputy Foreign Secretary Ian Gilmour, Education Secretary Mark Carilsle, and Employment Secretary James Prior.

Christopher Soames was created a Commander of the Order of the British Empire in 1955 and Knight Grand Cross of the Order of St. Michael and St. George in 1972. Queen Elizabeth II appointed him Knight Grand Cross of the Royal Victorian Order in 1973, and that same year he was created a Grand Officier de l'Ordre de la Legion d'Honneur by President Pompidou and awarded the Medal of the City of Paris. In 1974 he received the Norwegian Grand Cross of the Order of St. Olaf and an honorary doctorate from St. Andrews University in Scotland, and in 1975 he was awarded the Robert Schuman Prize. He was created a Companion of Honour in 1980. Soames served in 1973 as president of the Royal Agricultural Society of England. He is a member of White's Club in London.

Lord and Lady Soames, who have five grown children—Nicholas, Emma, Jeremy, Charlotte, and Rupert—divide their time between their apartment in the Kensington district of London and a converted mill house in Hampshire. Nicknamed "the Chimp" by members of his family, Soames, who is six feet four inches tall, is described by Laurence Marks in the London *Observer* (December 16, 1979) as "a large, cheerful man" with a "big personality," who is "short-fused but knows how to control his temper" and "bullies people who don't stand up to him." He is "no reader" but "a splendid cook," and he enjoys "country sports, racing . . . , and serious eating." His late Cabinet colleague Iain Macleod once said of him: "Behind that incredibly bluff exterior lies an incredibly bluff interior." Soames tends to be impatient with details and paperwork, preferring, according to an acquaintance quoted by Simon Hoggart in the *Guardian Weekly* (December 16, 1979), "the broad sweep of history" and "the grand panorama of world statesmanship."

References: Guardian p12 Ja 2 '73 por; Illus Lond N p28 N '72 por; London Sunday Times p5 D 9 '79 por; London Sunday Times Mag p71 Ap 27 '80 por; N Y Times p15 F 22 '69 por, A p7 D 13 '79; Britannica Book of the Year, 1973; International Who's Who, 1980-81; Who's Who, 1981-82; Who's Who in the World, 1980-81

Sovern, Michael I(ra)

Dec. 1, 1931- University president. Address: b. Office of the President, Columbia University, 116th St. and Broadway, New York City, N.Y. 10027; h. 32 E. 64th St., New York City, N.Y. 10021

When the trustees of Columbia University endorsed the selection of Michael I. Sovern as the university's seventeenth president in 1980, they looked for leadership to a renowned law scholar, a well-liked teacher, a skilled mediator and veteran of many New York City labor disputes, a long-time civil rights advocate, and an experienced academic administrator all in one. Since enrolling as a freshman in 1949, Sovern has spent only two years away from the Morningside Heights campus. While teaching there as professor of law in 1968, he took a crucial part in reuniting and reforming the university after it had been shocked by student demonstrations. His later appointments as dean of the law school, in 1970, and provost and vice-president for academic affairs, in 1979, turned out to be steppingstones to the presidency of the 17,900-student university, which, founded in 1754, is the oldest in New York State and the fifth oldest in the country.

Michael Ira Sovern was born in New York City's borough of the Bronx on December 1, 1931 to Jewish parents, Julius Sovern, a dress salesman, and Lillian (Arnstein) Sovern. He grew up on Jerome Avenue, just a few blocks

from Yankee Stadium, where his favorite baseball team played. After the death of his father, when Michael was twelve, his mother worked as a bookkeeper to support her son and her daughter, Denise. As a teenager, he was employed during summers and part time during the school year at a textile factory in Brooklyn and then as a garment-district warehouse checker in Manhattan. A brilliant student, he finished near the top of his class at the academically exacting Bronx High School of Science and graduated *summa cum laude* with the B.A. degree from Columbia University in 1953. Recalling his student days at the Ivy League college, he promised in his inaugural address as president of Columbia to give "close attention to Columbia's role as an open door to our society for promising young people . . . whose ability to learn is greater than their ability to pay." He went on to say, "If such a door had not been opened to me, I would not be here today."

Also excelling other students in his class at Columbia's School of Law, Sovern was awarded the James Ordronaux Prize along with his LL.B. degree in 1955. The following year he was admitted to the New York bar. Meanwhile, immediately after graduation, he had joined the law faculty of the University of Minnesota as an assistant professor. In Minneapolis he quickly advanced to associate professor, but when he returned, after two years there, to his alma mater for a year as visiting professor, he was asked to stay on and to become, in 1958, an associate professor of law at Columbia. With his promotion in 1960, he was made, at the age of twenty-eight, the youngest full professor in the university's modern history. He was also one of the most popular teachers.

Described in *Time* (April 20, 1970) as "an unapologetic liberal with a special interest in eliminating racial discrimination in employment," Sovern is the author of "The National Labor Relations Act and Racial Discrimination," which appeared in 1962 in the *Columbia Law Review*. From 1962 to 1965 he directed research for the Twentieth Century Fund's Project on Racial Discrimination in Employment and in 1966 completed the report *Legal Restraints on Racial Discrimination in Employment* (Twentieth Century Fund). His study found that state and federal attempts to end job bias were being impeded by the deficient enforcement powers, inadequate budgets, and weak administration of their commissions.

Another way in which Sovern applied his expertise beyond the classroom was by serving as chairman of the American Civil Liberties Union committee on labor and industry. He directed legal training institutes for the National Association for the Advancement of Colored People, for which he also worked in its successful opposition to President Richard Nixon's nomination of Clement F. Haynsworth Jr. and G. Harold Carswell as Associate Justices of the Supreme Court in 1970. Professor Sovern was also a founding director of the Mexican-American Legal Defense and Education Fund and the Puerto Rican Legal Defense and Education Fund, as well as of the Mobilization for Youth Legal Services, which provided legal advice to the poor. One of the courses that he taught at Columbia was in poverty law, a subject that he examined with other legal experts in *Cases and Materials on Law and Poverty* (West, 1969; second edition, 1973).

Among Sovern's special interests as a teacher were labor law and conflict resolution. Pointing to the need to train law students in methods of conciliation, he told M.A. Farber of the New York *Times* (April 8, 1970), "It's ironic that, at this time in our history, we don't give more attention in our law schools to how to bring people together." On many occasions during the 1960's and 1970's Sovern was called upon as fact finder, mediator, and arbitrator in contract disputes between the city of New York or private industry and unions representing police officers, fire fighters, transit workers, welfare workers, teachers, and telephone employees. Jared Kopel of the New York *Post* (October 26, 1976) credited him with playing "a critical role" in transit negotiations in New York in 1971 and 1974. As mediator in 1976 in a dispute between the city and the Patrolmen's Benevolent Association, he helped shape a compromise on a police contract within just one week.

"It's a wholly unstructured environment," Sovern once said of his experiences at the bargaining table, as quoted in the New York *Post*. "You can't compel people to do anything. The mediator's only weapons are his sensibility and his intelligence." The pressure involved in negotiating a police or transit strike in a city of more than 7,000,000 inhabitants exhilarated Sovern and incited him to greater effort. "It's like an athlete performing near the limit of his ability," he explained. "It's both an ethical and psychological matter. I just feel good."

Sovern's greatest challenge as a negotiator came in 1968 on the Columbia campus itself. In the spring of that year student strikes, demonstrations, and sit-ins brought the orderly operations of the university to a halt. The students were protesting Columbia's plans to build a new gymnasium on city-owned Morningside Heights Park—thus taking a chunk of park away from the neighborhood—and the university's ties with the Institute for Defense Analysis, a group of universities engaged in military research for the United States government that the students regarded as contributing to the fighting in Vietnam. At the height of the crisis, "an angry and demoralized faculty"—in the words of Gene I. Maeroff of the New York *Times* (January 8, 1980)—met to consider whether to go on strike also. But, as Maeroff further recalled, "a carefully reasoned speech at that meeting by a young law professor was considered a turning point in persuading the faculty not to strike and in helping to restore the dignity of the embattled campus." That young speechmaker was Michael I. Sovern.

The subsequent formation of the eighteen-member faculty executive committee, with Sovern as its chairman, helped substantially to relieve tensions on campus over the next six months. By the time the new academic year began, in September 1968, the faculty group had drawn up a set of rules for campus protests, permitting student demonstrations but prohibiting disruption of university life.

Sovern's committee also called for the creation of a university senate, a group designed to bring students, professors, administrators, alumni, and staff together to plan school policy.

Columbia's student riots, as recounted in *Newsweek* (January 21, 1980), "shattered its administration and shook the confidence of its faculty and alumni." But Sovern's efforts during the conflict won praise from all quarters. "In helping to heal Columbia after the 1968 crisis, Sovern applied the soothing humor and tough pragmatism that have earned him wide respect as a labor arbitrator and mediator," a writer for *Time* (April 20, 1970) pointed out. Sovern himself observed that the Columbia crisis was "a period of awakening" for him. It may also be considered a turning point in his career. When, in 1970, William C. Warren retired as dean of Columbia's School of Law, Sovern won unanimous endorsement as his successor. Announcing the appointment, which became effective on July 1, Andrew W. Cordier, the university's president, said, "He will bring to the school the energy, determination and fairness that he has exhibited in the classroom, in his professional specialization in labor and employment and, equally important, in his effective and far-reaching leadership of the executive committee of the faculty."

The new dean of the 1,000-student law school had some definite ideas about the direction legal education would take under his leadership. Sovern's conviction was that law graduates should be as knowledgeable about conciliation as they were about litigation. "The idea that we should spend all our time in law school teaching people how to win instead of how to settle is very damaging in this day and age," he said, as quoted in *Time* (April 20, 1970). He vowed to "pay more attention to what and how we teach" and to make Columbia "the best law school in the world." Six months after taking office, he told Israel Shenker of the New York *Times* (January 22, 1971), "You've got to like fund-raising, educational policy-making, budget planning, speechmaking and conference attending." He noted that the major difference between a dean and a professor is that "it's the dean's job to think full-time about the institution and innovation."

Assessing his accomplishments as dean of the law school in his 1976 interview with the New York *Post,* Sovern said that he was most proud of introducing curriculum changes that included cross-disciplinary studies and a clinic giving students a chance to work on actual cases. In 1978 Sovern was named provost and vice-president for academic affairs at Columbia, with the responsibilities of supervising the entire university curriculum and preparing the academic budget. When he assumed that post on January 15, 1979, he became the first top academic officer chosen from a professional school rather than from the arts and sciences faculty.

Since Sovern also had the task of acting as surrogate to President William J. McGill, the view soon prevailed on campus that his appointment as provost made him heir apparent to the Columbia presidency. In June 1979 McGill announced his intention to retire the following year. After a six-month search in which a nine-member committee of trustees, alumni, tenured and nontenured faculty members, and students reviewed some 700 nominations, on January 7, 1980 Sovern was chosen to be the university's nineteenth president. In their coverage of the selection for *Newsweek* (January 21, 1980) reporters quoted the comments of Henry Graff, head of Columbia's history department, concerning Sovern's qualifications for his new post: "He has good connections with the business community and he knows his way around government. He's imaginative and realistic."

In press interviews following his appointment, which became effective on July 1, 1980, Sovern outlined his priorities as president. His goals included boosting the university's resources through a $300,000,000, or more, fund-raising drive. The money would be used for endowments for faculty positions, increased financial aid to students, a new chemistry building, renovations to dormitories and classroom buildings, and other efforts to "reindustrialize" the university by updating its equipment and various assets so as to remain competitive. Sovern said he hoped to improve Columbia's relations with its affiliated women's college, Barnard, and also with the surrounding community, Morningside Heights. Inasmuch as Columbia owns one in five residential buildings in the neighborhood, the university could do more in its role as landlord, Sovern maintained, to make Morningside Heights more attractive. Concerned also about academic quality, he proposed to re-examine the undergraduate liberal arts program at Columbia, increasing scientific education for nonscientists and emphasizing broad learning combined with specialization in a major subject.

At his inaugural ceremony on September 28, 1980 President Sovern elaborated on his objectives in an address that called for enabling Columbia to face up to an array of challenging responsibilities. "Columbia's schools and colleges pride themselves on educating America's leaders," he said. "Generation after generation, the distinction of our alumni justifies that pride. Yet the quality of America's public leadership today seems cause more for self-flagellation than for self-congratulation." He thought it would be "grandiose" to assume that universities could "cure all of the failings of our society," but, he urged, "we can help, in our teaching and in our research." The following week as the keynote speaker at the annual conference of the Association of Graduate Schools in the Association of American Universities, Sovern proposed a government loan program that would allow doctoral students as many as forty years to pay back money borrowed for their graduate education. If universities fail to hold their best scholars, he argued, they would have to settle for "leftovers," persons whom private industry did not want, to be "the shapers of scholarship, the definers of excellence, the judges of merit in the twenty-first century."

While much occupied with teaching and negotiating, Sovern arranged and moderated a ten-part NBC-TV series in 1965-66 called *Due Process and the Accused*, which won an award from the American Bar Association. He served as special counsel to the New York State Joint Legislative Committee on Industrial Relations in 1962-63 and as special counsel to the governor of New Jersey from 1974 to 1977. He has been a member of the panel of arbitrators of the New Jersey Board of Mediation since 1960 and of the Federal Mediation and Conciliation Service since 1965. From 1965 to 1980, he was consultant on law to *Time* magazine. His professional societies include the Council on Foreign Relations, the New York State Bar Association, the Society of Professionals in Dispute Resolution, and the American Academy of Arts and Sciences. In 1980 Columbia awarded him an honorary LL.D. degree.

Michael I. Sovern has been married three times: to Lenore Goodman on February 21, 1952, to Eleanor Leen on August 25, 1963, and to Joan Wit on March 9, 1974. His first two marriages ended in divorce. There are six children in the family—Jeffrey Austin, Elizabeth Ann, and Douglas Todd (by his first marriage); Julie Danielle (by his second marriage); and David Wit and Hannah Wit (his present wife's children by her previous marriage). Sovern is a six-footer who keeps his weight at 185 pounds by playing tennis and working out on exercise machines in a gym. Because of his earlier negotiations in the public sphere and his more recent prominence at Columbia, he has often been interviewed in the press, where he appears as a sharp-witted man with an urbane manner and a good-humored outlook on his work.

References: Columbia Reports p4 Je '70 por; N Y Post p21 D 24 '71 por, p37 O 26 '76 por; N Y Times p39 Ap 8 '70 por, B p4 Ja 8 '80, B p3 F 22 '80 por; N Y Times Mag p38+ S 28 '80 por; Newsweek 95:85 Ja 21 '80 por; Time 95: 45+ Ap 20 '70 por, 115:69 Ja 21 '80 por; Who's Who in America, 1980-81

Sowell, Thomas

July 30, 1930- Economist. Address: b. c/o The Hoover Institution on War, Revolution, and Peace, Stanford University, Stanford, Calif. 94305

Abetted by a new wave of conservatism, the election of Ronald Reagan to the Presidency,

and the belief of many blacks that traditional civil rights strategies have failed them, Thomas Sowell is a leading contender in the bitter contest over who now speaks for American blacks. A brilliant polemicist and trenchant debater, Sowell is currently a senior fellow at Stanford University's Hoover Institution on War, Revolution, and Peace and a member of Reagan's economic policy advisory board. He is a distinguished social science professor who was trained at the University of Chicago's department of economics under the free-market economics experts Milton Friedman and George Stigler. His scholarly reputation derives from scores of well-documented articles and books that sometimes veer from his academic specialty of economics into such fields as education, ethnology, sociology, politics, and social decision making.

To a wider public Sowell is better known as an acerbic debunker of what he views as racial-economic myths propagated by a self-serving black leadership and the white liberal establishment. Because he has taken a stand against such liberal causes as forced busing, the minimum wage, affirmative action, quotas, desegregated schools, and government assistance programs, Sowell has been called a "house nigger" by enraged black civil rights leaders, but he is regarded as a challenging alternative by a Republican Administration attuned to his "bootstrap" philosophy of social advancement nurtured by free choice, self-reliance, work, and personal initiative.

Once described as a man who "zealously prizes his privacy," Thomas Sowell has revealed of his family origins only that he was born in Gastonia, North Carolina on July 30, 1930 to parents who were "low-skilled workers." After nine years of living mostly in Charlotte, North Carolina, his family moved to Harlem in New

York City, where, in an early encounter for him with Northern attitudes towards Southerners, he was almost demoted from fourth grade to third because the separate-but-equal schools from which he came were automatically considered to be backward. When Sowell's intelligence was finally recognized, he was placed in a class for gifted students, but he had to drop out of the tenth grade at Stuyvesant High School to work in a factory and as a grocery delivery boy and Western Union messenger. Those four years provided him with a painful lesson in what happens to blacks who lack education and skills. At seventeen, while attending night school but "losing in every way," he left home, only to be drafted in 1951 into the United States Marines. He was assigned for two years to Camp Lejeune, North Carolina as a photographer. After his discharge, Sowell used his benefits under the GI bill to enroll in night classes at Howard University in Washington, D.C., while he worked in the daytime as a civil service clerk in the General Acounting Office. At the age of twenty-four, after spending three semesters at Howard, he transferred to Harvard University in Cambridge, Massachusetts.

The difference in academic expectations between Harvard and Howard, a predominantly black institution, turned out to be a "nightmare" for Sowell. "The worst time I ever had was my first term at Harvard," he has said. "But thank God, there weren't any bleeding hearts around in those days, and I finally made it on my own." After submitting a senior honors thesis on Karl Marx, he graduated from Harvard in 1958 with a B.A. degree in economics, magna cum laude.

Although he had leftist sympathies while an undergraduate at Harvard, Sowell found himself moving gradually to the right while working at Columbia University towards his M.A. degree in economics, which he obtained in 1959. That trend continued when he studied economics under the Nobel laureate Milton Friedman and Professor George Stigler at the University of Chicago, where he obtained his Ph.D. degree in 1968. According to *Newsweek* (March 9, 1981), Stigler has discounted any influence he might have had on Sowell's thinking. "He's a self-instructed man," Stigler said. "You didn't tell him what to do." Sowell himself has said that at the University of Chicago, a center for conservative economic theory, he was neither "bamboozled" by Friedman nor co-opted by the Establishment. While working at a summer job in economics at the United States Department of Labor in 1960, he had simply observed "the futility of intelligence and articulation without a systematically developed theoretical framework."

From June 1961 until August 1962 Thomas Sowell worked as an economist at the Department of Labor. He spent the academic year 1962-63 as an instructor in economics at Douglass College, Rutgers University and during the following school year was a lecturer in economics at Howard University. He left teaching from June 1964 to August 1965 to become an economic analyst for American Telephone & Telegraph Company in New York City but returned to academic life in September 1965 as an assistant professor of economics at Cornell University, where for a while he was its only black professor during a period of rising black enrollment and black militancy.

Convinced that capable black students needed to remedy past educational deficiencies, in the summer of 1968 Sowell directed an intensive Rockefeller Foundation program in economic theory for students who had largely been recruited from Negro colleges. He tendered his resignation from Cornell in disgust after the summer session of 1968, when he dismissed a disruptive black student, only to be overruled by his chairman. His action was commended by the nationally syndicated columnist Joseph Alsop, who ranked Sowell among those few courageous educators who recognized that the paternalism and coddling of black students were more harmful than beneficial.

When black students at Cornell occupied a building and staged a notorious "guns on campus" crisis in April 1969, Sowell, then a lame duck faculty member, refused to join a faculty debate about educational "relevance," nor did he cancel classes. "The principle that a university should make its decisions without armed threats seemed too obvious to require discussion," he wrote later. Ideologically, Sowell was at a far remove from both black militants and liberal white faculty members about what he considered Cornell's watered-down black studies programs, relaxed academic standards, selection of unprepared ghetto blacks for admission rather than blacks demonstrably more capable, and rejection of traditional admissions tests to predict academic performance for black students. He finally left Cornell at the conclusion of the academic year 1968-69.

Promoted to the rank of associate professor of economics, Sowell taught at Brandeis University in Waltham, Massachusetts during the academic year 1969-70 and at the University of California at Los Angeles from 1970 to 1972. He then left teaching again to work from July 1972 to August 1974 as project director for the Urban Institute, a private Washington institution that studies urban problems. For the Urban Institute he edited *American Ethnic Groups*, a collection of essays to which he contributed one of his own, entitled "Race and IQ Reconsidered."

By the time that Thomas Sowell returned to the University of California at Los Angeles, he had edited or written five scholarly books on economics: *The Evolutionary Economics of Thorstein Veblen* (Oxford, 1967); *Readings in the History of Economic Thought* (Holt, 1970); *Economics: Analysis and Issues* (Scott, Foresman, 1971); *Say's Law: An Historical Analysis* (Princeton, 1972); and *Classical Economics Reconsidered* (Princeton, 1974). Although the last-named book created something of a stir because of its revisionist attempt to correct historical misconceptions, it was his *Black Education: Myths and Tragedies* (McKay, 1972), written a few years earlier, that first brought Sowell wide attention and established him as an audacious spokesman for unfashionable ideas.

Black Education was both the apologia of a conservative educator and a hard-nosed assessment of current history. In it, Sowell first recounted his own struggles through black schools and white schools and then addressed himself to black education, its special problems, and proposals for its improvement. His thesis was that blacks everywhere are poorly educated, and his main assault, as his subtitle suggested, was on myth-ridden educators who enrolled unqualified ghetto students in nonproductive black studies programs, with tragic results both for them and for the capable black scholars who were bypassed. Developed with admirable clarity, although often brash and superior in tone, the book was a ringing call for honesty, high standards, and such remedies as a network of precollege training centers in basic skills. Reviewers concurred that *Black Education* was an important document, but Thaddeus H. Spratlin accurately predicted in the *Journal of Negro Education* (Spring 1973) that it would be either roundly "rejected as an insensitive and disparaging commentary" or rousingly "praised as a no-nonsense assessment."

Reactions were uniformly more favorable to Sowell's *Race and Economics* (McKay, 1975), which reviewer Michael Novak in the *Wall Street Journal* (September 4, 1975) called "the most important book on politics and race in years." Written with detachment and with a sophistication bred of scholarship, *Race and Economics* studied the economic history of blacks, particularly during slavery, compared it with the history of other racial and ethnic groups, and arrived at some conclusions about the role of race in the American economy. Along the way, according to Novak, "Mr. Sowell shatters more icons and clichés per chapter than any heretic in recent memory," among them the ascription of economic failures solely to racial intolerance. Sowell attributed most lack of black progress to government programs like subsidies, affirmative action, and the minimum wage—all quick, unsuccessful solutions. "Perhaps the greatest dilemma in attempts to raise ethnic minority income," Sowell wrote in *Race and Economics*, "is that those methods which have historically proved successful—self-reliance, work skills, education, business experience—are all slow developing, while those methods which are direct and immediate—job quotas, charity, subsidies, preferential treatment—tend to undermine self-reliance and pride of achievement in the long run."

During the 1970's Sowell produced a spate of articles, some in widely circulated and in-

fluential newspapers and magazines, that focused national attention upon such ethnic issues as black studies programs, admissions and hiring quotas, forced busing, excellence in segregated schools, and the validity of IQ testing. On all of them Sowell invariably adopted the position of a conservative, defined by him as "nothing more than a dissenter from the prevailing liberal orthodoxy." "We 'know' a thousand things," he wrote in an article for the *American Scholar* (Summer 1976) entitled "Social Science: The Public Disenchantment," "for which there is no real evidence." Accusing liberals of covering up known facts, he predicted that their solution will invariably involve more money, power, and prestige for intellectuals. As an alternative, he called for intellectuals to test ideas in the open marketplace, and for "reforms that would enable the poor to make their own decisions and eliminate the caretakers."

In *Knowledge and Decisions* (Basic Books, 1980), Sowell combined his previous diverse interests in a unified treatise on political economy that dovetailed with free-market principles. Critics generally agreed that it was "an elegant and highly intellectual exercise," in which Sowell condemned American decision makers as incompetent "outsiders" from academia, government, the courts, and unions. Calling for a shift in the locus of decision making away from government and towards the individual, the family, and autonomous associations, Sowell maintained that the decision-making process should attend to such economic laws as scarcity of resources, costs and benefits, and diminishing returns. Writing in the *National Review* (May 30, 1980), E. C. Barfield called *Knowledge and Decisions* "a powerful polemic in defense of individual freedom," which Sowell defined in his final sentence as "above all, the right of ordinary people to find elbow room for themselves and a refuge from the rampaging presumptions of their 'betters.'"

In June 1980 Sowell took a leave from the economics department at UCLA to become a senior fellow at the Hoover Institution on War, Revolution, and Peace, the prestigious conservative think tank located at Stanford University. That same year, when Milton Friedman's ten-part television series *Free to Choose* appeared on PBS, Sowell took part in debates about Friedman's free-market principles and provided some of the program's most dramatic moments. Observers noted that Sowell was already riding the wave of conservatism that crested in November.

As early as September 29, 1980, the conservative New York *Times* columnist William Safire predicted that Thomas Sowell would be Ronald Reagan's choice for United States Secretary of Labor, and in December, when the President's transition team considered possible appointees, Sowell's name appeared high on the lists for Cabinet posts. Sowell had originally been considered for a federal government berth back in April 1976, when President Gerald R. Ford appointed him to the Federal Trade Commission, but he withdrew when the White House could not assure him a full seven-year term extending past the upcoming November election of that year.

To draw the attention of the incoming Administration to conservative spokesmen for the black community, in December 1980 Sowell helped to organize a landmark "Black Alternatives Conference" in San Francisco that was attended by 100 black Republican businessmen and educators. Acting on Sowell's keynote declaration that "a creative role for the federal government is almost a contradiction in terms," the delegates advocated a reorganization of federal social programs, a reduction in the minimum wage, and the abolition of rent control laws. Edwin Meese 3d, then the director of Reagan's transition team, pledged to the conferees that some Cabinet posts and other high-level executive positions in the Administration would go to blacks.

Honoring that commitment, on February 10, 1981 Ronald Reagan appointed Sowell to his economic policy advisory board, which is charged with advising the President on domestic and foreign policies. Headed by George P. Shultz, the former Secretary of the Treasury, and responsible to Donald Regan, the current incumbent in that post, the board consists of twelve Republicans outside government, among them Milton Friedman, Alan Greenspan, Arthur F. Burns, and Paul McCracken. A profile on Sowell that appeared in Newsweek (March 9, 1981) reported that he had turned down a Cabinet post because "such active participation . . . would only damage his scholarly reputation." In the same article George Stigler, his former mentor, was quoted as saying: "Tom Sowell's going to be a leader whether he wants to or not. He's honest and thorough, and he's doing a great service to the nation—even if he turns out to be wrong."

Sowell has often insisted that most blacks are conservative and are therefore misrepresented by such established civil rights spokesmen as former U.N. Ambassador Andrew Young, Benjamin L. Hooks, president of the NAACP, and Vernon Jordan, director of the Urban League. Since such leaders did not let Sowell's contentions go unchallenged, an open conflict ensued that at times descended to invective and name-calling. When Sowell seemed certain to obtain an important appointment from Reagan, the general counsel for the NAACP, Thomas I. Atkins, said, "We would view with considerable concern [his] appointment to HUD or, for that matter, to any other Cabinet position. He would play the same kind of role which historically the house niggers played for the plantation owners." In turn, Sowell charged in the Washington Post (February 21, 1981) that a "light-skinned elite" of blacks was using liberal policies to gain self-serving access to whites. Sowell's raising of "pigment politics" triggered fierce responses in the Washington Post by Dorothy Gilliam and former HEW Secretary Patricia Roberts Harris. Both sides in the running conflict have asserted that now is not the time for blacks to be fighting blacks, especially since the black community has to decide what kind of a future it should pursue. "It's a bankrupt, hackneyed, and unrealistic idea," Hooks has said of Sowell's conservatism, "that we should go back to the nineteenth-century idea of everyone pulling [himself up] by his own bootstraps without any help." But Edwin Meese 3d told the delegates to the Black Alternatives Conference in San Francisco: "Some of the people who purport to represent the black community [are] talking about the ideas of the last ten years. You are talking about the ideas of the next ten years and beyond."

According to the Newsweek profile of Thomas Sowell, "though friends find him witty and gregarious in private, he is generally aloof to the point of reclusiveness." Talking to him, one friend was quoted as saying in the same article, "is to be enlightened, occasionally incredulous, and always stimulated," and a former colleague at the University of California has described him as "a driven man, determined to make a substantial contribution." Blunt and impatient at times with his opponents, Sowell has gained a reputation for a brusque militancy. Divorced from the former Alma Jean Parr, Sowell recently remarried and has custody of one of his two children by his first marriage, a son. He spends his rare leisure moments with his family or indulges in his long-standing hobby of photography. His latest books, all of which appeared in 1981, are Ethnic America: A History and Markets and Minorities, published by Basic Books, and Pink and Brown People, and Other Controversial Essays, published by the Hoover Institution Press.

References: Newsweek 97:29+ Mr 9 '81 por; Washington Post A p2 D 6 '80 por, C p10+ O 1 '81 pors; Contemporary Authors 1st rev vols 41-44 (1979); Sowell, Thomas. Black Education (1972); Who's Who Among Black Americans, 1975-76

Spillane, Mickey

Mar. 9, 1918- Writer. Address: b. c/o New American Library, 1301 Ave. of the Americas, New York City, N.Y. 10019; h. Murrells Inlet, South Carolina

Refashioning a formula for hard-boiled detective stories developed earlier by such old masters of the genre as Dashiel Hammett and Raymond Chandler, in 1947 Mickey Spillane first mixed his own steamy brew of sex, sadism, and vigilante violence in I, the Jury,

Mickey Spillane

tained a kind of pristine innocence, even though he has become a familiar figure to viewers through his tough-guy roles in movies and television beer commercials. One reason for his indestructible appeal may be his simple creed that "murder's gonna last forever."

Mickey Spillane was born Frank Morrison Spillane on March 9, 1918 in Brooklyn, New York, the only child of an Irish-Catholic bartender, John Joseph Spillane, and a Presbyterian mother, Catherine Anne Spillane. "I was christened in two churches and neither took," Spillane once explained after his conversion to Jehovah's Witnesses in the early 1950's. From his crusty father, who once dismissed his son's books as "crud," came the nickname that stuck, Mickey. Spillane attended grammar school in Brooklyn and Roosevelt Junior High in the Bayway section of Elizabeth, New Jersey, which he looks back upon as "a very tough neighborhood." Although his playmates were battle-hardened street urchins, he used to "scare hell" out of them with his ghost stories, and he sold his first story to a "slick" magazine soon after he graduated from Erasmus High School in Brooklyn in 1935. To survive during the Depression, Spillane worked at odd jobs during the winters and spent his summers as a lifeguard at Breezy Point, Long Island. Ray Masters, who was the chief lifeguard there at the time, remembers him as "a very quiet boy, a very good boy," with a heart "as big as gold." Deciding to study law, in 1939 he briefly attended Fort Hays State College in Kansas, where he was on the swimming and football teams.

Spillane's professional writing career grew out of his friendship with a Brooklyn youth named Joe Gill, whom he met when both of them were working as temporary salesmen during the 1940 Christmas rush in the basement of Gimbel's department store. Through Joe's brother Ray, an editor at Funnies, Inc., which produced comic books in midtown Manhattan, Spillane got a job as scripter-assistant editor with the firm. Other writers needed a week to produce an eight-page story for *Bull's Eye Bill, The Human Torch,* or *Captain Marvel,* but Spillane churned out one a day. "I'd be telling a lie," Ray Gill told Richard W. Johnston, who wrote a profile of Spillane for *Life* magazine (June 23, 1952), "if I said that I had ever met a more fabulous or prolific writer than Mickey." That promising career was sidetracked, however, when Spillane joined the United States Air Force the day after the Japanese bombed Pearl Harbor. Although he thirsted for combat, he was made a cadet flight instructor, much to his chagrin, and had to spend his four years of service in Florida and Mississippi.

Discharged with the rank of captain at the end of World War II, Spillane joined Joe and Ray Gill in establishing a free-lance comic book factory in a rented store on Vandeveer Place in Brooklyn. Plagued by spiraling prices and the postwar housing shortage, he became restive and discontented. "I was fed up with

which introduced Mike Hammer, the most celebrated of his tough-guy sleuths. Although he occasionally changed heroes in the more than a score of novels that followed over the next twenty-five years, the basic ingredients remained the same. The titles alone of his books, published by E. P. Dutton, became talismans for some mystery buffs: *My Gun Is Quick* (1950); *The Big Kill* (1951); *Kiss Me, Deadly* (1952); *The Girl Hunters* (1962); *The Death Dealers* (1967); and *The Erection Set* (1972). Nobody can be quite certain how many people in the habitable parts of the globe have read Mickey Spillane, but it is estimated that there are between 70,000,000 and 130,000,000 copies of his works in print, including translations in about fourteen countries.

In view of his slapdash and cursory techniques when measured against traditional literary standards, nobody except Mickey Spillane himself seems able to account for his phenomenal commercial success. "There's a big difference between an author and a writer," he once explained to Jerry Cassidy during an interview for *Writer's Digest* (September 1976). "Writers are professionals who make money. Authors usually have one or two books to tell. . . . I was always a good storyteller. This is what makes a good writer. You have to be a good storyteller." Spillane's undisputed flair for moving his jet-propelled action from a dramatic opening chapter to a surprising or shocking "smash ending" has served him well in comic books, novels, films, television, and—most recently—paperback mysteries for children. Weathering the attacks by critics on what they see as the sadism, misogyny, lawlessness, paranoia, and rabid right-wing politics in his work, Spillane himself has main-

this business of being a veteran and everybody trying to cut you up," he has said of that period. Then, in 1946, he and his first wife, the former Mary Ann Pearce, whom he had married in Greenwood, Mississippi the year before, discovered four acres of land for sale near the Hudson River community of Newburgh, New York. Acting on his abiding principle that a writer works only when he needs money, Spillane announced to his comic book colleagues that he planned to raise the $1,000 needed to buy the property by writing a novel.

After laboring for three weeks in the comic book factory, Spillane emerged with the manuscript of his first novel, I, the Jury. Acting on the advice of Ray Gill, he passed the manuscript on to Jack McKenna, a printing salesman, who had dealings with the publishing house of E. P. Dutton & Co. In accepting it for publication, its editor-in-chief, Nicholas Wreden, conceded to the members of the editorial committee mulling over the possibilities of I, the Jury that the novel was not in the best taste, but predicted, with admirable understatement, that it would sell. By 1954, when Christopher LaFarge equated "Hammerism" with McCarthyism in the Saturday Review, 1,600,000 copies had been published, with millions more to come. Meanwhile, Spillane had constructed a four-room cinder block house, garage, and study on his Newburgh property and moved in.

Since I, the Jury fixed the mold for all of Spillane's later books, it merits a summary. Set in a darkling world of organized crime and mindless evil, it is the lightning-swift narrative of Mike Hammer, a 6-foot, 190-pound bruiser and private investigator whom one commentator has called "unquestionably the toughest, most sadistic detective in the annals of murder fiction." Heavily addicted to alcohol and nicotine, incredibly quick with his fists and a gun, and as irresistible as an aphrodisiac to the succession of full-bosomed, neatly packaged young women he encounters, Hammer pursues vengeance with his "killer's lust," in this case directed against a narcotics ring that murdered his army buddy. Although a loner, Hammer is emotionally supported by his beautiful female sidekick named Velda, and by Pat Chambers, a police captain in homicide who reluctantly agrees that Hammer's brand of justice outside the law is swifter and fitter than his own.

As reviewers of I, the Jury noted, Hammer's trail through New York City's lower depths takes him alternately from an impossibly lovely siren, who strips in her teasing effort to seduce him (sometimes successfully), to a Hammer orgy of mayhem inflicted on some hapless quarry. In the climax the two action lines converge when the mob's ringleader is revealed to be a woman, the beauteous psychiatrist Charlotte Manning, whom Hammer coolly shoots in the "belly" after she has stripped down to the bare essentials. Her often quoted death scene is vintage Spillane.

In the five years from 1947 to 1952 Mickey Spillane completed seven novels. All but one— The Long Wait (1951), whose hero was Johnny McBride—dealt with Hammer's adventures, and all of them reprised the pattern set in I, the Jury. Spillane had only to alter the motive for vengeance, and Hammer was off: in The Big Kill to right the murder of a child's father; in Kiss Me, Deadly to hunt down two Mafia hit men; in One Lonely Night (1951) to destroy a Communist ring that had stolen some secret documents and kidnapped the virtuous Velda. Critics pointed out that Spillane had succeeded in lifting the taboos on sex and violence that had governed tough-guy mysteries, and they toted up, with grim satisfaction and lavish quotation, the mistreated women, battered faces, splintered bones, and bloody corpses in Mike Hammer's wake. In six novels, according to one count, Mike Hammer had dispatched fifty-eight people.

Since Spillane's novels derived scant aid or comfort from literary reviewers, it took a while for the Hammer cult to gather momentum, and with a growing family to support, Spillane lived through some lean years at Newburgh. He tried without success to land a job with the local newspaper, worked in a downtown department store, and exercised his considerable brawn as a trampoline artist with Ringling Bros. and Barnum & Bailey, a fond memory for him still. He even deliberately lost weight so that he could be shot from a circus cannon.

Spillane's scorn for reviewers only deepened when his work continued to be greeted almost unanimously with curt dismissal or undisguised invective. The Saturday Review's summary judgment of I, the Jury was typical: "Lurid action, lurid characters, lurid plot, lurid finish." Anthony Boucher, the New York Times authority on mysteries, sniped away at Spillane in his columns: "plot (which is both strained and obvious) and writing (which often approaches parody)"; "a spectacularly bad book"; and "the best Spillane—which is the faintest praise this department has ever bestowed." But perhaps the most scathing article was that by Malcolm Cowley in the New Republic (February 11, 1952), in which he concluded that Hammer's sadism and misogyny marked him as "a homicidal paranoiac." Although some reviewers eventually recognized Spillane's crisp imagery, grip on narrative, and bravura endings, few took his work seriously. Meanwhile, Spillane responded in kind. "I pay no attention to those jerks who think they're critics," he said during one interview, and on another occasion, "I don't give a hoot about readin' reviews. What I want to read is the royalty checks."

By 1952, the year that ushered in a nine-year hiatus in his novel writing, Spillane finally found himself free of financial pressure, and in January 1953 he sold the film rights to his books to the British producer Victor Saville for $250,000. But some astute observers attributed Spillane's long silence not to his sudden affluence but to his conversion in 1951 to the sect of Jehovah's Witnesses, which occurred, he said, after one of its members convinced him that the theory of evolution was wrong. He soon converted his wife and mother, and reporters often described him as quoting from his pocket Bible and doing door-to-door missionary work.

Under the aegis of United Artists, Saville quickly finished four Spillane movies, starting in August 1953 with *I, the Jury*, a three-dimensional extravaganza that starred Biff Elliott as Hammer. *The Long Wait* followed in 1954; *Kiss Me, Deadly* was released in 1955, with Ralph Meeker as Hammer; and *My Gun Is Quick* appeared in 1957, with Robert Bray. When Spillane descended on Hollywood during the shooting of *I, the Jury*, he reportedly quarreled with Saville about casting and threatened to halt the series by rubbing out Mike Hammer in his next book. Saville later announced his intention to sue if Spillane carried out his rumored plans to film a novel on his own.

When, on a trip to Florida, Spillane stopped off to judge a beauty contest at the Sun-Fun Festival at Myrtle Beach, South Carolina, he was so impressed by the area that in 1953 he transported his first wife and their four children—Kathy, Ward, Mike, and Carolyn—to a beach house at nearby Murrells Inlet, where he has lived ever since. He wrote stories for such now defunct pulp magazines as *True* and *Cavalier*, began writing for television and movies, and appeared on television specials, including *The Milton Berle Show*, usually in comic spoofs of his macho characters. In 1954 he played himself as a detective hired by wild animal trainer Clyde Beatty to solve a circus mystery in Warner Brothers' *Ring of Fear*, a film that he heavily rewrote.

Indirectly, and involuntarily, Spillane may have caused the campaigns against violence in television that were mounted after a series called *Mickey Spillane's Mike Hammer* was scrutinized by the Television Review Board in 1958. Since he was not involved in the series, which starred David McGavin as Hammer, Spillane was embittered by the moral crusades. He has often blamed his undeserved unsavory reputation on the excesses of his imitators. Nevertheless, he appeared in an episode of *Columbo* in 1974, and in recent years he often turns up in the throng of blue collar workers, athletes, and entertainers who debate the merits of lightness versus taste in the Miller Lite Beer commercials.

In 1961 Mickey Spillane returned to the writing of novels with *The Deep*, in which a hoodlum known only as "The Deep" solved a murder and singlehandedly wiped out a crime machine. The public, however, clamored for another hero, and he obliged with *The Girl Hunters*, in which Mike Hammer was pitted against an international spy ring and a beautiful blonde enemy. Even before the novel appeared in 1962 Spillane had started work on a film, starring himself, with Colorama Features, Inc., which was shot in New York City and on the MGM lot at Elstree Studios outside London. Although the reviewer for *Time* (June 7, 1963) thought that Spillane neither looked nor sounded like a professional, he conceded that "As Mike Hammer, Actor Spillane is tremendous." "It was easy," Spillane might have responded, since he has often said, "I *am* Mike Hammer." One other Spillane novel, *The Delta Factor* (1967), was released as a film in 1971 by American Continental.

Into the steady flow of eighteen novels that he published between 1961 and 1973, Spillane occasionally introduced new tough-guy heroes: Tiger Mann in *The Day of the Guns* (1964), *Bloody Sunrise* (1965), *The Death Dealers* (1965), and *The By-Pass Control* (1966); "The Hood" in *Me, Hood* (1963) and *The Return of the Hood* (1964); Dogeron Kelly in *The Erection Set* (1972); and Gil Burke in *The Last Cop Out* (1973). But even more significant than the changes in name, as John G. Cawelti has pointed out in his *Adventure, Mystery, and Romance* (1976), was the fact that Spillane recruited his new breed of heroes either from the underworld itself, as in "The Hood" novels, or from intelligence circles, as in the case of Tiger Mann, enlisting them into a contest against the ultimate corruption, "the worldwide Communist conspiracy, with its American dupes." His latter-day protagonists are now dedicated to protecting wronged innocents from the menace of political monsters, both domestic and foreign.

Although Spillane has disavowed any political commitment, he has never concealed his sympathy with such representatives of the far right as the novelist Ayn Rand and governors George Wallace and Lester Maddox, nor has he tried to hide his displeasure with antiwar protesters, legal rights for criminals, welfare programs, the United Nations, and big government. In his novels, however, as Cawelti has demonstrated, Spillane is less a political advocate than a simple evangelist with "a passionate hatred" for evil, a spokesman for many Americans who feel "hostility toward the sinful city with its corrupt men of wealth, its degenerate foreigners, and its Scarlet Women."

"Of all the hard-boiled writers," Cawelti has noted, "Spillane's art is closest in its mythical simplicity to folktale," and it was that ability to spin an archetypal story about right and wrong that won Spillane a Junior Literary Guild award for his first children's book, *The Day the Sea Rolled Back* (Windmill, 1979). An adventure story about two boys who discover treasure aboard a shipwreck that is exposed when the sea mysteriously recedes, the book appropriated themes from his adult mysteries and employed some of his old techniques, including the "big, surprise" ending that he always writes first. Two more of his adventure books for children, *The Ship that*

Never Was and *The Shrinking Island,* are scheduled for publication in 1982.

For many years Mickey Spillane has given interviewers the impression of being a bantam-sized Mike Hammer, whom he has also portrayed in the photographs for the jackets of his books: a self-professed roughneck with chiseled facial features, set mouth, peering hazel eyes, and crew-cut hair, who wears a custom-made porkpie hat and tight-fitting clothes that show off his compact five-foot eight-inch frame and bulging muscles. He has proclaimed his toughness to journalists with reminiscences of how he beat up Brooklyn Communists and New York muggers, and how he bore bullet and knife wounds when he helped Federal agents to smash a narcotics ring. At the same time, interviewers have found him to be amiable, easy-going, gregarious, and "full of little-kid enthusiasms." Recently his manner has softened. "After all, [I'm] sixty-three, and I'm learning that there are a lot of things you can't do when you're older that you could do while you were young," he told Fred Ferretti of the New York *Times.* "And when you get to the end of your career you want to do things for fun."

Divorced from the former Mary Ann Pearce in 1962, Mickey Spillane married his second wife, the former Sherri Malinou, an actress and model who is twenty-four years his junior, in November 1964 in Malibu Beach, California. She once posed nude for the dustjacket of *The Erection Set.* Long a collector of guns, flier of private planes, and driver of souped-up automobiles, Spillane now spends most of his leisure time in fishing, crabbing, and skin-diving. He plans to continue to write children's adventure stories and is now working on a play.

References: Chicago Tribue Mag p28+ Ag 16 '81 pors; Life 32:79+ Je 23 '52 pors, 51:127+ S 8 '61 pors; Newsday L I p 19+ Jl 26 '81 por; People 16:52+ Jl 27 '81 pors; Washington Post B p1+ Je 8 '72 pors; Writer's Digest p18+ S '76; Cawelti, John G. Adventure, Mystery, and Romance (1976); Contemporary Authors vols 25-28 (1971); Who's Who in America, 1980-81

Stever, H(orton) Guyford

Oct. 24, 1916- Scientist; educator; former government official. Address: h. 1528 33rd St. NW, Washington, D.C. 20007

A scientist and educator who has helped to shape two decades of federal policies in the areas of science and technology, H. Guyford Stever has played respected, though occasionally criticized, roles in the highest echelons of government bureacracy. A physicist who made his major scientific contributions in aeronautical engineering during the 1940's and 1950's, Stever relinquished laboratory research first for university administrative posts and, beginning in the early 1970's, for full-time government service, including five years as director of the National Science Foundation and appointments as science adviser to presidents Richard Nixon and Gerald Ford. His generally noncontroversial stances resulted in a low public profile, which sometimes was criticized by the scientific community, and brought him a reputation for accommodation to the exigencies of government and politics, but Stever himself took a modest and pragmatic view, seeing his sundry roles as communicative, interpretative, and informative. Of his presidential advisership Stever said that "the whole object is to try to be the translator—take ideas welling up in the scientific community and see that the government takes action on them." In recent years, since leaving his White House post at the end of the Ford Administration, Stever has been self-employed as a corporate director and a consultant to corporations and institutions both in the United States and abroad.

Horton Guyford Stever was born on October 24, 1916, in the glass manufacturing city of Corning, New York, the son of Ralph Raymond Stever, a merchant, and Alma (Matt) Stever. Following his high school years, three of which he served as class president, Stever attended Colgate University in Hamilton, New York. Aided by scholarships and part-time jobs, Stever obtained his A.B. degree, with a major in physics, in 1938. He undertook graduate work, also in physics, at the California Institute of Technology, where he received his Ph.D. degree in 1941. He has explained that "physics was very exciting in those days.... I was interested in the most fundamental of physics."

Returning to the East Coast, Stever briefly held a staff position at the Massachusetts Institute of Technology radiation laboratory, where he taught and did research. With the United States entry into World War II, Stever joined the Office of Scientific Research and Development, a government agency headed by Vannevar Bush, the distinguished electrical engineer and physicist. Serving as a science liaison officer at the London Mission of the OSRD from 1942 through 1945, Stever analyzed developments in German and British radar systems, and strengthened Great Britain's defenses against the V-1 and V-2 missiles. After the invasion of Europe, he also was a member of several intelligence missions to Europe.

Following his return to the United States, Stever went back to the Massachusetts Institute of Technology as assistant professor in the department of aeronautical engineering. He served in that rank from 1946 to 1951, when he was promoted to associate professor. In 1956 he was appointed to a full professorship, and in that same year he became associate dean in the school of engineering. During the years from 1961 to 1965 he headed MIT's department of mechanical engineering and its department of naval architecture and marine engineering.

During the first two decades of Stever's career, from the onset of World War II in fields of space exploration and aeronautical engineering, he formulated and solved a broad spectrum of problems that helped to lead to the era of supersonic flight and laid the groundwork for the hypersonic and orbital speeds attained by aircraft and spacecraft during the past twenty years. Stever's main research contributions—which, although he had been trained in physics, were mainly in the field of aeronautical engineering—concerned the development of guided missile technology and the control of transonic aircraft. Some of his early experiments, conducted in about 1949, tested the aerodynamic properties of unmanned missiles with a view toward the development of their guidance and control. Practical problems that arose in the experimental situation—models of missiles and aircraft are tested in so-called "wind tunnels"— led Stever to explore the condensation nucleation process in high speed wind tunnels in order to improve the effectiveness of very high speed tunnel testing. In other experiments, Stever studied the aerodynamics of manned aircraft at transonic speeds (about 550 to 900 miles per hour) and thus contributed to the understanding of how to stabilize planes that approached and surpassed the speed of sound.

Concomitant with his teaching and research activities, Stever held a number of appointments to government and military advisory committees, which multiplied as technology helped to lead cold-war America into the space age. The United States Air Force, and later, NASA, often called upon his advisory services. From 1946 to 1948 Stever was a member of the Guided Missile Technological Evaluation Group, convened by the Research and Development Board of the Army and Navy. In 1947 he joined the Air Force's Science Advisory Board, on which he remained until 1969 and for which he served a number of years as chairman. Stever was chief scientist for the Air Force from 1955 to 1956. In 1957 he chaired an *ad hoc* committee that reported on the importance of space technology for the military and reacted to the Russian launch of *Sputnik* in that year by proposing the establishment of a program that eventually would lead to a moon landing. As chairman of the Special Committee on Space Exploration that was convened by the National Advisory Committee for Aeronautics at about the same time, Stever administered the report that provided the first guidelines for NASA in its development of a civilian space program. He also served on the executive committee of the Defense Science Board from 1956 to 1967, and on the steering committee of the Technical Advisory Panel to the Department of Defense.

In 1965 Stever left MIT to take over the presidency of the Carnegie Institute of Technology in Pittsburgh. His tenure there, which lasted until 1972, saw the merger during 1967-68 of Carnegie with the Mellon Institute. Under Stever's administration at what is now known as Carnegie-Mellon University, there was an emphasis on the integration of a science education with other disciplines; a school of urban and public affairs and a college of humanities and social sciences were established, and a new degree, that of Doctor of Arts, was granted for the first time. Stever presided over Carnegie-Mellon during a period of student turmoil and was praised for his evenhanded treatment of campus unrest. Although some members of the faculty were reportedly disturbed by the time and effort that Stever expended on the student disorders, he himself thought that a stern reexamination of the values taking shape in a technological society was eminently worthwhile.

Continuing his work in government advisory roles, from 1967 to 1970 Stever was a member of the Special Commission on the Social Sciences, administered by the National Science Foundation, the federal agency that supports scientific research with grants, awards, and contracts. During 1970 he served on two of President Richard Nixon's committees, the Ad Hoc Science Panel and the Task Force on Science Policy, and in that same year Nixon also appointed him to fill a vacancy on the National Science Board, the policy-making arm of the National Science Foundation. When, in February 1972, Stever became director of the National Science Foundation, few observers were surprised at the appointment, since he was, as Deborah Shapley of *Science* magazine (March 31, 1972) pointed out, "the favorite-son candidate of both the Administration and the science-government advisory system through which he has risen for twenty years." According to Deborah Shapley, Stever, "one of the few good Republican scientist-administrators," seemed a desirable choice because his opinions were not known to be at odds with those of the Nixon Administration, and he was said not to have any "missiles up his sleeves or airplanes in his pocket."

As head of the National Science Foundation under the faltering Nixon Administration, Stever became a party to controversy when the President eliminated the White House Office of Science and Technology in the spring of 1973 and failed to replace his science adviser, Edward E. David Jr., when the latter resigned in January of that year. Instead, Nixon named Stever his unofficial adviser, a move that both scientists and some congressmen viewed with alarm. To some critics, Stever's concomitant role as head of the National Science Foundation suggested a conflict of interest between his two positions; they also thought that Stever found it difficult to reach President Nixon and that even once he did, he proved somewhat ineffectual. In an article for the Washington *Post* (January 27, 1974) William Stockton wrote: "Congressional critics suggest Stever has little influence in the Administration. They contend he is reluctant to press ideas or enter controversial areas where sound advice might help resolve complex issues." But although Stever acknowledged that some conflict might exist, he did not consider his dual roles as head of the National Science Foundation and as science adviser to the President to be a major problem, and he felt that his views were given an adequate hearing by the Administration. "I have all the access I need to the President's top advisers," he asserted. "They listen quite a bit."

After the resignation of President Nixon on August 9, 1974, Stever remained in the dual role of director of the National Science Foundation and science adviser to the President under the Ford Administration until, in August 1976, he was confirmed as a full-time President's White House director of the Office of Science and Technology Policy, a move that, in effect, reestablished the official science adviof a position that had been abandoned under Nixon. Rumored for more than a year, Stever's appointment was not made until what turned out to be the closing months of the Ford Administration. The New York *Times* noted in an editorial (August 24, 1976) that "Science has now returned to the White House" and endorsed Stever's belief that his contributions to policy would best serve nondefense areas. At the time of his confirmation, Stever said that he would concentrate on energy-related problems, nuclear waste disposal, and exploitation of the oceans. "The space program has

proved our tremendous technological capability," he pointed out. "But we have not proven we can do as well in government with some of the civilian side of technology." He planned to devote more attention than had previously been given to such life sciences as biology, health, and agriculture. Stever also advocated the study of the merits of a "science court" that would pass judgment on controversial scientific issues related to the public good and safety, such as fluoridation of water and the use of pesticides.

At the end of the Ford Administration, H. Guyford Stever left his White House post and during the past several years has been happily self-employed as a consultant to various corporations and other organizations. He is a director of TRW, the electronics firm, and also of Schering Plough, and Goodyear Tire & Rubber Company. While he continues to be active in a variety of government-related functions, he says that he does not anticipate a return to government employment under the Reagan Administration. On June 29, 1946 Stever married Adelaide Louise Risley Floyd, and the couple has four children: Horton Guyford Jr., Sarah Newell, Margarette Risley (Margarette is also the name of Stever's older sister and and only sibling), and Roy Risley. Stever, who is about six feet tall and weighs about 190 pounds, has often been described by interviewers and associates as personable and well-liked. A fly fisherman and maker of flies for angling, Stever also likes to hike and play golf, and he enjoys opera and ballet. He is a member of several clubs, including the Bohemian Club, the Century Association, and the Cosmos Club.

Since he received the President's Certificate of Merit in 1948, Stever has been honored with many awards and medals. They include the Exceptional Civilian Service Award, United States Air Force, 1956; the Distinguished Public Service Medal, Department of Defense, 1968; and Commander Order of Merit, People's Republic of Poland, 1976. A member of both the National Academy of Science and the National Academy of Engineering, Stever is a fellow of the American Academy of Arts and Sciences, the American Association for the Advancement of Science, the American Institute of Aeronautics and Astronautics, and many other organizations. He has been awarded many honorary degrees by colleges and universities, including Notre Dame, Northwestern, Clark, Washington and Jefferson, Allegheny, Lafayette, and his alma mater, Colgate, in recognition of his contributions to science and technology.

References: N Y Times p37 N 16 '71; *Science* p1441+ Mar 31 '72; *American Men and Women of Science* 13 ed (1976); *International Who's Who, 1981-82*; *McGraw-Hill Modern Men of Science* (1966); *McGraw-Hill Modern Scientists and Engineers* (1980); *Who's Who in America, 1980-81*

Stockman, David (Alan)

Nov. 10, 1946- Director of the Office of Management and Budget. Address: b. Executive Office of the President, Office of Management and Budget, Washington, D.C. 20503

Under David Stockman's direction the Office of Management and Budget has become the pivotal agency of the United States government, while he himself has been recognized, at least during its crucial formative period, as one of the most influential men in the Reagan Administration. Dedicated to the goal of lesser government intrusion into the private sector of America, he has been the principal drafter and salesman of a plan to turn around the flow of federal spending on welfare and other social programs, which has steadily increased during the past thirty years. In his conformity to supply-side economics, furthermore, he has argued for a substantial tax cut over a three-year period to spur productivity by encouraging investment and entrepreneurship so that an eventual growth in revenues would attain a balanced budget. The post that Stockman, a former Republican Representative from Michigan, has held since January 20, 1981 may be among the most powerful in Washington, but it is also probably the least popular. Referring to Stockman's prominence in the Republican resumption of control, Robert G. Kaiser wrote in the Washington *Post* (February 5, 1981), "He is important to President Reagan as an architect of government policy and as a lightning rod to deflect the political outcry the policy will provoke."

The oldest of five children of Allen and Carol (Bartz) Stockman, David Alan Stockman was born in Camp Hood, Texas on November 10,

1946, when his father was serving in the Army. Shortly afterward the family moved to St. Joseph in southwest Michigan, where Allen Stockman took over the operation of a 150-acre fruit farm that had been in the Bartz family for generations. While growing up on the farm, David Stockman acquired his habit of sustained hard work and an interest in politics that was encouraged by his grandfather, William Bartz, who served as county chairman of the Republican party for thirty years. At the age of seventeen David took part in the local campaign effort for the unsuccessful Republican Presidential nominee, Barry M. Goldwater.

Also in 1964 Stockman graduated from Lakeshore High School in Stevensville, Michigan, where he had been president of the student council and a member of the football and basketball teams. Later, at Michigan State University, the political attitudes generated by his rural, middle-class conservative background were temporarily eclipsed as he became involved in the anti-Vietnam war movement then flourishing on American college campuses. In 1967 he was the leading spokesman, and only paid staff member, of Vietnam Summer, which came under the surveillance of the Michigan State Police intelligence unit. Many years later, in December 1980, the designated OMB director described Vietnam Summer as "basically a church group engaged in an entirely acceptable activity."

Stockman's association with the Edgewood United Church of Christ in East Lansing, Michigan, which had stimulated his antiwar feeling, also affected his religious views. Through its senior minister, the Reverend Truman Morrison, he became interested in the work of Reinhold Niebuhr, the Protestant theologian and non-Communist leftist. "I was trying to find a way intellectually out of the radical thicket I was in," Stockman has explained, as quoted in the Washington *Post Magazine* (February 8, 1981). "Niebuhr was sort of a bridge back to a more conventional view of the world."

Agriculture had been Stockman's intended major subject when he entered Michigan State University. He graduated *cum laude* in 1968 with a B.A. degree in American history. Although he did not plan to seek ordination, he accepted a scholarship to the Harvard University Divinity School, which gave him exemption from the draft and an opportunity to study the writings of Niebuhr. But because, as it turned out, some of his courses were in government and politics, his teachers included the political scientist James Q. Wilson and the sociologist Nathan Glazer, both of whom were former liberals who had become progenitors of a new conservatism. Stockman turned to them, as he had to Niebuhr, as a way out of radicalism. His most influential mentor was probably Daniel Patrick Moynihan, now Democratic Senator from New York, who at that time was teaching at Harvard and commuting to Washington, where he served as special assistant for domestic policy to President Richard Nixon. Hired to carry out various household chores and to baby-sit for the three children, Stockman boarded with the family and in evening discussions with Moynihan acquired a philosophical justification for adopting liberal Republicanism.

While attending a seminar at Harvard conducted by David S. Broder, then a columnist and now an associate editor of the Washington Post, Stockman came to the attention of Congressman John B. Anderson, Republican from Illinois, who was one of the guest lecturers. On the recommendation of Broder and Moynihan, Anderson soon afterward chose Stockman to be a staff member of the House Republican Conference, the policy-making committee for Republican Representatives, of which he was chairman. Without taking his divinity degree, in 1970 Stockman left Harvard to serve as Anderson's special assistant. Two years later he became executive director of the House Republican Conference. Despite their close relationship, the two men developed ideological differences. While Anderson was growing increasingly liberal, Stockman moved in an opposite direction, especially in regard to his conservative preferences in economics.

During 1974 Stockman returned to Harvard as a fellow of the John F. Kennedy School of Government of the Institute of Politics. In politics, however, as in economics, he is for the most part informally educated, having acquired much of what Hugh Sidey of Time called his "arsenal of knowledge" from the research and analysis of the complex operations of government that he undertook while serving on the Republican Conference. An opponent of big government, he championed deregulation in the interests of a free-market economy and urged curtailment of federally sponsored social programs. His article "The Social Pork Barrel," published in the neoconservative journal the Public Interest in 1975, charged that politicians and bureaucrats had been abusing well-intentioned programs like those advocated in President Lyndon B. Johnson's Great Society "to create self-perpetuating constituencies."

The attention that Stockman gained from that article, as well as from the commendation of it by the Public Interest's coeditor Irving Kristol that appeared in the Wall Street Journal, boosted his chances for an elective political office. Resigning in 1975 from the Republican Conference, he went back to Michigan to plan a primary campaign against Edward Hutchinson, the Republican incumbent Representative from the Fourth Congressional District. A local circuit court judge, Chester J. Byrns, who introduced Stockman to potential contributors to a campaign fund, told Walter Shapiro of the Washington Post (February 8, 1981). "Dave was wearing his hair long in those days, sort of a Prince Valiant haircut, and that didn't help. . . . [But] Stockman fascinated those

people because he was a walking computer. He was using facts and figures that these business leaders could look up. And they did, and they were impressed."

Soon after Stockman formally declared his candidacy, in early February 1976, Hutchinson announced his intention to retire from Congress. His withdrawal from the race in that solidly Republican district assured victory in the general election for Stockman, who won 61 percent of the vote to defeat Richard E. Daugherty by 107,881 to 69,655. Unchallenged in the 1978 primary, he took 71 percent of the vote from Democrat Morgan L. Hager Jr. Upon taking his seat in 1977 in the Ninety-fifth Congress, Stockman was assigned to the House Administration Committee and, more importantly, to the influential Interstate and Foreign Commerce Committee and to its subcommittees on energy and power and health and environment. He also represented House Republicans on the National Commission on Air Quality and served as chairman of the Republican economic policy task force, which had the responsibility of proposing alternatives to the economic programs of the Carter Administration.

Wherever practical, Representative Stockman appears to have tried to reduce the role of government in American life by refusing to vote funds for social programs. As early as February 1977, for instance, he opposed the bill to increase the authorization for the emergency public works jobs program that was part of President Carter's economic stimulus package. He rejected a 1978 bill to establish a consumer protection agency within the executive branch and the 1979 bill that created a separate Department of Education. Convinced that it is not the function of government to bail out private industry, he was the only Michigan Representative to vote against authorization of $1.5 billion in federal loan guarantees for the Chrysler Corporation. He also opposed the creation of 125,400,000 acres of national parks and forests in Alaska. On other domestic issues he voted for deregulation of natural gas and for delaying compliance with automobile-pollution controls.

An advocate of a strong military setup, Stockman approved 1977 and 1978 defense-spending measures that included production of B-1 bombers, in opposition to President Carter's position. He generally favored reduction in foreign aid appropriations and in 1980 supported a measure to cut contributions to international development banks. His voting record points to some willingness to vote on issues themselves without regard to conservative labels. For example, he objected to prohibiting the use of federal funds for abortions and agreed to extending the ratification date for the Equal Rights Amendment. Americans for Constitutional Action, nevertheless, gave his voting record a rating of 83 for 1977 and 80 for 1978, while he received from Americans for Democratic Action a rating of 25 and 20 for the respective years. In 1979 his percentage of conservative coalition support reached 65 and his party unity percentage, 69.

"As a new House member," Sidney Blumenthal wrote in the New York Times Magazine (March 15, 1981) of Stockman's performance in Congress, "his ascribed status was that of a back-bencher, but he quickly won a reputation as an aggressive intellectual gadfly pouring out a torrent of bills and research papers." During his two terms in Congress he contributed to the shaping of major legislation in energy, attacking the $88 billion synfuels-development program and the gasoline-allocation plan of the Carter Administration. He helped to defeat Carter's hospital-cost containment bill, and in 1980 he joined the Missouri Democratic Representative Richard A. Gephardt in sponsoring a health care reform bill that would offer tax-exclusion rewards to employees who chose low-cost options in health care plans. Also in 1980 he collaborated with Democratic Representative Phil Gramm of Texas in proposing to the House an alternative conservative budget containing spending cuts of $25 billion for fiscal 1981.

Even before Stockman entered Congress he had become an ally of Representative Jack Kemp, a New York Republican who instructed him in supply-side economics and introduced him to its exponents Arthur Laffer and Jude Wanniski. With Republican Senator William V. Roth of Delaware, Kemp collaborated on a proposal to cut personal income taxes by 33 percent over three years and to reduce corporate taxes to a lesser extent. The Kemp-Roth bill was defeated in 1978, but Stockman remained persuaded of the need for a long-range, comprehensive tax cut to invigorate the economy.

Shortly after the election of Ronald Reagan to the Presidency, in November 1980, Stockman began to draft in consultation with Kemp a document called "Avoiding a GOP Economic Dunkirk," a blueprint of 100 days of emergency action for the new Republican Administration. One of their recommendations was for the adoption of a large part of the Kemp-Roth tax-cut proposal. Other steps that they urged Reagan to take included deregulating the oil industry immediately so that prices would reduce usage while offering incentives to increase supply, relieving regulations in other industries, and achieving fiscal stability by progressive cutbacks in spending. The federal budget, they warned Reagan, was becoming an "automatic coast-to-coast soup line."

Disclosure of details of the Stockman-Kemp paper in the New York Times of December 11, 1980 coincided with Reagan's designation of Stockman as director of the Office of Management and Budget. Reagan had been enormously impressed by the keen-minded young Congressman during the Presidential campaign when Stockman substituted first for John Anderson and then for Jimmy Carter during Reagan's rehearsals for his televised debates with the two other Presidential candidates. Reagan's aides had reportedly slated Stockman for the post of Secretary of Energy. But with the backing of Kemp, Stockman openly sought the directorship of OMB, believing that through that agency he could best bring his ideas to bear on the process of government. As quoted in Business Week (December 15, 1980), he once pointed out, "OMB is the needle's eye through which all policy must pass. It has to be integrated into the Cabinet government structure."

On January 8, 1981, in a five-hour confirmation hearing on his appointment, Stockman told Senators that the Reagan Administration's remedy for the nation's economic plight would be a four-year plan to overcome lack of confidence in the government's handling of federal finances. It would include a "structural overhaul" of the budget together with a cut in taxes, which he argued was needed, despite an expected budget deficit, to generate revenues that would eventually balance the budget. At that time he was still a member of Congress, having been elected to a third term in 1980, but he resigned his seat after his confirmation.

Criticizing the budget for fiscal 1982 that Carter had submitted to Congress at the close of his Administration as a fiscal policy that "would only cause further deterioration of the economy," Stockman set about on an accelerated schedule to scrutinize every program in every agency in his search for ways to slash expenditures. The inevitable objection that he encountered from Cabinet officers included a protest from Secretary of State Alexander M. Haig Jr. over projected decreases in foreign aid programs. In his many appearances, moreover, before Congressional committees and subcommittees, he became the target of Democratic attack. At a Senate Budget Committee hearing on March 12, 1981, for instance, Senator Howard M. Metzenbaum of Ohio told him, "I think you've been brilliant. But I also think you've been cruel, inhumane and unfair. You're causing a perversion of justice for the poor, the middle class, the Northeast, and the Middle West." On that occasion Stockman replied, as he did similarly on others, that his proposals were not "carved in stone" and that he would be receptive to "superior ideas."

The "major surgery" that Stockman performed on almost all areas of government was obvious in the 1982 budget requests that Reagan submitted to Congress in February and March 1981, which together called for $48.6 billion in cuts from Carter's proposed budget. Reagan's insistence upon holding government spending to $695.3 billion in fiscal 1982 affected hundreds of programs, including federal administration costs, nutrition and commodity programs of the Department of Agriculture, youth training programs of the Labor Department, construction of hospitals by the Veterans Administration, federal loan and guarantee programs, urban grants, and legal aid for the poor and other "entitlements."

"The thundering herd of sacred cows has now been reduced to a handful," Stockman could claim. The Defense Department, however, remained unscathed. On May 14, 1981 the Senate approved Reagan's request for over $135 billion in defense spending for fiscal 1982, some $30 billion more than Carter had asked for. On the same day House-Senate conferees decided on a compromise $695.4 billion budget that followed Reagan's recommendations except for proposed additional cuts in Social Security. Gaining final Congressional approval on May 21, the budget resolution set the spending targets, but required the House and Senate committees to make the actual cuts in programs. Because of unforeseen circumstances, such as continued high interest rates that increased the government's cost of borrowing, well before the end of the year it became obvious that Reagan could not balance the budget on schedule by 1984 without further drastic reduction in spending. For political and other reasons, however, Stockman was generally discouraged in his efforts to explore two potential sources of saving—Social Security and the military buildup.

In many statements for television and the press Stockman reiterated that spending cuts alone, without tax cuts, would not achieve a balanced budget. He called the request for a three-year tax cut "nonnegotiable." Some members of Congress, however, feared that Reagan's appeal for a 25 percent tax cut over three years would be inflationary and firmly opposed it. But much the same coalition of Republicans and conservative Democrats that had secured passage of the budget resolution brought the President a victory in Congress on his tax plan in July 1981.

A startling challenge to Stockman's standing in Washington occurred with the publication in early November of the December issue of the *Atlantic Monthly*, which contained an article by William Greider based on eighteen interviews from December 1980 to September 1981. Quoted statements disclosing, among other matters, Stockman's private doubts about his own budget calculations and the effectiveness of the Reagan economic program in general created such a furor that on November 12 Stockman apologized for his "poor judgment and loose talk" and offered to resign. Reagan refused to accept the resignation, partly because, according to White House aides, he regarded Stockman as "too indispensable." Many Democrats and some Republicans on Capitol Hill, however, maintained that the credibility of the budget director had been severely damaged.

An earnest, intense man who has been described as appearing "to vibrate with energy," David Stockman is nevertheless cool and self-assured under close questioning in TV interviews and heated criticism in Capitol Hill hearings. He is the antithesis of a glad-hander, and to some Washington veterans he has seemed brash and intimidating. "His frail good looks

and boyish charm are potent catalysts for celebrity," writers for *Newsweek* (February 16, 1981) observed, however, ". . . and his buzzsaw intellect has helped him to stage a series of bravura performances before Congress." He wears conservatively tailored business suits and has a slender build, brown eyes, and prematurely graying brown hair. Except for an occasional hike or game of tennis, he reportedly leaves no time for recreation in his sixteen hour workday.

References: Bsns W p94+ F 16 '81 por; Chicago Tribune V p9 F 22 '81 por; Cong Q p3610+ D 20 '80 por; N Y Times Mag p22+ Mr 15 '81 pors; Newsweek 96:31+ D 8 '80 por, 97:24+ F 16 '81 pors; Time 117:11 F 16 '81 por; U S News 90:8 F 16 '81 por; Washington Post Mag p8+ F 8 '81 por; Almanac of American Politics, 1980; Congressional Directory, 1979

Stroessner, Alfredo

Nov. 3, 1912- President of Paraguay. Address: Casa Presidencial, Avenida Mariscal López, Asunción, Paraguay

NOTE: This biography supersedes the article that appeared in *Current Biography* in 1958.

The longest-ruling dictator in Latin America— and one of the most durable in the world—is Alfredo Stroessner, President of Paraguay. An army officer who rose through the ranks to become Commander in Chief before seizing power in a military coup d'etat in May 1954, General Stroessner has ruled his isolated and poverty-stricken nation ever since by maintaining a delicate balance between coercion and tolerance of a token opposition, and between modest economic development and a social structure that has remained fundamentally unchanged since the nineteenth century. A man of tremendous energy and political acumen, Stroessner is proud that he has brought more than two decades of "peace and tranquillity" to Paraguay, during which time many schools, roads, hospitals, bridges, and other public projects have been constructed. In fact, Paraguay enjoyed a high annual growth rate of about 8 percent during most of the 1970's and has now embarked on a massive project to develop its only notable natural resource, hydroelectric power. But the regime's critics, including some of the world's leading human rights organizations, charge that the benefits of the business boom have not reached most Paraguayans and that the regime has maintained the so-called "peace" through permanent suspension of civil guarantees and the wholesale jailing, torture, and deportation of its opponents.

Alfredo Stroessner was born in Encarnación, Paraguay on November 3, 1912, the son of a German immigrant, Hugo Stroessner, who established a successful brewery in Encarnación, and Heriberta (Mattiauda) Stroessner. After obtaining his early education in Asunción (the capital of Paraguay) and in Rio de Janeiro, Alfredo Stroessner entered the Military College in Asunción on March 1, 1929. Even before finishing his studies there, he distinguished himself in 1932, in an early battle of the Chaco War with Bolivia (1932-35), and achieved the rank of second lieutenant. Throughout the duration of that war, he proved outstanding as the commander of an artillery section and emerged with the rank of first lieutenant.

Although Paraguay won the Chaco War, it paid a heavy price for its victory. Landlocked, underpopulated (the nation today has only about 3,000,000 inhabitants), and lacking any significant mineral resources, Paraguay throughout its history has been one of the most backward and unstable countries on earth. The war, which exhausted the country's finances, led to nearly twenty years of political upheaval, with coups following each other in dizzying succession. The young Alfredo Stroessner, however, showed himself adept at maintaining his political balance and advanced briskly in his career. In 1936 he was promoted to captain, in 1940 to major, and in the latter year he was chosen for special artillery training in Brazil. In 1943 he was nominated to enter Paraguay's Superior War College, a high honor, and just a week after receiving his diploma from there in 1945 he was named to command the General Broguez Regiment, the country's key artillery unit. Only one month later he was promoted to lieutenant colonel.

"Ambitious and ruthless," Paul H. Lewis wrote in his *Paraguay Under Stroessner* (1980), "[Stroessner] plotted against every president he served under. . . ." After his success in crucial battles for the winning side in the Paraguayan Civil War of 1947, he was poised for power. In 1949, after backing the right side in a coup, he was promoted to brigadier general, and a few months later, in September, switched sides and helped bring Dr. Federico Chávez to the presidency. Chavez rewarded Stroessner handsomely by naming him commander of the nation's artillery in 1950, head of the first military region in 1951, and finally Commander in Chief of the armed forces that same year. But on May 5, 1954 Stroessner overthrew Chávez in a bloody coup, and an interim President was installed. It was announced that new elections would be held on July 11, 1954 with Stroessner as the Presidential candidate of the dominant Colorado party (also known as the National Republican Association). Running without opposition, Stroessner received 250,000 votes and took office on August 15, 1954.

When Stroessner took over, Paraguayan political life was a shambles. In classic Latin American fashion, the country had long been controlled by two parties, the Colorados and the Liberals, both ultraconservative, both based on the tiny oligarchy that owned most of the arable land and ran their huge ranches in an almost feudal fashion. But unlike some other Latin American nations, such as Argentina and Brazil, virtually no change had taken place in that century-old system by the 1950's. Having lost the 1947 Civil War, the party of the Liberals was much the weaker of the two faction-ridden parties, and every faction was headed by a potentate whose only concern was to maneuver himself or his friends into power. The Byzantine-like political life of Paraguay consisted of endless labyrinthine intrigues; elections were blatant frauds at best, held only to consecrate whatever dictator had attained momentary ascendancy in the Colorado party and the army.

During his first years in command, Stroessner therefore had every reason to feel highly insecure. At first he sought the counsel of his potential rivals but at the same time played them against each other, isolating them one by one and gradually monopolizing power. When, in 1958, he again ran for the Presidency without opposition, he was elected to a five-year term. Under pressure from the John F. Kennedy Administration, in 1963 Stroessner managed to persuade one group of Liberals to provide opposition in the elections, only the second time in the history of Paraguay that a Presidential vote had been contested. Of course he won, but the Liberals were handsomely rewarded with one third of the seats in the Chamber of Deputies.

While adroitly taming the Colorados, Stroessner simply suppressed all other opposition. During the late 1950's hundreds of members of the opposition were rounded up. Many languished for years in jail without trial, and reports of torture became commonplace. Stroessner justified his repression by citing the threat of Communist subversion, a claim lent some credence in the early 1960's when several groups of young Paraguayans made abortive attempts at rural guerrilla warfare. He pointed with some pride to the stability he had brought to Paraguay and to his other accomplishments. In an article for the *Nation* (February 23, 1963) Barry M. Lando noted that his achievements included "uncontaminated drinking water for the capital of Asunción, two major highways towards Bolivia and Brazil, the beginnings of a merchant marine . . . , a bridge on the Brazilian border and an extensive project to attract foreign investment." Stroessner boasted that he had built one school a week in Paraguay during his regime.

By the mid-1960's the rigid pattern of the regime was well established. Since then, it has altered remarkably little. Stroessner rules singlehandedly, rewarding his loyal party and military minions with patronage and requiring all civil servants to belong to the Colorado party. So long as it does not become unruly or threatening, opposition is tolerated, and periods of relative liberalization alternate unpredictably with crackdowns. The number of long-term political prisoners has rarely risen higher than 300, since the favored tactic of the powerful security forces, abetted by omnipresent government informers, has been to arrest opposition figures often, treat them roughly, and then release them. With the exception of about two months in 1959, a formal state of siege, renewed by Congress every ninety days, has been in effect for the entire period of Stroessner's rule.

In 1967 Stroessner managed to get through Congress a new Constitution for Paraguay, partly because the old one, adopted in 1940, prohibited presidents from serving for more than two terms. (Stroessner had already served almost three, but he explained that the first was merely the uncompleted portion of Chávez' term.) The new Constitution conveniently legalized two more terms for presidents, and in February 1968, after a campaign in which three opposition parties were allowed a modicum of political activity and press censorship was relaxed, Stroessner was reelected overwhelmingly, with about 70 percent of the vote; in 1973 he won again, with 80 percent. By 1977 he had almost outlasted his own Constitution, so the Colorados obligingly amended it again, granting him unlimited terms of office. In the 1978 Presidential elections his share of the vote was nearly 90 percent.

Stroessner's foreign policy throughout his Presidency has rested largely on three premises: fervent anti-Communism; careful diplomacy to maintain independence from Paraguay's two giant neighbors, Brazil and Argentina; and, above all, unwavering support of the United States. Stroessner promulgated the latter principle in a speech he made to the diplomatic corps of Paraguay in May 1956, when he proclaimed his "complete adherence to the policy of the United States, the great nation which for its culture, strength, and moral and material progress has earned the distinction of being the leading soldier and most important arsenal of the democracies." Paraguay consistently votes with the United States in the United Nations and in the Organization of American States. Stroessner supported American intervention in the Dominican Republic in 1965 and backed the American war effort in Vietnam. In 1968 he accepted an invitation from President Lyndon B. Johnson to spend five days in Washington. At a press conference held during his stay he denied that he was a dictator and asserted, according to the New York *Times* (March 22, 1968), that he had "never lifted a finger against anyone." He added, "It does no good to proclaim freedom of speech and of the press when the population can't read or when there are no roads to distribute newspapers, books, and magazines. . . . For this reason, my government has built thousands of roads, schools, colleges, universities and has created teaching staffs." Many of those improvements were made possible by United States aid, which totaled $160,000,000 between 1954 and 1976.

Stroessner's basic economic policy was made clear in a 1956 Stabilization Plan designed by the International Monetary Fund, which advocated strong but fiscally conservative state support for private businessmen through such measures as low taxes, devaluation of the local currency, a stable money supply, repression of labor unions, and incentives for foreign investment. Its achievements have been noteworthy. Per capita income rose from $200 in 1953 to $283 in 1973, inflation has been low by Latin American standards, and production and trade have expanded sharply, with exports rising from about $31,000,000 in 1953 to $279,000,000 in 1977. Since 1974 a boom has taken place in Paraguay whose driving force was Stroessner's agreement with Brazil in 1973 to build a $10 billion hydroelectric dam at Itaipú, on the Parana river, which, when completed in 1988, will be the largest in the world. Paraguay's sales of its surplus electricity to Brazil are expected to earn the country some $200,000,000 a year.

Critics note a darker side to the economic picture, however, pointing out that Paraguay's leading industry, after agriculture, is smuggling, and that the lucrative trade in everything from cigarettes to consumer goods to heroin is managed by the government, with each branch of the armed forces controlling specific routes. That is only one aspect of what is widely acknowledged to be an all-pervasive system of corruption. Even the Itaipú treaty may not be the blessing it appears, for it commits Paraguay to pay off the enormous construction costs of the dam by selling its electricity to Brazil for fifty years at a fixed low rate.

But perhaps the most telling criticism of Stroessner's fiefdom is that until very recently, it has held back any change in a social system that has usually been described by observers as "feudal" or, at best, "nineteenth-century." Although infant mortality has declined during his rule, and life expectancy has increased, the benefits of economic growth have been concentrated within the small ranching and business class. Serious agarian reform has been grossly neglected, and in 1976 the peasants who make up the majority of Paraguay's population still suffered an abysmally low per capital income of $85.

Inevitably, Stroessner has come into sharp conflict with the Catholic Church of Paraguay, which has increasingly aligned itself with struggles for social justice. Beginning in the late 1960's, the church's efforts to organize peasants have been savagely repressed by the army and police, and many liberal priests have been arrested, beaten, or deported. The church newspaper, *Comunidad,* was shut down in 1969, and in 1972 the Catholic University in Asunción was invaded and wrecked by the police. At one point the Archbishop of Paraguay took the unprecedented step of excommunicating the Minister of the Interior and the Chief of Police and prohibited the celebration of Mass throughout the nation as a protest, but Stroessner proved an implacable opponent, and the repression continued. The most sweeping crackdown came in late 1975 and early 1976, when the armed forces crushed the Catholic Agrarian Leagues. More than 1,000 Paraguayans were arrested, eight Jesuits were deported, and several prisoners died under torture.

After Jimmy Carter took over the American Presidency in 1977, Stroessner again came under pressure from the United States to liberalize his regime. As a result, Stroessner released four political prisoners who had been in jail for twenty years without trial and gradually liberated many of the hundreds of others who had remained incarcerated after the 1976 crackdown. When, in 1978, the State Department of the United States listed Paraguay as one of the Western hemisphere's worst human rights violators, Stroessner did not protest angrily or renounce American military aid, as did some other Latin American nations. (The Congress of the United States later suspended such aid.) But he did ventilate his opinions on the subject to a Brazilian magazine, according to the New York *Times* (February 15, 1978), with the statement, "The theme of human rights is a Trojan horse of international Communism and deserves only one response from us. All rights are respected by my government in accordance with the law and without discrimination."

As the 1980's began, Stroessner faced what was perhaps his greatest challenge, which came not from the terrorized and fragmented opposition but from social changes that had begun to affect even the somnolent backwater of Paraguay. With the increased investment resulting from the Itaipú dam and Stroessner's foreign borrowing, industry has begun to play a more important part in Paraguay's economy.

Migration from rural to urban areas has begun in earnest, and many of the estimated 600,000 Paraguayans who had emigrated to work elsewhere have returned to the country. A massive influx of Brazilians, buying great tracts of Paraguayan land, has also caused some concern. In 1980 Stroessner's government continued to repress attempts to organize peasants; Amnesty International reported that twenty peasants were killed and hundreds arrested in response to their demands for land and economic rights. But observers wondered how long an essentially anachronistic social system and government could continue to withstand present-day destabilizing pressures.

General Stroessner is a husky man, six feet tall, with light-colored hair and moustache and what one writer called "wary eyes." He is amiable and mild-mannered, but taciturn. His speaking style has been called "less than electrifying;" his speeches usually emphasize, besides paeans to tranquillity and economic progress, the sterling values of patriotism and family. His other salient qualities are those associated with the old-style Latin *caudillos,* or dictators, of which breed he may be the last: toughness, courage, boldness, and cunning. He rises before dawn for a workday that often runs from 4:30 A.M. to midnight. A stickler for detail, he insists on approving every promotion in the country's armed forces. Stroessner has fostered a modest cult of personality in Paraguay. The Asunción airport and a city are named for him, posters with his benign countenance are everywhere, and a neon sign in the central square of Asunción proclaims the message "Peace, Work, and Well-Being with Stroessner." But he appears genuinely popular and often can be seen driving about unaccompanied by bodyguards.

Alfredo Stroessner is married to a former schoolteacher, Eligia Mora Delgado. They have two sons, Gustavo Adolfo and Alfredo Hugo, and a daughter, Graciela Concepción. Gustavo, an air force officer, has been mentioned as a possible political heir. The general and his wife live unostentatiously. His hobbies include fishing, hunting, and chess, and he also enjoys flying planes and military helicopters. His state visits have included a second one to Washington in 1978, one to Japan in 1972, and one to Spain in 1973. Among the international leaders to visit Paraguay have been Richard Nixon in 1958 and Charles de Gaulle in 1964. Hospitable to fallen strongmen from other nations, Stroessner harbored Juan Perón in 1955 and Anastasio Somoza in 1978. His well-decorated chest at official military reviews sports the Paraguayan Cruz del Chaco, the Cruz del Defensor, and important medals from Argentina and Brazil.

References: Guardian Weekly 125:12+ O 25 '81 por; Harper's 258:20+ F '79; Newsweek 71:46 F 26 '68; Bourne, Richard. Political Leaders of Latin America (1970); Lewis, Paul H. Paraguay Under Stroessner (1980)

Sutherland, Donald

July 17, 1934- Canadian actor. Address: b.
760 N. La Cienega Blvd.,
Los Angeles, Calif. 90069

Lacking the golden-boy good looks or brooding matinee-idol handsomeness that Hollywood often demands of its leading men, Donald Sutherland established his reputation in the 1960's as a versatile character actor in a handful of horror films and thrillers. His big break came in 1970, when he played the irrepressible Hawkeye Pierce in M*A*S*H, Robert Altman's irreverent smash hit. Known for his attention to the details of characterization, Sutherland earned the best notices of his career for his delineation of the tortured father in Ordinary People, the domestic drama that won the New York Film Critics' award as best picture of 1980. "In movies it's not my character I'm creating. It's the character in the director's head," he said in a recent interview. "My job is to figure out what he wants and give it to him."

Donald McNichol Sutherland was born in St. John, New Brunswick, Canada on July 17, 1934, the son of Dorothy Isabel (McNichol) Sutherland, a mathematics teacher, and Frederick McLae Sutherland, a salesman. A few years later, the family moved to Bridgewater, Nova Scotia, and it was there that Donald Sutherland received his elementary and secondary education in the local public schools. As a boy, Sutherland enjoyed making puppets, and for a time, he dreamed of becoming a sculptor, but as he grew older, he developed an interest in radio broadcasting. By the time he was fourteen, he was a disc jockey on his own radio show.

Following his graduation from high school, Sutherland moved to Toronto, Ontario, where, at the behest of his father, he enrolled as an engineering student in the School of Practical Science at the University of Toronto. He soon discovered that engineering was not to his liking and switched his major to English. Accepting a fellow student's dare, he auditioned for and won a part in the Hart House Theatre staging of James Thurber's The Male Animal. He subsequently appeared at the theatre in productions of The Tempest and Electra. During vacations he played in summer stock at Port Carling, Ontario. Among his more demanding roles was that of the good-natured, slightly batty Elwood P. Dowd in Harvey. After taking his college degree in 1956, he decided to pursue his dramatic career in England. To earn pocket money while he studied acting at the London Academy of Music and Dramatic Art, he drove a gravel truck.

For the next few years Sutherland served an apprenticeship in provincial repertory companies in Nottingham, Chesterfield, Sheffield, Stratford, and Perth. He made his professional debut in London in a bit part in The Gimmick and followed that up with appearances in August for People, The Shewing-up of Blanco Posnet, and Two for the Seesaw. His stage work led to a number of roles in such British television series as The Saint, Gideon's Way, The Avengers, and Man in a Suitcase. The high point of his early television career was his portrayal of Fortinbras in the BBC's critically acclaimed production of Hamlet, which had been filmed on location in Denmark. In 1964, while appearing in a West End production of Spoon River Anthology, he was spotted by an Italian film director who offered him a job in the macabre film The Castle of the Living Dead (American-International, 1964). "I played a witch and a soldier," Sutherland recalled later, "and the last scene showed me fighting with myself." He subsequently took supporting roles in four low-budget horror films, including Dr. Terror's House of Horrors (Paramount, 1965), Die! Die! My Darling! (Columbia, 1965), and The Bedford Incident (Columbia, 1965), a Cold-War sea drama, before setting out for Hollywood in 1967. His first role in an American feature film was that of Vernon Pinkley, the psychopathic draftee who successfully impersonates an officer, in The Dirty Dozen (MGM, 1967), an action-packed adventure about twelve condemned military prisoners on a suicide raid behind Nazi lines.

Over the next few years Sutherland added to his rapidly growing list of credits secondary roles in television series, among them Court-Martial and Name of the Game, in the made-for-television movie The Sunshine Patriot, which was broadcast by NBC-TV on December 16, 1968, and in a few films. He was the authoritative voice of the computer in Billion Dollar Brain (United Artists, 1967), Ken Russell's self-indulgent adaptation of Len Deighton's best-selling spy novel; the Chorus Leader in Oedipus the King (Universal, 1968); a consumptive aristocrat in *Joanna* (Twentieth Century-Fox, 1968); a hired murderer in the brutal crime thriller *The Split* (MGM, 1968); and Lawrence, the well-meaning family friend in *Interlude* (Columbia, 1968), a sugary remake of the 1939 tearjerker *Intermezzo*.

By the end of the 1960's, Sutherland was one of the busiest actors in Hollywood. The year 1970 saw the release of no less than five motion pictures in which he played an important character, ranging from the small but juicy part of Oddball, the tank driver, in *Kelly's Heroes* (MGM), an inconsequential World War II action yarn, to the dual role of Charles and Pierre in Bud Yorkin's *Start the Revolution Without Me* (Warner Brothers), a period farce about two sets of twins who are accidentally reunited on the eve of the French Revolution after a thirty-year separation. In *Alex in Wonderland* (MGM), Paul Mazursky's plotless and almost embarrassingly autobiographical look at contemporary filmmaking, he played the thankless part of Alex Morrison, a promising motion picture director desperately searching for a meaningful story line, with such conviction and good humor that he "[yanked] the film behind him like some balky dog," according to Louise Sweeney, the otherwise unimpressed critic of the *Christian Science Monitor*. He also turned in an ingratiating performance as Father Michael Ferrier, the object of a young governess' misplaced affections, in the sentimental film *The Act of the Heart* (Universal).

The real turning point in Sutherland's career, however, came with the release of Robert Altman's antiestablishment comedy *M*A*S*H* (Twentieth Century-Fox, 1970), a smash hit, both critically and commercially. As Hawkeye Pierce, the cheerfully insolent battlefield surgeon assigned to a behind-the-lines mobile surgical hospital during the Korean war, Sutherland spiked his generally low-keyed characterization with what one critic has called a "dry-martini bite."

The underlying antiwar theme of *M*A*S*H* mirrored Sutherland's personal political views. An outspoken critic of the Vietnam War, he joined forces with Jane Fonda, the actress and antiwar activist, and other like-minded performers to found, in 1971, the Free Theatre Associates, a group dedicated to offering American soldiers an irreverent alternative to the traditional Bob Hope type of USO entertainment. Since they were banned from United States Army bases because of their political views, the troupers presented their program of rock music and withering political satire to enthusiastic audiences of servicemen in nearby theatres and public arenas. *F. T. A.* ("Free the Army"), a documentary film of the group's tour of military bases in Southeast Asia, was released by American International Pictures in 1972. "We must understand that war is finished," Sutherland said, in explaining his political activism to Guy Flatley for a New

York *Times* (February 15, 1970) profile. "War is like capital punishment. It never alters anything. . . . I may not have the precision or the intellect of an astute political critic, but I am concerned with social change. If you do not have some social and political commitment, you might as well give up."

Although he was a guaranteed box-office draw because of the phenomenal popularity of *M*A*S*H,* Sutherland continued to select his roles with care. He often preferred a pithy character part, like that of the Reverend Henry Dupas, the hippie minister, in Jules Feiffer's black comedy *Little Murders* (Twentieth Century-Fox, 1971) or Jesus Christ in *Johnny Got His Gun* (Cinemation Industries, 1971), an offbeat antiwar film, to the lead. "There is more than a challenge in character roles," he told Robert Mottley in an interview for the Washington *Post* (October 4, 1970). "There's longevity. A good character actor can show a different face in every film, and not bore the public."

Over the next few years, Sutherland showed audiences "a different face" in each of his starring roles, too. As the title character in *Klute* (Warner Brothers, 1971), Alan J. Pakula's psychological thriller, he was a diffident private investigator, and he played a laid-back, visionary ex-convict in *Steelyard Blues* (Warner Brothers, 1973), a counterculture comedy with a thin plot line. He took the part of an art historian with extrasensory perception in *Don't Look Now* (Paramount, 1973), a subtly sophisticated horror film directed by Nicholas Roeg; a fascist murderer in Bernardo Bertolucci's *1900;* an insurance company investigator in the routine *Lady Ice* (National General Pictures, 1973); and a bumbling secret agent in *S*P*Y*S* (Twentieth Century-Fox, 1974), a futile attempt to recapture the elusive magic of *M*A*S*H.*

Perhaps Sutherland's best role in the early 1970's was that of Homer Simpson, the sexually repressed accountant in *The Day of the Locust* (Paramount, 1975), John Schlesinger's film of Nathanael West's classic novel about Depression-era Hollywood hangers-on. Critical opinion divided on the merits of the film and on Sutherland's characterization. In his review for *New Times* (May 30, 1975), Frank Rich panned the picture, but he reserved the highest praise for Sutherland's "full-bodied" performance, adding that on a few occasions he came "miraculously close" to carrying the motion picture.

Intrigued by Sutherland's "erased face," Federico Fellini hired him, in 1975, to create the role of Casanova in his proposed adaptation of that legendary libertine's *Memoirs* for the screen. The year-long project was one of the most enriching acting experiences of Sutherland's career. "Fellini stretches you out and the pain can be incredible, but he never lets go, he always pulls you back." he told Martin Knelman of the Toronto *Globe and Mail* (February 12, 1977). When *Fellini's Casa-*

nova was finally released by Universal in 1977, the critics denounced the director for projecting his own image of the character as a shallow hedonist and for deliberately leaching the life out of the *Memoirs,* as both Jack Kroll, writing in *Newsweek,* and Christopher Porterfield, who commented on the film for *Time,* remarked. Most reviewers, however, gave Sutherland good marks for at least trying "to make something positive out of a negation," to use Porterfield's words.

After that fiasco, Sutherland achieved a degree of box-office success in two rip-roaring, old-fashioned adventure movies. His beguiling impersonation of Liam Devlin, an Irish patriot who collaborated with the Nazis during World War II, in *The Eagle Has Landed* (Columbia, 1977) was marred only by a stagey brogue, and in *The Great Train Robbery* (United Artists, 1979), a visually dazzling Victorian period piece, his broad caricature of a fast-fingered locksmith and pickpocket contrasted nicely with Sean Connery's resourceful gentleman thief.

Sutherland interrupted his film work in 1977 to play one of his heroes, Dr. Norman Bethune, a fiercely independent Canadian surgeon who had taken part in the long march in China and died there, a national hero, in 1938, in the Canadian Broadcasting Corporation's production *Bethune.* Returning to motion pictures, he appeared in Claude Chabrol's mystery *Blood Relatives* (1978), in the light comedy *Nothing Personal* (American International, 1979), one of the biggest box-office disappointments of the year, and in several Canadian films, including the thriller *Bear Island* and *A Man, A Woman, and a Bank,* a romantic comedy caper. The actor's credits also include cameos as a clumsy waiter in *Kentucky Fried Movie* (United Film, 1977), a college professor high on drugs in *National Lampoon's Animal House* (Universal, 1978), and a charismatic psychic in *Murder by Decree* (Avco Embassy, 1979).

In a conscious effort to change his image as a "stoned-out freak," Sutherland began, in the late 1970's, to seek out what he called "ordinary" or "straight" parts. "I don't see myself as Cary Grant or Clark Gable," he admitted to Jordan Young in an interview for the New York *Times* (September 23, 1977), "but I see myself playing roles where you can say, 'That's a perfect part for him'—not as a character actor, but as an actor performing a character which is close to one's self. . . . I have found gradually over the years that there is more truth in getting as close to the center of myself as I can. All the characters I've played were based on emotion, really gut-raw emotion. What I would like to achieve is moving them to an intellectual base."

Sutherland's first "ordinary" character was Matthew Bennell, the public health inspector in *Invasion of the Body Snatchers* (United Artists, 1978), an intelligent remake of the 1956 science fiction classic about an insidious takeover of the earth by extraterrestrial beings.

According to Sutherland, of all the characters he had played to date, Bennell was "the closest to the guy who lives in my house." "He was a lot like me," the actor told Young. "The character was straight on what I thought, straight on rationality, straight on observing people in crisis situations. I would like to develop that character and examine him further."

In his auspicious debut as a film director, Robert Redford gave Sutherland the opportunity to do just that when he chose the actor to portray Calvin Jarrett, the confused but loving father of an emotionally disturbed teenage son, in *Ordinary People* (Paramount, 1980). Sutherland's touching interpretation of Jarrett as a decent but befuddled man struggling to hold his family together stunned critics. To take a representative review, Vincent Canby, commenting on the film in the New York *Times* (September 19, 1980), said: "Mister Sutherland realizes his best film role in years, playing a fellow who, filled with love for both his wife and his son, is angrily accused by each of fence-sitting, of being weak and indecisive when he's really the only one in the family with some idea of what is wrong." Even Pauline Kael, who complained in the *New Yorker* (October 13, 1980) that Jarrett was "just a blob created to be tyrannized by Beth [his wife]," conceded that Sutherland gave "a rather graceful performance."

Sutherland, who has long harbored a desire to produce and direct his own films, formed a motion picture production company, McNichol Pictures, Inc., in the late 1970's. "There's an objective part of me that wishes to create movies," he told Sidney Fields of the New York *Daily News* (May 13, 1975). "I'm confident of my perception and ability to realize that. I want to direct because I can, and I'd enjoy it." In the meantime he completed work on two films: *Eye of the Needle* (United Artists, 1981), a World War II spy thriller, based on Ken Follett's best-selling novel, in which he gave a brilliantly understated performance as the ruthless Nazi assassin Faber, and a speculative drama, tentatively titled "Threshold," about a cardiologist who implants the first totally artificial heart. Sutherland made his New York stage debut in February 1981, as Humbert Humbert in Edward Albee's adaptation of Vladimir Nabokov's *Lolita.* The play, which was lambasted by critics, closed after twelve performances.

Once described as looking like a cross between "Christ at the Last Supper" and "Mick Jagger at Altamont," Donald Sutherland has graying blond hair and a long, thin, angular face with blue-green eyes and, according to one reporter, "oddly devilish features—arched eyebrows, pointy teeth, tiny mouth." He stands well over six feet tall (estimates vary from six feet two inches to six feet four inches) and usually weighs about 185 pounds. He keeps fit by running five miles daily. Friends find Sutherland to be complex and temperamental, and he himself concedes that he is, at times, "arrogant," "insensitive," and "self-centered." "I think it's part of the nature of being an actor," he told Ron Base in an interview for the Chicago *Tribune Magazine* (February 18, 1979). "There is a lot of coddling, a lot of self-importance. A lot of self-degradation." Insatiably inquisitive, he often ends up interviewing his interviewers. Although he is a self-confessed workaholic who does not "know how not to [work]," he occasionally takes time out to watch old movies on television, attend professional baseball games, or sail his boat, the *Black Duck.*

Sutherland has been married twice—to Lois May Hardwick, in 1959, and to Shirley Jean Douglas, an actress and the daughter of Thomas C. Douglas, the former premier of Saskatchewan, in 1966. Both marriages ended in divorce. Since 1974 he has lived with Francine Racette, a French-Canadian actress who has appeared as his costar in two Anglo-Canadian films, *Alien Thunder* and *The Disappearance.* The couple delivered their two sons—Roeg, who was named after Nicolas Roeg, and Rossif, the namesake of director Frédéric Rossif—themselves. Sutherland also has a son, Kiefer, and a daughter, Rachel, from his second marriage. He and Miss Racette and their two children have a house in the Brentwood area of Los Angeles, California, and an apartment in Paris, France.

References: Chicago Tribune VI p18+ O 26 '80 pors, mag p16+ F 18 '79; *Esquire* 95:49+ Mr '81 por; *Macleans* 83:40+ S '70 pors; *N Y Times* II p19+ S 23 '79; *Newsday* p12W Je 27 '70 pors; *Time* 95:41 F 2 '70 pors; *Toronto Globe and Mail* p12+ F 12 '77 pors; *Washington Post* G p1+ O 4 '70 por; *International Who's Who,* 1980-81

Suzuki, Zenko

Jan. 11, 1911- Prime Minister of Japan. *Address:* b. Office of the Prime Minister, Tokyo, Japan

Zenko Suzuki, a veteran political strategist known as a "fixer" behind the scenes and a man with virtually no enemies, was chosen Prime Minister of Japan on July 17, 1980, five weeks after the death of his predecessor, Masayoshi Ohira. A member of the lower house of Japan's national Diet since 1947, Suzuki had served the country's fisheries industry as an administrator, trade union organizer, and lobbyist. He attained a reputation as a mediator and conciliator when he was chairman of the executive council of Japan's dominant but much-divided Liberal Democratic party, a post that he occupied since 1968. Although he had served in three medium-level Cabinet posts—as Minister of Posts and Telecommunications, Minister of Health and Welfare, and Minister of Agriculture, Forestry, and Fisheries—the key ministries of foreign affairs, finance, and international trade, from which Prime Ministers had generally been chosen, had eluded him, and he lacked the connections with the business and bureaucratic elite that had traditionally determined national policy. But after a deadlock developed in the upper echelons of the party, Suzuki emerged as the logical candidate of the consensus.

Zenko Suzuki—whose given name means "good fortune"—was born on January 11, 1911 in the Pacific fishing port of Yamada, in Iwate Prefecture, on the northeastern coast of Honshu, Japan's main island. It was from his father, a fishery boss who owned several fishing boats and wielded considerable power locally in an industry noted for factional strife and resistance to change, that Suzuki learned the art of compromise at an early age. After graduating in March 1935 from the Imperial Fisheries Institute (now Tokyo University of Fisheries), he returned to his home district, where he worked for a government fishery agency and organized a national fishery workers' union. Over the years he was director of the fisheries department of the Iwate Prefectural Federation of Fishery Unions; manager and director of the planning department of the Central Fisheries Association; president of the Iwate Prefectural Fishing Port Association; director of the Iwate Prefectural Fisheries Promotion Association; and a member of the central committee of the federation of cooperative associations. Because of his employment in a vital food industry, Suzuki was not drafted into the military service until late in World War II

After World War II, Suzuki became a member of the Japanese Socialist party (Nihon Shakaito), and in Japan's first election under its postwar constitution, in April 1947, he ran successfully as its candidate for Iwate Prefecture in the House of Representatives (Shugiin), or lower chamber, in the national Diet (Kokkai), to which he was reelected thirteen times. In 1949, however, he changed his political affiliation to the more business-oriented Liberal party. He later revealed that his shift in allegiance was a move designed to bring him closer to the center of power, since the doctrinaire Marxist Socialists appeared to be relegated to the opposition for the foreseeable future. According to Suzuki, his constituents felt that as a Socialist he would have lacked the authority to obtain adequate reconstruction aid for his native region, which had recently been devastated by two disastrous typhoons.

Suzuki served in his first sub-Cabinet post, as Parliamentary Vice-Minister for Home Affairs, from November 1952 to May 1953. When, in 1955, the Democrats and Liberals decided to merge their parties, Suzuki was among the founders of the new Liberal Democratic party (Jiyu-Minshuto), which enjoyed strong rural support and favored private enterprise, the alliance with the United States, and the extension of Japanese interests in Asia, but generally regarded the organization and financial power as being more important than ideology. Within the faction-ridden LDP—which continues to dominate Japanese politics—Suzuki gradually rose to some prominence as the second-ranking member of the faction headed by Masayoshi Ohira. In June 1958 he began a year's tenure as chairman of the local administration committee in the House of Representatives. Concurrently with his political activities, Suzuki acted as chief lobbyist within the government for the prosperous and powerful fisheries industry, a function that enhanced his stature within the LDP and earned him the nickname "Mr. Fish."

From July 1960 until July 1961, Suzuki served in his first Cabinet position, as Minister of Posts and Telecommunications, in the government of Prime Minister Hayato Ikeada. In July 1964 he was appointed by Ikeada to the post of Chief Cabinet Secretary, which enabled him to act on occasion as official spokesman for the government. He remained in that position until November of that year, when Ikeada stepped down for reasons of health. In the government of Prime Minister Eisaku Sato, Suzuki served from June 1965 until December 1966 as Minister of Health and Welfare.

In December 1968 Suzuki was named chairman of the LDP executive council, the party's top policy-making body, and he was reappointed nine times between January 1970 and June 1980. The post enabled him to use his formidable skills as a moderator, political strategist, and backroom manipulator in resolving the party's factional struggles and mediating disputes on the national scene. He

is credited, for example, with having established a consensus within the LDP, after serious debate, for normalizing relations between Japan and the People's Republic of China in 1972. Another of his triumphs, for which he won national esteem, was his success in finding a suitable home port for the nuclear-powered freighter *Mutsu* after some two weeks of negotiations with fishermen who had objected to the possible release of radiation by the ship in their fishing grounds.

While serving as Minister of Agriculture, Forestry, and Fisheries in the Cabinet of Prime Minister Takeo Fukuda from December 1976 to November 1977, Suzuki put his negotiating skills to use in the long and difficult talks with the U.S.S.R. over fishing rights. In May 1977 he signed an interim agreement with Soviet officials in Moscow, determining the amount of fish that Japanese fishermen were permitted to catch for the remainder of the year within the Soviet Union's newly established 200-mile zone along its Pacific coast. Referring to the Moscow talks, Suzuki later said that he had "endured something unendurable and survived something unsurvivable." In early 1978 Suzuki—although no longer a member of the Cabinet—helped to negotiate a commercial agreement with New Zealand officials, under which Japan granted New Zealand certain trade advantages in return for access to New Zealand's fishing zone.

When Masayoshi Ohira won a four-way contest among LDP candidates for the Prime Ministership in December 1978, he named Suzuki, his closest aide, as his choice for general secretary of the party. But because of intraparty politics, Ohira was compelled to drop the nomination after it was vetoed by outgoing Prime Minister Takeo Fukuda, who had tried unsuccessfully to win reelection, and who continued to wield considerable power within the LDP as the leader of one of the rival factions.

Following the death of Prime Minister Ohira on June 12, 1980 as the result of a heart attack, Suzuki succeeded him as head of his faction within the LDP. Ohira's death had occurred in the midst of a leadership crisis that began on May 16, when his government failed to obtain a vote of confidence. Although the LDP increased its strength in the national elections of June 22, winning 284 seats in the 511-member lower house, it continued to be rent by factionalism. In the ensuing contest for the Prime Ministership, Suzuki refused to promote his own candidacy, insisting that he was better suited for the role of mediator within the party. But, as a man with few enemies and with a flair for reconciling hostile factions, he gradually emerged as the candidate of the consensus, especially after a deadlock developed between the two front-running candidates, Yasuhiro Nakasone and Toshio Komoto. The compromise choice, senior party leaders decided, was to come from the Ohira faction, since the late Prime Minister was believed to have sacrificed his health, and finally his life, in an effort to forge unity within the LDP.

Suzuki's nomination appeared to be a certainty after his endorsement by former Prime Ministers Takeo Fukuda and Kakuei Tanaka and by the powerful Federation of Economic Organization (Keidanren), representing Japan's leading industrialists. It cleared its final obstacle when no objection was raised at a meeting of the LDP's four supreme advisers on July 7, 1980. Suzuki began fortifying international ties for his forthcoming administration at a memorial service for Ohira on July 9, at which he met with President Jimmy Carter, Chinese Prime Minister Hua Guofeng, and other world leaders.

On July 15, 1980 the LDP's 424 elected members of the two houses of Parliament unanimously chose Suzuki as the party's president, thus ensuring his subsequent election as Prime Minister. With characteristic modesty, Suzuki declared in his three-minute acceptance speech that he knew he lacked the ability for the office but would do his utmost. Later, in a televised news conference, he pledged his continuing devotion to the "politics of harmony."

Suzuki was formally chosen Prime Minister by the two houses of Parliament on July 17, 1980, defeating his nearest rival, Socialist leader Ichio Asukata, by a vote of 291 to 106 in the House of Representatives and 134 to forty-nine in the House of Councillors, or upper house. In choosing his Cabinet, Suzuki demonstrated a masterly command of Japanese political realities, balancing faction against faction and placating potential rivals. The former Ohira faction, which he now headed, received six portfolios; the factions led by Tanaka and Fukuda obtained four each; the group headed by Nakasone was given three; that led by Komoto received two; and an additional two Cabinet seats were given to LDP independents. In a rare display of party harmony, three powerful factional leaders—Nakasone, Komoto, and Ichiro Nakagawa—agreed to accept relatively minor positions and thus retained greater freedom to criticize the government.

Members of the Suzuki faction obtained control of the key portfolios of foreign affairs and of foreign trade and industry, as well as the post of Chief Cabinet Secretary. The office of Foreign Minister went to Masayoshi Ito, a close associate of Ohira, who had served as caretaker Prime Minister in the weeks following the latter's death, and whose selection seemed to indicate Suzuki's commitment to the continuation of the late Prime Minister's foreign policies. The average age of members of the new Suzuki Cabinet was 63.5 years, and nearly two-thirds of them had headed ministries in previous administrations.

Although over the years Suzuki had acquired only limited experience in foreign affairs, trade, and finance, and little was known of his views

in those areas, informed observers predicted that he would become one of Japan's strongest heads of government because of his political expertise. Shortly after taking office, Suzuki assured newsmen that close ties with the United States would remain the cornerstone of his country's foreign policy and that he would try to meet American expectations in regard to military and economic policies. He also declared his government's intentions to maintain close contact with Middle Eastern and Southeast Asian nations, to increase economic and technical aid to resource-rich developing countries, and to cultivate better relations with the U.S.S.R., which had become strained after the Soviet invasion of Afghanistan. To improve the domestic economy, Suzuki indicated that he planned to reduce budget deficits by tightening administrative expenditures, and he proposed cuts in government subsidies, such as those given for rice production, instead of tax increases.

In answer to American demands that Japan assume more responsibility for its own national defense, Suzuki reaffirmed in his first major policy speech, on August 18, 1980, his predecessor's commitment to "steady and significant increases" in military expenditures to reduce his country's dependence on the United States for its security but stressed the strictly defensive nature of such an effort. "We are committed not to become a military power," he declared. The Prime Minister also called for a lessened dependence on public bonds to finance deficit spending, proposed diversification of energy sources to reduce Japan's reliance on imported oil, and promised to clean up corruption in the scandal-ridden LDP.

As 1980 drew to a close, problems facing the Suzuki government included a deadlock, in October, in economic talks with American representatives concerning Japanese automobile exports to the United States and other matters; the question of converting the 1976 political funds control law into a more effective weapon against corrupt practices; the persistence of political violence, much of it by radical student groups; and the Persian Gulf war, which posed the threat of a cutoff of Middle Eastern oil supplies to Japan. Reports from South Korea, a major trading partner of Japan, that the Korean dissident Kim Dae Jung had been sentenced to death, greatly disturbed Suzuki, not only as a gross violation of human rights, but also because the prospect of Kim's execution heightened the threat of mounting instability on the strategically important Korean peninsula. (The death sentence was later commuted to life imprisonment.) Suzuki's continuation as Prime Minister was assured on November 27, 1980, when he was formally reelected LDP president for a two-year term at a convention commemorating the party's twenty-fifth anniversary.

Several points of discord between Japan and the United States were ironed out in talks by Suzuki and President Ronald Reagan during the Japanese Prime Minister's first official visit to Washington, D.C., in May 1981. A joint communiqué issued after the talks included a pledge by Suzuki to step up his country's defense effort. But a reference to a Japanese-American "alliance" provoked criticism among those in Japan to whom any positive commitment to American foreign policy was anathema. Although Suzuki insisted that the statement merely referred to the two countries' "common political values," Suzuki's government was severely challenged, and Foreign Minister Masayoshi Ito was prompted to resign from the Cabinet.

Zenko Suzuki and his wife of some forty years, Sachi, have three daughters and a son. According to the *Guardian* (July 20, 1980), "the Japanese press has diligently researched Mr. Suzuki's personal habits and informed a public hungry for background that [he] is partial to raw fish, noodles, and Johnny Walker Red Label." He enjoys golf and the Japanese game *go*. Unable to converse in foreign languages and relatively unknown in world capitals, he has a reputation among those who know him in his own country for patience, amiability, modesty, good humor, and a proclivity for hard work. A profile in the New York *Times* (July 9, 1980) describes him somewhat unflatteringly as having "square, heavy features, solid jowls, and a rough, inarticulate manner." And Murray Sayle observed in the *New Republic* (September 27, 1980) that "any way you look at him Zenko Suzuki is no oil painting," but added: "The new Japanese Prime Minister is nonetheless what his countrymen call a *happo bijin*, an 'eight-direction beauty' —an expert at sensing the public mood, expressing views that he thinks will command maximum support, and thus looking good from all angles."

References: Asia Research Bulletin p707+ Jl 31 '80; Christian Sci Mon p2 Jl 8 '80 por; Far Eastern Economic R 109:9+ Jl 11-17 '80 por; N Y Times A p4 Jl 9 '80 por, A p10 My 8 '81; Wall St J p17 Jl 18 '80 por; Washington Post A p9 Jl 15 '80 por; International Who's Who, 1980-81; Japan Biographical Encyclopedia & Who's Who, 1964-65

Thomas, Franklin A(ugustine)

May 27, 1934- Foundation official; lawyer. Address: b. Ford Foundation, 320 E. 43d St., New York City, N.Y. 10017; h. 308 Lafayette Ave., Brooklyn, N.Y. 11238

On June 1, 1979 Franklin A. Thomas succeeded McGeorge Bundy as the seventh president of the Ford Foundation, becoming the first black person to head a major philanthropic organization. With assets of $2.8 billion, as of mid-1981, the Ford Foundation is the largest private institution of its kind in the United States, and since 1950 it has disbursed some $5 billion to organizations and individuals in about 100 countries. Thomas, who is a successful lawyer, previously served from 1967 to 1977 as president and chief executive officer of the Bedford-Stuyvesant Restoration Corporation in Brooklyn, New York, which was involved in one of the few successful urban renewal programs of recent years. Under his leadership, the Restoration Corporation helped to establish neighborhood businesses, renovated local residences, and created thousands of new jobs. At the Ford Foundation, Thomas has emphasized such major problem areas as urban decay, social inequality of blacks and women, and Third World poverty as primary targets of organizational activity.

Franklin Augustine Thomas was born in a relatively stable working-class area in the Bedford-Stuyvesant section of Brooklyn, New York on May 27, 1934. His father, James Thomas, a laborer, died when Franklin was twelve. His mother, Viola (Atherley) Thomas, who had emigrated from Barbados, worked as a waitress and housekeeper and went to night school during World War II to qualify as a machinist. The youngest of six children, Franklin Thomas was the only member of his family to go to college. As a boy he shunned street gangs, became active in the Boy Scouts, and developed skill in basketball on the black-top courts of his neighborhood. At Franklin K. Lane High School he was the captain and star of the basketball team and excelled as a student.

Thomas attributes his success to the attitudes instilled in him at home. As he explained to Paula Giddings in an interview for *Encore* (November 19, 1979): "I grew up in a family that just assumed that, one, you were smart and capable, two, that you were going to work hard, and, three, that the combination of these two meant that anything was possible, and no one should be allowed to impose any limitations on you—that the greatest limitation that someone *could* impose on you was if you took it in your head that something you were qualified for or wanted would be withheld. Once you start thinking that way it has to affect your performance."

Thanks to his ability as an athlete, Thomas received a number of college scholarship offers after his graduation from high school in 1952. He turned them down, however, and decided to enroll at Columbia University, where he received no athletic scholarship but was able to obtain a job waiting on tables to help pay his tuition. Thomas starred on Columbia's basketball team, was voted the Ivy League's most valuable player in 1955 and 1956, and became the first black student to serve as captain of an Ivy League varsity team. He still holds the university's record for rebounds in a single season. Thomas also joined the local chapter of the NAACP to campaign for the admission of more black students to the university. He graduated from Columbia with a B.A. degree in 1956.

After college, Thomas accepted an ROTC commission in the Air Force, and from 1956 to 1960 he served in the Strategic Air Command as a navigator on refueling flights from bases in Greenland, England, and Turkey. Several years later he still retained the rank of captain in the Air Force reserve. In 1960 Thomas enrolled in Columbia University Law School, where he was a member of the Phi Delta Phi legal fraternity. In 1962, while still a student, he worked as a legal assistant for the general counsel of the New York State Insurance Department. He obtained his LL.B. degree with moot court honors in 1963 and was admitted to the New York State Bar the following year.

In 1963 and 1964 Thomas worked as an adviser and attorney in the regional New York office of the Federal Housing and Home Finance Agency. In 1964 he was appointed assistant United States attorney for the Southern District of New York. One of the most noteworthy cases he handled in that post involved the prosecution of three men charged with attempting to blow up the Statue of Liberty. As one of three attorneys in the case, he called almost fifty witnesses before the grand jury in the process of building an intricate case of conspiracy. The three defendants were convicted in May 1965. Thomas also worked, in cooperation with Vincent L. Broderick, then chief assistant United States attorney for the Southern District of New

York, on a challenge to the appeal of Nelson C. Drummond, whose conviction on charges of espionage was subsequently upheld by the courts. In addition to his formal duties, Thomas was captain of a basketball team organized by himself and his co-workers, which won a number of victories over the rival teams of the FBI and other law enforcement agencies.

When Broderick became police commissioner of New York City in 1965 he offered Thomas the position of deputy police commissioner in charge of legal matters in the city police department. Thomas accepted the offer, succeeding Leonard E. Reisman in the $17,500-a-year post in October of that year, the fourth black man to serve as a deputy police commissioner of New York City. In his new job, Thomas headed a staff of thirty attorneys, served as legal adviser to the commissioner, and directed the department's legislative program.

By 1966, Bedford-Stuyvesant, the second-largest black community in the United States—exceeded only by Chicago's South Side—was, like many other American urban ghettos, plagued increasingly by social unrest, urban decay, and high unemployment. In an effort to remedy that situation, United States Senator Robert F. Kennedy assembled businessmen and civic leaders to form the experimental Bedford-Stuyvesant Restoration Corporation. Corporate administration was divided between the Development Services Board, made up largely of white business and community leaders through whom funds were raised, and the Restoration Corporation Board, composed mainly of black members, which supervised the local community activities of the organization. As the police department's representative at the early organizational meetings, Thomas soon caught Kennedy's attention, and it was not long before the latter asked him to become president and chief executive officer of the new corporation. Thomas accepted, resigning from his job at the police department early in 1967.

"A lot of tensions existed among some members of the community in Bedford-Stuyvesant," Thomas told an Associated Press reporter, as reported in the Houston *Post* (May 13, 1979), "the sense being that this was a new group coming in, imposing on the locals. It seemed the whole idea would go down the drain. One of the few things local factions agreed on was that I was O.K. because I was born and raised there." The factions in the 100-block community of some 450,000 inhabitants included feminists, blacks of varying economic strata, Puerto Ricans, and the so-called "poverty warlords" out to exploit racial tensions and offers of government assistance.

One of Thomas' first and most delicate tasks was to eliminate the distinction between the Development Services Board and the Restoration Corporation Board, an arrangement considered intolerable by many. Without any fanfare, the two boards were reorganized under his direction into a single governing unit. On April 1, 1968 Thomas announced that a $100,000,000 pool of mortgage funds had been pledged by a group of banks, insurance companies, and savings and loans institutions to hire unemployed youths to renovate homes in the crumbling neighborhood.

Thomas later described his early experience as head of the Restoration Corporation as "a crash course in management 101 to about postgraduate work," according to the *Wall Street Journal* (February 15, 1979). In the ten years he headed the Bedford-Stuyvesant Restoration Corporation, Thomas earned a nationwide reputation and compiled a long list of impressive achievements. A $6,000,000 plaza complex housing small shops, businesses, and the Billie Holliday Theater was constructed during his tenure; 125 businesses providing 3,300 jobs were established; several thousand people were placed in additional jobs or training programs; and the IBM Corporation was induced to build an $11,000,000 plant in the area. In addition, 3,337 homes were renovated, community service centers were set up, and mortagages were extended to some 1,100 home owners.

The Bedford-Stuyvesant Restoration Corporation spent some $63,000,000 in public and private funds under Thomas' guidance and earned an outstanding reputation for administering one of the country's rare successful urban renewal projects. One of the major contributors to the corporation was the Ford Foundation, which, under the leadership of McGeorge Bundy, devoted much of its attention to civil rights in the 1960's and 1970's and spent more than $8,000,000 on the Bedford-Stuyvesant project from 1967 on. In 1977 Thomas was named a trustee of the Ford Foundation. That same year he resigned from the presidency of the Restoration Corporation and resumed the practice of law. "I agreed to serve two years and stayed ten," Thomas told Roger B. May of the *Wall Street Journal* (February 15, 1979). He opened a law office in Manhattan in order to be able, in his words, to "reflect and think about being a lawyer." When Archibald L. Gillies, the president of the John Hay Whitney Foundation, ran unsuccessfully for a seat on the New York City Council in 1977, Thomas assumed Gillies' duties for a nine-month period. During that period he focused his attention primarily on questions of urban economic renewal.

Earlier, Thomas had turned down an offer from President-elect Jimmy Carter of the Cabinet post of Secretary of Housing and Urban Development, a fact that was reported by Carter at a news conference on December 16, 1976. Thomas later told John Kifner of the New York *Times* (January 30, 1979) that the HUD job was not "what the last ten years had positioned me to do." He added: "Two things went through my mind. Did I think I could make a unique difference? I didn't see that I could. And, as I envisioned how my time would be spent, it seemed to me I would be spending half my time or more testifying before committees of Congress about existing programs, a lot of which I have questions about."

McGeorge Bundy, national security adviser to Presidents John F. Kennedy and Lyndon B. Johnson, and president of the Ford Foundation since 1966, had announced as early as 1974 his intention to retire in 1979. Consequently, a seven-member search committee was established to seek out a qualified person to replace Bundy as the $120,000-a-year head of the world's largest and richest foundation. The panel placed ads in leading newspapers and solicited suggestions. It reviewed lists of Rhodes Scholars, members of minority groups, women, former White House fellows, and even United States Congressmen. After a year's deliberation and a review of over 300 applications for the job, the committee announced on January 30, 1979 the selection of Franklin A. Thomas to replace Bundy as president of the Ford Foundation effective June 1, 1979.

Reaction to the panel's choice was universally favorable. "Frank Thomas' appointment as head of a major bulwark of American institutional life heralds a new era of black inclusion, not only as soldiers in our society, but as generals commanding its heights," Vernon Jordan wrote in his syndicated column appearing in the Detroit *Free Press* (February 9, 1979). Thomas himself had some misgivings about the job, as he told Paula Gidding of *Encore*. "I was not sure how I would respond if the position were offered to me," he remarked. "I know that sounds strange, but I looked at my present job, the influence over the things I felt important, the privacy it afforded me, and I wasn't so sure that the Ford job would enhance these things, and if they did, at what cost."

The recession and a sharp decline in stock market values had caused the assets of the foundation to shrink from $4 billion in the mid-1960's to $2.2 billion by 1979, a figure that increased to $2.8 billion over the next two years. Its yearly program budget, which had been as high as $200,000,000 in the mid-1970's, had dropped to $98,700,000 by 1978. Thomas' first major decision as head of the Ford Foundation was to order a meticulous review of the organization's administrative structure, assets, and philanthropic activities. The review process, which lasted more than eighteen months, was described by Kathleen Teltsch in the New York *Times* (February 8, 1981) as "one of the longest transition periods for any large institution." Nevertheless, certain initiatives were taken during that period, one of the most important of which was the development of a closer working relationship between the foundation and business, taking the form of joint ventures to finance major projects. In 1980 the Ford Foundation and seven other organizations formed the Local Initiatives Support Corporation in an effort to revitalize American communities, and similar joint ventures were organized for overseas projects.

The foundation also adopted new policies with regard to relationships between the sexes. Financial grants were carefully examined to determine their effects on women and to eliminate what might be considered sexist biases. Within the administration, men were hired to fill clerical, secretarial, and other support positions, and the foundation introduced paid parental leave for fathers among its employees, on the theory that child-rearing should be a joint male-female enterprise. But Thomas' major emphasis was on reducing bureaucratic overhead, shoring up the fund's shrinking capital base, and encouraging joint ventures and local initiatives. "There is a terrible fear in the foundation world—and in society—of admitting that most change is incremental," he told an interviewer for U.S. News & World Report (March 23, 1981). "Somehow you gain your greatest credibility when you talk in terms of great vision."

The conservative mood that heralded the 1980's and the foundation's financial troubles were to some extent responsible for Thomas' relatively cautious approach. After the sharp decline in its capital assets in the mid-1970's, the trustees had drastically reduced spending commitments. Staff and budgets were sliced almost in half, and the board even considered ending the Ford Foundation altogether. During the first year of Thomas' presidency, however, the fund was for the first time in years able to maintain its spending level without dipping into its capital reserves.

One reason for the Foundation's greater solvency was Thomas' de-emphasis of expensive studies "leading to more studies," which he considered generally sterile, in favor of more dynamic, action-oriented programs. He also sharply reduced staff size. In May 1981, for example, Thomas allowed the contracts of some thirty of the fund's forty-five program officers to lapse and took additional steps to reduce management and salary costs. Large-scale support for world population control was phased out, and plans were made to close some overseas offices. "We cannot do everything," Thomas explained, as quoted in the New York Times (February 8, 1981).

Retrenchment activities caused some disaffection among Ford Foundation employees, and there were persistent press rumors of "staff malaise." Nevertheless, the cutbacks allowed the fund to earmark $240,000,000 for grants in 1981 and 1982, its largest allocation since the early 1970's. The 1981 budget included $43,400,000 for urban renewal and aid to the poor, $27,100,000 to fund human rights activities, $23,000,000 for Third World rural poverty programs, and lesser grants for education and studies on immigration and foreign policy.

Thomas has served as a director or trustee of several organizations, including the John Hay Whitney Foundation, the Foreign Policy Study Foundation, and the Columbia Law School Alumni Association, and he has sat on the boards of directors of such corporations as the Columbia Broadcasting System, the Aluminum Corporation of America, the Cummins Engine Company, Allied Stores Corporation, and the New York Life Insurance Corporation. In 1969 he and Dr. M. Moran Weston, rector of Harlem's St. Philip's Episcopal Church, were named the first black members of Columbia University's board of trustees. As the only black person sitting on Citicorp's twenty-six member board of directors, Thomas reportedly was instrumental in persuading that company to end its loans to the white supremacist government of South Africa. Thomas holds honorary degrees from several universities, including Yale, Fordham, Pace, Columbia, and the Pratt Institute. He received the Lyndon B. Johnson Foundation award for "contribution to the betterment of urban life" in 1974 and Columbia University's Medal of Excellence in 1976. In 1979 Thomas, who had visited South Africa with Vernon Jordan three years earlier, became chairman of the privately financed eleven-member Study Commission on United States Policy Toward Southern Africa, and he wrote the foreword to its report Time Running Out (1981), which urges the United States to persuade the South African government to give its nonwhite population its fair share of political power.

Franklin A. Thomas' marriage to the former Dawn Conrada, a schoolteacher and book editor, ended in divorce in 1972. Their oldest son, Keith, has been attending college, while the three younger children, Hillary, Kerrie, and Kyle, live with their mother in New Jersey. Thomas, who stands six feet four inches tall, lives in a restored brownstone building in Bedford-Stuyvesant and has a retreat in upstate New York. He socializes with a small group of friends, including Vernon Jordan, Eleanor Holmes Norton, Gloria Steinem, and John Hay Whitney. "The more conservative mood of the society means that it is necessary to make a different kind of case than used to be required to get public support for social needs," Thomas told the interviewer for U.S. News & World Report (March 23, 1981). "It is no longer enough to simply state that there is a particular need. . . . Today, a greater level of understanding of a problem and ways of addressing it are required, along with a greater sophistication in presenting it, so that you end up being inclusive of more of the values and interests in society."

References: Encore p34+ N 19 '79 pors; N Y Times p28 O 23 '65 por, B p3 Ja 30 '79; New Yorker 57:25+ Ag 31 '81; Newsweek 93:39 F 12 '79 por; Britannica Book of the Year, 1980; International Who's Who, 1981-82; 1,000 Successful Blacks (1973); Who's Who Among Black Americans, 1977-78; Who's Who in America, 1980-81

Thompson, Hunter S(tockton)

July 18, 1939- Writer. Address: h. "Owl Farm,"
Woody Creek, Colo. 81656

The "new journalism," described by Tom Wolfe, one of its original practitioners, as a nonfiction form with "the emotional impact usually found only in novels and short stories," has been carried to an idiosyncratic extreme, beyond any pretense of objectivity, by Hunter S. Thompson, the once and perhaps future "mad-dog prince of Gonzo journalism." "Unlike Tom Wolfe or Gay Talese," Thompson once explained, "I almost never try to *reconstruct* a story. . . . Gonzo is just a word I picked up because I liked the sound of it—which is not to say there isn't a basic difference between the kind of writing I do and the Wolfe/Talese style. They tend to go back and recreate stories that have already happened, while I get right in the middle of whatever I'm writing about—as personally involved as possible."

Thompson's first book, *Hell's Angels* (1966), about the notorious motorcycle gang, was fairly conventional in comparison with his bizarrely comic stream-of-consciousness socio-political writing in *Fear and Loathing in Las Vegas* (1972) and *Fear and Loathing: On the Campaign Trail '72* (1973). The central character in those wild, sprawling satires was "Dr. Thompson," a snarling, drug- and alcohol-crazed refugee from the failed psychedelic dream of the 1960's hurling creative vituperation at the greed and corruption of the alien society in which he found himself in the 1970's. After Thompson quit his position as national affairs editor of *Rolling Stone* magazine (where most of his Gonzo writing first appeared) in 1976, little was heard from the maniacal "doctor," and in

an author's note prefacing *The Great Shark Hunt* (1979), Thompson seemed to imply that he was looking for another literary persona. Whatever his future course, many critics believe that Thompson has already established a lasting place for himself in American literature on the strength alone of *Fear and Loathing in Las Vegas,* which some regard as the funniest American prose work since *Naked Lunch.*

Hunter Stockton Thompson was born in Louisville, Kentucky, on July 18, 1939, the son of Jack R. Thompson, an insurance agent, and Virginia (Ray) Thompson. After attending public schools in Louisville, he joined the United States Air Force, in which he did sports writing for a base newspaper in Florida. In 1958, two years before his term of enlistment was up, he was honorably discharged from the Air Force after a commanding officer reported that "his flair for invention and imagination" and "rebellious disregard for military dress and authority . . . sometimes seem to rub off on the other airmen."

After his discharge, Thompson took, and was soon fired from, a writing job with the Middletown (New York) *Record* and a traineeship at *Time* magazine, and he wrote for a bowling magazine in Puerto Rico until it failed. In 1960, at least partly in emulation of Jack Kerouac, he traveled across country to California, finished a never-published novel while living in Big Sur, and investigated the North Beach beatnik scene in San Francisco.

From California, Thompson went to South America, where he traveled for two years, from 1961 to 1963, and had his first success as a journalist, sending dispatches on such subjects as local Indian life, smuggling, tin mining, and jungle banditry to the now defunct Dow-Jones weekly, *National Observer,* from Colombia, Ecuador, and other countries. Returning to the United States, he continued to write for the *National Observer* on Western drifters crowded by technology, Indians in Washington state fighting for fishing rights, and other underdog or offbeat topics. He quit writing for the *National Observer* when it refused to let him cover the "Free Speech" movement at the University of California at Berkeley.

Settling in San Francisco, Thompson resumed his efforts at fiction while earning a bare subsistence driving a cab, doing odd jobs, and turning out an occasional article, such as one on Berkeley's radicals for the *Nation* in 1965 and another on the hippie drug culture of San Francisco's Haight-Ashbury for the New York *Times Magazine* in 1967. Following the publication of an article on the Hell's Angels by Thompson in the *Nation,* in May 1965, his mailbox piled up with book offers, and he accepted the one that came from Random House.

The first reporter to meet with the Hell's Angels on their own turf instead of relying on police information, Thompson rode with them for a year—an experience that culminated in his being badly beaten up in an internal gang brawl—in order to produce *Hell's Angels: A Strange and Terrible Saga.* While critical of the authorities and the media for exaggerating, for their own opportunistic reasons, both the numbers of Angels and the magnitude of their depredations (and thus enhancing their vaunted status as savage outlaws), he detailed their actual offenses and defined the real threat they represent. Thompson saw the Angels as "the first wave of a future that nothing in our history has prepared us to cope with," the avant-garde of a smoldering horde of uprooted unemployables. "Their lack of education has not only rendered them completely useless in a highly technical economy, but it has also given them the leisure to cultivate a powerful resentment . . . and to translate it into a destructive cult." Millions of more passive losers admire them, he wrote, because at least "they have banded together. . . . They may not have an answer, but at least they are still on their feet." Some critics were bothered by the cartoon quality given to violence in *Hell's Angels,* but most seemed to agree with the reviewer for *Choice* (June 1977) that there is in print no more "accurate a description or . . . plausible an analysis" of the Hell's Angels than Thompson's.

Not long after his experience with the Hell's Angels, Thompson's political consciousness was, as he put it, "really jerked around." When covering the Democratic Convention in Chicago in August 1968 as a straight reporter, he was caught in the clash of police with anti-Vietnam war demonstrators, saw "innocent people beaten senseless," and was himself struck with a billy club. He came away from the events in Chicago convinced, as he later told friends, that "we *have* to get into politics, if only in self-defense." Thus radicalized, he became a prime mover in the "freak politics" movement in Aspen, Colorado. He and many others from the counterculture had taken refuge in the Aspen area and, having seen commercialism destroy, in turn, the beatnik and hippie communities in such places as San Francisco, they were determined to prevent the ski and real estate industries from despoiling Aspen. On his return from Chicago, Thompson persuaded Joe Edwards, a lawyer and fellow "freak," to run for mayor of Aspen on an anti-development platform, and in a subsequent election Thompson himself ran for sheriff of Pitkin County on the same platform. (He promised to tear up the streets, replant them with grass, and scare off the "greedheads" by renaming Aspen "Fat City.") Edwards lost by six votes, and Thompson, while also losing overall, won three of the six major precincts in the county.

Apace with the growth of his interest in politics, Thompson's writing took on the intensely adversary, anti-Establishment quality that became one of the distinguishing characteristics of Gonzo journalism. He traces the genesis of the Gonzo style to one specific desperate situation, a deadline crisis when he was writing a story on the 1970 Kentucky Derby for *Scanlan's* magazine. "I'd blown my mind, couldn't work," he recounted in the *Playboy* interview. "So finally I just started jerking pages out of my notebook and numbering them and sending them to the printer. I was sure it was the last article I was ever going to do for anybody. Then when it came out, there were massive numbers of letters, phone calls, congratulations, people calling it a 'great breakthrough in journalism.' And I thought . . . , if I can write like this and get away with it, why should I keep trying to write like the New York *Times?* It was like falling down an elevator shaft and landing in a pool full of mermaids." He also said that his early experience in sportswriting, where "you get a tremendous leeway with the usage of words," was a natural preparation for Gonzo journalism. As for the name Gonzo, its source was one of the admiring notes Thompson received after the article on the Kentucky Derby appeared in *Scanlan's.* The note was from Bill Cardoso, a writer whom he had met when he was covering the 1968 Nixon campaign for the *National Observer.* Cardoso pronounced the Derby piece "real Gonzo," and the name stuck.

It was to their mutual benefit that Thompson and *Rolling Stone* magazine found each other in 1970. "*Rolling Stone* was the first place I had been where I could write exactly what I felt," Thompson has said. *Rolling Stone,* for its part, was trying to set a new course away from its original, narrow rock 'n' roll orientation, and Hunter's wide-open writing contributed more to that effort than any other innovation tried by the magazine's young publisher, Jann Wenner. Thompson's first article in *Rolling Stone,* "The Battle of Aspen: Freak Power in the Rockies," was followed by "Strange Rumblings in Aztlan" and the two-part "Fear and Loathing in Las Vegas," which became the book of the same name.

Fear and Loathing in Las Vegas: A Savage Journey to the Heart of the American Dream (Random House, 1971) began as a double assignment, to cover a motorcycle race and a national drug enforcement convention in Las Vegas. In executing the assignment, Thompson largely ignored both events to focus on his trip to the Nevada gambling capital and his sojourn there. In that nightmarish odyssey, Thompson and his traveling companion (an Hawaiian-shirted Samoan lawyer), "bent and twisted" on alcohol and assorted chemicals (from "high-powered blotter acid" to "uppers, downers, screamers, laughers"), were depicted in continual feverish flight from the consequences of driving infractions, wrecked rent-a-cars, unpaid hotel bills, and their own fits of paranoia. "I lost all track of the ratio between what was true and what was not," Thompson later said.

Underlying the madness in *Fear and Loathing in Las Vegas* was a serious theme, a message of wistfulness for the time in the 1960's when "the energy of a whole generation [came] to a head in a long fine flash." From the vantage point of 1971 he asserted, in contrast, "We are wired into a *survival* trip [and] uppers are going out of style. . . . 'Consciousness expansion' went out with [President Johnson] and it is worth noting, historically, that downers came in with Nixon." Within that context, Thompson became an heroic outlaw pitted against the hustlers of Las Vegas, a city of raw power and blatant wealth, of that extreme negation of the dream of the "flower children," the "shark ethic."

Reviewing *Fear and Loathing in Las Vegas* in the New York *Times Book Review* (July 23, 1972), Crawford Woods wrote: "The form that reached apotheosis in [Norman Mailer's] *Armies of the Night* reaches the end of its rope in *Fear and Loathing,* a chronicle of addiction and dismemberment so vicious that it requires a lot of resilience to sense that the author's purpose is more moralizing than sadistic. He is moving in a country where only a few cranky saviors—Jonathan Swift for one—have gone before. And he moves with the cool integrity of an artist indifferent to his reception."

It was Thompson who, against the resistance of most of the *Rolling Stone* staff, persuaded Jann Wenner to make the salutary venture into political reportage. In covering the 1972 Presidential campaign, Thompson, true to Gonzo form, was in a chronic, frantic rush to meet deadlines and never far from a nervous breakdown. Characteristically, he was as candid in his partiality for George McGovern as he was in his scorn for some of the other candidates, including Richard Nixon ("the Werewolf in us, the bully, the shyster").

Because "writing about politics would paralyze [his] brain if he couldn't have a slash of weird humor now and then," Thompson in his campaign coverage invented such stories as one about John Chancellor, the distinguished broadcast journalist, mischievously doctoring Thompson's drink with a "heavy hit of black acid" and another about a Brazilian doctor flying in "with an emergency packet of [the exotic drug] Ibogaine" for Edmund Muskie. The lunacy aside, Thompson's reportage was of a quality to prompt Dan Rather, the CBS newsman, to "wonder where [he, Rather, had] been as a journalist." Displaying a shrewd investigative and analytical ability, Thompson was the first to predict McGovern's capture of the Democratic nomination, and he uncovered plans for funneling mob money into the Humphrey campaign, noted the declining importance of party organization in the primaries, and revealed the intricate maneuvering behind a challenge to the South Carolina delegation at the Democratic Convention.

The respect Thompson had earned in the liberal political community was manifested after the campaign, when a number of important strategists from the Kennedy, McCarthy, and McGovern staffs (among them, Frank Mankiewicz,

Adam Walinsky, Patrick Caddell, and Richard N. Goodwin) responded to his convocation of a symposium to produce an agenda for "a change in politics in this country." The convention, held in Elko, Nevada, "descended into gibberish," as Thompson reported.

His work trying to organize a Washington office for *Rolling Stone* cut into Thompson's writing output, and when he did apply himself to the typewriter again, he hit a writer's block. (A friend and fellow *Rolling Stone* editor had a possible explanation: "It's a terrible responsibility to have to keep topping yourself when you have a reputation for being the nation's leading looney.") His 1973 article "Fear and Loathing at the Superbowl"—in which he discussed coach Vince Lombardi's winning-is-all approach to football and Richard Nixon's similar political philosophy as reflections of general violent competitiveness in the United States—had the old Gonzo touch, as did his articles on Watergate for *Rolling Stone,* but such instances became increasingly rare. Contracting malaria in Kinshasa, Zaire when he went there to cover the Muhammad Ali-George Foreman fight, he failed to attend the bout and produced no story at all. Sent to Saigon by *Rolling Stone* a few weeks before the final collapse of the American military intervention there, he produced nothing but several cables about such matters as his expense account and left safely before the fall of Saigon for Laos, where he wrote a lackluster two-page dispatch. After returning to the United States, he buried himself in research for a novel until the early summer of 1976, when he came forth with his last *Rolling Stone* article, a curious political piece favorable to Jimmy Carter, then the Democratic candidate for President. Thompson, who had been feuding off and on with Jann Wenner all along, became furious when Wenner ran as the cover line for the article, "An Endorsement, with Fear and Loathing." He left *Rolling Stone,* apparently for good.

The Great Shark Hunt (Summit Books, 1979) brought together a variety of pieces Thompson had written over the previous sixteen years. Regarding the author's note stating that Thompson had "finished the life I planned to live" so that "everything from now on will be a new life" and signed, "HST #1 R.I.P.," Nicholas Lemann wrote in *Esquire* (September 1979): 'To say what he wanted to say, [Thompson] turned himself into Dr. Thompson, Gonzo journalist, [a character who] is really a modern version of a classic kind of American hero—the rebellious, irreverent, drunken wanderer driven to wild misbehavior by the encroachments of civilization. . . . As for the death of Dr. Thompson, the proximate cause seems to have been his creator's bitter falling-out with the editor of *Rolling Stone.* But perhaps the good doctor was also a victim of changing times. He saw America as a simple place—gross and corrupt and ruled by evil men but simple nonetheless. Now . . . it seems more complicated."

The misadventures of Thompson and his old friend and attorney, Oscar Zeta Acosta, were the inspiration for the motion picture *Where the Buffalo Roam* (Universal, 1980), on which Thompson served as executive consultant and screenplay collaborator. In the film, set in the heyday of the counterculture in the late 1960's, Thompson was represented in his "Doctor" persona (portrayed by Bill Murray) and Acosta became Karl Lazlo (Peter Boyle), an "overweight, paranoid Chicano." The movie was generally panned for its "sophomoric slapstick" and "relentless mayhem."

Hunter S. Thompson is a lean but sturdy six feet three inches tall. His characteristic attire includes tennis shoes, shorts or jeans, a loud, untucked shirt, and dark aviator glasses. He facetiously attributes his loss of hair to overindulgence in alcohol and other mind-altering substances as well as tobacco. Thompson and Sandra Dawn, who were married on May 19, 1963, have a teenaged son, Juan. Thompson, who has several pets (a myna bird and some peacocks and Doberman pinschers), lives on a 100-acre farm in Woody Creek, Colorado, a few miles from Aspen. On a hillside near his home, Thompson has mounted a series of gongs as a shooting gallery for him and his .44 Magnum. In writing, Thompson usually speaks his first draft into a tape recorder and does the final draft on an electric typewriter. Under the name "Raoul Duke" the writer is a running character in Garry Trudeau's comic strip, *Doonesbury*. In Gonzo journalism, Raoul Duke is the alter ego of Dr. Thompson (whose doctorate is self-bestowed).

References: Esquire 92:92 S '79 por; N Y Times Bk R p54 O 14 '79 por; New Times 7:22+ D 10 '76 pors; Playboy 21:75+ N '74 pors; Contemporary Authors 1st rev vols 17-20 (1976); Who's Who in America, 1980-81

Tiger, Lionel

Feb. 5, 1937- Anthropologist; educator. Address:
b. Research Office, The Harry Frank
Guggenheim Foundation, 17 W. 9th St.,
New York City, N.Y. 10011

Lionel Tiger, who has been a professor of anthropology at Rutgers University since 1968, was trained as a sociologist, but he thinks of himself as a "comparative zoologist" whose subject is man. In five controversial books, including the best-selling *The Imperial Animal*, and over sixty professional articles on such subjects as the behavior of men in groups, sex-role patterns, and the roots of optimism, he has expounded the radical view that human behavior has evolutionary, genetic origins. Largely because he takes his evidence from the fields of ethology, primatology, zoology, and related disciplines, Tiger has been criticized by some of his colleagues, mainly the cultural determinists, for what they see as his shortcomings in methodology, but in recent years, he has won the support of many sociobiologists, among them Edward O. Wilson. His books, most recently *Optimism: The Biology of Hope*, have been compared to the informal, speculative essays of Charles Darwin as well as to the popular but academically suspect works of Desmond Morris and Robert Ardrey. "He creates a ferment of ideas," anthropologist Robin Fox, Tiger's longtime friend and collaborator said in a recent interview, "but sadly, he's had to pay a great penalty for being original."

The only child of Martin Tiger, a Latvian immigrant who operated a small grocery, and Lillian (Schneider) Tiger, Lionel Tiger was born on February 5, 1937, in Montreal, Canada. In interviews, he has frequently alluded to his stable childhood in the sizable Jewish community there, although he eventually rebelled against its dogmatic dictates. "It was probably a very special crucible, because it provided a kind of formal cynicism that you simply had to have," he explained years later to Dom Moraes in an interview for *Voices For Life: Reflections on the Human Condition* (1975). "It was a good way of becoming quickly skeptical about systems." Educated in Montreal's public schools, he attended Baron Byng High School, where he took part in intramural sports and such extracurricular activities as the film society and the literary magazine.

Following his graduation from high school in 1953, Tiger enrolled at McGill University in

Montreal, where he majored in sociology and English. He won the Chester McNaughton Prize for Creative Writing and served, successively, as managing editor and features editor of the *McGill Daily,* the campus newspaper, and as a script writer for the *Red and White Revue.* In his senior year he was chosen as McGill's Student Society's representative to the World University Senate Study Seminar in West Africa. After obtaining his B.A. degree, with distinction, in 1957, he remained at the university for graduate work in sociology. "I was a victim of the middle-class idea that you have to go to college, and then I just kept on getting scholarships," he told Jack Robbins of the New York *Post* (July 12, 1967). He earned his M.A. degree in sociology in 1959, after submitting a thesis on the relationship between bureaucratic structures and research and innovation in the Pulp and Paper Institute of Canada.

Continuing his graduate career at the London School of Economics and Political Science, Tiger received his Ph.D. degree in political sociology in 1963. His doctoral dissertation, *Bureaucracy and Charisma in Ghana,* was a study of the civil service in that newly independent African country. Tiger's field research in Ghana became a determining factor in his decision to turn his attention from sociology to anthropology. As he traveled around the country, he was struck by the many similarities between his native culture and that of the Ghanaians, resemblances that could not be explained by the "common British socialization," as Tiger put it. His observations, when added to the information that he picked up from talks with visiting archaeologists, paleontologists, and zoologists, led him to think more and more in the "generous terms" of biology. He told Dom Moraes: "The biological perspective seemed to me more generous because it permitted an expansion of sociological imagination to include all members of the species with equal validity. One ceased instantly talking about advanced or backward people."

Returning to North America in January 1963, Tiger taught briefly as a visiting lecturer in the department of sociology and anthropology at Western Washington State College (now Western Washington University, in Bellingham). He then accepted a post as assistant professor of sociology at the University of British Columbia in Vancouver. Most of his early professional articles, published in such journals as *Current History* and the *Bulletin of African Studies in Canada,* discussed the implications of his research in Ghana, and he was one of the authors of *Discipline and Discovery* (University of British Columbia Press, 1966), a proposal for arts education, but his interest in biology and its possible application to the study of social organizations and processes continued to grow. That interest intensified in 1965, when he met Robin Fox, a like-minded anthropologist, while both were attending a symposium of the Royal Society at the London Zoo. "Once the trivial novelty of the conjunction of our names wore off," the pair wrote later, "we became aware of the serious identity of our interests in the role of biology in the process of human social life." Their first collaboration, "The Zoological Perspective in Social Science," a paper published in the March 1966 issue of *Man: The Journal of the Royal Anthropological Institute,* was a kind of prolegomenon to a discipline that did not yet exist. In 1967 Fox accepted an appointment as chairman of the department of anthropology at Rutgers University, and the following year, Tiger joined the faculty there as well as an associate professor of anthropology.

Dissatisfied with the generally accepted sociological theory that most of the differences between men and women result from cultural patterning, in his first book, *Men in Groups* (Random House, 1969), Tiger proposed a hypothesis of biologically programmed "male bonding," an enduring term that he coined to explain the universal propensity of men to band together. Drawing on published research in biology, ethology, anthropology, and other related disciplines, he saw in armies, corporations, athletic teams, governments, and all-male secret societies a genetic vestige of the hunting parties of primitive man and of the male-dominated social systems of his primate relatives. Contending that "male bonding patterns reflect and arise out of man's history as a hunter," he suggested that aggression was "a 'normal' feature of the human biologically based repertoire, a type of behavior intrinsic to man's belief and his effective interaction with his social environment."

Commenting in *Life* magazine (June 20, 1969), Robert Ardrey hailed *Men in Groups* as "the first genuinely creative contribution to our understanding of human arrangements since David Riesman's *The Lonely Crowd."* While other reviewers occasionally faulted Tiger for his use of jargon and his manner of presentation, many acknowledged the important implications of both his thesis and his unorthodox, multidisciplinary approach. Because of its controversial nature, the book received wide attention. As Tiger facetiously remarked years later, it "didn't make me rich, just famous."

Because *Men in Groups* presented a well-documented, carefully reasoned case for biologically-based male dominance, it inevitably incurred the wrath of the nascent women's liberation movement. Although Tiger insisted that he personally deplored male chauvinism, he repeatedly defended his thesis against the feminists' accusation that it was ideologically constructed on television talk shows and in newspaper and magazine articles. Writing in the New York *Times Magazine* (October 25, 1970), for example, he took feminist leaders to task for ignoring the "biological factors" that made men better suited for certain political and social roles. "Our biological heritage is the product of years of successful adaptation and it recurs in each generation with only tiny alterations," he maintained. "It is simply prudent that those concerned with changing sex roles understand the possible biological importance of what they want to do, and take careful measure of what these phenomena mean. If they do not, the primary victims of their misanalysis, unfortunately, will be—as usual—women and their daughters."

Further study of the available data on early man and his primate predecessors led to Tiger's next book, *The Imperial Animal* (Holt, 1971), which was written in a collaboration with Robin Fox. Essentially an overview of human species-specific behavior and social patterns and relations examined in the light of recent studies in primatology, *The Imperial Animal* focused on man's inherited animal nature and argued that his "wired" behavioral patterns were just as much the product of his evolutionary development as his body. Inspired by linguist Noam Chomsky's theory of a universal grammar, the authors formulated the concept of a "biogrammar," which postulates that the "underlying structure of behavior" is "biogrammatical," that is, it is firmly "rooted in the biology of the species." Tiger and Fox used that "universal behavioral grammar" to examine man's transition from "the simple life to the symbol life" and traced its implications for the study of marriage and kinship, economics, politics, aggression, and demography, among other things.

As Konrad Lorenz, the Nobel Prize-winning ethologist, had predicted in his foreword to *The Imperial Animal*, the book raised "storms of emotional indignation" and caused considerable controversy in the academic community. Some behavioral scientists, like Lorenz, applauded the authors' effort as a convincing and provocative argument for the "scientific understanding" of man; others scoffed that Tiger and Fox had boarded "a bandwagon full of monkeys" and accused them of racism, sexism, neofascism, propagandism, and methodological irresponsibility. Speaking in their own defense in an article for the *Columbia Forum* (Fall 1973), Tiger and Fox explained that the book was a deliberate "attempt at breaching the barriers between disciplines in a manner flexible enough to engage the attention of people in all sciences concerned." "If the human sciences do not investigate the basic biological nature of man and its expression in social behavior," they warned, "then the way is open for any manipulators of behavior to define human nature to their own advantage and force all of us to conform to their definitions."

Although Tiger had used vast amounts of data from various disciplines to support his theory, he had not himself undertaken research that might help validate his views until the mid-1970's, when he and Joseph Shepher, an Israeli sociologist, began collecting data for *Women in the Kibbutz* (Harcourt, 1975). Using census results and their own questionnaires, the authors compiled statistics on the families, work patterns, politics, education, and military experience of three generations of Israeli women. The results lent substance to Tiger's hypothesis that biology, to a large extent, determined behavior. According to Tiger and Shepher, a majority of women in the kibbutz "acted against the principles of their socialization and ideology, against the wishes of the men of their communities, against the economic interest of the kibbutzim, in order to be able to devote more time and energy to private maternal activities rather than to economic and political public ones."

Despite its many pages of statistical charts and tables, *Women in the Kibbutz* was criticized for being "basically popular, not scholarly." Feminists questioned the statistical significance of the authors' findings and took exception to their attempt to extrapolate from a specific group of women in an unusual environment to all women, thus exercising "the very patterns of 'logic' that have underwritten sexism for centuries," to use Glenda Riley's words. Although he continued to assert that sex differences have a biological origin, Tiger believed that the feminist emphasis on equality gave "a well-needed jolt to the social sciences, which have assumed for too long that by studying men one was studying people." As he remarked in "The Female Imperative," a short article published in the Toronto *Globe and Mail* (September 30, 1978), "biological differences exist; the challenge is to prevent them from emerging as inequalities."

Ever since he had researched *Men in Groups*, Tiger had been fascinated by the peculiarly human trait of optimism. Concluding that a successful hunt depended, at least in part, on the hopeful confidence of the primitive hunters, Tiger reasoned that optimism was "central to the process of human evolution," that there was "an evolutionary advantage to be gained from expecting good things of the future." He plumbed the biological wellsprings of hope and its relationship to psychological depression, religion, reproduction, creativity, suicide, financial success, and even diet and exercise in *Optimism: The Biology of Hope* (Simon & Schuster, 1979).

As he had done in the past, Tiger buttressed his argument with data culled from a variety of scientific disciplines, from the theories of such disparate thinkers as William James, Noam Chomsky, Claude Lévi-Strauss, and Sigmund Freud, and from recent advances in neurochemistry, including the discovery of the endorphins—the "natural opiates" secreted by the brain in times of stress. He deduced that "making optimistic symbols and anticipating optimistic outcomes of undecided situations is as much part of human nature, of the human biology, as are the shape of the body, the growth of children, and the zest of sexual pleasure."

No less an authority than Edward O. Wilson, the Harvard biologist who is perhaps the leading proponent of sociobiology, congratulated Tiger for his "strikingly original" speculations on the genetic origins of hope, courage, and mental well-being. With a few exceptions, notably the New York *Times*'s Anatole Broyard, lay reviewers were dismayed to find that Tiger's latest effort was, as one of them put it, "more frankly personal than rigorously scientific." Terrence Des Pres, who reviewed the book for the *Saturday Review* (June 9, 1979), deplored its "rambling surfeit of guesses . . . , truisms, rhetorical questions, and gratuitous asides," and Jean Strouse, in her evaluation for *Newsweek* (May 7, 1979), reproached Tiger for his "smug tone" and "quantum leaps from quirky fact to cosmic truth." But even the dissenters conceded that his thesis was intriguing.

In 1972 Tiger was named professor of anthropology at the Graduate School of Rutgers University. That same year he joined the staff of the Harry F. Guggenheim Foundation as director of research. From 1975 to 1978 he served as co-principal investigator of that foundation's program in sociobiology. In the past decade he took part in more than a dozen professional meetings, conferences, and symposiums, and he became a familar figure on the academic lecture circuit. He was the script consultant for and narrator of four sixty-minute documentaries on the evolution and biology of behavior, which were broadcast on Canadian television in 1978. A regular contributor to scholarly and technical journals, he has, in recent years, published articles in such lay periodicals as *Psychology Today*, *Fortune*, and *Newsweek*. The indefatigable Tiger continues to do research as well, and in June 1980, he reported to the International Society of Primatologists the results of a study of the hidden effects of oral contraceptives on the mating patterns of stumptail macaque monkeys. The findings indicated that alterations in body chemistry profoundly affected the monkeys' behavior patterns. Tiger suspects that contraceptives have similar effects on human feelings and behavior.

A short, trim man, Lionel Tiger stands five feet six and one-half inches tall and keeps his weight at about 148 pounds by jogging and playing tennis. He has blue eyes, unruly gray hair, and a taste for stylish, well-tailored clothes. In his spare time, he enjoys growing vegetables, cooking, reading books on architecture and urban planning, and listening to "any mode of skillful music." Since his separation from his wife, Virginia Conner, a professor of English at Rutgers University, whom he married on August 19, 1964, Tiger has lived alone in the Greenwich Village section of New York City. The two share custody of their son, Sebastian Benjamin.

Although occasionally depressed by what he calls the "crushing structure of human problems," Tiger is convinced that the "broadly

scientific understanding" of those problems will eventually contribute to their solutions. He is further reassured by the world's seemingly "inexhaustible supply of jokes." In regard to his personal life, he told Barbara Rowe, in an interview for *People* magazine (May 28, 1979), "I've been lucky in having a variety of intense experiences, some having to do with my work, some with my personal life. These, of course, have not always been without bafflement and pain. Yet somehow I continue to hear an insistent tone that is beguiling and rather sweet, which, with predictable optimism, I take to be advance notice of a delightful future."

References: Macleans 92:42+ My 28 '79 por; N Y Post p25 Jl 12 '69 por; Psych Today 12:31+ Ja '79 por; Contemporary Authors 1st rev vols 25-28 (1971); Moraes, Dom. Voices For Life (1975); Who's Who in America, 1980-81

Timerman, Jacobo

Jan. 6, 1923- Journalist; author; social activist. Address: b. c/o Alfred A. Knopf, 201 E. 50th St., New York City, N.Y. 10022; c/o Ma'ariv, Tel Aviv, Israel

One of Argentina's most distinguished journalists, Jacobo Timerman became the focal point of an international human rights issue after he was seized in April 1977 by Argentine security forces and held captive for thirty months. He described that harrowing ordeal in his book *Prisoner Without a Name, Cell Without a Number* (Knopf, 1981). A Jew, a dedicated Zionist, and an outspoken defender of social justice, Timerman, as publisher of the liberal Buenos Aires daily *La Opinión* from 1971 to 1977, provoked controversy with his attacks on government corruption and repression, his allegations of officially-sanctioned anti-Semitism in Argentina, and his efforts to get to the bottom of the unexplained disappearances of an estimated 15,000 to 20,000 Argentines seized by official authorities or paramilitary death squads. More recently, Timerman, who is now a journalist in Israel, has challenged the human rights policy of the Administration of President Ronald Reagan and its tendency to tolerate right-wing "authoritarian" regimes while condemning those of the "totalitarian" left.

In the foreword to his book, Jacobo Timerman revealed that his family, "by way of those strange, biforked paths of Judaism, escaped the Spanish occupation of the Netherlands, and the Inquisition, and wound up in a small town of Vinnitsa Oblast in the Ukraine, called Bar." He was born there on January 6, 1923, the older of the two sons of Nathan and Eva (Berman) Timerman. Although his parents were poor, according to "family accounts" the Timermans "were prominent in the community and fought for Jewish rights." He was only five when his family left Bar for Argentina to escape the pogroms that were rampant in the Ukraine in the 1920's, but he remembered attending the town's Great Synagogue with his father, his uncles, and his cousins, and he bore away with him "a vague longing for those tall, bearded, unsmiling men."

When Jacobo Timerman was twelve his father died, leaving his mother with having to support him and his brother, Yoselle, who is now known as José. "His closeness to this strong woman is one of the grand tones of his character . . . ," Ted Solotaroff concluded in the *Nation* (June 13, 1981). "Her dream of a Jewish homeland became his Zionism." The Timermans lived in the Once (Eleventh) District of Buenos Aires, the heart of the Jewish quarter, in a one-room apartment they occupied rent-free in exchange for performing janitorial duties in their tenement building. While his mother worked as a street vendor selling clothes, Jacobo attended public schools, working afternoons as messenger boy for a jewelry store. A "neurotic obsessive" about the suffering of world Jewry, Timerman recalls, his mother constantly reminded her sons of it. After the rise of Hitler, she would ask them during meals: "How can we be eating while the Jews in Germany are being mistreated?"

Timerman had his first contact with Zionism at eight, when his mother enrolled him in the Jewish sports club Macabi. At fourteen he joined Avuca, a student group that organized discussions on Zionism and Jewish history. Later he learned the techniques of agriculture, hoping eventually to work on a kibbutz in Israel. A major influence on his life was his encounter, through Avuca, with two Jewish

Boy Scouts who were Socialist Zionists. "When I heard them speak," he wrote, "I became destined for that world I would never abandon and never try to abandon—a world that at times took the form of Zionism, at times the struggle for human rights, at times the fight for freedom of expression, and at other times again the solidarity with dissidents against all totalitarianisms."

Thereafter Timerman concentrated his reading on works by such socially committed writers as Jack London, Upton Sinclair, John Dos Passos, Henri Barbusse, and Erich Maria Remarque. He joined Socialist May Day demonstrations and identified with returning Jewish veterans of the Zionist organization Hashomer Hatzair who had fought against Franco in the Spanish Civil War. In 1944 he was arrested while attending a film festival of the Argentine League for Human Rights, allegedly a Communist affiliate, and was detained for twenty-four hours. He also became a member of the Youth League for Freedom, which supported the Allied cause at a time when the Argentine government backed the Germans and was eventually dissolved by police as a Communist front. On one occasion, Timerman was arrested and detained overnight after leading a group of young anti-fascists in an attack on the headquarters of a Nazi newspaper. Anxious to enlist as a volunteer in the struggle against the Axis, Timerman offered his services to the Free French Committee and the British and American embassies in Buenos Aires but was not accepted.

Although Timerman once told Richard Eder of the New York *Times* (December 15, 1979) that he did not "become a journalist" but "was born one," he originally started out on another course. For a year he went to the school of engineering in nearby La Plata. Among his teachers there was Ernesto Sábato, who eventually became one of Argentina's foremost novelists. Timerman began to make his mark in journalism in 1947, when he became a free-lance writer for several literary magazines. In the late 1950's he joined the staff of *La Razón*, then one of Buenos Aires' leading newspapers. His resourcefulness as a reporter became widely known, according to his long-time friend Jacob Kovadloff, after the February 1958 election of Arturo Frondizi as President of Argentina on a nationalist, anti-imperialist platform. Before Frondizi assumed office in May of that year, Timerman traveled with him by air on a series of visits to heads of state of other countries in Latin America. His front page dispatches for *La Razón* gave the nation up-to-date news about Frondizi's plans for governing.

Timerman's restless, inventive journalism carried him into radio, television, and publishing. In the early 1960's, with a group of young fellow journalists, he launched *Primera Plana*, a highly successful weekly news magazine patterned on the format of *Time* or *Newsweek* magazine. Timerman sold it and in 1969 founded *Confirmado,* another popular news-weekly. Having in turn sold it, he again joined other colleagues and founded the newspaper *La Opinión,* of which the first issue appeared on May 4, 1971.

Modeled on the liberal Parisian daily *Le Monde,* Timerman's newspaper was greeted, in Kovadloff's words, as a "breath of fresh air in Argentine life" by the intellectual, politically-minded readers to whom it catered. As its publisher-editor, Timerman announced that *La Opinión* would support Israel, that its stance would be left of center, and that it would give extensive coverage to the arts. *La Opinión* took no private advertising and, unlike other Argentine newspapers, it allowed its writers to sign their articles. When *La Opinión* prospered, attaining a circulation of some 150,000, Timerman sold a 45 percent share to David Graiver, a young Jewish financier. In 1974, with Graiver's help, he built a modern printing plant that serviced his newspaper. He also founded a small but successful book-publishing firm, Timerman Editores, which under the direction of his son Hector published works on contemporary issues, many of them especially commissioned from their authors.

From 1971 to 1977, the years in which Timerman published *La Opinión,* Argentina experienced one of the most trying and violent periods of its history. Always outspoken and politically aware, moving within the nation's most influential circles, Timerman was constantly involved in national affairs. Although *La Opinión* remained left of center it became a force for moderation and opposed extremism of all political shades. As a result, Timerman became the target of harassment and violence from both left and right. In July 1972 Timerman's home was among twenty places time-bombed by the Montoneros, an ultra-leftist faction of the Peronists, who remained a major political force in Argentina seventeen years after the forced exile of President Juan Perón. With the proliferation of terrorist groups, Timerman's life was in constant danger.

When in the spring of 1973 Argentina reverted to civilian government with the resignation of President General Alejandro Agustín Lanusse, Timerman supported the election of Hector Cámpora, whose undisguised function was to prepare the country for the return of Juan Perón. *La Opinión*'s Peronist allegiance continued after Perón returned and was overwhelmingly reelected President in September 1973. It ceased, however, after Perón's third wife, Isabel Martínez de Perón, who assumed the Presidency upon her husband's death in July 1974, proved completely unable to govern effectively.

Meanwhile, Timerman continued to champion democratic institutions and human rights, irrespective of ideological boundaries. Taking positions that later confounded his prison interrogators, he condemned the Soviet Union's persecution of dissidents, right-wing tendencies in Israel's government, terrorist acts of the Palestine Liberation Organization, and Fidel Castro's treatment of political prisoners and exportation of terrorism. On the other hand, Timerman supported the Marxist government of Salvador Allende, who was elected President of neighboring Chile in 1970, and after Allende's overthrow in a bloody military coup in 1973, he was named "public enemy number one" by the Chilean press because of *La Opinión*'s denunciations of human rights violations by that country's new dictatorship. In February 1976 Timerman urged in *La Opinión* that Argentina's military move against Isabel Perón's government, following twenty months of economic chaos, political corruption, and inability to prevent terrorist acts by the left-wing Montoneros and Trotskyite People's Revolutionary Army (ERP) and the far-right "death squads" of the Argentine Anticommunist Alliance. As a result, *La Opinión* was shut down for ten days.

When President Isabel Perón was overthrown in March 1976 by a three-man military junta headed by Lieutenant General Jorge Rafael Videla, who became President, Timerman's position was perilously ambiguous. On the one hand, he backed Videla's promises of national unity, economic reconstruction, and ultimate return to traditional constitutional processes. On the other, he deplored the government's free-market policies, the mounting violence, and the increasing numbers of *desaparecidos,* or missing persons, most of them abducted by extreme right-wing elements of the military. *La Opinión,* along with the English-language Buenos Aires *Herald,* edited by Robert Cox, soon were almost alone among periodicals in insisting upon cessation of all terrorism and upon *habeas corpus* proceedings for those taken into custody, whose stories and names Timerman published regularly in his paper.

Ironically, while the Videla government mounted pressures on *La Opinión* to stop marshalling public opinion, it pointed to the continued existence of that opposition organ as proof of its own moderation. As means of exerting pressure on *La Opinión,* the authorities at times withheld official government advertising from its pages and compelled the paper to bear excessive production costs. As the danger increased, some reporters quit, and a few loyal ones eventually joined the scores of journalists who disappeared. Timerman received many death threats, from both left and right, and published responses to some of them on the front page of *La Opinión.* In his editorials he insisted that the newspaper would maintain its standards and expressed curiosity about who would eventually claim his corpse. In answer to advice from friends that he leave Argentina, Timerman asserted: "I am one who belongs to Masada"—referring to a first-century Jewish community whose citizens chose to die rather than surrender to the Romans.

At 2:00 A.M. on April 15, 1977, twenty armed men in civilian clothes broke into Timerman's Buenos Aires home and, allegedly on orders from the Tenth Infantry Brigade, carried him off. His family did not learn of his whereabouts until six weeks later. In the months that followed, Timerman was moved about, to three clandestine places of confinement and two regular prisons. In *Prisoner Without a Name, Cell Without a Number* he recounted his experiences—a simulated execution, beatings, electric shock tortures, extended periods of solitary confinement under humiliating circumstances, and intense interrogations. Timerman concluded that although most of his fellow prisoners were not Jews, a Nazi-like element of the military looked towards a "final solution" for Argentina's more than 300,000 Jewish citizens and subjected Jewish prisoners to especially harsh treatment. When he openly admitted to his interrogators that *La Opinión* was a Zionist organ, his captors seemed determined to use him as showcase proof of an alleged worldwide Zionist plot to seize Patagonia in southern Argentina for a second Jewish state. Their futile plan, Timerman believes, may have saved his life.

Since no formal charges were filed, official motives for Timerman's imprisonment were never clear. The military at first spoke vaguely of "subversive acts" and "economic crimes." Eventually, however, Timerman was publicly linked with David Graiver, the part-owner of *La Opinión*, whose financial empire had grown to include banks in Brussels and New York. Following reports—not fully substantiated—of Graiver's mysterious death in August 1976 in a plane crash in Mexico, his empire collapsed. It was alleged that he had looted his own banks. Eight months later, shortly before Timerman's arrest, Argentine authorities alleged that Graiver was the financial agent through whom the Montoneros invested millions extorted through ransom. Timerman's connection with Graiver was presented as part of a Jewish-Marxist-Montonero conspiracy, and authorities tried to support that contention by reprinting leftist *La Opinión* articles in the press.

Timerman's release on September 25, 1979, following more than a year of imprisonment and seventeen months of house arrest, came after three judicial declarations of his innocence on all charges. In October 1977, after sixteen hours of questioning, he had been cleared by a military special war council of links with guerrilla forces. Then, in July 1978, Argentina's supreme court, acting on a writ of *habeas corpus* filed by Timerman's wife, decided that there was no legal basis for holding him. Nevertheless, Timerman remained under house arrest. The supreme court's unanimous second verdict of innocence on September 18, 1979 precipitated a face-off between military hard-liners and moderates, but after a few days of indecision Timerman was finally released, put on a plane with a visa to Israel, and stripped of his Argentine citizenship and his property.

During Timerman's incarceration, worldwide attention focused on his case. Cyrus Vance, Alexander Solzhenitsyn, and Henry Kissinger were among the many who spoke out for his release, as were Amnesty International, the Inter-American Press Association, and the human rights commission of the Organization of American States. In interviews and in his book, Timerman credited his life to those efforts, and particularly to those of the Vatican and the Administration of President Jimmy Carter, which withheld aid to Argentina because of human rights violations. Timerman singled out for special praise Patricia M. Derian, Carter's Assistant Secretary of State for Human Rights. On the other hand, he leveled increasingly harsh criticism at the lack of support he received from Argentine Jewish leaders. "I had not been humiliated by torture, by electric shocks on my genitals, but had been profoundly humiliated by [their] silent complicity," he wrote in his book. Their "panic," he continued, "constituted a nightmare within a tragedy."

When Timerman's eloquent story of his imprisonment, translated from the Spanish by Toby Talbot, appeared, in condensed form in the *New Yorker* (April 20, 1981), and as the book *Prisoner Without a Name, Cell Without a Number* (Knopf, 1981), the response was sympathetic. Many critics concurred with Barbara Amiel, who said in her *Maclean's* review (June 15, 1981) that the book was "both horrifying and hypnotic in its revelations," and that it reinforced an undeniable point: "no possible political system of the extreme left or right can offer human beings any degree of stability, prosperity and justice."

Soon, however, Timerman became once more a center of controversy. During a book-promotion visit to the United States he repeatedly criticized Argentine Jewish leadership and the Reagan Administration's policies on human rights. Appearing on *Bill Moyers' Journal*, presented over WNET-TV on May 29, 1981, Timerman vigorously condemned the State Department's low-keyed response to human rights violations in "authoritarian" nations like Argentina, and he compared Argentine Jewish leaders to members of a *Judenrat*, or Jewish council, of the kind that cooperated with the Nazis during World War II. Timerman attended confirmation hearings of the Senate Foreign Relations Committee in May 1981 on Ernest W. Lefever, President Reagan's nominee for Assistant Secretary of State for Human Rights. Although he did not testify against Lefever's policy of "quiet diplomacy" toward allies like Argentina that violated human rights, his presence at the hearings was regarded as a significant factor in mustering Congressional opposition that caused Lefever to withdraw from consideration.

Timerman's views were met by volleys of sometimes acerbic responses from such commentators as William F. Buckley Jr., Irving Kristol, and Norman Podhoretz. In the *Wall Street Journal* (May 29, 1981), Kristol suggested that the "Graiver Affair," rather than the fact that he was a Jew, was the cause of his imprisonment, while the former Israeli diplomat Benno Weiser Varon, in an article in *Midstream* (December 1980), refuted contentions that the Timerman case constituted another "Dreyfus affair." Disagreement with Timerman also came from Mario Gorenstein, president of the Jewish Associations of Argentina. On the other hand, Timerman had many supporters, including Argentine human rights leader Emilio Mingone, Rabbi Morton Rosenthal of the Anti-Defamation League of B'nai B'rith, and New York *Times* columnist Anthony Lewis. Ted Solotaroff observed in the *Nation* (June 13, 1981): "He is, quite simply, an extraordinary man: reflective, humane, righteous and withal extremely brave, resourceful and hardheaded."

Now a resident of Tel Aviv, Timerman is a columnist for the daily *Ma'ariv* and also has written for the newspaper *Davar*. In 1979 he was awarded the Hubert H. Humphrey Freedom Prize of the Anti-Defamation League of B'nai B'rith and the David Ben-Gurion Award of the United Jewish Appeal, in 1980 he received the Golden Pen of Freedom from the International Federation of Newspaper Publishers, and in 1981 he was presented the Maria Moors Cabot Prize for contributions to inter-American understanding. He holds the Arthur Morse Award of the Aspen Institute and has been honored by Hadassah, the United Synagogue of America, and the American Jewish Committee.

Jacobo Timerman and his wife Riche (or Risha), a former law student, whom he married on May 20, 1950, are grandparents and have three sons: Daniel, who works on a kibbutz in Israel; Hector, an editor at Random House in New York; and Javier, a student at Hebrew University in Jerusalem. Timerman has been described as robust and stocky, with thinning gray hair and a wide-mouthed, rugged face. He wears tinted glasses owing to an eye injury in his youth. When he appeared on television with Bill Moyers he spoke in fluent but accented English. To those who know him he is an admirable but difficult man with considerable ego, sometimes harsh in his judgments, and not inclined to mince words or shy from controversy in causes he has supported all his life.

References: Encounter 57:74+ N '81; Harpers 263:20+ N '81 por; Long Island Jewish Press 10:1+ N 6-12 '81 pors; N Y Rev of Books 28:10+ S 24 '81; N Y Times p2 D 15 '79 por; Pub W 219:16 My 1 '81 por; USA Today p30+ S '79 por; Timerman, Jacobo. Prisoner Without a Name, Cell Without a Number (1981)

Tsongas, Paul E(fthemios) (song'us)

Feb. 14, 1941- United States Senator from Massachusetts. Address: b. 342 Russell Senate Office Bldg., Washington, D.C. 20510

As the junior United States Senator from Massachusetts, Paul E. Tsongas, who is best described as a pragmatic liberal, operates in the shadow of his senior colleague, Edward M. Kennedy. Nevertheless, the young Democrat has made his own mark in his first term. In the Ninety-seventh Congress, Tsongas has added a seat on the powerful Committee on Foreign Relations to the post he had held on the Banking, Housing and Urban Affairs Committee since entering the Senate in 1979. He has also been gaining increasing attention from the media for his trenchant criticisms of his own liberal wing of the Democratic party, and he is expected to play a crucial role as the Democrats seek the fresh ideas and initiatives needed to return them to power.

Paul Efthemios Tsongas, the grandson of a Greek immigrant, was born on February 14, 1941 in the old textile manufacturing city of Lowell, Massachusetts to Efthemios George Tsongas, a dry cleaner, and his wife, Katina. He has a twin sister, Thalia Schlesinger, and

another sister, Victoria Peters. After graduating from Lowell High School in 1958, Tsongas worked his way through Dartmouth College, where he obtained a B.A. degree in history in

1962. He spent the next two years with the Peace Corps as a teacher in an Ethiopian village. "Nothing before or after that time has shaped my view of the world so deeply," he has recalled. On his return to the United States in 1964, Tsongas entered the Yale University Law School, and during the summers of 1966 and 1967 he worked as a Congressional intern for Republican F. Bradford Morse, who represented his home district in Congress. After obtaining his LL.B. degree from Yale in 1967, he was admitted to the Massachusetts bar.

Tsongas spent a year, in 1967-68, as a training coordinator for the Peace Corps in the West Indies. During 1968-69 he was on the Governor's Committee on Law Enforcement for the Commonwealth of Massachusetts, and from 1969 to 1971 he served the Bay State as a deputy assistant attorney general. In his first bid for public office, Tsongas was elected to the Lowell City Council in 1969 and served until 1972. While he was on the council, he and other local leaders developed the innovative Lowell Plan, which created a national park to preserve historic downtown buildings and, at the same time, stimulated private investment to revitalize the economically depressed city's business district. Elected on a reform slate, Tsongas served as a Middlesex County commissioner in 1973-74 but earned the ill will of party regulars because of his efforts to divest the county government of patronage. Concurrently with his public service, Tsongas engaged in private law practice from 1971 to 1974 and furthered his education at Harvard University's John F. Kennedy School of Government, where he obtained a master of public administration degree in 1973.

In 1974 Tsongas set his sights on the Congressional seat for his home district, the Fifth of Massachusetts. Under normal circumstances Tsongas' chances would have been extremely slender. A longtime Republican stronghold, the Fifth Congressional District sent Edith Nourse Rogers to Washington from 1924 to 1958. F. Bradford Morse, in whose office Tsongas had worked as an intern, succeeded her and held the seat until 1972. Two years later, however, the Republicans were laboring under the burden of President Richard Nixon's resignation. After taking 73 percent of the vote in the Democratic primary contest against William Madden, Tsongas easily defeated the one-term Republican incumbent, Paul W. Cronin, in November 1974 by a margin of almost 35,000 votes out of some 164,000 cast. He became the first Democrat to represent the district in about ninety years. "The people wanted a Democrat," Tsongas has explained. "We could not have won if Watergate had not taken place."

Taking his seat in the Ninety-fourth Congress in January 1975, Tsongas easily won reelection in 1976 and served on the Banking, Currency and Housing Committee and the Interior and Insular Affairs Committee during his two Congressional terms. He took a special interest in issues involving human rights, developing nations, international lending institutions, and the environment. His solidly liberal record earned him a rating of 100 percent from the Americans for Democratic Action for 1977, and the League of Conservation Voters gave him the same perfect score. The conservative Americans for Constitutional Action, on the other hand, rated him at only 4 percent for that year. Among other legislation, Tsongas voted for the common situs picketing bill desired by labor and in favor of the establishment of the Consumer Protection Agency. He opposed increased defense spending, construction of the B-1 bomber, delay in the implementation of auto emission controls, and deregulation of natural gas prices. He dismayed some liberals by his unsuccessful support in 1977 for a higher gasoline tax intended to curb fuel consumption. The young Congressman made his most notable legislative efforts as a member of the Subcommittee on Energy and the Environment, where he was an advocate for increased research on solar power. After a visit to Africa in December 1977, Tsongas favored a continued arms embargo against Ethiopia's repressive military regime but at the same time favored expanded contacts with that country to counter Soviet influence there.

In May 1978 Tsongas announced that he would seek the seat held in the United States Senate by Edward W. Brooke. A liberal Republican and the first black Senator since Reconstruction, Brooke was popular with Massachusetts voters. Tsongas, however, was unhappy that the Senator had wavered before supporting the Panama Canal accords. "Defeat of those treaties," he charged, "would have been a foreign policy disaster for the United States all over Latin America." He also indicated that he would emphasize the two-term incumbent's growing reputation for neglecting Massachusetts' interests. The Democrats gained an unanticipated additional advantage when the Boston *Globe* revealed that Brooke had misrepresented his financial affairs in a sworn statement taken in connection with his divorce.

To earn the right to face Brooke, Tsongas had to fend off several Democrats who entered the race after the Senator's personal problems became public knowledge. The young Congressman won 36 percent of the vote in a five-way race in the September 1978 primary. His chief rivals, Massachusetts Secretary of State Paul Guzzi and Boston school committee member Kathleen Sullivan Alioto, gained 31 percent and 19 percent respectively. With financial help from the Greek-American community and strong support from Senator Edward M. Kennedy, who had previously avoided confrontations with Brooke, Tsongas then turned his full attention to his Republican opponent. While avoiding mention of Brooke's private difficulties, the Congressman emphasized his own more liberal record on foreign affairs and on economic matters, his support for a national health insurance program, and his success in winning federal aid to restore the old cities of New England. On election day in November 1978 he tallied 1,093,283 votes to Brooke's 890,584. Tsongas proved to be a gracious victor. "I tried to dislike him, but I never could," he said of his opponent. "Brooke leaves some very large shoes to be filled, and I intend to fill them." Brooke, in turn, praised the manner in which Tsongas had conducted his campaign.

Maintaining his reputation for liberalism in the Senate, Tsongas received ratings of 89 percent from the Americans for Democratic Action and 12 percent from the Americans for Constitutional Action for his positions on the issues of 1980. As a member of the Energy and Natural Resources Committee in the Ninety-sixth Congress, he continued to support additional funding for the development of solar energy and joined Senator Henry M. Jackson in calling for tougher fuel economy standards for automobiles. Tsongas backed President Jimmy Carter's gasoline rationing program but was dismayed by the Administration's promises of special treatment for farmers and energy producers. As a member of the Banking, Housing and Urban Affairs Committee, he helped to defeat in 1979 a proposal by its Democratic chairman, William Proxmire, to cut $700,000,000 from the federally subsidized housing program. "It would appear that the Administration and the Congress have found a mutually agreeable scapegoat: urban affairs," Tsongas said at the time. "The cities of this country, and the people in those cities, are taking it on the chin."

During his brief time in the Senate, Tsongas has established a notable record on domestic legislation. In 1979 he and Republican Senator Richard G. Lugar of Indiana reacted angrily to a generous settlement made by the troubled Chrysler Corporation with the United Auto Workers. The two Banking Committee members price for supporting $4 billion in aid for the ailing company, and Congress eventually mandated major wage concessions. demanded a three-year wage freeze as their

Widely recognized as a leading spokesman for conservationist forces in the Senate, Tsongas played a crucial role in 1980 in shaping a compromise Alaska lands bill that would satisfy his environmentalist allies as well as Energy Committee leaders Henry M. Jackson and Mark O. Hatfield, while at the same time persuading Alaska's Republican Senator Ted Stevens to end his obstruction of such legislation. Although less stringent than the original bill passed by the House, the Tsongas version reserved about one-third of Alaska for wildlife refuges, national parks, and other conservation areas. President Carter, who signed it into law in December 1980, called it the "most important conservation measure to come before any Congress or any President in this century."

In the Ninety-sixth Congress Tsongas introduced legislation to establish a Presidential commission to study the creation of a national service program for youth. His proposal, which was incorporated in the Senate's draft of the domestic violence bill of 1980, was deleted in the final version, but Tsongas has not given up on it, convinced, on the basis of his own experience in the Peace Corps, that volunteer service helps the giver at least as much as the receiver. "A new commitment to service could be the right medicine for our ailing national spirit," Tsongas believes. "It might help turn our society away from the extremes of the 'me' generation of the 1970's, with many fashion-conscious young Americans growing up unconscious of other Americans who are struggling for basic needs."

When he entered the Senate, Tsongas had hoped to win a seat on the powerful Foreign Relations Committee. Its leadership, however, had already selected one Greek-American, Democrat Paul S. Sarbanes of Maryland, and thought it imprudent to name another at a time when the United States was seeking to improve relations with Greece's rival, Turkey. Nevertheless, Tsongas spoke frequently on matters relating to international affairs. He and Senator George S. McGovern of South Dakota sharply criticized a decision by Congress in 1979 to end the economic boycott of Rhodesia after the installation of the new black-led government of Bishop Abel T. Muzorewa. Tsongas charged that the white minorities in Rhodesia, Namibia, and South Africa were following a public-relations strategy of "staged elections involving black moderates, new constitutions establishing an illusion of majority rule, and the dismantling of petty segregation." He warned that, if the United States gave its blessing to such "internal settlements" before real majority rule was achieved, the Soviet Union would eventually emerge in African eyes as the only true friend of their nationalist aspirations.

Tsongas was one of the first liberals to speak out about the erosion of popular support that seemed to portend electoral disaster for his party in 1980. In an important speech delivered before the convention of the Americans for Democratic Action in June of that year, the Senator praised liberalism for its achievements in civil rights and other areas, but he warned that many young Americans had "never experienced the abuses and injustices that molded us" and took "for granted the social equities that we had to fight for." Tsongas advised liberals that, in order to survive, they had to respond flexibly to current concerns about such issues as energy, productivity, defense, and the environment. With an obvious allusion to Ronald Reagan's old Borax-sponsored *Death Valley Days* television series, the Senator forecast that a liberal failure would allow conservatives to lead the country on "a twenty-mule-team march into the past."

Recently, Tsongas has been urging liberals to rethink their positions on some basic issues. He has chastised them, for example, for opposing a ten-cent-a-gallon tax designed to discourage the use of gasoline. Such a levy would hurt consumers, he admits, but the rapid depletion of the world's oil supply would hurt them even more in the future. Likewise, Tsongas has asked liberals to accept the use of both nuclear and coal-based power generation, maintaining that an environmentally purist position may be self-defeating. "If we fail to adjust to the simple realities," he told an interviewer for *Esquire* (December 1980), "then those people we are most anxious to protect—the poor and the powerless—are precisely those who are going to get crushed when the shortage hits five years from now." Tsongas has also argued in favor of government assistance to the business community, where needed. The Senator, who sometimes refers to Japanese industry as "the enemy," has urged tax relief measures to help businesses to create employment and legislation to improve the competitive position of the United States in world markets. "We've spent the last few decades worrying about the distribution of the golden eggs," he says. "The time has come to worry about the health of the goose."

Despite his concessions to changing political realities, Tsongas remains a firm foe of President Ronald Reagan's policies. He has described the 1980 rush to the Reagan bandwagon as a short-sighted effort by Americans to find easy answers to difficult questions, and he is convinced that the Administration will ultimately be rejected. As a new member of the Senate Foreign Relations Committee in the Ninety-seventh Congress, he cast one of the two votes against the confirmation of Alexander M. Haig Jr. as Secretary of State in January 1981. He was also in the forefront among the challengers of Ernest W. Lefever, who finally stepped down in June 1981 as President Reagan's nominee for Assistant Secretary of State for Human Rights after his qualifications for the post were severely questioned. In March 1981 Tsongas joined Senator Kennedy and others in introducing a bill to halt United States military aid to El Salvador.

In Tsongas' view, the Reagan Administration's abandonment of the human rights initiative and its reliance on military solutions for such countries as El Salvador promises to generate substantial opposition. He also believes that the public may discover serious shortcomings in the logic behind the Kemp-Roth tax-cut plan favored by the White House. Therefore, the Senator believes that the Democrats' main tasks are to educate Americans about the complexity of the problems facing them and to develop alternative programs for the time when disillusionment with the Republicans' solutions taken hold. In his book *The Road From Here: Liberalism and Realities in the 1980's* (Knopf, 1981), Tsongas presents his ideas with what he has termed "nonideological, clear-eyed realism."

Senator Tsongas describes his as the "best job in the world," but he hopes never to suc-

cumb to the deadening fear of not being reelected. He does not deny occasionally entertaining thoughts of the Presidency. "I honestly believe—as immodest as this may sound—that I have a better sense of where this country ought to be going than almost anyone," he told the *Esquire* interviewer. But the Senator admits that he has not yet developed the capacity for the responsibility of the office, and he wonders whether an outspoken politician with his views could win a national election. "You know," he has said, "point men don't become generals; they get killed. If it turns out that my job in this business is to help provide direction—if that's what I end up being remembered for while someone else carries the ball—well, I could live with that. With a severe pang every now and then, but I could live with it."

Paul E. Tsongas is darkly handsome and of slight build. Commentators have noted that his quietly confident and unassuming manner has made him an effective campaigner. House Speaker Thomas P. O'Neill once described him as "the most low-key politician" he had ever met. Tsongas is one of the very few Senators whose financial worth is noticeably limited. While he was a Congressman, he devoted great effort to repaying education loans to Dartmouth and Yale, as well as to Boston University, where his wife was studying law. The Senator, whose religious affiliation is with the Greek Orthodox Church, married Nicola Sauvage on December 21, 1969. They have three daughters, Ashley, Katina, and Molly.

References: Cong Q 36:3507 D 30 '78 por; New Repub 185:29+ N 25 '81; Washington Post B p1+ S 23 '81 por; Congressional Directory, 1979; Who's Who in America, 1980-81; Who's Who in American Politics, 1979-80

Tyler, Anne

Oct. 25, 1941- Writer. Address: b. c/o Diarmuid Russell, 551 Fifth Ave., New York City, N.Y. 10017; h. 222 Tunbridge Rd., Baltimore, Md. 21212

Since the early 1960's Anne Tyler has been presenting her vision of the contemporary American South in witty, compassionate novels and short stories that are products of her imagination rather than the fictional translation of her personal experience. "I want to live other lives," she has explained. "I've never quite believed that one chance is all I get. Writing is my way of taking chances." Especially admired for its skilled characterization and pinpointed precision of detail, her straightforward and understated fiction focuses on eccentric individuals and chaotic families. The

Anne Tyler

heroes among them, Miss Tyler has pointed out, "are first the ones who manage to endure and second the ones who somehow are able to grant other people the privacy of the space around them and yet produce some warmth." Although she writes about the American South, Anne Tyler is definitely not a member of the Southern Gothic school. Her affectionately realized novels are free of grotesquerie, theological implications, and sudden eruptions of violence.

Anne Tyler was born in Minneapolis, Minnesota on October 25, 1941 to Lloyd Parry Tyler, an industrial chemist, and Phyllis (Mahon) Tyler, a social worker. Together with her parents and her three younger brothers, she spent her childhood living with rural Quaker communal groups throughout the Midwest and the South. After settling down for five years in Celo Community, in the mountains of North Carolina, the family moved to the outskirts of Raleigh, where Anne attended secondary school. At the age of sixteen she entered Duke University, where she took a freshman composition course from the novelist Reynolds Price, whom, along with Eudora Welty, she considers a major influence on her fiction. Although she devoted some of her energies to producing original work and twice won the Anne Flexner Award for creative writing, she majored in Russian.

In 1961, after spending only three years at Duke, she completed work for her bachelor of arts degree and earned a membership in the Phi Beta Kappa Society. Following a year of graduate study in Russian at Columbia University, she returned to Duke to serve as its library's Russian bibliographer in 1962 and 1963. In 1964 and 1965 she was assistant to the librarian at the law library of McGill University in Montreal. She abandoned library work in favor of a full-time writing career when she moved in 1967 to Baltimore, where she has lived ever since.

When she was only twenty-two, Anne Tyler wrote her first novel, *If Morning Ever Comes* (Knopf, 1964), to keep herself occupied before she found a job in Montreal. Her precocity and her polished, restrained style attracted the attention of several reviewers, including Rollene W. Saal of the New York *Times Book Review* (November 22, 1964), who called *If Morning Ever Comes* "a subtle and surprisingly mature story," and Katherine Gauss Jackson of *Harper's Magazine* (November 1964), who was impressed by its seriousness and sanity. Miss Tyler tells her story in third-person narration from the point of view of her protagonist, Ben Joe Hawkes, who impulsively heads home from Columbia Law School because he feels responsible for the household of women he has left down in Sandhill, North Carolina. But his visit reminds him that he cannot penetrate their private world: his past, which is so alive in his memory, eludes his grasp when he returns to the scenes of his boyhood. Because his own family does not need him, Ben Joe turns his attention to Shelley Domer, a simpler, more dependent female who was his high-school sweetheart. Much to his and Shelley's surprise, he ask her to elope and takes her back to New York City with him as "his own little piece of Sandhill transplanted."

Assuming that fiction must chronicle human growth or social flux, the detractors of *If Morning Ever Comes* protested that "the hero is hardly better defined at the end than he is at the beginning" and that Anne Tyler "has not yet shown that she can make a character develop or a situation crystallize." But Miss Tyler, who has often expressed her "utter lack of faith in change," had no intention of building a novel according to the pattern of "exposition, development, and resolution" that many critics expected to find.

Nor did Anne Tyler alter her attitude towards her characters in her second novel, *The Tin Can Tree* (Knopf, 1965), which describes from the alternating points of view of a photographer and his girlfriend the temporary disruption of life in the Pike household of Larksville, North Carolina after the death of six-year-old Janie Rose in a tractor accident. Because her characters regain their former equilibrium by the book's end, reviewers again complained that her fiction failed to convey what one of them termed "that sense of development which is the true novel's motive force." Nevertheless, they praised the effectiveness of her evocation of people and places, achieved with an economy of means. For example, Millicent Bell of the New York *Times Book Review* (November 21, 1965), calling *The Tin Can Tree* "a snapshot," felt obliged to observe that "the hand that has clicked its shutter has selected a moment of truth." Following the novel's publication, Anne Tyler received a writing award from *Mademoiselle* magazine.

Preoccupied with the responsibility of caring for her infant daughters, Anne Tyler did not publish her third novel, *A Slipping-Down Life* (Knopf), until 1970. Significantly, its protagonist, a dumpy and lonely high school girl from Pulqua, North Carolina named Evie Decker, resolves to seek maturity and stability when she realizes, near the novel's end, that she is pregnant. She finds it necessary to leave her unpredictable husband, the rock 'n' roll singer Drumstrings Casey, whose attention she originally captured by etching his surname across her forehead with a razor blade. Miss Tyler dispels the potential sensationalism of her tale, based on an actual incident involving a fan of Elvis Presley, with a calm narrative voice that reports the point of view of Evie. With ironic wit and a kind of distanced compassion, Anne Tyler orchestrates the themes of the pain of alienation, the difficulty of human communication, and the search for meaning in life.

To present her next unlikely heroine in *The Clock Winder* (Knopf, 1972), Anne Tyler splinters her third-person narrative into different points of view. Elizabeth Abbott, an artist of sorts, who has a penchant for carving austere wooden figures, wanders into a job as handyman for the Emerson family in Baltimore during a year off from college. Despite her resistance to accepting responsibility, Elizabeth becomes irrevocably enmeshed in the affairs of the Emersons and over a ten-year period discovers the perils and pleasures of influencing other people. Although she tries to escape from the burdensome Emerson brood, she ultimately comes to their rescue. As in her first novel, *If Morning Ever Comes,* Anne Tyler pits a lone central character against a chaotic, incomprehensible household.

Critics accorded considerable attention to *The Clock Winder.* Although some disapproved of its rambling plot or what they viewed as the insubstantiality of its story, others applauded its quiet comedy. Paul A. Doyle, writing in *Best Sellers* (June 15, 1972), spoke for several reviewers when he commended *The Clock Winder* for its "depth of perception, thoughtful analysis of life and people, and graceful, fresh prose style." Sara Blackburn raised the issue of regional writing when she called *The Clock Winder* a flawless Southern novel in her review for *Book World* (May 14, 1972). The book, she asserted, has "many of the virtues that we associate with 'Southern' writing—an easy, almost confidential directness, fine skill at quick characterization, a sure eye for atmosphere, and a special nostalgic humor—and none of its liabilities—sentimentality, a sometimes cloying innocence wise beyond its pretense, a tendency toward over-rich metaphor."

When Bruce Cook of *Saturday Review* (September 4, 1976) asked her during the course of an interview about being a Southern writer, Anne Tyler replied, "I don't actually consider myself Southern, though I suppose I'm that more than anything else. Because if I did consider myself Southern, then that would make me a Southern novelist—and I don't think there is any such thing." She feels no affinity with William Faulkner, who is generally considered the paradigmatic twentieth-century Southern novelist, because of his extremely masculine outlook and determinedly digressive style. She points instead to another Southern writer, Eudora Welty, as the strongest influence on her work. From her exemplar Miss Tyler learned that "there were stories to be written about the mundane life around me."

Despite Anne Tyler's dismissal of the concept of the Southern novelist, her former English professor, Reynolds Price, calls her "the nearest thing . . . to an urban novelist" among Southerners because she has used Baltimore and its environs as a principal setting in all her novels beginning with *The Clock Winder.* Her fifth novel, *Celestial Navigation* (Knopf, 1974), unfolds entirely in the Baltimore area, with most of it taking place in the boardinghouse belonging to its agoraphobic protagonist, Jeremy Pauling, who will not willingly leave his block. The most gifted of Anne Tyler's artist figures, Jeremy makes marvelous collages and sculptures, although he cannot drive a car or carry on a coherent conversation. His alienation from the rhythms of conventional American life brings about the failure of his relationship with Mary Tell, the only person, except his mother, whom he has ever loved.

As his admirer Miss Vinton observes in the novel, Jeremy steers his life by "celestial navigation": "He sees from a distance at all times, without trying, even trying not to. It is his condition. He *lives* at a distance. He makes pictures the way other men make maps—setting down the few fixed points that he knows, hoping they will guide him as he goes floating through this unfamiliar planet." The critical response to *Celestial Navigation* focused on Anne Tyler's presentation of Jeremy through a "collage-like" compilation of first-person accounts of him from the women in his life interspersed with segments that report his view of the world in an understated third-person voice. Some reviewers could see no point in that technique, but others found it an appropriate means of delineating Jeremy's character without violating his solitude. Eileen Kennedy spoke for the many reviewers who found the novel a convincing portrait of an artist when she wrote in *Best Sellers* (May 1, 1974) that "Anne Tyler has translated into words how the mind works with form, line, color: her achievement is extraordinary." *Celestial Navigation* is Anne Tyler's especial favorite among her novels.

In her next novel Anne Tyler expanded her scope from the interior landscape of a single mind to the geographic span of the Eastern United States and the time span of over a century. *Searching for Caleb* (Knopf, 1976), wider in compass than Miss Tyler's other novels, nevertheless shares their methods of delineating character through finely rendered details. An omniscient third-person voice weaves in and out of different points of view and periods of time to present the story of four generations of the Peck family of Baltimore. Beginning with Justin, a thriving sea merchant, the Pecks build themselves into an institution buttressed by good taste and a propriety based on repression. The rebellion of Caleb, the artist figure who leaves the family compound one day in 1912, is repeated less dramatically in the behavior of his great-niece and great-nephew, Justine and Duncan.

Searching for Caleb received virtually unanimous critical acclaim for its humorous yet sensitive handling of the theme of individual choice versus the grip of family custom and heredity. As Catherine Peters explained in the London *Times Literary Supplement* (August 27, 1976), "It becomes clear in the course of this robust, witty novel that Anne Tyler is concerned with an existential examination of the nature of freedom. The choices . . . are not as simple as they seem, perhaps not in themselves important: it is the use made of them that matters." Walter Sullivan, writing in the *Sewanee Review* (Winter 1977), echoed the praise bestowed on Anne Tyler for her controlled but exuberant style: "Miss Tyler has learned a great deal about her craft in the twelve years since her first novel was published, but she has retained a kind of innocence in her view of life, a sense of wonder at all the crazy things in the world and an abiding affection for her own flaky characters."

Anne Tyler once again narrowed her scope in her seventh novel, *Earthly Possessions* (Knopf, 1977), which presents the first-person narrative of Charlotte Emory's double journey: one to Florida as the hostage of bank robber Jake Simms and the other into her past through reminiscence. Charlotte is yet another minor figure in Anne Tyler's gallery of artists, a photographer who has taken over her dead father's studio. She is also a lone alien in a domestic environment cluttered by untidy people and too many possessions. Moreover, as John Updike pointed out in his review for the *New Yorker* (June 6, 1977), Charlotte Emory belongs to "a familiar class of Anne Tyler heroines: women admirably active in the details of living yet alarmingly passive in the large curve of their lives—riders on male-generated events." The critical consensus concerning *Earthly Possessions* was that it lacked the depth of *Celestial Navigation* and *Searching for Caleb*, but as Nicholas Delbanco assured readers of the *New Republic* (May 28, 1977), "Anne Tyler's average work is more than good enough." Evidently agreeing with that assessment, the American Academy and Institute of Arts and Letters in 1977 awarded Anne Tyler a citation "for literary excellence and promise of important work to come."

In another indication of her growing prestige, Anne Tyler's eighth novel, *Morgan's Passing* (Knopf, 1980), earned a nomination for the National Book Critics Circle Award in 1981. That same year, she won the Janet Heidinger Kafka Prize, an award bestowed by the University of Rochester for fiction written by an American woman, also for *Morgan's Passing*. It deals with Morgan Gower, an alien inmate of a messy household full of women, who is himself a maker of chaos as a creator and perpetrator of fictions. An impromptu artist at disguises, he awakens each morning, gazes at his image in the mirror, and decides what persona to take on. Nevertheless, Morgan seeks order and serenity, virtues he projects onto his beloved, the puppeteer Emily Meredith, who is much younger than he. The novel's third-person narration, fluctuating between Morgan's and Emily's points of view, develops its themes, which include the search for identity, the need for self-renewal, and life as improvisation, with deft humor.

Morgan's Passing generated spirited critical discussion, with most reviewers taking sides for or against its protagonist. In the contingent of those who disapproved was Edmund Fuller of the *Wall Street Journal* (April 21, 1980), who contended that Anne Tyler had failed in handling "the always delicate problem of persuading readers to have a tolerant affection for a type of person who is amusing to watch from a distance but who would drive you mad if you had to be closely involved with him." James Wolcott of the *New York Review of Books* (April 3, 1980) pointed to the characterization of Morgan as the novel's undoing, but an admiring Peter S. Prescott of *Newsweek* (March 24, 1980) praised Anne Tyler's characterization of Morgan for its comic skill, while Robert Towers of the *New Republic* (March 22, 1980) savored her clear-eyed comprehension of her characters' shortcomings.

In addition to her eight novels, Anne Tyler has published some forty short stories in magazines such as the *New Yorker*, the *Saturday Evening Post*, *McCall's*, *Ladies' Home Journal*, *Redbook*, *Mademoiselle*, *Seventeen*, *Southern Review*, and *Antioch Review* and has contributed many articles to the New York *Times Book Review*. In her short fiction Miss Tyler frequently focuses on a single character, reporting his or her point of view in an understated third-person voice and presenting a single incident or a single day in such a way that it adumbrates a whole life. As in her novels, the settings are usually Southern and the themes generally center on family relationships, alienation or loneliness, the failure of communication between individuals, and the search for meaning in life.

Anne Tyler shares her north Baltimore home with her husband, the Iranian-born child psychiatrist Taghi Mohammad Modarressi, whom she married on May 3, 1963, and her daughters, Tezh and Mitra. As a dedicated writer, Anne Tyler leads the kind of orderly and highly organized life that many of her characters long for, working at home during her children's school hours on Monday through Thursday and reserving Friday for errands and weekends for family. Shut away in her starkly plain study, she sits on a daybed and writes with a pen in longhand, so that, as she says, she can hear her characters speak, and she derives her ideas from boxes of index cards, many of which she prepares during her hours of habitual insomnia.

Anne Tyler's usual working method is to compose a first draft of each novel, read it to find out "what it means," and then revise it to unify and enhance her subconscious intentions. The end Anne Tyler always keeps in view is the writing of "serious" fiction. As she has explained, "A serious book is one that

removes me to another life as I am reading it. It has to have layers and layers, like life does. It has to be an extremely believable lie." The reward she seeks is the joy of sharing her fictive worlds with empathetic readers. "They in their solitude, and I in mine, have somehow managed to touch without either of us feeling intruded upon," she says of their rapport. "We've spent some time on neutral territory, sharing a life that belongs to neither of us."

References: N Y Times Bk R p13+ My 8 '77 pors; New Yorker 56:97+ Je 23 '80; Washington Post G p1+ Ag 15 '76; Contemporary Authors 1st rev vols 9-12 (1974); Who's Who in America, 1980-81; Who's Who of American Women, 1979-80; World Authors: 1970-1975 (1980)

Waitz, Grete (vītz)

Oct. 1, 1953- Runner. Address: b. c/o Larry DeFreitas, Libco/Adidas, 1 Silver Court, Springfield, N.J. 07081

Of all the women runners to emerge during the running boom of the 1970's, the most celebrated is Grete Waitz, an erstwhile Norwegian schoolteacher who has been competing internationally for eleven years. Mrs. Waitz has won races at all distances and on all surfaces, but her forte is not speed in sprinting but endurance in road running—that is, the ability to sustain a high percentage of her maximum pace over distance. She developed as a middle-distance runner, better at the mile and the 3,000 meters than the 1,500 meters, but

she finally hit her stride in the 1978 New York Marathon, in which she set a new record for women. In lowering her time in that 26-mile, 385-yard New York City event in the years following (to 2:25:42 in 1980), she narrowed the gap between the clocking of men and women for the distance to seventeen minutes and eight seconds. Between 1978 and 1981 she also won the women's international cross-country championship three times and set new world records for the 10,000 meters (30:59.8), 7.1 miles (37:12), and 15,000 meters (48:01). Suffering from shin splints, she dropped out of the 1981 New York Marathon at mid-course and cheered on New Zealand's Allison Roe, who set a new women's record of 2:25.28. In the same race Alberto Salazar lowered the time for men to 2:8.13.

Mrs. Waitz's success in distance running was undoubtedly a factor in the recent decision of the all-male International Olympic Committee —on the advice of the International Amateur Athletic Federation—to add 3,000-meter and marathon events to the women's Olympic track program, beginning in 1984. "In her concentration, her cool grace, her coiled-spring hardness, Waitz is a riveting symbol of uncompromised excellence," Kenny Moore observed in Sports Illustrated (October 22, 1979), "and the message is taking hold."

Grete Waitz acquired her current last name by her marriage to Jack Waitz, an accountant for an Oslo newspaper who has sacrificed his own avocation as a runner in order to serve as her coach and manager. She was born Grete Andersen in Oslo, Norway on October 1, 1953, the youngest of three children of John Andersen, a pharmacist, and Reidun Andersen, a grocery store clerk. Growing up in an athletic family in a country where athletes are not idolized but emulated, Grete became involved in sports early, starting with handball and moving on to gymnastics and track. Her potential as a runner was noticed by a neighbor, the Olympic javelin champion Terje

Pedersen, who recruited her for his track team when she was eleven. "He was my hero . . . ," she told Kenny Moore of *Sports Illustrated*. "I wanted to please him so much."

Running only the sprints at first, Grete soon graduated to 400 meters. She early realized that her strong point was distance, as she told Kenny Moore: "As I trained, I got no faster, only stronger. By 1972 I was running the 800 and the 1,500, and I saw that I was better in the 1,500, so I trained more and more but still got no faster, just stronger."

In 1972 Mrs. Waitz emerged without a medal from her first Olympic competition, the 1,500 meters, then the longest women's Olympic run. Women began competing in the Olympics in 1900, four years after the modern games began, but their progress against sexist paternalism was slow, and it suffered a serious setback in 1928, when two contestants in the 800 meters fainted at the finish line. Thereafter, women's Olympic events were limited to 200 meters until 1960, when the 800-meter race was reinstated. Similarly, women were excluded from the Boston Marathon until Katharine Switzer participated in that event disguised as a man in 1967. Women were not excluded from the New York City Marathon when it was inaugurated in 1970, but none finished in that event until 1972.

All along, Mrs. Waitz was philosophical about the acceptance, and the potential, of women in distance running. "Anything new takes getting used to," she observed in the *Sports Illustrated* interview with Kenny Moore. "In 1973 when we first ran the 3,000 here in Oslo, lots of journalists said it was terrible, it wasn't 'pretty' to see the women getting tired. That changed when I set a world record in it in 1975. Everybody loved it then."

In the 1974 European championships, Mrs. Waitz placed third in the 1,500 meters, and the following year she set a record of 8:46.6 in the 3,000 meters. She was eliminated in the semi-finals of the 1,500 meters in the Olympics in Montreal in 1976. In 1977 she won the World Cup at 3,000 meters, and in 1978 she finished fifth in the 1,500 meters in the European championships, with a time of 4:00.6, just 0.6 seconds away from the bronze medal.

Until 1978, Mrs. Waitz's career seemed fated to remain as stunted as those of previous women endurance runners unable to realize their potential fully within the distance limitations imposed on them in Olympic and International Amateur Athletic Federation events. Then came the invitation from the New York Road Runners Club, sponsor of the New York Marathon, which her husband and Knut Kvalheim, the Norwegian men's 10,000-meter record holder, persuaded her to accept.

Her strategy in her first marathon, the 1978 New York City race, was to try to conserve her strength in the beginning but still to keep up with the favorite, Germany's Christa Vahlensieck, and to hope for the best in the final miles. When she started the race she was only a face in a crowd of 11,000 and the number she was assigned—F1173—made clear that she was not among the officially projected leaders in the race. During the race she followed Miss Vahlensieck for the first nine miles and then pulled out in front and completed the unfamiliar course among a swarm of male competitors. Her time was two hours, thirty-two minutes, and thirty seconds, eighty-eighth overall and a new women's world record by more than two minutes. "I couldn't have gone much farther," she later confessed. "I couldn't run for three days afterward. I even had trouble *walking*. Maybe I ran well because I didn't know how terrible it is, the pain after [more than] thirty kilometers."

After returning to Norway and her job teaching physical education, Norwegian, and English at the Bjölsen School, a secondary school in Oslo, she decided that the diversion of her time and attention to running was "not good for the kids." She quit teaching—with the intention of returning to it in the future—and later became a consultant to a sporting goods company.

In both 1978 and 1979 Grete Waitz won the women's world cross-country championship, and in July 1979 she ran the 3,000 meters in 8:31.8, a time second only to the 8:27.1 world record of the U.S.S.R.'s Lyudmila Bragina. In New York City in June 1979 she set a world record of 31:14.4 in the 10,000-meter L'eggs Mini-Marathon in Central Park. Four months later she was back in New York for her second marathon there, this time wearing number F1. In the 1979 marathon she shaved five minutes and fifty-seven seconds off her 1978 record, finishing sixty-ninth overall with a time of two hours, twenty-seven minutes, and thirty-three seconds. Despite stomach cramps that forced her to take a rest during the race, she had become the first woman ever to run a marathon faster than two and a half hours, a time formerly seen as a barrier separating male and female runners. "The last time I saw her was at the starting gate," Gillian Adams, the women's runner-up, told Al Harvin of the *New York Times* (October 22, 1979). "She's just really, really fit. I've watched her a lot in races in Europe. She's well built for running —long legs, slim—and she's very determined. I'm not surprised she's run that fast."

The decision to go or not to go to Moscow for the 1980 Olympics weighed heavily on Mrs. Waitz, because she would have had to change her training schedule and pacing to concentrate on the 1,500 meters again. She was happy when the Norwegian Athletic Federation made her decision academic by choosing to support the American-led boycott of the Moscow Olympics, an action undertaken in protest of the Soviet intervention in Afghanistan.

As it turned out, 1980 was a banner year for Grete Waitz even without the Olympics. She won the women's international cross-country championship for the third straight year; set new world records for five miles, ten miles, 15,000 meters, and 20,000 meters; bettered her 10,000-meter mark by fifteen seconds; and again finished first among women in the New York Marathon, with an improvement of two minutes and twenty-five seconds in her time. Her clocking in the 1980 marathon would have beaten all the men who finished in the 1970 marathon, including Gary Muhrcke, who won in 2:31:38, and all male Olympic marathon gold medalists before 1952.

On May 30, 1981 Mrs. Waitz won her third consecutive L'eggs Mini-marathon, covering the 10,000 meters in thirty-two minutes and forty-three seconds, well over a minute slower than the record she set in 1980. "I didn't go for any record because it was much too hot," she explained to Al Harvin of the New York Times (May 31, 1981). "I don't like to run all the time against the clock. I just wanted to run to win today."

Mrs. Waitz usually trains twice a day, one hour early in the morning and one hour late in the afternoon, but she says that she "listens to [her] body," and if it tells her to go easy she will limit herself to one hour a day for perhaps one or two days a week. Her training is mostly speed work, with some medium-distance runs thrown in. "I never train more than ten kilometers at once," she explained when Lesley Visser interviewed her on the occasion of her being selected "sportswoman of the year" by Women's Sports (January 1981). "To be honest, anything more is boring. I train only for the 3,000." She said that the 3,000-meter limit held true even before marathons, and that she viewed the twenty-mile practice runs of many marathon trainees as extremely ill-advised. "The main difference between me and the other girls is simply that I have more speed, more tempo. Girls training now don't do enough speed or track training. They are running long all the time." She has no special training diet, although she places importance on the ordinary Norwegian practices of a light lunch (rather than a heavy hot meal) at noon and the eating of dark hardtack rather than white bread (the one dietary proscription she mentions in interview after interview).

Alluding to the Eastern European system of "total sport," her husband has said that Mrs. Waitz is "not easily molded." "She wouldn't have thrived in any more structured system. Hers must be as normal a life as possible. She is very bright, she always got the best marks in school and was the youngest applicant accepted for the teachers' college. She prepared for teaching as carefully as for running, and it [was] just as important to her." Her independence of spirit was demonstrated when she turned down a stipend from the Norwegian Amateur Athletic Federation because she did not want to feel under any pressure to perform well other than that of her own desire to win. "I race to win," she has said, "not to set records."

Jack and Grete Waitz, who were married in 1975, live in a modest apartment on a hill (her favorite training ground) in the Oslo suburb of Romsaas. Outside of the traveling that they reluctantly accept as a necessary part of an international running career, they are homebodies, content with each other's company, with watching some television, and with entertaining friends. "We do not like to go places where people will point at me," she told Lesley Visser in the interview for Women's Sports. "I do not need publicity. The travel and publicity is sometimes hard. It has meant that I spent Christmas in California, spring in New York, and hours on the telephone. And it makes it difficult to keep my nine o'clock curfew." Miss Visser found her to be "refreshingly demure" in a world where athletic celebrity is usually accompanied by an outsized ego.

Blond, blue-eyed Grete Waitz is five feet seven inches tall and weighs about 116 pounds. When she is running, her face is the impassive register of a drive and concentration that transcend pain, and at other times it is usually solemn and thoughtful. Because, as she has observed, she is "not always smiling and laughing," people mistakenly think she is sad. "I'm not sad . . . maybe a little cool . . . controlled. That's the word. Controlled." As for the future, she will take it a year at a time: "I'll never stop running, but the hard training and the competition call for intensity. Once you know international racing, you can't just ease off a bit. It has to be one or the other; as hard as you can, or just for fun."

References: N Y Times III p8 O 22 '79; People 14:36 D 29 '80 por; Sports Ill 51:42+ O 22 '79 pors; Women's Sports 1:32+ Ja '79 pors, 2:15+ Mr '80 pors, 3:35+ Ja '81 pors

---

Wałesa, Lech (va-wenz'a lek)

1943(?)- Polish labor leader. Address: b. Morski Hotel, Gdansk, Poland

When labor unrest erupted into massive strikes in Poland in July 1980, Lech Wałesa was an apparently obscure unemployed electrician known to authorities as an incorrigible labor "troublemaker." A mere three months later, as the organizer and chairman of the only independent trade union in the Communist world, Wałesa had become one of the three most powerful men in his country, on a par with the First Secretary of the Communist party and the Primate of the Roman Catholic church. Speaking the simple language of the workingman and identifying himself as a faithful son of the church, he has drawn 10,000,000 of Poland's 17,300,000 workers into his union, known as Solidarity. His achievement has alarmed the

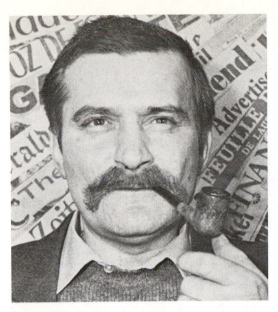

Lech Wałesa

The improvement of conditions under Gierek proved to be only temporary. By overextending itself in its plan to modernize industry, the Gierek regime ran up unexpectedly high international debts. At the same time, in an effort to right the balance of trade and to build up buying power with the West, it increased the export of goods, including such prized meat and meat products as Polish ham, and those commodities, accordingly, became scarcer at home. Worker discontent seethed, finally erupting in strikes and violent demonstrations at Ursus, near Warsaw, and Radom, in east central Poland, when Gierek attempted to end the five-year freeze on meat and other food prices on April 1976. To avert escalation of the crisis, the First Secretary quickly restored the freeze.

Gdansk was not directly affected by the events of April 1976, but Wałesa was fired from his job at the shipyard for his boldness in protesting the erosion of the concessions made to workers six years before. In the following years he lived inconspicuously, providing for his family as best he could despite successive job losses and jailings resulting from his labor agitation.

Although he was by comparison a moderate, Wałesa's development as a labor leader was strongly influenced by his contact with the radical Committee for Social Self-Defense (KOR). That organization was founded by the disaffected Communist sociologist Jacek Kuron and other dissident intellectuals to give medical, legal, and material aid to workers—and the families of those workers—who were fired, jailed, or under attack for having taken part in the April 1976 strikes and demonstrations. Partly through its clandestine bulletins and newspaper *Robotnik*, KOR came to serve an even more vital purpose—that of an information clearinghouse and communications system giving a sense of unity to workers who would otherwise have been isolated in their plight. It also served as an educational agency, a school of formation for an incipient labor leadership generally more moderate than its own leadership. While stressing the difference between his labor movement and KOR—"KOR does not direct us, it helps us"—Wałesa later came to the defense of KOR on those occasions when the state tried to suppress its "antisocialist" activities.

Two major events in recent Polish history favored the progress of Wałesa's work as a labor leader. One was the Soviet decision, following the signing of the Helsinki agreements of 1975, to make the most of the incorrigibility of Poland, the *enfant terrible* of the Eastern bloc, and let the country become a "showcase of détente." The other was the election in October 1978 of Karol Cardinal Wojtyla of Poland as the first Slavic pope in the history of the Roman Catholic Church. As Pope John Paul II, Wojtyla returned to his native country for a remarkable nine-day visit in June 1979. The joyous, and sometimes tearful, popular

rulers of the Soviet bloc because it is an implicit contradiction of the Communist party's claim to be the sole legitimate representative of the working class. But Wałesa wisely never makes the contradiction explicit, and by skillfully steering a course between militancy and moderation, he has succeeded thus far in satisfying the basic demands of Poland's aroused workers without provoking intervention by the Soviet Union, which naturally fears that the Polish example might inspire other Eastern bloc nations to do likewise. As one observer has quipped, "Wałesa has surpassed 'Wallenda in pulling off the biggest tightrope act in history."

One of eight children of a carpenter, Lech Wałesa was born in Popow, Poland during the German occupation of World War II. After his father died, his mother married her brother-in-law, Stanisław Wałesa. While visiting relatives in the United States with her second husband in 1973, Mrs. Wałesa was killed in a traffic accident. The stepfather, a lumberman, remained in the United States and now lives in Jersey City, New Jersey.

Wałesa attended a state vocational school in Lipno, near Popow, and after graduation he moved to Gdansk on the Baltic Coast to work as an electrician at the Lenin Shipyard there. In December 1970 the government's raising of food prices sparked violent protests in and around Gdansk. During the "bread riots" strikers at the Lenin Shipyard moved into the streets, where fifty-five of them were massacred by the police. As the violence continued for four days, Władisław Gomułka was forced to resign as First Secretary of the Polish Communist party and was succeeded by Edward Gierek, who made concessions to the workers.

reception accorded the Pope contrasted dramatically with the grudging protocol extended by the government. An international television audience suddenly saw a demoralized nation renewed in spirit, a whole people daring to assert a patriotism symbolically inseparable from religion and therefore in defiance of the Communist state. All that the solidarity needed was a capitalization of the "s."

Wałesa's cofounding of an embryonic free trade union on the Baltic Coast was signaled in January 1979 by the first issue of the bimonthly *The Worker of the Coast,* subtitled "the organ of the founding committee of the free trade unions." The following July he was among the signers of a charter of workers' rights published in *Robotnik.* Among the demands listed were an end to censorship, an eight-hour day, improved job safety conditions, higher wages, and legalization of the right to strike. But the most important statement in the charter was the following: "Strikes are useful short-term weapons, but free and independent trade unions are necessary to ensure that the gains won through a strike are not later lost. Only they will give us an equal footing in negotiations, a power the authorities cannot ignore."

When the Polish government, plagued by an enormous foreign debt and serious food shortages, doubled meat prices on July 1, 1980, scattered work stoppages followed in factories across Poland as workers demanded higher wages to compensate for the increased prices. On August 14 the Lenin Shipyard was seized by strikers, who immediately demanded and won the reinstatement of Wałesa and two other dismissed workers. Scaling the fence to join the workers occupying the yard, Wałesa became the leader of the strike, which differed from earlier ones in that the workers were making political as well as economic demands, including the right to form trade unions free of party control and greater freedom of expression. Wałesa was ready to call off the strike on August 16, when the management of the shipyard conceded two points—the rehiring of other fired union activists and raises in pay—but changed his mind when radicals on the strike committee insisted on continuing until the free union movement was recognized.

With the strike spreading across the Baltic Coast, an inter-factory strike committee headed by Wałesa was established on August 17. A week later Prime Minister Edward Babiuch and three other Politburo members were dismissed in a party shakeup, and party leader Gierek promised democratization of the official unions. But Wałesa articulated the strike committee's primary goal in his response to Gierek: "A change in personnel does not interest me. What I want is the freedom of the unions, and I don't care who negotiates that."

As the strike expanded beyond the Baltic region to involve over 300,000 workers, a government committee headed by Deputy Prime Minister Mieczysław Jagielski began negotiating with the strike committee led by Wałesa. On August 31 Wałesa and Jagielski signed an accord, known as the Gdansk agreement, granting workers the right to form independent unions and to strike, the first time such rights had ever been conceded in a Soviet bloc country. The government also pledged to grant wage increases and social benefits, relax censorship, open the state-controlled media to a wide variety of opinion, broadcast Roman Catholic Mass on Sundays, and release jailed members of KOR. The unions, in turn, acknowledged the supremacy of the Communist party in Polish society and accepted Poland's military alliances within the Soviet bloc.

Wałesa demonstrated his organization's strength and discipline when, on his order, workers in Poland's major cities staged a one-hour warning strike on October 3 to protest government procrastination in granting wage increases and greater press freedom as well as its obstruction of union organizing. Next, Wałesa successfully faced down the government on the issue of registration of the independent unions as legal entities. On October 14 a Warsaw court granted the unions the right to register as a single national entity known as Solidarity. But the tribunal added to the proposed charter clauses recognizing the leading role of the Communist party, affirming Poland's alliance system, and abjuring any intent of becoming a political party. Arguing that such items did not belong in a union charter, Wałesa threatened strike action while appealing to the Supreme Court. On October 31 he began discussions with Prime Minister Jozef Pinkowski, and on November 10 the court ruled in the union's favor. With Solidarity registered as a legal organization, party leader Stanisław Kania on November 14 met for the first time with Wałesa, the chairman of the union's national commission. The meeting was generally regarded as a formal indication of the government's acceptance of Solidarity as an integral part of the Polish socialist system.

When political arrests in Warsaw on November 21 prompted that city's Solidarity chapter to call for a general strike, a probe of the police, and a slashing of the state prosecutor's budget, Wałesa flew to Warsaw and warned workers that if extreme demands goaded the Soviet Union to intervene, "we might lose everything." After talks, the authorities released the arrested men and promised to discuss the other issues, and Wałesa called for a six-week moratorium on strikes.

Labor peace prevailed in December as the Soviet Union began a military buildup that put fifty-five divisions near Poland's borders. But in January 1981 worker militancy developed around the government's failure to implement its promised agreement, made in Gdansk, to establish a five-day work week by granting free Saturdays. Wałesa had no choice but to go along with a boycott of work on Saturday,

January 10. Following a visit to Italy (which included a private audience with the Pope), he himself started another such boycott, on January 24. Wildcat strikes on the issue helped persuade the government to meet with Wałesa, and under a pact concluded on January 31, workers were granted three out of four Saturdays off, and a five-day work week was planned for 1982. In addition, Solidarity was granted weekly radio and television time.

Except in regions of the south, the southeast, and the southwest, wildcat strikes by factory workers and coal miners on other issues ended with an agreement reached by the government and Solidarity early in February 1981. Agitation for full union recognition for Rural Solidarity was defused on February 10, 1981, when the Supreme Court issued a compromise ruling to the effect that the farmers had the right to register as "associations."

Amid increasing signals from Moscow that Warsaw must toughen its labor policy, General Wojciech Jaruzelski replaced Jozef Pinkowski as Premier of Poland on February 9, 1981. Wałesa persuaded striking workers in the southwest as well as student strikers to give the new government a chance, but his own patience wore thin when that government began prosecuting some militant unionists and dissidents, including leaders of the nationalist Confederation of Independent Poland (KPN). On March 10 he began talks with Premier Jaruzelski on the prosecutions, which he, Wałesa, viewed as "reprisals."

The largest organized protest in the history of Communist Poland occurred on March 27, 1981 when most of Poland's 13,000,000 industrial workers held a four-hour strike to protest the beatings of union activists in Bydgoszcz eight days before. Protests over food shortages erupted nationwide in late July and early August, and the national congress of Solidarity in its first session, in September, called for free elections in Poland and more workers' rights and urged other Soviet-bloc workers to form free unions. Despite the dissatisfaction of radical unionists with his moderation and "autocratic" rule, Wałesa was reelected chairman of Solidarity during the second session of the congress, on October 2.

With a mandate for tough action, General Jaruzelski became party leader—in addition to premier—on October 18, 1981. In a counter show of strength, Polish workers held a one-hour nationwide walkout on October 28 to protest food shortages and harassment of Solidarity members. In the first summit session of its kind in Poland, General Jaruzelski, Archbishop Jozef Glemp, and Wałesa met to seek a solution to the national economic crisis on November 5, 1981.

Denying charges that he is opposed to the Communist system, Wałesa answers, "We don't want to bring down this government or any other government." Reluctant to talk about politics, he describes himself as "a union man" who is simply trying to deal with workers'

problems. "Those who brought us to this present situation in our country are anti-socialist. We in the unions are the upholders of socialism." What he is opposed to is any system that "makes people forget they are human beings."

Speaking the simple, sometimes ungrammatical language of the common man, Wałesa has won the loyalty of millions of Polish workers, who at mass rallies follow the song "God Save Poland" with chants of "Long live Wałesa" and "May he live 100 years." Although he is not a powerful speaker, his direct, low-key, anecdotal style appeals to his audiences, as does his combining of nationalism with religion. A crucifix is displayed wherever he speaks and he always wears a lapel medallion of the Virgin Mary in her identity as the Black Madonna of Czestochowa. "These are not only symbols of devotion," Anna Wlentinowicz, another Solidarity leader, has explained. "These symbolize Poland reborn, the Poland of the movement."

Lech and Mirosława Wałesa were married in 1969. They have four sons and two daughters and have been reported to be expecting a seventh child. The gravelly-voiced Wałesa is five feet seven inches tall and has reddish brown hair and moustache and impish brown eyes. Although unpolished in his ways and informal in his manner, he is an adroit politician and diplomat, always well-groomed and polite in his confrontations with government leaders, delivering the harshest of criticism in the gentlest of voices. With his followers, he can be louder and sharper but, regardless of the occasion, his good humor is usually as unfailing as his air of authority.

The Solidarity leader has a union salary of equivalent to $333 a month, about the same as that of a shipyard worker. He admits that he is sometimes tempted by the offers of automobiles, villas, and other luxuries made by government officials who would perhaps like to corrupt him. "But then I go to church and pray and I'm able to reject them." (He is a daily communicant.) He has, however, accepted help and gifts from followers, including supplies of cigarettes and food. He now has four suits in addition to the rumpled suit he constantly wore when he first emerged on the world scene, and he has moved with his family from a two-room flat into a six-room apartment.

Wałesa always travels with two carloads of bodyguards, and more than arrest he fears death in an automobile "accident." Although he professes to be a reluctant leader, his wife has been quoted as saying "Leszek [little Lech] has always believed he is destined by God for something big."

References: N Y Times p16 Ag 31 '80 por; National R 33:32+ Ja 23 '81; Newsweek 96: 42+ D 8 '80 pors; People 14:28+ D 29 '80 por; Time 116:31 D 29 '80 pors, 117:38 Ja 5 '81 por; U S News 89:19 D 15 '80 por; International Who's Who, 1981-82

Waters, Muddy

Apr. 4, 1915- Musician; singer. Address: b. c/o Cameron Organization, 320 S. Waiola Ave., La Grange, Ill. 60525

The "gut singer"—as he calls himself—and electric slide guitarist Muddy Waters played a seminal role in the development of urban ensemble blues, which might be described as the down-home Mississippi delta sound with amplification and a beat. Although not widely appreciated in its raw form, the Chicago blues, as Waters' hard-driving idiom is also called, has been strongly influential in popular music. Waters migrated from the delta to Chicago in 1943, and during the 1950's his relentless phrasing and gritty instrumentation became models for his black contemporaries. During the past two decades his appeal has been chiefly to a white audience and he has markedly influenced a generation of white hard-rock musicians, including guitarist-singer Johnny Winter, who often concertizes and records with him, along with such old Chicago cronies of Waters' as the harmonica player James Cotton. Among the songs in Waters' repertoire are "Rollin' Stone," "Got My Mojo Workin'," "Tiger in Your Tank," "Deep Down in Florida," "Hoochie Coochie Man," "Funky Butt," "I Can't Be Satisfied," "Mule Kicking in My Stall," and "Whiskey Ain't No Good." Several of his albums, including *They Call Me Muddy Waters*, *The London Muddy Waters Sessions*, and *Muddy Waters: Woodstock Album*, have won Grammy awards in the ethnic/traditional category.

Muddy Waters was born McKinley Morganfield on April 4, 1915 in Rolling Fork, Mississippi, the second son of Ollie Morganfield, a farmer, and Bertha (Jones) Morganfield. After

his mother died, when he was about three, his maternal grandmother took him to live with her in her sharecropper's cabin on Stovall's plantation in Clarksdale, Mississippi. According to most accounts, his grandmother nicknamed him Muddy Waters because as a young child he liked to play in the muddy creek behind their cabin. Whatever its origin, the nickname endured, to become his professional name.

The late Big Bill Broonzy, a Mississippi delta bluesman who preceded Waters in migrating to Chicago, once said, "We sang the blues. In New Orleans they played jazz." The blues is an expression of the black person made mobile, rather than free, by the Emancipation Proclamation, as Arnold Shaw wrote in *The Rock Revolution* (1969): "The blues is a migratory music of men in search of work, food, money, sex, love, and self-respect. A music of nasal moans, spoken delivery, and on-the-beat phrasing, it originated in the delta region of Mississippi." Waters heard that music sung as he worked as a boy in the corn and cotton fields, and as far back as he can remember he was "beating on bucket tops and tin cans—anything with a sound." His first conventional instruments were, successively, the accordion, the jew's-harp, and the harmonica. Acquiring a guitar when he was seventeen, he was soon playing such traditional delta blues songs as "Walkin' Blues," "Dark Road Blues," "Catfish Blues," and "Pony Blues."

His chief models among older delta musicians were Charley Patton, Eddie ("Son") House, and Robert Johnson. House and Johnson were then the foremost practitioners of the "bottleneck" slide technique—in which an improvised fret is moved over the strings of the guitar as they are plucked—and Waters also admired "that preaching kind of singing" which House did. At the home of a neighbor who owned a phonograph, he would listen for hours on end to such blues records as the Mississippi Sheiks's "Sittin' on Top of the World," Leroy Carr's "How Long Blues," Lonnie Johnson's "Careless Love," and Memphis Minnie's "Bumble Bee."

All the records he heard, even the more urbane, were translated by Waters into the delta idiom, a harsh, strongly rhythmic music with sharp lyrical complexities that is more easily imitated instrumentally than vocally. "There are a lot of good youngsters around today, including whites," Waters has said, "who can *play* about as good as anybody you could name. But there is one thing they never can do: sing like a Son House or Robert Johnson. In order to sing like Robert Johnson, you got to *be* a Robert Johnson—grow and live and suffer like he did."

The delta style aside, Waters made songs in the public domain his own by change or embellishment. "Bumble Bee," for example, became "Honey Bee," and "Catfish Blues" became "Rollin' Stone," Waters' rambler's manifesto, the inspiration for Bob Dylan's "Like a Rolling Stone" and for the names of Mick

Jagger's rock group and of Jan Wenner's magazine. Rambler though he was, Waters remained at the Stovall plantation as long as he did mostly for his grandmother's sake. Weekdays he worked in the fields, and weekends he performed in town, at fish fries, in juke joints, or at parties. Ultimately he ran his own juke house, complete with moonshine whiskey and a gambling table.

The folk musicologist Alan Lomax, making field recordings for the Library of Congress archives, discovered Waters in 1941. Lomax had gone to Stovall's plantation looking for Robert Johnson, only to learn that Johnson had died years before, the victim of homicide. Instead, Lomax recorded Waters playing his steel-bodied acoustic guitar and singing such songs as "I Be's Troubled" and "Country Blues." In a return visit to the plantation, a year later, Lomax recorded him as a soloist with Son Sims and his string band. In those early recordings, Waters' voice comes across with urgency, to the accompaniment of hypnotic repetitive bass patterns and sharp slide treble figures. They can be heard on the Testament album *Down on Stovall's Plantation* (T-2210).

Encouraged by hearing himself on the Lomax pressings, and following an argument with the overseer at the plantation, Waters in 1943 joined the wartime migration northward to Chicago, where his married sister was living and where he planned to seek his musical fortune. Staying at his sister's apartment until he found one of his own, he earned a living working in a paper mill, driving a truck, and delivering Venetian blinds. Evenings and weekends, he began playing at parties and at taverns with other musicians from the delta, including the guitarists Baby Face Leroy, Jimmy Rogers, and Blue Smitty and the pianist Eddie Boyd, and soon he formed his own group.

The Southern bluesmen who had established themselves in Chicago in the prewar years, including John Lee ("Sonny Boy") Williamson, Big Bill Broonzy, and Tampa Red still dominated the blues scene there, but Waters and his associates, with their rawer down-home sound, were crucial factors in the crystallization of the hard, strident style that came to be identified with the Chicago blues. One distinguishing element in the new sound created by Waters was amplification, which he began to use to raise the decibel level of his music above the noise in the crowded and rowdy bars and nightclubs of Chicago's South Side in the postwar years. Another was a pepping up of the blues beat with metrical surprise, by introducing an irregular backbeat into the normal twelve bars.

In 1947 Leonard and Phil Chess, two brothers from Poland who owned a nightclub on Chicago's South Side, established Aristocrat Records to record the kind of "race" music popular with the patrons of their club. Two songs recorded by Waters that year for Aristocrat—"Little Anna Mae" and "Gypsy Wom-

an," his first "hoodoo" recording—were withheld from release by Leonard Chess, the production half of the fraternal team, because he was accustomed to a more jazz-like sound. In 1948 Waters cut two more sides for Aristocrat, "I Can't Be Satisfied" and "I Feel Like Going Home," accompanied by Big Crawford's string band as well as Waters' electric slide guitar. Leonard Chess was again dubious, but he released the record and, to his surprise, it became, by Artistocrat's specialized-audience standards, a hit. Even more successful was "Rollin' Stone," which Chess released two years later.

In 1950 the Chess brothers changed the name of their label from Aristocrat to Chess Records. In the early 1950's Waters brought into his recording sessions at Chess the band that gave postwar Chicago blues its definitive sound. It included Elgin Evans on drums, Jimmy Rogers on second guitar, and Little Walter Jacobs, whose innovative use of the amplifier made his harmonica one the most revolutionary ingredients of the sound Waters was creating. Among the other brilliant bluesmen who played with Waters over the years were bassist Willie Dixon (who wrote many of his songs), harmonica player Shakey Walter Horton, guitarist Buddy Guy, and pianist Otis Spann, who was Waters' right-hand man from the mid-1950's until his death in 1969.

The quality and coherence of Waters' recordings for the then predominantly black rhythm-and-blues audience in the early and mid-1950's brought him a kind of recognition rare for a blues singer. As Pete Welding observed in the *American Folk Music Occasional* (Oak, 1970), those recordings "possess an immediacy, force, lack of artifice, [and] surging rhythm" and were "largely responsible for lending vitality and passion—as well as direction—to the then emerging rhythm-and-blues form." Outstanding among the releases were "Louisiana Blues," "Long Distance Call," "Honey Bee," "She Moves Me," and "Still a Fool," in 1951; "Standing Around Crying," in 1952; "Hoochie Coochie Man," which was number eight on the r & b charts in 1953; and "Just Make Love to Me," which was number four in 1954. Waters' earliest Chicago recordings, including three sides cut for Columbia Records but withheld from release, are on *Chicago Blues: The Beginning* (Testament 2207) and *Sail On* (Chess 1539). Recordings made in the 1950's were collected on *Real Folk Blues* (Chess 1501) and *More Real Folk Blues* (Chess 1511).

From their base in Chicago, Waters and his band went on regular tours of the South and made less regular forays into the East, traveling from gig to gig in Waters' Cadillac. Recalling the impact of rock 'n' roll, beginning in the mid-1950's, Waters told Robert Palmer in an interview for *Rolling Stone* (October 5, 1978): "It hurt the blues pretty bad. People wanted to 'bug all the time and we couldn't play slow blues anymore. But we still hustled around and kept going. We survived."

His changeover to a white audience began in 1958, with a tour of Great Britain, the success of which only gradually became apparent. Waters' amplified sound brought complaints from English folk purists, but his volume and power impressed some British musicians, notably Alexis Korner and Cyril Davis, and that impression lasted. Following the lead of Korner, Davis, *et al.*, the Rolling Stones, Eric Clapton and the Yardbirds, and other white rock-blues groups sprang up in England in the 1960's, playing louder than Waters ever did. "Do I like them?" Waters responded when Tom Zito of the Washington *Post* (August 9, 1972) asked him what he thought of the Rolling Stones. "I mean, I better love them! You white people didn't know my name until those boys started recording my songs."

In the United States, Waters' transition to a white audience began with his appearance at the 1960 Newport Jazz Festival and the live album resulting therefrom. There were traces of the Chicago blues in such American rock groups and singers as Jefferson Airplane/Starship, Janis Joplin, Blood, Sweat, and Tears, and Led Zeppelin, and Waters' influence was direct and enormous with such young white musicians as Paul Butterfield and Mike Bloomfield.

Ironically, the popular white rock stars who owed so much to Waters' music artistically overshadowed their model and mentor commercially. In an effort to attract the psychedelic rock audience, Chess Records persuaded Waters to record with augmented Jimi Hendrix-type studio backing on such albums as *Electric Mud* (1968), but those accommodations to the vogue were failures, in which the guitar work seemed to have no meaningful relation to Waters' singing.

In contrast, as Geoffrey Cannon observed in the *Guardian* (February 4, 1969), *Muddy Waters: More Real Folk Blues* (Chess LPS 1511) was a simple recording on which Waters combined singing and guitar playing "so that they are one." "The folk blues music he sings and plays is majestic, sexual, male. It moves us because it is his own music [expressing] his experiences as he has lived them. . . . He masters both himself and his music through spare discipline, through exact, small differences between phrases and chords. Always, it's the same man talking."

Also much more effective than *Electric Mud* was another effort in a similar direction, the 1969 double-LP tribute to Waters' influence on younger, mainly white, rock-oriented musicians, *Fathers and Sons* (Chess LPS 127), the cover illustration of which was a cartoon version of the Sistine Chapel ceiling, with a black Jehovah extending his creative finger toward a white Adam in fig leaf and dark glasses. Contributing to the success of the collaboration was the willingness of the "sons"—Mike Bloomfield on guitar, Paul Butterfield on electric harmonica, and Donald ("Duck") Dunn on bass guitar—to serve for the most part as unassuming sidemen. Dunn, for example, provided a restrained

bass; Bloomfield laid down tasteful bass lines behind the master's guitar and treble riffs at the end of his vocal phrases, and his richly textured solos on such songs as "Walkin' Thru the Park," "Can't Lose What You Ain't Never Had," and "Standin' Round Crying" complemented Waters' funkier style; and Butterfield was powerful while remaining in Waters' mode in "Walkin' Forty Days and Forty Nights" and "Baby, Please Don't Go." The best of Waters' sides of the 1960's were brought together in the album *They Call Me Muddy Waters* (Chess 1553).

In an automobile accident in October 1969, a head-on collision in which the drivers of both cars were killed, Waters suffered a broken leg, fractured ribs, a sprained back, and a paralyzed right hand. He was hospitalized for three months, bedridden at home for several more months, and on crutches for six additional months. He thought he would never play again, but after therapy for his right hand he could again finger his guitar, although not with quite the old dexterity.

Fronting a six-piece band that featured Pinetop Perkins on piano and Willie Smith on drums, Waters resumed his concert tours in 1971. His engagements during the following years included performances at such clubs as the Bottom Line and Max's Kansas City in New York City, the Cellar Door in Washington, D.C., and Mr. Kelly's in Chicago, such houses as Radio City Music Hall in New York City, and the Montreux, Antibes, Nice, and Newport jazz festivals. During those years Chess Records was sold and sold again, and Waters was unhappy to find himself belonging to a succession of conglomerates. Under the new, shrewd management of Scott Cameron, he sued Arc Music, the publishing arm of Chess Records, for royalties due him for many compositions, and won an out-of-court settlement.

In 1976 Waters contracted with Blue Sky Records (which are distributed by Columbia Records) for a series of albums to be produced by the American rock star and virtuoso guitarist Johnny Winter. "The man understands things that I forgot," Waters said of Winter soon after the two began to work together. "He listened to me when I was a kid. My singing, from the deep part of Mississippi, the delta, it's so different it's hard for anybody to figure out—it's hard for the *musicians* to figure out. . . . This music isn't a clock thing, it don't go tick-tick-tick-tick. It goes four ticks and maybe two more ticks, and then the next time maybe it goes in the right order."

The first Waters album produced by Winter was *Hard Again* (1977), on which Waters was backed by Winter and harmonica player James Cotton in such old standards as "Mannish Boy" and six new songs, of which "The Blues Had a Baby and They Named It Rock 'n' Roll" became the most popular. Critics heard a "rejuvenated," "reaffirmed," "unleashed" Waters on *Hard Again*, whose sales exceeded 100,000, an unusual figure for a blues recording.

On *I'm Ready* (1978) Waters was joined by his old Chicago colleagues Walter Horton and Jimmy Rogers, both of whom had a salutary restraining effect on the exuberant Winter. Among the cuts were new versions of the title song as well as of "Rock Me," "Screamin' and Cryin'," and "Good Morning, Little Schoolgirl" and the originals "Thirty-three Years" and "Who Do You Trust?" Reviewing *I'm Ready* in *Rolling Stone* (April 6, 1978), Dave Marsh observed that Waters had found "the proper context" and the "right supporting players" for showing that he had never "lost his incredible sense of the blues, either as a guitarist or as a vocalist." "At this point, Muddy Waters is still singing like the true king of the blues, the last great original master of the form. Or, to put it another way, his mojo is working so well that it just might work on even you." *Hard Again* and *I'm Ready* brought Waters Grammy awards in the ethnic/traditional category.

Waters was among the guest performers in the concert film *The Last Waltz* (United Artists, 1978), Martin Scorsese's documentary about the final get-together of Bob Dylan and The Band. The 1979 Newport Jazz Festival included a tribute to Waters at Radio City Music Hall at which Waters, playing, as usual, with the verve of a much younger man, jammed with Johnny Winter, James Cotton, and B. B. King. After witnessing a performance by Waters at the Beacon Theatre in Manhattan in March 1981, Stephen Holden wrote in the New York *Times* (April 1, 1981): "Vocally, Mr. Waters is a raw blues shouter whose gruff attacks are completely unaffected. There is nothing pretty about his guttural baritone, and his direct phrasing communicates basic emotions with a harsh exuberance. Mr. Waters's guitar style is similarly primitive. Squealing and vibrant, it has a visceral intensity that perfectly matches his singing."

Muddy Waters is a big man of commanding presence who exudes macho self-confidence, retains his Mississippi drawl, and has a chronically bad back. By his wife, Geneva, who died in 1973, he has two grown sons. In an interview with Paul Hendrickson for the *Washington Post* (February 10, 1978), he spoke of a new love in his life: "She's twenty-four. I call her my little Sunshine. She's from Florida." Waters lives in a Chicago suburb, in a two-story frame house that swarms with his grandchildren and with the children of the neighborhood.

Waters is philosophical about blacks turning their backs on the blues, as he said in the Washington *Post* interview with Tom Zito: "I imagine that if I was a young black musician today, I'd go in for rock instead of blues. You can make $1,000,000 with one big hit. You have to go hungry on the blues for a long time. And as for the audience, so once they were black and now they're white. I guess you could say I raised two crops in one year now, couldn't you?"

References: *Chicago Tribune* VI p5 My 24 '81 por; *Ebony* 27:76+ Mr '72 pors; N Y *Daily News* p69 Ag 23 '77 por; N Y *Times* C p1+ Mr 27 '81 por; *Rolling Stone* p55+ O 5 '78 pors; *Time* 98:46 Ag 9 '71 por; *Washington Post* B p1+ S 24 '71, B p13 Ag 9 '72 por; Guralnick, Peter. *Feel Like Goin' Home* (1971); Harris, Sheldon. *Blues Who's Who* (1980); *Who's Who in America*, 1980-81

Will, George F(rederick)

1941- Journalist. Address: b. Washington Post, 1150 15th St. NW, Washington, D.C. 20071

George F. Will is a nationally syndicated, Pulitzer Prize-winning conservative columnist who probes below the surface of political issues for their broad philosophical significance. A former professor of political philosophy, Will worked as an aide to Senator Gordon Allott of Colorado before he became a columnist. Now regarded as the most intellectually substantial of the conservative columnists, he began his Washington *Post* column, currently appearing twice a week in over 300 newspapers, in 1973, and three years later started to contribute his biweekly column to *Newsweek* magazine. Although in agreement with other conservatives on most issues, Will rejects free-market economics on the ground that its antipolitical bias neglects the important role of the state in curbing naked self-interest in favor of national goals not attainable by individuals. Disturbed by what he considers to be an erosion of moral values and a sense of common purpose in America, Will viewed the Reagan Presidential campaign as a vehicle for countering that trend and enthusiastically backed the Republican candidate. He therefore emerged from the 1980 election campaign as a kind of informal intellectual adviser to President Ronald Reagan.

The son of Frederick L. and Louise 'Will, George Frederick Will was born into an academic environment in Champaign, Illinois, in 1941. His father was a professor of philosophy at the University of Illinois at Champaign; his mother taught in high school and later edited a children's encyclopedia. Although both parents were Democrats, they were essentially apolitical. When Frederick L. Will retired from the University of Illinois in 1977, his son paid a tribute to the decisive influence that his father had had upon his character in a column that he wrote for the Washington Post (April 3, 1977). Remembering an occasion when a sudden philosophic insight led his father to discard a manuscript that had been almost ten years in the making, Will observed that "there is no moral power like that of quiet example, and none more vivid to me than my father's."

At Trinity College in Hartford, Connecticut, Will was more interested in National League baseball than intellectual matters until his senior year, when he advanced from being sports editor to editor of the school's newspaper. A liberal during his undergraduate days, he served as a cochairman of Trinity Students for Kennedy in 1960. But after enrolling at Oxford University, Will found himself drawn into a circle of students who, under the influence of Friedrich von Hayek, advocated a free-market economy. "It was in Britain," David S. Broder quoted Will as saying in his The Changing of the Guard (Simon & Schuster, 1980), "that I began to see how a state fueled by unclear ideas about egalitarianism and a sort of reflexive, trendy, intellectual anticapitalism could suffocate the social energies of a country. . . . I became a quite thoroughly ideological capitalist." Returning to the United States, Will entered graduate school at Princeton University, where in 1964 he received a Ph.D. degree in political science after submitting a dissertation on the First Amendment. At Princeton, he gradually moved away from the laissez-faire brand of conservatism, eventually coming to the conclusion that advocates of the free market fail to appreciate the decisive role of politics in society. Along with Leo Strauss, the University of Chicago political philosopher whose disciple he had become, he decided that political institutions have a crucial function because the free play of market forces does not necessarily insure justice.

After leaving Princeton University, George F. Will taught political science at Michigan State University and the University of Toronto, but he left academic life in January 1970 to join the staff of Senator Gordon Allott of Colorado, the chairman of the Republican Policy Committee. During his first year in Washington, which he found "terrific" because, in his opinion, "bad times are always fun," he helped to plan a filibuster against the Cooper-Church amendment to restrict military activity in Cambodia and Laos, and he put his rhetorical skills to work to enhance the quality of Senator Allott's speeches. In the meantime, he had begun to contribute articles to William F. Buckley's conservative National Review, in which he deplored decreases in outlays for defense and increases in social spending. According to Will, the redistributionist policies of the welfare state not only eroded freedom but aided powerful, organized interests rather than the poor.

In spite of the eloquent speeches prepared by his aide, Senator Gordon Allott lost his bid for reelection in 1972, and when his term expired in January 1973, George F. Will lost his staff position. The same month he became Washington editor of the National Review, a post he held until 1975, and he began writing occasional columns for the op-ed page of the Washington Post, spurred on by the enthusiastic response of Meg Greenfield, who was then the deputy editor of its editorial page. In September 1973 the column was nationally syndicated by the Washington Post Writers Group, and in January 1974 it began appearing on a regular twice-a-week basis. Two years later, Will became a contributing editor of Newsweek, writing a biweekly column that appeared on its back page.

One of the youngest conservative columnists ever to gain national recognition, George F. Will was soon regarded as an outstanding practitioner of his craft and was especially admired for the lucidity and grace of his style. Displaying his impressive erudition without any signs of strain, he larded his columns with quotes from such varied and disparate sources as T. S. Eliot, Evelyn Waugh, Mark Twain, Dante, Grantland Rice, and the Bhagavadgita. His dry wit could prove devastating when applied to some of the most venerated figures of the literary establishment, as when in a Washington Post (April 22, 1975) piece on Jean-Paul Sartre, he wrote: "Existentialism often seems to be the belief that because life is absurd, philosophy should be, too."

But it was their intellectual depth, more than anything else, that gave George F. Will's columns their genuine distinction. As Ronald Dworkin observed in the New York Review of Books (October 12, 1978), Will is "the most ambitious" of the conservative columnists because "he wants to define the conservative position not as a matter of party or particular issues but as a general and distinct political theory." In his introduction to The Pursuit of Happiness and Other Sobering Thoughts, a collection of his columns published by Harper & Row in 1978, Will announced that his subject is "not what is secret, but what is latent, the kernel of principle and other significance that exists, recognized or not, inside events, actions, policies and manners." The result, as Carll Tucker pointed out in the *Saturday Review* (July 8, 1978), is that his columns "read as well after the heat of events as before. Sometimes better." In naming George F. Will one of America's 200 young leaders, *Time* magazine (July 15, 1974) reported that "almost overnight his perceptive political commentary made him a leader of conservative opinion." And in 1977 Will was awarded the Pulitzer Prize for distinguished commentary.

Because he is pessimistic about mankind's potential for moral progress and skeptical concerning the works of man, Will is wary of social transformations achieved by welfare state redistributionism or economic growth. "True conservatives," he wrote in *Newsweek* (November 1, 1976), "distrust and try to modulate social forces that work against the conservation of traditional values." "But for a century," Will continued, pitting himself against free-market conservatives, "the dominant conservatism has uncritically worshiped the most transforming force, the dynamism of the American economy." That brand of conservatism "conserves little," he argued, noting that economic growth had levied "a severe toll against small towns, small enterprises, family farms, local governments, craftsmanship, environmental values, a sense of community, and other aspects of humane living."

The economic dynamic and its accompanying free-market ethic had, Will believed, created a grave cultural crisis in which self-interest preempted all other values. He contended that, as beneficiaries of the extraordinary abundance created by economic progress, Americans harbored inordinate appetites for consumer goods and services. Influenced meanwhile by the free-market outlook, they believed that the efforts of individuals to satisfy those appetites, unrestrained by government, invariably redounded to the public good. As Will wrote in the Washington *Post* (August 27, 1975), Americans mistakenly felt that "self-interest could substitute for such virtues as public spiritedness in binding a community together." He argued that a society held together only by transient considerations of self-interest was inherently unstable, lacking in firm moral values and, perhaps, incapable of defending its national independence. An unabashed elitist, he believed that rampant egalitarianism was further weakening Americans' sense of common purpose because it discouraged individuals from respecting any standards external to themselves and led to the election of mediocre politicians who used their offices simply to pander to their constituents' demands.

Rejecting the disparagement of the state by free-market conservatives, Will held, like the classical philosophers long before him, that politics is a noble and essential calling and that government is needed to achieve common social goals beyond the reach of the individual. In his introduction to *The Pursuit of Happiness*

he maintained that "statecraft is, inevitably, soulcraft," meaning by that dictum that government must cultivate in its citizens the kind of character essential to the preservation of a free and civilized society capable of abstaining from self-indulgence for the collective well-being. Among the traits he considered essential for that kind of character were respect for law, public spiritedness, self-discipline, moderation, and reasonableness.

Nevertheless, George F. Will agreed with his fellow conservatives on a variety of issues. He stressed the need for a strong national defense, favored nuclear power, and opposed abortion, busing, affirmative action, the legalization of marijuana, and rights for homosexuals. But on some issues his philosophy took him down a different path. A backer of government fuel conservation regulations, he observed, for example, in the Washington *Post* (April 17, 1977) that "Government exists not merely to serve individuals' immediate preferences, but to achieve collective purposes for an ongoing nation. . . . The market has a remarkable ability to satisfy the desires of the day. But government has other, graver responsibilities, which include planning for the energy needs, military and economic, of the future." Auto safety requirements also met with his approval. With his early recognition and condemnation of President Richard Nixon's Watergate coverup, Will broke with most conservatives by viewing the Nixon Administration's clandestine activities as yet another link in America's recent history of self-indulgent, radical, anti-institutional outbreaks, going back to the civil rights and antiwar movements, in which immediate objectives were placed above respect for law.

Concerned about the prospects of an American society that seemed to him reluctant to make the sacrifices imperative for its future well-being, Will found little to assuage his fears in the policies of President Jimmy Carter in response to an unprecedented Soviet military buildup. In *Newsweek* (March 16, 1981) he wrote that the Carter Administration had "talked loudly about not needing big sticks," stalling or canceling key weapons programs in the hope that supplications and good intentions could substitute for national strength. In the meantime, according to Will, the Administration squandered its resources so lavishly on social programs that huge budget deficits were accumulated despite unparalleled tax increases.

In the conservative challenge to President Jimmy Carter that was mounted within the ranks of the Republican party, Will saw some cause for optimism. Late in 1979 his first preference for the Republican Presidential nomination was not the conservative Ronald Reagan but the more middle-of-the-road Howard Baker, the Senator from Tennessee. Believing that the evaluation of character was as important as issues in assessing the merits of candidates, he did not feel that Reagan had the requisite qualities to be President of the United States. But he was so impressed by Reagan's ability to cope with the crises of the 1980 primary campaign and his generosity following his victory that he came to the conclusion that the former California governor possessed the skill, flexibility, and openness needed to govern effectively. As for the Republican platform, he found it to be "to some extent, a noble rarity, commitment to mold rather than mere conformity to the mood of the moment," although he felt that its uncritical support of capitalism, with its tendency to erode traditional values, conflicted with the Republican party's commitment to halt moral decline.

Consequently, George F. Will ardently backed Ronald Reagan during the 1980 Presidential campaign. "Democrats think they can win," he wrote in his Washington *Post* column (August 24, 1980), "by mixing candor and hysteria —by saying Carter is dismal but Reagan is dangerous." Although he helped to groom Reagan for his debate with Carter, Will denied any conflict between that role and his function as a journalist, since he flatly rejected the view that journalists should adopt an adversary relationship with the government. As he argued in *Newsweek* (January 19, 1981): "A journalist's duty is to see politicians steadily and see them whole. To have intelligent sympathy with them, it helps to know a few as friends." Acting on that precept, Will associated with Reagan both politically and socially during the transitional period between the election and the inauguration, as a member of the President-elect's unofficial brain trust and as his host on at least one occasion.

Since 1974 George F. Will has appeared on public television on *Agronsky and Company*, a news discussion program presided over by Martin Agronsky. In 1975 he was also to be seen on public television as one of the correspondents for *Assignment America*, conducting an interview with Alf Landon, the 1936 Republican nominee for President, and reporting on the gaudy glories of Las Vegas, and in 1980 the American Broadcasting Company hired him as one of its outside commentators for its coverage of both the Democratic and Republican conventions.

George F. Will and Madeleine C. Marion were married on September 4, 1967. They have two sons and a daughter and live in a house in Chevy Chase, Maryland. Although his personality has been described as being chilly or distant, Carll Tucker contended in *Saturday Review* (July 8, 1978): "He would have one perceive him as a misanthrope, an owlish, cranky relic of some simpler era. His work reveals him as a decent, gentle, companionable man, aware of the complexity of events and pained by the pain of others." Will is an enthusiastic advocate of walking, which he has extolled in one of his columns as "the most civilized and civilizing exercise because it is the one most conducive to thinking." A rabid Chicago Cubs fan since the age of seven, he

has facetiously attributed his conservatism, with its concomitant bleak view of mankind, to the persistent failures of that ill-starred baseball club.

References: Broder, David S. *The Changing of the Guard* (1980); *Who's Who in America, 1980-81*

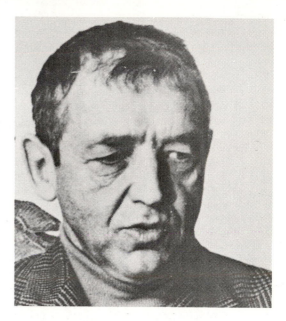

Wyeth, Andrew (Newell) (wī'ə th)

July 12, 1917- Painter. Address: Chadds Ford, Pa. 19317

NOTE: This biography supersedes the article that appeared in *Current Biography* in 1955.

A solitary figure for many years in contemporary American art, Andrew Wyeth is a representational watercolorist and tempera painter who ignored the taste of the art establishment during the heyday of abstract expressionism to win nationwide popularity, inspire countless imitators, and earn the highest prices ever paid for the work of a living American artist. Although he is generally regarded as a realist, he may also be thought of as an abstractionist in that his trees, birds, and kitchen stoves, which look precisely like trees, birds, and kitchen stoves, are likely to be metaphors for loneliness, violence, or decay. His pictures evoke in viewers moods with which they are familiar —often meditative or nostalgic or tranquil and sometimes unsettling—and his perception of the interiors of houses, landscapes, and people indigenous to his home environments in Pennsylvania and Maine—his only subjects—is distinctly personal. As a draughtsman, Wyeth has been compared to the Flemish masters, whom he also approaches, in the opinion of John Canaday of the New York Times (February 14, 1967), "in the exquisite adjustments of tone, color and emphasis that make the difference between the detailed reproduction of nature and a work of art."

Andrew Newell Wyeth was born in the idyllic Pennsylvania farming village of Chadds Ford, in the valley of the Brandywine River, on July 12, 1917, the youngest of five children of Newell Convers and Carolyn Brenneman (Bockius) Wyeth. His mother belonged to a Pennsylvania German, or Dutch, family from Lancaster County, and his father was descended from a Swiss family that had settled in Needham, Massachusetts in the mid-seventeenth century. When a young man, N. C. Wyeth moved from New England to study with the illustrator Howard Pyle in Chadds Ford, where he built his home and studio and where all his children were born. His older son, Nathaniel Convers, is an engineer; two of his daughters, Henriette (Mrs. Peter Hurd) and Carolyn, are painters; and another daughter, Ann (Mrs. John McCoy), is a composer of music.

As the son of the well-known mural painter and beloved illustrator of *Treasure Island*, *Robin Hood*, and other children's classics, Andrew Wyeth grew up in an atmosphere that encouraged his tendency toward the theatrical. The collection of historical costumes and props in his father's studio nourished his romantic fantasies, in which he was free to indulge because sinus trouble in childhood prevented him from attending school and private tutoring left him with time to fill in solitude. In his conversation with Thomas Hoving for the catalogue of his exhibition at the Metropolitan Museum of Art in 1976-77, he recalled, "I played alone, and wandered a great deal over the hills, painting watercolors that literally exploded, slapdash over my pages, and drew in pencil or pen and ink in a wild and undisciplined manner."

Impressed by the talent of Henriette and Carolyn, N. C. Wyeth had begun instructing them in drawing at an early age. Andrew received scant attention until he was about fifteen years old, when he showed his father a toy miniature theatre he had constructed. In his academic training in his father's studio, he gained an understanding of how to look carefully at and deeply into an object and to observe and seize its transient quality. N. C. Wyeth also taught his son the use of the materials and tools of painting, but did not impose on him his own technique.

The Wyeth family customarily spent the summer months in New England, at first in Needham, where, as a boy, Andrew acquired the feeling for pine trees apparent in his mature painting, and later, beginning about 1927, in Port Clyde, Maine. His watercolor landscapes and seascapes of Maine, somewhat

reminiscent of Winslow Homer, made up the greater part of his first one-man show, a sell-out, at the William Macbeth Gallery in New York City in October 1937. Immediate success, however, did not reassure Wyeth, an exceedingly self-critical artist. Feeling that his work was too facile and spontaneous, he returned to his father's studio to pursue realism by concentrating on the human figure and over a period of some months, at the suggestion of his father, drew a skeleton from all angles.

While continuing to paint his deft and flamboyant watercolors, such as his 1942 series of lobsters, Wyeth soon began working in egg tempera, a technique to which his brother-in-law, the painter Peter Hurd, introduced him. The medium of tempera, together with the drybrush method he often employed, forced Wyeth to slow down the execution of a painting and enabled him to achieve the superb textural effects that distinguish his work. He exhibited his temperas at a 1941 Macbeth Gallery show and at the "American Realists and Magic Realists" show in 1943 at the Museum of Modern Art in New York, where he was represented in the latter category. Although he admired the vigor of some abstract expressionists, who were then coming into dominance, Wyeth's statement in the show's catalogue made clear the difference between him and the avant-gardists: "My aim is to escape from the medium with which I work. To leave no residue of technical mannerism to stand between my expression and the observer. To seek freedom through significant form and design rather than through the diversion of so-called free and accidental brushwork. . . . Not to exhibit craft but rather to submerge it; and make it rightfully the handmaiden of beauty, power, and emotional content."

What Wyeth regards as the turning point in his life and career came with the death in October 1945 of his father, whose car was hit by a train at a railroad crossing in Chadds Ford. Wyeth's paintings in several solo shows at the Macbeth Gallery and various group shows had earned critical respect for their lyrical and imaginative characteristics and indications of steady development in brushwork, use of color, and treatment of light. But referring to the death of his father in an interview with Richard Meryman for *Life* (May 14, 1965), Wyeth said, "When he died, I was just a clever watercolorist—lots of swish and swash." The tragic accident left him with the resolve "to really do something serious" with his talent and training. "I had always had this great emotion toward the landscape," he told Meryman, "and so, with his death, . . . the landscape took on a meaning—the quality of him."

The increased importance of emotion in Wyeth's work is evident in the poignant but restrained tempera *Winter 1946*, on which he concentrated for several months following his father's death. He expressed his own feeling in the form of a boy running precipitously down a hill as the bright winter's sun casts an accompanying shadow in flight. While at work on the painting, Wyeth felt much remorse that he had never done a picture of his father, but, he said in the *Life* interview, "the hill finally became a portrait of him." It was at a crossing on the other side of the hill that his father had been killed.

Although the human figure does appear occasionally in Wyeth's early work, such as *Rum Runner* (1944), it was not until after his father's death that he began in earnest to paint people. Most of his portraits are of a single figure, unsmiling and reflective, transmitting a sense of loneliness. Mary Rose Beaumont suggested in *Arts & Artists* (August 1980) that he found a surrogate father in Karl Kuerner, a German-born Chadds Ford neighbor whose farm, of 150 or more acres, had fascinated Wyeth since childhood. In 1948, after making many preliminary drawings, he painted what he considers to be his best portrait, *Karl*. "Wyeth's 'photographic' realism is deceptively simple: it is built upon a many-dimensional relation to his work," Allen S. Weller wrote in regard to that painting in *Art USA Now* (1963). ". . . Karl's weather-beaten face corresponds to the weathered ceiling. The abstract flat surface aesthetics of the ceiling are brutally broken by the third visage of Karl, a juxtaposition as vivid in optical effect as a surrealist's psychic impact. The psychic is not omitted, however—much is hung on Karl's relation to the ceiling hooks."

Equivalents of ceiling hooks in some of Wyeth's other pictures often have the effect, among others, of avoiding the "sweetness" that he deplores in much realistic painting. The jagged, menacing edge of a sawed log, seen through the window of a sun-filled room in Kuerner's house, threatens the calm of *Groundhog Day* (1959), one of Wyeth's most widely admired works. Through such details as the log and the table set for one, the artist intended to capture what he called "the very essence of the man," Karl, who is not present in the picture.

Nor do cattle appear in *Brown Swiss* (1957), his landscape "portrait" of the Kuerner farm. The painting owes its title to a pencil sketch of a Brown Swiss, but its inspiration came from a sidelong glimpse that Wyeth once had of Kuerner's house reflected in a pond. In the process of abstracting and transmitting his impression, he made scores of painstaking drawings and watercolor sketches, eventually reducing the Brown Swiss to cattle tracks across the field and, as he explained to Hoving, making his predominant color "almost like the tawny brown pelt of a Brown Swiss bull." Other Wyeth pictures associated with Kuerner, who died in 1979, include the tempera *Spring Fed* (1967), an interior of the milk room; the drybrush watercolor landscape *Evening at Kuerners* (1970); the tempera portrait *Anna Kuerner* (1971); and the double portrait *The Kuerners* (1971).

Among Wyeth's many works that belong to his Pennsylvania experience, but not specifically the Kuerners, is *The Trodden Weed* (1951) —a picture reportedly admired by Nikita S. Khrushchev—depicting the booted legs of a man walking on a brown hill. He conceived the idea for the painting while recuperating from a severe illness, when he slowly roamed the fields wearing a pair of boots that had once been part of Howard Pyle's costume collection and watching his feet and the ground beneath. The painting may symbolize death itself or man's rejection of illness and death.

For Wyeth, the Pennsylvania countryside meant solid stone walls and soggy, rich earth, in contrast to Maine, which seemed to him "all dry bones and dessicated sinews," as he was quoted as saying in the catalogue of his Metropolitan Museum of Art show. But Maine appealed to him strongly because of a simplicity that he found to be disappearing elsewhere in America. He tried to epitomize the people and the land in portraits like *The Patriot* (1964) and scenes like *River Cove* (1958).

On his twenty-second birthday, while spending the summer in Maine, Wyeth met Betsy Merle James, the daughter of a newspaper editor. They were married the following year, on May 15, 1940. At their first meeting Betsy James had taken Wyeth to Cushing to introduce him to her long-time friend Christina Olson, who had been crippled by polio in childhood. It was her weather-beaten, three-story, steep-roofed clapboard house, built on a coastal promontory, rather than Christina herself, that attracted Wyeth's interest on that occasion. But Christina's personality and qualities that seemed to Wyeth to represent Maine gradually made her his favorite subject. The Olsons—Christina and her brother Alvaro, a blueberry farmer—were the Maine counterpart of the Kuerners. He was free to come and go in the Olson household, as he was at the Kuerners', and turned a second-story room in Christina's house into a studio.

Christina's World (1948), a tempera owned by the Metropolitan Museum of Art, has a haunting appeal and broad symbolism that account largely for its having become probably Wyeth's most popular work. Christina— whose crippled condition, like the peeling wallpaper of a Wyeth interior, does not immediately engage the viewer's attention—drags herself through a blueberry field toward her distant house. Only her pink dress relieves the bleakness of the landscape. Wyeth's tender, subtle portraits *Christine Olson* (1947), *Miss Olson* (1952), and *Anna Christina* (1967), as Mary Rose Beaumont pointed out, make it clear that "Christina is not the eager, young, yearning woman of *Christina's World*, but an ugly, hideously crippled middle-aged woman, whose quality of mind Wyeth admired to the point where the ugliness is transcended in the loving truth of his portrayal."

Among Wyeth's most memorable works are some of his interior and exterior paintings of

Christina's house, including *Wind from the Sea* (1947), *Seed Corn* (1948), and *Weather Side* (1965). *End of Olsons,* a view of part of the roof and chimney of the house, was painted in 1969, the year after Christina's death, and is the last of his pictures relating to the Olson environment. But among his neighbors in Maine, Wyeth found a quite different subject for his portraits in the teenage girl Siri, whose father, George Erickson, he painted in *The Finn* (1969). The seminude *Bikini* (1968), the topless *The Sauna* (1968), and the nude *The Virgin* (1969), *Indian Summer* (1970), and *Black Water* (1972) belong to a series that Robert Hughes in *Time* (September 3, 1973) placed among "the solidest and least theatrical of Wyeth's work." In his interview with Hoving, Wyeth contrasted his pictures of Siri, which represented "an invigorating, zestful, powerful phenomenon," with those of Christina, "which symbolize the deterioration and the dwindling of something."

Having rarely, if ever, looked beyond his Maine and Pennsylvania homes for his subject matter, Wyeth has long been confronted with critics' misgivings about narrowness of range. He insists upon painting what he knows best and what involves him emotionally. "Realism without emotion is dead painting. Like Norman Rockwell," he maintained in his discussion with Selden Rodman for *Conversations with Artists* (1957). Talking with Hoving, he coupled the emotional with the technical in assuring quality. "Emotion is my bulwark," he said. "I think that's the only thing that endures, finally."

Because of his emphasis on his feelings toward his subjects, Wyeth has occasionally been charged with lapsing into sentimentality, especially in his evocation of the past. Avantgarde and some other critics also deride the anecdotal references in paintings like *Distant Thunder* (1961), in which a woman, Betsy Wyeth, lies asleep in a blueberry field on a summer day, while the family dog nearby grows anxious about an ominous sound. But Wyeth is generally praised for lack of pathos in his treatment of old age and similar subjects and, to use Weller's words, "an almost animistic feeling for his rural milieu." Searching for a deeper meaning in whatever he paints, he strives to convey silence in the fall of snow, steadfastness in the flow of water. As he explores themes of distance, emptiness, endurance, timelessness, desolation, and loneliness, he pleases viewers with recognizable objects that have meaning for them. His subdued, nonsensual colors, primarily earth tones, suit his melancholy, or "thoughtful," the word he prefers, outlook. "It is really rather odd," John Russell wrote in the New York *Times* (October 24, 1976), "that a nation which rightly prides itself on its buoyancy of spirit should identify so firmly with an artist whose speciality is the study of wounded or inarticulate natures in an unforgiving landscape."

A major exhibition of Wyeth's work drew hundreds of thousands of visitors to the Pennsylvania Academy of Fine Arts in Philadelphia in 1966 and the Baltimore Museum of Art in 1966-67 and broke attendance records at the Whitney Museum in New York in 1967 before moving on to the Art Institute of Chicago. Enormous crowds also flocked to his retrospective at the Boston Museum of Fine Arts in 1970 and to his exhibition, "Two Worlds of Andrew Wyeth: Kuerners and Olsons," which included preliminary studies of his paintings, at the Metropolitan Museum of Art in New York in 1976-77. His paintings are included in the collections of many American museums, including the Brandywine River Museum in Chadds Ford. Twenty-six of his paintings that were once owned by the film producer Joseph E. Levine, the most extensive collection aside from the artist's own, are on permanent loan to the Greenville County Museum of Art in Greenville, South Carolina.

In a choice reflecting public taste in painting, President John F. Kennedy named Wyeth in 1963 as the first artist to receive the Presidential Freedom Award, the country's highest civilian award. Another President, Richard Nixon, honored Wyeth in 1970 with a dinner and private exhibition of his paintings at the White House. On that "first-time" occasion Nixon toasted him as the painter who had "caught the heart of America." Wyeth's other tributes include the gold medal for painting of the National Institutes of Arts and Letters for 1965 and scores of painting and watercolor prizes and honorary degrees. In 1977 he made his first trip to Europe, to be inducted into the French Academy of Fine Arts, becoming the only American artist since John Singer Sargent to be admitted to the academy. The Soviet Academy of the Arts elected him an honorary member in 1978.

Andrew and Betsy Wyeth, who helps her husband in business matters and with exhibitions, have two sons. A tempera profile of his older son, *Nicholas* (1955), in which Wyeth caught the evanescent quality of youth, was a favorite of President Dwight D. Eisenhower. James Browning (Jamie) Wyeth, a noted painter in his own right, was the daydreaming boy wearing a coonskin hat whom his father painted in the drybrush watercolor *Faraway* (1952). The Wyeth homestead in Chadds Ford consists of an eighteenth-century miller's house, a gristmill now used as a studio, and a converted granary, all of which have been carefully restored. In Cushing, Wyeth lives in a restored eighteenth-century clapboard house. His fondness for simple things does not mean that his tastes are ordinary or inexpensive, in houses, cars, or clothes. He often wears suits with Nehru collars made by Pennsylvania Germans. The rangy, blue-eyed artist dislikes intrusion into his private life and is apt to be reserved toward strangers. But his neighbors know him as a "down-to-earth guy" with a hearty laugh. "He's a tease and a mimic," Amei Wallach reported in *Newsday* (October 10, 1976), "good at telling stories and doing all the voices realistically. At one point he even thought about becoming an actor."

References: Art & Artists 15:22+ Ag '80; Biog N p918 Jl/Ag '75 por; Life 58:93+ My 14 '65 por; Newsday II p1+ O 10 '76 pors; Show 5:47+ My '65 pors; Time 102:54 S 2 '73 por; Contemporary Artists (1977); Logsdon, Gene. Wyeth People (1971); Meryman, Richard. The World of Andrew Wyeth (1968); Nordness, Lee, ed. Art USA Now vol 2 (1962); Rodman, Selden. Conversations with Artists (1957); Who's Who in America, 1980-81

Ziaur Rahman

Jan. 19, 1936- President of the People's Republic of Bangladesh. Address: Office of the President, Dacca, Bangladesh

BULLETIN: Ziaur Rahman was assassinated on May 30, 1981 at Chittagong in an attempted coup by army officers. *Obituary:* N Y Times p1+ My 31 '81

As President of Bangladesh, Major General Ziaur Rahman heads a nation that is among the most destitute and overpopulated in the world. Once described by Henry Kissinger as an "international basket case," the Bengal nation, which declared its independence from Pakistan in 1971, has long been plagued not only by such natural disasters as floods, famine, and drought, but by such man-induced problems as economic and political turmoil, corruption, and violence. Among its 90,000,000 people, crowded into an area smaller than

Wisconsin, a large proportion are illiterate, unemployed, or on the brink of starvation. But "General Zia"—who played a key role in the Bangladesh independence struggle, took power as a military strongman in 1975, and assumed the Presidency in 1977—represents a ray of hope to its people, combining his formidable military skills with a knack for grassroots politicking and an ability to grasp the problems of the Third World. "He has put vigor into the government," one European birth control expert has said, as quoted in the New York Times (June 7, 1978). "Things are steadily getting better in Bangladesh, as they have been ever since the day that he took over."

Ziaur Rahman was born on January 19, 1936 in the town of Bogra, about 100 miles northwest of Dacca, in Bengal, then a province of British India, and he grew up and was schooled in his native region. (As is the case with many Bengalis, the last two letters of Ziaur Rahman's first name form an article that is used with the second name.) In 1953, six years after Pakistan was carved out of the predominantly Moslem northeastern and northwestern regions of the newly independent Indian subcontinent, Zia, at seventeen, joined the Pakistani army, then as now one of the few avenues open to his countrymen for escaping a life of penury. Although competition was stiff, Zia seemed to display an early aptitude for military life.

Commissioned in 1955, within ten years Zia worked his way up to commander of a company in the First East Bengal Regiment. During the 1965 Indo-Pakistan War over Kashmir, the young officer fought in the Khemkaran sector. In 1966 he left the front to teach at the Pakistan Military Academy in Kakul and then at the Staff College in Quetta. The three years he spent as a teacher were a satisfying period in his life, and much of his later rapport with the roughhewn unemployed Bengali youth whom he tried as President of Bangladesh to organize into volunteer work units stems from that time.

In 1969 Zia was briefly posted as second-in-command of a regiment in Joydepur before leaving for extensive training in West Germany and several months with the British army. By October of 1970 he was back in his country as commander of the newly established Eighth East Bengal Regiment in the coastal city of Chittagong. Meanwhile, Zia had become increasingly active as a sympathizer of the Bengali national movement. Originating in Dacca in the 1960's and centering upon the Awami League, headed by Sheik Mujibur Rahman (popularly known as Mujib), the movement sought regional autonomy for culturally and geographically distinct and economically deprived East Pakistan from the politically dominant and more prosperous Western portion of the country.

Bengali discontent came to a full boil in March 1971, after Pakistan's Prime Minister, General A.M. Yahya Khan, indefinitely postponed the convening of a new national assembly that would have given East Pakistan a substantial degree of political autonomy. Amid futile negotiation efforts between Mujib and Yahya Khan, riots and strikes broke out in Dacca and elsewhere. In response, Pakistani troops moved against the civilian population with great force. An estimated 1,000,000 Bengalis were said to have been killed in the civil strife, and millions more fled to India. Meanwhile, Zia, then a major, led his forces in Chittagong in a revolt against the Pakistani army and in a radio broadcast on March 27, 1971 proclaimed the independence of Bangladesh (Bengal Nation), indicating his intention to become President of the new country. Although Zia's action made him something of a national hero, his triumph proved short-lived, because the Pakistani army soon reestablished its power and Yahya Khan reimposed martial law in East Pakistan.

As a leader of the rebel forces, Zia, who attained the rank of lieutenant colonel in August 1971, organized the First Brigade of the Bangladesh army later that year, with units of the first, third, and eighth Bengal regiments, which became known as the "Z-Force." The final liberation of Bangladesh took place on December 16, 1971 after allied Indian and East Bengali forces defeated the Pakistani army in a two-week war. Following the establishment of independent Bangladesh under the Prime Ministership of Sheik Mujib, who returned from imprisonment in West Pakistan in January 1972, Zia was named commander of the new nation's Comilla Brigade, and in June 1972 he was further rewarded with the post of army deputy chief of staff. But all was not well between him and Mujib, the temperamental "father of the nation," who had not taken kindly to Zia's action in proclaiming himself head of state in the March 1971 Chittagong broadcast.

Although in the beginning Sheik Mujib commanded wide popular support, by 1974 he had come increasingly under fire for his failure to resolve his country's immense economic problems, his efforts to establish one-man rule, his dependence on India and the Soviet Union, and allegations of corruption involving leading members of his Awami League and his own relatives. On August 15, 1975 Mujib was killed, along with his family, in a revolt by a group of right-wing Islamic pro-Pakistan officers. Ten days later, Zia—who in the meantime had advanced to major general, a rank he still holds—was named chief of staff of the army by the new President, Khandakar Moshtaque Ahmed, who had assumed the power to rule by martial law. When that government was in turn overthrown in early November 1975 in a coup led by the pro-Indian commander of the Dacca garrison, Zia was placed briefly under house arrest for alleged anti-Indian sentiments. That regime lasted only four days, however, and in the new government, headed by chief martial law administrator and President Abu Sadat Mohammed Sayed, a former supreme

court chief justice who took office on November 7, Zia was named deputy chief martial law administrator.

According to Denis Warner, writing in *Atlantic Monthly* (November 1978), Zia actually led the November 7, 1975 coup and as army chief of staff assumed the real power at the head of a ten-man military council, while Sayed's positions as chief martial law administrator and President were merely titular. In addition to his formal posts as deputy chief martial law administrator and army chief of staff, Zia served as Minister of Finance and Home Affairs from 1975 to 1978, as Minister of Commerce and Foreign Trade from 1975 to 1977, and as Minister of Information and Broadcasting in 1975-76. Meanwhile, to consolidate his power, he moved vigorously, with arrests and executions, against those in the military and in politics whom he considered potential threats. Among them was Lieutenant Colonel Mohammed Abu Taher, leader of a left-wing faction, and a former close associate of Zia and fellow war hero, who was executed in July 1976 on charges of plotting to overthrow the government.

On November 29, 1976, eight days after postponement of national elections scheduled for early 1977 on the ground that they would "endanger peace and tranquility" and "strengthen the hands of the enemy," Sayed formally relinquished the office of chief martial law administrator to Zia. Shortly thereafter, General Zia arrested eleven prominent members of Mujib's still popular Awami League on charges of being "prejudicial to the state." Zia's position as head of state was formalized on April 21, 1977, when he was sworn in as Bangladesh's seventh President in its six years of independence, after Sayed stepped down for reasons of ill health and nominated Zia as his successor in accordance with the 1972 constitution.

On the day after his inauguration Zia announced that he would seek to ascertain the confidence of the people through a nationwide referendum based on universal adult franchise and promised national elections for the coming year. He also called for an amendment to the 1972 constitution that would include "faith in Allah" as one of the four guiding principles of state policy, along with "nationalism, democracy, and socialism," thus in effect transforming Bangladesh from a secular to an Islamic state. Some 33,600,000 voters, or 85 percent of the electorate, went to the polls on May 30, 1977 to vote on the question: "Do you have confidence in President Ziaur Rahman and in the policies and programs enunciated by him?" Nearly 99 percent voted affirmatively, and although some skepticism was voiced by the opposition as to the honesty of the referendum, foreign observers maintained that the results substantially reflected public opinion in Bangladesh.

Although most of his countrymen agreed that since assuming power in 1975 Zia had given Bangladesh its best government during its brief history, and that he had met with some success in maintaining stability, cutting down corruption, and controlling inflation, opposition to his rule persisted. In early October 1977 a self-styled "people's army" of dissidents in the military staged a coup attempt that was promptly crushed by government forces. Although Zia at first dismissed the action as the work of "some undisciplined soldiers," he responded later that month by banning three political parties belived to be implicated in the plot, including the pro-Moscow Bangladesh Communist party.

Nevertheless, Zia permitted national elections to proceed on June 3, 1978. One of ten candidates, the President ran on the slogan "General Zia symbolizes national stability" as the candidate of the six-party National Front coalition. His only serious rival was Major General Ataul Ghany Osmany, a fellow war hero, representing the six-party United Democratic Front, supported by the Awami League and pro-Soviet elements. The main issue of the campaign was whether Bangladesh should continue under a Presidential system of government, as favored by Zia, or whether a parliamentary system, advocated by Osmany and others who feared one-man rule, should be adopted. Zia assured voters that even under a Presidential system, the parliament would be a sovereign body, with powers to enact legislation, amend the constitution, and remove the President. Campaigning throughout the country by plane, jeep, or helicopter, Zia stressed the importance of bringing "the people back into the process of government" and, in an allusion to the deficiencies of Sheik Mujib's administration, called for order and stability, and an end to "the corruption and mismanagement of the old days."

The election turned out to be an overwhelming victory for Zia, who received 77 percent of the 19,000,000 votes cast. Eight minor candidates polled less than 2 percent of the vote between them. Despite charges by opposition spokesmen of irregularities in the voting and contentions that Zia had won only because he had obtained an amendment in a law that had excluded active military officers from political candidacy, the election result was generally accepted, and Osmany did not contest it. Sworn in on June 12 for a five-year term, Zia appointed a twenty-eight-member council of ministers, or Cabinet, to replace the council of Presidential advisers established by his predecessor. In December 1978 Zia promised the repeal of all "undemocratic provisions" in effect since 1975 and announced that he would appoint a Prime Minister who would command a parliamentary majority, that the President would have no veto power over legislation, and that all fundamental rights of citizens would be restored.

In the parliamentary elections held after two postponements on February 18, 1979, all opposition parties were permitted to put up candidates. Zia's recently organized Bangladesh Nationalist party won 203 of the 300 legislative seats, while the opposition Awami League elected forty representatives. On the whole, Bangladesh seemed to have experienced marked progress in human rights under Zia's Presidency, for hundreds of political prisoners were released, and in April 1979 Zia abrogated all remaining martial law restrictions in favor of "civilian democratic rule and a sovereign parliament." Those developments in turn inspired confidence among foreign investors in the United States and elsewhere.

Zia is convinced that his direct and highly personal grassroots approach in far-flung hamlets and indigent villages is helping to bring the vast majority of his people from a harshly primitive rural existence into the twentieth century. On his frequent visits to all parts of the country, the President exhorts farmers to work harder to produce more food, instructs women on the urgent need for birth control, spends hours with villagers digging canals to deter flooding and encourage year-round crops, and drops in on schools to congratulate overworked teachers and volunteers struggling to raise the country's 25 percent literacy rate. He also engages in long talks with local Islamic mullahs, trying to break down their resistance to the use of fertilizer (most still prefer to ensure a good harvest with religious symbols) and to convince them of the necessity of permitting hitherto closeted women to work outside the home.

Urban intellectuals, labor leaders, and government workers have complained that the President was spending too much time in the countryside, and they have suggested that his motivation was to build a personality cult to bolster his own position. Zia is unperturbed by such criticism. "From now on anyone who wants to go into politics will have to go to the people," he told Kevin Rafferty of the *New Statesman* (January 6, 1978). "In the past the politicians did not bother with the people: they just fought one another for what they could get. This country has many resources if only we can release them. We have got to work hard, go to the villages, go to the people."

Through his efforts to conciliate pro-Pakistani and pro-Indian sentiment within Bangladesh's armed forces and among the general public, Zia has met with some success in bringing about the political stability his country needs if it is to meet its goals of doubling food production and reducing the birth rate from 2.5 to 2 percent by 1985. He is also aware that aid from abroad must be substantially increased if Bangladesh is to survive in the 1980's. Jute, the country's only major export and source of precious foreign exchange, is no longer in high demand, and there is little capital available to develop Bangladesh's unexplored natural gas and offshore oil reserves, since the modernization of agriculture and light industry receive first priority.

A familiar figure at Commonwealth heads of governments conferences and at meetings of such international agencies as the Food and Agricultural Organization, President Zia has made state visits to capitals throughout the world. In 1980 his government signed accords with India, Japan, the People's Republic of China, and other nations for improved trade and for scientific and technological cooperation. During a visit to Washington, D.C. in August of that year, he received assurances from President Jimmy Carter of "all possible cooperation" in the implementation of Bangladesh's economic development program. Zia's administration has been contemplating duty-free "export trading zones," similar to those Taiwan has set up successfully in recent years. The Bangladesh government still controls most industry, but in 1980-81 the statutory minimum price for jute was dropped for the first time in favor of a free-market system.

A realist about the world economy as well, Zia tends to agree with the assessment of United States Senator and former Ambassador to the U.N. Daniel Patrick Moynihan that the Organization of Petroleum Exporting Countries and the Soviet Union are just as responsible for the destitution of many of the non-industrialized nations as the United States and Western Europe. Unlike most of his peers in the U. N.'s "Group of 77," Zia is unafraid of denouncing OPEC for its skyrocketing prices or the Soviet Union and other socialist countries for what he feels are grossly inadequate foreign aid budgets. In his speech before the U.N. General Assembly on August 26, 1980 he asked all industrialized nations to double their development assistance funds and called on oil-producing countries in particular not only to "effect a 50 percent reduction in the price of oil for the least developed countries" but also to "invest a part of their assets in developing countries."

President Ziaur Rahman, who is married and has two sons, is an energetic and extraordinarily disciplined man. He sometimes works until 3:00 in the morning, reviewing new programs and catching up on paperwork. Then, after only a few hours of sleep, he flies off in his helicopter to some remote district. Not a brilliant public speaker, he feels more at home in face-to-face contact with people than on the podium. Time off with his family is rare. The dapper major general, who has forsaken his once famous camouflage uniform for well-tailored Western suits, plays squash and enjoys watching an occasional sports match on television when time permits. But for the present he seems preoccupied with little else besides his country's future and his role in it.

References: Atlan 242:6+ N '78; Cur World Leaders 24:14 Ja '81 por; N Y Times A p2 Je 7 '78 por, A p4 Jl 28 '80 por; New Statesm p8+ Ja 6 '78; International Who's Who, 1980-81; International Year Book and Statesmen's Who's Who, 1981

PHOTO CREDITS

Patricia Argiro, Jacob Druckman; © Eve Arnold, John Huston; *Bachrach*, Michael I. Sovern; *Blumensaadt/Matrix*, Thomas Sowell; *Cavouk Portraits*, Edward Richard Schreyer; *CBS News Photo*, Charles Kuralt; *Central Office of Information, London*, Elizabeth, Queen Mother of Great Britain, Michael Foot, Lord Soames; *Roland Coufort/Gamma Liaison*, Mengistu Haile Mariam; *Alain Dejean/Sygma*, Stanisław Kania; *P. J. Dolan, Courtesy of Acquavella Contemporary Art, Inc.*, Anthony Caro; *Epic Portrait Associated*, Muddy Waters; *Sigrid Estrada*, Lionel Tiger; *Ford Foundation/Georgiana Silk*, Franklin A. Thomas; *Mary Francis*, Dick Francis; *Information Service of the Consulate General of India*, N. Sanjiva Reddy; © *Israel Sun Ltd.*, Ariel Sharon; *Martha Kaplan*, Jacobo Timerman; *Keystone*, Alec Guinness, James Ivory; © *Keystone*, Yaacov Agam; *Max Koot*, Queen Beatrix; *T. Korody/Sygma*, Jodie Foster; © *Jill Krementz*, Margaret Drabble; *Bertrand Laforet/Gamma Liaison*, Adolfo Pérez Esquivel; *Bertrand Laforet-Daniel Simon/Gamma*, Isabelle Huppert; © *Laszlo*, Hans Selye; *John Lefebre*, Jean-Michel Folon; *Jorge Lewinski*, Bridget Riley; *Lumifot*, Leopoldo Calvo Sotelo; *Jacqueline McCord*, Wilfrid Sheed; © *Fred McDarrah*, Michael Cimino; *Robert R. McElroy/Newsweek*, Santo Loquasto; © *1953 Rollie McKenna*, Bill Brandt; *Jack Manning/The New York Times*, Mickey Spillane; *Duane Michals, Courtesy of Sidney Janis Gallery, New York*, Duane Michals;

Wayne C. O'Neill/U. S. Army Photograph, Frank Carlucci; *Al Satterwhite*, Hunter S. Thompson; *William E. Sauro/The New York Times*, Mary Gordon; © *Steven Sloman*, Nancy Graves; *Solters & Roskin, Inc.*, David Hartman; *Christian Steiner*, Samuel Ramey; *Pat Stone/Mother Earth News*, John Holt; *Allen Tannenbaum/Sygma*, Debbie Harry; *Nathaniel Tileston*, Joseph Chaikin; *Lia Troyanovsky*, Merrill Ashley; *Ian Tyas/Keystone*, Marie Rambert; *United Press International*, Tracy Austin, Abolhassan Bani-Sadr, Michael Bennett, Ingmar Bergman, Mike Bossy, Hodding Carter 3d, Warren M. Christopher, Johan Cruyff, Jim Dale, Blythe Danner, Angie Dickinson, José Napoleón Duarte, Jerry Falwell, David Garth, Sugar Ray Leonard, Marsha Mason, Toshiro Mifune, Kenny Rogers, Mark Russell, Sylvia Sidney, Donald Sutherland, Zenko Suzuki, Grete Waitz, Lech Wałęsa; *Thomas Victor*, Elizabeth Hardwick; © *1980 Thomas Victor*, James Merrill, Czesław Miłosz; © *Diana H. Walker*, Anne Tyler; *Chris Ware/Keystone*, Derek Jacobi; *Wide World*, Tim Conway, Francesco Cossiga, John Crosby, Neil Diamond, Samuel K. Doe, Barry Gibb, Philip Glass, Philip C. Habib, Abbie Hoffman, Barnard Hughes, Saddam Hussein, Babrak Karmal, Henry Kaufman, Edwin H. Land, Robert H. Michel, Milton Obote, Paul Schrader, David Stockman, Alfredo Stroessner, Andrew Wyeth; *Carey Winfrey/The New York Times*, Hilla Limann.

OBITUARIES

AGAR, HERBERT (SEBASTIAN) Sept. 29, 1897-Nov. 24, 1980 Author; journalist; won Pulitzer Prize in history for *The People's Choice* (1933), a study of American Presidents; also wrote, among other books on American history and the democratic heritage, *A Time for Greatness* (1942) and *The Price of Union* (1950); in addition, was author of literary studies and such works as *The Saving Remnant: An Account of Jewish Survival Since 1914* (1960) and *The Darkest Hour: England Alone, June 1940-June 1941* (1973); with Louisville *Courier-Journal*, was London correspondent (1929-34), columnist (1935-38), and editor (1940-42); founded Freedom House (1941); during World War II, was attaché at United States Embassy in London; after war, remained in Britain as publishing and television executive; died in Sussex, England. See *Current Biography* (March) 1944.

Obituary

N Y Times D p23 N 25 '80

AMALRIK, ANDREI (ALEKSEYEVICH) May 12, 1938-Nov. 11, 1980 Soviet writer; historian; human rights advocate; even among his fellow dissidents, was a maverick, taking his stands on purely moral, apolitical grounds; made clear in *Will the Soviet Union Survive Until 1984?* (1970) that he did not share optimism of Democratic Movement, mainstream of dissent within Soviet Union; also, scorned détente and spoke out against injustice as he perceived it in West; in *Involuntary Journey to Siberia* (1970), gave account of first of his two internal exiles; emigrated under pressure in 1976; lived in Netherlands, United States, and France; completed manuscript for last book, "Notebooks of a Revolutionary"; died in automobile accident near Guadalajara, Spain, on way to human rights conference organized by dissident groups in Madrid. See *Current Biography* (April) 1974.

Obituary

N Y Times B p12 N 13 '80

AMERASINGHE, HAMILTON SHIRLEY Mar. 18, 1913-Dec. 4, 1980 Sri Lanka diplomat and government official; foreign service posts included concurrent assignments of Ceylon's High Commissioner to India and Ambassador to Nepal and Afghanistan (1963-67); served as chief delegate to the United Nations (from 1967) and as president of the General Assembly (1976); directed prolonged U.N. negotiations to draft a law of the sea treaty (1973-80); died in New York City. See *Current Biography* (March) 1977.

Obituary

N Y Times B p11 D 5 '80

APPEL, JAMES Z(IEGLER) May 15, 1907-Aug. 31, 1981 Physician; former president of American Medical Association (1965-66); as president, was instrumental in fending off physicians' boycott of newly created Medicare despite personal antipathy for that Social Security-based medical insurance program for aged; was dedicated, old-fashioned general practitioner, working until month before his death out of office in home in which he had been born in Lancaster, Pennsylvania; died in Lancaster. See *Current Biography* (March) 1966.

Obituary

N Y Times A p17 S 2 '81

AUCHINLECK, SIR CLAUDE (JOHN EYRE) June 21, 1884-Mar. 23, 1981 British field marshal; began military career as subaltern in India, where he ultimately became commander of British forces; served in Egypt and Mesopotamia in World War I; as British commander in chief in Middle East in World War II, halted German offensive in Egypt's western desert; when Field Marshal Erwin Rommel's forces rallied to defeat British at Tobruk, refused to launch immediate counterattack, on ground that his men needed regrouping and reinforcing; for the refusal, was dismissed by Prime Minister Winston Churchill in August 1942; died in Marrakesh, Morocco. See *Current Biography* (February) 1942.

Obituary

N Y Times B p10 Mr 25 '81

BAGNOLD, ENID (ALGERINE) Oct. 27, 1889-Mar. 31, 1981 British writer; achieved celebrity when her novel *National Velvet* (1935) was made into a 1944 movie starring twelve-year-old Elizabeth Taylor; wrote five other novels and ten plays characterized by cultivated wit and unconventional turn of ideas, including *The Chalk Garden* (1955), a New York and London hit and a successful 1964 film, and *A Matter of Gravity*, in which Katharine Hepburn starred on Broadway in 1976; died in London. See *Current Biography* (June) 1964.

Obituary

N Y Times D p23 Ap 1 '81

BALDWIN, ROGER NASH Jan. 21, 1884-Aug. 26, 1981 Social activist; in 1920 founded American Civil Liberties Union, libertarian organization devoted to nonpartisan defense of principles of Bill of Rights; until 1950 was executive director of A.C.L.U., which came to the legal defense of such varied clients as Sacco and Vanzetti, John T. Scopes of "Monkey Trial" fame, the publishers of James Joyce's banned *Ulysses*, Japanese-Americans interned during World War II, and neo-Nazi groups; remained A.C.L.U.'s spiritual leader until his death; had previously operated A.C.L.U.'s predecessor, American Union Against Militarism's Civil Liberties Bureau, which provided legal representation for draft resisters and conscientious objectors in World War I; was himself jailed for a year for refusal to be drafted. See *Current Biography* (January-February) 1940.

Obituary

N Y Times D p18 Ag 27 '81

BARBER, SAMUEL Mar. 9, 1910-Jan. 23, 1981 Composer; wrote elegantly crafted, lyrically appealing music in a traditional idiom, sometimes described as "neo-Romantic," that was performed to acclaim by the world's leading orchestras, instrumentalists, and singers; won Pulitzer Prize in 1959 for his opera *Vanessa*, which had a libretto by his friend Gian Carlo Menotti, and again in 1963 for his formally exquisite First Piano Concerto; other works include *Dover Beach* (1931), Adagio for Strings (1936), and the ballets *Medea* (1946) and *Souvenirs* (1955); died in New York City. See *Current Biography* (September) 1963.

Obituary

N Y Times p1+ Ja 24 '81

BARR, ALFRED H(AMILTON), JR. Jan. 28, 1902-Aug. 15, 1981 Museum official; art historian; among most innovative, powerful, and controversial tastemakers in American, if not world, art; taught first American college course in modern art, at Wellesley College in 1926; was first, formative director of Museum of Modern Art, from 1929 to 1943; conceived MOMA's radical multi-departmental plan and built its collection of twentieth-century art into world's most important and most comprehensive, extending beyond traditional "fine arts" into architecture, film, photography, industrial and theatre design, and commercial and useful art; remained at museum as advisory director until 1947 and director of collections until 1961; died in Salisbury, Connecticut. See *Current Biography* (January) 1961.

Obituary

N Y Times B p15 Ag 17 '81

BENNETT, ROBERT RUSSELL June 15, 1894-Aug. 18, 1981 Composer; arranger; conductor; former musical director of National Broadcasting Company; was leading orchestrator of Broadway musicals of his time; between 1926 and 1960 scored some 300 shows, including *Rose Marie, Show Boat, Of Thee I Sing, Porgy and Bess, Anything Goes, Carmen Jones, Finian's Rainbow, Annie Get Your Gun, Kiss Me Kate, Carousel, South Pacific, The King and I, The Sound of Music, My Fair Lady,* and

Camelot; contributed orchestrations and original music to more than thirty motion pictures and many important television programs, including the *Victory at Sea* series; composed one full-length opera, two one-act operas, six symphonies, and many other orchestral works as well as chamber and solo pieces; died in New York City. See *Current Biography* (May) 1962.

Obituary

N Y Times D p19 Ag 20 '81

BERGEN, JOHN J(OSEPH) Aug. 7, 1896-Dec-11, 1980 Financier and industrialist; as chairman of the Graham-Paige Corporation, an investment company, initiated the relocation and replacement of Manhattan's old Madison Square Garden with a $100,000,000 sports and entertainment center, completed in 1968; promoted professional hockey, basketball, and baseball activity in New York City; served for many years in the Naval Reserve, in which he held the rank of rear admiral (retired); died in Cuernavaca, Mexico. See *Current Biography* (June) 1961.

Obituary

N Y Times B p5 D 12 '80

BERMAN, EMILE ZOLA Nov. 2, 1903-July 3, 1981 Lawyer; one of keenest legal minds in United States and a leading authority on negligence law; won national prominence in 1956 as defense attorney for Marine Corps Staff Sergeant Matthew C. McKeon, charged with causing deaths of six recruits on disciplinary night march; also was one of defense lawyers in widely publicized trial of Sirhan Sirhan for 1968 murder of Senator Robert F. Kennedy; died in New York City. See *Current Biography* (June) 1972.

Obituary

N Y Times p14 Jl 5 '81

BETANCOURT, RÓMULO Feb. 22, 1908-Sept. 28, 1981 Venezuelan statesman; a leading representative of non-Communist, democratic left in Latin America; organized Acción Democrática (1941); as provisional President of revolutionary junta that overthrew dictatorship of General Isaías Medina Angarita, instituted major economic and social reforms (1945-48); was ousted by military coup, but returned from exile after overthrow of General Marcos Pérez Jiménez (1958) and was elected President; as head of coalition government (1959-64), implemented democratic reforms and maintained friendly relations with United States; continued to serve his government as elder statesman and adviser in recent years; died in New York City. See *Current Biography* (May) 1960.

Obituary

N Y Times D p22 S 29 '81

BINNS, JOSEPH PATTERSON June 28, 1905-Nov. 23, 1980 Former hotel executive; rose from room clerk in an Atlantic City hotel (1928-31) to vice-president of Hilton Hotels Corporation (1946-62), in which post he served as general manager of the Palmer House, Chicago (1946-49) and executive vice-president and general manager of the Waldorf-Astoria, New York (1949-61); as president and chief executive officer of Rock-Hil-Uris Corporation (1961-64) was managing director of the New York Hilton and Washington Hilton hotels; died on Indian Creek Island, near Miami Beach, Florida. See *Current Biography* (June) 1954.

Obituary

N Y Times D p19 N 26 '80

BLISS, RAY C(HARLES) Dec. 16, 1907-Aug. 6, 1981 Politician; businessman; as chairman of Republican National Committee from 1966 to 1969, was largely credited with rebuilding Republican party, which had been fragmented by factionalism and demoralized by Barry Goldwater's landslide loss to Lyndon B. Johnson in 1964; helped elect Richard Nixon to Presidency in 1968; in power struggle, ceded national chairmanship to Nixon's choice, Rogers C. B. Morton, in 1969; had been effective Republican state chairman in Ohio for sixteen years; outside of politics, was founder and president of Tower Agencies Inc., general insurance and real estate firm in Akron; died in Akron. See *Current Biography* (January) 1966.

Obituary

N Y Times D p13 Ag 7 '81

BÖHM, KARL Aug. 28, 1894-Aug. 14, 1981 Austrian conductor; one of most esteemed musicians of his time; was noted for his interpretations of Mozart, Wagner, and Richard Strauss operas and for solid, sedate performances devoid of flourishes; conductor of Vienna Philharmonic Orchestra (from 1933); director of Dresden (Germany) Staatsoper (1934-43); general director of Vienna Staatsoper (1943-45, 1954-56); gave first of many performances at Metropolitan Opera in New York City in 1957; guest conductor in Paris, London, Berlin, Milan, Buenos Aires, and other locations; made many recordings; died in Salzburg. See *Current Biography* (June) 1968.

Obituary

N Y Times p47 Ag 15 '81

BOONE, RICHARD June 18, 1917-Jan. 10, 1981 Actor; director; performed in about 200 television programs and sixty-five films as well as several plays; was best known for role of Paladin, the cultured hired gunman in *Have Gun, Will Travel* (CBS-TV, 1957-63); was host of the less popular but critically admired *Richard Boone Show* (NBC-TV, 1963-64), a pioneering dramatic anthology patterned on repertory theatre, appearing also in half the plays presented; died in St. Augustine, Florida. See *Current Biography* (February) 1964.

Obituary

N Y Times D p11 Ja 12 '81

BRADLEY, OMAR N(ELSON) Feb. 12, 1893-Apr. 8, 1981 Five-star general of the United States Army; during World War II commanded the 2d Corps in the Northern Tunisian and Sicilian campaigns, the First Army during the assault landing in Normandy on June 6, 1944, and the 12th Army Group, comprising over 1,300,000 combat troops of four armies, through the fighting in France and Germany; was considered a master tactician in battle and was known as the "G.I.'s General" because of his concern for the welfare of the infantryman; chairman of the Joint Chiefs of Staff (1947-53); died in New York City. See *Current Biography* (July) 1943.

Obituary

N Y Times p1+ Ap 9 '81

BREUER, MARCEL (LAJOS) May 21, 1902-July 1, 1981 Hungarian-born architect; earned reputation as "form-giver" of twentieth century by adapting modern European style to American technology; while associated with Walter Gropius at Bauhaus in Germany during 1920's, designed tubular steel furniture, including Wassily chair; taught at Harvard University Graduate School of Design (1937-46) before opening architectural practice in New York City; designed, among other buildings, Paris headquarters of UNESCO (1953-58), IBM Research Center in La Gaude, France (1960-61), St. John's Abbey in Collegeville, Minnesota (1953-61), and Whitney Museum of American Art in New York City (1963-66); died at his New York City home. See *Current Biography* (June) 1960.

Obituary

N Y Times A p10 Jl 3 '81

CABOT, JOHN M(OORS) Dec. 11, 1901-Feb. 23, 1981 Former diplomat; foreign service officer who held the important post of chargé d'affaires in Belgrade in 1946-47, when a split between Yugoslavia and the Soviet Union was developing; served as Assistant Secretary of State for Inter-American Affairs (1953-54) and as Ambassador to Sweden (1954-57), Colombia (1957-59), Brazil (1959-61), and Poland (1962-65); as diplomat, advocated direct contact with people of other nations; author of *Towards Our Common American Destiny* (1955) and other books; died in Washington, D.C. See *Current Biography* (September) 1953.

Obituary

N Y Times B p6 F 25 '81

CAETANO, MARCELLO (JOSE) Aug. 17, 1906-Oct. 26, 1980 Prime Minister of Portugal (1968-74); university professor; protégé of dictator António de Oliveira Salazar, whom he succeeded as head of government; chief theoretician of Salazar's corporate state, known as Estado Novo; occupied various posts under Salazar, including that of deputy prime minister (1955-58); permitted some liberal reforms during his basically conservative regime; was ousted by revolution of Armed Forces Movement and went into exile in Brazil; died in Rio de Janeiro. See *Current Biography* (March) 1970.

Obituary

N Y Times D p13 O 27 '80

CÁMPORA, HÉCTOR JOSÉ Mar. 26, 1909-Dec. 19, 1980 Former Argentine government official; a dedicated adherent of the policies of Juan D. Perón, whose Presidency he supported as a member, and for seven years president, of the Chamber of Deputies (1946-55); served as President of Argentina for seven weeks (May-July 1973), having been elected as a stand-in candidate of the Justicialist Liberation Front for Perón, then in exile; resigned to allow Perón's return to power; died in exile in Mexico City. See *Current Biography* (October) 1973.

Obituary

N Y Times p49 D 20 '80

CELLER, EMANUEL May 6, 1888-Jan. 15, 1981 Former Congressman; lawyer; had one of the longest political careers in New York history as a Democratic member of the House of Representatives (1923-72) from a Brooklyn district; as the influential chairman of the House Judiciary Committee, beginning in 1949, wrote and guided to passage the Civil Rights Act of 1957, of 1960, and of 1964; sponsored other important liberal legislation and opposed the methods of the House Committee on Un-American Activities; died in Brooklyn. See *Current Biography* (November) 1966.

Obituary

N Y Times D p16 Ja 16 '81

CHAYEFSKY, PADDY Jan. 29, 1923-Aug. 1, 1981 Playwright; wrote realistic, intimate dramas about the joys and tribulations of ordinary people for stage, television, and motion pictures; achieved first major success with television play *Marty* (1953), which became an Academy Award-winning motion picture in 1955; won additional Oscars for *Hospital* (1971) and *Network* (1976); also wrote screenplays *The Catered Affair* (1956), *The Bachelor Party* (1957), *The Goddess* (1958), and *Altered States* (1979), and Broadway plays *Middle of the Night* (1956), *The Tenth Man* (1959), and *Gideon*

(1961); died in New York City. See *Current Biography* (September) 1957.

Obituary

N Y Times p1+ Ag 2 '81

CLAIR, RENÉ Nov. 11, 1891-Mar. 15, 1981 French filmmaker; in early experimental work such as the Dadaistic *Entr'acte* (1924) blended elements of absurdity and fantasy and developed the camera techniques and distinctive comedic style that shaped later masterpieces like *Sous les Toits de Paris* (1930) and *A Nous la Liberté* (1932); became noted for satiric treatment of social pretension, pursuit of wealth, and other aspects of human behavior; directed less successful films, including *It Happened Tomorrow* (1944), in Hollywood during World War II; was the first to gain membership in the French Academy solely for contributions to film; died in Neuilly, France. See *Current Biography* (November) 1941.

Obituary

N Y Times B p11 Mr 16 '81

CONNELLY, MARC Dec. 13, 1890-Dec. 21, 1980 Author; playwright; theatrical producer and director; collaborated with George S. Kaufman on several light comedies, including *Dulcy* (1921), before writing *The Green Pastures,* a depiction of the Old Testament as if by Southern plantation blacks, which won him a Pulitzer Prize and fame; directed Arthur Kober's *Having Wonderful Time* (1937), which he also coproduced, and other stage plays; wrote occasional scenarios, including *The Cradle Song* (Paramount, 1933); belonged to the Algonquin Round Table and other literary circles, as recorded in his memoir, *Voices Off-Stage* (1968); died in New York City. See *Current Biography* (November) 1969.

Obituary

N Y Times A p1+ D 22 '80

COON, CARLETON S(TEVENS) June 23, 1904-June 3, 1981 Anthropologist; archaeologist; university professor; best known for his eminently readable scientific works *The Story of Man* (1954) and *The Seven Caves* (1957); propounded theory that Homo sapiens is not descended from apes but rather that "apes are descended from ground-living primates that almost became men"; further argued that five major races of mankind are descended from five other groups of ground-living primates, all differentiated primordially, and that nonspecialization and openness to change are keys to evolutionary advance; also wrote, among other books, an autobiography completed shortly before his death; died at his home in Gloucester, Massachusetts; See *Current Biography* (September) 1955.

Obituary

N Y Times p19 Je 6 '81

CRONIN, A(RCHIBALD) J(OSEPH) July 19, 1896-Jan. 6, 1981 Writer; a Scottish physician who, beginning with *Hatter's Castle* (1931), turned to writing enormously popular novels, some of which were made into successful films, combining a concern for social problems and human values with melodramatic action, among them *The Stars Look Down* (1935), set in a North England mining town; *The Citadel* (1937), about a doctor who exchanges his work in a Welsh mining village for a fashionable London practice; and *The Keys of the Kingdom*, the story of a Roman Catholic missionary in China; became an American citizen after World War II; died in Glion, near Montreux, Switzerland. See *Current Biography* (July) 1942.

Obituary

N Y Times p16 Ja 10 '81

CROWTHER, (F.) BOSLEY July 13, 1905- Mar. 7, 1981 Film critic; journalist; on the staff of the New York *Times,* beginning in 1928, worked as a general reporter, feature writer, and re-write man before becoming, in 1940, that paper's film critic, a post that he held until 1967; wrote some 200 movie reviews and about fifty Sunday articles on film a year as well as several books, including *The Lion's Share: the Story of an Entertainment Empire* (1957), a history of MGM; was considered one of the country's most perceptive and influential authorities on motion picture art and industry; died in Mount Kisco, New York. See *Current Biography* (July) 1957.

Obituary

N Y Times p36 Mr 8 '81

CURRAN, JOSEPH E(DWIN) Mar. 1, 1906- Aug. 14, 1981 Labor leader; founder and former long-term president of National Maritime Union; a seaman since 1922, joined International Seaman's Union in 1935; the following year, led his first strike in defiance of I.S.U. leadership; in 1937, led 30,000 members of I.S.U. into new National Maritime Union, which grew in membership to peak of 100,000 during World War II and then declined to current 50,000; elected vice-president of Congress of Industrial Organizations in 1940 and retained that post after C.I.O. merged with American Federation of Labor in 1955; retired in 1973; died in Boca Raton, Florida. See *Current Biography* (April) 1945.

Obituary

N Y Times p47 Ag 15 '81

DAY, DOROTHY Nov. 8, 1897-Nov. 29, 1980 Roman Catholic social activist; author; major figure in American radicalism; seminal force in development of contemporary American Catholic social and economic consciousness; precursor of Catholic "New Left"; wrote autobiographies *From Union Square to Rome* (1938) and *The Long Loneliness* (1952), among other books; worked for Communist and Socialist publications before her conversion to Catholicism in 1927; with Peter Maurin, in 1933 founded Catholic Worker, anarcho-pacifist movement comprising urban "houses of hospitality" for destitute and rural communes; published *Catholic Worker,* penny monthly promoting "Green Revolution" combining direct action for social justice and nonviolent resistance to "warfare state" with Christian philosophy of voluntary poverty; lived what she preached, a life of self-abnegation among the poorest, joined to political agitation and the jailings resulting therefrom; died at Catholic Worker hospice on New York City's Lower East Side. See *Current Biography* (May) 1962.

Obituary

N Y Times D p12 D 1 '80

DEAN, WILLIAM F(RISHE) Aug. 1, 1899-Aug. 25, 1981 Major General, United States Army; highest ranking American to be taken prisoner during Korean war; during three years in prisoner-of-war camps, resisted all efforts by his Communist captors to extract military information from him; received Congressional Medal of Honor *in absentia* in 1950; after his liberation, in 1953, wrote *General Dean's Story* (1954) with William L. Worden; in World War II, had won Distinguished Service Cross for bravery under fire in France; retired in 1955. See *Current Biography* (September) 1954.

Obituary

N Y Times D p23 Ag 26 '81

DEWEY, CHARLES S(CHUVELDT) Nov. 10, 1882-Dec. 26, 1980 Former United States government official; banker; began his career in Washington in 1924 as Assistant Secretary of the Treasury, a post that he left in 1927 to become director for four years of the Bank of Poland; served as Republican member of the House of Representatives from Illinois (1941-45) and as agent general on the Joint Congressional Committee for Foreign Economic Co-operation (Marshall Plan) after World War II; died in Washington, D.C. See *Current Biography* (June) 1949.

Obituary

N Y Times p20 D 27 '80

DISALLE, MICHAEL V(INCENT) Jan. 6, 1908-Sept. 15, 1981 United States government official; director of Office of Price Stabilization (1950-52) and of Economic Stabilization Agency (1952-53); as Governor of Ohio (1959-63), promoted social legislation and was closely allied to President John F. Kennedy; from 1963 on, engaged in private law practice in Ohio and Washington, D.C.; died while vacationing in Italy. See *Current Biography* (January) 1951.

Obituary

N Y Times D p27 S 17 '81

DODDS, HAROLD W(ILLIS) June 28, 1889-Oct. 25, 1980 Educator; political scientist; was electoral adviser to various Latin American governments during 1920's; joined faculty of Princeton University as professor of municipal government and public administration in 1927; was president of Princeton from 1933 until his retirement in 1957; in addition, held high posts, including presidency, in National Municipal League, and served on numerous governmental consultative panels, including a Hoover Commission task force on civil service reform in the mid-1950's; died in Hightstown, New Jersey. See Current Biography (December) 1945.

Obituary

Washington Post B p4 O 27 '80

DOENITZ, KARL Sept. 16, 1891-Dec. 24, 1980 Former German grand admiral; as commander of the submarine fleet during World War II, directed the U-boat campaign against Allied shipping; in 1943 succeeded Grand Admiral Erich Raeder as Navy Commander in Chief; having been appointed by Adolf Hitler as his successor on April 30, 1945, presided over Germany's surrender on May 23; was convicted of war crimes at the Nuremberg trials in 1947 and sentenced to ten years in prison; died in Hamburg, West Germany. See Current Biography (November) 1942.

Obituary

N Y Times A p1+ D 26 '80

DOUGLAS, DONALD W(ILLS) Apr. 6, 1892-Feb. 1, 1981 Aeronautical engineer and airplane manufacturer; headed the Douglas Aircraft Company from the 1920's until its merger with the McDonnell Aircraft Corporation in 1967; dominated commercial aviation with a series of aircraft designs that included the twin-engine DC-3 and the DC-8 jetliner; during World War II produced in weight more military aircraft than any other manufacturer; died in Palm Springs, California. See Current Biography (December) 1950.

Obituary

N Y Times B p14 F 3 '81

DOUGLAS, MELVYN Apr. 5, 1901-Aug. 4, 1981 Actor; during career spanning more than fifty years, appeared in some seventy motion pictures, as well as in Broadway plays and on television, in the roles ranging from debonair leading men to cantankerous old codgers; won Oscar awards as best supporting actor in *Hud* (1963) and *Being There* (1980), and Oscar nomination for best actor in *I Never Sang for My Father* (1970); received Tony award for leading role in Broadway production of *The Best*

Man (1960) and Emmy award for television performance in *Do Not Go Gentle Into That Good Night* (1968); with his wife, the late United States Representative and former actress Helen Gahagan Douglas, championed liberal causes; died in New York City. See Current Biography (May) 1942.

Obituary

N Y Times A p21 Ag 2 '81

ECKSTEIN, GUSTAV Oct. 26, 1890-Sept. 23, 1981 Physiologist; wide-ranging scholar, whose fields of interest included medicine, psychology, philosophy, literature, music, Oriental art, and travel; was an authority on behavior of animals and birds; taught at University of Cincinnati (1917-61); wrote ten books, including best-selling *The Body Has a Head* (1969), an exploration of the study of the human body; was working on biography of Soviet physiologist Ivan Pavlov at time of his death, in Cincinnati, Ohio. See Current Biography (May) 1942.

Obituary

N Y Times B p14 S 25 '81

EDWARDS, JOAN Feb. 13, 1919-Aug. 27, 1981 Singer; songwriter; was featured vocalist with bands of Rudy Vallee and Paul Whiteman during late 1930's and 1940's; shared spotlight with Frank Sinatra on popular radio program *Your Hit Parade* (1941-46) and later starred in radio series *At Home With Joan* and in movie *Hit Parade of 1947*; composed a number of popular songs and advertising jingles and collaborated with Lyn Duddy on score for 1950 Broadway revue *Tickets, Please*; died in New York City. See Current Biography (October) 1953.

Obituary

N Y Times p11 Ag 29 '81

ETHRIDGE, MARK (FOSTER) Apr. 22, 1896-Apr. 5, 1981 Newspaper editor and publisher; was associated for twenty-seven years with the Louisville *Courier-Journal* and Louisville *Times*, as vice-president and general manager (1926-42), publisher (1942-62), and chairman of the board (1962-63); made those papers nationally known because of his advocacy of complete and honest news coverage and of racial justice and other progressive causes; vice-president and editor of *Newsday* (1963-65); taught journalism at the University of North Carolina (1965-68); died in Moncure, North Carolina. See Current Biography (January) 1946.

Obituary

N Y Times B p10 Ap 7 '81

FISHER, WELTHY (BLAKESLEY HONSINGER)
Sept. 18, 1879-Dec. 16, 1980 Missionary; educator; went to China in 1906 as a Methodist missionary and became principal of a girls' school in Nanchang; during 1940's traveled widely to continue the missionary work of her late husband, a Methodist minister; at the urging of Mohandas K. Gandhi that she work in Indian villages, founded Literacy House in Lucknow to train teachers in a program of literacy; was president until 1972 of Literacy House and World Education, Inc., which promotes education in undeveloped and developing nations; died in Southbury, Connecticut. See *Current Biography* (December) 1969.

Obituary

N Y Times A p33 D 17 '80

FISK, JAMES BROWN Aug. 30, 1910-Aug. 10, 1981 Physicist; former president (1959-73) and chairman (1973-74) of Bell Laboratories, research and development arm of American Telephone and Telegraph Company; before and after joining Bell Labs as researcher, in 1939, taught at various universities; during World War II, supervised work on development of microwave magnetron for use in high frequency radar; later assembled research teams responsible for such inventions as transistor, lasers, and satellite communications systems; on leave from Bell, served United States government as first director of research for the Atomic Energy Commission (1947) and as head of team that negotiated technical groundwork for nuclear test ban treaty (1958), among other such posts; died in Elizabethtown, New York. See *Current Biography* (January) 1959.

Obituary

N Y Times D p21 Ag 13 '81

FITZSIMMONS, FRANK E(DWARD) Apr. 7, 1908-May 6, 1981 Labor union official; president of the International Brotherhood of Teamsters; was loyal deputy of longtime Teamsters president Jimmy Hoffa, going back to the 1930's, when they were organizers together in Detroit; became acting president of union when Hoffa went to prison in 1967; remained in office in his own right after Hoffa's release from prison, in 1971, and his disappearance and presumed death, in 1975; died in San Diego, California. See *Current Biography* (May) 1971.

Obituary

N Y Times B p14 My 7 '81

FOX, CAROL June 15, 1926-July 21, 1981 Opera producer; cofounder and manager (from 1952) of Lyric Theatre of Chicago, reorganized in 1956 as Lyric Opera of Chicago and sometimes called "La Scala West" because of its inter-national reputation; introduced such top European artists as Tito Gobbi and Maria Callas to American audiences; founded apprentice artist program for American singers (1973); retired amid controversy in January 1981; died in Chicago. See *Current Biography* (July) 1978.

Obituary

N Y Times B p5 Jl 23 '81

FOX, VIRGIL (KEEL) May 3, 1912-Oct. 25, 1980 Organist; was master of five-manual Aeolian-Skinner at Riverside Church in New York City from 1946 to 1964; helped establish modern organ as concert instrument; in his concert itinerary, ranged from cathedrals of Europe to rock music auditoriums; attracted large numbers of people, especially the young, to organ concerts by his combination of musicianship, especially dazzling pedal technique, flamboyant showmanship typified by iridescent, rhinestone-studded clothes, free-wheeling apostrophes to audience, and blazing tours de force; died in West Palm Beach, Florida. See *Current Biography* (January) 1964.

Obituary

N Y Times D p13 O 27 '80

FRASER OF NORTH CAPE, BRUCE AUSTIN FRASER, 1st BARON Feb. 5, 1888-Feb. 12, 1981 British admiral; as commander in chief of the Home Fleet during World War II had charge of countering the German U-boat offensive; was credited with sinking the German battleship *Scharnhorst* off North Cape, Norway (1943); also commanded warships in Pacific battles; served as First Sea Lord and Chief of Naval Staff, the senior command of the British Navy (1948-51); died in London. See *Current Biography* (July) 1943.

Obituary

N Y Times A p16 F 13 '81

FREDERIKA (LOUISE), CONSORT OF PAUL I, KING OF THE HELLENES Apr. 18, 1917-Feb. 6, 1981 Member of a princely German family; was married on January 9, 1938 to Crown Prince Paul of Greece, who became King of the Hellenes in 1947; was known as a strong-willed Queen who played a conspicuous role in public life; became Queen Mother when her son, Constantine, ascended to the throne on March 6, 1969, following the death of King Paul; fled with Constantine to Rome in the wake of the 1967 Greek military coup d'état; lived in self-imposed exile after the overthrow of the monarchy in 1973; died in Madrid while visiting her daughter, Queen Sofia of Spain. See *Current Biography* (January) 1955.

Obituary

N Y Times p36 F 8 '81

FRINGS, KETTI (HARTLEY) 1920(?)-Feb. 11, 1981 Writer whose screenplays included *Hold Back the Dawn* (1941), based on a story that she also published as a novel, *Come Back, Little Sheba* (1952), adapted from William Inge's play, and *The Shrike*, adapted from Joseph Kramm's play; won the 1958 Pulitzer Prize in drama and the New York Drama Critics Circle Award for her dramatization of Thomas Wolfe's novel *Look Homeward, Angel*, which opened on Broadway in 1957; died in Los Angeles, California. See *Current Biography* (January) 1960.

Obituary

N Y Times A p16 F 13 '81

GOLDEN, HARRY (LEWIS) May 6, 1902-Oct. 2, 1981 Journalist; author; satirized bigotry and other human faults and foibles with irreverent folk humor, derived from his New York Lower East Side Jewish background, in his monthly *Carolina Israelite*, which he published and edited in Charlotte, North Carolina (1941-68), and in such anecdotal books as *Only in America* (1958), *For 2 Cents Plain* (1959), *Enjoy, Enjoy* (1960), and *Golden Book of Jewish Humor* (1972); also wrote such serious studies as *Jews in American History* (1950, with Martin Rywell), and anecdotal biography *Carl Sandburg* (1961), among other works; died at his home in Charlotte. See *Current Biography* (January) 1959.

Obituary

N Y Times p33 O 3 '81

GRASSO, ELLA T(AMBUSSI) May 10, 1919-Feb. 5, 1981 Former Governor of Connecticut; as protégée of John M. Bailey, Democratic state chairman, became influential in state and national politics; served as a member of the state House of Representatives (1953-57), secretary of state of Connecticut (1958-70), and member of the United States House of Representatives (1971-75); in 1974 was elected Governor of Connecticut, becoming first woman in the country to be Governor in her own right; considered a liberal legislator, but as Governor protected the status quo and practised frugality in welfare and other programs; was popular for her accessibility and expressions of personal concern; was reelected in 1979, but resigned on New Year's Eve 1980 because of illness; died in Hartford. See *Current Biography* (May) 1975.

Obituary

N Y Times A p1+ F 6 '81

GRIBBLE, HARRY WAGSTAFF (GRAHAM-) 1891(?)-Jan. 28, 1981 Playwright; director; noted for his versatility; began his career as an actor in his native England; wrote or collaborated on Broadway revues, including *Artists and Models* (1922), dramas, including *Elizabeth and Essex* (1930), and screenplays, including *Stella Dallas* (1937); was director of *The Taming of the Shrew* (1935), starring the Lunts, and producer-director of the play *Johnny Belinda* (1940) and of the hit comedy-drama *Anna Lucasta* (1944), which he also rewrote in part; died in New York City. See *Current Biography* (September) 1945.

Obituary

N Y Times D p15 Ja 30 '81

HAGERTY, JAMES C. May 9, 1909-Apr. 11, 1981 Former White House press secretary; journalist; reporter on the New York *Times* (1934-43); executive assistant (1943-50) and press secretary (1950-52) to New York Governor Thomas E. Dewey; as press secretary to President Dwight D. Eisenhower gained wide respect for tact, fair play, and efficiency; initiated regularly scheduled Presidential news conferences and allowed reporters to quote directly; vice-president of news, special events, and public affairs (1961-63) and vice-president for corporate relations (1963-75) of ABC; died in Bronxville, New York. See *Current Biography* (March) 1953.

Obituary

N Y Times D p10 Ap 13 '81

HANSON, HOWARD Oct. 28, 1896-Feb. 26, 1981 Composer; conductor; director of the Eastman School of Music in Rochester, New York (1924-64); promoted the growth of a distinctive modern American music through his teaching and his own post-Romantic, widely varied compositions, including the symphonic poem *North and West*, the choral work *Lament for Beowulf*, the opera *Merry Mount*, and seven symphonies, among them the Fourth Symphony, for which he won the 1944 Pulitzer Prize in music; was founder and conductor of the Eastman Philharmonia and guest conductor of many leading orchestras; died in Rochester. See *Current Biography* (September) 1966.

Obituary

N Y Times p19 F 28 '81

HARBURG, E(DGAR) Y(IPSEL) Apr. 8, 1896-Mar. 5, 1981 Lyricist; collaborated with leading American composers of popular music on stage and screen productions; for the revue *Americana* (1932) wrote the Depression-inspired *Brother, Can You Spare a Dime?*, which exemplifies his penchant for social comment; with Harold Arlen wrote Oscar-winning "Over the Rainbow" for *The Wizard of Oz* (1939); combined social satire with humor, romance, and fantasy in the Broadway musical *Finian's Rainbow* (1947), for which he supplied the lyrics and collaborated on the book; died in auto accident in Los Angeles. See *Current Biography* (July) 1980.

Obituary

N Y Times p17 Mr 7 '81

HAUGE, GABRIEL (SYLFEST) Mar. 7, 1914-July 24, 1981 Economist; banker; educator; administrative assistant (1953-56) and special assistant (1956-58) for economic affairs under President Dwight D. Eisenhower; helped to formulate United States post-World War II economic policies; as president (1963-71) and board chairman (1971-79) of Manufacturers Hanover Trust Company, supervised its growth into fourth-largest bank in United States; died in New York City. See *Current Biography* (October) 1953.

Obituary

N Y Times p20 Jl 25 '81

HIRSHHORN, JOSEPH H(ERMAN) Aug. 1, 1899-Aug. 31, 1981 Financier; art patron; mining tycoon; founder and benefactor of museum in Washington, D.C. that bears his name; rose from immigrant Brooklyn childhood to become self-made nine-figure millionaire through speculation in stock market and dealings in uranium and other geological lodes, chiefly in Canada; amassed one of world's largest private art collections, containing some 5,800 pieces, including sculpture ranging from Etruscan to Henry Moore and comprehensive representation of contemporary American painting; donated entire collection, valued at $50,000,000, to United States in 1966; died in Washington, D.C. See *Current Biography* (November) 1966.

Obituary

N Y Times A p17 S 2 '81

HOUGHTON, AMORY July 27, 1899-Feb. 21, 1981 Glass manufacturer; began his association with the Corning (New York) Glass Works in 1921, advancing to the presidency in 1930 and holding other executive titles before becoming chairman emeritus in 1971; through his commitment to basic research, collaborated with other companies to form the Pittsburg Corning Corporation, the Owens-Corning Fiberglas Corporation, and the Dow Corning Corporation; held various government posts during World War II, including chief mission officer for the Lend-Lease Administration; served as Ambassador to France (1958-61); died in Charleston, South Carolina. See *Current Biography* (January) 1947.

Obituary

N Y Times D p11 F 23 '81

HOWARD, ELSTON (GENE) Feb. 23, 1929(?)-Dec. 14, 1980 Baseball player; in 1955 became the first black to play for the New York Yankees; during fourteen seasons in the major leagues, thirteen with the Yankees and one with the Boston Red Sox, had a batting average of .274 with 167 home runs; named American League's most valuable player in 1963 and, as catcher, won Gold Glove awards in 1963 and 1964; played in ten World Series; after retirement as a player in 1968, coached for the Yankees; died in New York City. See *Current Biography* (April) 1964.

Obituary

N Y Times D p17 D 15 '80

ILG, FRANCES L(ILLIAN) Oct. 11, 1902-July 26, 1981 Pediatrician; educator; associate of Dr. Arnold Gesell, Dr. Louise Ames, and others at Yale University Clinic of Child Development (1933-50); cofounder (1950) and director of Gesell Institute of Child Development, later known as Gesell Institute of Human Development; coauthor of over twenty books on behavior patterns of children, including (with Gesell) *Infant and Child in the Culture of Today* (1943); with Dr. Ames, wrote syndicated newspaper column *Child Behavior*; continued to write and lecture after her retirement in 1970; died in Manitowish Waters, Wisconsin. See *Current Biography* (September) 1956.

Obituary

N Y Times B p8 Jl 28 '81

JENKINS, RAY H(OWARD) Mar. 18, 1897-Dec. 26, 1980 Lawyer; began practice in Knoxville, Tennessee in 1920, specializing in criminal law; managed the campaigns of several Republican candidates in Tennessee; gained considerable renown in 1954 for his dogged manner of questioning as special counsel to the Senate permanent subcommittee on investigations, which held televised hearings into the exchange of charges between Senator Joseph R. McCarthy and the United States Army; died in Knoxville. See *Current Biography* (June) 1954.

Obituary

N Y Times p30 D 28 '80

JESSEL, GEORGE (ALBERT) Apr. 3, 1898-May 24, 1981 Showman; comedian; "Toastmaster General of the United States"; claimed credit for inventing the celebrity "roast"; in his melodramatic after-dinner speeches and other stand-up routines, traded heavily on his patriotism and his Jewish rearing in New York City; began career as juvenile hoofer and singer in vaudeville; developed stage act featuring sentimental and funny simulated telephone conversation with his mother; starred in 1925 hit *The Jazz Singer*, among other Broadway shows; pursued Hollywood career, chiefly as producer, for ten years beginning in 1943; in recent decades concentrated on funeral eulogies, fund-raising for Israel and other causes, and banquet appearances; died in Los Angeles, California. See *Current Biography* (March) 1943.

Obituary

N Y Times D p12 My 26 '81

JOHNSON, PAMELA HANSFORD May 29, 1912-June 18, 1981 British writer; was noted for her witty, satirical fiction; published some twenty-five novels, including *This Bed Thy Centre* (1935), *An Impossible Marriage* (1954), *The Honors Board* (1970), and *A Bonfire* (1981); also wrote plays, such as *Corinth House* (1948), and literary studies, including works on Dickens, Proust, and Thomas Wolfe; died in London, almost one year after death of her husband, the noted author and scientist C. P. Snow. See *Current Biography* (Yearbook) 1948.

Obituary

N Y Times p21 Je 20 '81

KEMPER, JAMES S(COTT) Nov. 18, 1886-Sept. 17, 1981 Insurance executive; founder (1912) and president (1919-45) of Lumbermen's Mutual Casualty Company; retired in 1966 as chairman and chief executive officer of Kemper Group, comprising one of the world's largest fire and casualty underwriting organizations; president of United States Chamber of Commerce (1940-41); served as treasurer of Republican National Committee (1946-49) and in other party posts; United States Ambassador to Brazil (1953-54); died at his Chicago home. See *Current Biography* (April) 1941.

Obituary

N Y Times p21 S 19 '81

KINTNER, ROBERT E(DMONDS) Sept. 12, 1909-Dec. 20, 1980 Former broadcasting company executive; began career as a journalist with the New York *Herald Tribune;* as president of the American Broadcasting Company (1950-56) and National Broadcasting Company (1958-65) was criticized for succeeding financially by flooding television with crime, comedy and western programs, although his chief interest was news; served as special assistant and Cabinet secretary to President Lyndon B. Johnson (1966-67); died in Washington, D.C. See *Current Biography* (October) 1950.

Obituary

N Y Times B p15 D 23 '80

KNIGHT, JOHN S(HIVELY) Oct. 26, 1894-June 16, 1981 Newspaper publisher; parlayed Akron (Ohio) *Beacon-Journal,* which he inherited from his father in 1932, into Knight-Ridder Newspapers Inc., which by 1981 numbered thirty-two newspapers in seventeen states—including Miami *Herald,* Detroit *Free Press,* and Philadelphia *Inquirer*—with an aggregate weekly circulation of 25,000,000, the largest for a newspaper chain in the United States; won 1968 Pulitzer Prize for his weekly column, "The Editor's Notebook"; was a firm champion of editorial integrity and freedom of the press around the world; retired in 1976 as editorial

chairman of Knight-Ridder Newspapers Inc.; died in Akron, Ohio. See *Current Biography* (April) 1945.

Obituary

N Y Times B p14 Je 18 '81

KOSYGIN, ALEKSEI N(IKOLAYEVICH) Feb. 20, 1904-Dec. 18, 1980 Former Chairman of the U.S.S.R. Council of Ministers (Prime Minister); was a close aide to Joseph Stalin on industrial and financial matters in the 1940's; held various government posts during the regime of Nikita S. Khrushchev, including chairman of the State Planning Commission; member of the Politburo (1948-54 and from 1966); after the ouster of Khrushchev in 1964 shared leadership as Prime Minister with First Secretary of the Communist party Leonid I. Brezhnev and President Nikolai V. Podgorny; resigned because of illness on October 23, 1980. See *Current Biography* (September) 1965.

Obituary

N Y Times p1+ D 20 '80, p43 D 21 '80

LAMARSH, JUDY Dec. 20, 1924-Oct. 27, 1980 Canadian government official; lawyer; Liberal member of House of Commons; as Minister of National Health and Welfare (1963-65), was youngest member and only woman in Cabinet of Prime Minister Lester B. Pearson; helped to promote passage of national assistance plan for elderly, disabled, and unemployed, among other measures; also served as Secretary of State (1965-68), a post mainly concerned with cultural affairs; left government service in 1968 to return to private law practice; died at her home in Toronto, Ontario. See *Current Biography* (April) 1968.

Obituary

N Y Times A p32 O 28 '80

LEGER, JULES Apr. 4, 1913-Nov. 22, 1980 Canadian statesman; Governor-General of Canada (1974-79); previously served as Undersecretary of State for External Affairs (1954-58) and Undersecretary of State (1968-73); was Ambassador to Italy (1962-64) and to France (1964-68); also represented his country in Chile, Great Britain, Mexico, and the councils of NATO and OEEC; died in Ottawa. See *Current Biography* (November) 1976.

Obituary

N Y Times D p11 N 24 '80

LENNON, JOHN Oct. 9, 1940-Dec. 8, 1980 Singer; musician; songwriter; cultural hero; in 1960's was acknowledged leader of British rock group the Beatles, perhaps most popular and socially as well as musically influential act in show business history; intellectually and linguistically playful, was self-described "hip," "hallucinatory" side of Lennon-Paul McCartney composing team, with his hand most evident in such Beatle songs as "Help!" "Revolution," "Strawberry Fields," and "Lucy in the Sky with Diamonds"; after teaming with second wife, Yoko Ono, recorded demythologizing compositions ("The Dream Is Over") and political rallying cries ("Come Together," "Give Peace a Chance," "Imagine"); after five-year retreat, issued LP that included hit single "Starting Over" one month before his assassination in his adopted New York City—an event that set off international public mourning. See *Current Biography* (December) 1965.

Obituary

N Y Times p1+ D 9 '80, A p1+ D 10 '80

LESAGE, JEAN June 10, 1912-Dec. 11, 1980 Former Premier of Quebec, Canada; lawyer; member of the House of Commons (1945-58); leader of Quebec's Liberal party (1958-69); as Premier of Quebec (1960-66) and Minister of Finance and Minister of Federal-Provincial Affairs (1961-66), initiated a program of reforms that transferred responsibility in education and other institutions from the Roman Catholic Church to the government and radically changed the province's social and economic structure; died at his home near the city of Quebec. See *Current Biography* (November) 1961.

Obituary

N Y Times p34 D 13 '80

LEVIN, MEYER Oct. 8, 1905-July 9, 1981 Writer of novels and nonfiction, often on Jewish topics, as well as plays, documentary films, and scenarios; associate editor and film critic for *Esquire* (1933-39); as a journalist, covered Spanish Civil War and post-World War II illegal immigration of European Jews to Palestine; author of best-selling novel *Compulsion* (1956), about Leopold-Loeb murder case; most recently, wrote *The Architect,* a roman à clef about Frank Lloyd Wright, to be published posthumously; died in Jerusalem. See *Current Biography* (April) 1940.

Obituary

N Y Times p16 Jl 11 '81

LIEBMAN, MAX Aug. 5, 1902-July 21, 1981 Stage and television producer and director; as social director at Hotel Tamiment in Pennsylvania's Pocono Mountains (1932-47), discovered such budding talent as Danny Kaye, Jerome Robbins, and many others; introduced sophisticated Broadway-style variety shows to television as producer of Emmy-award-winning *Your Show of Shows* (1949-54), highlighted by comedy sketches featuring Sid Caesar and

Imogene Coca; later produced and directed television spectaculars; died in New York City. See *Current Biography* (April) 1953.

Obituary

N Y Times A p14 Jl 24 '81

LILIENTHAL, DAVID E(LI) July 8, 1899-Jan. 15, 1981 Former United States government official; lawyer; served as director in charge of the power program of the three-man board of the Tennessee Valley Authority from 1933 until becoming chairman in 1941; during World War II expanded power program to make TVA by 1944 the nation's largest producer of electricity; resigned from TVA in 1945 to work with State Department on plans for atomic energy control; as Atomic Energy Commission chairman (1947-50) aimed to increase United States lead in atomic energy and weapons production; chairman of the Development and Research Corporation (1953-79) for dam and power plant projects; died in New York City. See *Current Biography* (June) 1944.

Obituary

N Y Times A p1+ Ja 16 '81

LOEB, WILLIAM Dec. 26, 1905-Sept. 13, 1981 Publisher (since 1946) of nationally influential Manchester (New Hampshire) *Union Leader;* expressed right-wing views in front-page editorials, castigating liberal Democrats and moderate Republicans alike, but also sympathized with organized labor and instituted profit-sharing plan for his employees; backed Barry Goldwater and Ronald Reagan, but withdrew support from Richard Nixon after latter's rapprochement with China and the Soviet Union; owned several other New England newspapers; died in Burlington, Massachusetts. See *Current Biography* (March) 1974.

Obituary

N Y Times D p15 S 14 '81

LONGO, LUIGI Mar. 15, 1900-Oct. 16, 1980 Italian political leader and legislator; Secretary-General of Italian Communist party from 1964, when he succeeded the late Palmiro Togliatti, until 1972, when he retired in favor of Enrico Berlinguer; with Togliatti and others, helped to found Communist party of Italy (1921); spent era of Benito Mussolini's Fascist dictatorship largely in imprisonment or exile; was honored by United States for role in organizing underground guerrillas during World War II; died at clinic in Rome suburb. See *Current Biography* (February) 1966.

Obituary

N Y Times D p19 O 17 '80

LOOS, ANITA Apr. 26, 1893-Aug. 18, 1981 Writer; noted for her witty film scripts, plays, and novels; won international acclaim with her satirical novel *Gentlemen Prefer Blondes* (1925), featuring the ingenuous gold-digger Lorelei Lee, and worked on its adaptations as a play and a musical comedy; also wrote *But Gentlemen Marry Brunettes* (1928), *A Mouse Is Born* (1951), *No Mother to Guide Her* (1961), and her autobiographical *A Girl Like I* (1966) and *Kiss Hollywood Goodbye* (1974), among other books; died in New York City. See *Current Biography* (February) 1974.

Obituary

N Y Times D p19 Ag 19 '81

LOUIS, JOE May 13, 1914-Apr. 12, 1981 Former world heavyweight champion; was nicknamed the "Brown Bomber"; won the heavyweight crown from James J. Braddock on June 22, 1937 and defended the title twenty-five times, the last against Jersey Joe Walcott on June 25, 1948, before retiring undefeated as champion on March 1, 1949; a deadpan boxer noted for his fast, smashing fists, which compensated for slow footwork, and judged by many experts to be the best heavyweight fighter in history; despite personal reversals in later life was regarded affectionately as "the major black hero of his time"; died in Las Vegas, Nevada. See *Current Biography* (October) 1940.

Obituary

N Y Times A p1+ Ap 13 '81

McCAIN, JOHN S(IDNEY), JR. Jan. 17, 1911-Mar. 22, 1981 Admiral, United States Navy; was much-decorated submarine commander in World War II; alternated between ship commands and Washington desk jobs, including Navy's chief of legislative liaison in 1950's and its chief of information in early 1960's; as commander of Atlantic Fleet's amphibious force, led American occupation of Dominican Republic in 1965; later served as military adviser to United States Ambassador to the United Nations and as Navy's commander in chief in Europe and the Pacific; retired in 1972; died on military aircraft enroute from Europe. See *Current Biography* (June) 1970.

Obituary

N Y Times B p19 Mr 24 '81

MACDONALD, MALCOLM (JOHN) 1901- Jan. 11, 1981 British diplomat; served as Colonial Secretary (1935-40) and Minister of Health (1940-41) in various Labour governments; spent three decades (1941-69) in ambassadorial-level posts in Canada, Africa, and Asia; as Commissioner-General for the United Kingdom in Southeast Asia (1948-55), helped set up SEATO; author of several travel and bird-watching books; awarded Order of Merit, 1969; was

chancellor of University of Durham (1970-81); died at home in Sevenoaks, Kent. See *Current Biography* (November) 1954.

Obituary

N Y Times D p11 Ja 12 '81

McLEAN, ROBERT Oct. 1, 1891-Dec. 5, 1980 Former newspaper publisher; exerted a strong influence on journalism in the United States as publisher and president (1931-64) of the evening and Sunday Philadelphia *Bulletin* and as director (1924-68) and president (1938-57) of the Associated Press, the country's largest wire service; died in Montecito, California. See *Current Biography* (November) 1951.

Obituary

N Y Times p53 D 7 '80

McLUHAN, (HERBERT) MARSHALL July 21, 1911-Dec. 31, 1980 Canadian communications specialist; professor of English (beginning in 1952) and director of the Center for Culture and Technology (beginning in 1963) of the University of Toronto; a controversial prophet of electronic communications and the author of the much-quoted aphorism "The medium is the message," whose books *The Mechanical Bride* (1951), *Understanding Media* (1964), and others explore the ways in which the nature itself of television, tape recorders, telephone, and other technological means of imparting information have effected widespread social changes; died in Toronto. See *Current Biography* (June) 1967.

Obituary

N Y Times p1+ Ja 1 '81

McCORMACK, JOHN W(ILLIAM) Dec. 21, 1891-Nov. 22, 1980 United States Democratic Representative from Massachusetts (1928-71); lawyer; forty-fifth Speaker of House of Representatives (1962-71); one of most influential and colorful political figures in United States; champion of New Deal program; supported civil rights, antipoverty, and other social legislation, but also sponsored anti-Communist measures; was nicknamed "The Archbishop" because of his identification with Roman Catholic Church and "Rabbi John" because of ties to Jewish community; died at nursing home in Dedham, Massachusetts. See *Current Biography* (April) 1962.

Obituary

N Y Times p1+ N 23 '80

McQUEEN, STEVE Mar 24, 1930-Nov. 7, 1980 Actor; became one of the highest-paid motion picture stars of 1960's and 1970's through popularity of his portrayals of tough, cool loner with sex appeal; had first big break as Ben Gazzara's replacement in lead of *A Hatful* of *Rain* on Broadway in 1956; on television, starred as the bounty hunter in the series *Wanted—Dead or Alive* (1958-61); in films (where he did virtually all of his motor racing and dangerous stunt scenes himself) played, among other roles, a prisoner of the Germans in World War II in *The Great Escape* (1963), the unsuccessful upstart gambler in *The Cincinnati Kid* (1965), the inscrutable, alienated sailor in *The Sand Pebbles* (1966), the millionaire bank robber in *The Thomas Crown Affair* (1968), the independent cop taking on the syndicate in the box-office blockbluster *Bullitt* (1968), the race driver in *Le Mans* (1971), and the prison escapee in *Papillon* (1973); died in Juárez, Mexico. See *Current Biography* (October) 1960.

Obituary

N Y Times p28 N 8 '80

MEARNS, DAVID C(HAMBERS) Dec. 31, 1899-May 21, 1981 Librarian; during life-long career at Library of Congress, served as director of reference department (1943-49), assistant librarian (1949-51), and chief of manuscript division (1951-67); after retirement, acted as honorary consultant in humanities; was authority on Abraham Lincoln; edited *The Lincoln Papers* (1948) and wrote several books, including a history of Library of Congress; died in Alexandria, Virginia. See *Current Biography* (July) 1961.

Obituary

N Y Times p21 My 30 '81

MILLER, IRVING Dec. 24, 1903-Dec. 24, 1980 Former Jewish organization official; rabbi (1946-63) and later rabbi emeritus of Congregation Sons of Israel in Woodmere, Long Island, New York; secretary-general of World Jewish Congress (1942-45); president of Zionist Organization of America (1952-54); chairman of American Zionist Council (1954-63); died in Woodmere. See *Current Biography* (November) 1952.

Obituary

N Y Times p30 D 28 '80

MONTALE, EUGENIO Oct. 21, 1896-Sept. 12, 1981 Italian poet; journalist; won 1975 Nobel Prize for Literature; served as curator of Gabinetto Vieusseux library in Florence (1928-38) but was dismissed for refusing to join Fascist party; later worked as literary editor and then music critic for *Corriere della sera* in Milan (from 1948); published five volumes of verse—*Ossi di seppia* (Cuttlefish Bones, 1925), *Le occasioni* (The Occasions, 1939), *La bufèra e altro* (The Storm and Other Things, 1956), *Satura* (1963), and *Diario del '71 e del '72*

(Diary of '71 and '72, 1973)—as well as collections of stories and essays and translations of English literary works; died in Milan. See *Current Biography* (April) 1976.

Obituary

N Y Times D p15 S 14 '81

MONTGOMERY, ROBERT May 21, 1904-Sept. 27, 1981 Actor; began career on Broadway stage (1924); appeared as romantic hero in scores of Hollywood comedy films; received Oscar nomination for portrayal of psychopathic killer in *Night Must Fall* (1937) and also won acclaim for performances in serious roles in *Here Comes Mr. Jordan* (1941), *They Were Expendable* (1945), and *Lady in the Lake* (1946), and for work as director of *The Gallant Hours* (1960) and other films; producer and host of popular weekly television drama series *Robert Montgomery Presents* (1950-57); media consultant to President Dwight D. Eisenhower (1952-60); died in New York City. See *Current Biography* (January) 1948.

Obituary

N Y Times B p6 S 28 '81

MOSES, ROBERT Dec. 18, 1888-July 29, 1981 Public official; as New York's controversial "master builder," played major role in molding state's physical environment; occupied a variety of state and city posts, including president of Long Island State Park Commission and chairman of State Council of Parks (1924-63), New York City parks commissioner (1934-60), chairman of New York State Power Authority (1954-63), and chairman of Triborough Bridge and Tunnel Authority (1954-63); between 1924 and 1968, developed public works costing $27 billion, including eleven bridges, 481 miles of highway, 658 playgrounds, seventy-five state parks, and such projects as Jones Beach, Shea Stadium, the United Nations, and Lincoln Center; died in West Islip, New York. See *Current Biography* (February) 1954.

Obituary

N Y Times A p1+ Jl 30 '81

MOSLEY, SIR OSWALD (ERNALD) Nov. 16, 1896-Dec. 2, 1980 Former British politician; Member of Parliament—Conservative (1918-22), Independent (1922-24), Labour (1926-32); founded the British Union of Fascists (1932); organized a private army to attack London Jews; as an admirer of Adolf Hitler and Benito Mussolini, opposed Great Britain's role in World War II; spent the war years in prison and later chose exile in France; died in Orsay, France. See *Current Biography* (July) 1940.

Obituary

N Y Times D p23 D 4 '80

NEUMANN, EMANUEL July 2, 1893-Oct. 26, 1980 Zionist leader; lawyer; business executive; bank official; played key role in establishment of Israel; served in various executive positions in Zionist movement (from 1918); president of Jewish National Fund (1928-30) and of Zionist Organization of America (1947-49, 1956-58); member of Jewish Agency delegation to U.N. (1947); chairman of United States section of World Zionist Organization (1968-72); founder (1961) and first president of Tarbuth Foundation for the Advancement of Hebrew Culture; died in Tel Aviv, Israel. See Current Biography (March) 1967.

Obituary

N Y Times D p13 O 27 '80

NICOLSON, MARJORIE HOPE Feb. 18, 1894-Mar. 9, 1981 Educator; professor of English and dean of Smith College (1929-41); professor of English at Columbia University's Graduate School (1941-62); was known for research on the influence of science on literature, particularly in the seventeenth century; wrote The Microscope and English Imagination (1935) and Newton Demands the Muse (1946), among other books; in 1940 became the first woman to head Phi Beta Kappa; died in White Plains, New York. See Current Biography (April) 1940.

Obituary

N Y Times B p17 Mr 10 '81

NORTHROP, JOHN K(NUDSEN) Nov. 10, 1895-Feb. 18, 1981 Former aircraft company executive; aeronautical engineer; pioneer designer of the Lockheed Vega of 1927, which set speed and endurance records; formed a Northrop Corporation in 1932 as a division of Douglas Aircraft Company, for which he helped to design DC-1, DC-2, and DC-3 airliners; became in 1939 president and head of engineering and research of Northrop Aircraft, Inc., now Northrop Corporation, which produced the tailless Flying Wing, World War II military planes that included the night-flying Black Widow, and the postwar F-89 jet interceptor and intercontinental Snark missile; retired in 1952; died in Glendale, California. See Current Biography (March) 1949.

Obituary

N Y Times A p20 F 20 '81

OCHSNER, (EDWARD WILLIAM) ALTON May 4, 1896-Sept. 24, 1981 Physician; world-renowned chest surgeon; one of first, in 1940's, to present evidence that cigarette smoking was a major cause of lung cancer; professor and chairman of surgery department (from 1927) and professor emeritus (from 1961) at Tulane University in New Orleans, where he co-founded (1941) the Alton Ochsner Clinic, a unit of what eventually became the Ochsner Medical Institutions; author of Smoking and

Cancer (1954) and other works; died in New Orleans, Louisiana. See Current Biography (October) 1966.

Obituary

N Y Times B p14 S 25 '81

O'HARA, MARY (July 10, 1885-Oct. 15, 1980) Author; began career as screenwriter; after leaving Hollywood, ran dairy ranch in Wyoming, the setting for My Friend Flicka (1941), her best-selling novel about a boy and his horse, and its popular sequel, Thunderhead (1943); also wrote Green Grass of Wyoming (1946), which, like the earlier novels, was adapted for the screen, and Wyoming Summer (1963), a diary, among other books; died in Chevy Chase, Maryland. See Current Biography (January) 1944.

Obituary

N Y Times D p23 O 16 '80

O'NEIL, JAMES F(RANCIS) June 13, 1898-July 28, 1981 Veterans organization official; former police chief of Manchester, New Hampshire; publisher of American Legion Magazine (1950-78); as national commander of American Legion (1947-48), helped to establish group of selected legionnaires to "spot and counter" subversive activities; died in New York City. See Current Biography (November) 1947.

Obituary

N Y Times B p6 Jl 31 '81

OSBORN, FREDERICK (HENRY) Mar. 21, 1889-Jan. 5, 1981 Author; one-time successful businessman, turned to research in demography and eugenics in 1930's; wrote several books, including The Future of Human Heredity (1968) and Our Plundered Planet (1970); with temporary rank of general, headed Morale Branch of United States Army (1941-45); as United States delegate to U. N. Atomic Energy Commission (1947-50), fought for international control of atomic energy; served as chairman of Population Council (1930-68) and secretary-treasurer of American Eugenics Society (1959-70); died in New York City. See Current Biography (November) 1941.

Obituary

N Y Times B p12 Ja 7 '81

PADOVER, SAUL K(USSIEL) Apr. 13, 1905-Feb. 22, 1981 Historian; educator; served in the government as assistant to the Secretary of the Interior (1939-43) and as an investigator with the Office of Strategic Services (1944-45); wrote a column for the New York newspaper PM (1946-48); professor of political science (beginning in 1949) and dean of the School of Politics (1950-55) of the New School for Social Research; author of some thirty books, several of them on Thomas Jefferson and Karl Marx, including *Jefferson and the National Capital* (1945) and *Marx on America and the Civil War* (1973); died in New York City. See *Current Biography* (October) 1952.

Obituary

N Y Times N p12 F 24 '81

PAULEY, EDWIN W(ENDELL) Jan. 7, 1903-July 28, 1981 Industrialist; United States government official; founder (1928) of Petrol Corporation, later sold to Standard Oil Company; board chairman (from 1958) of Pauley Petroleum Inc.; coordinator for petroleum lend-lease supplies to Great Britain and Soviet Union at beginning of World War II; United States representative on Allied Reparations Commission (1945-46); adviser to Presidents Harry S. Truman, John F. Kennedy, and Lyndon B. Johnson; past treasurer and secretary of Democratic National Committee; died in Beverly Hills, California. See *Current Biography* (June) 1945.

Obituary

N Y Times B p17 Jl 30 '81

PELLA, GIUSEPPE Apr. 18, 1902-May 31, 1981 Italian economist and legislator; was Prime Minister of Italy for five months (1953-54) that were marked by crisis with Yugoslavia over Trieste; served in various top economic Cabinet posts, including Minister of Finance, Treasury, and Budget (1947-54, 1960-62), and as Minister of Foreign Affairs (1953-54, 1957-60); died in Rome. See *Current Biography* (November) 1953.

Obituary

N Y Times B p6 Je 1 '81

PRICE, BYRON Mar. 25, 1891-Aug. 6, 1981 Journalist; public official; staff member (from 1912) and executive news editor (1937-41) of Associated Press; as United States director of censorship (1941-45), administered largely voluntary regulatory code that sought to balance constitutional right of freedom of press with wartime security needs; chairman of Association of Motion Picture Producers (1946-47); Assistant Secretary General of United Nations in charge of administrative and budgetary affairs (1947-54); died in Hendersonville, North Carolina. See *Current Biography* (February) 1942.

Obituary

N Y Times p44 Ag 8 '81

ROGGE, O(ETJE) JOHN Oct. 12, 1903-Mar. 22, 1981 Lawyer; civil rights activist; as Assistant Attorney General in charge of the criminal division in the Department of Justice (1939-40) carried out investigations and prosecutions to break up the Louisiana political machine that survived the death of Huey Long; as assistant to the Attorney General (1943-46) helped to conduct sedition trial against thirty American pro-Nazis; opposed the House Un-American Activities Committee; author of *The First and the Fifth* (1960) and other books on civil liberties; died in New York City. See *Current Biography* (February) 1948.

Obituary

N Y Times B p14 Mr 23 '81

ROSZAK, THEODORE May 1, 1907-Sept. 3, 1981 Artist; as painter and lithographer, advanced from realism to an abstract expressionism that was modified by surrealism; as metal sculptor, moved from constructivist, geometrical forms to expressionistic, symbolic works; is best known for light yet forceful welded-steel sculptures brazed with brass, bronze, copper, and nickel and based on subjects drawn from literature, personal experience, and Existentialist philosophy; stirred controversy with thirty-seven-foot aluminum eagle he created for United States Embassy in London; died in St. Vincent's Hospital in New York City. See *Current Biography* (June) 1966.

Obituary

N Y Times A p12 S 4 '81

SADAT, ANWAR (EL-) Dec. 25, 1918-Oct. 6, 1981 President of Egypt (1970-81); widely regarded as one of world's great statesmen but condemned by militant Arab foes; was closely associated with Gamal Abdel Nasser and other army officers in overthrow of King Farouk (1952); occupied high government posts, including vice-presidency, under Nasser; after succeeding to Presidency on Nasser's death, turned increasingly toward West and away from Soviet bloc; waged war against Israel in 1973, but undertook one of major peace initiatives of all time when he went to Jerusalem in 1977 for talks that led to 1979 Egyptian-Israeli peace treaty; shared 1978 Nobel Peace Prize with Israeli Prime Minister Menachem Begin; was assassinated by Egyptian soldiers while watching a military parade in Cairo. See *Current Biography* (March) 1971.

Obituary

N Y Times A p1+ O 7 '81

SANDERS, HARLAND Sept. 9, 1890-Dec. 16, 1980 Businessman; founded the Kentucky Fried Chicken Corporation in 1956 as a franchise venture, parlaying his pressure cooker and secret blend of spices into an enterprise of more than 600 franchises by 1964, when he sold most of the business; helped promote subsequent growth of the company through his distinctive Southern gentleman image and honorary colonel's title, which he had acquired in 1935; died near Shelbyville, Kentucky. See *Current Biography* (April) 1973.

Obituary

N Y Times A p33 D 17 '80

SAROYAN, WILLIAM Aug. 31, 1908-May 18, 1981 Writer; in his novels, short stories, plays, and other writings drew directly on his experience as the son of Armenian immigrants and his savoring of the variety of American life but turned personal incidents into allegorical events in which readers could find their own meanings; had original, freewheeling style and exuberant spirit; first came to national attention with short story "The Daring Young Man on the Flying Trapeze" in 1934; reached his peak with Pulitzer Prize-winning play *The Time of Your Life* (1939); also wrote, among other works, the collection of short stories *My Name Is Aram* (1940) and the motion picture and novel *The Human Comedy* (1943); died in Fresno, California. See *Current Biography* (November) 1972.

Obituary

N Y Times A p1+ My 19 '81

SCOTT, HAZEL (DOROTHY) June 11, 1920-Oct. 2, 1981 Jazz pianist and singer whose repertoire included classical music, show tunes, blues, and rock; began professional career as a pianist at thirteen and made Carnegie Hall debut in 1940; appeared in Broadway musicals *Sing Out the News* (1938) and *Priorities of 1942*, at New York World's Fair (1939), and in such Hollywood films as *Rhapsody in Blue* (1945); gave many benefit performances in behalf of civil rights; was married (from 1945) to late United States Representative Adam Clayton Powell Jr.; continued to perform in nightclubs until shortly before her death, in New York City. See *Current Biography* (August) 1943.

Obituary

N Y Times p33 O 3 '81

SNEIDER, VERN Oct. 6, 1916-May 1, 1981 Author; on basis of his own experience in World War II, wrote *The Teahouse of the August Moon* (1951), the gently humorous novel about an American captain in command of Okinawan village that was later adapted to stage and screen with great success by John Patrick; also wrote novels *A Pail of Oysters* (1953) and *The King from Ashtabula* (1960) and volume of short stories *A Long Way from Home* (1956); died in Monroe, Michigan. See *Current Biography* (Yearbook) 1956.

Obituary

N Y Times p56 My 3 '81

SOYER, ISAAC Apr. 20, 1907-July 8, 1981 Painter; lithographer; with brothers Moses and Raphael, was a leading exponent of realist school in New York; taught at University of Buffalo and other institutions; was noted for portraits of family and friends, landscapes, and such vignettes of Depression-era working-class life as *Employment Agency;* died in New York City. See *Current Biography* (March) 1941.

Obituary

N Y Times B p6 Jl 16 '81

SPEER, ALBERT Mar. 19, 1905-Sept. 1, 1981 Architect; designed some of Nazi Germany's major buildings and monuments in 1930's; as Adolf Hitler's Minister for Armaments and War Production (1942-45), was considered Nazi regime's second-most powerful official; at Nuremberg trial (1945-46), was the only one of top Nazi leaders to admit responsibility for regime's war crimes; served prison term at Spandau fortress in Berlin (1947-66); author of *Inside the Third Reich* (1970) and *Spandau: The Secret Diaries* (1976), which provide considerable insight into Hitler's Germany and workings of Nazi mentality; also wrote *Infiltration: How Heinrich Himmler Schemed to Build an SS Industrial Empire* (1981): died in London, England. See *Current Biography* (October) 1976.

Obituary

N Y Times A p18 S 2 '81

STEIN, JULES (CAESAR) Apr. 26, 1896-Apr. 29, 1981 Business executive; gave up ophthalmologic practice in 1924 to found Music Corporation of America as band-booking agency; as president (1924-46) and chairman of the board (1946-73), presided over growth of that enterprise into MCA, Inc., the dominant entertainment talent agency in United States; established Research to Prevent Blindness, Inc. in 1960; led successful fight for federally funded National Eye Institute; was recipient of several humanitarian awards; died in Los Angeles, California. See *Current Biography* (May) 1967.

Obituary

N Y Times B p12 Ap 30 '81

SUN YAT-SEN, MME. 1890-May 29, 1981 Deputy chairman of People's Republic of China, a largely ceremonial position; widow of Sun Yat-sen, who founded Chinese Republic in 1911; sister of Mme. Chiang Kai-shek; broke with her family to become staunch Communist; maintained her government post despite denunciations of her by radical Red Guards during Cultural Revolution, in 1966; received foreign ambassadors in her palace in Peking when they officially presented their credentials upon arriving in the Chinese capital; died in Peking. See *Current Biography* (April) 1944.

Obituary

N Y Times p1+ My 30 '81

TEAGUE, OLIN E(ARL) Apr. 6, 1910-Jan. 23, 1981 Former Congressman; Democratic member from Texas of the United States House of Representatives (1946-77); became identified with veterans affairs and sponsored legislation providing educational benefits for veterans; was also an advocate of the nation's space program; died at the Bethesda Naval Hospital in Maryland. See *Current Biography* (March) 1952.

Obituary

N Y Times p16 Ja 24 '81

TEALE, EDWIN WAY June 2, 1899-Oct. 18, 1980 Naturalist; writer; illustrator; photographer; was staff writer with *Popular Science* for thirteen years beginning in 1928; with his first nature book, *Grassroot Jungles* (1937), about insects, set a Thoreauvian course combining scientific research and observation with a poet-philosopher's appreciation of beauty in the wild; won Pulitzer Prize for general nonfiction for *Wandering Through Winter* (1965), the final volume of his natural history of the four seasons in North America, a fifteen-year project; died in Norwich, Connecticut. See *Current Biography* (December) 1961.

Obituary

N Y Times B p10 O 21 '80

THOMAS, LOWELL (JACKSON) Apr. 6, 1892-Aug. 29, 1981 Radio and television news commentator; author; world traveler; with own slides and film, gave popular travelog "shows," as he called them, beginning in 1915; was unofficial United States on-the-spot historian of World War I; beginning in 1930, was longest continually operating newscaster in network radio history, with audience estimated at 70 billion over forty-six-year period; was also voice of *Movietone News* for seventeen years; on television, did thirty-nine-week PBS series *Lowell Thomas Remembers* in 1976; most recently, was taping five-minute syndicated radio series about older celebrities, *The Best Years;* wrote more than fifty books, including *With Lawrence in Arabia* (1924) and two volumes of autobiography, *Good Evening, Everybody* (1977) and *So Long Until Tomorrow* (1978); died at his home in Pawling, New York. See *Current Biography* (January) 1952.

Obituary

N Y Times p40 Ag 30 '81

THURMAN, HOWARD Nov. 18, 1900-Apr. 10, 1981 Clergyman; former educator; ordained a Baptist minister (1925); professor of systematic theology and dean of chapel at Howard University (1932-44); copastor of the Church for the Fellowship of All Peoples (1944-53), which he helped to found in San Francisco to bring members of the white, black, and Oriental races into a single congregation; professor of spiritual disciplines and resources at Boston University's School of Theology (1953-65), as the university's first full-time black professor; died in San Francisco. See *Current Biography* (June) 1955.

Obituary

N Y Times B p18 Ap 14 '81

TORRIJOS HERRERA, OMAR Feb. 13, 1929-July 31, 1981 Panamanian military officer and political leader; as commander of National Guard, overthrew President Arnulfo Arias in 1968 and occupied top position of power in Panama; assumed rank of brigadier general (1969) and held title of Chief of Government and Supreme Leader of the Panamanian Revolution (1972-78); instituted major economic, social, and political reforms; was a chief architect of Panama Canal treaties with the United States (1979); provoked some controversy by granting asylum to deposed Shah of Iran (1979-80); died in air crash in Western Panama. See *Current Biography* (July) 1973.

Obituary

N Y Times p1+ Ag 2 '81

TRIPPE, JUAN T(ERRY) June 27, 1899-Apr. 3, 1981 Airline executive; was a founder in 1927 of the company that in 1949 became known as Pan American World Airways; pioneered international commercial aviation, making Pan Am the first airline to provide service across the Atlantic and Pacific in the 1930's, expanding jet passenger travel in the 1950's, and inaugurating use of the Boeing 747 in the 1960's; extended global operations into an 80,000-air-mile network connecting the United States with eighty-five other countries by 1968, when he retired as chairman and chief executive officer; remained active in business enterprises, including real estate development; died in New York City. See *Current Biography* (February) 1955.

Obituary

N Y Times p1+ Ap 4 '81

UREY, HAROLD C(LAYTON) Apr. 29, 1893-Jan. 5, 1981 Scientist; professor of chemistry at several universities, including the University of California at La Jolla (1958-70); won the Nobel Prize for Chemistry in 1934 for his discovery of deuterium, or heavy hydrogen, which led to development of the H-bomb; opposed building both the bomb and nuclear reactors; was an advocate of world government; contributed to space exploration; offered chemical explanations for the origin and evolution of the universe and of life; died in La Jolla. See *Current Biography* (July) 1960.

Obituary

N Y Times A p1+ Ja 7 '81

URRUTIA LLEO, MANUEL Dec. 8, 1901-July 5, 1981 Former President of Cuba; as a judge in Santiago de Cuba in 1950's, became a staunch opponent of dictatorship of President Fulgencio Batista; served as provisional President of Cuba under revolutionary regime of Fidel Castro from January 1959 until his dismissal by Castro six months later; after coming to United States in 1963, headed anti-Castro Democratic Revolutionary Alliance and published book *Fidel Castro & Company, Inc.: Communist Tyranny in Cuba* (1964); died in Queens, New York City. See *Current Biography* (May) 1959.

Obituary

N Y Times D p7 Jl 6 '81

VAGNOZZI, EGIDIO CARDINAL Feb. 2, 1906-Dec. 26, 1980 Roman Catholic prelate; after twenty-eight years of service as a Vatican diplomat was appointed, in 1958, Apostolic Delegate in Washington, D.C.; as the Pope's official representative wielded considerable influence in United States Catholicism; was regarded as a conservative with a cautious attitude toward changes in church traditions introduced by Vatican II; was created a Cardinal in 1967, when he returned to the Vatican to work on economic affairs of the Holy See; died in Rome. See *Current Biography* (March) 1967.

Obituary

N Y Times D p15 D 30 '80

VAUGHAN, HARRY H(AWKINS) Nov. 26, 1893-May 20, 1981 Army major general; was military aide to Harry S. Truman during Truman's years as Vice-President and President of the United States, from 1945 to 1953; had served beside Truman in World War I and in Army Reserves between the world wars and under him on staff of Senate Armed Services subcommittee investigating arms procurement; was often engaged in heated public altercations with his critics, who accused him of "influence peddling"; died in Fort Belvoir, Virginia. See *Current Biography* (March) 1949.

Obituary

N Y Times B p6 My 22 '81

VERA-ELLEN Feb. 16, 1926-Aug. 30, 1981 Dancer; actress; rose to Broadway stardom as versatile leading dancer in such musical hits as *Panama Hattie* (1940) and *By Jupiter* (1942); in Hollywood, was paired with best dancers of the day, including Fred Astaire, in *Three Little Words* (1950) and *The Belle of New York* (1952), and Gene Kelly, in *On the Town* (1949) and *Words and Music* (1948), in which the two danced the famous "Slaughter on Tenth Avenue" sequence; perhaps best remembered for her role in Irving Berlin's *White Christmas* (1954);

died in Los Angeles, California. See *Current Biography* (February) 1959.

Obituary

N Y Times A p17 S 2 '81

VINSON, CARL Nov. 18, 1883-June 1, 1981 Former United States Democratic Representative from Georgia; after two terms in Georgia General Assembly, served fifty years (1914-64)—longer than anyone else to date—in the United States House of Representatives; as chairman of House Naval Affairs Committee (1932-47) and House Armed Services Committee (1950-64), was leading advocate of strong national defense and played crucial role in formulation and passage of military-related bills; died in Milledgeville, Georgia. See *Current Biography* (April) 1942.

Obituary

N Y Times B p10 Je 2 '81

WALLACE, DeWITT Nov. 12, 1889-Mar. 30, 1981 Retired editor; publisher; in 1922, with his wife, Lila Acheson Wallace, founded *Reader's Digest,* a pocket-size magazine of condensed "articles of lasting interest" chosen from well-known periodicals; later included articles—uplifting treatments of a variety of subjects, usually of public concern and conservative slant—by *Digest* authors and solicited contributions to special features like "Life in These United States"; increased circulation of *Digest* to 30,500,000 a month in sixteen languages, the largest in the world; retired in 1973; died in Mount Kisco, New York. See *Current Biography* (May) 1956.

Obituary

N Y Times D p23 Ap 1 '81

WANG SHIH-CHIEH Mar. 10, 1891-Apr.(?) 1981 Nationalist Chinese government official; diplomat; educator; was one of Generalissimo Chiang Kai-shek's most trusted advisers; president of National Wuhan University (1929-33); Minister of Education (1933-37); as Minister of Foreign Affairs (1945-48), took part in abortive peace talks between Nationalist regime and Communists under Mao Zedong; died in Taipeh. See *Current Biography* (September) 1945.

Obituary

Time 117:53 My 4 '81

WARD, BARBARA (MARY) May 23, 1914-May 31, 1981 British economist; author; journalist; was at various times editor of the *Economist,* president of International Institute for Environment and Development, governor of the British Broadcasting Corporation, and panelist on the BBC's popular discussion program *The Brains Trust;* exerted enormous influence as lecturer, adviser to statesmen, and author of such books as *The West at Bay* (1948) and *India and the West* (1961); eloquently argued interdependence of nations, stressing unity of the Western industrial countries and need for aid to Third World and accomodation with Communist bloc; also spoke and wrote on Catholicism in modern world; died at her home in southern England; See *Current Biography* (January) 1950.

Obituary

N Y Times B p6 Je 1 '81

WARREN, HARRY Dec. 24, 1893-Sept. 22, 1981 Songwriter; one of foremost composers of American popular music; during career spanning nearly sixty years, wrote more than 300 songs, in collaboration with lyricists Al Dubin, Johnny Mercer, Ira Gershwin, Billy Rose, and others; composed songs for Broadway musicals and for more than fifty· Hollywood films, including *42nd Street* (1933), *Sun Valley Serenade* (1941), and *Ziegfeld Follies* (1946); won Academy Awards for hit songs "Lullaby of Broadway," (1935), "You'll Never Know" (1940), and "On the Atchison, Topeka and the Santa Fe" (1946); also created choral works, piano vignettes, and other compositions; died in Los Angeles. See *Current Biography* (June) 1943.

Obituary

N Y Times D p23 S 23 '81

WEST, MAE Aug. 17, 1893-Nov. 22, 1980 Actress; playwright; was her own masterpiece, a self-packaged caricature of a *femme fatale* in the Gay Nineties tradition; as such, was American show business' bawdy personification of the brazen vamp for more than six decades; began career in vaudeville; reached her zenith on stage in title role of *Diamond Lil* (1928), one of her own plays; transferred Lil, a gold-digging saloon singer, to screen in *She Done Him Wrong* (1933); made eleven additional motion pictures, including *My Little Chickadee* (1940), with W. C. Fields, probably her best, and *Sextette* (1978), certainly her worst, a brave but futile defiance of physical decay; died in Los Angeles. See *Current Biography* (November) 1967.

Obituary

N Y Times p1+ N 23 '80

WHITEHEAD, DON(ALD FORD) Apr. 8, 1908-Jan. 12, 1981 Journalist; as a correspondent of the Associated Press covered the major World War II battles in Europe and North Africa; won the Pulitzer Prize for international reporting in 1951 for stories on the Korean War written while accompanying the American forces; won the Pulitzer Prize for national reporting in 1953 for day-to-day account of President-elect Dwight D. Eisenhower's trip to Korea; columnist of the Knoxville *News-Sen-*tinel (1959-78); author of *The F.B.I. Story* (1956) and other books; died in Knoxville, Tennessee. See *Current Biography* (December) 1953.

Obituary

N Y Times B p4 Ja 14 '81

WILDER, ALEC Feb. 16, 1907-Dec. 24, 1980 Composer; wrote hundreds of popular songs, including "I'll Be Around" and "While You're Young," and hundreds of formal compositions —operas, operettas, works for full orchestra, wind ensemble, and chamber groups like the Alec Wilder *Octet*; in popular and concert pieces and in compositions that blended elements of both, music was characterized by coloristic, lyrical, elusive qualities that set him apart; author of *American Popular Song* (1972), tracing the development of popular songs from 1900 to 1950; died in Gainesville, Florida. See *Current Biography* (July) 1980.

Obituary

N Y Times p33 D 25 '80

WILKINS, ROY Aug. 30, 1901-Sept. 8, 1981 Organization official; civil rights leader; was executive secretary of National Association for the Advancement of Colored People from 1955 to 1977; began career as newsman with black weekly Kansas City (Missouri) *Call*, of which he became managing editor; left *Call* in 1931 to join secretariat of NAACP as assistant to Walter White; in 1934 succeeded W. E. B. Du Bois as editor of *The Crisis*, official NAACP organ; as executive secretary, was "too" moderate by standards of black militants, but Presidents as well as middle- and working-class blacks respected his solid, thoughtful leadership in strategy of quiet, legal confrontation; died in New York City. See *Current Biography* (January) 1964.

Obituary

N Y Times A p1 S 9 '81

WILLIAMS, ERIC (EUSTACE) Sept. 25, 1911-Mar. 29, 1981 Prime Minister of Trinidad and Tobago; authority on the West Indies who taught for several years at Howard University in Washington, D.C. and served on the Caribbean Commission before returning to his native Trinidad to found the People's National Movement in 1955; helped guide the British colony to independence within the Commonwealth in 1962, when he began his eighteen years as Prime Minister of the independent state of Trinidad and Tobago; held simultaneous Cabinet posts, including Minister of Finance, Planning and Development (1967-71); died in Port of Spain, Trinidad. See *Current Biography* (February) 1966.

Obituary

N Y Times D p22 Mr 31 '81

WILLIAMS, MARY LOU May 8, 1910-May 28, 1981 Pianist; composer; arranger; "Queen of Jazz"; was an adventurous and original performer; had career spanning succession of jazz eras and styles; was rooted in blues and boogie-woogie; in swing era, wrote such songs as "Roll 'Em" and "Camel Hop" for Benny Goodman, "What's Your Story, Morning Glory?" for Jimmy Lunceford, and "Trumpets No End" for Duke Ellington; contributed to development of bebop in the 1940's; after conversion to Roman Catholicism, in 1957, wrote mostly religious music, including several Masses; became artist in residence at Duke University in 1977; died at her home in Durham, North Carolina. See *Current Biography* (November) 1966.

Obituary

N Y Times p21 My 30 '81

WYLER, WILLIAM July 1, 1902-July 28, 1981 Motion picture director and producer; one of most esteemed directors of Hollywood's golden age; began film career in 1925 as director of two-reel Westerns; won Academy Awards as best director for *Mrs. Miniver* (1942), *The Best Years of Our Lives* (1945), and *Ben Hur* (1958); also earned acclaim for his direction of such film classics as *Dead End* (1937), *Jezebel* (1938), *Wuthering Heights* (1939), *The Little Foxes* (1941), *Roman Holiday* (1953), *Friendly Persuasion* (1956), *The Big Country* (1958), *The Children's Hour* (1962), and *Funny Girl* (1968); died in Beverly Hills, California. See *Current Biography* (June) 1951.

Obituary

N Y Times A p1+ Jl 29 '81

WYSZYNSKI, STEFAN CARDINAL Aug. 3, 1901-May 28, 1981 Roman Catholic prelate; Primate of Poland; Archbishop of Gniezno and Warsaw; was autocratic, defiant personification of a nation and a church under siege; as protector of Poland's Catholic faith, astutely moved from hard-line opposition to atheistic Communistic regime under Stalinism to judicious cooperation with it in social and economic programs in recent years; had both an encouraging and a moderating influence on Lech Wałesa and Solidarity, Poland's independent labor union movement; died in Warsaw. See *Current Biography* (January) 1958.

Obituary

N Y Times p1+ My 29 '81

YOST, CHARLES W(OODRUFF) Nov. 6, 1907-May 21, 1981 Diplomat; career foreign service officer; scholar; in 1950's, served as United States Ambassador to Laos, Syria, and Morocco, successively; helped plan the founding of the United Nations and held several positions with the American U.N. delegation, including chief delegate (1969-71); was a fellow with several foreign-policy think tanks, including the Council on Foreign Relations; wrote *History and Memory* (1980), among other books; died in Washington, D.C. See *Current Biography* (March) 1959.

Obituary

N Y Times p21 My 23 '81

YUKAWA, HIDEKI Jan. 23, 1907-Sept. 8, 1981 Japanese physicist; received 1949 Nobel Prize in Physics for postulating existence, later confirmed, of subatomic particles called mesons; professor of physics at Kyoto University (from 1939); visiting professor at Institute for Advanced Study at Princeton, New Jersey (1948-49); professor at Columbia University (1951-53); director of Research Institute for Fundamental Physics at Kyoto University (1953-70); died in Kyoto. See *Current Biography* (January) 1950.

Obituary

N Y Times D p23 S 10 '81

ZULLI, FLOYD, JR. Sept. 22, 1922-Oct. 12, 1980 University professor; pioneer television teacher; taught Romance languages at New York University, beginning in 1946; won four local Emmy awards, including one for outstanding television personality of 1957-58 for his teaching of comparative literature on *Sunrise Semester* five mornings a week on CBS's channel 2 in New York City; died in Glen Cove, Long Island. See *Current Biography* (January) 1958.

Obituary

N Y Times D p23 O 15 '80

BIOGRAPHICAL REFERENCES

Almanac of American Politics, 1980

American Architects Directory, 1970

American Bar, 1965

American Catholic Who's Who, 1976-77

American Medical Directory, 1979

American Men and Women of Science 14th ed (1979)

Asia Who's Who (1960)

Biographical Directory of Librarians in the United States and Canada (1970)

Biographical Directory of the American Congress, 1774-1971 (1971)

Biographical Encyclopaedia & Who's Who of the American Theatre (1966)

Biographical Encyclopedia of Pakistan, 1971-72

Biographic Directory of the USSR (1958)

Burke's Peerage, Baronetage, and Knightage, 1970

Canadian Who's Who, 1980

Celebrity Register (1973)

Chi è? (1961)

China Yearbook, 1971-72

Chujoy, A., and Manchester, P. W., eds. Dance Encyclopedia (1967)

Concise Biographical Dictionary of Singers (1969)

Congressional Directory, 1981

Congressional Quarterly Almanac, 1981

Contemporary Artists (1977)

Contemporary Authors (1962-80)

Contemporary Dramatists (1973)

Contemporary Novelists (1976)

Contemporary Poets (1975)

Contemporary Poets of the English Language (1970)

Debrett's Peerage and Baronetage (1980)

Dictionary of Contemporary American Artists (1977)

Dictionary of International Biography, 1975

Dictionary of Latin American and Caribbean Biography (1971)

Dictionnaire de biographie française (1964)

Directory of American Judges (1955)

Directory of American Scholars (1974)

Directory of British Scientists, 1966-67

Directory of Medical Specialists, 1972-73

Encyclopedia of Pop, Rock and Soul (1974)

Episcopal Clergy Directory, 1972

Ewen, D., ed. Composers of Today (1936); Living Musicians (1940); First Supplement (1957); Men and Women Who Make Music (1949); American Composers Today (1949); European Composers Today (1954); The New Book of Modern Composers (1961); Popular American Composers (1962; First Supplement, 1972); Composers Since 1900 (1969); Musicians Since 1900 (1978)

Feather, Leonard. Encyclopedio of Jazz (1960); Encyclopedia of Jazz in the Sixties (1966)

Filmgoer's Companion (1977)

Football Register, 1980

Foremost Women in Communications (1970)

Grove's Dictionary of Music and Musicians (1955)

Hindustan Year Book and Who's Who, 1963

Hvem er Hvem? 1973

International Authors and Writers Who's Who, 1978

International Motion Picture Almanac, 1981

International Television Almanac, 1981

International Who's Who, 1981-82

International Who's Who in Art and Antiques, 1976

International Who's Who in Music, 1975

International Who's Who in Poetry (1974-75)

International Who's Who of the Arab World (1978)

International Year Book and Statesmen's Who's Who, 1981

Japan Biographical Encyclopedia & Who's Who, 1964-65

Jews in the World of Science (1956)

Junior Book of Authors (1951)

Katz, E. Film Encyclopedia (1979)

Kelly's Handbook to the Titled, Landed and Official Classes, 1964

Kleine Slavische Biographie (1958)

Kraks Bla Bog, 1964

Kürschners Deutscher Gelehrten-Kalender, 1970

Leaders in Education (1974)

Leaders in Electronics (1979)

Leaders in Profile (1975)

McGraw-Hill Modern Scientists and Engineers (1980)

Martindale-Hubbell Law Directory, 1979

Middle East and North Africa, 1978-79

More Junior Authors (1963)

Nalanda Year-Book and Who's Who in India and Pakistan, 1958

National Cyclopaedia of American Biography current vols A-M (1926-78)

New Century Cyclopedia of Names (1954)

Nordness, Lee, ed. Art USA Now (1963)

Notable Australians (1978)

Notable Names in the American Theatre (1976)

Nouveau Dictionnaire National des Contemporains (1968)

Offical Baseball Register, 1981
Official Catholic Directory, 1976
Oxford Companion to Film (1976)

Panorama Biografico degli Italiani d'Oggi (1956)
Political Profiles (1976-79)
Politics in America (1981)
Poor's Register of Directors and Executives, 1974
Prominent Personalities in the USSR (1968)

Quién es Quién en la Argentina, 1968-69
Quién es Quién en Venezuela, Panama, Ecuador, Colombia, 1956

Robinson, Donald. 100 Most Important People in the World Today (1972)

Slonimsky, Nicholas. Baker's Biographical Dictionary of Musicians (1978)
Something About the Author (1971-80)

Third Book of Junior Authors (1972)
Thomas, S. Men of Space (1960-68)
Thompson, K. A. Dictionary of Twentieth-Century Composers (1973)
Thompson, O., ed. International Cyclopedia of Music and Musicians, 1964
Thomson, D. Biographical Dictionary of Film (1976)
Twentieth Century Authors (1942; First Supplement, 1955)
Two Hundred Contemporary Authors (1969)

Vem är Det, 1973

Webster's Biographical Dictionary (1971)
Wer ist Wer? (1979)
Who is Who in Music (1951)
Who's Who, 1980-81
Who's Who among Black Americans, 1977-78
Who's Who in Advertising (1963)
Who's Who in Africa, 1973
Who's Who in America, 1980-81
Who's Who in American Art (1980)
Who's Who in American Education, 1967-68
Who's Who in American Politics, 1981-82
Who's Who in Art (1974)
Who's Who in Australia, 1971
Who's Who in Austria, 1971-72
Who's Who in Baseball, 1971
Who's Who in Belgium (1962)
Who's Who in California, 1965
Who's Who in Canada, 1969-70
Who's Who in Chicago and Illinois (1950)
Who's Who in Colored America, 1950
Who's Who in Communist China (1969)
Who's Who in Engineering, 1964
Who's Who in Finance and Industry, 1981-82
Who's Who in France, 1979-80
Who's Who in France (Paris), 1953-54
Who's Who in Germany (1972)
Who's Who in Hollywood, 1900-1976
Who's Who in Israel, 1978
Who's Who in Italy, 1957-58
Who's Who in Labor, 1976
Who's Who in Latin America Pts 1-7 (1945-51)
Who's Who in Library Service (1970)
Who's Who in Malaysia, 1967
Who's Who in Music, 1969
Who's Who in New York, 1960
Who's Who in New Zealand (1968)
Who's Who in Opera, 1976
Who's Who in Philosophy (1969)

Who's Who in Professional Baseball (1973)
Who's Who in Publishing (1971)
Who's Who in Railroading in North America (1959)
Who's Who in Saudi Arabia, 1978-79
Who's Who in Space, 1966-67
Who's Who in Spain, 1965
Who's Who in Switzerland, 1970-71
Who's Who in the Arab World, 1981-82
Who's Who in the East, 1979-80
Who's Who in the Midwest, 1980-81
Who's Who in the Netherlands, 1962-63
Who's Who in the South and Southwest, 1980-81
Who's Who in the Theatre (1977)
Who's Who in the United Nations (1975)
Who's Who in the USSR, 1972
Who's Who in the West, 1980-81
Who's Who in the World, 1974-75
Who's Who in World Aviation and Astronautics (1958)
Who's Who in World Jewry (1978)
Who's Who of American Women, 1981-82
Who's Who of British Engineers, 1970-71
Who's Who of British Scientists, 1971-72
Who's Who of Jazz (1972)
Who's Who of Rhodesia, Mauritius, Central and East Africa, 1965
Who's Who of Southern Africa, 1970
Wie is Dat? (1956)
Women Lawyers in the United States (1957)
World Authors: 1950-1970 (1975)
World Authors: 1970-75 (1980)
World Biography (1954)
World Who's Who in Science (1968)
World's Who's Who of Women (1974-75)

PERIODICALS AND NEWSPAPERS CONSULTED

ALA Bul–American Library Association Bulletin
After Dark
Am Artist–American Artist
Am Libs–American Libraries
Am Scholar–American Scholar
Am Sociol R–American Sociological Review
America
Américas
Arch Forum–Architectural forum (disc.)
Arch Rec–Architectural Record
Archaeology
Art N–Artnews
Arts
Arts & Arch–Arts & Architecture
Atlan–Atlantic Monthly
Aviation W–Aviation Week and Space Technology

Ballet N–Ballet News
Barron's
Ballet News
Biog N–Biography News
Book-of-the-Month Club N–Book-of-the-Month Club News
Book World
Broadcasting
Bsns W–Business Week

Cath World–Catholic World
Chicago Tribune
Christian Sci Mon–Christian Science Monitor
Columbia J R–Columbia Journalism Review
Commonweal
Cong Digest–Congressional Digest
Cong Q–Congressional Quarterly Weekly Report
Cosmop–Cosmopolitan
Crawdaddy
Cue (now incorporated into New York)
Cur Hist–Current History
Cur World Leaders–Current World Leaders

Dance Mag–Dance Magazine
Discover

Ebony
Ed & Pub–Editor & Publisher
Encounter
Esquire

Facts on File
Family Circle
For Affairs–Foreign Affairs
For Policy Bul–Foreign Policy Bulletin

Forbes
Fortune

Good H–Good Housekeeping
Guardian

Harper's
Hi Fi–High Fidelity
Hi Fi/Stereo R–Hi/Fi Stereo Review
Holiday
Horizon

Illus Lond N–Illustrated London News
Intellectual Digest (disc.)

Ladies Home J–Ladies' Home Journal
Lib J–Library Journal
Life
London Observer
Look (disc.)
Los Angeles Times

McCall's
Macleans Mag–Maclean's Magazine
Mlle–Mademoiselle
Modern Maturity
More (disc.)
Ms
Mus Am–Musical America
Mus Courier–Musical Courier (disc.)
Mus Mod Art–Museum of Modern Art Bulletin

N Y Daily News
N Y Tribune (disc.)
N Y Herald Tribune Bk R–New York Herald Tribune Book Review (disc.)
N Y Post
N Y Rev of Books–New York Review of Books
N Y Sunday News
N Y Times
N Y Times Bk R–New York Times Book Review
N Y Times Mag–New York Times Magazine
N Y World-Telegram–New York World-Telegram and Sun (disc.)
N Y World Journal Tribune (disc.)
Nat Geog Mag–National Geographic Magazine
Nat Observer–National Observer (disc.)
Nation
Nations Bsns–Nation's Business
Nature
New Leader
New Repub–New Republic

New Statesm–New Statesman
New Times (disc.)
New York–New York Magazine
New Yorker
Newsday
Newsweek

Omni
Opera N–Opera News

Penthouse
People
Philadelphia Inquirer
Playboy
Pop Sci–Popular Science Monthly
Psych Today–Psychology Today
Pub W–Publishers Weekly

Quest (disc.)

Read Digest–Reader's Digest
Redbook
Reporter–The Reporter (disc.)
Rolling Stone

Sat Eve Post–Saturday Evening Post
Sat R–Saturday Review
Sci Am–Scientific American
Sci Mo–Scientific Monthly
Sci N L–Science News Letter
Science
Science '81
Show Bus Illus–Show Business Illustrated (disc.)
Smithsonian
Spec–Spectator
Sport
Sports Illus–Sports Illustrated
Sr Schol–Senior Scholastic

Theatre Arts (disc.)
This Week–This Week Magazine (disc.)
Time–Time
Times Lit Sup–London Times Literary Supplement
Toronto Globe and Mail
TV Guide

U N Rev–United Nations Review
U S News–U.S. News & World Report

Variety
Village Voice
Vogue

Wall St J–Wall Street Journal
Washington M–Washington Monthly
Washington Post
Wilson Lib Bul–Wilson Library Bulletin

Yale R–Yale Review

CLASSIFICATION BY PROFESSION—1981

ARCHITECTURE
Pérez Esquivel, Adolfo

ART
Agam, Yaacov
Caro, Anthony
Chicago, Judy
De Montebello, Philippe
Folon, Jean-Michel
Graves, Nancy
Loquasto, Santo
Michals, Duane
Pérez Esquivel, Adolfo
Rexroth, Kenneth
Riley, Bridget
Wyeth, Andrew

BUSINESS
Brown, Charles L.
Calvo Sotelo, Leopoldo
Clausen, A. W.
Heinz, John
Kaufman, Henry
Land, Edwin H.
McColough, C. Peter

DANCE
Ashley, Merrill
Bennett, Michael
Loquasto, Santo
Rambert, Marie

DIPLOMACY
Christopher, Warren M.
Habib, Philip C.
Kirkpatrick, Jeane J.
Lord Soames

EDUCATION
Crosby, John
Druckman, Jacob
Holt, John
Kirkpatrick, Jeane J.
Miłosz, Czesław
Morrison, Philip
Pérez Esquivel, Adolfo

Sanger, Frederick
Sovern, Michael I.
Sowell, Thomas
Stever, H. Guyford
Tiger, Lionel

FINANCE
Clausen, A. W.
Kaufman, Henry
Regan, Donald T.
Seaga, Edward

GOVERNMENT AND POLITICS, FOREIGN
Bani-Sadr, Abolhassan
Queen Beatrix
Brundtland, Gro Harlem
Calvo Sotelo, Leopoldo
Chun Doo Hwan
Cossiga, Francesco
Doe, Samuel K.
Elizabeth, Queen Mother of Great Britain
Foot, Michael
Haughey, Charles J.
Hussein, Saddam
Kania, Stanisław
Karmal, Babrak
Limann, Hilla
Mengistu Haile Mariam
Obote, Milton
Reddy, N. Sanjiva
Schreyer, Edward Richard
Seaga, Edward
Sharon, Ariel
Lord Soames
Stroessner, Alfredo
Suzuki, Zenko
Wałesa, Lech
Ziaur Rahman

GOVERNMENT AND POLITICS, U.S.
Carlucci, Frank
Carter, Hodding, 3d
Christopher, Warren M.
Falwell, Jerry

Garth, David
Habib, Philip C.
Heinz, John
Jones, James R.
Kirkpatrick, Jeane J.
Meese, Edwin, 3d
Michal, Robert H.
Packwood, Bob
Regan, Donald T.
Sowell, Thomas
Stever, H. Guyford
Stockman, David
Tsongas, Paul E.

INTERNATIONAL RELATIONS
Christopher, Warren M.
Clausen, A. W.
Habib, Philip C.
Kirkpatrick, Jeane J.
Lord Soames

JOURNALISM
Brokaw, Tom
Carter, Hodding, 3d
Foot, Michael
Mudd, Roger
Sanders, Marlene
Sheed, Wilfrid
Thompson, Hunter S.
Timerman, Jacobo
Will, George F.

LABOR
Jones, James R.
Sovern, Michael I.
Thomas, Franklin A.
Wałesa, Lech

LAW
Christopher, Warren M.
Meese, Edwin, 3d
Packwood, Bob
Sovern, Michael I.
Tsongas, Paul E.

LITERATURE
Clavell, James
Drabble, Margaret
Francis, Dick
Gordon, Mary
Hardwick, Elizabeth
King, Stephen
Merrill, James
Miłosz, Czesław
Rexroth, Kenneth
Sheed, Frank
Sheed, Wilfrid
Spillane, Mickey
Thompson, Hunter S.
Tyler, Anne

MEDICINE
Brundtland, Gro Harlem
Dausset, Jean
Gajdusek, D. Carleton
Selye, Hans

MILITARY
Chun Doo Hwan
Doe, Samuel K.
Mengistu Haile Mariam
Sharon, Ariel
Stroessner, Alfredo
Ziaur Rahman

MOTION PICTURES
Bennett, Michael
Bergman, Ingmar
Cimino, Michael
Clavell, James
Conway, Tim
Dale, Jim
Danner, Blythe
Diamond, Neil
Dickinson, Angie
Foster, Jodie
Gibb, Berry
Guinness, Alec
Harry, Debbie
Hartman, David
Hughes, Barnard
Huppert, Isabelle
Huston, John
Ivory, James

Jacobi, Derek
Lansing, Sherry
Loquasto, Santo
Mason, Marsha
Mifune, Toshiro
Schrader, Paul
Sidney, Sylvia
Spillane, Mickey
Sutherland, Donald

MUSIC
Bonynge, Richard
Cotrubas, Ileana
Crosby, John
Diamond, Neil
Druckman, Jacob
Gibb, Barry
Glass, Philip
Harry, Debbie
Ramey, Samuel
Rogers, Kenny
Waters, Muddy

NONFICTION
Carter, Hodding, 3d
Drabble, Margaret
Foot, Michael
Gilder, George
Gordon, Mary
Hoffman, Abbie
Holt, John
King, Stephen
Kirkpatrick, Jeane J.
Kuralt, Charles
Rexroth, Kenneth
Schrader, Paul
Selye, Hans
Sheed, Frank
Sheed, 'Wilfrid
Sidney, Sylvia
Sowell, Thomas
Thompson, Hunter S.
Tiger, Lionel
Timerman, Jacobo

ORGANIZATIONS
Falwell, Jerry
Thomas, Franklin A.

PHOTOGRAPHY
Brandt, Bill
Land, Edwin H.
Michals, Duane

PSYCHOLOGY
Selye, Hans

PUBLISHING
Hardwick, Elizabeth
Sheed, Frank

RADIO
Kuralt, Charles
Russell, Mark
Sanders, Marlene

RELIGION
Falwell, Jerry
Sheed, Frank

SCIENCE
Dausset, Jean
Gajdusek, D. Carleton
Land, Edwin H.
Morrison, Philip
Sanger, Frederick
Stever, H. Guyford

SOCIAL ACTIVISM
Hoffman, Abbie
Pérez Esquivel, Adolfo
Timerman, Jacobo

SOCIAL SCIENCES
Bani-Sadr, Abolhassan
Gilder, George
Kaufman, Henry
Kirkpatrick, Jeane J.
Sowell, Thomas
Tiger, Lionel

SPORTS
Austin, Tracy
Bossy, Mike
Brett, George
Cruyff, Johan
Francis, Dick
Holmes, Larry
John, Tommy
Leonard, Sugar Ray
Waitz, Grete

TECHNOLOGY
Land, Edwin H.
Stever, H. Guyford

TELEVISION
Bennett, Michael
Bergman, Ingmar
Brokaw, Tom

Carter, Hodding, 3d
Clavell, James
Conway, Tim
Dale, Jim
Danner, Blythe
Diamond, Neil
Dickinson, Angie
Foster, Jodie
Jacobi, Derek
Harry, Debbie
Hartman, David
Hughes, Barnard
Huppert, Isabelle
Ivory, James
Kuralt, Charles
Mason, Marsha
Mifune, Toshiro
Mudd, Roger
Rogers, Kenny
Russell, Mark
Sanders, Marlene

Sidney, Sylvia
Spillane, Mickey
Sutherland, Donald
Will, George F.

THEATRE
Bennett, Michael
Bergman, Ingmar
Chaikin, Joseph
Dale, Jim
Danner, Blythe
Guinness, Alec
Hartman, David
Hughes, Barnard
Huppert, Isabelle
Huston, John
Jacobi, Derek
Loquasto, Santo
Mason, Marsha
Sidney, Sylvia
Sutherland, Donald

For the index to 1940-1970 biographies, see
Current Biography Cumulative Index 1940-1970
For the index to 1971-1980 biographies, see the 1980 yearbook.

Grasso, Ella T(ambussi) obit Mar 81

Graves, Nancy (Stevenson) May 81

Gribble, Harry Wagstaff (Graham-) obit Apr 81

Guinness, Alec Mar 81

Habib, Philip C(harles) Sep 81

Hagerty, James C. obit Jun 81

Hanson, Howard obit Apr 81

Harburg, E(dgar) Y(ipsel) obit Apr 81

Hardwick, Elizabeth Feb 81

Harry, Debbie Nov 81

Hartman, David Jun 81

Hauge, Gabriel (Sylfest) obit Sep 81

Haughey, Charles J(ames) Feb 81

Heinz, (Henry) John, (3d) Apr 81

Hirshhorn, Joseph H(erman) obit Oct 81

Hoffman, Abbie Apr 81

Holmes, Larry Aug 81

Holt, John (Caldwell) Jun 81

Houghton, Amory obit Apr 81

Howard, Elston (Gene) obit Feb 81

Hughes, Barnard Sep 81

Huppert, Isabelle Nov 81

Hussein, Saddam (al-Tikriti) Sep 81

Huston, John Mar 81

Ilg, Frances L(illian) obit Sep 81

Ivory, James Jul 81

Jacobi, Derek May 81

Jenkins, Ray H(oward) obit Feb 81

Jessel, George (Albert) obit Jul 81

John, Tommy Oct 81

Johnson, Pamela Hansford obit Aug 81

Jones, James R(obert) Oct 81

Kania, Stanislaw Jun 81

Karmal, Babrak Mar 81

Kaufman, Henry Aug 81

Kemper, James S(cott) obit Nov 81

King, Stephen Oct 81

Kintner, Robert E(dmonds) obit Feb 81

Kirkpatrick, Jeane (Duane) J(ordan) Jul 81

Knight, John S(hively) obit Aug 81

Kosygin, Aleksei N(ikolaye-vich) obit Feb 81

Kuralt, Charles Jul 81

LaMarsh, Judy obit Jan 81

Land, Edwin H(erbert) Mar 81

Lansing, Sherry (Lee) May 81

Léger, Jules obit Jan 81

Lennon, John obit Feb 81

Leonard, Ray See Leonard, Sugar Ray Feb 81

Leonard, Sugar Ray Feb 81

Lesage, Jean obit Feb 81

Levin, Meyer obit Sep 81

Liebman, Max obit Sep 81

Lilienthal, David E(li) obit Mar 81

Limann, Hilla Jun 81

Loeb, William obit Nov 81

Longo, Luigi obit Jan 81

Loos, Anita obit Oct 81

Loquasto, Santo Jun 81

Louis, Joe obit Jun 81

McCain, John S(idney), Jr. obit Jun 81

MacDonald, Malcolm (John) obit Mar 81

McLean, Robert obit Feb 81

McLuhan, (Herbert) Marshall obit Feb 81

McColough, C(harles) Peter Jan 81

McCormack, John W(illiam) obit Jan 81

McQueen, Steve obit Jan 81

Mason, Marsha Apr 81

Mearns, David C(hambers) obit Jul 81

Meese, Edwin, 3d Sep 81

Mengistu Haile Mariam Jul 81

Merrill, James (Ingram) Aug 81

Michals, Duane (Steven) Apr 81

Michel, Robert H(enry) Sep 81

Mifune, Toshiro Jun 81

Miller, Irving obit Feb 81

Milosz, Czeslaw Oct 81

Montale, Eugenio obit Nov 81

Montebello, (Guy-) Philippe (Lannes) de See De Montebello, Philippe Apr 81

Montgomery, Robert obit Nov 81

Morrison, Philip Jul 81

Moses, Robert obit Sep 81

Mosley, Sir Oswald (Ernald) obit Feb 81

Mudd, Roger (Harrison) Jan 81

Neumann, Emanuel obit Jan 81

Nicolson, Marjorie Hope obit Jun 81

Northrop, John K(nudsen) obit Apr 81

Obote, (Apollo) Milton Apr 81

Ochsner, (Edward William) Alton obit Nov 81

O'Hara, Mary obit Jan 81

O'Neil, James F(rancis) obit Sep 81

Osborn, Frederick (Henry) obit Mar 81

Packwood, Bob Jan 81

Padover, Saul K(ussiel) obit Apr 81

Pauley, Edwin W(endell) obit Sep 81

Pella, Giuseppe obit Aug 81

Pérez Esquivel, Adolfo Mar 81

Price, Byron obit Sep 81

Rambert, Marie Feb 81

Ramey, Samuel Jul 81

Reddy, N(eelam) Sanjiva Mar 81

Regan, Donald T(homas) Nov 81

Rexroth, Kenneth Apr 81

Riley, Bridget (Louise) Sep 81

Rogers, Kenny Jan 81

Rogge, O(etje) John obit Jun 81

Roszak, Theodore obit Oct 81

Russell, Mark Mar 81

Sadat, Anwar (el-) obit Nov 81

Sanders, Harland obit Feb 81

Sanders, Marlene Feb 81

Sanger, Frederick Jul 81

Saroyan, William obit Jul 81

Schrader, Paul Aug 81

Schreyer, Edward Richard Feb 81

Scott, Hazel (Dorothy) obit Nov 81

Seaga, Edward (Phillip George) Apr 81

Selye, Hans (Hugo Bruno) Jan 81

Sharon, Ariel Apr 81

Sheed, Frank (Joseph) Sep 81

Sheed, Wilfrid Aug 81

Sidney, Sylvia Oct 81

Sneider, Vern obit Jun 81

Soames, (Arthur) Christopher (John), Baron of Fletching Aug 81

Soong Ching-ling. See Sun Yat-sen, Mme. obit Jul 81
Sovern, Michael I(ra) Feb 81
Sowell, Thomas Jul 81
Soyer, Isaac obit Sep 81
Speer, Albert obit Oct 81
Spillane, Mickey Sep 81
Stein, Jules (Caesar) obit Jun 81
Stever, H(orton) Guyford Jan 81
Stockman, David (Alan) Aug 81
Stroessner, Alfredo Mar 81
Sun Yat-sen, Mme. obit Jul 81
Sutherland, Donald Feb 81
Suzuki, Zenko Jan 81

Teague, Olin E(arl) obit Apr 81
Teale, Edwin Way obit Jan 81
Thomas, Franklin A(ugustine) Oct 81
Thomas, Lowell (Jackson) obit Oct 81
Thompson, Hunter S(tockton) Mar 81
Thurman, Howard obit Jun 81

Tiger, Lionel Jan 81
Timerman, Jacobo Nov 81
Torrijos Herrera, Omar obit Sep 81
Trippe, Juan T(erry) obit May 81
Tsongas, Paul E(fthemios) Jul 81
Tyler, Anne Jun 81

Urey, Harold C(layton) obit Mar 81
Urrutia Lleo, Manuel obit Aug 81

Vagnozzi, Egidio Cardinal obit Feb 81
Vaughan, Harry H(awkins) obit Jul 81
Vera-Ellen obit Oct 81
Vinson, Carl obit Jul 81

Waitz, Grete Apr 81
Walesa, Lech Apr 81
Wallace, DeWitt obit May 81
Wang Shih-chieh obit Jun 81

Ward, Barbara (Mary) obit Jul 81
Warren, Harry obit Nov 81
Waters, Muddy May 81
West, Mae obit Jan 81
Whitehead, Don(ald Ford) obit Mar 81
Wilder, Alec obit Feb 81
Wilkins, Roy obit Oct 81
Will, George F(rederick) Sep 81
Williams, Eric (Eustace) obit May 81
Williams, Mary Lou obit Jul 81
Wyeth, Andrew (Newell) Nov 81
Wyler, William obit Sep 81
Wyszynski, Stefan Cardinal obit Jul 81

Yost, Charles W(oodruff) obit Jul 81
Yukawa, Hideki obit Nov 81

Ziaur Rahman Jun 81 obit Jul 81
Zulli, Floyd, Jr. obit Jan 81

2047